CULTURE AND VALUES

Culture and Values

A Survey of the Western Humanities

Alternate Volume

Third Edition

Lawrence S. Cunningham
University of Notre Dame

John J. Reich
Syracuse University, Italy

Harcourt Brace College Publishers
Fort Worth Philadelphia San Diego New York Orlando Austin San Antonio
Toronto Montreal London Sydney Tokyo

Publisher • Ted Buchholz
Acquisitions Editor • Barbara J. C. Rosenberg
Developmental Editor • Terri House
Project Editor • Laura J. Hanna
Production Manager • Debra A. Jenkin
Senior Art Director • Don Fujimoto
Photo/Permissions Editor • Elsa Peterson
Composition/Color Separation • Progressive Typographers Inc.
Printing and Binding • R. R. Donnelley & Sons

Cover image: Elisabeth Vigée LeBrun, Self Portrait.
St. Petersburg, Hermitage Museum. Scala/Art Resource, NY.

Address for Editorial Correspondence
Harcourt Brace College Publishers
301 Commerce Street, Suite 3700
Fort Worth, Texas 76102

Address for Orders
Harcourt Brace & Company
6277 Sea Harbor Drive
Orlando, FL 32887
1-800-782-4479, or 1-800-433-0001 (in Florida)

Printed in the United States of America

Library of Congress Catalog Card Number 92-75576

ISBN 0-15-500195-7

4567890123 048 987654321

Preface

In the first edition of this book we set out our aim: to create a readable and reliable textbook for college and university students in the integrated humanities that would satisfy the needs of the students and the standards of their instructors. We hoped to describe the most important landmarks of Western civilization's cultural heritage as enthusiastically as we could so that students would learn to love and appreciate them as we did when we first studied them ourselves.

We trust that our basic philosophy in preparing this book still shows forth in this third edition. We are still convinced of the need to use an historical approach to the humanities. We still believe that the text should focus fundamentally on the Western tradition, even if we try to remind ourselves that culture is not so neatly packaged. We are unapologetic about our focus on high culture—since that is the heritage which has shaped our civilization, for better or worse. Finally, we have held to our principle of selectivity both because we did not want this book to look like a catalogue and because we feel that fewer things understood well can stand as a springboard for broader understanding. Behind all of these convictions is our strong conviction that any textbook should be the first word and not the final one. We trust in the teacher to explain what we have left unexplained and to speak where we have been silent.

In the more than ten-year period since the first edition appeared we have enjoyed the contact with students and teachers who have used the books and given us their reactions, generous in their praise and pointed in their criticisms, as they have tried to make our book their own. In that period, as we have predicted in the first preface, we also anticipated that deficiencies, omissions, errors of fact, and unsubtle judgments would be found. And so they were. We are grateful for those criticisms just as we were chagrined by our mistakes. We trust that this new edition will respond to those criticisms and suggestions. We have taken them seriously and have tried to be responsive to them.

The decision to do a third edition of the book was made in late 1990 after the entire work was reviewed both by users and those who had no previous acquaintance with it. Their criticisms, our own discussions, and consultations with the Harcourt Brace editors form the critical background for this third edition. *Culture and Values* is still here, but some significant changes and additions have been made.

We have added new material on Islam. We have also added greater material to single out the role of women in our story and have attempted to respond to the needs of cultural diversity, especially in the later chapters. Many reviewers have requested more material on popular culture. We do not want our text to shift from a consideration of the humanistic tradition to one of social history, but we did add some boxes on "sports and games" to signal the ways in which we are near neighbors of our common ancestors. Our tendency is not to stray from the West because we cannot do full justice to the great civilization(s) which are not our own. We wish to be faithful to the subtitle of this work. To attempt a discussion of the other great civilizations of the world—whether those of Africa or the traditions of Asia—would not require a revision; it would require a new work; one which we do not feel competent to produce within the framework of what we present here.

We are now left with the happy task of expressing our gratitude to those who have helped us in preparing this third edition.

Special thanks go to Barbara Rosenberg, acquisitions editor; Terri House, developmental editor; Laura Hanna, project editor; Debra Jenkin, production manager; Don Fujimoto, senior art director; and Elsa Peterson, photo/permissions editor. We would also like to acknowledge the reviewers of the third edition: Deborah Patterson, Edison Community College; Timothy W. Ulman, Palomar College; Ira Holmes, Central Florida Community College; Stewart J. Day, Southwest State University; Kurt E. Blaugher, Mount Saint Mary's College; Gwen S. Sell, Macon College; John Wickersham, Maryville College; Armand E. Vorce, University of Southern Colorado; Sally Souder, St. Louis Community College; Arthur R. Bassett, Brigham Young University; Barbara Tomlinson, Kean College of New Jersey; Barbara Kramer, Santa Fe Community College; Charles H. Cudney, Walla Walla Community College; Jan De Cosmo, Florida A & M University; Gilbert Prince, California State University, Chico; Lillian Schanfield, Barry University; Phyllis J. Kozlowski, Moraine Valley Community College; Sandra Burns, San Diego Mesa College; Janice L. Allen, Seminole Community College; Barbara Van Sittert, Phoenix College; Gae Elder, Abraham Baldwin Agricultural College; Thomas Parker, California State University, Chico; Elizabeth F. Pennington, Santa Fe Community College; Catherine Cheal, California State University, Northridge; LaNelle Witt, Eastern New Mexico University, Roswell.

Finally, we are grateful to all of the teachers and students who have used *Culture and Values* over the years. In a very basic sense, this book is theirs.

LSC

JJR

Contents

THE ARTS:
AN INTRODUCTION

One way to see the arts as a whole is to consider a widespread mutual experience: a church or synagogue service. Such a gathering is a celebration of written literature done, at least in part, in music in an architectural setting decorated to reflect the religious sensibilities of the community. A church service makes use of visual arts, literature, and music. While the service acts as an integrator of the arts, considered separately, each art has its own peculiar characteristics that give it shape.

Music is primarily a temporal art, which is to say that there is music when there is someone to play the instruments and sing the songs. When the performance is over, the music stops.

The visual *arts* and *architecture* are spatial arts that have permanence. When a religious service is over, people may still come into the building to admire its architecture or marvel at its paintings or sculptures or look at the decorative details of the building.

Literature has a permanent quality in that it is recorded in books, although some literature is meant not to be read but to be heard. Shakespeare did not write plays for people to read but for audiences to see and hear performed. Books nonetheless have permanence in the sense that they can be read not only in a specific context but also at one's pleasure. Thus, to continue the religious service example, one can read the psalms for their poetry or for devotion apart from their communal use in worship.

What we have said about the religious service applies equally to anything from a rock concert to grand opera: artworks can be seen as an integrated whole. Likewise, we can consider these arts separately. After all, people paint paintings, compose music, or write poetry to be enjoyed as discrete experiences. At other times, of course, two arts may be joined when there was no original intention to do so, as when a composer sets a poem to music or an artist finds inspiration in a literary text or, to use a more complex example, when a ballet is inspired by a literary text and is danced against the background or sets created by an artist to enhance both the dance and the text that inspired it.

However we view the arts, either separately or as integrated, one thing is clear: they are the product of human invention and human genius. When we speak of *culture,* we are not talking about something strange or "highbrow"; we are talking about something that derives from human invention. A jungle is a product of nature, but a garden is a product of culture: human ingenuity has modified the vegetative world.

In this book we discuss some of the works of human culture that have endured over the centuries. We often refer to these works as *masterpieces,* but what does the term mean? The issue is complicated because taste and attitudes change over the centuries. Two hundred years ago the medieval cathedral was not appreciated; it was called Gothic because it was considered barbarian. Today we call such a building a masterpiece. Very roughly we can say that a masterpiece of art is any work that carries with it a surplus of meaning.

Having "surplus of meaning" means that a certain work not only reflects technical and imaginative skill but also that its very existence sums up the best of a certain age, which spills over as a source of inspiration for further ages. As one reads through the history of the Western humanistic achievement it is clear that certain products of human genius are looked to by subsequent generations as a source of inspiration; they have a surplus of meaning. Thus the Roman achievement in architecture with the dome of the Pantheon both symbolized their skill in architecture and became a reference point for every major dome built in the West since. The dome of the Pantheon finds echoes in 6th-century Constantinople (Hagia Sophia); in 15th-century Florence (the Duomo); in 16th-century Rome (St. Peter's); and in 18th-century Washington, D.C. (the Capitol building).

The notion of surplus of meaning provides us with a clue as to how to study the humanistic tradition and its achievements. Admittedly simplifying, we can say that such a study has two steps that we have tried to synthesize into a whole in this book:

1. **The work in itself.** At this level we are asking the question of fact and raising the issue of observation: What is the work and how is it achieved? This question includes not only the basic information about, say, what kind of visual art this is (sculpture, painting, mosaic) or what its formal elements are (Is it geometric in style? bright in color? very linear? and so on) but also questions of its function: Is this work an homage to politics? for a private patron? for a church? We look at artworks, then, to ask questions about both their form and their function.

This is an important point. We may look at a painting or sculpture in a museum with great pleasure, but that pleasure would be all the more enhanced were we to see that work in its proper setting rather than as an object on display. To ask about form and function, in short, is to ask equally about context. When reading certain literary works (such as the *Iliad* or the *Song of Roland*) we should read them aloud since, in their original form, they were written to be recited, not read silently on a page.

2. **The work in relation to history.** The human achievements of our common past tell us much about earlier cultures both in their differences and in their similarities. A study of the tragic plays that have survived from ancient Athens gives us a glimpse into Athenians' problems, preoccupations, and aspirations as filtered through the words of Sophocles or Euripides. From such a study we learn both about the culture of Athens and something about how the human spirit has faced the perennial issues of justice, loyalty, and duty. In that sense we are in dialogue with our ancestors across the ages. In the study of ancient culture we see the roots of our own.

To carry out such a project requires willingness really to look at art and closely read literature with an eye equally to the aspect of form/function and to the past and the present. Music, however, requires a special treatment because it is the most abstract of arts (How do we speak about that which is meant not to be seen but to be heard?) and the most temporal. For that reason a somewhat more extended guide to music follows.

HOW TO LOOK AT ART

Anyone who thumbs through a standard history of art can be overwhelmed by the complexity of what is discussed. We find everything from paintings on the walls of caves and huge sculptures carved into the faces of mountains to tiny pieces of jewelry or miniature paintings. All of these are art because they were made by the human hand in an attempt to express human ideas and/or emotions. Our response to such objects depends a good deal on our own education and cultural biases. We may find some modern art ugly or stupid or bewildering. We may think of all art as highbrow or elitist despite the fact that we like certain movies (film is an art) enough to see them over and over.

Our lives are so bound up with art that we often fail to recognize how much we are shaped by it. We are bombarded with examples of graphic art (television commercials, magazine ads, CD jackets, displays in stores) every day; we use art to make statements about who we are and what we value in the way we decorate our rooms and in the style of our dress. In all of these ways we manipulate artistic symbols to make statements about what we believe in, what we stand for, and how we want others to see us.

The history of art is nothing more than the record of how people have used their minds and imaginations to symbolize who they are and what they value. If a certain age spends enormous amounts of money to build and decorate churches (as in 12th-century France) and another spends the same kind of money on palaces (like 18th-century France) we learn about what each age values the most.

The very complexity of human art makes it difficult to interpret. That difficulty increases when we are looking at art from a much different culture and/or a far different age. We may admire the massiveness of Egyptian architecture but find it hard to appreciate why such energies were used for the cult of the dead. When confronted with the art of another age (or even our own art, for that matter) a number of questions we can ask of ourselves and of the art may lead us to greater understanding.

For what was this piece of art made? This is essentially a question of *context*. Most of the religious paintings in our museums were originally meant to be seen in churches in very specific settings. To imagine them in their original setting helps us to understand that they had a devotional purpose that is lost when they are seen on a museum wall. To ask about the original setting, then, helps us to ask further whether the painting is in fact devotional or meant as a teaching tool or to serve some other purpose.

Setting is crucial. A frescoed wall on a public building is meant to be seen by many people while a fresco on the wall of an aristocratic home is meant for a much smaller, more elite, class of viewer. A sculpture designed for a wall niche is going to have a shape different from one designed to be seen by walking around it. Similarly, art made under official sponsorship of an authoritarian government must be read in a far different manner than art produced by underground artists who have no standing with the government. Finally, art may be purely decorative or it may have a didactic purpose, but (and here is a paradox) purely decorative art may teach us while didactic art may end up being purely decorative.

What, if anything, does this piece of art hope to communicate? This question is one of *intellectual* or *emotional* context. Funeral sculpture may reflect the grief of the survivors or a desire to commemorate the achievements of the deceased or to affirm what the survivors believe about life after death or a combination of these purposes. If we think of art as a variety of speech we can then inquire of any artwork: What is it saying?

An artist may strive for an ideal ("I want to paint the most beautiful woman in the world" or "I wish my painting to be taken for reality itself" or "I wish to move people to love or hate or sorrow by my sculpture") or to illustrate the power of an idea or (as is the case with most primitive art) to "capture" the power of the spirit world for religious and/or magical purposes.

An artist may well produce a work simply to demonstrate inventiveness or to expand the boundaries of what art means. The story is told of Pablo Picasso's reply to a woman who said that her ten-year-old child could paint better than he. Picasso replied, "Congratulations, Madame. Your child is a genius." We know that before he was a teenager Picasso could draw and paint with photographic accuracy. He said that during his long life he tried to learn how to paint with the fresh eye and spontaneous simplicity of a child.

How was this piece of art made? This question inquires into both the materials and the skills the artist employs to turn materials into art. Throughout this book we will speak of different artistic techniques, like bronze casting or etching or panel painting; here we make a more general point. To learn to appreciate the *craft* of the artist is a first step toward enjoying art for its worth as art—to developing an "eye" for art. This requires *looking* at the object as a crafted object. Thus, for example, a close examination of Michelangelo's *Pietà* shows the pure smooth beauty of marble while his *Slaves* demonstrate the roughness of stone and the sculptor's effort to carve meaning from hard material. We might stand back to admire a painting as a whole, but then to look closely at one portion of it teaches us the subtle manipulation of color and line that creates the overall effect.

What is the composition of this artwork? This question addresses how the artist "composes" the work. Much Renaissance painting uses a pyramidal construction so that the most important figure is at the apex of the pyramid and lesser figures form the base. Some paintings presume something happening outside the picture itself (such as an unseen source of light); a cubist painting tries to render simultaneous views of an object. At other times, an artist may enhance the composition by the manipulation of color with a movement from light to dark or a stark contrast between dark and light, as in the *chiaroscuro* of Baroque painting. In all these cases the artists intend to do something more than merely "depict" a scene; they appeal to our imaginative and intellectual powers as we enter into the picture or engage the sculpture or look at their film.

Composition, obviously, is not restricted to painting. Filmmakers compose with close-ups or tracking shots just as sculptors carve for frontal or side views of an object. Since all these techniques are designed to make us see in a particular manner, only by thinking about composition do we begin to reflect on what the artist has done. If we do not think about composition, we tend to take an artwork at "face value" and, as a consequence, are not training our "eye."

What elements should we notice about a work of art? The answer to this question is a summary of what we have stated above. Without pretending to exclusivity, we should judge art on the basis of the following three aspects:

Formal elements. What kind of artwork is it? What materials are employed? What is its composition in terms of structure? In terms of pure form, how does this particular work look when compared to a similar work of the same or another artist?

Symbolic elements. What is this artwork attempting to "say"? Is its purpose didactic, propagandistic, to give pleasure, or what? How well do the formal elements contribute to the symbolic statement being attempted in the work of art?

Social elements. What is the context of this work of art? Who is paying for it and why? Whose purposes does it serve? At this level many different philosophies come into play. A Marxist critic might judge a work in terms of its sense of class or economic aspects, while a feminist might inquire whether it affirms women or acts as an agent of subjugation and/or exploitation.

It is possible to restrict oneself to formal criticism of an artwork (Is this well done in terms of craft and composition?), but such an approach does not do full justice to what the artist is trying to do. Conversely, to judge every work purely in terms of social theory excludes the notion of an artistic work and, as a consequence, reduces art to politics or philosophy. For a fuller appreciation of art, then, all the elements mentioned above need to come into play.

HOW TO LISTEN TO MUSIC

The sections of this book devoted to music are designed for readers who have no special training in musical theory and practice. Response to significant works of music, after all, should require no more specialized knowledge than the ability to respond to *Oedipus Rex,* say, or a Byzantine mosaic. Indeed, many millions of people buy recorded music in one form or another, or enjoy listening to it on the radio, without the slightest knowledge of how the music is constructed or performed.

The gap between the simple pleasure of the listener and the complex skills of composer and performer often prevents the development of a more serious grasp of music history and its relation to the other arts. The aim of this section is to help bridge that gap without trying to provide too much technical information. After a brief survey of music's role in Western culture we shall look at the "language" used to discuss musical works, both specific terminology, such as *sharp* and *flat,* and more general concepts, such as line and color.

Music in Western Culture

The origins of music are unknown, and neither the excavations of ancient instruments and depictions of performers nor the evidence from modern primitive societies gives any impression of its early stages. Presumably, like the early cave paintings, it served some kind of magical or ritual purpose. This is borne out by the fact that music still forms a vital part of most religious ceremonies today, from the hymns sung in Christian churches or the solo singing of the cantor in an Orthodox Jewish synagogue to the elaborate musical rituals performed in Buddhist or Shinto temples in Japan. The Old Testament makes many references to the power of music, most notably in the famous story of the battle of Jericho, and it is clear that by historical times music played an important role in Jewish life, both sacred and secular.

By the time of the Greeks, the first major Western culture to develop, music had become as much a science as an art. It retained its importance for religious rituals; in fact, according to Greek mythology the gods themselves invented it. At the same time the theoretical relationships between the various musical pitches attracted the attention of philosophers such as Pythagoras (c. 550 B.C.), who described the underlying unity of the universe as the "harmony of the spheres." Later 4th-century-B.C. thinkers like Plato and Aristotle emphasized music's power to affect human feeling and behavior. Thus for the Greeks music represented a religious, intellectual, and moral force. Once again, music is still used in our own world to affect people's feelings, whether it be the stirring sound of a march, a solemn funeral dirge, or the eroticism of much modern "pop" music (of which Plato would thoroughly have disapproved).

Virtually all the music—and art, for that matter—to have survived from the Middle Ages is religious. Popular secular music certainly existed, but since no real system of notation was invented before the 11th century, it has disappeared without trace. The ceremonies of both the Western and the Eastern (Byzantine) church centered around the chanting of a single musical line, a kind of music that is called *monophonic* (from the Greek "single voice"). Around the time musical notation was devised, composers began to become interested in the possibilities of notes sounding simultaneously—what we would think of as harmony. Music involving several separate lines sounding together (as in a modern string quartet or a jazz group) became popular only in the 14th century. This gradual introduction of *polyphony* ("many voices") is perhaps the single most important development in the history of music, since composers began to think not only horizontally (that is, melodically) but also vertically, or harmonically. In the process the possibilities of musical expression were immeasurably enriched.

The Experience of Listening

"What music expresses is eternal, infinite, and ideal. It does *not* express the passion, love, or longing of this or that individual in this or that situation, but passion, love, or longing in itself; and this it presents in that unlimited variety of motivations which is the exclusive and particular characteristic of music, foreign and inexpressible in any other language" (Richard Wagner). With these words one of the greatest of all composers described the power of music to express universal emotions. Yet for those unaccustomed to serious listening, it is precisely this breadth of experience that is difficult to identify with. We can understand a joyful or tragic situation. Joy and tragedy themselves, though, are more difficult to comprehend.

There are a number of ways by which the experience of listening can become more rewarding and more enjoyable. Not all of them will work for everyone, but over the course of time they have proved helpful for many newcomers to the satisfactions of music.

1. *Before listening* to the piece you have selected, ask yourself some questions:

What is the historical context of the music? For whom was it composed—for a general or for an elite audience?

Did the composer have a specific assignment? If the work was intended for performance in church, for example, it should sound very different from a set of dances. Sometimes the location of the performance affected the sound of the music: composers of masses to be sung in Gothic cathedrals used the buildings' acoustical properties to emphasize the resonant qualities of their works.

With what forces is the music to be performed? Do they correspond to those intended by the composer? Performers of medieval music, in particular, often have to reconstruct much that is missing or uncertain. Even in the case of later traditions, the original sounds can sometimes be only approximated. The superstars of the 18th-century world of opera were the *castrati,* male singers who had been castrated in their youth and whose voices had therefore never broken; contemporaries described the sounds they produced as incomparably brilliant and flexible. The custom, which seems to us so barbaric, was abandoned in the 19th century, and even the most fanatic musicologist must settle for a substitute today. The case is an extreme one, but it points the moral that even with the best of intentions, modern performers cannot always reproduce the original sounds.

Does the work have a text? If so, read it through before you listen to the music; it is easiest to concentrate on one thing at a time. In the case of a translation, does the version you are using capture the spirit of the original? Translators sometimes take a simple, popular lyric and make it sound archaic and obscure in order to convey the sense of "old" music. If the words do not make much sense to you, probably they would seem equally incomprehensible to the composer. Music, of all the arts, is concerned with direct communication.

Is the piece divided into sections? If so, why? Is their relationship determined by purely musical considerations—the structure of the piece—or by external factors, the words of a song, for example, or the parts of a Mass?

Finally, given all the above, what do you expect the music to sound like? Your preliminary thinking should have prepared you for the kind of musical experience in store for you. If it has not, go back and reconsider some of the points above.

2. *While you are listening* to the music:

Concentrate as completely as you can. It is virtually impossible to gain much from music written in an unfamiliar idiom unless you give it your full attention. Read written information before you begin to listen, as you ask yourself the questions above, not *while* the music is playing. If there is a text, keep an eye on it but do not let it distract you from the music.

Concentrating is not always easy, particularly if you are mainly used to listening to music as a background, but there are some ways in which you can help your own concentration. To avoid visual distraction, fix your eyes on some detail near you—a mark on the wall, a design in someone's dress, the cover of a book. At first this will seem artificial, but after a while your attention should be taken by the music. If you feel your concentration fading, do *not* pick up a magazine or gaze around; consciously force your attention back to the music and try to analyze what you are hearing. Does it correspond to your expectations? How is the composer trying to achieve an effect? By variety of instrumental color? Are any of the ideas, or tunes, repeated?

Unlike literature or the visual arts, music occurs in the dimension of time. When you are reading, you can turn backward to check a reference or remind yourself of a character's identity. In looking at a painting, you can move from a detail to an overall view as often as you want. In music, the speed of your attention is controlled by the composer. Once you lose the thread of the discourse, you cannot regain it by going back; you must try to pick up again and follow the music as it continues—and that requires your renewed attention.

On the other hand, in these times of easy access to recordings, the same pieces can be listened to repeatedly. Even the most experienced musicians cannot grasp some works fully without several hearings. Indeed, one of the features that distinguishes "art" music from more "popular" works is its capacity to yield increasing rewards. On a first hearing, therefore, try to grasp the general mood and structure and note features to listen for the next time you hear the piece. Do not be discouraged if the idiom seems strange or remote, and be prepared to become familiar with a few works from each period you are studying.

As you become accustomed to serious listening, you will notice certain patterns used by composers to give form to their works. They vary according to the styles of the day, and throughout this book there are descriptions of each period's musical characteristics. In responding to the general feeling the music expresses, therefore, you should try to note the specific features that identify the time of its composition.

3. *After you have heard the piece,* ask yourself these questions:

Which characteristics of the music indicated the period of its composition? Were they due to the forces employed (voices and/or instruments)?

How was the piece constructed? Did the composer make use of repetition? Was there a change of mood and, if so, did the original mood return at the end?

What kind of melody was used? Was it continuous or did it divide into a series of shorter phrases?

If a text was involved, how did the music relate to the words? Were they audible? Did the composer intend them to be? If not, why not?

Were there aspects of the music that reminded you of the literature and visual arts of the same period? In what kind of buildings can you imagine it being performed? What does it tell you about the society for which it was written?

Finally, ask yourself the most difficult question of all: What did the music express? Richard Wagner described the meaning of music as "foreign and inexpressible in any other language." There is no dictionary of musical meaning, and listeners must interpret for themselves what they hear. We all understand the general significance of words like *contentment* or *despair,* but music can distinguish between a million shades of each.

Concepts in Music

There is a natural tendency in talking about the arts to use terms from one art form in describing another. Thus most people would know what to expect from a "colorful" story or a painting in "quiet" shades of blue. This metaphorical use of language helps describe characteristics that are otherwise often very difficult to isolate, but some care is required to remain within the general bounds of comprehension.

Line. In music, *line* generally means the progression in time of a series of notes: the melody. A melody in music is a succession of tones related to one another to form a complete musical thought. Melodies vary in length and in shape and may be made up of several smaller parts. They may move quickly or slowly, smoothly or with strongly accented (stressed) notes. Some melodies are carefully balanced and proportional, others are irregular and asymmetrical. A melodic line dictates the basic character of a piece of music, just as lines do in a painting or the plot line does for a story or play.

Texture. The degree to which a piece of music has a thick or thin *texture* depends on the number of voices and/or instruments involved. Thus the monophonic music of the Middle Ages, with its single voice, has the thinnest texture possible. At the opposite extreme is a 19th-century opera, where half a dozen soloists, chorus, and a large orchestra were sometimes combined. Needless to say, thickness and thinness of texture are neither good nor bad in themselves, merely simple terms of description.

Composers control the shifting texture of their works in several ways. The number of lines heard simultaneously can be increased or reduced—a full orchestral climax followed by a single flute, for example. The most important factor in the texture of the sound, however, is the number of combined independent melodic lines; this playing (or singing) together of two or more separate melodies is called *counterpoint.* Another factor influencing musical texture is the vertical arrangement of the notes: six notes played close together low in the scale will sound thicker than six notes more widely distributed.

Color. The color, or *timbre,* of a piece of music is determined by the instruments or voices employed. Gregorian chant is monochrome, having only one line. The modern symphony orchestra has a vast range to draw upon, from the bright sound of the oboe or the trumpet to the dark, mellow sound of the cello or French horn. Some composers have been more interested than others in exploiting the range of color instrumental combinations can produce; not surprisingly, Romantic music provides some of the most colorful examples.

Medium. The *medium* is the method of performance. Pieces can be written for solo piano, string quartet, symphony orchestra, or any other combination the composer chooses. A prime factor will be the importance of color in the work. Another is the length and seriousness of the musical material. It is difficult, although not impossible, for a piece written for solo violin to sustain the listener's interest for half an hour. Still another is the practicality of performance. Pieces using large or unusual combinations of instruments stand less chance of being frequently programmed. In the 19th century composers often chose a medium that allowed performance in the home, thus creating a vast piano literature.

Form. *Form* is the outward, visible (or hearable) shape of a work as opposed to its substance (medium) or color. This structure can be created in a number of ways. Baroque composers worked according to the principle of unity in variety. In most Baroque movements the principal melodic idea continually recurs in the music, and the general texture remains consistent. The formal basis of much classical music is contrast, where two or more melodies of differing character (hard and soft, or brilliant and sentimental) are first laid out separately, then developed and combined, then separated again. The Romantics often pushed the notion of contrasts to extremes, although retaining the basic notions of classical form. Certain types of work dictate their own form. A composer writing a requiem mass is clearly less free to experiment with formal variation than one writing a piece for symphony orchestra. The words of a song strongly suggest the structure of the music, even if they do not impose it. Indeed, so pronounced was the Baroque sense of unity that the sung arias in Baroque operas inevitably conclude with a repetition of the words and music of the beginning, even if the character's mood or emotion has changed.

Thus music, like the other arts, involves the general concepts described above. A firm grasp of them is essential to an understanding of how the various arts have changed and developed over the centuries and how the changes are reflected in similarities—or differences—between art forms. The concept of the humanities implies that the arts did not grow and change in isolation from one another or from the world around. As this book shows, they are integrated both among themselves and with the general developments of Western thought and history.

HOW TO READ LITERATURE

"Reading literature" conjures up visions of someone sitting in an armchair with glasses on and nose buried in a thick volume—say, Tolstoy's *War and Peace.* The plain truth is that a fair amount of the literature found in this book was never meant to be read that way at all. Once that fact is recognized, reading becomes an exercise in which different methods can serve as a great aid for both pleasure and understanding. That becomes clear when we consider various literary forms and ask ourselves how their authors originally meant them to be encountered. Let us consider some of the forms that will be studied in this volume to make the point more specifically:

Dramatic literature. This is the most obvious genre of literature that calls for something more than reading the text quietly. Plays—ancient, medieval, Elizabethan, or modern—are meant to be acted, with living voices interpreting what the playwright wrote in the script. What seems to be strange and stilted language as we first encounter Shakespeare becomes powerful and beautiful when we hear his words spoken by someone who knows and loves language.

A further point: Until relatively recent times most dramas were played on stages nearly bare of scenery and, obviously, extremely limited in terms of lighting, theatrical devices, and the like. As a consequence, earlier texts contain a great deal of description that in the modern theater (and, even more, in a film) can be supplied by current technology. Where Shakespeare has a character say "But look, the morn in russet mantle clad/Walks o'er the dew of yon high eastward hill," a modern writer might simply instruct the lighting manager to make the sun come up.

Dramatic literature must be approached with a sense of its oral aspect as well as an awareness that the language reflects the intention of the author to have the words acted out. Dramatic language is meant to be *heard* and *seen.*

Epic. Like drama, epics have a strong oral background. It is a commonplace to note that before Homer's *Iliad* took its present form it was memorized and recited by a professional class of bards. Similarly, the *Song of Roland* was probably heard by many people and read by relatively few in the formative decades of its composition. Even epics that are more consciously literary echo the oral background of the epic; Vergil begins his elegant *Aeneid* with the words "Arms and the man I sing" not "Of Arms and the man I write."

The practical conclusion to be drawn from this is that these long poetic tales take on a greater power when they are read aloud with sensitivity to their cadence.

Poetry. Under this general heading we have a very complicated subject. To approach poetry with intelligence we need to inquire about the kind of poetry with which we are dealing. The lyrics of songs are poems, but they are better heard sung than read in a book. On the other hand, certain kinds of poems are so arranged on a page that not to see them in print is to miss a good deal of their power or charm. Furthermore, some poems are meant for the individual reader while others are public pieces meant for the group. There is, for example, a vast difference between a love sonnet and a biblical psalm. Both are examples of poetry, but the former expresses a private emotion while the latter most likely gets its full energy from use in worship: we can imagine a congregation singing a psalm but not the same congregation reciting one of Petrarch's sonnets to Laura.

In poetry, then, context is all. Our appreciation of a poem is enhanced once we have discovered where the poem belongs: with music? on a page? for an aristocratic circle of intellectuals? as part of a national or ethnic or religious heritage? as propaganda or protest or to express deep emotions?

At base, however, poetry is the refined use of language. The poet is the maker of words. Our greatest appreciation of a poem comes when we say to ourselves that this could not be said better. An authentic poem cannot be edited or paraphrased or glossed. Poetic language, even in long poems, is economical. One can understand that by simple experiment: take one of Dante's portraits in *The Divine Comedy* and try to do a better job of description in fewer words. The genius of Dante (or Chaucer in the *Prologue* to *The Canterbury Tales*) is his ability to sketch out a fully formed person in a few stanzas.

Prose. God created humans, the writer Elie Wiesel once remarked, because he loves a good story. Narrative is as old as human history. The stories that stand behind the *Decameron* and *The Canterbury Tales* have been shown to have existed not only for centuries but in widely different cultural milieus. Stories are told to draw out moral examples or to instruct or warn, but, by and large, stories are told because we enjoy hearing them. We read novels in order to enter into a new world and suspend the workaday world we live in, just as we watch films for the same purpose. The difference between a story and a film is that one can linger over a story, but in a film there is no "second look."

Some prose obviously is not fictional. It can be autobiographical like Augustine's *Confessions* or it may be a philosophical essay like Jean-Paul Sartre's attempt to explain what he means by existentialism. How do we approach that kind of writing? First, with a willingness to listen to what is being said. Second, with a readiness to judge: Does this passage ring true? What objections might I make to it? and so on. Third, with an openness that says, in effect, there is something to be learned here.

A final point has to do with attitude. We live in an age in which much of what we know comes to us in very brief "sound bites" via television and much of what we read comes to us in the disposable form of newspapers and magazines and inexpensive paperbacks. To read—*really* to read—requires that we discipline ourselves to cultivate a more leisurely approach to that art. There is merit in speed-reading the morning sports page; there is no merit in doing the same with a poem or a short story. It may take time to learn to slow down and read at a leisurely pace (leisure is the basis of culture, says Aristotle), but if we learn to do so we have taught ourselves a skill that will enrich us all our lives.

CULTURE AND VALUES

PREHISTORY	EGYPT

PREHISTORY

2,000,000 B.C.

Paleolithic Period (Old Stone Age)

c. 100,000 First ritual burying of dead

c. 30,000–25,000 *Venus of Willendorf;* worship of female creative power

c. 15,000–10,000 Cave art at Lascaux and Altamira

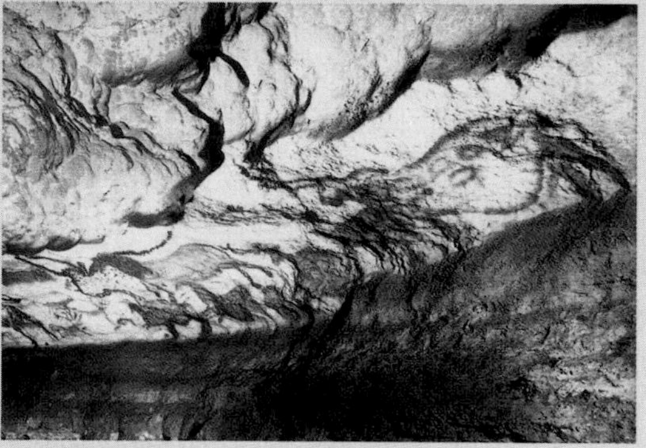

Hunting predominates

Stone weapons

8000

Neolithic Period (Late Stone Age)

Domestication of animals; cultivation of food

Villages formed

First wars

c. 5000 Beginnings of civilization. Pottery invented

First large-scale architecture; bronze tools

3000

Most dates are approximate

EGYPT

8000 B.C.

Neolithic Period

3200–2700 PREDYNASTIC PERIOD

c. 3100 Development of hieroglyphic writing

3000

Bronze Age

2700–2250 OLD KINGDOM: development of mummification ritual; art reflects confidence and certainty

c. 2650 Imhotep constructs first pyramid for King Zoser at Saqqara

2650–2514 Great Pyramids and Sphinx built at Giza

c. 2470 *Seated Scribe,* from Saqqara

2250–1990 FIRST INTERMEDIATE PERIOD

1990–1790 MIDDLE KINGDOM: art reflects new uncertainty

c. 1900 "Song of the Harper"

c. 1878–1841 Reign of Sesostris III; Portrait: *Sesostris III*

1790–1570 SECOND INTERMEDIATE PERIOD

1570–1185 NEW KINGDOM

1364–1347 Reign of Amenhotep IV (Akhenaton); religious and political reform; worship of single god Aton; capital moved from Thebes to Tel el-Amarna; naturalism in art

c. 1370 Portrait: *Nefertiti;* Akhenaton, "Hymn to Aton"

1361–1352 Reign of Tutankhamen; return to conservatism

1298–1232 Reign of Ramses II; colossal buildings constructed at Luxor, Karnak, Abu Simbel

1185–500 LATE PERIOD: Egypt's power declines; artists revert to Old Kingdom styles

1000

Iron Age

671–663 Assyrian occupation of Egypt

600

CHAPTER 1 THE BEGINNINGS OF CIVILIZATION

MESOPOTAMIA	AEGEAN WORLD
3500–2350 SUMERIAN PERIOD: development of pictographic writing; construction of first ziggurats; cult of mother goddess	**c. 6000** Introduction of new agricultural techniques from the East

MESOPOTAMIA

c. 3000 *Lady of Warka*

c. 2700 Reign of Gilgamesh

c. 2600–2400 *Ram in a Thicket,* from Royal Cemetery at Ur

2350–2150 AKKADIAN PERIOD: rule of Sargon and descendants; ended by invasion of Gutians from Iran

2330–2320 *Head of Akkadian King,* probably Sargon

c. 2300 *Stele of Naram-Sin*

2150–1900 NEO-SUMERIAN PERIOD

2100–2000 Construction of ziggurat at Ur

c. 2100 Gudea, governor of Lagash

c. 2000 Earliest version of *The Epic of Gilgamesh*

1900–1600 BABYLONIAN PERIOD

1792–1750 *The Law Code of Hammurabi*

c. 1760 *Stele of Hammurabi*

1600–1150 KASSITE PERIOD

1150–612 ASSYRIAN PERIOD

883–859 Reign of Assurnasirpal II; palace at Nimrud

668–626 Reign of Assurbanipal; palace at Nineveh

612 Fall of Nineveh

559–529 Reign of Cyrus the Great; expansion of Persian Empire

AEGEAN WORLD

2800–2000 Early Minoan Period on Crete; growth of Cycladic culture

c. 2500 Cycladic idol

2000–1600 Middle Minoan Period on Crete; construction of palace complexes; development of linear writing

c. 1700 Knossos Palace destroyed by earthquake and rebuilt on grander scale; *Wasp Pendant,* from Mallia

1600–1400 Late Minoan Period on Crete

c. 1600 First Mycenaean palace constructed; Royal Grave Circle at Mycenae

c. 1600 *Snake Goddess,* from Knossos

c. 1550 Gold death mask, from Mycenae

1500 Frescoes from House Delta, Thera

1400 Fall of Knossos and decline of Minoan civilization

1400–1200 Mycenaean empire flourishes

1250 Mycenaean war against Troy

1100 Final collapse of Mycenaean power

1100–1000 DARK AGE

1000–750 HEROIC AGE

c. 900–700 Evolution of Homeric epics *Iliad* and *Odyssey*

750–600 AGE OF COLONIZATION

CHAPTER

1 THE BEGINNINGS OF CIVILIZATION

AROUND 5000 B.C. humans began to lay the bases for the growth of civilization. After millennia of hunting and gathering, the development of agriculture made possible for the first time the formation of settled communities.

Civilization is so broad a term that it is not easy to define simply. Nonetheless, societies which qualify for the label "civilized" generally possess at least the majority, if not all, of the following characteristics:

1. Some form of urban life involving the construction of permanent settlements—cities, in short.
2. A system of government which regulates political relations.
3. The development of distinct social classes, distinguished from one another by two related factors, wealth and occupation.
4. Tools and specialized skills for the production of goods, leading to the rise of manufacturing and trade.
5. Some form of written communication, making it possible to share and preserve information.
6. A shared system of religious belief, whose officials—or priests—often play a significant role in community affairs.

It is important to realize, at the beginning of our survey of Western civilization, that the term "civilized," when used in this anthropological sense, implies no value judgment as to the merits of a particular society. So-called "primitive" peoples are capable of producing valuable and lasting works of art, and of living full and satisfying lives, while, as the 20th century has shown, some of the most "civilized" societies in history can be responsible for causing indescribable human suffering. Furthermore, at the century's end, advanced industrial civilization seems increasingly in danger of destroying the environment, and making the world uninhabitable for any form of life, human or animal. The pages that follow chronicle the high achievements of Western civilization, but the grim background against which many of them appeared should never be forgotten. As the 18th-century philosopher Giambattista Vico observed, "advanced" civilizations can be barbaric in ways far more terrible than preliterate peoples.

The basic advances that made possible the growth of Western civilization were first achieved by the earlier civilizations of the ancient Middle East. These ancient peoples were the first who systematically produced food, mined and processed metals, organized themselves into cities, and devised legal and moral codes of behavior, together with systems of government and religion. In all these areas they had a profound influence on later peoples. At the same time they produced a major artistic tradition which, quite apart from its high intrinsic interest, was to have a number of effects on the development of Western art.

To discover the origins of Western civilization, therefore, we must look at cultures that at first seem remote in both time and place. Yet these peoples produced the achievements described in this chapter—achievements that form the background to the history of our own culture.

THE EARLIEST PEOPLE AND THEIR ART

Even the earliest civilizations appeared relatively late in human history, at the beginning of the period known as the Neolithic or Late Stone Age (c. 8000 B.C.). The process of human evolution is long and confusing, and many aspects of it remain uncertain. Our first ancestors probably appeared

1.1 Hall of Bulls, left wall, Lascaux (Dordogne), France. c. 15,000–10,000 B.C. Paintings like these were not intended to be decorations, since they are not in the inhabited parts of the caves but in the dark inner recesses. They probably had magical significance for their creators, who may have believed that gaining control of an animal in a painting would help to defeat it in the hunt.

between a million and half a million years ago in the Paleolithic period or Old Stone Age. For most of the succeeding millennia, people were dominated by the physical forces of geography and climate, able to keep themselves alive only by a persistent search for food and shelter. Those who chose the wrong places or the wrong methods did not survive, while others were preserved by their instincts or good fortune.

Primitive conditions hardly encouraged the growth of civilization, yet there is some evidence of a kind of intellectual development. Archaeological evidence has shown that about one hundred thousand years ago the ancestors of *Homo sapiens* belonging to the type known as Neanderthal people were the first to bury their dead carefully and place funerary offerings in the graves—the earliest indication of the existence of religious beliefs.

Toward the end of the Paleolithic period, around 15,000 B.C., there was a major breakthrough. The human desire for self-expression resulted in the invention of visual art. The cave paintings of Lascaux and Altamira and statuettes like the *Venus of Willendorf* are among the earliest products of the human creative urge. Although the art of this remote age would be valuable for its historical significance alone, many of the paintings and statues can stand as masterpieces in their own right. The lines are concentrated but immensely expressive. In some cases artists used the surface on which they were painting to create an added sense of realism—a bulge on a cave wall suggested the hump of a bull [1.1]. The combination of naturalistic observation and abstraction can only be described as sophisticated, and since their discovery in our own century the paintings have served as a powerful inspiration to modern eyes.

The choice of subjects tells us something about the worldview of Paleolithic people. The earliest cave paintings show animals and hunting, which played a vital part in providing food and clothing. More significant, perhaps, is the fact that all the oldest known statuettes of human figures represent women, who are shown with their sexual characteristics emphasized or enlarged [1.2]. The Paleolithic world perhaps saw woman's practical role—the source of birth and life—as symbolic of a more profound feminine force that underlay the masculine world of the hunt. Worship of female creative power was also to play an important part in the religion of the ancient Middle East and of Bronze Age Greece. Even though the Greeks of a later period emphasized other aspects of human power, reverence for a mother goddess or Earth Mother was to live on.

1.2 ***Venus of Willendorf.*** **Lower Austria, c. 30,000–25,000 B.C. Limestone, height 4⅜" (11 cm). Natural History Museum, Vienna. This tiny statuette is one of a series of female figurines from the Upper Paleolithic period that are known as Venus figures. The statuette, which has no facial features, is evidently a fertility symbol.**

The Neolithic period (c. 8000 B.C.) represents in all aspects a major break with the past. After a million years of hunting, ways to domesticate animals and cultivate food were discovered. People began to gather together in villages where they could lead a settled existence. The development of improved farming techniques made it possible for a community to accumulate stores of grain and thereby become less dependent for their survival on a good harvest each year. But these stores provided a motive for raids by neighboring communities. Thus war, for the first time in human history, became profitable. Other more constructive changes followed at a rapid pace. Pottery was invented around 5000 B.C. and not long afterward metal began to replace stone as the principal material for tools and weapons. The first metal used was copper, but it was soon discovered that an alloy of copper and tin would produce a much stronger metal, bronze. The use of bronze became widespread, giving its name to the Bronze Age, which lasted from around 3000 B.C. to the introduction of iron around 1000 B.C.

At the beginning of the Bronze Age, large-scale architecture began to appear. The fortified settlements that had been established in Egypt and Mesopotamia now were able to develop those aspects of existence which entitle them to be called the first true civilizations.

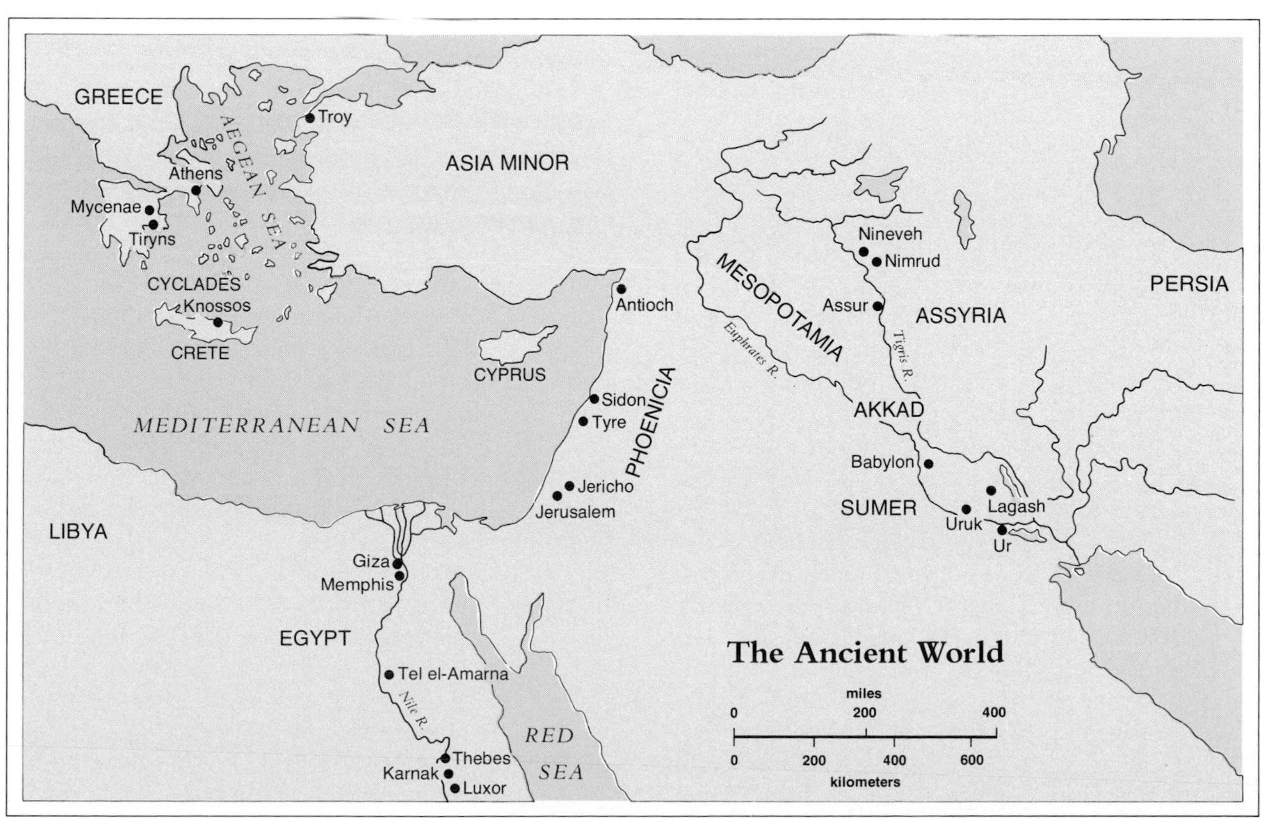

Egypt and Mesopotamia have much in common. Their climates are similar and both are dominated by great rivers, Egypt by the Nile and Mesopotamia by the Tigris and Euphrates (see map). Yet each was to develop its own distinct culture and make its own contribution to the history of civilization. Egypt is discussed first in the following account, but both areas developed over the same general time span.

Ancient Egypt

One major determinant in the development of ancient Egyptian culture was geography. In total area, ancient Egypt was only a little larger than the state of Maryland. At the delta of the Nile was Lower Egypt, broad and flat, within easy reach of neighboring parts of the Mediterranean. Upper Egypt, more isolated from foreign contacts, consisted of a long narrow strip of fertile soil, hemmed in by high cliffs and desert, running on either side of the Nile for most of its 1250 miles (2000 kilometers). Since rainfall was very sparse along the Nile, agriculture depended on the yearly flooding of the river.

The immensely long span of Egyptian history was divided into 31 dynasties by an Egyptian priest, Manetho, who wrote a *History of Egypt* in Greek around 280 B.C. Modern scholars still follow his system, putting the dynasties into four groups and calling the period that preceded them the Predynastic. The four main divisions, with their approximate dates, are: the Old Kingdom, c. 2700 B.C.; the Middle Kingdom, c. 1990 B.C.; the New Kingdom, c. 1570 B.C.; and the Late Period, c. 1185 B.C. until Egypt was absorbed into the Persian Empire around 500 B.C. The periods were separated from one another by intermediate times of disturbances and confusion.

During the last centuries of the Late Period, Egypt was invaded by the Nubians of the upper Nile, a black people whom the Egyptians called Cush. Overrunning first Upper Egypt in 750 B.C. and then Lower Egypt around 720 B.C., they and their successors, the Nobatae, helped to preserve Egyptian culture through the periods of foreign rule. The role played by these black peoples in the formation of the Western cultural tradition, in particular their influence on the Greeks, has recently become the focus of much scholarly discussion.

In spite of its long history, the most striking feature of Egyptian culture is its unity and consistency. Nothing is in stronger contrast to the process of dynamic change initiated by the Greeks and still characteristic of our own culture than the relative absence of change of Egyptian art, religion, language, and political structure over thousands of years. Naturally, even the Egyptians were subject to outside influences, and events at home and abroad affected their worldview. It is possible to trace a mood of increasing pessimism from the vital, life-affirming spirit of the Old Kingdom to the New Kingdom vision of death as an escape from the grim realities of life. Nevertheless, the Egyptians maintained a strong resistance to change. Their art, in particular, remained conservative and rooted in the past.

In a land where regional independence already existed in the natural separation of Upper from Lower Egypt, national unity was maintained by a strong central government firmly controlled by a single ruler, the pharaoh. He was regarded as a living god, the equal of any other deity. He had absolute power, although the execution of his orders depended on a large official bureaucracy whose influence tended to increase in time.

Beneath the pharaoh were the priests, who saw as their responsibility the preservation of traditional religious beliefs. One of the most fundamental of these was the concept of divine kingship involving the pharaoh himself, a belief that reflected the Egyptian view of creation. The first great god of Egyptian religion, the sun god Aton-Ra, had created the world by imposing order on the primeval chaos of the universe; in the same way, the pharaoh ordered and controlled the visible world.

The most striking aspect of Egyptian religious thought, however, is its obsession with immortality and the possibilities of life after death. All Egyptians, not only the ruling class, were offered the hope of survival in the next world as a reward for a good life in a form that was thought of in literal, physical terms. Elaborate funeral rituals at which the dead would be judged and passed as worthy to move on to the afterlife began to develop. The funeral rites, together with their meaning, were described in a series of sacred texts known collectively as the *Book of the Dead*. The god who presided over these ceremonies was Osiris [1.3]. The worship of Osiris, his wife Isis, and their son, the falcon god Horus, which came in time to symbolize a sense of spiritual afterlife, as opposed to simple material survival, represented the mystical side of Egyptian religion. Osiris himself, according to the myth, had been killed and then reborn; he owed his resurrection to the intervention of Isis, the dominant mother goddess of Egyptian religion, protectress of the living and dead. The worship of Isis became one of the most important and durable of Egyptian cults—a temple to her was found among the ruins of Roman Pompeii—while the return to life of Osiris provided a divine parallel to

1.3 Painted relief from the funerary temple of Sethos I at Abydos. c. 1300 B.C. Sethos in the guise of the god Osiris, standing at left, is conversing with Thoth, the ibis-headed god of writing.

the annual rebirth of the land caused by the flooding Nile.

At the same time the Egyptians worshiped a host of other deities, subdeities, and nature spirits whose names were often confused and sometimes interchangeable. These gods, responsible for all aspects of existence, inspired mythology and ritual that affected the daily life of every Egyptian. They included Hathor, the goddess of beauty and love, often represented as a cow; Bes, the god of war; and Hapi, the god of the Nile. A number of animals, like the jackal and the cat, also had special sacred significance (Table 1.1).

Traditional Egyptian religion involved, then, a bewildering confusion of figures whose rights and privileges were jealously guarded by their priests. One of the ways to worship them was to give them visible form in works of art—a principal function of Egyptian artists. In addition to producing images of deities, artists were required to provide temples and shrines where they could be honored. Even the buildings that commemorated the names and deeds of real people served religious purposes. Thus the same central authority that controlled religion affected the development of the arts. The pharaoh's court laid down the standards applied throughout Egypt. Individual artists had little opportunity to exercise their own ingenuity by deviating from them.

The Old and Middle Kingdoms

The huge scale of many Egyptian works of art is at least in part the result of the easy availability of stone, the most frequently used material from the early Old Kingdom to the Late Period. In the Third Dynasty, the architect Imhotep used stone to construct the earliest pyramid as a tomb for his master, the pharaoh Zoser. This began the tradition of building massive funerary monuments that would serve to guarantee immortality for their occupants. At the same time, the practice of mummification developed. The body was embalmed to maintain its physical form, since Egyptian religious belief held that preservation of the body was necessary for the survival of the soul. Imhotep himself, the first architect known to history, was in later ages regarded as the epitome of wisdom and was deified.

The great age of the pyramid came in the Fourth Dynasty with the construction of the three colossal pyramids at Giza for the pharaohs Cheops, Chefren, and Mycerinus [1.4]. In size and abstract simplicity, these structures show Egyptian skill in

TABLE 1.1 Principal Egyptian Deities

Aton-Ra	Sun God	Creator of Heaven and Earth
Osiris	King of the Underworld	Judge of the Dead
Isis	Sister and Wife of Osiris	Mourner of the Dead
Horus	Son of Isis and Osiris	God of the Morning Sun
Chensu	Moon God	Human-headed with crescent moon
Ptah	Father of the Gods	Created humans
Thoth	Ibis (bird) God	The Scribe of the Gods
Set	Brother of Osiris	Personification of Evil
Anubis	Jackal God	God of the Dead
Hapi	God of the Nile	Fertility God
Hathor	Cow Goddess	Sky Goddess
Seker	Hawk God	God of the Night Sun

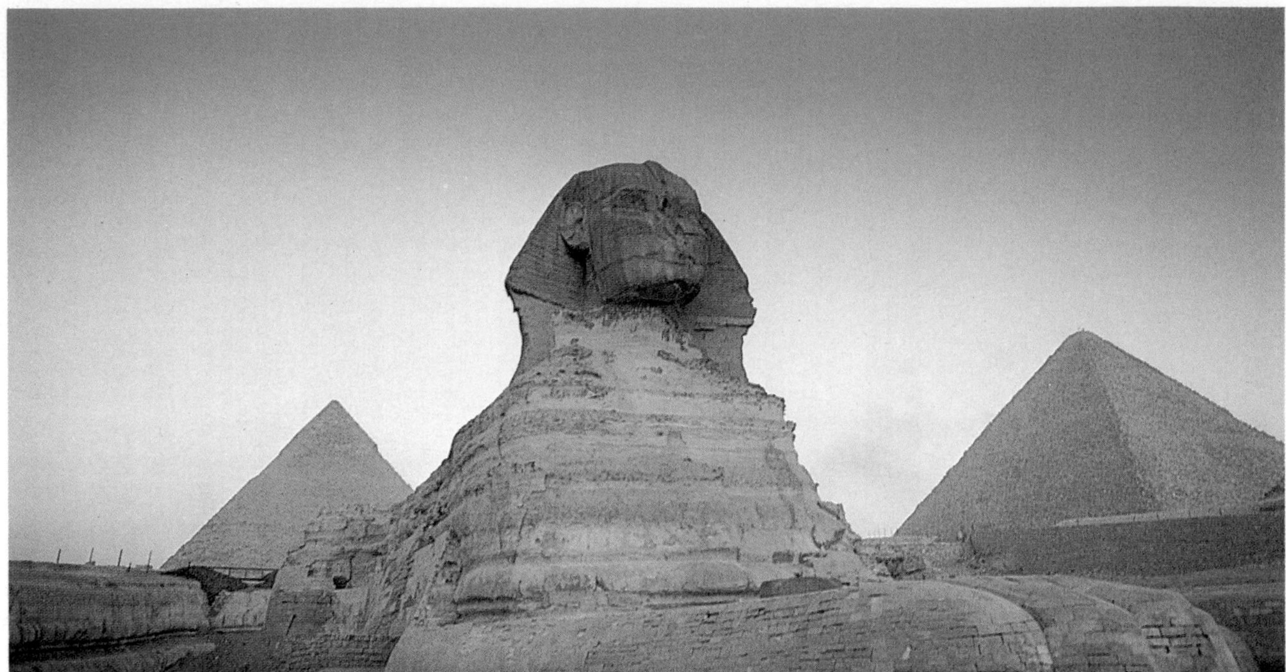

1.4 Sphinx at Giza. c. 2540–2514 B.C. Limestone, length 240' (73.2 m), height 65' (19.83 m). The lion's body symbolizes immortality. The pharaohs were often buried in lion skins. About 500 yards (457 meters) away is the Pyramid of Chefren.

design and engineering on a massive scale—an achievement probably made possible by slave labor, although some scholars believe that the building of the great monuments was essentially the work of farmers during the off season. In any case, the pyramids and almost all other Egyptian works of art perpetuate the memories of members of the upper classes, and bear witness to a life-style which would not have been possible without slaves.

We still know little about the slaves or the poor Egyptians who were farm laborers. Many of the slaves were captured prisoners, who were forced to labor in the government quarries and on the estates of the temples. Over time, the descendants of slaves could enlist in the army; as professional soldiers they could take their place in Egyptian society.

The construction of the pyramids was an elaborate and complex affair. Stone quarried on the spot formed the core of each structure, but the fine limestone blocks originally used for facing, now stripped away, came from across the Nile. These were quarried in the dry season; then when the floods came they were ferried across the river, cut into shape, and dragged into place. At the center of each pyramid was a chamber in which was placed the mummified body of the pharaoh, surrounded by the treasures that were to follow him into the next life. These massive constructions the pharaohs planned as their resting places for eternity and as monuments that would perpetuate their names. Their success was partial. Four and a half thousand years later, their names are remembered—their pyramids, still dominating the flat landscape, symbolize the enduring character of ancient Egypt. As shelters for their occupants and their treasures, however, the pyramids were vulnerable. The very size of the pyramids drew attention to the riches hidden within them, and robbers were quick to tunnel through and plunder them, sometimes only shortly after the burial chamber had been sealed.

Chefren, who commissioned the second of the three pyramids at Giza, was also responsible for perhaps the most famous of all Egyptian images, the colossal Sphinx [1.4], a guardian for his tomb. The aloof tranquility of the human face, perhaps a portrait of the pharaoh, set on a lion's body, made an especially strong impression fifteen hundred years later on the Classical Greeks, who saw it as a divine symbol of the mysterious and enigmatic. Greek art makes frequent use of the sphinx as a motif, and it also appears in Greek mythology, most typically in the story of how Oedipus solved its riddle and thereby saved the Greek city of Thebes from disaster.

The appearance of Chefren himself is preserved for us in a number of statues that are typical of Old Kingdom art [1.5]. The sculptor's approach to anatomy and drapery is realistic, and details are shown with great precision. But the features of the

1.5 ***Chefren.*** **Giza, c. 2560 B.C. Dark green diorite, height 5' (1.52 m). Egyptian Museum, Cairo.**

1.6 ***Sesostris III.*** **c. 1878–1841 B.C. Black granite, height 4'10½" (1.5 m). Egyptian Museum, Cairo.**

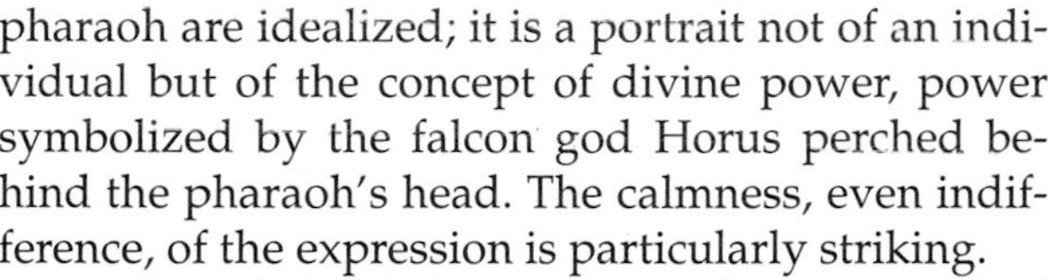

pharaoh are idealized; it is a portrait not of an individual but of the concept of divine power, power symbolized by the falcon god Horus perched behind the pharaoh's head. The calmness, even indifference, of the expression is particularly striking.

The art of the Old Kingdom reflects a mood of confidence and certainty that was brought to an abrupt end around 2200 B.C. by a period of violent disturbance. Divisions between the regions began to strengthen the power of local governors. By the time of the Middle Kingdom, it was no longer possible for pharaoh, priests, or nobles to face the future with complete trust in divine providence. Middle Kingdom art reflects this new uncertainty in two ways. On the one hand, the Old Kingdom came to represent a kind of Golden Age; artists tried to recapture its lofty serenity in their own works. At the same time, the more troubled spirit of the new period is reflected in the massive weight and somber expressions of some of the official portraits. The furrowed brow and grim look of Sesostris III convey the impression that to be a Middle Kingdom pharaoh was hardly a very relaxing occupation [1.6].

The New Kingdom

In spite of increasing contacts with foreign cultures, New Kingdom artists continued basically to work within age-old traditions. Like virtually all artists in the ancient world they depicted the idea of what they wanted to show rather than its actual appearance; an eye in a profile carving, for example, would be depicted as if seen from the front. This approach is often called "conceptual," as opposed to the "descriptive" style the Greeks were to develop. In the Eighteenth Dynasty, however, there was a remarkable change. The pharaoh Amenhotep IV, who ruled from 1379 to 1362 B.C., singlehandedly attempted a total reform of Egyptian religious and political life. He replaced the numberless deities of traditional religion with a single one, the sun god Aton, and changed his own name to Akhenaton, or "the servant of Aton." The most complete expression of his devotion to Aton survives in the form of a hymn to the god, which movingly expresses his sincerity: "Thou appearest beautifully on the horizon of Heaven, thou living Aton, the beginning of life! When thou art risen on

1.7 *Akhenaton, Nefertiti, and Three of Their Children.* Amarna, c. 1370–1350 B.C. Limestone relief, height 17" (43 cm). Egyptian Museum, State Museums, Berlin. The naturalism of this relief, verging on sentimentality, is typical of late Amarna art.

1.8 *Queen Nefertiti.* Tel el-Amarna. c. 1370 B.C. Painted limestone, height 20" (51 cm). State Museums, Berlin. Though the portrait is not exaggerated, it is idealized.

the eastern horizon, thou hast filled every land with thy beauty. . . ." In order to make these revolutionary moves more effective and to escape the influence of the priests at the royal court of Thebes, he transferred the capital to a new location, known today as Tel el-Amarna.

Here a new kind of art developed. The weight and idealism of the traditional conceptual style gave way to a new lightness and naturalism. For the first time physical characteristics are depicted in detail, and scenes are relaxed and even humorous. A stone relief showing the royal couple and three of their children sitting quietly under the rays of the sun disc is an astonishing departure from the dignified style of the preceding thousand years [1.7]. Queen Nefertiti herself is the subject of perhaps the most famous of all Egyptian portraits [1.8], a sculpture that shows none of the exaggeration to which Amarna art is sometimes prone, but a grace and elegance very different from earlier official portraits.

All these artistic changes were, of course, the result of Akhenaton's sweeping and revolutionary religious reforms. They did not last long. Akhenaton's belief in a single god who ruled the universe was threatening to the priests, who had a vested interest in preserving the old polytheistic traditions. Not surprisingly, Akhenaton's successors branded him a heretic and fanatic and cut his name out of all the monuments that survived him.

The reaction against Akhenaton's religious policy and the Amarna style was almost immediate. His successor, Tutankhamen, however, is remembered not for leading the opposition—or indeed for any event in his short life. He owes his fame to the treasures found intact in his unrobbed tomb. These sumptuous gold objects, enriched with ivory and precious stones, still show something of the liveliness of Amarna art, but a return to conservatism is beginning; in fact by the Nineteenth and Twentieth Dynasties Akhenaton had been completely forgotten.

In any case, it is not so much for what they reveal about the trends in art that the treasures of Tutankhamen are significant. The discovery of the tomb is important for a different reason. Our knowledge of the cultures of the ancient world is constantly being revised by the work of archaeologists; many of their finds are minor, but some are major and spectacular. In the case of excavations such as the tomb of Tutankhamen the process of uncovering the past sometimes becomes as exciting and significant as what is discovered. The long search conducted by Howard Carter in the Valley of the Kings that culminated in the opening of the inner chamber of the sealed tomb of Tutankhamen

on February 17, 1923, and the discovery of the intact sarcophagus of the king has become part of history [1.9].

The excavations of Knossos and Mycenae, discussed later in this chapter, and the discovery of Pompeii (Chapter 4) are also major turning points

1.9 The first view of the treasures of Tutankhamen. Egyptian. Dynasty XVIII. Thebes: Valley of the Kings. Antechamber: west side. This is what Howard Carter saw when he opened the doorway of the antechamber of the tomb of Tutankhamen on November 26, 1922. The objects include three gilt couches in the form of animals and, at the right in back, the pharaoh's golden throne. The tomb itself was opened three months later.

SPORTS AND GAMES

Checkers beyond the Grave

The ancient Egyptians' enthusiasm for playing board games extended to the next world: the *Book of the Dead* tells us that playing a game called *senet* was one of the occupations of the deceased person in the afterlife, and in the sketches which appear in some of the texts a player is shown sitting at a board, accompanied by his wife. As early as the Old Kingdom, painted scenes in tombs show checkerboards in use, sometimes accompanied by music and other kinds of entertainment.

Tutankhamen was evidently a keen player, since his tomb contained no less than four game boards. Nothing in their character or decoration suggests that they were religious or funerary in function; the games were probably the ones he used in life. They have inscriptions wishing the pharaoh long life and prosperity, and calling him "Fair of laws, he who pacifies the Two Lands" (that is, Upper and Lower Egypt).

1.10 Game board from the tomb of Tutankhamen. c. 1325 B.C. Ebony and ivory, partly gilded, length 6" (46 cm). Egyptian Museum, Cairo.

The largest of them (1.10) is made of ebony and ivory, covered in places with gold leaf, with thirty squares on its surface. Five of the squares are inscribed. The pieces, now missing, were moved about the board by throwing knucklebones or casting sticks—the ancient Egyptian equivalent of dice; sets of both were found in the tomb. The aim of each of the two players was probably to be the first to reach the square labeled "happiness, beauty." The square immediately in front of this one, inscribed "water," may have been a danger point.

in the growth of our knowledge of the past. But sensational finds like these are exceptions. Understanding the cultural achievements of past civilizations involves a slow and painstaking series of minor discoveries, each of which adds to the knowledge that thus must be constantly revised and reinterpreted.

By the end of the New Kingdom the taste for monumental building had returned. The temples constructed during the reign of Ramses II (1298–1232 B.C.) at Luxor, Karnak, and Abu Simbel are probably the most colossal of all Egyptian constructions [1.11]. Within a century, however, internal dissensions and foreign events had produced a sharp decline in Egypt's power. Throughout the Late Period, artists reverted again to the styles of earlier periods. Tombs were once again constructed in the shape of pyramids, as they had been in the Old Kingdom, and sculptors tried to recapture the realism and sense of volume of Old and Middle Kingdom art. Even direct contacts with the Assyrians, Persians, and Greeks—during the period between the Assyrian occupation of 671–633 B.C. and Alexander's conquest of Egypt in 331 B.C.—produced little effect on late Egyptian art. To the end of their history, the Egyptians remained faithful to their three-thousand-year-old tradition. Probably no other culture in human history has ever demonstrated so strong a conservatism and determination to preserve its separate traditions.

THE CULTURES OF MESOPOTAMIA

The unity so characteristic of ancient Egyptian culture has no parallel in the history of ancient Mesopotamia. A succession of different peoples, each with their own language, religion, and customs, produced a wide variety of achievements. This makes it far more difficult to generalize about Mesopotamian culture than about ancient Egyptian. The picture is further complicated by the presence of a series of related peoples on the periphery of the Mesopotamian territory. The Hittites,

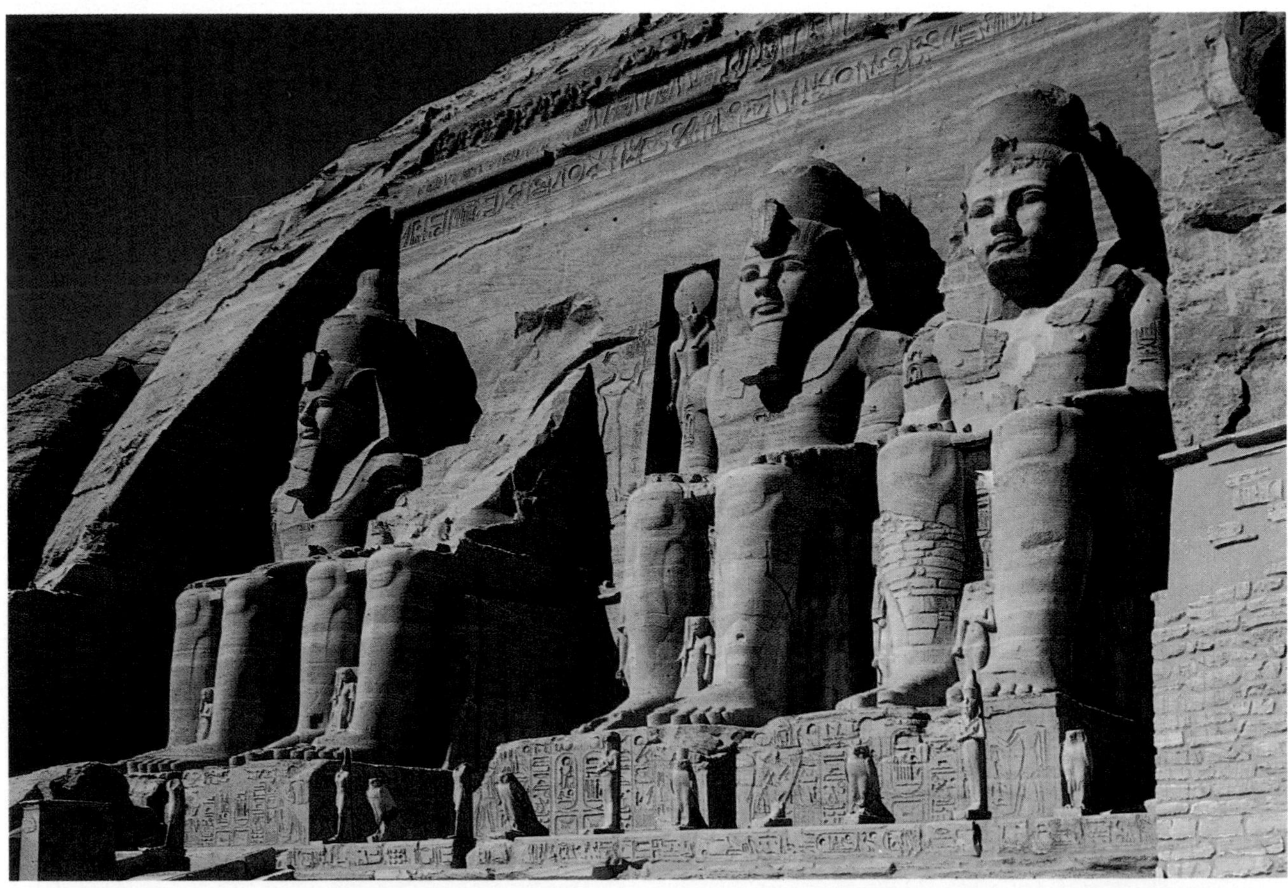

1.11 Temple of Ramses II at Abu Simbel, c. 1257 B.C. Height of statues about 60' (18.3 m). These four huge statues, erected in commemoration of Ramses' military victories, are all of the pharaoh himself. Between and near the feet are small statues of Ramses' mother, wife, and children. Below are statues of the pharaoh as the god Osiris and the falcon god Horus, to whom the temple was dedicated.

CONTEMPORARY VOICES

Love, Marriage, and Divorce in Ancient Egypt

A young man's love song:

Seven days from yesterday I have not seen my beloved,
And sickness has crept over me,
And I am become heavy in my limbs
And am unmindful of mine own body.
If the master-physicians come to me,
My heart has no comfort of their remedies,
And the magicians, no resource is in them,
My malady is not diagnosed.

Better for me is my beloved than any remedies,
More important is she for me than the entire compendium of medicine.

My salutation is when she enters from without.
When I see her, then am I well;
Opens she her eye, my limbs are young again;
Speaks she, and I am strong;
And when I embrace her, she banishes evil,
And it passes from me for seven days.

Quoted in Leonard Cottrell, *Life Under the Pharaohs* (New York: Holt, Rinehart and Winston, 1960), p. 84.

A young girl's song to her beloved:

Oh, flower of henna!
My heart stands still in thy presence.
I have made mine eyes brilliant for thee with kohl.
When I behold thee, I fly to thee, oh my Beloved!
Oh, Lord of my heart, sweet is this hour. An hour passed with thee is worth an hour of eternity!
Oh, flower of marjoram!
Fain would I be to thee as the garden in which I have planted flowers and sweet-smelling shrubs! the garden watered by pleasant runlets, and refreshed by the north breeze!
Here let us walk, oh my Beloved, hand in hand, our hearts filled with joy!
Better than food, better than drink, is it to behold thee.
To behold thee, and to behold thee again!

Quoted in Amelia B. Edwards, *Pharaohs, Fellahs, and Explorers* (New York: Harper, 1891), p. 225.

A father's advice to his son:

Double the food which thou givest thy mother, carry her as she carried thee. She had a heavy load in thee, but she did not leave it to me. After thou wert borne she was still burdened with thee; her breast was in thy mouth for three years, and though thy filth was disgusting, her heart was not disgusted. When thou takest a wife, remember how thy mother gave birth to thee, and her raising thee as well; do not let thy wife blame thee, nor cause that she raise her hands to the god.

Quoted in Barbara Mestz; *Temples, Tombs and Hieroglyphics* (New York: Coward-McCann, 1964), p. 333.

How a wife can obtain a divorce:

If she shall stand up in the congregation and shall say, "I divorce my husband," the price of divorce shall be on her head; she shall return to the scales and weigh for the husband five shekels, and all which I have delivered into her hand she shall give back, and she shall go away whithersoever she will.

Quoted in Leonard Cottrell, *Life Under the Pharaohs* (New York: Holt, Rinehart and Winston, 1960), p. 94.

the Syrians, and the peoples of early Iran all had periods of prosperity and artistic greatness, although in general they were overshadowed by the more powerful nations of Mesopotamia and Egypt. A description of their achievements would be beyond the scope of this book.

Sumer

The history of Mesopotamia can be divided into two major periods, the Sumerian (c. 3500–2350 B.C.) and the Semitic (c. 2350–612 B.C., when Nineveh fell). The Sumerians and Semitic peoples differed in their racial origins and languages; the term "Semitic" is derived from the name of Shem, one of the sons of Noah, and is generally used to refer to people speaking a Semitic language. In the ancient world, these included the Akkadians, Babylonians, Assyrians, and Phoenicians. The most common association of "Semitic" is with the Jewish people, whose traditional language, Hebrew, falls into the same group; they also originated in the region of Mesopotamia (for a discussion of the early history of the Jews, see Chapter 5). Arabic and certain other Mediterranean languages—including Maltese—are also Semitic.

The earliest Sumerian communities were agricultural settlements on the land between the Tigris and Euphrates rivers, an area known as the Fertile Crescent. Unlike Upper Egypt, the land here is flat, and so dikes and canals were needed to prevent

1.12 *Top:* Picture writing: Copy of a limestone tablet from Kish. c. 3200 B.C. Ashmolean Museum, Oxford; original in Baghdad Museum. Center: Hieroglyphics: detail of a pillar of a festival building of Sesostris I, Karnak. c. 1940 B.C. Egyptian Museum, Cairo. *Bottom:* Cuneiform: detail of the *Stele of Hammurabi* (see figure 1.18). c. 1760 B.C. The limestone tablet is the oldest known example of picture writing. Among the signs are several representing parts of the human body, including a head, hand, and foot. This writing system later developed into cuneiform. The Egyptians, however, continued to use hieroglyphics throughout their history.

flooding during the rainy season and to provide water during the rest of the year. When the early settlers found that they had to undertake these large-scale construction projects in order to improve their agriculture, they began to merge their small villages to form towns.

By far the most important event of this stage in the development of Sumerian culture was the invention of the first system of writing, known as cuneiform [1.12]. The earliest form of writing was developed at Uruk (now Warka), one of the first Mesopotamian settlements, around the middle of the fourth millennium B.C. It consisted of a series of simplified picture signs that represented the objects they showed and, in addition, related ideas. Thus a leg could mean either a leg itself or the concept of walking. The signs were drawn on soft clay tablets which were then baked hard.

These pictorial signs evolved into a series of wedge-shaped marks that were pressed in clay with a split reed. The cuneiform system (*cuneus* is the Latin word for wedge) had the advantage of being quick and economical, and the inscribed clay tablets were easy to store. The ability to write made it possible to trade and to administer on a wider scale, and with the increasing economic strength this more highly organized society brought, a number of powerful cities began to develop.

The central focus of life in these larger communities was the temple, the dwelling place of the particular god who watched over the town. Religion, in fact, played a central part in all aspects of Sumerian culture. The gods themselves were manifest in natural phenomena, sky and earth, sun and moon, lightning and storm. The chief religious holidays were closely linked to the passage of the seasons. The most important annual event was the New Year, the crucial moment when the blazing heat of the previous summer and the cold of winter gave way to the possibility of a fertile spring. The fertility of the earth was symbolized by the Great Mother and the sterility of the winter by the death of her partner, Tammuz. Each year his disappearance was mourned at the beginning of the New Year festival. When his resurrection was celebrated at the end of the festival, hope for the season to come was expressed by the renewal of the sacred marriage of god and goddess.

1.13 *Lady of Warka.* Uruk, c. 3000 B.C. White marble, height 7⅞" (20 cm). Iraq Museum, Baghdad. Originally the hair was probably gold leaf and the eyes and eyebrows were colored inlays.

As in the Paleolithic period, the importance of female creative power is reflected in Sumerian art. Among its finest achievements is the so-called *Lady of Warka* [1.13], a female head from the city of Uruk. It is not clear whether the head is of a divine or mortal figure. The face shows an altogether exceptional nobility and sensitivity.

The governing power in cities like Uruk was in the hands of the priests, who controlled and administered both religious and economic affairs. The ruler himself served as the representative on earth of the god of the city but, unlike the pharaoh, was never thought of as divine and never became the center of a cult. His purpose was to watch over his people's interests by building better temples and digging more canals rather than acquiring personal wealth or power. Over the centuries rulers began to detach themselves increasingly from the control of the priests, but the immense prestige of the temples assured the religious leaders a lasting power.

The most famous of all Sumerian rulers was Gilgamesh, who ruled at Uruk about 2700 B.C. Around his name grew up a series of legends that developed into one of the first great masterpieces of poetic expression. *The Epic of Gilgamesh* begins with the adventures of Gilgamesh and his warrior friend Enkidu. Gilgamesh himself is courted by the queen of heaven, the goddess Ishtar. He rejects her advances and later kills a bull sent against him as a punishment. In revenge, the gods kill Enkidu; his death marks the turning point of the poem's mood. With the awareness of death's reality even for the bravest, Gilgamesh now sets out to seek the meaning of life. Toward the end of his journey he meets Utnapishtim, the only person to whom the gods have given everlasting life; from him Gilgamesh seeks the secrets of immortality. Utnapishtim, in the course of their conversation, tells him the story of the flood as it was known in Babylonia. By the end of the epic, Gilgamesh fails to achieve immortality and returns home to die.

Originally composed in Sumerian c. 2000 B.C., the epic was eventually written down on clay tablets in their own languages by Babylonians, Hittites, and others. The poem was widely known. The story of the flood, recorded in tablet eleven, bears a striking resemblance to that of the biblical story in Genesis; both accounts have parallel accounts of the building of boats, the coming of torrential rain, and the sending out of birds. The tone is very different, however. The God of the Hebrews acts out of moral disapproval, while the divinities in the epic were disturbed in their sleep by noisy mortals.

The Epic of Gilgamesh is a profoundly pessimistic work. Unlike the ancient Egyptians, the

Mesopotamians saw life as a continual struggle whose only alternative was the bleak darkness of death. Dying Egyptians—if they were righteous—could expect a happy existence in the next life, but for the Mesopotamian there was only the dim prospect of eternal gloom.

The story of Gilgamesh rises to a supreme level in the section that describes the last stages of his journey. Then the epic touches on universal questions: Is all human achievement futile in the face of death? Is there a purpose in human existence? If so, how can it be discovered? The quest of Gilgamesh is the basic human search.

Only at the end of Gilgamesh's journey do we sense that the purpose of the journey may have been the journey itself and that what was important was to have asked the questions. Weary as he was on his return he was wiser than when he left, and in leaving us an account of his experiences, "engraved on a stone," he communicates them to us, a powerful and moving illustration of the power of the written word.

1.14 Head of a king (Sargon?), from Nineveh. Akkadian, c. 2330 B.C. Bronze, height 14¼" (37 cm). Iraq Museum, Baghdad. Originally, the eyes were probably precious stones.

1.15 *Stele of Naram-Sin,* from Susa, Iran. Akkadian, c. 2300 B.C. Red sandstone, height 6'6" (2 m). Louvre, Paris. The king, wearing a horned crown, stands beneath symbols of the gods. The diagonal composition is well suited to the triangular shape of the stele.

Akkadian and Babylonian Culture

In the years from 2350 to 2150 B.C. the whole of Mesopotamia fell under the control of the Semitic king Sargon and his descendants. The art of this Akkadian period (named for Sargon's capital city, Akkad) shows a continuation of the trends of the Sumerian age, although total submission to the gods is replaced by a more positive attitude to human achievement. A bronze head from Nineveh

[1.14], perhaps a portrait of Sargon himself, expresses a pride and self-confidence that recur in other works of the period like the famous *Stele of Naram-Sin* (*stele:* stone slab), showing a later Akkadian king standing on the bodies of his enemies [1.15].

When Akkadian rule was brought to an abrupt and violent end by the invasion of the Gutians from Iran, the cities of Mesopotamia reverted to earlier ways. As in the early Sumerian period, the chief buildings constructed were large brick platforms with superimposed terraces, known as *ziggurats*. These clearly had religious significance; the one built at Ur around 2100 B.C. [1.16] had huge staircases that led to a shrine at the top. The same return to traditional beliefs is illustrated by the religious inscriptions on the bases of the many surviving statues of Gudea, the governor of the city of Lagash around 2100 B.C., as well as by his humble attitude [1.17].

By around 1800 B.C., Mesopotamia had once again been unified, this time under the Babylonians. Their most famous king, Hammurabi, was the author of a law code that was one of the earliest attempts to achieve social justice by legislation—a major development in the growth of civilization. The laws were carved on a stele, with Hammurabi himself shown at the top in the presence of the sun god Shamash [1.18]. Many of the law code's provisions deal with the relationship between husbands, wives, and other family members, as the following shows:

from The Law Code of Hammurabi

131. If a man accuse his wife and she have not been taken in lying with another man, she shall take an oath in the name of god and she shall return to her house.

142. If a woman hate her husband and say, "Thou shalt not have me," her past shall be inquired into for any deficiency of hers; and if she have been careful and be without past sin and her husband have been going out and greatly belittling her, that woman has no blame. She shall take her dowry and go to her father's house.

145. If a man take a wife and she do not present him with children, and he set his face to take a concubine,

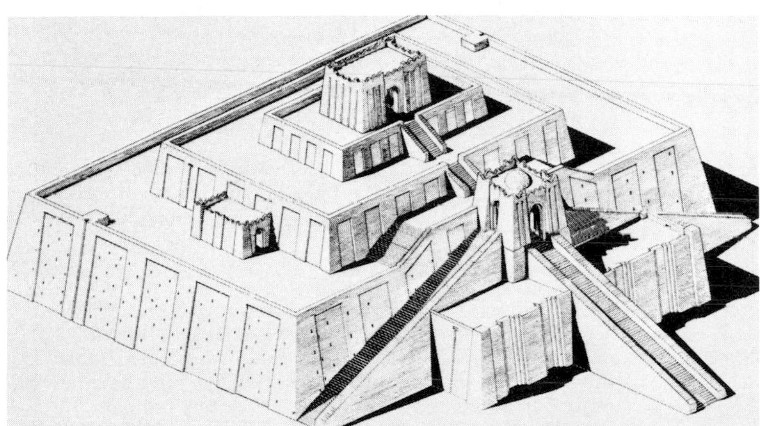

1.16 Ziggurat at Ur. Neo-Sumerian, c. 2100–2000 B.C. Mudbrick faced with baked brick laid in bitumen. The drawing shows the probable original appearance. The photograph shows the ziggurat now, partially restored. The Akkadian word *ziggurat* means "pinnacle" or "mountaintop"—a place where the gods were thought to reveal themselves. These plains dwellers made artificial mountains surmounted by shrines.

1.17 *Gudea.* c. 2100 B.C. Diorite, height 41" (105 cm). Louvre, Paris. Gudea is shown in an attitude of devotion, hands tightly clasped, as he stands before the gods.

1.18 *Stele of Hammurabi.* c. 1760 B.C. Basalt, height 7'3¾" (2.25 m). Louvre, Paris. The sun god is dictating the law to the king, who is listening reverently. They are shown on a mountain, indicated by the irregular ridges beneath the god's feet. Below is *The Law Code of Hammurabi,* carved in cuneiform.

that man may take a concubine and bring her into his house. That concubine shall not take precedence of his wife.

162. If a man take a wife and she bear him children and that woman die, her father may not lay claim to her dowry. Her dowry belongs to her children.

The Assyrians

By 1550 B.C. Babylon had been taken over by the Kassites, a formerly nomadic people who had occupied Babylonia and settled there, but they too would fall in turn under the domination of the Assyrians, who evolved the last great culture of ancient Mesopotamia. The peak of Assyrian power was between 1000 and 612 B.C.—the time when Greek civilization was developing, as described in Chapter 2. But Assyrian achievements are the culmination of the culture of ancient Mesopotamia.

A huge palace constructed at Nimrud during the reign of Assurnasirpal II (883–859 B.C.) was decorated with an elaborately carved series of relief slabs. The subjects are often religious, but a number of slabs that show the king on hunting expeditions have a vigor and freedom that are unusual in Mesopotamian art. The palaces of later Assyrian kings were decorated with similar reliefs. At Nineveh the palace of Assurbanipal (668–626 B.C.) was filled with scenes of war appropriate to an age of increasing turmoil. The representations of dead

1.19 Detail, relief from the Palace of Assurbanipal at Nineveh, [illegible]–[illegible] B.C. Gypsum slab carved in low relief, height 19" (50 cm). British Museum, London (reproduced by courtesy of the Trustees). Wild asses are being hunted by mastiffs. The mare below turns in her flight to look back for her foal.

and dying soldiers on the battlefields are generally conventional, if highly elaborate. But again the hunting scenes are different—they show a genuine and moving identification with the suffering animals [1.19].

With the fall of Nineveh in 612 B.C. Assyrian domination ended. The Assyrian Empire fell into the hands of two tribes, first the Medes and then the Persians; the great age of Mesopotamia was over. The Persians, like the Medes whom they subsequently conquered and absorbed, were originally a nomadic warrior people. In the century following their victory over the Assyrians, they continued to expand; by the death of the Persian ruler Cyrus the Great (c. 590–529 B.C.), their empire stretched from the Mediterranean to the Indus River. After an unsuccessful attempt to conquer Greece (see Chapter 2), the Persians were finally themselves conquered by Alexander the Great around 330 B.C.

Lacking the unifying elements provided in Egypt by the pharaoh and a national religion, the peoples of Mesopotamia perhaps never equaled Egyptian achievements in the arts. However, they formed ordered societies within independent city-states that anticipated the city-states of the Greeks. They also evolved a comparatively enlightened view of human relationships, as shown by *The Law Code of Hammurabi.*

AEGEAN CULTURE IN THE BRONZE AGE

Neither the Egyptians of the Old Kingdom nor the Sumerians seem to have shown any interest in their contemporaries living to the west of them, and with good reason. In Greece and the islands of the Aegean Sea, though the arrival of immigrants from farther east in the early Neolithic period (c. 6000 B.C.) had brought new agricultural techniques, in general life continued there for the next three thousand years almost completely untouched by the rise of organized cultures elsewhere.

Yet, beginning in the early Bronze Age, there developed in the area around the Aegean Sea a level of civilization as brilliant and sophisticated as any other in Europe or western Asia. (The same period saw the appearance of a similarly urban culture in the Indus Valley on the Indian subcontinent.) Then around 1100 B.C., after almost two thousand years of existence, this Bronze Age Aegean civilization disappeared as dramatically as it had arisen. The rediscovery in the 20th century of these peoples, the Minoans of Crete and the Mycenaeans of mainland Greece, is perhaps the most splendid achievement in the history of archaeology in the Mediterranean—and one that has opened up vast new perspectives in the study of the later Greeks.

What connection is there between Greek culture and the magnificent civilization of the Bronze Age? Did much of later Greek religion, thought, and art have its origins in this earlier period, even though the Greeks themselves seemed to know nothing about it? Or was the culture of the Minoans and Mycenaeans an isolated phenomenon, destroyed utterly near the end of the Bronze Age, lost until it was found again in our own time? The Aegean culture is important not only for the possible light it throws on later times. Its existence also shows that the ancient world could reach beyond the monumentality and earnestness of the Egyptians and Mesopotamians, that it could attain a way of life that valued grace, beauty, and comfort—a life that could truly be called civilized.

Cycladic Art

During most of the Bronze Age the major centers of Aegean culture were on Crete or the mainland, but in the early phase there were settlements on a group of islands of the central Aegean, the Cyclades. Little is known about these Cycladic people. They used bronze tools. They also produced pottery which, though less finely made than that produced elsewhere in the Aegean at the time, sometimes shows remarkable imagination and even humor [1.20]. The chief claim to fame of Cycladic art—a considerable one—lies in the marble statues, or idols, that were produced in large quantities and in many cases buried with the dead.

1.20 Cycladic vase in the shape of a hedgehog drinking from a bowl. Syros, c. 2500–2200 B.C. Painted clay, height 4¼" (11 cm). National Archaeological Museum, Athens.

1.21 Cycladic idol. c. 2500 B.C. Marble, height 19¾" (50 cm). British Museum, London (reproduced by courtesy of the Trustees).

The statues range in height from a few inches to almost life-size; the average is about a foot (30.5 centimeters) high. Most of the figures are female; the most common type shows a naked woman standing or, more probably, lying, with her arms folded and head tilted back [1.21]. The face is indicated only by a central ridge for the nose. The simplic-

EAST MEETS WEST

The Indus Valley People

In the 1920s another ancient civilization was first discovered, that of the Indus Valley, in what is now Pakistan. Like the Minoans, the Indus Valley people must have had myths involving bulls, since the bull appears frequently on their carved seal stones. There is no direct evidence of contact between the two cultures, but we do know that the Indus Valley people traded with the Akkadians in the time of Sargon, a period during which the Minoans were active in the eastern Mediterranean.

Originally founded around 3000 B.C., the two principal centers of Indus culture, Harappa and Mohenjo-daro, became large-scale flourishing cities. They were built of baked bricks and had elaborate drainage systems. At Mohenjo-daro a great bath, an assembly hall, and other monumental public buildings have been excavated. Farming seems to have been the principal occupation; wheat, barley, and rice were grown, and the Indus Valley dwellers were the first people known to cultivate cotton.

A standardized writing system that makes use of picture-signs and has not been deciphered was widely used throughout Indus territory. The Indus people were not great metalworkers; the finest of their surviving statues are of stone [1.22]. Pottery was mass-produced and its general distribution as well as a standard system of weights and measures suggest a powerfully centralized state.

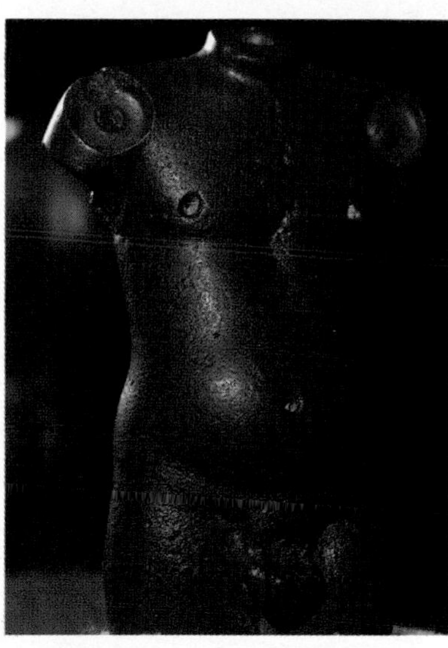

1.22 Torso of a man from Mohenjo-daro. 3rd millennium B.C. Red stone. National Museum, New Delhi. Museum of Central Asiatic Antiquities, New Delhi.

Like that of the Minoans, the collapse of the Indus civilization is still not fully understood. By around 1700 B.C. most of the Indus Valley centers were in decline, in part due to a series of disastrous floods of the river. Another factor was probably overexploitation of the land; huge amounts of wood and other vegetation must have been used to stoke the fires that baked the bricks of which the cities were constructed. The final blow was the invasion of a new people, the Aryans, who moved southeast into India at the end of the second millennium B.C.

Thus, like the Minoans, the Indus Valley people were forgotten for some three thousand years before being rediscovered by modern archaeologists. We now know that Indus culture represents one of the high points in the development of civilization in the Orient.

ity of the form and the fine working of the marble—stone of superb quality—often produce an effect of great beauty.

The purpose of the Cycladic idols remains uncertain. The fact that most of them have been found in graves suggests that they had a religious function in the funeral ritual. The overwhelming preponderance of female figures seems to indicate that they were in some way connected with the cult of the mother goddess, which was common in Mesopotamia and which dominated Aegean Bronze Age religion. Whether the figures actually represent goddesses remains uncertain.

We now know that the period of the production of the Cycladic idols was one of increasing development on Crete. Yet for the classical Greeks of the 5th century B.C. Crete was chiefly famous as the home of the legendary King Minos, who ruled at Knossos. Here, according to myth, was a Labyrinth that housed the Minotaur, a monstrous creature, half man and half bull, the product of the union of Minos' wife Pasiphae with a bull. Minos exacted from Athens a regular tribute of seven boys and seven girls who were sent to be devoured by the Minotaur. According to the myths, after this had been going on for some time, the Athenian hero Theseus volunteered to stop the grisly tribute. He went to Knossos with the new group of intended victims and, with the help of the king's daughter Ariadne (who had fallen in love with him) killed the Minotaur in its lair in the middle of the Labyrinth. He then escaped with Ariadne and the Athenian boys and girls. Theseus later abandoned Ariadne on the island of Naxos, but the god Dionysus discovered her there and comforted her. The story had many more details, and other myths describe other events. The important point is that the later Greeks had a mythological picture of

Knossos as a prosperous and thriving community ruled by a powerful and ruthless king from his palace. Nor was Knossos the only center mentioned in Greek stories of Crete. In the *Odyssey* Homer even refers to "Crete of a hundred cities."

These, however, were legends. By the time of Classical Greece no evidence whatever for the existence of the Palace of Minos or the other cities could be seen. It is not surprising that the Greeks themselves showed no inclination to try to find any hidden traces. Archaeology, after all, is a relatively modern pursuit, and there is little indication of any serious enthusiasm in classical antiquity for the material remains of the past. Later ages continued to accept the Greeks' own judgment. For many centuries the story of Minos and the Labyrinth was thought to be a good tale with no foundation in fact.

The Excavation of Knossos

By the end of the 19th century, however, things had changed. Heinrich Schliemann had proven that the stories of the war against Troy and the Mycenaeans who had waged it were far from mere legends (see page 25). Was it possible that the mythical palace of King Minos at Knossos also really existed?

In 1894 the English archaeologist Arthur Evans first went to Crete to see if he could discover something of its history in the Bronze Age. At Knossos he found evidence of ancient remains, some of them already uncovered by amateur enthusiasts. He returned in 1899 and again in 1900, this time with a permit to excavate. On March 23, 1900, serious work began at Knossos, and within days it became apparent that the finds represented a civilization even older than that of the Mycenaeans. The quantity was staggering: pottery, frescoes, inscribed tablets, and, on April 13, a room with elaborate paintings and a raised seat with high back—the throne room of King Minos. Evans' discoveries at Knossos (and finds later made elsewhere on Crete by other archaeologists) did much to confirm legendary accounts of Cretan prosperity and power. Yet these discoveries did far more than merely give a true historical background to the myth of the Minotaur.

Evans had in fact found an entire civilization, which he called Minoan after the legendary king. Evans himself is said to have once remarked modestly, "Any success as an archaeologist I owe to two things: very short sight, so I look at everything closely, and being slow on the uptake, so I never leap to conclusions." Actually, the magnitude of his achievement can scarcely be exaggerated. All study of the Minoans has been strongly influenced by his initial classification of the finds, especially the pottery. Evans divided the history of the Bronze Age in Crete into three main periods—Early Minoan, Middle Minoan, and Late Minoan—and further subdivided each of these into three. The precise dates of each period can be disputed, but all the excavations of the years following Evans have confirmed his initial description of the main sequence of events.

Life and Art in the Minoan Palaces

The Early Minoan period was one of increasing growth. Small towns began to appear in the south and east of Crete, and the first contacts were established with Egypt and Mesopotamia. Around 2000 B.C., however, came the first major development in Minoan civilization, marking the beginning of the Middle Minoan period. The earlier scattered towns were abandoned and large urban centers evolved. These are generally called palaces, although their function was far more than just to provide homes for ruling families.

The best known of these centers is Knossos (other important ones have been excavated at Phaistos, Mallia, and Zakro). The main palace building, constructed around an open rectangular courtyard, contained rooms for banquets, public receptions, religious ceremonies, and administrative work. In addition, there were living quarters for the royal family and working areas for slaves and craftsmen [1.23, 1.24]. Around the palace were the private houses of the aristocrats and chief religious leaders. The technical sophistication of these great centers was remarkable. There were elaborate drainage systems, and the palaces were designed and constructed to remain cool in summer and be heated easily in winter.

Few aspects of the Minoan achievement are more impressive than the development of an architectural style appropriate for these great structures. Unlike the carefully, almost obsessively planned Egyptian building complexes, Minoan palaces seem at first disorganized in plan. In practice, however, the division between the various functions of a palace—official, residential, religious—was achieved by a careful division of space. In the construction of the buildings themselves, rough stonework was hidden behind plaster and frescoes. Minoan columns tapered downwards; their narrowest point was at their base, unlike Greek columns, whose widest point is at their base, or

1.23 Plan of the Palace of Minos at Knossos. c. 1600–1400 B.C. Each Cretan palace had a central court oriented north-south, state apartments to the west, and royal living apartments to the east.

1.24 Throne Room, Palace of Minos at Knossos. The room was reconstructed about 1450 B.C., shortly before the final destruction of the palace. The frescoes around the throne show sacred flowers and griffins—mythological beasts with lion bodies and bird heads.

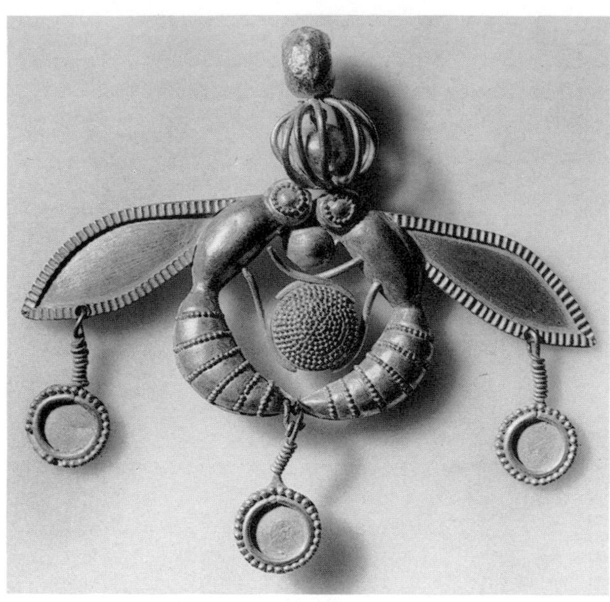

1.25 ***Wasp Pendant,*** **from Mallia. c. 1700 B.C. Gold, width 1⅞" (5 cm). Archaeological Museum, Heraklion. This enlarged view shows the exquisite craftsmanship, using the techniques of granulation and wire-working. Two wasps (or perhaps hornets) are curved around a honeycomb.**

Egyptian columns, most of which retain the same width from top to bottom. Minoan architects used these columns to provide impressive entrances, and to construct "light-wells" (vertical shafts running down through the buildings to carry light to the lower stories).

Middle Minoan art shows great liveliness and color. The brilliantly painted pottery, superb jewelry such as the famous *Wasp Pendant* from Mallia [1.25], and the many exquisitely carved seal stones all attest to the Minoans' love of beauty and artistic skill. Unlike their contemporaries in Egypt and Mesopotamia, the Minoans showed little interest in monumental art. Their greatest works are on a small, even miniature, scale. At the same time, they invented a writing system of hieroglyphic signs that was used in the archives of the palace for administrative purposes.

Toward the end of the Middle Minoan period (c. 1700 B.C.) the palaces were destroyed, probably by an earthquake, then rebuilt on an even grander scale. There was further reconstruction about a century later, perhaps because of another earthquake. These palaces of the Late Minoan period represent the high point of Minoan culture. The wall paintings of this period are among the greatest treasures of all. Their spontaneity and freedom create a mood very different from Egyptian and Mesopotamian art, and they show a love of nature expressed with brilliant colors and vivid observation. Most of the best examples of these later paintings are from Knossos, but some particularly enchanting scenes have been found in the recent excavation of a Minoan colony on the island of Thera [1.26].

Although the rulers of the palaces seem to have been male, the central figure of Minoan religion was a mother goddess who was connected with fertility. She seems to have taken on different forms, or rather the function of female divinity was divided among several separate deities. Sometimes

1.26 Room with landscape frescoes, House Delta, Thera. Minoan, c. 1500 B.C. National Archaeological Museum, Athens. A springtime scene—bright flowers and soaring birds—covers three sides of a small room.

1.27 *Snake Goddess,* from the Temple Repository at Knossos. c. 1600 B.C. Faïence, height 11½" (30 cm). Archaeological Museum, Heraklion. The bare breasts are typical for Minoan court ladies, but the apron indicates a religious function. The figure probably represents a priestess serving the goddess, not the goddess herself.

when she is shown flanked by animals, as the Mistress of the Beasts, she seems to be the ancestor of the Greek goddess Artemis. Other depictions show goddesses of vegetation. The most famous Minoan figurine is the so-called *Snake Goddess* [1.27].

Throughout the last great age of the palaces, the influence of Minoan artistic styles began to spread to the mainland. But Minoan political and military power was on the wane, and Knossos seems to have been invaded and occupied by mainlanders around 1450 B.C. Shortly afterward, both at Knossos and elsewhere, there is evidence of widespread destruction. By 1400 B.C., Minoan culture had come to an abrupt end. The causes are mysterious and have been much argued; we shall probably never know exactly what happened. The eruption of a volcano on Thera a century earlier, about 1500 B.C., may have played some part in changing the balance of power in the Aegean. In any case, there is no doubt that throughout the last period of the palaces a new power was growing, the Mycenaeans. These people may well have played a part in the destruction of Knossos.

Schliemann and the Discovery of Mycenae

The Mycenaeans, the people of mainland Greece in the Bronze Age, are named after the largest of their settlements, Mycenae. Most of the Mycenaean centers were in the southern part of Greece known as the Peloponnesus, although there were also some settlements farther north, of which the two most important were Athens and Thebes. Like the Minoans, the Mycenaeans were familiar from Greek myths long before their material remains were excavated. They were famous in legend mainly for launching an expedition against Troy, across the Aegean Sea. The Trojan War (c. 1250 B.C.) and its aftermath provided the material for many later Greek works, most notably the *Iliad* and the *Odyssey*, the two great epic poems of Homer, but for a long time it was believed that the war and even the very existence of Troy were myths.

Heinrich Schliemann dedicated his life and work to proving that the legends were founded on reality. Born in Germany in 1822, Schliemann was introduced to the Homeric poems as a child by his father and was overwhelmed by their incomparable vividness. He became determined to discover Homer's Troy and prove the poet right. Excavation has always been expensive, and Schliemann therefore decided to make his fortune in business, retire early, and devote his profits to the pursuit of his goal. By 1863, this remarkable man had accumulated a considerable amount of money from trading in, among other things, tea and was ready to devote himself to his second career. After a period of study and travel, in 1870 he finally began excavations on the site where he had decided the remains of Homer's Troy lay buried beneath the Roman city of Ilium. By 1873 he had found not only walls and the gate of the city but quantities of gold, silver, and bronze objects.

Inspired by the success of his Trojan campaign, Schliemann moved on to the second part of his task: to discover the Mycenaeans who had made war on Troy. In 1876 he began to excavate within the walls of Mycenae itself, and there he almost immediately came upon the Royal Grave Circle with

1.28 "Mask of Agamemnon," from Shaft Grave V, Mycenae. c. 1550 B.C. Beaten gold, height 10⅛" (26 cm). National Archaeological Museum, Athens. This death mask is actually a portrait of a Mycenaean ruler of three centuries earlier than Agamemnon.

its stupendous quantities of gold treasures [1.28]. Homer had described Mycenae as "rich in gold," and Schliemann was always convinced that the royal family whose graves he had unearthed was that of Agamemnon, leader of the Mycenaean expedition against Troy. We now know that the finds date to an even earlier period, and later excavations both at Mycenae and at other mainland sites have provided a much more exact picture of Mycenaean history. This does not diminish Schliemann's achievement. However unscientific his methods, he had proved the existence of a civilization in Bronze Age Greece that surpassed in splendor even the legends; he had opened a new era in the study of the past.

Mycenaean Art and Architecture

Like the Minoans, the Mycenaeans centered their life around great palace complexes. In Mycenae itself, the palace probably was first built around 1600 B.C., and the graves found by Schliemann date to shortly thereafter. Until the fall of Knossos in 1400 B.C., the Mycenaeans were strongly under the influence of Minoan culture, but with the end of Minoan power they became the natural leaders in the Aegean area. From 1400 to 1200 B.C., Mycenaean traders traveled throughout the Mediterranean, from Egypt and the Near East as far west as Italy. The Mycenaean Empire grew in power and prosperity. Toward the end of this period, around 1250 B.C., the successful expedition was launched against Troy, perhaps for reasons of trade rivalry. A short time later, around 1200 B.C., the Mycenaean Empire itself fell, its major centers destroyed and most of them abandoned. Invasion by enemies, internal strife, and natural causes have all been suggested, but the fall of the Mycenaeans still remains mysterious.

1.29 Reconstruction of the Citadel of Mycenae as it would have looked around 1300 B.C. The very thick walls are visible. The palace has a commanding position at the summit.

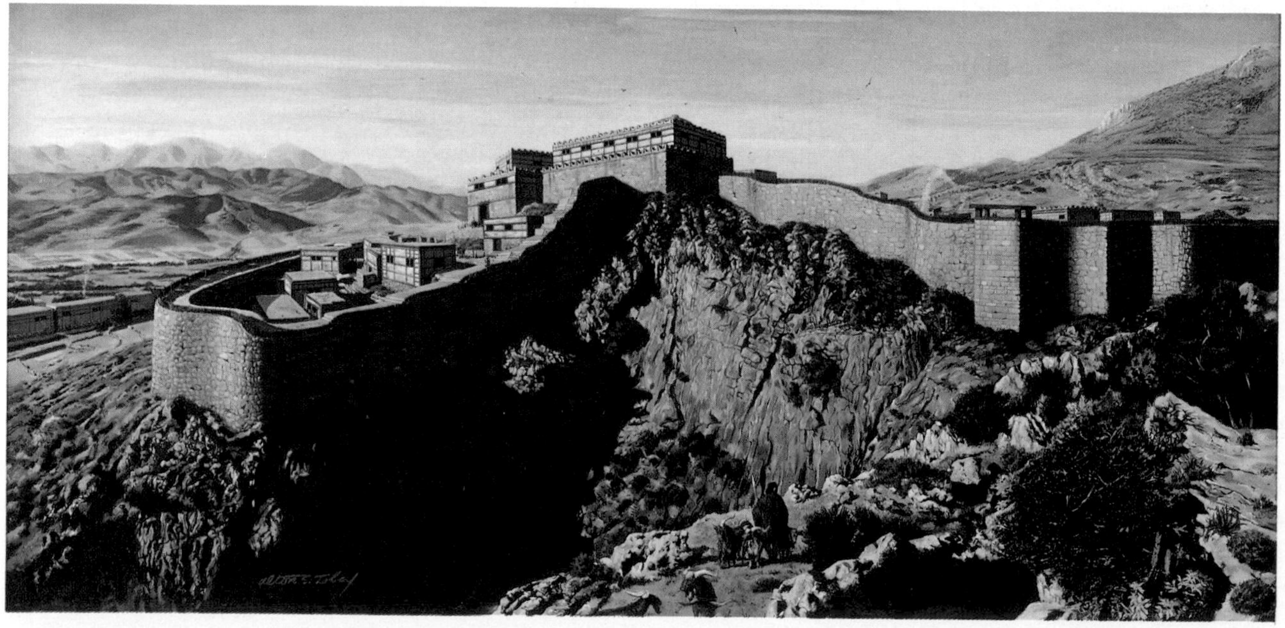

Their collapse is made even more incomprehensible by the massive fortifications that protected most of the palaces. At Mycenae itself, the walls are 15 feet (4.6 meters) thick and probably were 50 feet (15.3 meters) high. As in the case of other Mycenaean centers, the actual location was chosen for its defensibility [1.29]. The somber character of these fortress-palaces is reflected in the general tone of Mycenaean civilization. Unlike the relaxed culture of the Minoans, Mycenaean culture as reflected in its art was preoccupied with death and war. It is no coincidence that many of the richest finds have come from tombs. Like the Minoans, the Mycenaeans decorated their palaces with frescoes, although the Mycenaean paintings are more solemn and dignified than their Minoan counterparts.

The disaster of 1200 B.C. brought a violent end to the Mycenaeans' political and economic domination of the Mediterranean, but their culture lingered on for another hundred years. A few of the palaces were inhabited again, and some Mycenaeans fled eastward, where they settled on the islands of Rhodes and Cyprus. By 1100 B.C., however, renewed violence had extinguished the last traces of Bronze Age culture in Greece. A century later, after a period our lack of information forces us to call the Dark Age, the story of Western culture truly begins with the dawning of the Iron Age.

Before leaving the rich achievements of the Bronze Age world, both in Greece and farther afield, it is worth asking how much survived to be handed down to our own civilization. For the Greeks themselves, the Iron Age brought a new beginning in most material respects. At the same time, however, there are links with the earlier era in less tangible areas. In particular, although Greek religion never placed as strong an emphasis on worship of the mother goddess as the Bronze Age did, she remained a potent force in traditional beliefs. Behind the official reverence for Zeus, father of the gods and mortals, there lay a profound respect for goddesses like Hera, patroness of the family, Artemis, Mistress of the Beasts and goddess of childbirth, and Demeter, the goddess of fertility and agriculture. The continued worship of these goddesses, which was to last under different guises for centuries, represents a reverence for female creative power that is one of the oldest legacies from the period before our culture began—we saw it as far back as the Paleolithic period—and perhaps one of the most significant.

As for Egypt and Mesopotamia, their impact on later culture remains the subject of debate. In the course of their growth and development, the Greeks were brought into contact with the black Cushite culture of Egypt, and Greek art and architecture were decisively influenced by it. Although the Greeks retained their artistic independence, the style they developed under the inspiration of eastern models, including those of Mesopotamia, has conditioned the entire history of Western art. The cultures of ancient Egypt and the Middle East had very little firsthand influence on the formation of our civilization, partly because Greek culture had a vitality that was by this time lacking in the older peoples and at least partly because of historical accident. Egypt and Assyria, powerful though they were, fell to the Persians, while Greece managed not only to survive but even to inflict an ignominious defeat on its Persian invaders.

Yet even if ancient Egypt and Mesopotamia lie outside the mainstream of our cultural tradition, they continue to exert a powerful influence on the Western imagination, as the Tutankhamen exhibitions and their accompanying "Tut mania" showed in the 1970s. In part their fascination lies in their exoticism and in the excitement of their rediscovery in our own day. The pharaoh who can curse his excavator from beyond the grave is certainly a dramatic, if fictional, representative of his age. At the same time, the artistic achievements of those distant times need no historical justification. Created in a world very remote from our own, they serve as a reminder of the innate human urge to give expression to the eternal problems of existence.

SUMMARY

The early civilizations of the ancient Middle East laid the basis for the development of Western culture. In Egypt and Mesopotamia, in the period around 3000 B.C., the simple farming communities of the earlier Neolithic (New Stone) Age were replaced by cities, the product of agricultural discoveries that provided the food supply for relatively large numbers of people to live together.

Many of the characteristics of urban life developed during the following centuries: large-scale buildings, trade and commerce, systems of government and religion. The people of the Mesopotamian city of Uruk invented the earliest known writing system in the world.

Egyptian society was dominated by a strong central monarchy, with the pharaoh (the Egyptian king) presiding over a large bureaucracy that administered the affairs of state. Egyptian religious life was controlled by the priests, who sought to maintain old traditions, and Egyptian art generally reflected the policy of state control. Periods of political uncertainty were reflected in contemporary art. The confidence and stability of Old Kingdom sculpture, for example, disappeared in the unsettled conditions of the Middle Kingdom.

In the reign of the New Kingdom pharaoh Amenhotep IV, better known as Akhenaton (1379–1362 B.C.), there was a change: The numberless deities of Egyptian religion were replaced by a single sun god, and Egyptian art became naturalistic for the first time in its history. Akhenaton's successors, however, restored the traditional system of deities and the artistic conventions of former times.

The chief characteristic of Egyptian religious thought was the belief in survival after death for those who had led a good life. Elaborate funeral rituals were devised, in which the god Osiris, Judge of the Dead, was invoked. From early in Egyptian history monumental tombs were constructed for the ruling classes, the most famous of which are the Great Pyramids at Giza.

Mesopotamian culture lacked the unity of Egyptian life: A series of different peoples had their own languages, religions, and customs. The Sumerians, the earliest, lived in cities dominated by great temples built on artificial platforms. The temple priests administered both religious and economic affairs, sharing their duties with local civic rulers. Unlike the Egyptian pharaohs who were thought of as gods, Sumerian rulers never became the focus of a cult. They represented their city's god and served the interests of their people by overseeing government projects. Among the earliest of Sumerian kings was Gilgamesh, whose legendary deeds are described in the epic poem that bears his name.

Mesopotamia was ruled by the Akkadians, a Semitic people, from 2350 to 2150 B.C. Their kingdom was invaded and destroyed, and in a brief period of Neo-Sumerian revival the principal religious monument at Ur, the Ziggurat, was built. Around 1800 B.C. Mesopotamia was reunified by the Babylonians, whose most famous king, Hammurabi, was the author of an important law code.

The last people to rule Mesopotamia were the Assyrians, the peak of whose power was between 1000 B.C. and 612 B.C., the year in which their capital Nineveh was sacked by the Persians. Successive royal palaces, first at Nimrud and then at Nineveh, were decorated with massive stone relief carvings that showed aspects of life at court (royal processions, hunting scenes) with considerable realism.

The first urban culture in the West, known as Minoan, developed on the Mediterranean island of Crete. Around 2000 B.C. large towns were constructed; these served as centers for the ruling families and the chief religious leaders. The largest Minoan community, Knossos, was destroyed several times by earthquakes and each time was rebuilt on a grander scale. Like the other Minoan palaces, Knossos was decorated with vivid wall paintings depicting religious ceremonies and scenes from daily life. Many examples have been found of the elaborate jewelry worn by figures in the paintings; one of the richest is the gold Wasp Pendant from Mallia.

Around 1400 B.C. Knossos was abandoned for reasons that remain mysterious, and power passed to mainland Greece, where a people called the Mycenaeans had appeared by 1600 B.C. Most of our information about the Mycenaeans comes from their tombs. The earliest ones, at Mycenae itself, were dug into the ground within a circular enclosure; vast quantities of gold treasure, including death masks, jewelry, and weapons were buried with the bodies of the dead. The Mycenaeans traded widely in the Mediterranean area, and around 1250 B.C. they sacked the city of Troy, an economic rival. Shortly after, however, their own cities were destroyed. Within a century Mycenaean culture had vanished, although it was to have important influence upon later Greek civilization.

Pronunciation Guide

Akhenaton: Ak-en-AH-tun
Akkadian: Ak-AY-di-un
Amarna: Am-AR-nuh
Assurbanipal: As-er-BAN-i-pal
Assurnasirpal: A-ser-na-SEER-pal
Chefren: KEF-ren
Cheops: KEE-ops
Cuneiform: CUE-ni-form
Cyclades: SIK-la-dees
Euphrates: You-FRAY-tees
Gilgamesh: GIL-gum-esh
Hammurabi: Ham-oo-RA-bee
Hieroglyph: HIGH-ro-glif
Knossos: KNO-sos
Lascaux: Lasc-OWE
Mallia: MAR-lia
Mesopotamia: Mes-o-pot-AIM-i-a
Minos: MY-nos
Mycenae: My-SEEN-ee
Nefertiti: Nef-er-TEE-TEE
Phaistos: FES-tos
Pharaoh: FARE-owe
Schliemann: SHLEE-man

Stele: STAY-lay
Sumerian: Soo-MEE-ri-an
Tutankhamen: Tut-an-KA-mun
Uruk: Oo-ROOK
Willendorf: VIL-en-dorf
Zakro: ZAK-roe
Ziggurat: ZIG-oo-rat

Exercises

1. Compare the religious beliefs of the Egyptians and the Mesopotamians. What do their differences tell us about the cultures involved?
2. How did the development of Egyptian society affect their art? What were the principal subjects depicted by Egyptian artists?
3. What evidence is there for the role of women in the cultures discussed in this chapter?
4. What information do the excavations at the Palace of Knossos provide about Minoan daily life?
5. If you could return in time to visit one of the peoples described in the chapter, which would you choose?

Further Reading

Aldred, C. *The Egyptians.* New York: Praeger, 1961. A short but comprehensive account of Egyptian culture by one of the leading Egyptologists of the century.

Childe, V. Gordon. *What Happened in History.* Baltimore: Penguin, 1942. One of the most important books on the early development of civilization. The author's account is strongly influenced by his political views but is fundamental to an understanding of modern research on early Mesopotamia.

Frankfort, H. *The Art and Architecture of the Ancient Orient.* Baltimore: Penguin, 1970. The best single-volume guide to its subject. Technical in places but written with immense breadth of knowledge and fully illustrated.

———, et al. *Before Philosophy.* Baltimore: Penguin, 1949. Subtitled "The Intellectual Adventure of Ancient Man," this book discusses Egyptian and Mesopotamian views on life, death, the function of the state, and the nature of the world. Not easy to read, but well worth the effort.

Hood, S. *The Arts in Prehistoric Greece.* Baltimore: Penguin, 1978. An up-to-date introduction to Minoan and Mycenaean art. The author, who has himself dug both in Crete and at Mycenae, includes evidence from the most recent excavations.

Johnson, R. *The Civilization of Ancient Egypt.* London: Thames and Hudson, 1978. A good, well-balanced account that gives a general picture of Egyptian art and society.

Marinatos, S., and M. Hirmer. *Crete and Mycenae.* New York: Abrams, 1960. Chiefly valuable for its pictures, although Marinatos' commentary is authoritative and informative.

Roux, G. *Ancient Iraq,* 2nd ed. Baltimore: Penguin, 1980. A history of the ancient Near East from the Paleolithic period to Roman times.

Seton Lloyd, H. *Archaeology of Mesopotamia.* London: Methuen, 1978. An authoritative survey of recent archaeological discoveries in Mesopotamia and their significance for our knowledge of the cultures involved.

Smith, W. S., revised by W. K. Simpson. *The Art and Architecture of Ancient Egypt,* 2nd ed. Baltimore: Penguin, 1981. A thorough survey of all aspects of Egyptian art, with numerous photographs and diagrams.

Warren, P. *The Aegean Civilizations.* Oxford: Elsevier-Phaidon, 1975. A good general account of Bronze Age Aegean culture, especially well illustrated. The author includes an interesting account of his own excavations in Crete.

Willetts, R. F. *The Civilization of Ancient Crete.* London: Methuen, 1977. Deals with the Minoans and their successors on Crete and concludes with a section on Crete in the 20th century.

	GENERAL EVENTS	LITERATURE & PHILOSOPHY	ART
3000 B.C. BRONZE AGE Mycenaean Period	**c. 1184** Fall of Troy		
1100 Dark Age	**1100** Collapse of Mycenaean Empire		
1000 IRON AGE Heroic Age	**1000** Development of Iron Age culture at Athens **800–700** Greeks begin colonizing in East and Italy **776** First Olympic Games **c. 775** First Greek colony in Italy founded at Pithekoussai	**c. 900–700** Evolution of Homeric epics *Iliad* and *Odyssey* **8th cent.** Hesiod, *Works and Days* and *Theogony*	**1000–900** Protogeometric pottery decoration: bold circular shapes similar to Mycenaean motifs 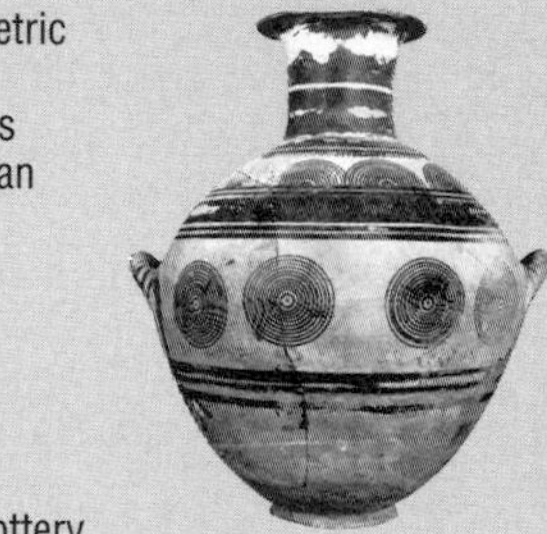 **900–700** Geometric pottery decoration: linear designs of zigzags, triangles, diamonds, meanders
750 Age of Colonization	**750–600** Greeks found colonies throughout Mediterranean, from Egypt to Black Sea	**c. 700** Greeks adapt Phoenician alphabet for their own language **c. 650** Archilochus, earliest Greek lyric poet, active	**8th cent.** Geometric pottery incorporates stylized human figure in painted design; Dipylon amphora **c. 650** Large freestanding sculpture evolves **late 7th cent.** Orientalizing styles in vase painting; Corinthian aryballos **c. 600** *New York Kouros;* Athenians develop narrative style in black-figure vase painting; increased naturalism in Greek art 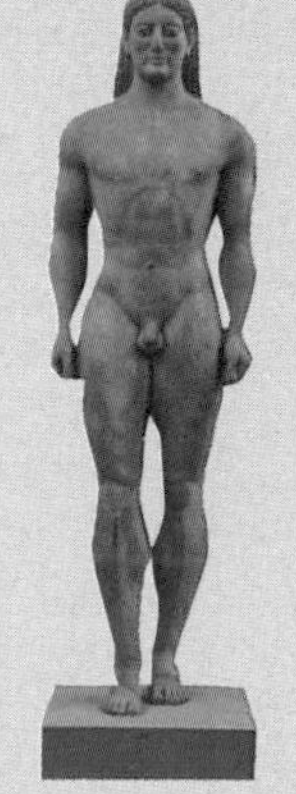
600 Archaic Period	**c. 590** Solon reforms Athenian constitution **546** Rule of Pisistratus begins growth of Athenian power; Persian Empire expands to take over Greek colonies in Asia Minor **510** Restoration of democracy at Athens **490** Start of the Persian Wars; forces of King Darius defeated at Marathon	**early 6th cent.** Sappho, *Poems* **6th cent.** Development of Presocratic schools of philosophy: Materialists, Pythagoreans, Dualists, Atomists **c. 540–480** Heraclitus of Ephesus teaches his theory of "impermanence" **late 6th cent.** Playwriting competition begins **after 525** First official version of Homeric epics written	**c. 550** *Calf-Bearer* **c. 540** *Peplos Kore* **c. 530** *Anavysos Kouros* **c. 525** Exekias, *Suicide of Ajax,* amphora **late 6th cent.** Red-figure style of vase painting introduced; *Euphronios Vase,* krater 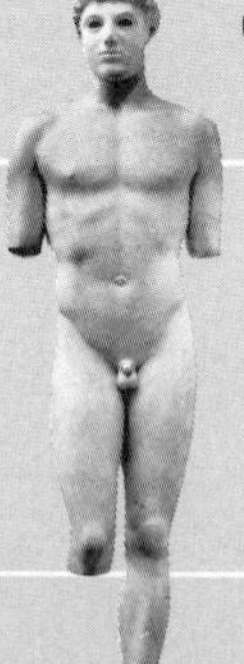 **c. 490** *Critian Boy;* turning point between Archaic and Classical periods
480 Classical Period	**480** Xerxes leads a second expedition against Greece; wins battle of Thermopylae and sacks Athens; Greeks defeat Persians decisively at Salamis **479** Greek victories at Plataea and Mycale end Persian Wars	**c. 475** Parmenides writes on his theory of knowledge **c. 440** Herodotus begins *History of the Persian Wars*	
323			

Many dates are approximate

CHAPTER 2 EARLY GREECE

ARCHITECTURE	MUSIC

Early music primarily vocal with instrumental accompaniment; use of flute and simple lyre popular

c. 600 Form of Doric temple fully established, derived from early wooden structures; Temple of Hera at Olympia

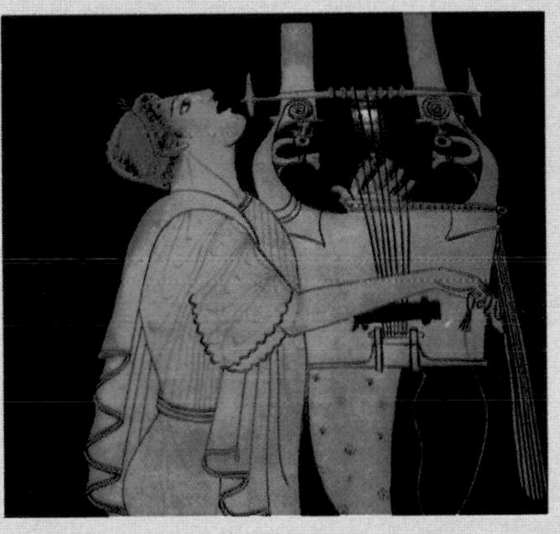

7th cent. Development of aulos (double flute), used to accompany songs

c. 675 Terpander of Lesbos introduces cithara

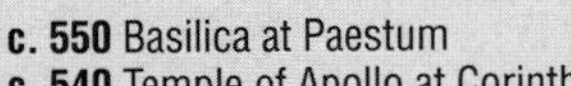

c. 550 Basilica at Paestum
c. 540 Temple of Apollo at Corinth

c. 500 Temple of Aphaia, Aegina

586 Sacadas of Argos composes first known purely instrumental work for performance on aulos at Pythian Games in Delphi

c. 550 Pythagoras discovers numerical relationship of music harmonies and our modern musical scale

5th cent. First widespread use of Ionic order

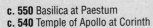

late 5th cent. Earliest surviving fragment of Greek music

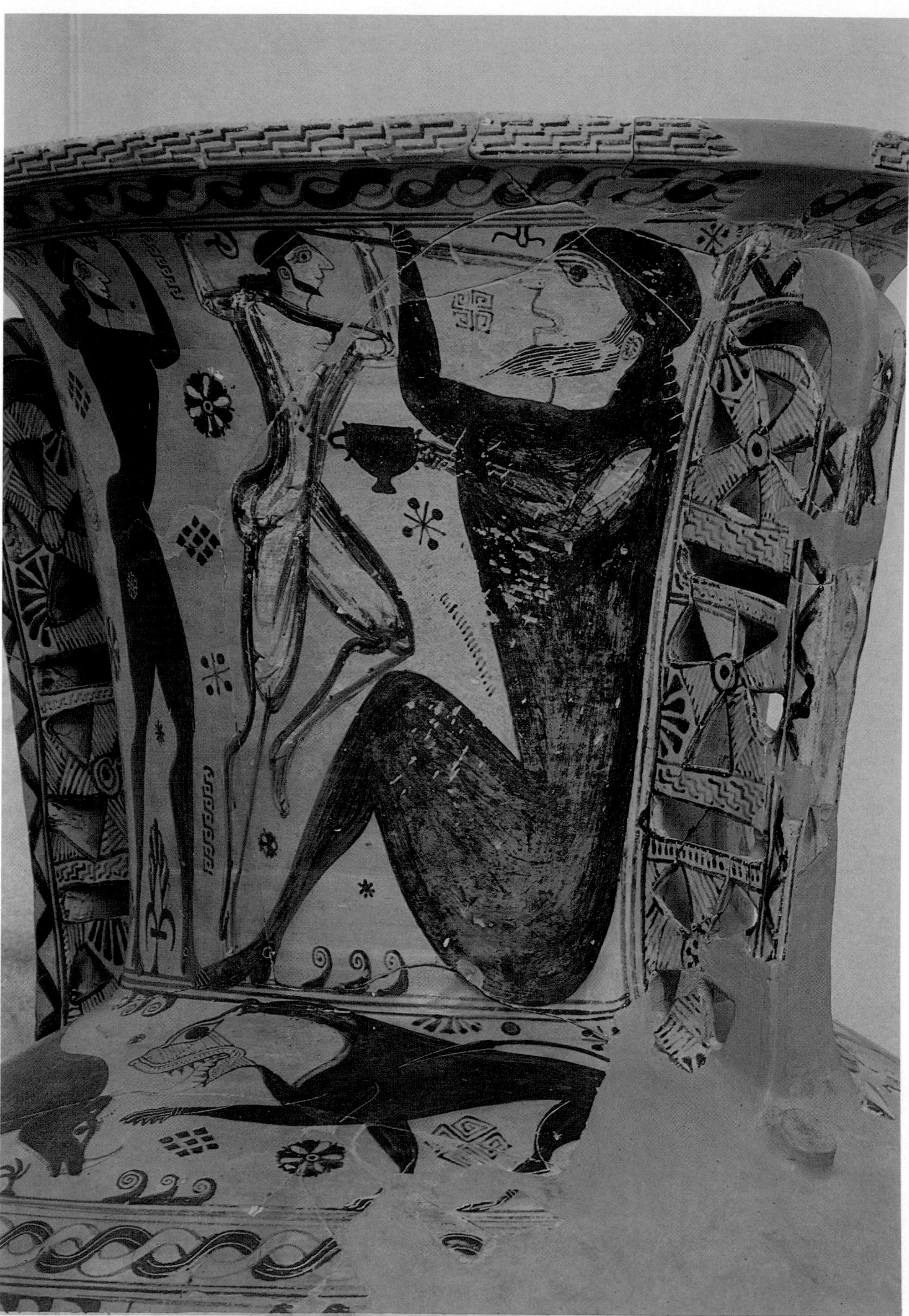

C H A P T E R

2
EARLY GREECE

One of the major turning points of history is the period around 1000 B.C., the change from the Bronze Age to the Iron Age throughout the Mediterranean area. In the following centuries a culture developed in a small corner of southeastern Europe, Greece, which was to form the foundation of Western civilization. By the 5th century B.C. this culture had produced one of the greatest eras of human achievement.

In certain basic ways, of course, there was some continuity between the Bronze Age and the Iron Age. For example, Athens, which in the 5th century B.C. became the intellectual center of Classical Greece, had been a Mycenaean city long before the Iron Age began. In most significant respects, however, the Iron Age Greeks had to discover for themselves almost all the cultural skills associated with civilization—the visual arts, architecture, literature, philosophy, even the art of writing. The Mycenaeans had known how to write and build and create art. However, their abrupt and violent end around 1100 B.C. was followed by a century of disturbance and confusion that cut off the Bronze Age from the new world of the Iron Age. To follow the first attempts of these Iron Age people to develop an artistic style, organize their societies, and question the nature of the universe is to witness the birth of Western culture.

The history of early Greece falls naturally into three periods, each marked by its own distinctive artistic achievement. During the first three hundred years or so of the Iron Age, development was slow and the Greeks had only limited contact with other Mediterranean peoples. During this period the first great works of literature were created—the epic poems known as the *Iliad* and the *Odyssey*. Because these works treat heroic themes, the early Iron Age in Greece is sometimes known as the Heroic Age. The visual art of the period used a style known as Geometric.

By the beginning of the 8th century B.C., Greek travelers and merchants had already begun to explore the lands to the east and west. In the next 150 years (c. 750–600 B.C.), called the Age of Colonization, many new ideas and artistic styles were brought to Greece.

These foreign influences were finally absorbed in the third era of early Greece known as the Archaic period (c. 600–480 B.C.). This period, the culmination of the first five hundred years of Greek history, paved the way for the Classical period, discussed in Chapter 3. The Greeks' relationship to the world around them took a decisive turn at the very end of the Archaic period with their victory over the Persians in the wars that lasted from 490 to 479 B.C. The events of the Persian Wars thus end this chapter.

HOMER AND THE HEROIC AGE

During the Mycenaean period most of Greece had been united under a single influence. When the Mycenaeans fell, however, Greece split up into a series of independent regions that corresponded to the geographically separated areas created by the mountain ranges and high hills that crisscross the terrain. Within each of these geographically discrete areas there developed an urban center that controlled the surrounding countryside. Thus Athens became the dominating force in the geographical region known as Attica; Thebes controlled Boeotia; Sparta controlled Laconia, and so on (see map, page 35). A central urban community of this kind was called by the Greeks of a later period a *polis*, a term generally translated as "city-state."

The polis served as focal point for all political, religious, social, and artistic activities within its region. Its citizens felt toward their own individual city a loyalty that was far stronger than any generalized sense of community with their fellow Greeks over the mountains. Each of the leading cities developed its own artistic style, which led to fierce competition and in time bitter and destructive rivalries. The polis was, therefore, both the glory and the ruin of Greek civilization, producing on the one hand an unequaled concentration of intellectual and cultural development, on the other a tendency to internal squabbling at the least provocation.

The fragmentation of social and cultural life had a marked effect on the development of Greek mythology and religion. Religion played an important part in Greek life, as Greek art and literature demonstrate, but it was very different in nature from the other systems of belief that influenced our culture, Judaism and Christianity. For one thing, Greek mythology offers no central body of information or teaching corresponding to the Old or New Testaments. Often there are varying versions of the same basic story; even when these versions do not actually contradict one another, they are difficult to reconcile. For another thing, the very characters of the Greek gods and goddesses often seem confused and self-contradictory. For example, Zeus, President of the Immortals and Father of gods and humans, generally represented the concept of an objective moral code to which both gods and mortals were expected to conform; Zeus imposed justice and supervised the punishment of wrongdoers [2.1]. Yet this same majestic ruler was also involved in many love affairs and seductions, in the course of which his behavior was often undignified and even comical. How could the Greeks have believed in a champion of morality whose own moral standards were so lax?

2.1 *Zeus (Poseidon?)*. c. 465 B.C. Bronze, height 6'10" (2.08 m). National Archaeological Museum, Athens. Whether this striding god is Zeus or Poseidon, god of the sea, the combination of majestic dignity and physical strength reflects the Greeks' view of their gods as superior beings with definitely human attributes. This statue, found in the sea off Cape Artemisium, comes from the end of the period covered in this chapter; it may have been intended to commemorate the Greek victory over the Persians.

The answer lies in the fact that Greek myth and religion of later times consist of a mass of folk tales, primitive customs, and traditional rituals that grew up during the Heroic Age and were never developed into a single unified system. Individual cities had their own mythological traditions, some of them going back to the Bronze Age, others gradually developing under the influence of neighboring peoples. Poets and artists felt free to choose the versions that appealed to their own tastes or helped them to express their ideas. Later Greeks, it is true, tried to organize all these conflicting beliefs into something resembling order. Father Zeus ruled from Mount Olympus, where he was surrounded by the other principal Olympian deities. His wife Hera was the goddess of marriage and the protectress of the family. His daughter Athena symbolized intelligence and understanding. Aphrodite was the goddess of love, Ares, her lover, the god of war, and so on. But the range and variety of the Greek imagination defied this kind of categorization. The Greeks loved a good story, and so tales that did not fit the ordered scheme continued to circulate.

These contradictions were, of course, perfectly apparent to the Greeks themselves, but they used their religion to illuminate their own lives, rather than to give them divine guidance. One of the clearest examples is the contrast that Greek poets drew between the powers of Apollo and Dionysus, two of the most important of their gods. Apollo represented logic and order, the power of the mind; Dionysus was the god of the emotions, whose influence, if excessive, could lead to violence and disorder. By worshiping both these forces, the Greeks were acknowledging their obvious dual existence

in human nature and trying to strike a prudent balance between them.

The Greek deities served many purposes, therefore, but these purposes were very different from those of the other Western religions. No Greek god, not even Zeus, represents supreme good. At the other end of the moral scale, there is no Greek figure of supreme evil corresponding to the Christian concept of Satan. The Greeks turned to their deities for explanations of both natural phenomena and psychological characteristics they recognized in themselves. At the same time they used their gods and goddesses as yet another way of enhancing the glory of their individual city-states, as in the case of the cult of Athena at Athens. Problems of human morality required human, rather than divine, solutions. The Greeks turned to art and literature, rather than prayer, as a means of trying to discover them (Table 2.1).

At the beginning of Greek history stand two epic poems which even the quarrelsome Greeks themselves saw as national, indeed universal, in their significance. The *Iliad* and the *Odyssey* have, from that early time, been held in the highest esteem. Homer, their accepted author, is generally regarded as not only the first figure in the Western literary tradition but also one of the greatest. Yet even though Homer's genius is beyond doubt, little else about him is clear. In fact, the many problems and theories connected with the Homeric epics and their creator are generally summed up under the label "the Homeric Question."

The ancient Greeks themselves were not sure who had composed the *Iliad* and the *Odyssey*, when

TABLE 2.1 The Principal Greek Deities

Zeus	Father of Gods and Men
Hera	Wife of Zeus, Queen of Heaven
Poseidon	Brother of Zeus, God of the Sea
Hephaestus	Son of Zeus and Hera, God of Fire
Ares	God of War
Apollo	God of Prophecy, Intellect, Music, and Medicine
Artemis	Goddess of Chastity and the Moon
Demeter	Earth Mother, Goddess of Fertility
Aphrodite	Goddess of Beauty, Love, and Marriage
Athena	Goddess of Wisdom
Hermes	Messenger of the Gods, God of Cleverness
Dionysus	God of Wine and the Emotions

and where the author had lived, or even if one person was responsible for both of them. In general, tradition ascribed the epics to a blind poet called Homer; almost every city worthy of the name claimed to be his birthplace. Theories about when he had lived ranged from the time of the Trojan War, around 1250 B.C., to 500 years later.

The problem of who Homer was, and even whether he existed at all, continues to vex scholars to this day. In any case, most experts would probably now agree that the creation of the *Iliad* and the *Odyssey* was a highly complex affair. Each of the epics basically consists of a number of shorter folk tales that were combined, gradually evolving over a century or more into the works as we now know them.

These epic poems were almost certainly composed and preserved at a time before the introduction of writing in Greece, poets passing them down by word of mouth. Professional bards—storytellers—probably learned a host of ready-made components: traditional tales, stock incidents, and a whole catalog of repeated phrases and descriptions. In the absence of any written text the works remained fluid, and individual reciters would bring their own contributions. On the other hand, both the Homeric epics show a marked unity of style and structure.

The first crystallization of these popular stories had probably occurred by around 800 B.C., but the poems were still not in their final form for more than a century. The first written official version of each epic was probably not made before the late 6th century B.C. The edition of the poems used by modern scholars was made by a scribe working at Alexandria in the 2nd century B.C.

Where, then, in this long development must we place Homer? He may perhaps have been the man who first began to combine the separate tales into a single whole; or perhaps he was the man who sometime after 800 B.C. imposed an artistic unity on the mass of remembered folk stories he had inherited. The differences between the *Iliad* and the *Odyssey* have suggested to a number of commentators that a different "Homer" may have been responsible for the creation or development of each work, but here we are in the realm of speculation. Perhaps after all it would be best to follow the ancient Greeks themselves, contenting ourselves with the belief that at some stage in the evolution of the poems they were filtered through the imagination of the first great genius of the Western literary tradition, without being too specific about which stage it was.

Both works show evidence of their long evolution by word of mouth. All the chief characters are given standardized descriptive adjectives as "epithets," that are repeated whenever they appear: Achilles is "swift-footed" and Odysseus "cunning." Phrases, lines, and entire sections are often repeated. There are also minor inconsistencies in the plots.

Furthermore, the heroic world of warfare is made more accessible to the poem's audience by the use of elaborate similes, which compare aspects of the story to everyday life in the early Iron Age—

CONTEMPORARY VOICES

Daily Life in the World of Homer

From the description of scenes on the shield of Achilles:

> Next he showed two beautiful cities full of people. In one of them weddings and banquets were afoot. They were bringing the brides through the streets from their homes, to the loud music of the wedding-hymn and the light of blazing torches. Youths accompanied by flute and lyre were whirling in the dance, and the women had come to the doors of their houses to enjoy the show. But the men had flocked to the meeting-place, where a case had come up between two litigants, about the payment of compensation for a man who had been killed. The defendant claimed the right to pay in full and was announcing his intention to the people; but the other contested his claim and refused all compensation. Both parties insisted that the issue should be settled by a referee; and both were cheered by their supporters in the crowd, whom the heralds were attempting to silence. The Elders sat on the sacred bench, a semicircle of polished stone; and each, as he received the speaker's rod from the clear-voiced heralds, came forward in his turn to give his judgment, staff in hand. Two talents of gold were displayed in the center: they were the fee for the Elder whose exposition of the law should prove the best.

Homer, *Iliad*, trans. E. V. Rieu (Baltimore: Penguin, 1950), Book XVII, p. 349.

the massing of the Greek forces, for example, is likened to a swarm of flies buzzing around pails of milk.

Although the two poems are clearly the result of a single tradition, they are very different in spirit. The *Iliad* is somber, taut, direct. The concentration of its theme makes it easier to understand, and certainly easier to explain, than the more digressive and lighthearted *Odyssey*. But the *Odyssey* is certainly not a lesser work; if anything, its range and breadth of humanity are even greater, and its design is more elaborate.

The action of the *Iliad* takes place during the final year of the Greeks' siege of Troy, or Ilium. Its subject is only indirectly concerned with the Trojan War, however, and the poem ends before the episode of the wooden horse and the fall of the city. Its principal theme is stated in the opening lines of Book I, which establish the tragic mood of the work. Here the poet invokes the goddess of poetic inspiration: "Sing, goddess, of the anger of Peleus' son Achilles, which disastrously inflicted countless sufferings on the Greeks, sending the strong souls of many heroes to Hades and leaving their bodies to be devoured by dogs and all birds. . . ."

The subject of the *Iliad*, then, is the anger of Achilles and its consequences. Its message is a direct one: We must be prepared to answer for the results of our own actions and realize that when we act wrongly we will cause suffering both for ourselves and, perhaps more important, for those we love. Although the setting of the *Iliad* is heroic, even mythic, the theme of human responsibility is universal. This relevance to our own experience is underlined by the realism in the scenes of battles and death, which are characteristic of epic literature's interest in heroic warfare.

The story of Achilles' disastrous mistake is told in a basically simple and direct narrative. It begins with a quarrel between Agamemnon, commander-in-chief of the Greek forces, and Achilles, his powerful ally, who resents Agamemnon's overbearing assertion of authority. After a public argument, Achilles decides to punish Agamemnon by withdrawing his military support and retiring to his tent, in the hope that without his aid the Greeks will be unable to overcome the Trojans. In the battles that follow he is proved correct; the Trojans inflict a series of defeats on the Greeks, killing many of their leading warriors.

Agamemnon eventually (Book IX) admits that he behaved too high-handedly and offers Achilles, through intermediaries, not only a handsome apology but a generous financial inducement to return to the fighting and save the Greek cause. Achilles, however, rejects this attempt to make amends and stubbornly nurses his anger as the fighting resumes and Greek casualties mount. Then his dearest friend Patroclus is killed by the Trojan leader Hector, son of their king (Book XVI). Only now does Achilles return to battle, his former anger against Agamemnon now turned against the Trojans in general and Hector in particular.

After killing Hector in single combat (Book XXII), Achilles abuses Hector's corpse in order to relieve his own sense of guilt at having permitted Patroclus' death. Finally, Priam, the old king of Troy, steals into the Greek camp by night to beg for the return of his son's body (Book XXIV). In this encounter with Priam, Achilles at last recognizes and accepts the tragic nature of life and the inevitability of death. His anger melts and he hands over the body of his dead enemy. The *Iliad* ends with the funeral rites of Hector, "tamer of horses."

As is clear even from this brief summary, there is a direct relationship between human actions and their consequences. The gods appear in the *Iliad* and frequently play a part in the action, but at no time can divine intervention save Achilles from paying the price for his unreasonable anger. Furthermore, Achilles' crime is committed not against a divine code of ethics but against human standards of behavior. All his companions, including Patroclus, realize that he is behaving unreasonably.

From its earliest beginnings, therefore, the Greek view of morality is in strong contrast to the Judeo-Christian tradition. At the center of the Homeric universe is not God but human beings, who are at least partly in control of their own destiny. If they cannot choose the time when they die, they can at least choose how they live. The standards by which human life will be judged are those established by one's fellow humans. In the *Iliad* the gods serve as divine "umpires." They watch the action and comment on it and at times enforce the rules, but they do not affect the course of history. Humans do not always, however, fully realize the consequences of their behavior. In fact, they often prefer to believe that things happen "according to the will of the gods" rather than because of their own actions. Yet the gods themselves claim no such power. In a remarkable passage at the beginning of Book I of the *Odyssey* we see the world for a moment through the eyes of Zeus as he sits at dinner on Mount Olympus: "How foolish men are! How unjustly they blame the gods! It is their lot to suffer, but because of their own folly they bring upon themselves sufferings over and above what is fated for them. And then they blame the gods." These are hardly words we can imagine coming from the God of the Old Testament.

The principal theme of the *Odyssey* is the return home of the Greek hero Odysseus from the war against Troy. Odysseus' journey, which takes ten years, is filled with adventures involving one-eyed giants, monsters of various kinds, a seductive enchantress, a romantic young girl, a floating island, a trip to the underworld, and many other fairy-tale elements. Into this main narrative is woven a description of the wanderings of Odysseus' son, Telemachus, who, searching for his missing father, visits many of the other Greek leaders who have returned safely from Troy.

In the last half of the poem Odysseus finally returns home in disguise. Without revealing his identity to his ever-faithful wife Penelope, he kills the suitors who have been pestering her for ten years to declare her husband dead and remarry. Homer keeps us waiting almost to the very end for the grand recognition scene between husband and wife. All ends happily, with Penelope, Odysseus, and his aged father Laertes peacefully reunited.

It is worth examining the Homeric world at some length, because the *Iliad* and the *Odyssey* formed the basis of education and culture throughout the Greek and Roman world; children learned the two poems by heart at school. Ideas changed and developed, but reverence for Homer remained constant.

2.2 Protogeometric amphora. c. 950 B.C. Height 21¾" (56 cm). Kerameikos Museum, Athens. Photo DAI Athens, Ker 7750. The circles and semicircles typical of this style were drawn with a compass.

ART AND SOCIETY IN EARLY GREECE

Geometric Art

Our impressions of the first three hundred years of Greek art (1000–700 B.C.) are based largely on painted pottery, hardly a major art form even in later times, for little else has survived. Of architecture there is almost no trace. Although small bronze and ivory statuettes and relief plaques were being made from the 9th century B.C. on, the earliest surviving large stone sculptures date to the mid-7th century B.C.

Painted vases, therefore, are our major source of information about artistic developments. It comes as something of a surprise to find that Homer's contemporaries decorated their pots with abstract geometric designs, with no attempt at the qualities most typical of their literature, vividness and realism. This style has given its name to the two subdivisions of the period, the Protogeometric (1000–900 B.C.) and the Geometric (900–700 B.C.).

For the first hundred years, artists decorated their vases with simple, bold designs consisting mainly of concentric circles and semicircles [2.2]. In some ways this period represents a transition from the end of the Mycenaean age, but the memory of Mycenaean motifs soon gave way to a new style. If Protogeometric pottery seems a long way from Greek art of later centuries, it does show qualities of clarity and order that reappear later, although in a very different context.

In the Geometric pottery of the following two centuries (900–700 B.C.) the use of abstract design continued, but the emphasis changed. Circles and semicircles were replaced by linear designs, zigzags, triangles, diamonds, and above all the *meander* (a maze pattern). There is something strangely obsessive about many of these vessels—a sense of artists searching for a subject, meanwhile working out over and over the implications of mathematical formulas. Once again we seem a long way from the achievements of later Greek artists, with their emphasis on realism, yet precise mathematical relationships lie behind the design of much of the greatest Greek art.

By the 8th century B.C., artists had begun to find their way toward the principal subject of later Greek art, the human form. Thus human and animal figures begin to appear among the meanders and zigzags. This is a moment of such importance in the history of Western art that we should not take it for granted. We have been so conditioned by the art of the ancient Greeks that from the late Geometric period until our own time Western art has been primarily concerned with the depiction of human beings. Landscapes are a popular subject, it is true, and in our own century art has become abstract again. Yet most paintings and sculptures deal with the human form, treated in a more or less realistic way.

This realism may seem so obvious as to be hardly worth stating, but it must be remembered that the art of peoples who were not influenced by the Greeks is very different. Islamic art, for example, deals almost exclusively in abstract design. Indian sculptors depicted their gods and heroes in human form, but they certainly did not treat them realistically. The Hindu god Shiva, for example, is often shown with many arms. It is a tribute to the Greeks' overwhelming influence on our culture that, from the Roman period to the 20th century, artists have accepted the Greeks' decision to make the realistic treatment of the human form the central focus of art, whether the forms were those of mortal people or divine gods and goddesses.

The Greeks themselves did not achieve this naturalism overnight. The first depictions of human beings, which appear on Geometric vases shortly after 800 B.C., are highly stylized. They are painted in silhouette, and a single figure often combines front and side views, the head and legs being shown in profile while the upper half of the body is seen from the front. A number of the vases decorated with stick figures of this kind are of immense size. One of them, the *Dipylon Amphora*, is almost 5 feet (1.24 meters) tall [2.3]. These vases were set up over tombs to serve as grave markers; they had holes in their bases so that offerings poured into them could seep down to the dead below. The scenes on them frequently show the funeral ceremony. Others show processions of warriors, both on foot and in chariots.

2.3 *Dipylon Amphora.* c. 750 B.C. Height 4'11" (1.24 m). National Archaeological Museum, Athens. This immense vase originally was a grave marker. The main band, between the handles, shows the lying-in-state of the dead man on whose grave the vase stood; on both sides of the bier are mourners tearing their hair in grief. Note the two bands of animals, deer and running goats, in the upper part of the vase.

The Age of Colonization

Throughout the period of Homer and Geometric art, individual city-states were ruled by small groups of aristocrats who concentrated wealth and power in their own hands. Presumably, it is their graves that were marked with great amphoras like the *Dipylon* vase. By the 8th century B.C., however, two centuries of peace had allowed the individual city-states to become quite prosperous. The ruling classes became increasingly concerned with the image of their city-states. They began to function as patrons of the arts as well as military leaders. Great international festivals began to develop at Olympia, Delphi, and other sacred sites, at which athletes and poets—representing their city—could compete with one another.

During the 7th century, as trade with both fellow Greeks and other Near Eastern peoples increased, economic success became a crucial factor in the growth of a *polis* (or city-state); individual cities began to mint their own coins shortly before 600 B.C. Yet political power remained in the hands of a small hereditary aristocracy, leaving a growing urban population increasingly frustrated. Both the

SPORTS AND GAMES

The Olympics

The Olympic Games are the oldest international sporting contests still in existence in the world. Founded in 776 B.C., they were held at Olympia every four years up to 394 A.D., when the growth of cheating induced Emperor Theodosius I to abolish them. They were revived again in 1896; the first modern Olympics took place in Athens. The 1992 Games were held in Barcelona, Spain, and the 1996 competitions are scheduled for Atlanta, Georgia.

At the very first Games, the principal event was a foot race in honor of Zeus, whose worship formed one of the chief cults at Olympia; over the following years, other contests would be added, including boxing, wrestling, long jump, chariot racing, and discus and javelin throwing. Although the Olympic and other festivals retained their important association with religion, their fundamental significance lay in the competition between athletes: the word *athletics* is Greek in origin, and means contest or struggle.

The element of effort and strain, the sheer physical suffering, provided some of the satisfaction, and the poet Pindar (515–438 B.C.) describes the ideal athlete as "one who delights in the toil and the cost." For the Greeks, the honor of victory was a sufficient prize, symbolized at Olympia by the awarding of a simple wreath of wild olive. On the other hand, winners of important events received lavish treatment on their return home; the jubilant citizens would sometimes knock down part of the walls of the town to make a special entrance, and provide the victor with free meals at state expense for the rest of his life.

The competitions were confined to boys and men, who performed nude. (The only city where women regularly took part in athletic events was Sparta.) Married women could not attend the Olympic Games, and it is probable that few unmarried women availed themselves of their right to be present. By classical times, the course of the festival was standardized. The first of the five days was dedicated to religious ceremonies and to various "fringe" events: poetry readings, sculpture exhibitions, and the like. The next day began with one of the most exciting and dangerous contests, the four-horse chariot race; this involved 24 laps of the race course, over a total distance of almost nine miles, each lap involving a hair-raising turn around the turning-post at the end of the course. A horse race followed, with the jockeys wearing neither shoes nor stirrups, and the day's competitions ended with the pentathlon—each competitor took part in five events, the foot race, long jump, discus and javelin throwing, and finally wrestling.

After a day marked by solemn sacrifices at the altar of Zeus and a great banquet, the fourth day saw the remaining athletic events, foot racing, wrestling, and boxing. The closing ceremonies took place on the last day, and the winners celebrated their victories with a final dinner.

Over time, unfairness and corruption tended to increase, and led eventually to the abolition of the festival. Nonetheless, for over a thousand years the Olympic spirit represented an ideal in Greek life, whereby physical prowess was devoted to peace and not war; for three months beforehand, and then during the Games themselves, a Sacred Truce operated throughout Greece, and even the bitterest of opponents suspended their fighting in the name of the Olympic festival.

accumulation of wealth and the problem of overpopulation produced a single result: colonization.

Throughout the 8th and 7th centuries, enterprising Greeks went abroad either to make their fortunes or to increase them. To the west, Italy and Sicily were colonized and Greek cities established there. Some of these, like Syracuse in Sicily or Sybaris in southern Italy, became even richer and more powerful than the mother cities from which the colonizers had come. Unfortunately if inevitably, the settlers took with them not only the culture of their polis but their intercity rivalries, often with disastrous results. To the south and east, cities were also established in Egypt and on the Black Sea.

The most significant wave of colonization was that which moved eastward to the coast of Asia Minor, in some cases back to territory that had been inhabited by the Mycenaeans centuries earlier. From here the colonizers established trade contacts with peoples in the ancient Near East, including the Phoenicians and the Persians. Within Greece itself the effect on art and life of this expansion to the east was immense. After almost three hundred years of cultural isolation, in a land cut off from its neighbors by mountains and sea, the Greeks were brought face to face with the immensely rich and sophisticated cultures of the ancient Near East. Oriental ideas and artistic styles were seen by the colonizers and carried home by the traders. A growing quantity of eastern artifacts, ivories, jewelry, and metalwork was sent back to the mother cities and even to the Greek cities of Italy. So great was the impact of Near Eastern art on the Greeks from the late 8th century to around 600 B.C. that this period and its style are generally known by the name *Orientalizing*.

2.4 **Aryballos. Middle Corinthian, c. 625 B.C. State Museums, Berlin. The black-figure technique and the very Eastern-looking panther are characteristic of the Orientalizing style. Also characteristic are the flowerlike decorations, which are blobs of paint scored with lines. The musculature and features of the panther are also the result of scoring.**

THE VISUAL ARTS AT CORINTH AND ATHENS

Different Greek cities reacted to Oriental influences in different ways, although all were strongly influenced. In particular, the growing hostility between the two richest city-states, Athens and Corinth, which two centuries later led to the Peloponnesian War and the fall of Athens, seems already symbolized in the strong differences between their Orientalizing pottery. The Corinthian artists developed a miniature style that made use of a wide variety of eastern motifs—sphinxes, winged human figures, floral designs—all of them arranged in bands covering almost the entire surface of the vase. White, yellow, and purple were often used to highlight details, producing a bold and striking effect. After the monotony of Geometric pottery the variety of subject and range of color come as a welcome change.

The small size of the pots made them ideal for export. Corinthian vases have in fact been discovered not only throughout Greece but also in Italy, Egypt, and the Near East. Clearly, any self-respecting woman of the 7th century B.C. wanted an elegant little Corinthian flask [2.4] for her perfume, oil, or makeup. The vases are well made, the

EAST MEETS WEST

The Phoenicians

The Phoenicians, a Semitic people, inhabited the narrow coastal plain of what is now Lebanon and western Syria; their principal cities were Tyre and Sidon. Famous throughout the ancient world as merchants and traders, they controlled a string of trading stations and colonies that ran from western Spain to Mesopotamia. Great seafarers, they explored the Atlantic coast of Europe and are reputed to have sailed around Africa. In order to organize their commercial activities they developed an alphabet that was borrowed, in a modified form, by the Greeks. The Romanized version of this Greek form was used by all Western European languages (including, of course, English) as they developed.

In 574 B.C. they were conquered by the Babylonians, but their colony of Carthage in North Africa (about eight miles from the modern city of Tunis) remained independent and developed its own trading empire. Phoenician influence in the western Mediterranean ended only when the Carthaginians became embroiled in a series of wars with Rome that ended with the destruction of Carthage in 146 B.C.

For a people with so long a history and so important a role in the ancient world, the Phoenicians remain little known. The generally unsympathetic picture they present is in part a result of the fact that most of our knowledge of Phoenician culture comes from Greek and Roman sources. The Greeks' dislike and mistrust for the Phoenicians appears as early as the *Odyssey*, where Odysseus describes a Phoenician merchant as "a man who knew all the tricks, always swallowing up what he could, a real troublemaker."

2.5 *The Blinding of Polyphemus,* detail of proto-Attic amphora. c. 650 B.C. Height of frieze 17" (43 cm). Museum, Eleusis. The technique is crude, but the artist shows imagination and even humor in depicting an episode from the *Odyssey.* At the center is Odysseus himself, guiding a sharpened, heated pole into the single eye of Polyphemus, the Cyclops, seated drunkenly at the right—note the wine cup in his hand.

figures lively, and the style instantly recognizable as Corinthian—an important factor for commercial success. Corinth's notable political and economic strength throughout the 7th and early 6th centuries B.C. was, in fact, built on the sale of these little pots and their contents.

In Athens, potters were slower to throw off the effects of the Geometric period and less able to develop an all-purpose style like the Corinthian. The vases remain large and the attempts to depict humans and animals are often clumsy. The achievements of later Athenian art are nonetheless clearly foreshadowed in the vitality of the figures and the constant desire of the artists to illustrate events from mythology [2.5] or daily life rather than simply to decorate a surface in the Corinthian manner.

By 600 B.C. the narrative style had become established at Athens. As the Athenians began to take over an increasing share of the market for painted vases and their contents, Corinth's position declined, and the trade rivalry that later had devastating results began to develop.

The Beginnings of Greek Sculpture

The influence of Near Eastern and Egyptian models on Greek sculpture and architecture is more consistent and easier to trace than on pottery. The first Greek settlers in Egypt were given land around the mid-7th century B.C. by the Egyptian

2.6 *Kore* from Delos, dedicated by Nikandre. c. 650 B.C. Marble. National Archaeological Museum, Athens. Photo DAI Athens, Hege 1100. Unlike the *kouros,* the figure is completely clothed, though both have the same rigid stance, arms by sides, and wiglike hair.

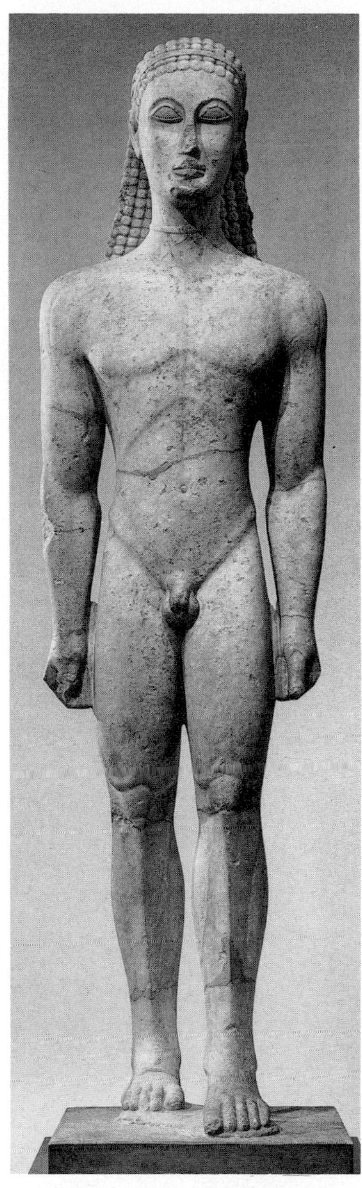

2.7 *Kouros*. c. 615 B.C. Marble, height 6'1½" (1.87 m). Metropolitan Museum of Art, New York (Fletcher Fund, 1932).

pharaoh Psammetichos I. It is surely no coincidence that the earliest Greek stone sculptures, which date from about the same period, markedly resemble Egyptian cult statues and were placed in similarly grandiose temples. (The earliest surviving temple, that of Hera at Olympia, dates at least in part to this period.) These stone figures consist of a small number of types repeated over and over. The most popular were the standing female, or *kore*, clad in drapery [2.6], and the standing male, or *kouros*, always shown nude [2.7]. This nudity already marks a break with the Egyptian tradition in which figures wore loincloths and foreshadows the heroic male nudity of Classical Greek art. The stance of the *kouros* figures, however, was firmly based on Egyptian models. One foot (usually the left) is forward, the arms are by the sides, and the hands are clenched. The elaborate wiglike hair is also Egyptian in inspiration.

By 600 B.C., only a few years after the first appearance of these statues, Greek art had reached a critical stage. After the slow and cautious progress of the Geometric period, the entire character of painting and sculpture had changed, and within the century following 700 B.C. Greek artists had abandoned abstract design for increasing realism. At this point in their development the Greek spirit of independence and inquiry asserted itself. Instead of following their eastern counterparts and repeating the same models and conventions for centuries, Greek painters and sculptors allowed their curiosity to lead them in a new direction, one that changed the history of art. The early stone figures and painted silhouettes had represented human beings, but only in a schematic, stylized form. Beginning in the Archaic period artists used their work to try to answer such questions as: What do human beings really look like? How do perspective and foreshortening work? What in fact is the true nature of appearance? For the first time in history they began to reproduce the human form in a way true to nature rather than merely to echo the achievements of their predecessors.

Sculpture and Painting in the Archaic Period

It is tempting to see the works of art and literature of the Archaic period (600–480 B.C.) as steps on the road that leads to the artistic and intellectual achievement in the Classical Age of the 5th and 4th centuries B.C. rather than to appreciate them for their own qualities. This would be to underestimate seriously the vitality of one of the most creative periods in the development of our culture. In some ways, in fact, the spirit of adventure, of striving toward new forms and new ideas, makes the Archaic achievement more exciting, if less perfected, than that of the Classical period. It is better to travel hopefully than to arrive, as Robert Louis Stevenson put it.

The change in Archaic art is a reflection of similar social developments. The hereditary aristocrats were beginning to lose their commanding status. At Athens, Solon (c. 639–559 B.C.), the legislator and poet, reformed the legal system in 594 B.C., and divided the citizens into four classes; members of all four could take part in the debates of the Assembly and sit in the law courts.

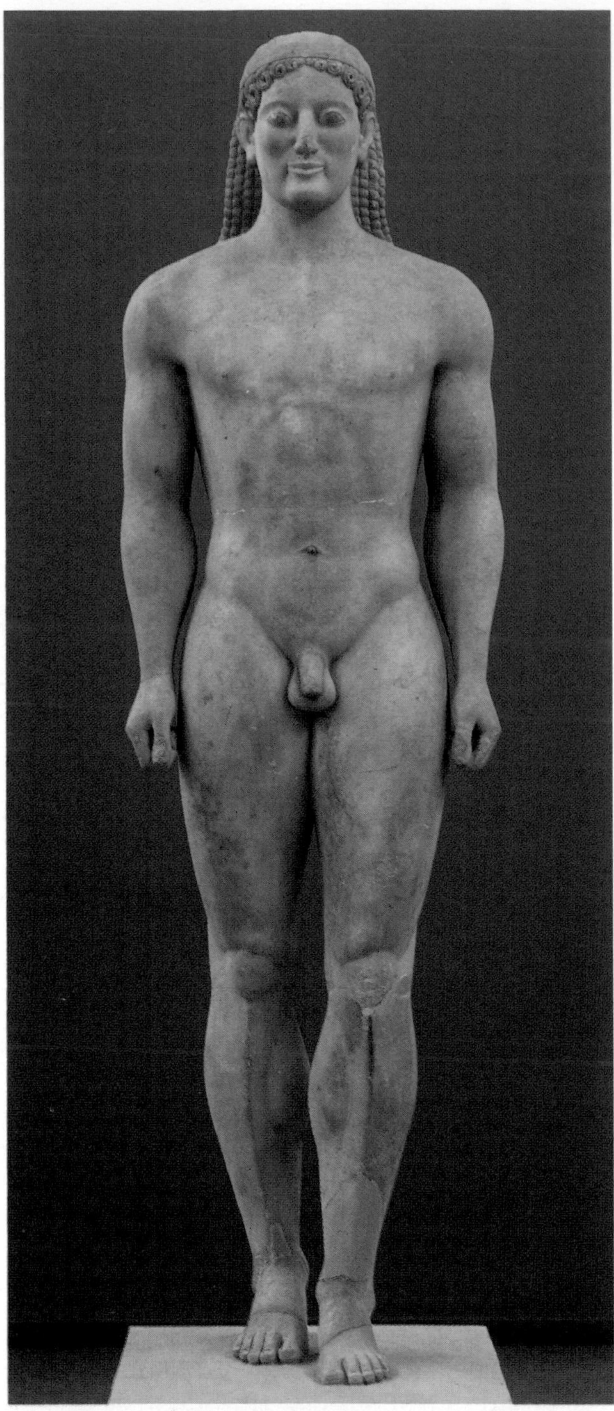

2.8 *Kouros* from Anavysos. c. 530 B.C. Marble, height 6'4" (1.93 m). National Archaeological Museum, Athens. Note the realism of the muscles and the new sense of power. According to an inscription on the base, this was the funerary monument to a young man, Kroisos, who had died heroically in battle.

2.9 *Calf-Bearer.* c. 550 B.C. Marble, height 5'5" (1.65 m). Acropolis Museum, Athens. The archaic smile is softened in this figure. Realism appears in the displacement of the man's hair by the animal's legs and in the expression of the calf.

In place of the old aristocratic clans, a new class of rich merchant traders, who had made their fortunes in the economic expansion, began to dominate, winning power by playing on the discontent of the oppressed lower classes. These new rulers were called "tyrants"—although the word had none of the unfavorable sense that it now has. Many of them, in fact, were patrons of the arts. The most famous of them all was Pisistratus, who ruled Athens from 546 B.C. until 528 B.C. Clearly, revolutions like those that brought him and his fellow

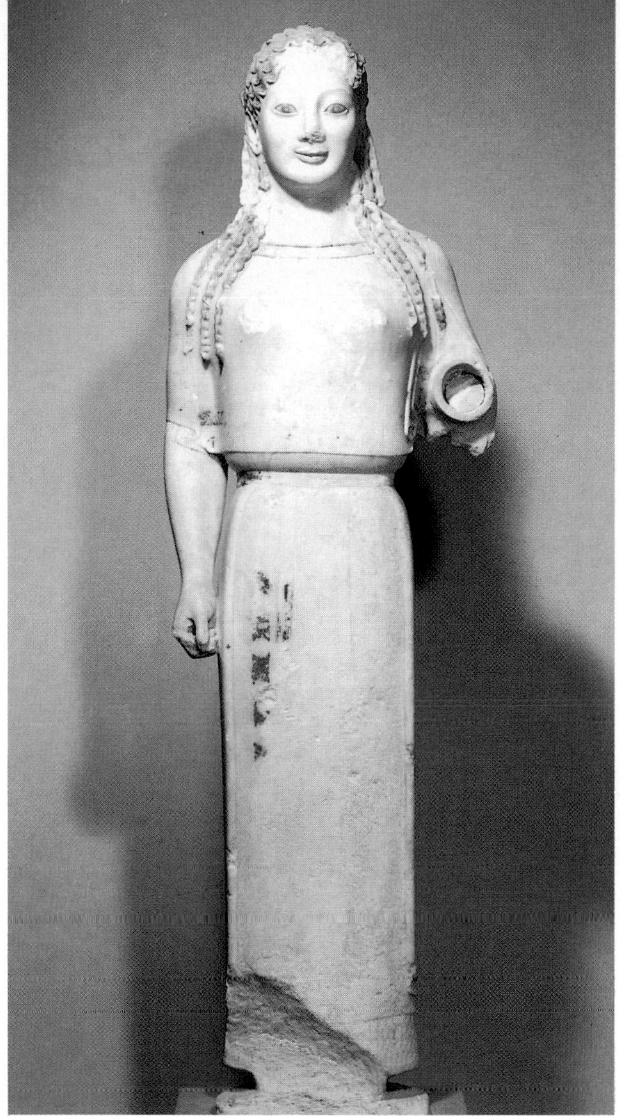

2.10 ***Peplos Kore.*** **c. 540 B.C. Marble, height 4' (1.21 m). Acropolis Museum, Athens. The statue is identified by the woolen *peplos* or mantle the woman is wearing over her dress. The missing left arm was extended. The Greeks painted important parts of their stone statues; traces of paint show here.**

tyrants to power were likely to produce revolutionary changes in the arts.

In sculpture there was an astounding progress from the formalized *kouroi* of the early Archaic period, with their flat planes and rigid stances, to the fully rounded figures of the late 6th century, toward the end of the period. Statues like the *Anavysos Kouros* [2.8] show a careful study of the human anatomy. The conventions remain the same, but the statues have a new life and vigor.

Although most of the male figures are shown in the traditional stance, there are a few important exceptions. The finest is perhaps the famous *Calf-Bearer* [2.9] from the Athenian Acropolis (the hill that dominated the center of ancient Athens). The essential unity between man and beast is conveyed simply but with great feeling by the diagonals formed by the man's hands and the calf's legs and by the alignment of the two heads.

The finest female figures of the period also come from the Acropolis. The Persians broke them when they sacked Athens in 480 B.C., and then the Athenians buried them when they returned to their city the next year after defeating the Persians. Rediscovered by modern excavators, the statues are among the most impressive of Archaic masterpieces. They show a gradual but sure development from the earliest *korai* (the plural form of *kore*) to the richness and variety of the work of the late 6th century [2.10].

In addition to these freestanding figures, two other kinds of sculpture now appeared: large-scale statues made to decorate temples and carved stone slabs. In both cases sculptors used the technique of *relief* carving: figures do not stand freely, visible from all angles, but are carved into a block of stone, part of which is left as background. In *high relief* the figures project from the background so much as to seem almost three-dimensional. In *low relief* the carving preserves the flat surface of the stone. Temple sculpture, or as it is often called, architectural sculpture, was frequently in high relief, as in the depiction of the decapitation of Medusa from Selinus [2.11]. Individual carved stone slabs are generally in low relief. Most that have survived

2.11 Metope showing the decapitation of Medusa. Selinus, c. 540 B.C. Archaeological Museum, Palermo. Medusa was a gorgon whose look turned anyone to stone. Perseus is cutting off Medusa's head with the encouragement of Athena, who stands at left. The gorgon's son Pegasus, the winged horse, leaps up at her side. Medusa is shown in the conventional pose indicating rapid motion.

2.12 Aristokles. *Stele of Aristion.* c. 510 B.C. Height without base 8' (2.44 m). National Archaeological Museum, Athens. The leather jacket contrasts with the soft folds of the undershirt.

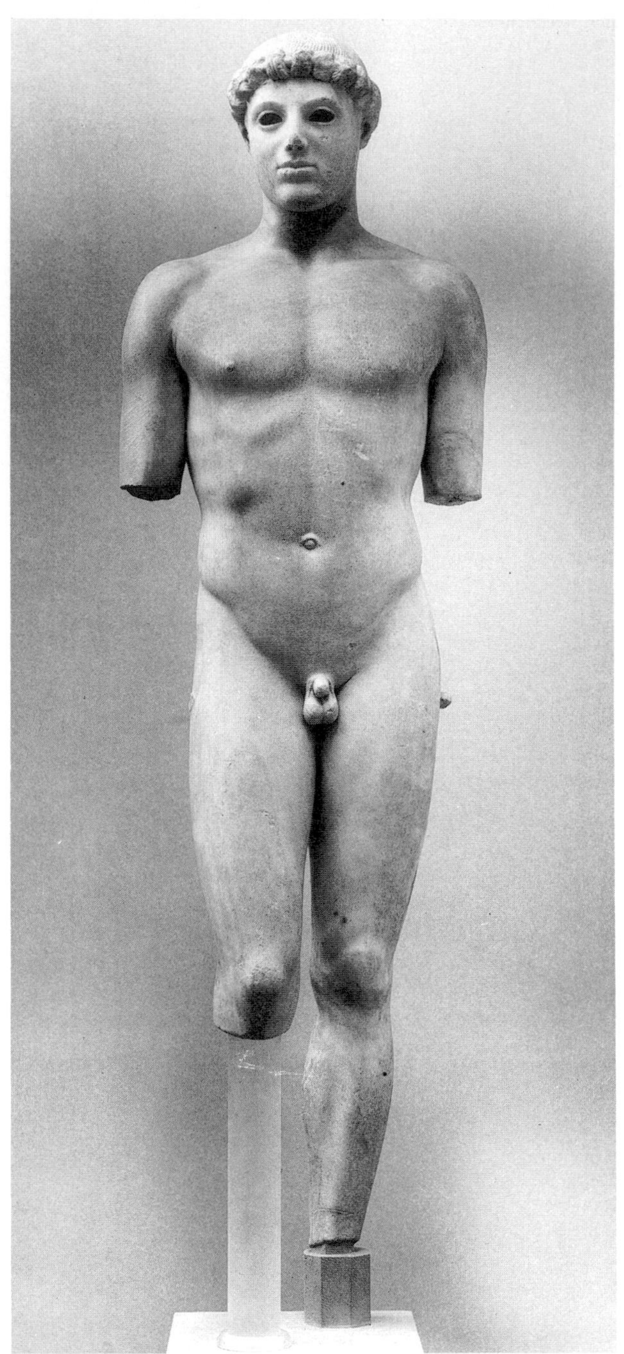

2.13 *Critian Boy.* c. 490 B.C. Marble, height 34" (86 cm). Acropolis Museum, Athens. The archaic smile has been superseded by a more natural expression.

were used as grave markers. The workmanship is often of a remarkable subtlety, as on the grave stele, or gravestone, of Aristion [2.12].

The range of Archaic sculpture is great, and the best pieces communicate something of the excitement of their makers in solving new problems. Almost all of them, however, have in common one feature that often disturbs the modern viewer—the famous "archaic smile." This facial expression, which to our eyes may seem more like a grimace,

2.14 Exekias. *The Suicide of Ajax.* c. 525 B.C. Black-figure vase, height 21¼" (54 cm). Musée des Beaux-Arts, Boulogne. Ajax buries his sword in the ground so that he can throw himself on to it. The pathos of the warrior's last moments is emphasized by the empty space around him, the weeping tree, and his now useless shield and helmet.

has been explained in a number of ways. Some believe that it is merely the result of technical inexperience on the part of the sculptors. Others see it as a reflection of the Archaic Greeks' sense of certainty and optimism in facing a world that they seemed increasingly able to control. Whatever its cause, by the end of the 6th century B.C., and with the increasing threat posed by the Persians, the archaic smile had begun to fade. It was replaced by the more somber expression of works like the *Critian Boy* [2.13]. This statue marks a literal "turning point" between the late Archaic world and the early Classical period. For the first time in ancient art the figure is no longer looking or walking straight ahead. The head and the upper part of the body turn slightly; as they do so, the weight shifts from one leg to the other and the hips move. Having solved the problem of representing a standing figure in a realistic way, the sculptor has tackled a new and even more complex problem—showing a figure in motion. The consequences of this accomplishment were explored to the full in the Classical period.

By the mid-6th century B.C. the art of vase painting had also made great progress. Works like those of Exekias, perhaps the greatest of black-figure painters, combine superb draftsmanship and immense power of expression [2.14]. For so restricted a medium, vase painting shows a surprising range. If Exekias' style is serious, somber, sometimes even grim, the style of his contemporary, the Amasis painter, is relaxed, humorous, and charming.

The end of the 6th century B.C. marks a major development in vase painting with the introduction of the new *red-figure style*. This showed the figures in the red color of the clay, with details filled in with the brush. The increased subtlety made possible by this style was used to develop new techniques of foreshortening, perspective, and three-dimensionality.

Although some artists continued to produce black-figure works, by the end of the Archaic period, around 525 B.C., almost all had turned to the new style. The last Archaic vase painters are among the greatest red-figure artists. Works like the *Euphronios Vase* [2.15] have a solidity and monumentality that altogether transcend the usual limitations of the medium.

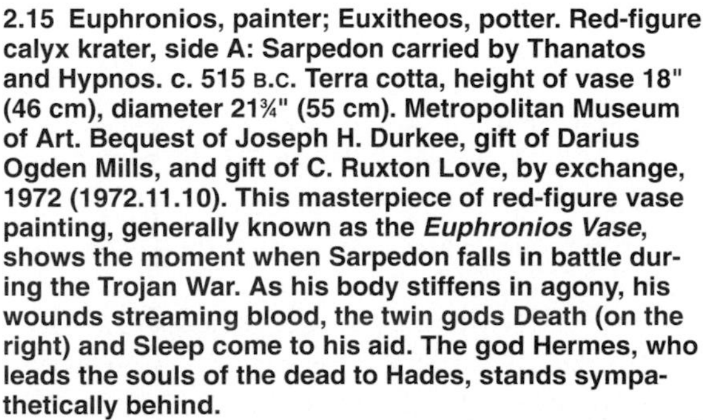

2.15 Euphronios, painter; Euxitheos, potter. Red-figure calyx krater, side A: Sarpedon carried by Thanatos and Hypnos. c. 515 B.C. Terra cotta, height of vase 18" (46 cm), diameter 21¾" (55 cm). Metropolitan Museum of Art. Bequest of Joseph H. Durkee, gift of Darius Ogden Mills, and gift of C. Ruxton Love, by exchange, 1972 (1972.11.10). This masterpiece of red-figure vase painting, generally known as the *Euphronios Vase*, shows the moment when Sarpedon falls in battle during the Trojan War. As his body stiffens in agony, his wounds streaming blood, the twin gods Death (on the right) and Sleep come to his aid. The god Hermes, who leads the souls of the dead to Hades, stands sympathetically behind.

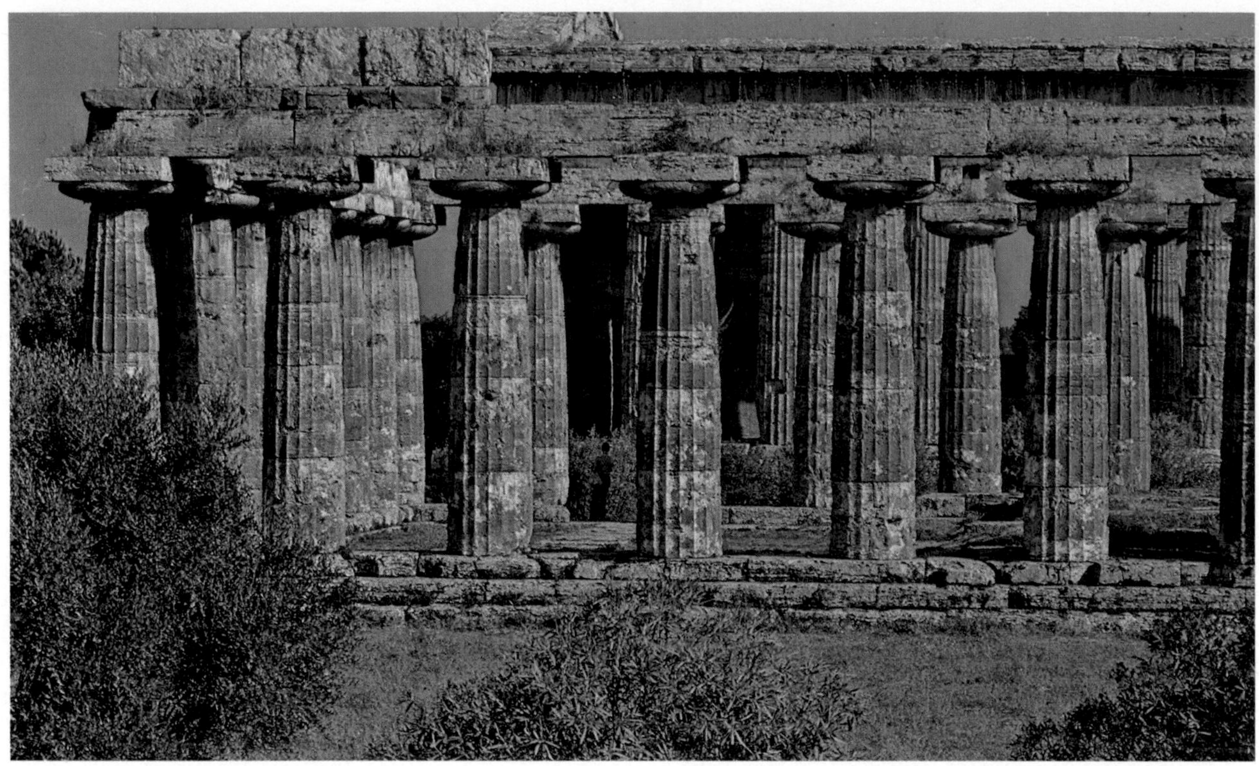

2.16 Basilica at Paestum. c. 550 B.C. This temple to Hera is one of the earliest surviving Greek temples. The bulging columns and spreading capitals are typical of Doric architecture in the Archaic period. (Visible through the columns and above the entablature are columns and part of the pediment of a second temple of Hera beyond, built a century later.)

Architecture: The Doric and Ionic Orders

In architecture, the Archaic period was marked by the construction of a number of major temples in the Doric style or order. As in the case of sculpture, Egyptian models played an important part in the early development of the Greek style. The first architect in history whose name has come down to us was the Egyptian Zoser. The earliest Egyptian buildings made use of bundles of papyrus to form posts; from these there soon developed the stone post-and-lintel constructions characteristic of Egyptian architecture. Buildings in this style probably inspired the first Greek temples.

The Doric order seems to have been firmly established by 600 B.C., though none of the earlier examples of the evolving style have survived. Important Doric temples include the Temple of Hera at Olympia, the Temple of Apollo at Corinth, and the earliest of the three Doric temples at Paestum, often called the Basilica (meeting hall), though it is now known to have been dedicated to the goddess Hera [2.16]. The Ionic style of temple architecture, which was widely used in Classical Greece, did not become fully established until later. In the Archaic period, Ionic buildings were constructed at such sites as Samos and Ephesus, but most Ionic temples date to the 5th century B.C. and later. For the sake of convenience both the Doric and Ionic orders [2.17] are described here. A later

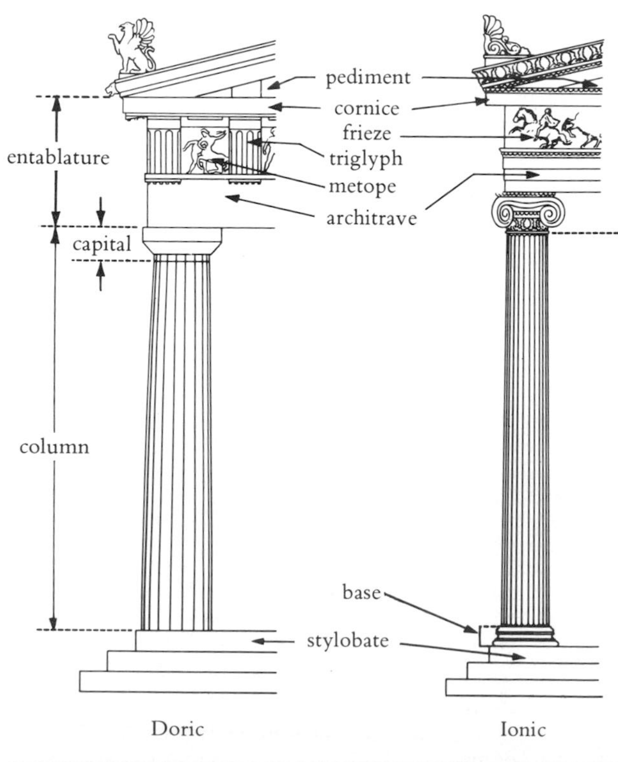

2.17 The Doric and Ionic orders.

order, the Corinthian, is principally of interest for its popularity with Roman architects and is discussed in that context in Chapter 4.

The Doric order is the simpler and the grander of the two. Some of its characteristics seem directly derived from construction methods used in earlier wooden buildings, and its dignity is perhaps in part related to the length of its history. Doric columns have no base but rise directly from the floor of a building. They taper toward the top and have twenty flutes, or vertical grooves. The *capital*, which forms the head of each column, consists of two sections, a spreading convex disc (the *echinus*) and, above, a square block (the *abacus*). The upper part of the temple, or *entablature*, is divided into three sections. The lowest, the *architrave*, is a plain band of rectangular blocks, above which is the *frieze*, consisting of alternating *triglyphs* and *metopes*. The triglyphs are divided by grooves into three vertical bands. The metope panels are sometimes plain, sometimes decorated with sculpture or painting. The building is crowned by a *cornice*, or projecting upper part, consisting of a horizontal section and two slanting sections meeting at a peak. The long extended triangle thus formed is the *pediment*, often filled with sculptural decoration.

In contrast, the Ionic order is more graceful and more elaborate in architectural details. Ionic columns rise from a tiered base and have twenty-four flutes. These flutes do not meet at a sharp angle as Doric flutes do but are separated by narrow vertical bands. The capitals consist of a pair of spirals, or *volutes*. The architrave is not flat as in the Doric order but composed of three projecting bands. In place of the Doric triglyphs and metopes is a continuous band often decorated with a running frieze of sculpture.

The two orders produced different effects. The Doric order suggested simple dignity; the absence of decorative detail drew attention to the weight and massiveness of the Doric temple itself. Ionic temples, on the other hand, conveyed a sense of lightness and delicacy by means of ornate decorations and fanciful carving. The surface of an Ionic temple is as important as its structural design.

MUSIC AND DANCE IN EARLY GREECE

In comparison with the visual arts, the history of Greek music is highly problematic. The very small quantity of evidence is as confusing as it is helpful. Although the frequent references to musical performance make it clear that music played a vital role in all aspects of Greek life, less than a dozen fragments of actual Greek music have survived; the earliest of these dates from the late 5th century B.C. Unfortunately, the problem of understanding the system of notation makes authentic performance of these fragments impossible.

Our inability to recreate even the examples we have is particularly frustrating because from the earliest times music was renowned for its emotional and spiritual power. For the Greeks music was of divine origin; the gods themselves had invented musical instruments: Hermes or Apollo the lyre, Athena the flute, and so on. Many of the earliest myths told of the powerful effect of music. Orpheus could move trees and rocks and tame wild beasts by his song; the lyre playing of Amphion brought stones to life. Nor was music making reserved for professional performers or women, as so often in later centuries. When, in Book IX of the *Iliad*, Agamemnon's ambassadors arrive at the tent of Achilles they find the great hero playing a lyre, "clear-sounding, splendid and carefully wrought," and entertaining himself by singing "of men's fame." How one would like to have heard that song!

The Greek belief that music could profoundly affect human behavior meant that it played an important part in both public and private life and was especially important in a religious context. Greek musical theory was later summarized by the two great philosophers of the 4th century B.C., Plato and Aristotle, both of whom discuss the doctrine of *ethos* and give music an important place in their writings. An understanding of doctrines of musical theory was also considered fundamental to a good general education.

Greek music was built up of a series of distinct modes, or scale types, each of which had its own name (see page 69). According to the doctrine of ethos, the characteristic, or ethos, of each mode was so powerful that it gave music written in it the ability to affect human behavior in a specific way. Thus the *Dorian* mode expressed firm, powerful, even warlike feelings, while the *Phrygian* mode produced passionate, sensual emotions. This identification of specific note patterns with individual human reactions seems to reach back to the dawn of Greek music history. The legendary founder of Greek music was Olympus, who was believed by the Greeks to have come from Asia Minor; it is surely no coincidence that two of the modes—the Phrygian and the Lydian—bear names of places in Asia Minor.

The first figure in music about whose existence we can be relatively certain was Terpander, who came from the island of Lesbos. Around 675 B.C. he used the *kithara*, an elaborate seven-string lyre, to accompany vocal music on ceremonial occasions. The simple lyre, relatively small and easy to hold, had a sounding box made of a whole tortoise shell and sides formed of goat horns or curved pieces of wood. On the other hand, the kithara had a much larger sounding box made of wood, metal, or even ivory, and broad, hollow sides, to give greater resonance to the sound. The player had to stand while performing on it; the instrument had straps to support it, leaving the player's hands free [2.18].

Another musical instrument developed about this time was the *aulos*, a double-reed instrument [2.19] similar to the modern oboe, which according to the traditional account had first been brought

2.18 Berlin Painter. Detail of red-figure amphora. Nola, c. 490 B.C. Terra cotta, height of vase 16⅝" (42 cm). Metropolitan Museum of Art, New York (Fletcher Fund, 1956). This vase gives a good idea of the Greeks' enthusiasm for music in general and the cithara in particular. The young musician is singing to his own accompaniment.

2.19 Karneia Painter. Detail of red-figure krater. Ceglie del Campo, c. 410 B.C. Terra cotta. Museo Nazionale, Taranto. A young woman plays the aulos for the god Dionysus. The flowing lines of the dress accentuate her figure. The necklace and bracelets are in low relief.

into Greece by Olympus. Like the kithara and lyre, the aulos was generally used to accompany songs.

The little evidence we have suggests that early Greek music was primarily vocal—the instruments were used mainly to accompany the singers. The breakthrough into purely instrumental music seems to have come at the beginning of the Archaic period. We know that in 586 B.C. Sacadas of Argos composed a work to be played on the aulos for the Pythian Games at Delphia—a piece that remained well known and popular for centuries. Also, its character confirms the Greek love of narrative, for it described in music Apollo's fight with the dragon that the Pythian Games commemorated. The information is tantalizing indeed, since this first piece of "program music," the remote ancestor of Richard Strauss' *Till Eulenspiegel* and *Don Quixote*, must have been highly effective for its appeal to have lasted so long.

We know little more of the music of the Archaic period than these odd facts. The lyrics of some of the songs have survived, including some of the choral odes performed in honor of various gods. Apollo and his sister Artemis were thanked for delivery from misfortune by the singing of a *paean*, or solemn invocation to the gods, while the *dithyramb*, or choral hymn to Dionysus, was sung in his honor at public ceremonies.

Also closely tied to music was dance, which played a significant part as well in the development of drama. We know both more and less about the early stages of Greek dance than we do about music. On the one hand, we have from as early as the late Geometric period actual depictions of dances in progress [2.20], whereas the sound of music of the same period is entirely lost to us. On the other hand, in the Classical period the function of dance remained religious and social, whereas a vast literature on music theory developed, with philosophical implications that became explicit in the writings of Plato and Aristotle; through this literature some information on early music has been preserved.

What we do know about dancing and individual dances suggests that here, as in music and visual arts, telling a story was important. One famous dance was called the *geranos*, from the word for "crane." The dancers apparently made movements like those of the bird, but the steps of the dance had a more specific meaning. According to tradition, it was first performed by Theseus outside the Labyrinth with the boys and girls he had saved by killing the Minotaur (see pages 21–22). The intricate patterns of the dance were supposed to represent the Labyrinth itself. Having accomplished two dangerous feats—killing the Minotaur and finding his way out of the Labyrinth—Theseus stayed around long enough to lead a complicated performance. Dancing was obviously of great importance to the Greeks.

2.20 Geometric bowl showing dancing. c. 740 B.C. Diameter 6¼" (16 cm). National Archaeological Museum, Athens. Photo DAI Athens, NM 3278. The dancers include both women and men, three playing lyres.

EARLY GREEK LITERATURE AND PHILOSOPHY

Our knowledge of literary developments between the time of Homer and the Archaic period is very limited. An exception is Hesiod, who probably lived shortly before 700 B.C. He is the author of a poetic account of the origins of the world called the *Theogony* and a rather more down-to-earth work, the *Works and Days*, which mainly concerned the disadvantages in being a poor, oppressed (and depressed) farmer in Boeotia, where the climate is "severe in winter, stuffy in summer, good at no time of year." In the Archaic period, however, the same burst of creative energy that revolutionized the visual arts produced a wave of new poets. The medium they chose was lyric verse.

Lyric Poetry

The emergence of lyric poetry was, like developments in the other arts, a sign of the times. The heroic verse of Homer was intended for the ruling class of an aristocratic society, who had the leisure and the inclination to hear of the great and not so great deeds of great men and who were interested in the problems of mighty leaders like Agamemnon and Achilles. Lyric verse is concerned above all else with the poet's own feelings, emotions, and opinions. The writers of the 6th century B.C. do not hesitate to tell us what they themselves feel about life, death, love, drinking too much wine, or anything else that crosses their minds. Heroes and the glories of battle are no longer the ideal.

Above all other Greek lyric poets, Sappho has captured the hearts and minds of the following ages. She is the first woman to leave a literary record that reflects her own personal experiences. Her poems have survived only in fragmentary form, and the details of her life remain confused and much disputed. We must be grateful, then, for what we have and not try to overinterpret it.

Sappho was born around 612 B.C. on the island of Lesbos, where she spent most of her life. She seems to have been able to combine the roles of wife and mother with those of poet and teacher; within her own lifetime she was widely respected for her works and surrounded by a group of younger women who presumably came to Lesbos to finish their education, in much the same way that Americans used to go to Paris for a final cultural polish.

The affection between Sappho and her pupils was deep and sincere and is constantly reflected in her poems. The nature of this affection has been debated for centuries. The plain fact is that apart from her poetry we know almost nothing about Sappho herself. Even her appearance is debatable; she is described by one ancient authority as "beautiful day" and by another as short, dark, and ugly. Her fellow poet Alcaeus calls her "violet-haired, pure, and honey-smiling." Thus those who read Sappho must decide for themselves what the passion of the poems expresses, for passionate they certainly are.

Perhaps Sappho's greatest quality lies in her ability to probe the depths of her own responses and by describing them to understand them. Just as contemporary sculptors and painters sought to understand the workings of their own bodies by depicting them, so Sappho revealed both to herself and to us the workings of her emotions.

The First Philosophers: The Presocratics

The century that saw the expression of the intimate self-revelations of lyric poetry was marked by the development of rational philosophy, which challenged the traditional religious ideas of Homer and Hesiod and scoffed at gods who took human form. If horses and cows had hands and could draw, they would draw gods looking like horses and cows, wrote Xenophanes of Colophon in the second half of the 6th century B.C.

The word "philosophy" literally means "love of wisdom," but in the Western tradition it usually refers to inquiries into the nature and ultimate significance of the human experience. Ever since the Archaic period philosophers have spent some two and a half millennia debating the question: "What is philosophy?" Some of its branches are Logic (the study of the structure of valid arguments); Metaphysics (investigation into the nature of ultimate reality); Epistemology (theory of knowledge); Ethics (moral philosophy); Aesthetics (the philosophy of the arts, and, more generally, taste); and political philosophy.

For the first time in history, the philosophers of the Archaic period turned away from religious teachings; they used the power of human reason to try to discover how the world came into being and how it works, and to understand the place of humans in it. A wide variety of schools of thought developed, which is collectively described by the somewhat confusing label *Presocratics*. The label is accurate in that they all lived and died before the time of Socrates (469–399 B.C.), who, together with his pupil Plato (c. 427–347 B.C.), is the greatest name in Greek philosophy. On the other hand, these 6th-century philosophers had little in common with one another except the time when they lived. Thus it is important to remember that the term "Presocratic" does not describe any single philosophical system. Indeed, many of the so-called Presocratic philosophers, with their studies into the origins of the world and the workings of nature, were examining questions which we would consider scientific rather than philosophical. The various schools were united principally by their use of logic and theoretical reasoning to solve practical questions about the world and human existence.

The earliest school to develop was that of the *Materialists*, who sought to explain all phenomena in terms of one or more elements. Thales of Miletus (c. 585 B.C.), for example, thought that water alone underlay the changing world of nature. However absurd Thales' theory was, his notion that the world had evolved naturally, rather than as the result of divine creation, was a revolutionary one. He also began the Greek tradition of free discussion of ideas in the marketplace and other public places. Intellectual exchange was no longer limited to an educated elite or a priestly class. In this way, as with his rejection of traditional religion, Thales and his successors created a fundamental breakaway from the traditional values of Homeric society.

Later, Empedocles of Acragas (c. 495 B.C.) introduced four elements—fire, earth, air, water. The various combinations (through love) and separations (through strife and war) of these elements in a cyclical pattern explained how creatures as well as nations were born, grew, decayed, and died. Anaxagoras of Clazomenae (c. 500 B.C.) postulated an infinite number of small particles, which, however small they might be, always contained not only a dominant substance (for example, bone or water) but also stray bits of other substances in lesser quantities. Unity in nature, he claimed, came from the force of Reason.

The Presocratic philosopher who had the greatest influence on later times was Pythagoras of Samos (c. 550 B.C.). He left his home city for political reasons and settled in southern Italy, where he founded a school of his own. He required his followers to lead pure and devout lives, uniting together to uphold morals and chastity, as well as order and harmony, for the common good. These apparently noble principles did nothing to win him favor from the people among whom he had settled; according to one account he and three hundred of his followers were killed.

It is difficult to know which of the principles of *Pythagoreanism* can be directly attributed to Pythagoras himself and which were added later by his disciples. His chief religious doctrines seem to have been belief in the transmigration of souls and the kinship of all living things, teachings that led to the development of a religious cult that bore his name. In science, his chief contribution was in mathematics. He discovered the numerical relationship of musical harmonies. Our modern musical scale, consisting of an *octave* (a span of eight tones) divided into its constituent parts, derives ultimately from his researches. Inspired by this discovery, Pythagoras went on to claim that mathematical relationships represented the underlying principle of the universe and of morality, the so-called "harmony of the spheres." He is chiefly remembered today for a much less cosmic discovery, the geometrical theorem that bears his name.

In contrast to Pythagoras' belief in universal harmony, the *Dualists* claimed that there existed two separate universes, the world around us, subject to constant change, and another ideal world, perfect and unchanging, which could only be realized through the intellect. The chief proponent of this school was Heraclitus of Ephesus (c. 500 B.C.) whose cryptic pronouncements won him the label "the Obscure." He summed up the unpredictable, and therefore unknowable, quality of Nature in the well-known saying, "It is not possible to step twice into the same river." Unlike his predecessors who had tried to understand the fundamental nature of matter, Heraclitus thus drew attention instead to the process whereby matter changed.

Parmenides of Elea (c. 510 B.C.), on the other hand, went so far as to claim that true reality can only be apprehended by reason and is all-perfect and unchanging, without time or motion. Our mistaken impressions come from our senses, which are flawed and subject to error. As a result, the world which we perceive through them, including the processes of time and change, is a sham and a delusion. His younger pupil, Zeno (c. 490 B.C.), presented a number of difficult paradoxes in support of their doctrines. These paradoxes were later discussed by Plato and Aristotle.

The last and perhaps the greatest school of Presocratic philosophy was that of the *Atomists*, led by Leucippus and Democritus (c. 460 B.C.), who believed that the ultimate, unchangeable reality consisted of atoms (small "indivisible" particles not obvious to the naked eye) and the void (nothingness). Atomism survived into Roman times in the later philosophy of Epicureanism and into the 19th century in the early Atomic Theory of John Dalton. Even in our own times, the great physicist Werner Heisenberg (1901–1976), who astonished the world of science with his discoveries in quantum mechanics, derived his initial inspiration from the Greek Atomists.

The various schools of Presocratic philosophers are often complex and difficult to understand. In part this is due to the kind of questions they addressed, in part to the fragmentary nature of the texts in which their ideas have survived. Furthermore, unlike all subsequent philosophers, they had no predecessors on whom to base their ideas or methods. Yet, through the cryptic phrases and often mysterious arguments, there shines a love of knowledge and a passionate search for answers to questions which still perplex humanity. And in their emphasis on the human rather than the divine they prefigure many of the most important stages in the development of the Western tradition, from Classical Athens to the Renaissance to the 18th-century Age of Reason. In the words of Protagoras (c. 485–415 B.C.), "Man is the measure of all things, of the existence of those that exist, and of the non-existence of those that do not."

Herodotus, The First Greek Historian

At the beginning of the 5th century B.C. the Greeks had to face the greatest threat in their history. Their success in meeting the challenge precipitated a decisive break with the world of Archaic culture. In 499 B.C. the Greek cities of Asia Minor, with Athenian support, rebelled against their Persian rulers. The Persian king, Darius, succeeded in checking this revolt; he then resolved to lead a punitive expedition against the mainland Greek cities that had sent help to the eastern cities. In 490 B.C. he took a massive army to Greece; to everyone's surprise, the Persians were defeated by the Athenians at the Battle of Marathon. After Darius' death in 486 B.C., his son Xerxes launched an even more grandiose expedition in 480 B.C. Xerxes defeated the Spartans at Thermopylae and then attacked and sacked Athens itself. While the city was falling, the Athenians took to their ships, obeying an oracle that enjoined them to "trust to their wooden walls." Eventually they inflicted a crushing defeat on the Persian navy at nearby Salamis. In 479 B.C., after being conquered on land and sea, at Plataea and Mycale, the Persians returned home, completely beaten.

The great historian Herodotus (484–420 B.C.) has left us, in the nine books of his *History of the Persian Wars,* a detailed account of the closing years of the Archaic period. He also, however, has two other claims on our attention. He is the first writer in the Western tradition to devote himself to historical writing rather than epic or lyric poetry, a fact that has earned him the title Father of History. At the same time he is one of the greatest storytellers, always sustaining the reader's interest, in both the main line of his narrative and the frequent and entertaining digressions. One of these, the tale of Rhampsinitus and the thief, has been described as the first detective story in Western literature.

Herodotus was not a scientific historian in our terms—he had definite weaknesses. He never really understood the finer points of military strategy. He almost always interpreted events in terms of personalities, showing little interest in underlying political or economic causes. His strengths, however, were many. Although his subject involved conflict between Greeks and foreigners, he remained remarkably impartial and free from national prejudice. His natural curiosity about the world around him and about his fellow human beings was buttressed by acute powers of observation. Above all, he recorded as much information as possible, even when versions conflicted. He also tried to provide a reasonable evaluation of the reliability of his sources so later readers could form their own opinions.

Herodotus' analysis of the Greek victory was based on a serious philosophical, indeed theological, belief—that the Persians were defeated because they were morally in the wrong. Their moral fault was *hubris,* excessive ambition; thus the Greeks' victory was at the same time an example of right over might and a demonstration that the gods themselves would guarantee the triumph of justice. In Book VII, Xerxes' uncle, Artabanus, warns him in 480 B.C. not to invade Greece: "You know, my lord, that amongst living creatures it is the great ones that God smites with his thunder, out of envy of their pride. It is God's way to bring the lofty low. For He tolerates pride in none but Himself."

Modern readers, however, less influenced by Herodotus' religious beliefs, will be more inclined to draw a political message from the Persian defeat. The Greeks were successful at least partly because for once they had managed to unite in the face of a common enemy. Their victories inaugurated the greatest period in Greek history, the Classical Age.

SUMMARY

Shortly after 1000 B.C. Greek civilization began to develop. From the beginning, the Greek world was divided into separate city-states among which fierce rivalries would grow. For the first two centuries the Greeks had little contact with other peoples, but around 800 B.C. Greek travelers and merchants began to explore throughout the Mediterranean. The visual arts during these early centuries are principally represented by pottery decorated with geometric designs. The period also saw the creation of two of the greatest masterpieces of Western literature, the *Iliad* and the *Odyssey*.

During the Age of Colonization (c. 750–600 B.C.) the Greeks came in contact with a wide range of foreign peoples. The ancient Near East, in particular, played a large part in influencing the development of Greek art and architecture. The decoration of pottery became Orientalizing in style, while large freestanding sculpture based on Egyptian models began to evolve. Important Greek colonies began to develop in southern Italy and Sicily.

The period from 600 B.C. to 480 B.C., known as the Archaic Age, was marked by political and cultural change. A new literary form, lyric poetry, became popular; one of its leading practitioners was the poetess Sappho. The so-called Presocratics began to develop a wide range of philosophical schools. Sculpture and vase painting both became increasingly naturalistic. The aristocratic rulers of earlier times were supplanted by "tyrants," rich merchant traders who depended on the support of the lower classes. In Athens, Solon's reform of the constitution introduced a form of democracy, which was overthrown by the tyrant Pisistratus in 546 B.C.

Democratic government was restored at Athens in 510 B.C., and shortly thereafter the Greeks became embroiled with the mighty Persian Empire to their east. In 499 B.C. the Greek cities of western Asia, established more than a century earlier, rebelled against their Persian rulers; the Athenians sent help. The Persians crushed the revolt, and in 490 B.C. the Persian king, Darius, led an expedition against the Greeks to punish them for their interference.

Against all odds, the Persians were defeated at the Battle of Marathon. Darius, humiliated, was forced to withdraw, but ten years later Xerxes, his son, mounted an even more grandiose campaign to restore Persian honor. In 480 B.C. he invaded Greece, defeated Spartan troops at Thermopylae, and sacked Athens. The Athenians took to their ships, however, and destroyed the Persian navy at the Battle of Salamis.

The following year combined Greek forces defeated Xerxes' army on land, and the Persians returned home in defeat. Faced by the greatest threat in their history, the Greeks had managed to present a united front. Their victories set the scene for the Classical Age of Greek culture. A detailed account of the Greeks' success can be found in the *History of the Persian Wars* written by Herodotus, the first Greek historian and the earliest significant prose writer in Western literature.

Pronunciation Guide

Achilles: A-KILL-ees
Agamemnon: A-ga-MEM-non
Amphora: AM-fo-ra
Aphrodite: Af-ro-DIE-tee
Boeotia: Bee-OWE-sha
Dionysus: Di-on-EES-us
Darius: Dar-I-us
Dithyramb: DITH-ee-ram
Euphronius: You-FRO-ni-us
Hera: HERE-a
Herodotus: Her-ODD-ot-us
Kore: KO-ray
Laconia: La-CONE-ee-a
Metope: MET-owe-pe
Paestum: PIE-stum
Peloponnesian: Pel-op-on-EASE-i-an
Phoenician: Fun-EESH-i-an
Priam: PRY-am
Sappho: SAF-owe
Stele: STAY-lay
Thales: THAY-lees
Thermopylae: Ther-MOP-u-lee
Triglyph: TRIG-lif
Xerxes: ZER-ksees

Exercises

1. What are the main features of the Homeric world-view? What effect do they have on the style of the Homeric epics?
2. Describe the development of Greek sculpture from the mid-7th century to the end of the Archaic period.
3. What evidence has survived as to the nature of Greek music? What does it tell us about the Greeks' attitude to music?
4. Discuss the principal schools of Presocratic philosophy.
5. What are the chief differences between the Doric and Ionic orders of architecture?

Further Reading

Boardman, J. *The Greek Overseas.* Baltimore: Penguin, 1973. A vivid and informative account of the development and effects of Greek colonization.

Bury, J. B., and R. Meiggs. *A History of Greece to the Death of Alexander the Great*, 4th ed. New York: St. Martin's, 1975. The best single-volume history of ancient Greece.

Coldstream, J. N. *Geometric Greece.* London: Methuen, 1977. A technical but readable account of all aspects of life in Geometric Greece.

Cook, R. M. *Greek Art.* Baltimore: Penguin, 1976. The best single-volume survey of all the visual arts in Greece, this book places them in their historical context.

Hooker, J. T. *The Ancient Spartans.* London: Methuen, 1980. A detailed study of a still relatively neglected subject that collects and interprets recent discoveries.

Johnston, A. *The Emergence of Greece.* Oxford: Elsevier-Phaidon, 1976. Primarily an up-to-date account of the archaeology of early Greece, the book also gives an excellent synthesis of history and art.

Luce, J. V. *Homer and the Heroic Age.* New York: Harper & Row, 1975. A masterly account of the historical background of the Homeric epics, although the author's view that Homer's world chiefly reflects that of the Mycenaeans is by no means universally shared.

Schups, K. *Economic Rights of Women in Ancient Greece.* Edinburgh: Edinburgh University Press, 1979. By using modern research techniques to analyze a wide range of material, this book significantly enlarges our view of Greek society.

Snodgrass, A. *Archaic Greece.* Berkeley: University of California Press, 1980. An important survey of the historical and archaeological evidence for a rich and complex period.

Vermeule, E. *Aspects of Death in Early Greek Art and Poetry.* Berkeley: University of California Press, 1981. In a sensitively written study, the author uses the visual arts and poetry to deal with themes that are, by their nature, difficult to pin down.

Period	Date	GENERAL EVENTS	LITERATURE & PHILOSOPHY	ART
	500 B.C.			**c. 490** *Critian Boy;* turning point between Archaic and Classical Periods
CLASSICAL PERIOD	480	**478** Formation of Delian League; beginning of Athenian empire **461** Pericles comes to prominence at Athens **454** Treasury of Delian League moved to Athens	**458** Aeschylus, *Oresteia* trilogy wins first prize in drama festival of Dionysus	**480–323** First naturalistic sculpture and painting appear **c. 460** Sculptures at Temple of Zeus, Olympia
CLASSICAL PERIOD — Golden Age	450	**443–430** Pericles in full control of Athens **432** Peloponnesian War begins **429** Pericles dies of plague that devastates Athens **421** Peace of Nicias **413** Renewed outbreak of Peloponnesian War	**441** Sophocles, *Antigone* **c. 429** Sophocles, *Oedipus the King* **c. 421** Euripides, *The Suppliant Women* **c. 420–c. 399** Thucydides, *History of Peloponnesian War* **414** Aristophanes, *The Birds* **411** Aristophanes, *Lysistrata*	**c. 450** Myron, *Discus Thrower* **c. 440** Polyclitus, *Doryphorus*, treatise *The Canon* **432** Phidias completes Parthenon sculptures **late 5th cent**. Funerary relief sculpture and white-ground vase painting; lekythos, *Warrior Seated at His Tomb* 
CLASSICAL PERIOD — Late Classical Period	404	**404** Fall of Athens and victory of Sparta **404–403** Rule of Thirty Tyrants **387** King's Peace signed **371–362** Ascendancy of Thebes **359–336** Philip II, king of Macedon **338** Macedonians defeat Greeks at Battle of Chaeronea **336–323** Alexander the Great, king of Macedon **331** City of Alexandria founded	**399** Trial and execution of Socrates **before 387** Plato, *Republic* **387** Plato founds Academy **c. 385** Xenophon chronicles teachings of Socrates **c. 347–c. 399** Aristotle, *Politics, Metaphysics* **335** Aristotle founds Lyceum	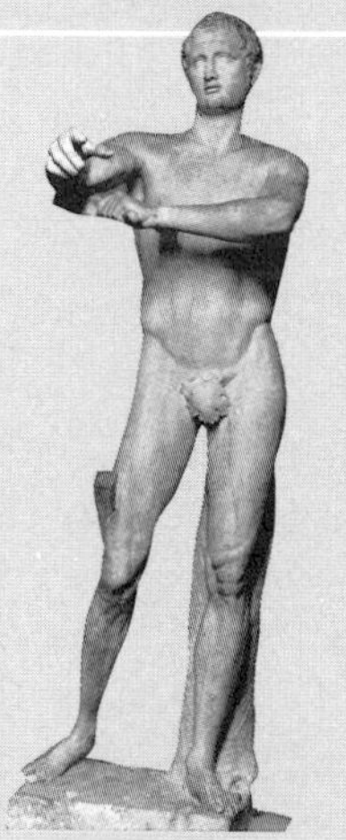 **c. 350** Scopas, *Pothos* **c. 350** Frescoes, Royal Cemetery at Vergina **c. 340** Praxiteles, *Hermes with Infant Dionysus* **c. 325** Lysippus, *Apoxymenos*
HELLENISTIC PERIOD	323	**323–281** Wars of Alexander's successors **262** Pergamum becomes independent kingdom **197–156** Eumenes II, king of Pergamum **146** Romans sack Corinth; Greece becomes Roman province		**323–146** Development of realistic portraiture  **c. 150** *Laocoön;* mosaic, House of Masks, Delos
	146			

CHAPTER 3 CLASSICAL GREECE AND THE HELLENISTIC PERIOD

ARCHITECTURE	MUSIC
470–456 Libon of Elis, Temple of Zeus at Olympia	**c. 500–425** Music serves as accompaniment in dramatic performances
449 Pericles commissions work on Acropolis **447–438** Ictinus and Callicrates, Parthenon **437–432** Mnesicles, Propylaea **c. 427–424** Callicrates, Temple of Athena Nike **421–406** Erechtheum	
356 Temple of Artemis at Ephesus destroyed by fire and rebuilt **c. 350** Theater at Epidaurus	**c. 400** Music dominates dramatic performances **4th cent.** Instrumental music becomes popular
323–146 *Tholos* and other new building forms appear **279** Lighthouse at Alexandria **c. 180–160** Menocrates of Rhodes, Pergamum Altar	**late 2nd cent.** Earliest surviving Greek music

LA 2

CHAPTER

3 CLASSICAL GREECE AND THE HELLENISTIC PERIOD

THE VICTORIES in the Persian Wars produced a new spirit of optimism and unity in Greece. Divine forces, it appeared, had guaranteed the triumph of right over wrong. There seemed to be no limit to the possibilities of human development. The achievements of the Classical period, which lasted from 479 B.C. to the death of Alexander the Great in 323 B.C., do much to justify the Greeks' proud self-confidence. They certainly represent a level of civilization that has rarely, if ever, been reached since—a level that has been a continuing inspiration to our culture.

Classical civilization reached its high point in Athens during the last half of the 5th century B.C., a time of unparalleled richness in artistic and intellectual achievement that is often called the Golden Age of Greece. To some extent, the importance of the great figures who dominated this period lies in the fact that they were the first in their fields. There are, in fact, few areas of human thought in which the 5th-century Greeks were not pioneers. In subjects as diverse as drama and historiography, town planning and medicine, painting and sculpture, mathematics and government, they laid the foundations of later achievements. Even more astonishing, often they were not merely the first in their fields but also among the greatest of all time. Greek tragedies, for example, are still read and performed today because they give experiences that are as intense emotionally and intellectually as anything in the Western dramatic tradition.

In the Late Classical period, from 404 to 323 B.C., artists and writers continued to explore ideas and styles first outlined in the century before, though in different ways. Greek cultural life was no longer dominated by Athens; a single center no longer governed artistic developments. This 4th-century period was therefore one of greater variety, with individual artists following their own personal visions. The greatest of all Late Classical contributions to our cultural tradition was in the field of philosophy. The works of Plato and Aristotle became the basis of Western thought for the next two thousand years.

Even after the death of Alexander the Great in 323 B.C. and the end of the Classical Age, the Hellenistic period that followed was characterized by an artistic vitality that ultimately drew its inspiration from Classical achievements. Only when Greece was conquered by the Romans in the late 2nd century B.C. did Greek culture cease to have an independent existence.

THE CLASSICAL IDEAL

Although the Roman conquest of Greece ended the glories of the Classical Age, in a way it also perpetuated them by contributing to the melding of Greek culture into the Western humanistic tradition. It was not the Greeks themselves but their conquerors who spread Greek ideas throughout the ancient world and thus down in time to our own day. These conquerors were first the Macedonians and then, above all, the Romans, possessors of practical skills that they used to construct a world sufficiently at peace for ideas to have a place in it. The Greeks did not live in such tranquility; we must always remember that the Athenians of the Golden Age existed not in an environment of calm contemplation but in a world of tension and violence. Their tragic inability to put into practice their own noble ideals and live in peace with other Greeks—the darker side of their genius—proved fatal to their independence; it led to war with the rest of Greece in 431 B.C. and to the fall of Athens in 404 B.C. In this context, the Greek search for order takes on an added significance.

It was the belief that the quest for reason and order could succeed that gave a unifying ideal to the immense and varied output of the Classical Age. The central principle of this Classical Ideal was that existence can be ordered and controlled, that human ability can triumph over the apparent chaos of the natural world and create a balanced society. In order to achieve this equilibrium, individual human beings should try to stay within what seem to be reasonable limits, for those who do not are guilty of *hubris*, excessive pride—the same hubris of which the Persian leader Xerxes was guilty and for which he paid the price (see page 53). The aim of life should be a perfect balance: everything in due proportion and nothing in excess. "Nothing too much" was one of the most famous Greek proverbs.

The emphasis that the Classical Greeks placed on order affected their spiritual attitudes. Individuals can achieve order, they believed, by understanding why people act as they do and, above all, by understanding the motives for their *own* actions. Thus confidence in the power of both human reason and human self-knowledge was as important as belief in the gods. The greatest of all Greek temples of the Classical Age, the Parthenon, which crowned the Athenian Acropolis [3.1], was planned not so much to honor the goddess Athena as to glorify Athens and thus human achievement. Even in their darkest days, the Classical Greeks never lost sight of the magnitude of human capability and, perhaps even more important, human potential—a vision that has returned over the centuries to inspire later generations and has certainly not lost its relevance in our own times.

The political and cultural center of Greece during the first half of the Classical period was Athens. Here, by the end of the Persian Wars in 479 B.C., the Athenians had emerged as the most powerful people in the Greek world. For one thing, their role in the defeat of the Persians had been a decisive one. For another, their democratic system of government, first established in the late 6th century B.C., was proving to be both effective and stable. All male Athenian citizens were not only entitled but were required to participate in the running of the state, either as members of the General Assembly, the *ecclesia*, with its directing council, the *boulé*, or by holding individual magistracies. They were also eligible to serve on juries.

Under Athenian leadership in the years following the wars a defensive organization of Greek city-states was formed to guard against any future attack from outside. The money collected from the participating members was kept in a treasury on the island of Delos, sacred to Apollo and politically neutral. This organization became known as the Delian League.

Within a short time a number of other important city-states, including Thebes, Sparta, and Athens' old trade rival Corinth, began to suspect that the League was serving not so much to protect all of Greece as to strengthen Athenian power. They believed the Athenians were turning an association of free and independent states into an empire of subject peoples. Their suspicions were confirmed when in 454 B.C. the funds of the League were transferred from Delos to Athens and some of the money was used to pay for Athenian building projects, including the Parthenon. The spirit of Greek

3.1 The Acropolis, Athens, from the northwest. The Parthenon, temple to Athena, is at the highest point. Below it spreads the monumental gateway, the Propylaea. At far left is the Erechtheum.

unity was starting to dissolve; the Greek world was beginning to divide into two opposing sides: on the one hand Athens and her allies (the cities that remained in the League) and, on the other, the rest of Greece. Conflict was inevitable. The Spartans were finally persuaded to lead an alliance against Athens to check her "imperialistic designs." This war, called the Peloponnesian War after the homeland of the Spartans and their supporters, began in 431 B.C. and dragged on until 404 B.C.

Our understanding of the Peloponnesian War and its significance owes much to the account by the great historian Thucydides, who himself lived through its calamitous events. Born around 460 B.C., Thucydides played an active part in Athenian politics in the years before the war. In 424 B.C. he was elected general and put in charge of defending the city of Amphipolis in northern Greece. When the city fell to Spartan troops, Thucydides was condemned in his absence and sentenced to exile. He did not return to Athens until 404 B.C.

Thucydides intended his *History of the Peloponnesian War* to describe the entire course of the war up to 404 B.C., but he died before completing it; the narrative breaks off at the end of 411 B.C. The work is extremely valuable for its detailed description of events, for, although its author was an Athenian he managed to be both accurate and impartial. At the same time, however, Thucydides tried to write more than simply an account of a local war. The *History* was an attempt to analyze human motives and reactions so that future generations would understand how and why the conflict occurred and, in turn, understand themselves. The work was not meant to entertain by providing digressions and anecdotes but to search out the truth and use it to demonstrate universal principles of human behavior. This emphasis on reason makes Thucydides' work typical of the Classical period.

The hero of Thucydides' account of the years immediately preceding the war is Pericles, the leader whose name symbolizes the achievements of the Athenian Golden Age [3.2]. An aristocrat by birth, Pericles began his political career in the aftermath of the transfer of the Delian League's funds to Athens. By 443 B.C. he had unofficially assumed the leadership of the Athenian democracy, although he continued democratically to run for reelection every year. Under his guidance the few remaining years of peace were devoted to making visible the glory of Athens by constructing on the Acropolis the majestic buildings that still, though in ruins, evoke the grandeur of Periclean Athens (Table 3.1).

Had Pericles continued to lead Athens during the war itself, the final outcome might have been

3.2 Kresllas. *Pericles.* Roman copy after original of c. 440 B.C. Marble. Vatican Museum, Rome. Pericles is wearing a helmet, pushed up over his forehead, because his official rank while leader of Athens was that of general.

TABLE 3.1 Athens in the Age of Pericles (ruled 443–429 B.C.)

Area of the city	7 square miles
Population of the city	100,000–125,000
Population of the region (Attica)	200,000–250,000
Political institution	General Assembly, Council of 500, Ten Generals
Economy	Maritime trade; Crafts (textiles, pottery); Farming (olives, grapes, wheat)
Cultural life	History (Thucydides); Drama (Aeschylus, Sophocles, Euripides, Aristophanes); Philosophy (Socrates); Architecture (Ictinus, Callicrates, Mnesicles); Sculpture (Phidias)
Principal buildings	Parthenon, Propylea (the Erechtheum, the other major building on the Athenian Acropolis, was not begun in Pericles' lifetime)

different, but in 430 B.C. the city was ravaged by disease, perhaps bubonic plague, and in 429 B.C. Pericles died. No successor could be found who was capable of winning the respect and support of the majority of his fellow citizens. The war continued indecisively until 421 B.C., when an uneasy peace was signed. Shortly thereafter the Athenians made an ill-advised attempt to replenish their treasury by organizing an unprovoked attack on the wealthy Greek cities of Sicily. The expedition proved a total disaster; thousands of Athenians were killed or taken prisoner. When the war began again in 411 B.C. the Athenian forces were fatally weakened. The end came in 404 B.C. After a siege that left many people dying in the streets, Athens surrendered unconditionally to the Spartans and their allies.

DRAMA AND PHILOSOPHY IN CLASSICAL GREECE

The Drama Festivals of Dionysus

The tumultuous years of the 5th century B.C., passing from the spirit of euphoria that followed the ending of the Persian Wars to the mood of doubt and self-questioning of 404 B.C., may seem unlikely to have produced the kind of intellectual concentration characteristic of Classical Greek drama. Yet it was, in fact, in the plays written specifically for performance in the theater of Dionysus at Athens in these years that Classical literature reached its most elevated heights. The tragedies of the three great masters, Aeschylus, Sophocles, and Euripides, not only illustrate the development of contemporary thought but also contain some of the most memorable scenes in the history of the theater.

Tragic drama was not itself an invention of the 5th century B.C. It had evolved over the preceding century from choral hymns sung in honor of the god Dionysus, and the religious character of its origins was still present in its fully developed form. The plays that have survived from the Classical period at Athens were all written for performance at one of the two annual festivals sacred to Dionysus before an audience consisting of the entire population of the city. (Like the Egyptian god, Osiris, Dionysus died and was reborn, and the festivals held in his honor may be related to earlier ceremonies developed in Egypt.) To go to the theater was to take part in a religious ritual; the theaters themselves were regarded as sacred ground [3.3].

Each of the authors of the works given each year normally submitted four plays to be performed consecutively on a single day—three tragedies, or a "trilogy," and a more lighthearted play called a *satyr* play (a satyr was a mythological figure: a man with an animal's ears and tail). The "trilogies" sometimes narrated parts of a single story, although often the three works were based on differ-

3.3 Polyclitus. Theater, Epidaurus. c. 350 B.C. Diameter 373' (113.69 m), orchestra 66' (20.12 m) across.

ent stories with a common theme. At the end of each festival the plays were judged and a prize awarded to the winning author.

The dramas were religious not only in time and place but also in nature. The plots, generally drawn from mythology, often dealt with the relationship between the human and the divine. To achieve an appropriate seriousness, the style of performance was lofty and dignified. The actors, who in a sense served as priests of Dionysus, wore masks, elaborate costumes, and raised shoes.

The chorus, whose sacred dithyrambic hymn had been the original starting point in the development of tragedy, retained an important function throughout the 5th century B.C. In some plays (generally the earlier ones) the chorus forms a group centrally involved in the action, as in Aeschylus' *Suppliants* and *Eumenides*. More often, as in Sophocles' *Oedipus the King* or *Antigone*, the chorus represents the point of view of the spectator, rather than that of the characters participating directly in the events on stage; in these plays the chorus reduces to more human terms the intense emotions of the principals and comments on them. Even in the time of Euripides, when dramatic confrontation became more important than extended poetic or philosophical expression, the chorus still retained one important function, that of punctuating the action and dividing it into separate episodes by singing lyric odes whose subject was sometimes only indirectly related to the action of the play.

These aspects of Classical tragedy are a reminder that the surviving texts of the plays represent only a small part of the total experience of the original performances. The words—or at least some of them—have survived; but the music to which the words were sung and which accompanied much of the action, the elaborate choreography to which the chorus moved, indeed the whole grandiose spectacle performed out-of-doors in theaters located in sites of extreme natural beauty before an audience of thousands—all of this can only be recaptured in the imagination. It is perhaps relevant to remember that when, almost two thousand years later, around A.D. 1600, a small group of Florentine intellectuals decided to revive the art of Classical drama, they succeeded instead in inventing opera. Similarly, in the 19th century the German composer Richard Wagner was inspired by Greek tragedy to devise his concept of a *Gesamtkunstwerk* (literally "total work of art"), a work of art that combined all the arts into one; he illustrated this concept by writing his dramatic operas.

The Athenian Tragic Dramatists

Even if some elements of the surviving Greek dramas are lost, we do have the words. The differing worldviews of the authors of these works vividly illustrate the changing fate of 5th-century-B.C. Athens. The earliest of the playwrights, Aeschylus (525–456 B.C.), died before the lofty aspirations of the early years of the Classical period could be shaken by contemporary events. His work shows a deep awareness of human weakness and the dangers of power (he had himself fought at the Battle of Marathon in 490 B.C.), but he retains an enduring belief that in the end right will triumph. In Aeschylus' plays the process of being able to recognize what is right is painful: One must suffer to learn one's errors; yet the process is inevitable, controlled by a divine force of justice personified under the name of Zeus.

The essential optimism of Aeschylus' philosophy must be kept in mind because the actual course of the events he describes is often violent and bloody. Perhaps his most impressive plays are the three that form the *Oresteia* trilogy. This trilogy, the only complete one that has survived, won first prize in the festival of 458 B.C. at Athens. The subject of the trilogy is nothing less than the growth of civilization, represented by the gradual transition from a primitive law of "vendetta" and blood for blood to the rational society of civilized human beings.

The first of the three plays, the *Agamemnon*, presents the first of these systems in operation. King Agamemnon returns to his homeland, Argos, after leading the Greeks to victory at Troy. Ten years earlier, on the way to Troy, he had been forced to choose either to abandon the campaign because of unfavorable tides or to obtain an easy passage by sacrificing his daughter Iphigenia. (The situation may seem contrived, but it clearly symbolizes a conflict between public and personal responsibilities.) After considerable hesitation and self-doubt he had chosen to sacrifice his daughter. On his return home at the end of the Trojan War, he pays the price for her death by being murdered by his wife Clytemnestra [3.4]. Her ostensible motive is vengeance for Iphigenia's death, but an equally powerful, if less noble, one is her desire to replace Agamemnon both as husband and king by her lover Aegisthus. Thus Aeschylus shows us that even the "law of the jungle" is not always as simple as it may seem, while at the same time the punishment of one crime creates in its turn another crime to be punished. If Agamemnon's murder of his

3.4 ***Attic Red Figured Calyx Krater.*** **The Dokimasia Painter, about 460 B.C. Side A:** ***The Murder of Agamemnon by Aegisthus.*** **Clay, H: 0.51 m. Diam: 0.51 m. Museum of Fine Arts, Boston. Aegisthus strikes the blow in this version of the story, with Clytemnestra standing behind him grasping an axe. Agamemnon, killed as he was about to take a bath, is wearing only a light robe.**

daughter merits vengeance, then so does Clytemnestra's murder of her husband. Violence breeds violence.

The second play, *The Libation Bearers,* shows us the effects of the operation of this principle on Agamemnon and Clytemnestra's son, Orestes. After spending years in exile Orestes returns to Argos to avenge his father's death by killing his mother. Although a further murder can accomplish nothing except the transfer of blood guilt to Orestes himself, the primitive law of "vendetta" requires him to act. With the encouragement of his sister Electra, he kills Clytemnestra. His punishment follows immediately. He is driven mad by the Furies, the implacable goddesses of vengeance, who hound him from his home.

The Furies themselves give their name to the third play, in which they are tactfully called *The Eumenides,* or "the kindly ones." In his resolution of the tragedy of Orestes and his family, Aeschylus makes it clear that violence can only be brought to an end by the power of reason and persuasion. After a period of tormented wandering, Orestes comes finally to Athens where he stands trial for the murder of his mother before a jury of Athenians, presided over by Athena herself. The Furies insist on his condemnation on the principle of blood for blood, but Orestes is defended by Apollo, the god of reason, and finally acquitted by his fellow human beings. Thus the long series of murders is brought to an end, and the apparently inevitable violence and despair of the earlier plays is finally dispelled by the power of persuasion and human reason, which—admittedly with the help of Athena and Apollo—have managed to bring civilization and order out of primeval chaos.

In spite of all of the horror of the earlier plays, therefore, the *Oresteia* ends on a positive note. Aeschylus affirms his belief that progress can be achieved by reason and order. This gradual transition from darkness to light is handled throughout the three plays with unfailing skill. Aeschylus matches the grandeur of his conception with majestic language. His rugged style makes him sometimes difficult to understand, but all the verbal effects are used to dramatic purpose. The piling up of images and complexity of expression produce an emotional tension that has never been surpassed.

The life of Sophocles (496–406 B.C.) spanned both the glories and the disasters of the 5th century B.C. Of the three great tragic poets, Sophocles was the most prosperous and successful; he was a personal friend of Pericles. He is said to have written 123 plays, but only seven have survived, all of them from the end of his career. They all express a much less positive vision of life than that of Aeschylus. His philosophy is not easy to extract from his work, since he is more concerned with exploring and developing the individual characters in his dramas than with expounding a point of view; in general, he seems to combine an awareness of the tragic consequences of individual mistakes with a belief in the collective ability and dignity of the human race.

The consequences of human error are vividly depicted in his play *Antigone,* first performed around 440 B.C. Thebes has been attacked by forces under the leadership of Polynices; the attack is beaten off and Polynices killed. In the aftermath Creon, king of Thebes, declares the dead warrior a traitor and forbids anyone to bury him on pain of death. Antigone, Polynices' sister, disobeys, claiming that her religious and family obligations override those to the state. Creon angrily condemns her to death. He subsequently relents, but too late: Antigone, his son (betrothed to Antigone), and his wife have all committed suicide. Creon's stubbornness and bad judgment thus bring tragedy for him as well as for Antigone.

3.5 The ancient theater at Delphi. 1951. The columns in the background are the ruins of the Temple of Apollo.

Paradoxically, however, the choice between good and evil is never clear or easy and is sometimes impossible. More than any of his contemporaries, Sophocles emphasizes how much lies outside our own control, in the hands of destiny or the gods. His insistence that we respect and revere the forces that we cannot see or understand makes him the most traditionally religious of the tragedians. These ambiguities appear in his best-known play, *Oedipus the King,* which has stood ever since Classical times as a symbol of Greek tragic drama [3.5]. A century after it was first performed, around 429 B.C., Aristotle used it as his model when, in the *Poetics,* he discussed the nature of tragedy. Its unities of time, place, and action, the inexorable drive of the story with its inevitable yet profoundly tragic conclusion, the beauty of its poetry—all these have made *Oedipus the King* a true classic, in all senses. Its impact has lasted down to our own times; it had a notable effect on the ideas of Sigmund Freud. Yet in spite of the universal admiration the play has excited, its message is far from clear.

The story concerns Oedipus, doomed even before his birth to kill his father and marry his mother, his attempts to avoid fate, and his final discovery that he has failed. If the play seems, in part, to be saying that we cannot avoid our destiny, it leaves unanswered the question of whether we deserve that destiny or not. Certainly Oedipus does not choose deliberately to kill his father and marry his mother, even though unknowingly everything he does leads to this end. Then why does he deserve to suffer for his actions?

One of the traditional answers to this question can be found in Aristotle's analysis of tragedy in the *Poetics.* Referring particularly to *Oedipus,* Aristotle makes the point that the downfall of a tragic figure is generally the result of a flaw (the Greek word is *hamartia*) in his character. Thus Oedipus' pride and stubbornness in insisting on discovering who he is and the anger he shows in the process bring about the final disastrous revelation. In this way the flaws, or weaknesses, in his character overcome his good points and destroy him.

As a description of Oedipus' behavior, this explanation is convincing enough, but it fails to provide a satisfactory account of the original causes of his condition. Perhaps the message of the play is, in fact, that there are some aspects of existence beyond our understanding, aspects that operate by principles outside our range of experience. If this is so, and many literary critics would deny it, Sophocles seems to be describing the final helplessness of humanity in the face of forces that we cannot control and warning against too great a belief in self-reliance.

The significance for the Athenians themselves of Oedipus' fall from greatness emerges in full force in the work of Euripides (c. 484–406 B.C.). Although only a little younger than Sophocles, Euripides expresses all the weariness and disillusion of the war-torn years at the end of the 5th century B.C. Of all the tragedians he is perhaps the closest to our own time, with his concern for realism and his determination to expose social, political, and religious injustices.

Although Euripides admits the existence of irrational forces in the universe that can be personified in the form of gods and goddesses, he certainly does not regard them as worthy of respect and worship. This skepticism won him the charge of impiety. His plays show characters frequently pushed to the limits of endurance; their reactions show a new concern for psychological truth. In particular, Euripides exhibits a profound sympathy and understanding for the problems of women who live in a society dominated by men. Characters like Medea and Phaedra challenged many of the basic premises of contemporary Athenian society.

Euripides' deepest hatred is reserved for war and its senseless misery. Like the other dramatists he draws the subject matter of his plays from traditional myths, but the lines delivered by the actors must have sounded in their hearers' ears with a terrible relevance. *The Suppliant Women* was probably written in 421 B.C., when ten years of indecisive fighting had produced nothing but an uneasy truce. Its subject is the recovery by Theseus, ruler of Athens, of the bodies of seven chiefs killed fighting at Thebes in order to return them to their families for burial. He yields to their mothers—the women of the title—who beg him to recover the corpses. The audience would have little need to be reminded of the grief of wives and mothers or of the kind of political processes that produced years of futile fighting.

If Aeschylus' belief in human progress is more noble, Euripides is certainly more realistic. Although unpopular in his own time, he later became the most widely read of the three tragedians. As a result, more of his plays have been preserved (nineteen in all), works with a wide range of emotional expression. They extend from romantic comedies like *Helen* and *Iphigenia in Taurus* to the profoundly disturbing *Bacchae,* his last completed play, in which Euripides the rationalist explores the inadequacy of reason as the sole approach to life. In this acknowledgement of the power of emotion to overwhelm the order and balance so typical of the Classical ideal, he is most clearly speaking for his time.

Aristophanes and Greek Comedy

Euripides was not, of course, the only Athenian to realize the futility of war. The plays of Aristophanes (c. 450–385 B.C.), the greatest comic poet of 5th-century-B.C. Athens, deal with the same theme. His work combines political satire with a strong vein of fantasy.

In *The Birds,* produced in 414 B.C., two Athenians decide to leave home and find a better place to live. They join forces with the birds and build a new city in midair called Cloudcuckooland, which cuts off contact between gods and humans by blocking the path of the smoke rising from sacrifices. The gods are forced to come to terms with the new city and Zeus hands over his scepter of authority to the birds.

This is simple escapism, but *Lysistrata,* written a few years later, in 411 B.C., deals with the problem of how to prevent war in a more practical fashion. In the course of the play the main protagonist, Lysistrata, persuades her fellow women of Athens to refuse to make love with their husbands until peace is negotiated. At the same time her followers seize the Acropolis. The men, teased and frustrated, finally give in and envoys are summoned from Sparta. The play ends with the Athenians and Spartans dancing together for joy at the new peace.

With the end of the Peloponnesian War in 404 B.C. and the fall of Athenian democracy, both art and political life were to be affected by an atmosphere of considerable confusion. Though Athens had been removed as the dominating force in Greece, there was no successor among her rivals. The vacuum was not filled until the mid-4th century with the appearance on the scene of Philip of Macedon. Earlier, a disastrous series of skirmishes between Sparta, Thebes, Athens, Corinth, and Argos had been temporarily suspended by the intervention of the Great King of the Persians himself, and the so-called King's Peace was signed in 387 B.C. But after a brief respite, the Thebans decisively defeated the Spartan forces at Leuctra in 371 B.C. and remained for a few years the leading force in Greek political life.

With the accession of Philip in Macedon in 359 B.C., however, the balance of power in Greece began to change. The hitherto backward northern kingdom of Macedon began to exert a new unifying influence, despite opposition in Thebes and in Athens, where the great Athenian orator Demosthenes led the resistance. In 338 B.C., at the Battle of Chaeronea (see map, page 35), Philip defeated Athenian and Theban forces and unified all the cities of Greece, with the exception of Sparta, in an alliance known as the League of Corinth.

Even before his assassination in 336 B.C., Philip had developed schemes for enlarging his empire by attacking Persia. His son and successor, Alexander, carried them out. He spent the ten years from 333 B.C. until his own death in 323 B.C. in an amazing series of campaigns across Asia, destroying the Persian Empire and reaching as far as India. The effects of the breakup of this new Macedonian empire after the death of Alexander were to be felt throughout the Hellenistic period that followed.

Philosophy in the Late Classical Period

The intellectual and cultural spirit of the new century was foreshadowed in its very first year in an event at Athens. In 399 B.C. the philosopher Socrates was charged with impiety and corruption of the young, found guilty, and executed. Yet the ideas that Socrates represented—concern with the fate of the individual and the questioning of traditional values—could not be killed so easily. They had already begun to spread at the end of the 5th century B.C. and came to dominate the culture of the 4th century B.C.

Socrates is one of the most important figures in Greek history. He is also one of the most difficult to understand clearly. Much of the philosophy of the Greeks and of later ages and cultures has been inspired by his life and teachings. Yet Socrates himself wrote nothing; most of what we know of him comes from the works of his disciple, Plato. Socrates was born around 469 B.C., the son of a sculptor and a midwife; in later life he claimed to have followed his mother's profession in being a "midwife to ideas." He seems first to have been interested in natural science, but he soon turned to the problems of human behavior and morality. Unlike the sophists, the professional philosophers of the day, he never took money for teaching, nor did he ever found a school. Instead he went around Athens, to both public places like the markets and the gymnasia and private gatherings, talking and arguing, testing traditional ideas by subjecting them to a barrage of questions—as he put it, "following the argument wherever it led." Socrates gradually gained a circle of enthusiastic followers, drawn mainly from the young. At the same time he acquired many enemies, disturbed by both his challenge to established morality and the uncompromising persistence with which he interrogated those who upheld it. Socrates was no respecter of the pride or dignity of others, and his search for the truth inevitably exposed the ignorance of his opponents.

Among Socrates' supporters were a number who had taken part in an unpopular and tyrannical political coup at Athens immediately following the Peloponnesian War. The rule of the so-called Thirty Tyrants lasted only from 404 to 403 B.C.; it ended with the death or expulsion of its leading figures. The return of democracy gave Socrates' enemies a chance to take advantage of the hostility felt toward those who had "collaborated" with the tyrants; thus in 399 B.C. he was put on trial.

It seems probable that to some degree the proceedings were intended for show and that those who voted for the death sentence never seriously thought it would be carried out. Socrates was urged by his friends to escape from prison, and the authorities themselves offered him every opportunity. However, the strength of his own morality and his reverence for the laws of his city prohibited him from doing so. After a final discussion with his friends he was put to death by the administration of a draught of hemlock.

Many of Socrates' disciples tried to preserve his memory by writing accounts of his life and teachings. The works of only two have survived. One of these is the Greek historian Xenophon, whose *Apology, Symposium,* and *Memorabilia* are interesting, if superficial. The other is Plato, who, together with his pupil Aristotle, stands at the forefront of the whole intellectual tradition of Western civilization.

The dialogues of Plato claim to record the teachings of Socrates. Indeed, in almost all of them Socrates himself appears, arguing with his opponents and presenting his own ideas. How much of Plato's picture of Socrates is historical truth and how much is Plato's invention, however, is debatable. The Socratic problem has been almost as much discussed as the identity of Homer. In general, modern opinion supports the view that in the early dialogues Plato tried to preserve something of his master's views and methods, while in the later ones he used Socrates as the spokesman for his own ideas.

There can certainly be no doubt that Plato was deeply impressed by Socrates' life and death. Born in 428 B.C., he was drawn by other members of his aristocratic family into the Socratic circle. Plato was present at the trial of Socrates, whose speech in his own defense Plato records in the *Apology,* one of three works that describe Socrates' last days. In the *Crito,* set in prison, Socrates explains why he refuses to escape. The *Phaedo* gives an account of his last day spent discussing with his friends the immortality of the soul and his death.

After Socrates' death, Plato left Athens, horrified at the society that had sanctioned the execution, and spent a number of years traveling. He returned in 387 B.C. and founded the Academy, the first permanent institution in Western civilization devoted to education and research, and thus the forerunner of all our universities. Its curriculum concentrated on mathematics, law, and political theory. Its purpose was to produce experts for the service of the state. Some twenty years later, in 368 B.C., Plato was invited to Sicily to put his political theories into practice by turning Syracuse into a model kingdom and its young ruler, Dionysius II, into a philosopher king. Predictably, the attempt was a dismal failure, and by 366 B.C. he was back in Athens. Apart from a second visit to Syracuse in 362 B.C., equally unsuccessful, he seems to have spent the rest of his life in Athens, teaching and writing. He died there in 347 B.C.

Much of Plato's work deals with political theory and the construction of an ideal society. The belief in an ideal is, in fact, characteristic of most of his thinking. It is most clearly expressed in his Theory of Forms, according to which in a higher dimension of existence there are perfect Forms of which all the phenomena we perceive in the world around us represent pale reflections. There can be no doubt that Plato's vision of an ideal society is far too authoritarian for most tastes, involving among other restrictions the careful breeding of children, the censorship of music and poetry, and the abolition of private property. In fairness to Plato, however, it must be remembered that his works are intended not as a set of instructions to be followed literally but as a challenge to think seriously about how our lives should be organized. Furthermore, the disadvantages of democratic government had become all too clear during the last years of the 5th century B.C. If Plato's attempt to redress the balance seems to veer excessively in the other direction, it may in part have been inspired by the continuing chaos of 4th-century Greek politics.

Plato's most gifted pupil, Aristotle (384–322 B.C.), continued to develop his master's doctrines, at first wholeheartedly and later critically, for at least twenty years. In 335 B.C., Aristotle founded a school in competition with Plato's Academy, the Lyceum, severing fundamental ties with Plato from then on. Aristotle in effect introduced a rival philosophy—one that has attracted thinking minds ever since. Indeed, in the 19th century the English poet Samuel Taylor Coleridge was to comment, with much truth, that one was born either a "Platonist" or an "Aristotelian."

The Lyceum seems to have been organized with typically Aristotelian efficiency. In the morning Aristotle himself lectured to the full-time students, many of whom came from other parts of Greece to attend his courses and work on the projects he was directing. In the afternoon the students pursued their research in the library, museum, and map collection attached to the Lyceum, while Aristotle gave more general lectures to the public. His custom of strolling along the Lyceum's circular walkways, immersed in profound contemplation or discourse, gained his school the name *Peripatetic,* or the "walking" school.

As a philosopher Aristotle was the greatest systematizer. He wrote on every topic of serious study of the time. Many of his classifications have remained valid to this day, although some of the disciplines, such as psychology and physics, have severed their ties with philosophy and have become important sciences in their own right.

The most complex of Aristotle's works is probably the *Metaphysics,* in which he deals with his chief dispute with Plato, which concerned the Theory of Forms. Plato had postulated a higher dimension of existence for the Ideal Forms and thereby created a split between the apparent reality that we perceive and the genuine reality that we can only know by philosophical contemplation. Moreover, knowledge of these forms depended on a theory of "remembering" them from previous existences. Aristotle, on the other hand, claimed that the forms were actually present in the objects we see around us, thereby eliminating the split between the two realities.

Elsewhere in the *Metaphysics* Aristotle discusses the nature of God, whom he describes as "thought thinking of itself" and "the Unmoved Mover." The nature of the physical world ruled over by this supreme being is further explored in the *Physics,* which is concerned with the elements that compose the universe and the laws by which they operate.

Other important works by Aristotle include the *Rhetoric,* which prescribes the ideal model of oratory, and the *Poetics,* which does the same for poetry and includes the famous definition of tragedy mentioned earlier (see page 65). Briefly, Aristotle's formula for tragedy is as follows: The tragic hero, who must be noble, through some undetected "tragic flaw" in character meets with a bad end involving the reversal of fortune and sometimes death. The audience, through various emotional and intellectual relations with this tragic figure, undergoes a "cleansing" or "purgation" of the soul, called *catharsis*. Critics of this analysis sometimes complain that Aristotle was trying to read his own very subjective formulas into the Greek tragedies of the time. This is not entirely just, since Aristotle was probably writing for future tragedians, prescribing what ought to be rather than what was.

Aristotle's influence on later ages was vast, although not continuous. Philip of Macedon employed him to tutor young Alexander, but the effect on the young conqueror was probably minimal. Thereafter his works were lost and not recovered until the 1st century B.C., when they were used by the Roman statesman and thinker Cicero (106–43 B.C.). During the Middle Ages, they were translated into Latin and Arabic and became a philosophical basis for Christian theology. Saint Thomas Aquinas' synthesis of Aristotelian philosophy and Christian doctrine still remains the official philosophical position of the Roman Catholic Church.

In philosophy, theology, and scientific and intellectual thought as a whole, many of the distinctions first applied by Aristotle were rediscovered in the early Renaissance and are still valid today. Indeed, no survey such as this can begin to do justice to one described by Dante as "the master of those who know." In the more than two thousand years since his death only Leonardo da Vinci has come near to equaling his creative range.

GREEK MUSIC IN THE CLASSICAL PERIOD

Both Plato and Aristotle found a place for music in their ideal states; their comments on it provide some information on the status of Greek music in the Classical period. Throughout the 5th century B.C. music played an important part in dramatic performances but was generally subordinated to the poetry. By the end of the Peloponnesian War, however, the musical aspect of tragedy had begun to predominate. It is interesting to note that Euripides was criticized by his contemporaries for the lack of form and symmetry and the overemotionalism of his music, not of his verse. With its release from the function of mere accompaniment, instrumental music became especially popular in the 4th century B.C.

The belief in the doctrine of *ethos* (page 49) whereby music had the power to influence human behavior, meant that the study of music played a vital part in the education and life style of Classical Greeks. In Plato's view, participation in musical activities molded the character for better or worse—thus the ban on certain kinds of music, those with the "wrong" ethos, in his ideal Republic. At the same time the musical scale, with its various ratios of pitches, reflected the proportions of the cosmos; music thereby provided a link between the real world and the abstract world of Forms.

For Aristotle music held a more practical, less mystical, value in the attainment of virtue. As a mathematician he believed that the numerical relationships which linked the various pitches could be used by a musician to compose works which imitated the highest state of reason, and thus virtue. Furthermore, just as individuals could create works with a virtuous, moral ethos, so too the State would be served by "ethical" music.

For all its importance in Greek life and thought, however, the actual sound of Greek music and the principles whereby it was composed are not easy to reconstruct or understand.

The numerical relationship of notes to one another established by Pythagoras (see page 53) was used to divide the basic unit of an octave (series of eight notes) into smaller intervals named after their positions in relation to the lowest note in the octave. The interval known as a *fourth*, for example, represents the space between the lowest note and the fourth note up the octave. The intervals were then combined to form a series of scales, or *modes*. Each was given a name and was associated with a particular emotional range. Thus the Dorian mode was serious and warlike, the Phrygian exciting and emotional, and the Mixolydian plaintive and pathetic.

The unit with which Greek music was constructed was the *tetrachord*, a group of four notes of which the two outer ones are a perfect fourth apart and the inner ones variably spaced. The combination of two tetrachords formed a mode. The Dorian mode, for example, consisted of the following two tetrachords:

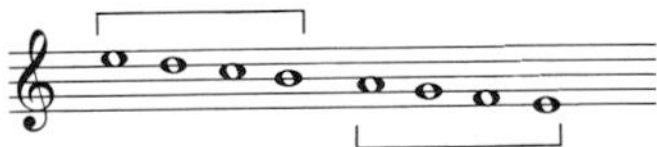

The Lydian mode was composed of two different tetrachords:

The origin of the modes and their relationship to one another is uncertain; it was disputed even in ancient times. The situation has not been made easier by the fact that medieval church music adopted the same system of mathematical construction and even some of the same names, but applied them to different modes.

The word *harmony* is Greek in origin; literally it means a "joining together," and in a musical context the Greeks used it to describe various kinds of scales. There is nevertheless no evidence that Greek music contained any element of harmony in a more modern sense—that is, of groups of notes (chords) sounded simultaneously. Throughout the fifth century B.C. musical rhythm was tied to that of the words or dance steps the music accompanied. Special instruments such as cymbals and tambourines were used to mark the rhythmical patterns, and Greek writers on music often discussed specific problems presented to composers by the nature of the Greek language and its accent system.

Although few traces have survived, a system of musical notation was used to write down compositions; the Greeks probably borrowed it, like their alphabet, from the Phoenicians. Originally used for lyre music, it used symbols to mark the position of fingers on the lyre strings, rather like modern guitar notation (tablature). The system was then adapted for vocal music and for nonstringed instruments such as the *aulos*. The oldest of the few examples to survive dates to around 250 B.C.

THE VISUAL ARTS IN CLASSICAL GREECE

Sculpture and Vase Painting in the 5th Century B.C.

3.6 Myron. *Discobolos (Discus Thrower).* Roman copy after bronze original of c. 450 B.C. Marble, life-size. National Museum, Rome.

Like the writers and thinkers of their time, artists of the mid-5th century B.C. were concerned with ideas of balance and order. Very early Classical works like the *Critian Boy* [2.13] revealed a new interest in realism, and the sculptors who came later began to explore the exciting possibilities of representing the human body in motion.

Among the most famous 5th-century sculptors working at Athens was Myron. Although none of his sculptures has survived, there are a number of later copies of one of his most famous pieces, the *Discus Thrower* [3.6]. The original, made around 450 B.C., is typical of its age in combining realistic treatment of an action with an idealized portrayal of the athlete himself.

While striving for naturalism, artists like Myron tried also to create a new standard of human beauty by controlling the human form according to principles of proportion, symmetry, and balance. Among the finest examples of mid-5th-century-B.C sculpture are two bronze statues found off the coast of southeast Italy in the 1980s [3.7]. Known as the Riace Bronzes, they were probably the work of a master sculptor on the Greek mainland. They represent warriors, although their precise subject, together with the reason for their presence in Italian water, remains a mystery. Around 440 B.C., one of the greatest of Classical sculptors, Polyclitus of Argos, devised a mathematical formula for representing the perfect male body, an ideal canon of proportion, and wrote a book about it. The idea behind *The Canon* was that ideal beauty consisted of a precise relationship between the various parts of the body. Polyclitus' book must have set forth the details of his system of proportion. To illustrate his theory, he also produced a bronze statue of a young man holding a spear, the *Doryphoros*. Both book and original statue are lost; only later copies of the *Doryphoros* survive [3.8].

3.7 Warrior. 5th century B.C. Bronze with glass, bone, silver, and copper inlay, height 6'6" (2 m). Museo Nazionale, Reggio Calabrio, Italy.

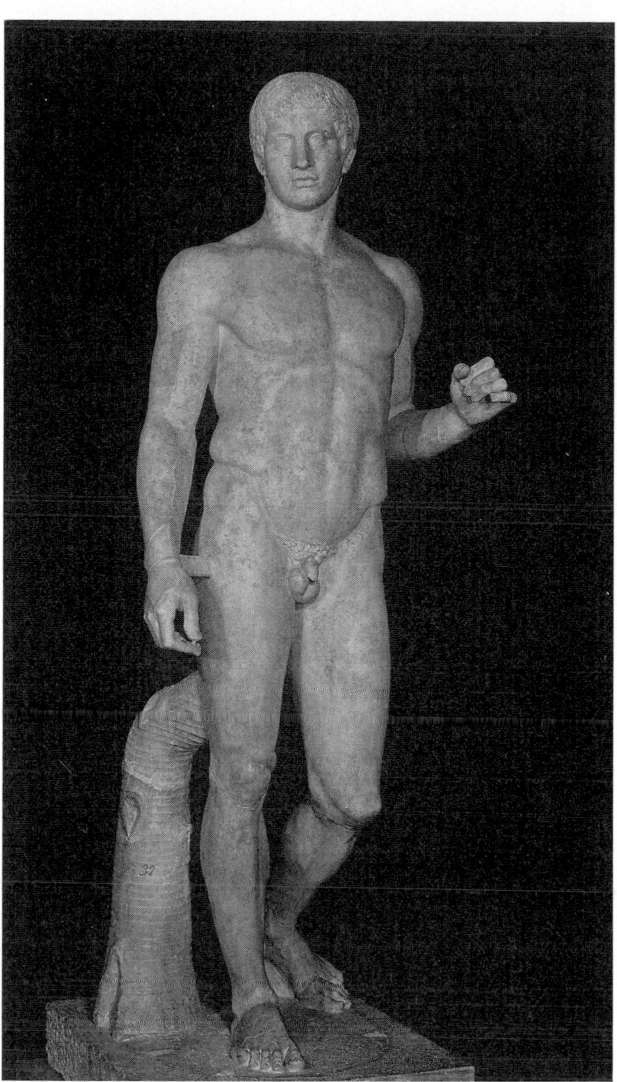

3.8 Polyclitus. *Doryphoros (Spear Bearer).* Roman copy after bronze original of c. 450 B.C. Marble, life-size. Archaeological Museum, Naples.

We do not know, therefore, exactly what Polyclitus' system was. Nevertheless, we have some indication in the writings of a later philosopher, Chrysippus (c. 280–207 B.C.), who wrote that "beauty consists of the proportion of the parts; of finger to finger; of all the fingers to the palm and the wrist; of those to the forearm; of the forearm to the upper arm; and of all these parts to one another, as set forth in *The Canon* of Polyclitus." Even if the exact relationships are lost, what was important about Polyclitus' ideal—and what made it so characteristic of the Classical vision as a whole—was that it depended on precisely ordered and balanced interrelationships of the various parts of the human body. Furthermore, the ideal beauty this created was not produced by nature, but by the power of the human intellect.

In the late 5th century B.C., as the Greeks became embroiled in the Peloponnesian War, sculpture and vase painting were characterized by a growing concern with the individual rather than a generalized ideal. Artists began to depict the emotional responses of ordinary people to life and death instead of approaching these responses indirectly through the use of myths. Thus, death and mourning became increasingly common subjects.

Among the most touching works to survive from the period are a number of oil flasks used for funerary offerings [3.9]. They are painted with mourning or graveside scenes on a white rather than red background. The figures are depicted with

3.9 **Reed Painter.** ***Warrior Seated at His Tomb.*** **Late 5th century B.C. White-ground lekythos, height 18⅞" (48 cm). National Archaeological Museum, Athens. A youth is at one side. On the other side is a young woman who holds the warrior's shield and helmet.**

3.10 Grave stele of Crito and Timarista. c. 420 B.C. Marble. Museum, Rhodes.

quiet and calm dignity but with considerable feeling. This personal rather than public response to death is found also on the gravemarkers of the very end of the 5th century B.C., which show a grief that is perhaps resigned but still intense [3.10].

Architecture in the 5th Century B.C.

In architecture, as in sculpture, designers were concerned with proportion and the interrelationship of the various parts that constitute a complete structure. Nowhere is this more apparent than in the Temple of Zeus at Olympia [3.11], the first great artistic achievement of the years following the Persian Wars, begun in 470 B.C. and finished by 456 B.C. By the time of its completion it was also the largest Doric temple in mainland Greece; it was clearly intended to illustrate the new Classical preoccupation with proportion. The distance from the center of one column to the center of the next was the unit of measurement for the whole temple. Thus the height of each column is equal to two units, and the combined length of a triglyph and a metope equals half a unit.

The theme of order, implicit in the architecture of the temple, became explicit in the sculpture that decorated it. At the center of the west pediment, standing calmly amidst a fight raging between Lapiths and Centaurs, was the figure of Apollo, the god of reason, exerting his authority by a single confident gesture [3.12].

Like the works of Aeschylus, the sculptures from Olympia express a conviction that justice will triumph and that the gods will enforce it. The art of the second half of the 5th century B.C., however, is more concerned with human achievement than with divine will. Pericles' building program for the Acropolis, or citadel of Athens, represents the supreme expression in visual terms of Classical ideals [3.13].

This greatest of all Classical artistic achievements has a special grandeur and poignancy. The splendor of its conception and execution has survived the vicissitudes of time; the great temple to Athena, the Parthenon, remains to this day an incomparable symbol of the Golden Age of Greece. Yet it was built during years of growing division and hostility in the Greek world—the last sculpture was barely in place before the outbreak of the Peloponnesian War in 431 B.C. Pericles died in 429 B.C., but fighting and building both dragged on. The Erechtheum, the final temple to be completed, was not finished until 406 B.C., two years before the end of the war and the fall of Athens. Pericles had intended the whole program to perpetuate the memory of Athens' glorious achievements, but instead it is a reminder of the gulf between Classical high ideals and the realities of political existence in 5th-century-B.C. Greece.

3.11 Reconstruction drawing of east façade, Temple of Zeus, Olympia. c. 470–456 B.C. The pediment shows Zeus between two contestants prior to a chariot race.

3.12 Apollo intervenes in the battle between the Lapiths and Centaurs, from the west pediment of the Temple of Zeus, Olympia. c. 470–456 B.C. Museum, Olympia.

3.13 Model reconstruction of the Acropolis. Royal Ontario Museum, Toronto. Most of the smaller buildings no longer exist, leaving an unobstructed view of the Parthenon that was not possible in ancient times.

Even the funding of the Parthenon symbolizes this gap, since it was paid for at least in part from the treasury of the Delian League (see page 61). The transfer of the League's funds to Athens in 454 B.C. clearly indicated Pericles' imperialist intentions, as did the use to which he put them. In this way the supreme monument of Periclean Athens was built with money originally intended for a pan-Hellenic League. It is even more ironic that Athens' further high-handed behavior created a spirit of ill feeling and distrust throughout the Greek world that led inevitably to the outbreak of the Peloponnesian War—a war that effectively destroyed the Athenian glory the Parthenon had been intended to symbolize.

The great outcrop of rock that forms the Acropolis was an obvious choice by Pericles for the Parthenon and the other buildings planned with it. The site, which towers above the rest of the city, had served as a center for Athenian life from Mycenaean times, when a fortress was built on it. Throughout the Archaic period a series of temples had been constructed there, the last of them destroyed by the Persians in 480 B.C.

Work on the Acropolis was begun in 449 B.C. under the direction of Phidias, the greatest sculptor of his day and a personal friend of Pericles. The Parthenon [3.14] was the first building to be constructed (the name of the temple comes from the Greek *parthenos,* or virgin; that is, the goddess Athena). It was built between 447 and 438 B.C.; its sculptural decoration was complete by 432 B.C. Even larger than the Temple of Zeus at Olympia, the building combines the Doric order of its columns (seventeen on the sides and eight on the ends) with some Ionic features, including a continuous running frieze inside the outer colonnade, at the top of the temple wall and inner colonnades. The design incorporates a number of refinements intended to prevent any sense of monotony or heaviness and gives to the building an air of richness and grace. Like earlier Doric columns, those of the Parthenon are thickest at the point one-third from the base and then taper to the top, a device called *entasis.* In addition, all the columns tilt slightly toward each other (it has been calculated that they would all meet if extended upward for 2 miles, or 3.2 kilometers). The columns at the corners are thicker and closer together than the others and the entablature leans outwards. The flat floor is not really flat at all but convex. All these refinements are, of course, extremely subtle and barely

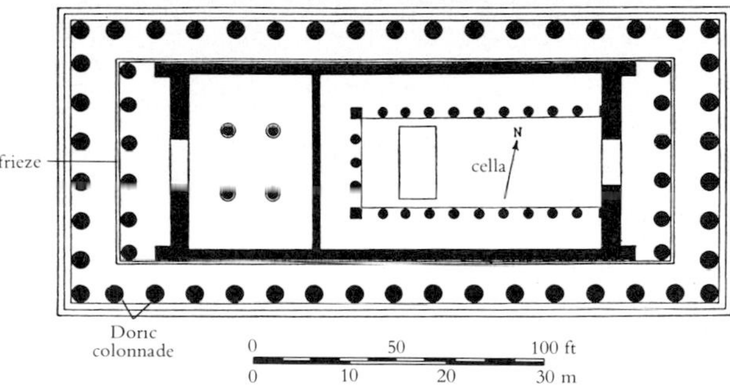

3.14 Ictinus and Callicrates. The Parthenon, Athens. 447–432 B.C. Height of columns 34' (10.36 m). Below is a plan of the temple.

visible to the naked eye. The perfection of their execution, requiring incredible precision of mathematical calculation, is the highest possible tribute to the Classical search for order.

The sculptural decoration of the Parthenon occupied three parts of the building and made use of three different techniques of carving. The figures in the pediments are freestanding; the frieze is carved in low relief; the metopes are in high relief (see page 45). The Ionic frieze, 520' (158.6 meters) long, is carved in low relief; it depicts a procession that took place every four years on the occasion of the Great Panathenaic Festival. It shows Athenians walking and riding to the Acropolis in a ceremony during which an ancient wooden statue of Athena was presented with a new robe. The variety of movement, gesture, and rhythm achieved in the relatively limited technique of low relief makes the frieze among the greatest treasures of Greek art [3.15]. At the beginning of the 19th century, most of the frieze, together with other Parthenon sculptures, was removed from the building by the British Ambassador to Constantinople, Lord Elgin; these are now in the British Museum. (All the sculptures from the Parthenon that are in the British Museum are generally known as the Elgin Marbles.)

Equally impressive are the surviving figures from the east and west pediments, which are freestanding. They show, respectively, the birth of Athena and her contest with Poseidon, god of the sea, to decide which of them should be patron

3.15 Equestrian group, detail of Parthenon frieze (north face). c. 442–432 B.C. Pentelic marble, height 41⅞" (106 cm). British Museum, London (reproduced by courtesy of the Trustees). The composition is elaborate but clear. The riders, with their calm, typically Classical expressions, are shown in various positions: note especially the last figure on the right.

deity of the city. They are badly damaged; even so, statues like the group of three goddesses [3.16], from the east pediment, show a combination of idealism and naturalism that has never been surpassed. The anatomy of the figures and the drapery, which in some cases covers them, are both treated realistically, even in places where the details of the workmanship would have been barely visible to the spectator below. The realism is combined, however, with a characteristically Classical preoccupation with proportion and balance; the result is sculptures that achieve an almost perfect blend of the two elements of the Classical style: ideal beauty represented in realistic terms.

In contrast to the frieze, the technique employed on the metopes is high relief, so high, in fact, that some of the figures seem almost completely detached from their background. These metopes, which illustrate a number of mythological battles, represent a lower level of achievement, although some are more successful than others at reconciling scenes of violence and Classical idealism. The most

3.16 ***Three Goddesses*, from Parthenon east pediment. c. 438–432 B.C. Marble, over life-size. British Museum, London (reproduced by courtesy of the Trustees). The robes show the sculptor's technical virtuosity in carving drapery.**

3.17 ***Lapith and Centaur*, metope from Parthenon (south face). c. 448–442 B.C. Pentelic marble, height 4'4¼" (1.34 m). British Museum, London (reproduced by courtesy of the Trustees). The assailed Lapith has dropped to one knee.**

impressive ones show episodes from the battle between Lapiths and Centaurs [3.17], the same story we saw on the west pediment at Olympia.

The monumental entrance to the Acropolis, the Propylaea [3.18], was begun in 437 B.C. and finished on the eve of the outbreak of war, although probably only by a modification of the architect Mnesicles' original plan. An unusual feature of its design is that both Doric and Ionic columns are used, the Doric ones visible from the front and the back and the Ionic ones lining the passageway through the outer porch.

The other major building on the Acropolis is the Erechtheum, an Ionic temple of complex design, which was begun in 421 B.C. but not completed until 406 B.C. The chief technical problem facing the architect, whose identity is unknown, was the uneven ground level of the site. The problem was solved by creating a building with entrances on different levels. The nature of the building itself produced other design problems. The Erechtheum had to commemorate a whole series of elaborate religious events and honor a number of different deities. One of its four chambers housed the ancient wooden statue of Athena that was at the center of the Great Panathenaic Festival shown on the Parthenon frieze. Elsewhere in the temple were altars to Poseidon and Erechtheus, an early Athenian king; to the legendary Athenian hero Butes; and to Hephaistos, the god of the forge. Furthermore, the design had to incorporate the marks in the ground made by Poseidon's trident during the competition with Athena, as shown on the west pediment of the Parthenon, and the site of the grave of another early and probably legendary Athenian king, Cecrops. The result of all this was a building whose complex plan is still not fully understood. In fact, the exact identification of the inner chambers remains in doubt.

The decoration of the temple is both elaborate and delicate, almost fragile. Its best-known feature is the South Porch, where the roof rests not on columns but on the famous *caryatids,* statues of young women [3.19]. These graceful figures, which stand gravely upright with one knee slightly bent as if to sustain the weight of the roof, represent the most complete attempt until then to conceal the structural functions of a column behind its form.

In many respects innovations such as these make the Erechtheum as representative of the mood of the late 5th century B.C. as the confident Parthenon is of the mood of a generation earlier. The apparent lack of a coherent overall plan and the blurring of traditional distinctions between architecture and sculpture, structure and decoration, seem to question traditional architectural values in a way that parallels the doubts of Euripides and his contemporaries.

3.18 Mnesicles. Propylaea, Athens (west front). 437–431 B.C. This is the view from the Temple of Athena Nike. Note the contrast between the simple Doric columns of the façade and the Ionic columns that line the center passageway.

3.19 *Porch of the Maidens,* Erechtheum, Athens. 421–406 B.C. Height of caryatids 7' 9" (2.30 m).

The Visual Arts in the 4th Century B.C.

As in the case of literature and philosophy, the confusion of Greek political life in the years following the defeat of Athens in 404 B.C. affected the development of the visual arts. In general, the idealism and heroic characters of High Classical art were replaced with a growing interest in realism and emotion. Our knowledge of the visual arts in the 4th century B.C. is, however, far from complete. Greek fresco painting of the period has been entirely lost, though recent discoveries in northern Greece at the Royal Cemetery of Vergina suggest that some of it may yet be found again [3.20]. In sculpture, fortunately, Roman copies of lost original statues enable us to form a fairly good estimate of the main developments. It is clear that Plato's interest in the fate of the individual soul finds its parallel in the sculptural treatment of the human form. Facial expressions become more emotional, often characterized by a mood of dreamy tenderness. Technical skill in depicting drapery and the anatomy beneath are put to the service of a new virtuosity. The three sculptors who dominated the art of the 4th century B.C. are Praxiteles, Scopas, and Lysippus.

The influence of Praxiteles on his contemporaries was immense. His particular brand of gentle melancholy is well illustrated by the *Hermes* at Olympia [3.21] that is generally attributed to him. Equally important is his famous statue of Aphrodite nude [3.22], of which some fifty copies have survived. This represents the discovery of the female body as an object of beauty in itself; it was also one of the first attempts in Western art to introduce the element of sensuality into the portrayal of the female form.

3.20 *Pluto Seizing Persephone,* detail of wall painting from Royal Tomb I, Vergina. Mid-4th century B.C. This unique example of Late Classical monumental painting was discovered by the Greek archaeologist Manolis Andronikos in 1977. It shows a remarkable fluency and freedom of technique.

EAST MEETS WEST

The Greeks in India

The earliest known contact between Greeks and Indians occurred long before the time of Alexander, on Greek soil: According to Herodotus, a detachment of Indians fought in the Persian army during the Persian War of 480–479 B.C. Later, as Alexander drove his way across Asia in the decade preceding his death in 323 B.C., Indian troops continued to provide support to the Persians; their most valuable assets were the elephants they had trained for warfare.

By 326 B.C., Alexander's army had arrived in the Punjab in northwest India. There they fought, and barely defeated, the army of King Poros (probably a tribal name), which was equipped with no fewer than two hundred elephants. On hearing that the next kingdom, the Ganges, had a force of five thousand elephants, Alexander's men flatly refused to go on; even his charisma could not make them change their minds. Most returned westward, although some stayed on in the region known as Bactria in what is now Afghanistan and northwest India.

The Greek cities of Bactria served as a bridge between East and West in two ways. They lay astride the principal central Asian trade routes and thus controlled commercial exchange; some of the most splendid of Greek coins were minted by Bactrian Greeks. Secondly—and more significantly in the long run—they carried Western art and culture into India. In addition to the influence of Greek styles on Buddhist sculpture, Indian Sanskrit drama may well have been inspired by Classical Greek models. Western theories of science and medicine also passed east. Long after these scientific ideas had been forgotten in the West, that is almost a thousand years later, they were reimported into medieval Europe by Muslim explorers.

3.21 Praxiteles. *Hermes with the Infant Dionysus.* c. 340 B.C. Marble, height 7'1" (2.16 m). Museum, Olympia. Hermes' missing right arm held a bunch of grapes just out of the baby's reach.

3.22 Praxiteles. *Aphrodite of Cyrene.* Roman copy of c. 100 B.C. Marble, height 5' (1.52 m). National Museum, Rome. This copy was found by chance in the Roman baths at Cyrene, North Africa. The statue is also called *Venus Anadyomene,* the Roman name for Aphrodite and a Greek word meaning "rising up from the sea," often used in referring to Aphrodite because she was supposed to have arisen from the sea at her birth. The porpoise is a reminder of the goddess' marine associations.

3.23 Scopas. *Pothos.* Roman copy after original of c. 350 B.C. Marble. Palazzo dei Conservatori, Rome.

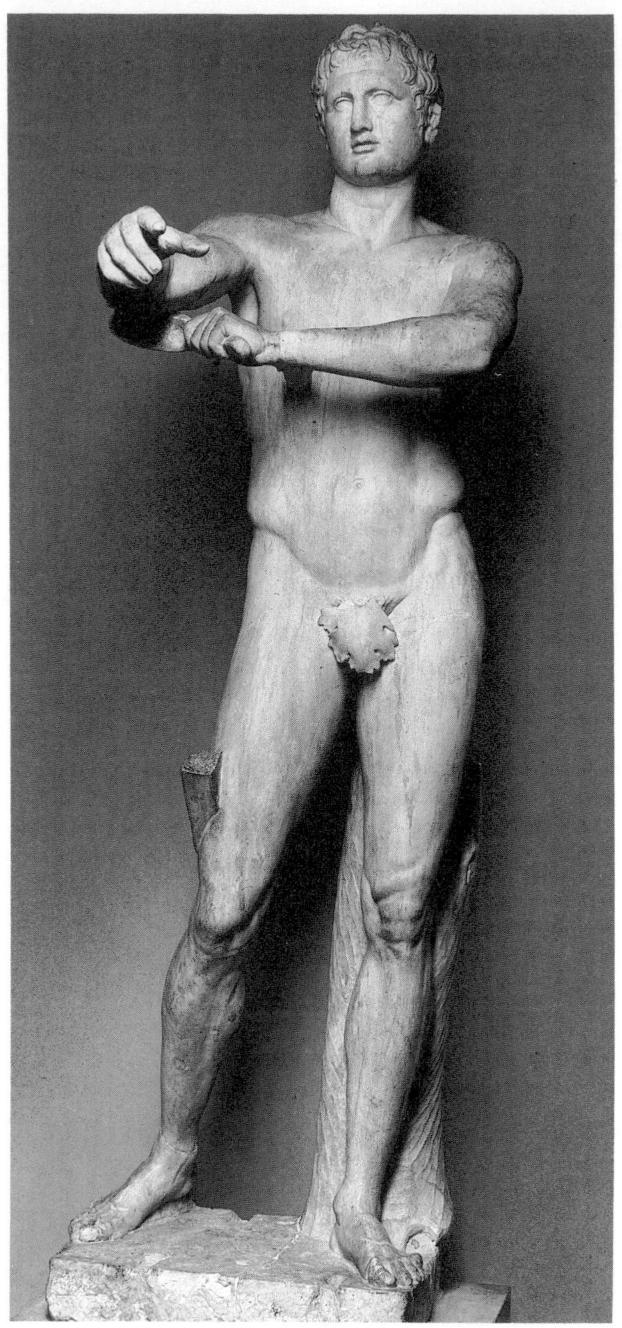

3.24 Lysippus. *Apoxyomenos (The Scraper).* Roman copy after bronze original of c. 330 B.C. Marble, height 6'9" (2.06 m). Vatican Museums, Rome. The young athlete is cleaning off sweat and dirt with a tool called a strigil.

The art of Scopas was more dramatic, with an emphasis on emotion and intensity. Roman copies of his statue of *Pothos,* or Desire [3.23], allow comparison of this yearning figure with Praxiteles' more relaxed *Hermes.*

The impact of Lysippus was as much on succeeding periods as on his own time. One of his chief claims to fame was as the official portraitist of Alexander the Great. Lysippus' very individual characteristics—a new, more attenuated system of proportion, greater concern for realism, and the large scale of many of his works—had a profound effect later on Hellenistic art [3.24].

In architecture, as in the arts generally, the Late Classical period was one of innovation. The great sanctuaries at Olympia and Delphi were expanded and new cities were laid out at Rhodes, Cnidus, and Priene, using Classical principles of town planning.

The 4th century B.C. was also notable for the invention of building forms new to Greek architecture, including the *tholos,* or circular building [3.25]. The most grandiose work of the century was probably the Temple of Artemis at Ephesus, destroyed by fire in 356 B.C. and rebuilt on the same massive scale as before.

CONTEMPORARY VOICES

Kerdo the Cobbler

Step lively: open that drawer of sandals.

Look first at this, Metro; this sole, is it not adjusted like the most perfect of soles? Look, you also, women, at the heel-piece; see how it is held down and how well it is joined to the straps; yet, no part is better than another: all are perfect. And the color!—may the Goddess give you every joy of life!—you could find nothing to equal it. The color! neither saffron nor wax glow like this! Three minæ, for the leather, went to Kandas from Kerdo, who made these. And this other color! it was no cheaper. I swear, by all that is sacred and venerable, women, in truth held and maintained, with no more falsehood than a pair of scales—and, if not, may Kerdo know life and pleasure no more!—this almost drove me bankrupt! For enormous gains no longer satisfy the leathersellers. They do the least of the work, but our works of art depend on them and the cobbler suffers the most terrible misery and distress, night and day. I am glued to my stool even at night, worn out with work, sleepless until the noises of the dawn. And I have not told all: I support thirteen workmen, women, because my own children will not work. Even if Zeus begged them in tears, they would only chant: "What do you bring? What do you bring?" They sit around in comfort somewhere else, warming their legs, like little birds. But, as the saying goes, it is not talk, but money, which pays the bills. If this pair does not please you, Metro, you can see more and still more, until you are sure that Kerdo has not been talking nonsense.

Pistos, bring all those shoes from the shelves.

You must go back satisfied to your houses, women. Here are novelties of every sort: of Sykione and Ambrakia, laced slippers, hemp sandals, Ionian sandals, night slippers, high heels, Argian sandals, red ones:—name the ones you like best. (How dogs—and women—devour the substance of the cobbler!)

A WOMAN: And how much do you ask for that pair you have been parading so well? But do not thunder too loud and frighten us away!

KERDO: Value them yourself, and fix their price, if you like; one who leaves it to you will not deceive you. If you wish, woman, a good cobbler's work, you will set a price—yes, by these gray temples where the fox has made his lair—which will provide bread for those who handle the tools. (O Hermes! if nothing comes into our net now, I don't know when our sauce-pan will get another chance as good!)

Herondas, trans. George Howe and Gustave Adolphus Harrer, *Greek Literature in Translation* (New York: Harper, 1924), p. 542. Herondas was a Greek poet of the 3rd century B.C. whose mimes, from one of which this passage comes, were probably written for performance in public.

Although the Greeks of the 4th century B.C. lacked the certainty and self-confidence of their predecessors, their culture shows no lack of ideas or inspiration. Furthermore, even before Alexander's death the Macedonian Empire had spread Greek culture throughout the Mediterranean world. If Athens itself had lost any real political or commercial importance, the ideas of its great innovators began to affect an ever-growing number of people.

When Alexander died in the summer of 323 B.C., the division of his empire into separate independent kingdoms spread Greek culture even more

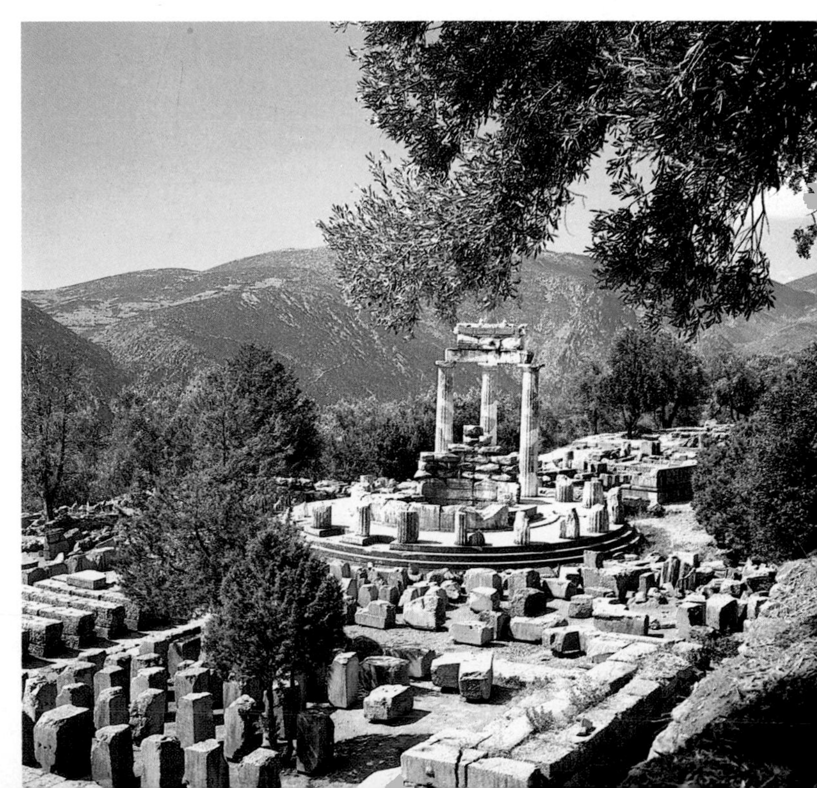

3.25 Theodoros of Phokaia. Tholos of the Sanctuary of Athena Pronaia, Delphi. c. 390 B.C. Marble and limestone; diameter of cella 28'2⅝" (8.6 m), present height 27'2½" (8.29 m). This is one of the first circular designs in Greek architecture. Originally, twenty Doric columns encircled the temple and ten Corinthian columns were set against the wall of the cella within.

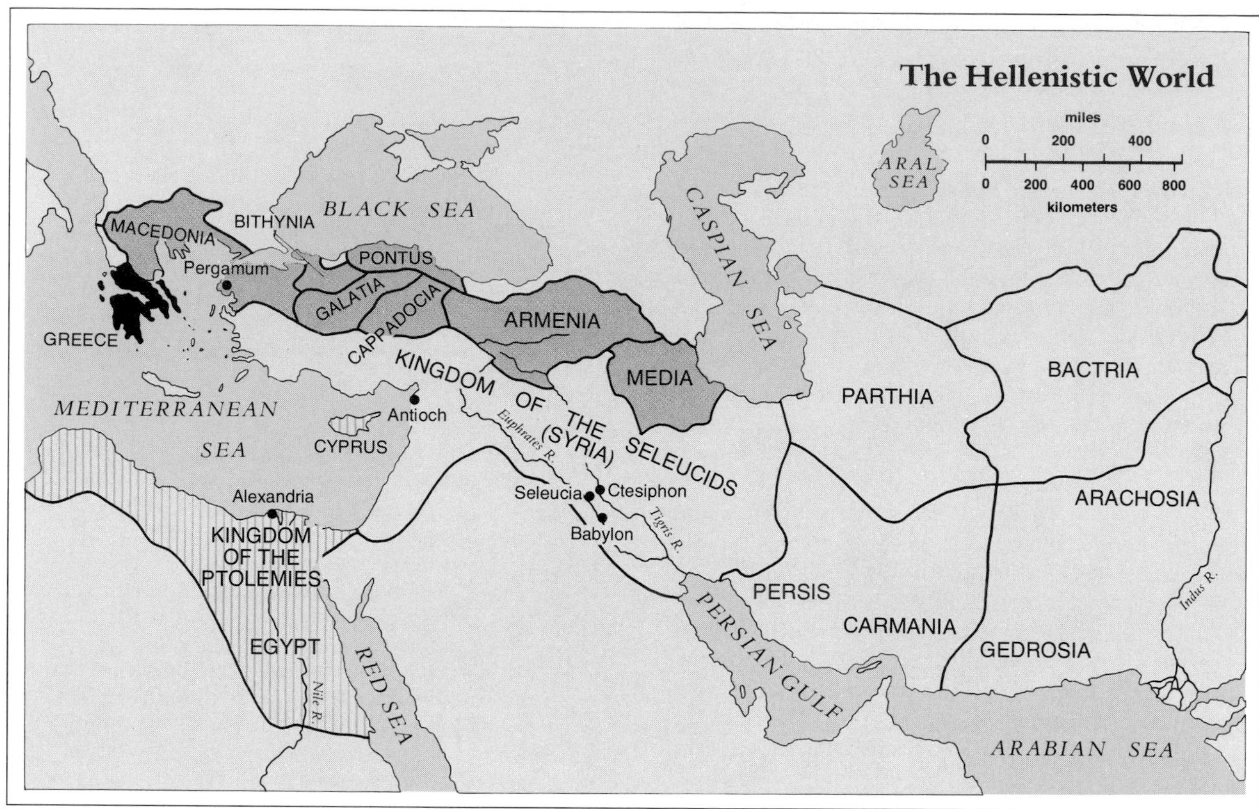

widely. The kingdoms of the Seleucids in Syria and the Ptolemies in Egypt are the true successors to Periclean Athens. Even as far away as India sculptors and town planners were influenced by ideas developed by Athenians of the 5th and 4th centuries B.C.

In due course, the cultural achievement of Classical Greece was absorbed and reborn in Rome, as Chapter 4 will show. Meanwhile, in the period known as the Hellenistic Age, which lasted from the death of Alexander to the Roman conquest of Greece in 146 B.C., that achievement took a new turn.

THE HELLENISTIC PERIOD

Alexander's generals' inability to agree on a single successor after his death made the division of the Macedonian Empire inevitable. The four most important kingdoms that split off, Syria (the kingdom of the Seleucids), Egypt, Pergamum, and Macedonia itself (see map, above), were soon at loggerheads and remained so until they were finally conquered by Rome. Each of them, however, in its own way continued the spread of Greek culture, as the name of the period implies (it is derived from the verb "to Hellenize," or to spread Greek influence).

The greatest of all centers of Greek learning was in the Egyptian city of Alexandria, where King Ptolemy, Alexander's former personal staff officer and bodyguard, planned a large institute for scholarship known as the Temple of the Muses, or the Museum. The Library at the Museum contained everything of importance ever written in Greek, up to seven hundred thousand separate works, according to contemporary authorities. Its destruction by fire when Julius Caesar besieged the city in 47 B.C. must surely be one of the great intellectual disasters in the history of Western culture.

In Asia Minor and farther east in Syria the Hellenistic rulers of the new kingdoms fostered Greek art and literature as one means of holding foreign influences at bay. Libraries were built at Pergamum and the Syrian capital of Antioch, and philosophers from Greece were encouraged to visit the new centers of learning and lecture there. In this way Greek ideas not only retained their hold but began to make an impression on more remote peoples even farther east. The first Buddhist monumental sculpture, called Gandharan after the Indian province of Gandhara where it developed, made use of Greek styles and techniques. There is even a classic Buddhist religious work called *The Questions of King Milinda* in which a local Greek ruler, probably called Menandros, is described exchanging ideas with a Buddhist sage, ending with the ruler's conversion to Buddhism—one example of the failure of Greek ideas to convince those exposed to them.

Yet, however much literature and philosophy could do to maintain the importance of Greek culture, it was primarily to the visual arts that Hellenistic rulers turned. In doing so they inaugurated the last great period of Greek art.

The most powerful influence on the period immediately following Alexander's death was the memory of his life. The daring and immensity of his conquests, his own heroic personality, the new world he had sought to create—all these produced a spirit of adventure and experiment. Artists of the Hellenistic period sought not so much to equal or surpass their Classical predecessors in the familiar forms as to discover new subjects and invent new techniques. The development of realistic portraiture dates to this period [3.26], as does the construction of buildings like the Lighthouse at Alexandria [3.27], in its day the tallest tower ever built and one of the Seven Wonders of the World.

The all-pervading spirit of the Classical Age had been order. Now artists began to discover the delights of freedom. Classical art was calm and restrained, but Hellenistic art was emotional and expressive. Classical artists sought clarity and balance even in showing scenes of violence, but Hellenistic artists allowed themselves to depict riotous confusion involving strong contrasts of light and shade and the appearance of perpetual motion. It is not surprising that the term *baroque*, originally used to describe the extravagant European art of the 17th century A.D., is often applied to the art of the Hellenistic period.

3.27 Reconstruction of the Lighthouse on Pharos, north of Alexandria harbor, 279 B.C. Original height 440' (134.2 m). The beam of light from the lantern at top was intensified by a system of reflectors. The name of the island, Pharos, became, and still is, another word for lighthouse or beacon.

3.26 *Alexander the Great.* Pergamum, c. 160 B.C. Marble. Archaeological Museum, Istanbul. Note the emotional fire of the eyes and mouth, emphasized by the set of the head.

The artists responsible for these innovations created their works for a new kind of patron. Most of the great works of the Classical period had been produced for the state, with the result that the principal themes and inspirations were religious and political. With the disintegration of the Macedonian Empire and the establishment of prosperous kingdoms at Pergamum, Antioch, and elsewhere, there developed a group of powerful rulers and wealthy businessmen who commissioned works either to provide lavish decoration for their cities or to adorn their private palaces and villas. Artists were no longer responsible to humanity and to the gods, but to whoever paid for the work. Their patrons encouraged them to develop new techniques and surpass the achievements of rivals.

At the same time, the change in the artist's social role produced a change in the function of the work. Whereas in the Classical period architects had devoted themselves to the construction of temples and religious sanctuaries, the Hellenistic age is notable for its marketplaces and theaters, as well as for scientific and technical buildings like the Tower of the Winds at Athens and the Lighthouse at Alexandria [3.27].

3.28 Reconstruction model of Upper City, Pergamum. State Museums, East Berlin. The steeply sloping theater is at left; the altar to Zeus is in the center foreground.

Among the rich cities of Hellenistic Asia, none was wealthier than Pergamum, ruled by a dynasty of kings known as the Attalids. Pergamum was founded in the early 3rd century B.C. and reached the high point of its greatness in the reign of Eumenes II (197–159 B.C.). The layout of the chief buildings in the city represents a rejection of the Classical concepts of order and balance. Unlike the Periclean buildings on the Athenian Acropolis, the buildings in Pergamum were placed independently of one another with a new and dramatic use of space. The theater itself, set on a steep slope, seemed to be falling headlong down the hillside [3.28].

The chief religious shrine of Pergamum was the immense altar to Zeus erected by Eumenes II around 180 B.C. to commemorate the victories of his father, Attalus I, over the Gauls. Its base is decorated with a colossal frieze depicting the battle of the gods and giants. The triumphant figure of Zeus presumably stands as a symbol for the victorious king of Pergamum. The drama and violence of the battle find perfect expression in the tangled, writhing bodies, which leap out of the frieze in high relief, and in the intensity of the gestures and facial expressions [3.29]. The immense emotional impact of the scenes may prevent us from appreciating the remarkable skill of the artists, some of whom were brought from Athens to work on the project. However, the movement of the figures is very far from random and the surface of the stone has been carefully worked to reproduce the texture of hair, skin, fabric, metal, and so on.

The Altar of Zeus represents the most complete illustration of the principles and practice of Hellenistic art. It is, of course, a work on a grand, even grandiose, scale, intended to impress a wide public. But many of its characteristics occur in freestanding pieces of sculpture like the *Laocoön* [3.30]. This famous work shows the Trojan priest Laocoön, punished by the gods for his attempt to warn his people against bringing into their city the wooden horse left by the Greeks. To silence the priest, Apollo sends two sea serpents to strangle him and his sons. The large piece is superbly composed, with the three figures bound together by the sinuous curves of the serpents; they pull away from one another under the agony of the creatures' coils.

By the end of the Hellenistic period both artists and public seemed a little weary of so much richness and elaboration and returned to some of the

3.29 *Athena Slaying Giant.* Detail of Altar to Zeus frieze, Pergamum. c. 180 B.C. Marble, height 7'6" (2.29 m). State Museums, Berlin. Athena is grasping the giant Alcyoneus by the hair to lift him off the ground, source of his strength. His mother Ge, the earth goddess, looks on despairingly from below.

3.30 Agesander, Athenodorus, and Polydorus of Rhodes. *Laocoön Group.* c. 150 B.C. Marble, height 8' (2.44 m). Vatican Museums, Rome. This statue was uncovered in 1506 in the ruins of Nero's Golden House. Note the similarity between Laocoön's head and the head of the giant Alcyoneus on the Pergamum frieze.

principles of Classical art. At the same time the gradual conquest of the Hellenistic kingdoms by Rome and their absorption into the Roman Empire produced a new synthesis in which the achievements of Classical and Hellenistic Greece fused with the native Italian culture and passed on to later ages.

SUMMARY

The period covered in this chapter falls into three parts. The first, the years from 479 B.C. to 404 B.C., saw the growth of Athenian power and the consequent mistrust on the part of the rest of the Greek world of Athens' intentions. The same period was marked by major cultural developments at Athens. Sculptors such as Myron and Phidias created the High Classical blend of realism and idealism. Tragic drama, in which music played an important role, reached its highest achievement in the works of Aeschylus, Sophocles, and Euripides. In 449 B.C. work was begun on the buildings on the Athenian Acropolis planned by Pericles, Athens' ambitious leader. The Parthenon and the Propylea were completed in an atmosphere made increasingly tense by the deteriorating relations between Athens and the other leading Greek states, particularly Corinth and Sparta.

In 431 B.C. the Peloponnesian War broke out, with Athens and her few remaining allies on one side, and the rest of the Greek world on the other. In 429 B.C. Pericles was killed by a plague that ravaged the city. In the absence of firm leadership the war dragged on, and during a period of truce the Athenians launched a disastrous campaign against the Greek cities of Sicily. When hostilities resumed, the Athenians were fatally weakened, and in 404 B.C. they surrendered to the Spartans and their allies.

The years of fighting profoundly affected cultural developments at Athens. Both the sculpture and the vase painting of the late 5th century B.C. show a new and somber interest in funerary subjects. In the theater the later plays of Euripides depicted the horrors of war, while the comedies of Aristophanes mocked the political leaders responsible for the turmoil. Thucydides wrote his *History of the Peloponnesian War* to try to analyze the motives and reactions of the participants. Socrates began to question his fellow Athenians about their moral and religious beliefs in a similar spirit of inquiry.

The second period, from 404 B.C. to 323 B.C., was marked by considerable upheaval. Athens was no longer the dominating force in the Greek world, but there was no successor among her rivals. First Sparta and then Thebes achieved an uneasy control of Greek political life. With the collapse of the optimism of the High Classical period the Late Classical age was marked by a new concern with the individual. The dreamy melancholy of Praxiteles' statues is in strong contrast to the idealism of a century earlier, while his figure of Aphrodite naked was one of the first examples in the Western tradition of sensuous female nudity. The most complete demonstration of the new interest in the fate of the individual can be found in the works of Plato, Socrates' disciple, who spent much of his life studying the relationship between individuals and the state. Aristotle, Plato's younger contemporary, also wrote on political theory as well as on a host of other topics.

In 359 B.C. the northern kingdom of Macedon passed under the rule of Philip II and began to play an increasing part in Greek affairs. Despite Athenian resistance, led by the orator Demosthenes, Philip succeeded in uniting the cities of Greece in an alliance known as the League of Corinth; the only important city to remain independent was Sparta.

When Philip was assassinated in 336 B.C. he was succeeded by his son Alexander, who set out to expand the Macedonian Empire. After defeating the Persians, he set out in an amazing series of campaigns across Asia that brought him to the borders of India. Only the revolt of his weary troops prevented him from going farther. In 323 B.C., in the course of the long journey home, Alexander died of fever.

The period from 323 B.C. to 146 B.C., marked by the spread of Greek culture throughout the parts of Asia conquered by Alexander, is known as the Hellenistic Age. In the confusion following his death, four kingdoms emerged: Syria, Egypt, Pergamum, and Macedon itself. Prosperous and aggressive and frequently at war with one another, they combined Greek intellectual ideas and artistic styles with native Eastern ones.

The chief characteristics of Hellenistic art were virtuosity and drama. Works such as the Altar of Zeus at Pergamum were commissioned by Hellenistic rulers to glorify their reigns. Artists were encouraged to develop elaborate new techniques and employ them in complex and dramatic ways. The principal buildings of the age were public works like markets and theaters or scientific constructions such as the Lighthouse at Alexandria.

The inability of the Hellenistic kingdoms to present a united front caused them to fall victim one by one to a new force in the eastern Mediterranean: Rome. By the end of the 3rd century B.C. the Romans had secured their position in the western

Mediterranean and begun an expansion into Asia that was to bring all the Hellenistic kingdoms under their control.

In 146 B.C. Roman troops captured the city of Corinth, center of the League of Corinth founded by Philip and symbol of Greek independence. Greece was made into a Roman province, and its subsequent history followed that of the Roman Empire. If Greece was under Roman political control, however, Greek art and culture dominated much of Roman cultural life and were passed on by the Romans into the Western tradition.

Exercises

1. Explain the chief differences between the three principal Greek tragic dramatists. Illustrate with episodes in particular plays.
2. Discuss the contributions of Plato and Aristotle to the development of philosophy.
3. Describe Greek musical theory in the 5th and 4th centuries B.C.
4. How was sculpture used to decorate the buildings on the Athenian Acropolis? What is the significance of the myths it illustrates?
5. What are the features of a work of art that indicate it is Hellenistic? How does the Hellenistic style contrast with that of the Classical period?

Pronunciation Guide

Aegisthus: Ee-GISTH-us
Aeschylus: EESK-ill-us
Antigone: Ant-IG-owe-nee
Aristophanes: A-rist-OFF-an-ease
Caryatid: Ca-ree-AT-id
Catharsis: Cath-ARE-sis
Chaeronaea: Kai-ron-EE-a
Clytemnaestra: Klit-em-NESS-tra
Demosthenes: Dem-OSTH-en-ease
Doryphorus: Dor-IF-or-us
Elgin: EL-ghin
Entasis: ENT-ass-iss
Erechtheum: Er-EK-thee-um
Eumenides: You-MEN-id-ease
Euripides: You-RIP-id-ease
Ictinus: Ic-TINE-us
Laocoön: La-OK-owe-on
Mnesicles: MNEE-sik-lees
Oedipus: ED-ip-us
Panathenaic: Pan-ath-e-NAY-ic
Parthenon: PARTH-en-on
Pericles: PE-rik-lees
Phaedo: FEE-doe
Phidias: FID-i-ass
Polyclitus: Po-lic-LIE-tus
Propylea: Pro-pie-LEE-a
Ptolemy: PTOL-em-ee
Satyr: SAY-tr
Scopas: SKOWE-pass
Seleucids: Sell-YOU-sids
Thucydides: Thyou-SID-id-ease

Further Reading

Barnes, J. *Aristotle.* Oxford: Oxford University Press, 1982. In a mere eighty pages this remarkable book provides an excellent general introduction to Aristotle's vast range of works.

Casson, L. *Travel in the Ancient World.* New York: New York University Press, 1974. An absorbing description of the part played by travel and communication throughout antiquity.

Cawkwell, G. *Philip of Macedon.* Boston: Houghton Mifflin, 1978. A lively account, incorporating new discoveries, of the career of one of the most influential figures in Greek history.

Finley, M. I. (ed.) *The Legacy of Greece: A New Appraisal.* Oxford: Oxford University Press, 1981. A collection of essays by various authors who discuss Greek achievements in various fields—philosophy, art, literature, among others—and evaluate their relevance to the late 20th century.

Hammond, N. G. L. *Alexander the Great: King, Commander, and Statesman.* London: Methuen, 1981. Alexander is still a controversial figure. The author of this scholarly study, clearly an admirer, provides a vivid account of Alexander's life.

Lefkowitz, M. R. and M. B. Fant. *Women in Greece and Rome.* Toronto: University of Toronto Press, 1978. A collection of writings from Classical antiquity by, about, sometimes even against women.

Lesky, A. *Greek Tragic Poetry,* 3rd ed.; trans. M. Dillon. New Haven: Yale University Press, 1983. The latest version of one of the standard works on Greek tragedy, analyzing it as literature rather than as theater.

Morford, M. P. O. and P. J. Lenardon. *Classical Mythology.* New York: Longman, 1977. A useful reference source for the many myths found in Greek art and literature, this book also discusses Greek religion and the Greeks' views of the afterlife.

Staveley, E. S. *Greek and Roman Voting and Elections.* London: Methuen, 1972. An absorbing introduction to the world of ancient politics and political practices.

Walbank, F. W. *The Hellenistic World.* Cambridge: Harvard University Press, 1982. This book describes the various Hellenistic kingdoms and evaluates their cultural achievements. Includes a good section on Hellenistic science and technology.

Wycherley, R. E. *The Stones of Athens.* Princeton: Princeton University Press, 1978. An authoritative description of the monuments of Classical Athens that includes an individual description as well as a bibliography for each important building.

			GENERAL EVENTS	LITERATURE & PHILOSOPHY
		753 B.C.	**753 B.C.** Founding of Rome (traditional date) **c. 700** Development of Etruscan culture	
ROMAN REPUBLIC	Conquest of Italy and Mediterranean	509	**509** Expulsion of Etruscan kings and foundation of Roman Republic **450** Promulgation of the *Twelve Tables* of laws **c. 390** Sack of Rome by Gauls **287** Hortensian Law reinforces plebeian power **264–241** First Punic War: Roman conquest of Sicily, Sardinia, Corsica **218–201** Second Punic War: Roman conquest of Spain **146** Destruction of Carthage: Africa becomes Roman province. Sack of Corinth: Greece becomes Roman province	**c. 200–160 B.C.** Ennius, *Annales,* epic poem; Plautus, *Mostellaria,* Roman comedy; Terence, Roman comedies **2nd cent.** Epicureanism and Stoicism imported to Rome
ROMAN REPUBLIC	Political Crisis at Rome	133	**90–88** Social War **82–81** Sulla dictator at Rome **60** First Triumvirate: Pompey, Caesar, Crassus **58–56** Caesar conquers Gaul **48** Battle of Pharsalus: war of Caesar and Pompey ends in death of Pompey. Caesar meets Cleopatra in Egypt **46–44** Caesar rules Rome as dictator until assassinated **43** Second Triumvirate: Antony, Lepidus, Octavian	**c. 65–43** Lucretius, *On the Nature of Things,* Epicurean poem; Cicero, orations and philosophical essays; Catullus, lyric poems; Caesar, *Commentaries,* on Gallic wars
ROMAN EMPIRE	Stability	31	**31** Battle of Actium won by Octavian **30** Death of Antony and Cleopatra **27–14** Octavian under name of Augustus rules as first Roman emperor **c. 6** Birth of Jesus; crucified c. A.D. 30	**c. 27 B.C.–A.D. 14** Horace, *Odes* and *Ars Poetica;* Vergil, *Aeneid, Georgics, Eclogues;* Ovid, *Metamorphoses,* mythological tales; Livy, *Annals of the Roman People*
ROMAN EMPIRE	Stability	B.C. / A.D.	**A.D. 14–68** Julio-Claudian emperors: Tiberius, Caligula, Claudius, Nero **69–96** Flavian emperors: Vespasian, Titus, Domitian **70** Capture of Jerusalem by Titus; destruction of Solomon's Temple **79** Destruction of Pompeii and Herculaneum **96–138** Adoptive emperors: Nerva, Trajan, Hadrian, et al. **138–192** Antonine emperors: Antoninus Pius, Marcus Aurelius, et al.	**c. A.D. 100–150** Tacitus, *History;* Juvenal, *Satires;* Pliny the Younger, *Letters;* Suetonius, *Lives of the Caesars;* Epictetus, *Enchiridion,* on Stoicism **c. 166–179** Marcus Aurelius, *Meditations,* on Stoicism
ROMAN EMPIRE	Disintegration	180	**193–235** Severan emperors: Septimius Severus, Caracalla, et al. **212** Edict of Caracalla	
ROMAN EMPIRE	Reconstruction and Decline	284	**284–305** Reign of Diocletian; return of civil order **301** Edict of Diocletian, fixing wages and prices **307–337** Reign of Constantine; sole emperor after 324 **330** Founding of Constantinople **392** Paganism officially suppressed; Christianity made state religion **409–455** Vandals and Visigoths invade Italy, Spain, Gaul, Africa **476** Romulus Augustulus forced to abdicate as last Western Roman emperor	
		A.D. 476		

CHAPTER 4

THE ROMAN LEGACY

ART	ARCHITECTURE	MUSIC
c. 650–500 B.C. Influence of Greek and Orientalizing styles on Etruscan art **late 6th cent.** Etruscan *Apollo,* from Veii 	**c. 616–509 B.C.** Etruscans drain marshes, build temples, construct roads	Extension of Greek trumpet into Roman tuba, used in games, processions, battles
		c. 2nd cent B.C. Greek music becomes popular at Rome
 **1st cent.** Realistic portraiture; *Portrait of Cicero* **c. 30 B.C.–A.D. 30** Villa of Mysteries frescoes, Pompeii	**1st cent.** Discovery of concrete **c. 82** Sulla commissions Sanctuary of Fortuna Primagenia, Praeneste 	
c. 20 *View of a Garden,* fresco from Augustus' villa, Prima Porta **13–9** *Ara Pacis*	Use of arch, vault, dome, principles of stress/counterstress	
 **c. A.D. 14** *Augustus of Prima Porta*	**1st cent. A.D.** Pont du Gard, Nîmes; atrium-style houses at Pompeii **c. 126** Pantheon, Rome  	
 Decline of realism **324–330** Colossal head from Basilica of Constantine, Rome	**300–305** Diocletian's palace, Split **306–315** Basilica of Constantine, Rome	

C H A P T E R

4
THE ROMAN LEGACY

THE IMPORTANCE OF ROME

IF THE ORIGINS of our intellectual heritage go back to the Greeks and, less directly, to the peoples of Egypt and the Near East, the contribution of Rome to the wider spreading of Western civilization was tremendous. In fields like language, law, politics, religion, and art Roman culture continues to affect our lives. The road network of modern Europe is based on one planned and built by the Romans some two thousand years ago; the alphabet we use is the Roman alphabet; and the division of the year into twelve months of unequal length is a modified form of the calendar introduced by Julius Caesar in 45 B.C. Even after the fall of the Roman Empire the city of Rome stood for centuries as the symbol of civilization itself; later empires deliberately shaped themselves on the Roman model.

The enormous impact of Rome on our culture is partly the result of the industrious and determined character of the Romans themselves, who very early in their history saw themselves as the divinely appointed rulers of the world. In the course of fulfilling their mission they spread Roman culture from the north of England to Africa, from Spain to India (see map). This Romanization of the entire known world permitted the spread of ideas the Romans had drawn from other peoples. It was through the Romans that Greek art and literature were handed down into the Western tradition, not from the Greeks themselves. The rapid spread of Christianity in the 4th century A.D. was a result of the decision of the Roman emperors to adopt it as the official religion of the Roman Empire. In these and in other respects, the legacy Rome was to pass on to Western civilization had been inherited from its predecessors.

The Romans themselves were surprisingly modest about their own cultural achievements, in fact, believing that their strengths lay in good government and military prowess rather than in artistic and intellectual attainments. It was their view that Rome should get on with the job of ruling the world and leave luxuries like sculpture and astronomy to others.

It is easy but unfair to accept the Romans' estimate of themselves as uncreative without questioning it. True, in some fields the Roman contribution was not very impressive. What little we know about Roman music, for example, suggests that its loss is hardly a serious one. It was intended mainly for performance at religious events like weddings and funerals, and as a background for social occasions. Musicians were often brought into aristocratic homes to provide after-dinner entertainment at a party, and individual performers, frequently women, would play before small groups in a domestic setting. Small bands of traveling musicians, playing on pipes and such percussion instruments as cymbals and tambourines, provided background music for the acrobats and jugglers who performed in public squares and during gladiatorial contests [4.1].

Nonetheless, for the Romans music certainly had none of the intellectual and philosophical significance it bore for the Greeks, and when Roman writers mention musical performances it is often to complain about the noise. The only serious development in Roman music was the extension of the Greek trumpet into a longer and louder bronze instrument known as the *tuba,* which was used on public occasions like games and processions and in battle, when an especially powerful type some 4' (1.2 meters) long gave the signals for attack and retreat. The sound was not pleasant.

4.1 Gladiatorial contest with orchestra of hydraulic organ, trumpet, and horn players. Mosaic from villa near Zliten, North Africa, c. A.D. 70. Museum of Antiquities, Tripoli.

In general, Roman music lovers contented themselves with Greek music played on Greek instruments. Although serious music began to grow in popularity with the spread of Greek culture, it always remained an aristocratic rather than popular taste. The emperor Nero's love of music, coupled with his insistence on giving public concerts on the lyre, may even have hastened his downfall.

In areas other than music, the Roman achievement is considerable. There is no doubt that Roman art and literature rarely show the originality of their Greek predecessors, but originality is not the only artistic virtue, nor is its absence always a defect. The Roman genius, in fact, lay precisely in absorbing and assimilating influences from outside and going on to create from them something typically Roman. The lyric poetry of 1st-century-B.C. writers like Catullus was inspired by the works of Sappho, Alcaeus, and other Greek poets of the 6th century B.C., but nothing could be more Roman in spirit than Catullus' poems. In architecture, the Romans achieved a style that is one of the most impressive of all our legacies from the ancient world.

It is useful to emphasize the very real value of Roman art and literature because there has been a tendency since the 19th century to exalt the Greek cultural achievement at the expense of the Roman. All agree on the superior quality of Roman roads, sewers, and aqueducts; Roman sculpture or drama has in general been less highly rated, mainly because of comparisons with that of the Greeks. Any study of Roman culture inevitably involves examining the influences that went to make it up, and it is necessary always to remember the Roman ability to absorb and combine outside ideas and create something fresh from them.

Rome's history was a long one, beginning with the foundation of the city in the 8th century B.C. For the first two and a half centuries of its existence it was ruled by kings. The rest of the vast span of Roman history is divided into two long periods: Republican Rome (509–31 B.C.), during which time democratic government was first developed and then allowed to collapse; and Imperial Rome (31 B.C.–A.D. 476), during when the Roman world was ruled, at least in theory, by one man—the Emperor. The date A.D. 476 marks the deposition of the last Roman Emperor in the West; it forms a convenient, if artificial, terminus to the Imperial period (see page 116).

Shortly after the foundation of the Republic, the Romans began their conquest of neighboring peoples, first in Italy, then throughout Europe, Asia, and North Africa. As their territory grew, Roman civilization developed along with it, assimilating the cultures of the peoples who fell under Roman domination. But long before the Romans conquered Greece or anywhere else, they were themselves conquered by the Etruscans, and the story of Rome's rise to power truly begins with the impact on Roman life made by Etruscan rule there.

THE ETRUSCANS AND THEIR ART

The late 8th century B.C. was a time of great activity in Italy. The Greeks had reached the south coast and Sicily. In the valley of the Tiber, farmers and herdsmen of a group of tribes known as the Latins (origin of the name of the language spoken by the Romans) were establishing small village settlements, one of which was to become the future imperial city of Rome. The most flourishing area at the time, however, was to the north of Rome, where in central Italy a new culture—the Etruscan—was appearing.

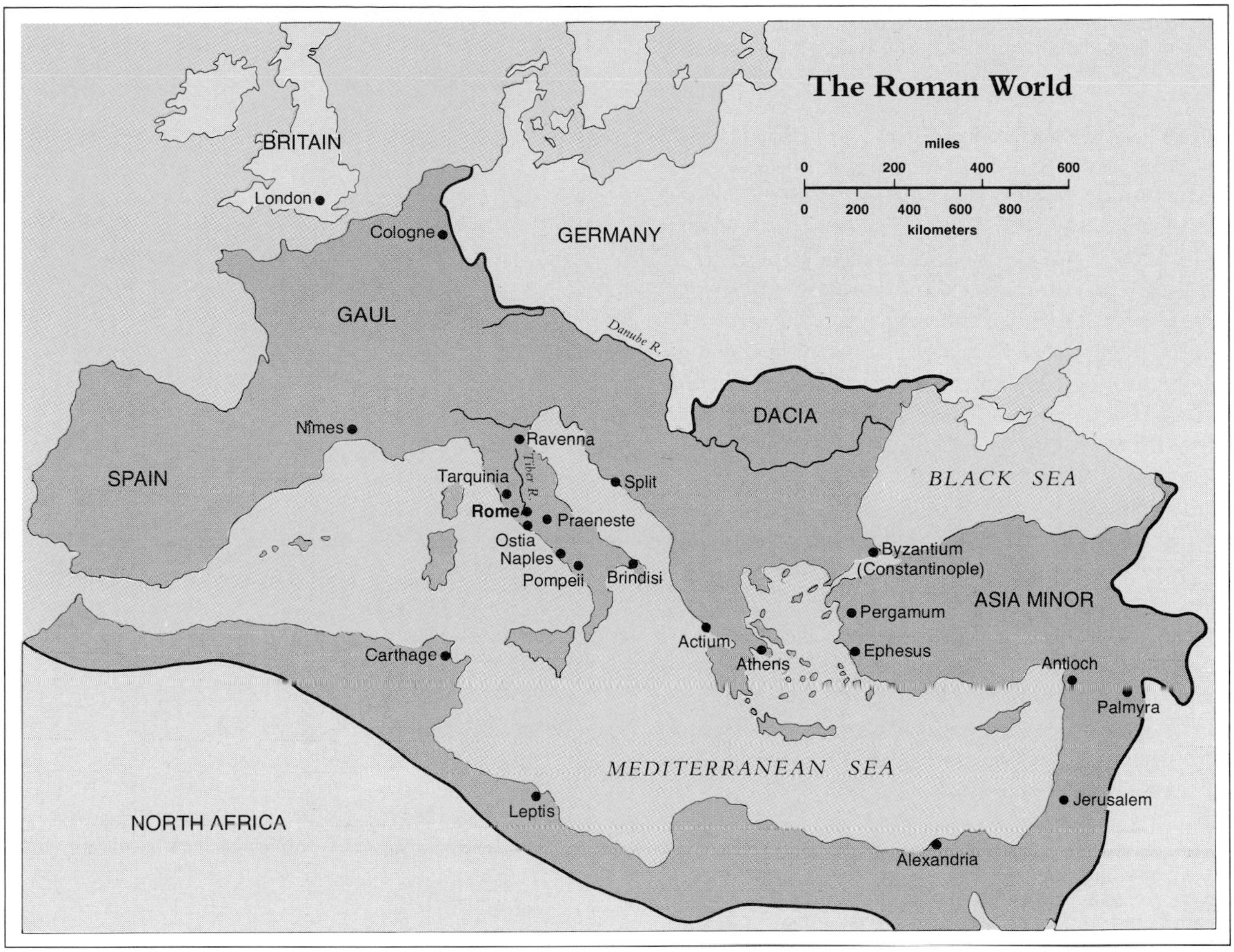

The Etruscans are among the most intriguing of ancient peoples, and ever since early Roman times scholars have argued about who they were, where they came from, and what language they spoke. Even today, in spite of the discoveries of modern archaeologists, we still know little about the origins of the Etruscans and their language has still not been deciphered. By 700 B.C. they had established themselves in the part of Italy named for them, Tuscany; but it is not clear whether they arrived from abroad or whether their culture was a more developed form of an earlier Italian one. The ancient Greeks and Romans believed that the Etruscans had come to Italy from the East, perhaps from Lydia, an ancient kingdom in Asia Minor. Indeed, many aspects of their life and much of their art have pronounced Eastern characteristics. In other ways, however, the Etruscans have much in common with their predecessors in central Italy. Even so, no other culture related to the Etruscans' has ever been found. Whatever their origins, they were to have a major effect upon Italian life, and on the growth of Rome and its culture [4.2].

4.2 *Capitoline She-Wolf.* Etruscan, late 6th or early 5th century B.C. Bronze, length 4'4" (1.32 m). Capitoline Museum, Rome. Although this statue or one very like it became the mascot of Rome, it was probably made by an Etruscan craftsman. The twins Romulus and Remus, legendary founders of the city, were added during the Renaissance.

4.3 *Apollo of Veii.* Etruscan, late 6th or early 5th century B.C. Terra cotta, height 5'10" (1.78 m). Museo Nazionale di Villa Giulia, Rome.

From the very beginning of their history the Etruscans showed an outstanding sophistication and technological ability. The sumptuous gold treasures buried in their tombs are evidence both of their material prosperity and of their superb craftsmanship. The commercial contacts of the Etruscans extended over most of the western Mediterranean, and in Italy itself Etruscan cities like Cerveteri and Tarquinia developed rich artistic traditions. Etruscan art has its own special character, a kind of elemental force almost primitive in spirit, although the craftsmanship and techniques are highly sophisticated. Unlike the Greeks, the Etruscans were less interested in intellectual problems of proportion or understanding how the human body works than in producing an immediate impact upon the viewer. The famous statue of Apollo found in 1916 at Veii [4.3] is unquestionably related to Greek models, but the tension of the god's pose and the sinister quality of his smile produce an effect of great power in a typically Etruscan way. Other Etruscan art is more relaxed, showing a love of na-

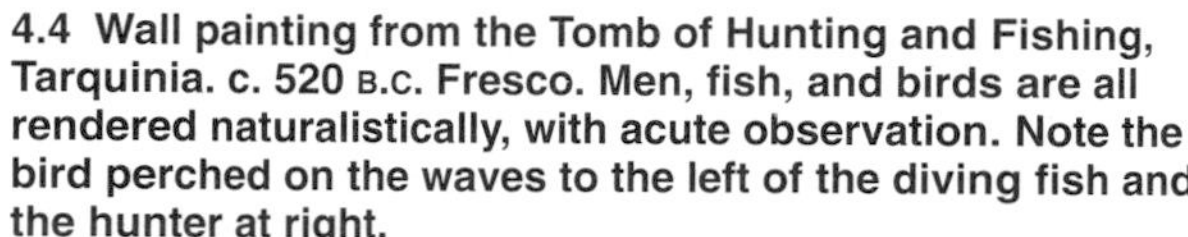

4.4 Wall painting from the Tomb of Hunting and Fishing, Tarquinia. c. 520 B.C. Fresco. Men, fish, and birds are all rendered naturalistically, with acute observation. Note the bird perched on the waves to the left of the diving fish and the hunter at right.

4.5 Lid of a funerary urn showing the dead couple whose ashes it contains. Etruscan, 1st century B.C. Terra cotta, length 18½" (47 cm). Museo Guarnacci, Volterra.

ture rarely found in Greek art. The paintings in the Tomb of Hunting and Fishing at Tarquinia [4.4] convey a marvelous sense of light and air, the hazy blue background evoking the sensations of sea and spray.

This gifted people was bound to exert a strong influence on the development of civilization in Italy; Etruscan occupation of Rome from 616 to 510 B.C. marks a turning point in Roman history. According to later tradition, the city of Rome had been founded in 753 B.C. and was ruled in its earliest days by kings (in actual fact Rome was probably not much more than a small country town for most of this period). The later Romans' own grandiose picture of the early days of their city was intended to glamorize its origins, but only with the arrival of the Etruscans did anything like an urban center begin to develop. Etruscan engineers drained a large marshy area, previously uninhabitable, which became the community's center, the future Roman Forum. They built temples and shrines and constructed roads. Among other innovations, the Etruscans introduced a number of things we are accustomed to think of as typically Roman, including public games like chariot racing and even the toga, the most characteristic form of Roman dress.

Most important, however, was the fact that under Etruscan domination the Romans found themselves for the first time in contact with the larger world. Instead of being simple villagers living in a small community governed by tribal chiefs, they became part of a large cultural unit with links throughout Italy and abroad. Within a hundred years Rome had learned the lessons of Etruscan technology and culture, driven the Etruscans back to their own territory, and begun her unrelenting climb to power.

The rise of Rome signaled the decline of the Etruscans throughout Italy. In the centuries following their expulsion from Rome in 510 B.C., their cities were conquered and their territory taken over by the Romans. In the 1st century B.C. they automatically received the right of Roman citizenship and became absorbed into the Roman Empire. The gradual collapse of their world is mirrored in later Etruscan art. The wall paintings in the tombs become increasingly gloomy, suggesting that for an Etruscan of the 3rd century B.C. the misfortunes of this life were followed by the tortures of the next. The old couple from Volterra whose anxious faces are so vividly depicted on the lid of their sarcophagus [4.5] give us some idea of the troubled spirit of the final days of Etruscan culture.

REPUBLICAN ROME (509–31 B.C.)

With the expulsion of the Etruscans in 510 B.C., the Romans began their climb to power, free now to rule themselves. Instead of choosing a new king, Rome constituted itself a republic, governed by the people somewhat along the lines of the Greek city-states, although less democratically. Two chief magistrates or consuls were elected for a one-year term by all the male citizens, but the principal assembly, the Senate, drew most of its members from Roman aristocratic families. From the very beginning, therefore, power was concentrated in the hands of the upper class, the patricians, although the lower class (the plebeians) was permitted to form its own assembly. The leaders elected by the plebeian assembly, the tribunes, represented the plebeians' interests and protected them against state officials who treated them unjustly. The meeting place for both the Senate and the assemblies of

4.6 The Roman forum—center of the political, economic, and religious life of the Roman world—as it appears today.

the people was the *forum,* the large open space at the foot of the Palatine and Capitoline hills that had been drained and made habitable by the Etruscans [4.6].

From the founding of the Roman Republic to its bloody end in the civil wars following the murder of Julius Caesar in 44 B.C., its history was dominated by agitation for political equality. Yet the first major confrontation, the conflict between patricians and plebeians, never seriously endangered political stability in Rome or military campaigns abroad. Both sides showed a flexibility and spirit of compromise that produced a gradual growth in plebeian power while avoiding any split disastrous enough to interrupt Rome's growing domination of the Italian peninsula. The final plebeian victory came in 287 B.C. with the passage of the Hortensian Law, which made the decisions of the plebeian assembly binding on the entire Senate and Roman people. By then most of Italy had already fallen under Roman control.

Increasing power brought new problems. In the 3rd and 2nd centuries B.C. Rome began to build its empire abroad. By the 1st century B.C. the whole Hellenistic world had been conquered. From Spain to the Middle East stretched a vast territory consisting of subject provinces, protectorates, and nominally free kingdoms, all of which depended on Roman good will and administrative efficiency.

Unfortunately, the Romans had been too busy in acquiring their empire to think very hard about how to rule it; the results were frequently chaotic. Provincial administration was incompetent and often corrupt. The long series of wars had hardened the Roman character, leading to insensitivity and, frequently, brutality in the treatment of conquered peoples. This situation was not helped by increasing political instability at home. The old balance of power struck between the patricians and plebeians was being increasingly disturbed by the rise of a middle class, many of whom were plebeians who had made their fortunes in the wars. Against this background were fought bitter struggles that eventually caused the collapse of the Republic.

By the 1st century B.C. it was apparent that the political system that had been devised for a thriving but small city five hundred years earlier was hopelessly inadequate for a vast empire. Discontent among Rome's Italian allies led to open revolt. Although the Romans were victorious in the Social War of 90–88 B.C., the cost in lives and economic stability was tremendous. The ineffectiveness of the Senate and the frustration of the Roman people led to a series of struggles among the leading statesmen for supreme power. The Roman general Sulla ruled as dictator for a brief and violent period beginning in 82 B.C., but suddenly resigned three years later, in 79 B.C. There followed a long-drawn-out series of political skirmishes between Pompey, the self-appointed defender of the Senate, and Julius Caesar, culminating in Caesar's withdrawal to Gaul and subsequent return to Rome in

49 B.C. After a short but bitter conflict Caesar defeated Pompey in 48 B.C. at the Battle of Pharsalus and returned to Rome as dictator, only to be assassinated himself in 44 B.C. The civil wars that followed brought the Republic to its unlamented end.

The years of almost uninterrupted violence had a profound effect upon the Roman character, and the relief felt when a new era dawned under the first emperor, Augustus, can only be fully appreciated in this light.

Literary Developments During the Republic

The Romans put most of their energy into political and military affairs, leaving little time for art or literature. By the 3rd century B.C., when most of the Mediterranean was under their control and they could afford to relax, they were overwhelmed intellectually and artistically by the Greeks. Conquest of the Hellenistic kingdoms of the East and of Greece itself brought the Romans into contact with Hellenistic Greek culture (see pages 82–86). Thus, from the 3rd century B.C. most Roman works of art followed Greek models in form and content. Roman plays were based on Greek originals, Roman temples imitated Greek buildings, and Roman sculpture and painting depicted episodes from Greek mythology.

Greek influence extends to the works of Ennius (239–169 B.C.), known to later Romans as the father of Roman poetry. Almost all of his works are lost, but from later accounts Ennius' tragedies appear to have been adapted from Greek models. His major work was the *Annals*, an epic chronicle of the history of Rome, in which for the first time a Greek metrical scheme was used to write Latin verse.

The two comic playwrights Plautus (c. 254–184 B.C.) and Terence (c. 195–159 B.C.) are the first Roman writers whose works have survived in quantity. Their plays are adaptations of Greek comedies; whereas the Greek originals are comic satires, the Roman versions turn human foibles into pure comedy. Plautus, the more boisterous of the two, is fond of comic songs and farcical intrigues. Terence's style is more refined and his characters show greater realism. It says something about the taste of the Roman public that Plautus was by far the more successful. In later times, however, Terence's sophisticated style was much admired. His plays were studied and imitated both during the Middle Ages and more recently. Both authors were fond of extremely elaborate plots involving mistaken identities, identical twins, and general confusion, with everything sorted out in the last scene.

In general, however, when educated Romans of the late Republic stopped to think about something other than politics it was likely to be love. Roman lyric poetry, often on a romantic theme, is one of the most rewarding genres of Latin literature. The first great Roman lyric poet, Catullus (c. 80–54 B.C.), is one of the best-loved of all Roman authors. Instead of philosophical or historical themes, he returned to a traditional subject from Sappho's time—personal experience—and charted the course of his own love affair with a woman whom he calls Lesbia. Among his works are twenty-five short poems describing the course of his relationship that range from the ecstasy of its early stages to the disillusionment and despair of the final breakup. The clarity of his style is the perfect counterpart to the direct expression of his emotions.

These poems, personal though they are, are not simply an outpouring of feelings. Catullus makes his own experiences universal. However trivial one man's unhappy love affair may seem in the context of the grim world of the late Republic, Lesbia's inconstancy has achieved a timelessness unequaled by many more serious events.

Two of the principal figures who dominated those events also made important contributions to Republican literature. Julius Caesar (100–44 B.C.) is perhaps the most famous Roman of them all. Brilliant politician, skilled general, expert administrator and organizer, he was also able to write the history of his own military campaigns in his *Commentaries*, in a simple but gripping style. In the four years during which he ruled Rome he did much to repair the damage of the previous decades. His assassination on March 15, 44 B.C., at the hands of a band of devoted republicans served only to prolong Rome's agony for another thirteen years—as well as provide Shakespeare with the plot for one of his best-known plays.

Perhaps the most endearing figure of the late Republic was Marcus Tullius Cicero (106–43 B.C.), who first made his reputation as a lawyer. He is certainly the figure of this period about whom we know the most, for he took part in a number of important legal cases and embarked on a political career. In 63 B.C. he served as consul. A few years later, the severity with which he had put down a plot against the government during his consulship earned him a short period in exile as the result of the scheming of a rival political faction. He returned in triumph, however, and in the struggle between Pompey and Caesar supported Pompey. Although Caesar seems to have forgiven him, Cicero never really trusted Caesar, in spite of his admiration for the dictator's abilities. His mixed feelings are well expressed in a letter to his friend Atticus after he had invited Caesar, by then the ruler of the Roman world, to dinner:

> Quite a guest, although I have no regrets and everything went very well indeed. . . . He was taking medicine for his digestion, so he ate and drank without worrying and seemed perfectly at ease. It was a lavish dinner, excellently served and in addition well prepared and seasoned with good conversation, very agreeable, you know. What can I say? We were human beings together. But he's not the kind of guest to whom you'd say "it's been fun, come again on the way back." Once is enough! We talked about nothing serious, a lot about literature: he seemed to enjoy it and have a good time. So now you know about how I entertained him—or rather had him billeted on me. It was a nuisance, as I said, but not unpleasant.

From letters like these we can derive an incomparably vivid picture of Cicero and his world. Almost nine hundred were published, most of them after his death. If they often reveal Cicero's weaknesses—his vanity, his inability to make a decision, his stubbornness—they confirm his humanity and sensitivity. For his contemporaries and for later ages his chief fame was nevertheless as an orator. Although the cases and causes that prompted his speeches have ceased to have any but historical interest, the power of a Ciceronian oration can still thrill the responsive reader, especially when it is read aloud.

Roman Philosophy and Law

The Romans produced little in the way of original philosophical writing. Their practical nature made them suspicious of professional philosophers and unable to appreciate the rather subtle delights involved in arguing both sides of a complex moral or ethical question. In consequence most of the great Roman philosophical writers devoted their energies to expounding Greek philosophy to a Roman audience. The two principal schools of philosophy to make an impact at Rome, *Epicureanism* and *Stoicism,* were both imported from Greece.

Epicureanism never really gained many followers, in spite of the efforts of the poet Lucretius (99–55 B.C.), who described its doctrines in his brilliant poem *On the Nature of Things (De Rerum natura).* A remarkable synthesis of poetry and philosophy, this work alone is probably responsible for whatever admiration the Romans could muster for a system of thought so different from their own traditional virtues of simplicity and seriousness. According to Epicurus (341–271 B.C.), the founder of the school, the correct goal and principle of human actions is pleasure. Although Epicureanism stresses moderation and prudence in the pursuit of pleasure, the Romans insisted on thinking of the philosophy as a typically Greek enthusiasm for self-indulgence and debauchery.

Lucretius tried to correct this impression by emphasizing the profoundly intellectual and rational aspects of Epicureanism. Its principal teaching was that the gods, if they exist, play no part in human affairs or in the phenomena of nature; as a result we can live our lives free from superstitious fear of the unknown and the threat of divine retribution. The Epicurean theory of matter explains the world in purely physical terms. It describes the universe as made up of two elements: small particles of matter, or atoms, and empty space. The atoms are completely solid, possessing the qualities of size, shape, and mass, and can be neither split nor destroyed. Their joining together to form complex structures is entirely caused by their random swerving in space, without interference from the gods. As a result, human life can be lived in complete freedom; we can face the challenges of existence and even natural disasters like earthquakes or plagues with complete serenity, since their occurrence is random and outside our control. According to Epicurus, at death the atoms that make up our body separate, and neither body, mind, nor soul survives. Since no part of us is in any way immortal, we should have no fear of death, which offers no threat of punishment in a future world but brings only the complete ending of any sensation.

Epicureanism's rejection of a divine force in the world and its campaign against superstition probably appealed to the Romans as little as its claim that the best life was one of pleasure and calm composure. The hardheaded practical moralizing of the Roman mentality found far more appeal in the other school of philosophy imported into Rome from Greece, Stoicism. The Stoics taught that the world was governed by Reason and that Divine Providence watched over the virtuous, never allowing them to suffer evil. The key to becoming virtuous lay in willing or desiring only that which was under one's own control. Thus riches, power, or even physical health—all subject to the whims of Fortune—were excluded as objects of desire. For the Stoic all that counted was that which was subject to the individual's will.

Although Stoicism had already won a following at Rome by the 1st century B.C. and was discussed

TABLE 4.1 Principal Roman Deities and Their Greek Equivalents

Roman	Greek	Roman	Greek
Jupiter	Zeus	Diana	Artemis
Juno	Hera	Ceres	Demeter
Neptune	Poseidon	Venus	Aphrodite
Vulcan	Hephaestus	Minerva	Athena
Mars	Ares	Mercury	Hermes
Apollo	Apollo	Bacchus	Dionysus

by Cicero in his philosophical writings, its chief literary exponents came slightly later. Seneca (8 B.C.–A.D. 65) wrote a number of essays on Stoic morality. He had an opportunity, and the necessity, to practice the moral fortitude about which he wrote when his former pupil, the emperor Nero, ordered him to commit suicide, since the taking of one's own life was fully sanctioned by Stoic philosophers. Perhaps the most impressive of all Stoic writers is Epictetus (c. A.D. 50–134), a former slave who established a school of philosophy in Rome and then in Greece. In his *Encheiridion (Handbook)* he recommends an absolute trust in Divine Providence to be maintained through every misfortune. For Epictetus the philosopher represented the spokesman of Providence itself "taking the human race for his children."

Epictetus' teachings exerted a profound influence on the last great Stoic, the emperor Marcus Aurelius A.D. 121–180), who was constantly plagued with the dilemma of being a Stoic and an emperor at the same time. Delicate in health, sentimental, inclined to be disillusioned by the weaknesses of others, Marcus Aurelius struggled hard to maintain the balance between his public duty and his personal convictions. While on military duty he composed his *Meditations,* which are less a philosophical treatise than an account of his own attempt to live the life of a Stoic. As many of his observations make clear, this was no easy task: "Tell yourself every morning 'Today I shall meet the officious, the ungrateful, the bullying, the treacherous, the envious, the selfish. All of them behave like this because they do not know the difference between good and bad.' "

Yet, even though Stoicism continued to attract a number of Roman intellectuals, the great majority of Romans remained immune to the appeal of the philosophical life. Both in the 1st century B.C. and later, the very superstition both Stoicism and Epicureanism sought to combat remained deeply ingrained in the Roman character. Festivals in honor of traditional deities were celebrated until long after the advent of Christianity (Table 4.1). Rituals that tried to read the future by the traditional examination of animals' entrails and other time-honored methods continued to be popular. If the Romans had paused more often to meditate on the nature of existence, they would probably have had less time to civilize the world.

Among the most lasting achievements of Julius Caesar's dictatorship and of Roman culture in general was the creation of a single unified code of civil law, the *Ius Civile.* The science of law is one of the few original creations of Roman literature. The earliest legal code of the Republic was the so-called Law of the Twelve Tables of 451–450 B.C. By the time of Caesar, however, most of this law had become either irrelevant or out of date and had been replaced by a mass of later legislation, much of it contradictory and confusing.

Caesar's *Ius Civile,* produced with the help of eminent legal experts of the day, served as the model for later times, receiving its final form in 533 A.D., when it was collected, edited, and published by the Byzantine emperor Justinian (527–565 A.D.). Justinian's *Corpus Iuris Civilis* remained in use in many parts of Europe for centuries, and profoundly influenced the development of modern legal systems. Even at the end of the 20th century, millions of people live in countries whose legal systems derive from that of ancient Rome; one eminent British judge has observed of Roman law that "there is not a problem of jurisprudence which it does not touch: there is scarcely a corner of political science on which its light has not fallen."

According to the great Roman lawyer Ulpian (died 228 A.D.), "Law is the art of the good and the fair." The Romans developed this art over the centuries during which they built up their empire of widely differing peoples. Roman law was international, adapting Roman notions of law and order to local conditions, and changing and developing in the process. Many of the jurists responsible for establishing legal principles had practical administrative experience from serving in the provinces. Legal experts were in great demand at Rome; the state encouraged public service, and problems of home and provincial government frequently occupied the best minds of the day.

Many of these jurists acquired widespread reputations for wisdom and integrity. The emperor Augustus gave to some of them the right to issue "authoritative opinions," while a century or so later the emperor Hadrian formed a judicial council to guide him in matters of law. Their general aim was to equate human law with that of Nature by developing an objective system of natural justice. By using this, the emperor could fulfill his duty to serve his subjects as Benefactor, and bring all peoples together under a single government.

Thus over the centuries the Romans built up a body of legal opinion that was comprehensive, concerned with absolute and eternal values, and valid for all times and places; at its heart lay the principle of "equity"—equality for all. By the time Justinian produced his codification, he was able to draw on a thousand years of practical wisdom.

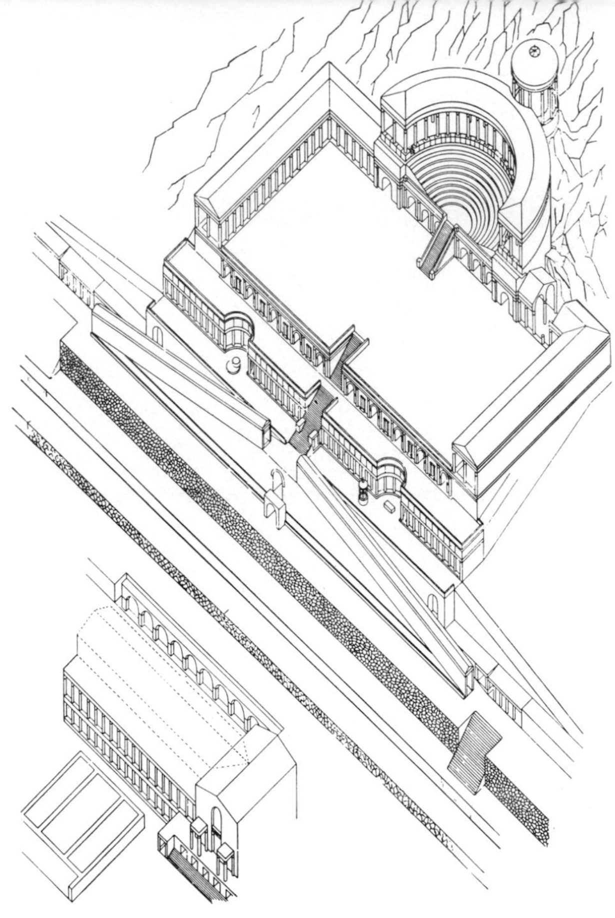

4.8 Plan of the Sanctuary of Fortuna Primigenia, Praeneste (Palestrina). This vast complex, constructed by Sulla after his destruction of the city in 82 B.C., is a series of six immense terraces crowned by a semicircular structure in front of which stood an altar.

Republican Art and Architecture

In the visual arts as in literature, the late Republic shows the translation of Greek styles into new Roman forms. The political scene was dominated by individuals like Cicero and Caesar; their individualism was captured in portrait busts that were both realistic and psychologically revealing. To some extent these realistic sculptures are based on such Etruscan models as the heads of the old couple on the Volterra sarcophagus [see 4.5] rather than on Hellenistic portraits, which idealized their subjects. However, the subtlety and understanding shown in portraits like those of Cicero and Caesar represent a typically Roman combination and amplification of others' styles. In many respects, indeed, Roman portraiture represents Roman art at its most creative and sensitive. It certainly opened up new expressive possibilities, as artists discovered how to use physical appearance to convey something about character. Many of the best Roman portraits serve as revealing psychological documents, expressing, for example, Cicero's self-satisfaction as well as his humanity [4.7]. Realistic details like the lines at the corners of the eyes and mouth, the hollows in the cheeks, or the set of the lips are used to express both outer appearance and inner character. The new skill, as it developed, could of course be put to propaganda use, and statesmen and politicians soon learned that they could project their chosen self-image through their portraits.

4.7 *Bust of Cicero.* Roman, 1st century B.C. Uffizi, Forence. This portrait of one of the leading figures of the late Republic suggests the ability of Roman sculptors of the period to capture both likeness and character. Cicero is portrayed as thoughtful and preoccupied.

The powerful political figures of the period also used the medium of architecture to express their authority. The huge sanctuary constructed by Sulla at Praeneste (modern Palestrina) around 82 B.C. [4.8] has all the qualities of symmetry and grandeur we associate with later Roman imperial architecture, although it took its inspiration from massive Hellenistic building programs such as that at Pergamum. Caesar himself had a large area in the center of Rome cleared for the construction of a forum, or public meeting place, to be named after him. In time it was dwarfed by later monumental fora, but it had initiated the construction of public buildings for personal display and glory.

IMPERIAL ROME (31 B.C.–A.D. 476)

With the assassination of Julius Caesar a brief respite from civil war was followed by further turmoil. Caesar's lieutenant, Mark Antony, led the campaign to avenge his death and punish the conspirators. He was joined in this by Caesar's young great-nephew, Octavius, who had been named by Caesar as his heir and had recently arrived in Rome from the provinces. It soon became apparent that Antony and Octavius (or Octavian, to use the name he now took) were unlikely to coexist very happily. After the final defeat of the conspirators in 42 B.C. a temporary peace was obtained by putting Octavian in charge of the western provinces and sending Antony to the East. A final confrontation could not be long delayed, and Antony's fatal involvement with Cleopatra alienated much of his support at Rome. The end came in 31 B.C. at the Battle of Actium. The forces of Antony, reinforced by those of Cleopatra, were routed, and the couple committed suicide. Octavian was left as sole ruler of the Roman world, a world that was now in ruins. His victory marked the end of the Roman Republic.

When Octavian took supreme control after the Battle of Actium, Rome had been continuously involved both in civil and external wars for much of a century. The political and cultural institutions of Roman life were beyond repair, the economy was wrecked, and large areas of Italy were in complete turmoil. By the time of Octavian's death in A.D. 14, Rome had achieved a peace and prosperity unequaled in its history before or after. The art and literature created during his rule represents the peak of the Roman cultural achievement. To the Romans of his own time it seemed that a new Golden Age had dawned, and for centuries afterward his memory was revered. As the first Roman emperor, Octavian inaugurated the second great period in Roman history—the Empire, which lasted technically from 27 B.C., when he assumed the title Augustus, until A.D. 476, when the last Roman emperor was overthrown. In many ways, however, the period began with the Battle of Actium and continued in the subsequent western and Byzantine empires (Table 4.2).

TABLE 4.2 The Principal Roman Emperors

Emperor	Reign	Dynasty
Augustus	27 B.C.–A.D. 14	Julio-Claudians
Tiberius	14–37	
Gaius (Caligula)	37–41	
Claudius	41–54	
Nero	54–68	
Year of the Four Emperors	69	
Vespasian	69–79	Flavians
Titus	79–81	
Domitian	81–96	
Nerva	96–98	Adoptive Emperors
Trajan	98–117	
Hadrian	117–138	
Antoninus Pius	138–161	Antonines
Marcus Aurelius	161–180	
Commodus	180–193	
Septimius Severus	193–211	
Alexander Severus	222–235	
Decius	249–251	
Diocletian	284–305	
Constantine	306–337	

Augustus' cultural achievement was stupendous, but it could only have been accomplished in a world at peace. In order to achieve this, it was necessary to build a new political order. A republican system of government suitable for a small state had long since proved woefully inadequate for a vast and multi-ethnic empire. Augustus tactfully, if misleadingly, claimed that he "replaced the State in the hands of the Senate and Roman people." In fact, he did the reverse: While maintaining the appearance of a reborn republic, he took all effective power into the hands of himself and his imperial staff.

From the time of Augustus, the emperor and his bureaucracy controlled virtually all decisions. A huge civil service developed, with various career paths. A typical middle-class Roman might begin with a period of military service, move on to a post as fiscal agent in one of the provinces, then serve in a government department back in Rome, and end up as a senior official in the imperial postal service or the police.

Augustus also began the reform of the army, which the central government had been unable to control during the last chaotic decades of the Republic. Its principal function now became to guard the frontiers. It was made up of some 250,000 Roman citizens, and about the same number of local recruits. The commanders of these half a million soldiers looked directly to the emperor as their general-in-chief. The troops did far more than fight. They served as engineers, building roads and bridges. They sowed crops and harvested them. They surveyed the countryside and helped to police it. In the process, they won widespread respect and gratitude from Rome's provincial subjects.

Protected by the army, and administered by the civil service, the empire expanded economically. With freedom of travel and trade, goods circulated with no tariffs or customs duties; traders only had to pay harbor dues. From the time of Augustus, the Roman road system carried increasing numbers of travelers—traders, officials, students, wandering philosophers, the couriers of banks and shipping agencies—between the great urban centers. Cities like Alexandria or Antioch were self-governing to some degree, with municipal charters giving them constitutions based on the Roman model.

4.9 View of a garden, from the villa of Livia and Augustus at Prima Porta. c. 20 B.C. Fresco, detail, Museo delle Terme, Rome. The peaceful scene, with its abundance of fruit and flowers, reflects the interest in country life expressed in Vergil's *Eclogues* and *Georgics*.

Not all later emperors were as diligent or successful as Augustus. Caligula, Nero, and some others have become notorious as monsters of depravity. Yet the imperial system which Augustus founded was to last for almost five hundred years.

Augustan Literature: Vergil

Augustus himself played an active part in supporting and encouraging the writers and artists of his day; many of their works echo the chief themes of Augustan politics—the return of peace, the importance of the land and agriculture, the putting aside of ostentation and luxury in favor of a simple life, and above all the belief in Rome's destiny as world ruler. Some of the greatest works of Roman sculpture commemorate Augustus and his deeds; Horace and Vergil sing his praises in their poems. It is sometimes said that much of this art was propaganda, organized by the emperor to present the most favorable picture possible of his reign. Even the greatest works of the time do relate in some way or other to the Augustan worldview, and it is difficult to imagine a poet whose philosophy differed radically from that of the emperor being able to give voice to it. But we have no reason to doubt the sincerity of the gratitude felt toward Augustus or the strength of what seems to have been an almost universal feeling that at last a new era had dawned. In any case, from the time of Augustus art at Rome became in large measure official. Most of Roman architecture and sculpture of the period was public, commissioned by the state, and served state purposes.

The greater the artist, the more subtle the response to the Augustan vision. The greatest of all Roman poets, Publius Vergilius Maro (70–19 B.C.), devoted the last ten years of his life to the composition of an epic poem intended to honor Rome, and, by implication, Augustus. The result was the *Aeneid*, one of the great poems of the world, not completely finished at the poet's death. For much of the Middle Ages, Vergil himself was held in the highest reverence. A succession of great poets has regarded him as their master—Dante, Tasso, and Milton, among others. Probably no work of literature in the entire tradition of Western culture has been more loved and revered than the *Aeneid*—described by T. S. Eliot as *the classic* of Western society—yet its significance is complex and by no means universally agreed upon.

The *Aeneid* was not Vergil's first poem. The earliest authentic works that have survived are ten short pastoral poems known as the *Eclogues* (or sometimes the *Bucolics*) which deal with the joys and sorrows of the country and the shepherds and herdsmen who live there. Vergil himself was the son of a farmer; his deep love of the land emerges also in his next work, the four books of the *Georgics* (29 B.C.). Their most obvious purpose is to serve as a practical guide to farming, and they offer helpful advice on such subjects as cattle breeding and beekeeping as well as a deep conviction that the strength of Italy lies in its agricultural richness. In a great passage in the second book of the *Georgics* Vergil hails the "ancient earth, great mother of crops and men." He does not disguise the hardships of the farmer's life, the poverty, hard work, and frequent disappointments, but still feels that only life in the country brings true peace and contentment [4.9].

The spirit of the *Georgics* clearly matched Augustus' plans for an agricultural revival. Indeed, it was probably the emperor himself who commissioned Vergil to write an epic poem that would be to Roman literature what the *Iliad* and *Odyssey* were for Greek: a national epic. The task was immense. Vergil had to find a subject that would do appropriate honor to Rome and its past as well as commemorate the achievements of Augustus. The *Aeneid* is not a perfect poem (on his deathbed Vergil ordered his friends to destroy it), but in some ways it surpasses even the high expectations Augustus must have had for it. Vergil succeeded in providing Rome with its national epic and stands as a worthy successor to Homer. At the same time, he created a profoundly moving study of the nature of human destiny and personal responsibility.

The *Aeneid* is divided into twelve books. Its hero is a Trojan prince, Aeneas, who flees from the ruins of burning Troy and sails west to Italy to found a new city, the predecessor of Rome. Vergil's choice was significant: Aeneas' Trojan birth establishes connections with the world of Homer; his arrival in Italy involves the origins of Rome; and the theme of a fresh beginning born, as it were, out of the ashes of the past corresponds perfectly to the Augustan mood of revival. We first meet Aeneas and his followers in the middle of his journey from Troy to Italy, caught in a storm that casts them up on the coast of North Africa. They make their way to the city of Carthage, where they are given shelter by the Carthaginian ruler, Queen Dido. At a dinner in his honor Aeneas describes the fall of Troy (Book II) and his wanderings from Troy to Carthage (Book III), in the course of which his father Anchises had died.

In Book IV, perhaps the best known, the action resumes where it had broken off at the end of Book

I. The tragic love that develops between Dido and Aeneas tempts Aeneas to stay in Carthage and thereby abandon his mission to found a new home in Italy. A divine messenger is sent to remind Aeneas of his responsibilities. He leaves after an agonizing encounter with Dido, and the distraught queen kills herself.

Book V brings the Trojans to Italy. In Book VI, Aeneas journeys to the underworld to hear from the spirit of his father the destiny of Rome. This tremendous episode provides the turning point of the poem. Before it we see Aeneas, and he sees himself, as a man prone to human weaknesses and subject to personal feelings. After Anchises' revelations, Aeneas' humanity is replaced by a sense of mission and the weary, suffering Trojan exile becomes transformed into a "man of destiny."

In Books VII and VIII, the Trojans arrive at the river Tiber and Aeneas visits the future site of Rome while the Italian peoples prepare to resist the Trojan invaders. The last four books describe in detail the war between the Trojans and the Latins, in the course of which there are losses on both sides. The *Aeneid* ends with the death of the great Italian warrior Turnus and the final victory of Aeneas.

It is tempting to see Aeneas as the archetype of Augustus; certainly Vergil must have intended for us to draw some parallels. Other historical analogies can also be found: Dido and Cleopatra, for example, have much in common. The *Aeneid* is, however, far more than an allegorical retelling of the events leading up to the foundation of the empire. Put briefly, Aeneas undertakes a responsibility for which initially he has no real enthusiasm and which costs him and others considerable suffering. It would have been much easier for him to have stayed in Carthage, or settled somewhere else along his way, rather than push forward under difficult circumstances into a foreign land where he and his followers were not welcome.

Once he has accepted his mission, however, he fulfills it conscientiously and in the process learns to sublimate his own personal desires to a common good. If this is indeed a portrait of Augustus, it represents a much more complex view of his character than we might expect. And Vergil goes further. If greatness can only be acquired by sacrificing human individuals, is it worth the price? Is the future glory of Rome a sufficient excuse for the cruel and unmanly treatment of Dido? Readers will provide their own answers. Vergil's might have been that the sacrifices were probably worth it, but barely. Much, of course, depends on individual views on the nature and purpose of existence, and for Vergil there is no doubt that life is essentially tragic. The prevailing mood of the poem is one of melancholy regret for the sadness of human lives and the inevitability of human suffering.

Augustan Sculpture

Many of the characteristics of Vergil's poetry can also be found in contemporary sculpture. In a relief from one of the most important works of the period, the *Ara Pacis* (Altar of Peace), Aeneas himself

4.10 Aeneas sacrificing, from the *Ara Pacis*, Rome. 13–9 B.C. Marble. Aeneas is depicted in the manner of a Classical Greek god; the landscape and elaborate relief detail are typical of late Hellenistic art.

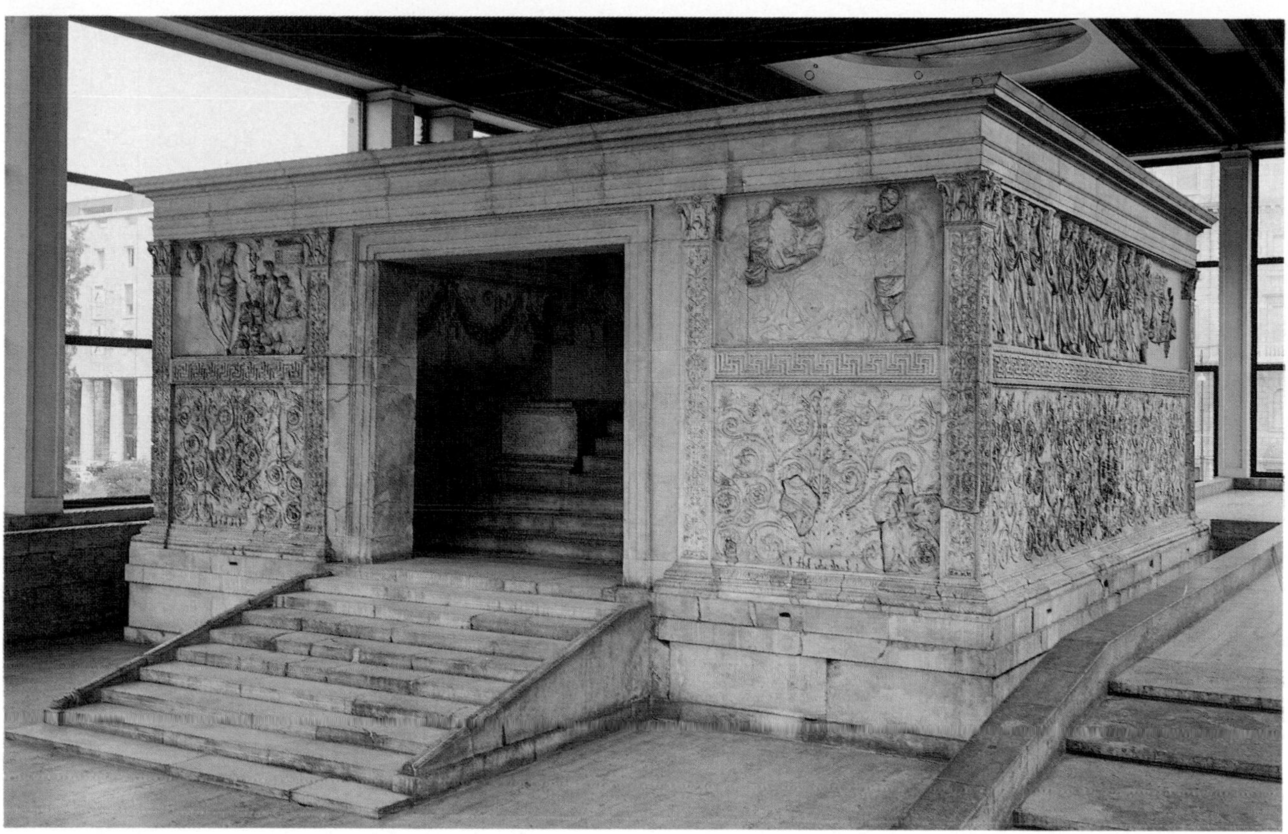

4.11 ***Ara Pacis*** **of Augustus, Rome. 13–9 B.C. Marble, 36 × 33' (11 × 10 m). The central doorway, through which the altar itself is just visible, is flanked by reliefs showing Romulus and Remus and Aeneas. On the right-hand side is the procession led by Augustus. The altar originally stood on the ancient Via Flaminia. Fragments were discovered in the 16th century; the remaining pieces were located in 1937 and 1938 and the structure was reconstructed near the mausoleum of Augustus.**

performs a sacrifice on his arrival in Italy before a small shrine that contains two sacred images brought from Troy [4.10]. More significantly, the *Ara Pacis* depicts the abundance of nature that could flourish again in the peace of the Augustan age. The altar, begun on Augustus' return to Rome in 13 B.C. after a visit to the provinces, was dedicated on January 30, 9 B.C., at a ceremony that is shown in the surrounding reliefs [4.11]. The procession making its way to the sacrifice is divided into two parts. On the south side Augustus leads the way, accompanied by priests and followed by the members of his family; the north side shows senators and other dignitaries. The lower part of the walls is decorated with a rich band of fruit and floral motifs, luxuriantly intertwined, amid which swans are placed. The actual entrance to the altar is flanked by two reliefs—on the right, the one showing Aeneas, and on the left, Romulus and Remus.

The *Ara Pacis* is perhaps the single most comprehensive statement of how Augustus wanted his contemporaries—and future generations—to see his reign. The altar is dedicated neither to Jupiter or Mars nor to Augustus himself but to the spirit of Peace. Augustus is shown as the first among equals rather than supreme ruler; although he leads the procession, he is marked by no special richness of dress. The presence of Augustus' family indicates that he intends his successor to be drawn from among them, and that they have a special role to play in public affairs. The reliefs of Aeneas and of Romulus and Remus relate the entire ceremony to Rome's glorious past. Further scenes at the back showing the Earth Mother and the goddess of war emphasize the abundance of the land and the need for vigilance. The rich vegetation of the lower band is a constant reminder of the rewards of agriculture that can be enjoyed once more in the peace to which the whole altar is dedicated.

Amazingly enough, this detailed political and social message is expressed without pretentiousness and with superb workmanship. The style is deliberately and self-consciously "classical," based on works like the Parthenon frieze. To depict the New Golden Age of Augustus, his artists have chosen the artistic language of the Golden Age of Athens, although with a Roman accent. The figures in the procession, for instance, are portrayed far more realistically than those in the sculpture of 5th-century-B.C. Athens.

The elaborate message illustrated by the *Ara Pacis* can also be seen in the best-preserved statue of the emperor himself, the *Augustus of Prima Porta,* so called after the spot where an imperial villa containing the sculpture was excavated [4.12]. The statue probably dates from about the time of the emperor's death; the face is in the full vigor of life, calm and determined. The stance is one of quiet authority. The ornately carved breastplate recalls one of the chief events of Augustus' reign. In 20 B.C. he defeated the Parthians, an eastern tribe, and recaptured from them the Roman standards that had been lost in battle in 53 B.C. On that former occasion Rome had suffered one of the greatest military defeats in its history, and Augustus' victory played an important part in restoring national pride. The breastplate shows a bearded Parthian handing back the eagle-crowned standard to a Roman soldier. The cupid on a dolphin at Augustus' feet serves two purposes. The symbol of the goddess Venus, it connects Augustus and his family with Aeneas (whose mother was Venus) and thereby with the origins of Rome. At the same time it looks to the future by representing Augustus' grandson Gaius, who was born the year of the victory over

4.12 *Augustus of Prima Porta.* c. A.D. 14. Marble, height 6'8" (2.03 m). Vatican Museums, Rome.

EAST MEETS WEST

Roman Traders in the Far East

Wealthy upper-class Romans provided a constant market for luxury goods imported from outside Italy. Some items could be found within the Empire: Spain supplied rare fruits such as dates or figs, and silk was imported from the Greek island of Cos. Yet the exotic always has a special appeal, and during the Augustan Age Roman merchants traveled as far as China to supply the demand for luxuries.

In the 1st century B.C. Roman navigators discovered for the first time that if they traveled during the monsoon season, when the winds blew favorably, they could sail from Egypt to India in about forty days. Commercial trading posts were set up on the Indian coast, where goods such as spices, ivory, incense, and pearls were paid for with Roman goods and money (hoards of Augustan coins have been found at Indian sites), and transported back to Rome. One of the hottest-selling items was pepper, for which the Romans developed an inordinate taste; great warehouses for its storage were built along the river Tiber.

The Indian connection provided access overland to an even more exotic and desirable market: that of China. The high quality of Chinese silk was already familiar to fashion-conscious Romans, but the overland Central Asian trade route passed through the hostile territory of the Parthians, whom Augustus had conquered but by no means subdued. Now it became possible to transport Chinese silks through Afghanistan and down the river Indus to the Indian Ocean; from there they and other luxury items were shipped back to Rome. On the outward voyage the Roman ships carried copper, lead, and Italian wine to trade with their new Chinese contacts. On the trip back to Rome many ships stopped off at the Horn of Africa (modern Ethiopia and Somalia) to pick up tortoise shell and ivory.

The trade route to China remained in use until the collapse of the Roman Empire. Even in the most troubled times Roman high society demanded a constant supply of the latest in luxury Chinese silks.

the Parthians and was at one time considered a possible successor to his grandfather.

The choice of his successor was the one problem that Augustus never managed to solve to his own satisfaction. The death of other candidates forced him to fall back reluctantly on his unpopular stepson Tiberius—the succession was a problem that was to recur throughout the long history of the empire, since no really effective mechanism was ever devised for guaranteeing a peaceful transfer of power. (As early as the reign of Claudius [A.D. 41–54], the right to choose a new emperor was seized by the army.) In every other respect the Augustan age was one of high attainment. In the visual arts, Augustan artists set the styles that dominated succeeding generations, while writers like the poets Vergil, Horace, Ovid, and Propertius, and the historian Livy established a Golden Age of Latin literature.

Curiously enough, perhaps the only person to have any real doubts about the Augustan achievement may have been Augustus himself. The Roman writer and gossip Suetonius (A.D. c. 69–c. 140) tells us that as the emperor lay dying he ordered a slave to bring a mirror so that he could comb his hair. He looked at himself, then turned to some friends standing by and asked, "Tell me, have I played my part in the comedy of life well enough?"

The Evidence of Pompeii

The 1st and 2nd centuries A.D. are probably the best-documented times in the whole of classical antiquity. From the many literary sources and the wealth of art and architecture that has survived, it is possible to reconstruct a detailed picture of life in imperial Rome. Even more complete is our knowledge of a prosperous but unimportant little town some 150 miles (240 kilometers) south of Rome that owes its worldwide fame to the circumstances of its destruction [4.13]. On August 24 in the year A.D. 79, the volcano Vesuvius above the Gulf of Naples erupted and a number of small towns were buried, the nearer ones under flowing lava and those some distance away under pumice and ash. By far the most famous is Pompeii, situated some 10 miles (16 kilometers) southeast of the erupting peak. Excavation first began there more than two hundred years ago. The finds preserved by the volcanic debris give us a rich and vivid impression of the way of life in a provincial town of the early empire—from the temples in which the Pompeians

4.13 Aerial view of the excavated portion of Pompeii as it appears today. The long, open rectangular space in the lower center is the forum. The total area is 166 acres (67.23 hectares). Although excavations at Pompeii have been in progress for more than two hundred years, some two-fifths of the city is still buried.

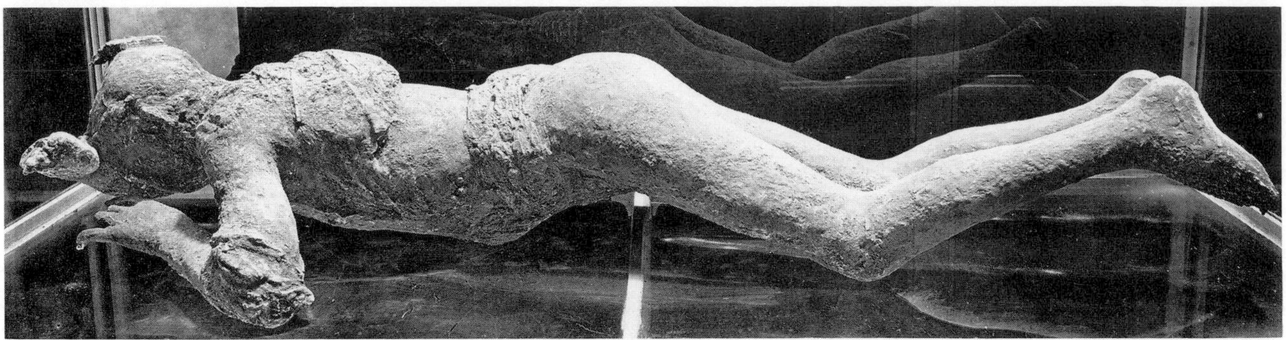

4.14 Cast of a woman trapped in volcanic pumice during the eruption of Mount Vesuvius at Pompeii, A.D. 79. Museo Nazionale, Naples.

4.15 Carbonized dates, walnuts, sunflower seeds, and bread from Pompeii, August 24, A.D. 79. Museo Nazionale, Naples.

worshiped and the baths in which they cleaned themselves to their food on the fatal day [4.14, 4.15].

An eyewitness report about the eruption comes from two letters written by the Roman politician and literary figure Pliny the Younger (A.D. 62–before 114)—so called to distinguish him from his uncle, Pliny the Elder (A.D. 23–79). The two were in fact together at Misenum on the Bay of Naples on the day of the eruption. Pliny's uncle was much interested in natural phenomena (his chief work was a *Natural History* in 37 volumes); to investigate for himself the nature of the explosion he made his way toward Vesuvius, where he was suffocated to death by the fumes. The younger Pliny stayed behind with his mother and in a letter to the historian Tacitus a little while later described the events of the next few hours:

PLINY THE YOUNGER
Letter to Tacitus on the Eruption of Vesuvius

You say that the letter I wrote at your request about the death of my uncle makes you want to hear about the terrors, and dangers as well, which I endured, having been left behind at Misenum—I had started on that topic but broken off. "Though my mind shudders to remember, I shall begin." After my uncle departed I spent the rest of the day on my studies; it was for that purpose I had stayed. Then I took a bath, ate dinner, and went to bed; but my sleep was restless and brief. For a number of days before this there had been a quivering of the ground, not so fearful because it was common in Campania. On that night, however, it became so violent that everything seemed not so much to move as to be overturned. My mother came rushing into my bedroom; I was just getting up, intending in my turn to arouse her if she were asleep. We sat down in the rather narrow courtyard of the house lying between the sea and the buildings. I don't know whether I should call it iron nerves or folly—I was only seventeen: I called for a book of Titus Livy and as if at ease I read it and even copied some passages, as I had been doing. Then one of my uncle's friends, who had recently come from Spain to visit him, when he saw my mother and me sitting there, and me actually reading a book, rebuked her apathy and my unconcern. But I was as intent on my book as ever.

It was now the first hour of day, but the light was still faint and doubtful. The adjacent buildings now began to collapse, and there was great, indeed inevitable, danger of being involved in the ruins; for though the place was open, it was narrow. Then at last we decided to leave the town. The dismayed crowd came after us; it preferred following someone else's decision rather than its own; in panic that is practically the same as wisdom. So as we went off we were crowded and shoved along by a huge mob of followers. When we got out beyond the buildings we halted. We saw many strange and fearful sights there. For the carriages we had ordered brought for us, though on perfectly level ground, kept rolling back and forth; even when the wheels were checked with stones they would not stand still. Moreover the sea appeared to be sucked back and to be repelled by the vibration of the earth; the shoreline was much farther out than usual, and many specimens of marine life were caught on the dry sands. On the other side a black and frightful cloud, rent by twisting and quivering paths of fire, gaped open in huge patterns of flames; it was like sheet lightning, but far worse. Then indeed that friend from Spain whom I have mentioned spoke to us more sharply and insistently: "If your brother and uncle still lives, he wants you to be saved; if he has died, his wish was that you should survive him; so why do you delay to make your escape?" We replied that we would not allow ourselves to think of our own safety while still uncertain of his. Without waiting any longer he rushed off and left the danger behind at top speed.

Soon thereafter the cloud I have described began to descend to the earth and to cover the sea; it had encircled Capri and hidden it from view, and had blotted out the promontory of Misenum. Then my mother began to plead, urge, and order me to make my escape as best I could, for I could, being young; she, weighed down with years and weakness, would die happy if she had not been the cause of death to me. I replied that I would not find safety except in her company; then I took her hand and made her walk faster. She obeyed with difficulty and scolded herself for slowing me. Now ashes, though thin as yet, began to fall. I looked back; a dense fog was looming up behind us; it poured over the ground like a river as it followed. "Let us turn aside," said I, "lest, if we should fall on the road, we should be trampled in the darkness by the throng of those going our way." We barely had time to consider the thought, when night was upon us, not such a night as when there is no moon or there are clouds, but such as in a closed place with the lights put out. One could hear the wailing of women, the crying of children, the shouting of men; they called each other, some their parents, others their children, still others their mates, and sought to recognize each other by their voices. Some lamented their own fate, others the fate of their loved ones. There were even those who in fear of death prayed for death. Many raised their hands to the gods; more held that there were nowhere gods any more and that this was that eternal and final night of the universe. Nor were those lacking who exaggerated real dangers with feigned and lying terrors. Men appeared who reported that part of Misenum was buried in ruins, and part of it in flames; it was false, but found credulous listeners.

It lightened a little; this seemed to us not daylight but a sign of approaching fire. But the fire stopped some distance away; darkness came on again, again ashes, thick and heavy. We got up repeatedly to shake these off; otherwise we would have been buried and crushed by the weight. I might boast that not a groan, not a cowardly word, escaped from my lips in the midst of such dangers, were it not that I believed I was perishing along with everything else, and everything else along with me; a wretched and yet a real consolation for having to die. At last the fog dissipated into smoke or mist, and then vanished; soon there was real daylight; the sun even shone, though wanly, as when there is an eclipse. Our still trembling eyes found everything changed, buried in deep ashes as if in snow. We returned to Misenum and attended to our physical needs as best we could; then we spent a night in suspense between hope and fear. Fear was the stronger, for the trembling of the earth continued, and many, crazed by their sufferings, were mocking their own woes and others' by awful predictions. But as for us, though we had suffered dangers and anticipated others, we had not even then any thought of going away until we should have word of my uncle.

You will read this account, far from worthy of history, without any intention of incorporating it; and you must blame yourself, since you insisted on having it, if it shall seem not even worthy of a letter.

With a few exceptions, like the frescoes in the Villa of the Mysteries [4.16], the works of art unearthed at Pompeii are not masterpieces. Their importance lies precisely in the fact that they show us how the ordinary Pompeian lived, worked, and played [4.17]. The general picture is very impressive. Cool, comfortable houses were decorated with charming frescoes and mosaics and included quiet gardens, remote from the noise of busy streets and watered by fountains. The household silver and other domestic ornaments found in the ruins of houses were often of very high quality. Although the population of Pompeii was only twenty thousand, there were no fewer than three sets of public baths, a theater, a concert hall, an amphitheater large enough to seat the entire population, and a more-than-adequate number of brothels. The forum was closed to traffic, and the major public buildings ranged around it include a splendid

4.16 Wall paintings from the Villa of the Mysteries, Pompeii. c. 60 B.C. Frescoes. Probably no ancient work of art has been more argued about than these paintings. They seem to relate to the cult of the Greek god Dionysus and the importance of the cult for girls approaching marriage, but many of the details are difficult to interpret. There is no argument, however, about the high quality of the paintings.

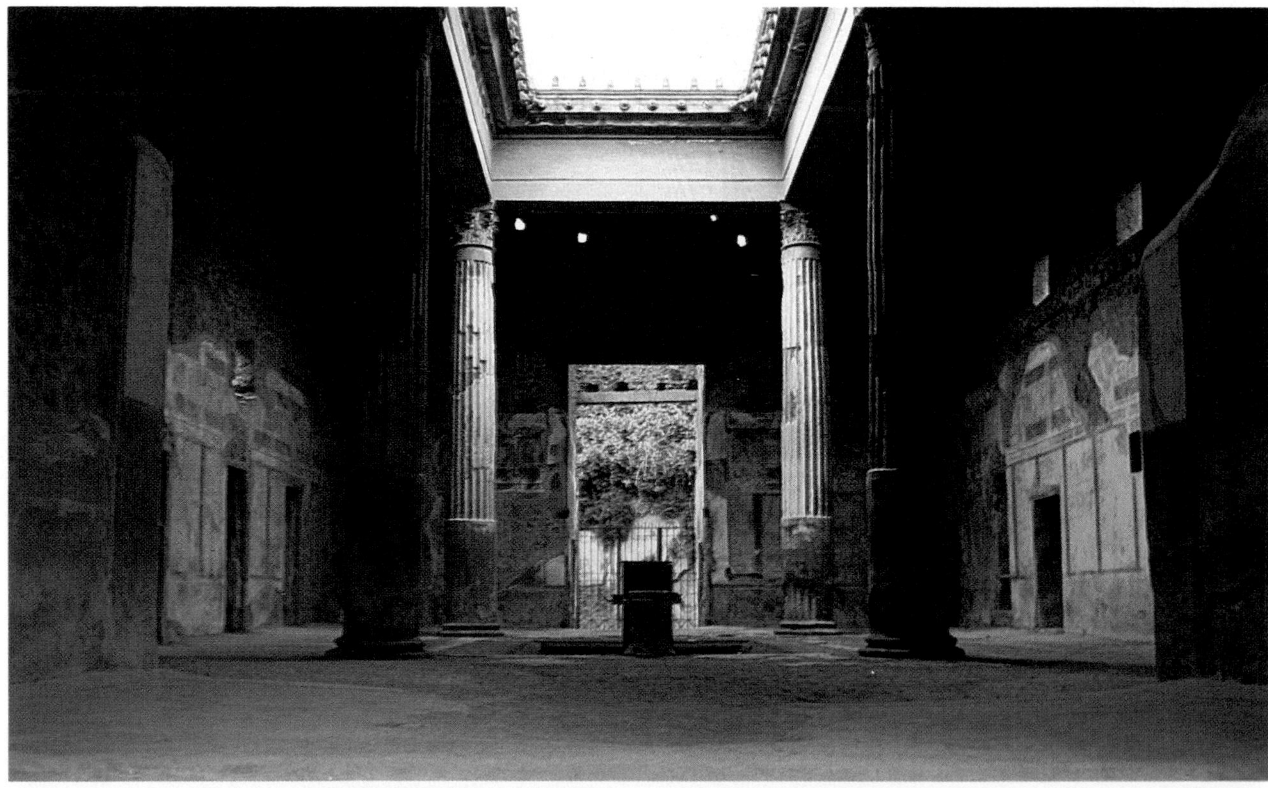

4.17 Peristyle of the House of the Silver Wedding, Pompeii. 1st century A.D. The open plan of substantial houses such as this helped keep the interior cool in summer; the adjoining rooms were closed off by folding doors in winter.

4.18 Model of ancient Rome as it was in about A.D. 320. Museo della Civiltà Romana, Rome. In the right center is the emperor's palace on the Palatine Hill, with the Colosseum above and the mammoth Basilica of Constantine at the upper left.

basilica or large hall that served as both stock exchange and law courts. Life must have been extremely comfortable at Pompeii, even though it was by no means the most prosperous of the towns buried by Vesuvius. Although only a small part of Herculaneum has been excavated, some mansions found there far surpass the houses of Pompeii. In the last few years work has begun at Oplontis, where a superbly decorated villa has already come to light.

Apart from its historic importance, the excavation of Pompeii in the 18th and 19th centuries had a profound effect on contemporary writers and artists. Johann Wolfgang von Goethe visited the site in 1787 and wrote of the buried city that "of all the disasters there have been in this world, few have provided so much delight to posterity." Johann Winckelmann (1717–1768), sometimes called the father of archaeology and art history, used material from the excavations in his *History of Ancient Art*. Artists like Ingres, David, and Canova were influenced by Pompeian paintings and sculptures; on a more popular level a style of Wedgwood china was based on Pompeian motifs. Countless poets and novelists of the 19th century either set episodes in the excavations at Pompeii or tried to imagine what life there was like in Roman times.

Roman Imperial Architecture

All the charm and comfort of Pompeii pale before the grandeur of imperial Rome itself, where both public buildings and private houses were constructed in numbers and on a scale that still remains impressive [4.18]. The Roman achievement in both architecture and engineering had a lasting effect on the development of later architectural styles. In particular their use of the arch, probably borrowed from the Etruscans, was widely imitated, and pseudo-Roman triumphal arches have sprung up in such unlikely places as the Champs Élysées in Paris and Washington Square in New York. The original triumphal arches commemorated military victories [4.19]; each was a permanent version of the temporary wooden arch erected to celebrate the return to the capital of a victorious general.

4.19 Arch of Titus, Rome. A.D. 81. Height 47'4" (14.43 m). This structure commemorates the Roman capture of Jerusalem in A.D. 70.

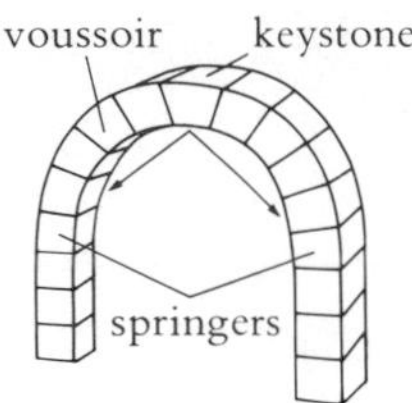

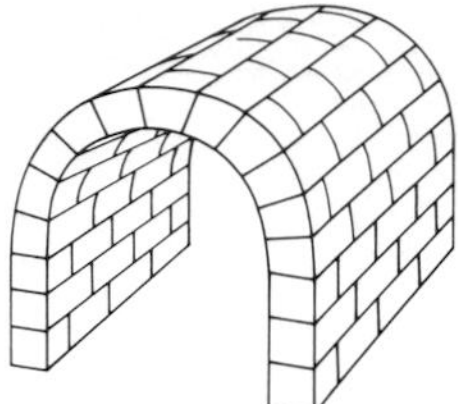

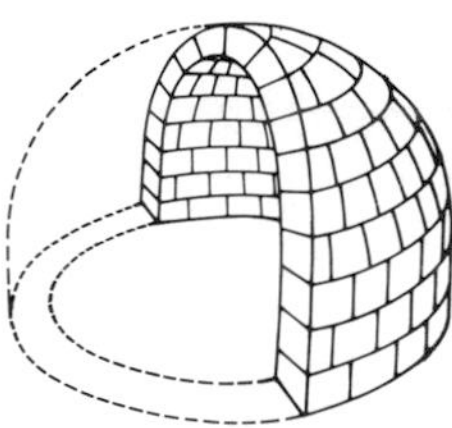

4.20 ***Top:*** **Simple arch composed of wedge-shaped blocks (or** ***voussoirs*****) and** ***keystone;*** **the curve of the arch rises from the** ***springers*** **on either side.** ***Center:*** **Tunnel or barrel vault composed of a series of arches.** ***Bottom:*** **Dome composed of a series of arches intersecting each other around a central axis.**

4.21 Pantheon, Rome. c. A.D. 126. Height of portico 59' (17.98 m).

Equally important was the use of internal arches and vaults [4.20] to provide roofs for structures of increasing size and complexity. Greek and Republican Roman temples had been relatively small, partly because of the difficulties involved in roofing a large space without supports. With the invention of concrete in the 1st century B.C. and growing understanding of the principles of stress and counterstress, Roman architects were able to experiment with elaborate new forms, many of which—like the barrel vault and the dome—were to pass into the Western architectural tradition.

The Greeks had rarely built arches, but the Etruscans used them as early as the 5th century B.C., and the Romans may well have borrowed the arch form from them. From the 2nd century B.C. on, stone arches were regularly used for bridges and aqueducts. Vaults of small size were often used for domestic buildings, and by the time of Augustus architects had begun to construct larger-scale barrel vaults, semicylindrical in shape, two or more of which could intersect to roof a large area. The dome, which is really a hemispherical vault, became increasingly popular with the building of the vast public baths of imperial Rome. Using both bricks and concrete, architects could combine vaults, barrel vaults, and domes to construct very elaborate buildings capable of holding thousands of people at a time. The inside and outside surfaces of the buildings were then covered with a marble

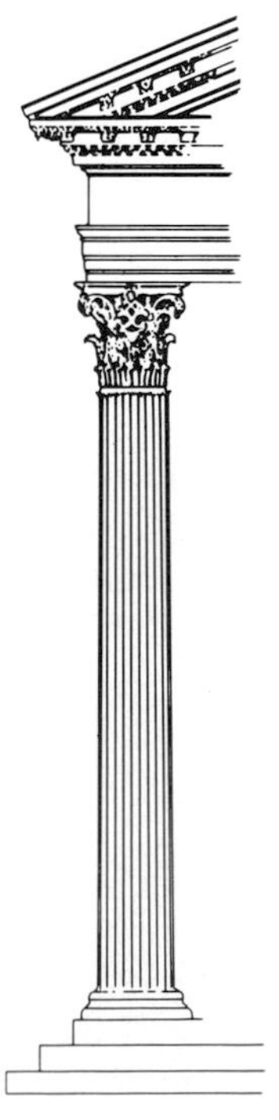

4.22 Corinthian capital. This elaborate bell-shape design, decorated with acanthus leaves, first became commonly used in Hellenistic times. It was especially popular with Roman architects, who in general preferred it to both the Doric and Ionic styles.

SPORTS AND GAMES

A Day at the Colosseum

Modern observers, impressed by the Roman genius for organization and efficiency, are almost universally horrified by the Romans' most popular form of entertainment: the spectacle of humans and animals fighting to the death. The enthusiasm for the bloodletting was not limited to the lower classes, although regular free performances undoubtedly helped to win the support of the urban mob; more than one emperor sought popularity by giving his people "bread and circuses."

The chief performers were the gladiators. Many of these were robbers and murderers, who faced a death sentence in any case; others were prisoners of war. The evening before a contest, the gladiators involved were served a lavish dinner—for many of them their last meal—which curious members of the public could attend. The next morning the gladiators paraded before the emperor's box, greeting him with the words "Those who are about to die salute you." Weapons were then examined, and blunt swords weeded out, and the fighters divided into pairs. In some cases the two would have the same arms, in other cases a fully armored fighter with a heavy sword would be matched against an unarmed gladiator whose weapons were a small sharp dagger and a net. On one occasion, at a performance offered by the emperor Domitian in 90 A.D., a dwarf fought a woman.

As the fights followed one another, the spectators would take sides, betting on their favorites. When a gladiator succeeded in killing his opponent, he retired and—literally—lived to fight another day. Attendants dragged out the dead body and turned over the bloodstained sand; our modern word "arena" is derived from the Latin word for sand, *harena.* In some cases, to the disappointment of the crowd, the two duellists were equally skillful; the contest was declared a draw, and the next pair was called. If a gladiator was seriously but not fatally wounded, he laid down his weapons, stretched himself on his back, and raised his left arm for mercy. His opponent then had the right either to spare him or to deliver the decisive blow. If the emperor were present, however, that right passed to the imperial box, and the emperor in turn often consulted the wishes of the spectators. When the public thought the defeated fighter had put on a good show, they waved their handkerchiefs, raised their thumbs, and shouted *"Mitte!"* (Let him go!). When they were less satisfied, they called out *"Iugula!"* (Cut his throat!), and turned their thumbs down. The emperor duly passed on the appropriate signal.

facing to conceal the elaborate internal support structures.

Much of the work of these architects was destroyed during the barbarian invasions of the 5th and 6th centuries A.D. and more was wrecked in the Renaissance by builders looking for bricks or marble. By great good fortune one of the most superb of all imperial structures has been preserved almost intact. The Pantheon [4.21] was built around 126, during the reign of Hadrian (117–138) to a design by the emperor himself. An austere and majestic exterior portico is supported on granite columns with Corinthian capitals [4.22]. It leads into the central rotunda, an astonishing construction approximately 142 feet (43.3 meters) high and wide in which a huge concrete dome rests on a wall interrupted by a series of niches. The building's only light source is a huge *oculus* (eye) at the top of the dome, an opening 30' (9.2 meters) across. The proportions of the building are very carefully calculated and contribute to its air of balance. The height of the dome from the ground, for example, is exactly equal to its width.

The Pantheon was dwarfed by the huge complex of buildings that made up the imperial fora. Completed by the beginning of the 2nd century A.D., they formed a vast architectural design unsurpassed in antiquity and barely equaled since [4.23]. Elsewhere in the city, baths, theaters, temples, race tracks, and libraries catered to the needs and fancies of a huge urban population. In many of these structures builders continued to experiment with new techniques of construction, and architectural principles developed in Rome were applied throughout the Roman Empire. From Spain to the Middle East, theaters, amphitheaters, and other public buildings were erected according to the same basic designs, leaving a permanent record of construction methods for later generations.

Urban life on such a scale required a constant supply of one of the basic human necessities, water. Their system of aqueducts is one of the most impressive of the Romans' engineering achievements. A vast network of pipes brought millions of gallons of water a day into Rome, distributing it to public fountains and baths and to the private villas of the

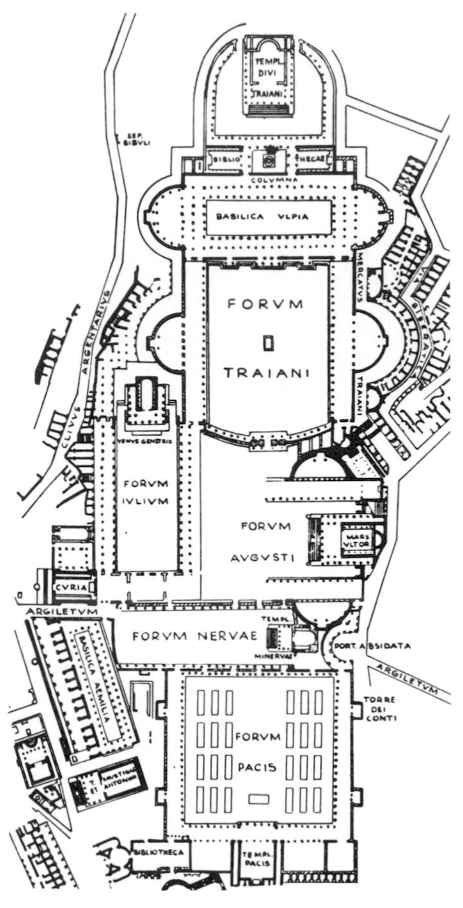

4.23 Plan of the imperial fora, Rome. Unlike the Republican forum, which served as a public meeting place, these huge complexes were constructed as monuments to the emperors who commissioned them.

wealthy. At the same time a system of covered street drains was built, eliminating the open sewers that had been usual before Roman times. These open drains were to return during the medieval period, when many of the Roman engineering skills were gone.

With the passage of time, most of the aqueducts that supplied ancient Rome have been demolished or have collapsed. Elsewhere in the Roman Empire, however, examples have survived that give some idea of Roman engineering skill. The famous Pont du Gard [4.24], which can still be seen in southern France, was probably first constructed during the reign of Augustus. It carried the aqueduct that supplied the Roman city of Nîmes with water—a hundred gallons (387.5 liters) a day for each inhabitant—and was made of uncemented stone. The largest blocks weigh 2 tons (1.8 metric tons).

Even with the provision of such facilities, imperial Rome suffered from overcrowding. The average Roman lived in an apartment block, of which there were some 45,000. Most of these have long since disappeared, although their appearance can be reconstructed from examples excavated at Ostia, Rome's port [4.25]. The height of the apartment blocks was controlled by law to prevent the construction of unsafe buildings, but it was not unheard of for a building to collapse and fire was a constant danger. No doubt the grandeur of the public buildings in Rome was intended at least in part to distract the poorer Romans from thoughts of their humble private residences.

4.24 Pont du Gard, near Nîmes in southern France. Late 1st century B.C. Length 902' (274.93 m), height 161' (49.07 m). Note the careful positioning of the three rows of arches along the top of which ran the water channel. The whole aqueduct was 25 miles (40 kilometers) long. This section carried the water over the river Gard.

4.25 Reconstruction drawing of the garden façade of the Insula dei Dipinti, an apartment block in Ostia, the seaport of ancient Rome.

Rome as the Object of Satire

Life in this huge metropolis had many of the problems of big-city living today: Noise, traffic jams, dirty streets, and overcrowding were all constant sources of complaint. A particularly bitter protest comes from the Roman satirist Juvenal (A.D. c. 60–c. 130). Born in the provinces, he came to Rome, where he served as a magistrate and irritated the current emperor, Domitian—not a difficult task. After a period of exile, probably in Egypt, he returned to Rome and lived in considerable poverty. Toward the end of his life, however, his circumstances improved. His sixteen *Satires* make it perfectly clear that Juvenal liked neither Rome nor Romans. He tells us that he writes out of fierce

CONTEMPORARY VOICES

A Dinner Party in Imperial Rome

At the end of this course Trimalchio left the table to relieve himself, and so finding ourselves free from the constraint of his overbearing presence, we began to indulge in a little friendly conversation. Accordingly Dama began first, after calling for a cup of wine. "A day! what is a day?" he exclaimed, "before you can turn round, it's night again! So really you can't do better than go straight from bed to board. Fine cold weather we've been having; why! even my bath has hardly warmed me. But truly hot liquor is a good clothier. I've been drinking bumpers, and I'm downright fuddled. The wine has got into my head."

Seleucus then struck into the talk: "I don't bathe every day," he said; "your systematic bather's a mere fuller. Water's got teeth, and melts the heart away, a little every day; but there! when I've fortified my belly with a cup of mulled wine, I say 'Go hang!' to the cold. Indeed I couldn't bathe today, for I've been to a funeral. A fine fellow he was too, good old Chrysanthus, but he's given up the ghost now. He was calling me just this moment, only just this moment; I could fancy myself talking to him now. Alas! alas! what are we but blown bladders on two legs? We're nor worth as much as flies; they are some use, but we're no better than bubbles." "He wasn't careful enough in his diet?" "I tell you, for five whole days not one drop of water, or one crumb of bread, passed his lips. Nevertheless he has joined the majority. The doctors killed him,—or rather his day was come; the very best of doctors is only a satisfaction to the mind. Anyhow he was handsomely buried, on his own best bed, with good blankets. The wailing was first class,—he did a trifle manumission before he died; though no doubt his wife's tears were a bit forced. A pity he always treated her so well. But woman! woman's of the kite kind. No man ought ever to do 'em a good turn; just as well pitch it in the well at once. Old love's an eating sore!"

From Petronius, *The Satyricon,* trans. attributed to Oscar Wilde (privately printed, 1928), p. 81.

outrage at the corruption and decadence of his day, the depraved aristocracy, the general greed and meanness. "At such a time who could *not* write satire?" His fiercest loathing is reserved for foreigners, although in the sixth *Satire* he launches a particularly virulent attack against women in one of the archetypal documents of misogyny.

Juvenal himself does not emerge as a very pleasant character and his obsessive hatred frequently verges on the psychopathic. As a satirical poet, though, he is among the greatest in Western literature, and strongly influenced many of his successors, including Jonathan Swift. Few other writers can make better or more powerful use of biting sarcasm, irony, and outright invective.

THE END OF THE ROMAN EMPIRE

Few historical subjects have been as much discussed as the fall of the Roman Empire. It is not even possible to agree on when it fell, let alone why. The traditional date, A.D. 476, marks the deposition of the last Roman emperor, Romulus Augustulus. By that time, however, the political unity of the empire had already disintegrated. Perhaps the beginning of the end was A.D. 330, when the emperor Constantine moved the capital from Rome to a new city on the Bosporus, Constantinople, although in another sense the transfer represented a new development as much as a conclusion. It might even be possible to argue that Constantine's successors in the East, the Byzantine emperors, were the successors of Augustus and that there is a continuous tradition from the beginning of the empire in 31 B.C. to the fall of Constantinople in A.D. 1453.

Fascinating though the question may be, in a sense it is theoretical rather than practical. The Roman Empire did not fall overnight. Many of the causes for its long decline are obvious though not always easy to order in importance. One crucial factor was the growing power and changing character of the army. The larger it became, the more necessary it was to recruit troops from the more distant provinces—Germans, Illyrians, and others, the very people the army was supposed to be holding in check. Most of these soldiers had never been anywhere near Rome. They felt no loyalty to the empire, no reason to defend Roman interests. A succession of emperors had to buy their support by raising their pay and promising gifts of lands. At the same time, the army came to play an increasingly prominent part in the choice of a new emperor, and, since the army itself was largely non-Roman, so were many of the emperors chosen. Rulers of the 3rd and 4th centuries included Africans, Thracians, a Syrian, and an Arab, men unlikely to feel any strong reason to place the interests of Rome over those of themselves and their own men.

Throughout this late period the empire was increasingly threatened from outside. To the west, barbarian tribes like the Huns, the Goths, and the Alemanni began to penetrate farther and farther into its defenses and even to sack Rome itself.

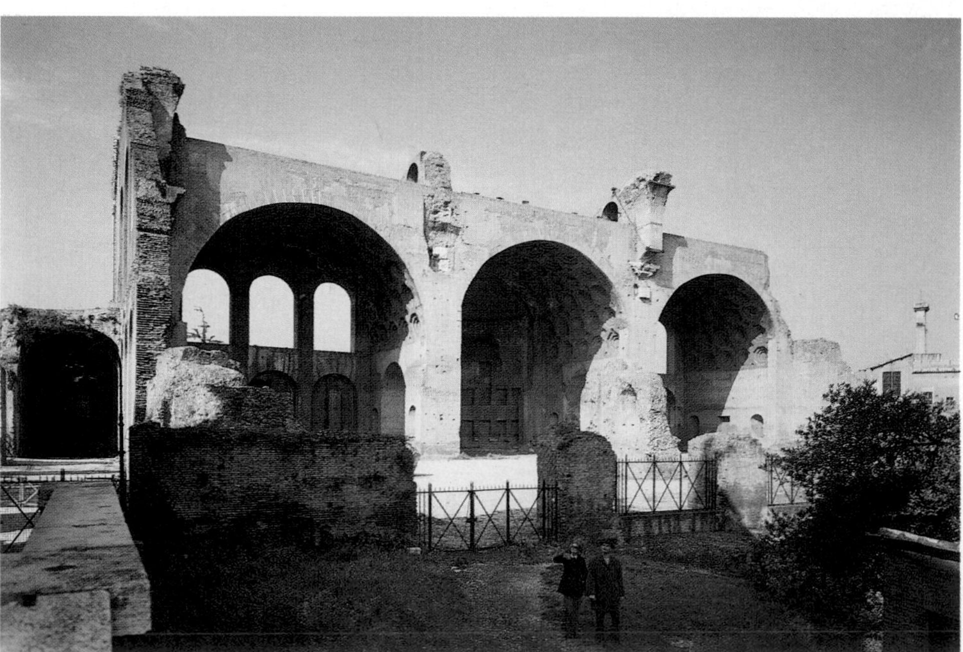

4.26 Basilica of Constantine, the last great imperial building in Rome. Begun in A.D. 306 by Maxentius, it was finished by Constantine after 315. Only the northern side is still standing; the central nave and south aisle collapsed during antiquity.

4.27 Head of the colossal statue of Constantine that stood in the Basilica of Constantine, Rome. A.D. 324–330. Marble, height 8'6" (2.59 m). Palazzo dei Conservatori, Rome. The massive and majestic simplicity of this portrait is very different from the detailed observation of earlier, much smaller Roman portraits like that of Cicero (Figure 4.7), illustrating the new belief in the emperor as God's regent on earth.

Meanwhile, in the East, Roman armies were continually involved in resisting the growing power of the Persians. In many parts of the empire it became clear that Rome could provide no help against invaders, and some of the provinces set themselves up as independent states with their own armies.

Problems like these inevitably had a devastating effect on the economy. Taxes increased and the value of money declined. The constant threat of invasion or civil war made trade impossible. What funds there were went for the support of the army, and the general standard of living suffered a steady decline. The eastern provinces, the old Hellenistic kingdoms, suffered rather less than the rest of the empire, since they were protected in part by the wealth accumulated over the centuries and by their long tradition of civilization. As a result, Italy sank to the level of a province rather than remain the center of the imperial administration.

Total collapse was prevented by the efforts of two emperors: Diocletian, who ruled from A.D. 284 to 305, and Constantine, who ruled from 306 to 337. Both men were masterly organizers who realized that the only way to save the empire was to impose the most stringent controls on every aspect of life—social, administrative, and economic. In 301 the Edict of Diocletian was passed, establishing fixed maximums for the sale of goods and for wages. A vast bureaucracy was set up to collect taxes and administer the provinces. The emperor himself became once again the focal point of the empire, but to protect himself from the dangers of coups and assassinations, he never appeared in public. As a result, an elaborate court with complex rituals developed, and the emperor's claim to semidivine status invested him with a new religious authority.

Late Roman Art and Architecture

Even if the emperor did not show himself to his subjects, he could impress them in other ways, and the reigns of Diocletian and Constantine marked the last great age of Roman architecture. The immense Basilica of Constantine [4.26], with its central nave rising to a height of 100' (30.5 meters), is now in ruins, but in its day this assembly hall must have been a powerful reminder of the emperor's authority. It also contained a 30' (9.2-meter) statue of the emperor himself [4.27]. The palace Diocletian had built for him at Split, on the Adriatic coast, is constructed on the plan of a military camp, with enormous central avenues dividing it into four quarters [4.28]. The decoration makes use of

4.28 **Reconstruction model of the Palace of Diocletian at Split, Yugoslavia. A.D. 300–305. Museo della Civiltà Romana, Rome. Note the octagonal dome of the emperor's mausoleum.**

Eastern motifs, and the whole design is far from the classical style of earlier times.

In sculpture, too, classical forms and styles were increasingly abandoned. Realistic portraiture and naturalistic drapery were neglected, and sculptors no longer tried to express depth or reality in their relief carving. The lack of perspective and precision in their work foreshadows the art of the early Middle Ages [4.29]. The general abandonment of classical ideas these artistic changes indicate went along with a waning of interest in Stoicism and Epicureanism and a new enthusiasm for Eastern religious cults. Traditional Roman religion had always been organized by the state, and from the time of the late Republic some Romans had sought a more personal religious satisfaction in the worship of Eastern deities. During the last stages of the empire, strong cults developed around the Phrygian goddess Cybele, the Egyptian Isis, and the sun god Mithras.

The appearance and eventual triumph of Christianity is outside the scope of this account, but its emergence as the official religion of the empire played a final and decisive part in bringing to an end the classical era. Pagan art, pagan literature, and pagan culture as a whole represented forces and ideals Christianity strongly rejected, and the art of the early Christians is fundamentally different in its inspiration. Yet even the fathers of the early Church, implacable opponents of paganism, could not fail to be moved by the end of so great a cultural tradition.

The memory of Rome's greatness lived on through the succeeding ages of turmoil and achievement and the classical spirit survived, to be reborn triumphantly in the Renaissance.

SUMMARY

The vast extent of ancient Roman history—more than twelve hundred years—can be conveniently divided into three chief periods: the Monarchy (753

4.29 *Constantine Receiving Homage from the Senate,* frieze on the Arch of Constantine, Rome. A.D. 315. Marble, 3'4" × 17'6" (1.02 × 5.33 m). On both sides of the emperor (seated in the center) his officials distribute money to the crowds below. The simplified style, in which most of the puppetlike figures are shown frontally, foreshadows Byzantine and medieval art and is certainly very different from the style of earlier reliefs (Figures 4.10, 4.11).

B.C.–510 B.C.); the Republic (509 B.C.–31 B.C.); and the Empire (31 B.C.–A.D. 476).

The city was founded in the mid-8th century, around the time the Greeks were setting up colonies in southern Italy and Sicily. Rome's first inhabitants were Latins, an Italian people native to central Italy, after whom the Roman language is named. Traditional accounts of the city's origins claimed that its first rulers were a series of seven kings. The first four were Latin, but in 616 B.C. Rome fell under Etruscan control. The Etruscans had developed in the region of central Italy to the north of Rome, although their origins are uncertain; they may have migrated to Italy from western Asia.

Etruscan art was strongly influenced by Greek and Orientalizing styles. Among the most striking works to survive are the tomb paintings at Tarquinia, one of the principal Etruscan cities, and the sculpture from the temple of Apollo at Veii. Although many Etruscan inscriptions can be deciphered, no Etruscan literature has been discovered. For the century during which they ruled Rome, the Etruscans expanded its trade contacts and introduced important technological innovations. In 510 B.C. the Romans drove out the last Etruscan king.

In 509 B.C. the Roman Republic was declared. The political system of the new state evolved from the need to achieve a balance of political power between the two classes of citizens: the aristocratic patricians and the people, or plebeians. There gradually developed two political institutions, the Senate and the Assembly of the people, while plebeians eventually won the right to run for election to virtually all offices of state. The growth of internal political stability was accompanied by the spread of Roman power throughout Italy. Among those to fall under Roman domination were the Etruscans, their former rulers. Little in the way of art or literature has survived from this early period, and most of what was produced seems to have been inspired by Etruscan or, more generally, Greek models.

In 264 B.C. there began a series of wars (the Punic wars) between Rome and her chief rival in the western Mediterranean, Carthage. By 201 B.C. the Romans had proved victorious, and Roman colonies were established in Spain and North Africa. Throughout the following century Roman power spread eastward. In 146 B.C. Greece was absorbed into the Roman Empire, and the Hellenistic kingdom of Pergamum was bequeathed to Rome by its last king, Attalus III, on his death in 133 B.C. The 2nd century B.C. also saw the beginnings of the development of an independent Roman culture, although Greek influence remained strong. The Roman poet Ennius composed his epic, the *Annales,* while Plautus and Terence wrote comedies based on Greek originals. Greek music became popular at Rome, and the two chief schools of Greek philosophy, Stoicism and Epicureanism, began to attract Roman adherents.

With such vast territorial expansion, strains began to appear in Roman political and social life. The growth of a middle class, the *equites,* disturbed the old equilibrium, and the last century of the republic (133 B.C. to 31 B.C.) was beset by continual crisis. A succession of powerful figures—Marius, Sulla, Pompey, Caesar—struggled to assume control of the state. The last of these proved victorious in 48 B.C. only to be assassinated four years later. Amid bitter fighting between Mark Antony, Caesar's lieutenant, and Octavius, the late dictator's nephew and heir, the republic collapsed.

The political confusion of the republic's last century was accompanied by important cultural developments. Among the major literary figures of the age were the Epicurean poet Lucretius, the lyric poet Catullus, and the orator and politician Cicero. Caesar himself combined his political and military career with the writing of accounts of his campaigns. In the visual arts realistic portrait sculpture became common, while the invention of concrete was to have enormous consequences both for Roman building and for the history of all later architecture in the West. Sulla's great Sanctuary at Praeneste inaugurated the tradition of large-scale public building projects that was to become common during the empire.

In 31 B.C. Octavius defeated the combined forces of Antony and Cleopatra to emerge as sole ruler of the Roman world; in 27 B.C., under the name Augustus, he became its first emperor. The Augustan Age marked the high point of Roman art and literature, and many of its finest achievements were produced to celebrate the Augustan revolution. Vergil was commissioned to write a Roman national epic: The result was the *Aeneid*. Augustus himself was portrayed in numerous statues and portraits, including the *Augustus of Prima Porta,* and in the reliefs on the Ara Pacis. Important public works included the Pont du Gard near Nîmes, France.

From the time of Augustus until A.D. 476, the empire was ruled by a series of emperors who were increasingly dependent on an elaborate state bureaucracy. Augustus and his first four successors were from a single family, but with time emperors either seized power for themselves or were imposed by the army. The empire continued to expand until the reign of Hadrian (A.D. 117–138), who fixed its borders to achieve stability abroad.

Some idea of the character of provincial daily life in the empire can be gained from the excavations at Pompeii and the other cities around the Bay of Naples, which were destroyed by an eruption of the volcano Vesuvius in A.D. 79. Writers of the early empire include the historian Tacitus and the satirist Juvenal. Among the most impressive works of architecture of the period is the Pantheon, designed by Hadrian himself, which makes bold use of concrete.

The 3rd century was marked by continual struggles for imperial power. A brief peace was imposed in the reign of Aurelian (A.D. 270–275), but it proved temporary. Only the Emperor Diocletian (A.D. 284–305) managed to restore order by massive administrative and economic reform. After Diocletian's retirement to his palace at Split, one of his successors, Constantine (A.D. 307–337), transferred the imperial capital from Rome to the new city of Constantinople in A.D. 330, and the western part of the empire began its final decline. During this last period Roman art became less realistic as classical forms and styles were abandoned in favor of simpler, more massive effects. Finally Rome itself was shaken by barbarian assaults, and the last western emperor was forced to abdicate in A.D. 476.

Pronunciation Guide

Aeneid: Ee-NEE-id
Anchises: Ank-ICE-ease
Ara Pacis: ARE-a PAH-kiss
Ceres: SEAR-ease
Cerveteri: Cher-VET-er-ee
Cicero: SISS-er-owe
Cybele: KIB-e-lee
Dido: DIE-doe
Diocletian: Die-owe-KLEE-shan
Epictetus: Ep-ic-TEE-tus
Epicureanism: Ep-ik-you-REE-an-ism
Etruscans: Et-RUSK-ans
Gaius: GUY-us
Ius Civile: YUS kiv-EE-lay
Lydia: LID-i-a
Pantheon: PAN-thi-on
Plautus: PLOR-tus
Plebeians: Pleb-EE-ans
Pliny: PLIN-ee
Praeneste: Pry-NEST-ee
Stoicism: STOW-i-sism
Tacitus: TASS-it-us
Tarquinia: Tar-QUIN-i-a
Veii: VAY-ee
Winckelmann: VIN-kel-man

Exercises

1. What are the chief features of Etruscan culture and religion? What light do they cast on the problem of the Etruscans' origins?
2. "Roman art and culture are late and debased forms of Hellenistic art." Discuss.
3. In what ways does the *Aeneid* fulfill its aim to provide the Romans with a national epic? Compare it in this respect with the Greek epics, the *Iliad* and *Odyssey*, discussed in Chapter 2.
4. Describe in detail Augustus' use of the visual arts as instruments of propaganda. Are there comparable examples of the arts used for political purposes in recent times?
5. What do the discoveries at Rome and Pompeii tell us about daily life in the Roman Empire? In what significant respects did it differ from life today?

Further Reading

Brendel, O. J. *Etruscan Art.* Baltimore: Penguin, 1978. The most up-to-date survey of Etruscan painting and sculpture, with numerous illustrations.

Commager, S., ed. *Virgil, a Collection of Critical Essays.* Englewood Cliffs: Prentice-Hall, 1966. The literature on Vergil is immense and wide-ranging, but this volume of essays provides a useful survey of modern critical approaches and suggests some further directions for the interested reader to explore.

Crawford, M. *The Roman Republic.* Cambridge: Harvard University Press, 1982. An excellent survey of Republican history and culture, particularly good on coinage.

Grant, M. *Cities of Vesuvius: Pompeii and Herculaneum.* New York: American Heritage Press, 1971. This well-illustrated account describes the rediscovery of the buried cities, and analyzes the evidence they provide about Roman daily life.

Graves, Robert. *I, Claudius* and *Claudius the God.* Baltimore: Penguin, 1977. These two historical novels, originally published in 1934, are recreations of the Roman world that are both scholarly and thoroughly absorbing. Highly recommended.

Hanfmann, G. M. A. *Roman Art.* New York: Norton, 1975. The best introduction to the subject, with a very full selection of illustrations, sensitive comments, and up-to-date bibliographical notes.

Hooper, F. *Roman Realities.* Detroit: Wayne State University Press, 1980. A useful introduction to recent scholarship in Roman studies.

McKay, A. *Houses, Villas, and Palaces in the Roman World.* New York: Thames and Hudson, 1975. A guide to Roman domestic architecture, covering all parts of the Roman world. Good illustrations and diagrams.

Pallottino, M. *The Etruscans.* Baltimore: Penguin, 1975. A revised version of the standard work by the most eminent Etruscologist of our time, covering all aspects of Etruscan culture. Especially good on the language.

Potter, T. *The Changing Landscape of Southern Etruria.* New York: St. Martin's Press, 1979. A study of the material remains of central Italy, from the Etruscans and earlier to the present. An engrossing look at new archaeological techniques in action.

Scullard, H. H. *From the Gracchi to Nero.* 3rd edition. London: Methuen, 1970. A useful survey of the history of the late republic and the early empire, reflecting the state of modern scholarly opinion.

Vermeule, C. *Greek Sculpture and Roman Taste.* Ann Arbor: University of Michigan Press, 1977. This book casts considerable light on Roman attitudes toward Greek culture by describing how the Romans used Greek sculpture, both originals and copies, in their own public buildings and private estates.

Ward-Perkins, J. B. *Cities of Ancient Greece and Italy.* New York: Braziller, 1974. A magisterial account of city planning in the ancient world, distilled to a mere 128 pages.

Vickers, M. *The Roman World.* Oxford: Elsevier/Phaidon, 1977. A fully illustrated account of Roman art and archaeology, also valuable for its discussion of the rediscovery of classical antiquity in the Renaissance.

	GENERAL EVENTS	LITERATURE & PHILOSOPHY
3000 B.C.		
BRONZE AGE — Before 1260 B.C.	**1800–1600** Age of the Hebrew Patriarchs: Abraham, Isaac, Jacob **1600** Israelite tribes in Egypt **1280** Exodus of Israelites from Egypt under leadership of Moses	
1260 — Period of the Judges	**1260** Israelites begin to penetrate land of Canaan	
1040	**1040–1000** Reign of Saul, first king of Israel	
1000 — Age of the Monarchy	**1000–961** Reign of King David **961–922** Reign of Solomon; use of iron-tipped plow and iron war chariots; height of ancient Israel's cultural power: achievements form basis of Judaic, Christian, and Islamic religions	**c. 1000** Formation of the Scriptures in written form **c. 950** Book of Psalms **10th–9th cent.** Book of Kings
922 — Age of the Two Kingdoms	**922** Civil war after death of Solomon; split of Northern Kingdom (Israel) and Southern Kingdom (Judah); classical prophetic period begins **721** Northern Kingdom destroyed by Assyria	**8th–6th cent.** Old Testament books of Isaiah, Jeremiah, and Ezekiel
IRON AGE — **587** — Age of Exile, Return, and Occupations	**587** Southern Kingdom defeated; Jews driven into captivity in Babylonia **539** Cyrus the Persian permits Jews to return to Jerusalem **516** Dedication of Second Temple in Jerusalem **332** Conquest of Jerusalem by Alexander the Great **2nd cent.** Cult of Mithra in Rome	**after 5th cent.** Book of Job **end of 2d cent.** Apocryphal Book of Judith
63	**63** Conquest of Jerusalem by Romans under Pompey **37 B.C.–A.D. 4** Reign of Herod the Great under Roman tutelage **c. 6 B.C.** Birth of Jesus	
B.C. / A.D. — Roman Period	**c. A.D. 30** Death of Jesus; beginnings of Christianity in Palestine **45–49** First missionary journeys of Saint Paul **66–70** Jewish rebellions against Romans **c. 70** Titus destroys Jerusalem and razes the Temple; Jews sent into exile	**c. A.D. 70** "Sermon on the Mount" in Gospel of Saint Matthew, New Testament **c. A.D. 150** Justin Martyr *Apology*
A.D. 324		

Dates before the 10th cent. B.C. are approximate and remain controversial

CHAPTER 5 JERUSALEM AND EARLY CHRISTIANITY

ART	ARCHITECTURE	MUSIC

c. 961–c. 922 Hiram of Tyre constructs bronze "sea" in courtyard of Solomon's Temple

c. 961–c. 922 Building of Temple of Solomon; city of Megiddo rebuilt by Solomon

Music often accompanied the Psalms; musical instruments in use: drums, reed instruments, lyre, harp, horns

Depiction of divinity in art prohibited in Jewish religion

734 Oxen from bronze "sea" given to King of Assyria by King Achaz

587 Solomon's Temple destroyed by Babylonians

c. 536–515 Second Temple of Solomon constructed

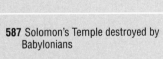

19 Herod the Great begins rebuilding Third Temple of Solomon

A.D. 70 Herod's Temple destroyed by the armies of Titus under Emperor Vespasian

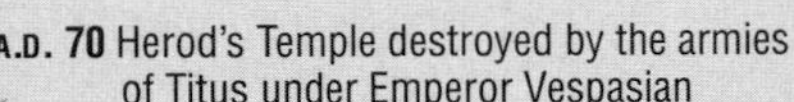

c. A.D. 81 Reliefs from Arch of Titus, Rome, commemorate Roman victory in Jerusalem

c. 81 Arch of Titus, Rome, commemorates victory of Roman army in Jerusalem

c. A.D. 230–240 Synagogue and House Church at Dura Europos

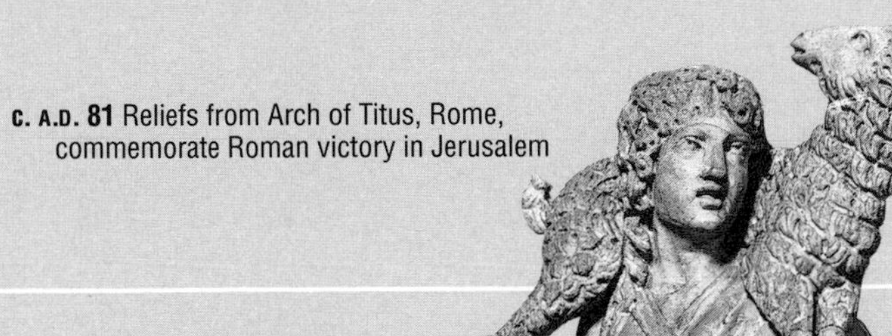

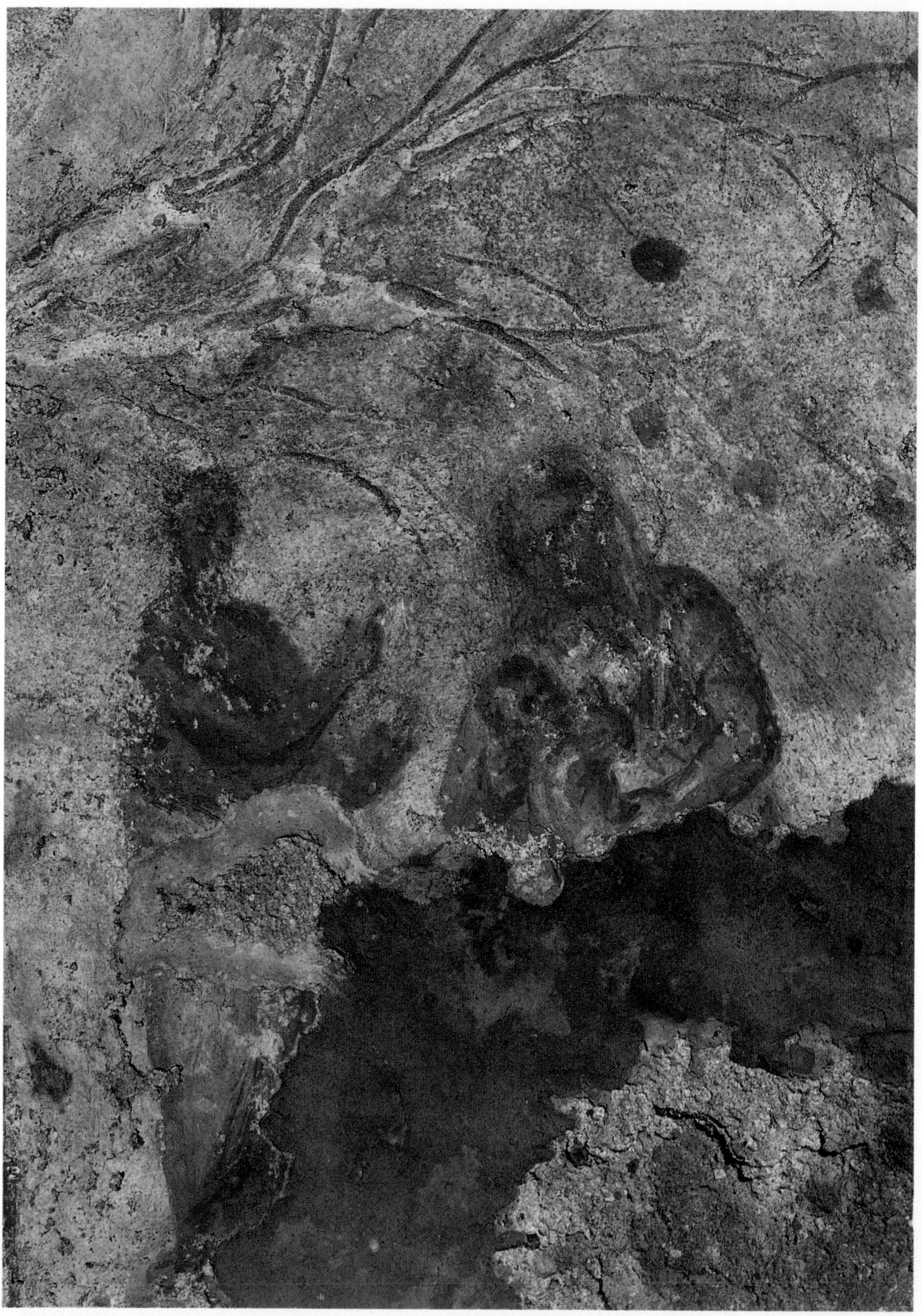

CHAPTER

5
JERUSALEM AND EARLY CHRISTIANITY

JUDAISM AND EARLY CHRISTIANITY

ONE OF THE interesting ironies of history is the fact that, more than three thousand years ago in the Middle East, a small tribe-turned-nation became one of the central sources for the development of Western civilization. The fact is incontestable: The marriage of the biblical tradition and Graeco-Roman culture has produced, for better or worse, the West as we know it today.

The irony is all the more telling because this ancient biblical people did not give to the world great art, significant music, philosophy, or science. Their language did not have a word for science. Their religion discouraged the plastic arts. We have the texts of their hymns, canticles, and psalms but we can only speculate how they were sung and how they were accompanied by instruments. What these people did give us was a book; more precisely, a collection of many different books we now call the Bible.

These people called themselves the Children of Israel or Israelites; at a later time they became known as the Jews (from the area around Jerusalem known as Judaea). In the Bible they are called Hebrews (most often by their neighbors), the name now most commonly used to describe the biblical people.

The history of the Hebrew people is long and complex, but the stages of their growth can be outlined as follows:

- **The Period of the Patriarchs.** According to the Bible, the Hebrew people had their origin in Abraham, the father (patriarch) of a tribe who took his people from ancient Mesopotamia to the land of Canaan on the east coast of the Mediterranean about 2000 B.C. After settling in this land, divided into twelve tribal areas, they eventually went to Egypt at the behest of Joseph, who had risen to high office in Egypt after his enslavement there.
- **The Period of the Exodus.** The Egyptians eventually enslaved the Hebrews (perhaps around 1750 B.C.), but they were led out of Egypt under the leadership of Moses. This "going out" (exodus) is one of the central themes of the Bible; this great event also gives its name to one of the books of the Bible.
- **The Period of the Conquest.** The biblical books of Joshua and Judges relate the struggles of the Hebrews to conquer the land of Canaan as they fought against the native peoples of that area and the competing "Sea People" (the Philistines) who came down from the north.
- **The United Monarchy.** The high point of the Hebrew political power came with the consolidation of Canaan and the rise of a monarchy. There were three kings: Saul, David, and Solomon. An ambitious flurry of building during the reign of Solomon (c. 961–922 B.C.) culminated in the construction of the great temple in Jerusalem [5.1].
- **Divided Kingdom and Exile.** After the death of Solomon a rift over the succession resulted in the separation of the Northern Kingdom and the Southern, the center of which was Jerusalem. Both were vulnerable to pressure from the surrounding great powers. The Northern Kingdom was destroyed by the Assyrians in the 8th century B.C. and its inhabitants (the so-called Lost Tribes of Israel) were swept away by death or exile. In 587 B.C. the Babylonians conquered the Southern Kingdom, destroyed Solomon's temple

5.1 Reconstruction drawing of Solomon's Temple. The description in the Bible of this destroyed temple was an inspiration for sacred architecture well into the Middle Ages. The two bronze columns in front may have represented the columns of fire and smoke that guided the Israelites while they were in the desert.

in Jerusalem, and carried the Hebrew people into an exile known to history as the Babylonian Captivity.

- **The Return.** The Hebrews returned from exile about 520 B.C. to rebuild their shattered temple and to resume their religious life. Their subsequent history was marked by a series of foreign (Greek, Egyptian, and Syrian) rulers, one brief period of political independence (c. 165 B.C.), and, finally, rule by Rome after the conquest of 63 B.C. In A.D. 70, after a Jewish revolt, the Romans destroyed Jerusalem and razed the rebuilt temple [5.2]. One small band of Jewish rebels that held off the Romans for two years at a mountain fortress called Masada was defeated in A.D. 73. Except for pockets of Jews who lived there over the centuries, not until 1948, when the state of Israel was established, would Jews hold political power in their ancestral home.

The Hebrew Bible and Its Message

The English word *bible* comes from the Greek name for the ancient city of Byblos, from which the papyrus reed used to make books was exported. As

5.2 *The Spoils of Jerusalem,* from the Arch of Titus, Rome. c. A.D. 81. Passageway relief. The seven-branched candelabrum (a *menorah*) is carried as part of the booty after the Romans sacked the city of Jerusalem.

already noted, the Bible is a collection of books that took its present shape over a long period of time.

The ancient Hebrews divided the books of their Bible into three large groupings: the Law, the Prophets, and the Writings. The Law referred specifically to the first five books of the Bible, called the *Torah* (from the Hebrew for "instruction" or "teaching"). The Prophets consists of writings attributed to the great moral teachers of the Hebrews who were called prophets because they spoke with the authority of God (*prophet* derives from a Greek word for "one who speaks for another"). The Writings contain the wisdom literature of the Bible, prose or poetry (like the book of Psalms) or a mixture of the two, as in the book of Job.

The list of books contained in the modern Bible was not established until A.D. 90, when an assembly of rabbis drew up such a list or *canon* even though its main outline had been known for centuries. The Christians in turn accepted this canon and added the twenty-seven books that make up what we know as the Christian scriptures of the New Testament. (Roman Catholics and Orthodox Christians also accept as canonical some books of the Old Testament that are not in the Hebrew canon but are found in an ancient Greek version of the Hebrew scriptures known as the *Septuagint*, a version of the Bible widely used in the ancient world.)

One fundamental issue about the Bible must be emphasized: Both ancient Israel, subsequent Jewish history, and the Christian world have made the Bible *the* central document not only for worship and the rule of faith but also as moral guide and anchor for ethical and religious stability. The Bible, directly and indirectly, has shaped our law, literature, language, ethics, and social outlook. It permeates our culture. To cite one single example: At Solomon's temple the people sang hymns of praise (psalms) to God just as they are sung in Jewish synagogues today. Those same psalms were sung by Jesus and his followers in their time just as they are sung and recited in Christian churches in every part of the world. That ancient formulation is, in a deep sense, part of our common religious culture.

The Bible is not a philosophical treatise; it is a sacred book. It is, nonetheless, a book that contains ideas; those ideas have had an enormous impact on the way we think and the way we look at the world. Some of the basic motifs of the Bible have been so influential in our culture that they should be considered in some detail. We will examine three such motifs that run like strands throughout the Hebrew scriptures.

1. *Biblical monotheism.* A central conviction of biblical religion is that there is one God, that this God is good, and (most crucially) that this God is involved in the arena of human history. This God is conceived of as a person and not as some impersonal force in the world of nature. *Monotheism* (the belief in one god) can thus be distinguished both from *henotheism* (the belief that there may be other gods, although only one is singled out for worship) and *polytheism* (the belief that there are many gods).

The opening pages of the Bible set out a creation story (see Genesis 1:1–2:4a) that, properly understood, provides us with a rather complete vision of what the Bible believes about God. The creation story of Genesis makes three basic assertions about God. First, God exists before the world and called it into existence by the simple act of utterance. God, unlike the gods and goddesses of the Hebrews' ancient neighbors, is not born out of the chaos that existed before the world. God is not to be confused with the world, nor did God have to struggle with the forces of chaos to create. Second, God pronounces each part of creation and creation as a whole as "good." Thus the book of Genesis does not present the material universe as evil or, as certain Eastern religions teach, an illusory world that conceals the true nature of reality. Finally, God creates human beings as the apex and crown of creation. The material world is a gift from God and human beings are obliged to care for it and be grateful for it. A basic motif of biblical prayer is gratitude to God for the gift of creation.

Biblical monotheism must not be thought of as a theory that simply sees God as the starting point or originator of all things after the fashion of a craftsperson who makes a chair and then forgets about it. The precise character of biblical monotheism is its conviction that God creates and sustains the world in general and chose a particular people to be both vehicle and sign of divine presence in the world. The precise character of that relationship can be found in the biblical notion of covenant.

Covenant is the crucial concept for setting out the relationship of God and the Hebrew people. The covenant can be summed up in the simple biblical phrase "I will be your God; you will be my people." In Hebrew history, the Bible insists, God has always been faithful to that covenant which was made with the people of Israel while the people must learn and relearn how to be faithful to it. Scholars have pointed out that the biblical covenant may be based on the language of ancient marriage covenants (e.g., "I will be your husband; you will be my wife"); if that is true it gives us an even deeper understanding of the term: The relationship of God and Israel is as close as the relationship of husband and wife.

This strong portrait of a single, deeply involved God who is beyond image or portrayal has had a profound impact on the shape of the Jewish-Christian worldview. The notion of covenant religion not only gave form to Hebrew religion; the idea of a renewed covenant became the central claim of Christianity. (Remember that another word for covenant is *testament*; hence the popular Old/New Testament split Christianity insists upon.) The idea has even spilled over from synagogues and churches into our national civil religion, where we affirm a belief in "One nation under God" and "In God we trust"—both sentiments rooted in the idea of a covenant.

2. *Ethics.* The Bible is not primarily an ethical treatise; it is a theological one even though it does set out a moral code of behavior both for individuals and society. The Bible has a large number of rules for worship and ritual but its fundamental ethical worldview lies in the idea that humans are created in "the image and likeness of God" (see Genesis 1:26). The more detailed formulation of that link between God and individual and social relationships is contained in the Ten Commandments, which the Bible depicts as being given by God to Moses after the latter brings the people out of the bondage of Egypt and before they reach the Promised Land (see Exodus 20). These commandments, consisting of both prohibitions (against murder, theft, idolatry, etc.) and positive commands (for worship, honoring of parents, etc.), are part of the larger ethical commands of all civilizations. The peculiarly monotheistic parts of the code appear in the first cluster, with the positive command to worship God alone and the prohibition of graven images and their worship.

Ancient Israel's ethics take on a more specific character in the writings of the prophets. The prophet (Hebrew *nabi*) speaks with God's authority. In Hebrew religion the prophet was not primarily concerned with the future (prophet and seer are thus not the same thing) even though the prophets do speak of a coming of peace and justice in the age of the messiah (the Hebrew word *messiah* means "anointed one."). The main prophetic task was to call people back to the observance of the covenant and to warn them about the ways in which they failed that covenant. The great 8th-century prophets who flourished in both the North and the South after the period of the monarchy left a great literature. They insisted that worship of God, for example, in the worship of the temple, was insufficient if that worship did not come from the heart and include love and compassion for others. The prophets were radical critics of social injustice and defenders of the poor. They linked worship with a deep concern for ethics. They envisioned God as a God of all people and insisted on the connection between worship of God and just living.

Prophets were not a hereditary caste in ancient Israel, as the priests were. Prophets were called to preach. In many instances they even resisted that call and expressed reluctance to undertake the prophetic task. The fact that they had an unpopular message explains both why many of them suffered a violent end and why some were reluctant to undertake the task of preaching.

The prophetic element in religion was one of Israel's most enduring contributions to the religious sensibility of the world. The idea that certain people are called directly by God to preach peace and justice in the context of religious faith would continue beyond the biblical period in Judaism and Christianity. It is not accidental, to cite one modern example, that the great civil rights leader Martin Luther King, Jr. (1929–1968) often cited the biblical prophets as exemplars for his own struggle in behalf of African Americans. That King died a violent death in 1968 is an all-too-ready example of how disquieting the prophetic message can be.

3. *Models and types.* Until modern times relatively few Jews or Christians actually read the Bible on an individual basis. Literacy was rare, books expensive, and leisure at a premium. Bibles were read to people most frequently in public gatherings of worship in synagogues or churches. The one time that the New Testament reports Jesus as reading is from a copy of the prophet Isaiah kept in a synagogue (Luke 4:16ff.). The biblical stories were read over the centuries in a familial setting (as at the Jewish Passover) or in formal worship on the Sabbath. The basic point, however, is that for more than three thousand years the stories and (equally important) the persons in these stories have been etched in the Western imagination. The faith of Abraham, the guidance of Moses, the wisdom of Solomon, the sufferings of Job, and the fidelity of Ruth have become proverbial in our culture.

These events and stories from the Bible are models of instruction and illumination; they have taken on a meaning far beyond their original significance. The events described in the book of Exodus, for example, are often invoked to justify a desire for freedom from oppression and slavery. It is not accidental that Benjamin Franklin suggested depicting the crossing of the reed sea (not the Red Sea as is often said) by the Children of Israel as the centerpiece of the Great Seal of the United States. Long before Franklin's day, the Pilgrims saw themselves as the new Children of Israel who had fled the oppression of Europe (read: Egypt) to find freedom in the land "flowing with milk and honey" that was America. At a later period in history the enslaved blacks of this country saw themselves as the oppressed Israelites in bondage. The desire of African Americans for freedom was couched in the language of the Bible as they sang "Go down, Moses. . . . Tell old Pharaoh: Let my people go!"

No humanities student can ignore the impact of the biblical tradition on our common culture. Our literature echoes it; our art is saturated in it; our social institutions are shaped by it. Writers in the Middle Ages said that all knowledge came from God in the form of two great books: the book of nature and the book called the Bible. We have enlarged that understanding today but, nonetheless, we have absorbed much of the Hebrew scriptures into the very texture of our culture.

The Beginnings of Christianity

The fundamental fact with which to study the life of Jesus is to remember that he was a Jew, born during the reign of the Roman emperor Augustus in the Roman-occupied land of Judaea. What we know about him, apart from a few glancing references in pagan and Jewish literature, comes from the four gospels (*gospel* derives from the Anglo-Saxon word meaning "good news") attributed to Matthew, Mark, Luke, and John. These gospels began to appear more than a generation after the death of Jesus, which probably occurred in A.D. 30. The gospels are religious documents, not biographies, but they contain historical data about Jesus as well as theological reflections about the meaning of his life and the significance of his deeds.

Jesus must also be understood in the light of the Jewish prophetical tradition discussed above. He preached the coming of God's kingdom, which would be a reign of justice and mercy. Israel's enemies would be overcome. Until that kingdom arrived, Jesus insisted on a life of repentance, an abandonment of earthly concerns, love of God and neighbor, compassion for the poor, downcast, and marginalized, and set forth his own life as an example. His identification with the poor and powerless antagonized his enemies—who included the leaders of his own religion and the governing authorities of the ruling Romans. Perhaps the most characteristic expression of the teachings of Jesus is

EAST MEETS WEST

Mithraism

About a hundred years before the time of Christ a new religious deity began to be worshiped in the Roman Empire. Brought from Persia (modern Iran), the divinity was Mithra, a god who had been worshiped in Persia for centuries although the cult of Mithra probably came into Persia itself from India.

Mithra was identified with the sun (like the Greek god Apollo) and his birthday was celebrated on December 25th—just after the winter solstice, when the sun was "reborn" for another year. The Christian decision to celebrate the birth of Christ on that date was probably a strategy to combat Mithra worship.

The cult of Mithra had a strong appeal for the Roman military, who saw in the warrior figure killing a bull a model for their own life of masculine achievement. Archaeologists have found sites of Mithra worship (a *Mithraeum*) all over the Roman Empire from the eastern Mediterranean to Italy and as far north as England and in what is present-day Hungary (ancient Pannonia).

Because the worship of Mithra was open only to those who had been initiated into its rites (a so-called mystery religion, it revealed mysteries concerning the gods) we do not have firm evidence concerning its ceremonies and their meaning. The rites did include the sacrifice of bulls, symbolic bathing, and communal meals. Because the rites of Mithra were connected with the signs of the Zodiac it is believed that the ceremonies were meant to act out a symbolic ascent into the heavens, where the devotees were freed from the bonds of fate and the influence of the stars.

Mithraism was a competitor of Christianity for the allegiance of the Romans. The cult died out in the 4th century under the pressure of an increasingly Christianized empire. While this Oriental religion had a wide appeal in the Roman period, it was hampered by its unremittingly masculine aspect. It did not permit women to be initiated into its mysteries. Nonetheless, its superficial resemblance to Christianity (a dying and reborn god; a kind of baptism; a ceremonial meal, and so on) made it a prime target for Christian polemicists who saw it as a demonic parody of their own religion. In many places churches were built over the remains of the sites of a Mithraeum as a symbol of the Christian victory over this pagan religion.

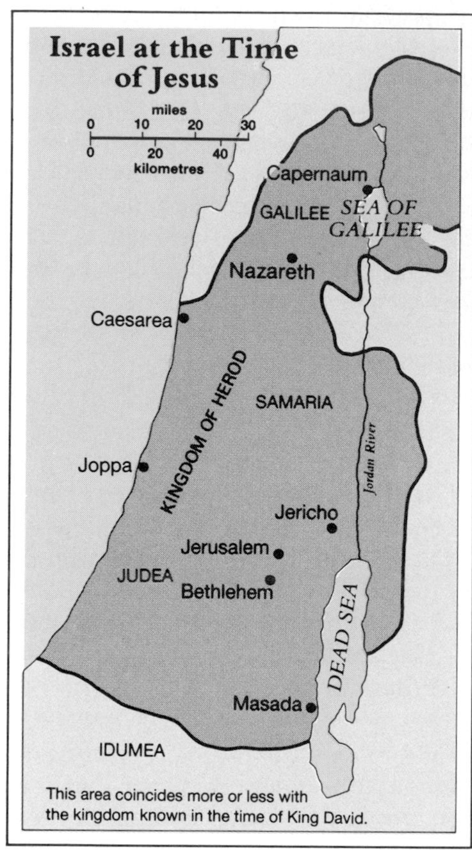

This area coincides more or less with the kingdom known in the time of King David.

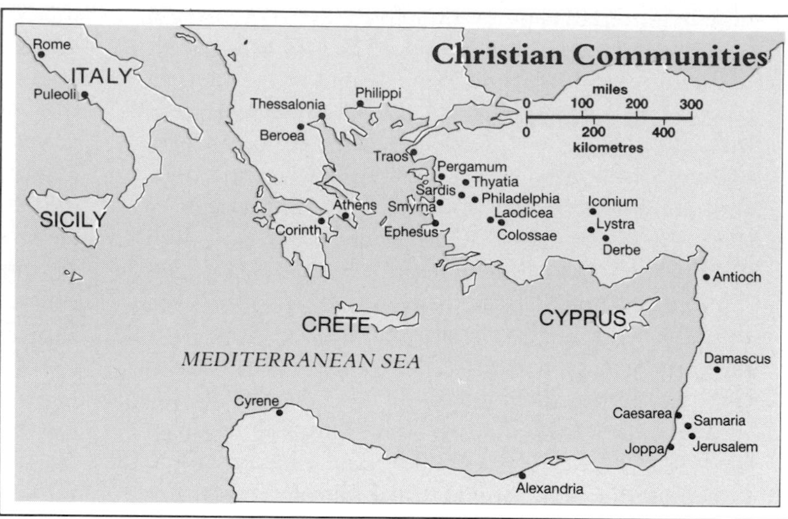

to be found in his parables and in the moral code he expressed in what is variously called The Beatitudes or The Sermon on the Mount.

All of the teachings of Jesus reflect a profound grasp of the piety and wisdom of the Jewish traditions, but the Gospels make a further claim for Jesus, depicting him as the *Christ* (a Greek translation of the Hebrew *messiah,* "anointed one")—the savior promised by the ancient biblical prophets who would bring about God's kingdom. His tragic death by crucifixion (a punishment so degrading that it could not be inflicted on Roman citizens) would seem to have ended the public career of Jesus. The early Christian church, however, insisted that Jesus overcame death by rising from the tomb three days after his death. This belief in the resurrection became a centerpiece of Christian faith and preaching and the basis on which early Christianity proclaimed Jesus as Christ.

Christianity Spreads

The slow growth of the Christian movement was given an early boost by the conversion of a Jewish zealot, Saul of Tarsus, around the year A.D. 35 near Damascus, Syria. Paul (his post-conversion name)

Table 5.1 Books of the Old and New Testaments

Genesis
Exodus
Leviticus
Numbers
Deuteronomy
Joshua
Judges
Ruth
I and II Samuel
I and II Kings
I and II Chronicles
Ezra
Nehemiah
Esther
Job
Psalms
Proverbs
Ecclesiastes
Song of Solomon
Isaiah
Jeremiah
Lamentations
Ezekiel
Daniel
Hosea
Joel
Amos
Obadiah
Jonah
Micah
Nahum
Habakkuk
Zephaniah
Haggai
Zechariah
Malachi

The Gospels:
- Matthew
- Mark
- Luke
- John

The Acts of the Apostles

The Letters of Paul:
- Romans
- I Corinthians
- II Corinthians
- Galatians
- Ephesians
- Philippians
- Colossians
- I Thessalonians
- II Thessalonians
- I Timothy
- II Timothy
- Titus
- Philemon
- Hebrews

The Letters of:
- James
- I Peter
- II Peter
- I John
- II John
- III John
- Jude

The Book of Revelation
(also called *The Apocalypse*)

won a crucial battle in the early Christian church, insisting that non-Jewish converts to the movement would not have to adhere to all Jewish religious customs, especially male circumcision. Paul's victory was to change Christianity from a religious movement within Judaism to a religious tradition that could embrace the non-Jewish world of the Roman Empire. One dramatic example of Paul's approach to this pagan world was a public sermon he gave in the city of Athens in which he used the language of Greek culture to speak to the Athenians with the message of the Christian movement (see Acts 17:16–34).

Paul was a tireless missionary. He made at least three long journeys through the cities on the northern shore of the Mediterranean (and may once have gotten as far as Spain). On his final journey he reached Rome itself, where he met his death at the hands of a Roman executioner around the year A.D. 62. In many of the cities he visited he left small communities of believers. Some of his letters (to the Romans, Galatians, Corinthians, and so on) are addressed to believers in these places and provide details of his theological and pastoral concerns.

By the end of the 1st century communities of Christian believers existed in most of the cities of the vast Roman Empire. Their numbers were sufficient enough that by A.D. 64 the emperor Nero could make Christians scapegoats for a fire that destroyed the city of Rome (probably set by the emperor's own agents). The Roman writer Tacitus provides a vivid description of the terrible tortures meted out against the Christians:

> . . . Nero charged, and viciously punished, people called Christians who were despised on account of their wicked practices. The founder of the sect, Christus, was executed by the procurator Pontius Pilate during the reign of Tiberius. The evil superstition was suppressed for a time but soon broke out afresh not only in Judea where it started but also in Rome where every filthy outrage arrives and prospers. First, those who confessed were seized and then, on their witness, a huge number was convicted, less for arson than for their hatred of the human race.
>
> In their death they were mocked. Some were sewn in animal skins and worried to death by dogs; others were crucified or burned so that, when daylight was over, they could serve as torches in the evening. Nero provided his own gardens for this show and made it into a circus. He mingled with the crowd dressed as a charioteer or posed in his chariot. As a result, the sufferers guilty and worthy of punishment although they were, did arouse the pity of the mob who saw their suffering resulted from the viciousness of one man and not because of some need for the common good. [*Annales* xv]

Two questions arise at this point: Why were the Christians successful in spreading their religion? Why did they become the object of persecution at the hands of the Romans?

A number of social factors aided the growth of Christianity: There was peace in the Roman Empire; a good system of safe roads made travel easy; there was a common language in the empire (a form of common Greek called *koine:* the language of the New Testament) and Christianity was first preached in a network of Jewish centers. Scholars have also offered some religious reasons: the growing interest of pagans in monotheism; the strong Christian emphasis on salvation and freedom from sin; the Christian custom of offering mutual aid and charity for its members; and its relative freedom from class distinctions. Paul wrote that in this faith there was "neither Jew nor Gentile; male nor female; slave or free person."

This new religion met a good deal of resistance. The first martyrs died before the movement spread outside Jerusalem because of the resistance of the Jewish establishment. Very quickly, too, the Christians gained the enmity of the Romans. Even before Nero's persecution in 64, the Christians had been expelled from the city of Rome by the emperor Claudius. From those early days until the 3rd century there were sporadic outbreaks of persecutions. In 250 under the emperor Decius there was an empire-wide persecution, with two others coming in 257 (under Valerian) and under Diocletian in 303. Finally, in 312 the emperor Constantine issued a decree in Milan allowing Christianity toleration as a religion.

What was the basis for this long history of persecution?

The reasons are complex. Ordinarily, Rome had no interest in the religious beliefs of its subjects as long as these beliefs did not threaten public order. The Christian communities seemed secretive; they had their own network of communication in the empire; they kept away from active life in the political realm; most telling of all, they refused to pay homage to the state gods and goddesses. A common charge made against them was that they were atheists: They denied the existence of the Roman gods. Romans conceived of their society as bound together in a seamless web of *pietas,* a virtue that meant a combination of love and reverential fear. The Romans felt that one should express *pietas* to the parents of a family; the family should express that *pietas* toward the state, and the state in turn owed *pietas* to the gods. That brought everything into harmony, and the state would flourish. The Christian refusal to express *pietas* to the gods

SPORTS AND GAMES

Sport as Metaphor

Apart from an allusion to a wrestling match turned violent in the Old Testament (II Samuel 2:12–17) there is little mention of sports in the Bible in any direct manner. What is striking, however, is the number of times Saint Paul, in his New Testament letters, makes reference to sporting events to drive home a religious point. What is obvious from these references is that Paul was quite familiar with the athletics practiced in the Roman world of the Mediterranean basin.

In Paul's letter to the church at Corinth, in fact, Paul mixes his athletic metaphors when he speaks of the Christian life. He notes that many race but only one receives first prize and encourages the Corinthian Christians to train to win, not a perishable, but an imperishable award. He then adds a personal note which invokes not only running but boxing: "I do not run aimlessly, I do not box as one beating the air but I pommel my body and subdue it, lest after preaching to others, I myself should be disqualified" (I Cor. 9:26). Paul uses that same mixture of metaphors in describing his own career as a missionary: "I have fought the good fight, I have finished the race, I have kept the faith" (II Tim. 4:7).

There is a little clue in a speech of Paul (Acts 24:16) that may explain his frequent use of athletic metaphors. He speaks of exercising himself; the Greek word *askein* meant training or exercise in an athletic sense. Paul may well have used the terminology of sport to speak of the rigor and discipline needed to be a Christian since his religion was a subject for persecution.

It is also interesting that from the Greek word *askein* there came the religious word *asceticism* which means the practices of self-control and self-denial which mark the dedicated religious. It was quite common in the early centuries for people to call the ascetic monks of the desert athletes for Christ. Thus the borrowed language of sport became part of the standard vocabulary of biblical and post-biblical Christianity.

seemed to the Romans to strike at the heart of civic order. The Christians, in short, were traitors to the state.

Christian writers of the 2nd century tried to answer these charges by insisting that the Christians wished to be good citizens and, in fact, could be. These writers (called *apologists*) wrote about the moral code of Christianity, about their beliefs and the reasons they could not worship the Roman deities. Their radical monotheism, inherited from Judaism, forbade such worship. Furthermore, they protested their roles as ready scapegoats for every ill, real and imagined, in society. The acid-tongued North African Christian writer Tertullian (c. 160–225) provided a sharp statement concerning the Christian grievance about such treatment: "If the Tiber floods its banks or the Nile doesn't flood; if the heavens stand still or the earth shakes, if there is hunger or drought, quickly the cry goes up, 'Christians to the lions!'"

One of the most important of the early Christian apologists was Justin Martyr. Born around A.D. 100 in Palestine, he converted to Christianity and taught, first, at Ephesus, and later in Rome. While in Rome he wrote two lengthy apologies to the emperors asking for toleration and attempting, at the same time, to explain the Christian religion. These early writings are extremely important since they provide a window on early Christian life and Christian attitudes towards both Roman and Jewish culture. Justin's writings, however, did not receive the audience for which he had hoped. In A.D. 165 he was scourged and beheaded in Rome under the anti-Christian laws.

Early Christian Art

Little significant Christian art or architecture dates from before the 4th century because of the illegal status of the Christian church and the clandestine life it was forced to lead. We do have art from the cemeteries of Rome and some other cities that were maintained by the Christian communities. These cemeteries (known as catacombs from the name of one of them, the *coemeterium ad catacumbas*) were the burial places of thousands of Christians. Contrary to romantic notions, these underground galleries, cut from the soft rock known as *tufa,* were never hiding places for Christians during the times of persecution, nor were they secret places for worship. Such ideas derive not from fact but from 19th-century novels. Similarly, only a minuscule number of the tombs contained the bodies of martyrs; none do today, since the martyrs were reburied inside the walls of the city of Rome in the early Middle Ages.

CONTEMPORARY VOICES

Vibia Perpetua

Another day, while we were dining at noonday, we were summoned away to a hearing at the forum. At once, rumors swept the neighborhoods and a huge crowd assembled. We mounted the tribune. The others, when questioned, confessed. Then it was my turn. My father arrived with my infant son and pulled me down saying, "Sacrifice! Have mercy on your child!" The governor Hilarianus, who held judicial power in place of the preconsul Minucius Timianus, chimed in: "Pity your father's old age! Have mercy on your infant child! Perform the imperial rituals for the well-being of the emperor." And I answered, "I will not perform it." Hilarianus: "You are a Christian?" And I answered, "I am a Christian." And as my father still stood by trying to change my mind, Hilarianus ordered him expelled from his sight; he was struck with a rod. I wept for my father's misfortune as if I had been hit myself; I grieved for his old age.

Then the governor read out the sentence: condemned to the beasts of the arena.

Cheerfully, we returned to prison.

Since my child was an infant and accustomed to breast feeding in prison, I sent the deacon Pomponius to my father imploring that my child be returned to me. But my father refused to give the child up. Somehow, through the will of God, the child no longer required the breast nor did my breasts become sore. I was neither tortured with grief over the child or with pain in my breasts.

Excerpt from the narrative of Vibia Perpetua, who was martyred in Carthage in A.D. 203, when she was twenty-two years old. The last line of her narrative, written the day before her death, says simply, "If anyone wishes to write of my outcome, let him do so."

These underground cemeteries are important, however, because they provide us some visual evidence about early Christian beliefs and customs. This artistic material falls into categories:

Frescoes (wall paintings done on fresh plaster). These are found frequently in the catacombs. Most depict biblical subjects that reflect the Christian hope of salvation and eternal life. Thus, for example, common themes like the story of Jonah or the raising of Lazarus from the dead allude to the Christian belief that everyone would be raised at the end of time. Another common motif is the communion meal of Jesus at the Last Supper as an anticipation of the heavenly banquet that awaited all believers in the next life [5.3]. These frescoes herald the beginnings of artistic themes which would continue down through the centuries. In the catacombs of Priscilla in Rome, for example, we find the first known depiction of the Virgin and Child, a subject which would become, in time, commonplace [5.4].

5.3 *Christ Teaching the Apostles.* c. A.D. 300. Wall painting. 1'3" × 4'3" (.38 × 1.3 m). Catacomb of Domitilla, Rome. The beardless Christ and the use of the Roman toga are characteristic. Partially destroyed; the original setting was meant to depict a eucharistic banquet.

5.4 *Virgin and Child.* c. A.D. 250 (?). Wall painting. Cemetery of Priscilla. The figure to the left has been identified as a prophetic figure, perhaps the prophet Isaiah.

5.5 *Good Shepherd.* c. A.D. 300. Marble, height 39" (99 cm). Vatican Museums, Rome. This depiction of Christ is very common in early Christian art, although sculptural examples are rather rare.

5.6 *Jonah Sarcophagus.* 4th century. Limestone. Museo Pio Cristiano, The Vatican. Besides the Jonah cycle there are other biblical scenes: at the top left, the raising of Lazarus; to the right of the sail at top, Moses striking the rock; at the far top right, a shepherd with a sheep.

5.7 *Chi-Rho Monogram.* 9th century A.D. Detail of sarcophagus of Saint Theodorus. Ravenna. The Vatican Museum, Rome. The first letters of Christ's name in Greek are in the center of the Roman military standard. The figure represents the Risen Christ; note the sleeping guards at the tomb under the arms of the cross.

Glass and sculpture. Although sculpture is quite rare before the 4th century, a statue of Christ as Good Shepherd [5.5], unbearded and with clearly classical borrowings, may be dated from this period. The figure repeats a common theme in the catacomb fresco art of the period. More common are the glass disks with gold paper cutouts pressed in them that are found in both Jewish and Christian catacombs as a decorative motif on individual tomb slots. After the period of Constantine carved sarcophagi also became both common and elaborate [5.6], [5.7].

Inscriptions. Each tomb was covered by a slab of marble that was cemented in place. On those slabs would be carved the name and death date of the buried person. Quite frequently, there was also a symbol such as an anchor (for hope) or a dove with an olive branch (peace) for decoration. One of the most common symbols was a fish. The Greek letters that spell out the word *fish* were considered an anagram for the phrase "Jesus Christ, Son of God and Savior" so that the fish symbol became a shorthand way of making that brief confession of faith [5.8].

Dura-Europos

5.8 *Fish and Chalice.* 3rd century. Floor mosaic. Ostia Antica (Rome). This mosaic, and other evidence, led scholars to believe that a house excavated in the Roman port city of Ostia was a house church with a baptistery. The fish was a common symbol of Christ. This is one of the earliest uses of the symbol.

Despite the persecutions of the Christians and the hostility of the Romans to the Jews, the religions managed to coexist and, to a certain extent, to thrive in the Roman Empire. One small indication of this fact can be seen in the spectacular archaeological finds made in the 1930s at a small town in present-day Syria called Dura-Europos. This small Roman garrison town, destroyed by Persian armies in A.D. 256, was covered by desert sands for nearly seventeen hundred years. The scholars who excavated it found a street that ran roughly north and south along the city wall (they called it Wall Street) and contained a Christian house church with some intact frescoes, a temple to a Semitic god called Aphlad, a temple to the god Zeus (Roman Jupiter), a meeting place for the worshipers of the cult of Mithra, and a Jewish synagogue with more than twenty well-preserved fresco paintings of scenes from the Hebrew scriptures [5.9].

The Dura-Europos discoveries revealed both the mingling of many religious cultures and demonstrated that the usual Jewish resistance to the visual arts was not total. Furthermore, the evidence of a building for Christian worship (part of a papyrus of the four gospels harmonized into one whole was found at the site) in place sixty years before Constantine's edict of toleration and in use during

5.9 *The Crossing of the Red Sea.* Fresco. c. A.D. 245. Dura-Europos. National Archaeological Museum, Damascus, Syria. This extraordinary scene shows Moses and Aaron with Egyptian soldiers on their right and the drowning armies on their left. This is part of a huge wall mural depicting scenes from the Hebrew scriptures.

a time when there were empire-wide persecutions of Christians is a significant discovery.

Scholars see in the art of Dura-Europos the mingling of both Eastern and Roman styles that might be the source for the art that would emerge more fully in the Byzantine world. Most significantly, the finds at Dura-Europas demonstrate how complex the religious situation of the time really was and how the neat generalizations of historians do not always correspond to the complicated realities of actual life.

Constantine and Early Christian Architecture

Two of the most famous churches in Christendom are associated with the reign of the emperor Constantine (306–337). The present Saint Peter's

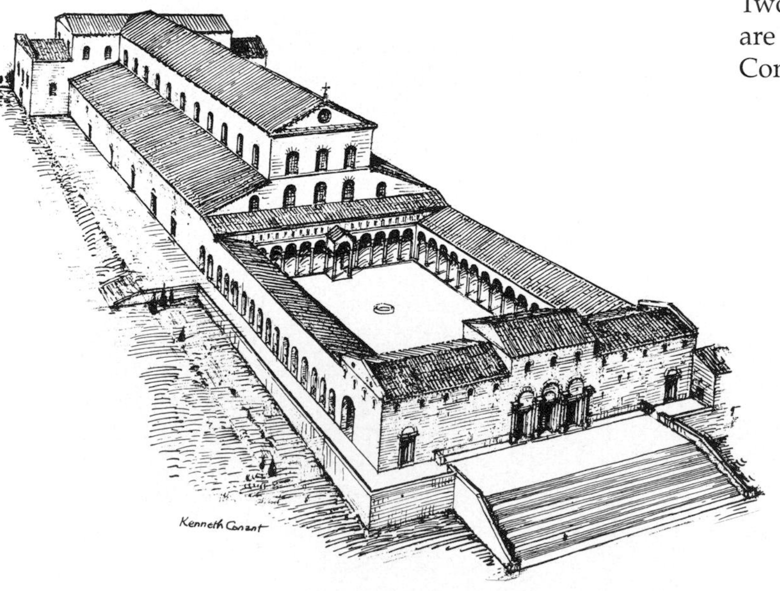

5.10 Old Saint Peter's Basilica. Rome. c. A.D. 333. Length of grand axis 835' (254.5 m), width of transept 295' (86.87 m). Reconstruction study by Kenneth J. Conant. Note the open atrium area and the basilica-style church behind it. The church was demolished in the 16th century when the new basilica was constructed.

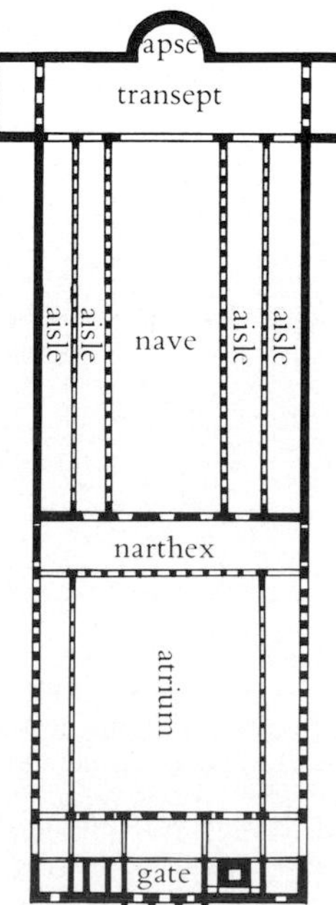

5.11 Floor plan of Old Saint Peter's Basilica.

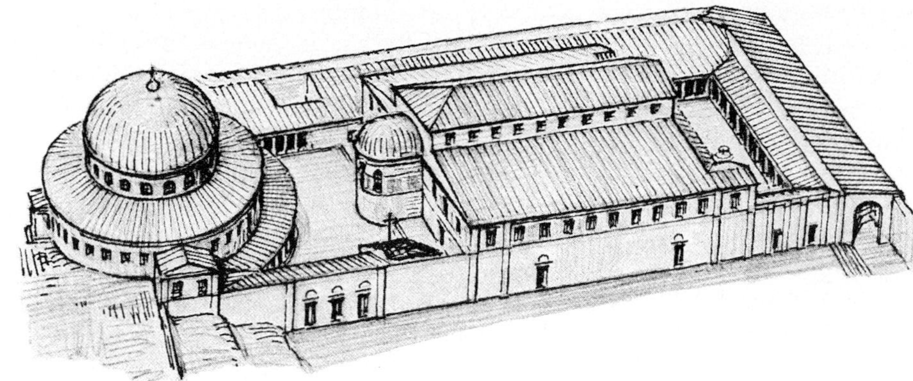

5.12 Church of the Holy Sepulchre, Jerusalem, as it appeared c. A.D. 345. Reconstruction by Kenneth J. Conant. In this drawing, both the domed area which covered the burial place of Christ and the detached basilica in front of it can be seen. In the present church there is no separation between the domed area and the basilica.

Basilica in the Vatican rests on the remains of a basilica built by Constantine and dedicated in A.D. 326. We do not have a fully articulated plan of that church, but its main outlines are clear. The faithful would enter into a courtyard called an *atrium* around which was a colonnaded arcade and from there through a vestibule into the church proper. The basilica, modeled after secular counterparts in Rome, featured a long central *nave* with two parallel side aisles. The nave was intersected at one end by a *transept*, the roof of which was pitched with wooden trusses and supported by the outer walls and the columned interiors. High up on the walls above the arches and below the roof was the so-called *clerestory*, windows that provided most of the interior illumination. This basilica-type church [5.10, 5.11] became a model from which many of the features of later church architecture evolved.

The other famous church built in the Constantinian period is the church of the Holy Sepulchre in Jerusalem [5.12]. This church was also built in the basilica style, its atrium in front of the basilica hall, but with a significant addition. Behind the basilica was a domed structure that covered—it was believed—the rocky place where the body of Christ had been buried for three days. The domelike structure was utilized in Christian architecture as an adaptation of existing domed structures in pagan Rome, most notably the Pantheon and some of the vast baths.

Early Christian Music

If the visual arts of early Christianity turned to Graeco-Roman models for inspiration, the music of the early church drew on Jewish sources. The tradition of singing (or, rather, chanting) sacred texts at religious services was an ancient Jewish custom that appears to go back to Mesopotamian sources. What little we know of Jewish music, in fact, suggests that it was strongly influenced by the various peoples with whom the Jews came into contact. The lyre used by Jewish musicians was a common Mesopotamian instrument, while the harp for which King David was famous came to the Jews from Assyria by way of Egypt [5.13].

By early Christian times Jewish religious services consisted of a standardized series of prayers

5.13 *The Blind Harper of Leiden,* detail from the tomb of Paatenemmheb, Saqqara. c. 1340–1330 B.C. Limestone bas-relief, height 11½" (29 cm). Rijksmuseum van Oudheden, Leiden, Netherlands. It is quite possible that the lyre depicted here is similar to those mentioned in the book of Psalms.

and scriptural readings organized in such a fashion as to create a cycle that fit the Jewish calendar. Many of these readings were taken over by early Christian congregations, particularly those where the number of converted Jews was high. In chanting the psalms the style of execution often depended on how well they were known by the congregation. Where the Jewish component of the congregation was strong the congregation would join in the chant. Increasingly, however, the singing was left to trained choruses with the other congregants joining in only for the standard response of *Amen* or *Alleluia*. As the music fell more into the hands of professionals it became increasingly complex.

This professionalization proved unpopular, however, with church authorities, who feared that the choirs were concerned more with performance than with worship. In 361 a provincial council of the Christian church in Laodicea ordered that there should be only one paid performer (a *cantor*) for each congregation. In Rome, the authorities discouraged poetic elaboration on the liturgical texts, a practice common among the Jews and the Christians of the East.

Part of the early Christian suspicion of music, in the West at least, was a reaction against the Greek doctrine of *ethos* in music, which claimed that music could have a profound effect on human behavior. That music might induce moods of passion or violence or might even be an agreeable sensation in itself was not likely to appeal to a church that required the *ethos* of its music to express religious truth alone. For this reason instrumental music was rejected as unsuitable for the Christian liturgy. Such instrumentation was, in the minds of many Christians, too reminiscent of pagan customs.

By the 4th century, then, the standard form of music in Christian churches was either *responsorial* singing, with a cantor intoning lines from the psalms and the congregation responding with a simple repeated refrain, or *antiphonal* singing, with parts of the congregation (or the cantor and the congregation) alternating verses of a psalm in a simple chant tone. By the beginning of the 5th century there is evidence of nonscriptural hymns being composed. Apart from some rare fragments, we have no illustration of music texts with notation before the 9th century.

SUMMARY

This chapter traces a very long history from the beginnings of the biblical tradition to the emergence of Christianity as a state religion in the Roman Empire, a history so complex that one hesitates to generalize about its shape and significance. Nonetheless, certain points deserve to be highlighted both because they are instructive in their own right and because of their continuing impact on the shape of Western culture.

First, the biblical tradition reflects the emergence of monotheism (a belief in one God) as a leading idea in Western culture. Judaism held the ideal of the uniqueness of God against the polytheistic cultures of Babylonia, Assyria, and Egypt. That idea carried over into Christianity and became a point of conflict with Roman culture. The Roman charge that Christians were atheists meant not that they denied the existence of God but that they rejected the Roman gods.

Second, the entire biblical tradition had a very strong ethical emphasis. The prophets never ceased to argue that the external practice of religion was worthless unless there was a "pure heart." Jesus preached essentially the same thing in his famous criticisms of those who would pray publicly but secretly, in his words, "devour the substance of widows."

This ethic was rooted in the biblical notion of *prophetism*—the belief that people could be called by God to denounce injustice in the face of hostility either from their own religious establishment or from equally hostile civil governments. Such prophetic protest, inspired by the biblical message, was always a factor in subsequent Judaism and Christianity.

Both Judaism and Christianity insisted on a personal God who was actively involved with the world of humanity to the degree that there was a *covenant* between God and people and that the world was created and sustained by God as a gift for humans. This was a powerful doctrine that flew in the face of the ancient belief in impersonal fate controlling the destiny of people or a pessimism about the goodness or reliability of the world as we have it and live in it.

The biblical belief in the providence of God would have an enormous impact on later Western culture in everything from shaping its philosophy of history (that history moves in a linear fashion and has a direction to it) to an optimism about the human capacity to understand the world and make its secrets known for the benefit of people. Western culture never accepted, at least as a majority opinion, that the physical world itself was sacred or an illusion. It was, rather, a gift to be explored and at times exploited.

Finally, the Jewish and Christian tradition produced a work of literature: the Bible. The significance of that production can best be understood in the subsequent chapters of this book. It will soon become clear that a good deal of what the humanistic tradition of art, literature, and music produced until well into the modern period is unintelligible if not seen as an ongoing attempt to interpret that text in various artistic media according to the needs of the age.

Pronunciation Guide

Constantine: CON-stan-tine
catacombs: CAT-ah-combs
covenant: KUV-e-nent
Decius: DAY-see-us
Diocletian: Die-oh-KLE-shun
Dura-Europos: Dew-rah You-ROPE-us
Exodus: X-oh-dus
Laodicea: Lay-oh-de-SEE-ah
Messiah: Mess-EYE-ah
Mithraism: MYTH-rah-is-im
pietas: PEA-ah tas
Torah: TOE-rah
tufa: TOO-fa

Exercises

1. Hebrew religion begins in a patriarchal culture (a tribe headed by a "father") and much of its language derives from that fact. What are the common titles for God that reflect that masculine dominance? Do some feminists have a case in their criticism of the overly patriarchal nature of biblical religion?
2. Biblical religion insists that God has no name and cannot be depicted in art. What do you think were the reasons behind that attitude (almost unique in the ancient world) and what were its cultural consequences?
3. The biblical covenant is summed up in "I will be your God; you will be my people." Can you suggest a short phrase to sum up a marriage covenant? a covenant between citizens and the state? What are the essential characteristics of a covenant?
4. Reread the Ten Commandments. Which of them make sense only to religious believers? Which have general applications? Could you suggest other commandments for inclusion in a modern version?
5. How would you characterize Jesus as a cultural type: teacher? philosopher? prophet? hero? martyr? other?
6. It is said that The Beatitudes are at the heart of the teaching of Jesus. Paraphrase those beatitudes in contemporary language. Which of them sound strangest to our ears?
7. Do you see any lessons about religious tolerance today from the history of the persecution of the Christians in the Roman Empire?
8. Constantine extended the aid of the state to Christians. What are the benefits of state support for religion? What are the problems?
9. In his famous praise of the virtue of love, Paul the Apostle says that love outlives both faith and hope. What kind of love is he talking about? How does love outlive both hope and faith?

Further Reading

Achtemeier, Paul, ed. *Harper's Bible Dictionary.* San Francisco: Harper & Row, 1985. Best one-volume reference work.

Alter, Robert. *The World of Biblical Narrative.* New York: Basic Books, 1992. An excellent work by a literary critic.

Alter, Robert and Frank Kermode. *The Literary Guide to the Bible.* Cambridge: Harvard University Press, 1987. Uneven but useful literary essays on all of the books of the Bible.

Anderson, Bernhard. *Understanding the Old Testament.* Englewood Cliffs: Prentice-Hall, 1975. The standard college-level introduction to the Hebrew scriptures. Many editions.

Freedman, David N., ed. *The Anchor Bible Dictionary.* Garden City: Doubleday, 1992. This six-volume work is a standard reference work.

Frend, W. H. C. *The Rise of Christianity.* Philadelphia: Fortress, 1983. An exhaustive treatment by an outstanding scholar.

Frye, Northrop. *The Great Code: The Bible and Literature.* New York: Harcourt Brace Jovanovich, 1981. A dense but rewarding study of biblical genre and Western literature.

Lane-Fox, Robert. *Pagans and Christians.* New York: Knopf, 1987. A brilliant study of the relationship of Roman culture and the emerging Christian movement in the first four centuries of the common era.

May, Herbert. *Oxford Bible Atlas.* New York: Oxford University Press, 1974. Invaluable for biblical geography.

Milburn, Robert. *Early Christian Art and Architecture.* Berkeley: University of California Press, 1988. Useful survey with many illustrations.

Pelikan, Jaroslav. *Jesus Through the Centuries: His Place in the History of Culture.* New Haven: Yale University Press, 1985. An account of the cultural interpretations of Jesus in Western culture by an eminent scholar.

Pritchard, J. B. *Ancient Near Eastern Texts Relating to the Old Testament.* Princeton: Princeton University Press, 1969. An indispensable collection of texts for biblical study taken from the cultures of those who were in contact with the biblical peoples. A standard reference work.

Weitzmann, Kurt. *Age of Spirituality: Late Antique and Early Christian Art.* New York: Metropolitan Museum of Art, 1979. An exhaustive catalogue based on the definitive exhibit of the roots of Christian art.

Wilken, Robert. *The Christians as the Romans Saw Them.* New Haven: Yale University Press, 1984. A well-written account of the rise of Christianity from the Roman point of view.

Era	Period	Dates	GENERAL EVENTS	LITERATURE & PHILOSOPHY
EARLY CHRISTIAN ERA	Period of Persecution	A.D. 64–313	**250** Persecution of Christians under Decius **286** Diocletian divides Roman Empire into East and West parts ruled by himself and Maximian **305** Abdication of Diocletian and Maximian; Constantius and Galerius rule as joint emperors **307–327** Reign of Constantine	**c. 67** Apostle Paul, bearer of Christian message throughout Mediterranean, martyred at Rome
	Period of Recognition	313–395	**313** Edict of Milan, giving Christians freedom of religion **324** Constantine convenes Council of Nicaea **330** Constantine dedicates new capital of Roman Empire on site of Byzantium, naming it Constantinople **337** Constantine is baptized a Christian on his deathbed **383** Ostrogoths accept Christianity	**c. 350** *Codex Sinaiticus,* earliest extant Greek codex of New Testament **c. 374–404** Saint John Chrysostom active as writer and preacher **c. 386** Saint Jerome translates Bible into Latin
BYZANTINE ERA	Growth of Empire	395–565	**395** Division of Roman Empire begun by Diocletian becomes total separation **4th–5th cent.** Decline of Western Roman Empire **410** Visigoths sack Rome **455** Vandals sack Rome **476** Romulus Augustulus forced to abdicate as last Western Roman emperor; Ostrogoths rule Italy **493–526** Theodoric the Ostrogoth reigns in Italy **527–565** Reign of Justinian as Eastern Roman emperor in Constantinople **532** Nika revolt; civil disorders in Constantinople **c. 533** Justinian codifies Roman Law **540** Belisarius conquers Ostrogoths in Italy for Justinian; Ravenna comes under Byzantine rule	**397** Augustine of Hippo, *The Confessions* **413–426** Augustine of Hippo, *The City of God* **c. 522–524** Boethius, *The Consolation of Philosophy,* allegorical treatise; translation of Aristotle's writings **524** Execution of Boethius by Theodoric the Ostrogoth **c. 562** Procopius, *History of the Wars, The Buildings, Secret History*
	Territorial Decline	565–900	**570** Muhammad born; dies 632 **730–843** Iconoclastic Controversy: ban on religious imagery **800** Pope Leo III crowns first Western Roman emperor (Charlemagne) at Rome since 5th cent.	**c. 620** Qur-an develops
	Second Growth	900–1100	**988–989** Russians accept Christianity **1054** Eastern and Western Church formally split	
	Final Decline	1100–1453	**1204** Crusaders sack Constantinople on way to Holy Land **1453** Constantinople falls to Ottoman Turks, ending Byzantine Empire; Church of Hagia Sophia becomes a mosque	

CHAPTER

6 BYZANTIUM AND THE RISE OF ISLAM

ART	ARCHITECTURE	MUSIC
c. 390 Obelisk of Theodosius erected in Hippodrome at Constantinople	**c. 324** Constantine has stadium in Constantinople enlarged to form Hippodrome **c. 326** Holy Sepulchre, Jerusalem **c. 333** Old Saint Peter's Basilica, Vatican Use of basilica plan and central plan with dome	**after 350** Beginnings of Byzantine music, based probably on Syriac and Hebrew music **386** Saint Ambrose of Milan begins use of vernacular hymns in church
c. 415 Theodosius II moves gilded horses and chariot from Rome to Hippodrome **c. 425** Mosaics at Mausoleum of Galla Placidia, Ravenna **c. 450** Dome mosaic in Orthodox Baptistery, Ravenna   **6th cent.** Art tied to theological doctrine and liturgical practice of Orthodox Church **c. 547** Ivory throne of Archbishop Maximian, given by Justinian for San Vitale **c. 550** Mosaics at Sant' Apollinare Nuovo and San Vitale, Ravenna; *Metamorphosis of Christ,* apse mosaic from Katholikon, Monastery of Saint Catherine, Mount Sinai	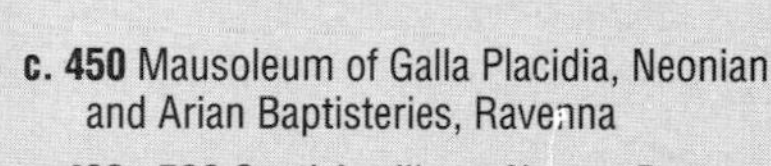 **c. 450** Mausoleum of Galla Placidia, Neonian and Arian Baptisteries, Ravenna **c. 493–526** Sant' Apollinare Nuovo, Ravenna **c. 526–547** San Vitale, Ravenna **526** Theodoric's Tomb, Ravenna **527** Hagia Eirene, Constantinople, begun **532–537** Anthemius of Tralles and Isidore of Miletus rebuild Hagia Sophia, Constantinople, combining basilica plan and central plan with dome **549** Sant' Apollinare in Classe **c. 550** Stephanos, Monastery of Saint Catherine, Mount Sinai 	
730–843 Ban on religious imagery; most earlier pictographic art destroyed		**590–602** Gregorian Chant established at Rome during papacy of Gregory the Great **7th cent.** Golden Age of Byzantine hymnody
Renewal of icon tradition	**1063** Saint Mark's, Venice, begun	**11th cent.** Codification of Greek liturgy; musical modifications decline
12th cent. Mosaics at Palermo, Sicily **c. 1410** Rublev active as painter of icons in Moscow	**c. 1166** Church of the Intercession of the Virgin, near Vladimir, Russia; "onion dome" adapted from central dome	

MAXIMIANVS

CHAPTER

6
BYZANTIUM AND THE RISE OF ISLAM

THE DECLINE OF ROME

BY THE EARLY 4th century the Roman Empire already had severe economic, political, and social problems. In 330 the emperor Constantine dedicated a Greek trading town on the Bosporus as his eastern capital, changing its name from Byzantium to Constantinople. It was to be a New Rome. Constantinople had some obvious advantages for a major city: It straddled the most prominent land route between Asia and Europe. It had a deepwater port with natural shelter. It guarded the passage between the Mediterranean and the Black Sea. The surrounding countryside was rich in forests and water. The neighboring areas of both Europe (Thrace) and Asia (Bithynia) were rich agricultural areas that could supply the city's food needs.

Because of the tumultuous conditions in Rome, the emperors spent less time there. By the beginning of the 5th century (in A.D. 402), the emperor Honorius moved the capital of the Western empire to the northern Italian city of Ravenna on the Adriatic coast. Seventy-four years later, in A.D. 476, the last Roman emperor in the West would die there. Goths would occupy the city; they in turn were defeated by the imperial forces from Constantinople.

In the waning decades of the 4th and 5th centuries Christianity continued to grow and expand in influence. During that period, in far different places, two writers would live who saw the decline of the West: Augustine in Roman North Africa and Boethius in the city of Ravenna. Their writings were to have an enormous impact on the culture of Europe. Each deserves consideration.

LITERATURE AND PHILOSOPHY

Augustine of Hippo

The greatest writer of the Christian Latin West, Augustine of Hippo, was a witness to the decline of Roman power. Born in 354 in North Africa (then part of the Roman provinces), Augustine received a thorough classical education in Africa and in Rome. He was converted to Christianity in Milan and soon afterward returned to his native country, where he was named bishop of Hippo in 390. When the Visigoths sacked Rome in 410, the pagan world was aghast and many blamed the rise of Christianity for this event. Partially as a response to this charge, Augustine wrote *The City of God* as an attempt to show that history had a direction willed by God and that "in the end" all would be made right as the city of man gave way to the city of God. Augustine's work, packed with reflections on scripture, philosophy, and pagan wisdom, is often cited as one of the most influential philosophies of history written in the Western world.

Indeed, it is difficult to overestimate the intellectual impact of Augustine of Hippo on the subsequent cultural history of the West. His influence within Christianity is without parallel. Until Thomas Aquinas in the 13th century, all Christian theologians in the West started from explicitly Augustinian premises. Even Thomas did not shake off his debt to Augustine, although he replaced Augustine's strong Platonic orientation with a more empirical Aristotelian one. Augustine emphasized the absolute majesty of God, the immutability of God's will, and the flawed state of the human condition (notions derived from Saint

Paul). These tenets received a powerful reformulation in the Protestant Reformation by Martin Luther (who as a Catholic friar had lived under the rule of Saint Augustine) and by John Calvin, a profound student of Augustine's theological writings.

Augustine also made a notable impact beyond theology. *The City of God,* begun about 412, was an attempt to formulate a coherent and all-embracing philosophy of history, the first such attempt in the West. For Augustine, history moves on a straight line in a direction from its origin in God until it ends, again in God, at the consummation of history in the Last Judgment. Augustine rejected the older pagan notion that history repeats itself endlessly in cycles. His reading of the Bible convinced him that humanity had an origin, played out its story, and would terminate. The city of man would be judged and the city of God would be saved. Subsequent philosophers of history have secularized this view but, with very few exceptions (Vico, a 17th-century Italian philosopher, was one), have maintained the outlines of Augustine's framework to some extent. "A bright future," "an atomic wasteland of the future," and "classless society" are all statements about the end of history, all statements that echo, however dimly, the worldview of Augustine.

Augustine also invented the genre of self-reflective writing in the West. "I would know myself that I might know Thee," Augustine writes of God in *The Confessions.* Before Augustine's time, memoirs related a life in terms of social, political, or military affairs (as, for example, Caesar's *Gallic Wars* did), but Augustine's intimate self-scrutiny and inquiry into the significance of life were new in Western culture. There would not be another work like *The Confessions* until Petrarch, an indefatigable student of Augustine, wrote his *Letter to Posterity* in the mid-14th century. The Renaissance writers, an extremely self-conscious generation, were devoted students of Augustine's stately Latin prose; even the great later autobiographies of our inherited culture—those of Gibbon, Mill, Newman—are literary and spiritual descendants of Augustine.

Augustine's *The Confessions* is a compelling analysis of his spiritual and intellectual development from his youth until the time of his conversion to Christianity and readiness to return to his native Africa. The title must be understood in a triple sense—a confession of sin, an act of faith in God, and a confession of praise—so it is appropriate that Augustine began his book as a prayer directed to God.

Although strongly autobiographical, *The Confessions* is actually a long meditation by Augustine on the hidden grace of God as his life is shaped toward its appointed end. Augustine "confesses" to God (and the reader) how his early drive for fame as a teacher of rhetoric, his flirtation with the Manichean sect and its belief in gods of evil and good, his liaison with a woman that resulted in the birth of a son, and his restless movement from North Africa to Rome and Milan were all part of a seamless web of circumstance that made up an individual life. Interspersed in the narrative line of his early life are Augustine's reflections on the most basic philosophical and theological questions of the day, always linked to his own experience.

If *The Confessions* can be said to be the beginning of autobiography, beyond that historic importance it is classic and singular in its balance of immense learning, searching speculation, and intense self-scrutiny. It is a work concerned first of all with meaning at the deepest philosophical level, and its full power is evident only to the reader who will take the time to enter Augustine's line of argument.

Boethius

In the twilight period in Ravenna between the death of the last Roman emperor and the arrival of Justinian's troops an important figure who bridged the gap between classical paganism and Christianity lived and died. Anicius Manlius Severinus Boethius was a highly educated Roman who entered the service of the Goth king Theodoric in 522. Imprisoned for reasons that are not clear, Boethius wrote a treatise called *The Consolation of Philosophy* while awaiting execution. Cast as a dialogue between Lady Philosophy and the author on the philosophical and religious basis for human freedom, the work blends the spirit of the Book of Job with Roman stoicism. Attempting to console him for his sad state of disgrace and imprisonment, Lady Philosophy demands that the author avoid self-pity, that he face his troubles with serenity and hope. Insisting that a provident God overcomes all evil, Philosophy insists that blind fate has no control over humanity. She explains that human freedom exists along with an all-knowing God and that good will triumph. Although Christian themes permeate the work, there is no explicit mention of Christian doctrine. What one does sense is the recasting of Roman thought into Christian patterns. In a way, *The Consolation of Philosophy* is one of the last works of the late Roman period. It reflects the elegance of Roman expression, the burgeoning hope of Christianity, and the terrible sadness that must have afflicted any sensitive Roman in this period.

The Consolation of Philosophy was one of the most widely read and influential works of the Middle Ages (Chaucer made an English translation of it from an already-existing French version). Its message of hope and faith was liberally quoted by every major medieval thinker from Thomas Aquinas to Dante Alighieri.

Boethius sets out a basic problem and provides an answer that would become normative Christian thought for subsequent centuries. In *The Consolation* Boethius asks how one can reconcile human freedom with the notion of an all-knowing God. To put it another way: If God knows what we do before we do it, how can we be said to be free agents who must accept responsibility for personal acts? The answer, Boethius insists through Lady Philosophy, is to look at the problem from the point of view of God, not from the human vantage point. God lives in eternity. Eternity does not mean a "long time" with a past and a future. Eternity means "no time": God lives in an eternal moment that for Him is a "now." In that sense God does not "foresee" the future. There is no future for God. God sees everything in one simple moment that is only past, present, and future from the human point of view. Boethius says that God does not exercise *praevidentia* (seeing things before they happen) but *providence* (seeing all things in the simultaneity of their happening). Thus God, in a single eternal, ineffable moment, grasps all activity, which exists for us as a long sequence of events. More specifically, in that moment, God sees our choices, the events that follow from them, and the ultimate consequences of those choices.

The consolation of Boethius, as Lady Philosophy explains it, rests in the fact that people do act with freedom, that they are not in the hands of an indifferent fate, and that the ultimate meaning of life rests with the all-seeing presence of a God, not a blind force. Lady Philosophy sums up her discussion with Boethius by offering him this "consolation." It is her assurance that his life, even while awaiting execution in a prison cell, was not the product of a blind fate or an uncaring force in the universe.

The language of Boethius, with its discussion of time, eternity, free will, and the nature of God, echoes the great philosophical tradition of Plato and Aristotle (Boethius had translated the latter's works) as well as the stoicism of Cicero and the theological reflections of Augustine. It is a fitting end to the intellectual tradition of the late Roman Empire in the West.

THE ASCENDANCY OF BYZANTIUM

The city of Constantinople became the center of imperial life in the early 5th century and reached its highest expression of power in the early 6th century with the ascension of Justinian to the throne in 527. His stated intention was to restore the empire to a state of grandeur. In this project he was aided by his wife Theodora. A former dancer and prostitute, Theodora was a tough-minded and capable woman who added strength and resolve to the grandiose plans of the emperor. She was Justinian's equal, and perhaps more.

The reign of Justinian and Theodora was impressive, if profligate, by any standard. The emperor encouraged Persian monks residing in China to bring back silkworms for the introduction of the silk industry into the West. Because the silk industry of China was a fiercely guarded monopoly, the monks accomplished this rather dangerous mission by smuggling silkworm eggs out of the country in hollow tubes, and within a decade the silk industry in the Western world rivaled that of China.

Justinian also revised and codified Roman law, a gigantic undertaking of scholarship and research. Roman law had evolved over a thousand-year period, and by Justinian's time was a vast jumble of disorganized and often contradictory decisions, decrees, statutes, opinions, and legal codes. Under the aegis of the emperor, a legal scholar named Tribonian produced order out of this chaos. First a *Code* that summarized all imperial decrees from the time of Hadrian (in the 2nd century) to the time of Justinian was published. The Code was followed by the *Pandects* (digest), which synthesized a vast quantity of legal opinion and scholarship from the past. Finally came the *Institutes,* a legal collection broken down into four categories by which the laws concerning persons, things, actions, and personal wrongs (in other words, criminal law) were set forth. The body of this legal revision became the basis for the law courts of the empire and, in later centuries, the basis for the use of Roman law in the West.

Justinian and Theodora were fiercely partisan Christians who took a keen interest in theology and ecclesiastical governance. Justinian's fanatical devotion prompted him to shut down the last surviving Platonic academy in the world on the grounds that its paganism was inimical to the true religion. His own personal life—despite evidences of cruelty and capriciousness—was austere and abstemious, influenced by the presence of so many monks in the city of Constantinople. His generosity to the church was great, with his largess shown most clearly in openhanded patronage of church building. Hagia Sophia, his most famous project, has become legendary for the beauty and opulence of its decoration.

Hagia Sophia: Monument and Symbol

Hagia Sophia (Greek for "Holy Wisdom") was the principal church of Constantinople. It had been destroyed twice, once by fire and—during Justinian's reign—during the terrible civil disorders of the Nika revolt in 532 that devastated most of the European side of the city. Soon afterward Justinian decided to rebuild the church using the plans of two architects, Anthemius of Tralles and Isidore of Miletus. Work began in 532 and the new edifice was solemnly dedicated five years later in the presence of Justinian and Theodora.

The church of Hagia Sophia was a stunning architectural achievement that combined the longitudinal shape of the Roman basilica with a domed central plan. Two centuries earlier Constantine had

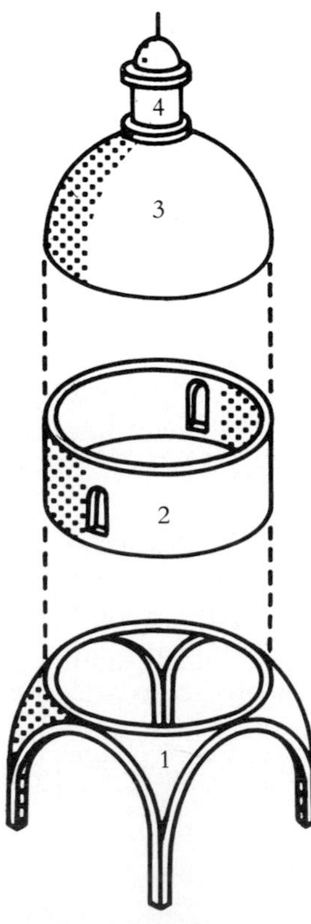

6.1 Dome construction: 1. pendentive; 2. drum; 3. cupola; 4. lantern.

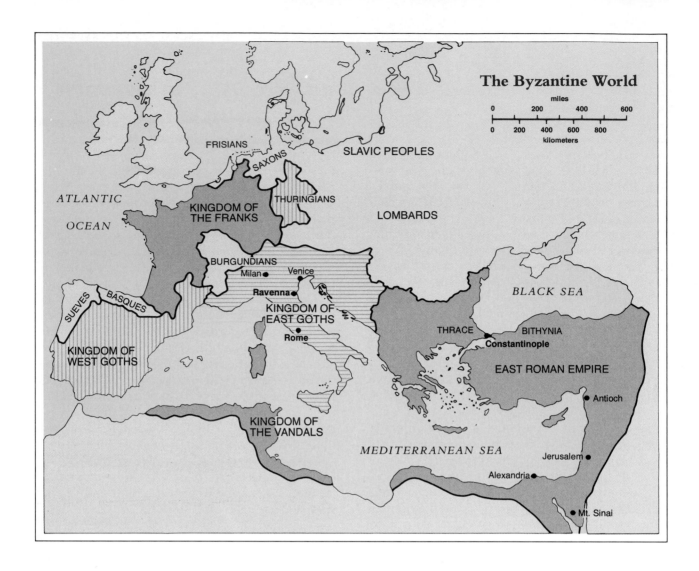

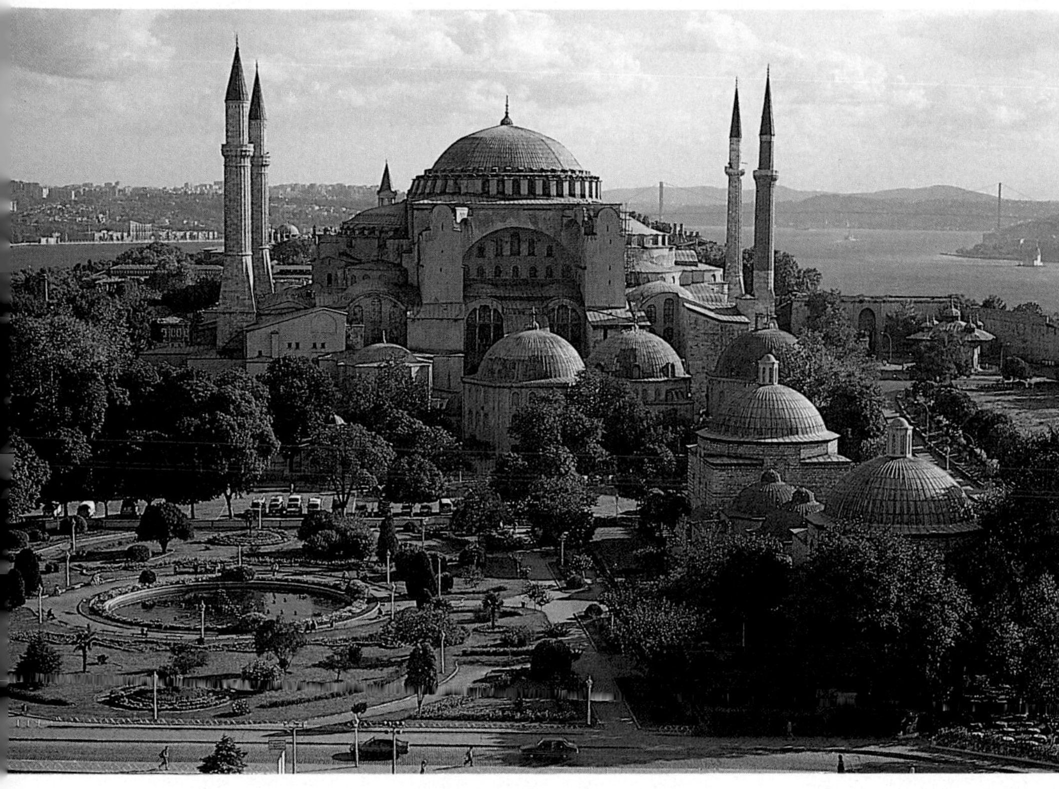

6.2 Anthemius of Tralles and Isidore of Miletus. Hagia Sophia, Constantinople (Istanbul). Exterior view from the southeast. The towers, of Turkish origin, are a later addition.

used both the dome and basilica shapes in the church of the Holy Sepulchre in Jerusalem, as we have seen, but he had not joined them into a unity. In still earlier domed buildings in the Roman world such as the Pantheon and Santa Costanza, the dome rested on a circular drum. This gave the dome solidity but limited its height and expansiveness. Anthemius and Isidore solved this problem by the use of *pendentives* [6.1], triangular masonry devices that carried the weight of the dome on massive piers rather than straight down to the drum. In the church of Hagia Sophia the central dome was abutted by two half-domes so that a person looking down at the building from above might see a nave in the form of an oval instead of a quadrangle [6.2].

The church—184' (55.2 m) high, 41' (12.3 m) higher than the Pantheon—retained a hint of the old basilica style as a result of the columned side aisles and the gallery for female worshipers in the triforium space above the arches of the aisles, but the overwhelming visual impression came from the massive dome. Since the pendentives reduced the weight of the dome, the area between drum and dome could be pierced by forty windows that made the dome seem to hang in space. Light streamed into the church from the windows and refracted off the rich mosaics and colored marbles that covered the interior [6.3].

6.3 Anthemius of Tralles and Isidore of Miletus. Hagia Sophia, Constantinople (Istanbul). An interior view, looking toward the apse, shows how the windows between drum and dome give an impression of floating lightness that continues down to the floor.

CONTEMPORARY VOICES

Procopius of Caesarea

The whole ceiling is overlaid with pure gold . . . yet the light reflecting from the stones [of the mosaics] prevails, shining out of rivalry with the gold. There are two colonnades, one on each side, not separated in any way from the church itself. . . . They have vaulted ceilings and are decorated with gold. One of these is designated for men-worshipers and the other for women but they have nothing to distinguish them nor do they differ in any way. Their very equality serves to beautify the church and their similarity to adorn it.

Who can recount the beauty of the columns and the stones with which the church is decorated? One might imagine that he had come upon a meadow with its flowers in full bloom. For he would surely marvel at the purple of some, the green tint of others, and at those from which the white flashes, and again, at those which Nature, like some painter, varies with contrasting colors.

And whenever anyone enters this church to pray . . . his mind is lifted up toward God and is exalted, feeling that He cannot be very far away, but must especially love to dwell in this place which He has favored. And this does not happen only to one who sees the church for the first time, but the same experience comes to him on each successive occasion, as though the sight were new each time. Of this spectacle no one ever has a surfeit, but when present in the church people rejoice in what they see, and when they depart they take enormous delight in talking about it.

[Procopius of Caesarea, The Buildings, Book 1.1. Procopius was in the service of the emperor Justinian. His *Secret History* was a bitterly critical portrait of the emperor and the empress.]

Light, in fact, was a key theoretical element behind the entire conception of Hagia Sophia. Light is the symbol of divine wisdom in the philosophy of Plato and in the New Testament. A common metaphor in pagan and biblical wisdom had the sun and its rays represent the eternity of God and his illumination of mortals. The suffusion of light was an element in the Hagia Sophia that went far beyond the functional need to illuminate the interior of the church. Light refracting in the church created a spiritual ambiance analogous to that of heaven, where the faithful would be bathed in the actual light of God.

The sequence of the various parts of the worship service at Constantinople—the *liturgy*—was developed from the inspiration of Saint John Chrysostom (345–407), patriarch of the city in the century before Justinian. The official liturgy of Byzantine Christianity is still the Divine Liturgy of Saint John Chrysostom, modified and added to over the centuries. In that liturgy, the worshiping community visualized itself as standing in the forecourt of heaven when it worshiped in the church. Amid the swirling incense, the glittering light, and the stately chants of the clergy and people comes a sense of participation with the household of heaven standing before God. A fragment from the liturgy—added during the reign of Justinian's successor Justin II (565–578)—underscores the point dramatically. Note the characteristic cry of *Wisdom!* and the description of the congregation as mystically present in heaven:

> PRIEST Wisdom! That ever being guarded by Thy power, we may give glory to Thee, Father, Son, and Holy Spirit, now and forevermore.
>
> CONGREGATION Amen. Let us here who represent the mystic Cherubim in singing the thrice holy hymn to the life-giving Trinity now lay aside every earthly care so that we may welcome the King of the universe who comes escorted by invisible armies of angels. Alleluia. Alleluia. Alleluia.

Hagia Sophia was enriched by subsequent emperors, and after repairs were made to the dome in 989 new mosaics were added to the church. After the fall of Constantinople in 1453 the Turks turned the church into a mosque; the mosaics were whitewashed or plastered over since the Qur-an prohibited the use of images. When the mosque was converted to a museum by the modern Turkish state, some of the mosaics were uncovered, so today we can get some sense of the splendor of the original interior.

Other monuments bear the mark of Justinian's creative efforts. His church of the Holy Apostles, built on the site of an earlier church of the same name destroyed by an earthquake, did not survive the fall of the city in 1453 but did serve as a model for the church of Saint Mark in Venice. Near the church of the Hagia Sophia is the church of *Hagia Eirene* (Holy Peace), now a mosque, whose architecture also shows the combination of basilica and dome. The church, dedicated to the martyr saints Sergius and Bacchus and begun in 527, was a pre-

6.4 The so-called Mausoleum of Galla Placidia, Ravenna. Early 5th century. This building has sunk more than a meter (c. 4') into the marshy soil, thus making it seem rather squat in appearance.

liminary study for the later Hagia Sophia. In all, Justinian built more than twenty-five churches and convents in Constantinople. His program of secular architecture included an impressive water conduit system that still exists.

RAVENNA

Art and Architecture

Ravenna is a repository of monuments that reflect its late Roman, barbarian Gothic, and Byzantine history. The mausoleum (burial chapel) of Galla Placidia (who reigned as regent from 430 to 450) was built at the end of the Roman period of Ravenna's history [6.4]. Once thought to be the tomb of the empress (hence its name), it is more likely a votive chapel to Saint Lawrence originally attached to the nearby church of the Holy Cross. The huge sarcophagi in the building are probably medieval. This small chapel in the shape of a cross, very plain on the outside, shows the architectural tendency to combine the basilica-style nave with the structure of a dome (it even uses a modified pendentive form) used later in monumental structures like Hagia Sophia.

The importance of Galla Placidia rests in the complete and breathtakingly beautiful mosaics that decorate the walls and ceiling. The north niche, just above the entrance, has a *lunette* (a small arched space) mosaic depicting Christ as the Good Shepherd [6.5]. Clothed in royal purple and with a gold staff in his hand, the figure of Christ has a courtly, almost languid elegance that refines the more rustic depictions of the Good Shepherd theme in earlier Roman Christian art. The vaulting of both the *apse* (the altar end of the church) and the dome is covered with a deep blue mosaic interspersed with stylized sunbursts and stars in gold. This "Persian rug" motif symbolized the heavens, the dwelling place of God. Since the *tesserae,* the small cubes that

6.5 *The Good Shepherd* from the mausoleum of Galla Placidia, Ravenna. 5th century. Mosaic. The "Persian rug" motif can be seen in the vault. Note the beardless Christ dressed in a Roman toga.

6.6 ***The Martyrdom of Saint Lawrence,*** **from the mausoleum of Galla Placidia, Ravenna. 5th century. Mosaic. The window, a modern one, is made of alabaster. Saint Lawrence, with the gridiron on which legend said he was roasted, is at the lower right.**

6.7 Ceiling mosaic of the Orthodox Baptistery, Ravenna. Mid-5th century.

make up the mosaic, are not set fully flush in the wall, the surfaces of the mosaic are irregular. These surfaces thus refract and break up the light in the chapel, especially from flickering lamps and candles. (The translucent alabaster windows now in the chapel were installed in the 20th century.)

Opposite the lunette of the Good Shepherd is another lunette that depicts the deacon martyr of the Roman Church, Saint Lawrence, who stands next to the gridiron that was the instrument of his death. Beyond the gridiron is an open cabinet containing codices of the four gospels [6.6]. The spaces above these mosaics are filled with figures of the apostles. Between these are symbols of the search for religious understanding—deer, doves, fountains. In the arches, more spectacular and often overlooked are the abstract interlocking designs with their brightness and *trompe l'œil* (trick-the-eye) quality.

The two baptisteries of Ravenna represent a major religious division of the time between the Orthodox Christians, who accepted the divinity of Christ, and the Arian Christians, who did not. The Neonian Baptistery, built by Orthodox Christians in the early 5th century next to the ancient cathedral of the city, is octagonal—as were most baptisteries, because of their derivation from Roman bathhouses. The ceiling mosaic, directly over the baptismal pool, is particularly striking. The lower register of the mosaic, above the windows, shows floral designs based on common Roman decorative motifs. Just above are a circle of empty thrones interspersed with altars with biblical codices open on them [6.7]. In the band above are the apostles, who seem to be walking in a stately procession around the circle of the dome. In the central disc is a mosaic of the baptism of Christ by John the Baptist in the Jordan River. The spirit of the river is depicted as Neptune.

The mosaic ensemble in the ceiling was designed to reflect the beliefs of the participants in the ceremonies below. The circling apostles reminded the candidates for baptism that the church was founded on the apostles; the convert's baptism was a promise that one day he or she would dwell with the apostles in heaven. Finally, the codices on the altars taught of the sources of their belief, while the empty thrones promised the new Christians a place in the heavenly Jerusalem. The art, then, was not merely decorative but, in the words of a modern Orthodox thinker, "theology in color."

The Arian Baptistery, built by the Goths toward the end of the 5th century, is much more severely decorated. Again the traditional scene of Christ's baptism is in the central disc of the ceiling mosaic.

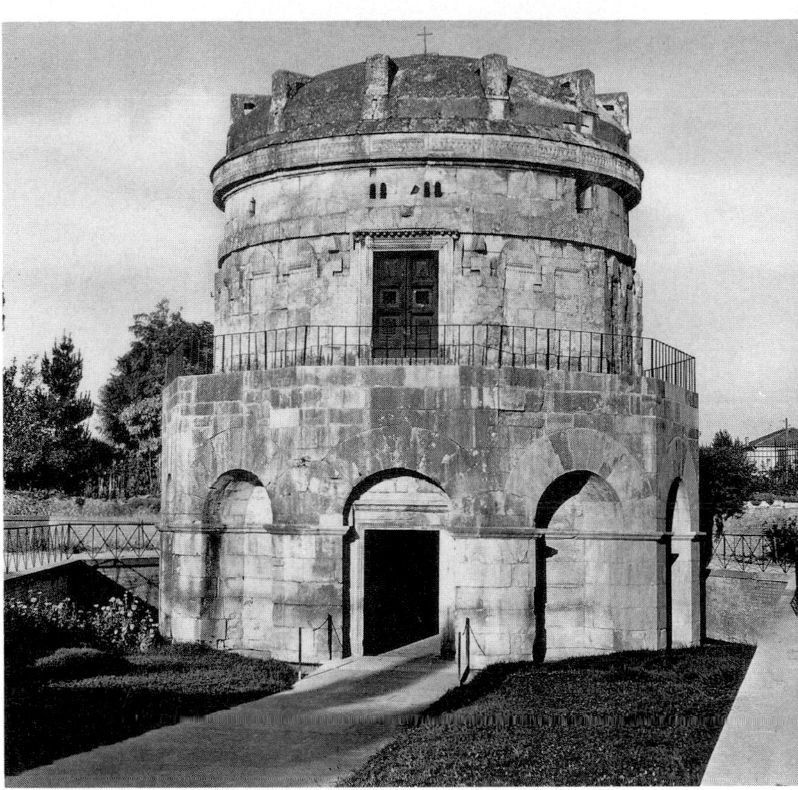

6.8 Tomb of Theodoric, Ravenna. Early 6th century. The cap of the mausoleum is a huge stone that measures 36' × 10' (11 × 3 m). The great porphyry tomb inside the mausoleum was pillaged in the early Middle Ages.

Here the figure of the River Jordan has lobster-like claws sprouting from his head—a curiously pagan marine touch. The twelve apostles in the lower register are divided into two groups, one led by Peter and the other by Paul. These two groups converge at a throne bearing a jeweled cross (the crucifix with the body of Christ on the cross is very uncommon in this period) that represents in a single symbol the passion and the resurrection of Christ.

Theodoric, the emperor of the Goths who had executed Boethius and reigned from 493 to 526, was buried in a massive mausoleum that may still be seen on the outskirts of Ravenna [6.8]. The most famous extant monument of Theodoric's reign aside from his mausoleum is the church of Sant' Apollinare Nuovo, originally called the Church of the Redeemer, the palace church of Theodoric. This church is constructed in the severe basilica style: a wide nave with two side aisles partitioned off from the nave by double columns of marble. The apse decorations have been destroyed, but the walls of the basilica, richly ornamented with mosaics, can be seen. The mosaics, however, are of two different dates and reflect in one building both the Roman and Byzantine styles of art. On each side of the

6.9 South wall mosaic, Sant' Apollinare Nuovo, Ravenna. Early 6th century. The procession of male saints is in the lower register. The prophets and apostles are placed between the windows. Scenes from the gospels are in the upper register. Detail appears in Figure 6.11.

6.10 North-wall mosaic, Sant' Apollinare Nuovo, Ravenna. Early 6th century. Note the procession of female saints oriented behind the Three Magi, who all approach the enthroned Madonna. Details appear in Figures 6.12 and 6.13.

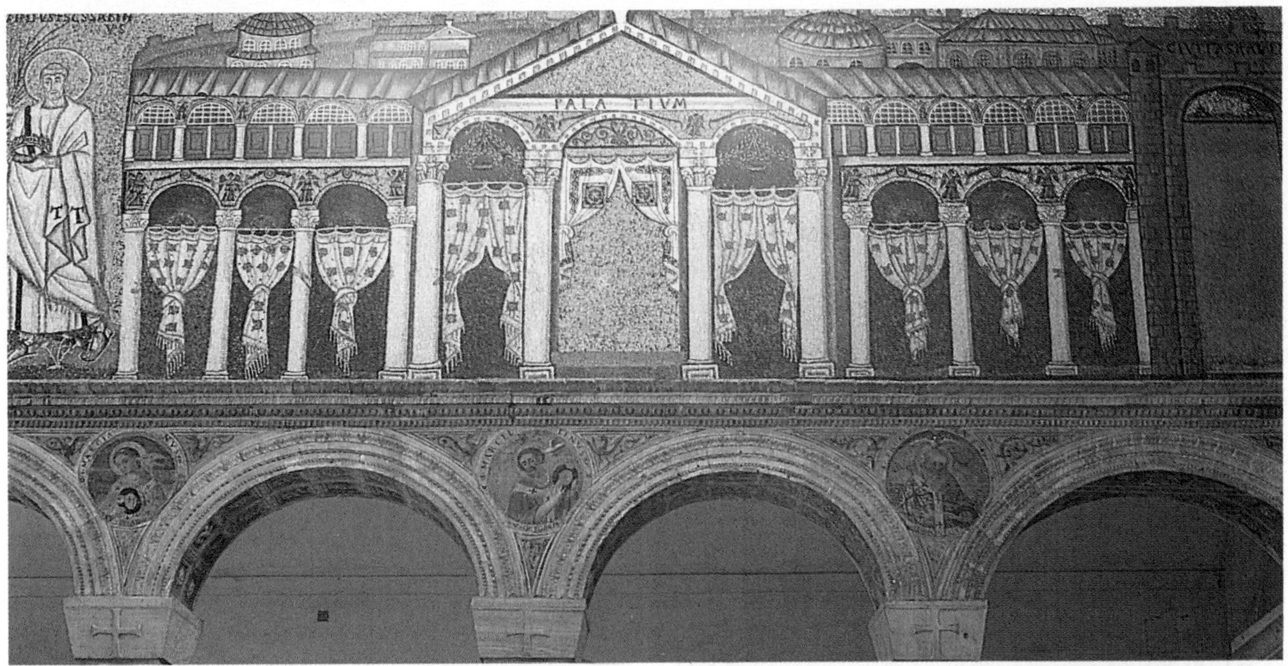

6.11 Theodoric's palace; detail of south wall mosaic, Sant' Apollinare Nuovo, Ravenna.

aisles, in the spaces just above the aisle arches, are processions of male and female saints, each procession facing toward the apse and main altar [6.9]. They move to an enthroned Christ on one side and toward a Madonna and Child on the other. These mosaics were added to the church when the building passed from the Goths into Byzantine hands in the reign of Justinian. The depiction of Theodoric's palace [6.10], in fact, still shows evidence of Orthodox censorship. In the arched spaces one can still see traces of halos of now-excised Arian saints (or perhaps members of Theodoric's court). On several columns of the mosaic can be seen the hands of figures that have now been replaced by decorative twisted draperies. The next register above has a line of prophetic figures. At the level of the clerestory windows are scenes from the New Testament—the miracles of Christ on one side [6.11–6.13] and scenes from his passion on the other. These mosaics are very different in style from the procession of sainted martyrs on the lower level. The gospel sequence is more Roman in

6.12 Jesus calls the apostles Peter and Andrew. North wall upper-register mosaic, Sant' Apollinare Nuovo, Ravenna. Note the Christ figure in the royal purple toga and his beardless appearance.

6.13 The Magi bearing gifts; detail of north wall mosaic, Sant' Apollinare Nuovo, Ravenna. Christian legend had already named these figures Balthasar, Melchior, and Caspar, which names can be seen inscribed on the mosaic. Bishop Apollinaris was a 2nd-century apologist for Christianity who defended his faith in a treatise addressed to the emperor, Marcus Aurelius.

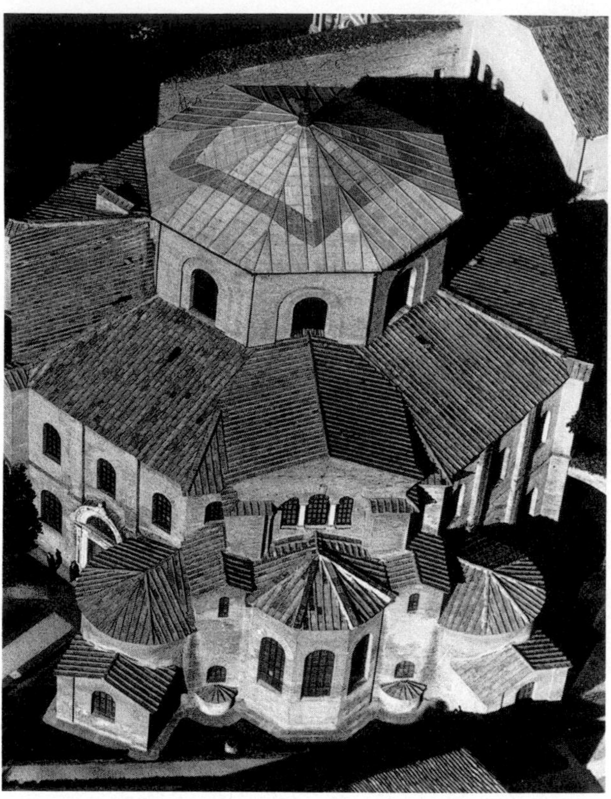

6.14 San Vitale, Ravenna. c. 530–548. Aerial view. This complex building, the inspiration for Charlemagne's church at Aachen, gives little exterior evidence that it is done in the basilica style.

inspiration, more severe and simple. Certain themes of earlier Roman Christian iconography are evident. The procession of saints, most likely erected by artists from a Constantinople studio, is much more lush, reverent, and static in tone. The Orientalizing element is especially noteworthy in the depiction of the Three Magi (with their Phrygian caps) who offer gifts to the Christ Child.

The church of San Vitale most clearly testifies to the presence of Justinian in Ravenna [6.14]. Dedicated by Bishop Maximian in 547, it had been begun by Bishop Ecclesius in 526, the year Justinian came to the throne, while the Goths still ruled Ravenna. The church is octagonal, with only the barest hint of basilica length. How different it is may be seen by comparing it with Sant' Apollinare in Classe (the ancient seaport of Ravenna), built at roughly the same time [6.15]. The octagon has another octagon within it. This interior octagon, supported by columned arches and containing a second-story women's gallery, is the structural basis for the dome. The dome is supported on the octagonal walls by small vaults called *squinches* that cut across the angles of each part of the octagon.

The most arresting characteristic of San Vitale, apart from its intricate and not fully understood architectural design, is its stunning program of mosaics. In the apse is a great mosaic of Christ the Pantocrator, the one who sustains all things in his

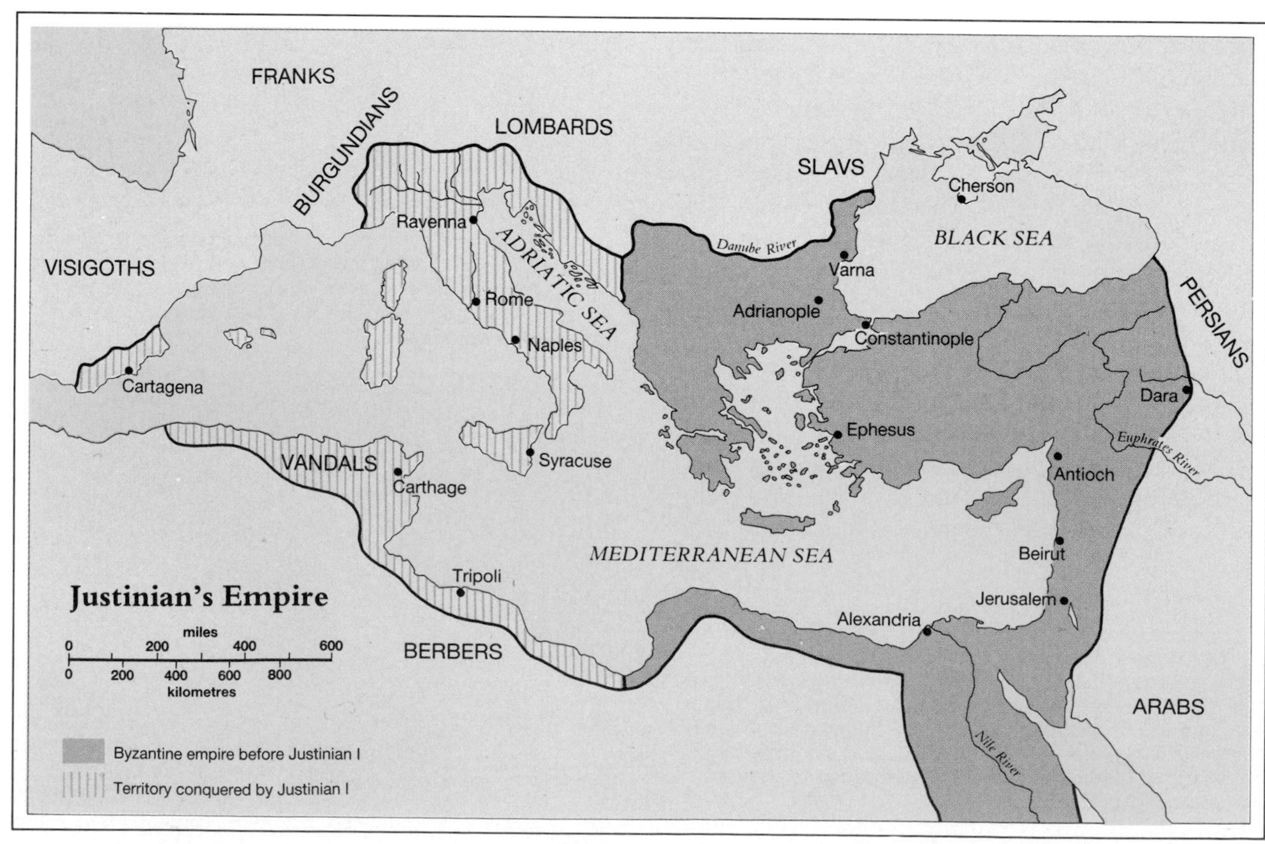

6.15 Sant' Apollinare in Classe, Ravenna. c. 549. The tower is a medieval addition. The clear outlines of the basilica style, with its side aisles, can be clearly seen in this photograph.

hands [6.16]. Christ is portrayed as a beardless young man, clothed in royal purple. He holds in his left hand a book with seven seals (a reference to the book of Revelation) and offers the crown of martyrdom to Saint Vitalis with his right. Flanked by the two archangels, Christ is offered a model of the church by the bishop, Ecclesius, who laid its foundations. Above the figures are symbolic representations of the four rivers of paradise.

Mosaics to the left and right of the apse mosaic represent the royal couple as regents of Christ on earth. On the left wall of the sanctuary is a mosaic depicting Justinian and his attendants [6.17]. It is

6.16 Christ enthroned, with Saint Vitalis and Bishop Ecclesius, ceiling mosaic, San Vitale, Ravenna. c. 530. The bishop holds a model of the church at the extreme right while Christ hands the crown of martyrdom to the saint on the left.

6.17 Emperor Justinian and courtiers, wall mosaic, San Vitale, Ravenna. c. 547. The church authorities stand at the emperor's left; the civil authorities at the right.

6.18 Empress Theodora and retinue, wall mosaic, San Vitale, Ravenna. c. 547. Note the Three Magi on the hem of the empress' gown.

6.19 Empress Theodora; detail of figure 6.18, San Vitale, Ravenna, c. 547. Note the irregular placement of the tesserae in this mosaic.

not merely accidental nor an exercise of simple piety that the soldiers carry a shield with *chi* and *rho* (the first Greek letters in the name of Christ) or that there are twelve attendants or that the figure of the emperor divides clergy and laity. The emperor considered himself the regent of Christ, an attitude summed up in the *iconographic*, or symbolic, program: Justinian represents Christ on earth and his power balances both church and state. The only figure identified in the mosaic is Bishop (later Archbishop) Maximian flanked by his clergy, who include a deacon with a jeweled gospel and a subdeacon with a chained incense pot.

Opposite the emperor's retinue, the Empress Theodora and her attendants look across at the imperial group [6.18–6.19]. Theodora holds a chalice to complement the bread basket *(paten)* held by the emperor. At the hem of Theodora's gown is a small scene of the Magi bringing gifts to the Christ Child. Scholars disagree whether the two mosaics represent the royal couple bringing the eucharistic gifts for the celebration of the liturgy or the donation of the sacred vessels for the church. It was a custom for the rulers to give such gifts to the more important churches of their realm. The fact that the empress seems to be leaving her palace (two male functionaries of the court are ushering her out) makes the latter interpretation the more probable one. The women at Theodora's left are striking; those to the extreme left are stereotyped, but the two closest to the empress appear more individualized, leading some art historians to suggest that they are idealized portraits of two of Theodora's closest friends: the wife and daughter of the conqueror of Ravenna, Belisarius.

The royal generosity extended not only to the building and decoration of the church of San Vitale. An ivory throne, now preserved in the episcopal museum of Ravenna, was a gift of the emperor to Bishop Maximian, the ecclesiastical ruler of Ravenna when San Vitale was dedicated [6.20]. A close stylistic analysis of the carving on the throne has led scholars to see the work of at least four different artists on the panels, all probably from Constantinople. The front of the throne bears portraits of John the Baptist and the four Evangelists,

6.20 Bishop's *cathedra* (throne) of Maximian. c. 546–556. Ivory panels on wood frame. Height 4'11" (1.5 m), width 1'11⅝" (.6 m). Archepiscopal Museum, Ravenna. Maximian is portrayed with his name in the Justinian mosaic (see 6.17).

while the back has scenes from the New Testament with sides showing episodes from the Old Testament of the life of Joseph. The purely decorative elements of trailing vines and animals show the style of a different hand, probably Syrian. The bishop's throne (*cathedra* in Latin; a cathedral is a church where a bishop presides) bears a small monogram: *"Maximian, Bishop."*

The entire ensemble of San Vitale, with its pierced capitals typical of the Byzantine style, its elaborate mosaic portraits of saints and prophets, its lunette mosaics of Old Testament prefigurements of the Eucharist, and monumental mosaic scenes, is a living testimony to the rich fusion of imperial, Christian, and Middle Eastern cultural impulses. San Vitale is a microcosm of the sociopolitical vision of Byzantium fused with the religious worldview of early Christianity.

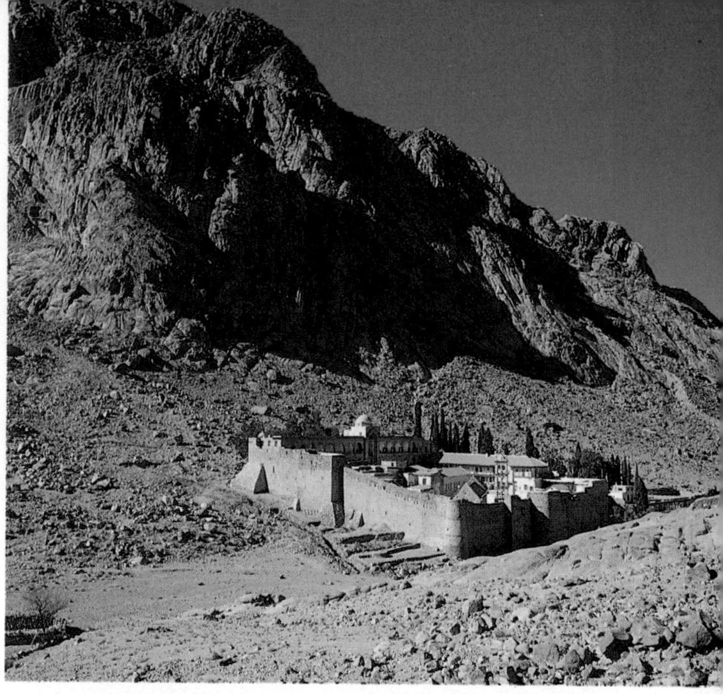

6.21 The fortress monastery of Saint Catherine in the Sinai Desert. 6th century. The church (called the *Katholikon*) from Justinian's time can be seen in the lower center of the walled enclosure, flanked by a belltower.

SAINT CATHERINE'S MONASTERY AT MOUNT SINAI

Justinian is remembered not only in Constantinople and Ravenna but also in the Near East, where he founded a monastery that is still in use some fifteen hundred years later—a living link back to the Byzantine world.

In her *Peregrinatio,* that wonderfully tireless traveler of the 4th century, Etheria, describes a visit to

SPORTS AND GAMES

Unruly Fans

Our papers are full of stories about fans at athletic events getting out of control after a game and rioting within the stadium or, more commonly, trashing an area of the city in order to express either their disgust at a loss or, more typically, their jubilation at victory. More recently, we have had the phenomenon of fans (e.g., British soccer fans) who riot and fight as a signature of their status as a fan even though they might not realize that "fan" is merely a shortened form of the word "fanatic"! Some of these "fan riots" have caused panic and large loss of life.

That the unruly behavior of athletic fans is not a new phenomenon is clear from 6th-century Byzantine history. In the time of the emperor Justinian the followers of chariot racing in Constantinople's hippodrome were divided into the Greens and the Blues. Oddly enough these factions also separated over the issue of theology; the Greens were monophysites who thought that Christ had only one nature while the Blues held the orthodox position that there were two natures in Christ, human and divine. They further divided themselves over the kind of clothes they wore and how they cut their hair, with the Greens shaving the front of their head and wearing their hair long in back after the fashion of the barbarian Huns to the north.

Here is what Procopius, Justinian's court historian, wrote in his *History of the Wars* about these factions: "They subject themselves to the most bitter physical violence. . . . They fight against those sitting opposite them. . . . They have a senseless hatred of their neighbors which is perpetual and never ending. . . . They care for nothing, human or divine, except winning their engagements. . . . They do not think it their affair even if they are short of food and in desperate straits as long as it goes well with their 'party,' which is the name they give their fellow insurgents." Procopius then concludes: "For my part, I can only call this a disease of the soul."

One might think Procopius unduly harsh in his judgment except for the fact that the Greens and the Blues rioted in January 532 and nearly destroyed the city in the process. That riot, called the *Nika* Revolt because some of the rioters shouted the slogan *Nika* (victory, in Greek), almost ended by dethroning the emperor and was, in fact, ended by a merciless and bloody battle of the imperial army against the rioters. It was that state of anarchy which prompted Procopius to be so severe in his judgment of the horse-racing fans of Byzantium.

the forbidding desert of the Sinai to pray at the site where God appeared to Moses in a burning bush (that, Etheria assures us, "is still alive to this day and throws out shoots") and to climb the mountain where the Law was given to Moses. She says that there was a church at the spot of the burning bush with some hermits living nearby to tend it and see to the needs of pilgrim visitors. More than a century later, the emperor Justinian built a monastery fortress at the foot of Mount Sinai and some pilgrimage chapels on the slopes of the mountain [6.21]. An Arabic inscription over one of the gates tells the story:

> The pious king Justinian, of the Greek Church, in the expectation of divine assistance and in the hope of divine promises, built the monastery of Mount Sinai and the Church of the Colloquy [a church over the spot where Moses spoke to God in the burning bush] to his eternal memory and that of his wife, Theodora, so that all the earth and all its inhabitants should become the heritage of God; for the Lord is the best of masters. The building was finished in the thirtieth year of his reign and he gave the monastery a superior named Dukhas. This took place in the 6021st year after Adam, the 527th year [by the calendar] of the era of Christ the Savior.

Because of the number of factors—most important its extreme isolation and the very dry weather—the monastery is an immense repository of ancient Byzantine art and culture. It preserves, as well as the oldest icons in Christianity, some of Justinian's architecture. The monastery is also famous as the site of the rediscovery of the earliest Greek codex of the New Testament hitherto found. Called the *Codex Sinaiticus,* it was discovered in the monastery by the German scholar Konstantin von Tischendorf in the 19th century. The codex—from the middle of the 4th century—was given by the monks to the Tsar of Russia. In 1933 the Soviet government sold it for £100,000 to the British Museum, where it remains today, a precious document.

The monastery is surrounded by heavy, fortified walls, the main part of which date from before Justinian's time. Within those walls are some modern buildings, including a fireproof structure that houses the monastery's library and icon collections. The monastic church, the *Katholikon,* dates from the time of Justinian, as recently discovered inscriptions carved into the wooden trusses in the ceiling of the church prove. Even the name of the architect—Stephanos—was uncovered. This church thus is unique: signed 6th-century ecclesiastical architecture.

One of the more spectacular holdings of the monastery is its vast collections of religious icons. Because of the iconoclastic controversies of the 8th and 9th centuries in the Byzantine Empire, almost no pictorial art remains from the period before the 8th century. Sinai survived the purges of the "image-breakers" (iconoclasts) that engulfed the rest of the Byzantine world because of its extreme isolation. At Sinai, a range of icons that date from Justinian's time to the modern period can be seen. In a real sense, the icons of the monastery of Saint Catherine show the entire evolution of icon painting.

The Greek word *icon* means image. In the Byzantine Christian tradition, icon refers to a painting of a religious figure or a religious scene that is used in the public worship (the liturgy) of the church. Icons are not primarily decorative and they are didactic only in a secondary sense: For the Orthodox Christian faithful the icon is a window into the world of the sacred. Just as Jesus Christ was in the flesh but imaged God in eternity, so the icon is a "thing," but it permits a glimpse into the timeless world of religious mystery. One stands before the icon and speaks through its image to the

6.22 ***Christ Pantocrater.*** **c. 500–530. Encaustic on wood panel. 32¼" × 17¾" (84 × 46 cm). Monastery of Saint Catherine, Mount Sinai. The book is a complex symbol that symbolizes the Bible, Christ as the Word of God, and the record of human secrets that will be opened on the Last Day.**

reality beyond it. This explains why the figures in an icon are usually portrayed full-front with no shadow or sense of three-dimensionality. The figures "speak" directly and frontally to the viewer against a hieratic background of gold.

This iconic style becomes clear by an examination of an icon of Christ that may well have been sent to his new monastery by Justinian himself [6.22]. The icon is done by the *encaustic* method of painting (a technique common in the Roman world for funerary portraits): painting with molten wax that has been colored by pigments. Christ, looking directly at the viewer, is robed in royal purple; in his left hand he holds a jeweled codex and with his right hand he blesses the viewer.

This icon is an example from a large number found at Sinai that can be dated from before the 10th century. The entire corpus represents a continuous tradition of Byzantine art and piety. Mount Sinai is unique in its great tradition of historical continuity. Despite the rise of Islam, the harshness of the atmosphere, the vicissitudes of history, and the changing culture of the modern world, the monastery fortress at Sinai is living testimony to a style of life and a religiosity with an unbroken history to the time of Justinian's building program.

THE PERSISTENCE OF BYZANTINE CULTURE

It is simplistic to describe Byzantine art as unchanging—it underwent regional, intellectual, social, and iconographic changes—but a person who visits a modern Greek or Russian Orthodox church is struck more by the similarities than by the dissimilarities with the art of early medieval Constantinople. Furthermore, the immediately recognizable Byzantine style can be found in the history of art in areas as geographically diverse as Sicily in southern Italy and the far-eastern reaches of Russia. What explains this basic persistence of style and outlook?

First of all, until it fell to the Turks in 1453, Constantinople exerted an extraordinary cultural influence over the rest of the eastern Christian world. Russian emissaries sent to Constantinople in the late 10th century to inquire about religion brought back to Russia both favorable reports about Byzantine Christianity and a taste for the Byzantine style of religious art. It was the impact of services in Hagia Sophia that most impressed the delegates of Prince Vladimir, the first Christian ruler in Russia. Although art in Christian Russia was to develop its own regional variations, it was still closely tied to the art of Constantinople; Russian "onion-dome" churches, for example, are native adaptations of the central-dome churches of Byzantium.

Russia, in fact, accepted Christianity about 150 years after the ban on icons was lifted in Constantinople in 843. By this time the second "golden age" of Byzantine art was well under way. By the 11th century, Byzantine artists were not only working in Russia but had also established schools of icon painting in such centers as Kiev. By the end of the century these schools had passed into the hands of Russian monks, but their stylistic roots remained the artistic ideas of Byzantium. Even after the Mongol invasions of Russia in 1240, Russian religious art continued to have close ties to the Greek world, although less with Constantinople than with the monastic centers of Mount Athos and Salonica in Greece.

Byzantine influence was also very strong in Italy. We have already seen the influence of Justinian's court on Ravenna. Although northern Italy fell to Lombard rule in the 8th century, Byzantine influence continued in the south of Italy for the next five hundred years. During the iconoclastic controversy in the East many Greek artisans went into exile in Italy, where their work is still to be seen. Even while the Kingdom of Sicily was under Norman rule in the 12th century, Byzantine artisans were still active—as the great mosaics of Monreale, Cefalù, and Palermo testify. In northern Italy, especially in Venice, the trade routes to the East and the effects of the Crusades permitted a strong presence of Byzantine art, as the mosaics of the church of Saint Mark (as well as Byzantine art looted when the Crusaders entered Constantinople in 1204) and the cathedral on the nearby island of Torcello attest. We shall see in later chapters the impact of this artistic presence on panel painting in Italy. Until the revolutionary changes by Cimabue and Giotto at the end of the 13th century, the pervasive influence of this style was so great that Italian painting up to that time is often characterized as Italo-Byzantine.

There is another reason that Byzantine aesthetics seem so changeless over the centuries. From the time of Justinian (and even more so after controversies of the 8th and 9th centuries) Byzantine art was intimately tied to the theology and liturgical practices of the Orthodox church. The use of icons, for example, is not merely a pious practice but a deep-rooted part of the faith. Each year the Orthodox church celebrated a feast commemorating the triumph of the Icon party called the Feast of the Triumph of Orthodoxy.

Art, then, is tied to theological doctrine and liturgical practice. Because of the innate conservatism of the theological tradition, innovation either in theology or in art was discouraged. The ideal of the artist was not to try something new but to infuse his work with a spirit of deep spirituality and unwavering reverence. This art, while extremely conservative, was never stagnant. The artists strove for fidelity to the past as their aesthetic criterion. As art historian André Grabar has noted, "Their role can be compared to that of musical performers in our day, who do not feel that their importance is diminished by the fact that they limit their talent to the interpretation of other people's work, since each interpretation contains original nuances."

This attitude of theological conservatism and aesthetic stability helps explain why, for example, the art of icon painting is considered a holy occupation in the Eastern Orthodox church. Today, when a new Orthodox church is built the congregation may commission from a monk or icon painter the necessary icons for the interior of the church. The expeditions of scholars who went to Saint Catherine's monastery to study the treasures there recall the sadness they felt at the funeral of a monk, Father Demetrios, in 1958. The last icon painter in the monastery, he marked the end of a tradition that stretched back nearly fifteen hundred years.

Travelers to Mount Athos in Greece can visit (with some difficulty) the small monastic communities *(sketes)* on the south of the peninsula, where monastic icon painters still work at their art. In our century there has been a renaissance of the appreciation of this style of painting. In Greece there has been a modern attempt to purge icon painting of Western influences (especially those of the Renaissance and the Baroque periods) in order to recover a more authentic link with the great Byzantine tradition of the past. In Russia there has been a surge of interest in the treasures of past religious art. This has resulted in careful conservation of the icons in Russia, exhibits of the art in the museums of Russia and abroad, and an intense scholarly study of this heritage as well as a revival of interest in the Orthodox church itself.

Byzantine culture was not confined to artistic concerns. We have already seen that Justinian made an important contribution to legal studies. Constantinople also had a literary, philosophical, and theological culture. Although Justinian closed the pagan academies, later Byzantine emperors encouraged humanistic and theological studies. While the links between Constantinople and the West were strained over the centuries, those links did remain. At first a good deal of Greek learning came into the West (after having been lost in the early Middle Ages) through the agency of Arabic sources. The philosophical writings of Aristotle became available to Westerners in the late 12th and early 13th centuries in the form of Latin translations or Arabic translations of the Greek: Aristotle came to the University of Paris from the Muslim centers of learning in Spain and northern Africa. Not until the 15th century did Greek become a widely known language in the West; in the 14th century Petrarch and Boccaccio had a difficult time finding anyone to teach them the language. By the 15th century this had changed. One factor contributing to the Renaissance love for the classics was the presence of Greek-speaking scholars from Constantinople in Italy.

The importance of this reinfusion of Greek culture can be seen easily enough by looking at the great libraries of 15th-century Italy. Of the nearly four thousand books in the Vatican library listed in a catalogue of 1484, a thousand were in Greek, most of them from Constantinople. The core of the great library of Saint Mark's in Venice was Cardinal Bessarion's collection of Greek books, brought from the East when he went to the Council of Ferrara–Florence to discuss the union of the Greek and Latin churches in 1438. Bessarion brought with him, in addition to his books, a noted Platonic scholar, Genistos Plethon, who lectured on Platonic philosophy for the delighted Florentines. This event prompted Cosimo de' Medici to subsidize the collection, translation, and study of Plato's philosophy under the direction of Marsilio Ficino. Ficino's Platonic Academy, supported by Medici money, became a rallying point for the study of philosophical ideas.

The fall of Constantinople to the Turks in 1453 brought a flood of émigré Greek scholars to the West, in particular to Italy. The presence of these scholars enhanced the already considerable interest in Greek studies. Greek refugee scholars soon held chairs at the various *studia* (schools) of the leading Italian cities. These scholars taught language, edited texts, wrote commentaries, and fostered an interest not only in Greek pagan learning but also in the literature of the Greek Fathers of the Church. By the end of the 15th century the famous Aldine press in Venice was publishing a whole series of Greek classics to meet the great demand for such works. This new source of learning and scholarship spread rapidly throughout Western Europe so that by the early 16th century the study of Greek was an ordinary but central part of both humanistic and theological education.

The cultural worldview of Justinian's Constantinople is preserved directly in the conservative traditionalism of Orthodox religious art and indirectly by Constantinople's gift of Greek learning to Europe during the Renaissance. The great social and political power of the Byzantine Empire ended in the 15th century although it had been in decline since the end of the 12th century. Only the great monuments remain to remind us of a splendid and opulent culture now gone but once active and vigorous for nearly a thousand years.

THE RISE OF ISLAM

The splendor of the Byzantine world would be strenuously challenged by a new religion which arose in 6th-century Arabia. In the year 570 Muhummad was born in Mecca to a merchant family. Around the year 610 he began to receive revelations from God through the agency of the archangel Gabriel. These revelations or "recitations" form the basis for the Muslim scriptures called the *Qur-an*. Despite his best efforts, his Meccan neighbors were not sympathetic to his religious message and Muhammad fled to the city of Medina in 622. That flight (called the *Hegira*) is so important that it marks the beginning of the Islamic calendar. In 630, Muhammad returned to Mecca, purged it of its polytheism, and established the city as the center of his new religious movement. Muhammad died in 632 but within a decade after his death, Islam had already spread to Damascus in Syria, to Jerusalem, to Egypt, and to Persia.

The religion itself claims to rest on five basic "pillars":

(1) A rigorous monotheism which claims that there is but one God (Allah) and that Muhammad is his prophet or messenger who proclaims this sacred truth.
(2) An obligation to pray five times a day. Public prayer, following on the call to assembly from a mosque tower, is a characteristic of Islam.
(3) An obligation to observe a rigorous fast (no food or drink from sunup to sundown) during the month of Ramadan.
(4) The obligation to give alms to the poor.
(5) The obligation to make at least one pilgrimage (called the *Haj*) to Mecca at least once during one's lifetime [6.23].

At the core of Islamic belief is the central conviction that everyone is called upon to submit (Islam means "submission" or "surrender") to God who is responsible for the creation and sustenance of the world. Muhammad is not looked upon as divine but as the last definitive messenger in a tradition

6.23 The *Sanctuary at Mecca*. This is the central focus of the Islamic pilgrimage in Mecca. Pious pilgrims circle the draped black stone (Ka'ba) upon which, it is believed, one can see the footprints of Abraham. To the left and front of the Ka'ba is the tomb of Ishmael from whom Muslims trace their descent.

that goes back to Jesus and Moses who are both honored in Islam as prophets in a line that would end with Muhammad. Traditions about Muhammad (called *Hadith*) see him as the model of surrender to God and the paradigm for every faithful Muslim.

The Qur-an sums up God's definitive revelation to the world so that its proclamation is, as it were, the voice of God in the world. The Qur-an was compiled about a decade after Muhammad's death. It is almost impossible to distinguish which utterances come from the Medina or Mecca period. The Qur-an is divided into *suras* based on the length of the utterance; after the first, introductory sura, the longest ones come first and the last of the suras is the shortest. Along with the Qur-an, one must also take note of the tradition of law *(Hadith)* which gave shape to the culture of Islam in its concern both for personal and social behavior.

Islamic tradition has a panoply of customs which give it its own particular shape. Muslim males are circumcised. Dietary restrictions are common: no pork is eaten and alcoholic beverages are forbidden. There are major religious festivals like the holy month of fasting called Ramadan and the celebration of the birthday of the prophet. Muslim ethics frown on interest taking (usury) and gambling. Polygamy is permitted but not universally practiced.

The Culture of Islam

The basic religious ideas dictated, as they do for every religion, the cultural and artistic paths which they would pursue. Islam, for instance, is ferociously resistant to any hint of polytheism or idolatry because of its central monotheistic bias. Hence its religious art tends to be abstract because of its fear of idol making. Secondly, the Qur-an is so central to Islamic religion that it should not be surprising that arts connected with the reproductions of books (bindings, fine calligraphy, etc.) should be a central concern. Indeed, the art of fine writing or the art of Qur-anic recitation is a highly prized skill; even today, in Islamic countries, there are national contests of Qur-an recitation [6.24]. This emphasis on the literal word of God in the Qur-an explains why Islam, which is an aggressively missionary religion, does not use translations of its scriptures. Every pious Muslim is expected to learn the Qur-an in its original Arabic.

The most important building in Islam is the *mosque*. The mosque serves as a place of prayer, especially Friday prayer, and for the hearing of sermons. Since there is no formal liturgy beyond that of prayer, the mosque tends to emphasize spaciousness so that the community at prayer (exclusively male) may gather in order to face East, indicated by a niche in the mosque called a *mihrab* (i.e., "in the direction of Mecca") to pray. The great mosques of the Islamic world [6.25] tend to blend both arts we have spoken of here: spacious architecture in order to create a unified space for worship decorated by an abstract art and fine calligraphy in order to give a sense of beauty without falling into the sin of idolatry.

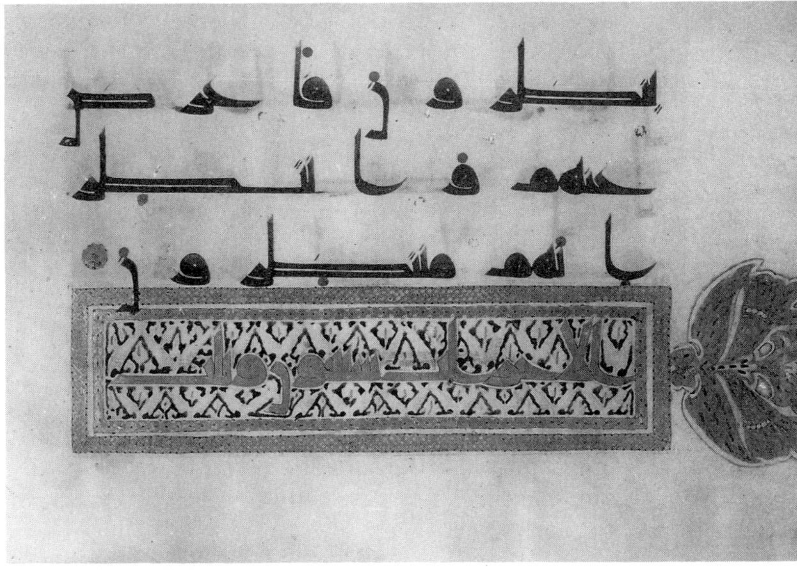

6.24 ***Page from the Qur-an.*** **Iraq? 8th. century? 8½" × 13" (21.6 × 32.5 cm). Museum of Islamic Art, Berlin. The highly stylized calligraphy is known as Kufic script; it is one of the earliest and most beautiful of Arabic calligraphy styles.**

In its long history Islam has had a great intellectual tradition which combined Islamic learning and philosophy. In fact, the recovery of Greek philosophers like Aristotle in the West is due, mainly, to editions which came to the West in translations done from the Arabic. The Muslim penetration into the West in which its culture touched Europe in the West in Spain and in the East in what is present-day Eastern Europe had a profound effect on the language, culture, and art of the West as visitors in places as diverse as Budapest (Hungary) and Cordova (Spain) can attest.

SUMMARY

This chapter traces briefly the slow waning of Roman power in the West by focusing on two late Roman writers who are both Christians: Boethius, who wrote in provincial Ravenna, and Augustine, who lived in Roman North Africa.

As the wheel of fortune turned Rome down, Byzantium began its ascent as the center of culture. Our focus was on the great builder and patron of Byzantine culture, the emperor Justinian and his consort, Theodora. The central feature of their reign is its blending of their political power with the Christian church so that church and state became a seamless whole. Christianity, which had been a despised and persecuted sect, now became the official religion of the state.

Byzantine Christianity had a readily recognizable look to it, a look most apparent in its art and architecture. It was an art that was otherworldly and formal and profoundly sacred. A contemporary Orthodox theologian has said that the proper attitude of a Byzantine worshiper is *gazing*. The mosaics and icons of this tradition were meant to be seen as windows through which the devout might see the eternal mysteries of religion. No conscious attempt was made to be innovative in this art. The emphasis was always on deepening the experience of sacred mystery.

The influence of this art was far-reaching. Italo-Byzantine styles of art persisted in the West up to the beginnings of the Italian Renaissance. The same styles entered Russia in the end of the 10th century and still persist. Contemporary students can visit Greek or Russian churches today and see these art forms alive as part of traditional Christian orthodox worship and practice.

Because Byzantium (centered in the city of Constantinople) was Greek-speaking, the culture

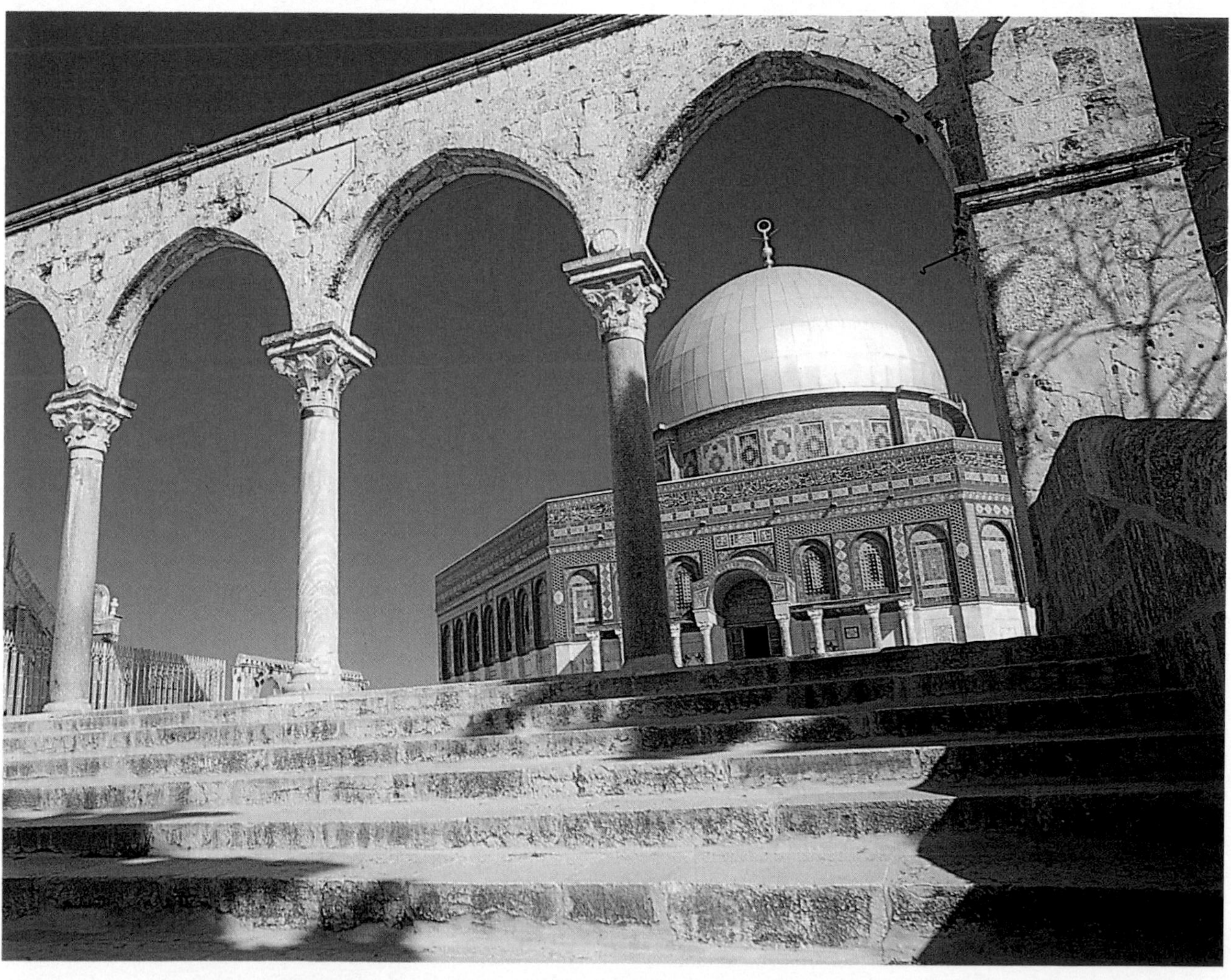

6.25 *Dome of the Rock.* Jerusalem. Late 7th century. This great mosque in Jerusalem, the second holiest site in Islam, was built to cover the place where Abraham is supposed to have sacrificed Isaac. Tradition says that the scales of justice will hang from the arched gate on the Day of Judgment to weigh the good and evil done by each person.

EAST MEETS WEST

Silk Comes to the West

The Chinese invented the weaving of silk long before the Christian era. Some sources trace its production back to the third millenium before the common era. The Chinese exported silk but forbade, under penalty of death, the export of silkworms out of the country. Imported Chinese silk was sold during both Greek and Roman days for fabulous prices but the West did not know the techniques involved in its production. It was the Byzantine emperor Justinian who broke the Chinese monopoly.

According to Procopius, Justinian's court historian, it was in A.D. 561 that two Christian monks who had lived in China were persuaded by the emperor to bring back the materials needed for the making of silk. The two smuggled back to Constantinople both the cocoons of silkworms and the seeds of the mulberry tree (on whose leaves the worms feed) in their hollowed-out walking staffs. With these materials, Justinian encouraged a flourishing silk trade that provided costly clothes and religious vestments for Europe.

Nearly a century later, Muslims, quite independently learned the secret of silk and introduced the trade both in North Africa and in Sicily and Spain. By the middle ages, there was a flourishing silk industry in Italy which lasted right down into modern times.

Interestingly enough, the European silk industry was exported to Colonial America (by, among others, Benjamin Franklin). Areas from Georgia to Pennsylvania produced large quantities of raw and finished silk before the 19th century. The American industry collapsed, however, because silk production was so labor-intensive that the industry could not be sustained on a profitable basis. The widespread presence of the mulberry tree is the only remnant left of that industry.

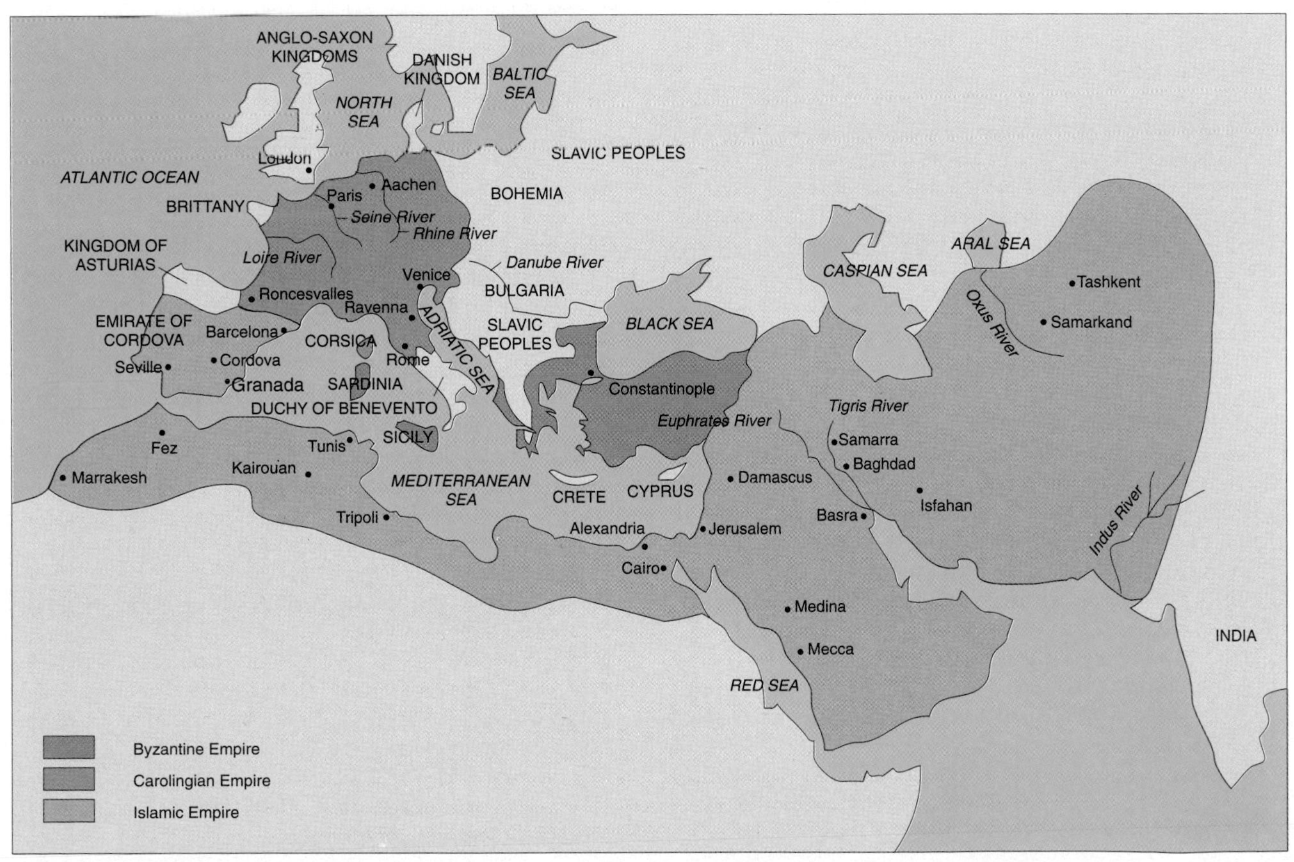

of ancient Greece was kept alive in that center until the middle of the 15th century, when the city fell to the Ottoman Turks. The removal of much of that culture to the West was a strong influence on the development of the Renaissance, as we shall see in subsequent chapters.

One other factor to be noted in this chapter is the rise of Islam. Islam grew in the 7th century to be a shaping force on Western culture both because it supplanted traditional Roman/Christian areas of influence in North Africa and in the Middle East (especially the Holy Land) and because the growth of this alternative culture would exert pressure on Europe as it penetrated into the Iberian peninsula of present-day Spain and Portugal. That penetration would have both political consequences and a vast cultural influence on the West.

Exercises

1. Augustine understood the word *confessions* to mean both an admission of sin and a statement of belief. Why is that term so useful and correct for an autobiography? Do most modern autobiographies constitute a confession in Augustine's sense of the term?
2. In *The City of God* Augustine defines peace as "the tranquillity of order." What does he mean? Is that definition a good one?
3. The outstanding art of the Byzantine period is the mosaic. What made mosaic such a desirable art form for the period? What do you see as its limitations?
4. Take a long look at the Ravenna mosaics of Justinian and Theodora and their court. What political and social values show through in the composition of the scenes, taken as a whole?
5. Look carefully at the various depictions of Christ found in Byzantine mosaics and icons. What religious values are underscored in those depictions? What values are neglected?
6. Define the term *icon* and be sure you understand its function in Orthodox Christianity. Is there anything comparable in contemporary art in terms of function?
7. Byzantine art prided itself on not changing its style but in preserving and perfecting it. Is there something to be said for continuity rather than change in artistic styles? What are the more apparent objections to such a philosophy?
8. The Byzantine Empire saw and, ultimately, succumbed to the rise of Islam. What are the most obvious points of tension between Islam and the Orthodox church of Byzantium?
9. Can you imagine what difficulties, if any, a Muslim may have in understanding the religion of the Byzantine Empire?

Pronunciation Guide

Anthemius: An-THEE-me-us
Boethius: Bow-A-thee-us
Galla Placidia: Gala Plah-SID-e-ah
Hadith: Ha-deeth
Hagia Sophia: Ha-GE-ah So-FEE-ah
Honorius: Ho-NOR-e-us
John Chrysostom: Jon CHRIS-o-stam
Justinian: Jus-TIN-e-an
Maximian: Max-IM-e-an
Pantocrater: Pan-TAW-craw-ter [also: Pan-TOE-crater]
Qur-an: Kuh-ran
Ramadan: RAH-mah-dawn
Ravenna: Raw-VEN-ah
San Apollinare: Sawn Ah-pole-in-ARE-a
San Vitale: Sawn Vee-TALL-a
Theodora: Thee-ah-DOOR-ah
Theodoric: Thee-AH-door-ick
Tribonian: Tree-BONE-e-an

Further Reading

Armstrong, Karen, *Muhammad: A Western Attempt to Understand Islam.* San Francisco: HarperCollins, 1992. A popular and sympathetic study.

Beckwith, John, *The Art of Constantinople.* New York: Phaidon, 1961. A brief survey of Byzantine art from A.D. 330 to 1453 with good illustrations.

Brown, Peter. *Augustine of Hippo: A Biography.* Berkeley: University of California Press, 1967. Brilliant, definitive, and readable.

Esposito, John *Islam: The Straight Path* (New York: Oxford, 1991). A very readable introduction.

Gibbon, Edward. *The Decline and Fall of the Roman Empire.* Many editions; the standard version is in 9 vols., edited by J. Bury in 1914. This monumental work, first published in 1776, is still the single best work on the period of Rome's decline. For a panoramic view of the period in this chapter and an example of how English should be written, it is unparalleled.

Grabar, André. *Byzantium: Byzantine Art in the Middle Ages.* London: Methuen, 1966. A sensitive and original study of Byzantine art and culture by an acknowledged expert in the field.

Kazhdan, Alexander (ed.), *The Oxford dictionary of Byzantium* 3 vol. New York: Oxford, 1991. The definitive reference work.

MacDonald, William. *Early Christian and Byzantine Architecture.* New York: Braziller, 1967. A handy survey with good photographs and schematics of important buildings.

Simson, Otto von. *The Sacred Fortress.* Chicago: University of Chicago Press, 1948. The best book on the artistic heritage of Ravenna.

Talbot Rice, David, and Tamara Talbot Rice. *Icons and Their History.* London: Thames and Hudson, 1974. Fine scholarship with good bibliographies and beautiful plates.

Watt, W. M. *Muhammad: Statesman and Prophet.* New York: Oxford, 1974. A classic study.

Vidal, Gore. *Julian.* New York: Vintage, 1977. This novel, originally published in 1964, is a brilliant evocation of Christianity and Classicism in conflict toward the end of the Roman Empire.

Ware, Timothy. *The Orthodox Church.* Baltimore: Penguin, 1969. A reliable, nontechnical survey.

		GENERAL EVENTS	LITERATURE & PHILOSOPHY
EARLY MIDDLE AGES	Rise of the Franks (650–768)	**711** Muslims invade Spain **714–741** Charles Martel, grandfather of Charlemagne, reigns as first ruler of Frankish kingdom **732** Charles Martel defeats Muslims at Battle of Poitiers **741–768** Reign of Pepin the Short, father of Charlemagne	**735** Death of Venerable Bede, author of *Ecclesiastical History of the English People* and other religious writings
	Carolingian Period (768–1000)	**768** Charlemagne ascends Frankish throne **772–778** Charlemagne's military campaigns against Muslim Emirates **778** Battle of Roncesvalles **c. 790** Charlemagne settles his court at Aachen (Aix-la-Chapelle) **800** Charlemagne crowned Holy Roman emperor at Rome by Pope Leo III **814** Death of Charlemagne **910** Founding of monastery at Cluny **987–996** Reign of Hugh Capet in France ends Carolingian line of succession	**after 780** Carolingian minuscule form of lettering developed **781** Charlemagne opens palace school, importing such scholars as Theodulf of Orléans and Alcuin of York **785** Alcuin, *Sacramentary* **after 814** Carolingian monasteries adopt *Rule* of Saint Benedict of Nursia (480–547?) **821** Einhard, *Vita Caroli (Life of Charlemagne)* **after 950** Hrosvitha's *Thais*
	Romanesque Period (1000–1140)	**11th cent.** Pilgrimages become very popular **1066** Norman invasion of England by William the Conqueror **1096–1099** First Crusade; capture of Jerusalem by Christians	**c. 1098** *Song of Roland, chanson de geste* inspired by Battle of Roncesvalles, written down after 300 yrs. of oral tradition **12th cent.** Development of liturgical drama **c. 1125** Saint Bernard of Clairvaux denounces extravagances of Romanesque decoration
GOTHIC PERIOD	(1140–1400)	**1165** Charlemagne canonized at Cathedral of Aachen **1187** Sultan Saladin conquers Jerusalem **1202–1204** Fourth Crusade; sack of Constantinople by crusaders **1270** Eighth Crusade **1291** Fall of Acre, last Christian stronghold in Holy Land	**14th–15th cent.** Play cycles performed outside the church; *Everyman* (15th cent.), morality play

CHAPTER

7 CHARLEMAGNE AND THE RISE OF MEDIEVAL CULTURE

ART

8th–9th cent. Irish *Book of Kells*

Illuminated manuscripts and carved ivories prevalent

c. 775 *Centula Evangeliary* and *Ďagulf Psalter*

800–810 *Gospel Book of Charlemagne*

early 9th cent. *Crucifixion Ivory,* done at palace school of Charlemagne

c. 820–830 *Utrecht Psalter*

1100–1125 Sculptures at Abbey Church of Saint-Pierre, Moissac

1120–1132 Sculptures at Abbey Church of La Madeleine, Vézelay

c. 1140 Portal sculptures at Priory Church, Saint-Gilles-du-Gard

c. 1165 Reliquary of Charlemagne and candelabra commissioned for Aachen cathedral by Frederick Barbarossa for canonization of Charlemagne

ARCHITECTURE

Monastic complexes become important centers in rural life

c. 795 Palace and chapel of Charlemagne at Aachen

c. 820 Plan for Abbey of Saint Gall, the "ideal" monastery

Use of massive walls and piers, rounded arches, and minimal windows

c. 1071–1112 Pilgrimage church at Santiago de Compostela, Spain

c. 1080–1130 Church of Saint Sernin, Toulouse, pilgrimage center

1088–1130 Great Third Church at Cluny

1096–1120 Abbey Church of La Madeleine, Vézelay

MUSIC

c. 800 Monasteries become centers for encouragement of sacred music; theoretical study of music at Charlemagne's palace school

9th cent. Use of semi-dramatic trope in liturgical music; *Quem Quaeritis* trope introduced into Easter Mass

c. 810 Gregorian plain chant *(cantus planus)* obligatory in Charlemagne's churches

822 Earliest documented church organ

11th–12th cent. Gregorian chant codified

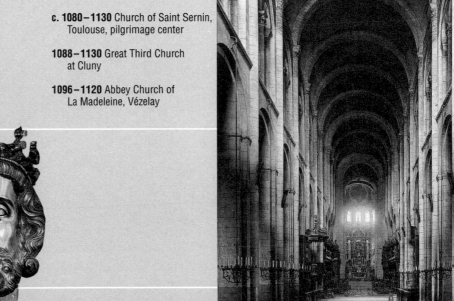

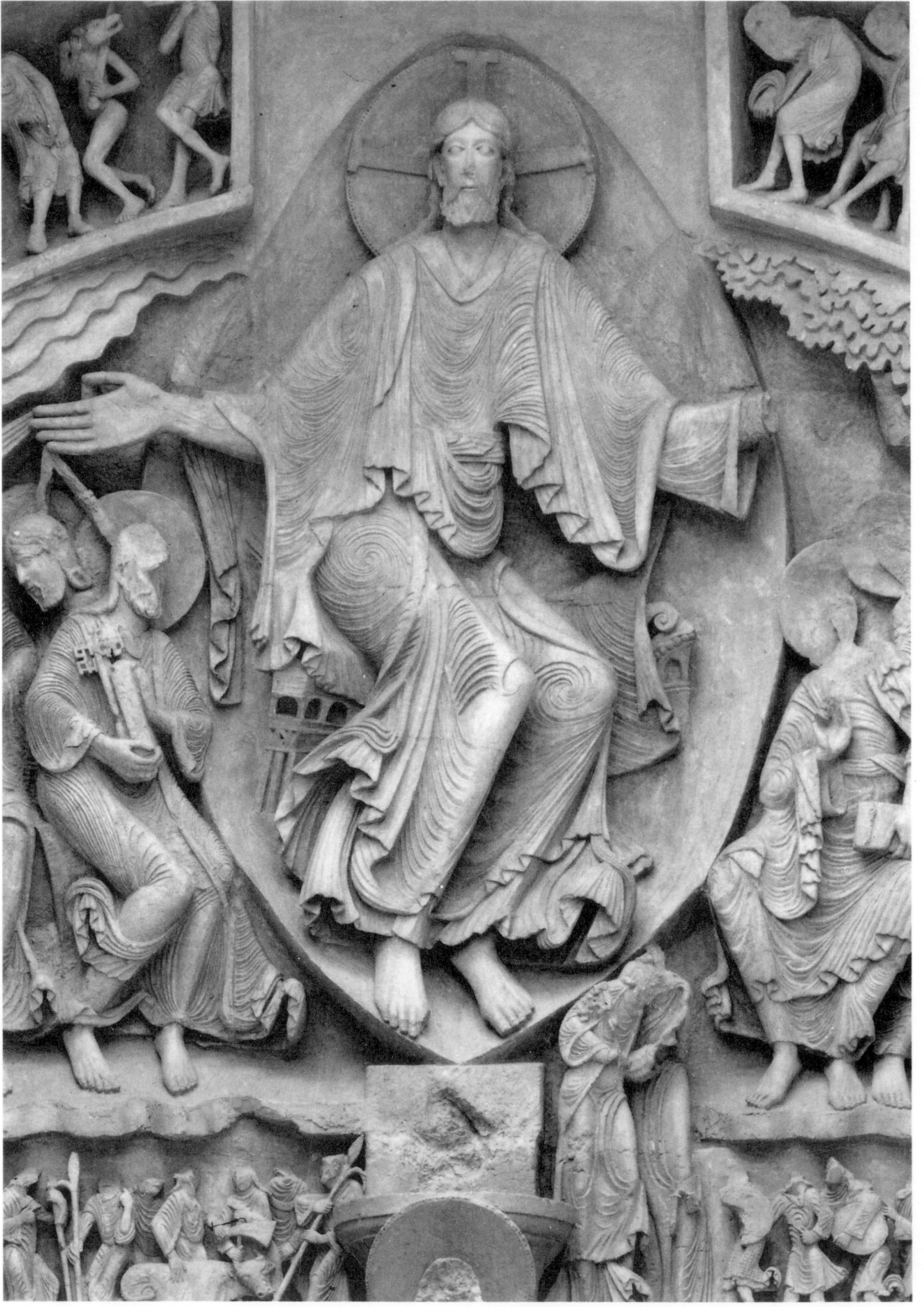

CHAPTER

7

CHARLEMAGNE AND THE RISE OF MEDIEVAL CULTURE

CHARLEMAGNE AS RULER AND DIPLOMAT

Charles the Great (742?–814)—known to subsequent history as Charlemagne—was crowned emperor of the Roman Empire in Saint Peter's Basilica in Rome on Christmas Day A.D. 800 by Pope Leo III, in the first imperial coronation in the West since the late 6th century. The papal coronation was rebellion in the eyes of the Byzantine court, and the emperor in Constantinople considered Charlemagne a usurper, but this act marked the revival of the Roman Empire in the West.

Charlemagne was an able administrator of lands brought under his subjugation. He modified and adapted the classic Roman administrative machinery to fit the needs of his own kingdom. Charlemagne's rule was essentially feudal—structured in a hierarchical fashion, with lesser rulers bound by acts of fealty to higher ones. Lesser rulers were generally large landowners who derived their right to own and rule their land from their tie to the emperor. Charlemagne also maintained a number of vassal dependents at his court who acted as counselors at home and as legates to execute and oversee the imperial will abroad. From his palace the emperor regularly issued legal decrees modeled on the old imperial Roman decrees [7.1]. These decrees were detailed sets of instructions that touched on a wide variety of secular and religious issues. Those that have survived give us some sense of what life was like in the very early medieval period. The legates of the emperor carried the decrees to the various regions of the empire and reported back on their acceptance and implementation. This burgeoning bureaucratic system required a class of civil servants with a reasonable level of literacy, an important factor in the cultivation of letters that was so much a part of the so-called Carolingian Renaissance.

The popular view of the early Middle Ages—often referred to as the Dark Ages—is of a period of isolated and ignorant peoples with little contact outside the confines of their own immediate surroundings, and at times that was indeed the general condition of life. Nonetheless, it is important to note that in the late 8th and early 9th centuries Charlemagne not only ruled over an immense kingdom (all of modern-day France, Germany, the Low Countries, and Italy as far south as Calabria) but also had extensive diplomatic contact outside that kingdom. Charlemagne maintained regular, if

7.1 Charlemagne's seal. 9th century. Archives Nationales, Paris. This Roman gem with the head of a philosopher or an emperor was used by Charlemagne to impress on wax on official documents. The inscription reads *Christ protect Charles King of the Franks.*

somewhat testy, diplomatic relations with the emperor in Constantinople (at one point he tried to negotiate a marriage between himself and the Byzantine empress Irene in order to consolidate the two empires). Envoys from Constantinople were regularly received in his palace at Aachen, and Charlemagne learned Greek well enough to understand the envoys speaking their own tongue.

Charlemagne's relationship with the rulers of Islamic kingdoms is interesting. Islam had spread all along the southern Mediterranean coast in the preceding century. Arabs were in complete command of all the Middle East, North Africa, and most of the Iberian peninsula. Charlemagne's grandfather Charles Martel (Charles the Hammer) had defeated the Muslims decisively at the battle of Poitiers in 732, thus halting an Islamic challenge from Spain to the rest of Europe. Charlemagne himself had fought the Muslims of the Córdoba caliphate on the Franco-Spanish borders; the battle of Roncesvalles (778) was the historical basis for the later epic poem the *Song of Roland.*

Despite his warlike relationship with Muslims in the West, Charlemagne had close diplomatic ties with the great Harun al-Rashid, the caliph of Baghdad. In 787 Charlemagne sent an embassy to the caliph to beg protection for the holy places of the Christians in Muslim-held Palestine. The caliph (of *A Thousand and One Nights* fame) received the Frankish legates and their gifts (mainly bolts of the much-prized Frisian cloth) with welcome and sent an elephant back to the emperor as a gesture of friendship. This gift actually arrived at Aachen and lived there for a few years before succumbing to the harsh winter climate. Charlemagne's negotiations were successful. From a pair of Palestinian monks he received the keys to the church of the Holy Sepulchre and other major Christian shrines, an important symbolic act that made the emperor the official guardian of the holiest shrines in Christendom.

Charlemagne's reign was also conspicuous for its economic developments. He stabilized the currency system of his kingdom. The silver *denier* struck at the royal mint in Frankfurt after 804 became the standard coin of the time; its presence in archaeological finds from Russia to England testifies to its widespread use and the faith traders had in it.

Trade and commerce were vigorous. Charlemagne welcomed Jewish immigration into his kingdom to provide a merchant class for commerce. There were annual trade fairs at Saint Denis near Paris, at which English merchants could buy

EAST MEETS WEST

Muslim Spain

In 711 Islamic troops from North Africa crossed the straits of Gibraltar and conquered what is now a large portion of Spain. They called these lands *Al Andalus,* from which we get the name *Andalusia* for that part of modern Spain. These followers of Mohammed attempted to reach into what is present-day southern France until they were defeated by the grandfather of Charlemagne, Charles Martel, at the battle of Poitiers in 732. The Muslims ruled Spain until overcome by Christian forces in the 13th century in a series of battles that have the generic name *Reconquista.*

What is most significant about the Muslim occupation of Spain is not the fact that they were there but that they were there when Islam as a whole was undergoing a dramatic cultural renaissance. Spanish cities like Cordoba, Seville, and Toledo still reflect the architectural influence of this period, while Islamic buildings like the Alcazar in Seville, and the Alhambra in Granada demonstrate how successfully the Muslims used Arab and Byzantine architectural styles to create a stunningly beautiful architecture. Despite the strong antipathy between the Christian West and Islamic Spain (reflected so vividly in the *Song of Roland*) a vigorous trade existed between the two cultures. Toledo steel for the making of swords and Cordoba leather are only two of the products highly prized in the West.

Most significantly of all for medieval culture, Islamic Spain became a conduit to the West for Greek learning. In the city of Toledo translators turned Greek writers like Euclid, Ptolemy, Galen, Hippocrates, and Aristotle into Latin for scholars. One indelible reminder of this work is the number of words that entered European languages as a direct result of this intellectual labor in the scientific learning of the time; our English words *zero, cipher, algebra, algorithm,* and *alcohol* (among many) are directly traceable back to Arabic. As we shall see in the next chapter, the university revolution of the 12th and 13th centuries would not have been possible without the flow of Aristotle's works which came to the West from translations done in Spain. Thomas Aquinas, for example, read Aristotle in a Latin translation done from Arabic manuscripts that had been, in turn, translated by Islamic scholars from the Greek originals.

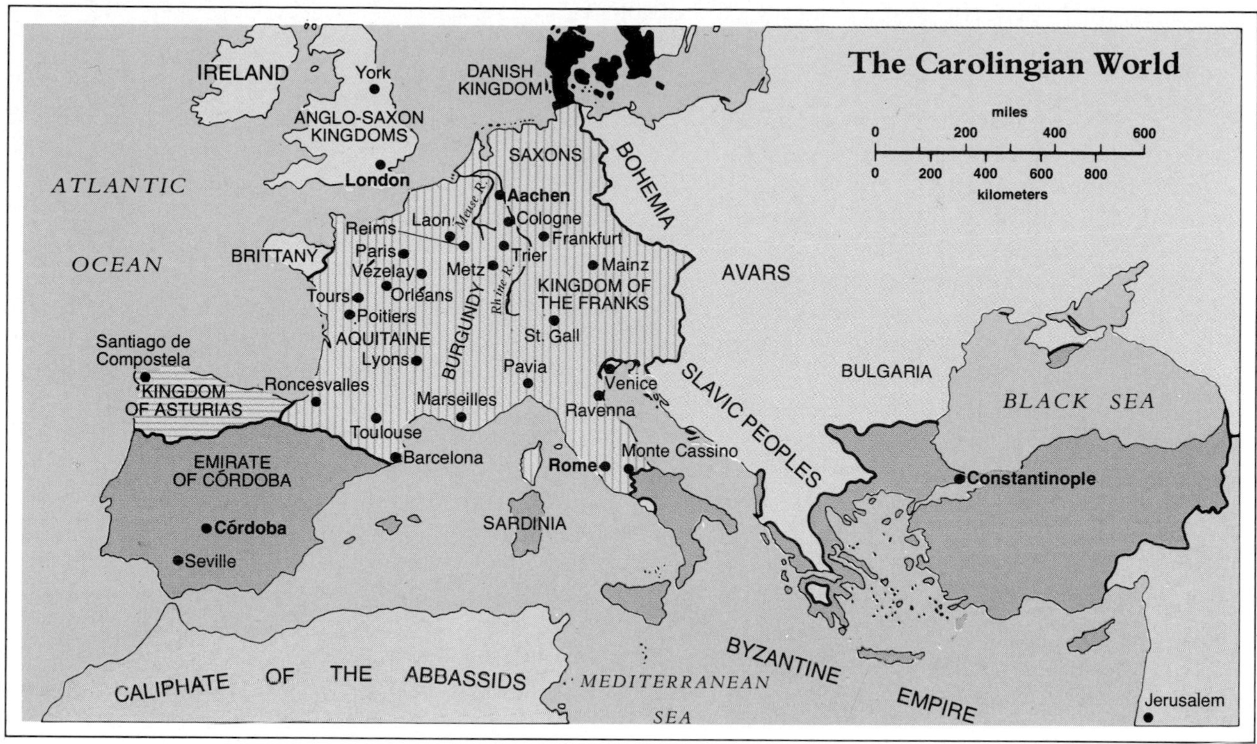

foodstuffs, honey, and wine from the Carolingian estates. A similar fair was held each year at Pavia, an important town of the old Lombard kingdom of northern Italy. Port cities such as Marseilles provided mercantile contracts with the Muslims of Spain and North Africa. Jewish merchants operated as middlemen in France for markets throughout the Near East. The chief of Charlemagne's mission to Harun al-Rashid's court was a Jew named Isaac who had the linguistic ability and geographic background to make the trip to Baghdad and back—with an elephant—at a time when travel was a risky enterprise. Rivers such as the Rhine and the Moselle were utilized as important trade routes. One of the most sought-after articles from the Frankish kingdom was the iron broadsword produced from forges in and around the city of Cologne and sold to Arabs in the Middle East through Jewish merchants at the port cities. Vivid testimony to their value can be read in the repeated embargoes (imposed under penalty of death) decreed by Charlemagne against their export to the land of the Vikings, who put them too often to effective use against their Frankish manufacturers in coastal raids on North Sea towns and trading posts.

LEARNING IN THE TIME OF CHARLEMAGNE

At Aachen Charlemagne opened his famous "palace school," an institution that was a prime factor in initiating what has been called the Carolingian Renaissance. Literacy in Western Europe before the time of Charlemagne was rather spotty; it existed, but hardly thrived, in certain monastic centers that kept alive the old tradition of humanistic learning taken from ancient Rome. Original scholarship was rare, although monastic copyists did keep alive the tradition of literary conservation. Charlemagne himself could not write.

The scholars and teachers Charlemagne brought to Aachen provide some clues as to the various locales in which early medieval learning had survived. Peter of Pisa and Paul the Deacon (from Lombardy) came to teach grammar and rhetoric at his school since they had had contact with the surviving liberal arts curriculum in Italy. Theodulf of Orleans was a theologian and poet. He had studied in the surviving Christian kingdom of Spain and was an heir to the encyclopedic tradition of Isadore of Seville and his followers. Finally and most importantly, Charlemagne brought an Anglo-Saxon, Alcuin of York, to Aachen after meeting him in Italy in 781. Alcuin had been trained in the English intellectual tradition of the Venerable Bede (died 735), the most prominent intellectual of his day, a monk who had welded together the study of humane letters and biblical scholarship. These scholar-teachers were hired by Charlemagne for several purposes.

First, Charlemagne wished to establish a system of education for the young of his kingdom. The primary purpose of these schools was to develop literacy; Alcuin of York developed a curriculum for them. He insisted that humane learning should consist of those studies which developed logic and science. It was from this distinction that later medieval pedagogues developed the two courses of studies for all schooling prior to the university: the *trivium* (grammar, rhetoric, and dialectic) and the *quadrivium* (arithmetic, geometry, music, and astronomy). These subjects remained at the heart of the school curriculum from the medieval period until modern times. (The now much-neglected "classical education" has its roots in this basic plan of learning.)

Few books were available and writing was done on slates or waxed tablets since parchment was expensive. In grammar, some of the texts of the Latin grammarian Priscian might be studied and then applied to passages from Latin prose writers. In rhetoric, the work of Cicero was studied, or Quintilian's *Institutio Oratoria*, if available. For dialectic, some of the work of Aristotle might be read in the Latin translation of Boethius. In arithmetic, multiplication and division were learned and perhaps there was some practice on the *abacus,* since the Latin numerals were clumsy to compute with pen and paper. Arithmetic also included some practice in chronology as students were taught to compute the variable dates of Easter. They would finish with a study of the allegorical meaning of numbers. Geometry was based on the study of Euclid. Astronomy was derived from the Roman writer Pliny, with some attention to Bede's work. Music was the theoretical study of scale, proportion, the harmony of the universe, and the "music of the spheres." Music at this period was distinguished from *cantus,* which was the practical knowledge of chants and hymns for church use. In general, all study was based largely on the rote mastery of texts.

Beyond the foundation of schools, Charlemagne needed scholars to reform existing texts and to halt their terrible corruption, especially those used in church worship. Literary revival was closely connected with liturgical revival. Part of Charlemagne's educational reform envisioned people who would read aloud and sing in church from decent, reliable texts. Literacy was conceived a necessary prerequisite for worship.

It was mainly Alcuin of York who worked at the task of revising the liturgical books. Alcuin published a book of Old and New Testament passages in Latin for public reading during Mass. He sent for books from Rome in order to publish a *sacramentary,* a book of prayers and rites for the administration of the sacraments of the church. Alcuin's sacramentary was made obligatory for the churches of the Frankish kingdom in 785. Charlemagne made the Roman chant (called *Gregorian* after Pope Gregory the Great, who was said to have initiated such chants in the end of the 6th century) obligatory in all the churches of his realm. Alcuin also attempted to correct scribal errors in the Vulgate Bible (the Latin version of Saint Jerome) by a comparative reading of manuscripts, a gigantic task he never completed.

Beyond the practical need for literacy there was a further aim of education in this period. It was generally believed that all learning would lead to a better grasp of revealed truth—the Bible. The study of profane letters (by and large the literature of Rome) was a necessary first step toward the full study of the Bible. The study of grammar would set out the rules of writing, while dialectic would help distinguish true from false propositions. Models for such study were sought in the works of Cicero, Statius, Ovid, Lucan, and Vergil. These principles of correct writing and argumentation could then be applied to the study of the Bible in order to get closer to its truth. The pursuit of analysis, definition, and verbal clarity are the roots from which the scholastic form of philosophy would spring in the High Middle Ages. Scholasticism, which dominated European intellectual life until the eve of the Renaissance, had its first beginnings in the educational methodology established by Alcuin and his companions.

These educational enterprises were not centered exclusively at the palace school at Aachen. Under Charlemagne's direction Alcuin developed a system of schools throughout the Frankish Empire, schools centered in both monasteries and towns. Attempts were also made to attach them to parish churches in the rural areas. The monastic school at Metz became a center for singing and liturgical study; schools at Lyons, Orleans, Mainz, Tours, and Laon had centers for teaching children rudimentary literary skills and offered some opportunity for further study in the liberal arts and the study of scripture. The establishment of these schools was accomplished by a steady stream of decrees and capitularies emanating from the Aachen palace. A circular letter, written most likely by Alcuin, called *On the Cultivation of Learning,* encouraged monks to study the Bible and to teach the young to do the same. A decree of 798 insisted that prelates and country clergy alike start schools for children.

This program of renewal in educational matters was an ideal set forth at a time when education was at a low ebb in Europe. Charlemagne tried to reverse the trend and in so doing encouraged real hope for an educated class in his time. His efforts were not entirely successful; many of his reforms came to naught in the generations after him when Europe slipped back into violence and ignorance.

CONTEMPORARY VOICES

An Abbot, an Irish Scholar, and Charlemagne's Biographer

Even as the sailor, fatigued with his labors, rejoices when he sights the familiar shore toward which he has long aspired, so does the scribe rejoice who sees the long-desired end of the book which has so overcome him with weariness. The man who does not know how to write makes light of the scribes' pains, but those who have done it know how hard is this work.

[A 9th-century monk-copyist describing labor in the scriptorium]

I love, better than all glory, to sit in diligent study over my little book. Pangur Ben has no envy of me, for he finds a mouse in his snares while only a difficult argument falls into mine. He bumps against the wall and I against the rigors of science. . . . He rejoices when he has a mouse in his paw as I rejoice when I have understood a difficult question. . . . Each of us loves our art.

[An Irish scholar and his cat]

He paid the greatest attention to the liberal arts. He had great respect for men who taught them, bestowing high honors on them. When he was learning the rules of grammar he received tuition from Peter the Deacon of Pisa who, by then, was an old man. For all other subjects he was taught by Alcuin, surnamed Albinus, a man of the Saxon race who came from Britain and was the most learned man anywhere to be found. Under him, the emperor spent much time and effort in studying rhetoric, dialectic, and especially astrology. He applied himself to mathematics and traced the course of the stars with great attention and care. He also tried to learn to write. With this end in view he used to keep writing tablets and notebooks under the pillows of his bed, so that he could try his hand at forming letters during his leisure moments; but, although he tried very hard, he had begun late in life and he made very little progress.

[Einhard in his biography of Charlemagne]

Most of those who were educated were young men although there is some evidence of learning among the aristocratic women of Charlemagne's court. The only book written by a Frankish woman in his time was a sort of manual for Christian living written by Dhouda for her own son. We do know however that there had to be a certain level of literacy for women who participated in the religious life of the monasteries and there is also some evidence that illuminated manuscripts that have come to us were done by women in such convents.

BENEDICTINE MONASTICISM

Monasticism—from the Greek *monos* (alone)—was an integral part of Christianity from the 3rd century on. Monasticism came into the West from the great Eastern tradition of asceticism (self-denial) and eremitism (the solitary life). Its development in the West was very complex, and we cannot speak of any one form of monasticism as predominant before the time of Charlemagne.

Celtic monasticism in Ireland was characterized both by austere living and by a rather lively intellectual tradition. Monasticism in Italy was far more simple and rude. Some of the monasteries on the continent were lax, and Europe was full of wandering monks. No rule of life predominated in the 6th and 7th centuries. Monastic life-styles varied not only from country to country but also from monastery to monastery.

The Rule of Saint Benedict

One strain of European monasticism derived from a rule of life written in Italy by Benedict of Nursia (480–547?) in the early 6th century. Although it borrows from earlier monastic rules and was applied only to a small proportion of monasteries for a century after its publication, the Rule of Saint Benedict eventually became the Magna Carta of monasticism in the West. Charlemagne had Alcuin of York bring the Rule to his kingdom and impose it on the monasteries of the Frankish kingdom to reform them and impose on them some sense of regular observance. In fact, the earliest copy of the Rule of Saint Benedict we possess today (a 9th-century manuscript preserved in the Swiss monastery of Saint Gall) is a copy of a copy Charlemagne had made in 814 from Saint Benedict's autograph copy then preserved at the abbey of Monte Cassino in Italy (now lost).

The Rule of Saint Benedict consists of a prologue and seventy-three chapters (some only a few sentences long), which set out the ideal of monastic life. Monks (the brethren) were to live a family life in community under the direction of a freely elected father (the abbot) for the purpose of being schooled in religious perfection. They were to possess nothing of their own (poverty); they were to live in one monastery and not wander (stability); their life was to be one of obedience to the abbot; and they were to remain unmarried (chastity). Their daily life was to be a balance of common prayer, work, and study. Their prayer life centered around duly appointed hours of liturgical praise of God that were to mark the intervals of the day. This prayer, called the "Divine Office," consisted of the public recitation of psalms, hymns, and prayers with readings from the Holy Scriptures. The offices were interspersed throughout the day and were central to the monks' life. The periods of public liturgical prayer themselves set off the times for reading, study, and the manual labor that was done for the good of the community and its sustenance. The life-style of Benedictine monasticism can be summed up in its motto: "pray and work." The rule was observed by both men and women.

The daily life of the monk was determined by sunrise and sunset (as it was for most people in those days). Here is a typical day—called the *horarium*—in an early medieval monastery. The italicized words designate the names for the liturgical hours of the day:

Horarium Monasticum

2:00 A.M.	Rise
2:10–3:30	*Nocturns* (later called *Matins*; the longest office of the day)
3:30–5:00	Private reading and study
5:00–5:45	*Lauds* (the second office; also called "morning prayer")
5:45–8:15	Private reading and *Prime* (the first of the short offices of the day); at times, there was communal Mass at this time and, in some places, a light breakfast, depending on the season
8:15–2:30	Work punctuated by short offices of *Tierce*, *Sext*, and *None* (literally the third, sixth, and ninth hours)
2:30–3:15	Dinner
3:15–4:15	Reading and private religious exercises
4:15–4:45	*Vespers*—break—*Compline* (night prayers)
5:15–6:00	To bed for the night

This daily regimen changed on feast days (less work and more prayer) and during the summer (earlier rising, work later in the day when the sun was down a bit, more food, and so on). While the schedule now seems harsh, it would not have surprised a person of the time. Benedict would have found it absurd for people to sleep while the sun is shining and then stay up under the glare of artificial light. When we look at the horarium closely we see a day in which prayer and reading get four hours each, while there are about six hours of work. The rest of the day was devoted to personal chores, eating, and the like.

The triumph of the Benedictine monastic style of life (the early Middle Ages has been called the Benedictine centuries by some historians) is to be found in its sensible balance between the extreme asceticism of Eastern monastic practices and the unstructured life of Western monasticism before the Benedictine reforms. There was an even balance of prayer, manual labor, and intellectual life.

Women and the Monastic Life

While we tend to think of monasticism as a masculine enterprise, it should be remembered that the vowed religious life was open to both men and women. The entire early history of Christianity records a flourishing monastic life for women. In the late Roman period groups of religious women flourished all over the Roman Empire. Saint Benedict's own sister, Scholastica (died c. 543), was head of a monastery not far from her brother's establishment at Monte Cassino. Her contemporary, Brigid of Ireland (died c. 525), was such a powerful figure in the Irish church that legends grew up about her prowess as a miracle worker and teacher. Her reputation as a saint was such that churches dedicated to her dotted Ireland, England, and places on the continent where Irish monasticism took root. In England, in the seventh century, Hilda, abbess of Whitby (614–680), not only ruled over a prominent monastery which was a center of learning (many Anglo-Saxon bishops were educated there) but she held a famous episcopal gathering (synod) to determine church policy. Hilda also encouraged lay learning. It was she who fostered the talents of the cowherd poet Caedmon who produced vernacular poetry concerned with Christian themes.

Since monasticism presumed a certain degree of literacy, it was possible for women to exercise their talents in a way that was not possible within the confines of the more restricted life of the court or the family. The Benedictine tradition produced great figures like that of Hildegard of Bingen (1098–1179) who wrote treatises on prayer, philosophy, medicine, and devotion. She was also a painter, illustrator, musician, critic, and a preacher.

Out of this great tradition we possess a number of edifying lives written by the contemporaries of these women which laud their decision to give up marriage in order to serve God. These lives of the saints were extremely popular since they served as exemplars of holy living. They were read publicly in churches (hence they were called *legends*—things read aloud) and for private devotion.

MONASTICISM AND GREGORIAN CHANT

The main occupation of the monk was the *Opus Dei* (work of God)—the liturgical common prayer of the monasteric horarium; life centered around the monastic church where the monks gathered seven times a day for prayer. The centrality of the liturgy also explains why copying, correcting, and illuminating manuscripts was such an important part of monastic life. Texts were needed for religious services as well as for spiritual reading. The monks were encouraged to study the scriptures as a lifelong occupation. For monks this study was *lectio divina* (divine reading) and was central to their development as a monk. This monastic imperative encouraged the study of the Bible and such ancillary disciplines (grammar, criticism, and the like) as necessary for the study of Scripture. From the 7th century on, monastic scriptoria were busily engaged in copying a wealth of material, both sacred and profane.

The monasteries were also centers for the development of sacred music. We have already seen that Charlemagne was interested in church music. His biographer Einhard tells us that the emperor "made careful reforms in the way in which the psalms were chanted and the lessons read. He was himself an expert at both of these exercises but he never read the lesson in public and he would sing only with the rest of the congregation and then in a low voice." Charlemagne's keen interest in music explains why certain monasteries of his reign—notably those at Metz and Trier—became centers for church music.

Charlemagne brought monks from Rome to stabilize and reform church music in his kingdom as part of his overall plan of liturgical renovation. In the earlier period of Christianity's growth quite diverse traditions of ecclesiastical music developed in various parts of the West. Roman music represented one tradition—later called *Gregorian* chant after Pope Gregory the Great (540–604), who was believed to have codified the music in the late 6th century. Milan had its own musical tradition, known as *Ambrosian* music—in honor of Saint Ambrose, who had been a noted hymn writer, as Saint Augustine attests in the *Confessions*. There was a peculiar regional style of music in Spain known as *Mozarabic* chant, while the Franks also had their own peculiar style of chant. All of these styles derive from earlier models of music which have their roots in Hebrew, Greco-Roman, and Byzantine styles. Lack of documentation permits only an educated reconstruction of this early music and its original development.

Gregorian chant as we know it today was not codified until the 11th and 12th centuries, so it is rather difficult to reconstruct precisely the music of Charlemagne's court. It was probably a mixture of Roman and Frankish styles of singing. It was *monophonic*—that is, one or many voices sang a single melodic line—and more often than not lacked musical accompaniment in the monastic churches. Most scholars believe that the majority of the music consisted of simple chants for the recitation of the psalms at the Divine Office; more elaborate forms were used for the hymns of the Office and the Mass chants. The music was simply called *cantus planus*, plainsong or plainchant.

In its more elementary form the chant consisted of a single note for each syllable of a word. The basic symbols used to notate Gregorian chant were called *neums*. Using the Gregorian notational system with its four-line staff and the opening line of Psalm 109, *Dixit Dominus Domino Meo, sede a dextris meis* (The Lord said to my Lord: sit on my right hand), a line of syllabic chant would look like this:

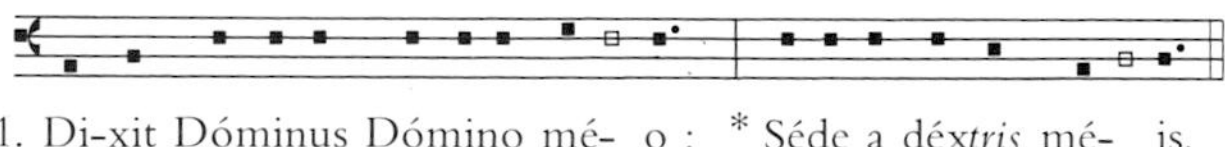
1. Di-xit Dóminus Dómino mé- o : * Séde a déxtris mé- is.

Even in the earliest form of chants, a cadence was created by emphasizing the final word of a phrase with the addition of one or two extra notes, as above. Later, more notes were added to the final words or syllables for elaboration and variation. For example:

1. Di-xit Dóminus Dómino mé- o : *Séde a déxtris mé- is.
D
D2
f
g
or : mé- is.
or : mé- is.
or : mé- is.
or : mé- is.

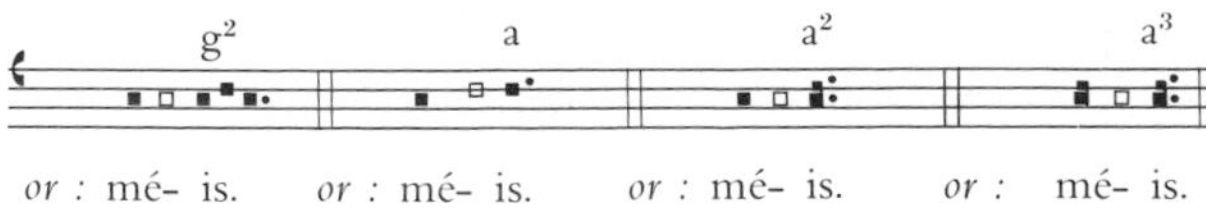

The simplicity of syllabic chant should not be regarded as useful only for the monotonous chanting of psalm verses. Very simple yet hauntingly melodic Gregorian compositions still exist that do not use elaborate cadences but rely on simple syllabic notes. A fine example is the Gregorian melody for the Lord's Prayer, reproduced here in modern notation. No rests are indicated in the musical text; the singer should simply breathe on a skipped note (it is presumed that not all would skip the same note) so that the music flows without pause. Ordinarily, these chants would be sung *a capella* (without musical accompaniment).

Certain phrases, especially words of acclamation (like *Alleluia*) or the word at the end of a line, were elaborated beyond the few notes provided in syllabic chant. This extensive elaboration of a final syllable (or any syllable) by a chain of intricate notes was called a *melisma*. An example of melismatic chant may be noted in the elaboration of the final *ia* of the Easter *Alleluia* sung at the Easter Mass:

LITURGICAL MUSIC AND THE RISE OF DRAMA

The Liturgical Trope

One development connected with melismatic chant which evolved in the Carolingian period was the *trope*. Since books were scarce, monks memorized a great deal of liturgical chant. As an aid to memorization and, also, to provide some variety in the chant, words would be added to the long melismas. These words, tropes, would be verbal elaborations of the content of the text. Thus, for example, if there was a melismatic *Kyrie Eleison* (the Greek "Lord, have mercy on us" retained in the Latin Mass) with an elaboration of notes for the syllables *rie* of Kyrie, it became customary to add words such as *sanctus* (holy), *dominus* (lord), and the like, which were sung to the tune of the melisma. The use of tropes grew rapidly and became standard in liturgical music until they were removed from the liturgy at the time of the Counter-Reformation in the 16th century.

Scholars have pointed to the introduction of tropes into liturgical music as the origin of drama in the Western world. There had been drama in the classical and Byzantine worlds, of course, but drama in Europe developed from the liturgy of the medieval church after it largely had been lost (or suppressed) in the very early Middle Ages.

A 9th-century manuscript (preserved at the monastery of Saint Gall) preserves an early trope that was added to the music of the Easter entrance hymn (the *Introit*) for Mass. It is in the form of a short dialogue and seems to have been sung by either two different singers or two choirs. It is called the *Quem Quæritis* trope from its opening lines:

The *Quem Quæritis* Trope

De Resurrectione Domini	Of the Lord's Resurrection
Int[errogatio]: *Quem quæritis in sepulchro, {o} Christicolæ?*	Question [of the angels]: *Whom seek ye in the sepulchre, O followers of Christ?*
R[esponsio]: *Jesum Nazarenum crucifixum, o cœlicolæ.*	Answer [of the Marys]: *Jesus of Nazareth, which was crucified, O celestial ones.*
[Angeli:] *Non est hic; surrexit, sicut prædixerat.*	[The angels:] *He is not here; he is risen, just as he foretold.*

Ite, nuntiate quia surrexit de sepulchro.	*Go, announce that he is risen from the sepulchre.*

Very shortly after the introduction of this trope into the Easter Mass the short interrogation began to be acted, not at Mass but at the end of the night services preceding Easter dawn. The dialogue of the *Quem Quæritis* was not greatly enlarged but the directions for its singing were elaborated into the form of a short play. By the 11th and 12th centuries the dialogue was elaborated beyond the words of the Bible and more persons were added. By the 12th century the stories took on greater complexity.

It was a logical step to remove these plays from the church and perform them in the public square. By the 14th century sizable cycles of plays were performed in conjunction with various feast days and underwritten by the craft or merchants' guilds. Some of these cycles acted out the major stories of the Bible, from Adam to the Last Judgment. The repertory also began to include plays about the lives of the saints and allegorical plays about the combats of virtue and vice, such as the 15th-century work *Everyman*. These plays were a staple of public life well into the 16th century. William Shakespeare, for example, may well have seen such plays in his youth.

THE MORALITY PLAY: *EVERYMAN*

Everyman is a 15th-century play that may well be a translation from a much earlier Dutch play. The subject is no longer a redoing of a biblical theme but rather the personification of abstractions representing a theme dear to the medieval heart: the struggle for the soul. The unprepared reader of *Everyman* will note the heavy-handed allegorizing and moralizing (complete with a "Doctor" who makes a final appearance to point up the moral of the play) with some sense of estrangement, but with a closer reading, students will also note the stark dignity of the play, the earnestness with which it is constructed, and the economy of its structure. Written in rather spare rhyming couplets, *Everyman* is a good example of the transitional play that forms a link between the earlier liturgical drama and the more secular drama that was to come at the end of the English medieval period.

The plot of *Everyman* is simplicity itself; it is quickly summarized by the messenger who opens the play. Everyman must face God in final judgment after death. None of the aids and friends of this life will support Everyman, as the speeches of the allegorical figures of Fellowship and others make clear. The strengths for Everyman come from the aiding virtues of Confession, Good Deeds, and Knowledge. The story, however, is not the central core of this play; the themes that run through the entire play are what should engage our attention. First is the common medieval notion of life itself as a pilgrimage, a notion that comes up again and again. It is embedded not only in the medieval penchant for pilgrimage but the use of that term (as one sees, for example, in Chaucer) as a metaphor. Second, the notion of the inevitability of death as the defining action of human life is omnipresent in medieval culture. *Everyman* has an extremely intense *memento mori* ("Keep death before your eyes!") motif. Finally, medieval theology puts great emphasis on the will of the human being in the attainment of salvation. It is not faith (this virtue is presumed) that will save Everyman; his or her willingness to learn (Knowledge), act (Good Deeds), and convert (Confession) will make the difference between salvation and damnation.

The Messenger says that *Everyman* is "By figure a moral play." It is meant not merely to instruct on the content of religion (as does a mystery play) but to instruct for the purposes of moral conversion. The earlier mystery plays usually point out a moral at the end of the performance. The morality uses its resources to moralize throughout the play.

The one lingering element from the liturgy in a play like *Everyman* is its pageant quality: The dramatic force of the presentation is enhanced by the solemn wearing of gowns, the stately pace of the speeches, and the seriousness of the message. The play depends less on props and place. Morality plays did not evolve directly out of liturgical drama (they may owe something to the study of earlier plays based on the classics studied in schools) but the liturgical overtones are not totally absent.

Nonliturgical Drama

At the end of the early Middle Ages we also have evidence of plays that were not dependent on liturgical worship. Thus a German nun-poet named Hrosvitha (or Roswitha; the name is spelled variously) who lived at the aristocratic court of Gandersheim and died around the year 1000 has left us both a collection of legends written in Latin and six plays modeled on the work of the Roman dramatist Terence. What is interesting about this well-educated woman is the broad range of her learning and her mastery of classical Latin in an age that did not put a high premium on education of females. Scholars also point out that her prose legend called *Theophilus* is the first known instance

7.2 Woodcut of *Pafnutius and Thaïs* from the 16th-century edition of her plays by Conrad Celtis. Celtis, an early German humanist (died 1508), made an edition of Hrosvita's plays as a part of his program to exalt German contributions to literature.

in German literature of the Faust theme—the selling of one's soul to the devil for material gain and public glory.

Hrosvitha's plays were probably meant to be read aloud by a small circle of literate people, but there is some internal evidence that they may also have been acted out in some rudimentary fashion. They are heavily moralistic (typically involving a religious conversion or steadfastness in faith during a time of persecution) and very didactic. In the play *The Conversion of the Harlot Thaïs*, for example, the holy man Pafnutius begins with a long conversation with his disciples on a liberal education and the rules of musical proportion and harmony. Such a discussion would seem a wild digression to us today, but for her audience it would be a way not only of learning about the liberal arts but a reminder that their study leads, inevitably, to a consideration of God [7.2]. That her plays do not have a finished dramatic quality underscores the fact that she was the *first* dramatist writing in Germany (as well as Germany's first female poet). Her model was the ancient drama of Rome as far as style was concerned, but her intention was to use that style to educate and convert. She was a direct heir of the humane learning that developed in the Carolingian and Ottonian periods.

THE LEGEND OF CHARLEMAGNE: *SONG OF ROLAND*

Charlemagne's kingdom did not long survive intact after the death of the emperor. By the 10th century, the Frankish kingdom was fractured and Europe reduced to a state worthy of the name "Dark Ages." Anarchy, famine, ignorance, war, and factionalism were constants in 10th-century Europe; Charlemagne's era was looked back to as a long-vanished Golden Age. By the 12th century, Charlemagne's reputation was such that he was canonized (in Aachen on December 29, 1165) by the Emperor Frederick Barbarossa. Charlemagne's cult was immensely popular throughout France—especially at the royal abbey of Saint Denis in Paris, which made many claims of earlier links with the legendary emperor.

A 15th-century oil painting in Aachen depicts an idealized Charlemagne as saint, wearing the crown of the Holy Roman Emperor and carrying a model of the church he had built at Aachen. Frederick Barbarossa commemorated the canonization by commissioning a great wrought bronze candelabrum to hang in the Aachen cathedral. He also ordered a gold reliquary (now in the Louvre in Paris) to house the bones of one of his saintly predecessor's arms [7.3]; another reliquary, in the form of a portrait bust that contains fragments of Charlemagne's skull, is in the cathedral treasury at Aachen.

The memory of Charlemagne and his epoch was kept more vividly alive, however, in cycles of epic poems and in tales and memoirs developed, embroidered, and disseminated by poets and singers throughout Europe from shortly after Charlemagne's time until the late Middle Ages. These are the famous *chansons de geste* (songs of deeds) or, as some were called, *chansons d'histoire* (songs of history). Of these songs, the oldest extant—as well as the best and most famous—is the *Song of Roland*.

The *Song of Roland* was written sometime late in the 11th century, but behind it lay some three hundred years of oral tradition and earlier poems cele-

7.3 Reliquary of Charlemagne. Bust of Charlemagne after 1349; crown before 1349. Cathedral Treasury, Aachen. Reliquaries of this type are containers for some relic of the person depicted by the statue.

brating a battle between Charlemagne's army and a Muslim force at the Spanish border. Charlemagne did indeed campaign against the emirate of Spain in 777 and 778, without conclusive result. In August 778 Charlemagne's rear guard was ambushed by the Basques while making its way through the Pyrenees after the invasion of Spain. The real extent of that battle (later placed, on not too much evidence, at the town of Roncesvalles) is unclear. Some experts maintain that it was a minor skirmish, remembered in the area in local legends later told and retold (and considerably embroidered in the process) by monks of the monasteries and sanctuaries on the pilgrimage routes to the great shrine of Saint James at Santiago de Compostela in Spain. Other historians insist that the battle was a horrendous bloodbath for the army of Charlemagne and that the tale was carried back to the Frankish cities; the legend was transformed as it was repeated by the descendants of the few survivors.

In any event, by the 11th century the tale was widely known in Europe. Excerpts from the *Song of Roland* were sung to inspire the Norman army before the Battle of Hastings in 1066, and in 1096 Pope Urban II cited it in an appeal to French patriotism when he attempted to raise armies for a crusade to free the Holy Land. Medieval translations of the poem into German, Norse, and Italo-French attest to its widespread popularity outside the French-speaking area.

The *Song of Roland* is an epic poem; its unknown writer or writers had little interest in historical accuracy or geographic niceties. Its subject matter is the glory of the military campaign, the chivalric nature of the true knight, the constant possibility of human deviousness, and the clash of good and evil. The poem, although set in the 8th century, reflects the military values and chivalric code of the 11th century.

The story is simple: Muslims attack the retreating rear portion of Charlemagne's army (through an act of betrayal) while it is under the command of Roland, a favorite nephew of the emperor. Roland's army is defeated, but not before he sounds his ivory horn to alert the emperor to the peril. The emperor in turn raises a huge army from throughout Christendom while the Muslims also raise a great force. An epic battle follows; Charlemagne, with divine aid, is victorious.

The *Song of Roland* is some four thousand lines long; it is divided into stanzas, and each line contains ten syllables. It is impossible to reproduce the rhyme in English, since each stanza ends with an assonance, so the poem is best read in blank verse translation—although that sacrifices the recitative quality of the original.

This poem was meant to be heard, not read. It was recited by wandering minstrels—*jongleurs*—to largely illiterate audiences. This fact explains the verse style, the immediacy of the adjectives describing the characters and the situations, and the somewhat repetitive language. The still-unexplained AOI at the end of many stanzas may have something to do with the expected reaction of the *jongleur* as he uttered that particular sound to give emphasis to a stanza. (Some sense of the immediacy of the original may be gained by a reader today who declaims some of these stanzas with gestures and appropriate pauses.)

Certain details of the poem merit particular attention. A portion of the poem recounts Charlemagne's arrival on the scene and his victory over the Saracens who are beleaguering the forces commanded by Roland. Most striking is the mixture of military and religious ideals, not an uncommon motif in the medieval period. This mixture is reflected not only in the imagery and in the plot (Charlemagne's prayer keeps the sun from setting in order to allow time for victory, an echo of the biblical siege of Jericho by Joshua) but also in the bellicose Archbishop Turpin. Christian valor is contrasted with Saracen wickedness and treachery; the anti-Muslim bias of the poem is clear. The Muslim Saracens are pagans and idolaters—an odd way to describe the rigidly monotheistic followers of Islam. The *Song of Roland,* like much of the epic tradition from which it springs, is nevertheless devoted to the martial virtues of courage and strength, the comradeship of the battlefield, and the power of great men as well as the venality of evil ones.

The *Song of Roland* was immensely popular in its own time. It spawned a number of other compositions like the *Pseudo Turpin* and the *Song of Aspremont* in order to continue the story or elaborate portions of it. At a much later time in Italy the story was redone in the telling of the exploits of Orlando (Roland). To this day, children in Sicily visit the traditional puppet shows in which the exploits of brave Roland and his mates are acted out with great clatter and verve. Spectators at those shows witness stories that go back to the beginnings of the medieval period.

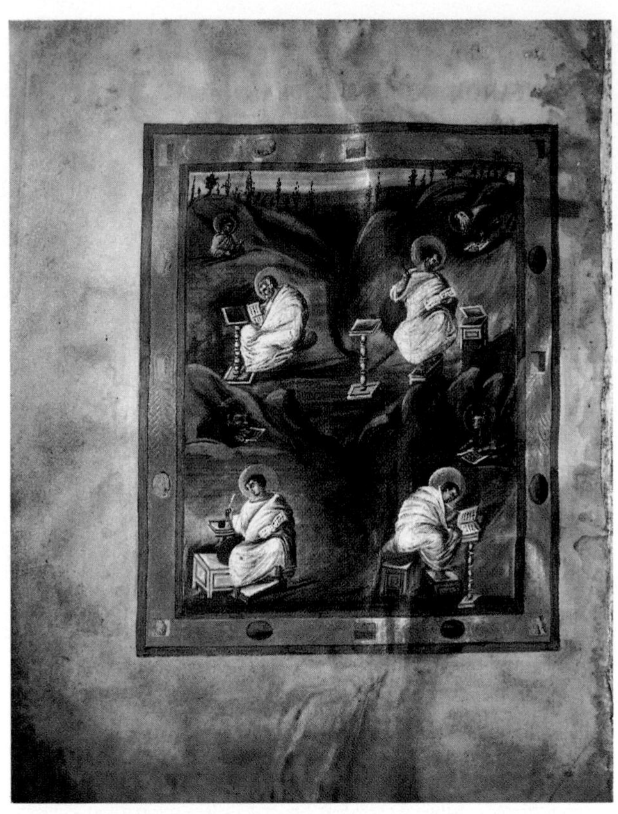

7.4 The four evangelists and their symbols, from the *Gospel Book of Charlemagne*. Palace School of Charlemagne, Aachen. Early 9th century. Manuscript illustration. Cathedral Treasury, Aachen.

THE VISUAL ARTS

The Illuminated Book

Given Charlemagne's preoccupation with literary culture, it should not be surprising that a great deal of artistic effort should have been expended on the production and illumination of manuscripts. Carolingian manuscripts were made of parchment (treated animal skins, mainly from cows and sheep) since papyrus was unavailable and the technical process of making paper was not known during this period. For very fine books the parchment was dyed purple and the letters were painted on with silver and gold pigments.

While a good deal of decoration of Carolingian manuscripts shows the influence of Irish models, the illustrations often show other influences. This is strikingly apparent in the illustrations of the *Gospel Book of Charlemagne* (800–810), where it is clear that the artists were conscious of the Roman style [7.4]. The page showing the four evangelists with their symbolic emblems is strikingly classical: the four evangelists are toga-clad like ancient Roman consuls. There is some evidence that the artists attempted some experiments in three-dimensionality. The wooded background in the receding part of the upper two illustrations tends to bring the evangelists forward and thus diminish the flatness we associate both with Byzantine and Celtic illustrations.

The *Utrecht Psalter* (so called because its present home is the University of Utrecht in Holland) has been called the masterpiece of the Carolingian Renaissance. Executed at Rheims sometime around 820 to 840, it contains the whole psalter with wonderfully free and playful pen drawings around the text of the psalms. The figures are free from any hieratic stiffness; they are mobile and show a nervous energy. The illustration for Psalm 149, for example, has a scene at the bottom of the page showing various figures "praising God with horn and cymbals" [7.5]. There are two other interesting aspects of the same illustration. One is that the figures are in the act of praising Christ, who stands at the apex of the illustration with the symbols of his resurrection (the staff-like cross in his hand). Although the psalms speak of the praise of God, for the medieval

7.5 Page from the *Utrecht Psalter*. Hautvillers (near Reims). c. 820–840. Pen and ink on vellum. 12⅞ × 10" (33 × 26 cm). University Library, Utrecht. This page is typical of the quick nervous style of the unknown illustrator who did similar symbolic drawings for the entire psalter of 150 psalms.

7.6 *Crucifixion*. Palace School of Charlemagne. Early 9th century. Ivory, 9⅞ × 6½" (25 × 16 cm). Cathedral Treasury of Saint Just, Narbonne. Such ivories were often used as covers for Gospel books and other liturgical works. They were often produced as gifts for special occasions.

Christian the "hidden" or true meaning of the scriptures was that they speak in a prefigurative way of Christ. Thus the psalmist who praises God is a "shadow" of the church that praises Christ. A second thing to note in this illustration is the bottom-center scene of an organ with two men working the bellows to supply the air.

The style of the *Utrecht Psalter* has much in common with early Christian illustration. The lavish purple and silver manuscripts show a conscious imitation of Byzantine taste. We have also noted the influence of Celtic illustration. Carolingian manuscript art thus had a certain international flavor, and the various styles and borrowings give ample testimony to the cosmopolitan character of Charlemagne's culture. This universality diminished in the next century; not until the period of the so-called International Style in the 14th century would such a broad eclecticism again be seen in Europe.

One other art form that developed from the Carolingian love for the book is ivory carving. This technique was not unique to Charlemagne's time; it was known in the ancient world and highly valued in Byzantium. The ivories that have survived from Charlemagne's time were used for book covers. One beautiful example of the ivory carver's art is a crucifixion panel made at the palace workshop at Aachen sometime in the early 9th century [7.6]. Note the crowded scenes that surround the crucifixion event. Reading clockwise from the bottom left, one sees the Last Supper, the betrayal in the garden, and, at the top, a soldier piercing Jesus' side. As a balance at the top right another soldier offers Jesus a vinegar-soaked sponge on a lance. Below that scene is one of the women at the tomb and, at the bottom, the incredulity of Thomas. Framing these scenes above are the ascension of Christ on the left and the Pentecost on the right, the two scenes separated by a stylized sun and moon. The entire ivory is framed with geometric and abstract floral designs. The composition indicates that the carver had seen some examples of early Christian carving, while the beardless Christ and the flow of the drapery indicate familiarity with Byzantine art.

One surviving Carolingian manuscript that allows us to see both illumination and ivory work is the *Dagulf Psalter*, made as a gift for Pope Hadrian I, who reigned from 772 to 795. The psalms are not illustrated like the ones in the *Utrecht Psalter*; instead, the illustrator begins a tradition that will be fairly normal for psalters in the future: he enlarges and illuminates the initial letter of the first, fifty-first, and hundred-first psalms. The *B* of the first word of Psalm 1, *Beatus vir qui* (Blessed is the man who), is enlarged and decorated in the swelling style of Celtic illumination; the same patterns are echoed on the page margin [7.7].

The ivory covers of the psalter have been preserved and are now in the Louvre [7.8]. Rather than the usual crowded scenes of most of these covers, the ivories from the *Dagulf Psalter* are composed of two scenes on each of the panels; the scenes make references to both the psalter and the papal connection. The panel on the left shows, above, David and his court; below, David is shown singing one of his psalms to the accompaniment of his lyre. The right

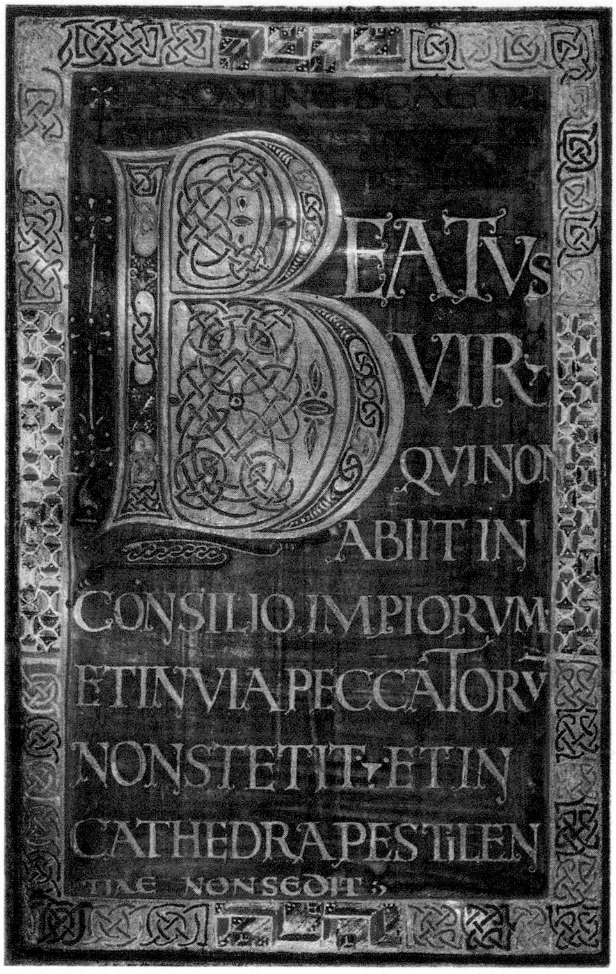

7.7 Beginning of Psalm 1 from the *Dagulf Psalter*. Late 8th century. Manuscript illustration, 7½ × 4⅝" (19 × 12 cm). Austrian National Library. This psalter may well have been produced by a woman's hand at a convent.

7.8 Cover panels for the *Dagulf Psalter*. Late 8th century. Ivory, 6⅛ × 3⅛" (17 × 8 cm). Louvre, Paris. Jerome correcting the psalter (lower right panel) reflects common work in the monasteries of the Carolingian period.

SPORTS AND GAMES

Athletics and Warfare

For the aristocratic males of Carolingian Europe, early adolescence was a period of rigorous athletic training which had one sole aim: to create a knight of arms. Rhabanus Maurus, a contemporary writer, said that it was expected that the youth of the great houses be trained to endure heat, cold, adversity, and pain as part of the normal education and upbringing needed to produce warriors.

Three elements went into that training: swordsmanship, riding skills, and the hunt. Swords had an almost religious significance for early medievals; even in works as late as the *Song of Roland* we see them named, praised, and even studded with relics. Skill with the use of the great Carolingian swords was an art that every potential knight had to acquire.

Furthermore, the knight fought on horseback (that is what separated the knight from the soldier) which meant that he had to learn the equestrian arts not only to ride well but to ride with enough ease that his weapons could be used to full advantage. The *quintain*—a device that pivoted and hit the rider should he not strike a target squarely with a lance—was a common form of practice which had a long and continuing history of use (it is mentioned, for example, in Trollope's 19th-century novel *Barchester Towers* as being part of a day's entertainment).

It was in hunting, especially hunting on horseback, that the knight honed his skills. Carolingian literature is full of tales of the hunt in which the skills of horsemanship and the use of arrows and lances, are combined. The hunting parties (especially the chase) could be dangerous, even lethal, but were seen as part of knightly training and as a prelude for what one scholar has called the "greatest hunt": warfare.

One other aspect of hunting in this period was the use of falcons. Falconry came into Europe from the East (via the Muslims?) where it had been known in both ancient China and Persia. These carefully trained and pampered birds were highly prized, jealously protected, and formed, along with the horse and armor, a central part of the aristocratic patrimony. The use of falcons for hunting would remain as an integral part of rural aristocratic culture well into the late renaissance period. It is still a popular (and aristocratic) part of life among the desert sheiks of the Middle East.

panel depicts Saint Jerome receiving a letter from Pope Damasus instructing him to correct the psalter; the scene below depicts Jerome in the act of working on the psalter while a grateful clergy looks on.

One other advance in manuscript production during the Carolingian period was in the area of fine handwriting or, as it is more technically known, calligraphy. Handwriting before the Carolingian period was cluttered, unformed, and cramped. It was very hard to read because of its erratic flourishes and its lack of symmetry. After 780 scribes in Carolingian scriptoria began to develop a precise and rounded form of lettering that became known as the Carolingian *minuscule*, as opposed to the *majuscule* or capital letter. This form of lettering was so crisp and legible that it soon became a standard form of manuscript writing. Even in the 15th century, the Florentine humanists preferred the minuscule calligraphy for their manuscripts. When printing became popular in the early 16th century, printers soon designed type fonts to conform to Carolingian minuscule. It superseded Gothic type in popularity and is the ancestor of modern standard lettering systems.

CHARLEMAGNE'S PALACE AT AACHEN

Beyond his immediate commercial, military, and political goals, Charlemagne had an overwhelming desire to model his kingdom on that of ancient Rome. His coronation in Rome symbolized the fusion of the ancient imperial ideal with the notion of Christian destiny. It was not accidental that Charlemagne's favorite book—he had it read to him frequently at meals—was Augustine's *The City of God*. One highly visible way of making this ideal concrete was to build a capital.

At Aachen (in French it is called Aix-la-Chapelle) Charlemagne built his palace and royal chapel [7.9]. Except for the chapel (incorporated into the present cathedral), all the buildings of Charlemagne's palace have been destroyed and the Aachen city hall (itself built in the 14th century) covers the palace site. The palace itself was a long one-story building; its main room was the large royal hall, which measured roughly 140 × 60' (42.7 × 18.3 m). So richly decorated that even the fastidious and sophisticated Byzantine legates were favorably impressed, the room had as its focal point

7.9 Model reconstruction of Charlemagne's palace at Aachen. Römisch-Germanisches Zentral Museum, Mainz. The royal hall with its long gallery is in the foreground. The octagonal royal chapel in the background should be compared with San Vitale in Ravenna.

at the western end the emperor's throne. In front of the palace was an open courtyard around which were outbuildings and apartments for the imperial retinue. Around the year 800 the courtyard held a great bronze statue of Theodoric, once king of the Ravenna Ostrogoths, that Charlemagne had brought back from Ravenna to adorn his palace.

The royal hall was joined to Charlemagne's chapel by a long wooden gallery. This royal chapel was probably built around 795. With sixteen exterior walls, the chapel was a central-plan church based on an octagon [7.10]; its model undoubtedly was the church of San Vitale in Ravenna, which Charlemagne had visited and admired. The oc-

7.10 Interior of chapel of Charlemagne, Aachen. This view, toward the east, shows the emperor's tribune in the second story. The ceiling mosaics on the ceiling and the lower-level inscriptions are modern.

tagon formed the main nave of the church, which was surrounded by *cloisters;* the building itself was two-storied. At the eastern end of the chapel was an altar dedicated to the Savior, with a chapel dedicated to the Virgin directly below it. The central space was crowned with an octagonal cupola, the lower part of which was pierced by windows, the main source of light in the church. The outside of the church was plain and severe; the inside was richly ornamented with marbles brought to Aachen from Ravenna and Rome. The interior of the cupola was decorated with a rich mosaic depicting Christ and the twenty-four elders of the Apocalypse (now destroyed; the present mosaics in the chapel are modern copies) while the other planes of the interior were covered with frescoes (now also destroyed). The railing of the upper gallery was made from bronze screens that are still in place, wrought in geometrical forms.

The chapel included two objects that emphasized its royal status: the most important relic of the kingdom, Saint Martin of Tours' cape, and a throne. Charlemagne's throne was on the second floor, opposite the chapel of the Savior. From this vantage point the emperor could observe the liturgical services being conducted in the Savior chapel and at the same time view the Virgin chapel with its rich collection of relics.

Charlemagne's throne, with its curved back and armrests, was mounted by six stone steps. This arrangement was obviously taken from King Solomon's throne as described in the Bible (I Kings 10: 18–19). Charlemagne was to be thought of as the "new Solomon" who, like his ancient prototype, was an ambitious builder, a sagacious lawgiver, and the symbol of national unity. That this analogy was not an idle fancy is proved by a letter from Alcuin, Charlemagne's friend and tutor, to the emperor in anticipation of his return to Aachen: "May I soon be allowed to come with palms, accompanied with children singing psalms, to meet your triumphant glory, and to see once more your beloved face in the Jerusalem of our most dear fatherland, wherein is the temple set up to God by this most wise Solomon."

The Carolingian Monastery

In the period between Saint Benedict and Charlemagne the Benedictine monastery underwent a complex evolution. Originally the monasteries were made up of small communities with fewer than fifteen members who led a life of prayer and work in a rather simple setting. With the decline of city life and the disorders brought on by the repeated invasions of the barbarians after the 5th century, the monastery became increasingly a center of life for rural populations. Monasteries not only kept learning alive and worship intact but were also called upon to serve as shelters for the traveler, rudimentary hospitals for the sick, places of refuge in time of invasion, granaries for the farmer, centers of law for both religious and civil courts, and places that could provide agricultural services such as milling and brewing.

This expansion of services, making the monastery into what has been called a "miniature civic center," inevitably changed the physical character of the monastery compound itself. By Charlemagne's time the monastery was an intricate complex of buildings suitable for the many tasks it was called upon to perform [Table 7.1]. One vivid example of the complexity of the Carolingian monastery can be gained by a study of a plan for

TABLE 7.1 The Major Parts of the Monastery

The Monastic Church	Site of the major religious services.
The Chapter House	Ordinary meeting room of the monastic community; the name comes from the custom of reading a chapter of the rule of Saint Benedict aloud each day to the community.
The Cloister	Technically, the enclosed part of the monastery; more commonly, the enclosed garden and walkway in the interior of the monastery.
The Scriptorium	Library and copying area of the monastery.
The Refectory	Monks' dining hall.
The Novitiate	Quarters for aspirant monks not yet vowed in the community.
The Dormitory	Sleeping area for the monks.
The Infirmary	For sick, retired, and elderly monks.
The Guest House	For visitors, retreatants, and travelers.
The Outbuildings	Buildings for the farms and crafts of the monastery. Small buildings far from the main monastery that housed farmer monks were called *granges.*

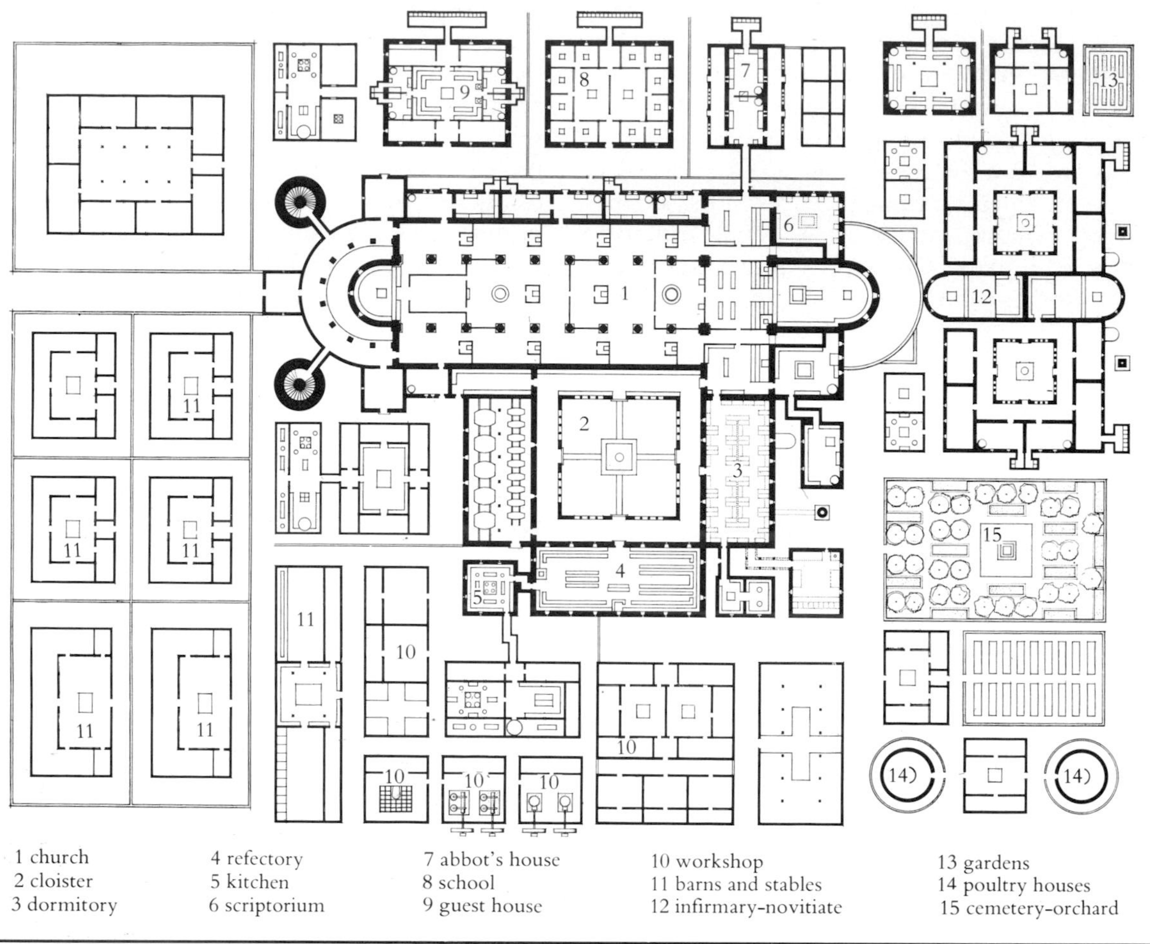

7.11 Plan for an ideal monastery. c. 820. Reconstruction by Walter Horn and Ernest Born from the manuscript in the library of the monastery of Saint Gall in Switzerland. The original plan, 3'8" (1.12 m) across, was drawn to scale on vellum. The monastery site would have been 480' × 640' (146 × 195 m) which would have housed 120 monks and 170 serfs. It was a plan for future monasteries and exerted, over the centuries, considerable influence on monastery construction.

an ideal monastery developed about 820 at the Benedictine abbey of Saint Gall in present-day Switzerland [7.11].

In the Saint Gall plan the monastic church dominated the area. Set off with its two round towers, it was a basilica-style church with numerous entrances for the use of the monks. To the south of the church was a rectangular garden space surrounded by a covered walkway (the *cloister*) from which radiated the monk's dormitory, dining hall *(refectory)*, and kitchens. To the north of the church were a copying room *(scriptorium)*, a separate house for the abbot, a school for youths and young novices, and a guest house. To the extreme south of the church were ranged workshops, barns, and other utilitarian outbuildings. To the east beyond the church were an infirmary and a separate house for aspirant monks (the *novitiate*), gardens, poultry houses, and the community cemetery.

The Romanesque Style

The plan of Saint Gall was never realized in stone, but the Benedictines did participate in ambitious architectural works after the Carolingian period. In the 11th century, after a long period of desolation and warfare, Europe began to stir with new life. Pilgrimages became very popular as travel became safe. Pilgrimage routes—in particular to sites in Spain, England, and Italy—crisscrossed Europe. Crusades were mounted to free the holy places of the Middle East from the Muslims so that pilgrims could journey in peace to the most desired goal of the pilgrim: Jerusalem. In this period monks built and maintained pilgrimage churches and hostels on the major routes of the pilgrims.

The building style of this period (roughly from 1000 to 1200) is called Romanesque because the architecture was larger and more "Roman"-looking than the work done in the earlier medieval centuries. The two most striking characteristics of this architecture were the use of heavy stone arches and generous exterior decoration, mainly sculpture. The Romanesque style had two obvious advantages. One was that the use of heavy stone and masonry walls permitted larger and more spacious interiors. Secondly, the heavy walls could support stone arches (mainly the Roman barrel arch), at least in France and Spain, which in turn permitted fireproof stone and masonry roofs. Long experience had shown that basilica-style churches, with their wooden trusses and wooden roofs, were notoriously susceptible to destruction by fire.

Romanesque architecture sprouted all over Europe, and while it showed great regional variation, its main lines are clear enough. The Benedictine pilgrimage church of Saint Sernin in Toulouse was designed to accommodate the large number of pilgrims as they made their way to the famous shrine of Santiago de Compostela in Spain. A glimpse at the floor plan [7.12] and the interior [7.13] shows clearly that the generous interior space was articulated in such a manner that large numbers of persons besides the monastic community could move freely through the building. For example, the floor plan allows for an aisle parallel to the nave to go completely around the church. In that fashion the monastic choir, which extended out into the nave, was circumvented by the faithful—who could make a complete circle of the church without disturbing the monks.

Exterior church decoration was almost unknown in the Carolingian period, but during the Romanesque period there was a veritable explosion of exterior sculpture. The lack of interior light (precluded by the thick solid walls needed for the roof vaulting) drove the artist outside, in a sense. A favorite area of decoration was the *portal* or doorway, since the crowds would pass through the doors to

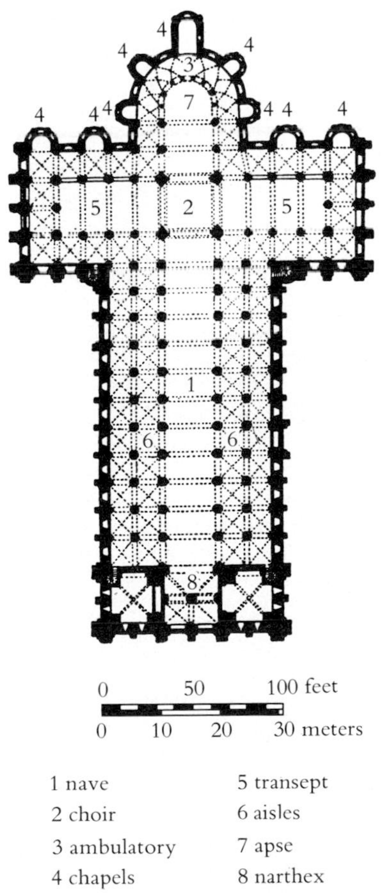

7.12 Floor plan of the church of Saint Sernin, Toulouse. Notice the ample aisles for easy passage of pilgrim groups around the entire church. The radiating chapels around the ambulatory permitted many priests to celebrate Mass simultaneously.

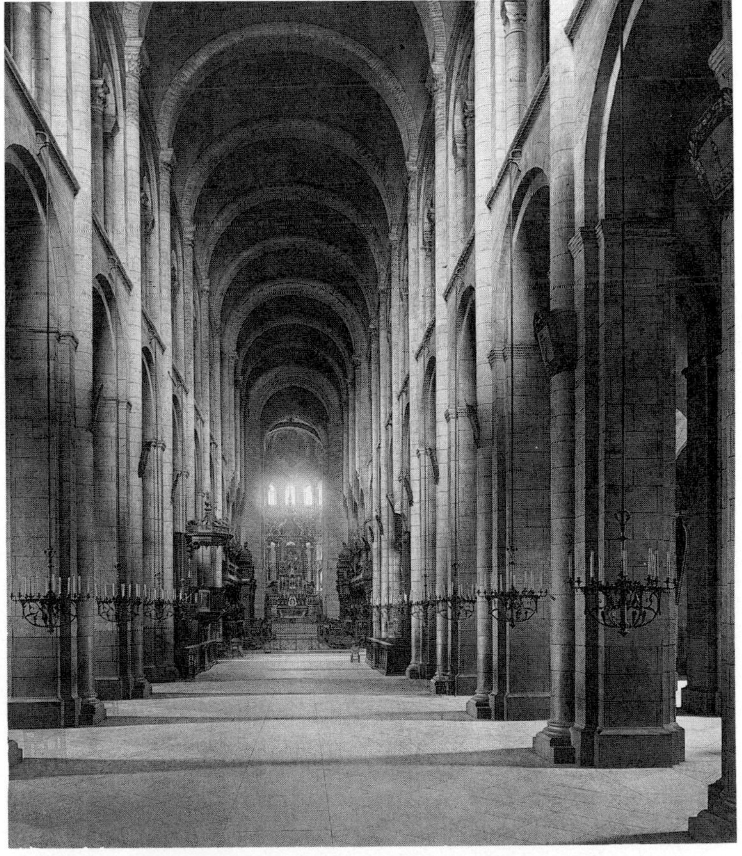

7.13 Interior of the church of Saint Sernin, Toulouse. c. 1080–1120. The massive ceiling vaults are called barrel or tunnel vaults. This heavy stonework required heavy walls to support the weight of the vaults. The galleries, with their own vaults, also helped with the support of the cut-stone ceiling vaults.

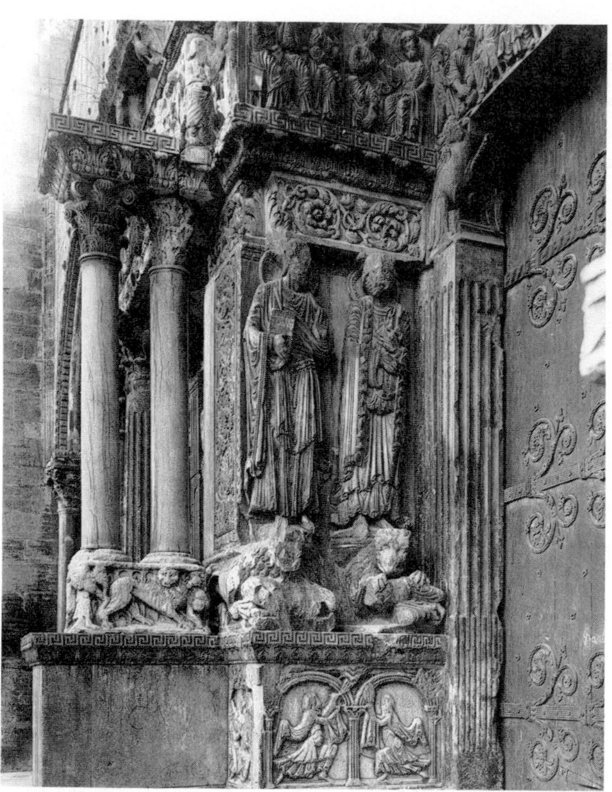

7.14 Jamb on the central portal, Saint Gilles du Gard, France. c. 1140. Notice the echoes of classical column capitals and low-relief carving on the jambs.

7.15 *Demon of Luxury,* nave capital sculpture, abbey church of La Madeleine, Vézelay. c. 1130. This kind of extravagant figure would be criticized by monastic reformers of the 12th century.

7.16 *Jeremiah the prophet,* trumeau of south portal, Saint Pierre, Moissac, France. Early 12th century. The serpentine figure of the prophet leans toward the church as he holds the scroll of his biblical book. The lions probably reflect the influence of Islamic art from Spain.

enter the church and receive edifying instruction in the process. The artist might decorate a door jamb [7.14], a captal [7.15], or the central supporting post of a portal, the *trumeau* [7.16].

The fullest iconographic program of the Romanesque sculptor can usually be found in the half-moon-shaped space called the *tympanum* over the portal; Romanesque churches in France offer many splendid examples of this elaborated art. The sculptural program over the inner west door of the Benedictine abbey church of Sainte Madeleine at Vézelay is representative of the elaborated art in stone [7.17].

7.17 *Pentecost*, tympanum, abbey church of La Madeleine, Vézelay. c. 1120–1132. The lower band of figures reflects all of the peoples of the earth called to salvation by the central figure of Christ.

The Vézelay tympanum depicts Christ, ascending into heaven, giving his church the mission to preach the gospel to the entire world. Christ, in the center almond shape called the *mandorla*, sends the power of the Holy Spirit into the apostles who cluster on either side and just below with copies of the gospel in their hands. Below the apostles the lintel stone depicts the peoples of the world, including fanciful races known to the sculptor only through the legendary travel books and encyclopedias that circulated in Europe. The theme of the exotic peoples to be healed by the gospel is repeated in the eight arching compartments above the central scene, which depict strange peoples, lepers, cripples, and others who need to hear the gospel. The outer arches, or *archivolts*, depict the signs of the zodiac and the symbolic seasons of the year, a reminder that the gospel depicted in the central scene is to be preached "in season and out"; these symbolic medallions are interspersed with mythical and fantastic beasts. The outer archivolts are purely decorative, derived perhaps from Islamic sources known to the artists through the Muslim architecture of Spain.

Romanesque style was a European phenomenon—its variant forms in Italy, Germany, and England give ample testimony—and a summing-up of much of European culture between the end of the Carolingian period and the rise of city life and the Gothic style in the late 12th century. The roots of the Romanesque were in the Benedictine tradition of service, scholarship, and solidity. Churches like Vézelay also manifest the period's concern with travel, expansion, and the attendant knowledge that comes from such mobility. When reaction came against the more extravagant forms of Romanesque decoration it came from Bernard of Clairvaux (1090–1153), who was primarily a monastic reformer. Bernard was horrified by the fantastic nature of Romanesque sculpture since he felt so many "and so marvelous are the varieties of diverse shapes that we are more tempted to read in the marbles than in the Book and to spend our whole day wondering at these things rather than meditating on the Law of God." Even Bernard's strictures testify to the close relationship between the Benedictines and the Romanesque (especially the French Romanesque), which is another reason the period after Charlemagne and before the primacy of the city can be called simply the Benedictine Age.

SUMMARY

Our attention in this chapter shifted from Byzantium to the west and, more specifically, to the rise of the kingdom of the Franks under Charlemagne. The so-called Carolingian Renaissance rekindled the life of culture after the dark period following the fall of the last Roman emperor in the West in the late 5th century and the rise of the so-called barbarian tribes.

Charlemagne's reign saw the standardization of monasticism, worship, music, and education in the church. Those reforms would give general shape to western Catholicism that, in some ways, endured into the modern period. Equally important was Charlemagne's assumption of the title of Holy Roman Emperor. That act would establish a political office that would exist in Europe until the end of World War I in the 20th century. It also became a cause for friction between Rome and Constantinople because the Byzantine emperors saw Charlemagne's act as an intrusion on their legitimate claim to be the successors of the old Roman Empire.

The Carolingian world was essentially rural and feudal. Society was based on a rather rigid hierarchy with the emperor at the top, the nobles and higher clergy below him, and the vast sea of peasants bound to the land at the bottom of the pyramid. There was little in the way of city life on any scale. The outpost of rural Europe was the miniature town known as the monastery or the stronghold of the nobles. The rise of the city and increased social mobility would eventually destroy the largely agricultural and feudal society as the High Middle Ages emerged in the 11th century.

Finally there was Charlemagne as a mythic figure who eventually became drawn larger than life in the *Song of Roland*. The growth of such myths always occurs because they have some deep desires behind them. In the case of Charlemagne, the desire was to describe the ideal warrior who could perform two very fundamental tasks for Europe: vanquish the Islamic powers which threatened Christian Europe and provide a model for a unified empire (the Holy Roman Empire) that would be both a perfect feudal society and one strong enough to accomplish the first task of destroying Islam. Not without reason was the *Song of Roland* a central poem for the first Crusaders who turned their faces to the east.

Pronunciation Guide

Aachen: Ah-ken
Aix-la-Chapelle: Eye-lah-shap-el
Alcuin: Al-quin
Dagulf: Dah-gulf
Harun al-Rashid: Haw-RUNE all-raw-sheed
horarium: hoar-ARE-e-um
Hroswitha: Haw-ros-WITH-ah *or* Ross-WITH-ah
psalter: SALT-er
Quem Quæritis: kwem-QUAY-re-tus
Roland: ROLL-on
Roncesvalles: Ron-sa-vals
trope: TROP
Utrecht: YOU-trek(t)
Vézelay: Vez-e-LAY

Exercises

1. The "seven liberal arts" are divided into the trivium and the quadrivium. How much of the trivium lingers in primary education today? What has been added to those "trivial" subjects?
2. Two subjects studied in the quadrivium were music and astronomy. Those subjects were quite different from what we understand them to be today. How were they understood and how do we understand them?
3. One feature of the Carolingian period was the central place of monasticism. Why was monasticism exceptionally suited to a time when there was little urban life?
4. Many scholars have argued that monasticism is the living out of a utopian ideal. How is monasticism a "utopian" behavior and to what degree is it also a form of countercultural living?
5. Why is plainchant (Gregorian chant) ideally suited for congregational singing, especially for the unaccompanied voice?
6. Contrast the place of books in early medieval culture and in our own beyond the obvious issue of our better production technologies.
7. Drama evolved out of worship in the early medieval period just as Greek tragedy evolved out of worship in its time. Speculate on why there should be this connection between worship and drama.
8. Byzantine churches tended to lavish their decorative efforts on the insides of churches while Romanesque churches tended to decorate the outsides, more especially the façades. Suggest reasons for this widely observable fact.

Further Reading

Brault, Gerald. *The Song of Roland*. 2 vols. University Park: University of Pennsylvania Press, 1978. Critical edition with notes. Essential.

Brondsted, Johannes. *The Vikings*. Translated by Kalle Skov. New York: Penguin Books, 1960. A basic survey of the Northmen; with some illustrations in black and white.

Bullough, Donald. *The Age of Charlemagne*. New York: Putnam, 1966. Well-written and lavishly illustrated.

Dunbabin, Jean. *France in the Making*. New York: Oxford University Press, 1985. An account of how the Frankish kingdom evolved into what we know as France.

Folz, Robert. *The Coronation of Charlemagne: 25th December 800*. Translated by J. E. Anderson. London: Routledge & Kegan Paul, 1974. A detailed but readable study of Charlemagne's imperial ideals.

Henderson, George. *Early Medieval*. New York: Penguin Books, 1972. Part of the "style and civilization" series; an extremely readable and thorough study of artistic styles in the early medieval period with 150 illustrations and a thorough bibliography.

Knowles, David. *Christian Monasticism*. New York: McGraw-Hill, 1969. A readable survey of the history of Christian monasticism by a distinguished monastic historian.

McNamara, Jo Ann, ed. *Sainted Women Of the Dark Ages*. Durham: Duke University Press, 1992. Anthology of saintly lives. Important.

Price, Lorna. *The Plan of St. Gall in Brief*. Berkeley: University of California Press, 1982. An inexpensive condensed edition of the definitive study of Walter Horn and Ernest Born. Excellent drawings and floor plans. Very valuable.

Riche, Pierre. *Daily Life in the World of Charlemagne*. Translated by Jo Ann McNamara. Philadelphia: University of Pennsylvania Press, 1978. A fascinating and indispensable study of all facets of Carolingian life.

Thorpe, Lewis (trans.). *Einhard and Notker the Stammerer: Two Lives of Charlemagne*. New York: Penguin Books, 1969. Basic sources from the period with a good introduction.

Wallace-Hadrill, J. M. *The Frankish Church*. Oxford: The Clarendon Press, 1983. The definitive study of ecclesiastical life in the age of Charlemagne.

		GENERAL EVENTS	LITERATURE & PHILOSOPHY	ART
EARLY MIDDLE AGES	768	**987** Paris made center of feudal kingdom of Hugh Capet		
	1000 Romanesque Period	**11th cent.** Capetian kings consolidate power and expand French kingdom **1096–1099** First Crusade; capture of Jerusalem by Christians	**12th cent.** Golden Age of University of Paris under scholastic masters **1113** Abelard begins teaching in Paris; meets Heloise **1121** Abelard, *Sic et Non;* birth of Scholasticism	**12th cent.** *Notre Dame de Belle Verrière,* stained glass window at Chartres
	1140 Early Gothic Period	**1141** Saint Bernard of Clairvaux leads condemnation of Abelard at Council of Sens **c. 1150** Universities of Paris and Bologna founded **c. 1163** Oxford University founded **1180** Philip Augustus assumes throne of France; promotes Paris as capital	**after 1150** Recovery of lost texts by Aristotle and others via Arabic translations **c. 1190** Maimonides, *Guide for the Perplexed*	**c. 1145–1170** Tympanum of right door, Royal Portal, Chartres
HIGH MIDDLE AGES	1194 Mature Gothic Period	**1202–1204** Fourth Crusade; crusaders sack Constantinople on way to Holy Land **c. 1209** Cambridge University founded **1215** Magna Carta, limiting powers of king, signed in England **c. 1220** Growth begins of mendicant friars: Franciscans, Dominicans **1258** Robert de Sorbon founds Paris hospice for scholars, forerunner of Sorbonne **1270** Eighth Crusade; death of Saint Louis of France **c. 1271–1293** Marco Polo travels to China and India **1291** Fall of Acre, last Christian stronghold in Holy Land **1348–1367** Universities based on Paris model founded in Prague, Vienna, Cracow, Pecs	**13th cent.** Era of secular poems; Goliardic verse **c. 1224–1226** Saint Francis of Assisi, "Canticle of Brother Sun" **c. 1267–1273** Aquinas, *Summa Theologica* **1300** Dante exiled from Florence **c. 1303–1321** Dante, *Divine Comedy* **c. 1385–1400** Chaucer, *The Canterbury Tales*	**c. 1200** Charlemagne window at Chartres **c. 1215** *Christ Blessing,* trumeau, south porch, Chartres **c. 1215–c. 1250** Guild windows at Chartres
	1400			

CHAPTER

8 HIGH MIDDLE AGES: THE SEARCH FOR SYNTHESIS

ARCHITECTURE	MUSIC
	10th cent. Organum develops
 **c. 1130** Halt of construction at Great Third Abbey Church of Cluny	**11th cent.** Guido of Arezzo invents musical notation used today **12th cent.** Notre Dame School of Paris is center of music study and composition
1140 Abbot Suger begins rebuilding Abbey Church of Saint Denis; Gothic style evolves: use of pointed arch, flying buttress, window tracery **c. 1163–1250** Cathedral of Notre Dame, Paris **c. 1180** Philip Augustus commissions Louvre as royal residence and treasury	**12th–13th cent.** French troubadours and trouvères flourish **1160** Léonin of Paris, *Magnus Liber Organi* **1181** Pérotin "the Great," director of Notre Dame School of Paris
1194 Chartres cathedral destroyed by fire; rebuilding begins 1195 (ends 1260) **1220–1269** Cathedral of Amiens **c. 1235** Honnecourt, notebook **1243–1248** Sainte Chapelle, Paris **1247–1568** Cathedral of Beauvais; cathedral of Strasbourg **1399–1439** Spire of Strasbourg cathedral erected	**13th cent.** German minnesingers flourish **c. 1250** Polyphonic motets are principal form of composition

C H A P T E R

8

HIGH MIDDLE AGES: THE SEARCH FOR SYNTHESIS

THE SIGNIFICANCE OF PARIS

FROM ABOUT 1150 TO 1300 Paris could well claim to be the center of Western civilization. Beyond its position as a royal seat, it was a strong mercantile center. Its annual trade fair was famous. In addition, Paris gave birth to Gothic architecture, the philosophical and theological traditions known as scholasticism, and the educational community that in time became known as the university. These three creations have their own distinct history but they sprang from a common intellectual impulse: the desire to articulate all knowledge in a systematic manner.

The culture of the Middle Ages derives from the twin sources of all Western high culture: the humane learning inherited from the culture of Greece and Rome and the accepted faith of the West, which has its origin in the worldview of the Judeo-Christian scriptures and religious worldview.

The flowering of a distinct expression of culture in and around medieval Paris was made possible by a large number of factors. There was a renewed interest in learning, fueled largely by the discovery of hitherto lost texts from the classical world—especially the writings of Aristotle—which came to the West via the Muslim world. The often ill-fated Crusades begun in the 11th century to recover the Holy Land and the increasing vogue for pilgrimages created a certain cosmopolitanism that, in turn, weakened the static feudal society. Religious reforms initiated by new religious orders like that of the Cistercians in the 12th century and the begging friars in the 13th breathed new life into the church.

Beyond these more generalized currents one can also point to individuals of genius who were crucial in the humanistic renaissance of the time. The University of Paris is inextricably linked with the name of Peter Abelard just as scholasticism is associated with the name of Thomas Aquinas. The Gothic style, unlike most art movements, can be pinpointed to a specific time at a particular place and with a single individual. Gothic architecture began near Paris at the Abbey of Saint Denis in the first half of the 12th century under the sponsorship of the head of the abbey, the Abbot Suger (1080–1151).

THE GOTHIC STYLE

Suger's Building Program for Saint Denis

The Benedictine Abbey of Saint Denis over which Abbot Suger presided from 1122 until his death nearly twenty-nine years later was the focal point for French patriotism. The abbey church—built in Carolingian times—housed the relics of Saint Denis, a 5th-century martyr who had evangelized the area of Paris before his martyrdom. The crypt of the church served as burial place for Frankish kings and nobles from before the reign of Charlemagne, although it lacked the tomb of Charlemagne himself. One concrete link between the Abbey of Saint Denis and Charlemagne came through a series of literary works. The fictitious *Pélerinage de Charlemagne* claimed that the relics of the Passion housed at the abbey had been brought there by Charlemagne himself when he returned from a pilgrimage-crusade to the Holy Land. Another work, the *Pseudo-Turpin,* has Charlemagne returning to the Abbey of Saint Denis after his Spanish campaign and proclaiming all France to be under the protection and tutelage of the saint. These two legends were widely believed in the Middle Ages; there is fair evidence that Suger himself accepted their authenticity. The main themes of the legends—pilgrimages, crusades, and the mythical presence of Charlemagne—created a story about the abbey that made it a major Christian shrine as well as one worthy of the royal city of Paris.

Pilgrims and visitors came to Paris to visit Saint Denis either because of the fame of the abbey's relics or because of the annual *Lendit,* the trade fair held near the precincts of the abbey. Accordingly, in 1124 Suger decided to build a new church to accommodate those who flocked to the popular pilgrimage center. This rebuilding program took the better part of fifteen years and never saw completion. Suger mentions as models two sacred buildings that by his time already had archetypal significance for Christianity. He wanted his church to be as lavish and brilliant as Hagia Sophia in Constantinople, which he knew only by reputation, and as loyal to the will of God as the Temple of Solomon as it was described in the Bible.

The first phase of Suger's project was basically a demolition and repair job; he had to tear down the more deteriorated parts of the old church and replace them. He reconstructed the western façade of the church and added two towers. In order better to handle the pilgrimage crowds and the increasingly elaborate processions called for in the medieval liturgy, the entrance was given three portals. The *narthex,* the part of the church one enters first (before the nave) was rebuilt and the old nave was to be extended by about 40' (12.2 m). In about 1140 Suger abruptly stopped work on the narthex to commence work at the opposite end—the *choir,* the area of the church where the monks sang the Office. By his own reckoning, he spent three years and three months at this new construction. The finished choir made a revolutionary change in architecture in the West.

Suger's choir was surrounded by a double *ambulatory,* an aisle around the apse and behind the high altar. The outer ambulatory had seven radiating chapels to accommodate the increasing number of monks who were priests and thus said Mass on a daily basis. Two tall windows pierced the walls of each chapel so that there was little external masonry wall in relation to the amount of space covered by windows. The chapels were shallow enough to permit the light from the windows to fall on the inner ambulatory [8.1].

Although Suger's nave was never completed, there is some evidence that it would have had characteristics similar to that of the choir: crossed rib vaults with an abundance of stained-glass windows to permit the flooding of light into the church. We can get some idea of what that nave might have looked like by looking at churches directly inspired by Saint Denis: the cathedrals of Senlis and Noyons [8.2] (their bishops were both at the consecration of Saint Denis in 1144), begun respectively in 1153 and 1157, as well as the cathedral of Notre Dame in Paris, the first stone of which was laid in 1163. This quick emulation of the style of Saint Denis blossomed by the end of the century

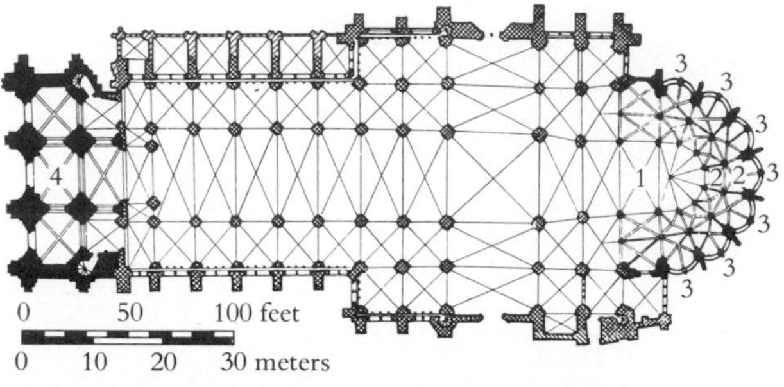

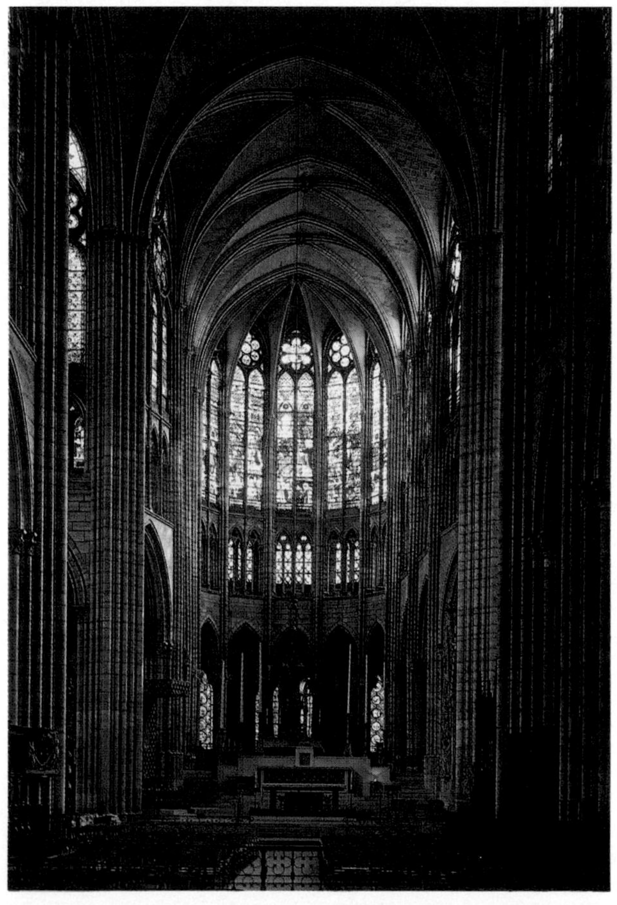

8.1 Plan of the abbey church of Saint Denis, built around 1140, and photograph of the ambulatory. Parts of the existing church shaded black in the plan are those rebuilt by Abbot Suger. The photograph shows how use of the ribbed vault and pointed arches gives scope for the passage of light through the lancet windows.
1. choir 3. radiating chapels
2. ambulatory 4. narthex

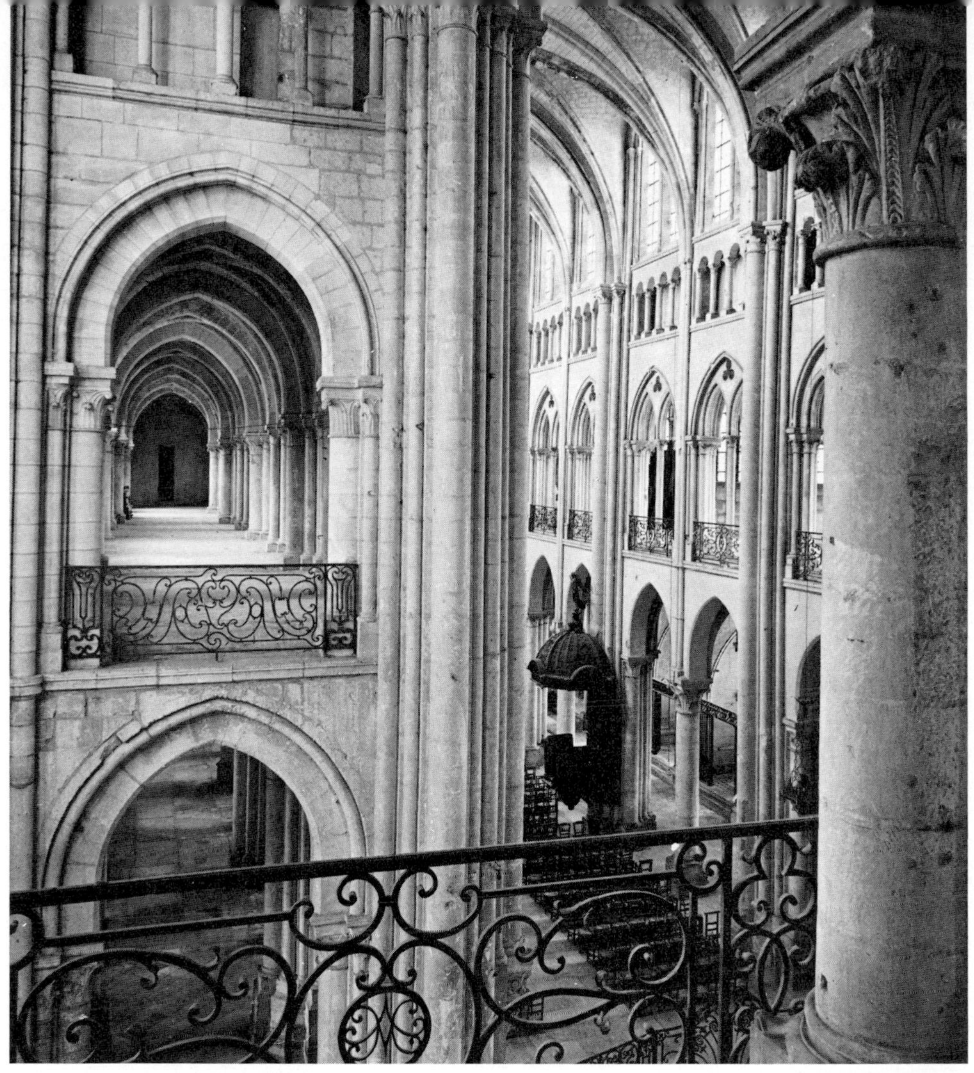

8.2 Interior of Noyons Cathedral. The nave was finished between 1285 and 1330. A fine example of the older style of Gothic architecture. The walls have four rather than the typical three levels: the nave arcade at floor level; the tribune gallery; a triforium; the clerestory with its windows. The rather thick walls of the triforium level would give way, in other Gothic churches, to thinner walls and more pointed arches.

into a veritable explosion of cathedral building in the cities and towns radiating out from Paris, the so-called Île-de-France. The Gothic impulse so touched other countries as well that by the end of the 13th century there were fine examples of Gothic architecture in England, Germany, and Italy.

The term *Gothic* merits a word of explanation. It was used first in the 17th century as a pejorative term meaning "barbarous" or "rude" to distinguish buildings that did not follow the classical models of Greece and Rome, a use still current in the mid-18th century. It was only as a result of the reappraisal of the medieval period in the last century that the word lost its negative meaning.

It is tempting to say that the common characteristic of these cathedrals was the desire for verticality. We tend to identify the Gothic style with the pointed arch, pinnacles and columns, and increasingly higher walls buttressed from the outside by flying arches to accommodate the weight of a pitched roof and the sheer size of the ascending walls [8.3]. It is a truism that the medieval builders seem to engage in contests to build higher and higher almost as a matter of civic pride: Chartres (begun in 1194) reached a height of 122' (37.2 m);

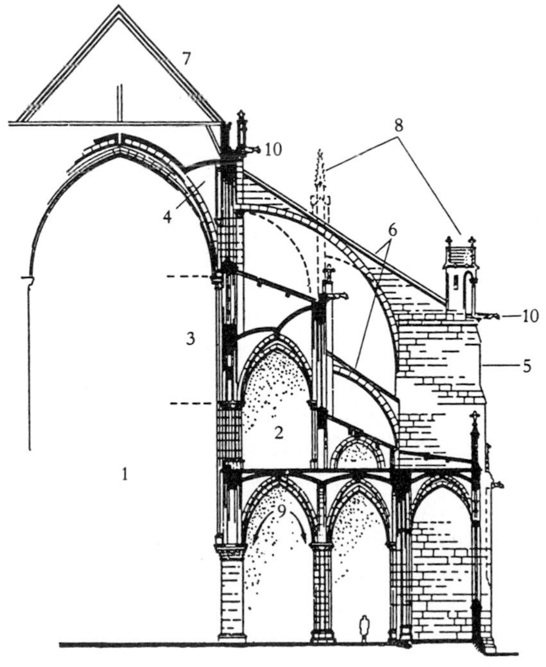

8.3 Transverse half-sectional drawing of the cathedral of Notre Dame in Paris. The height is about 140' (42.7 m). The tiny figure at the lower right gives some sense of scale.

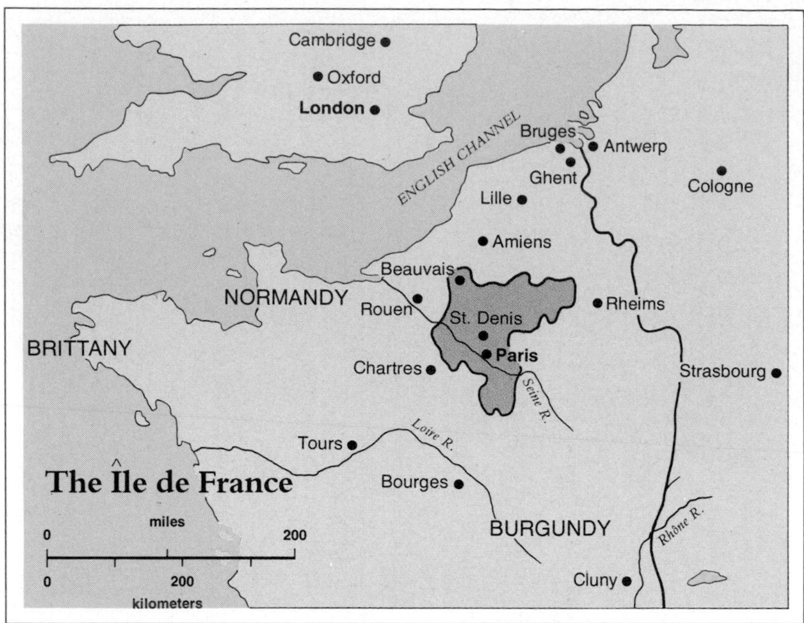

almost as a response, the builders of Amiens (begun 1220) stretched that height to 140' (42.7 m), while Beauvais (begun 1247) pushed verticality almost to the limit with a height of 157' (47.9 m) from the cathedral pavement to the roof arch; indeed, Beauvais had a serious collapse of the roof when the building was barely completed.

That verticality typified Gothic architecture is indisputable, yet Romanesque architects only a generation before Suger had attempted the same verticality, as is evident in such churches as the proposed third abbey church of Cluny or the pilgrimage church at Santiago de Compostela in Spain. What prevented the Romanesque architect from attaining greater verticality was not lack of desire but insufficient technical means. The pointed arch was known in Romanesque architecture but not fully understood. It distributed weight more thoroughly in a downward direction and lessened the need for the massive interior piers of the typical Romanesque church. The size of the piers was further reduced by using buttresses outside the building to prop the interior piers and absorb some of the downward thrust. Furthermore, the downward thrust of the exterior buttresses themselves could be increased by the addition of heavy decorative devices such as spires.

The net result of these technical innovations was to lessen the thickness, weight, and mass of the walls of the Gothic cathedral. This reduction provided an opportunity for greater height with less bulk to absorb the weight of the vaulted roof. Such a reduction made the walls more available as framing devices for the windows that are so characteristic of the period. It has been said, perhaps with some exaggeration, that walls in Gothic cathedrals were replaced by masonry scaffolding for windows [8.4]. In any case, the basic characteristic of Gothic architecture is not verticality but luminosity. The Gothic may be described as transparent—diaphanous—architecture.

The Mysticism of Light

Abbot Suger wrote two short booklets about his stewardship of the abbey and his ideas about the building and decorating program he initiated for the abbey church—extremely important sources for our understanding of the thought that stood behind the actual work of the builder and artist. Underlying Suger's description of the abbey's art treasures and architectural improvements was a theory or (perhaps better) a theology of beauty. Suger was heavily indebted to his reading of certain mystical treatises written by Dionysius the Areopagite (whom Suger and many of his contemporaries assumed was the Saint Denis for whom the abbey was named), a 5th-century Syrian monk whose works on mystical theology were strongly influenced by neo-Platonic philosophers as well as by Christian doctrine. In the doctrine of the Pseudo-Dionysius (as later generations have called him), every created thing partakes, however imperfectly, of the essence of God. There is an ascending hierarchy of existence that ranges from inert min-

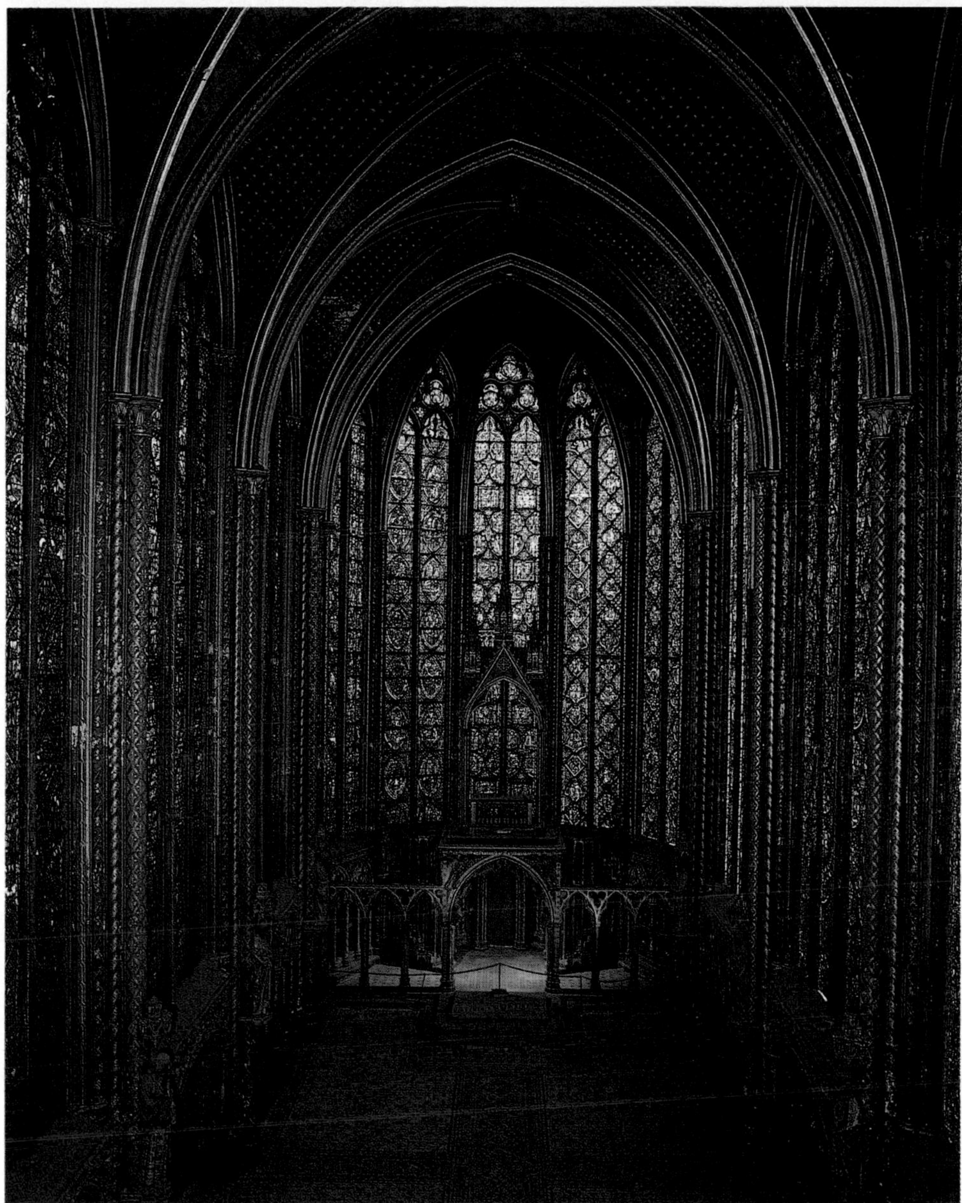

8.4 Interior of the upper chapel of La Sainte Chapelle, Paris. 1243–1248. Built to house relics of Christ's passion, this is an exquisite example of Gothic luminosity. Restored heavily, the overall effect is nonetheless maintained of skeletal architecture used as a frame for windows.

eral matter to the purity of light, which is God. The Pseudo-Dionysius described all of creation under the category of light: Every created thing is a small light that illumines the mind a bit. Ultimately, as light becomes more pure (as one ascends the hierarchy) one gets closer to pure light, which is God.

The high point of this light mysticism is expressed in the stained-glass window. Suger himself believed that when he finished his nave with its glass windows (never completed in fact) to complement his already finished choir, he would have a total structure that would make a single statement: "Bright is that which is brightly coupled with the bright, and bright is the noble edifice which is pervaded by the new light [*lux nova*]." The *lux nova* is an allusion to the biblical description of God as the God of light. Suger did not invent stained glass but he fully exploited its possibilities both by encouraging an architecture that could put it to its most advantageous employment and at the same time providing a theory to justify and enhance its use.

No discussion of light and glass in this period can overlook the famous windows of the cathedral of Chartres, a small but important commercial town just south of Paris. When the cathedral was rebuilt after a disastrous fire in 1194 (which destroyed everything except the west façade of the church), the new building gave wide scope to the glazier's art.

8.5 ***Notre Dame de Belle Verrière,*** **Chartres Cathedral. Early 13th century. The heavy vertical and horizontal lines are iron reinforcing rods to hold the window in place. The thinner lines are the leading. Details such as the Virgin's eyes, nose, and mouth are painted in. The red is a distinctive characteristic of the Chartres stained-glass workshops.**

When the walls were rebuilt, more than 173 windows were installed covering an area of about 2000 square yards (1672 square meters) of surface. It is important to note that, except for some fine details like facial contours, the glass is not painted. The glaziers produced the colors (the blues and reds of Chartres are famous and the tones were never again reproduced exactly) by adding metallic salts to molten glass. Individual pieces were fitted together like a jigsaw puzzle and fixed by leading the pieces together. Individual pieces were rarely larger than 8' (2.4 m) square, but 30' (9.2 m) sections could be bonded together safely in the leading process. The sections were set into stone frames (mullions) and reinforced in place by the use of iron retaining rods. Windows as large as 60' (18.3 m) high could be created in this fashion.

It would be useful at this point to compare the aesthetics of the stained-glass window to the mosaics discussed in Chapter 6. There was a strong element of light mysticism in the art of Byzantine mosaic decoration, derived from some of the same sources later utilized by Abbot Suger: neo-Platonism and the allegorical reading of the Bible. The actual perception of light in the two art forms, however, was radically different. The mosaic refracted light off an opaque surface. The "sacred" aura of the light in a Byzantine church comes from the oddly mysterious breaking up of light as it strikes the irregular surface of the mosaic tesserae. The stained-glass window was the medium through which the light was seen directly, even if it was subtly muted into diverse colors and combinations of colors.

You can only "read" the meaning of the window by looking at it from the inside with an exterior light source—the sun—illuminating it. It was a more perfectly Platonic analogy of God's relationship to the world and its creatures. The viewer sees an object (the illustrated window) but "through it" is conscious of a distant unseen source (the sun—God) that illumines it and gives it its intelligibility. (*Read* is not a rhetorical verb in this context. It was a commonplace of the period to refer to the stained-glass windows as the "Bible of the Poor" since the illiterate could "read" the biblical stories in their illustrated form in the cathedral.)

A close examination of one window at Chartres will illustrate the complexity of this idea. The *Notre Dame de Belle Verrière* (Our Lady of the Beautiful Window) [8.5], one of the most famous works in the cathedral, is a 12th-century work saved from the rubble of the fire of 1194 and reinstalled in the south choir. The window, with its characteristic pointed arch frame, depicts the Virgin enthroned with the Christ Child surrounded by worshiping angels bearing candles and censers. Directly above her is the dove that represents the Holy Spirit and at the very top a stylized church building representing the cathedral built in her honor.

To the simple viewer the window honored the Virgin, to whom one prayed in time of need and to whom the church was dedicated. The person of some theological sophistication would further recognize the particular scene of the Virgin enthroned as the symbol of Mary as the Seat of Wisdom, a very ancient motif in religious art. The window also has a conceptual link with the exterior sculptural program. In the tympanum of the portal is an enthroned Madonna and Christ Child with two censer-bearing angels. This scene is surrounded by sculptured arches, called *archivolts,* in which there are symbolic representations of the Seven Liberal Arts [8.6], which together constitute a shorthand version of the window.

The Blessed Virgin depicted as the Seat of Wisdom would be an especially attractive motif for the town of Chartres. The cathedral school was a flourishing center of literary and philosophical studies, studies which emphasized that human learning became wisdom only when it led to the source of wisdom, God. The fact that Mary was depicted here in glass would also call to mind an oft-repeated *exemplum* (moral example) used in medieval preaching and theology: Christ was born of a virgin. He passed through her body as light passes through a window, completely intact without changing the glass. The Christ/light—Mary/glass analogy is an apt and deepened metaphor to be seen in the *Belle Verrière* of Chartres.

8.6 Scenes from the life of the Virgin Mary. Tympanum of the right door of the royal portal, west façade, Chartres Cathedral. Done between 1145 and 1170, the central panel shows the Virgin and Child as an almost mirror image of the Belle Verrière (Figure 8.5). The arch has adoring angels while the outer arch (the archivolt) depicts the Seven Liberal Arts. At the lower left is Aristotle dipping his pen in ink with the female figure of Dialectic above him. Under the central figure of the Virgin are scenes from the life of Mary and the young Christ. At the lower left one can see the scene of the Annunciation.

8.7 Grotesques and a gargoyle waterspout on a tower terrace of the cathedral of Notre Dame, Paris. Many of these figures are modern representations of originals that were badly damaged during the French Revolution.

That kind of interpretation can be applied profitably to many aspects of Gothic art and architecture. Builders and theologians worked closely together while a cathedral was under construction. The church authorities felt it a primary duty not only to build a place suitable for divine worship but also to utilize every opportunity to teach and edify the participating worshiper. The famous Gothic gargoyles [8.7] are a good example of this blend of functionality and didacticism. These carved beasts served the practical purpose of funneling rainwater off the roofs while, in their extended and jutting positions on the roofs and buttresses, signifying that evil flees the sacred precincts of the church. At a far more ambitious level, the whole decorative scheme of a cathedral was an attempt to tell an integrated story about the history of salvation, a story alluded to in both profane and divine learning. The modern visitor may be overwhelmed by what appears a chaotic jumble of sculptures depicting biblical scenes, allegorical figures, symbols of the labors of the month, signs of the Zodiac, representatives of pagan learning, and panoramic views of Last Judgments; for the medieval viewer the variegated scenes represented a patterned whole. The decoration of the cathedral was, as it were, the common vocabulary of sermons, folk wisdom, and school learning fleshed out in stone.

The Many Meanings of the Gothic Cathedral

Some theological and philosophical background is crucial for an appreciation of the significance of the Gothic cathedral, but it is a serious oversimplification to view the cathedral only in the light of its intellectual milieu. The cathedral was, after all, the preeminent building in the episcopal towns of the Île-de-France, as a view of any of the towns shows. The cathedral overwhelms the town either by crowning a hilly site, as at Laon, or rising up above the town plain, as at Amiens. The cathedrals were *town* buildings (Saint Denis, a monastic church, is a conspicuous exception) and one might well inquire into their functional place in the life of the town. It is simplistic to think that their presence in the town reflected a credulous faith on the part of the populace or the egomania of the civil and religious builders. In fact, the cathedral served vital social and economic functions in medieval society.

A modern analogy illustrates the social function of architecture and building. Many small towns in America, especially those in rural areas of the South and the Northeast, center their civic and commercial life around a town square. The courthouse symbolically emanates social control (justice), social structures (births, weddings, and deaths are registered there), power (the sheriff, commissioners or aldermen, and the mayor are housed there), and—to a degree—culture, with its adjacent park and military or civic monuments to the founders and war dead. The better stores, the "uptown" churches, and the other appurtenances of respectability—banks, lawyers' and physicians' offices—cluster about the square. (The urbanization and suburbanization of America has steadily destroyed this basic symmetry, replacing it with a far more diffuse city or suburban pattern where the concept of "center" is less easy to identify.) The cathedral square of the typical European or Latin American town is the ancestor of the courthouse square. The difference is that the medieval cathedral exercised a degree of social control and integration more comprehensive than that of the courthouse.

The cathedral and its power were a serious force that shaped both individual and social life in the town. The individual was baptized in, made a communicant of, married in, and buried from, the cathedral. Schooling was obtained from the cathedral school and social services (hospitals, poor relief, orphanages, and so on) directed by the decisions of the cathedral staff (the *chapter*). The daily and yearly round of life was regulated by the horarium of the cathedral. People rose and ate and went to bed in rhythm with the tolling of the cathedral bell just as they worked or played in line with the feast days of the liturgical calendar of the church year. Citizens could sue and be sued in the church courts, and those same courts dispensed justice on a par with the civil courts; the scenes of the Last Judgment over the central portals of medieval cathedrals referred to more than divine justice.

Far more significant than the social interaction of town and cathedral was the economic impact of the cathedral on the town. The building of a cathedral was an extremely expensive enterprise. When the people of Chartres decided to rebuild their cathedral in 1194 the bishop pledged all of the diocesan revenues for three years (three to five million dollars!) simply to initiate the project [8.8]. It should be remembered that a town like Chartres was very small in the late 12th century, with no more than ten to fifteen thousand residents in the town itself. Some economic historians have attempted to show that the combination of civic pride and religious enthusiasm that motivated the town to build a cathedral was economically ruinous in the long run. The majority of scholars, however, insist that it was precisely economic gain that was the significant factor in construction. This was surely the case with Chartres.

From the late 9th century Chartres had been a major pilgrimage site. The cathedral possessed a relic of the Virgin (the tunic she wore when Jesus was born) given by Charles the Bald, the great-grandson of Charlemagne, in 876. Relics were very popular throughout the Middle Ages and this particular one was specially important to the pilgrims

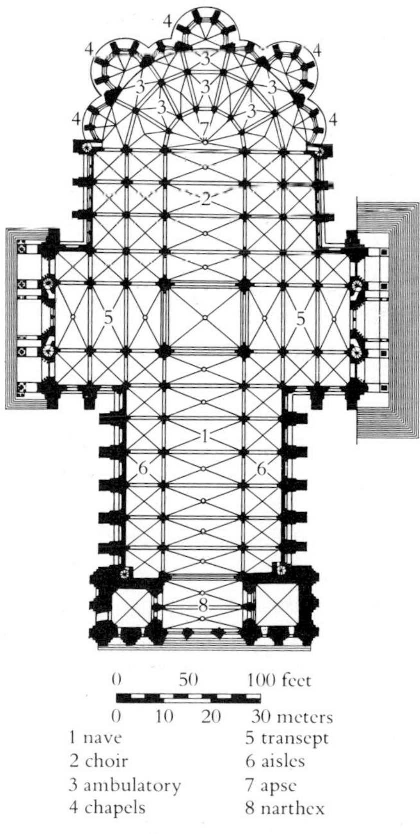

8.8 West Front and floor plan of Chartres Cathedral. 1194–1240. The towers were done at different times and reflect quite different styles of architecture.

8.9 Vintner's window, detail of stained-glass window, Chartres. c. 1215. This panel from a window donated by the winemakers of the area shows a carter taking wine casks to market.

of the time. The relic had not been destroyed by the fire of 1194, a sure sign in the eyes of the populace that the Virgin wished the church rebuilt. Furthermore, the four great feasts of the Blessed Virgin in the liturgical year (the Purification of Mary on February 2, the Annunciation on March 25, the Assumption on August 15, and the Nativity of the Virgin on September 8) were celebrated in Chartres in conjunction with large trade fairs that drew merchants and customers from all over Europe.

These fairs were held in the shadow of the cathedral and their conduct was protected by legislation issued by the cathedral chapter. Regulations from the chapter, for example, stated that the prized textiles of the area were to be sold near the north portal while the purveyors of fuel, vegetables, fruit, and wine were to be located by the south portal. There were also sellers of images, medals, and other religious objects (forerunners of the modern souvenir) to the pilgrims who came both for the fair and for reasons of devotion. The church, then, was as much a magnet for outsiders as it was a symbol for the townspeople.

The patrons who donated the windows of Chartres Cathedral also give some indication of the economics of the place. It was only natural that some of the large windows—like a rose window—would be the gift of a royal family or that a tall, pointed *lancet* window like those in the choir would be given by the nobility or the higher clergy. A large number of the windows, however, were donated by the members of the various craft and commercial guilds in the town; their "signature frames" can be found at the bottoms of the windows. The fact that the five large windows in honor of the Virgin in the *chevet*, the east end of the cathedral, were donated by merchants—principally the bakers, butchers, and vintners—indicates the significant power of the guilds [8.9].

The guild, a fraternal society of craftsmen or merchants, was a cross between a modern-day union and a fraternal organization like the Elks or the Knights of Columbus. Members of the guilds put themselves under the patronage of a saint, promised to perform certain charitable works, and acted as a mutual-aid society. Many of the economic guilds appear to have developed out of earlier, more purely religious confraternities. One had to belong to a guild to work at any level beyond day labor. The guild accepted and instructed apprentices; certified master craftsmen; regulated prices, wages, working conditions; and maintained funds for the care of older members and the burial of their dead. The guilds were a crucial part of town life and would remain so well into the modern period. And, as we shall see, the university developed from the guild idea in the 12th century.

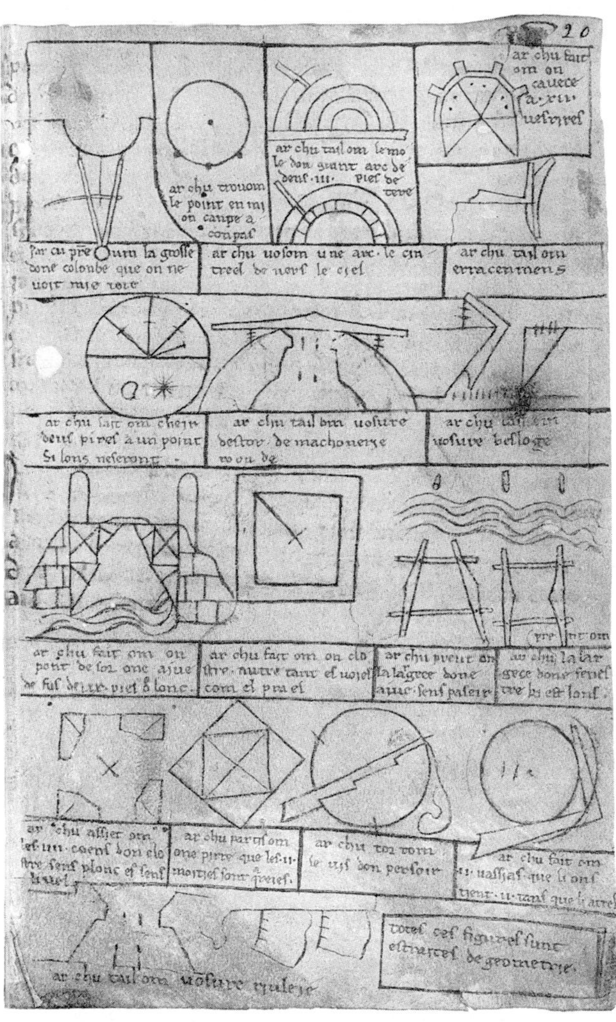

8.10 Villard de Honnecourt. Page on "practical geometry" from his *Album.* c. 1275. Pen and ink. Bibliothèque Nationale, Paris. *Top row:* Measuring the diameter of a partially visible column; finding the middle of a circle; cutting the mold of an arch; arching a vault with an outer covering; making an apse with twelve windows; cutting the spring stone of an arch. *Second row:* Bringing together two stones; cutting a voussoir for a round building; cutting an oblique voussoir. *Third row:* Bridging a stream with timbers; laying out a cloister without plumb line or level; measuring the width of river without crossing it; measuring the width of a distant window. *Bottom row:* Cutting a regular voussoir.

The motivation for the building of a medieval cathedral, then, came from the theological vision, religious devotion, civic pride, and socioeconomic interest. The actual construction depended on a large number of people. The cathedral chapter decided to construct a building, raised the money, and hired the master builder–architect. He in turn was responsible for hiring the various master craftsmen, designing the building, and creating the decorative scheme from ideas generated and approved by the theologians or church officials of the chapter. A great workshop was set up near the proposed site, with each master (mason, stonecutter, glazier) hiring his crew, obtaining his material, and setting up work quarters. Manual and occasional labor was recruited from the local population, but the construction crews were usually migratory groups who traveled from job to job.

The names of a number of master builders, including the builder of Chartres, have been lost, but others have survived in funerary inscriptions, commemorative plaques, and building records. Notes intended for students of buildings written by Villard de Honnecourt (about 1235), an architect from northern France, preserved in a unique copy at the Bibliothèque Nationale in Paris, provide us a rare glimpse into the skills of a medieval cathedral builder. Villard says in his book that he could teach a willing apprentice a wide range of skills ranging from carpentry and masonry to the more demanding skills of practical geometry [8.10] and plan drafting. The notebook also has random sketches and ideas jotted down for his own personal use; they include religious figures to serve as models for stonecarvers; animals and buildings that caught his eye; a perpetual motion machine (which didn't work); the first example of clockwork in the West; and a self-operating saw for cutting huge timbers for buttressing and roofing, among others. He visited Rheims and made sketches of the cathedral. He tells of traveling as far as Hungary to get work. While not as complete and wide-ranging as the Renaissance notebooks of Leonardo da Vinci (with which they have often been compared), Villard's notebook reveals a highly skilled, persistently inquisitive, and very inventive man.

A look through Villard's notebook forcefully reminds us that because our tendency is to emphasize the religious and social significance of a cathedral (as that is what first strikes us about it), we easily overlook the basic fact that a cathedral is a stunning technological achievement. A prime example of the technological virtuosity of such buildings is the elegant spire of Strasbourg Cathedral. Finished in 1439, the spire is 466' (142.1 m) high

8.11 Christ in the act of blessing. Figure on trumeau of main portal, Chartres Cathedral. c. 1215. This statue symbolically blesses all pilgrims who pass through the door, the "Gates of Heaven."

from pavement to tip—as high as a forty-story building. This stone structure remained the tallest in Europe until the mid-1960s, when the London Post Office Tower was completed.

The Gothic cathedral is an almost perfect artifact for the study of the humanistic enterprise since it may be approached from so many angles and at so many levels. It was first an architectural and technological achievement. Its ensemble of walls, windows, sculpture, and decoration demonstrated a peculiar way of combining human knowledge and religious faith that provides a basic aesthetic experience to the viewer. It had a fundamental economic and social significance for the community in which it was located. Finally, it was, for those who entered it in faith, a transcendental religious experience of passing from the profane to the sacred world. Henry Adams, in his wonderfully eccentric book *Mont-Saint-Michel and Chartres,* says that only a person coming to Chartres as a pilgrim could understand the building. The pilgrim is a central metaphor for the period whether one speaks of the actual pilgrim on the road to Santiago de Compostela or Canterbury or life itself as a pilgrimage toward God. Pilgrims to Chartres or the other cathedrals were pilgrims in both senses: They traveled to visit a real monument and, at the same time, hoped to find rest and salvation through the act [8.11]. It is no wonder Abbot Suger should have called Saint Denis the "Gate of Heaven": that is exactly what it was meant to be.

Music: The School of Notre Dame

It should not be surprising that in an age of artistic and architectural development such as the Gothic the rather austere music of the early church should also undergo development and change. From the time Charlemagne introduced Gregorian chant into the church life of the Frankish kingdom there had been further developments of that musical form. In the 11th century, Guido di Arezzo had worked out a system of musical notation that provided the basis for the development of the musical notation used today. Church musicians from the 10th century on also experimented with a single melodic line of plainchant by adding parallel voices at different musical intervals above the line of chant. This first step toward *polyphony,* a musical term for "many voices," is called *organum.* Outside the church, the knightly classes also composed and performed secular music. Some of the melodies of the *troubadours* and *trouvères* have survived, giving us an idea of secular music in the 12th and 13th centuries. The German *minnesingers* (*minne* means "love") of the 13th century utilized traditional church modes and melodies to create both secular and sacred songs.

The school of Notre Dame in Paris was the center of systematic musical study and composition in the 12th century. Léonin's *Magnus Liber Organi* (c. 1160) is an important source for our knowledge of music in the period of the Gothic cathedral. Léonin's book was a collection of organum compositions for use during the liturgical services

SPORTS AND GAMES

Sports and Animal Cruelty

One of the more common "sports" in the medieval period was the baiting of wild animals with dogs; a sport found in most cities and towns especially on market days. From the 12th century on, for instance, it was common to tether a large bull with a rope to a ring allowing the animal enough space to move in a circle of about thirty feet. People would bring their dogs and for a fee would be allowed to let the dogs worry the bull who, naturally enough, would fight the dogs by attempting to kick and gore them. The tenacious bulldog may have originally been bred to engage in such contests.

The same sport was practiced with captured bears with the notable difference that the bears were somewhat protected; they were not allowed to be severely wounded. Bulls, on the other hand, would be handed over to the butcher after they failed to give satisfactory sport to the spectators.

It seems hard for us to imagine but the practice of baiting large animals like bulls and bears was wildly popular well into modern times. In England, for instance, the spectacle was not banned by Parliament until 1835 and even then as eminent a figure as the essayist Lord MacCauley thought that it was a puritanical impulse which, as he noted sarcastically, forbade the sport not because of pain given to animals but to take away the pleasure of the spectators.

One other medieval animal sport which still enjoys a vogue among certain segments of our own population was that of cockfighting. The setting of one cock against another seems not to be of European origin but evidence of its practice as early as the 12th century is attested in the records. It was the custom of London schoolboys to bring cocks to school to fight on Shrove Tuesday (the day before Lent began—Mardi Gras day).

Some historians have suggested that cockfighting was introduced into England by Roman soldiers during the occupation of England at the beginning of the common era. Others have seen the practice (like that of dogfighting) as simply part of ancient rural blood sports which are to be found in various parts of the world.

---

throughout the church year. Léonin's work was carried on by the other great composer of the century, Pérotin, who assumed the directorship of the music school of Notre Dame sometime around 1181.

In Pérotin's music, the Notre Dame organum utilized the basic melodic line of the traditional chant (the *cantus firmus*) while a second melodic line (the *duplum*), a third (*triplum*), and in some cases a fourth (*quadruplum*) voice was added above the melody. These added lines mirrored the rhythmic flow of the cantus firmus. It was soon learned, however, that pleasing and intricate compositions could be created by having the duplum and triplum move in opposition to the cantus firmus. This *counterpoint* (from *contrapunctum,* against the note) meant, at its most basic level, that a descending series of notes in the cantus firmus would have an ascending series of notes in the melodic lines above it.

One development in the Gothic period deriving from the polyphony of organum was the motet. The *motet* usually had three voices (in some cases, four). The tenor—from the Latin *tenere* (to hold), another term for *cantus firmus*—maintained the traditional line, usually derived from an older ecclesiastical chant. Since some of the manuscripts from the period show no words for this tenor position, it has been thought that for many motets the tenor line was the musical accompaniment (perhaps the organ, then an instrument of increasing popularity). Above the tenor were two voices who sang interweaving melodies. In the early 13th century, these melodies were invariably in Latin and were exclusively religious in content. In the late 13th century it was not uncommon to sing the duplum in Latin and the triplum in French. Indeed, the two upper voices could be singing quite distinct songs: a hymn in Latin with a love lyric in French with a tenor voice (or instrument) maintaining an elaborated melody based on the melismas of Gregorian chant.

This increasingly sophisticated music, built on a monastic basis but with a new freedom of its own, is indicative of many of the intellectual currents of the period. It is a technically complex music rooted in the distant past but open to new and somewhat daring innovation, a blend of the traditional and the vernacular—all held together in an intellectually complicated balance of competing elements. Gothic music was an aural expression of the dynamism inherent in the medieval Gothic cathedral.

SCHOLASTICISM

The Rise of the Universities

A number of our contemporary institutions have roots in the Middle Ages. Trial by jury is one, constitutional monarchy another. By far the best-known and most widely diffused cultural institution that dates from the Middle Ages, however, is the university. In fact, some of the most prestigious centers of European learning today stand where they were founded eight hundred years ago: Oxford and Cambridge in England; the University of Paris in France; the University of Bologna in Italy. There is also a remarkable continuity between the organization and purposes of the medieval university and our own, except that we have coeducation. The medieval student would be puzzled, to be sure, by the idea of football games, coeducation, degrees in business or agriculture, and well-manicured campuses, were he to visit a modern American university. Such a student would find himself at home with the idea of a liberal arts curriculum, the degrees from the baccalaureate through the master's to the doctorate, and the high cost of textbooks. At a less serious level, he would be well acquainted with drinking parties, fraternities, and friction between town and gown (the phrase itself has a medieval ring). The literature that has come down to us from the period is full of complaints about poor housing, high rents, terrible food, and lack of jobs after graduation. Letters from the Middle Ages between students and parents have an almost uncanny contemporaneity about them except for the fact that women did not study in the medieval universities.

European universities developed in the late 12th and early 13th centuries along with the emergence of city life. In the earlier medieval period schools were most often associated with the monasteries, which were perforce situated in rural areas. As cities grew in importance, schools also developed at urban monasteries or, increasingly, under the aegis of bishops whose cathedrals were in the towns. The episcopal or cathedral school was a direct offshoot of the increasing importance of towns and the increasing power of bishops, the spiritual leaders of town life. In Italy, where town life had been relatively strong throughout the early Middle Ages and where feudalism never took hold, there was also a tradition of schools controlled by the laity. The center of medical studies in Salerno and the law faculty of Bologna had been in secular hands since the 10th century.

A number of factors help to explain the rapid rise of formal education institutions in the 12th

8.12 Laurencius de Voltolina (School of Bologna). A university lecture; from the *Lecture of Henricus de Alemania.* Second half of 14th century. Manuscript illumination. State Museums, Berlin. The professor expounds his text from the professorial chair *(cathedra).* Note the sleeping student at the lower right.

CONTEMPORARY VOICES

A Medieval Parent and a Student

I have recently discovered that you live dissolutely and slothfully, preferring license to restraint and play to work and strumming a guitar while the others are at their studies, whence it happens that you have read but one volume of law while more industrious companions have read several. I have decided to exhort you herewith to repent utterly of your dissolute and careless ways that you may no longer be called a waster and that your shame may be turned to good repute.

[parent to a son at the university in Orleans, 14th century]

We occupy a good and comely dwelling, next door but one from the schools and market place, so that we can go to school each day without wetting our feet. We have good companions in the house with us, well advanced in their studies, and of excellent habits—an advantage which we appreciate for, as the psalmist says "with an upright man thou wilt show thyself upright." Wherefore, lest production should cease for lack of material, we beg your paternity to send us by the bearer money for the purchase of parchment, ink, a desk, and the other things which we need, in sufficient amount that we may suffer no want on your account (God forbid!) but finish our studies and return home with honor. The bearer will also take charge of the shoes and stockings which you will send us, and any news at all.

[scholar to his father, Orleans, 14th century]

century. First, the increasing complexity of urban life created a demand for an educated class who could join the ranks of administrators and bureaucrats. Urban schools were not simply interested in providing basic literacy. They were designed to produce an educated class who could give support to the socioeconomic structures of society. Those who completed the arts curriculum of a 12th-century cathedral school (like the one at Chartres) could find ready employment in either the civil or the ecclesiastical bureaucracy as lawyers, clerks, or administrators.

There were also intellectual and cultural reasons for the rise of the universities. In the period from 1150 to 1250 came a wholesale discovery and publication of texts from the ancient world. Principal among these were lost books by Aristotle that came to the West through Muslim sources in Spain. Aristotle's writings covered a vast range of subjects ranging from meteorology and physics to logic and philosophy. Furthermore, with a closer relationship between Christian and Arabic scholars, a large amount of scientific and mathematical material was coming into Europe [8.12]. There was also a renaissance of legal studies centered primarily at Bologna, the one intellectual center that could nearly rival Paris. Finally, there was a new tool being refined by such scholars as Peter Abelard and Peter Lombard: dialectics. Theologians and philosophers began to apply the principles of logic to the study of philosophy and theology. Abelard's book *Sic et Non* (1121) put together conflicting opinions concerning theological matters with contradictory passages from the Bible and the Church Fathers and then attempted to mediate and reconcile the apparent divergences. This method was later refined and stylized into the method which was to become *scholasticism*, so called because it was the philosophical method of the schools, the communities of scholars at the nascent universities.

The most famous and representative university to emerge in the Middle Ages was the University of Paris. The eminence of Paris rested mainly on the fame of the teachers who came there to teach. At this state of educational development, the teacher really was the school. Students in the 12th century flocked from all over Europe to frequent the lectures of teachers like William of Champeaux (1070–1121) and, later, his formal student and vehement critic, Peter Abelard (1079–1142). Besides these famous individual teachers Paris also had some established centers of learning that enjoyed a vast reputation. There was a cathedral school attached to the cathedral of Notre Dame, a theological center associated with the canons of the church of Saint Victor, and a school of arts maintained at the ancient monastery of Sainte Geneviève.

Although it is difficult to assign precise dates, it is safe to say that the university at Paris developed in the final quarter of the 12th and early part of the 13th centuries. Its development began with the masters (*magistri,* teachers) of the city forming a corporation after the manner of the guilds. At this time the word *universitas* simply meant a guild or corporation. The masters formed the universitas in Paris in order to exercise some "quality control" over the teaching profession and the students entrusted to their care. At Bologna the reverse was true. The students formed the universitas in order to hire the teachers with the best qualifications and according to the most advantageous financial terms.

The universitas soon acquired a certain status in law with a corporate right to borrow money, to sue (and be sued), and to issue official documents. As a legal body it could issue stipulations for the conduct of both masters and students. When a student finished the course of studies and passed his examinations, the universitas would grant him a teaching certificate that enabled him to enter the ranks of the masters: He was a master of arts (our modern degree has its origin in that designation). After graduation a student could go on to specialized training in law, theology, or medicine. The completion of this specialized training entitled one to be called *doctor* (from the Latin *doctus,* learned) in his particular field. The modern notion that a professional person (doctor, lawyer, and the like) should be university-trained is an idea derived directly from the usages of the medieval university.

Since the Carolingian period—indeed, earlier—the core of education was the arts curriculum. In the late 12th century in Paris the arts began to be looked on as a prelude to the study of theology. This inevitably caused a degree of tension between the arts faculty and the theology masters. This tension resulted in 1210 in a split, with the masters and students of arts moving their faculty to the Left Bank of the Seine, where they settled in the area intersected by the rue du Fouarre (Straw Street—so named because the students sat on straw during lectures). That part of the Left Bank has traditionally been a student haunt. The name Latin Quarter reminds us of the old language that was once the only tongue used at the university.

By the end of the 12th century Paris was the intellectual center of Europe. Students came from all over Europe to study there. We do not have reliable statistics about their number, but an estimate of five to eight thousand students would not be far from the mark for the early 13th century. The students were organized into *nationes* by their place of national origin. By 1294 there were four recognized *nationes* in Paris: the French, the Picard, the Norman, and the Anglo-German. Student support came from families, pious benefactors, church stipends, or civic grants to underwrite an education. Certain generous patrons provided funds for hospices for scholars, the most famous of which was that underwritten by Robert de Sorbon in 1258 for graduate students in theology; his hospice was the forerunner of the Sorbonne in Paris.

By our standards, student life in the 13th century was harsh. Food and lodging were primitive, heating scarce, artificial lighting nonexistent, and income sporadic. The daily schedule was rigorous, made more so by the shortage of books and writing material. An "ideal" student's day, as sketched out in a late medieval pamphlet for student use, now seems rather grim:

A Student's Day at the University of Paris

4:00 A.M.	Rise
5:00–6:00	Arts lectures
6:00	Mass and breakfast
8:00–10:00	Lectures
11:00–12:00	Disputations before the noon meal
1:00–3:00 P.M.	"Repetitions"—study of morning lectures with tutors
3:00–5:00	Cursory lectures (generalized lectures on special topics) or disputations
6:00	Supper
7:00–9:00	Study and repetitions
9:00	Bed

The masters' lectures consisted of detailed commentaries on certain books the master intended to cover in a given term. Since books were expensive, emphasis was put on note taking and copying so that the student might build up his own collection of books. Examinations were oral, before a panel of masters. Students were also expected to participate in formal debates (called disputations) as part of their training.

Geoffrey Chaucer provides us an unforgettable, albeit idealized, portrait of the medieval student (the clerk or cleric—many of the students were members of the minor clerical orders of the church) in his Prologue to the *Canterbury Tales:*

> A clerk from Oxford was with us also,
> Who'd turned to getting knowledge, long ago.
> As meagre was his horse as is a rake,
> Nor he himself too fat, I'll undertake,
> But he looked hollow and went soberly.
> Right threadbare was his overcoat; for he
> Had got him yet no churchly benefice,
> Nor was so worldly as to gain office.
> For he would rather have at his bed's head
> Some twenty books, all bound in black and red,
> Of Aristotle and his philosophy
> Than rich robes, fiddle, or gay psaltery.
> Yet, and for all he was philosopher,
> He had but little gold within his coffer;

But all that he might borrow from a friend
On books and learning he would swiftly spend,
And then he'd pray right busily for the souls
Of those who gave him wherewithal for
schools.
Of study took he utmost care and heed.
Not one word spoke he more than was his
need;
And that was said in fullest reverence
And short and quick and full of high good
sense.
Pregnant of moral virtue was his speech;
And gladly would he learn and gladly teach.

Chaucer's portrait of the lean, pious, poor, zealous student was highly idealized to create a type. We get probably a far more realistic picture of what students were actually doing and thinking about from the considerable amount of popular poetry that comes from the student culture of the medieval period. This poetry depicts a student life we are all familiar with: a poetry of wine, women, song, sharp satires at the expense of pompous professors or poor accommodations, and the occasional episodes of cruelty that most individuals are capable of only when banded into groups.

The student subculture had also invented a mythical Saint Golias, who was the patron saint of wandering scholars. Verses (called Goliardic verse) were written in honor of the "saint." The poems that have come down to use are a far cry from the sober commentaries on Aristotle's *Metaphysics* that we usually associate with the medieval scholar.

One of the more interesting collections of these medieval lyrics was discovered in a Bavarian monastery in the early 19th century. The songs in this collection were written in Latin, Old French, and German and seem to date from the late 12th and the 13th centuries. Their subject range was wide but, given the nature of such songs, predictable. There were drinking songs, laments over the loss of love or the trials of fate, hymns in honor of nature, salutes to the end of winter and the coming of spring, and cheerfully obscene songs of exuberant sexuality. The lyrics reveal a shift of emotions ranging from the happiness of love to the despair of disappointment just as the allusions range from classical learning to medieval piety. One famous song, for example, praises the beautiful powerful virgin in language that echoes the piety of the church. The last line reveals, however, that the poem salutes not Mary but generous Venus.

In 1935 and 1936 the German composer Carl Orff set a number of these poems to music under the title *Carmina Burana*. His brilliantly lively blending of heavy percussion, snatches of ecclesiastical chant, strong choral voices, and vibrant rhythms have made this work a modern concert favorite. The listener gets a good sense of the vibrancy of these medieval lyrics by the use of the modern setting. Since the precise character of student music has not come down to us, Orff's new setting of these lyrics is a fine beginning for learning about the musicality of this popular poetry from the medieval university.

Did women study at the university? By and large they did not. Medieval customs sheltered women in a manner we find hard to imagine. Women were educated either privately (Heloise was tutored by her uncle in Paris when she met Abelard) or within the cloister of the convent. Furthermore, most of university life was tied to the church. The masters were clerics (except at Bologna) and most students depended on ecclesiastical pensions (benefices) to support them. There are exceptions to this rule. There seem to have been women in universities in both Italy and Germany, but they were the exception. At Salerno, famous for its faculty of medicine, there may have been woman physicians who were attached to the faculty. We do know that by the 14th century the university was licensing women physicians. There is also a tradition that Bologna had a woman professor of law who, according to the story, was so beautiful that she lectured from behind a screen so as not to dazzle her students! It is well to remember that the universities were very conservative and traditional institutions. It was not until this century, for example, that provisions were made for women's colleges at Oxford that enjoyed the full privileges of university life. The discrimination against women at the university level was something, for example, that moved the bitter complaints of the English novelist, Virginia Woolf, as late as the 1930s.

Francis of Assisi

In Italy, at the end of the 12th century, a young man would be born who would reshape medieval religious and cultural life. Giovanni Bernadone, born in 1181 in the Umbrian hill town of Assisi, was renamed "Francesco" (the "Little Frenchman") by his merchant father. Francis grew up the son of wealthy parents as a popular, somewhat spendthrift, and undisciplined youth. He joined the volunteer militia as a youth to do battle against the neighboring city of Perugia only to be captured and put into solitary confinement until a ransom could be found.

That incident seems to have marked a turning point in his life. He dropped out of society and began to lead a life of prayer and self-denial. Eventually he came to the conclusion that the life of perfect freedom demanded a life of total poverty. He gave away all of his goods and began a life of itinerant preaching that took him as far away as the Middle East. His simple life style attracted followers who wished to live in imitation of his life. By 1218, there were over three thousand "Little Brothers" (as he called them) who owed their religious allegiance to him. Francis died in 1226 when the movement he started was already a powerful religious order in the church [8.13].

8.13 Saint Francis of Assisi. Fresco. Santo Specchio. This may be the earliest portrait of Saint Francis; some scholars believe that it was executed during the saint's lifetime.

8.14 Saint Francis Preaching to the Birds. Detail of Berlingheri Altarpiece. Pescia. This is a detail from an altarpiece depicting incidents from the saint's life taken from early *legenda* written about him.

If we know Francis of Assisi today, it is because of garden shop statues of him with a bird on his shoulder. That he preached to the birds is a fact [8.14] but to think of him only as a medieval Doctor Doolittle speaking to animals is to trivialize a man who profoundly altered medieval culture. First, his notion of a mendicant (begging) brotherhood that would be mobile and capable of preaching in the newly emerging cities of Europe was a worthy substitute for the more rural, land-bound monasteries of the past. Secondly, Francis believed that the gospels could be followed literally and this led him to identify closely with the humanity of Christ. It is said that in 1224 he had so meditated on the passion of Christ that his own body parts had on them the crucifixion marks of Christ (the so-called *stigmata*). This emphasis on Christ's humanity would have a powerful impact in making religious art more realistic and vivid. Finally, Francis's attitude towards religious faith was powerfully affirmative. He praised the goodness of God's creation; he loved the created world; he preached concern for the poorest of the poor; he felt that all creation was a gift and that everything in creation praised God in its own way. Some scholars have argued that the impact of the Franciscan vision on the imagination of European culture was a remote cause of the Renaissance preoccupation with the natural world and the close observation of nature.

The early part of the 13th century, in fact, saw that rise of two complementary impulses that would energize late medieval culture: the intellectualism of the schools epitomized in someone like Thomas Aquinas (below) and the affective and emotional religion of a Francis of Assisi. Those two impulses were best synthesized in the masterpiece that summed up high medieval culture: the *Commedia* of Dante Alighieri.

Thomas Aquinas

The Golden Age of the University of Paris was the 13th century, since in that period Paris could lay fair claim to being the intellectual center of the Western world. It is a mark of the international character of medieval university life that some of its most distinguished professors were from outside France: Albert the Great was German; Alexander of Hales was English; Bonaventure and Thomas Aquinas were Italian.

Thomas Aquinas (1225?–1274) was the most famous and influential of the Parisian masters of the 13th century [8.15]. His intellectual influence went far beyond the lecture halls of Paris and is felt to the present. Born of noble parentage in southern Italy, Thomas joined the Preaching Friars of Saint Dominic (the Dominicans) in 1243. From 1245 to 1248 he studied with Albert the Great at both Paris and Cologne. He was made a *magister* of theology

8.15 Andrea di Buonaiuto. *The Triumph of Saint Thomas Aquinas.* c. 1365. Fresco. Santa Maria Novella, Florence. The saint is enthroned between figures of the Old and New Testaments with the personification of the Virtues, Sciences, and Liberal Arts below. This Florentine church had a school of studies attended by Dante Alighieri in his youth.

in 1258 after completing his doctoral studies. During this same period (from roughly 1256 to 1259) he lectured on theology in Paris. From 1259 to 1268 he was back in Italy, where he lectured and wrote at Orvieto (the papal court for a time), Rome, and Naples. From 1268 to 1272 he held a chair of theology again, when he returned to Naples to teach there. He died two years later on his way to a church council at Lyons in France.

Thomas Aquinas' life ended before he was fifty, but in that span he produced a vast corpus of writings (they fill forty folio volumes) on theology, philosophy, and biblical studies. It is a mark of his mobility that his masterpiece—the *Summa Theologica*—was composed at Rome, Viterbo, Paris, and Naples, although it was left unfinished at his death. While his writings touched on a wide variety of subjects, at root Thomas Aquinas was interested in and made a lifetime study of a very basic problem: How does one harmonize those things that are part of human learning (reason) with those supernatural truths revealed by God in the Bible and through the teaching of the church (revelation)? Aquinas' approach was to steer a middle path through two diametrically opposed opinions, both of which had avid supporters in the Middle Ages: the position of *fideism,* which held that religious faith as an absolute is indifferent to the efforts of human reason (*credo quia absurdum est,* I believe because it is absurd) and *rationalism,* which insists that everything, revelation included, must meet the test of rational human scrutiny. Aquinas wanted to demonstrate what the Gothic cathedral illustrated: that the liberal arts, the things and seasons of the world, and the mysteries revealed by God could be brought into some kind of intellectual harmony based on a single criterion of truth.

For Aquinas, reason finds truth when it sees evidence of truth. The mind judges something true when it has observed a sufficient number of facts to compel it to make that judgment. The mind gives assent to truth on the basis of evidence. Aquinas was convinced that there was a sufficient amount of observable evidence in the world to conclude the existence of God. He proposed five arguments in support of such a position. Still he recognized that such argumentation only yields a very limited understanding of God. Aquinas did not believe that the naked use of reason could ever discover or prove the mysteries about God revealed in the Bible: that God became a man in Jesus Christ or that there was a Trinity of persons in God. God had to tell us that. Our assent to it is not based on evidence, but on the authority of God who reveals it

EAST MEETS WEST

Islamic Medicine and Science

In the early Middle Ages the Muslims not only translated and commented on Greek learning in the fields of philosophy, medicine, science, and mathematics but also produced new advances in those fields.

It is safe to say that until the High Middle Ages Muslim scholars kept the art of medicine alive. Doctors like Rhazes (d. 932) gave a clinical description of measles and smallpox, while others like Avicenna (d. 1037) and Averröes (d. 1198) wrote influential medical treatises whose translations formed the basis for medicine in the West. The great Jewish physician Moses Maimonides (d. 1204) was trained in the Islamic tradition. He insisted on the value of personal and social hygiene (not always appreciated in those days) and was an expert on poisons. He would be an influential figure for the development of medicine among the Jews. (The popes in Rome used Jewish physicians exclusively well into the Renaissance period because of their great reputation in medicine.) Maimonides left his native Spain to serve as the personal physician to the Sultan of Baghdad, Saladin, which says something about the cross-fertilization of cultures in this period.

Muslim scholars centered in Baghdad after the year 800 did extremely influential work. They adapted the numerical system we use today from the Hindus of India, who invented it. We still refer to Arabic numerals. The sheer utility of this system can be seen by taking a sheet of paper and multiplying 55 by 40, then trying to do the same exercise by using Roman numerals (which lack the zero): LV × XL! The most famous of the Muslim mathematicians was Al Khwarizmi (c. 825), whose treatise gave us the word *algebra* and from whose name we get the word *algorithm.*

Mention should also be made of certain technological advances that came to the West from the world of Islam. Two such developments were of incalculable importance: From the Chinese the Muslims learned the art of making paper and the chemical composition of gunpowder. Finally, the Egyptian scholar Al Hazen (d. 1038) did important work on optics and became expert in the theory of lenses.

to us. If we could prove the mysteries of faith, there would have been no need for revelation and no need of faith.

Thus for Aquinas there is an organic relationship between reason and revelation. Philosophy perfects the human capacity to know and revelation perfects one beyond self by offering salvation and eternal life. Aquinas stated this relationship between reason and revelation at the very beginning of his great work of theology, the *Summa Theologica*.

When we read Aquinas today we get some sense of his stark and rigorous attempt to think things through. For one thing, he offers no stylistic adornment to relieve his philosophical and rational discourse. For another, he makes clear that philosophical reasoning is difficult; it is not a pastime for the incompetent or the intellectually lazy. Yet Aquinas was not a mere machine for logic. He had the temperament of a mystic. Some months before he died he simply put down his pen; when his secretary asked him why he had stopped writing, Aquinas simply said that in prayer and quiet he had had a vision and that what he had written "seemed as straw." Aquinas was a rare combination of intellectual and mystic.

The philosophical tradition Aquinas used in his writing was that of the Greek philosopher Aristotle. He first knew Aristotle's work in Latin translations based on Arabic texts done by Muslim scholars in the south of Spain and North Africa. Later Aquinas was able to use texts translated directly out of Greek by a Flemish friar and sometime companion, William of Moerbeke. Aquinas' use of Aristotle was certainly not a novelty in the Middle Ages. Such Arabic scholars as Avicenna (980–1036) and Averröes of Córdova (1126–1198) commented on Aristotle's philosophy and its relationship to the faith of Islam. Jewish thinkers like the famous Moses Maimonides (born in Córdova in 1135, died in Egypt in 1204) made similar attempts to bridge Greek thought and their own religious faith. Maimonides wrote his famous *Guide for the Perplexed* to demonstrate the essential compatibility of the Hebrew scriptures with the thought of Aristotle. Maimonides was determined that essentials of the biblical message not be compromised, but he likewise felt that in nonessentials there was room for human reflection. In this task of distinguishing the place of intellect and faith Maimonides anticipated the work of Thomas Aquinas by two generations.

Two other characteristics of the thought of Aquinas should be noted. First, his worldview was strongly hierarchical. Everything has its place in the universe, and that place is determined in relationship to God. A rock is good because it *is* (to Aquinas existence was a gift), but an animal is more perfect because it has life and thus shares more divine attributes. In turn, men and women are better still because they possess mind and will. Angels are closer yet to God because they, like God, are pure spirit.

This hierarchical worldview explains other characteristics of Aquinas' thought in particular and medieval thought in general: It is wide-ranging, it is encyclopedic, and in interrelating everything it is synthetic. Everything fits and has its place, meaning, and truth. That a person would speak on psychology, physics, politics, theology, and philosophy with equal authority would strike us as presumptuous, just as any building decorated with symbols from the classics, astrology, the Bible, and scenes from everyday life would now be considered a hodgepodge. Such was not the case in the 13th century, since it was assumed that everything ultimately pointed to God.

DANTE'S *DIVINE COMEDY*

In any discussion of the culture of the High Middle Ages two descriptive adjectives come immediately to mind: hierarchical and synthetic. It is a commonplace, for example, to compare the Gothic cathedral and the systematic treatises on philosophy and theology like the *Summa Theologica* of Saint Thomas Aquinas. On close inspection such comparisons may be facile, but they point to the following truths about this period that are relatively secure: Both the Gothic cathedral and the theology of Aquinas, for example, started from the tangible and sensual ("Nothing comes to the mind except through the senses" is a basic axiom for Aquinas) in order to mount in a hierarchical manner to the light that is God. Again, both writer and architect felt it possible to be universal in their desire to synthesize all human knowledge as prelude and pointer to the full revelation of God. Finally, they both constructed their edifices by the juxtaposition of tensions and syntheses.

If the Gothic cathedral and the *Summa* represent two masterpieces of the hierarchical and synthetic religious humanism of the Middle Ages, *The Divine Comedy* of Dante Alighieri (1265–1321) represents the same masterly achievement in literature. Dante [8.16] was a Florentine. He was nonetheless deeply influenced by the intellectual currents that emanated from the Paris of his time. As a comfortably fixed young man he devoted himself to a rigorous

8.16 Sandro Botticelli. *Dante* c. 1480–1485. Oil on canvas, 24¼ × 18½" (54 × 47 cm). Collection Dr. Martin Bodmer, Cologny/Geneva. Like most portraits of Dante, Botticelli's depicts him wearing the traditional laurel wreath of the poet.

TABLE 8.1 The Structure of Dante's Comedy

Hell

The Anteroom of the Neutrals

Circle 1:	*The Virtuous Pagans (Limbo)*
Circle 2:	*The Lascivious*
Circle 3:	*The Gluttonous*
Circle 4:	*The Greedy and the Wasteful*
Circle 5:	*The Wrathful*
Circle 6:	*The Heretics*
Circle 7:	*The Violent against Others, Self, God/ Nature/ and Art*
Circle 8:	*The Fraudulent (subdivided into ten classes, each of which dwells in a separate ditch)*
Circle 9:	*The Lake of the Treacherous against kindred, country, guests, lords and benefactors. Satan is imprisoned at the center of this frozen lake.*

Purgatory

Ante-Purgatory: The Excommunicated/The Lazy/The Unabsolved/Negligent Rulers
The Terraces of the Mount of Purgatory

1. *The Proud*
2. *The Envious*
3. *The Wrathful*
4. *The Slothful*
5. *The Avaricious*
6. *The Gluttonous*
7. *The Lascivious*

The Earthly Paradise

Paradise

1. *The Moon: The Faithful who were inconstant*
2. *Mercury: Service marred by ambition*
3. *Venus: Love marred by lust*
4. *The Sun: Wisdom; the theologians*
5. *Mars: Courage; the just warriors*
6. *Jupiter: Justice; the great rulers*
7. *Saturn: Temperance; the contemplatives and mystics*
8. *The Fixed Stars: The Church Triumphant*
9. *The Primum Mobile: The Order of Angels*
10. *The Empyrean Heavens: Angels, Saints, The Virgin, and the Holy Trinity*

program of philosophical and theological study in order to enhance his already burgeoning literary talent. His published work gives evidence of a profound culture and a deep love for study. He wrote on the origin and development of language *(De Vulgari Eloquentia)*, political theory *(De Monarchia)*, and generalized knowledge *(Convivio)* as well as his own poetic aspirations *(Vita Nuova)*. His masterpiece is the *Divine Comedy*.

Dante was exiled from Florence for political reasons in 1300. In his bitter wanderings in the north of Italy he worked on—and finally brought to conclusion—a long poem to which he gave a bitingly ironical title: *The Comedy of Dante Alighieri, A Florentine by Birth but Not in Behavior.* Dante called his poem a comedy since, as he noted, it had a happy ending and it was written in the popular language of the people. The adjective *divine* was added later; some say by Boccaccio, who in the next generation lectured on the poem in Florence and wrote one of the first biographies of the great poet.

The Divine Comedy relates a symbolic journey that the poet begins on Good Friday, 1300, through Hell, Purgatory, and Heaven [Table 8.1]. In the first two parts of his journey, Dante is guided by the ancient Roman poet Vergil, whose *Aeneid* was such an

QVI COELVM CECINIT MEDIVMQVE IMVMQVE TRIBVNAL LVSTRAVITQVE ANIMO CVNCTA POETA SVO DOCTVS ADEST DANTES SVA QVEM FLORENTIA SAEPE
SENSIT CONSILIIS AC PIETATE PATREM NIL POTVIT TANTO MORS SAEVA NOCERE POETAE QVEM VIVVM VIRTVS CARMEN IMAGO FACIT

8.17 Domenico di Michelino. *Dante and His Poem.* 1465. Fresco. Florence Cathedral. Dante, with an open copy of *The Comedy,* points to Hell with his right hand. The mount of Purgatory with its seven terraces is behind him. Florence's cathedral (with its newly finished dome) represents Paradise on the poet's left.

inspiration to him and from which he borrowed (especially from Book VI, which tells of Aeneas' own journey to the Underworld). From the border at the top of the Mount of Purgatory to the pinnacle of heaven where Dante glimpses the "still point of light" that is God, Dante's guide is Beatrice, a young woman Dante had loved passionately if platonically in his youth [8.17].

Every significant commentator on *The Comedy* has noted its careful organization. The poem is made up of one hundred cantos. The first canto of the *Inferno* serves as an introduction to the whole poem. There are then 33 cantos for each of the three major sections (*Inferno, Purgatorio,* and *Paradiso*). The entire poem is written in a rhyme scheme called *terza rima* (*aba, bcb, cdc,* and so on) that is almost impossible to duplicate in English because of the shortage of rhyming words in our language. The number three and its multiples, symbols of the Trinity, occur over and over. The *Inferno* is divided into nine regions plus a vestibule, and the same number is found in the *Purgatorio.* Dante's *Paradiso* is constituted by the nine heavens of the Ptolemaic system plus the Empyrean, the highest heaven. This scheme mirrors the whole poem of ninety-nine cantos plus one. The sinners in the *Inferno* are arranged according to whether they sinned by incontinence, violence, or fraud (a division Dante derived from Aristotle's *Ethics*), while the yearning souls of purgatory are divided in three ways according to how they acted or failed to act in relation to love. The saved souls in the *Paradiso* are divided into the lay folk, the active, and the contemplative. Nearest the throne of God, but reflected in the circles of heaven, are the nine categories of angels.

8.18 Hell, detail of mosaic in vault of baptistery of Florence Cathedral. 13th century. As a young man Dante would have seen this mosaic, which adorned the baptistery ("My beautiful San Giovanni," he calls it in his poem) of his native city.

Dante's interest in the symbolic goes beyond his elaborate manipulation of numbers. In the *Inferno* sinners suffer punishments that have symbolic value; their sufferings both punish and instruct. The gluttonous live on heaps of garbage under driving storms of cold rain, while the flatterers are immersed in pools of sewage and the sexually perverse walk burning stretches of sand in an environment as sterile as their attempts at love. Conversely, in the *Paradiso,* the blessed dwell in the circles most symbolic of their virtue. The theologians are in the circle of the sun since they provided such enlightenment to the world, and the holy warriors dwell in the sphere of Mars.

We can better appreciate the density and complexity of Dante's symbolism by looking at a single example. Our common image of Satan is that of a sly tempter (in popular art he is often in formal dress whispering blandishments in a willing ear with just a whiff of sulphur about him) after the manner of Milton's proud, perversely tragic, heroic Satan in *Paradise Lost.* For Dante, Satan is a huge, stupid beast, frozen in a lake of ice in the pit of hell. He beats six batlike wings (a demonic leftover from his angelic existence; see Isaiah 6:1–5) in an ineffectual attempt to escape the frozen pond that is watered by the four rivers of hell. He is grotesquely three-headed (a parody of the Trinity) and his slavering mouths remorselessly chew the bodies of three infamous traitors from sacred and secular history (Judas, Cassius, and Brutus).

Why does Dante portray Satan so grotesquely? It is clear that Dante borrowed some of the picture of Satan from Byzantine mosaics with which he would have been familiar in the baptistery of Florence [8.18]. Beyond that, the whole complex of Satan is heavily weighted with symbolic significance. Satan lies in frozen darkness at a point in the universe farthest from the warmth and light of God. He is the fallen angel of light (Lucifer means "light-bearer"), now encased in a pit in the center of the earth excavated by the force of his own fall from heaven. Satan is immobile in contrast to God who is the mover of all things in the universe. He is totally inarticulate and stupid because he represents, par excellence, all of the souls of hell who have lost what Dante calls "the good of intellect." Satan, and all of the souls in hell, will remain totally unfulfilled as created rational beings because they are cut off from the final source of rational understanding and fulfillment: God. Intellectual estrangement from God is for Dante, as it was for Thomas Aquinas, the essence of damnation. This estrangement is most evident in the case of Satan, who symbolizes in his very being the loss of rationality and all that derives from that fact.

Dante, following a line of thought already developed by Suger and Aquinas, conceived the human journey as a slow ascent to the purity of God by means of the created things of this world. To settle for less than God was, in essence, to fail to return to the natural source of life, God. This explains why light is such a crucial motif in *The Divine Comedy* as it had been in the theories of Abbot Suger. Neither light nor the sources of light (the sun) is ever mentioned in the *Inferno*. The overwhelming visual impression of the *Inferno* is darkness—a darkness that begins when Dante is lost in the "dark wood" of Canto I and continues until he climbs from hell and sees above his head the *stars* (the word stars ends each of the three major parts of the poem) of the Southern Hemisphere. In the ascent of the mountain of purgatory, daylight and sunset are controlling motifs to symbolize the reception and rejection of divine light. In the *Paradiso* the blessed are bathed in the reflected light that comes from God. At the climax of the *Paradiso* the poet has a momentary glimpse of God as a point of light and rather obscurely understands that God, the source of all intelligibility, is the power that also moves the "sun and the other stars."

Within the broad reaches of Dante's philosophical and theological preoccupations the poet still has the concentrated power to sketch unforgettable portraits: the doomed lovers Paolo and Francesca—each of the tercets that tell their story starts with the word *amore* (love); the haughty political leader Farinata degli Umberti; the pitiable suicide Pier delle Vigne; or the caricatures of gluttons like Ciacco the Hog. Damned, penitent, or saved, the characters are by turns both symbols and persons. Saint Peter represents the church in the *Paradiso* but also explodes with ferociously human anger at its abuses. Brunetto Latini in the *Inferno* with "his brown-baked features" is a condemned sodomite but still anxious that posterity at least remember his literary accomplishments.

It has been said that a mastery of *The Divine Comedy* would be a mastery of all that was significant about the intellectual culture of the Middle Ages. It is certainly true that the poem, encyclopedic and complex as it is, would provide a primer for any reader interested in the science, political theory, philosophy, literary criticism, and theology of the 13th century as well as a detailed acquaintance with the burning questions of Dante's time. The very comprehensiveness of the poem has often been its major obstacle for the modern reader. Beyond that hurdle is the strangeness of the Dantean world, so at variance with our own: earth-centered, manageably small, sure of its ideas of right and wrong, orthodox in its theology, prescientific in its outlook, Aristotelian in its philosophy. For all that, Dante is not only to be read for his store of medieval lore; he is, as T. S. Eliot once wrote, the most universal of poets. He had a deeply sympathetic appreciation of human aspiration, love and hate, the destiny of humanity, and the meaning of nature and history.

SUMMARY

The High Middle Ages saw the growth of a number of institutions that stood in sharp contrast to those of the Carolingian period. Foremost was the rise of the city. Urbanization brought with it a lessening of the importance of monastic life as a cultural center and the emergence of the influence of the bishop and the cathedral school. The increased need for a "knowledge class" triggered an expansion in education that would eventually lead to the university of scholars. Urbanization also warred against the old feudal values; it fostered trade and commerce; it made possible the growth of what today we would call a "middle class" who stood on the social ladder between the rural peasant/city worker and the landed royalty or hereditary aristocracy.

The 12th and 13th centuries were times of intense intellectual ferment and advance. New sources of knowledge came through Arabic sources either as original contributions (e.g., in medicine and science) or in the form of lost works of the classical past (e.g., the writings of Aristotle) to fuel the work of scholars. Advances in technology as "spinoffs" from the ambitious plans of both Romanesque and Gothic architects had their impact. The increase of a money economy aided the growth of artistic and musical culture.

One conspicuous characteristic of medieval culture was its belief that everything knowable could be expressed in a manageable and rational whole. Whether it appeared in stone (Chartres) or technical prose (Thomas Aquinas) or in poetry (Dante), the medieval mind saw hierarchy, order, intelligibility, and, above all, God in all of observable creation. This hierarchy expressed itself in its emphasis on advancing steps of understanding. The sculptural program of Chartres, for example, is a revelation of the Old Testament figures who point us to their proper fulfillment in the New. In the theology of Aquinas we move from the plane of natural reason to a fuller truth taught by revelation. In Dante we progress from an awareness of our sinful nature to an intuition into the nature of God. In all of these cases the emphasis is on harmony and gradation and a final purpose of all knowledge, which is to become aware of God. In that sense, at least, much of medieval culture could be said to be oriented in an otherworldly manner.

Exercises

1. Is it possible to think of a building or complex of buildings serving as an organizing metaphor for a contemporary city in the way a cathedral served in the Middle Ages?
2. What positive and/or negative outcomes do you see deriving from the medieval cult of the Virgin?
3. Compare the use and role of light in the atmosphere of Hagia Sophia and the cathedral of Chartres.
4. Set out some of the technological problems medieval builders had to solve in an age with limited power sources, no tempered metals, no computers or slide rules for calculations, and so on.
5. The medieval university was organized around the body of scholars who made up the faculty. To what degree does that model hold up today? What is the organizing principle of the modern college or university?
6. A good deal of medieval education utilized *dialectics.* What does that term mean? Where do dialectics, broadly understood, find their usefulness today?
7. Thomas Aquinas had no doubt that all knowledge was both interrelated and capable of being synthesized into a whole. Everything from science and philosophy to theology would fit into that synthesis. Would that view find many supporters today? If not, why not?
8. If you were to organize a contemporary hell for the great villains of our day, would you use Dante's classification or would you construct another schema? On what basis would it be organized?
9. Dante looks back to Vergil as the model for his great work of poetry. If we were to write a work today to celebrate our culture and destiny, would we feel the need to invoke a past model to do so? Who might it be?

Pronunciation Guide

Abelard: AB-eh-lard
Alighieri (Dante): Al-e-GARY
Aquinas: Ah-KWI-nas
Averroes: Av-ER-row-es
Avicenna: Av-e-CHENA
Carmina Burana: CAR-me-nah Bur-RAN-ah
Chartres: CHART-reh
Divina Commedia: Dee-VEE-nah Com-EH-dee-ah
Guido di Arezzo: GWE-dough deh Ah-RET-so
Leonin: LEE-oh-nin
Maimonides: my-MON-id-eze
Pérotin: PEAR-oh-tin
Pseudo-Dionysius: SUE-dough Die-oh-NY-sius
Suger: SUE-jay
Universitas: u-knee-VER-see-tas
Villard de Honnecourt: VEE-yard deh HO-knee-cor

Further Reading

Adams, Henry. *Mont-Saint-Michel and Chartres.* Garden City: Doubleday, 1959. A brilliant albeit eccentric work on the culture of the Gothic world. While its scholarship has been superseded in this century, it is still an aesthetic classic.

Aubert, Marcel. *Gothic Cathedrals of France and Their Treasures.* London: Nicholas Kaye, 1959. A handy encyclopedia of Gothic architecture by a noted French scholar of the era.

Bony, Jean. *French Gothic Architecture of the 12th and 13th Centuries.* Berkeley: University of California Press, 1983. Authoritative and lavishly illustrated.

Cunningham, Lawrence S. *Saint Francis of Assisi.* San Francisco: Harper & Row, 1981. Readable essays on the saint and his culture with profuse illustrations.

Daly, Lowrie. *The Medieval University: 1200–1400.* New York: Sheed & Ward, 1961. A handy and readable introduction.

Gilson, Etienne. *Reason and Revelation in the Middle Ages.* New York: Scribner, 1966. A brief but excellent survey of the intellectual milieu of the period by one of the foremost authorities of our century.

Gimpel, Jean. *The Medieval Machine: The Industrial Revolution of the Middle Ages.* New York: Penguin, 1977. A wonderful introduction to technology in medieval times.

Golding, William. *The Spire.* New York: Harcourt, 1964. A brilliant fictional evocation of medieval cathedral building.

Holmes, Urban T. *Daily Living in the Twelfth Century.* Madison: University of Wisconsin, 1966. An extremely readable account of ordinary life in medieval London and Paris drawn from documentary evidence.

Knowles, David. *The Evolution of Medieval Thought.* New York: Vintage, 1962. A classic study of medieval thought from Augustine to the eve of the Reformation.

Macauley, David. *Cathedral: The Story of Its Construction.*

Boston: Houghton Mifflin, 1973. A book for young and old readers on the construction of a cathedral, with pen-and-ink drawings by the author. A fascinating and lovely work that is simple but richly informative.

Panofsky, Erwin. *Abbot Suger.* Princeton: Princeton University Press, 1946. A translation of Suger's booklets on Saint Denis with an important introduction and full notes. Indispensable for the period.

Simson, Otto von. *The Gothic Cathedral.* New York: Harper & Row, 1964. A classic work on the aesthetics of the Gothic era in the Île-de-France. The work is quite valuable for its study of Saint Denis and Chartres.

Singleton, Charles. *The Divine Comedy of Dante Alighieri.* 6 vols. Princeton: Princeton University Press, 1972. With a commentary in English by the foremost authority on Dante in America. There are separate volumes of the poem in English with companion volumes of commentary. Excellent and indispensable.

Weisheipl, James. *Friar Thomas D'Aquino: His Life, Thought, and Work.* Garden City: Doubleday, 1974. Reflects the current state of Thomistic studies; scholarly, with good notes and bibliography.

LATE MIDDLE AGES / PROTO-RENAISSANCE

	GENERAL EVENTS	LITERATURE & PHILOSOPHY
1280		
	1299 Ottoman Turk dynasty founded	
	1300 Pope Boniface VIII proclaims first Jubilee Year (“Holy Year”)	
	1303 Philip the Fair of France humiliates Pope Boniface VIII	**c. 1303–1321** Dante, *Divine Comedy*
1309 “Babylonian Captivity” of the Papacy		
	1309 “Babylonian Captivity” of the papacy at Avignon begins	
	1326 Earliest known use of cannon	
	1337–1453 “Hundred Years’ War” between France and England	
	1346–1378 Reign of Charles IV, Holy Roman emperor	
	1346 English defeat French at Crécy	
	1348 Bubonic plague depopulates Europe	**1348–1352** Boccaccio, *Decameron,* collection of tales
	1356 English defeat French at Poitiers	**after 1350** Petrarch compiles *Canzoniere,* collection of poems
	1358 Revolt of lower classes *(Jacquerie)* in France	
	1363–1404 Reign of Philip the Bold, duke of Burgundy	**c. 1370** Saint Catherine of Siena urges end of “Babylonian Captivity”
	1376 Popes return to Rome from Avignon	**1373** Petrarch, *Letter to Posterity,* autobiography
1377 The Great Schism		
	1377–1399 Reign of Richard II in England	**c. 1377** Wycliff active in English church reform; translates Bible into English
	1378 “Great Schism” begins	
	1381 Peasant riots (“Wat Tyler Rebellion”) in England	
		c. 1385–1400 Chaucer, *The Canterbury Tales,* collection of tales
	1399–1413 Reign of Henry IV in England	**c. after 1389** Christine de Pisan, *The City of Women*
	1413 English defeat French at Agincourt	
	1417 Council of Constance ends “Great Schism” with election of Pope Martin V	
1417		

CHAPTER

9 THE 14TH CENTURY: A TIME OF TRANSITION

ART

13th cent. Dependence on Byzantine models in Italian painting

c. 1280–1290 Cimabue, *Madonna Enthroned; Crucifix,* Arezzo

c. 1300 New naturalism in Italian painting appears with work of Giotto

1305–1306 Giotto, Arena Chapel frescoes

c. 1308–1311 Duccio, *Maestà* altarpiece, Siena

c. 1310 G. Pisano completes Pisa Cathedral pulpit; Giotto, *Madonna Enthroned*

1333 Martini, *Annunciation*

1338–1339 A. Lorenzetti, *Good Government* fresco, Siena

c. 1347–1360 Prague, as residence of Charles IV, becomes major art center

c. 1350–1360 Unknown Bohemian Master, *Death of the Virgin*

c. 1363 Court of dukes of Burgundy at Dijon becomes important center of International Style

c. 1377–1413 *Wilton Diptych*

1395–1399 Broederlam, *Presentation in the Temple and Flight into Egypt*

1395–1406 Sluter, *Well of Moses*

1413–1416 Limbourg Brothers, illustrations for *Très Riches Heures du Duc de Berry*

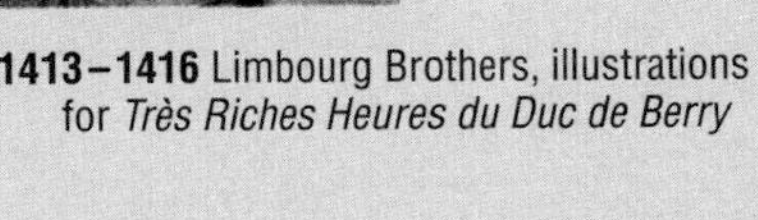

ARCHITECTURE

1288–1309 Palazzo Pubblico, Siena

1295 Santa Croce, Florence, begun

1296 Florence Cathedral (Duomo) begun

1298 Palazzo Vecchio, Florence, begun

1332–1357 Gloucester Cathedral choir ("Perpendicular" style)

c. 1345–1438 Doge's Palace, Venice

1386 Duomo of Milan begun

MUSIC

14th cent. Secular music flourishes

1325 Vitry, *Ars Nova Musicae,* treatise describing new system of musical notation

after 1337 Machaut, *Messe de Notre Dame,* polyphonic setting of the Ordinary of the Mass

c. 1350 Landini famous in Florence as performer and composer of madrigals and ballads

C H A P T E R

9
THE 14TH CENTURY: A TIME OF TRANSITION

CALAMITY, DECAY, AND VIOLENCE

THE 14TH CENTURY (often called the *Trecento,* Italian for "three hundred") is usually described by historians as the age that marks the end of the medieval period and the beginning of the Renaissance in Western Europe. If we accept this rather neat description of the period we should expect to see strong elements of the medieval sensibility as well as some stirrings of the "new birth" *(Renaissance)* of culture that was the hallmark of 15th-century European life. We must be cautious, however, about expecting the break between "medieval" and "Renaissance" to be clean and dramatic. History does not usually work with the precision employed by the historians. Nor should we expect to see cultural history moving upward in a straight line toward greater modernity or greater perfection. In fact, the 14th century was a period of unparalleled natural calamity, institutional decay, and cruel violence.

The Black Death

Midway through the century, in 1348, bubonic plague swept through Europe in a virulent epidemic that killed untold numbers of people and upset trade, culture, and daily life in ways hard for us to imagine. It has been estimated that some cities in Italy lost as much as two-thirds of their population in that year.

One prominent figure who lived through that devastation was the Italian writer Giovanni Boccaccio (1313–1375). His great collection of stories, the *Decameron,* has a plague setting. A group of young men and women flee Florence to avoid the plague; during their ten days' sojourn in the country (*Decameron* is Greek for "ten days") they amuse each other by telling stories. Each of the ten young people tells a story on each of the ten days. The resulting one hundred stories constitute a brilliant collection of folk tales, *fabliaux* (ribald fables), *exempla* (moral stories), and romances Boccaccio culled from the oral and written traditions of Europe. Because of their romantic elements, earthiness, and somewhat shocking bawdiness the *Decameron* has often been called the "Human Comedy" to contrast it with the lofty moral tone of Dante's epic work of an earlier generation.

However delightful and pleasing those stories are to read, they stand in sharp contrast to the horrific picture Boccaccio draws of the plague in his introduction to the *Decameron.* Boccaccio's account has the ring of authenticity. He had been an eyewitness to the events he describes. His vivid prose gives some small sense of what the plague must have been like for a people who possessed only the most rudimentary knowledge of medicine and no knowledge at all about the source of illness and disease.

The Great Schism

Nature was not the only scourge to affect the stability of Europe. The medieval Christian church, that most powerful and permanent large institution in medieval life, underwent convulsive changes in the 14th century, changes that were distant warning signals of the Reformation at the beginning of the 16th century.

A quick look at some dates indicates clearly the nature of these changes. In 1300 Pope Boniface VIII celebrated the great jubilee year at Rome that brought pilgrims and visitors from all over the Christian West to pay homage to the papacy and the church it represented and headed. This event

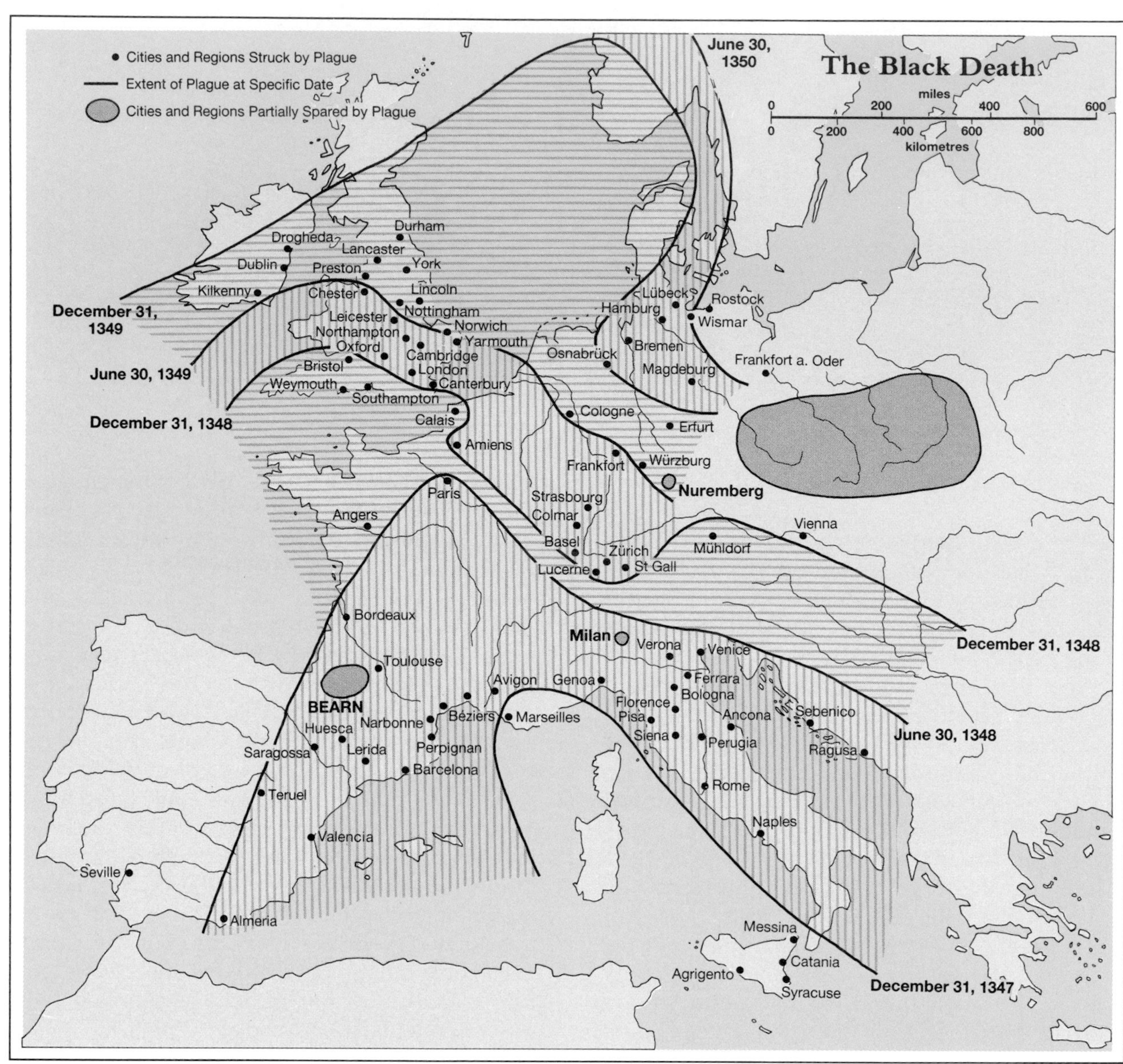

was one of the final symbolic moments of papal supremacy over European life and culture. Within the next three years Philip the Fair of France imprisoned and abused the same pope at the papal palace of Anagni. The pope died as a result of his humiliating encounters with royal power; even Dante's implacable hatred of Boniface could not restrain his outrage at the humiliation of the office of the pope. By 1309 the papacy, under severe pressure from the French, had been removed to Avignon in southern France, where it was to remain for nearly seventy years. In 1378 the papacy was further weakened by the Great Schism, which saw European Christianity divided into hostile camps, each of which pledged allegiance to a rival claimant to the papacy. Not until 1417 was this breach in church unity healed; a church council had to depose three papal pretenders to accomplish the reunification of the church.

The general disarray of the church in this period spawned ever more insistent demands for church reforms. Popular literature (as both Boccaccio and, in England, Geoffrey Chaucer, clearly demonstrate) unmercifully satirized the decadence of the church. Great saints like the mystic Catherine of Siena (1347–1380) wrote impassioned letters to the popes at Avignon in their "Babylonian Captivity" demanding that they return to Rome free from the political ties of the French monarchy. In England, John Wyclif's cries against the immorality of the higher clergy and the corruption of the church fueled indignation at all levels. The famous Peasant

CONTEMPORARY VOICES

John Ball

Good people; things cannot go right in England and never will, until goods are held in common and there are no more villeins [peasants] and gentlefolk. . . . In what way are those whom we call lords greater masters than ourselves? How have they deserved it? If we all spring from a common mother and father, Adam and Eve, how can they claim or prove that they are lords more than us except by making us produce and grow the wealth which they spend?

They are clad in velvet and camlet lined with squirrel and ermine, while we go dressed in coarse cloth.

They have the wines, the spices, and the good bread; we have the rye, the husks, and the straw and we drink water.

They have shelters and ease in their fine manors and we have hardship and toil, the winds and the rains in the fields.

And from us must come, from our labor, the things which keep them in luxury.

We are called serfs and beaten if we are slow in service to them, yet we have no sovereign lord we can complain to; none to hear us and do us justice.

Let us go to the king—he is young—and show him how we are oppressed and tell him how we want things changed or else we will change them ourselves. If we go in good earnest and all together, very many people who are called serfs and are held in subjection will follow us to get their freedom.

When the king hears us he will remedy the evil, willingly or otherwise!

[Sermon of the priest John Ball, a leader in the English Peasant Revolt of 1381, recorded in *The Chronicles* of Froissart]

EAST MEETS WEST

The Rise of the Ottoman Empire

The problems faced by church leaders in the 14th century were not limited to putting their own affairs in order. The preceding century had seen Western forces involved in the Crusades; in theory these "holy wars" were intended to capture Jerusalem for the West, although their principal practical result was to cause lasting damage to the Byzantine Empire. By 1261 Byzantium, center of the Eastern church, was reduced to Constantinople and the land around it.

With the fall of Constantinople in 1291, the last Christian stronghold in the Holy Land, to Egyptian troops, the former Byzantine territories fell into the hands of a new force, that of the Ottoman Turks. The Ottoman dynasty was founded in 1299, and from the beginning the Ottoman sultans showed themselves equally good at winning wars and building a strong, effectively administered state. By the mid-14th century they had conquered most of western Asia Minor (modern Turkey) and had begun to form permanent settlements on the European side of the straits of the Bosporus. Neither Eastern nor Western Christians presented any resistance, and in 1365 the Turks established their capital on European soil at Adrianople.

Within a few years the Turks had driven to the borders of Hungary, and in alarm the pope declared a crusade. A large disorganized Christian army was routed at the battle of Nicopolis in 1396. The Turks might well have gone on to besiege Central Europe, but they themselves were attacked from the east by nomad Mongol troops. It took a generation for the Ottoman rulers to regain control and complete their capture of the Byzantine Empire by taking Constantinople in 1453.

Thus in the course of the 14th century a powerful Islamic empire (the Turks had been converted to Islam around A.D. 1000) became established within all too easy reach of the European powers. Most of the connections between Europe and Turkey were to take the form of trade. Venice, in particular, soon developed strong economic ties with Constantinople. Cultural influences were mainly transmitted from West to East, since the Ottoman Turks were more interested in effective organization and in maintaining traditional religious modes than in philosophy, science, or the arts. Indeed, the most profound effect on the West of the Ottoman conquests was that the last generation of Byzantine scholars fled to Western Europe carrying with them their precious manuscripts of Greek texts, which did much to inspire the Renaissance of the 15th century.

Revolt of 1381 was greatly aided by the activism of people aroused by the ideas of Wyclif and his followers.

The 1381 revolt in England was only the last in a series of lower-class revolutions that occurred in the 14th century. The frequency and magnitude of these revolts (like that of the French peasants beginning in 1356) highlight the profound dissatisfactions with the church and the nobility in the period. It is not accidental that the story of Robin Hood, with its theme of violence toward the wealthy and care for the poor, began in the 14th century.

The Hundred Years' War

The terrible violence of the 14th century was caused not only by the alienation of the peasants but also by the Hundred Years' War between France and England. While the famous battles of the period—Poitiers, Crécy, Agincourt—now seem romantic and distant, it is undeniable that they brought unrelieved misery to France for long periods. Between battles, roaming bands of mercenaries pillaged the landscape to make up for their lack of pay. The various battles were terrible in themselves. One example must suffice. According to Jean Froissart's *Chronicles,* the English King Edward III sent a group of his men to examine the battlefield after the battle of Crécy (1346), in which the English longbowmen slaughtered the more traditionally armed French and mercenary armies: "They passed the whole day upon the field and made a careful report of all they saw. According to their report it appeared that 80 banners, the bodies of 11 princes, 1200 knights, and 30,000 common men were found dead on the field." It is no wonder that Barbara Tuchman's splendid history of life in 14th-century France, *A Distant Mirror* (1978) should have been subtitled "The Calamitous Fourteenth Century."

LITERATURE IN ITALY, ENGLAND, AND FRANCE

Amid the natural and institutional disasters of the 14th century there were signs of intense human creativity in all the arts, especially in literature. In Italy, Dante's literary eminence was secure at the time of his death (1321) and the reputation of Italian letters was further enhanced by two other outstanding Tuscan writers: the poet Francesco Petrarch and Giovanni Boccaccio, famed for the *Decameron.* In England, one of the greatest authors in the history of English letters was active: Geoffrey Chaucer. His life spanned the second half of the 14th century; he died, almost symbolically, in 1400.

Petrarch

It is appropriate to begin a discussion of 14th-century culture with Petrarch. His life spanned the better part of the century (1304–1374) and in that life we can see the conflict between the medieval and early Renaissance ideals being played out.

Petrarch (Petrarca in Italian) was born in Arezzo, a small town in Tuscany, south of Florence. As a young man, in obedience to parental wishes, he studied law for a year in France and for three years at the law faculty in Bologna. He abandoned his legal studies immediately after the death of his father to pursue a literary career. To support himself he accepted some minor church offices but was never ordained to the priesthood.

Petrarch made his home at Avignon (and later at a much more isolated spot near that papal city, Vaucluse), but for the greater part of his life he wandered from place to place. He never could settle down; his restlessness prevented him from accepting lucrative positions that would have made him a permanent resident of any one place. He received invitations to serve as secretary to various popes in Avignon and, through the intercession of his close friend Boccaccio, was offered a professorship in Florence. He took none of these positions.

Petrarch was insatiably curious. He fed his love for the ancient classics by searching out and copying ancient manuscripts that had remained hidden and unread in the various monasteries of Europe. It is said that at his death he had one of the finest private libraries in Europe. He wrote volumes of poetry and prose, carried on a vast correspondence, advised the rulers of the age, took a keen interest in horticulture, and kept a wide circle of literary and artistic friends. We know that at his death he possessed pictures by both Simone Martini and Giotto, two of the most influential artists of the time. In 1348 he was crowned poet laureate of Rome, the first artist so honored since the ancient days of Rome.

One true mark of the Renaissance sensibility was a keen interest in the self and an increased thirst for personal glory and fame. Petrarch surely is a 14th-century harbinger of that spirit. Dante's *The Divine Comedy* was totally oriented to the next life; the apex of Dante's vision is that of the soul rapt in the vision of God in eternity. Petrarch, profoundly religious, never denied that such a vision was the ultimate goal of life. At the same time, his work exhibits a tension between that goal and his thirst for earthly success and fame. In his famous prose work *Secretum (My Secret)*, written in 1343, the artist imagines himself in conversation with Saint Augustine. In a dialogue extraordinary for its sense of self-confession and self-scrutiny, Petrarch discusses his moral and intellectual failings, his besetting sins, and his tendency to fall into fits of depression. He agrees with his great hero Augustine that he should be less concerned with his intellectual labors and the fame that derives from them and more with salvation and the spiritual perfection of his life. However, Petrarch's argument has a note of ambivalence: "I will be true to myself as far as it is possible. I will pull myself together and collect my scattered wits, and make a great endeavor to possess my soul in patience. But even while we speak, a crowd of important affairs, though only of this world, is waiting for my attention."

The inspiration for the *Secretum* was Augustine's *Confessions*, a book Petrarch loved so much that he carried it with him everywhere. It may well have been the model for Petrarch's *Letter to Posterity*, one of the few examples of autobiography we possess after the time of Augustine. That Petrarch would have written an autobiography is testimony to his strong interest in himself as a person. The *Letter* was probably composed in 1373, a year before his death. Petrarch reviews his life up until 1351, where the text abruptly breaks off. The unfinished work is clear testimony to Petrarch's thirst for learning, fame, and self-awareness. At the same time, it is noteworthy for omitting any mention of the Black Death of 1348, which carried off the woman he loved. The letter is an important primary document of the sensibility of the 14th-century "proto-Renaissance."

Petrarch regarded as his most important works the Latin writings over which he labored with devotion and in conscious imitation of his most admired classical masters: Ovid, Cicero, and Vergil. Today, however, only the literary specialist or the antiquarian is likely to read his long epic poem in Latin called *Africa* (written in imitation of Vergil's *Aeneid*), or his prose work in praise of the past masters of the world *(De Viris Illustris)*, or his meditations on the benefits of the contemplative life *(De Vita Solitaria)*. What has assured the literary reputation of Petrarch is his incomparable vernacular poetry, which he considered somewhat trifling but collected carefully into his *Canzoniere (Songbook)*. The *Canzoniere* contains more than three hundred sonnets and 49 *canzoni* (songs) written in Italian during the span of his adult career.

The subject of a great deal of Petrarch's poetry is his love for Laura, a woman with whom he fell immediately in love in 1327 after seeing her at church in Avignon. Laura died in the plague of 1348. The poems in her honor are divided into those written during her lifetime and those mourning her untimely death. Petrarch poured out his love for Laura in over three hundred *sonnets*, fourteen-line poems he typically broke into an octave and a sestet. Although they were never actually lovers (Petrarch says in the *Secretum* that this was due more to her honor than to his; Laura was a married woman), his Laura was no mere literary abstraction. She was a flesh-and-blood woman whom Petrarch genuinely loved. One of the characteristics of his poetry, in fact, is the palpable reality of Laura as a person; she never becomes (as Beatrice does for Dante) a symbol without earthly reality.

The interest in Petrarch's sonnets did not end with his death. Petrarchism, by which is meant the Petrarchan form of the sonnet and particularly the poet's attitude to his subject matter—praise of a woman as the perfection of human beauty and the object of the highest expression of love—was introduced into other parts of Europe before the century was over. In England, Petrarch's sonnets were first imitated in form and subject by Sir Thomas Wyatt in the early 16th century. Although the Elizabethan poets eventually developed their own English form of the sonnet, the English Renaissance tradition of poetry owes a particularly large debt to Petrarch, as the poetry of Sir Philip Sidney (1554–1586), Edmund Spenser (1552–1599), and William Shakespeare (1564–1616) shows. Their sonnet sequences follow the example of Petrarch in linking together a series of sonnets in such a way as to indicate a development in the relationship of the poet to his love.

Petrarch's Sonnet 15

Backwards at every weary step and slow
These limbs I turn which with great pain I bear;
Then take I comfort from the fragrant air
That breathes from thee, and sighing onward
go.
But when I think how joy is turned to woe,
Remembering my short life and whence I fare,
I stay my feet for anguish and despair,
And cast my tearful eyes on earth below.
At times amid the storm of misery
This doubt assails me: how frail limbs and poor
Can severed from their spirit hope to live.
Then answers Love: Hast thou no memory
How I to lovers this great guerdon give,
Free from all human bondage to endure?

(trans. John Addington Symonds)

Chaucer

While it is possible to see the beginning of the Renaissance spirit in Petrarch and other Italian writers of the 14th century, the greatest English writer of the century, Geoffrey Chaucer (1340–1400), still reflects the culture of his immediate past. The new spirit of individualism discernible in Petrarch is missing in Chaucer. He is still very much a medieval man. Only in the later part of the 15th century, largely under the influence of Italian models, can we speak of the Renaissance in England. This underscores the valuable lesson about history that movements do not necessarily happen immediately and everywhere.

Scholars have been able to reconstruct Chaucer's life with only partial success. We know that his family had been fairly prosperous wine merchants and vintners and that he entered royal service early in his life, eventually becoming a squire to King Edward III. After 1373 he undertook various diplomatic tasks for the king, including at least two trips to Italy to negotiate commercial contracts. During these Italian journeys Chaucer came into contact with the writings of Dante, Petrarch, and Boccaccio. There has been some speculation that he actually met Petrarch, but the evidence is tenuous. Toward the end of his life Chaucer served as the customs agent for the port of London on the river Thames. He was thus never a leisured "man of letters"; his writing had to be done amid the hectic round of public affairs that engaged his attention as a highly placed civil servant.

Like many other successful writers of the late medieval period, Chaucer could claim a widespread acquaintance with the learning and culture of his time. This was still an age when it was possible to read most of the available books. Chaucer spoke and wrote French fluently, and his poems show the influence of many French allegories and "dream visions." That he also knew Italian literature is clear from his borrowings from Dante and Petrarch and from his use of stories and tales in Boccaccio's *Decameron* (although it is not clear that he knew that work directly). Chaucer also had a deep knowledge of Latin literature, both classical and ecclesiastical. Furthermore, his literary output was not limited to the composition of original works of poetry. He made a translation from Latin (with an eye on an earlier French version) of Boethius' *Consolation of Philosophy* as well as a translation from French of the 13th-century allegorical erotic fantasy the *Romance of the Rose*. He also composed a short treatise on the astrolabe and its relationship to the study of astronomy and astrology (two disciplines not clearly distinguished at that time).

The impressive range of Chaucer's learning pales in comparison with his most memorable and noteworthy talents: his profound feeling for the role of the English language as a vehicle for literature; his efforts to extend the range of the language (the richness of Chaucer's vocabulary was not exceeded until Shakespeare); and his incomparable skill in the art of human observation. Chaucer's characters are so finely realized that they have become standard types in English literature: His pardoner is an unforgettable villain, his knight the essence of courtesy, his wife of Bath a paradigm of rollicking bawdiness.

These characters, and others, are from Chaucer's masterpiece, *The Canterbury Tales,* begun sometime after 1385. To unify this vast work, a collection of miscellaneous tales, Chaucer used a typical literary device: a narrative frame, in this case a journey during which people tell each other tales. As noted, Boccaccio had used a similar device in the *Decameron*.

Chaucer's plan was to have a group of thirty pilgrims travel from London to the shrine of Thomas à Becket at Canterbury and back. After a general introduction, each pilgrim would tell two tales on the way and two on the return trip in order to pass the long hours of travel more pleasantly. Between tales they might engage in perfunctory conversation or prologues of their own to cement the tales further into a unified whole.

Chaucer never finished this ambitious project; he died before half of it was complete. The version we possess has a General Prologue in which the narrator, Geoffrey Chaucer, describes the individual pilgrims, his meeting with them at the Tabard Inn in London, and the start of the journey. Only twenty-three of the thirty pilgrims tell their tales (none tells two tales) and the group has not yet reached Canterbury. There is even some internal evidence that the material we possess was not meant for publication in its present form.

Although *The Canterbury Tales* is only a draft of what was intended to be Chaucer's masterwork, it is of incomparable literary and social value. A close reading of the General Prologue, for instance—with its representative, although limited, cross section of medieval society (no person lower in rank than a plowman or higher in rank than a knight appears)—affords an effortless entry into the complex world of late-medieval England. With quick, deft strokes Chaucer not only creates verbal portraits of people who at the same time seem both typical and uniquely real but also introduces us to a world of slowly dying knightly values, a world filled with such contrasts as clerical foibles, the desire for knowledge, the ribald taste of the lower social classes, and an appetite for philosophical conversation.

After the General Prologue, the various members of the pilgrim company begin to introduce themselves and proceed to tell their tales. Between the tales they engage in small talk or indulge in lengthy prologues of their own. In the tales that he completed, we see that Chaucer drew on the vast treasury of literature, both written and oral, that was the common patrimony of medieval culture. The Knight's Tale is a courtly romance; the miller and reeve tell stories that spring from the ribald *fabliaux* tradition of the time; the pardoner tells an *exemplum* such as any medieval preacher might employ; the prioress draws from the legends of the saints; the nun's priest uses an animal fable, while the parson characteristically enough provides a somewhat tedious example of a medieval prose sermon.

At places, as in the prologue to the tale of the Wife of Bath, we get from Chaucer a long meditation on some of the problems of the age. The Wife of Bath introduces her tale, for instance, with a discourse explaining why the persistent tradition against women *(misogyny)* is unjust and contrary to authentic Christian theology. She also makes a passionate plea for seeing sexual relations as a good given by God. This may strike us as unnecessary but in an age that prized the unmarried state (e.g., for monks, nuns, priests, etc.) it was a necessary corrective.

Christine de Pisan

Christine de Pisan (1365–1428?) is an extraordinary figure in late medieval literature if for no other reason than her pioneering role as one of Europe's first women professional writers to make her living with the power of her pen.

Born in Venice, Christine accompanied her father Thomas de Pizzano to the French court of Charles V when she was still a small child. Thomas was the king's physician, astrologer, and close adviser. He evidently gave his daughter a thorough education: she was able to write in both Italian and French and probably knew Latin well enough to read it. At fifteen she married Eugene of Castel, a young nobleman from Picardy. That same year (1380) the king died and the family fell on hard times with the loss of royal patronage. Five years

SPORTS AND GAMES

Recreation in a Medieval Village

For all the grim aspects of 14th-century life, characters such as those who took part in the pilgrimage described by Chaucer had a variety of ways of enlivening their leisure time back home in their villages. Many of their sports and pastimes, in fact, remain popular today.

Some activities provided a combination of spectator and participatory sport. While the young men played various ball games, "the ancient men came forth on horseback to see their sport," and "the maidens danced as long as they could well see." In northern Europe, ice skating was popular. As soon as the rivers froze, the young people would tie skates made of bone to their feet, "and shoving themselves by a little pointed staff, slide as swiftly as a bird flieth in the air, or an arrow out of a crossbow."

Other sports, especially those involving animal contests, make less appeal to modern tastes. Bull- and bearbaiting inevitably accompanied any holiday feast or celebration, and all classes and ages enjoyed cockfighting. Contests to the death between young roosters, generally blindfolded, took place in specially built cockpits, while children would take their prize birds to school with them, to show them off and trade them, rather as modern children do with baseball and other card sets.

Much of our information about medieval peasant sports and games comes from the work of John Stow (1525–1605), a prosperous tailor in Renaissance London, who collected and transcribed earlier medieval manuscripts: The passages quoted above are taken from an account by William Fitzstephen—an English cleric in the service of Thomas à Becket—written around 1200. While Stow himself had something of a tendency to romanticize the pleasures of village life, many of his descriptions have the ring of truth, and cast a gentler light on existences which must on the whole have been poverty-stricken and violent. "In the month of May, everyone would walk into the sweet meadows and green woods, there to rejoice their spirits with the beauty and savor of sweet flowers, and with the harmony of birds praising God in their kind." Today's walkers and hikers, fleeing to the country from city noise and pollution, will sympathize.

later her father and her husband were both dead, leaving Christine the sole support of her mother, niece, and three young children. To maintain this large family, Christine hit on an almost unheard-of solution for a woman of the time: She turned to writing and the patronage such writing could bring to earn a living.

Between 1399 and 1415 she composed fifteen books—which, as one of her translators has noted, is a staggering record in an age which had neither typewriters nor word processors. In 1399 she entered a famous literary debate about the *Romance of the Rose.* The *Romance,* a long and rather tedious poem, had been written in the preceding century and was immensely popular (Chaucer did an incomplete English translation of it). In 1275 Jean de Meung had written an addition to it that was violently critical of women. Christine attacked this misogynistic addition in a treatise called *A Letter to the God of Love.* In 1404 she wrote her final word on this debate in a long work entitled *The Book of the City of Ladies.*

The Book of the City of Ladies is indebted in its structure to Augustine's *The City of God,* and for its sources, a Latin treatise by Boccaccio entitled *De Claris Mulieribus.* Through use of stories of famous women *(clarae mulieres)* Christine demonstrates that they possessed virtues precisely opposite those vices imputed to women by Jean de Meung.

The following year (1405) Christine wrote *The Treasure of the City of Ladies,* a book of etiquette and advice to help women survive in society. What is extraordinarily interesting about this book (one of the few available in English translation) is its final section, in which Christine pens advice for every class of women from young brides and wives of shopkeepers to prostitutes and peasant women.

Around 1418 Christine retired to a convent in which her daughter was a nun, where she continued to write. Besides a treatise on arms and chivalry and a lament about the horrors of civil war, she also composed prayers and seven allegorical psalms. Of more enduring interest was *The Book of Peace,* a handbook of instruction for the Dauphin who was to become Charles VII and a short hymn in honor of the great Joan of Arc. Whether Christine lived to see the bitter end of Joan is uncertain, but her hymn is one of the few extant works written while Joan was alive.

Immensely popular in her own time (the Duc de Berry owned copies of every book she wrote), her reputation waned in the course of time, to be revived only in the last decade or so as scholars have tried to do justice to the forgotten heroines of our common history.

ART IN ITALY

Giorgio Vasari's *Lives of the Artists* (1550), the earliest account of the rebirth of Italian art in the Renaissance, treats first of all the great Florentine painter Giotto da Bondone (1266 or 1267–1337). In his *Life of Giotto* Vasari pays tribute to Giotto's work and also gives him credit for setting painting once again on to the right path, from which it had strayed.

Later generations have accepted Vasari's assessment and have seen Giotto as a revolutionary figure not for the 14th century alone but for the entire history of European art, making a major break with the art of the Middle Ages. Like all revolutionary figures, Giotto was more intimately linked with his past than his contemporaries and immediate successors realized, and to understand the magnitude of his achievements we must first see something of their context.

The Italo-Byzantine Background

Throughout the later Middle Ages art in Italy showed little of the richness and inventiveness of the great centers of northern Europe. Not only in France, where the University of Paris formed the intellectual capital of the Western world, but also in England and Germany, construction of the great Gothic cathedrals provided opportunities for artists to refine and develop their techniques. Sculptured decorations like *The Death of the Virgin* from Strasbourg Cathedral [9.1] are stylistically far more advanced than contemporary work in Italy. One of the reasons for this is that northern Gothic artists were beginning to return for inspiration not to their immediate predecessors but to classical art, with its realistic portrayal of the body and drapery. In Italy, however, artists were still rooted in the Byzantine tradition. Italian churches were generally decorated not with lifelike sculptural groups like the one from Strasbourg but with solemn and stylized frescoes and mosaics, a style called Italo-Byzantine.

There are notable exceptions to the generally conservative character of Italian art in the 13th century. Nicola Pisano (1220/1225–1284?) and his son Giovanni (1245/1250–1314) have been described as the creators of modern sculpture. Nicola's first major work was a marble pulpit for the baptistery in Pisa completed in 1260, clearly influenced by the Roman sarcophagi the sculptor could see around him in Pisa. By crowding in his figures and filling the scene with lively detail Nicola recaptured much of the vitality and realism of late Roman art while

9.1 *The Death of the Virgin,* tympanum of the south transept portal, Strasbourg Cathedral. c. 1220. The expressive faces and elaborate drapery show the influence of classical sculpture.

9.2 Nicola Pisano. *Annunciation and Nativity,* detail of pulpit. 1259–1260. Marble. Baptistery, Pisa. By crowding his figures together Nicola was able to combine the scene of the Nativity with the Annunciation and the shepherds in the fields.

9.3 Giovanni Pisano. *Nativity and Annunciation to the Shepherds,* detail of pulpit. 1302–1310. Marble. Cathedral, Pisa. The slender figures and sense of space create an effect very different from that of the work of the artist's father.

retaining the expressive qualities of Gothic sculpture. The work of his son Giovanni was less influenced by classical models than by his contemporaries in northern Europe—so much so that some scholars believe he must have spent some time in France. In his pulpit for the cathedral at Pisa, finished in 1310, the figures are more elegant and less crowded than those of his father, and show an intensity of feeling typical of northern late Gothic art [9.2, 9.3]. Both of these great sculptors foreshadowed major characteristics in the art of the Renaissance, Nicola by his emphasis on classical models and Giovanni by the naturalism and emotionalism of his figures and by his use of space.

While some Italian sculptors were responding to influences from outside, painting in Italy remained

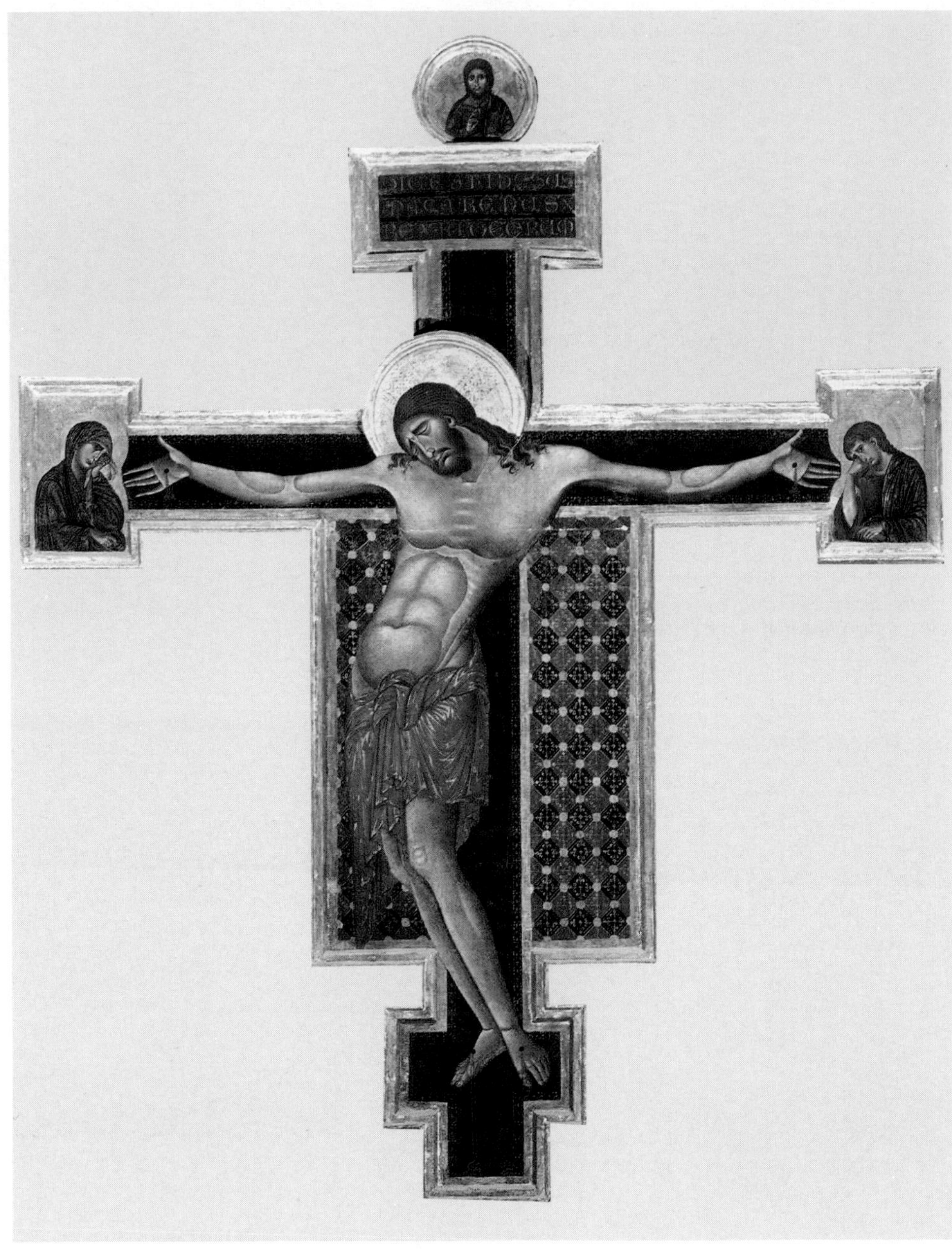

9.4 Cimabue. *Crucifixion.* c. 1240–1302. San Domenico, Arezzo.

firmly grounded in the Byzantine tradition. Byzantine art was originally derived from classical art. Although its static and solemn characteristics seem a long way away from Greek or Roman styles, Byzantine painters and mosaicists inherited the late Hellenistic and Roman artists' ability to give their figures a three-dimensional quality and to represent foreshortening. With these techniques available to him, Giotto was better able to break away from the stereotyped forms of Italo-Byzantine art and bring to painting the same naturalism and emotional power that appear in Giovanni Pisano's sculptures.

Giotto's predecessor as the leading painter in Florence, and perhaps also his teacher, was Cimabue (1240?–1302?). Not enough of his work has survived for us to have a clear impression of how much Giotto owed to Cimabue's influence, but the crucifix he painted for the church of San Domenico in Arezzo shows a remarkable realism and sophistication in the depiction of Christ's body [9.4]. Cimabue shows a genuine if incomplete un-

9.5 Cimabue. ***Madonna Enthroned.*** **1270–1285. Tempera on panel, 12'6" × 7'4" (3.81 × 2.24 m). Uffizi, Florence. Although much of the detail is Byzantine in inspiration, the scale of this painting has no Byzantine counterpart.**

derstanding of the anatomy of the figure and, more important, uses it to enhance the emotional impact of his painting by emphasizing the sense of strain and weight. At the same time the draped loincloth is not merely painted as a decorative design but as naturalistically soft folds through which the limbs beneath are visible. If in other works, like the immense Santa Trinità *Madonna* [9.5], Cimabue is more directly in the Italo-Byzantine tradition, here at least he seems directly to prefigure the impact of Giotto's art.

The works of Cimabue's contemporary Duccio di Buoninsegna (1255/60–1318/19) are more directly Byzantine in inspiration, but here too the new spirit of the times can be felt [Table 9.1]. His greatest achievement was the huge *Maestà*, painted between 1308 and 1311, for the high altar of the cathedral of Siena, his native city. The majestic Madonna who gives the work its name faced the congregation [9.6], while both the front and back of the altarpiece were covered with small compartments filled with scenes from the lives of Christ and the Virgin. The episodes themselves

TABLE 9.1 Siena in the Age of Duccio (1255/60–1318/19)

Population	20,000
Political Institutions	Council of the Nine, rotating Consistory (Magistracy)
Economy	Banking, wool manufacture, jewelry, and goldwork
Cultural Life	Painting (duccio, Martini); Sculpture (della Quercia); *Laudi*, or sacred songs (Bianco da Siena); Theology (St. Catherine)
Principal Buildings	Cathedral, Palazzo Pubblico (Town Hall)
Divine Protectress	The Virgin Mary, Queen of Siena

9.6 Duccio. *Madonna Enthroned,* detail of front panel of *Maestà* Altar. c. 1308–1311. Tempera on panel, height 6'10½" (2.1 m). Cathedral Museum, Siena. Notice the greater gentleness of the faces and the softer, flowing robe of the Virgin here than in Cimabue's painting.

9.7 Duccio. *The Annunciation of the Death of the Virgin*, from the *Maestà* Altar. c. 1308–1311. Tempera on panel. Cathedral Museum, Siena. One of the episodes from the *Maestà* altarpiece, this scene demonstrates Duccio's ability to create a convincing architectural space around his figures.

are familiar from earlier painters, but the range of emotional expression is new and astonishing, as Duccio reveals to us not only the physical appearance of each of his subjects but their emotional states as well. In a number of the scenes the action takes place within an architectural setting that conveys a greater sense of space than we find in any earlier paintings, including those from the ancient world [9.7].

Giotto's Break with the Past

Great as was Duccio's contribution to the development of painting, it was achieved without any decisive break with the tradition in which he worked. Even if we can now see the roots of some of Giotto's achievements in the works of Cimabue, the boldness of his vision, and the certainty with which he communicates it to us, represent one of the supreme achievements of Western art.

Giotto's preeminent characteristic was his realism. The Byzantine style had aimed for a rich, glowing surface, with elaborate linear designs. Now for the first time figures were painted with a sense of depth, their volume represented by a careful use of light and dark, so that they took on the same strength and presence as works of sculpture. Instead of being confronted with an image, spectators saw the living and breathing figures before them. In his great altarpiece of the Madonna enthroned, painted in 1310, Giotto brings us into the presence of the Virgin herself [9.8]. We see the ma-

9.8 Giotto. *Madonna Enthroned.* c. 1310. Tempera on panel, 10'8" × 6'8" (3.25 × 2.03 m). Uffizi, Florence. Although contemporary with Duccio's Madonna from the *Maestà* altarpiece, Giotto's painting has a much greater sense of weight and volume.

jestic solidity of her form, an impression enhanced by the realistic throne on which she sits. This is achieved not only by the three-dimensional modeling of the figures but also by the sense of space that surrounds the Virgin and Child and separates them from the worshiping angels.

But Giotto's greatness lay not so much in his ability to create realistic images—to "imitate Nature," as his contemporaries called it—as in using these images for dramatic effect. Rather than confining himself to single subjects in individual panel paintings, like that of the Madonna enthroned, he preferred to work on a more complex and monumental scale. His chief claim to fame is the great cycle of frescoes that fills the walls of the Arena Chapel in Padua. In these panels, which illustrate the lives of the Virgin and of Christ, Giotto used the new naturalistic style he had developed to express an almost inexhaustible range of emotions and dramatic situations. In the scene depicting the meeting of Joachim and Anna, the parents of the Virgin, the couple's deep affection is communicated to us with simplicity and humanity [9.9]. The quiet restraint of this episode is in strong contrast to the cosmic drama of the lamentation over the dead body of Christ [9.10]. Angels wheel overhead, screaming in grief, while below Mary supports her dead son and stares fiercely into his face. Around her are the other mourners, each a fully characterized individual. If the disciple John is the most

9.9 Giotto. *The Meeting of Joachim and Anna.* c. 1305. Fresco. Arena Chapel, Padua.

9.10 Giotto. Pietà *(Lamentation).* 1305–1306. Fresco, 7'7" × 7'9" (2.31 × 2.36 m). Arena Chapel, Padua.

passionate in the expression of his sorrow, as he flings his arms out, no less moving are the silent hunched figures in the foreground.

The Franciscans also engaged the talents of Giotto to pay honor to their patron, Francis of Assisi. While there is no scholarly consensus that Giotto painted the great cycle on the life of Francis once attributed to him in the upper basilica at Assisi (most scholars now attribute those works to an unknown artist called the "Master of the St. Francis Cycle") there is no doubt that in the second decade of the 14th century he did the fresco cycle in the Bardi chapel in the church of Santa Croce in Florence.

Giotto interpreted the deeds of Francis based on the life of the saint written by Saint Bonaventure (died 1274) who had been a contemporary of Thomas Aquinas. The narratives are not as simple as they first seem. The scene depicting Francis renouncing all of his earthly goods [9.11] shows a dramatic confrontation set before the palace of the local bishop. On the left is Pietro Bernadone holding the clothes of the saint who had stripped himself nude as a sign of renunciation. To the viewer's right is Bishop Guido, covering the nakedness of the saint with his episcopal cope (symbolizing his entry into the life of the church) while Francis assumes an attitude of prayer. Bonaventure's *Life*

9.11 Giotto. ***Saint Francis Renounces His Worldly Goods.*** **Santa Croce, Bardi Chapel in Florence, Scala.**

says that on that occasion Francis said, "Once I was called the son of Pietro Bernadone; now I say 'Our Father, who art in heaven'." Giotto frames this dramatic scene with little children, at opposite ends of the line of figures, reacting to the confrontation of father and son.

Painting in Siena

Giotto's appeal was direct and immediate, and at Florence his pupils and followers continued to work under his influence for most of the rest of the 14th century, content to explore the implications of the master's ideas rather than devise new styles. As a result, the scene of the most interesting new developments in the generation after Giotto was Siena, where Duccio's influence (although considerable) was much less overpowering. Among Duccio's pupils was Simone Martini (c. 1285–1344), a close friend of Petrarch, who worked for a time at Naples for the French king Robert of Anjou and spent the last years of his life at the papal court of Avignon. In Martini's work we find the first signs of the last great development of Gothic art, the so-called International Style. The elegant courts of France and the French kingdoms of Italy had developed a taste for magnificent colors, fashionable costumes, and rich designs. Although Simone's Sienese background preserved him from the more extreme effects, his *Annunciation* has an insubstantial grace and sophistication that are in strong contrast to the solid realism of Giotto [9.12]. The resplendent robe and mantle of the angel Gabriel and the deep blue dress of the Virgin, edged in gold, produce an impression of great splendor, while their willowy figures approach the ideal of courtly elegance.

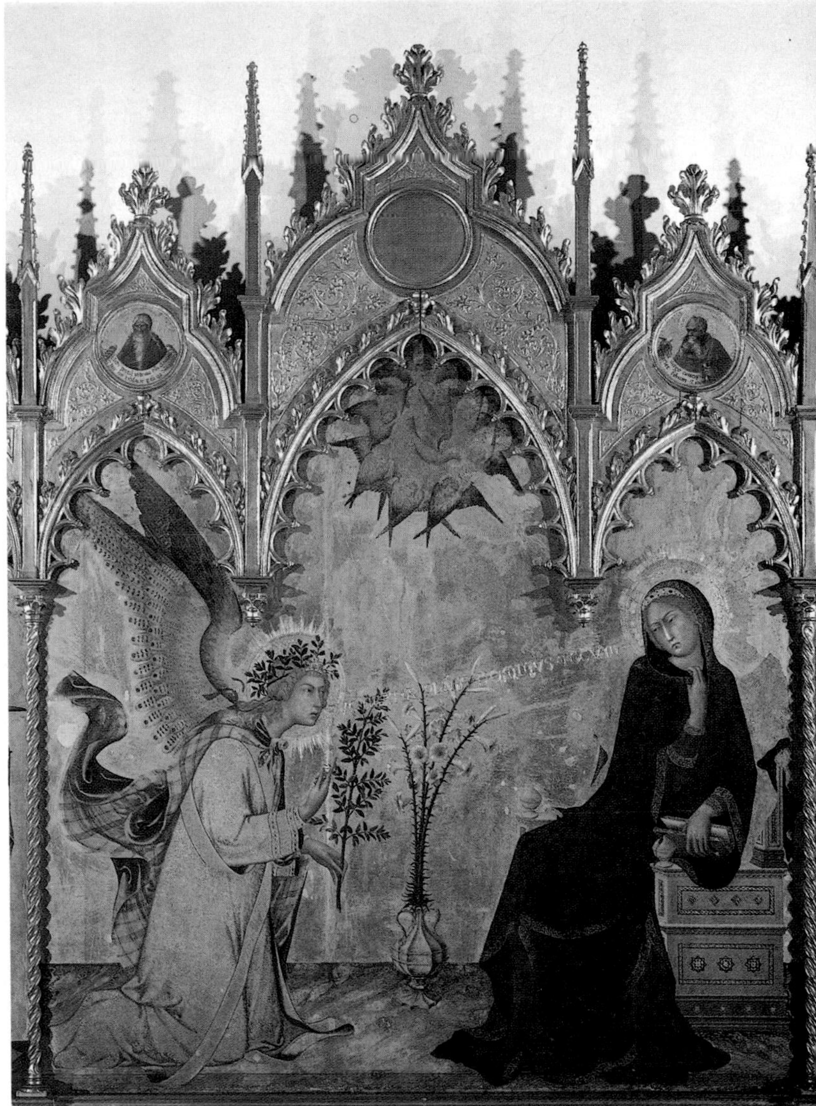

9.12 Simone Martini. *Annunciation.* 1333. Tempera on panel, 8'8" × 10' (2.64 × 3.05 m). Uffizi, Florence. The courtly elegance of the figures is in strong contrast to the massive realism of Giotto's Madonna.

9.13 Ambrogio Lorenzetti. *Effects of Good Government* (scenes in the city). 1337–1339. Fresco. Sala dei Nove, Palazzo Pubblico, Siena. Note the skillful use of perspective.

If Simone Martini was willing to sacrifice naturalism to surface brilliance, two of his contemporaries in Siena were more interested in applying Giotto's discoveries to their own work. Pietro Lorenzetti was born around 1280, his brother Ambrogio around 1285; both probably died in 1348, the year of the Black Death. The younger brother's best-known work is a huge fresco that decorates an entire wall in Siena's city hall, the Palazzo Pubblico; it was painted between 1338 and 1339 and illustrates the effects of good government on the city of Siena and the surrounding countryside [9.13]. The streets and buildings, filled with scenes of daily life, are painted with elaborate perspective. Richly dressed merchants with their wives, craftsmen at work, and graceful girls who dance in the street preserve for us a vivid picture of a life style that was to be abruptly ended by the Black Death. The scenes in the country, on the other hand, show a world that survives even today in rural Tuscany: peasants at work on farms and in orchards and vineyards [9.14].

9.14 Ambrogio Lorenzetti. *Effects of Good Government* (scenes in the countryside). 1337–1339. Fresco. Sala dei Nove, Palazzo Pubblico, Siena.

ART IN NORTHERN EUROPE

By the middle of the 14th century the gulf between artists in Italy and those north of the Alps had been reduced considerably. Painters like Simone Martini carried the latest developments in Sienese art to

France, were in turn influenced by styles they found there, and subsequently brought them back to Italy. The growing tendency toward a unity of artistic language throughout Western Europe was further increased by political developments. When, for example, in 1347 the city of Prague became the residence of the emperor Charles IV, it became a major art center rivaling even Paris in importance. Around 1360 an unknown Bohemian master working there painted a panel showing the death of the Virgin that combines the rich colors and careful architecture of Sienese painting with the strong emotional impact of northern Gothic art [9.15]. By the end of the century it was no longer possible to identify an artist's origins from the work. The *Wilton Diptych* was painted in England sometime after 1377 [9.16]. One of the two panels shows the young king Richard II accompanied by his

9.15 Unknown Bohemian Master, 2nd quarter, 14th century. *Death of the Virgin.* 1325–1350. Tempera on panel, 100 × 71 cm (39⅜ × 28"). Museum of Fine Arts, Boston (William Francis Warden Fund; Seth K. Sweetser Fund, The Henry C. and Martha B. Angell Collection, Juliana Cheney Edwards Collection, Gift of Martin Brimmer, and Gift of Reverend and Mrs. Frederick Frottingham, by exchange.)

9.16 French School. *Richard II Presented to the Virgin and Child by His Patron Saints (Wilton Diptych).* c. 1395. Oak panels, each 18 × 11½" (46 × 29 cm). National Gallery, London (reproduced by courtesy of the Trustees).

9.17 Claus Sluter. *The Well of Moses.* 1395–1406. Marble, height of figures about 6' (1.83 m). Chartreuse de Champmol, Dijon. The horns represent rays of light (a usage based on a Bible mistranslation).

patron saints, while on the other the Virgin and Child appear before the praying king, accompanied by eleven angels. They probably commemorate Richard's coronation in 1377, since he was eleven years old at the time. The wonderfully delicate yet rich colors and the careful use of shading have no parallel in English art of the period. The artist seems to have been familiar with the work of painters like Duccio and Simone Martini, but the elegance of the paintings and technique are neither simply Italian nor French. The painter of the *Wilton Diptych* was working in a style that can only be called International.

One of the first great centers of the International Style was the court of the Duke of Burgundy at Dijon, where sculptors like the Dutchman Claus Sluter and painters like the Flemish Melchior Broederlam served Duke Philip the Bold, who ruled there from 1364 to 1404, and his brother John, Duc de Berry. Sluter (active about 1380–1406) was commissioned to provide sculpture for a monastery, the Chartreuse de Champmol, founded near Dijon by Duke Philip. His most impressive work there is the so-called *Well of Moses,* designed for the monastery's cloister [9.17]. Not really a well at all, it consists of an elaborate base surrounded by stat-

9.18 Limbourg Brothers. February page from the *Trés Riches Heures du Duc de Berry.* 1416. Manuscript illumination, 8⅞ × 5⅜" (22 × 14 cm). Musée Condé, Chantilly. The chart above the painting represents the signs of the zodiac for the month of February.

ues of Moses and five other Old Testament prophets on which originally stood a crucifixion, now missing. At first glance the style of the figures is reminiscent of earlier Gothic statues, like those at Strasbourg, but a more careful look shows a host of carefully depicted details. In the figure of Moses the textures of the heavy drapery, the soft beard, and the wrinkled face are skillfully differentiated, and the expression has the vividness of a portrait. Equally realistic is the sense of weight and mass of the body beneath the drapery.

But for the most attractive details in all of late Gothic art we must turn to the *Trés Riches Heures du Duc de Berry,* an illustrated prayerbook commissioned by Philip the Bold's brother and completed in 1416. It was painted by the Limbourg brothers—Pol, Hennequin, and Herman. They were Flemish in origin, may have spent some time in Italy, and finally settled in France. Twelve illuminated pages are included in the book; these illustrate the twelve months of the year. These paintings are filled with an almost inexhaustible range of details that combine to depict the changing seasons of the year with poetry and humanity. On the page representing February the farm workers warming themselves inside the cottage, and the sheep huddling together outside, attract our attention immediately, but the whole scene is filled with marvelously painted details, from the steamy breath of the girl on the far right, stumbling back through the snow toward a warm fireside, to the snow-laden roofs of the frozen village in the far distance [9.18]. In May we move from the world of peasants to that of the aristocracy as a gorgeously dressed procession of lords and ladies rides out in the midst of the fresh greenery of springtime with the roof and turrets of a great castle in the background [9.19]. The sense of idleness and the delightful conceits of chivalry seem to evoke the world of Chaucer, while stylistically the sense of perspective and elegance of the figures is still another reminder of the influence of Sienese art.

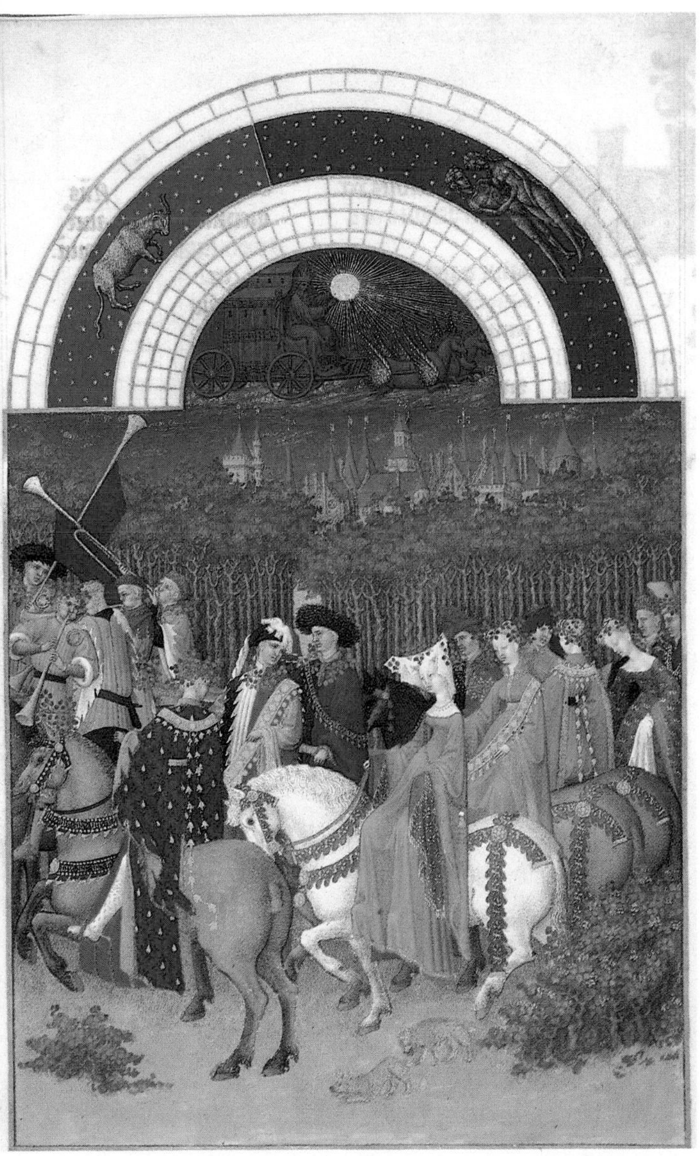

9.19 Limbourg Brothers. May page from the *Trés Riches Heures du Duc de Berry.* 1416. Manuscript illumination, 8⅞ × 5⅜" (22 × 14 cm). Musée Condé, Chantilly. The hunters blow their horns, but the courtiers are more interested in the ladies.

LATE GOTHIC ARCHITECTURE

As in the case of painting and sculpture, the generally unified style of northern Gothic architecture never really crossed the Alps into Italy. Although some of the most important Italian buildings of the 14th century are generally labeled Gothic, their style is very different from their northern counterparts. Two of the century's greatest churches illustrate this, both begun at Florence at the end of the 13th century—Santa Croce around 1295 and the cathedral (better known by the Italian word for cathedral, *duomo*) in 1296. Neither has buttresses and in both most of the wall surface is solid rather than pierced with the typical Gothic windows. The Duomo's most outstanding feature does not even date to the 14th century: Its magnificent dome was built by the great early Renaissance architect Filippo Brunelleschi between 1420 and 1436 [9.20].

More self-consciously Gothic is the Duomo in Milan, begun in 1386, which perhaps makes one feel relieved that Italian architects in general avoided the chief features of northern Gothic style. The immensely elaborate façade, bristling with spires, and the crowded piers of the sides seem to

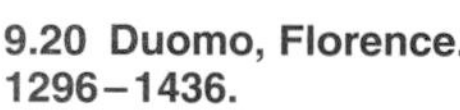

9.20 Duomo, Florence. 1296–1436.

be stuck on rather than integrated into the design. The presence of classical elements in the decorations is a reminder that by the time the Milan Duomo was completed the Renaissance had dawned [9.21].

Far more attractive are the secular public buildings of the age. The town halls of Florence and Siena, the Palazzo Vecchio (begun 1298) and the Palazzo Pubblico (begun 1288), convey the sense of strong government and civic pride that characterized life in these cities during the Trecento [9.22]. The towers served the double purpose of providing a lookout over the city and surrounding countryside while they expressed the determination of the city rulers to resist attack. The most beautiful of all government centers is probably the Doge's Palace in Venice, a city where more than anywhere else Gothic architecture took on an almost magical quality of lightness and delicacy. The Doge's Palace (begun about 1345) is composed of a heavy upper story that seems to float on two arcades, the lower a short and sturdy colonnade and the upper composed of tall, slender columns. The effect is enhanced by the way in which the whole building seems suspended in space between sky and sea [9.23].

For a final look at the late Gothic architecture at its most typical we must turn to England, where the style of this period is generally known as Perpendicular. The choir of Gloucester Cathedral, built between 1332 and 1357, illustrates the reason for the label [9.24]. The vertical line is emphasized, and our eyes are carried up to the roof, where a complex web of ribs decorate the vault. Unlike the ribs in earlier buildings, these serve no structural purpose but have become purely decorative. Their delicacy seems an apt reflection in stone of the graceful precision of the *Wilton Diptych* and the *Très Riches Heures*.

MUSIC: *ARS NOVA*

While Giotto was laying the foundations of a new naturalistic style of painting and writers like Petrarch and Chaucer were breathing fresh life into

9.21 Duomo, Milan. Begun 1368. The classical moldings over the windows and doorways of the façade are a reminder that the Duomo was not completed until the Renaissance.

9.22 Palazzo Pubblico, Siena. 1288–1309. The slits around the base of the gallery at the top of the tower were used for firing through on attackers below.

literary forms, composers in France and Italy were changing the style of music. To some extent this was the result of social changes: Musicians had begun to break away from their traditional role as servants of the church and to establish themselves as independent creative figures; most of the music that survives from the 14th century is secular. Much of it was written for singers and

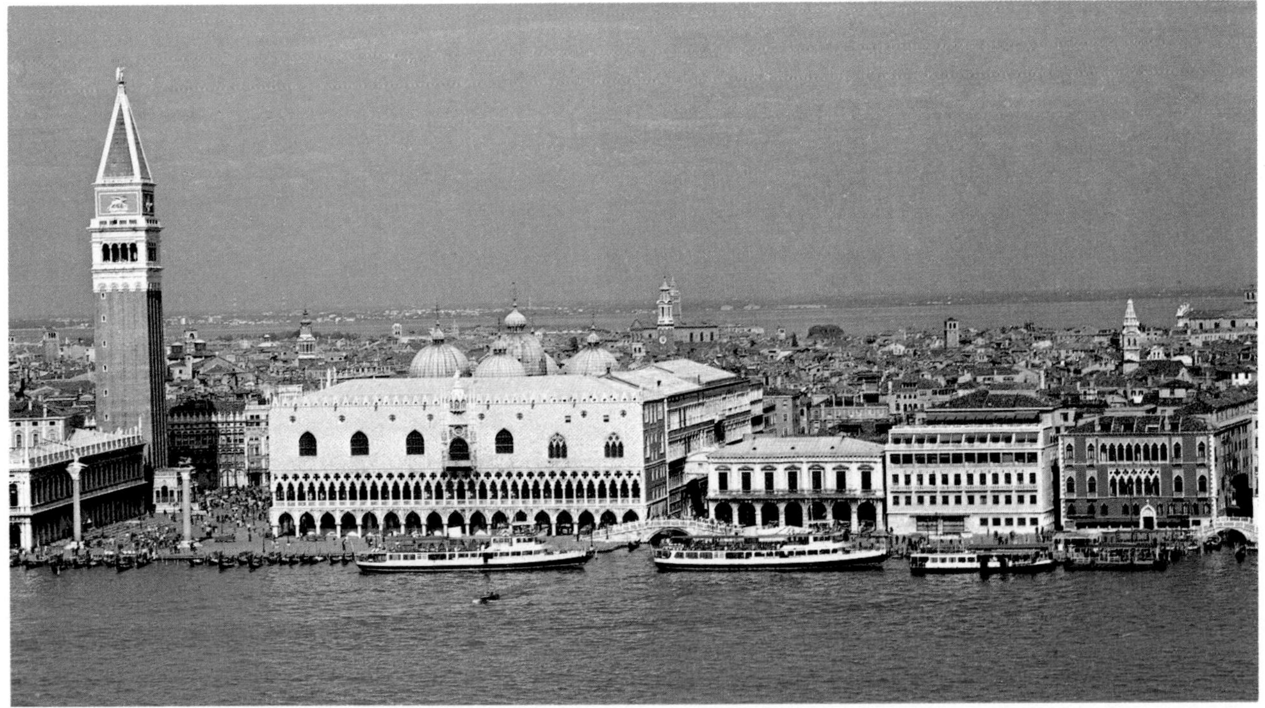

9.23 Doge's Palace, Venice. 1345–1438. Unlike the heavily fortified Palazzo Pubblico at Siena, this palace of the rulers of Venice, with its light, open arches, reflects the stability and security of the Venetian Republic.

9.24 Choir, Gloucester Cathedral. 1332–1357. The strong vertical lines show why the style of such buildings is called Perpendicular.

instrumentalists to perform at home for their own pleasure [9.25], or for the entertainment of aristocratic audiences like those depicted in the *Trés Riches Heures.* The texts composers set to music were increasingly varied; ballads, love songs, even descriptions of contemporary events, in contrast to the religious settings of the preceding century.

As the number of people who enjoyed listening to music and performing it began to grow, so did the range of musical expression. The term generally used to describe the sophisticated musical style of the 14th century is *Ars Nova,* derived from the title of a treatise written by the French composer Philippe de Vitry (1291–1361) around 1325. The work was written in Latin and called *Ars Nova Musicae (The New Art of Music).* Although it is really concerned with only one aspect of composition and describes a new system of rhythmic notation, the term *ars nova* has taken on a wider use and is applied to the new musical style that began to develop in France in the early 14th century and soon spread to Italy.

Its chief characteristic is a much greater richness and complexity of sound than before. This was partly achieved by the use of richer harmonies; thirds and sixths were increasingly employed and the austere sounds of parallel fifths, unisons, and octaves were generally avoided. Elaborate rhythmic devices were also introduced, including the method of construction called *isorhythm* (from the Greek word *isos,* which means equal). Isorhythm consisted of allotting to one of the voices in a polyphonic composition a repeated single melody. The voice was also assigned a repeating rhythmical pat-

9.25 A knight playing and singing to a lady, manuscript illumination illustrating the *Romance of the Rose.* Flemish, 14 × 10" (36 × 25 cm). British Library, London. The romantic interlude is enhanced by the idyllic surroundings; a walled garden with a fountain playing.

tern. Since the rhythmical pattern was of a different length from the melody, different notes would be stressed on each repetition. The purpose of this device was twofold: It both created a richness and variety of texture and imparted an element of unity to the piece.

The most famous French composer of this period was Guillaume de Machaut (1304?–1377), whose career spanned the worlds of traditional music and of the *Ars Nova.* He was trained as a priest and took holy orders, but much of his time was spent traveling throughout Europe in the service of the kings of Bohemia, Navarre, and France. Toward the end of his life he retired to Rheims, where he spent his last years as a canon. His most famous composition, and the most famous piece of music from the 14th century, is the *Messe de Notre Dame.* A four-part setting of the Ordinary of the Mass, it is remarkable chiefly for the way in which Machaut gives unity to the five sections that make up the work by creating a similarity of mood and even using a single musical motive that recurs throughout:

Machaut's *Messe de Notre Dame* is the first great example of the entire Ordinary of the Mass set to polyphonic music by a single composer. The Ordinary of the Mass refers to those parts of the Roman Catholic liturgy that do not change from day to day in contrast to the Propers (the readings from the Gospel or Epistles), which change daily. The parts of the Ordinary are:

1. The *Kyrie Eleison:* the repeated Greek phrases that mean "Lord have mercy on us!" and "Christ have mercy on us!"
2. The *Gloria:* a hymn of praise sung at all masses except funerals and masses during Lent and Advent.
3. The *Credo:* the Profession of Faith sung after the Gospel.
4. The *Sanctus* and *Benedictus:* a short hymn based on the angelic praise found in Isaiah 6, sung at the beginning of the eucharistic prayer.
5. The *Agnus Dei:* the prayer that begins "Lamb of God," sung before Communion.

Machaut's *Messe de Notre Dame,* then, stands at the head of a long tradition of musical composition in which composers use the Ordinary of the Mass to express in their own cultural idiom the timeless words of the liturgy. Machaut's Mass, in that sense, is the ancestor of the Renaissance compositions of Palestrina in the 16th century, the Baroque masses of Johann Sebastian Bach in the 18th century, and the frenetically eclectic modern *Mass* of Leonard Bernstein.

Machaut also contributed to another great musical tradition, that of secular song. With the increasing use of polyphony, composers began to turn their attentions to the old troubadour songs and write new settings that combined several different voices. Machaut's polyphonic secular songs took a number of forms. His *ballades* were written for two or three voices, the top voice carrying the melody while the others provided the accompaniment. These lower voices were probably sometimes played by instruments rather than sung. As in the ballades of earlier times the poems consisted of three stanzas, each of seven or eight lines, the last one or two lines being identical in all the stanzas to provide a refrain.

Many of these secular songs, both by Machaut and by other composers, deal with amorous topics, and often are addressed to the singer's beloved. The themes are predictable—the sorrow of parting, as in Machaut's *Au départir de vous*—reproaches for infidelity, protestations of love, and so on, but the freshness of the melodies and Machaut's constant inventiveness prevent them from seeming artificial.

The other important composer of the 14th century was the Italian Francesco Landini (1325–1397), who lived and worked in Florence. Blinded in his youth by smallpox, he was famous in his day as a virtuoso performer on the organ, lute, and flute. Among his surviving works are a number of *madrigals,* a form of word settings involving two or three verses set to the same music and separated by a refrain set to different music. In addition, he wrote a large number of *ballate* (ballads) including many for solo voice and two accompanying instruments. The vocal lines are often elaborate, and Landini makes use of rich, sonorous harmonies. But in the case of these and other works of the period, there is no specification of the instruments intended, or, indeed, of the general performance style Landini would have expected [9.26]. We know from contemporary accounts that in some cases performers would have changed the written notes by sharpening or flattening them, following the convention of the day. This practice of making sounds other than those on the page was called *musica ficta* (fictitious music), but no systematic description of the rules followed has been handed down to us. As a result, modern editors and performers often have only their own historical research and instincts to guide them. Although the

9.26 Music and musicians, manuscript illumination illustrating a treatise, *De Musica*. 14th century. Biblioteca Nazionale, Naples. Some of the instruments of the time are shown. The goddess Music is at the center, playing a small organ. Grouped around her are musicians with stringed instruments, percussion, and wind instruments.The inset shows David, founder of church music, plucking a psaltery.

Ars Nova of the 14th century marks a major development in the history of music, our knowledge of it is far from complete.

The 14th century was a time of stark contrast between the horrors of natural and social disasters and the flowering of artistic and cultural movements that were the harbingers of the 15th-century Renaissance in Italy. Chaucer, as we have seen, died in 1400, the year that may be taken as the close of the medieval period. By that time, some of the prime figures of the Italian Renaissance—Donatello, Fra Angelico, and Ghiberti—were already in their teens. The great outburst of cultural activity that was to mark Florence in the 15th century was near, even though it would not make a definite impact on England until the end of the century. The calamitous 14th century was a costly seedbed for rebirth and human renewal.

SUMMARY

The 14th century marks the painful transition from the medieval period to the world of the Renaissance. Its beginning saw the construction of several major buildings in Italy, including Florence's Duomo and Siena's Palazzo Pubblico, seat of city government. Music flourished throughout the century, especially in France, where Machaut was the leading composer of his day. In the years shortly after 1300 the new naturalistic style of Giotto revolutionized the art of painting, while the works of the Pisano family proved equally important for the history of sculpture. Yet the age was fraught with disasters and racked by war: the Hundred Years' War between France and England (1337–1453) was barely under way when in 1348 Europe was devastated by bubonic plague—the Black Death. Among the works of literature to reflect the effects of the terrible plague is Boccaccio's *Decameron*.

As the century began, the church appeared to be at the height of its influence. In 1300 Pope Boniface VIII proclaimed the first holy year, and pilgrims flocked to Rome. Yet within a few years the French had forced the transfer of the papacy to Avignon in southern France. Among those who accompanied the papal court was the poet Petrarch, many of whose sonnets deal with his love for Laura, killed by the Black Death. The "Babylonian Captivity" lasted from 1309 to 1376, and the pope's return to Rome was embittered by the Great Scism, which saw the Western powers locked in a struggle to impose rival claimants.

One of the artistic consequences of the papal move from Rome was that Italian styles were carried north of the Alps. The resulting blend of Italian and Northern elements is called the International style, which quickly spread throughout Europe; two of its main centers were at Prague and at Dijon. The more cosmopolitan spirit of the age is also illustrated by the career of the greatest English writer of the time, Chaucer, who traveled to Italy and to France and may actually have met Petrarch.

In an age of such ferment the pressure for reform intensified. In England, John Wyclif's charges of church corruption heightened dissatisfaction among the lower classes, leading to peasant riots in 1381. Similar popular protests against both the church and the aristocracy occurred in France in 1356, while in 1378 the poor woollen workers of

Florence revolted against the city authorities. These manifestations of general discontent brought no immediate radical changes in government, but they prepared the way for the social mobility of the Renaissance.

The greatest struggle of the century, the Hundred Years' War, was supposedly fought over the right of succession to the French throne. In fact, its underlying cause was the commercial rivalry between France and England and the attempts of both countries to gain control of the wool-manufacturing region of Flanders. The war's early stages were marked by a series of English victories, culminating in the battle of Poitiers of 1356. By 1380 the French had reversed the tide, and the last years of the century saw inconclusive skirmishes, with both sides resigned to a stalemate.

Thus a century in which political, economic, and religious strife and revolutionary artistic developments were accompanied by the disaster of plague produced deep changes in the fabric of European society and made possible the renewal of the Renaissance.

Pronunciation Guide

Arezzo: a-RET-so
Avignon: AV-een-yon
Boccaccio: Bo-KACH-owe
Chaucer: CHAW-ser
Cimabue: Chim-a-BOO-ay
Crécy: CRAY-see
Duccio: DO-chowe
Duomo: DWO-mo
Froissart: FRWAS-are
Giotto: JOT-toe
Guillaume Machaut: Ghee-OHM Mash-OWE
Lorenzetti: Lo-ren-ZETT-i
Maestà: Ma-ey-STAH
Palazzo Vecchio: Pa-LAT-so VEK-ee-owe
Petrarch: PET-rark
Pisano: Pee-ZAN-owe
Poitiers: PWAH-tee-ay
Santa Croce: SAN-ta CROW-chay
Schism: SISM
Trecento: Tray-CHEN-toe
Vasari: Vaz-ARE-ee

Exercises

1. Compare the literary achievements of Boccaccio and Petrarch. What light do they throw on the history of their times?
2. How does Chaucer characterize the participants in *The Canterbury Tales?* Select two and describe their chief features.
3. Describe Giotto's contribution to the history of painting and compare him to his predecessors.
4. What are the principal characteristics of northern European art in the 14th century? How does it differ from Italian art?
5. How did musical styles change in the 14th century? Discuss the contribution of Guillaume Machaut.

Further Reading

Gottfried, Robert S. *The Black Death: Natural and Human Disaster in Medieval Europe.* New York: Free Press, 1983. An important cultural study of the plague and its impact on late medieval culture.

Howard, Donald. *The Idea of Canterbury Tales.* Berkeley: University of California Press, 1977. An important study of the structure of Chaucer's greatest work.

Kane, George. *Chaucer.* New York: Oxford University Press, 1984. A brief, well-written study; part of the "Past Masters" series.

Lerner, Robert. *The Age of Adversity: The Fourteenth Century.* Ithaca: Cornell University Press, 1968. A brief but readable survey of the period covering both historical and cultural events of the century.

Martindale, Andrew. *The Complete Paintings of Giotto.* New York: Abrams, 1966. After a brief introduction the book offers a fully illustrated catalogue of Giotto's paintings with some excellent detail photographs.

Meiss, Millard. *Painting in Florence and Siena after the Black Death.* New York: Harper & Row, 1964. A brilliant work of scholarship that treats "The arts, religion and society in the mid-Fourteenth Century."

Pope-Hennessy, John. *Italian Gothic Sculpture.* London: Phaidon, 1972. An excellent illustrated survey. The comprehensive bibliography is especially valuable.

Stubblebine, James (ed.). *The Arena Chapel Frescoes.* New York: Norton, 1969. A collection of essays on Giotto's frescoes, illustrated.

Tuchman, Barbara. *A Distant Mirror: The Calamitous Fourteenth Century.* New York: Knopf, 1978. A brilliant work by one of our best popular writers on history. The book focuses almost exclusively on France and as a result lacks some balance. A joy to read and very revealing nevertheless.

White, John. *Art and Architecture in Italy 1250–1400.* Baltimore: Pelican, 1966. A useful single-volume survey, comprehensive yet detailed. Highly recommended.

Wilkins, Ernest H. *Life of Petrarch.* Chicago: University of Chicago Press, 1961. An exemplary biography valuable for its discussion of Italy in the 14th century and Petrarch's relationship with such figures as Boccaccio, Giotto, Simone Martini, and Chaucer.

	GENERAL EVENTS	LITERATURE & PHILOSOPHY	ART
FLORENTINE RENAISSANCE The First Phase 1400	**15th cent.** Florence center of European banking system; renaissance in exploration outside Europe begins **1417** Council of Constance ends "Great Schism" **1432** Florentines defeat Sienese at San Romano		**1401** Competition for North Doors of Florence Baptistery won by Ghiberti's *Sacrifice of Isaac* **1403** Ghiberti begins Baptistery doors; Brunelleschi, Donatello study Roman ruins **c. 1416–1417** Donatello, *Saint George* **1423** Fabriano, *The Adoration of the Magi,* International Style altarpiece **1425** Masaccio begins frescoes for Brancacci Chapel, Santa Maria del Carmine, Florence; *The Tribute Money* (1425), *Expulsion from the Garden* (c. 1425) **c. 1425–c. 1452** Ghiberti sculpts panels for East Doors of Florence Baptistery; *The Story of Jacob and Esau* (1435) Use of linear perspective to create three-dimensional space; naturalistic rendering of figures; return to classical ideals of beauty and proportion: Masaccio, *The Trinity,* Santa Maria Novella, Florence (c. 1428) **c. 1430–1432** Donatello, *David,* first free-standing nude since antiquity
The Medici Era 1434	**1434** Cosimo de' Medici becomes de facto ruler of Florence **1439–1442** Ecumenical Council of Florence deals with proposed union of Greek and Roman churches **1453** Fall of Constantinople to Turks; scholarly refugees bring Greek manuscripts to Italy **1464** Piero de' Medici takes power in Florence after death of Cosimo **1469** Lorenzo de' Medici rules city after death of Piero **1478** Pazzi conspiracy against the Medici fails **1489** Savonarola begins sermons against Florentine immorality **1492** Death of Lorenzo de' Medici	**1446–1450** Gutenberg invents movable printing type **1456** *Gutenberg Bible* printed at Mainz **1462** Cosimo de' Medici founds Platonic Academy in Florence, headed by Marsilio Ficino **1465** First Italian printing press, at Subiaco **1470–1499** Laura Cetera's humanist writings **1470–1527** Height of humanist learning **1475** *Recuyell of the Historyes of Troye,* printed by William Caxton, first book published in English **c. 1476–1477** Lorenzo de' Medici begins *Comento ad Alcuni Sonetti* **1482** Ficino, *Theologia Platonica* **1486** Pico della Mirandola, *Oration on the Dignity of Man* **1490** Lorenzo de' Medici, *The Song of Bacchus* **1491** Lorenzo de' Medici, *Laudi*	**1445–1450** Fra Angelico, *Annunciation,* fresco for Convent of San Marco, Florence **c. 1455** Donatello, *Mary Magdalene;* Uccello, *Battle of San Romano* **1459–1463** Gozzoli, *The Journey of the Magi* **c. 1467–1483** Leonardo works in Florence **1475** The Medici commission Botticelli's *Adoration of the Magi* for Santa Maria Novella **1478–c. 1482** Botticelli, *La Primavera, The Birth of Venus, Pallas and the Centaur* 
1494	**1494** Medici faction in exile; Savonarola becomes de facto ruler of Florence; Charles VIII of France invades Italy, beginning foreign invasions **1498** Savonarola burned at stake by order of Pope	**c. 1494** Aldus Manutius establishes Aldine Press in Venice **1496** Burning of books inspired by Savonarola **1502** Erasmus, *Enchiridion Militis Christiani*	**1498–1499** Michelangelo, *Pietà* **late 15th–early 16th cent.** Leonardo, *Notebooks* **c. 1495–1498** Leonardo, *Last Supper* **c. 1496** Botticelli burns some of his work in response to Savonarola's sermons
ROMAN RENAISSANCE 1503	**1512** Medici power restored in Florence; Machiavelli exiled	**1506** Erasmus travels to Italy **1509** Erasmus, *The Praise of Folly* **1513** Machiavelli, *The Prince* **1516** Erasmus, *Greek New Testament*	**c. 1503–1505** Leonardo, *Mona Lisa* **1506** Ancient *Laocoön* sculpture discovered
1520			

C H A P T E R

10 THE EARLY RENAISSANCE

TOWARD THE RENAISSANCE

THE 14TH CENTURY was a period of great social strife and turmoil as well as a time in which new stirrings were abroad in Europe. It was the century of Dante, Petrarch, Boccaccio, and Chaucer. The entrenched scholastic approach to learning was being tempered by renewed interest in classical literature. The long-cherished Byzantine art style was being challenged by the new realism of such Italian artists as Cimabue and Giotto in Florence, Simone Martini, and the Lorenzetti brothers, among others. Renewed interest in the world of nature was fueled by the enormous impact of Saint Francis of Assisi (1181–1226), who taught Europeans to see God in the beauty of the world and its creatures.

Europe was slowly recovering from the fearful plague-stricken years around 1348, a rebirth aided by a new growth in economics and trade. Wealth was being created by an emerging class whose claim to eminence was based less on noble blood than on ability to make money.

In the 15th century the center of this new vitality was Florence in Italy. No city its size has in its day exerted more influence on culture at large than this focus of banking and commerce. From roughly the 1420s until the end of the century a collaborative effort of thinkers, artists, and wealthy patrons enriched the city, in the process making it a magnet for all Europe. To that city and its cultural development we now turn.

THE FIRST PHASE: MASACCIO, GHIBERTI, AND BRUNELLESCHI

At the beginning of the 15th century Florence had every reason to be a proud city. It stood on the main road connecting Rome with the north. Its language—known at the time as the Tuscan dialect or the Tuscan idiom—was the strongest and most developed of the Italian dialects; its linguistic power had been demonstrated more than a century earlier by Dante Alighieri and his literary successors, Petrarch and Boccaccio. The twelve great *Arti* or trade guilds of Florence were commercially important for the city; in addition, representatives of the seven senior guilds formed the body of magistrates that ruled the city from the fortress-like town hall, the Palazzo Vecchio. This "representative" government, limited though it was to the prosperous guilds, preserved Florence from the rise of the terrible city tyrants who plagued so many other Italian cities.

Florence had been one of the centers of the wool trade since the late Middle Ages. In the 15th century it was also the center of the European banking system. In fact, our modern banks (the word *bank* is from the Italian *banco,* which means a counter or

TABLE 10.1 Major Social Events of the 15th Century

1439—Council of Florence attempts to reconcile Catholic and Orthodox churches
1453—End of the Hundred Years' War
1453—Constantinople (Byzantium) falls to the Turks
1469—Spain united under Ferdinand and Isabella
1485—Henry VIII begins reign as first Tudor king of England
1486—First European voyage around Cape of Good Hope
1492—Columbus discovers America
1492—Last Islamic city in Spain (Granada) falls to Ferdinand and Isabella
1494—Spain and Portugal divide spheres of influence in the New World
1497—Vasco da Gama begins first voyage to India
1498—Savonarola executed in Florence

table—the place where money is exchanged) and their systems of handling money are based largely on practices developed by the Florentines. They devised advanced accounting methods, letters of credit, and a system of checks; they were the first to emphasize the importance of a stable monetary system. The gold florin minted in Florence was the standard coin in European commerce for centuries.

Great Florentine banking families made and lost fortunes in trading and banking. These families—the Strozzi, Bardi, Tornabuoni, Pazzi, and Medici—were justly famous in their own time. They, in turn, were justly proud of their wealth and their city. The visitor to Florence today walks on streets named for these families and past palaces built for them. They combined a steady sense of business conservatism with an adventuresome pursuit of wealth and fame. No great Florentine banker would have thought it odd that one of this group began his will with the words "In the name of God and profit. Amen."

For all their renown and wealth, it was not the bankers who really gave Florence its lasting fame. By some mysterious stroke of good fortune Florence and its immediate surroundings produced, in the 15th century, a group of artists who revolutionized Western art to such an extent that later historians refer to the period as a time of rebirth *(renaissance)* in the arts.

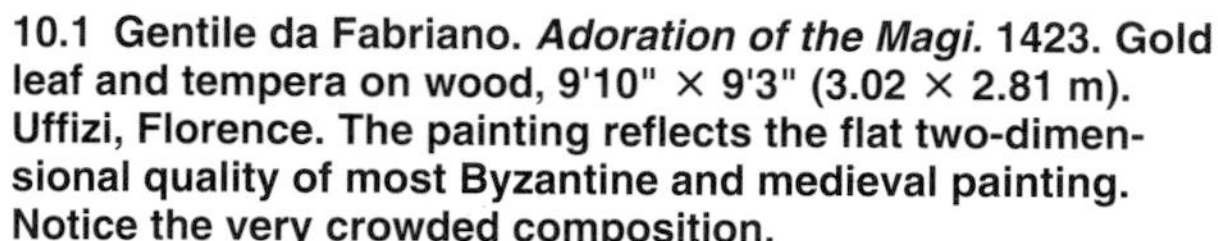

10.1 Gentile da Fabriano. *Adoration of the Magi.* 1423. Gold leaf and tempera on wood, 9'10" × 9'3" (3.02 × 2.81 m). Uffizi, Florence. The painting reflects the flat two-dimensional quality of most Byzantine and medieval painting. Notice the very crowded composition.

10.2 Masaccio. *The Holy Trinity.* 1428. Fresco, 21'10½" × 10'5" (6.66 × 3.19 m). Santa Maria Novella, Florence. The donors of the panel kneel at bottom left and right. The Trinity, with the Holy Spirit symbolized as a dove, is set in a classical Roman architectural frame.

The character of this revolutionary change in art is not easy to define, but we can evolve a partial definition by comparing two early 15th-century Florentine paintings. Sometime before 1423 a wealthy Florentine banker, Palla Strozzi, commissioned Gentile da Fabriano (c. 1385–1427) to paint an altarpiece for the Florentine church of Santa Trinità. The *Adoration of the Magi* [10.1], completed in 1423, is ornately framed in the style of Gothic art, with evidence of influences from the miniature painting of Northern Europe and from the older painting tradition of Italy itself. The altarpiece is in the style called "International" because it spread far beyond the area of its origins in France. This style reflects the old-fashioned tendency to fill up the spaces of the canvas, to employ the brightest colors on the palette, to use gold lavishly for halos and in the framing, and to ignore any strict proportion between the characters and the space they occupy. Gentile's altarpiece is, in fact, a strikingly beautiful painting that testifies to the lush possibilities of the conservative International Gothic style.

Only about five years later Tommaso Guidi (1401–1428), known as Masaccio, the precocious genius of Florentine painting, painted for the Dominican Church of Santa Maria Novella in Florence a fresco, *The Holy Trinity* [10.2], that is strikingly different from the kind of painting by Gentile. The most apparent difference is in the utilization of space. In *The Holy Trinity* the central figures of God the Father, the Holy Spirit, and the crucified Christ seem to stand in the foreground of deep three-dimensional space created by the illusionistically painted architectural framing of the Trinity. The character of the architecture is Roman, its barrel vaulting and coffering sustained by Corinthian columns and pilasters. At the sides, and slightly lower, Mary looks out at the viewer, while Saint John looks at Mary. At the edge of the scene, members of the donor family kneel in profile. The entire scene has an intense geometrical clarity based on the pyramid, with God as the apex of the triangle formed with the line of donors and saints at the ends of the base line.

In this single fresco appear many of the characteristics of Florentine Renaissance painting that mark it off from earlier painting styles: clarity of line, a concern for mathematically precise perspective, close observation of "real people," concern for psychological states, and an uncluttered arrangement that rejects the earlier tendency in painting to produce crowded scenes to fill up all the available space.

Masaccio's earlier frescoes in the Brancacci Chapel of the Church of the Carmine in Florence also show his revolutionizing style. His 1425 fresco called *The Tribute Money* [10.3] reflects his concern with realistic depiction of human beings. The central scene portrays Christ telling Peter that he can find the tax money for the temple in the mouth of a fish; at the left Peter recovers the coin of tribute; at the right he makes the tribute payment (Matthew 17:24–27). The clusters of figures surrounding Christ reflect a faithfulness to observed humanity that must have been startling to Masaccio's contemporaries, who had never seen anything quite like that in painting. The figures are in a space made believable by the receding lines of the buildings to the right. The fresco of the expulsion of Adam and Eve from Eden [10.4] in the same chapel shows not only realism in the figures but also a profound sense of human emotions: the shame and dismay of the first human beings as they are driven from the Garden of Paradise.

The revolutionary character of Masaccio's work was recognized in his own time. His influence on any number of Florentine painters who worked later in the century is clear. Two generations after Masaccio's death the young Michelangelo often crossed the Arno River to sketch the frescoes in the

10.3 Masaccio. *The Tribute Money.* c. 1425. Fresco, 8'4" × 19' (2.54 × 5.9 m). Brancacci Chapel, Santa Maria del Carmine, Florence. Three moments of the story are seen simultaneously: Jesus instructs Peter to find the coin of tribute, at center; at the left, Peter finds it in the mouth of a fish; at the right, Peter pays the tribute money. The story is in Matthew 17:24–27.

10.4 Masaccio. *The Expulsion from Paradise.* 1425–1428. Fresco, 7'¼" × 2'11" (2.14 × .90 m). Brancacci Chapel, Santa Maria del Carmine, Florence. The artist manages to convey both a sense of movement and a sense of the deep psychological distress and shame of the expelled couple.

10.5 Filippo Brunelleschi. *The Sacrifice of Isaac.* 1401. Gilt bronze, 21 × 17½" (53 × 44 cm). Museo Nazionale del Bargello, Florence. Note the figures spilling over the bottom part of the frame.

10.6 Lorenzo Ghiberti. *The Sacrifice of Isaac.* 1401. Gilt bronze, 21 × 17½" (53 × 44 cm). Museo Nazionale del Bargello, Florence. This was the winning panel in the competition.

Brancacci chapel. In the next century Giorgio Vasari (1511–1574) in his *Lives of the Artists* would judge Masaccio's influence as basic and crucial: "The superb Masaccio . . . adopted a new manner for his heads, his draperies, buildings, and nudes, his colors, and foreshortening. He thus brought into existence the modern style which, beginning during his period, has been employed by all of our artists down to the present day. . . ."

The innovative character of 15th-century art was not limited to painting. Significant changes were occurring in sculpture and architecture as well. A famous competition was announced in 1401 for the right to decorate the doors of the Florence Baptistery, dedicated to Saint John the Baptist and a focal point of Florentine life. The baptistery is an ancient octagonal Romanesque building, which in the 15th century had such a reputation for antiquity that some thought it had originally been a Roman temple. Vasari tells us that an eminent group of artists including Lorenzo Ghiberti (1378–1455) and Filippo Brunelleschi (1377–1466) were among the competitors. Ghiberti won.

A comparison of Brunelleschi's and Ghiberti's panels shows the differences between the two and allows us to infer the criteria used to judge the winner. The assigned subject for the competition was Abraham's sacrifice of Isaac (Genesis 22:1–14). Brunelleschi's version [10.5] has a certain vigor, but it is a busy and crowded composition. The figures of the servants spill out of the four-leaf or quatrefoil frame while the major figures (the ram, the angel, and the two principals) are in flattened two-dimensional profile with little background space.

By contrast, Ghiberti's panel on the same subject [10.6] is divided dramatically by a slashing diagonal line separating the two sets of actors into clearly designated planes of action. The drastically foreshortened angel appears to be flying into the scene from deep space. Furthermore, as a close examination of the cast shows, Ghiberti's panel is a technical tour de force. Except for the figure of Isaac and Abraham's left foot (and part of the rock it rests on), the entire scene was cast as a single unit. Demonstrating his strong background as a goldsmith, Ghiberti finely modeled and skillfully finished his panel. It is a piece of fierce sentiment, mathematical perspective, and exquisite work.

Ghiberti worked for almost a quarter of a century on the North Doors, completing twenty panels. Just as he was finishing, the Cathedral authorities commissioned him in 1425 to execute another set of panels for the East Doors, those facing the Cathedral itself. This commission occupied the next quarter of a century (from roughly 1425 to 1452 or 1453), and the results of these labors were so striking that Michelangelo later in the century said Ghiberti's East Doors were not unworthy to be called the "Gates of Paradise," and so they are called to this day.

The panels of the East Doors [10.7] were radically different in style and composition from the North Door panels. The Gothic style quatrefoils were replaced by more classically severe rectangular frames. The complete set of panels was framed, in turn, by a series of portrait busts of prophets and sybils.

Although Filippo Brunelleschi lost to Ghiberti in the sculpture competition of 1401, he made a major

10.7 Lorenzo Ghiberti. East Doors of the Baptistery of the Cathedral of Florence. 1425–1432. Gilt bronze, height 17' (5.18 m). "The Gates of Paradise."

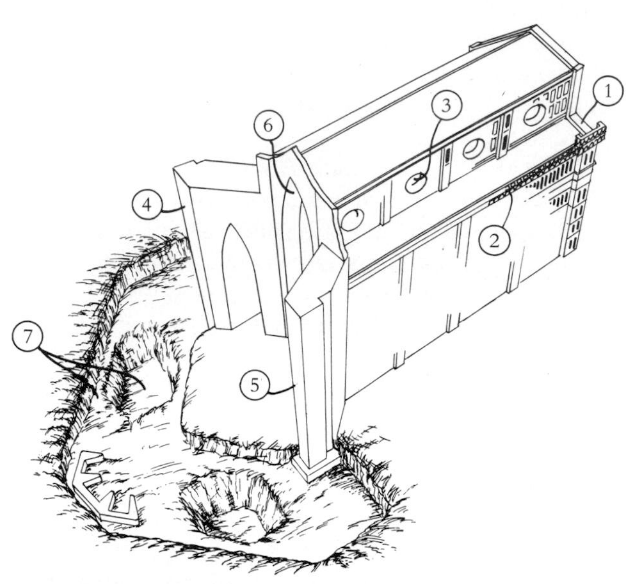

10.8 **Florence Cathedral in 1390. An artist's reconstruction of the cathedral as Brunelleschi would have found it when he began his work. (1) Façade and side wall. (2) Gallery. (3) Circular windows. (4) Armature under construction. (5) Vaulting under construction. (6) Sacristy piers. (7) Excavations for buttresses.**

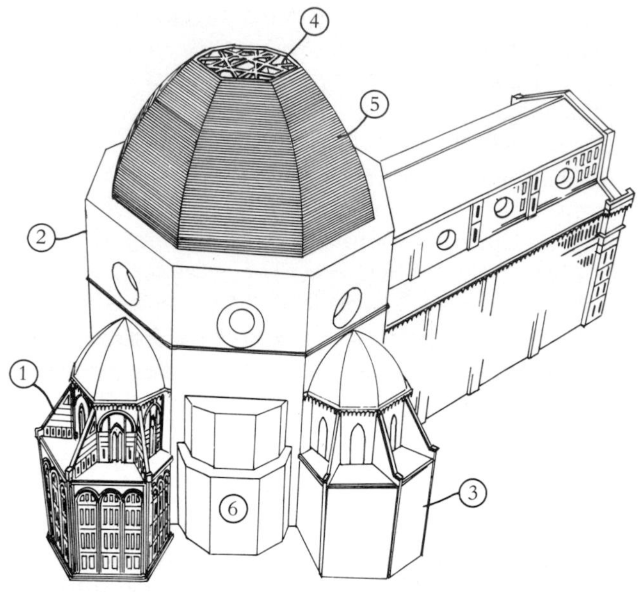

10.9 **Florence Cathedral in 1418. (1) Buttressing. (2) Completed drum (tambour). (3) Side tribunes under construction. (4) Armature under construction. (5) Vaulting under construction. (6) Sacristy piers.**

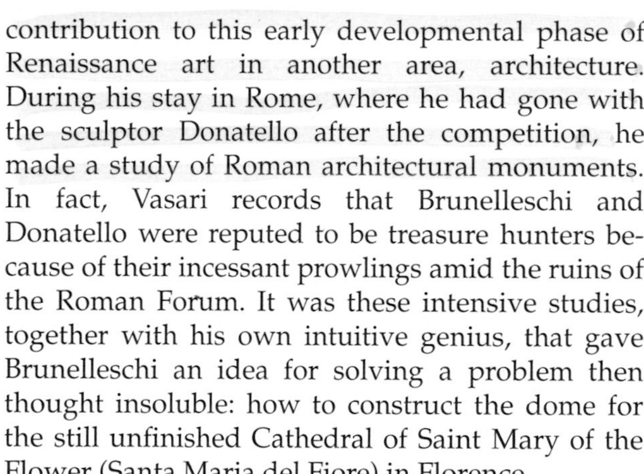

contribution to this early developmental phase of Renaissance art in another area, architecture. During his stay in Rome, where he had gone with the sculptor Donatello after the competition, he made a study of Roman architectural monuments. In fact, Vasari records that Brunelleschi and Donatello were reputed to be treasure hunters because of their incessant prowlings amid the ruins of the Roman Forum. It was these intensive studies, together with his own intuitive genius, that gave Brunelleschi an idea for solving a problem then thought insoluble: how to construct the dome for the still unfinished Cathedral of Saint Mary of the Flower (Santa Maria del Fiore) in Florence.

The Cathedral of Florence had been built by Arnolfo di Cambio in the previous century over the remains of the older church of Santa Reparata. In the early 15th century, however, the church was still unfinished, although the nave was already complete [10.8]. No one had quite figured out how to span the great area without immense buttresses on the outside and supporting armatures on the inside. Brunelleschi worked on this problem between 1417 and 1420, trying, simultaneously, to solve the technical aspects of doming the building and convincing the skeptical cathedral overseers that it could be done. He eventually won the day, but work on the dome was not completed until 1436.

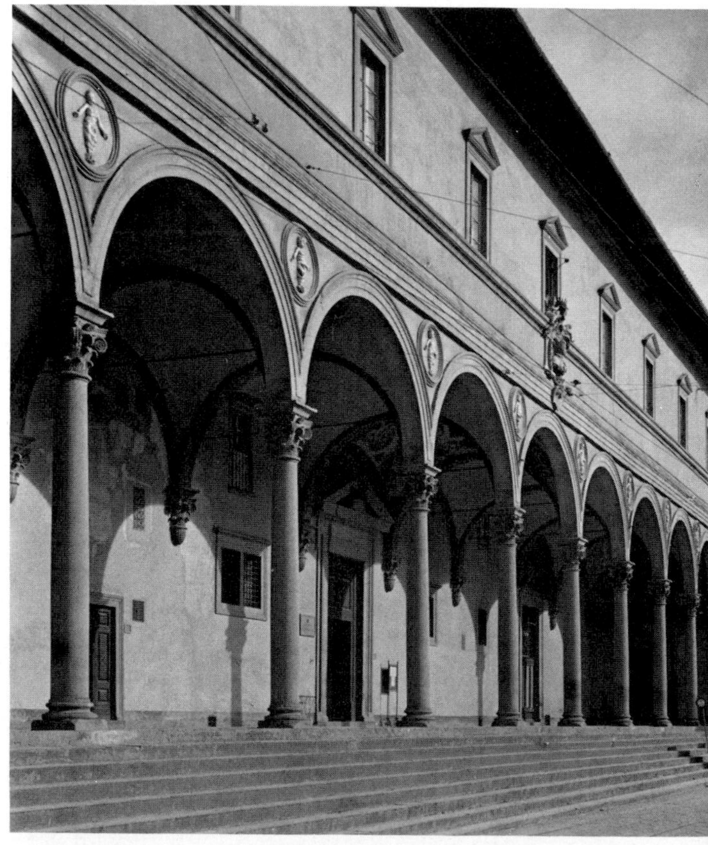

10.10 **Filippo Brunelleschi. Foundling Hospital, Florence. 1419–1426. The glazed terra-cotta medallions of the swaddled children are from the della Robbia workshop in Florence.**

His solution, briefly, was to combine the buttressing methods of the Gothic cathedral and classical vaulting techniques that he had mastered by his careful study of the Roman Pantheon and other buildings from antiquity. By putting a smaller dome within the larger dome to support the greater weight of the outside dome, he could not only cover the great *tambour* or drum [10.9] but also free the inside of the dome from any need for elaborate armatures or supporting structures. This dome was strong enough to support the lantern that eventually crowned the whole construction. It was a breathtaking technical achievement, as well as an aesthetic success, as any person viewing Florence from the surrounding hills can testify. Years later, writing about his own work on the dome of Saint Peter's in the Vatican, Michelangelo had Brunelleschi's dome in mind when he said "I will create your sister; bigger but no more beautiful."

The technical brilliance of Brunelleschi's dome cannot be overpraised, but his real architectural achievement lies in his designs for buildings that make a break with older forms of architecture. His Foundling Hospital [10.10], with its open-columned loggias and their graceful Corinthian pillars, arches, and entablature, is, despite its seeming simplicity, a highly intricate work, its proportions calculated with mathematical rigor. The building is an open departure from the heaviness of the Romanesque so common in the area of Tuscany as well as a rejection of the overly elaborate Gothic exteriors.

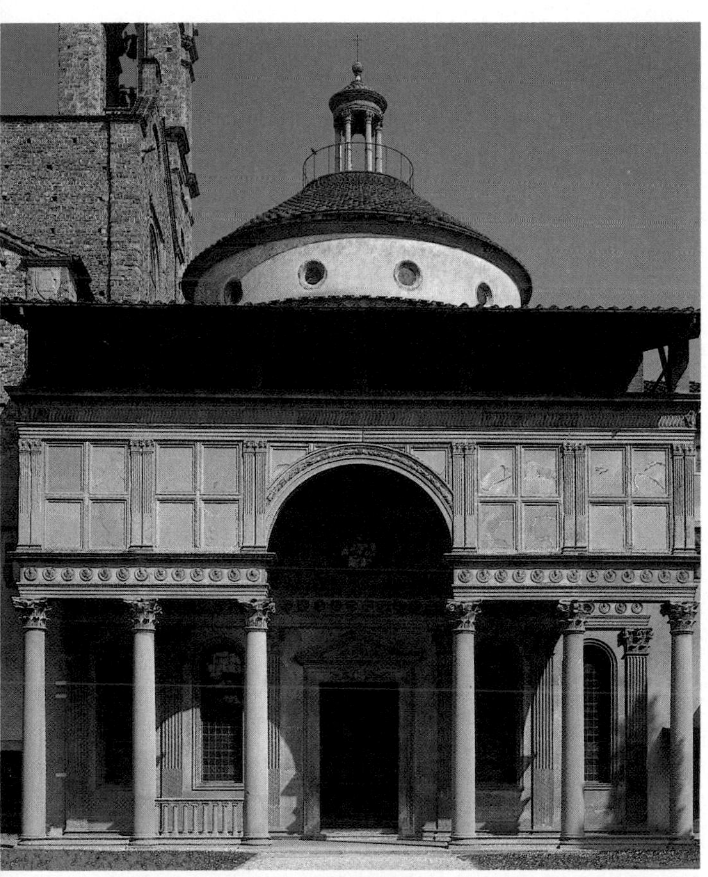

10.11 Filippo Brunelleschi. Pazzi Chapel, Florence. 1430–1433. Part of the Franciscan church of Santa Croce can be seen in the left background.

This same concern with classical order, proportion, and serenity can be seen in Brunelleschi's finest work, the chapel he designed for the Pazzi family next to the Franciscan Church of Santa Croce in Florence [10.11]. Its exterior evokes Roman austerity with its delicate columns, severe façade, and small dome reminiscent of the lines of Rome's Pantheon.

In this very brief look at three different art forms and artists in the early 15th century certain recurring words and themes give a rough descriptive outline of what the Florentine Renaissance style reflects: a concern with, and the technical ability to handle, space and volume in a believable way; a studious approach to models of art from ancient Rome; a departure from the more ethereal mode of medieval otherworldliness to a greater concern for human realism. The Florentine artistic temperament leaped over its medieval heritage (although not completely) in order to reaffirm what it considered the classical ideal of ancient Rome and Greece.

THE MEDICI ERA

The Florentine Republic was governed by representatives of the major trade guilds. This control by a very select group of people who represented commercial power and wealth inevitably led to domination by the most wealthy of the group. From 1434 until 1492 Florence was under the control of one family: the Medici.

The Medici family had old, though up to then undistinguished, roots in the countryside around Florence. Their prosperity in the 15th century rested mainly on their immense banking fortune. By the middle of that century Medici branch banks existed in London, Naples, Cologne, Geneva, Lyons, Basel, Avignon, Bruges, Antwerp, Lübeck, Bologna, Rome, Pisa, and Venice. The great Flemish painting by Jan van Eyck, *Giovanni Arnolfini and His Bride* [10.12], in fact, commemorates van Eyck's witnessing of the marriage of this Florentine representative of the Medici bank in 1434 in Bruges. While it is more usual to look at the painting

10.12 Jan van Eyck. *Giovanni Arnolfini and His Bride.* 1434. Oil on panel, 33 × 22½" (83.82 × 57.15 cm). National Gallery, London (by courtesy of the Trustees). The artist, reflected in the mirror, stands in the doorway. The Latin words on the wall read "Jan van Eyck was here." The pair of sandals at the lower left symbolizes a sacred event; the dog is a symbol of fidelity and domestic peace.

because of its exquisite technique, its rich symbolism, and its almost microscopic concern for detail, it is also profitable to view it sociologically as a testimony to how far the influence of the Medici extended.

Cosimo de' Medici

Cosimo de' Medici (de facto ruler of Florence from 1434 to 1464) was an astute banker and a highly cultivated man of letters. His closest friends were professional humanists, collectors of books, and patrons of the arts. Cosimo himself spent vast sums on the collecting and copying of ancient manuscripts. He had his copyists work in a neat cursive hand that would be the later model for the form of letters we call *italic.* His collection of books (together with those added by later members of his family) formed the core of the great humanist collection housed today in the Laurentian library in Florence.

Although Cosimo never mastered Greek to any degree, he was intensely interested in Greek philosophy and literature. He financed the chair of Greek at the *Studium* of Florence. When Greek prelates visited Florence during the ecumenical council held in 1439 (the council sought a union between the Greek and Latin churches), Cosimo took the opportunity to seek out scholars in the retinue of the prelates from Constantinople. He was particularly struck with the brilliance of Genisthos Plethon (c. 1355–1452), who lectured on Plato. Cosimo persuaded Plethon to remain in the city to continue his lectures.

Cosimo's most significant contribution to the advancement of Greek studies was the foundation and endowment of an academy for the study of Plato. For years Cosimo and his heirs supported a priest, Marsilio Ficino, in order to allow him to translate and comment on the works of Plato. In the course of his long life (he died in 1499), Ficino translated into Latin all of Plato, Plotinus, and other Platonic thinkers. He wrote his own compendium of Platonism called the *Theologia Platonica.* These translations and commentaries had an immense influence on art and intellectual life in Italy and beyond the Alps.

Cosimo often joined his friends at a suburban villa to discuss Plato under the tutelage of Ficino. This elite group embraced Plato's ideas of striving for the ideal good and persistently searching for truth and beauty. This idealism became an important strain in Florentine culture. Ficino managed to combine his study of Plato with his own understanding of Christianity. It was Ficino who coined the term "Platonic love"—the spiritual bond between two persons who were joined together in the contemplative search for the true, the good, and the beautiful. Cosimo, a pious man in his own right, found great consolation in this Christian platonism of Ficino. "Come and join me as soon as you possibly can and be sure to bring with you Plato's treatise *On the Sovereign Good,*" Cosimo once wrote his protégé; "there is no pursuit to which I would devote myself more zealously than the pursuit of truth. Come then and bring with you the lyre of Orpheus."

Cosimo, a fiercely patriotic Florentine, known to his contemporaries as *Pater Patriae* (Father of the Homeland), lavished his funds on art projects to

10.13 Donatello. *Saint George*. 1416–1417. Marble, height 6'5" (1.96 m). Museo Nazionale del Bargello, Florence. Originally, the saint grasped a spear in his right hand.

10.14 Donatello. *David*. c. 1430–1432. Bronze, height 5'2½" (1.58 m). Museo Nazionale del Bargello, Florence. The killing of Goliath is shown at three stages in this book. Michelangelo's *David* is shown as he sees his foe (Figure 10.27). Bernini's *David* is shown in the exertion of his attack (Figure 13.9). Donatello's *David* reposes after the attack as he leans on the sword of the giant and rests his other foot on Goliath's severed head.

enhance the beauty of the city, at the same time glorifying his family name and atoning for his sins, especially usury, by acts of generous charity. He befriended and supported many artists. He was a very close friend and financial supporter of the greatest Florentine sculptor of the first half of the 15th century, Donato di Niccolò di Betto Bardi (1386–1466), known as Donatello. Donatello was an eccentric genius who cared for little besides his work; it was said that he left his fees in a basket in his studio for the free use of his apprentices or whoever else might be in need.

Even today a leisurely stroll around the historic center of Florence can, in a short time, give an idea of the tremendous range of Donatello's imaginative and artistic versatility. One need only compare his early *Saint George* [10.13], fiercely tense and classically severe, with the later bronze *David* [10.14].

10.15 Donatello. *Saint Mary Magdalene*. 1455. Polychromed wood, height 6'2" (1.88 m). Museo dell' Opera del Duomo, Florence. Cleaned and restored after flood damage in 1966, this statue now reveals some traces of the original polychrome. It was originally in the baptistery of the Florence Cathedral.

The *Saint George* is a niche sculpture originally executed for the church of Orsanmichele, while the *David* is meant to be seen from all sides. The *David*, a near-life-size figure, is the first freestanding statue of a nude figure sculpted since Roman antiquity. It also marks a definite step in Renaissance taste: In spite of its subject, it is more clearly "pagan" than biblical in spirit. The sculptor obviously wanted to show the beauty of form of this adolescent male clothed only in carefully fashioned military leg armor and a Tuscan shepherds's hat. The figure was most likely made for a garden. Some scholars have speculated that the commission was from Cosimo himself, although clear documentary proof is lacking.

Donatello's over-life-size wooden figure of Mary Magdalene [10.15] seems light years away from the spirit of *David*. Carved around 1455, it shows the Magdalene as an ancient penitent, ravaged by time and her own life of penance. The viewer is asked, mentally, to compare this older woman with the younger sinner described in the Bible. The statue, then, is a profound meditation on the vanity of life, a theme lingering in Florentine culture from its medieval past, and, at the same time, a hymn to the penitential spirit that made the Magdalene a saint.

Cosimo de' Medici had a particular fondness for the Dominican Convent of San Marco in Florence. In 1437 he asked Michelozzo, the architect who designed the Medici palace in Florence, to rebuild the convent for the friars. One of the Dominicans who lived there was a painter of established reputation, Fra Angelico (1387–1455). When Michelozzo's renovations were done, Fra Angelico decorated many of the convent walls and most of the cells of the friars with paintings, executing many of these works under the watchful eye of Cosimo, who stayed regularly at the convent. Fra Angelico's famous *Annunciation* fresco [10.16] shows his indebtedness to the artistic tradition of Masaccio: the use of architecture to frame space, a sense of realism and drama, and a close observation of the actual world.

Another painter who enjoyed the Medici largesse was Paolo Uccello (1397–1475), who did a series of three paintings for the Medici palace commemorating the earlier battle of San Romano (1432) in which the Florentines defeated the Sienese. The paintings (now dispersed to museums in London, Florence, and Paris) show Uccello's intense fascination with perspective [10.17]. The scenes are marked by slashing lines, foreshortened animals, receding backgrounds, and seemingly cluttered landscapes filled with figures of different proportions. When the three paintings were together as a unit they gave a panoramic sweep of the battle running across 34' (10.3 m) of the wall space.

Cosimo's last years were racked with chronic illness and depression brought on by the premature deaths of his son Giovanni and a favorite grandson, as well as the physical weakness of his other son, Piero. Toward the end of his life Cosimo's wife once found him in his study with his eyes closed. She asked him why he sat in that fashion. "To get them accustomed to it," he replied. Cosimo de' Medici died on August 1, 1464. His position as head of the family and as first citizen of the city was taken by his son Piero, called "the Gouty" in reference to the affliction of gout from which he suffered all his life.

10.16 Fra Angelico. *Annunciation.* 1445–1450. Fresco, 7'6" × 10'5" (2.29 × 3.18 m). Monastery of San Marco, Florence. Note how the architecture frames the two principal figures in the scene. Botanists can identify the flowers in the garden to the left.

10.17 Paolo Uccello. *The Battle of San Romano.* 1455. Tempera on wood, 6'10" × 10'7" (1.83 × 3.22 m). Uffizi, Florence. The upraised spears and javelins give the picture a sense of frantic complexity.

10.18 Sandro Botticelli. *Adoration of the Magi.* 1475. Tempera on wood, 3'7½" × 4'4¾" (1.1 × 1.34 m). Uffizi, Florence. Cosimo de' Medici kneels in front of the Virgin; Lorenzo is in the left foreground; Giuliano is at right against the wall. The figure in the right foreground looking out is thought to be the artist.

10.19 Benozzo Gozzoli. *The Journey of the Magi,* detail. 1459. Fresco, length (entire work), 12'4½" (3.77 m). Medici Palace Chapel, Florence. The horseman, representing one of the Magi, is thought to be an idealized portrait of the Byzantine emperor John VII Paleologus, who visited Florence at the invitation of Cosimo de' Medici for a church council in 1439.

Piero de' Medici

Piero's control over the city lasted only five years. It was a time beset by much political turmoil as well as continued artistic activity. Piero continued to support his father's old friend Donatello and maintained his patronage of Ficino's platonic labors and his generous support of both religious and civic art and architecture.

One new painter who came under the care of Piero was Alessandro di Mariano dei Filipepi (1444–1510), known more familiarly as Sandro Botticelli. Botticelli earlier had been an apprentice of the painter Fra Filippo Lippi (c. 1406–1469), but it was Piero and his aristocratic wife Lucrezia Tornabuoni (a highly cultivated woman who was a religious poet) who took Botticelli into their home and treated him as a member of the family. Botticelli stayed closely allied with the Medici for decades.

One tribute to the Medici was Botticelli's painting *Adoration of the Magi* [10.18], a work commissioned for the Florentine church of Santa Maria Novella. The Magi are shown as three generations of the Medici family; there are also portraits of Lorenzo and Giuliano, the sons of Piero. The painting was paid for by a friend of the Medici family. Many scholars think it was a votive offering to the church in thanksgiving for the safety of the family during the political turmoil of 1466.

The theme of the Magi was a favorite of the Medici. They regularly took part in the pageants in the streets of Florence celebrating the Three Kings on the feast of the Epiphany (January 6). It is for that reason, one assumes, that Piero commissioned a fresco of that scene for the chapel of his own palace. The painter was Benozzo Gozzoli (1420–1495), once an apprentice of Fra Angelico. Gozzoli produced an opulent scene filled with personages of Oriental splendor modeled on the Greek scholars who had come to Florence during the ecumenical council and who stayed on to teach Greek. The fresco also included some contemporary portraits, including one of the artist himself [10.19].

Lorenzo the Magnificent

Piero de' Medici died in 1469. The mantle of power settled on the shoulders of his son Lorenzo, who accepted the responsibility with pragmatic resignation, since, as he said, "It bodes ill for any wealthy man in Florence who doesn't control political power." Lorenzo, a rather ugly man with a high raspy voice, became the most illustrious of the family; in his own day he was known as "the magnificent"—Lorenzo il Magnifico. His accomplishments were so many and varied that the last half of the 15th century in Florence is often called the Laurentian Era.

Lorenzo continued the family tradition of art patronage by supporting various projects and by adding to the Medici collection of ancient gems, other antiquities, and books. He was also more directly involved in the arts. Lorenzo was an accomplished poet, but his reputation as a political and social leader has made us forget that he was an important contributor to the development of vernacular Italian poetry. He continued the sonnet tradition begun by Petrarch. One of his most ambitious projects—done in conscious imitation of Dante's *Vita Nuova*—was a long work that alternated his own sonnets with extended prose commentaries; this was the *Comento ad alcuni sonetti* (*A Commentary on Some Sonnets*, begun around 1476–1477). In addition to this very ambitious work, Lorenzo wrote hunting songs, poems for the carnival season, religious poetry, and occasional burlesque poems with a cheerfully bawdy tone to them.

The poem for which Lorenzo is best known is "The Song of Bacchus." Written in 1490, its opening stanzas echo the old Roman dictum of living for the present because of the shortness of life and the uncertainty of the future.

The Song of Bacchus

How beautiful is youth,
That flees so fleetingly by.
Let him be who chases joy
For tomorrow there is no certainty.

Look at Bacchus and Ariadne
So beautiful and much in love.
Since deceitful time flees
They are always happy.

Joyful little satyrs
of the nymphs enamored,
In every cave and glade
Have set traps by the hundred;
Now, by Bacchus intoxicated,
Dance and leap without end.

Let him be who chases joy
For tomorrow there is no certainty.

Lorenzo's interests in learning were deep. He had been tutored as a youth by Ficino and as an adult he continued the habit of spending evenings with an elite group of friends and Ficino. He often took with him his friend Botticelli and a young sculptor who worked in a Medici-sponsored sculpture garden, Michelangelo Buonarroti.

10.20 Sandro Botticelli. *La Primavera (Springtime).* c. 1478. Tempera on canvas, 6'8" × 10'4" (2.03 × 3.14 m). Uffizi, Florence. This work and *The Birth of Venus* (Figure 10.21) are the best examples of Botticelli's fusion of pagan symbolism, Neoplatonic idealism, and the quest for the ideal feminine.

The Laurentian patronage of learning was extensive. Lorenzo contributed the funds necessary to rebuild the University of Pisa and designated it the principal university of Tuscany (Galileo taught there in the next century). He continued to underwrite the study of Greek at the *Studium* of Florence.

The Greek faculty at Florence attracted students from all over Europe. Indeed, this center was a principal means by which Greek learning was exported to the rest of Europe, especially to countries beyond the Alps. English scholars like Thomas Linacre, John Colet, and William Grocyn came to Florence to study Greek and other classical disciplines. Linacre was later to gain fame as a physician and founder of England's Royal College of Physicians. Grocyn returned to England to found the chair of Greek at Oxford. Colet used his training to become a biblical scholar and a founder of Saint Paul's School in London. The two greatest French humanists of the 16th century had, as young men, come under the influence of Greek learning from Italy. Guillaume Budé (died 1540) founded, under the patronage of the French kings, a library at Fontainebleau that was the beginning of the Bibliothèque Nationale of Paris. He also founded the Collège de France, still the most prestigious center of higher learning in France. Jacques Lefèvre d'Étaples had also studied in Florence and became the greatest intellectual church reformer of 16th-century France.

Lorenzo was less interested in painting than either his father Piero or his grandfather Cosimo. Nevertheless, some of the paintings done in his lifetime have come to epitomize the spirit of the age because of their close familial and philosophical links to Lorenzo's family. This is especially true of the work of Botticelli and, more specifically, his paintings *Primavera* and *The Birth of Venus.*

Botticelli painted *La Primavera (Springtime)* [10.20] for a cousin of Lorenzo named Lorenzo di' Pierfrancesco. One of the most popular paintings in the history of Western art, *La Primavera* is an elaborate mythological allegory of the burgeoning fertility of the world. The allegory itself has never been fully explicated, but the main characters are clearly discernible: At the extreme right the wind god

Zephyr pursues a nymph who is transformed into the goddess Flora (next figure), who scatters her flowers; at the left are the god Mercury and three dancing Graces. Over the Graces and the central female figure (who represents Spring) is blind Cupid ready to launch an arrow that will bring love to the one he hits. The rich carpeting of springtime flowers and the background of the orange grove provide luxuriant surroundings.

In the 16th century Vasari saw *La Primavera* in Lorenzo di' Pierfrancesco's villa together with another painting by Botticelli, *The Birth of Venus* (1480). A gentle, almost fragile work of idealized beauty, *The Birth of Venus* [10.21] shows the wind gods gently stirring the sea breezes as Venus emerges from the sea and an attendant waits for her with a billowing cape. The Venus figure is inspired by the *Venus pudica* (the Modest Venus) figures of antiquity. The most significant aspect of the painting (and of *La Primavera*) is the impulse, motivated by Platonism, to idealize the figures. Botticelli is trying to depict not a particular woman but the essential ideal of female beauty. The Venus of this painting reflects a complex synthesis of Platonic idealism, Christian mysticism relating to the Virgin, and the classical ideal of the female figure of Venus.

Two other artists who lived in Laurentian Florence are of worldwide significance: Leonardo da Vinci (1452–1519) and Michelangelo Buonarroti. Leonardo came from a small Tuscan town near Florence called Vinci. He lived in Florence until the 1480s, when he left for Milan; from there he moved restlessly from place to place until his death in France. Leonardo has been called *the* genius of the Renaissance not so much for what he left in the way of art (although his *Last Supper* and *Mona Lisa* are surely among the more famous set pieces of all time) as for the things that he dreamed of doing and the problems he set himself to solve and the phenomena he observed and set down in his *Notebooks*.

If we had nothing but the *Notebooks*, we would still say that Leonardo had one of humanity's most fertile minds. He left sketches for flying machines, submarines, turbines, elevators, ideal cities, and machines of almost every description [10.22]. His knowledge of anatomy was unsurpassed (he came

10.21 Sandro Botticelli. *The Birth of Venus*. 1480. Tempera on canvas, 6'7" × 9'2" (2.01 × 2.79 m). Uffizi, Florence. Scholars have made great exertions to unlock the full meaning of this work and *La Primavera*. A comparison of the two shows some close similarity in the figures.

10.22 Leonardo da Vinci. *Helicopter or Aerial Screw.* c. 1485–1490. Bibliothèque de l'Institut de France, Paris. Leonardo's "code writing" is decipherable only when held against a mirror.

very close to discovering the circulation path of blood), while his interest in the natural worlds of geology and botany was keen. The *Notebooks,* in short, reflect a restlessly searching mind that sought to understand the world and its constituent parts. Its chosen fields of inquiry are dominated by many of the characteristics common to the period: a concern with mathematics, a deep respect for seeing the natural world, and a love for beauty.

Leonardo's *The Last Supper* [10.23] is a good example of these characteristics. Leonardo chooses the moment when Jesus announces that someone at the table will betray him. The apostles are arranged in four distinct groups. The central figure of Christ is highlighted by the apostles who either look at him or gesture toward him. Christ is haloed by the central window space behind him, with the lines of the room all converging toward that point. The painting has great emotional power even though it is one of the most carefully mathematical paintings ever executed.

Leonardo's expressive power as a painter is ably illustrated in his striking *Madonna of the Rocks* [10.24], begun shortly after his arrival in Milan in 1483, a decade before he painted *The Last Supper.* The Virgin drapes her right arm over the figure of the infant Saint John the Baptist while her hand hovers in protective blessing over the Christ child. An exquisitely rendered angel points to the scene. The cavern-like space in the background would

10.23 Leonardo da Vinci. *The Last Supper.* 1495–1498. Fresco, 14'5" × 28'¼" (4.39 × 8.61 m). Refectory, Santa Maria delle Grazie, Milan. Below the figure of Christ one can still see the doorway cut into the wall during the Napoleonic period by soldiers who used the monastery as a military headquarters.

10.24 Leonardo da Vinci. *Madonna of the Rocks*. Begun 1483. Panel painting transferred to canvas, 78 × 48". Louvre, Paris. There is another version of this painting in London's National Gallery, but this one is thought to be completely from the hand of Leonardo. It was to be part of a large altarpiece, never completed, in honor of the Virgin.

10.25 Michelangelo. *Madonna of the Stairs*. 1489–1492. Marble, 21¾ × 15¾" (55 × 40 cm). Casa Buonarroti, Florence. A very fine example of low-relief (bas-relief) carving, with its figures nearly flush to the marble surface.

10.26 Michelangelo. *Pietà*. 1498–1499. Marble, height 5'9" (1.75 m). Saint Peter's, Vatican, Rome. One of the most "finished" of Michelangelo's sculptures, its high sheen is the result of intense polishing of the marble.

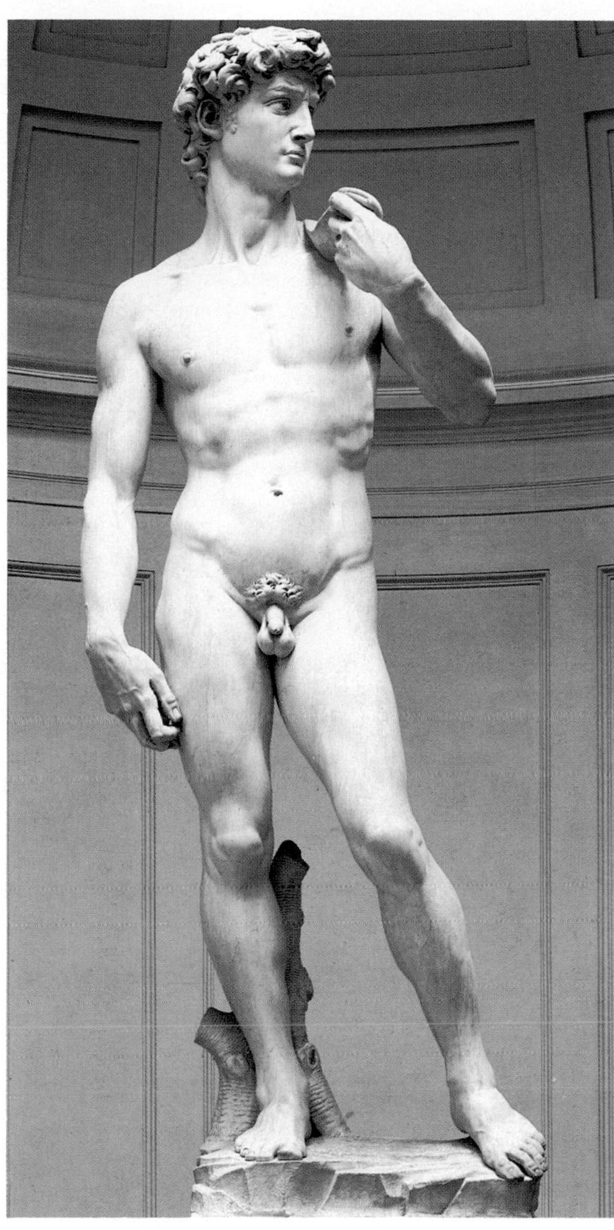

10.27 Michelangelo. *David*. 1501–1504. Marble, height 18' (5.49 m). Accademia, Florence. Much of the weight of this figure is borne by David's right leg (with the stylized tree trunk in the rear) in a position called *contraposto* in Italian.

remind the perceptive viewer both of the cave at Bethlehem where Christ was born and the cave in which he would be buried. Leonardo's rendering of the jagged rocks stands in sharper relief because of the misty light in the extreme background. The particular beauty of the painting derives at least partially from the juxtaposition of the beautifully rendered persons in all their humanity with the wildly mysterious natural frame in which they are set.

The other great genius of the late 15th century is Michelangelo Buonarroti (1476–1564). After his early days in the sculpture garden of Lorenzo, he produced many of his greatest works in Rome; they are considered in the next chapter. However, even a few examples of his early works show both the great promise of Michelangelo's talent and some of the influences he absorbed in Florence under the Medici. The *Madonna of the Stairs* [10.25], an early marble relief, reflects his study of ancient reliefs or cameo carving (which he may well have seen in Lorenzo's collection). By 1498 his style had matured enough for him to carve, for a French cardinal in Rome, the universally admired *Pietà* [10.26], which combines his deep sensitivity with an idealism in the beauty of the Madonna's face that is reminiscent of Botticelli.

Finally, this early period of Michelangelo's work includes a sculpture that has become almost synonymous with Florence: the *David* [10.27], carved in 1501–1504 from a massive piece of Carrara marble that had lain behind the cathedral in Florence since the middle of the preceding century. The sculpture's great size and its almost photographically realistic musculature combine to make it one of Michelangelo's clearest statements of idealized beauty. The statue was intended to be seen from below with the left arm (the one touching the shoulder) facing the viewer and the right side turned back toward the Cathedral. In fact, it was placed outside the Palazzo Vecchio as a symbol of the civic power of the city, where it remained until weathering and damage required its removal to a museum in the 19th century.

It has been said that Botticelli's paintings, the *Davids* of both Donatello and Michelangelo, and the general skepticism of a mind like Leonardo's are all symptoms of the general pagan tone of Laurentian Florence—that Athens and Rome, in short, seemed far more important to 15th-century Florence than Jerusalem did. There is no doubt that the classical revival was central to Florentine culture. Nor is there any doubt that the times had little patience with, or admiration for, medieval culture. However, the notion that the Renaissance spirit marked a clean break with medieval ideals must take into account the life and career of the Dominican preacher and reformer Fra Savonarola (1452–1498).

Savonarola lived at the Convent of San Marco in Florence from 1490 until his execution in 1498. His urgent preachings against the vanities of Florence in general and the degeneracy of its art and culture in particular had an electric effect on the populace. His influence was not limited to the credulous masses of the workers of the city. Lorenzo called him to his own deathbed in 1492 to receive the last sacraments even though Savonarola had been a bitter and open enemy of Medici control over the city. Savonarola, in fact, wanted a restored Republic with a strong ethical and theocratic base. Botticelli was so impressed by Savonarola that he burned some of his more worldly paintings, and scholars see in his last works a more profound religiosity derived from the contact with the reforming friar. Michelangelo, when an old man in Rome, told a friend that he could still hear the words of Savonarola ringing in his ears. Pico della Mirandola (1463–1494), one of the most brilliant humanists of the period, turned from his polyglot studies of Greek, Hebrew, Aramaic, and Latin to a devout life under the direction of the friar; only his early death prevented him from joining Savonarola as a friar at San Marco.

Savonarola's hold over the Florentine political order (for a brief time he was the de facto ruler of the city) came to an end in 1498 when he defied papal excommunication and was then strangled and burned in the public square before the Palazzo Vecchio. By that time, Lorenzo had been dead for six years and the Medici family had lost power in Florence. They were to return in the next century, but the Golden Age of Lorenzo had ended with a spasm of medieval piety. The influence of the city and its ideals, however, had already spread far beyond its boundaries.

CONTEMPORARY VOICES

Fra Savonarola

Creatures are beautiful insofar as they share in and approach the beauty of the soul. Take two women of like bodily beauty, and if one is holy and the other is evil, you will notice that the holy one is more loved by everyone than the evil one, so all eyes will rest on her. The same is true of men. A holy man, however deformed bodily, pleases everyone because, no matter how ugly he may be, his holiness shows itself and makes everything he does gracious.

Think how beautiful the Virgin was, who was so holy. She shines forth in all she does. St. Thomas [Aquinas] says that no one who saw her ever looked on her with evil desire, so evident was her sanctity.

But now think of the saints as they are painted in the churches of the city. Young men go about saying "This is the Magdalen and that is Saint John," and only because the paintings in the church are modeled on them. This is a terrible thing because the things of God are undervalued.

You fill the churches with your own vanity.

Do you think that the Virgin Mary went about dressed as she is shown in paintings? I tell you she went about dressed like a poor person with simplicity and her face so covered that it was hardly seen. The same is true of Saint Elizabeth.

You would do well to destroy pictures so unsuitably conceived. You make the Virgin Mary look like a whore. How the worship of God is mocked!

From a sermon of Fra Savonarola to a congregation in the Cathedral of Florence.

EAST MEETS WEST

The Renaissance in Exploration

Travel outside Europe had persisted throughout the Middle Ages, but the 15th century saw a renaissance in exploration because of some technological advances. Although both the compass and the astrolabe (for measuring latitudes) had been known for centuries, under Islamic influence they were greatly refined in this period. Furthermore, it was in the 15th century that the first three-masted ships, with their great advance in power, came into common use. In 1410 there appeared a Latin translation of the astronomical and geographical works of Ptolemy, the late-Latin writer whose writings had been lost to the West but known in the Muslim world. This translation provided further impetus for better maps and other navigational aids.

The Portuguese can claim star billing for 15th-century exploration. Under Prince Henry the Navigator (1390–1460), explorations down the west coast of Africa were undertaken in an effort to find a sea route to the fabled land of India. By mid-century the Portuguese had trading centers on the coast of Africa, where they engaged in a lucrative commerce in pepper, ivory, and gold. By 1446 these explorers and traders had pushed fifteen hundred miles down the African coast and passed the Cape Verde Islands. The motives for such risky travel were complex: partly a matter of expanded economics, partly an attempt to outflank the Muslims who controlled all of North Africa, and partly, a desire to extend Christian influence in the world.

By the last decade of the century Vasco da Gama had rounded the tip of Africa, proving that there was a sea route to India. In 1499 da Gama returned to Lisbon and a tumultuous welcome with a cargo of spices and precious stones. India had been reached by sea. The stranglehold of the Venetians and the Muslims (with their ports on the Mediterranean) had been broken. Europe now looked to the Atlantic—which would have enormous consequences, as Christopher Columbus proved in the same decade.

As early as 1441, however, Portuguese traders had sent back captured Africans to the European homeland. These merchants soon realized that Africa could supply cheap labor by the simple expedient of enslaving people. The explorers of Portugal, then, have the dubious honor of having begun the African slave trade.

THE CHARACTER OF RENAISSANCE HUMANISM

Jules Michelet, a 19th-century French historian, first coined the word *Renaissance* specifically to describe the cultural period of 15th-century Florence. The broad outline of this rebirth is described by the Swiss historian Jakob Burckhardt in his massive *The Civilization of the Renaissance in Italy,* first published in 1860, a book that is the beginning point for any discussion of the topic. Burckhardt's thesis is simple and persuasive. European culture, he argued, was reborn in the 15th century after a long dormant period that extended from the fall of the Roman Empire until the beginning of the 14th century.

The characteristics of this new birth, Burckhardt said, were first noticeable in Italy and were the foundation blocks of the modern world. It was in late 14th- and 15th-century Italy that new ideas about the nature of the political order developed, of which the Republican government of Florence is an example, as well as the consciousness of the artist as an individual seeking personal fame. This pursuit of glory and fame was in sharp contrast to the self effacing and world-denying attitude of the Middle Ages. Burckhardt also saw the thirst for classical learning, the desire to construct a humanism from that learning, and an emphasis on the good life as an intellectual repudiation of medieval religion and ethics.

Burckhardt's ideas have provoked strong reactions from historians and scholars, many of whom reject his theory as simplistic. Charles Homer Haskins, an American scholar, attacked Burckhardt's ideas in 1927 in a book whose title gives away his line of argument: *The Renaissance of the Twelfth Century*. Haskins pointed out that everything Burckhardt said about Florentine life in the 15th century could be said with equal justification about Paris in the 12th century. Furthermore (as noted in Chapter 7), scholars have also spoken of a Carolingian Renaissance identified with the court of the emperor Charlemagne.

What is the truth? Was there a genuine Renaissance in 15th-century Italy? Many scholars today try to mediate a position between Burckhardt and his detractors. They admit that something new was happening in the intellectual and cultural life of 15th-century Italy and that contemporaries were conscious of it. "May every thoughtful spirit thank God that it has been given to him to be born in this new age, so filled with hope and promise, which already enjoys a greater array of gifted persons than the world has seen in the past thousand years," wrote Matteo Palmieri, a Florentine businessman, in 1436. Yet this "new age" of which Palmieri spoke did not spring up overnight. The roots must be traced to Italy's long tradition of lay learning, the Franciscan movement of the 13th century, the relative absence of feudalism in Italy, and the long maintenance of Italian city life. In short, something new was happening precisely because Italy's long historical antecedents permitted it.

The question remains, however: What was new in the Renaissance? The Renaissance was surely more than a change in artistic taste or an advance in technological artistic skill. We need to go deeper. What motivated the shift in artistic taste? What fueled the personal energy that produced artistic innovation? What caused flocks of foreign scholars to cross the Alps to study in Florence and in other centers where they could absorb the "new learning"?

The answer to these questions, briefly, is this: There arose in Italy, as early as the time of Petrarch (1304–1372), but clearly in the 15th century, a strong conviction that humanist learning would not only ennoble and perfect the individual but could also serve as a powerful instrument for social and religious reform. Very few Renaissance humanists denied the need for God's grace, but all felt that human intellectual effort should be the first concern of anyone who wished truly to advance the good of self or society. The career of Pico della Mirandola, one of the most brilliant and gifted Florentine humanist scholars, illustrates this humanist belief.

Pico della Mirandola

Pico della Mirandola (1463–1494) was an intimate friend of Lorenzo de' Medici and a companion of the Platonic scholar Marsilio Ficino. Precociously brilliant, Pico once bragged, not totally implausibly, that he had read every book in Italy. He was deeply involved with the intellectual life of his day.

Pico was convinced that all human learning could be synthesized in such a way as to yield basic and elementary truths. To demonstrate this, he set out to master all the systems of knowledge that then existed. He thoroughly mastered the Latin and Greek classics. He studied medieval Aristotelianism at the University of Paris and learned Arabic and the Islamic tradition. He was the first Christian in his day to take an active interest in Hebrew culture; he learned Hebrew and Aramaic and studied the Talmud with Jewish scholars.

At the age of twenty Pico proposed to defend at Rome his nine hundred *theses* (intellectual propositions), which he claimed summed up all current learning and speculation. Church leaders attacked some of his propositions as unorthodox; Pico left Rome and the debate was never held.

The preface to these theses, called the *Oration on the Dignity of Man,* has often been cited as the first and most important document of Renaissance humanism. Its central thesis is that humanity stands at the apex of creation in such a way as to create the link between the world of God and that of the creation. Pico brings his wide learning to bear on this fundamental proposition: Humanity is a great miracle. He not only calls on the traditional biblical and classical sources but also cites, from his immense reading, the opinions of the great writers of the Jewish, Arabic, and Neoplatonic traditions. The enthusiasm of the youthful Pico for his subject is as apparent as his desire to display his learning.

Scholars disagree on Pico's originality as a thinker. Many argue that his writings are a hodgepodge of knowledge without any genuine synthesis. There is no disagreement, however, about Pico's immense ability as a student of languages and culture to open new fields of study and, in that way, contribute much to the enthusiasm for learning in his own day. His reputation attracted students to him. The most influential of these was a German named Johann Reuchlin (1455–1522), who came to Florence to study Hebrew with him. After mastering that language and Greek as well, Reuchlin went back to Germany to pursue his studies and to apply them to biblical scholarship. In the early 16th century he came under the influence of Martin Luther (see Chapter 12) but never joined the Reformation. Reuchlin passionately defended the legitimacy of biblical studies oriented to the original languages. When his approach was attacked in one of those periodic outbursts of anti-Semitism so characteristic of European culture of the time, Reuchlin, true to his humanist impulses, not only defended his studies as a true instrument of religious reform but also made an impassioned plea for toleration that was not characteristic of his time.

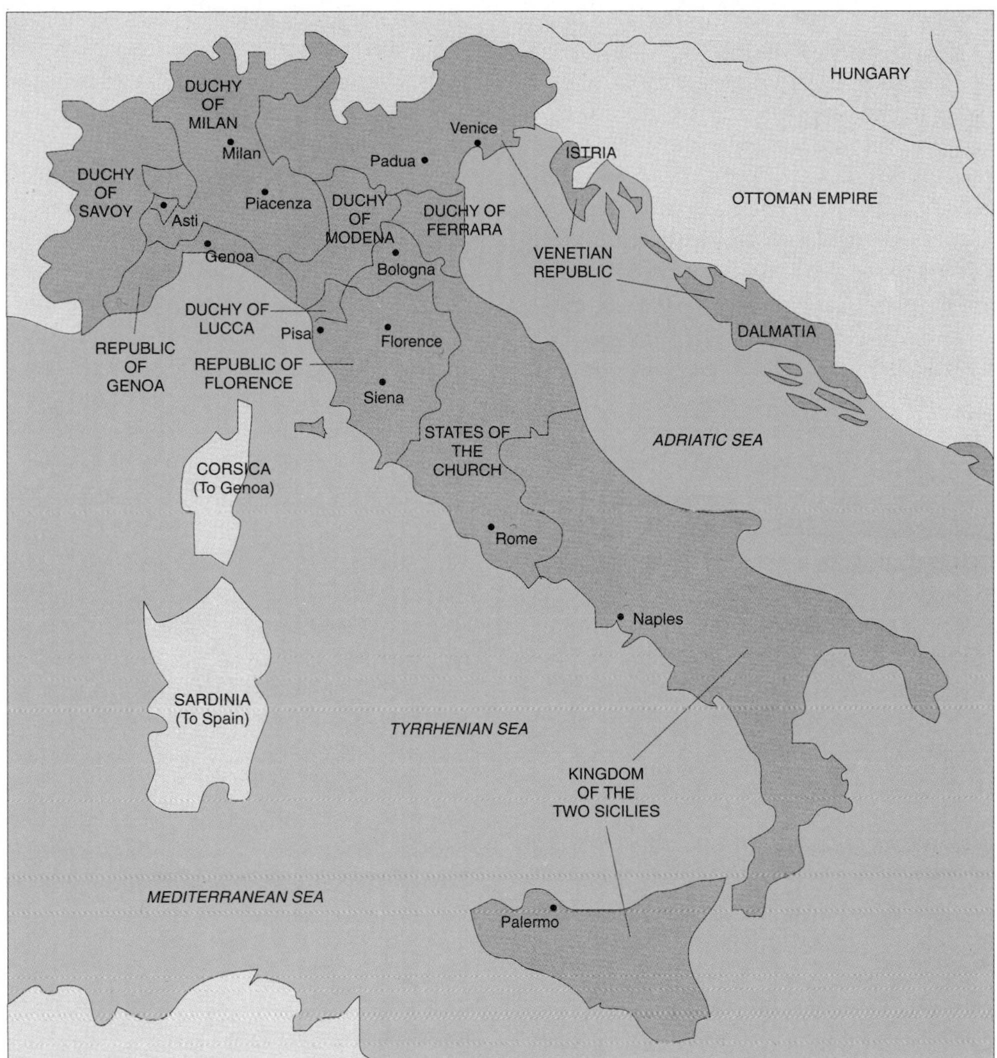

Printing Technology and the Spread of Humanism

The export of humanist learning was not restricted to the exchange of scholars between Italy and the countries to the north. Printing had been invented in the early 15th century, so books were becoming more accessible to the educated classes. The most famous humanist printer and publisher of the 15th century was Aldus Manutius (1449–1515), whose Aldine Press was in Venice, his native city (see map above). Aldus was a scholar in his own right; he learned Greek from refugee scholars who settled in Venice after the fall of Constantinople in 1453. Recognizing the need for competent and reliable editions of the classical authors, he employed professional humanists to collate and correct manuscripts. Erasmus, the greatest of the northern humanists, was, for a time, in his employ.

Aldus was also a technical innovator. He designed Greek typefaces, created italic type fonts (modeled after the scribal hand used for copying Florentine manuscripts), developed new inks, and obtained new paper from the nearby town of Fabriano, still a source of fine papers for artists and printmakers. His books were near pocket-size, easily portable, and inexpensive. The scope of the press's activities was huge: After 1494 Aldus (and, later, his son) published, in about twenty years, the complete works of Aristotle and the works of Plato, Pindar, Herodotus, Sophocles, Aristophanes, Xenophon, and Demosthenes. Aldus reissued the Latin classics in better editions and published vernacular writers like Dante and Petrarch as well as contemporary poets like Poliziano, the Florentine friend of Lorenzo.

The Aldine Press was not an isolated phenomenon. Germany, where Western printing really started, already had an active printing and publishing tradition. Johannes Gutenberg (c. 1395–1468) originated the method of printing from movable type that was then used with virtually no change until the late 19th century. Gutenberg finished printing a Bible at Mainz in 1455. The first book printed in English, *The Recuyell* (collection) *of the Historyes of Troye,* was published by William Caxton in 1475. Historians have estimated that before 1500 European presses produced between six and nine million books in thirteen thousand different editions. Nearly fifty thousand of these books survive in libraries throughout the world.

This conjunction of pride in humanist learning and technology of printing had profound consequences for European culture. It permitted the wide diffusion of ideas to a large number of people in a relatively short time. There is no doubt that vigorous intellectual movements—one thinks immediately of the Protestant Reformation—benefited immensely from printing. This communications revolution was as important for the Renaissance period as radio, film, and television have been for our own.

Women and the Renaissance

It has been asked: Did women have a renaissance? It is clear that women, as the idealization of certain images and ideas, were central to the renaissance conception of beauty (think of Botticelli's *Primavera* or *Venus*) but it is equally true that very little provision was made for women to participate in the new learning which constituted the heart of humanism. A recent generation of scholars, however, have recovered for us voices that have been hitherto silent. When women did get a humanist education it was either because they came from aristocratic families that allowed women the leisure and means to get an education or they were children of families who highly prized learning and saw nothing amiss with educating women as well as men.

A recently published anthology of texts (see King and Rabil, bibliography) by women humanists in Italy demonstrates that most of them came from the more illustrious families of the time. Thus Ippolita Sforza (of the Milan Sforzas) actually delivered an oration before the renaissance humanist and pope Pius II in 1459. Others, like Isotta Nogarola, had to swim against the tide and choose a life of letters while resisting both marriage and pressure to enter a convent. Others, like Cecilia Gonzaga, entered into convent life for the precise reason of finding the shelter and leisure to advance their studies in the "New Learning."

It is instructive that a determined humanist named Laura Cereta (died 1499) from Brescia constinued her scholarly life throughout her mature years against a tide of criticism from both men who were her peers and from women. Out of those struggles came two letters which were penned to answer both critics: a defense of learning aimed at male humanists and a defense of her vocation directed towards her female critics. Those two documents testify to the difficulty of her life apart from the roles expected of her in society.

TWO STYLES OF HUMANISM

In the generation after the death of Lorenzo de' Medici the new learning made its way north, where it was most often put to use in attempts to reform the religious life of the area; in Italy, however, the learning remained tied to more worldly matters. The double usage of humanist learning for secular and spiritual reform can be better appreciated by a brief consideration of the work of the two most important writers of the period after the golden period of the Medicean Renaissance: Niccolò Machiavelli and Desiderius Erasmus.

Machiavelli

Niccolò Machiavelli (1469–1527), trained as a humanist and active as a diplomat in Florence, was exiled from the city when the Medici reassumed power in 1512. In his exile, a few miles from the city which he had served for many years, Machiavelli wrote a political treatise on politics called *The Prince* that was published only after his death.

The Prince is often considered the first purely secular study of political theory in the West. Machiavelli's inspiration is the government of Republican Rome (509–31 B.C.). He sees Christianity's role in politics as a disaster that destroys the power of the state to govern. For that reason, Machiavelli asserts, the state needs to restrict the power of the church, allowing it to exercise its office only in the spiritual realm. The prince, as ruler of the state, must understand that the key to success in governing is in the exercise of power. Power is to be used with wisdom and ruthlessness. The prince, in a favorite illustration of Machiavelli, must be as sly as the fox and as brutal as the lion.

Above all, the prince must not be deterred from his tasks by any consideration of morality beyond that of power and its ends. In this sense, cruelty or hypocrisy is permissible; judicious cruelty consolidates power and discourages revolution. Senseless cruelty is, however, counterproductive.

The basic theme of *The Prince* is the pragmatic use of power for state management. Previously the tradition of political theory had always invoked the transcendent authority of God to ensure the stability and legitimacy of the state. For Machiavelli it was power, not the moral law of God, that provided the state with its ultimate sanction. The final test of the successful ruler was the willingness to exercise power judiciously and freedom from the constraints of moral suasion. "A prince must not keep faith when by doing so it would be against his self-interest," Machiavelli says in one of the most famous passages from his book. His justification is ". . . If all men were good this precept would not be a good one but as they are bad and would not observe their faith with you, so you are not bound to keep faith with them." This bold pragmatism explains why the Catholic Church put *The Prince* on its *Index of Prohibited Books* and why the adjective "Machiavellian" means, in English, devious or unscrupulous in political dealings. Machiavelli had such a bad reputation that many 16th-century English plays had a stock evil character—an Italian called "Old Nick." The English phrase "to be filled with the Old Nick," meaning to be devilish, derives from Machiavelli's reputation as an immoral man. But Machiavelli's realistic pragmatism also explains why Catherine the Great of Russia and Napoleon read him with great care.

10.28 Albrecht Dürer. *Erasmus of Rotterdam.* 1526. Intaglio print, 9¾ × 7½" (25 × 19 cm). Detail: Writing stand and monogram. Metropolitan Museum of Art, New York (Fletcher Fund, 1919). The Latin inscription says that Erasmus was drawn from life by the artist; the Greek epigram praises the written word. The stylized letters *AD* are the signature letters of the artist and appear in all his engravings and prints.

In the last analysis, however, it is the figure of the Prince which best defines a view of politics that looks to a leader who understands that power is what keeps a political person as a strong ruler. Such a leader uses a simple rule of thumb: How does one exercise power in order to retain power? Such a ruler does not appeal to eternal rules but to simple calculations: Will the exercise of power in this or that particular fashion guarantee the stability of the state? If ruthlessness or violence is needed, let there be ruthlessness or violence (or terror!). Machiavelli did not want to create a monster and he certainly did not want violence for its own sake. He did favor, however, whatever means it took to keep the state intact and powerful by whatever means necessary. That is the deepest meaning of the adjective "Machiavellian."

Erasmus

Desiderius Erasmus (1466–1536) has been called the most important Christian humanist in Europe [10.28]. Educated in Holland and at the University of Paris, Erasmus was a monk and priest who soon tired of his official church life. He became aware of humanist learning through his visits to England, where he met men like John Colet and Thomas More. Fired by their enthusiasm for the new learning, Erasmus traveled to Italy in 1506, with lengthy stays in both Rome and Venice. Thereafter he led the life of a wandering scholar, gaining immense fame as both scholar and author.

Erasmus' many books were attempts to combine classical learning and a simple interiorized approach to Christian living. In the *Enchiridion Militis Christiani* (1502) he attempted to spell out this Christian humanism in practical terms. The title has a typical Erasmian pun; the word *enchiridion* can mean either "handbook" or "short sword";

thus the title can mean the handbook or the short sword of the Christian knight. His *Greek New Testament* (1516) was the first attempt to edit the Greek text of the New Testament by a comparison of extant manuscripts. Because Erasmus used only three manuscripts, his version is not technically perfect, but it was a noteworthy attempt and a clear indication of how a humanist felt he could contribute to ecclesiastical work.

The most famous book Erasmus wrote, *The Praise of Folly* (1509), was dashed off almost as a joke while he was a house guest of Sir Thomas More in England. Again the title is a pun; *Encomium Moriae* can mean either "praise of folly" or "praise of More"—Thomas More, his host. *The Praise of Folly* is a humorous work, but beneath its seemingly lighthearted spoof of the foibles of the day there are strong denunciations of corruption, evil, ignorance, and prejudice in society. Erasmus flailed away at the makers of war (he had a strong pacifist streak), venal lawyers, and fraudulent doctors, but, above all, he bitterly attacked religious corruption: the sterility of religious scholarship and the superstitions in religious practice. Reading *The Praise of Folly* makes one wonder why Luther never won Erasmus over to the Reformation (Erasmus debated Luther, in fact). Erasmus remained in the old Church, but as a bitter critic of its follies and an indefatigable proponent of its reform.

This sweeping social criticism struck an obvious nerve. The book delighted not only the great Sir Thomas More (who was concerned enough about religious convictions to die for them later in the century) but also many sensitive people of the time. *The Praise of Folly* went through twenty-seven editions in the lifetime of Erasmus and outsold every other book except the Bible in the 16th century.

Comparing Machiavelli and Erasmus is a bit like comparing apples and potatoes, but a few points of contact can be noted that help us to generalize about the meaning of the Renaissance. Both men were heavily indebted to the new learning coming out of 15th-century Italy. Both looked back to the great classical heritage of the past for their models of inspiration. Both were elegant Latinists who avoided the style and thought patterns of the medieval world. Machiavelli's devotion to the Roman past was total. He saw the historic development of Christianity as a threat and stumbling block to the fine working of the state. Erasmus, by contrast, felt that learning from the past could be wedded to the Christian tradition to create an instrument for social reform. His ideal was a Christian humanism based on this formula. It was a formula potent enough to influence thinking throughout the 16th century.

The tug-of-war between classicism and Christianity may be one key to understanding the Renaissance. It may even help us understand something about the character of almost everything we have discussed in this chapter. The culture of the 15th century often was, in fact, a dialectical struggle: At times classical ideals clashed with biblical ideals; at other times, the two managed to live either in harmony or in a temporary marriage of convenience. The strains of classicism and Christianity interacted in complex and subtle ways. This important fact helps us to understand a culture that produced, in a generation, an elegant scholar like Ficino and a firebrand like Savonarola, a pious artist like Fra Angelico and a titanic genius like Michelangelo—and a Machiavelli and an Erasmus.

MUSIC IN THE 15TH CENTURY

By the early 15th century the force of the Italian *Ars Nova* movement in music had spent itself. The principal composers of the early Renaissance were from the North. Strong commercial links between Florence and the North ensured the exchange of ideas, and a new musical idiom that had been developed to please the ear of the prosperous merchant families of the North soon found its way to Italy.

Guillaume Dufay

Guillaume Dufay (c. 1400–1474), the most famous composer of the century, perfectly exemplifies the tendency of music to cross national boundaries. As a young man Dufay spent several years in Italy studying music and singing in the papal choir at Rome. He later served as music teacher in the French (Burgundian) court of Charles the Good. The works he composed there included masses and motets; he was one of the first composers after Machaut to write complete settings of the Mass. His secular works include a number of charming *chansons* (songs) that are free in form and expressive in nature.

Among the changes introduced into music by Dufay and his Burgundian followers (many of whom went to Italy for employment) was the secularization of the motet, a choral work that had previously used a religious text. Motets were now written for special occasions like coronations or no-

SPORTS AND GAMES

Gambling

Gambling is as old as humanity itself. Board games and dice have been found in archaeological digs all over the civilized world. Judging from the popular sermons and moralistic treatises that have survived from late medieval and early Renaissance Italy, gambling was especially popular (and problematic!) in the cities. Court records of 15th-century Florence document civic struggles with the problem; here is a not untypical example: Domenico Shartera of the Via San Gallo keeps "a band of thieves who play with loaded dice and swindle . . . he is a fine healthy man who is neither sick nor crippled; he is able to do something better than gamble with dice. Fined 50 lire."

Gambling booths were common in the main squares of most Italian cities. The owners, called *barattieri,* were licensed and often were employed in unsavory tasks like flogging criminals, thus giving us a sense of how little they were esteemed. While cards and chess were common in the family, the most common form of gambling in public involved dice, a board, and the use of "men" in games somewhat like backgammon or games involving dice alone. A three-dice game called *zara* (from which comes *azzardo* and, finally, the English word "hazard") was especially popular.

The moralists of the day railed against the public gambling but not because they objected to games of chance in their own right. Preachers like Siena's 15th-century San Bernardino pointed out how often people lost their income and ended up either blaspheming God for their ill fortune or ending up impoverished, in despair, and on occasion, suicides. What was even more worrisome for the public officials was the linkage between public gambling and violence. A contemporary poet (Antonio Pucci) caught the situation perfectly: "One may see the loser cursing with great sighs/With his hand to a jaw, giving and receiving great blows/And then comes the knife and they kill each other/And the whole public square is in turmoil."

It is for that reason that a popular preacher like Saint Bernardino would encourage people to bring their gaming boards, dice, and cards to him (he would burn them on bonfires called "the devil's castle") and, in return, promise to pray every day for the person when celebrating Mass.

ble marriages and the conclusions of peace treaties. Composers who could supply such motets on short notice found welcome in the courts of Renaissance Italian city-states.

Dufay was also one of the first composers to introduce a familiar folk tune into the music of the Mass, the best-known example being his use of the French folk tune *"L'homme armé"* ("The Man in Armor") in a mass that is now named for it. Other composers followed suit and the so-called *chanson masses* were composed throughout the 15th and 16th centuries. The *"L'homme armé"* alone was used for more than thirty different masses, including ones by such composers as Josquin and Palestrina. The intermingling of secular with religious elements is thoroughly in accordance with Renaissance ideals.

Among Dufay's most prominent pupils was the Flemish composer Johannes Ockeghem (c. 1430–1495), whose music was characterized by a smooth-flowing but complex web of contrapuntal lines generally written in a free style (the lines do not imitate one another). The resulting mood of the music is more serious than Dufay's, partly because of the intellectual complexity of the counterpoint and partly because Ockeghem sought a greater emotional expression. The combination of intellect and feeling is characteristic of the Renaissance striving for classical balance. Ockeghem's Requiem Mass is the oldest of the genre to survive (Dufay wrote one that has not been preserved).

Music in Medici Florence

The fact that Italian composers were overshadowed by their northern contemporaries did not in any way stifle Italian interest in music. Lorenzo de' Medici founded a school of harmony that attracted musicians from many parts of Europe; he himself had some skill as a lute player. Musical accompaniment enlivened the festivals and public processions of Florence. Popular dance tunes for the *saltarello* and the *pavana* have survived in lute transcriptions.

We know that the platonist writer Marsilio Ficino played the lyre before admiring audiences, although he had intentions more serious than mere entertainment. Unlike the visual artists who had models from classical antiquity for inspiration, students of music had no classical models to follow: no Greek or Roman music had survived in any significant form. Still, the ideas about music expressed by Plato and other writers fascinated Ficino and others. Greek music had been patterned after the meter of verse and its character carefully controlled by the mode in which it was composed. The Greek doctrine of "characteristic" or *ethos* is still not fully understood today, but Ficino and his friends realized that Plato and Aristotle regarded music as of the highest moral (and hence political) significance. The closest they could come to imitating ancient music was to write settings of Greek and Roman texts in which they tried to follow the meter as closely as possible. Among the most popular works was Vergil's *Aeneid*: The lament of Dido was set to music by no fewer than fourteen composers in the 15th and 16th centuries.

A more popular musical form was the *frottola,* probably first developed in Florence although the earliest surviving examples come from the Renaissance court of Mantua. The *frottola* was a setting of a humorous or amorous poem for three or four parts consisting of a singer and two or three instrumentalists. Written to be performed in aristocratic circles, the *frottola* often had a simple folk quality. The gradual diffusion of *frottole* throughout Europe gave Italy a reputation for good simple melody and clear vigorous expression.

The carnival song *(canto carnascialesco)* was a specifically Florentine form of the *frottola.* Written to be sung during the carnival season preceding Lent, such songs were very popular. Even the great Flemish composer Heinrich Issac wrote some during his stay with Lorenzo de' Medici around 1480. With the coming of the Dominican reformer Savonarola, however, the carnivals were abolished because of their alleged licentiousness. The songs also disappeared. After the death of Savonarola the songs were reintroduced but died out again in the 16th century.

SUMMARY

The main focus of this chapter is on the city of Florence in the 15th century. There are two basic reasons for this attention, one rooted in economics and the other in something far more difficult to define.

Florence was not a feudal city governed by a hereditary prince; it had a species of limited participatory government that was in the hands of its landed and moneyed peoples. It was the center of European banking in the 15th century and the hub of international wool and cloth trade. The vast monies in Florentine hands combined with a great sense of civic pride to give the city unparalleled opportunities for expansion and public works. The results can be seen in the explosion of building, art, sculpture, and learning that stretched throughout the century. The great banking families of Florence built and supported art to enhance their reputations, that of their cities, and, partly, as a form of expiation for the sin of taking interest on money, a practice forbidden by the Church. We tend to see Florence today from the perspective of their generosity.

Other forces were, of course, at work. The urban workers were exploited; they had rioted during the end of the 14th century and were ready for further protest. An undercurrent of medieval religiosity in the city manifested itself most conspicuously in the rise of Savonarola, who not only appealed to the common people but who had a reputation for sanctity that could touch the lives of an educated man like Pico della Mirandola and a powerful one like Lorenzo the Magnificent. Every Florentine could visit the Duomo or see the art in the city's churches, but not everyone was equally touched by the great renaissance in ideas and art that bubbled up in Florence.

Most puzzling about Florence in this period is the sheer enormity of artistic talent it produced. Florence was not a huge city; it often portrayed itself as a David in comparison to a Roman or Milanese Goliath. Yet this relatively small city produced a tradition of art that spanned the century: In sculpture Donatello and Michelangelo bridged the generations, as did Masaccio and Botticelli in painting. Part of the explanation, of course, was native talent, but part of it also lies in the character of a city that supported the arts, nurtured artists, and enhanced civic life with beauty and learning.

Pronunciation Guide

Botticelli: Boh-tee-CHEL-ee
Brunelleschi: Brew-ne-LESS-ki
Cosimo: CAH-ze-mow
de' Medici: deh-MED-e-chee
Donatello: don-ah-TELL-oh
Dufay: dew-FAY
duomo: dwo-mow
Ficino: Fee-CHEE-no
Ghiberti: Ghee-BAIR-tee
Lorenzo: Lo-WREN-zo
Machiavelli: Ma-key-ah-VEL-ee
Manutius: Mah-KNEW-tee-us
Masaccio: Mah-SA-cho
Pico della Mirandola: PEE-ko dell-ah Mee-RAN-dough-la
Piero: Pea-A-row
Savonarola: Sa-van-ah-ROLL-ah

Exercises

1. Choose one of the major paintings of this period and analyze it closely in terms of composition, gradations of color, and use of perspective.
2. List the chief problems of construction involved in raising the dome of the Florence Cathedral in an age that did not have today's building technologies.
3. To what artistic and cultural enterprises would wealthy people most likely contribute today if they had the resources and the power of a Medici family in a contemporary city?
4. What does the word *humanism* mean today and how does that meaning differ from its use in the 15th century?
5. If Erasmus were writing today, what would be his most likely targets of satire? What are the great follies of our age?
6. What advice would a contemporary Machiavelli give a contemporary "prince" (powerful political leader)? Why do political philosophers still study Machiavelli?
7. Many say that computers are changing learning as radically as did printing in its age. How are computer technologies changing learning?

Further Reading

Brucker, Gene. *Renaissance Florence.* New York: Wiley, 1969. A readable introduction to the city and its institutions.

Burckhardt, Jakob. *The Civilization of the Renaissance in Italy.* 2 vols. New York: Harper, 1958. The point of departure for all Renaissance study. A classic.

Hale, J. R. (ed). *A Concise Encyclopedia of the Italian Renaissance.* New York: Oxford University Press, 1982. A useful reference tool for Renaissance studies.

Hartt, Frederick. *A History of Italian Renaissance Art.* London: Thames and Hudson, 1970. The standard work; many fine illustrations.

King, Margaret, and Albert Rabil, eds. *Her Immaculate Hand: Selected Works by and about the Women Humanists of Quattrocento Italy.* Binghamton: Medieval & Renaissaance Texts, 1983. Valuable for original sources.

King, Margaret. *Women Of the Renaissance.* Chicago: University of Chicago Press, 1991. Pathbreaking work.

Kristeller, Paul O. *Renaissance Essays I and II.* New York: Harper & Row, 1968. Classic studies of Italian humanism.

Rice, Eugene. *Saint Jerome in the Renaissance.* Baltimore: Johns Hopkins, 1985. A brilliant book that shows how Jerome became a symbol of humanism. Interdisciplinary scholarship at its finest.

Simon, Kate. *A Renaissance Tapestry: The Gonzaga of Mantua.* New York: Harper & Row, 1988. A readable history with fine profiles of Renaissance figures and a good bibliography.

Trinkaus, Charles. *In Our Image and Likeness.* 2 vols. Chicago: University of Chicago Press, 1970. A brilliant study of humanism in the Renaissance.

	GENERAL EVENTS	LITERATURE & PHILOSOPHY	ART
1400			
FLORENTINE RENAISSANCE	**1471–1484** Reign of Pope Sixtus IV (della Rovere) **1492** Columbus discovers America **1494** Foreign invasions of Italy begin	**c. 1494** Aldine Press established in Venice	**1471–1484** Perugino, Botticelli, and others decorate Sistine Chapel side walls **1493–1506** Ancient frescoes and statues uncovered in Rome; *Laocoön* found 1506 **c. 1494** Decline of Medici power in Florence causes artists to migrate to Rome **1494–1495** Dürer's first trip to Venice
1503			
HIGH RENAISSANCE IN ITALY	**1503–1513** Reign of Pope Julius II (della Rovere) **c. 1510** Decline of Venetian trade as a result of new geographic discoveries **1513–1521** Reign of Pope Leo X (de' Medici) **1517** Reformation begins in Germany with Luther's 95 Theses, challenging the practice of indulgences		**c. 1500–1505** Giorgione, *Enthroned Madonna with Saint Liberalis and Saint Francis,* altarpiece **1505** Michelangelo called to Rome by Julius II to begin Pope's tomb; *Moses* (1513–1515), *Captives* (1527–1528) **1505–1508** Raphael works in Florence; *Madonna of the Meadows* (1505) **1508** Raphael begins frescoes for rooms in Vatican Palace; *The School of Athens,* Stanza della Segnatura (1510–1511) **1508–1511** Michelangelo, Sistine Chapel ceiling **c. 1510** Giorgione, *Fête Champêtre* **1511** Raphael, *Portrait of Julius II* **1515–1547** Francis I lures Leonardo and other Italian artists to France Painting in Venice emphasizes brilliant color and light; less linear than in Rome and Florence; Titian, *The Assumption of the Virgin* (1518) **1519** Death of Leonardo **1519–1534** Michelangelo works on Medici Chapel sculptures
1520			
MANNERISM AND LATE RENAISSANCE	**1523–1534** Reign of Pope Clement VII (de' Medici) **1527** Sack of Rome by Emperor Charles V **1534** Churches of Rome and England separate **1545** Council to reform Catholic Church begins at Trent	**c. 1524–1534** Strozzi, poem on Michelangelo's *Night* **1527** Luther translates Bible into German **1528** Castiglione, *The Courtier,* dialogue on ideal courtly life **1550** Vasari, *Lives of the Painters* **1558–1566** Cellini, *Autobiography of Benvenuto Cellini* **1561** *The Courtier* translated into English by Sir Thomas Hoby	**1520** Death of Raphael **c. 1520** Mannerism emerges as artistic style **c. 1528** Pontormo, *Deposition,* Capponi Chapel, Santa Felicitá, Florence **c. 1534** Parmigianino, *Madonna of the Long Neck* **1534–1541** Michelangelo, *Last Judgment* fresco, Sistine Chapel **1538** Titian, *Venus of Urbino* 
1603			

CHAPTER

11 THE HIGH RENAISSANCE IN ITALY

	ARCHITECTURE	MUSIC
	1473–1480 Sistine Chapel built for Pope Sixtus IV	**1473** Sistine Choir established by Sixtus IV **1486–1494** Josquin des Préz intermittently in service of Sistine Choir as composer of masses and motets; *Tu Pauperum Refugium*
	**1504** Bramante, Tempietto, San Pietro in Montorio, Rome **1506** Pope Julius II commissions Bramante to rebuild Saint Peter's Basilica	
	**1514** Death of Bramante; Raphael, Sangallo, and others continue work on Saint Peter's	**1512** Julian Choir established by Julius II for Saint Peter's Basilica
	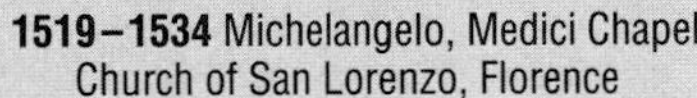 **1519–1534** Michelangelo, Medici Chapel, Church of San Lorenzo, Florence	
	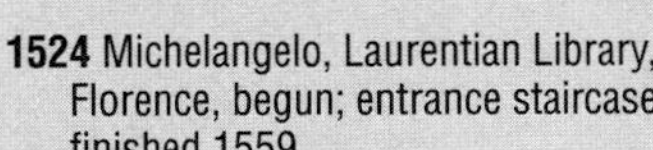 **1524** Michelangelo, Laurentian Library, Florence, begun; entrance staircase finished 1559	**1527** Adrian Willaert becomes choirmaster of Saint Mark's, Venice; multiple choirs and addition of instrumental music are Venetian innovations to liturgical music
	1547 Michelangelo appointed architect of Saint Peter's; apse and dome begun 1547	
1554 Cellini casts bronze *Perseus* in Florence **1564** Death of Michelangelo **1576** Titian dies of plague	**1592** Michelangelo's dome for Saint Peter's finished by Giacomo della Porta	**1567** Palestrina, *Missa Papae Marcelli* **1571–1594** Palestrina, choirmaster of Sistine Choir, in charge of musical reform for Vatican **1603** Victoria, *Requiem Mass for the Empress Maria*

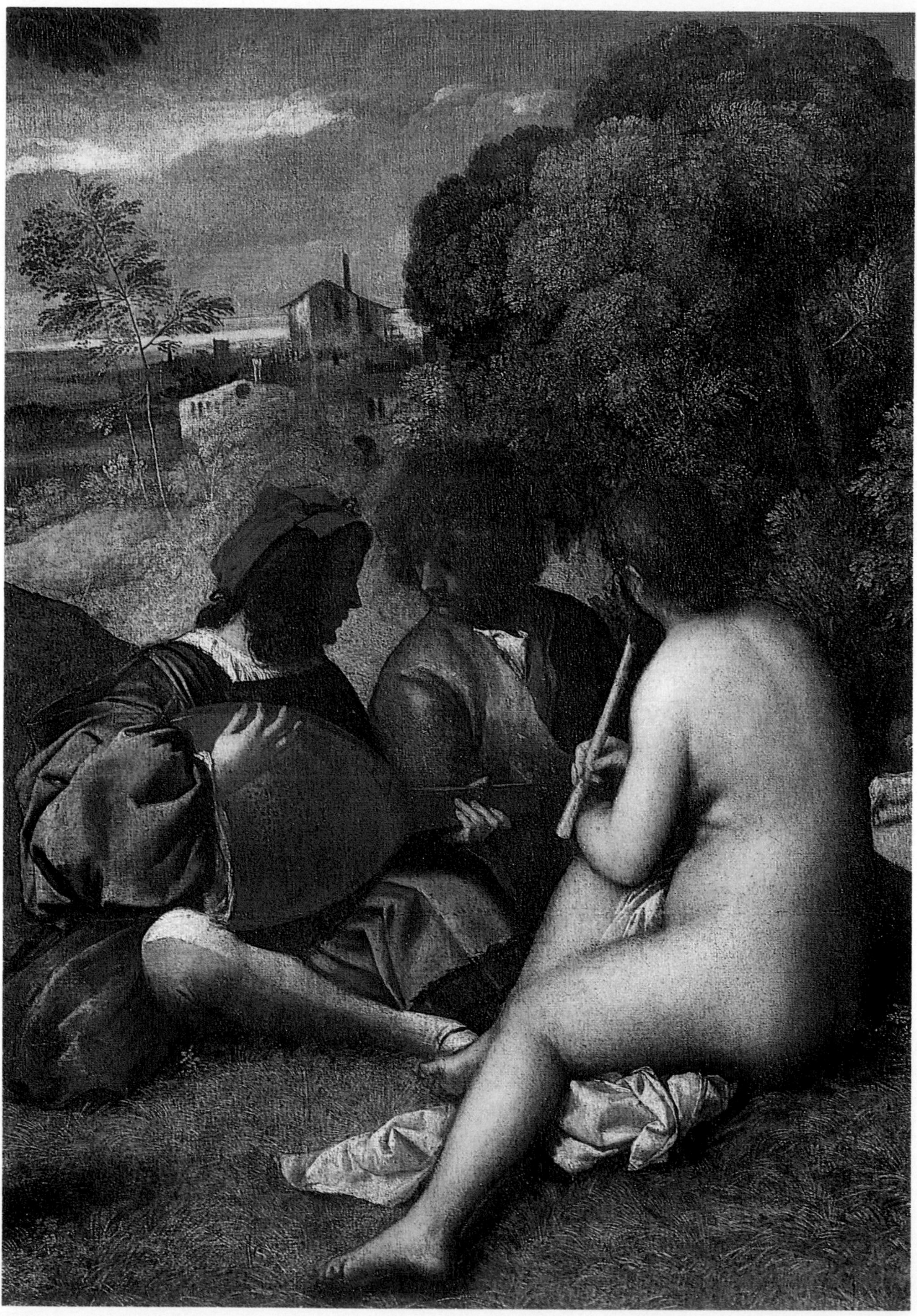

C H A P T E R

11
THE HIGH RENAISSANCE IN ITALY

POPES AND PATRONAGE

ARTISTS MUST WORK where their art is appreciated and their labors rewarded. Florence in the 15th century, shaped by the generous and refined patronage of the Medici and others, was an extremely congenial place for the talented artist. But when the political power of the Medici declined in the last decade of the century, many major artists inevitably migrated or were summoned to other centers of wealth and stability. The papal court at the Vatican in Rome was preeminently such a center.

In the 15th century (and even earlier) artists found rewarding work at the Vatican. Pope Sixtus IV (reigned 1471–1484) commissioned many artists famous in Florence—among them Ghirlandaio, Botticelli and Perugino—to fresco the side walls of the Sistine Chapel, named for himself, as well as work on other projects that caught his artistic fancy. Not the least of these projects was the enlargement and systematization of the Vatican Library.

The period known as the High Renaissance really began, however, in 1503, when a nephew of Sixtus IV became Pope Julius II (died 1513); both were members of the della Rovere family. Pope Julius was a fiery man who did not hesitate to don full military armor over his vestments and lead his papal troops into battle. Thanks to the influence of his papal uncle, he appreciated the fine arts, indulging his artistic tastes with the same single-mindedness that characterized his military campaigns. It was Pope Julius—called by his contemporaries *il papa terribile* (the awesome pope)—who summoned both Raphael Sanzio and Michelangelo Buonarroti to Rome.

Raphael

Raphael Sanzio (1483–1520) was born in Urbino, a center of humanist learning east of Florence dominated by the court of the Duke of Urbino. His precocious talent was first nurtured by his father, a painter, whose death in 1494 cut short the youth's education. The young Raphael then went to Perugia as an apprentice to the painter Perugino. Here his talents were quickly recognized. In 1505, at the age of twenty-two, he moved on to Florence, where he worked for three years.

During his stay in Florence, Raphael painted a large number of madonnas in a style that has

TABLE 11.1 Some Renaissance Popes of the 16th Century

Julius II (1503–1513). Of the della Rovere family; patron of Raphael and Michelangelo.

Leo X (1513–1521). Son of Lorenzo the Magnificent; patronized Michelangelo. Excommunicated Martin Luther.

Hadrian VI (1522–1523). Born in the Netherlands; a ferocious reformer and the last non-Italian pope until the 1970s.

Clement VII (1523–1534). Bastard grandson of Lorenzo de' Medici; commissioned the Medici tombs in Florence. Excommunicated Henry VIII. Commissioned *The Last Judgment* for the Sistine Chapel just before his death.

Paul III (1534–1549). Commissioned Michelangelo to build the Farnese Palace in Rome. Called the reform Council of Trent, which first met in 1545.

Julius III (1550–1555). Patron of the composer Palestrina. Confirmed the Constitutions of the Jesuits in 1550. Appointed Michelangelo as chief architect of St. Peter's.

Marcellus II (1555). Reigned as pope twenty-two days. Palestrina composed the *Missa Papae Marcelli* in his honor.

Paul IV (1555–1559). Began the papal reaction against the Renaissance spirit. A fanatical reformer; encouraged the Inquisition and instituted the *Index of Forbidden Books* in 1557.

11.1 Raphael. *Madonna of the Meadow.* 1506. Oil on panel, 44½" × 34¼" (113 × 87 cm). Kunsthistorisches Museum, Vienna. The infant John the Baptist kneels at the left of the picture in homage to the Christ child, who stands before his mother.

become almost synonymous with his name. The *Madonna of the Meadow* [11.1] is typical. In this painting Raphael arranged his figures in a pyramidal configuration to create a believable and balanced space. This geometrical device, which had already been popularized by Leonardo da Vinci, was congenial to the Renaissance preoccupation with rationally ordered composition. More important than the arrangement of shapes, however, is the beautiful modeling of the human forms, especially the figures of the two children, and the genuine sweetness and warmth conveyed by the faces. The head of the Madonna is peaceful and luminous, while the infant Christ and Saint John convey a somewhat more playful mood. The very human quality of the divine figure is Raphael's trademark.

11.2 Raphael. *School of Athens.* 1510–1511. Fresco, 26 × 18' (7.92 × 5.48 m). Stanza della Segnatura, Vatican Palace, Rome.

Raphael left Florence for Rome in 1508. By the following year, Pope Julius, whom Raphael later caught in an unforgettably fine portrait, had him working in the Vatican on a variety of projects. The pope, who genuinely loved Raphael, commissioned him to decorate various rooms of his palace. Raphael spent the rest of his brief life working on these projects and filling assorted administrative posts for the papacy, including, at one time, the office of architect of Saint Peter's Basilica and at another time superintendent of the Vatican's collection of antiquities.

One of Raphael's most outstanding works and certainly one of the most important for defining the meaning of the 16th-century Renaissance in Rome is a large fresco executed in 1510–1511 on the wall of the Stanza della Segnatura, an office in the Vatican Palace where documents requiring the pope's signature were prepared. Called now the *School of Athens* [11.2], the fresco is a highly symbolic homage to philosophy that complements Raphael's similar frescoes in the same room that symbolize poetry, law, and theology.

The *School of Athens* sets the great philosophers of antiquity in an immense illusionistic architectural framework that must have been at least partially inspired by the impressive ruins of Roman baths and basilicas, and perhaps by the new Saint Peter's, then under construction. Raphael's fresco depicts Roman barrel vaulting, coffered ceilings, and broad expanses not unlike the still-existing baths of ancient Rome. Occupying the center of the fresco, in places of honor framed by the receding lines of the architecture as a device to focus the viewer's eye, are the two greatest ancient Greek philosophers, Plato and Aristotle. Plato holds a copy of the *Timaeus* in one hand and with the other points to the heavens, the realm of ideal forms. Aristotle holds a copy of his *Ethics* and points to the earth, where his science of empirical observation must begin. Clustered about the two philosphers in varying poses and at various distances are other great figures of antiquity. Diogenes sprawls in front of the philosophers, while Pythagoras calculates on a slate and Ptolemy holds a globe. At the right, the idealized figure of Euclid with his compass is actually a portrait of Raphael's Roman protector, the architect Bramante. Raphael himself, in a self-portrait, looks out at the viewer at the extreme lower-right corner of the fresco.

Raphael's *School of Athens* reflects a high degree of sensitivity to ordered space, a complete ease with classical thought, obvious inspiration from the Roman architectural past, a brilliant sense of color and form, and a love for intellectual clarity—characteristics that could sum up the Renaissance ideal. That such a fresco should adorn a room in the Vatican, the center of Christian authority, is not difficult to explain. The papal court of Julius II shared the humanist conviction that philosophy is the servant of theology and that beauty, even if derived from a pagan civilization, is a gift of God and not to be despised. To underscore this point, Raphael's homage to theology across the room, his fresco called the *Disputà*, shows in a panoramic form similar to the *School of Athens* the efforts of theologians to penetrate divine mystery.

The Transfiguration was Raphael's last work, left unfinished at his death [11.3]. A great scene, evenly divided between the airy transcendence of the transfigured Christ, flanked by Old Testament figures, and overpoweringly blinded apostles and the rest of the world on the darker level of the earth is still held together with a great sense of balanced activity. This painting is usually seen as one of the great moments of the Roman High Renaissance.

11.3 Raphael. *The Transfiguration.* 1517. Tempera panel. 15'1½" × 9'1½" (4.6 × 2.8 m). Vatican Museum, Rome.

Michelangelo

In the lower center of Raphael's *School of Athens* is a lone figure leaning one elbow on a block of marble and scribbling, taking no notice of the exalted scene about him. Strangely isolated in his stonecutter's smock, the figure has recently been identified, at least tentatively, as Michelangelo. If the identification is correct, this is the younger artist's act of homage to the solitary genius who was working just a few yards away from him in the Sistine Chapel.

Michelangelo Buonarroti (1475–1564) was called to Rome in 1505 by Pope Julius II to create for him a monumental tomb. We have no clear sense of what the tomb was to look like, since over the years it went through at least five conceptual revisions. Certain features, however, at least in the initial stages, are definite. It was to have three levels; the bottom level was to have sculpted figures representing Victory and bound slaves. The second level was to have statues of Moses and Saint Paul as well as symbolic figures of the active and contemplative life—representative of the human striving for, and reception of, knowledge. The third level, it is assumed, was to have an effigy of the deceased pope.

The tomb of Pope Julius II was never finished. Michelangelo was interrupted in his long labors by both Pope Julius himself and, after the pope's death, the popes of the Medici family, who were more concerned with projects glorifying their own family. What was finished of the tomb represents a twenty-year span of frustrating delays and revised schemes. Even those finished pieces provide no sense of the whole, but they do represent some of the highest achievements of world art.

One of the finished pieces is the *Moses* [11.4] begun after the death of Julius in 1513. We easily sense both the bulky physicality of Moses and the carefully modeled particulars of musculature, drapery, and hair. The fiercely inspired look on the face of Moses is appropriate for one who has just come down from Mount Sinai after seeing God. The face radiates both divine fury and divine light. It is often said of Michelangelo that his works can overwhelm the viewer with a sense of awesomeness; Italians speak of his *terribilità*. If any single statue has this awesomeness, it is the *Moses*.

The highly finished quality of the *Moses* should be compared with the roughness of the *Captives* [11.5], the four figures Michelangelo worked on for the tomb of Julius in Florence in 1527–1528. There is no evidence that Michelangelo intended to leave these figures in so crude a state. Nevertheless, these magnificent works give a visual demonstration of the sculptor's methods. Michelangelo sometimes said that a living figure was concealed in a block of marble and that only the excess needed to be carved away to reveal it. The truth of the Neoplatonic notion that ideal form struggles to be freed from the confines of gross matter can almost be seen in these figures. A close examination reveals the bite marks of the sculptor's chisel as he worked to reveal each living figure by removing hard marble. Seldom do we have a chance, as we do here, to see the work of a great artist still unfolding.

11.4 Michelangelo. *Moses.* 1513–1515. Marble, height 8'4" (2.54 m). San Pietro in Vincoli, Rome. The horns on the head of Moses represent rays of light; the use of horns instead of rays is based on a mistranslation in the Latin Vulgate Bible.

It is not clear where the *Captives* fit into the overall plan of the tomb of Julius. It is most likely that

11.5 Michelangelo. Boboli *Captive.* 1527–1528. Marble, height 7'6½" (2.3 m). Accademia, Florence. These captives once stood in the Boboli Gardens of Florence, hence their name.

11.6 Drawing of tomb of Julius II. After Michelangelo, by his pupil Giacomo Rocchetti. Brown ink, 22½ × 15¼" (57 × 39 cm). Kupferstichkabinett, State Museums, Berlin. This is only one of many projected plans for the tomb of Julius. Note the slaves/captives at the bottom level and Moses on the right at the second level. The semirecumbent figure of the deceased pope is supported by angelic figures with an allegorical figure of Victory overhead in the center.

they were meant to serve as corner supports for the bottom level of the tomb, writhing under the weight of the whole [11.6]. Whatever was the ultimate plan for these figures, they are a stunning testament to the monumentally creative impulse of Michelangelo the sculptor.

Michelangelo had hardly begun work on the pope's tomb when Julius commanded him to fresco the ceiling of the Sistine Chapel to complete the work done in the previous century under Sixtus IV. But Michelangelo resisted the project (he actually fled Rome and had to be ordered back by papal edict). He considered himself a sculptor, and there were technical problems presented by the shape of the ceiling. Nevertheless, he gave in and in three years (1508–1511) finished the ceiling. He signed it "Michelangelo, Sculptor" to remind Julius of his reluctance and his own true vocation.

The ceiling [11.7] is as difficult to describe as it is to observe when standing in the Sistine Chapel. The overall organization consists of four large triangles at the corners; a series of eight triangular spaces on the outer border; an intermediate series of figures; and nine central panels (four larger than the other five), all bound together with architectural motifs and nude male figures. The corner tirangles depict heroic action in the Old Testament (Judith beheading Holofernes; David slaying Goliath; Haman punished for his crimes; the rod of Moses changing into a serpent), while the other eight triangles depict the biblical ancestors of Jesus Christ. The ten major intermediate figures are alternating portraits of pagan sibyls (prophetesses) and Old Testament prophets. The central panels are scenes from the book of Genesis. The one closest to the altar shows God dividing darkness from light and the one at the other end shows the

11.7 Michelangelo. Ceiling, Sistine Chapel. 1508–1512. Fresco, 44 × 128' (13.41 × 39.01 m). Vatican Palace, Rome.

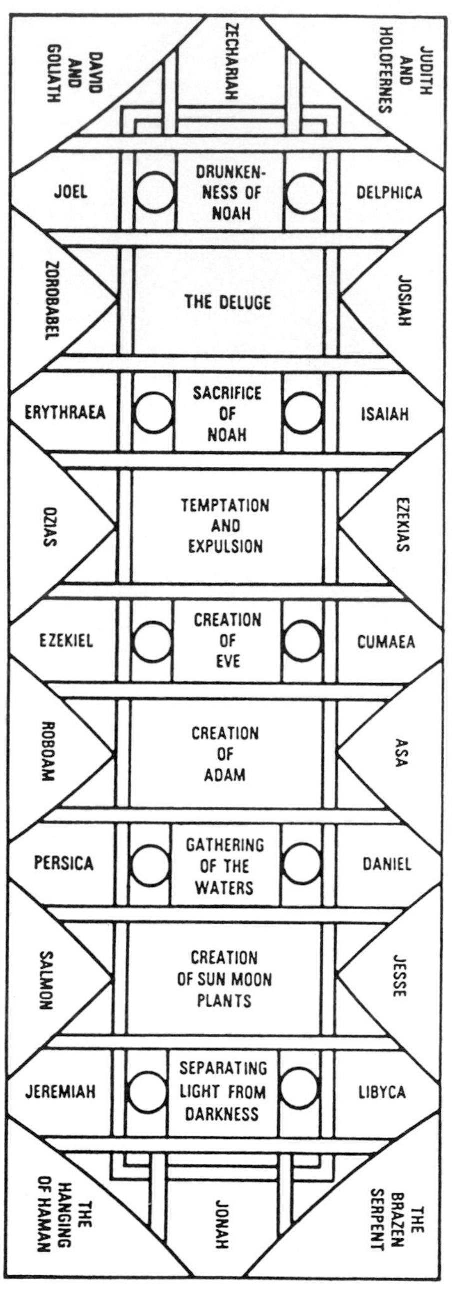

11.8 Schematic drawing of the iconographic plan of the Sistine ceiling. The corner triangles are called the *vele* (Italian "sails").

drunkenness of Noah (Genesis 9:20–27). This bare outline oversimplifies what is actually a complex, intricate design [11.8].

Michelangelo conceived and executed this huge work (128 × 44', or 39 × 13.4 m) as a single unit. Its overall meaning is a problem. The issue has engaged historians of art for generations without satisfactory resolution. Any attempt to formulate an authoritative statement must include a number of elements:

1. Michelangelo's interest in the Neoplatonism he had studied as a youth in Florence. Many writers have noted the Neoplatonic roots of his interest in the manipulation of darkness and light (the progression of darkness to light from the outer borders to the center panels; the panel of God creating light itself), the liberation of spirit from matter (the souls represented by nudes; the drunkenness of Noah, symbolic of humanity trapped by gross matter and thereby degraded),

11.9 Michelangelo. *Creation of Adam*, detail of the Sistine ceiling. 1508–1512. Compare the figure of Adam with the figure of David (p. 21) to get a sense of Michelangelo's concept of musculature.

and the numerous geometrical allusions done in triads, a triple division being much loved in Neoplatonic number symbolism.

2. The Christian understanding of the Old Testament as a work pointing to the coming of Christ, combined with the notion that even pagan prophets were dimly prophetic figures of Christ.
3. The complex tree symbolism in seven of the nine central panels, which refer to the symbolism of the tree in the Bible (the tree of good and evil in the Genesis story, the tree of the Cross, and so forth), as well as being allusions to the pope's family name, which happened to be della Rovere (of the oak tree).
4. The traditional theories of the relationship of the world of human wisdom (represented by the sibyls) and God's revelation (represented by the prophets).

In the panel depicting the *Creation of Adam* [11.9], to cite one specific example, many of these elements come together. A majestically muscular Adam rises, as if from sleep, from the bare earth as God stretches forth his creative finger to call him into being. God's left arm circles a woman and child who represent simultaneously Eve and her children and, by extension, the New Eve, who is the Blessed Virgin. Adam is a prefigurement of Christ. Below Adam a youth holding a cornucopia spilling forth leaves and acorns (symbols of the della Rovere family) stands just above the Persian sibyl. Stylistically, the fresco demonstrates Michelangelo's intense involvement with masculine anatomy seen as muscular monumentality. His ability to combine great physical bulk with linear grace and a powerful display of emotion fairly well defines the adjective *Michelangelesque,* applied to many later artists who were influenced by his style.

The full force of that Michelangelesque style can be seen in the artist's second contribution to the Sistine Chapel: a *Last Judgment* he painted on the wall behind the main altar between the years 1534 and 1541 [11.10]. A huge fresco marking the end of the world when Christ comes back as judge, *The Last Judgment* shows the Divine Judge standing in the upper center of the scene with the world being divided into the Dantean damned at the bottom and those who are called to glory above. Into that great scene Michelangelo poured both his own intense religious vision and a reflection of the troubled days within which he lived. It was, after all, a Rome which had already been sacked in 1527 and a church which had been riven by the Protestant Reformation in the North.

Under the patronage of Popes Leo X and Clement VII—both from the Medici family—Michelangelo worked on another project, the Medici Chapel in the Florentine church of San Lorenzo. This chapel is particulary interesting because Michelangelo designed and executed both the sculptures and the chapel in which they were to be placed. Although Michelangelo first conceived the project in 1519, he worked on it only in fits and

11.10 Michelangelo. *The Last Judgment,* Sistine Chapel, the Vatican. (1534–1541). The loincloths on the figures were added later to appease the puritan sensibilities of post-Reformation Catholicism. The figure in the flayed skin of Saint Bartholomew is a self-portrait of the painter.

11.11 Michelangelo. Medici Chapel. 1519–1534. Church of San Lorenzo, Florence. It is not clear that the statues of the Madonna and saints were finished by Michelangelo himself.

starts from 1521 to 1534. He never completely finished the chapel. In 1545 some of his students put the statues into place.

The interior of the Medici Chapel [11.11] echoes Brunelleschi's Pazzi Chapel with its dome, its use of a light greyish stone called *pietra serena,* its classical decoration, and its very chaste and severe style. The plan envisioned an altar at one end of the chapel and opposite it, at the other end, statues of the Madonna and Child with Saints Cosmas and Damian. The saints were the patrons of physicians, an allusion to the name *Medici,* which means "the doctor's family." At the base of these statues are buried in utter simplicity the bodies of Lorenzo the Magnificent and his brother Giuliano. On opposite walls are niches with idealized seated figures of relatives of Lorenzo the Magnificent, the Dukes Lorenzo and Giuliano de' Medici, in Roman armor. Beneath each are two symbolic figures resting on a sarcophagus, *Night* and *Day* and *Dawn* and *Dusk.*

This great complex, unfinished like many of Michelangelo's projects, is a brooding meditation on the shortness of life, the inevitability of death, and the Christian hope for resurrection. Both the stark decoration of the chapel and the positioning of the statues (Duke Lorenzo seems always turned to the dark with his head in shadow while Duke Giuliano seems more readily to accept the light) form a mute testament to the rather pessimistic and brooding nature of their creator. When Michelangelo had finished the figure of *Night* [11.12], a Florentine poet named Strozzi wrote a poem in honor of the statue, with a pun on the name Michelangelo:

11.12 Michelangelo. *Night,* detail of the tomb of Giuliano de' Medici. 1519–1534. Marble, length 6'4½" (1.94 m). The owl and the mask under the recumbent figure are emblems of night and dreams.

The Night you see sleeping in sweet repose
Was carved in stone by an angel.
Because she sleeps, she has life.
If you do not believe this, touch her and
She will speak.

Michelangelo, an accomplished poet in his own right, answered Strozzi's lines with a pessimistic rejoinder:

Sleep is precious; more precious to be stone
When evil and shame are abroad;
It is a blessing not to see, not to hear.
Pray, do not disturb me. Speak softly!

The New Saint Peter's

In 1506 Pope Julius II, in a gesture typical of his imperious nature, commissioned the architect Donato Bramante (1444–1514) to rebuild Saint Peter's Basilica in the Vatican. Old Saint Peter's had stood on the Vatican hill since it was first constructed more than a thousand years earlier, during the time of the Roman emperor Constantine. By the early 16th century it had suffered repeatedly from roof fires, structural stresses, and the simple ravages of time. In the minds of the Renaissance "moderns" it was a shaky anachronism.

Bramante's design envisioned a central domed church with a floor plan in the shape of a Greek cross with four equal arms [11.13]. The dome would have been set on a columned arcade with an exterior columniated arcade, called a *peristyle,* on the outer perimeter of the building. Any of the four main doors was to be directly across from a *portal* or door on the opposite side. This central plan was not executed in Bramante's lifetime, but a small chapel he built in 1502 next to the Church of San Pietro in Montorio, Rome, may give us a clue as to what Bramante had in mind. This *tempietto* (little temple) is believed to have been done in a style similar to what Bramante wanted later for Saint Peter's.

After Bramante's death a series of architects, including Raphael and Sangallo, worked on the mas-

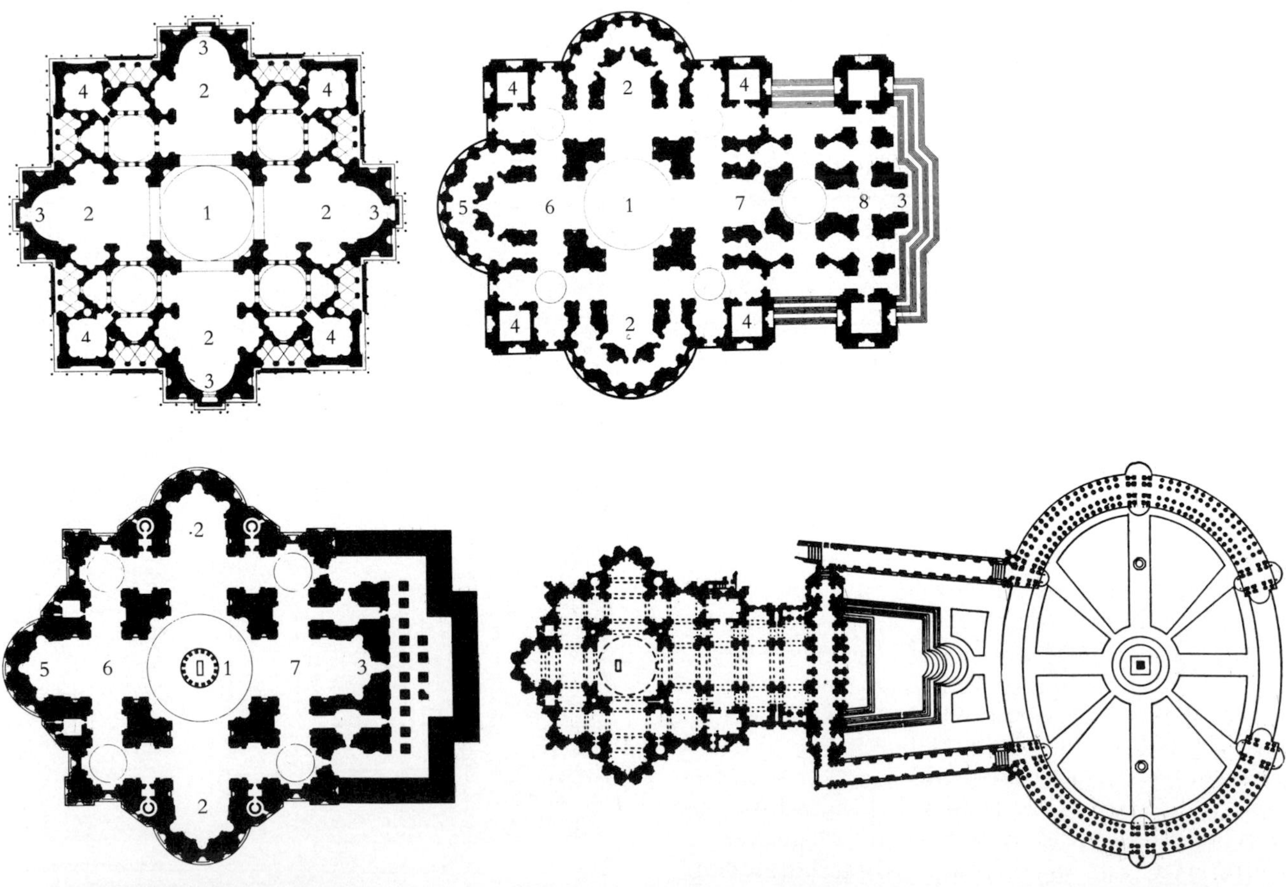

11.13 Floor plans for the new Saint Peter's Basilica, Rome. Maderna's final additions, especially the elongated nave, narthex, and large façade, obscured Michelangelo's original design. (1) Area of papal altar under dome. (2) Transept. (3) Portal. (4) Chapel (not all are identified). (5) Apse. (6) Choir. (7) Nave. (8) Narthex. (a) Bernini's *piazza,* done in 1656.

CONTEMPORARY VOICES

Donna Vittoria and Michelangelo

Donna Vittoria Colonna to Michelangelo:

Most honored Master Michelangelo, your art has brought you such fame that you would perhaps never have believed that this fame could fade with time or through any other cause. But the heavenly light has shone into your heart and shown you that, however long earthly glory may last, it is doomed to suffer the second death.

Michelangelo's poem on this theme:

I know full well that it was a fantasy
That made me think that art could be made into
An idol or a king. Though all men do
This, they do it half-unwillingly.
The loving thoughts, so happy and so vain,
Are finished now. A double death comes near—
The one is sure, the other is a threat.

An exchange between Michelangelo's friend and spiritual adviser (for whom he made some small sculptures and drawings, according to Vasari) and the artist. She was the recipient of a number of his poems.

sive project. Both these architects added a nave and aisles. In 1546 Michelangelo was appointed architect, since the plans previously drawn up seemed unworkable. Michelangelo returned to Bramante's plan for a central domed Greek cross church but envisioned a ribbed arched dome somewhat after the manner of the cathedral in Florence but on a far larger scale.

The present Saint Peter's seen from the front gives us no clear sense of what Michelangelo had in mind when he drew up his plans. Michelangelo's church had a long nave and a façade added by Carlo Maderna in the early 17th century. The colonnaded piazza was completed under the direction of Gian Lorenzo Bernini in 1663, almost a century after Michelangelo's death. Michelangelo lived to see the completion of the drum which was to support his dome. The dome itself was raised some thirty years after his death by Giacomo della Porta. The best way to understand what Michelangelo intended is to view Saint Peter's from behind, from the Vatican Gardens, where one can see the great dome looming up over the arms of the Greek cross design [11.14].

THE HIGH RENAISSANCE IN VENICE

The brilliant and dramatic outbreak of artistic activity in 16th-century Rome and Florence does not diminish the equally creative art being done in the Republic of Venice to the north. While Rome excelled in fresco, sculpture, and architecture, Venice was famous for its tradition of easel painting. Venice's impressive cosmopolitanism derived from its position as a maritime port and its trading tradition.

Because of the damp atmosphere of their watery city, Venetian painters quickly adopted oil painting, which had first been popularized in the north. Oil painting gave the artist unparalleled opportunities to enrich and deepen color by the application of many layers of paint. Oil painting in general, and

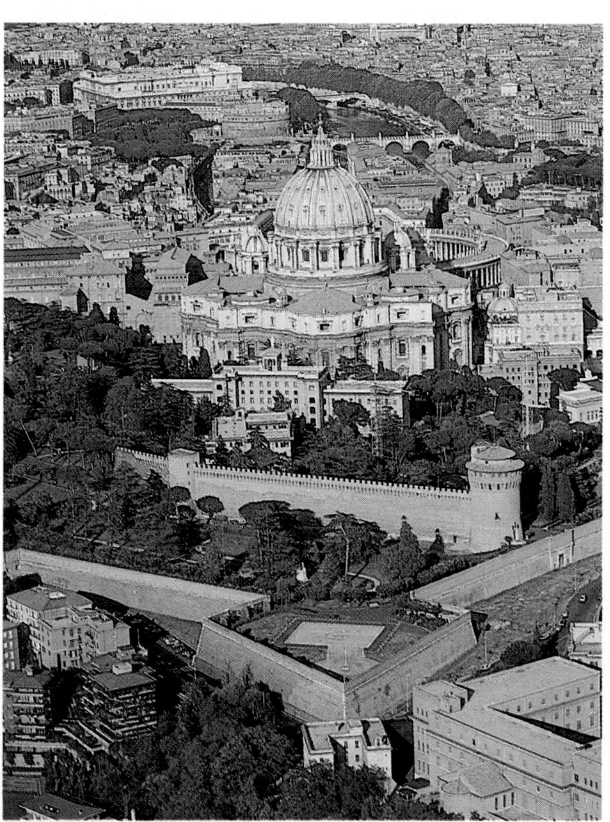

11.14 Michelangelo. Saint Peter's Basilica, Rome, from the southwest. 1546–1564; completed 1590 by Giacomo della Porta. The Vatican Gardens are behind the basilica visible at the lower center of this aerial photograph.

11.15 Giorgione. ***Enthroned Madonna with Saints Liberalis and Francis of Assisi.*** **c. 1500–1505. Oil on panel, 6'6¾" × 5' (1.99 × 1.52 m). Cathedral, Castelfranco. Saint Francis shows the wounds (the so-called *stigmata*) of Christ that he bore on his body.**

Venetian painting in particular, put great emphasis on the brilliance of its color and the subtlety of its light. The sunny environment of Venice, with light reflecting off the ever-present waterways, further inspired the Venetian feel for color and light. Although the generalization is subject to refinement, there is truth in the observation that Venetian painters emphasized color while painters in the south were preoccupied with line. Venetian painters, like their counterparts in northern Europe, had an eye for close detail and a love for landscape (an ironic interest, since Venice had so little of it).

Giorgione

The most celebrated and enigmatic painter in early 16th-century Venice was Giorgio di Castelfranco (c. 1477–1510), more commonly known as Giorgione. His large altarpiece, *Enthroned Madonna with Saints Liberalis and Francis of Assisi* [11.15], painted for the cathedral of his home town of Castelfranco, illustrates many of the characteristics of the Venetian Renaissance style. It is a highly geometric work (using the now-conventional form of the triangle with the Madonna at the apex) typical of Renaissance aesthetics of form. At the same time it shows some idiosyncratic characteristics—the luminous quality of the armor of Saint Liberalis and the minutely rendered landscape. This landscape,

11.16 Giorgione, *Le Concert Champêtre.* c. 1510. Oil on canvas, 3'7¼" × 4'6⅛" (1.05 × 1.38 m). Louvre, Paris. Giorgione's robust nude figures would be much imitated by later baroque painters like Peter Paul Rubens. Giorgione died before he finished the painting, which was completed by Titian.

with its two soldiers in the bend of the road and the receding horizon, echoes painters from the north like Jan van Eyck.

Far more typical of Giorgione's work are his paintings without religious content or recognizable story line or narrative quality. Typical of these is *Le Concert Champêtre* [11.16], done in the last year of the painter's life. The two voluptuous nudes frame two young men who are shadowed but also glowing in their richly rendered costumes. The sky behind threatens a storm, but Giorgione counterposes the storm to a serene pastoral scene that includes a distant farmhouse and shepherds with their flock. What does the painting hope to convey? Why does one woman pour water into the well? Is the lute in the hand of one man or the recorder in the hand of the other woman a clue? We do not know. It may be an elaborate allegory on music or poetry. What is clear is that the painting is a frankly secular homage to the profane joy of life rendered with the richness and lushness of concept and color.

Titian

If Giorgione's life was short, that of his onetime apprentice Tiziano Vecelli (c. 1488–1576), known as Titian, was long. Titian brought the Venetian love for striking color to its most beautiful fulfillment. His work had an impact not only on his contemporaries but also on later Baroque painters in other countries, such as Peter Paul Rubens in Antwerp and Diego Velázquez in Spain.

Titian's artistic output during seventy years of activity was huge. His reputation was such that he was lionized by popes and princes. He was a particular favorite of the Holy Roman emperor Charles V, who granted him noble rank after having summoned him on a number of occasions to work at the royal court. From this tremendous body of work two representative paintings, emblematic of the wide range of his abilities, provide a focus.

The huge panel painting in the Venetian Church of the Frari called *Assumption of the Virgin* [11.17] shows Titian at his monumental best. The swirling color in subtly different shadings and the dramatic gestures of the principals, all of which converge on the person of the Madonna, give a feeling of vibrant upward movement; color and composition define the subject of the assumption of Mary into heaven. The energy in the panel, however, should not distract the viewer from its meticulous spatial relationships. The use of a triangular composition, the subtle shift from dark to light, the lines converging on the Madonna from both above and below are all part of carefully wrought ideas that give the work its final coherence.

11.17 Titian. *Assumption of the Virgin.* 1516–1518. Oil on canvas, 22'6" × 11'8" (6.86 × 3.56 m). Church of the Frari, Venice. Note the three distinct levels in the composition of the painting.

Contrast this *Assumption* with Titian's work of twenty years later, the *Venus of Urbino* [11.18]. The religious intensity of the *Assumption* gives way to the sensual delight of the *Venus* done in homage to feminine beauty from a purely human perspective. The architectural background, evenly divided between light and dark coloration, replaces Giorgione's natural landscapes. The lushness of the

11.18 Titian. *Venus of Urbino.* 1538. Oil on canvas, 3'11" × 5'5" (1.19 × 1.62 m). Uffizi, Florence.

nude figure is enhanced by the richness of the brocade, the small bouquet of flowers, the little pet dog, and the circumspect maids at their tasks around a rich clothes chest in the background. The *Venus of Urbino* reflects a frank love of the human body, which is presented in a lavish artistic vocabulary. It is obvious that Titian painted this work for an aristocratic and wealthy patron.

SPORTS AND GAMES

Carnival

The custom of having festivities just before the beginning of the penitential season of Lent began in the early Middle Ages and endures even to this day in places as diverse as Rio in Brazil and New Orleans in Louisiana. The term *Mardi Gras* is French for "Fat Tuesday"—the last day for eating of meat before the forty-day fast that ends at Easter; the word carnival itself is from the Latin *carnem levare*—to take away meat.

The center of carnival in the papal Rome of the 16th century was the Piazza Navona which was built over what had been a Roman race course. In earlier times the carnival celebrations were held elsewhere in Rome but consisted mainly of licensed delinquency in which, for example, pigs were sent down from a hill for the common people to chase with the winners getting enough pork for a last meal of meat. This was done in an atmosphere of eating, parades, and quasi-sporting events. By 1545 these rustic events gave way to other forms of carnival entertainment.

The humanist popes of the 16th century demanded something far more genteel; they were to serve as a distraction for a city which had been sacked by the soldiers of Charles V in 1527. In the Piazza Navona there were long and elaborate processions (like our contemporary carnival parades) featuring mock Roman chariots or floats, usually displaying a classical motif. These elaborate displays were financed both by the papal court and, it seems, by the guilds and other lay organizations which were in the city. The symbolism was often pedagogical. One float depicted the pope as the mythical Androcles who befriended a lion by pulling a thorn from its paw. The thorn in the Roman pageant represented the pope removing heresy from the world!

Like our carnival parades today, the spectators were often dressed in elaborate costumes as they mingled in the crowd hoping to catch the trinkets thrown from the displays. Carnival was a time for masks to be worn (a particular fancy of the Venetian carnival but also found in Rome) in order to disguise the participants as they let loose with an orgy of celebration prior to the time of austere penance which was enforced both by custom and law. The older tradition of dances, games, and athletic events had given way to formal festivities not unlike those found today on the streets of New Orleans' French Quarter in the period just before Ash Wednesday.

Tintoretto

The last of the Venetian giants was Jacopo Robusti (1518–1594) known more familiarly as Tintoretto (the "little Dyer"—named for his father's occupation). After a short apprenticeship with Titian, Tintoretto worked in his own studio in Venice, a city from which he rarely strayed. It was said that over his studio door he wrote the words "The drawing of Michelangelo and the color of Titian." His most famous work was a huge cycle of frescoes done for the confraternity (called a *scuola*) of San Rocco in Venice. He began work on the frescoes in 1564 and in 1577 was named the Scuola's official painter. The oil painting depicting *The Last Supper* [11.19], done for the church of San Giorgio Maggiore in the last years of his life is a good example of Tintoretto's energetic and dramatic style as well as providing an opportunity for contrasting Tintoretto's work with that of Leonardo. After 1577 Tintoretto was called to decorate the ducal palace in Venice as part of a restoration project following on a terrible fire. Besides allegorical work celebrating the grandeur of the city, Tintoretto and his son Domenico worked on the frescoes of the great hall of the palace contributing a huge oil painting of paradise which is more famous for its size (it covered an 80' wall) than for its beauty.

MANNERISM

There is general agreement that at the end of the second decade of the 16th-century High Renaissance art in Italy, under severe intellectual, psychological, and cultural pressure, gave way to an art style that seemed to be an exaggeration of Renaissance form and a loosening of Renaissance intellectuality. It is not so much that a new school of artists arose but that a mood touched some artists at some point in their careers and captivated others totally. An earlier generation of art historians saw this tendency, called *Mannerism*, as a sign of decadence and decay. Scholarly opinion is less harsh today, viewing Mannerism as a distinct aesthetic to be judged on its own terms.

Mannerism is hard to define and the term is often used without any precise sense. The schema proposed by art historian Frederick Hartt might serve in place of a strict definition:

11.19 Tintoretto. *The Last Supper.* 1592–1594. Oil on canvas. 12' × 18'8" (3.66 × 5.69 m). San Giorgio Maggiore, Venice.

High Renaissance

Content:	Normal, supernormal, or ideal; appeals to universal
Narrative:	Direct, compact, comprehensible
Space:	Controlled, measured, harmonious, ideal
Composition:	Harmonious, integrated, often centralized
Proportions:	Normative, idealized
Figure:	Easily posed, with possibility of motion to new position
Color:	Balanced, controlled, harmonious
Substance:	Natural

Mannerism

Content:	Abnormal or anormal; exploits strangeness of subject, uncontrolled emotion, or withdrawal
Narrative:	Elaborate, involved, abstruse
Space:	Disjointed, spasmodic, often limited to foreground plane
Composition:	Conflicting, acentral, seeks frame
Proportions:	Uncanonical, usually attenuated
Figure:	Tensely posed; confined or overextended
Color:	Contrasting, surprising
Substance:	Artificial

Using Hartt's schema we can detect Mannerist tendencies in some of Michelangelo's later work. The figures of *Night, Day, Dawn,* and *Du*[illegible] seem to reflect the exaggerations of the Mannerist style Hartt describes. The entrance to the Laurentian Library [11.20] in Florence, begun by Michelangelo in 1524 to rehouse the Medici book collection, shows some of these characteristics. Its windows are not windows, its columns support nothing, its staircases with their rounded steps seem agitated and in motion, its dominant lines break up space in odd and seemingly unresolved ways.

Mannerist characteristics show up in only some of Michelangelo's works (*The Last Judgment* fresco in the Sistine Chapel might also be analyzed in this fashion), but some of his contemporaries quite clearly broke with the intellectual unity of the High Renaissance. Two in particular deserve some attention because they so clearly illustrate the Mannerist imagination.

Jacopo Carucci da Pontormo (1494–1557) was an eccentric and reclusive painter who had studied with Leonardo da Vinci in his youth. Pontormo's greatest painting is the *Deposition* [11.21] painted around 1528 for the church of Santa Felicità in Florence. The most striking feature of this work is its shocking colors: pinks, apple greens, washed-

11.20 Michelangelo. Vestibule of the Laurentian Library, Florence. Begun 1524; stairway completed 1559. This library today contains many of the books and manuscripts collected by the Medici family.

11.21 Jacopo Carucci da Pontormo. *Deposition.* c. 1528. Oil on panel, 11' × 6'6" (3.5 × 1.98 m). Capponi Chapel, Church of Santa Felicità, Florence. The twisted figures seem suspended in an airy space of no definite location. Note the odd palette the painter used to emphasize the horror and strangeness of the facial expressions.

11.22 Parmigianino. *Madonna of the Long Neck.* c. 1534. Oil on panel, 7'1" × 4'4" (2.15 × 1.32 m). Uffizi, Florence. Note the odd prophetic figure and the elongated column in the background.

out blues. It is very hard to think of any other painting in the Renaissance to which this stunningly original and exotic work can be compared.

An even more dramatic example of the Mannerist aesthetic is by Francesco Mazzola (1503–1540), called Parmigianino. He painted the *Madonna of the Long Neck* [11.22] for a church in Bologna. The gigantic proportions in the picture space are made all the more exaggerated by forcing the eye to move from the tiny prophetic figure in the background to the single column and then to the overwhelmingly large Madonna. The infant almost looks dead; in fact, his hanging left arm is reminiscent of the dead Christ in Michelangelo's *Pietà.* The Virgin's figure is rendered in a strangely elongated, almost serpentine, fashion. There is something oddly erotic and exotic about her due to the shape of her body, the long fingers, and the great curving "S" of her neck. The implied eroticism is reinforced by the partially clad figures clustered at her side.

How and under what circumstances Mannerism grew and matured is the subject of much debate. Some elements of that debate must include the intellectual and social upheavals of the time (everything from wars to the Protestant Reformation) and the human desire and need to innovate once the problems and potential of a given art style have been fully worked out. In a sense, Mannerism is a testament to the inventiveness and restlessness of the human spirit.

MUSIC IN THE 16TH CENTURY

Music at the Papal Court

The emphasis in this chapter on painting, sculpture, and architecture makes it easy to forget that many of these artistic creations were intended for the service of Roman Catholic worship. It should be no surprise that fine music was subsidized and nurtured in Rome at the papal court. In fact, the active patronage of the popes for both the creation and the performance of music dates back to the earliest centuries of the papacy. Gregorian chant, after all, is considered a product of the interest of Pope Gregory and the school of Roman chant. In 1473 Pope Sixtus IV established a permanent choir for his private chapel, which came to be the most important center of Roman music. Sixtus' nephew Julius II endowed the choir for Saint Peter's, the Julian Choir.

The Sistine Choir used only male voices. Preadolescent boys sang the soprano parts, while older men, chosen by competition, sang the alto, tenor, and bass parts. The number of voices varied then from sixteen to twenty-four (the choir eventually became, and still is, much larger). The Sistine Choir sang *a cappella* (without accompaniment), although we know that the popes enjoyed instrumental music outside the confines of the church. Cellini, for example, mentions that he played instrumental motets for Pope Clement VII.

While Botticelli and Perugino were decorating the walls of the Sistine Chapel, the greatest composer of the age, Josquin des Prez (c. 1440–1521), was in the service of the Sistine Choir, composing and directing music for its members from 1486 to 1494. From his music we can get some sense of the quality and style of the music of the time.

Josquin, who was Flemish, spent only those eight years in Rome, but his influence was widely felt in musical circles. He has been called the bridge figure between the music of the Middle Ages and the Renaissance. Although he wrote madrigals and many masses in his career, it was in the *motet* for four voices, a form not held to traditional usages in the way the masses were, that he showed his true genius for creative musical composition. Josquin has been most praised for homogeneous musical structure, a sense of balance and order, a feel for the quality of the word. These are all characteristics common to the aspirations of the 16th-century Italian humanists. In that sense, Josquin combined the considerable musical tradition of northern Europe with the new intellectual currents of the Italian south.

The Renaissance motet uses a sacred text sung by four voices in polyphony. Josquin divided his texts into clear divisions but disguised them by using overlapping voices so that one does not sense any break in his music. He also took considerable pains to marry his music to the obvious grammatical sense of the words while still expressing their emotional import by the use of the musical phrase. A portion of the motet *Tu Pauperum Refugium* ("Thou Refuge of the Poor") illustrates both points clearly. The text shows the principle of overlapping (look at the intervals at which the voices enter with, for example, the end of the phrase *obdormiat in morte*). Likewise, the descending voices underscore the sense of the words *ne unquam obdormiat in morte anima mea* ("lest my soul sleep in death") in a way that to one musicologist suggests death itself is entering.

ne un-quam ob - dor - mi - at in mor - te
ne un-quam ob-dor - mi - at in mor - te a -
ne un-quam ob - dor - mi - at in mor - te a -
ne un-quam ob - dor - mi - at in mor -
a - ni-ma me - - a.
- ni - ma, a - ni-ma me - - a.
ni-ma me - a.
te a - ni - ma me - - a.

The 16th-century composer most identified with Rome and the Vatican is Giovanni Pierluigi da Palestrina (1525–1594). He came from the Roman hill town of Palestrina as a youth and spent the rest of his life in the capital city. At various times in his career he was the choirmaster of the choir of Saint Peter's (the *cappella Giulia*), a singer in the Sistine Choir, choirmaster of two other Roman basilicas (Saint John Lateran and Saint Mary Major). Finally, from 1571 until his death he directed all music for the Vatican.

Palestrina flourished during the rather reactionary period in which the Catholic Church tried to reform itself in response to the Protestant Reformation by returning to the simpler ways of the past. It should not surprise us, then, that the more than one hundred masses he wrote were very conservative. His polyphony, while a model of order, proportion, and clarity, is nonetheless tied very closely to the musical tradition of the ecclesiastical past. Rarely does Palestrina move from the Gregorian roots of church music. For example, amid the polyphony of his *Mass in Honor of Pope Marcellus (Missa Papae Marcelli)* one can detect the traditional melodies of the Gregorian *Kyrie, Agnus Dei,* and so on. Despite that conservatism, he was an extremely influential composer whose work is still regularly heard in the Roman basilicas. His music was consciously imitated by the Spanish composer Victoria (or Vittoria—c. 1548–1611), whose motet *O Vos Omnes* is almost traditional at Holy Week Services in Rome, and by William Byrd (c. 1543–1623), who brought Palestrina's style to England.

Venetian Music

The essentially conservative character of Palestrina's music can be contrasted with the much more adventuresome situation in Venice, a city less touched by the ecclesiastical powers of Rome. In 1527 a Dutchman, Adrian Willaert, became choirmaster of the Church of Saint Mark's. He in turn trained Andrea Gabrieli and his more famous nephew, Giovanni Gabrieli, who became the most renowned Venetian composer of the 16th century.

The Venetians pioneered the use of multiple choirs for their church services. Saint Mark's regularly used two choirs, called split choirs, which permitted greater variation of musical composition in that the choirs could sing to and against each other in increasingly complex patterns. The Venetians also were more inclined to add instrumental music to their liturgical repertoire. They pioneered in the use of the organ for liturgical music.

EAST MEETS WEST

The Discovery of the New World

When Genoese sailor and explorer Christopher Columbus (1451–1506) died after four voyages to the New World, he was still convinced that he had discovered a sea route to Asia—the goal and dream of many explorers from the Middle Ages on. For all his navigational genius, Columbus was still gripped by the power of the medieval dream of the mythical lands of the East, ruled by the imaginary emperor Prester John.

Columbus' desire to sail westward was fueled in part by the maps and writings of a Florentine humanist named Paolo Toscanelli (1397–1482), who had argued that such a voyage would provide a route to Asia. When Columbus sailed in 1492, in three ships financed by the King and Queen of Spain, he finally reached land in the West (precisely where is still controversial) on October 12 of that year. In the course of his own further voyages he explored much of what we know today as the Caribbean and parts of Central America. Another Florentine, Amerigo Vespucci (1451–1512), in 1504 described these new lands as a continent. A German mapmaker inscribed those lands with his name, from which we get the word *America*.

North America was discovered in this same period from two different directions. John Cabot (1461–1498) sailed from Bristol, England, in 1497 and made landfall the same year at what is present-day Newfoundland in Canada. Juan Ponce de Leon (1460–1521), a member of Columbus' later voyages, sailed out of Puerto Rico in search of gold and a fabled Fountain of Youth. During the Easter season *(Pascua Florida)* of 1513 he sighted and then explored a land he called La Florida. Despite subsequent explorations, the Spanish did not colonize Florida until 1556, when a permanent settlement was made at what is now Saint Augustine.

The explorations of these new lands, fueled by imagination, greed, commercial interest, and religious zeal, would occupy the European powers for subsequent centuries. Their very existence and their vast expanse would change irrevocably the culture of Europe and, in the process, destroy or significantly modify the original peoples, the Europeans not quite understanding where they were, called *Indians*.

The independent possibilities of the organ gave rise to innovative compositions that highlighted the organ itself. These innovations became, in time, standard organ pieces: the prelude, the music played before the services began (called in Italy the *intonazione*), and the virtuoso prelude called the *toccata* (from the Italian *toccare,* "to touch"). The *toccata* was designed to feature the range of the instrument and the dexterity of the performer.

Both Roman and Venetian music were deeply influenced by the musical tradition of the North. Josquin des Prez and Adrian Willaert were, after all, both from the Low Countries. In Italy their music came in contact with the intellectual tradition of Italian humanism. Without pushing the analogy too far it could be said that Rome gave the musician the same Renaissance sensibility that it gave the painter: a sense of proportion, classicism, and balance. The Venetian composers, much like Venetian painters of the time, were interested in color and emotion.

CONTRASTING RENAISSANCE VOICES

Early 16th-century Renaissance culture was a study in contrasts. The period marked a time when some of the most refined artistic accomplishments were achieved, but it was also a period of great social upheaval. The lives of both Raphael and Leonardo ended at precisely the time Luther was struggling with the papacy. In 1527 Rome was sacked by the soldiers of the emperor Charles V in an orgy of rape and violence the city had not seen since the days of the Vandals in the 5th century. It would be simplistic to reduce the period of the High Renaissance to a contrast between cool intellectual sophistication and intensely violent passion; nevertheless, it is true that two of the most interesting writers of the period in Italy do reflect rather precisely those opposing tendencies.

Castiglione

Baldassare Castiglione (1478–1529) served in the diplomatic corps of Milan, Mantua, and Urbino. He was a versatile man—a person of profound learning, equipped with physical and martial skills, and possessed of a noble and refined demeanor. Raphael's famous portrait of Castiglione [11.23] faithfully reflects both Castiglione's aristocratic and intellectual qualities.

While serving at the court of Urbino from 1504 to 1516 Castiglione decided to write *The Courtier,* a task that occupied him for the next dozen years. It

11.23 Raphael. *Baldassare Castiglione.* 1515–1516. Oil on panel, transferred to canvas. 29½ × 25½" (75 × 65 cm). Louvre, Paris. Raphael would have known the famous humanist through family connections in his native Urbino.

was finally published by the Aldine Press in Venice in 1528, a year before the author's death. In *The Courtier,* cast in the form of an extended dialogue and borrowing heavily from the style and thought of ancient writers from Plato to Cicero, Castiglione has his learned friends discuss a range of topics—the ideals of chivalry, classical virtues, the character of the true courtier, the ideals of Platonic love. Posterity remembers Castiglione's insistent plea that the true courtier should be a person of humanist learning, impeccable ethics, refined courtesy, physical and martial skills, and fascinating conversation. He should not possess any of these qualities to the detriment of any other.

The *uomo universale*—the well-rounded person—should do all things with what Castiglione calls *sprezzatura. Sprezzatura,* which is almost impossible to translate into a single English word, means something like effortless mastery. The courtier, unlike the pedant, wears learning lightly, while his mastery of sword and horse has none of the fierce clumsiness of the common soldier in the ranks. The courtier does everything equally well but with an air of unhurried and graceful effortlessness.

Castiglione's work was translated into English by Sir Thomas Hoby in 1561. It exercised an immense influence on what the English upper classes thought the educated gentleman should be. We can detect echoes of Castiglione in some of the plays of Ben Jonson as well as in the drama of William Shakespeare. When in *Hamlet* (III, i), for example, Ophelia cries out in horror at the lunatic behavior of Hamlet (at his loss of *sprezzatura?*) the influence of Castiglione is clear:

Oh, what a noble mind is here o'erthrown!
The courtier's, soldier's, scholar's eye, tongue, sword:
The expectancy and rose of the fair state,
The glass of fashion and the mould of form,
The observed of all observers . . .

The most common criticism of Castiglione's courtier is that he reflects a world that is overly refined, too aesthetically sensitive, and excessively preoccupied with the niceties of decorum and dec-

11.24 Benvenuto Cellini. *Perseus.* 1545–1554. Bronze, height 18' (5.48 m). Loggia dei Lanzi, Florence. Earlier models of this statue, including a first effort in wax, are preserved in the Bargello Museum in Florence.

oration. The courtier's world, in short, is the world of the very wealthy, the very aristocratic, and the most select of the elite. If the reader shares that criticism when reading Castiglione, the *Autobiography of Benvenuto Cellini* should prove a bracing antidote to the niceties of Castiglione.

Cellini

Benvenuto Cellini (1500–1571) was a talented Florentine goldsmith and sculptor whose life, frankly chronicled, was a seemingly never-ending panorama of violence, intrigue, quarrel, sexual excess, egotism, and political machination. His *Autobiography,* much of it dictated to a young apprentice who wrote while Cellini worked, is a vast and rambling narrative of Cellini's life from his birth to the year 1562. We read vignettes about popes and commoners, artists and soldiers, cardinals and prostitutes, assassins and artists, as well as a gallery of other characters from the Renaissance demimonde of Medicean Florence and papal Rome.

Above all, we meet Benvenuto Cellini, who makes no bones about his talent, his love of life, or his taste for violence. Cellini is not one of Castiglione's courtiers. Cellini fathered eight legitimate and illegitimate children; he was banished from Florence for sodomy; imprisoned for assault; fled Rome after murdering a man; and fought on the walls of the Castel Sant' Angelo in Rome during the seige of 1527 in defense of the Medici pope Clement VII. Anyone who thinks of the Renaissance artist solely in terms of proportion, love of the classics, Neoplatonic philosophy, and genteel humanism is in for a shock when encountering Cellini's *Autobiography.*

One particular part of Cellini's book is interesting not for its characteristic bravado or swagger but for its insight into the working methods of an artist. In a somewhat melodramatic account Cellini describes the process of casting the bronze statue of Perseus that actually turned out to be his most famous work [11.24]. It now stands in the Loggia dei Lanzi next to the Palazzo Vecchio in Florence.

Cellini does not belong to the first rank of sculptors, although nobody has denied his skill as a craftsman. The *Perseus,* finished in 1554 for Duke Cosimo I de' Medici, is a highly refined work made more interesting because of Cellini's record of its genesis.

SUMMARY

Art follows patronage, as we have noted. The "high" Renaissance is summed up in the lives and works of three artists: Michelangelo, Raphael, and Leonardo da Vinci. The first two did their most famous work in the Vatican in the 16th century while Leonardo, true to his restless spirit, sojourned there only for a time before he began his wanderings through the courts of Europe. It is their work that gives full meaning to the summation of Renaissance ideals.

When we look at the work of Raphael and Michelangelo under the patronage of the popes, we should not forget that this explosion of art and culture was taking place while a new and formidable revolution was in the making: the Protestant Reformation. While it would be overly simplistic to think that the Renaissance caused the Reformation, it certainly must be seen as a factor—as we will see in the next chapter. Even so, there is a marked shift in the atmosphere in which Michelangelo worked in Rome before 1521 and afterward, when the full force of the Protestant revolt in the North was making itself felt in Rome.

The artistic work in Rome can be profitably contrasted with that which took place in Venice during roughly the same period. The Roman Renaissance was under the patronage of the church. Venetian art and music enjoyed the same patronage source as did Florence in the preceding century: commerce and trade. Venice made its fortune from the sea: The shipping of its busy port looked to both Europe and the Middle East. It was fiercely protective of its independence (including its independence from papal Rome) and proud of its ancient traditions. Even the religious art of Venice had a certain freedom from the kind of art being produced in Rome in the same century because Venice had less contact with the seething ideas current in the century.

Renaissance ideas had also penetrated other areas of Italy. Florence still had its artistic life (although somewhat diminished from its great days in the 15th century) but provincial cities like Parma and Mantua were not without their notables. Much of this artistic activity rested in the courts of the nobility who supplied the kind of life and leisure that made possible the courtier and the court life-style immortalized in the book by Castiglione. The insufficiencies of this court culture would become clear when the religious wars of the 16th century broke out and humanism had to confront the new realities coming from the increasingly Protestant North.

Pronunciation Guide

Bramante: bra-MAHN-tay
Buonarroti: bwon-ah-ROH-tee
Castiglione: KAS-til-YOH-nay
Cellini: che-LEE-nee
Le Concert Champêtre: leh kon-CER sham-PET-reh
Giorgione: jor-JOAN-eh
Josquin des Pres: Joss-KIN-day-PRAY
Laurentian: law-WREN-shen
Palestrina: pal-es-TRIN-ah
Parmigianino: PAR-me-jan-EE-no
Pontormo: pon-TOR-mo
***sprezzatura:*:** spreh-za-TOUR-ah
Strozzi: STROH-zee
tempietto: tem-PYET-toe
Titian: TEA-shan

Exercises

1. If you were to transpose Raphael's *School of Athens* into a contemporary setting, what kind of architecture would you use to frame the scene and whom would you include among the personages in the picture?
2. Critics use the adjective *Michelangeloesque.* Now that you have studied his work, what does that adjective mean to you? Give an all-inclusive definition of the term.
3. Michelangelo's Medici Chapel represents the artist's best attempt to express a permanent tribute to the dead. How does it differ in spirit from such monuments today? (You might begin by comparing it with the Vietnam Memorial in Washington, D.C., or some other such public monument.)
4. Castiglione's concept of *sprezzatura* was an attempt to summarize the ideal of the educated courtier. Is there a word or phrase that would best sum up the character of the well-rounded person today? Do we have a similar ideal? How would you characterize it?
5. Mannerism as an art style contains an element of exaggeration. Can you think of any art form with which we are familiar that uses exaggeration to make its point?
6. Art patronage in the 16th century came mainly from the church and from the wealthy. Are they equally sources of patronage today? What has replaced the church as a source of art patronage today? What does that say about our culture?

Further Reading

D'Amico, John F. *Renaissance Humanism in Papal Rome.* Baltimore: Johns Hopkins, 1983. Good background reading for the art of the period.

Kelly, J. N. D. (ed.). *The Oxford Dictionary of Popes.* New York: Oxford, 1986. A handy compendium of the papacy that includes material about papal patronage of the arts.

Levey, Michael. *High Renaissance.* New York: Penguin, 1975. A handy survey of the period.

Logan, Oliver. *Culture and Society in Venice: 1470–1790.* New York: Scribner's, 1972. A readable and well-illustrated survey.

Morris, James. *The World of Venice.* New York: Harcourt Brace Jovanovich, 1974. One of the best travel books on Venice. Readable, entertaining, and informative.

Partner, Peter. *Renaissance Rome: 1500–1559.* Berkeley: University of California Press, 1976. An excellent paperback social history of the city.

Rosand, David. *Painting in Cinquecento Venice.* New Haven: Yale University Press, 1982. Studies of Titian, Veronese, and Tintoretto.

Stinger, Charles. *The Renaissance in Rome.* Bloomington: Indiana University Press, 1985. A good cultural history.

Summers, David. *Michelangelo and the Language of Art.* Princeton: Princeton University Press, 1982. A scholarly study of the relationship between artistic language and Michelangelo's works.

Wohl, Alice, and Helmut Wohl (eds. and trans.). *Ascanio Condivi's Life of Michelangelo.* Baton Rouge: Louisiana State University Press, 1976. Translation of an early life of Michelangelo with clear illustrations and excellent notes.

	GENERAL EVENTS	LITERATURE & PHILOSOPHY	ART
1494–1500	**1498** da Gama lands in India		**1494–1495** Dürer visits Italy
1500–1525 GENESIS OF THE REFORMATION	**1515–1547** Reign of Francis I in France **1517** Reformation begins in Germany with Luther's 95 Theses, challenging the practice of indulgences **1519–1556** Reign of Charles V as Holy Roman Emperor **1521** Excommunication of Luther by Pope Leo X **1524–1525** Peasants' War in Germany	**1506–1532** Ariosto active in Italy **1509** Erasmus, *The Praise of Folly* **1516** More, *Utopia* **1521** Luther begins translation of Bible into German, published 1534 **1524** Erasmus, *De Libero Arbitrio (On Free Will)*	**1500** Dürer, *Self-Portrait* **early 16th cent.** Italian Renaissance art and thought spread northward **c. 1505–1510** Bosch, *Garden of Earthly Delights*, triptych **1508–1511** Dürer, *Adoration of the Trinity* **1513** Dürer, *Knight, Death and the Devil*, engraving **1515** Grünewald, *Isenheim Altarpiece*
1525–1550 SPREAD OF PROTESTANTISM	**1525** Francis I defeated by Charles V at Pavia **1527** Sack of Rome by Charles V **1534** Henry VIII founds Anglican Church in England when Parliament passes Act of Supremacy **1539** Society of Jesus (Jesuits) founded by Saint Ignatius of Loyola **1545–1564** Council of Trent initiates Counter-Reformation under Jesuit guidance	**1525** Luther, *De Servo Arbitrio (On the Bondage of the Will)* **1530** Budé persuades Francis I to found Collège de France as center for humanism **16th cent.** Humanism spreads, along with interest in scientific inquiry; availability of books increases literacy **1543** Copernicus, *On the Revolution of Celestial Bodies;* Vesalius, *Seven Books on the Structure of the Human Body*	**1525** Altdorfer, *Landscape*, early example of pure landscape painting **1528** Dürer, *Four Books on Human Proportions* **1529** Altdorfer, *Battle of Alexander and Darius* **c. 1530** Clouet, *Portrait of Francis I* **c. 1530–1550** Sacred art denounced as idolatry by reforming iconoclasts **c. 1533–1540** Decorations by Rosso Fiorentino for Palace at Fontainebleau **1539–1540** Holbein the Younger, *Portrait of Henry VIII* **1540–1543** Cellini, *Salt-Cellar*, commissioned by Francis I
1550–1575 GROWTH OF COUNTER-REFORMATION	**1550–1555** Wars between Lutheran and Catholic princes in Germany; ended by Peace of Augsburg in 1555 **1556** Retirement of Charles V **1556–1598** Reign of Philip II in Spain and Netherlands **1558–1603** Reign of Elizabeth in England **1572** Saint Bartholomew's Day Massacre in France	**1559** Pope Paul IV publishes first Index of Prohibited Books	**c. 1562–1567** Bruegel the Elder, *The Triumph of Death, Hunters in the Snow, Peasant Wedding*
1575–1620 RELIGIOUS AND NATIONALISTIC UNREST	**1581** United Provinces of Netherlands declare independence from Spain **1585** England sends troops to support Netherlands against Spain **1588** Philip's Spanish Armada defeated by English **1598** Edict of Nantes establishes religious toleration in France **1600** British found East India Tea Company **1602** Duelling banned in France **1607** English found colony of Virginia in New World **1609** Independence of Netherlands recognized by Spain	**1580** Montaigne's first *Essays* **c. 1587** Marlowe, *Tamburlaine*, tragedy **1590** Sidney, *Arcadia* **1590–1596** Spenser, *The Faerie Queene*, allegorical epic **1590–1610** Drama at height in Elizabethan England **1593** Marlowe, *Dr. Faustus*, tragedy **late 16th–early 17th cent.** Cervantes active in Spain, Jonson in England, Tasso in Italy **c. 1600** Shakespeare, *Hamlet* **c. 1604–1605** Shakespeare, *Othello, King Lear, Macbeth* **1611** *Authorized Version* of Bible **1620** Francis Bacon, *Novum Organum*	**c. 1600** Patronage for sacred art wanes in Reformation countries, fluorishes in Counter-Reformation countries

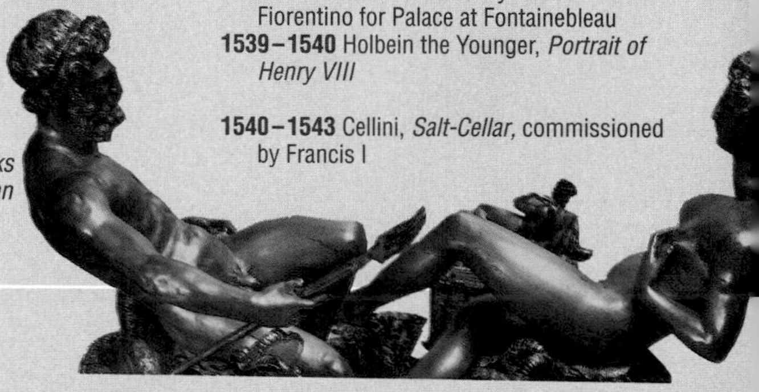

CHAPTER 12

THE RENAISSANCE IN THE NORTH

1548–1549 Goujon, *Fountain of the Innocents,* Louvre, Paris

c. 1590 Hilliard, *Portrait of a Youth,* miniature

ARCHITECTURE

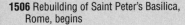

1506 Rebuilding of Saint Peter's Basilica, Rome, begins

1519 Château of Chambord built by Francis I

1546 Lescot and Goujon, Square Court of Louvre, begun

c. 1550 Reformation ends building of elaborate churches in Protestant countries

MUSIC

Vernacular hymns stressed by Reformers; musical elements in Protestant services simplified by Luther to increase comprehension

c. 1510 Isaac and Sendl active in Northern Europe

c. 1520 Marot and Janequin compose *chansons*

c. 1525–1530 *Ein' Feste Burg ist Unser' Gott (A Mighty Fortress Is Our God)*

1544 Gregorian chant is basis for first English-language litany in England

1549 Merbecke, *The Book of Common Praier Noted*

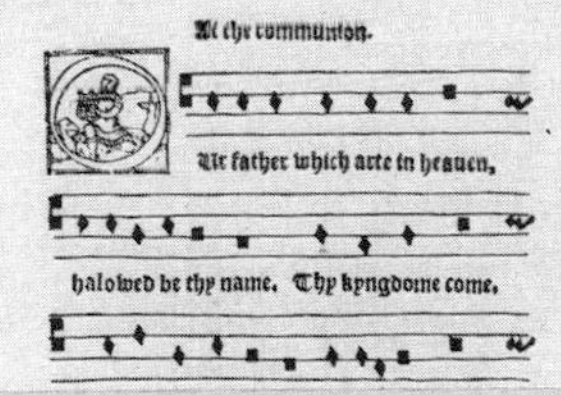

c. 1570 Tallis, English court organist, composes *Lamentations of Jeremiah*

1588 *Musica Transalpina* translated into English

1591 Byrd, *My Ladye Nevells Booke*

late 16th–early 17th cent. English madrigals by Byrd, Morley, and Weelkes follow Italian models; ayres by Dowland

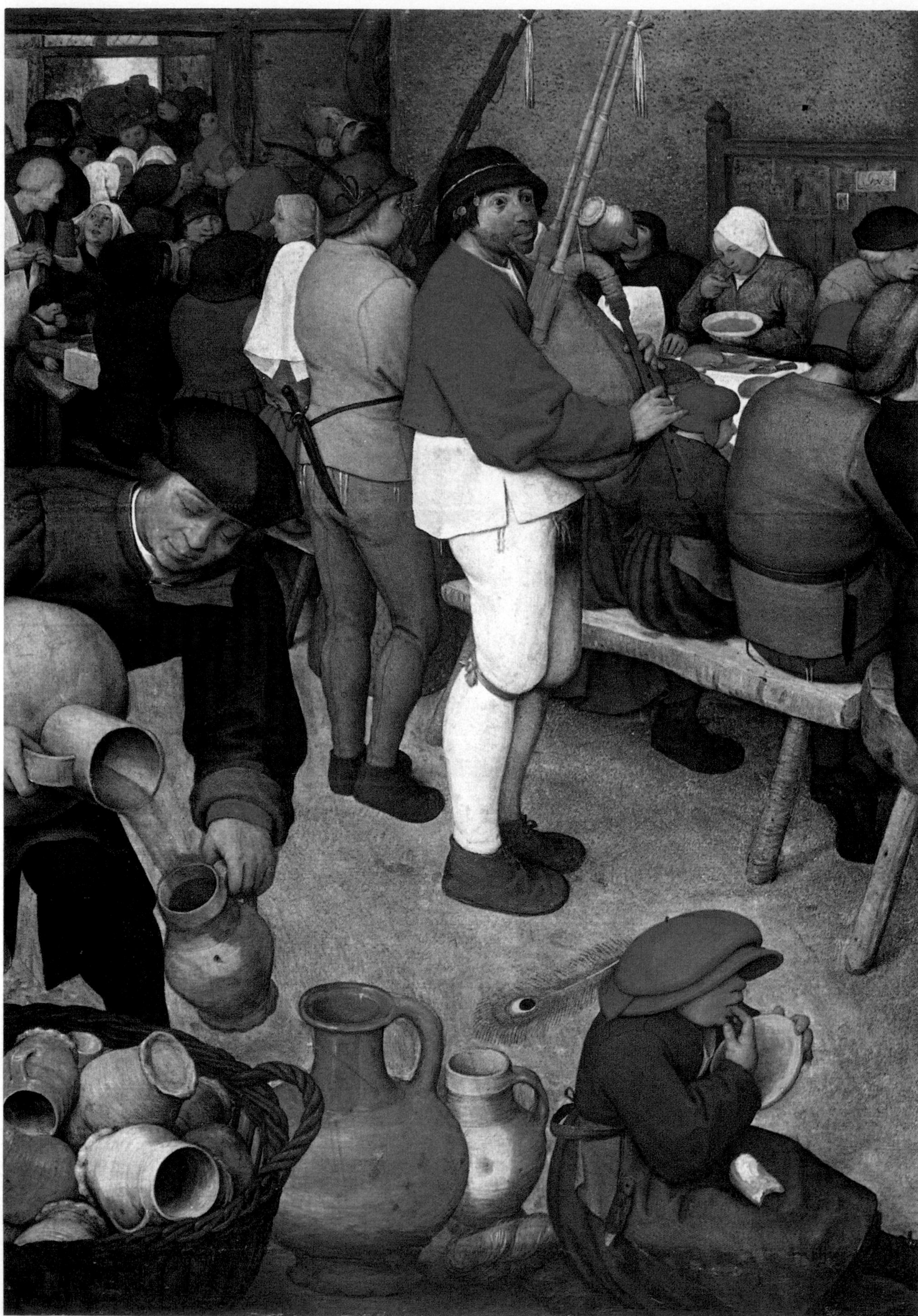

CHAPTER

12 THE RENAISSANCE IN THE NORTH

The ideas and artistic styles that developed in Italy during the 15th and 16th centuries produced immense changes in the cultural life of England, France, Germany, and the Netherlands. As the Renaissance spread beyond the Alps, the new humanism it carried roused northern Europe from its conservative intellectual patterns and offered an alternative to traditional religious doctrines. The infusion of Italian ideas produced a new breadth of vision that was responsible for some of the greatest northern painting and for important developments in music. By the end of the 16th century, under the influence of humanism, a brilliant cultural life had developed in Elizabethan England, where Renaissance English drama achieved its greatest glory in the work of William Shakespeare.

This was not the first time northern Europe and Italy had come into contact. During the 14th century a style of late-Gothic painting reflecting the grace and elegance of courtly life on both sides of the Alps had developed. Known as the International Style, it was popular in both Italy and northern Europe. Furthermore, as early as the beginning of that century German scholars who had gone to study in Italy returned home with a new enthusiasm for classical antiquity. Nor was the northern Renaissance a purely imported phenomenon, the filling of a cultural void by the wholesale adoption of foreign ways and styles. Northern artists drew upon a rich native past and were able to incorporate exciting new ideas from Italy into their own vision of the world. One of the chief characteristics of northern Renaissance art, in fact, was its emphasis on individualism; painters like Albrecht Dürer and Albrecht Altdorfer are as different from each other as they are from the Italian artists who initially influenced them.

The spread of Italian Renaissance ideas to the north was in many respects political rather than cultural. Throughout most of the 16th century the great monarchs of northern Europe vied with one another for political and military control over the states of Italy, and in the process were brought into contact with the latest developments in Italian artistic and intellectual life—and often based their own courts on Italian models. Francis I, who ruled France from 1515 to 1547, made a deliberate attempt to expose French culture to Italian influences by doing everything he could to attract Italian artists to the French court; among those who came were Leonardo da Vinci, Andrea del Sarto (1486–1530), and Benvenuto Cellini [12.1]. Francis and his successors also esteemed literature and scholarship highly. Francis' sister, Marguerite of Navarre, herself a writer of considerable gifts, became the center of an intellectual circle that included many of the finest minds of the age.

The history of Germany is intimately bound up with that of the Hapsburg family. In the first half of the 16th century the same Hapsburg who ruled Germany (under the old name of the Holy Roman Empire) as Charles V ruled Spain at the same time as Charles I. Charles was the principal competitor of Francis I for political domination of Italy, and although his interest in the arts was less cultivated than that of his rival, his conquests brought Italian culture to both Spain and the north [12.2]. On his abdication in 1556 he divided his vast territories between his brother Ferdinand and his son Philip. The Austrian and Spanish branches of the Hapsburg family remained the principal powers in Europe until the 1650s.

For most of the Renaissance, England remained under the dominion of a single family, the Tudors, whose last representative was Elizabeth I. Like her

12.1 Benvenuto Cellini. *The Saltcellar of Francis I.* 1539–1543. Gold, 10¼ × 13⅛" (26 × 33 cm). Kunsthistorisches Museum, Vienna. The male figure is Sea; the female is Land. "Both figures were seated with their legs interlaced, just as the arms of the sea run into the land," Cellini said.

EAST MEETS WEST

Spice Trading in Asia

The Hapsburgs and other rulers and bankers in northern Europe during the 15th and 16th centuries became increasingly powerful through a new source of wealth: trade with Asia. Fine silks, rugs, and spices such as ginger and nutmeg had been imported into Europe throughout the Middle Ages, but always through Muslim middlemen who sold the goods in the principal port cities of the eastern Mediterranean like Alexandria and Constantinople. The first European nation to conquer and occupy territory in Asia was Portugal: In 1498 the Portuguese navigator Vasco da Gama landed on the southwest coast of India. By 1509 fortified trading stations had been built along the Indian coast. From these Portuguese traders traveled to China and the Spice Islands of the Western Pacific.

For all their imperialist determination, however, the Portuguese lacked both the natural resources and the wealth to exchange for the cinnamon and cloves that were becoming increasingly sought after in northern Europe. Many of the Portuguese missions were thus financed by German and Flemish bankers, like the Fuggers of Augsburg. These northern investors provided either loans of cash or supplied in advance, on credit, cargoes of goods to be traded for spices. The gold, silver, copper, lead, and mercury carried to the East was produced mainly in Germany.

The bankers expected a return on their investment in the form of interest. Throughout the Middle Ages, however, the taking of interest was condemned as *usury.* The Catholic Church continued to hold to this prohibition, and Martin Luther in his turn warned against Fuggerism. Nonetheless, the practice was impossible to stop. Theologians began to distinguish between "usury" and "legitimate return." With this development of commerce, patterns of industrial life that lasted until the Industrial Revolution of the 19th century were established throughout northern Europe. The imperialist example of Portugal was soon imitated by other countries; the British East India Tea Company, for example, was founded in 1600.

12.2 Leone Leoni. *Bust of Emperor Charles V.* 1533–1555. Bronze, height 44" (112 cm). Kunsthistorisches Museum, Vienna. The sculptor deliberately portrayed the German ruler as a Roman emperor, thus associating Charles with both Italy and classical antiquity.

fellow rulers, in the course of her long reign (1558–1603) Elizabeth established her court as a center of art and learning. Although the influence of Italian models on the visual arts was less marked in England than elsewhere, revived interest in classical antiquity and the new humanism it inspired is reflected in the works of Shakespeare and other Elizabethan writers.

Although the art of the great northern centers drew heavily on Italy for inspiration, another factor was equally important. The 15th century was a period of almost unparalleled intellectual ferment, in which traditional ideas on religion and the nature of the universe were shaken and often permanently changed. Many of the revolutionary movements of the age were, in fact, northern in origin, and not surprisingly they had a profound effect on the art, music, and literature being produced in the same place and time. While northern artists were being influenced by the styles of their fellow artists south of the Alps, their cultural world was being equally shaped by theologians and scientists nearer home. The intellectual developments of this world form a necessary background to its artistic achievements.

THE REFORMATION

On the eve of All Saints' Day in 1517, a German Augustinian friar, Martin Luther (1483–1546), tacked a parchment containing ninety-five academic propositions (theses) written in Latin on the door of the collegiate church of Wittenberg—the usual procedure for advertising an academic debate [12.3]. Luther's theses constituted an attack on the Roman Catholic doctrine of indulgences (forgiveness of punishment for sins, usually obtained either through good works or prayers along with the payment of an appropriate sum of money); a timely topic since an indulgence was currently

12.3 Lucas Cranach. *Portrait of Martin Luther.* c. 1526. Oil on panel, 15 × 9" (38 × 24 cm). Uffizi Gallery, Florence.

12.4 Hans Holbein the Younger (1497–1543). ***Henry VIII in Wedding Dress.*** **1540. Oil on panel, 32½ × 29" (83 × 74 cm). Galleria Barberini, Rome. Weddings were not uncommon events in Henry's life. This wedding, when he was in his 49th year, as the inscription says, was probably the ill-fated one to his fourth wife, Anne of Cleves (see Figure 12.25).**

being preached near Wittenberg to help raise funds for the rebuilding of Saint Peter's in Rome.

Luther's act touched off a controversy that went far beyond academic debate. For the next few years there were arguments among theologians, while Luther received emissaries and directives from the Vatican as well as official warnings from the pope. Luther did not waver in his criticisms. On June 15, 1520, Pope Leo X (Giovanni de' Medici, son of Lorenzo the Magnificent) condemned Luther's teaching as heretical and on January 3, 1521, excommunicated him from the Catholic Church. The Protestant Reformation had been born.

Luther's reformation principles began to be applied in churches throughout Germany and a rapid and widespread outbreak of other reforming movements was touched off by Luther's example. By 1523 radical reformers far more iconoclastic than Luther began to agitate for a purer Christianity free from any trace of "popery." These radical reformers are often called *anabaptists* because of their insistence on adult baptism even if there had been baptism in infancy (the word means "baptized again"). Many of these anabaptist groups had radical social and political ideas, including pacifism and the refusal to take oaths or participate in civil government, which appealed to the discontent of the lower classes. One outcome was the Peasants' War in Germany, put down with ferocious bloodshed in 1525.

The Reformation was not confined to Germany. In 1523 Zurich, Switzerland, accepted the reformation ideal for its churches. Under the leadership of Ulrich Zwingli (1484–1531) Zurich, and later Berne and Basel, adopted Luther's reforms, including the abolition of statues and images and the right of the clergy to marry. In addition, the system of sacraments was greatly modified and reduced to include only baptism and the Lord's Supper. In Geneva, John Calvin (1509–1564) preached a brand of Protestantism even more extreme than that of either Luther or Zwingli. Calvin's doctrines soon spread north to the British Isles, especially Scotland, under the Calvinist John Knox, and west to the Low Countries, especially Holland. In England, King Henry VIII (born 1491, reigned 1509 –1547), formerly a stout opponent of Lutheranism, broke with Rome in 1534 after he failed to obtain a marital annulment from the pope [12.4]. In 1534 Henry issued the Act of Supremacy, declaring the English sovereign head of the church in England.

By the middle of the 16th century, therefore, Europe—for centuries solidly under the authority of the Church of Rome—was divided in a way that has remained essentially unaltered ever since. Spain and Portugal, Italy, most of France, southern Germany, Austria, parts of eastern Europe (Poland, Hungary, and parts of the Balkans), and Ireland remained Catholic, while most of Switzerland, the British Isles, all of Scandinavia, northern and eastern Germany, and other parts of eastern Europe gradually switched to Protestantism (see map).

Causes of the Reformation

What conditions permitted this rapid and revolutionary upheaval in Europe? The standard answer is that the medieval church was so riddled with corruption and incompetence that it was like a house of cards waiting to be toppled. This answer, while containing some truth, is not totally satisfactory since it does not explain why the Reformation did not happen a century earlier, when similar or worse conditions prevailed. Why had the Reformation not taken place during the 14th century, when there were such additional factors as plague, schisms, and wars as well as incipient reformers clamoring for change?

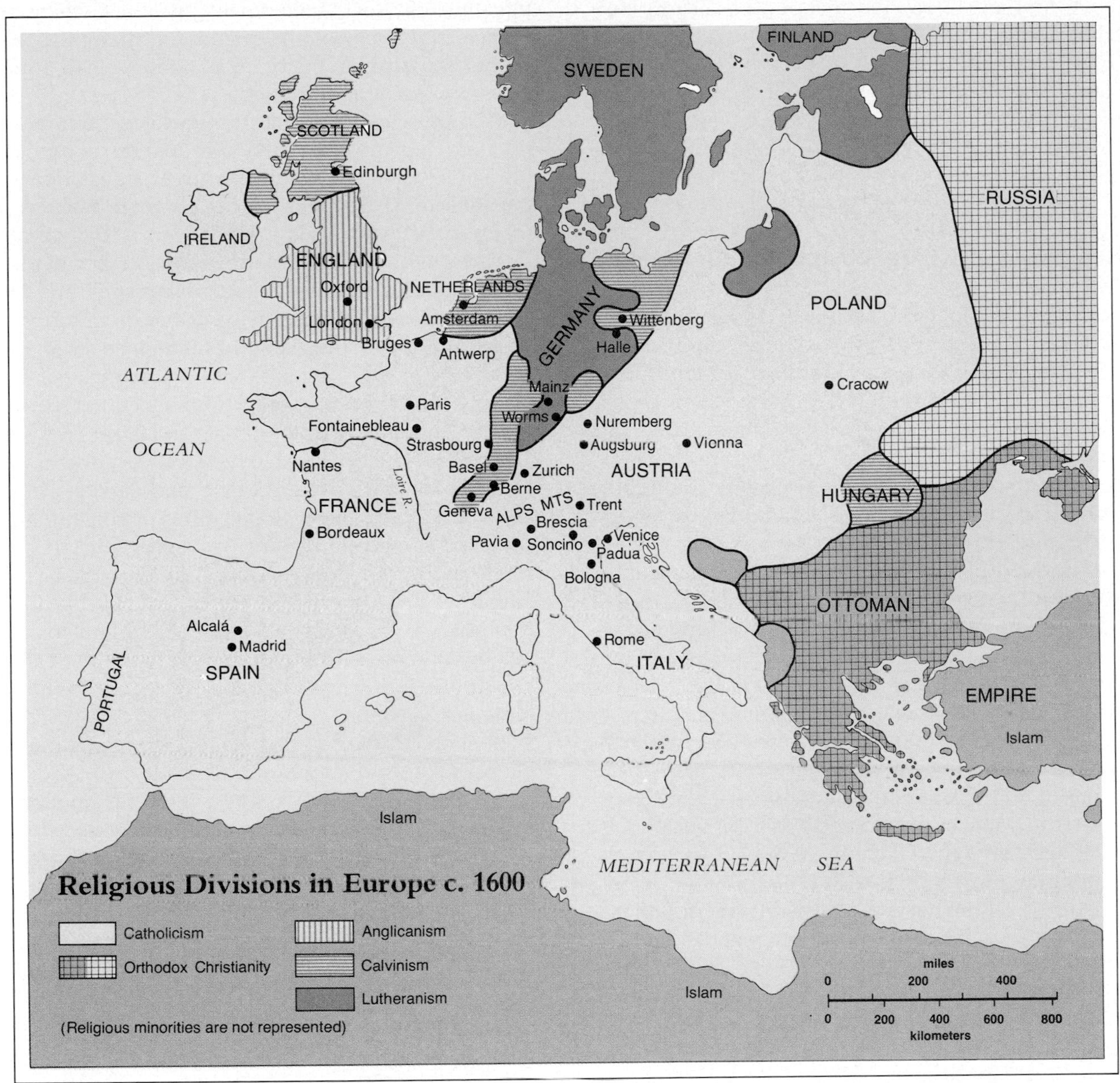

Religious Divisions in Europe c. 1600

The exact conditions that permitted the Reformation to happen are hard to pinpoint, but any explanation must take into account a number of elements that were clearly emerging in the 16th century. First, there was a rising sense of nationalism in Europe combined with increasing resentment at the economic and political demands made by the papacy, many of which ignored the rights of individual countries. Thus Luther's insistence that the German rulers reform the Church because the Church itself was impotent to do so appealed to both economic and nationalistic self-interests.

Second, the idea of reform in the Church had actually been maturing for centuries, with outcries against abuses and pleas for change. Some of the great humanists who were contemporaries of Luther, including Erasmus of Rotterdam, Thomas More in England, and Jacques Lefèvre d'Étaples in France, had also pilloried the excesses of the church. These men, and many of their followers and devoted readers, yearned for a deeper, more interior piety, free from the excessive pomp and ceremony that characterized so much of popular medieval religion. Luther's emphasis on personal conversion and his rejection of much of the ecclesiastical superstructure of Catholicism appealed to the sensibilities of many people. That the reformers to the left of Luther demanded even more rejection of Catholic practices shows how widespread was the desire for change.

Third, there were a number of other factors clustered around the two already mentioned: The low moral and intellectual condition of much of the clergy was a scandal; the wealth and lands of the monastic and episcopal lords were envied. In short, a large number of related economic and political factors fed the impulses of the Reformation.

Renaissance Humanism and the Reformation

The relationship between Renaissance humanism and the Protestant Reformation is significant if complex. With the single exception of John Calvin, none of the major church reformers was a professional humanist, although all of them came into contact with the movement. Luther himself had no early contact with the "new learning," though he utilized its fruits. Nevertheless, humanism as far back as the time of Petrarch shared many intellectual and cultural sentiments with the Reformation. We should note these similarities before treating the wide differences between the two movements.

The reformers and the humanists shared a number of religious aversions. They were both fiercely critical of monasticism, the decadent character of most popular devotion to the saints, the low intellectual preparation of the clergy, and the general venality and corruption of the higher clergy, especially the papal *curia* (the body of tribunals and assemblies through which the pope governed the Church).

Both the humanists and the reformers felt that the scholastic theology of the universities had degenerated into quibbling arguments, meaningless discussions, and dry academic exercises bereft of any intellectual or spiritual significance. In a common reaction both rejected the scholastics of the medieval universities in favor of Christian writers of an earlier age. John Calvin's reverence in the 16th century for the writings of the early Christian church father and philosopher Augustine (354–430) echoed the equal devotion of Petrarch in the 14th century.

Humanists and reformers alike spearheaded a move toward a better understanding of the Bible based not on the authority of theological interpretation but on close, critical scrutiny of the text, preferably in the original Hebrew and Greek. Indeed, the mastery of the three biblical languages (Latin, Greek, and Hebrew) was considered so important in the 16th century that schools were founded especially for the specific purpose of instruction in them. Some famous academic institutions, including Corpus Christi College, Oxford, the University of Alcalá, Spain, and the Collège de France in Paris, were founded for that purpose. Luther's own University of Wittenberg had three chairs for the study of biblical languages.

We can see the connection between humanist learning and the Reformation more clearly by noting some aspects of Luther's great translation of the Bible into German. Although there had been many earlier vernacular translations into German, Luther's, which he began in 1521, was the first produced entirely from the original languages, and the texts he used illuminate the contribution of humanist learning. For the New Testament he used the critical Greek edition prepared by Erasmus. For the book of Psalms he used a text published in Hebrew by the humanist printer Froben at Basel in 1516. The other Hebrew texts were rendered from a Hebrew version published by Italian Jewish scholars who worked in the Italian cities of Soncino and Brescia. His translations of the Apocrypha (books not found in the Hebrew canon) utilized the Greek edition of the Apocrypha printed in 1518 by Aldus Manutius at his press in Venice. As an aid for his labors Luther made abundant use of grammars and glossaries published by the humanist scholar Johannes Reuchlin.

In short, Luther's great achievement was possible only because much of the spadework had already been done by a generation of humanist philologists. This scholarly tradition endured: In 1611, when the translators of the famous English King James Version (see page 383) wrote their preface to the Bible, they noted that they had consulted commentaries and translations as well as translations or versions in Chaldee, Hebrew, Syriac, Greek, Latin, Spanish, French, Italian, and Dutch.

Although there were similarities and mutual influences between humanists and reformers, there were also vast differences. Two are of particular importance. The first relates to concepts of the nature of humanity. The humanist program was rooted in the notion of human perfectibility. This was as true of the Florentine humanists with their strong Platonic bias as it was of northern humanists like Erasmus. The humanists put great emphasis on the profoundly Greek (or, more accurately, Socratic) notion that education can produce a moral person. Both humanist learning and humanist education had a strong ethical bias: learning improves and ennobles. The reformers, by contrast, felt that humanity was hopelessly mired in sin and could only be raised from that condition by the free grace of God. For the reformers, the humanists' position that education could perfect a person undercut the notion of a sinful humanity in need of redemption.

CONTEMPORARY VOICES

Katherine Zell

Many of the Reformation's most active figures were women. Katherine Zell (1497–1562) was the wife of Matthew Zell, one of the first priests to demonstrate his break from the Church by marrying. When he died, she continued his teaching and pastoral work. She wrote this letter in 1558 to an old friend who was suffering from leprosy:

> My dear Lord Felix, since we have known each other for a full 30 years I am moved to visit you in your long and frightful illness. I have not been able to come as often as I would like, because of the load here for the poor and the sick, but you have been ever in my thoughts. We have often talked of how you have been stricken, cut off from rank, office, from your wife and friends, from all dealings with the world which recoils from your loathsome disease and leaves you in utter loneliness. At first you were bitter and utterly cast down till God gave you strength and patience, and now you are able to thank him that out of love he has taught you to bear the cross. Because I know that your illness weighs upon you daily and may easily cause you again to fall into despair and rebelliousness, I have gathered some passages which may make your yoke light in the spirit, though not in the flesh. I have written meditations on the 51st Psalm: 'Have mercy upon me, O God, according to thy loving-kindness,' and the 130th, 'Out of the depths have I cried unto thee, O Lord.' And then on the Lord's Prayer and the Creed.

From R. H. Bainton, *Women of the Reformation in Germany and Italy* (Boston: Beacon, 1974), p. 69.

The contrast between these two points of view is most clearly evident in a polemical debate between Luther and Erasmus on the nature of the human will. In a 1524 treatise called *De Libero Arbitrio (On Free Will)*, Erasmus defended the notion that human effort cooperates in the process of sanctification and salvation. Luther answered in 1525 with a famous tract entitled *De Servo Arbitrio (On the Bondage of the Will)*. The titles of the two pamphlets provide a shorthand description of the severe tensions between the two points of view.

A second difference between the humanists and the reformers begins with the humanist notion that behind all religious systems lies a universal truth that can be detected by a careful study of religious texts. Pico della Mirandola, for example, thought that the essential truth of Christianity could be detected in Talmudic, Platonic, Greek, and Latin authors. He felt that a sort of universal religion could be constructed from a close application of humanist scholarship to all areas of religion. The reformers, on the other hand, held to a simple yet unshakable dictum: *Scriptura sola* (the Bible alone). While the reformers were quite ready to use humanist methods to investigate the sacred text, they were adamant in their conviction that only the Bible held God's revelation to humanity.

As a result of the translation of the Bible into the vernacular language of millions of northern Europeans, Reformation theologians were able to lay stress on the Scriptures as the foundation of their teachings. Luther and Calvin furthermore encouraged lay education, urging their followers to read the Bible for themselves and find there—and only there—Christian truth. In interpreting what they read, individuals were to be guided by no official religious authority but were to make their own judgment following their own consciences. This doctrine is known as universal priesthood, since it denies a special authority to the clergy. All these teachings, although primarily theological, were to have profound and long-range cultural impacts.

We can see that there was an intense positive and negative interaction between humanism and the Reformation—a movement energized by books in general and the Bible in particular. The intensely literary preoccupations of 14th- and 15th-century humanism provided a background and impetus for the 16th-century Reformation. As a philosophical and cultural system, however, humanism was in general too optimistic and ecumenical for the more orthodox reformers. In the later 16th century humanism as a worldview found a congenial outlook in the Christian humanism of Cervantes and the gentle skepticism of Montaigne, but in Reformation circles it was used only as an intellectual instrument for other ends.

Cultural Significance of the Reformation

Cultural historians have attributed a great deal of significance to the Reformation. Some have argued, for example, that with its strong emphasis on individuals and their religious rights, the Reformation was a harbinger of the modern political world. However, with equal plausibility one could make the case that with its strong emphasis on social discipline and its biblical authoritarianism, the Reformation was the last great spasm of the medieval world. Likewise, in a famous thesis developed in the early 20th century by the German sociologist Max Weber, Calvinism was seen as the seedbed and moving force of modern capitalism. Weber's proposition has lingered in our vocabulary in phrases like *work ethic* or *Puritan ethic,* although most scholars now see it as more provocative than provable. Regardless of the scholarly debates about these large questions, there are other, more clearly defined ways in which the Protestant Reformation changed the course of Western culture.

First, the Reformation gave a definite impetus to the already growing use of books in European life. The strong emphasis on the reading and study of the Bible produced inevitable concern for increased literacy. Luther, for example, wanted free education to be provided for all children of all classes in Germany.

The central place of the Bible in religious life made an immense impact on the literary culture of the time. Luther's Bible in Germany and the King James Version in England (to say nothing of the Anglican *Book of Common Prayer*) exercised an inestimable influence on the very shape of the language spoken by their readers. In other countries touched by the Reformation the literary influence of the Bible in translation was absolutely fundamental. In the Scandinavian countries, vernacular literature really begins with translations of the Bible. In Finland, a more extreme example, Finnish was used as a written language for the first time in translating the Bible.

The Bible was not the only book to see widespread diffusion in this period. Books, pamphlets, and treatises crisscrossed Europe as the often intricate theological battles were waged for one or another theological position. It is not accidental that the Council of Trent (1545–1564), a prime instrument of the Catholic counter-reform, stringently legislated the manner in which Bibles were to be translated and distributed. The fact that a list of forbidden books (the infamous *Index*) was instituted by the Catholic Church at this time is evidence that the clerical leadership recognized the immense power of books. The number of books circulating in this period is staggering: Between 1517 and 1520 (even before his break with Rome) Luther's various writings sold about three hundred thousand copies in Europe.

Nolite ergo aſſimilari eis. Scit enim
pater ueſter quid opus ſit uobis: an-
tequā petatis eum. Sic ergo uos ora-
bitis. Pater noſter qui es in celis ſan-
ctificetur nomē tuū. Adueniat regnū
tuū. Fiat uolūtas tua: ſicut in celo et
in terra. Panē noſtrū ſupſubſtātialē
da nobis hodie. Et dimitte nobis de-
bita noſtra: ſicut et nos dimittimus
debitoribus noſtris. Et ne nos indu-
cas in temptationē: ſed libera nos a
malo. Si enim dimiſeritis hominibꝫ
peccata eoꝝ: dimittet et uobis pater
ueſter celeſtis delicta ueſtra. Si autem
non dimiſeritis hominibus: nec pa-

12.5 Portion of a page from the Gutenberg Bible. 1455. Rare Books and Manuscripts Division, New York Public Library. The Latin text of the Lord's Prayer (Matthew 6:9–13) begins on the fourth line with *Pater noster.* The first edition of this Bible, printed at Mainz, was probably 150 copies.

None of this, of course, would have been possible before the Reformation for the simple reason that printing did not exist in Europe. The invention of the printing press and movable type revolutionized Renaissance culture north and south of the Alps in the same way that films, radio, and television changed the 20th century [12.5]. There were two important side effects. The early availability of "book learning" undermined the dominance of universities, which had acted as the traditional guardians and spreaders of knowledge. Also, Latin began to lose its position as the only language for scholarship, since many of the new readers did not understand it. Luther fully grasped the implications of the spread of literacy, and his use of it to advance his cause was imitated countless times in the following centuries.

A second cultural fact about the Reformation, closely allied to the first, is also noteworthy. The reformers put a great emphasis on the *Word.* Besides reading and listening there was also singing, and the reformers—especially Luther—stressed the vernacular hymn. The hymn was seen as both a means of praise and an instrument of instruction. Luther himself was a hymn writer of note. The famous *"Ein' Feste Burg Ist Unser' Gott"* ("A Mighty

12.6 Luther's German Psalter. Lutherhalle, Wittenberg. The book is open at Luther's hymn *"Ein' Feste Burg,"* which is taken from one of the Psalms. The Latin words above Luther's name mean "God our refuge and strength." The hymn itself is printed in German.

Fortress Is Our God"), one of the best-loved hymns in Christianity, is generally attributed to him [12.6]. Indeed, the German musical tradition, which ultimately led to Johann Sebastian Bach in the 17th century, was very much the product of the Lutheran tradition of hymnody.

On the other hand, the 16th-century reformers had little need or sympathy for the plastic arts. They were in fact, militantly iconoclastic. One of the hallmarks of the first reformers was their denunciation of paintings, statues, and other visual representations as forms of papist idolatry. The net result of this iconoclastic spirit was that by the beginning of the 17th-century patronage for the sacred visual arts had virtually died in countries where the Reformation was strong. With the single exception of Rembrandt (and the exception is a gigantic one) it is difficult to name any first-rate painter or sculptor who worked from a Reformation religious perspective after the 16th century, although much secular art was produced.

The attitude of the 16th-century reformers toward the older tradition of the visual arts may be best summed up by the church of Saint Peter in Geneva, Switzerland. Formerly a Romanesque Catholic cathedral of the 12th century, Saint Peter's became Calvin's own church. The stained glass was removed, the walls whitewashed, the statues and crucifixes taken away, and a pulpit placed where the high altar once stood. The church of Saint Peter is a thoroughly reformed church, a building whose entire function is for the hearing of the preached and read word. Gone is the older notion (represented, for example, by the Cathedral of Chartres) of the church reflecting the otherworldly vision of heaven in the richness of its art. Reformation culture was in short an *aural,* not a *visual,* culture.

INTELLECTUAL DEVELOPMENTS

Montaigne's *Essays*

Michel Eyquem de Montaigne (1533–1593) came from a wealthy Bordeaux family. His father, who had been in Italy and was heavily influenced by Renaissance ideas, provided his son with a fine early education. Montaigne spoke nothing but Latin with his tutor when he was a child, so that when he went to school at the age of six he spoke Latin not only fluently but with a certain elegance. His later education (he studied law for a time) was a keen disappointment to him because of its pedantic narrowness. After a few years of public service, in 1571, Montaigne retired with his family to a rural estate to write and study. There, with the exception of a few years traveling and some further time of public service, he remained until his death.

The times were not happy. France was split over the religious issue, as was Montaigne's own family. He remained a Catholic, but his mother and sisters became Protestants. Only a year after his retirement came the terrible Saint Bartholomew's Day Massacre (August 24, 1572), in which thousands of French Protestants were slaughtered in a bloodbath

12.7 Giulio Campagnola. *The Astrologer.* 1509. Engraving, 3¾ × 6" (9.5 × 15 cm). British Museum, London (reproduced by courtesy of the Trustees). The old-fashioned astrologer is shown with all the paraphernalia of his craft, immersed in mystical speculation and apparently accompanied by his pet monster.

unequaled in France since the days of the Hundred Years' War. In the face of this violence and religious bigotry, Montaigne returned to a study of the classics and wrote out his ideas for consolation.

Montaigne's method was to write on a widely variegated list of topics gleaned either from his readings or from his own experiences. He called these short meditations *essays.* Our modern form of the essay is rooted in Montaigne's first use of the genre in Europe. The large numbers of short essays Montaigne wrote share certain qualities characteristic of a mind wearied by the violence and religious bigotry of the time: a sense of Stoic calmness (derived from his study of Cicero and Seneca), a tendency to moralize (in the best sense of that abused word) from his experiences, a generous nondogmatism, a vague sense of world-weariness.

The Growth of Science

The 16th century was not merely a turning point in the history of religions; it was a decisive age in the history of science. In earlier times a scientist was likely enough to be an ingenious tinkerer with elaborate inventions who dabbled in alchemy, astrology, and magic [12.7]. The new Renaissance scientist, a person of wide learning with a special interest in mathematics and philosophy, would develop bold and revolutionary ideas but always subject them to the test of practical experience [12.8].

The age produced many advances in science. In England alone William Gilbert (1540–1603) discovered that the earth was a large magnet whose pole

12.8 Hans Holbein the Younger. *Nikolaus Kratzer.* 1528. Tempera on panel, 32 × 26" (83 × 67 cm). Louvre, Paris. The new scientists are represented here by Kratzer, official astronomer to the court of Henry VIII and a friend of Dürer. The tools used in the calculation he is making are devised for maximum precision, and the room in which Kratzer is working is equipped as a laboratory.

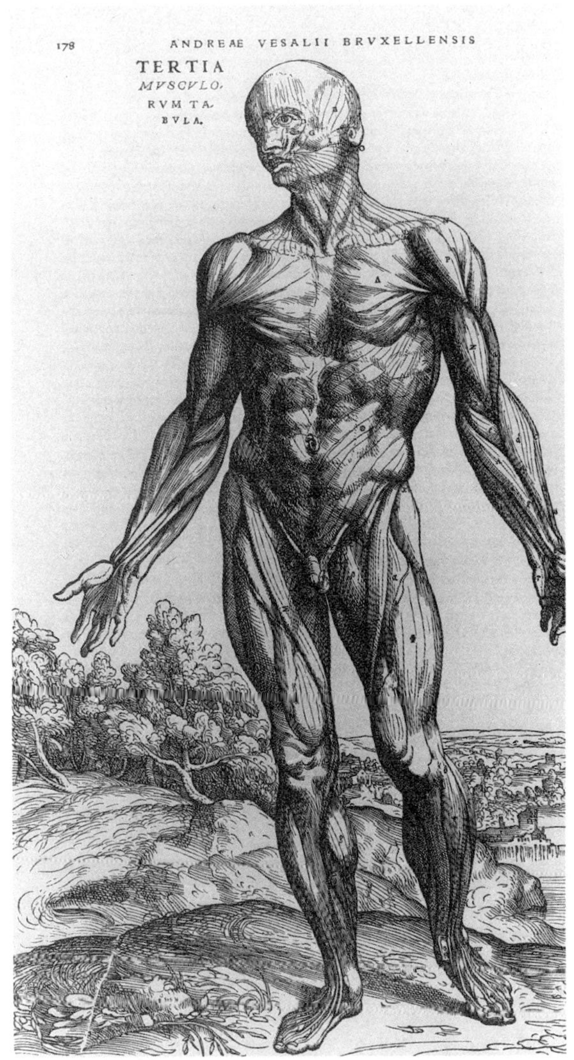

12.9 Andreas Vesalius. *Third Musculature Table* from *De humani corporis fabrica.* Brussels, 1543. National Library of Medicine, Bethesda, Maryland.

points approximately northward; Sir William Harvey (1578–1657) solved the problem of how the blood could "circulate"—get from the arteries to the veins and return to the heart—by postulating the existence of the then-undiscovered channels we now call capillaries; John Napier (1550–1615) discovered the very practical mathematical tool called the logarithm, which greatly reduced the time and effort needed to solve difficult equations. Elsewhere in Europe, the German Paracelsus (1493–1541) laid the foundations of modern medicine by his decisive rejection of traditional practices. Although his own theories were soon rejected, his insistence on observation and inquiry had important consequences, one of which can be seen in the work of Andreas Vesalius (1514–1564), who was born in Brussels and studied in Padua. Vesalius' *Seven Books on the Structure of the Human Body*, published in 1543, comprise a complete anatomical treatise, illustrating in minute detail and with impressive accuracy the human form [12.9].

The philosophical representative of the "new science" was Francis Bacon (1561–1626), who combined an active and somewhat disreputable political career with the writing of works intended to demolish traditional scientific views. The chief of these books was the *Novum Organum* (1620), which aimed to free science from the two-thousand-year-old grasp of Aristotle while at the same time warning against the unrestrained use of untested hypotheses.

Science and religion came into direct conflict in the work of the Polish astronomer Nicholas Copernicus (1473–1543), who studied at the universities of Cracow and Bologna. In 1543, the same year Vesalius' work appeared, he published *On the Revolutions of Celestial Bodies*, a treatise in which he denied that the sun and the planets revolve around the earth, and reverted instead to a long-dead Greek theory that the earth and planets orbit the sun. Catholic and Protestant theologians found themselves for once united in their refusal to accept an explanation of the universe that seemed to contradict the teaching of the Bible, but Copernicus' work, though not a complete break with the past, provided stimulus for Galileo's astronomical discoveries in the following century.

Furthermore, the general principle behind Copernicus' method had important repercussions for the entire history of science. Up to his time scientists had taken the position that, with certain exceptions, reality is as it appears to be. If the sun appears to revolve about the earth, that appearance is a "given" in nature, not to be questioned.

TABLE 12.1 Principal Discoveries and Inventions in the 16th Century

1486	Diaz rounds Cape of Good Hope
1492	Columbus discovers America
1493–1541	Paracelsus pioneers the use of chemicals to treat disease
1513	Balboa sights the Pacific Ocean
1516	Portuguese reach China
1520–22	First circumnavigation of globe, by Magellan
1530–43	Copernicus refutes geocentric view of universe
1533	Gemma Frisius invents principle of triangulation in surveying
1542	Leonhart Fuchs publishes herbal guide to medicine
1543	Vesalius publishes anatomical treatise
1546	Agricola publishes guide to metallurgy
1569	Mercator devises system of mapmaking
1572	Tycho Brahe observes first supernova and produces first modern star catalogue
1582	Pope Gregory XIII reforms the calendar
c. 1600	First refracting telescope constructed in Holland
1600	William Gilbert publishes treatise on magnetism

Copernicus questioned the assumption, claiming that it was equally plausible to take the earth's mobility as a given, since everything that had been explainable in the old way was fully explainable in the new [Table 12.1]. Copernicus' position on scientific matters was thus the equivalent of Luther's stand on the fallibility of the church.

THE VISUAL ARTS IN NORTHERN EUROPE

Painting in Germany: Dürer, Grünewald, Altdorfer

The conflict between Italian humanism, with its belief in human perfectibility, and the Reformation, which emphasized sin and the need for prayer, is reflected in the art of the greatest German painters of the early 16th century. It might even be said that the intellectual and religious battles of the times stimulated German art to its highest achievements, for both Albrecht Dürer (1471–1528) and Matthias Grünewald (about 1500–1528) are, in very different ways, towering figures in the development of European painting. In spite of his sympathy with Luther's beliefs. Dürer was strongly influenced by Italian artistic styles and, through Italian models, by classical ideas. Grünewald, on the other hand, rejected almost all Renaissance innovations and turned instead to traditional northern religious themes, treating them with new passion and emotion. Other artists, meanwhile, chose not to wrestle with the problems of the times. Some, including Albrecht Altdorfer (1480–1538), preferred to stand back and create a worldview of their own.

Dürer was born in Nuremberg, the son of a goldsmith. Even as a child he showed remarkable skill in drawing. His father apprenticed him to a wood engraver, and in 1494–1495—after finishing his traning—Dürer made the first of two visits to Italy. In Italy he saw for the first time the new technique of *linear perspective,* whereby all parallel lines converge at a single vanishing point, and came into contact with the growing interest in human anatomy. Quite as important as these technical discoveries, however, was his perception of a new function for the artist. The traditional German—indeed, medieval—view of the artist was as an artisan whose task was humbly, if expertly, to reproduce God's creations. Dürer adopted Renaissance humanism's conception of the artist as an inspired genius, creating a unique personal world. It is not by chance that a first glance at his *Self-Portrait* of 1500 [12.10] suggests a Christ-like figure rather than a prosperous German painter of the turn of the century. The effect is intentional. The lofty gaze of the eyes underlines the solemn, almost religious nature of the artist's vision, while the prominent hand draws attention to his use of the pen and the brush to communicate it to us.

In his paintings Dürer shows a fondness for precise and complex line drawing rather than the softer use of mass and color typical of Italian art. In fact, much of his greatest work appears in the more linear woodcuts and engravings. In 1498 he published a series of fifteen woodcuts illustrating the Revelation of Saint John, known as the *Apocalypse*

12.10 Albrecht Dürer. *Self-Portrait.* 1500. Panel, 25⅝ × 18⅞" (64 × 48 cm). Alte Pinakothek, Munich. The frontal pose and solemn gaze convey Dürer's belief in the seriousness of his calling.

series. Woodcut engravings are produced by drawing a design on a block of soft wood, then cutting away the surrounding wood to leave the lines of the drawing standing in relief. The blocks of wood can then be coated with ink and used to print an impression on paper. In the hands of Dürer this relatively simple technique was raised to new heights of expressiveness, as in his depiction of Saint Michael's fight against the dragon from the *Apocalypse* series [12.11]. In the upper part of the scene Michael and other angels, all of them with long hair curiously like Dürer's own, do battle with a gruesome horde of fiends, while the peaceful German landscape below seems untouched by the cosmic fight in progress. Dürer's vision of an apocalyptic struggle between good and evil reflected the spirit of the time and copies of the *Apocalypse* series sold in large quantities. Growing discontent with the Church was, as we have seen, one of the causes of Luther's Reformation; the general sense of forthcoming trouble and upheaval gave Dürer's woodcuts a particular aptness.

The medium of *line engraving* was also one to which Dürer brought an unsurpassed subtlety and expressiveness. Unlike a woodblock, where the artist can complete the drawing before cutting away any material, the copper plate from which a line engraving is printed has to be directly incised with the lines of the design by means of a sharp-pointed steel instrument called a *burin.* The richness of effect Dürer achieved in this extremely difficult medium, as in his engraving of *Adam and Eve* [12.12], is almost incredible. The engraving furthermore demonstrates not only his technical brilliance but also the source of much of his artistic inspiration. The carefully shaded bodies of Adam and Eve reflect the influence of contemporary Italian ideals of beauty, while the proportions of the figures are derived from classical literary sources. Dürer made up for the lack of actual Greek and Roman sculpture in Germany by a careful reading of ancient authors, from which he derived a system of proportion for the human figure.

12.11 Albrecht Dürer. *Saint Michael Fighting the Dragon,* from the *Apocalypse* series. 1498. Woodcut, 15½ × 11⅛" (39 × 28 cm). British Museum, London (reproduced by courtesy of the Trustees). Note Dürer's characteristic signature in the center bottom.

12.12 Albrecht Dürer. *Adam and Eve.* XVI Century (1504). Engraving, first state, 9⅞ × 7⅝" (25 × 19 cm). Metropolitan Museum of Art, New York (Fletcher Fund, 1919). The animals represent the sins and diseases that resulted from Adam and Eve's eating of the tree of knowledge: the cat, pride and cruelty; the ox, gluttony and sloth; and so on.

In 1505–1507 Dürer returned to Italy, where he spent most of his time in Venice, discussing theoretical and practical aspects of Renaissance art with Bellini and other Venetian artists. It was inevitable that the rich color characteristic of Venetian painting would make an impression on him, and many of his works of this period try to outdo even the Venetians in splendor.

His renewed interest in painting was, however, brief. For almost the rest of his life he devoted himself to engraving and to writing theoretical works on art. Between 1513 and 1515 he produced his three greatest engravings. The earliest of these, *Knight, Death, and the Devil* [12.13], again reflects contemporary religious preoccupations with its symbolic use of the Christian knight, accompanied by a dog who represents untiring devotion, and beset by the temptations of the devil (in a particularly untempting guise, it must be admitted). Neither this fearsome creature nor the appearance of Death, armed with an hourglass, can shake the knight's steadfast gaze.

By the end of his life Dürer was acknowledged one of the great figures of his time. Like Luther, he made use of the new possibilities of the printing press to spread his ideas. At the time of his death he was working on *Four Books on Human Proportions*. This work, in Latin, aimed to accomplish for art what Vesalius' did for medicine. It was inspired by two of the great intellectual concerns of the Renaissance: a return to classical ideals of beauty and proportion and a new quest for knowledge and scientific precision.

Although the work of Grünewald represents the other high point in German Renaissance art, very little is known about his life. Only in the 20th century did we discover his real name, Mathis Gothart Neithart; the date of his birth and early years of his career are still a mystery. Grünewald seems to have worked for a while at the court of the Cardinal Archbishop of Mainz, but in the 1525 Peasants' War he sided with the German peasants in their revolt against the injustices of their rulers, after which his enthusiasm for Luther's new ideas kept him from returning to the Cardinal's service. He retired to Halle, where he died in 1528.

12.13 Albrecht Dürer. *Knight, Death, and the Devil.* 1513. Engraving, 9¾ × 7½" (25 × 19 cm). British Museum, London (reproduced by courtesy of the Trustees). The knight's calm determination reflects Dürer's confidence in the ability of the devout Christian to resist temptation. This engraving may have been inspired by Erasmus' book *Handbook of the Christian Knight.*

12.14 Matthias Grünewald. *Crucifixion* from the *Isenheim Altarpiece,* exterior. Completed 1515. Panel (with framing) c. 9'9½" × 10'9" (2.98 × 3.28 m). Musée d'Unterlinden, Colmar. Behind Mary Magdalene, who kneels in grief, stand Mary and John, while on the other side John the Baptist points to Christ's sacrifice. Beside him, in Latin, are inscribed the words "He must increase, but I must decrease." Above Christ are the initial letters of the Latin words meaning "Jesus of Nazareth, King of the Jews."

What we know about his political and religious sympathies—his support for the oppressed and for the ideals of the Reformation—is borne out by the characteristics of his paintings. Unlike Dürer, Grünewald never went to Italy, and he showed no interest in the new styles developed there. The Renaissance conception of ideal beauty and the humanist interest in classical antiquity left him unmoved. Instead, he turned again and again to the traditional religious themes of German medieval art, bringing to them a passionate, almost violent intensity that must at least in part reflect the religious heart-searchings of the times. Yet it would be a mistake to see Grünewald's unforgettable images as merely another product of the spirit of the age, for an artist capable of so unique and personal a vision is in the last analysis inspired by factors that cannot be explained in historical terms. All that can safely be said is that no artist, before or since, has depicted the Crucifixion as a more searing tragedy or Christ's Resurrection as more radiantly triumphant.

Both these scenes occur in Grünewald's greatest work, the *Isenheim Altarpiece,* finished in 1515, which was commissioned for the church of a hospital run by members of the Order of Saint Anthony. The folding panels are painted with scenes and figures appropriate to its location, including saints associated with the curing of disease and events in the life of Saint Anthony himself. In particular, the patients who contemplated the altarpiece were expected to meditate on Christ's Crucifixion and Resurrection and derive from them comfort for their own sufferings.

In his painting of Christ in the Crucifixion panel [12.14], Grünewald uses numerous details to depict the intensity of Christ's anguish—from his straining hands, frozen in the agony of death, to the

12.15 Matthias Grünewald. *Resurrection* from the *Isenheim Altarpiece,* first opening. Completed 1515. Panel, 8'2½" × 3'½" (2.45 × .93 m). Musée d'Unterlinden, Colmar. Note the absence of any natural setting and the confused perspective, which give the scene an otherworldly quality.

thorns stuck in his festering body, to the huge iron spike that pins his feet to the cross. It is difficult to imagine anything further from the Italian Renaissance and its concepts of ideal beauty than this tortured image. Grünewald reveals an equal lack of interest in Renaissance or classical theories of proportion or perspective. The figure of Christ, for example, is not related in size to the other figures but dominates the panel, as a glance at the comparative size of the hands will show. Yet the sheer horror of this scene only throws into greater relief the triumph of the Resurrection [12.15]. Christ seems almost to have exploded out of the tomb, in a great burst of light that dazzles the viewers as well as the soldiers stumbling below. No greater contrast can be imagined than between that of the drooping body on the cross and this soaring weightless image that suggests a hope of similar resurrection to the sufferers in the hospital.

The drama of Grünewald's spiritual images is in strong contrast to the quiet, poetic calm of the work of Albrecht Altdorfer. Although closer in style to Grünewald than to Dürer, Altdorfer found his favorite subject not in religious themes but in landscapes. *Danube Landscape near Regensburg* [12.16], probably dating from around 1525, is one of the first examples in the Western tradition of a painting without a single human figure. From the time of the Greeks, art had served to tell a story, sacred or secular, or to illustrate some aspect of human behavior. Now for the first time the contemplation of the beauties of nature was in itself deemed a worthy subject for an artist. In this painting Altdorfer depicts a kind of ideal beauty very different from Dürer's *Fall of Man* but no less moving. Part of his inspiration may have come from the landscapes that can be seen in the background of paintings by Venetian artists like Giorgione, although there is no

12.16 Albrecht Altdorfer. *Danube Landscape near Regensburg.* c. 1522–1525. Panel, 11 × 8⅝" (28 × 22 cm). Alte Pinakothek, Munich. The only traces of human existence here are the road and the distant castle to which it leads.

12.17 Hieronymus Bosch. *Garden of Earthly Delights.* c. 1505–1510. Panel; center 7'2⅝" × 6'4¾" (2.2 × 1.95 m), each wing 7'2⅝" × 3'2¼" (2.2 × .97 m). Prado, Madrid. **Perhaps surprisingly, this catalogue of the sins of the flesh was among the favorite works of the gloomy King Philip II of Spain.**

evidence that Altdorfer ever visited Italy. Even if he did, his sympathy with the forces of nature, its light and scale and sense of life, seems more directly inspired by actual contact.

PAINTING IN THE NETHERLANDS: BOSCH AND BRUEGEL

The two greatest Netherlandish painters of the Renaissance, Hieronymus Bosch (c. 1450–1516) and Pieter Bruegel (1525–1569), are linked both by their pessimistic view of human nature and by their use of satire to express it. Bosch furthermore drew upon an apparently inexhaustible imagination to create a fantasy world that alternately fascinates and repels as the eye wanders from one bizarre scene to another. Although modern observers have interpreted Bosch's work in a variety of ways, it is generally agreed that, contrary to appearances, he was in fact a deeply religious painter. His chief subject is human folly in its innumerable forms, his theme that the inevitable punishment of sin is Hell. Salvation is possible through Christ, but few, according to Bosch, have the sense to look for it. His paintings show us the consequences.

Almost nothing is known of Bosch's life, and his works must speak for themselves. The most elaborate in its fantasy is a *triptych* (a painting made up of three panels) known as the *Garden of Earthly Delights* [12.17], which was probably finished around 1510. Into it are crowded hundreds of nude figures engaged in activities that range from the unimaginable to the indescribable, all in pursuit of erotic pleasure. The movement from the apparently innocent scene of the creation of Eve on the left to the fires of Hell on the right illustrates Bosch's belief that the pleasures of the body lead to damnation along a road of increasing depravity. Even in the Garden of Eden we sense what is to come, as Adam sits up with excited enthusiasm on being presented with the naked Eve, while God seems to eye him nervously.

The bright world of the middle panel, in which the pallid, rubbery figures seem to arrange themselves (and one another) in every conceivable position and permutation, gives way on the right to a hallucinatory vision of eternal damnation.

Bosch's symbolism is too complex and too private to permit a detailed understanding of the scene, yet his general message is clear enough: Hell is not terrifying so much as it is sordid and pathetic. The frantic scenes of activity are as senseless and futile as those of worldly existence, but in Hell their monstrous nature becomes fully apparent.

The sources of Bosch's inspiration in this and other works are unknown. Many of his demons and fantastic animals seem related to similar

12.18 Pieter Bruegel the Elder. *The Triumph of Death.* c. 1562–1564. Oil on panel, 3'10" × 5'3¾" (1.17 × 1.62 m). Prado, Madrid. Note the huge coffin on the right, guarded by rows of skeleton-soldiers, into which the dead are being piled.

manifestations of evil in medieval art, but no medieval artist ever devised a vision such as this or had the technique to execute it. To modern eyes some of his creations, like the human-headed monster on the right-hand panel turning both face and rear toward us, seem to prefigure the surrealist art of the 20th century. There is a danger, however, in applying labels from the art of later times to that of an earlier period. Bosch must simply be allowed to stand on his own as one of the great originals in the history of painting.

Pieter Bruegel, often called the Elder to distinguish him from his son of the same name, represents the culmination of Renaissance art in the

12.19 Pieter Bruegel the Elder. *Peasant Wedding Feast.* 1566–1567. Oil on panel, 3'8⅞" × 5'4⅛" (1.14 × 1.63 m). Kunsthistorisches Museum, Vienna. The composition of the painting is based on the diagonal line of the receding table that leads the eye past the bride and the bagpiper to the back of the room.

Netherlands. Like that of Bosch, his work is often fantastic, and his crowded canvases are frequently filled with scenes of grotesque activity. Some of his paintings suggest that he shared Bosch's view of the apparent futility of human existence and the prevalence of sin. In many of his pictures, however, the scenic backgrounds reveal a love and understanding of nature very different from Bosch's weird view of the world and represent one of the keys to understanding his work. For Bruegel, the full range of human activity formed part of a world in which there existed an underlying order. The beauty of nature forms the background not only to his pictures but actually to the lives of us all, he seems to say; by seeing ourselves as part of the natural cycle of existence we can avoid the folly of sin. If this interpretation of his work is correct, it places Bruegel with the humanists, who believed in the possibilities for human good, and there is some evidence to suggest that his friends did include members of a group of humanist philosophers active at Antwerp.

Although Bruegel's best-known paintings are scenes of peasant life, it is a mistake to think of him as unsophisticated. On the contrary, during the last years of his life, which he spent in Brussels, he was familiar with many of the leading scholars of the day and seems to have been a man of considerable culture. He certainly traveled to Italy, where he was apparently unaffected by the art but deeply impressed by the beauty of the landscape. Back home, he may well have supported the move to free the Netherlands from Spanish rule; some of his paintings seem to contain allusions to Spanish cruelties.

Bruegel's vision is so rich and so understanding of the range of human experience that it almost rivals that of Shakespeare, who was born in 1564, five years before Bruegel's death. In his great painting *The Triumph of Death* [12.18], Bruegel looks with uncompromising honesty at the universal phenomenon of death—which comes eventually to all, rich and powerful or poor and hopeless. Unlike Bosch, who reminds us that the righteous (if there are any) will be saved, Bruegel seems to offer no hope. Yet the same artist painted the *Peasant Wedding Feast* [12.19], a scene of cheerful celebration. True, Bruegel's peasants find pleasure in simple rather than sophisticated delights, in this case chiefly food and drink, but he reminds us that some are luckier than others. The little boy in the foreground, so completely engrossed in licking up every last delicious morsel of food, is counterbalanced by the bagpiper who looks wistfully and wanly over his shoulder at the tray of pies going by. Nor should we be too hasty to think of Bruegel's peasants as unthinking creatures, content with a brutish existence. The bride certainly does not seem either bright or beautiful, but she radiates happiness, and the general air of merriment is very attractive.

Bruegel's most profound statements are perhaps to be found in a cycle of paintings intended to illustrate the months of the year, rather like the *Trés Riches Heures* of the Limbourg brothers a century earlier. Bruegel finished only five of them, including the magnificent *Hunters in the Snow* of 1565 [12.20]. In the background tower lofty peaks, which represent Bruegel's memory of the Alps, seen on

12.20 Pieter Bruegel the Elder. *Hunters in the Snow*. 1565. Oil on panel, 3'10" × 5'3¾" (1.17 × 1.62 m). Kunsthistorisches Museum, Vienna. Note Bruegel's careful use of color to suggest a cold, clear, sunless day. From his first crossing of the Alps in the 1530s Bruegel was inspired by mountain scenery, and it reappeared throughout his work. In this painting, the panoramic sweep from the foreground to the lofty peaks behind makes the scene appear a microcosm of human existence. Thus Bruegel's "world landscapes" or *Weltlandschaften* are both literal depictions of scenes from nature and symbolic representations of the relationship between human beings and the world around them.

12.21 Jean Clouet (?). *Francis I.* c. 1525–1530. Tempera and oil on panel, 37¾ × 29⅛" (96 × 74 cm). Louvre, Paris. This famous work is now thought to be by an unknown artist rather than Clouet himself, but its style is very similar to that of his many official portraits of the king.

his trip to Italy. From the weary hunters in the foreground a line of barren trees leads the eye to fields of snow where peasants are hard at work. The scene can hardly be called a happy one, but neither is it unhappy. There is an inevitability in the way humans, animals, birds, and nature are all bound into a unity, expressive of a sense of order and purpose. The lesson of Italian humanism has been translated into a very different language, spoken with a highly individual accent, but Bruegel's northern scene seems in its own way inspired by a similar regard for human dignity.

Art and Architecture in France

France of the 16th century has little to compare with the artistic achievements of Germany and the Netherlands. The influence of Italian art on France was so strong, due in great part to the actual presence at the French court of Italian artists, that French painting was almost completely overwhelmed. The only native artist of note was Jean Clouet (c. 1485–1541), who was retained by Francis I chiefly to serve as his official portrait painter. Among the many portraits of the king attributed to Clouet is one of around 1530 [12.21] that does full justice to the sensual but calculating character of his master.

More interesting than French painting during the 16th century is French architecture. The series of luxurious châteaux that Francis I had built along the valley of the river Loire combined the airiness of the earlier French Gothic style with decorative motifs imported from Italian Renaissance architecture. The result was buildings like the beautiful Château of Chambord [12.22].

The love of decoration shown by the builders of Chambord emerges even more strongly as a feature

12.22 Château of Chambord. Begun 1529. Although the turrets and pinnacles are reminiscent of French medieval architecture, the central block and much of the decorative detail suggest Italian Renaissance models.

12.23 Pierre Lescot and Jean Goujon. Façade of the Square Court of the Louvre, Paris. Begun 1546. The architectural and sculptural decoration is Italian in origin but used here as typically French elaborate ornamentation.

of French architectural style in the design of the Square Court of the Louvre [12.23]. This structure was begun in 1546 by the architect Pierre Lescot (1510–1578) and the sculptor Jean Goujon (c. 1510–1568), working for once without Italian guidance. The façade of the court is a compendium of classical forms, from the window moldings to the Corinthian columns to the decorative motifs. The total effect, however, is very different from Italian buildings using the same features. Instead of being grand or awe-inspiring the building seems graceful and harmonious, perhaps even a little fussy, and the emphasis on decoration became a prominent characteristic of French art in the following two centuries.

Art in Elizabethan England

Throughout the 16th century English political and cultural life followed a path notably different from that of continental Europe, as it did so often in its previous history. The social unrest that had marked the later Middle Ages in England was finally brought to an end in 1485 by the accession of Henry VII, the first of the Tudor dynasty. For the entire 16th century, England enjoyed a new stability and commercial prosperity on the basis of which it began to play an increasingly active part in international politics. Henry VIII's final break with the Catholic Church in 1534 led to the later development of ties between England and the other countries of the Reformation, particularly the Netherlands. When years of tension between the Netherlanders and their Spanish rulers finally broke into open rebellion, England—by now ruled by Queen Elizabeth I (born 1533, reigned 1558–1603)—supplied help secretly. Relations between Elizabeth and the Spanish king, Philip II, were already strained, and English interference in the Spanish Netherlands was unlikely to help. In 1585, a new Spanish campaign of repression in the Netherlands, coupled with the threat of a Spanish invasion of England, drove the queen to take more open action, and she sent six thousand troops to fight alongside the Netherlanders. Their presence proved decisive.

Philip's anger at his defeat and at the progress of the campaign for an independent Netherlands was turned in fury against England. The massive Spanish Armada, the largest fleet the world had ever seen, was ready early in 1588 and sailed majestically north, only to be met by a fleet of much lighter, faster English ships commanded by Sir Francis Drake. The rest is part history, part legend. Even before the expedition sailed, Drake had "singed the beard of the King of Spain" by sailing into Cadiz harbor and setting fire to some of the

12.24 Nicholas Hilliard(?). *Ermine Portrait of Queen Elizabeth I.* 1585. Oil on canvas, 41¾ × 35" (106 x 89 cm). Hatfield House, England (collection of the Marquess of Salisbury). The ermine on the queen's sleeve is a symbol of virginity. The portrait as a whole is a symbol of her majesty, not intended to show her actual appearance.

Spanish galleons waiting there. The rest of the Armada reached the English Channel, where it was destroyed, partly by superior English tactics, partly by a huge storm promptly dubbed (by the victors, at least) the Protestant Wind. The subsequent tales told of English valor and daring brought a new luster to the closing years of the Elizabethan Age [12.24].

In view of England's self-appointed position as bulwark of Protestantism against the Catholic Church in general and Spain in particular, it is hardly surprising that Renaissance ideas developed south of the Alps took some time to affect English culture. Few Italian artists were tempted to work at the English court or, for that matter, were likely to be invited there. Furthermore, England's geographic position inevitably cut it off from intellectual developments in continental Europe and produced a kind of psychological insularity that was bolstered in the late 16th century by a wave of national pride. The finest expression of this is probably to be found in the lines William Shakespeare put into the mouth of John of Gaunt in Act II, scene i of *Richard II,* a play written some six years after the defeat of the Spanish Armada:

This royal throne of kings, this sceptered isle,
This earth of majesty, this seat of Mars,
This other Eden, demi-Paradise,
This fortress built by Nature for herself
Against infection and the hand of war,
This happy breed of men, this little world,
This precious stone set in the silver sea,
Which serves it in the office of a wall
Or as a moat defensive to a house
Against the envy of less happier lands—
This blessed plot, this earth, this realm, this
England. . . .

On the other hand, the same spirit of nationalism was bound to produce a somewhat narrow-minded rejection of new ideas from outside. English sculpture and painting suffered as a result.

The only foreign painter to work in England was himself a northerner, Hans Holbein the Younger (1497/8–1543), whose portrait of Henry VIII appears earlier in this chapter (see Figure 12.4). A magnificent portraitist, Holbein found himself sent by Henry to paint prospective brides so that the

12.25 Hans Holbein the Younger. *Anne of Cleves.* c. 1539–1540. Vellum applied to canvas, 25⅝ × 18⅞" (65 × 48 cm). Louvre, Paris. Viewing this portrait, Henry VIII sent for Anne of Cleves and made her his fourth queen. Note the formal pose and the suitably modest downturned gaze.

king could make his choice with at least some idea of their appearance—an effective if rather tedious method before photography. It must be added that the artist seems to have done his work rather too well, since his picture of Anne of Cleves [12.25] inspired Henry to marry the princess only to divorce her within six months, contemptuously dismissing her as his "Flanders Mare."

Apart from Holbein, English artists were virtually cut off from the new ideas current elsewhere. The only English painter of note during the 16th century was Nicholas Hilliard (1547–1619), best known for his miniatures, small portraits often painted in watercolor. The finest is of an unidentified young man who has something of the poetic melancholy of a Shakespearean lover [12.26]. When Hilliard turned to larger works, specifically to portraits of Queen Elizabeth, he was inevitably inhibited by his monarch's demand for a painting that would look regal and imposing rather than realistic. The result [see Figure 12.24] is a symbolic representation of majesty rather than a mere portrait.

12.26 Nicholas Hilliard. *Portrait of a Youth.* c. 1590. Parchment, 5⅜ × 2¾" (14 × 7 cm). Victoria and Albert Museum, London. Crown copyright. The thorns of the wild rose growing in the foreground may represent friendship in adversity. (The miniature is shown here at almost exactly its actual size.)

MUSIC OF THE NORTHERN RENAISSANCE

As in the visual arts, the Renaissance produced major stylistic changes in the development of music; nonetheless, in general, musical development in the Renaissance was marked by a less severe break with medieval custom than was the case with the visual arts. Although 16th-century European composers began to increase the complexity of their style, making frequent use of polyphony (several musical parts combined and sounding together), they continued to use forms developed in the High Middle Ages and the early Renaissance. In religious music the motet remained popular; this was a short choral piece for three or more voices, generally unaccompanied, set to a religious text. Composers also continued to compose *madrigals,* songs for three or more solo voices based generally on secular poems. For the most part these were intended for performance at home, and the skill of the singers was often tested by elaborate, interweaving polyphonic lines. The difficulty of the parts often made it necessary for the singers to use an instrumental accompaniment. This increasing complexity produced a significant change in the character of madrigals, which were especially popular in Elizabethan England. Nonetheless, 16th-century musicians were recognizably the heirs of their 13th- and 14th-century predecessors.

Music in France and Germany

The madrigal form was originally devised in Italy for the entertainment of courtly circles. By the early 16th century French composers, inspired by such lyric poets as Clement Marot (1496–1544), were writing more popular songs known as *chansons.*

The best-known composer of chansons was Clement Janequin (c. 1485–c. 1560), who was famous for building his works around a narrative program. In "La Guerre" ("The War") the music imitates the sound of shouting soldiers, fanfares, and rattling guns; other songs feature street cries and birdsongs. Frequently repeated notes and the use of nonsense syllables help to give Janequin's music great rhythmic vitality although it lacks the harmonic richness of Italian madrigals.

The same tendency to appeal to a general public characterized German and Flemish songs of the period with texts that were romantic, military, or sometimes even political in character. Among the great masters of the period was the Flemish composer Heinrich Isaac (c. 1450–1517), who composed songs in Italian and French as well as German. His style ranges from simple chordlike settings to elaborately interweaving lines that imitate one another. Isaac's pupil, the German Ludwig Senfl (c. 1690–c. 1542), was, if anything, more prolific than his teacher; his music is generally less complex and graceful—almost wistful—in mood.

Elizabethan Music

English music suffered far less than the visual arts from the cultural isolationism of Elizabethan England; the Elizabethan Age, in fact, marks one of the high points in its history. Almost two hundred years earlier the English musician John Dunstable (c. 1385–1453) had been one of the leading composers in Europe. By bringing English music into the mainstream of continental developments, he helped prepare the way for his Elizabethan successors.

A number of other factors were also responsible for the flourishing state of English music. To begin with, in England there had always been a greater interest in music than in the visual arts.

Also, the self-imposed ban on the importation of foreign art works and styles did not extend to printed music, with the result that by the early years of the reign of Elizabeth, Italian secular music began to circulate in English musical circles. A volume of Italian songs in translation was published in 1588 under the title *Musica Transalpina (Music from Across the Alps).*

As for sacred music, when Henry VIII staged his break with the pope in 1534, he was not at all ready to convert wholeheartedly to Lutheranism or Calvinism and discard the sung parts of the liturgy. The services, psalms, and hymns the new Anglican Church had to devise generally (although by no means invariably) used English rather than Latin texts, echoing Luther's use of the vernacular, but continued for the most part to follow Catholic models.

Thus, when the first official version of the English litany was issued in 1544 by the Archbishop of Canterbury, Thomas Cranmer, it made use of the traditional Gregorian chant, simplified so that only one note was allocated to each syllable of the text. This innovation preserved the flavor of the original music, while making it easier for a listener to follow the meaning of the words and thereby participate more directly in the worship. The tendency to simplify is also visible, literally [12.27], in the first published musical setting of the words of the *Book of Common Prayer,* which had appeared in 1549. This first musical edition, *The Book of Common Praier Noted* [set to music] by John Merbecke (c. 1510–c. 1585), again used only one note to each syllable, and his settings followed the normal accentuation of the English words. This work is still used by the Episcopal Church.

In more elaborate music the effects of the Reformation were even less evident. Most of the professional composers of the day, after all, had been brought up in a Catholic musical tradition, and while the split with Rome affected religious dogma (and of course permitted Henry to marry and divorce at will), it did not alter their freedom to compose as they wished. They continued to write pieces that alternated and combined the two chief styles of the day: blocks of chords in which every voice moved at the same time and the elaborate interweaving of voices known as *counterpoint.*

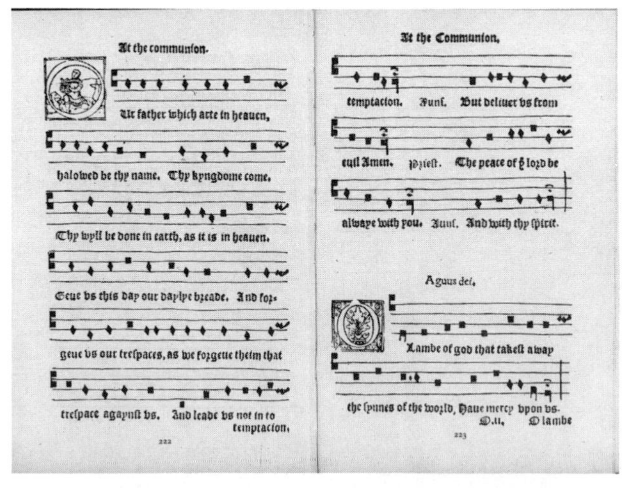

12.27 John Merbecke. ***The Book of Common Praier Noted.*** **British Library, London (reproduced by courtesy of the Trustees). The Lord's Prayer is on the left page and part of the right page. The words are in English, but note the Latin title *Agnus Dei (Lamb of God)* retained on the right page.**

The musical forms also remained unchanged except in name. Among the most popular compositions throughout Europe were motets, short choral works, the words of which were often in Latin. English composers continued to write works of this kind but used English texts and called them *anthems.* A piece that used the full choir throughout was called a *full anthem* and one containing passages for solo voice or voices a *verse anthem.* English musicians nevertheless did not entirely abandon the use of Latin. A number of the greatest figures of the period continued to write settings of Latin texts as well as ones in the vernacular.

The dual nature of Elizabethan music is well illustrated by the career of Thomas Tallis (c. 1505–1585), who spent more than forty years of his life as organist of the Chapel Royal at the English Court. Although his official duties required him to compose works for formal Protestant occasions, he also wrote Latin motets and Catholic masses. Tallis was above all a master of counterpoint, bringing the technique of combining and interweaving a number of vocal lines to a new height of complexity in one of his motets, *Spem in Alium (Hope in Another),* written for no less than forty voices, each moving independently. In his anthems, however, he adopted a simpler style with a greater use of chord passages, so that the listener could follow at least part of the English text. His last works combine both techniques to achieve a highly expressive, even emotional effect, as in his setting of the *Lamentations of Jeremiah.*

Among Tallis' many pupils was William Byrd (c. 1543–1623), the most versatile of Elizabethan composers and one of the greatest in the history of English music. Like Tallis, he produced both Protestant and Catholic church music, writing three Latin masses and four English services, including the so-called Great Service for five voices. Byrd also composed secular vocal and instrumental music, including a particularly beautiful elegy for voice and strings, *Ye Sacred Muses,* inspired by the death of Tallis himself. The concluding bars, setting the words "Tallis is dead and music dies," demonstrate his ability to achieve considerable emotional pathos with simple means, in this case the rise of an octave in the next-to-last bar:

And mu______ sic dies, And__ mu__ sic dies.

Much of Byrd's instrumental music was written for the virginal, an early keyboard instrument in the form of an oblong box small enough to be placed on a table or even held in the player's lap. It was once believed that the instrument was so called because of its popularity at the court of Elizabeth, the self-styled Virgin Queen, but references have been found to the name before her time, and its true origin is unknown. Forty-two pieces written for the virginal by Byrd were copied down in 1591 in an album known as *My Ladye Nevells Booke.* They include dances, variations, and fantasias and form a rich compendium of Byrd's range of style.

Byrd also wrote madrigals, songs performed by a small group of singers, often for their own entertainment at home. The madrigal had begun its life in Italy, where the words themselves were as important as the music, and Italian composers often chose poems that reflected the Renaissance interest in classical antiquity. The English madrigal was less concerned with Renaissance ideas of refinement than with the expression of emotional extremes. Many of the madrigals of Thomas Morley (1557–1602) are lighthearted in tone and fast moving, making use of refrains like "Fa la la." Among the best-known are "Sing we and chaunt it" and "Now is the Month of Maying," settings of popular verses rather than literary texts, intended not for an elite but for domestic performance by an increasingly prosperous middle class.

Other madrigals were more serious, even mournful. Both Morley and his younger contemporary Thomas Weelkes (c. 1575–1623) composed madrigals in memory of Henry Noel, an amateur musician who was a favorite at the court of Queen Elizabeth. Weelkes' piece "Noel, adieu" is striking for its use of extreme dissonances to express grief. In the following bars, the clash of C against C# seems strikingly modern in its harshness:

The most melancholy works of all Elizabethan music are the *ayres* of John Dowland (1562–1626), simple songs for one voice accompanied either by other voices or instruments. Dowland is the rare example of an Elizabethan musician who traveled widely. Irish by birth, he visited France, Germany, and Italy and even worked for a while at the court of King Christian IV of Denmark; ultimately he settled in England.

Dowland was the greatest virtuoso of his day on the lute, a plucked string instrument that is a relative of the guitar, and used it to accompany his ayres. Dowland's gloomy temperament was given full expression both in the ayres and in his solo pieces for lute, most of which are as obsessively depressed and woeful as Morley's madrigals are determinedly cheerful. Popular in his own day, in more recent times Dowland's music has undergone something of a revival with the growth of interest in the guitar and other similar instruments.

ENGLISH LITERATURE: SHAKESPEARE

English literature in the 16th century, unlike the visual arts and to a greater extent even than music, was strongly affected by new currents of Renaissance thought. One reason for this is purely practical. Soon after the invention of printing in Germany (see page 320), William Caxton (c. 1421–1491) introduced the printing press into England, and during the first half of the 16th century books became increasingly plentiful and cheap. With the spread of literature an increased literacy developed, and the new readers were anxious to keep in touch with all the latest ideas of their day.

The development of humanism in England undoubtedly influenced Erasmus of Rotterdam, who was brought into contact with humanist ideas during his visits there. In addition to teaching at Cambridge, Erasmus formed a warm personal friendship with the English statesman Sir Thomas More (1478–1535), who became Lord Chancellor in 1529.

More's *Utopia,* a philosophical romance in Latin describing an ideal world resembling that of Plato's *Republic,* was written under Erasmus' influence and was firmly based on humanistic ideals. Once introduced, these ideas caught on, and so did the use of classical or Italian models to express them. Sir Philip Sidney (1554–1586), the dashing youth who has been described as Castiglione's courtier come to life, wrote a series of sonnets in imitation of Petrarch and a romance, *Arcadia,* of the kind made popular in Italy by Lodovico Ariosto (1474–1533). Edmund Spenser (1552–1599), the greatest nondramatic poet of Elizabethan England, was also influenced by Ariosto and by Torquato Tasso (1544–1595), Ariosto's Italian successor in the production of massive epic poems. In *The Faerie Queene* Spenser combined the romance of Ariosto and the Christian allegory of Tasso to create an immensely complex epic. Its chivalrous hero, the Knight of the Red Cross, represents both Christianity and, through his resemblance to Saint George, England. At the same time the tests he undergoes make him a Renaissance version of the medieval figure of Everyman. The epic takes place in the imaginary land of Faerie, where the knight's path is frequently blocked by dragons, witches, wizards, and other magical creatures. All this mythological paraphernalia not only advances the plot but also provides a series of allegorical observations on moral and political questions of the day. The result has, in general, been more admired than read.

The greatest of all English achievements in the Renaissance were in drama. The classical models of English drama were the Latin tragedies of Seneca and the comedies of Plautus and Terence, which, with the introduction of printing, became more frequently read and performed. These ancient Roman plays created a taste for the theater that English dramatists began to satisfy in increasing quantities.

At the same time the same prosperity and leisure that created a demand for new madrigals produced a growing audience for drama. To satisfy this audience, traveling groups of actors began to form, often attaching themselves to the household of a noble who acted as their patron. These companies gave performances in public places, especially the courtyards of inns. When the first permanent theater buildings were constructed, their architects imitated the form of the inn courtyards, with roofs open to the sky and galleries around the sides. The stage generally consisted of a large platform jutting out into the center of the open area known as the *pit* or *ground* [12.28].

The design of these theaters allowed—indeed, encouraged—people of all classes to attend performances regularly since the price of admission varied for different parts of the theater. The more prosperous spectators sat in the galleries, where they had a clear view of the stage, while the poorer spectators stood around the stage in the ground. Dramatists and actors soon learned to please these so-called *groundlings* by appealing to their taste for noise and spectacle.

Not all performances were given in public before so democratic an audience. The most successful companies were invited to entertain Queen Elizabeth and her court. The plays written for these state occasions were generally more sophisticated in both content and style than those for more general performance. The works written for the court of James I, Elizabeth's successor, are among the more elaborate of all.

In general, English drama developed from a relatively popular entertainment in the mid-16th century to a more formal artificial one in the early 17th century. It is probably no coincidence that the greatest of all Elizabethan dramatists, Shakespeare

12.28 The Globe Playhouse, London. 1599–1613. This conjectural reconstruction by C. Walter Hodges shows the playhouse during the years when *Hamlet, King Lear,* and other Shakespearean plays were first performed there.

and Marlowe, wrote their best works at about the midpoint in this development, from about 1590 to 1610. Their plays reflect the increasing appreciation and demand for real poetry and high intellectual content without losing the "common touch" that has given their work its continual appeal.

Christopher Marlowe (1564–1593) was born two months before Shakespeare. Had he not been killed in a fight over a tavern bill at the age of 29, he might well have equaled Shakespeare's mighty achievements. It is certainly true that by the same age Shakespeare had written relatively little of importance, while Marlowe's works include the monumental two-part *Tamburlaine,* a vast tragic drama that explores the limits of human power; exuberant erotic verse like his *Hero and Leander;* and his greatest masterpiece, *Dr. Faustus.* Marlowe's use of *blank verse* for dramatic expression was imitated by virtually every other Elizabethan playwright, including Shakespeare. It consists of nonrhyming lines of iambic pentameter—lines of five metrical feet in which each foot has two syllables, the second one generally bearing the rhythmic stress. In style Marlowe's works reflect the passion and violence of his own life, their heroes striving to achieve the unachievable by overcoming all limits, only to be defeated by destiny.

Regret at the loss of what Marlowe might have written had he lived longer is balanced by gratitude for the many works William Shakespeare (1564–1616) left us. Shakespeare [12.29] is universally acknowledged the greatest writer in the English language, and one of the very greatest ever in any tongue. His position is best summarized in the words of his leading contemporary and rival playwright Ben Jonson (1572–1637): "He was not of an age, but for all time!"

Surprisingly little is known about Shakespeare's life. He was born at Stratford-upon-Avon; his early years and education seem to have been typical of

Mr. WILLIAM
SHAKESPEARES
COMEDIES,
HISTORIES, &
TRAGEDIES.
Publiſhed according to the True Originall Copies.

LONDON
Printed by Iſaac Iaggard, and Ed. Blount. 1623.

12.29 Title page of the First Folio, the first collected edition of Shakespeare's works, which was prepared by two of the playwright's fellow actors, London, 1623. Rare Books and Manuscripts Division, New York Public Library.

provincial England, although no details are known. In 1582 he married Anne Hathaway; over the next three years they had three children. By 1592, he was established in London as an actor and playwright. Exactly how he became involved in the theater and what he did from 1585 to 1592 remain a mystery.

From the beginning of his time in London Shakespeare was associated with the leading theatrical company of the day, the Lord Chamberlain's Men, which changed its name to the King's Men at the accession of James I in 1603.

Shakespeare's earliest plays followed the example of classical models in being carefully constructed, although their plots seem sometimes unnecessarily overcomplicated. In *The Comedy of Errors* (1592–1593), for example, Shakespeare combined two plays by the Roman comic writer

SPORTS AND GAMES

From the Duel to Fencing

Like a number of Shakespeare's plays, *Romeo and Juliet* includes a scene involving swordplay, but the most famous of all Shakespearean fights is probably the duel between Hamlet and Laertes at the end of *Hamlet.* The modern sport of fencing is derived from the custom of duels, which developed in northern Europe in the late Middle Ages. A duel was an armed combat between two persons, usually prearranged and in the presence of witnesses, for the purpose of settling a quarrel, avenging an insult, real or imagined, or vindicating the honor of one of the combatants or a third party. Although not all duels were intentionally fought to the death, the inexperience of the participants and the frequent absence of immediate medical aid often led to fatalities. By the 17th century, pistols provided an alternative to swords, with the person challenged having the right to choose.

The earliest form of contest was the judicial duel. If a man alleged in the presence of a judge that another had committed a crime, and the other denied it, the judge ordered them to meet in a duel. A woman accused in such a way had the right to name a champion. Since those involved believed that God supported the right cause, a loser who survived was executed in criminal cases or penalized in civil claims.

By Shakespeare's time, the law officially prohibited such contests, and in 1602 Henry IV banned duelling in France. Nevertheless skill in swordsmanship and a sensitive sense of honor were both marks of a gentleman, and the custom continued until well into the 19th century. Like other aspects of European culture, duelling spread to the United States. Perhaps the most famous case was the duel in which Aaron Burr killed Alexander Hamilton in 1804.

The notion of a contest in which the aim is to touch the opponent rather than to inflict wounds led to the sport of fencing. The match between Hamlet and Laertes is in theory intended to be just such a demonstration of skill; the "hits" only prove fatal because the King has poisoned the tip of Laertes' sword. In modern contests three different swords are used, ranging from the light foil to the medium épée to the heavy saber. In men's bouts, whoever touches his opponent five times is the winner; four hits are sufficient in women's matches.

Plautus (c. 254–184 B.C.) to create a series of situations racked by mistaken identities and general confusion. The careful manipulation of plot in the early plays is achieved at the expense of characterization, and the poetry tends to use artificial literary devices. Even Shakespeare's first great tragedy, *Romeo and Juliet* (1595), is not altogether free from an excessive use of puns and plays on words, although the psychological depiction of the young lovers is convincing and the play contains some magnificent passages.

The comedies of the next few years, including both *The Merchant of Venice* (c. 1596) and *Twelfth Night* (c. 1600), are more lyrical. The brilliant wit of the earlier plays often is replaced by a kind of wistful melancholy.

Twelfth Night, in fact, is often regarded as Shakespeare's supreme achievement in the field of comedy. Although the plot hinges on a series of well-worn comic devices—mistaken identities, separated twins, and so on—the characters are as vivid and individual as in any of his plays. Furthermore, the work's principal subject, romantic love, is shown from an almost infinite number of points of view. Yet at the same time Shakespeare was attracted to historical subjects, generally drawn from English history, as in *Henry IV, Parts I and II* (1597–1598), but also from Roman history, as in *Julius Caesar.*

Julius Caesar (1599) is notable for a number of reasons. It shows that Shakespeare shared the renewed interest of his contemporaries in classical antiquity. It is, in fact, based directly on the *Lives* of Caesar, Brutus, and Mark Antony by the Greek historian Plutarch (c. 46–c. 127), which had appeared in a new translation by Sir Thomas North in 1579. *Julius Caesar* also illustrates Shakespeare's growing interest in psychological motivation rather than simply the sequence of events. The playwright tells us not so much what his characters do as why they do it, making use of the *soliloquy,* a kind of speech in which characters utter their thoughts out loud, without addressing them to anyone else, and thereby reveal to the audience the inner workings of their minds.

The use of this device becomes increasingly common in Shakespeare's supreme achievements, the series of tragedies he wrote between 1600 and 1605: *Hamlet* (c. 1600), *Othello* (c. 1604), *King Lear* (c. 1605), and *Macbeth* (c. 1605). In dramatic truth, poetic beauty, and profundity of meaning these four plays achieve an artistic perfection equaled only by the tragic dramas of Classical Greece. Through his protagonists, Shakespeare explores the great problems of human existence—the many forms of love, the possibilities and consequences of human error, the mystery of death—with a subtlety and yet a directness that remain miraculous through countless readings or performances and continue to provide inspiration to artists and writers.

Shakespeare's later plays explore new directions. *Antony and Cleopatra* (c. 1607–1608) returns to Plutarch and to ancient Rome, but with a new richness and magnificence of language. The conciseness of his great tragedies is replaced by a delight in the sound of words, and the play contains some of the most musical of all Shakespearean verse. His very last works examine the borderline between tragedy and comedy with a sophistication that was perhaps intended to satisfy the new aristocratic audience of the court of King James I. *The Tempest* (1611), set on an enchanted island, blends high romance and low comedy to create a world of fantasy unlike that of any of the other plays.

In the year he wrote *The Tempest,* Shakespeare left London and retired to Stratford to live out the remaining years of his life in comparative prosperity. Although he continued to write, it is tempting to see in the lines he gave to Prospero toward the end of *The Tempest* (IV, i, 148–158) his own farewell to the theater, and to the world he created for it:

Our revels now are ended. These our actors,
As I foretold you, were all spirits, and
Are melted into air, into thin air.
And, like the baseless fabric of this vision,
The cloud-capped towers, the gorgeous palaces,
The solemn temples, the great globe itself
Yea, all which it inherit—shall dissolve
And, like this insubstantial pageant faded,
Leave not a rack behind. We are such stuff
As dreams are made on, and our little life
Is rounded with a sleep.

SUMMARY

The political and cultural life of northern Europe was profoundly changed by the Reformation. After centuries of domination by the Church of Rome, many northern countries gradually switched to one of the various forms of Protestantism, whose ideas and teachings were rapidly spread by the use of the newly invented printing press. The consequences of this division did much to shape modern Europe, while the success of the Reformation movement directly stimulated the Counter-Reformation of the 17th century.

The growth of literacy both north and south of the Alps made possible by the easy availability of books produced a vast new reading public. Among the new literary forms to be introduced was that of the essay, first used by Montaigne. Epic poems were also popular; the works of Lodovico Ariosto and Torquato Tasso circulated widely and were imitated by a number of writers, including Edmund Spenser. The revival of interest in classical drama produced a new and enthusiastic audience for plays; those written by Elizabethan dramatists like Christopher Marlowe combined high poetic and intellectual quality with popular appeal. The supreme achievement in English literature of the time—and perhaps of all time—can be found in the works of William Shakespeare. Furthermore, in an age when the importance of education was emphasized, many advances in science were made and important scientific publications appeared. They included Vesalius' work on anatomy and Copernicus' revolutionary astronomical theories.

In the visual arts the 16th century saw the spread of Italian Renaissance ideas northward. In some cases they were carried by Italian artists like Benvenuto Cellini, who went to work in France. Some major northern artists, like Albrecht Dürer, actually traveled to Italy. Dürer's art was strongly influenced by Italian theories of perspective, proportion, and color, although he retained the strong interest in line typical of northern art. But not all his contemporaries showed the same interest in Italian styles. Matthias Grünewald's paintings do not show Renaissance concerns for humanism and ideal beauty; instead, they draw on traditional medieval German art to project the artist's own passionate religious beliefs, formed against the background of the bitter conflict of the Peasants' War.

The two leading Netherlandish artists of the century, Hieronymus Bosch and Pieter Bruegel the Elder, were also influenced by contemporary religious ideas. Their work has other characteristics in common: a pessimistic attitude toward human nature and the use of satire—yet the final effect is very different. Bosch's paintings are complex and bizarre; Bruegel shows a broader range of interest in human activities, together with a love of nature.

Elsewhere in northern Europe artistic inspiration was more fitful. The only English painter of note was the miniaturist Nicholas Hilliard, while in France the principal achievements were in the field of architecture. Even in Germany and the Netherlands, by the end of the century the Reformation movement's unsympathetic attitude to the visual arts had produced a virtual end to official patronage for religious art.

Music, on the other hand, was central to Reformation practice: Luther himself was a hymn writer of note. In England, after Henry VIII broke with Rome to form the Anglican Church, the hymns devised by the new church generally followed Reformation practice by using texts in the vernacular rather than in Latin. The music, however, retained the complexity of the Italian style; as a result the religious works of musicians like Tallis and Byrd are among the finest of northern Renaissance compositions.

Secular music also had a wide following throughout northern Europe, particularly as the printing of music became increasingly common. The form of the madrigal, originally devised in Italy, spread to France, Germany, the Netherlands, and England. Many of the works of the leading composers of the day, including the French Clement Janequin and the Flemish Heinrich Isaac, were intended for a popular audience and dealt with romantic or military themes.

Thus the combination of new Renaissance artistic ideas and new Reformation religious teachings roused northern Europe from its conservative traditions and stimulated a series of vital cultural developments.

Pronunciation Guide

Altdorfer: ALT-door-fer
Apocalypse: ah-POC-a-lips
Bosch: BOSH
Bruegel: BROY-gull
Byrd: BIRD
Chambord: Sham-BORE
Chanson: Shans-ON
Copernicus: Cop-EARN-ik-us
Dürer: DUE-rer
Grünewald: GROON-ee-vald
Guttenberg: GOOT-en-burg
Holbein: HOLE-bine
Isenheim: IZ-en-hime
Janequin: ZHAN-u-can
Loire: LWAR
Luther: LOO-ther
Montaigne: Mont-ANE
Polyphonic: Pol-i-FON-ic

Exercises

1. Discuss the career of Albrecht Dürer and compare his work with that of his contemporaries in Germany and Italy.
2. What were the principal causes of the Reformation? What was its impact on the development of the arts?
3. Describe the effect of the spread of humanism in northern Europe. What part was played by the invention of printing?

4. What are the main features of musical development during the 16th century? Discuss the relationship between sacred and secular music.
5. Describe Shakespeare's development as a dramatist and analyze the plot of one of his plays.

Further Reading

Campbell, O. J., and E. G. Quinn (eds.). *A Shakespeare Encyclopedia.* New York: Crowell, 1966. A valuable source of information on a wide variety of Shakespearean topics.

Davis, N. *Society and Culture in Early Modern France.* Stanford: Stanford University Press, 1975. A study of popular culture in the 16th and 17th centuries that makes use of much fascinating material.

Dickens, A. G. *Reformation and Society in Sixteenth Century Europe.* New York: Harcourt Brace Jovanovich, 1966. A traditional account of social trends in Reformation Europe.

Eisenstein, E. *The Printing Press as an Instrument of Change.* Cambridge: Cambridge University Press, 1979. An important book on an important subject; discusses conventional books and also woodcuts, broadsheets, and printed illustrations.

Hitchcock, H. R. *German Renaissance Architecture.* Princeton: Princeton University Press, 1981. A well-illustrated study of a surprisingly neglected field; provides a background to contemporary achievements in other artistic fields.

Leech, C. *Twelfth Night and Shakespearian Comedy.* Toronto: University of Toronto Press, 1968. An analysis of the play that sets it in context among Shakespeare's other comedies.

Newman, J. *Renaissance Music.* Englewood Cliffs: Prentice-Hall, 1965. A handy and compact account of the main developments in Renaissance music throughout Europe.

Ozment, S. *Reformation Europe: A Guide to Research.* St. Louis: St. Louis University Press, 1982. This very useful collection of essays deals with a variety of aspects of Reformation life: art, society and the sexes, and others.

Panofsky, E. *The Life and Art of Albrecht Dürer.* Princeton: Princeton University Press, 1971. A magisterial account by one of the greatest of all art historians. Difficult at times but immensely rewarding.

Rose, M. B. *Women in the Middle Ages and the Renaissance.* Syracuse: Syracuse University Press, 1986. An anthology of readings that brings together a great deal of remarkable material and casts light on a subject that has only recently begun to be studied in its own right.

Snyder, J. *Northern Renaissance Art.* Englewood Cliffs: Prentice-Hall, 1985. The most up-to-date general survey of painting, sculpture, and the graphic arts in northern Europe from 1350 to 1575.

	GENERAL EVENTS	LITERATURE & PHILOSOPHY	ART
1560			
DECLINE OF SPANISH POWER	**1603–1625** Reign of James I in England **1609** Holland and Flanders given virtual independence in truce with Spain **1610–1643** Reign of Louis XIII in France; Marie de' Medici is regent during his minority	**1565** Teresa of Avila, *Autobiography* **1582–1584** John of the Cross, *The Dark Night* **1605–1615** Cervantes, *Don Quixote* **1611** Publication of *Authorized Version* of Bible, commissioned by King James I	**1595–1600** El Greco, *The Baptism of Christ* **1597–1604** Caravaggio and the Carracci at work in Rome **c. 1600–1602** Caravaggio, *The Doubting of Thomas, The Calling of Saint Matthew, The Martyrdom of Saint Matthew* **1604** A. Carracci, *The Flight into Egypt;* decorations for Palazzo Farnese Galleria completed **1616** Hals, *Banquet of the Officers of the Saint George Militia Company* **c. 1616–1617** Rubens, *The Rape of the Daughters of Leucippus*
1618			
THIRTY YEARS' WAR	**1618** Thirty Years' War begins in Germany **1620** English Pilgrims land at Plymouth **1621–1665** Reign of Philip IV in Spain **1643** Five-year-old Louis XIV ascends throne of France under regency of his mother **1648** Peace of Westphalia	**1621** Donne appointed Dean of Saint Paul's, London **1632** Galileo, founder of modern physics, submits *Dialogue Concerning the Two Chief World Systems* to Pope Urban VIII; is tried and condemned in 1633 **1637** Descartes, "Father of Modern Philosophy," publishes *The Discourse on Method* **1638** Galileo, *Dialogues Concerning Two New Sciences* **c. 1640** French Classical comedy and tragedy at height **1640–1643** Corneille, *Horace, Polyeucte,* tragedies **1641** Descartes, *Meditations* **1646** Crashaw, *Steps to the Temple*	**c. 1620** Artemisia Gentileschi, *Judith and Holofernes* **1622–1625** Rubens paints cycle of 21 paintings glorifying Marie de' Medici; Bernini, *The Rape of Proserpine* **1623** Bernini, *David;* Velázquez appointed court painter to Philip IV **c. 1625** Van Dyck, *Portrait of the Marchesa Cattaneo* **1627** Caravaggio's influence spreads northward when Louis XIII summons Vouet back from Rome to become court artist **c. 1630** A. Gentileschi, *Self-Portrait as "La Pittura"* **1631** Claude Lorrain, *The Mill* **1632** Van Dyck court painter to Charles I **c. 1639** Ribera, *The Martyrdom of Saint Bartholomew* **1642** Rembrandt, *The Night Watch* **1645–1652** Bernini, *Saint Teresa in Ecstasy*
1649			
PURITAN RULE	**1649** Execution of Charles I of England; Cromwell rules 1649–1658	**c. 1650** Locke active in England, Pascal in France, Spinoza in Holland **1651** Hobbes, *Leviathan* **c. 1659–1699** Poet and dramatist John Dryden active in England	**c. 1650** Poussin, *The Arcadian Shepherds;* Georges de La Tour, *Saint Sebastian Attended by Saint Irene* **1656** Velázquez, *Las Meninas*
1660			
AGE OF LOUIS XIV AND XV	**1660** Restoration of monarchy in England under Charles II **1661** Louis XIV assumes full control of France **1682** Louis XIV moves court to newly remodeled Versailles **1688** Parliamentary enemies of James II invite William of Orange to invade England **1689** Declaration of Rights establishes English constitutional government; William and Mary rule **1715** Louis XIV dies after 72-year reign; Louis XV ascends throne	**1664** Molière, *Tartuffe,* comedy **1667** Milton, *Paradise Lost,* epic poem in tradition of Homer and Vergil **1677** Racine, *Phèdre,* tragedy **1690** Locke, *Concerning Human Understanding* **1694** Voltaire born in Paris	**1662–1664** Vermeer, *Woman in Blue Reading a Letter* **1669** Death of Rembrandt; last *Self-Portrait* **1701** Rigaud, *Louis XIV*
1774			

CHAPTER 13 THE BAROQUE WORLD

ARCHITECTURE	MUSIC

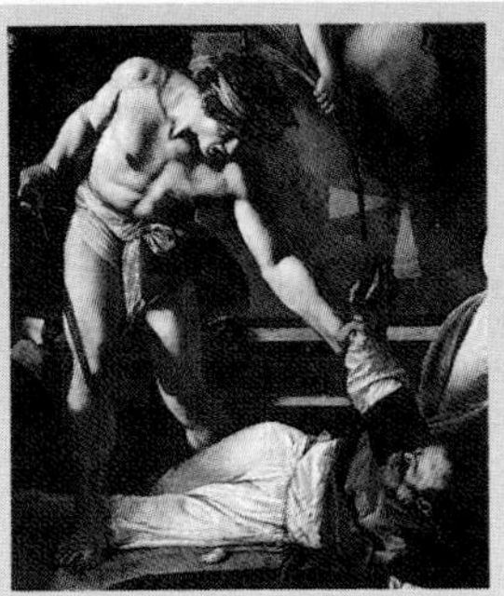

late 16th cent. Birth of opera in Florence, development of *monody*

1594–1595 Peri, *Dafne,* first play set to music, performed in Florence

1600 Peri, *Euridice*

Opera, concerto grosso, oratorio, cantata, and sonata established as musical forms; virtuoso tradition begins

1607 Monteverdi, *L'Orfeo*

1619 Schütz, *Psalms of David*

Retention of classical vocabulary of Renaissance but on grandiose scale; civic planning and private-house construction also prevalent because of rise of middle classes

1629 Bernini appointed official architect of Saint Peter's, Rome

1631–1687 Longhena, Santa Maria della Salute, Venice

1638–1641 Borromini, Church of San Carlo alle Quattro Fontane, Rome; façade added 1665–1667

1634 Frescobaldi active at Rome

1652 Lully enters service of Louis XIV

1663 Bernini, piazza and colonnades for Saint Peter's, Rome; church proper completed by Carlo Maderno 1607–1615

1669–1685 Le Vau and Hardouin-Mansart, Garden façade Versailles

1678 Le Brun and Hardouin-Mansart begin Hall of Mirrors, Palace of Versailles

1668 Buxtehude becomes organist at Lübeck

1674 Lully's *Alceste* first performed at Versailles

1685 Births of Bach, Handel, Scarlatti

c. 1720 Vivaldi, *The Four Seasons,* violin concertos

1721 J. S. Bach, *Brandenburg Concertos*

1723 Bach appointed Kantor of St. Thomas', Leipzig

1729 J. S. Bach, *St. Matthew Passion*

c. 1735 Rameau, *Les Indes Galantes*

1742 Handel's *Messiah* first performed

CHAPTER

13 THE BAROQUE WORLD

THE COUNTER-REFORMATION SPIRIT

By about 1600 the intellectual and artistic movements of the Renaissance and Reformation had taken a new turn. Although the cultural activity of the next hundred and fifty years was the natural outgrowth of earlier developments, the difference in spirit—already signaled by the middle of the 16th century—was striking.

The chief agent of the new spirit was the Roman Catholic Church. After initial shock at the success of Protestantism, the Catholic Church decided that the best defense was a well-planned attack. Switching to the offensive, the Church relied in great measure on new religious orders like the Jesuits to lead the movement known as the Counter-Reformation. Putting behind them the anxieties of the past, the chief representatives of the Counter-Reformation gave voice to a renewed spirit of confidence in the universality of the Church and the authority of its teachings.

The official position of the Church was newly stated at the Council of Trent, which met sporadically from 1545 to 1563. Under the leadership of Pope Paul III, the council redefined Catholic doctrines, and reaffirmed those dogmas which Protestantism had challenged. Transubstantiation, the apostolic succession of the priesthood, the belief in purgatory, and the rule of celibacy for the clergy were all confirmed as essential to the Catholic system of faith. The pope remained as monarchical ruler of the Church. At the same time, the Council tried to eliminate abuses by the clergy, and to tighten discipline. Bishops and priests could no longer hold more than one benefice, and theological seminaries were set up in every dioscese to improve the educational level of the priesthood.

One of the key instruments in the campaign to reestablish the authority of the Church was the Society of Jesus, an order of priests and brothers dedicated to the defense of the faith. The order was founded in 1534 by Ignatius Loyola (1491–1556), a Spanish nobleman. After spending the first part of his career as a soldier, he became converted to the religious life after suffering a serious wound. His *Spiritual Exercises* (begun 1522–1523) express a mystical, even morbid spirit of introspection, inspired by visions of Satan, Jesus, and the Trinity. A similarly heightened spiritual sense and attempt to describe mystical experiences occurs in the writings of other Spanish Catholics of the Counter-Reformation, most notably Saint Teresa of Avila (1515–1582) and Saint John of the Cross (1542–1591); the latter wrote powerfully of the soul's emergence from the "dark night" to attain union with God.

The Order which Ignatius Loyola founded soon became the most militant of the various religious movements to appear during the 16th century, Its members, the Jesuits, fought not with swords or guns, but with eloquence and the power of persuasion. The Jesuits were organized on the model of a military company, led by a general as their chief commander, and required to exercise iron discipline. Their duty was simple: to promote the teachings of the Church unquestioningly—Loyola taught that if the Church ruled that black was white, its followers were obliged to believe it. They reinforced this position by vigorous missionary work throughout Europe and in the Americas and the Far East, while improving educational institutions throughout Catholic Europe.

At the same time, the Council of Trent called on artists to remind Catholics of the power and splendor of their religion by commissioning a massive quantity of works of art dedicated to underlining the chief principles of Counter-Reformation teachings. Now it was the task of religious leaders and, under their guidance, of the artists to make this

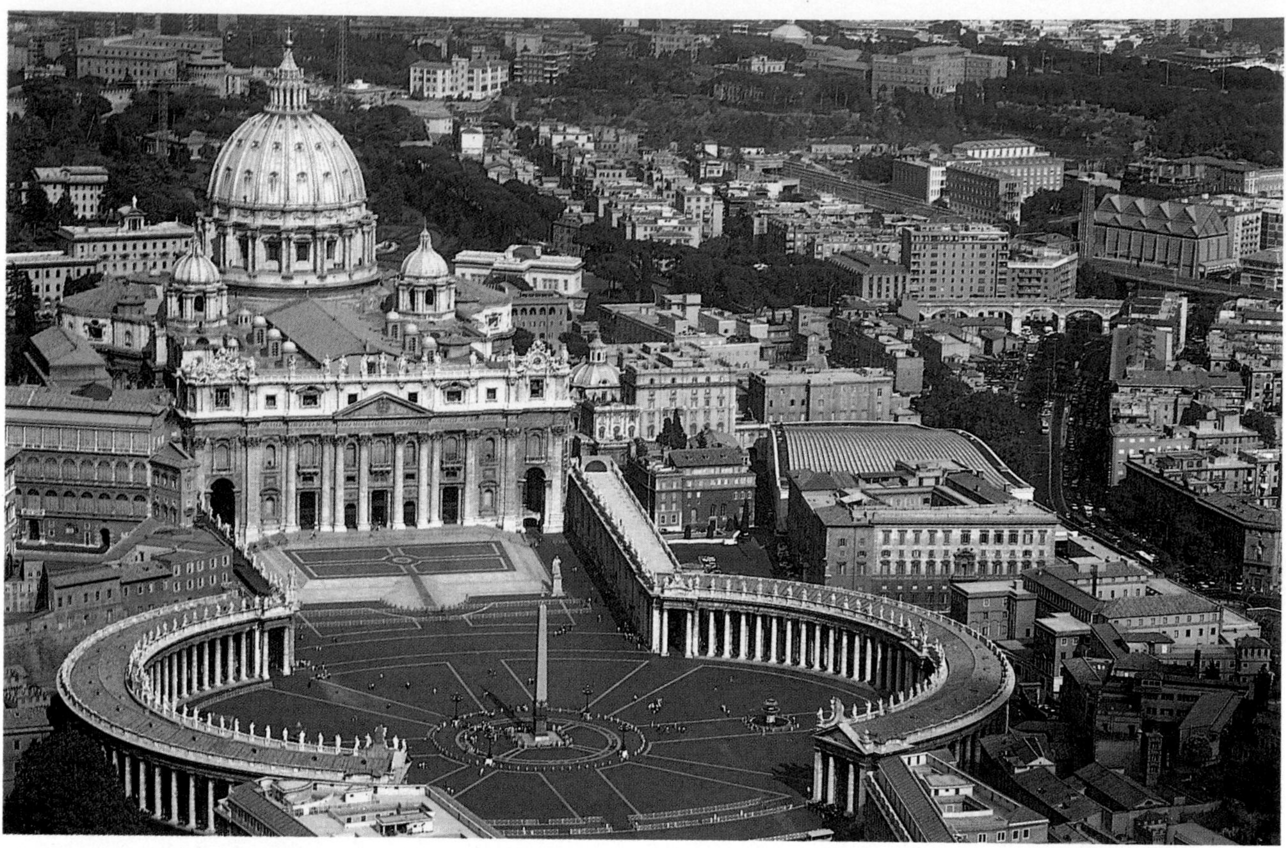

13.1 Aerial view of Saint Peter's, Rome. Height of façade 147' (44.81 m), width 374' (114 m). The nave and façade were finished by Carlo Maderna (1556–1629) between 1606 and 1612, and the colonnades around the square were built between 1656 and 1663 to the design of Bernini (see page 358). The completion of Saint Peter's was one of the first great achievements of baroque architecture.

position known to the faithful. New emphasis was placed on clarity and directness. The impression of the Church's triumphant resurgence was further reinforced by a new emphasis on material splendor and glory. In Rome itself the construction of a number of lavish churches was crowned by the completion at last of Saint Peter's and the addition of Bernini's spectacular *piazza*, or square, in front of it [13.1], while throughout Catholic Europe there developed a rich and ornate art that could do justice to the new demands for expressive power and spectacle.

The term used to describe the new style, at first in derision but since the 19th century simply as a convenient label, is *baroque*. The word's origins are obscure. It may be related to the Portuguese *barroco*, which means an irregularly shaped pearl, or perhaps to *baroco*, an Italian term used to describe a complicated problem in medieval logic. In any case, baroque came to be applied in general to anything elaborate and fanciful, in particular to the artistic style of the 17th and early 18th centuries.

Although strictly speaking baroque is a term applied only to the visual arts, it is frequently used to describe the entire cultural achievement of the age. To extend its use to literature, music, and even intellectual developments of the same period inevitably implies that all the arts of the Baroque period had certain characteristics in common. In fact, a close comparison between the visual arts, music, and literature of the 17th and early 18th centuries does reveal a number of shared ideas and attitudes. It is important to remember from the outset, however, that this artistic unity is by no means obvious. A first glance at the cultural range of the period actually reveals a quite astonishing variety of styles, developing individually in widely separated places and subject to very different political and social pressures.

In this respect the Baroque period marks a significant break with the Renaissance, when Italy had been the center of virtually all artistic development. In spite of the impact of the Counter-Reformation, the Reformation itself had begun an irreversible process of decentralization. By the beginning of the 17th century, although Rome was still the artistic capital of Europe, important cultural changes were taking place elsewhere. The economic growth of countries like Holland and England, and the increasing power of France, produced a series of artistic styles that developed locally rather than being imported wholesale from south of the Alps. Throughout northern Europe the rise of the middle class continued to create a new public for the arts, which in turn affected the development of painting, architecture, and music. For the first time European culture began to spread across the Atlantic, carried to the Americas by Counter-Reformation missionaries.

The much greater geographic spread of artistic achievement was accompanied by the creation of new artistic forms in response to new religious and social pressures. In music, for instance, the 17th century saw the birth of opera and of new kinds of instrumental music, including works for orchestra like the *concerto grosso*. Painters continued to depict scenes from the Bible and from classical mythology but they turned increasingly to other subjects including portraits, landscapes, and scenes from everyday life. Architects constructed private town houses and started to take an interest in civic planning instead of devoting themselves exclusively to churches and palaces.

A similar richness and variety can be found in the philosophical and scientific thought of the period, which managed temporarily to reconcile its own pursuit of scientific truth with traditional theological and political attitudes. By the end of the 17th century, however, the practical discoveries of science had begun to undermine long-accepted ideas and to lay the basis for the new skepticism that came to dominate the 18th century.

It would be unwise to look for broad general principles operating in an age of such dynamic and varied change. Nonetheless, to understand and appreciate the baroque spirit as it appears in the individual arts it is helpful to bear in mind the chief assumptions and preoccupations shared by most baroque artists. Whatever the medium in which they worked, baroque artists were united in their commitment to strong emotional statements, to psychological exploration, and to the invention of new and daring techniques.

Perhaps the most striking of these is the expression of intense emotions. In the Renaissance artists had generally tried to achieve the calm balance and order they thought of as typically classical: In the Baroque period artists were attracted by extremes of feeling. Sometimes these strong emotions were personal. Painters and poets alike tried to look into their own souls and reveal by color or word the depths of their own psychic and spiritual

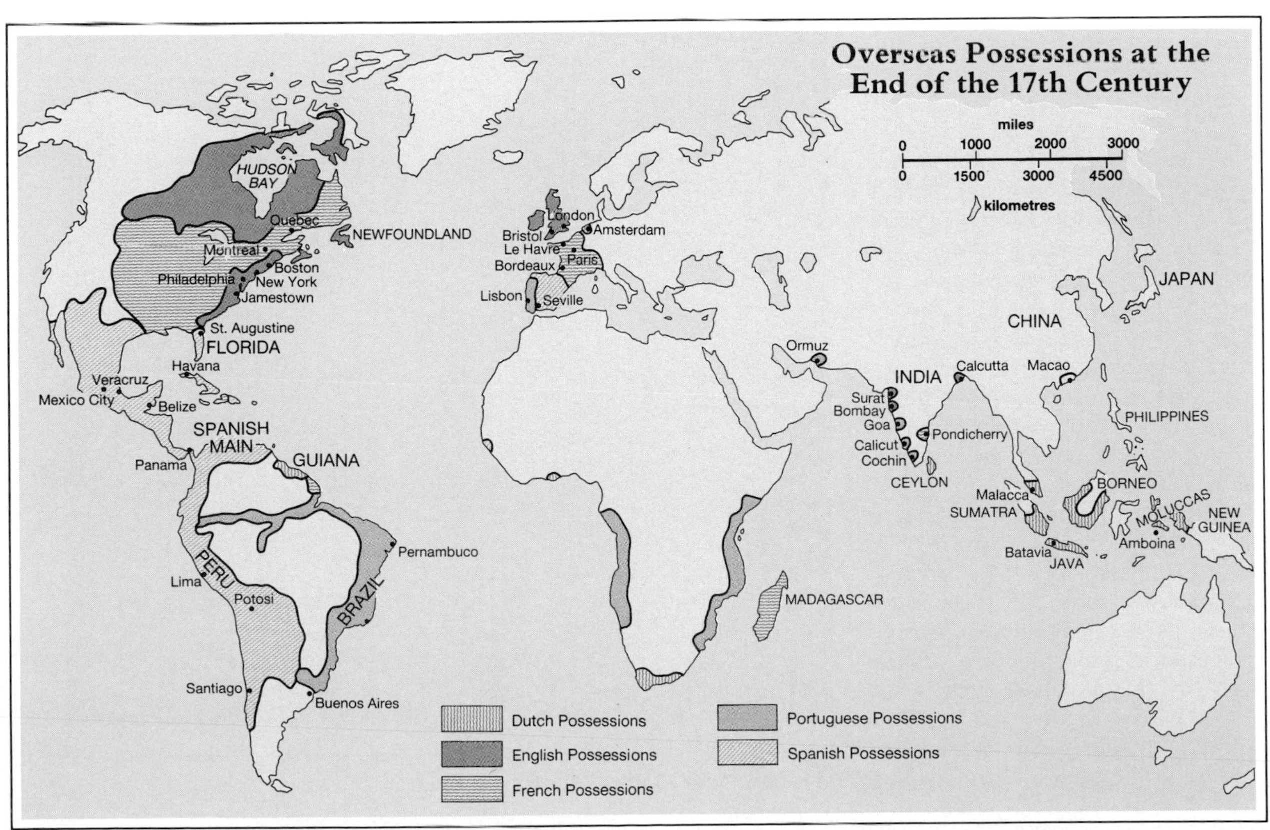

experience. More often artists tried to convey intense religious emotions. In each case, far from avoiding painful or extremely emotional states as subjects, their works sought out and explored them.

The concern with emotion produced in its turn an interest in what came to be called psychology. Baroque artists tried to explain how and why their subjects felt as strongly as they did by representing their emotional states as vividly and analytically as possible. This is particularly evident in 17th-century opera and drama, where music in the one case and words in the other were used to depict the precise state of mind of the characters.

EAST MEETS WEST

The Spanish Empire in America

The expedition of Christopher Columbus that discovered America in 1492 had been funded by the Spanish Queen Isabella in the hope that it would beat the Portuguese to the East. America was a consolation prize, and one which the *conquistadores* were quick to exploit. Mines were opened for precious metals, in which native Indians were put to forced labor; many of them died. Church leaders saw the new territories as ripe for missionary campaigns of conversion, and throughout the 16th and 17th centuries churches were built in the principal centers of Latin (or Spanish) America [13.2].

By the end of the 16th century the Spanish possessions in America were divided into two great viceroyalties: Mexico and Peru. A small white governing class of Castilian Spanish ruled the Indian population and a growing number of *mestizos* (people of mixed white and Indian descent). American-born whites, or Creoles, were regarded by the Spanish as inferior. Slaves were imported from Africa, and in general received better status and protection in Spanish America than those employed in the later Dutch, French, and English colonies of North America.

Counter-Reformation missionaries introduced the Spanish language and the faith of the Spanish Church, and with them other aspects of European culture. A printing press was functioning in Mexico City by the mid-16th century. By 1636, when Harvard College (the oldest university in the United States) was founded, there were already five European-style universities in Spanish America, including those of Mexico City and Lima.

Many of the most elaborate of Counter-Reformation projects and building schemes in Europe were funded by precious metals mined in Mexico and Peru. It has been calculated that for years half a million pounds of silver and ten thousand pounds of gold were transported annually from America to Spain.

Thus by the 17th century Europe had become transformed from a self-contained world to the center of a global navigation network from which America, Asia, and Africa were all within reach. The consequences for European culture were profound.

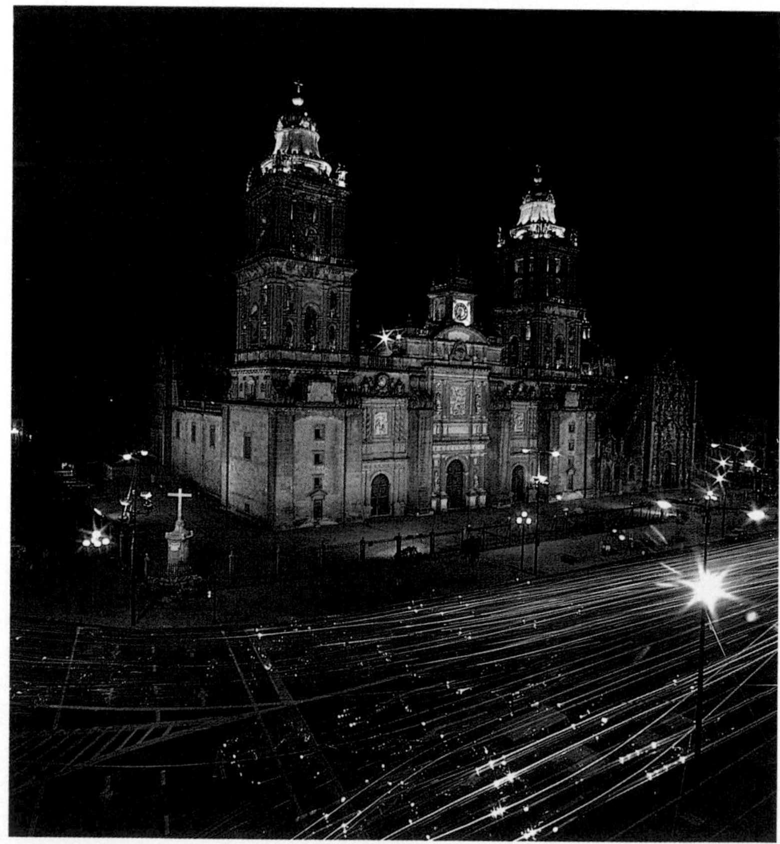

13.2 Mexico City Cathedral. 1656–1671.

The desire to express the inexpressible required the invention of new techniques. As a result, baroque art put great emphasis on virtuosity. Sculptors and painters achieved astonishing realism in the way in which they handled their media. Stone was carved in such a way as to give the effect of thin, flowing drapery, while 17th-century painters found ways to reproduce complex effects of light and shade [Table 13.1]. Baroque writers often used elaborate imagery and complicated grammatical structure to express intense emotional states. In music, both composers and performers began to develop new virtuoso skills; composers in their ability to write works of greater and greater complexity, and performers in their ability to sing or play music in the new style. In fact some pieces, like *toccatas*—free-form rhapsodies for keyboard—were principally intended to allow instrumentalists to demonstrate their technique, thus inaugurating the tradition of the virtuoso performer that reached a climax in the 19th century.

TABLE 13.1 Characteristics and Examples of Baroque Art

Characteristic	Example
Emotionalism	Caravaggio, *The Martyrdom of Saint Matthew* [13.4]
	Rubens, *Rape of the Daughters of Leucippus* [13.26]
Illusionism	Bernini, *David* [13.9]
	Rembrandt, *The Night Watch* [13.31]
Splendor	Bernini, Saint Peter's Square [13.1]
	Versailles [13.19, 20]
	Carracci, *The Triumph of Bacchus and Ariadne* [13.7]
Light and Shade	Caravaggio, *The Conversion of Saint Paul* [13.3]
	Velázquez, *Las Meninas* [13.24]
	Vermeer, *Woman Reading a Letter* [13.30]
	de La Tour, *The Lamentation over Saint Sebastian* [13.13]
Movement	El Greco, *Burial of Count Orgaz* [13.22]
	Borromini, *Façade for San Carlo* [13.12]
Religious Fervor	Ribera, *The Martyrdom of Saint Bartholomew* [13.23]
	El Greco, *The Martyrdom of Saint Maurice* [13.21]
Domestic Intimacy	Caravaggio, *Madonna of Loreto* [13.5]
	Rubens, *Hélène Fourment* [13.25]
	Rembrandt, *Jacob Blessing the Sons of Joseph* [13.33]

THE VISUAL ARTS IN THE BAROQUE PERIOD

Painting in Rome: Caravaggio and the Carracci

The foundations of baroque style, which was to dominate much of European painting for one hundred and fifty years, were laid in Rome around 1600 by two artists whose work at first glance seems to have little in common. Michelangelo Merisi (1573–1610), better known as Caravaggio—the name of his home town in northern Italy—explored the darker aspects of life and death in some of the most naturalistic and dramatic pictures ever painted. Annibale Carracci (1560–1609) preferred to paint light and elegant depictions of the loves of gods and goddesses and charming landscapes. That both artists exerted an immense influence on their successors says something for the extreme range of baroque painting.

Of the two painters, Caravaggio was certainly the more controversial in his day. His own life-style did little to recommend him to the aristocratic and ecclesiastical patrons on whom he depended. From his first arrival in Rome around 1590 Caravaggio seems to have lived an unconventional and violent life, in continual trouble with the police and alienating potential friends by his savage temper.

Any chances Caravaggio had for establishing himself successfully in Rome were brought to an abrupt end in 1606 when he quarreled violently with an opponent in a tennis match and stabbed him to death. He avoided punishment only by fleeing to Naples and then to Malta, where he was thrown into prison for attacking a police officer. Escaping, he made his way to Sicily and then back to Naples, where yet again he got involved in a violent quarrel, this time in a sleazy inn. Seriously wounded, he heard of the possibility of a pardon if he were to return to Rome, but on the journey back he died of a fever (brought on, it was said, by a final attack of rage at some sailors he mistakenly thought had robbed him). The pardon from the pope arrived a few days later.

The spirit of rebellion that governed Caravaggio's life can be seen in his art. In his depiction of religious scenes he refused to accept either the traditionally idealizing versions of earlier artists or the Counter-Reformation demands for magnificent display. Furthermore, instead of placing his figures in an elaborate setting in accordance with Counter-Reformation principles, Caravaggio surrounded them with shadows, a device that emphasizes the drama of the scene and the poverty of the participants.

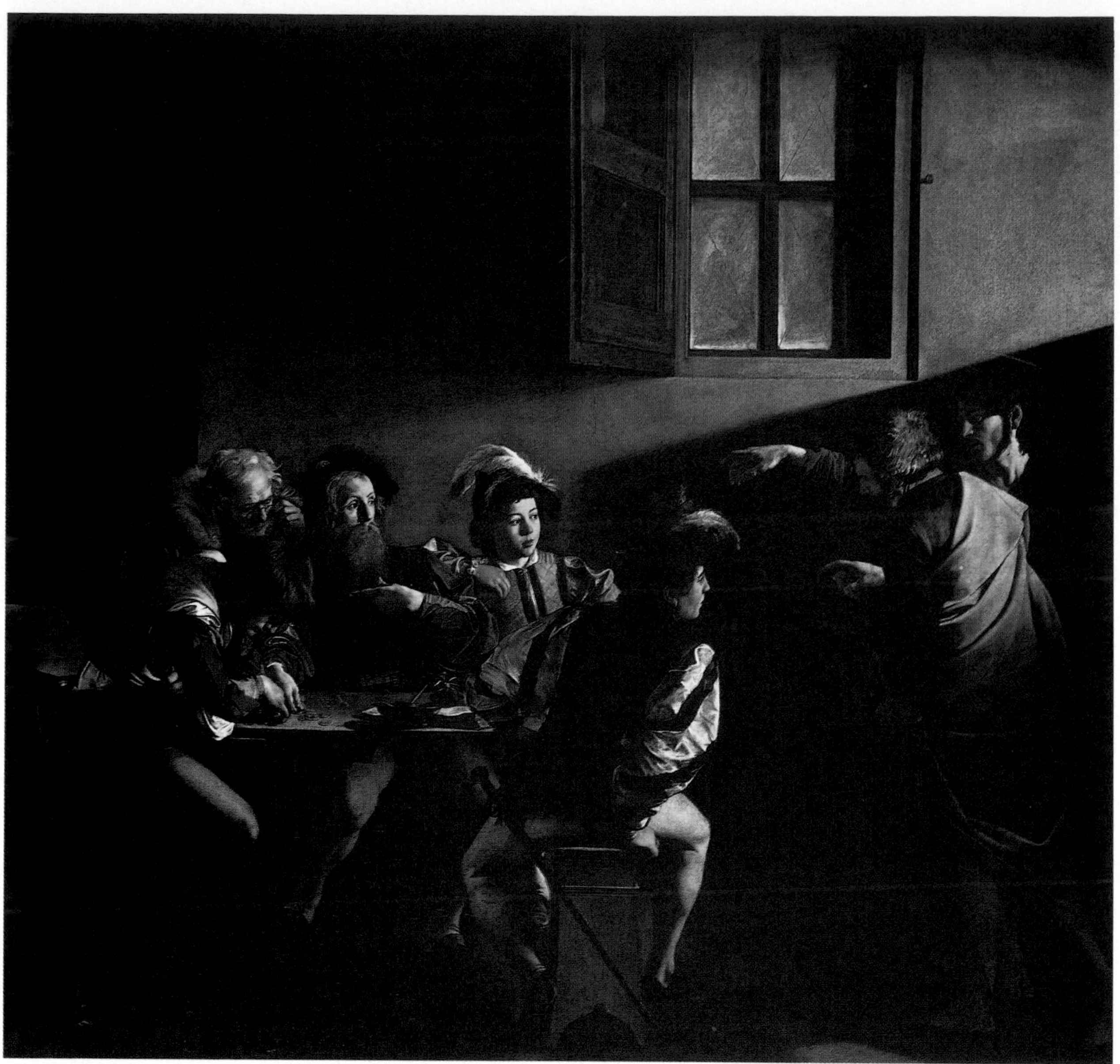

13.3 Caravaggio. *The Calling of Saint Matthew.* 1597–1598. Oil on canvas, 11'½" × 11'5" (3.38 × 1.48 m). Contarelli Chapel, San Luigi dei Francesi, Rome. The artist produces a highly dramatic effect by letting the bright light emanating from the half-hidden figure of Jesus to the right strike the head of Matthew. The future saint draws back from the glare in fear.

Caravaggio's preference for extreme contrasts between light and dark, described by the Italian word *chiaroscuro,* was one of the aspects of his style most imitated by later painters. When not handled by a master, the use of heavy shadows surrounding brightly lit figures in the foreground tends to become artificial and overtheatrical, but in Caravaggio's works it always serves a true dramatic purpose. In his painting *The Calling of St. Matthew* [13.3], one of three pictures painted between 1597 and 1603 for the Contarelli Chapel in the Church of San Luigi dei Francesi at Rome—Caravaggio's first important Roman commission — the stern hand of Jesus summoning the future apostle is emphasized by the beam of light which reveals the card players at the table; Matthew, awed and fearful, tries to shrink back into the darkness.

In his painting of *The Martyrdom of Saint Matthew* [13.4], Caravaggio used his own experience of suffering to portray it with painful realism, while the painting tells us as much about the reactions of the onlookers as about Matthew himself. They range from the sadistic violence of the executioner to the apparent indifference of the figures in shadow on

SPORTS AND GAMES

Cards and Dice

The scene of the calling of St. Matthew draws on one of the commonest forms of recreation in the 16th and 17th centuries, especially among the poorer classes, the playing of games with cards and dice. Both devices first appeared centuries earlier—dice were found in Tutankhamen's tomb—but the development of urban life produced increasing numbers of taverns and other public places where players could gamble and drink at the same time.

Playing cards were in use in Europe by the 14th century; they were probably introduced from the Orient. The first decks, known as tarot cards, had seventy-eight cards, divided into four suits; cups, pentacles, swords and wands, with another group of twenty-two cards, the major arcana, which functioned as permanent trumps (they ranked higher than any of the suit cards). From their earliest introduction, tarot cards were used as much for fortune telling as for playing games, and with the introduction of printing in the mid-15th century books began to circulate which interpreted the significance of various card combinations. Dice, six-sided cubes with their sides numbered from one to six, were perhaps even more popular, serving for board games and for games of chance.

Both cards and dice naturally lent themselves to gambling, and a tavern such as the one in Caravaggio's painting was often the scene of noisy games leading to accusations of cheating. While cheating at cards required sleight of hand, professional dice players often used false dice. One trick was to set a small bristle on one face of a die, which was intended to prevent the cube from ever landing on that face. Others were to hollow out one side, or to weight the cube—load the dice—so that the same face would always finish on the table.

Games with cards and dice retained their popularity over the centuries, and even the inventions of modern popular culture have not displaced them. With the development of the fifty-two card, four-suit deck in the early 18th century, whist became among the most widely known games. The modern form of whist, contract bridge, was perfected in the United States in 1925–1926 by Harold S. Vanderbilt. Bridge games range from simple domestic matches and social gatherings to international championship contests in which teams from many parts of the world compete.

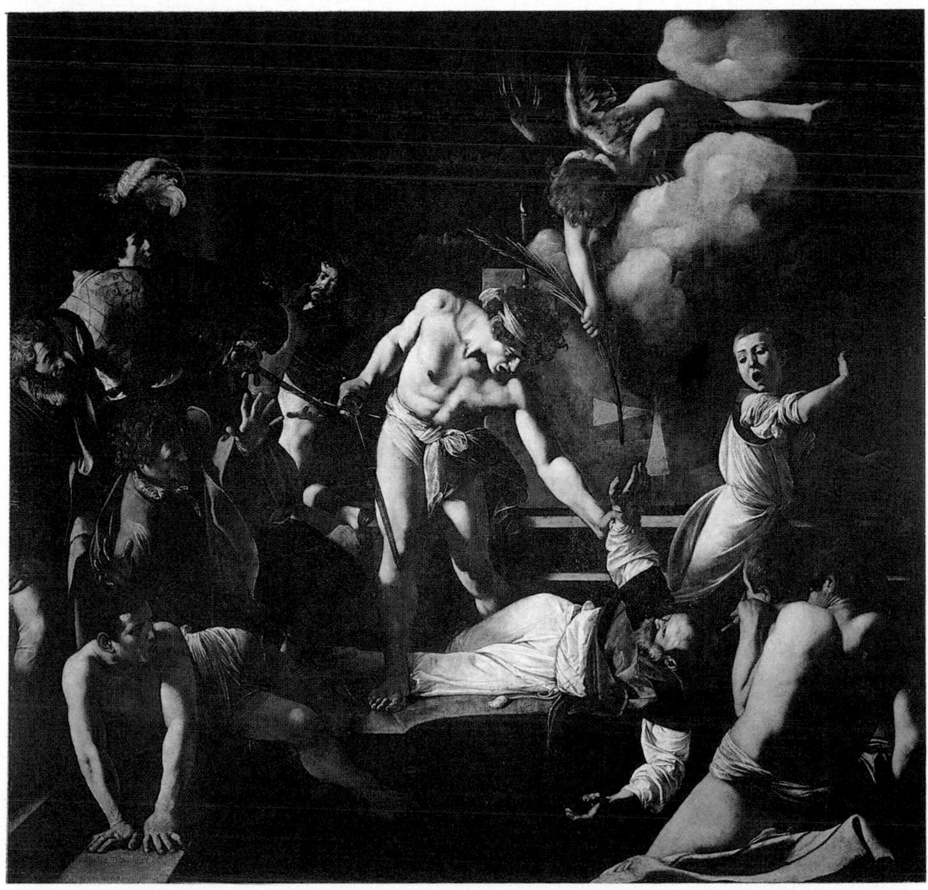

13.4 Caravaggio. *The Martyrdom of Saint Matthew.* c. 1602. Oil on canvas, 10'9" × 11'6" (3.3 × 3.5 m). Contarelli Chapel, San Luigi dei Francesi, Rome. The deeply moved onlooker at the very back of the scene is, according to one tradition, a self-portrait of the artist.

the left; only the angel swooping down with the palm of martyrdom relieves the brutality and pessimism of the scene.

It would be a mistake to think of Caravaggio's work as without tenderness. In the *Madonna of Loreto* [13.5] he shows us not the remote grace of a Botticelli Virgin or the sweet, calm beauty of a Raphael Madonna but a simple Roman mother. As she stands gravely on the doorstep of her back-street house where the plaster is falling away from the walls, two humble pilgrims fall to their knees in confident prayer. They raise their loving faces to the Virgin and Christ Child while turning toward us their muddy, travel-stained feet. It is perhaps not surprising that some of Caravaggio's contemporaries, brought up on the elegant and well-nourished Madonnas and worshipers of the Renaissance and surrounded by the splendor of Counter-Reformation art, should have found pictures like these disrespectful and lacking in devotion. It should be equally unsurprising that once the initial shock wore off, the honesty and truth of Caravaggio's vision made a profound impact on both artists and the public.

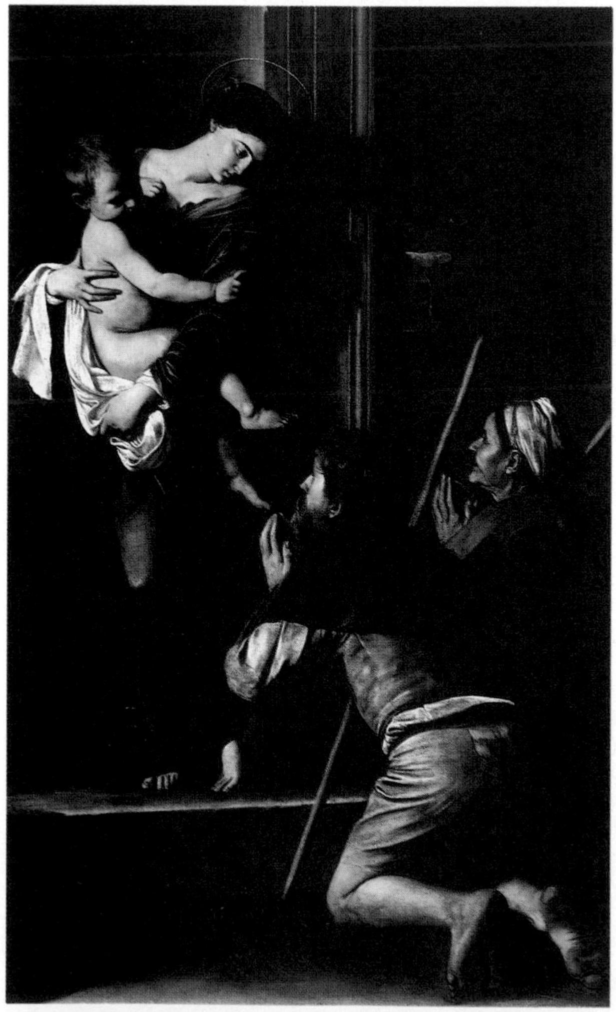

13.5 Caravaggio. *Madonna of Loreto.* c. 1604. Oil on canvas, 8'6½" × 4'10½" (2.6 × 1.5 m). Cavaletti Chapel, San Agostino, Rome. The shabby clothes show the poverty of the two pilgrims.

Among the painters working at Rome who fell under the spell of Caravaggio's works was Orazio Gentileschi (1563–1639), who was born in Pisa and studied in Florence. Much impressed by Caravaggio's dramatic naturalism and concern for psychological truth, Gentileschi based his own style on that of his younger contemporary. Since he spent the last eighteen years of his life traveling and living in northern Europe, first in France and then in England, he played an important part in spreading a knowledge of Caravaggio's style outside Italy. At the same time, moreover, he handed on his enthusiasm to a painter nearer home, his own daughter Artemisia (1592–1652/1653).

Artemisia Gentileschi has been described as the first woman in the history of the Western world to make a significant contribution to the art of her time. The question of why so few women achieved eminence in the visual arts before recent times is a complicated one, and the chief answers are principally social and economic rather than aesthetic. Certainly, Artemisia was typical of the few women painters of the Renaissance and Baroque periods who did become famous in that she was the daughter of a painter and therefore at home in the world of art and artists.

Gentileschi's most famous painting is *Judith and Holofernes* [13.6]. Done in chiaroscuro, the painting conveys a tremendous sense of violence as Judith and her maid loom over the drastically foreshortened body of Holofernes. There is a stark contrast between the realistic violence of the beheading and the sensual richness of the silken bed, the jewelry, and the cunning drapery. It is not inconceivable that the painter, herself a rape victim in her youth, poured her own passionate protest into this painting of a woman taking retribution against a would-be defiler. This work depicts a scene from the biblical story of the Jewish heroine Judith, who used her charms to save her people from an invading Assyrian army; she won the confidence of its general, Holofernes, and then beheaded him in the privacy of his tent.

It is a far cry from the dark, emotional world of Caravaggio and his followers to the brilliant, idealized world of Annibale Carracci, his brother Agostino, and his cousin Ludovico, all often spoken of collectively as the Carracci. The most gifted

13.6 Artemisia Gentileschi. *Judith and Holofernes.* c. 1620. Oil on canvas, 78⅓" × 64" (199 × 162.5 cm). Uffizi, Florence.

member of this Bolognese family was Annibale, whose earliest important work in Rome, the decoration of the *galleria* or formal reception hall of the Palazzo Farnese, was painted between 1597 and 1604, precisely the years when Caravaggio was working on the Contarelli Chapel. The many scenes in the galleria constitute a fresco cycle based on Greek and Roman mythology, depicting the

13.7 Annibale Carracci. *The Triumph of Bacchus and Ariadne.* 1597–1600. Fresco. Farnese Palace, Rome. The god's chariot, drawn by tigers, is accompanied by a wild procession of cupids, nymphs, and satyrs.

loves of the gods, including *The Triumph of Bacchus and Ariadne* [13.7]. The sense of exuberant life and movement and the mood of unrestrained sensual celebration seem at the farthest remove from Caravaggio's somber paintings, yet both artists share the baroque love of extreme emotion, and both show the same concern for realism of detail.

The same blend of ideal proportion and realistic detail emerges in Annibale's landscape paintings, of which the best-known is probably *The Flight into Egypt* [13.8]. The scene is the countryside around Rome, with the river Tiber in the foreground and the Alban hills in the distance. The tiny human figures are carefully related in proportion to this natu-

13.8 Annibale Carracci. *The Flight into Egypt.* c. 1604. Oil on canvas, 3' × 7'5⅝" (.9 × 2.3 m). Doria-Pamphili Gallery, Rome. In spite of the Holy Family in the center foreground, the painting is not so much religious as a depiction of the landscape around Rome.

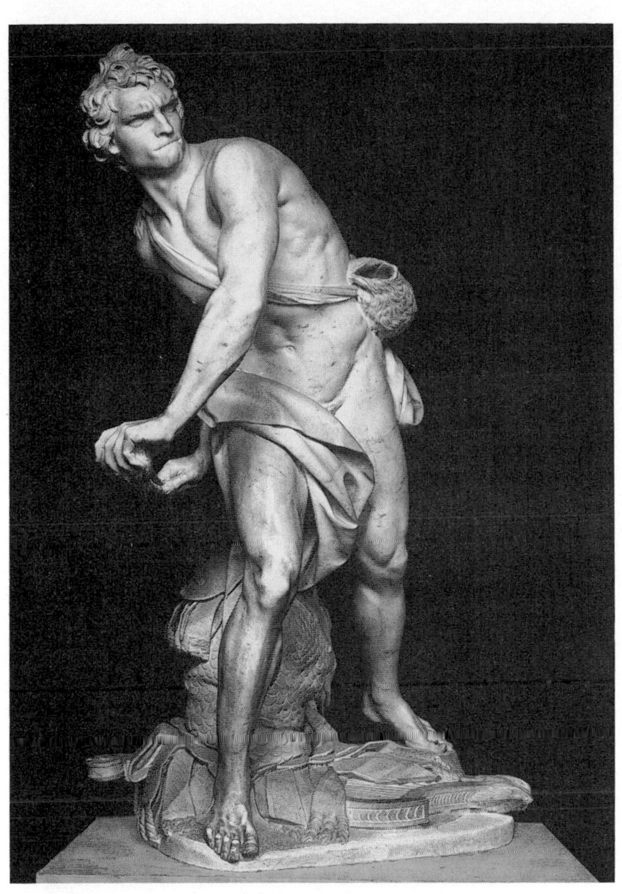

13.9 Gian Lorenzo Bernini. *David.* 1623–1624. Marble, height 5'6¼" (1.7 m). Borghese Gallery, Rome. It is said that Bernini carved the face while looking at his own in a mirror. The expression reinforces the tension of the pose.

ral setting, precisely balanced by the distant castle, and located just at the meeting point of the diagonal lines formed by the flock of sheep and the river. As a result, we perceive a sense of idyllic classical order while being convinced of the reality of the landscape.

Roman Baroque Sculpture and Architecture: Bernini and Borromini

The most influential of all Italian baroque artists of the Counter-Reformation was a sculptor and architect, not a painter. The sculptural achievement of Gian Lorenzo Bernini (1598–1680), of seemingly unlimited range of expression and unbelievable technical virtuosity, continued to influence sculptors until the 19th century; as the chief architect of Counter-Reformation Rome he permanently changed the face of that venerable city.

Born the son of a Florentine sculptor in Naples, Bernini showed signs of his extraordinary abilities from an early age. One of his first important works, a statue of *David* [13.9], seems to have been deliberately intended to evoke comparison with works by his illustrious predecessors. Unlike the *David*s of Donatello (see Figure 10.14) or Michelangelo (see Figure 10.27) which show the subject in repose, Bernini's figure is very definitely in the midst of action. From the bitten lips to the muscular tension of the arms to the final detail of the clenched toes of the right foot, this *David* seems to personify energy, almost exploding through space. Bernini gives the figure additional expressive power by his deep cuts in the stone, producing a strong contrast between light and dark. In its expression of violent emotion, its communication of the psychological state of its subject, and its virtuoso technique, this *David* is a truly baroque figure.

Some of Bernini's sculptures depict his aristocratic patrons with the same mastery he applied to less obviously spectacular subjects. The bust of Cardinal Scipione Borghese [13.10], with its quizzical expression and almost uncanny sense of movement, conveys the personality of the sitter with

13.10 Gian Lorenzo Bernini. *Cardinal Scipione Borghese.* 1632. Marble, height 30¾" (78 cm). Borghese Gallery, Rome. Breaking with the tradition of Renaissance portraiture, which showed the subject in repose, Bernini portrays the Cardinal, his first patron, with a sense of lively movement.

13.11 Gian Lorenzo Bernini. *Saint Teresa in Ecstasy.* 1645–1652. Marble and gilt bronze, life-size. Cornaro Chapel, Santa Maria della Vittoria, Rome. One of the supreme masterpieces of baroque art, this famous work shows Bernini's virtuoso skill in the expression of heightened religious emotion.

sympathy and subtlety. Most of his finest masterpieces, however, deal with religious themes, and draw their inspiration from Counter-Reformation teachings.

The most spectacular of these is *Saint Teresa in Ecstasy,* which uses a combination of architecture, sculpture, and natural light to convey the saint's ecstatic vision of an angel [13.11]. Gilded bronze shafts of light are further illuminated by light from a concealed window, as Saint Teresa, torn by violent emotion, awaits the blow of the angel, about to pierce her to the heart. The scene is set into an almost theatrical context, in which at the sides cardinals and members of the Cornaro family (in whose chapel the work is set) seem to watch from stage boxes.

Works such as these would have been more than sufficient to guarantee Bernini's immortality, but his architectural achievements are equally impressive. The physical appearance of baroque Rome was enriched by numerous Bernini fountains, Bernini palaces, and Bernini churches. Most important of all was his work on Saint Peter's, where he created in front of the basilica a vast piazza with its oval colonnade, central obelisk, and fountains, an ensemble (see Figure 13.1) that rivals in grandeur even the fora of Imperial Rome.

Bernini's expansive personality and his success in obtaining important commissions brought him tragically if inevitably into conflict with the other great architect of baroque Rome, Francesco Borromini (1599–1667). Brooding and melancholy much of the time, Borromini spent most of his career in constant competition with his brilliant rival and finally committed suicide. Whereas Bernini was concerned with the broad sweep of a design and grandiose effects, Borromini concentrated on elaborate details and highly complex structures.

13.12 Francesco Borromini. Façade, San Carlo alle Quattro Fontane, Rome. Begun 1638, façade finished 1667. Length 52' (15.86 m), width 34' (10.36 m), width of façade 38' (11.58 m). The curves and countercurves of the façade, together with the rich, almost cluttered, decoration, mark a deliberate rejection of the classical style.

CONTEMPORARY VOICES

Giambattista Passeri

In this passage the 17th-century painter and biographer Giambattista Passeri describes the suicide of Francesco Borromini. In the summer of 1667, tormented by Bernini's triumphant successes, Borromini

> . . . was assailed again with even greater violence by hypochondria which reduced him within a few days to such a state that nobody recognized him any more for Borromini, so haggard had his body become, and so frightening his face. He twisted his mouth in a thousand horrid ways, rolled his eyes from time to time in a fearful manner, and sometimes would roar and tremble like an irate lion. His nephew [Bernardo] consulted doctors, heard the advice of friends, and had him visited several times by priests. All agreed that he should never be left alone, nor be allowed any occasion for working, and that one should try to make him sleep at all costs, so that his spirit might calm down. This was the precise order which the servants received from his nephew and which they carried out. But instead of improving, his illness grew worse. Finding that he was never obeyed, as all he asked for was refused him, he imagined that this was done in order to annoy him rather than for his good, so that his restlessness increased and as time passed his hypochondria changed into pains in his chest, asthma, and a sort of intermittent frenzy. One evening, during the height of summer, he had at last thrown himself into his bed, but after barely an hour's sleep he woke up again, called the servant on duty, and asked for a light and writing material. Told by the servant that these had been forbidden him by the doctors and his nephew, he went back to bed and tried to sleep. But unable to do so in those hot and sultry hours, he started to toss agitatedly about as usual, until he was heard to exclaim "When will you stop afflicting me, O dismal thoughts? When will my mind cease being agitated? When will all these woes leave me? . . . What am I still doing in this cruel and execrable life?" He rose in a fury and ran to a sword which, unhappily for him and through carelessness of those who served him, had been on a table, and letting himself barbarously fall on the point was pierced from front to back. The servant rushed in at the noise and seeing the terrible spectacle called others for help, and so, half-dead and covered in blood, he was put back to bed. Knowing then that he had really reached the end of his life, he called for the confessor and made his will.

From R. and M. Wittkower, *Born Under Saturn* (New York: Norton, 1963), p. 141.

Borromini's greatest and most influential achievement was the church of San Carlo alle Quattro Fontane. The inside, designed between 1638 and 1641, was his first important work; the façade, which he added in 1665–1667, was his last [13.12]. On a relatively small exterior wall space Borromini has placed a wide range of decorative elements—columns, niches, arches, statues—while the façade itself flows in sinuous curves. The almost obsessive elaboration of design is in strong contrast to the clarity of many of Bernini's buildings, but its ornateness represents another baroque approach to architecture, one that was to have a continual appeal.

Baroque Art in France and Spain

In general, the more extravagant aspects of Italian baroque art never appealed greatly to French taste, which preferred elegance to display and restraint to emotion. Indeed, the conservative nature of French art found expression before the end of the century in the foundation of the Académie des Beaux-Arts, or Academy of the Fine Arts. The first of the special exhibitions organized by the Academy took place in 1667, under the patronage of Louis XIV. Both then and through the succeeding centuries Academy members saw their function as the defense of traditional standards and values rather than the encouragement of revolutionary new developments. Their innate conservatism affected both the works selected for exhibition and those awarded prizes. The tension between these self-appointed guardians of tradition and those artists who revolted against established ideas lasted well into the 19th century.

The closest parallel in French baroque painting to the intensity of Caravaggio is to be found in the strangely moving paintings of Georges de La Tour (1590–1652), whose candlelit scenes and humbly dressed figures are reminiscent in some aspects of

13.13 Georges de La Tour. *The Lamentation over Saint Sebastian.* 1645. Oil on canvas, c. 5'3" × 4'3" (1.6 × 1.3 m). Gemäldegalerie Staatliche Museen. Preussischer Kulturbesitz, Berlin. The influence of Caravaggio is obvious. Nevertheless, the simplification of details and the distaste for violence (there is no blood around the arrow) are typical of the restraint of de La Tour's paintings.

13.14 Nicolas Poussin. *Et in Arcadia Ego.* c. 1630. Oil on canvas, c. 40 × 32" (102 × 81 cm). Devonshire Collection, Chatsworth Settlement. Although influenced by classical sources, this early version of the subject has a poetic character that owes much to the art of Titian.

13.15 Nicolas Poussin. *Rape of the Sabine Women.* c. 1636–1637. Oil on canvas, 5'1" × 6'10½" (1.55 × 2.1 m). Metropolitan Museum of Art, New York (Harris Brisbane Dick Fund, 1946). By the time of this painting, Poussin was strongly influenced by the ancient sculptures he had studied in Rome, most notably in the careful depiction of the muscular structure of his figures.

the Italian's work. Yet the mood of such paintings as *The Lamentation over Saint Sebastian* [13.13] is much more restrained—the emotions are not stressed.

The greatest French painter of the 17th century, Nicolas Poussin (c. 1593–1665), echoed this French preference for restraint when he decisively rejected the innovations of Caravaggio, whose works he claimed to detest. He saw his own work as a kind of protest against the excesses of the baroque; a strong dislike of his Roman contemporaries nevertheless did not prevent his spending most of his life in Rome. It may seem strange that so French an artist should have chosen to live in Italy, but what drew him there was the art of ancient, not baroque, Rome. Poussin's only real and enduring enthusiasm was for the world of classical antiquity. His friends at Rome included the leading antiquarians of the day, and his paintings often express a nostalgic yearning for a long-vanished past.

Among Poussin's most poignant early works is *Et in Arcadia Ego* [13.14], in which four country dwellers gather at a large stone tomb amid an idyllic landscape. The inscription they struggle intently to decipher says *Et in Arcadia Ego* ("I am also in Arcadia"), a reminder that death exists even in the midst of such beauty and apparently simple charm. (Arcadia, although an actual region in Greece, was also used to refer to an imaginary land of perfect peace and beauty.) That charm is not altogether so simple, however. Poussin's rustic shepherds and casually dressed shepherdess seem to have stepped straight from some actual antique scene, such as Poussin often incorporated into his paintings, while the rich landscape is reminiscent of Venetian painting. The whole work therefore represents not so much the authentic representation of an actual past as the imaginative creation of a world that never really existed.

As his career developed, Poussin's style changed. The poetry of the earlier works was replaced by a grandeur that sometimes verges on stiffness. The *Rape of the Sabine Women* [13.15] is conceived on a massive scale and deals with a highly dramatic subject, yet the desperate women and violent Roman soldiers seem almost frozen in motion. Every figure is depicted clearly and precisely, as in Carracci's *The Triumph of Bacchus and Ariadne* (see Figure 13.7), yet with none of the exuberance of the earlier artist. The artificial, contrived air is deliberate.

By the end of his life, Poussin had returned to the simplicity of his earlier style, but it was drained of any trace of emotion. Another version of the subject of *Et in Arcadia Ego* [13.16], painted some ten years after the earlier one, makes a revealing contrast. The same four figures study the same tomb, but in a mood of deep stillness. Gone is the urgency of the earlier painting—and much of the poetry. In its place Poussin creates a mood of philosophical calm and tries to recapture the lofty spirit of antiquity, most notably in the noble brow and

13.16 Nicolas Poussin. *Et in Arcadia Ego.* 1638–1639. Oil on canvas. 33½ × 47⅝" (85 × 121 cm). Louvre, Paris. In comparison with Figure 13.14, an earlier version, this treatment is calmer and less dramatic. The group is seen from the front rather than diagonally, and both faces and poses are deliberately unemotional.

13.17 Claude Gellee (called Le) Lorrain. French (worked in Rome), 1600–1682. *Mill on a River*. 1631. Museum of Fine Arts, Boston (Seth K. Sweetser Fund). Oil on canvas, 61.5 × 84.2 cm (24¼ × 33¼"). Although this is one of Lorrain's early paintings, it already shows his ability to create a sense of infinite space and depth, in part by calculated contrasts between light and dark.

13.18 Hyacinthe Rigaud. *Louis XIV*. 1701. Louvre, Paris. (2.77 × 1.94 m). Louis was 63 when this portrait was painted. The swirling ermine-lined robes are a mark of the king's swagger. The ballet pose of the feet is a reminder of the popularity of dancing at the French court.

solemn stance of the shepherdess. Compensating for the loss of warmth is the transcendent beauty of the image.

Even had Poussin been prepared to leave Rome and return to the French court, the austere nature of his art would hardly have served to glorify that most autocratic and magnificent of monarchs, Louis XIV (born 1638, reigned 1643–1715). For the most part the king had only second-rate artists available to him at court: Like Poussin, the other great French painter of the day, Claude Lorrain (1600–1682) spent most of his life in Rome, and in any case was only really interested in painting landscapes [13.17].

Although most official court painters achieved only mediocre respectability, an exception must be made for Hyacinthe Rigaud (1659–1743), whose stunning portrait of Louis XIV [13.18] epitomizes baroque grandeur. It would be difficult to claim the intellectual vigor of Poussin or the emotional honesty of Caravaggio for this frankly flattering image of majesty. The stilted pose and the gorgeous robes might even suggest an element of exaggeration, almost of parody; yet a glance at the king's sagging face and stony gaze immediately puts such an idea to flight. Rigaud has captured his patron's outward splendor while not hiding his increasing weakness, due in great part to his decadent life-style. The signs of physical collapse are visible—*Et in Versailles Ego.*

13.19 Aerial view, Palace of Versailles. 1661–1688. Width of palace 1935' (589.79 m). The chief architects for the last stage of construction at Versailles were Louis le Vau (1612–1670) and Jules Hardouin-Mansart (1646–1708). Although the external decoration of the palace is classical in style, the massive scale is characteristic of baroque architecture.

Louis XIV's most lasting artistic achievement was the Palace of Versailles, built a few miles outside Paris as a new center for the court [13.19]. The history of its construction is long and complicated, and the final result betrays some of the uncertainties that went into its planning.

Louis XIV, an acute politician and astute judge of human psychology, was well aware of the fact that the aristocratic courtiers who surrounded him were likely to turn on him at the faintest sign of weakness or hesitation on his part. By constructing at Versailles an elaborate setting in which he could consciously act out the role of Grand Monarch, Louis conveyed the image of himself as supreme ruler and thereby retained his mastery over the aristocracy.

The Palace of Versailles was therefore conceived by the king in political terms. The architects' task, both inside and out, was to create a building that would illustrate Louis XIV's symbolic concept of himself as the Sun King. Thus each morning the king would rise from his bed, make his way past the assembled court through the Hall of Mirrors [13.20] where the seventeen huge mirrors reflected both the daylight and his own splendor, and enter the gardens along the main wing of the palace—which was laid out in an east–west axis to follow the path of the sun. At the same time both the palace and its gardens, which extend behind it for some two miles, were required to provide an appropriate setting for the balls, feasts, and fireworks displays organized there.

Given the grandiose symbolism of the ground plan and interior decorations, the actual appearance of the outside of the Palace of Versailles, with its rows of Ionic columns, is surprisingly modest. The simplicity of design and decoration is another demonstration of the French ability to combine the extremes of baroque art with a more classical spirit.

13.20 Jules Hardouin-Mansart and Charles Lebrun. Hall of Mirrors, Palace of Versailles. Begun 1676. Length 240' (73.15 m), width 34' (10.36 m), height 43' (13.11 m). The interior decoration was by Charles Lebrun (1619–1690), who borrowed the idea of a ceiling frescoed with mythological scenes from Carracci's painted ceiling in the Farnese Palace (see Figure 13.7).

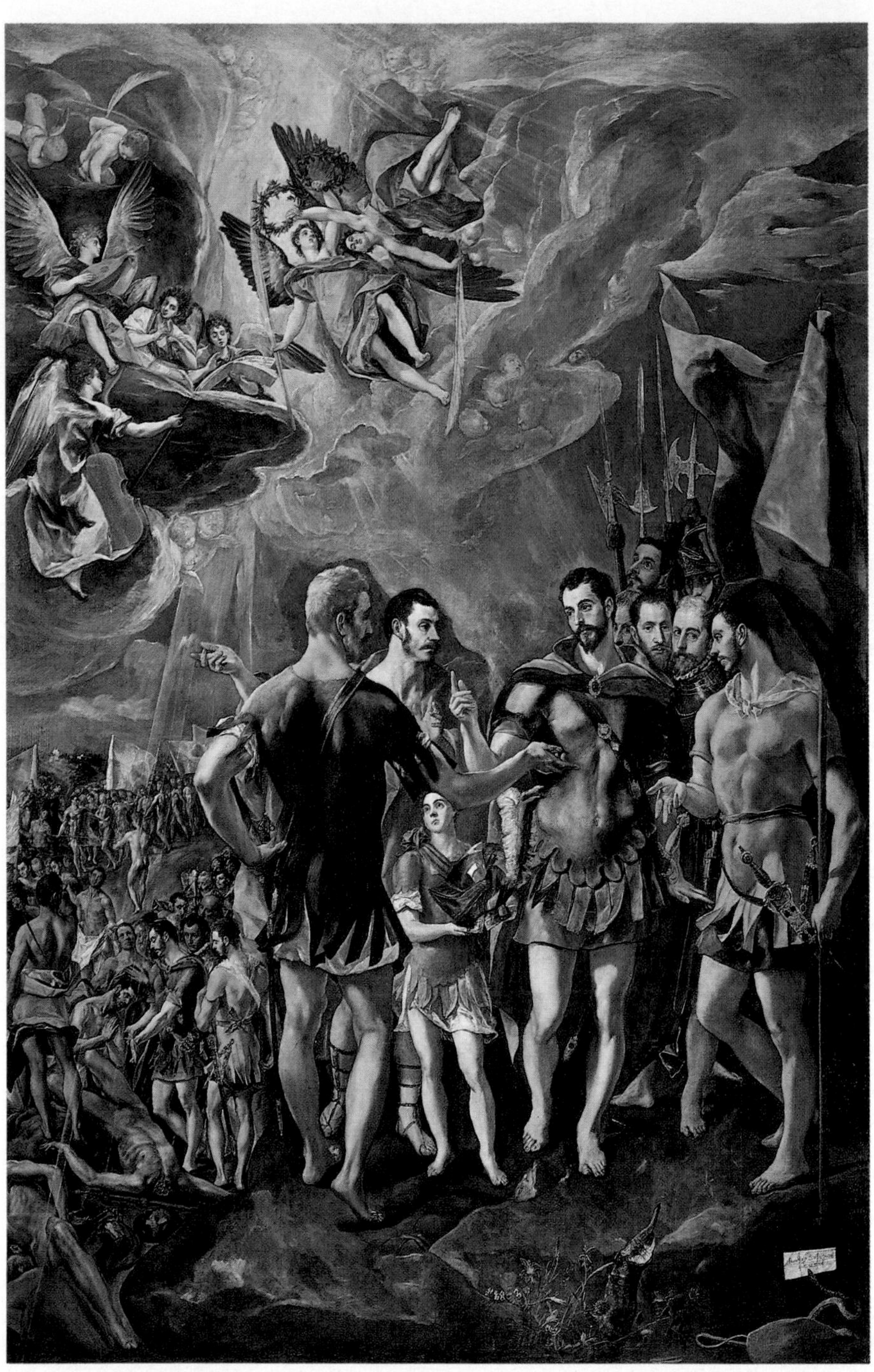

13.21 El Greco. *Martyrdom of Saint Maurice and the Theban Legion.* 1581–1584. Oil on canvas, 14'6" × 9'10" (4.42 × 3 m). Escorial Palace. The saint is facing the viewer, pointing up to the heavenly vision he sees.

The Spanish reaction to the baroque was very different. Strong religious emotion had always been a characteristic of Spanish Catholicism, and the new possibilities presented by baroque painting were foreshadowed in the work of the greatest painter active in Spain in the late 16th century, El Greco (1541–1614)—"the Greek." Domenikos Theotokopoulos (his original name) was born on the Greek island of Crete, which was at the time under Venetian rule. He seems to have traveled to Venice, where he was influenced by Titian, and to Rome. It is not known why he went to Spain, but he is recorded as having lived in Toledo from 1577 until his death.

Although he tried to obtain court patronage, the violence of contrasts in his works—clashes of color, scale, and emotion—did not appeal to official taste: his first royal commission, the *Martyrdom*

13.22 El Greco. *Burial of Count Orgaz.* 1586. Oil on canvas, 16' × 11'10" (4.88 × 3.61 m). San Tomé, Toledo, Spain. Note the elongated proportions of the figures in the heavens and the color contrasts between the upper and lower sections of the painting.

of Saint Maurice and the Theban Legion [13.21], was his last. The painting illustrates the theme of moral responsibility and choice. The Roman soldier Maurice, faced with a conflict between the demands of Roman law and of his Christian faith, chooses the latter, together with his fellow Theban and Christian legionnaires. The hallucinatory brightness of the colors is probably derived from Italian Mannerist painting of earlier in the 16th century, as are the elongated proportions, but the effect, underlined by the asymmetrical composition, is incomparably more fierce and disturbing.

In the absence of court patronage, El Greco produced many of his works for Toledo, his city of residence. Among the most spectacular is the *Burial of Count Orgaz* [13.22], a local benefactor who was rewarded for his generosity by the appearance of Saint Augustine and Saint Stephen at his funeral in 1323. They can be seen in the lower center of the painting, burying the count while his soul rises; the small boy dressed in black in the left-hand corner is the artist's eight-year-old son, identified by an inscription. The rich, heavy robes of the saints are balanced by the swirling drapery of the heavenly figures above, while the material and spiritual worlds are clearly separated by a row of grave, brooding local dignitaries.

The same religious fervor appears in the work of Jusepe Ribera (1591–1652) but is expressed in a far more naturalistic style. Like Caravaggio, Ribera used peasants in his religious scenes, which were painted with strong contrasts of light and dark. In his *The Martyrdom of Saint Bartholomew* [13.23] Ribera spares us nothing in the way of realism as the saint is hauled into position to be flayed. The muscular brutality of his executioners and the sense of impending physical agony are almost masochistic in their vividness. Only in the

13.23 Jusepe de Ribera. ***The Martyrdom of Saint Bartholomew.*** **c. 1638. Oil on canvas, 7'7¼" (2.34 m) square. Prado, Madrid. Unlike La Tour (see Figure 13.13), Ribera refuses to soften the subject by idealizing his figures.**

compassionate faces of some onlookers do we find any relief from the torment of the scene.

Although paintings like Ribera's are representative of much of Spanish baroque art, the work of Diego Velázquez (1599–1660), the greatest Spanish painter of the Baroque period, is very different in spirit. Velázquez used his superlative technique to depict scenes brimming with life, preferring the court of Phillip IV (where he spent much of his career) and the lives of ordinary people to religious or mythological subjects.

The finest and most complex work of Velázquez is *Las Meninas*, or *The Maids of Honor* [13.24]. Unlike Louis XIV, the Spanish king was fortunate enough to have one of the greatest painters in history to preserve the memory of his court. It is to Philip IV's credit that he treated Velázquez with respect and honor. In return Velázquez produced a number of superb portraits of the monarch and his family.

Las Meninas is an evocation of life in the royal palace. The scene is Velázquez' own studio there; the five-year-old Princess Margarita has come, with her two maids, to visit the painter at work on a huge painting that must surely be *Las Meninas* itself. Despite the size of the picture, the mood is quiet, even intimate: two figures in casual conversation, a sleepy dog, a passing court official, who raises a curtain at the back to peer into the room. Yet so subtle is Velázquez' use of color that we feel the very presence of the room as a three-dimensional space filled with light, now bright, now shadowy. The reality of details like the little princess' hair or dress never distracts from the overall unity of color and composition. That Velázquez was justifiably proud of his abilities is shown by the two distinguished visitors whose presence is felt rather than seen, reflected as they are in the mirror hanging on the back wall: the king and queen themselves, come to honor the artist by visiting him in his own studio.

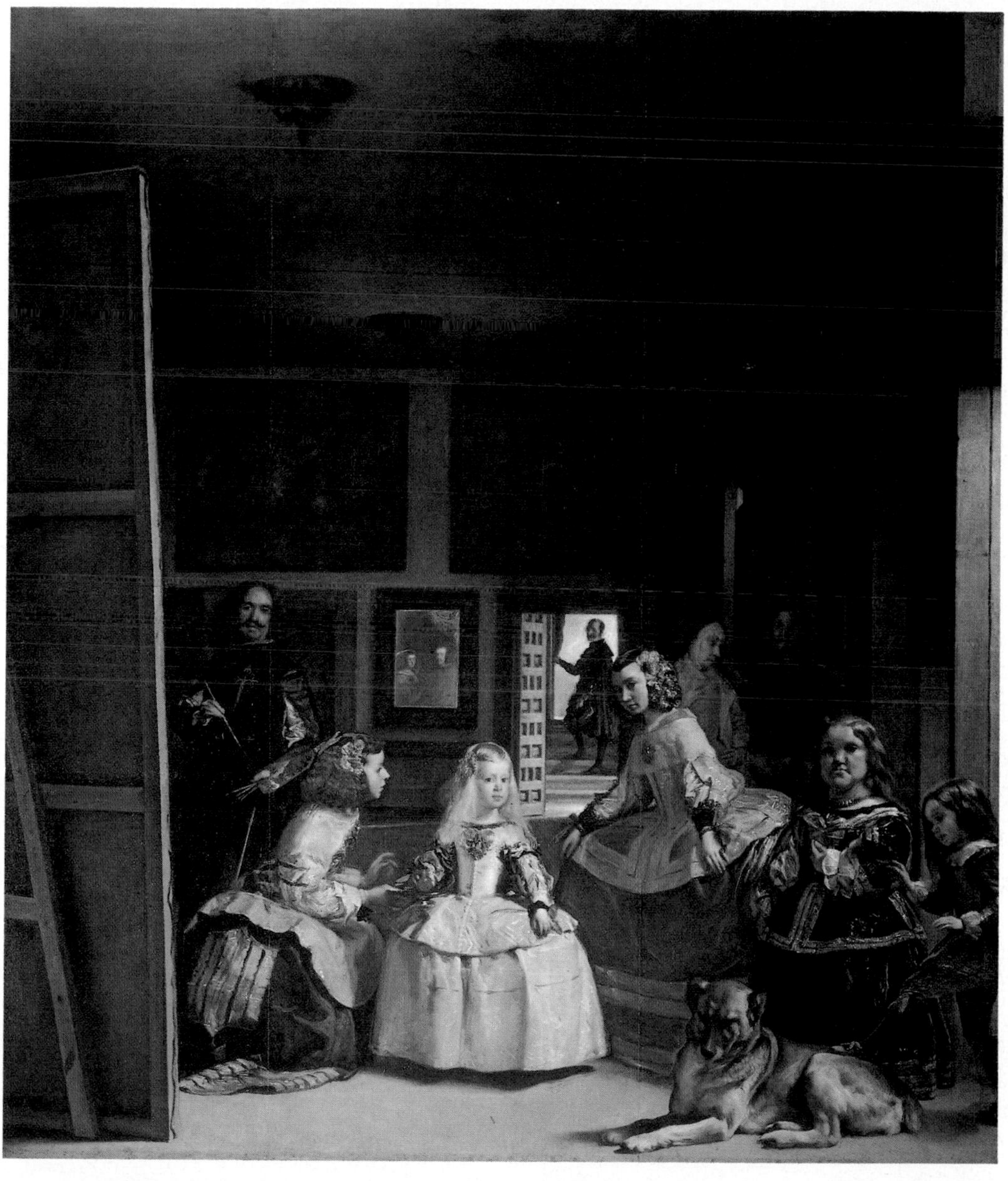

13.24 Diego Velázquez. *Las Meninas (The Maids of Honor).* 1651. Oil on canvas, 10'5" × 9' (3.18 × 2.74 m). Prado, Madrid. The red cross on the artist's breast, symbol of the noble Order of Santiago, was painted there after his death by the king's command. Velázquez regarded his nomination to the order in 1658 as recognition both of his own nobility and that of his art. He thus became one of the first victors in the war that artists had waged ever since the Renaissance for a social status equal to that of their patrons. Throughout the 16th and 17th centuries their aristocratic and ecclesiastical employers regarded them as little better than servants; only by the end of the 18th century were artists and musicians able to assert their social and political independence.

Baroque Art in Northern Europe

Most baroque art produced in northern Europe was intended for a middle-class rather than an aristocratic audience, as in Italy, France, and Spain. Before examining the effects of this, however, we must look at two very notable exceptions, Peter Paul Rubens (1577–1640) and his assistant and later rival, Anthony van Dyck (1599–1641), both Flemish by birth.

Rubens is often called the most universal of painters because he produced with apparent ease an almost inexhaustible stream of works of all kinds—religious subjects, portraits, landscapes, mythological scenes—all on the grandest of scales. Certainly he must have been among the most active artists in history: in addition to running the workshop used for the production of his commissions, he pursued a career in diplomacy, which involved considerable traveling throughout Europe, and still had time for academic study. He is said to have spoken and written six modern languages and to have read Latin fluently. He was also versed in theology. Further, in contrast to solitary and gloomy figures like Caravaggio and Borromini, Rubens seems to have been contented in his personal life. After the death of his first wife he remarried, at the age of fifty-three, a girl of sixteen, Hélène Fourment, with whom he spent an ecstatically happy ten years before his death. The paintings of his last decade are among the most intimate and tender of all artistic tributes to married love [13.25].

13.25 Peter Paul Rubens. *Hélène Fourment and Her Children.* 1636–1637. Oil on canvas, 44½ × 32¼" (118 × 85 cm). Louvre, Paris. In this affectionate portrait of his young wife and two of their children, Rubens achieves a sense of immediacy and freshness by his lightness of touch.

For the most part, however, intimacy is not the quality most characteristic of Rubens' art. Generally his pictures convey something of the restless energy of his life. In *The Rape of the Daughters of Leucippus* [13.26] every part of the painting is filled with movement as the mortal women, divine riders, and even the horses are drawn into a single pulsating spiral. The sense of action, so characteristic of Rubens' paintings, is in strong contrast to the frozen movement of Poussin's depiction of a similar episode (see Figure 13.15). Equally typical of the artist is his frank delight in the women's sensuous nudity and ample proportions—the slender grace of other artists' nudes was not at all to Rubens' taste.

Perhaps the most extraordinary achievement of Rubens' remarkable career was his fulfillment of a commission from Marie de' Medici, widow of Henry IV and mother of Louis XIII, to decorate an entire gallery with paintings illustrating her life. In a mere three years, from 1622 to 1625, he created twenty-four enormous paintings commemorating the chief events in which she played a part, with greater flattery than truth. The splendid *Journey of Marie de' Medici* [13.27] shows the magnificently attired queen on horseback at the Battle of Ponts-de-Cé, accompanied by the spirit of Power, while Fame and Glory flutter around her head. It hardly matters that the queen's forces were ignominiously defeated in the battle, so convincingly triumphant does her image appear.

Paintings on this scale required the help of assistants, and there is no doubt that in Rubens' workshop much of the preliminary work was done by his staff. One of the many artists employed for this purpose eventually became as much in demand as his former master for portraits of the aristocracy. Anthony van Dyck spent two years, 1618 to 1620, with Rubens before beginning his career as an independent artist. Although from time to time he painted religious subjects, his fame rests on his formal portraits, many of them produced during the years he spent in Italy and England.

13.26 Peter Paul Rubens. *The Rape of the Daughters of Leucippus.* c. 1618. Oil on canvas, 7'3" × 6'10" (2.21 × 2.08 m). Alte Pinakothek, Munich. According to the Greek legend, Castor and Pollux, twin sons of Zeus, carried off King Leucippus' two daughters, who had been betrothed to their cousins. The myth here becomes symbolic of physical passion.

13.27 Peter Paul Rubens. 1577–1640. *The Journey of Marie de' Medici.* 1622–1625. Oil on canvas, 14'11" × 9'6" (3.94 × 2.95 m). Louvre, Paris. This painting focuses on the triumphant figure of the queen. As in many of his large works, Rubens probably painted the important sections and left other parts to his assistants.

13.28 Anthony van Dyck. *Marchesa Elena Grimaldi, Wife of Marchese Nicola Cataneo.* c. 1623. Oil on canvas, 2.464 × 1.727 m (97 × 68"). National Gallery of Art, Washington (Widener Collection, 1942). Painted fairly early in van Dyck's career during a stay in Genoa, the portrait emphasizes the aristocratic bearing of its subject by somber colors and an artificial setting.

Van Dyck's refined taste equipped him for satisfying the demands of his noble patrons that they be shown as they thought they looked rather than as they actually were. It is certainly difficult to believe that any real-life figure could have had quite the haughty bearing and lofty dignity of the Marchesa Cataneo [13.28] in Van Dyck's portrait of her, although the Genoese nobility of which she was a member was known for its arrogance.

International celebrities like Rubens and Van Dyck, at home at the courts of all Europe, were far from typical of northern artists. Indeed, painters in the Netherlands in particular found themselves in a very different situation from their colleagues elsewhere. The two most lucrative sources of commissions, the Church and the aristocracy, were unavailable to them because the Dutch Calvinist Church followed post-Reformation practice in forbidding the use of images in church, and because Holland had never had its own powerful hereditary nobility. Painters therefore depended on the tastes and demands of the open market.

One highly profitable source of income for Dutch artists in the 17th century was the group portrait, in particular that of a militia, or civic guard company. These bands of soldiers had originally served a practical purpose in the defense of their country, but their regular reunions tended to be social gatherings, chiefly for the purpose of eating and drinking. A group of war veterans today would hire a photographer to commemorate their annual reunion; the militia companies engaged the services of a portrait painter. If they were lucky or rich enough they might even get Frans Hals (c. 1580–1666), whose group portraits capture the in-

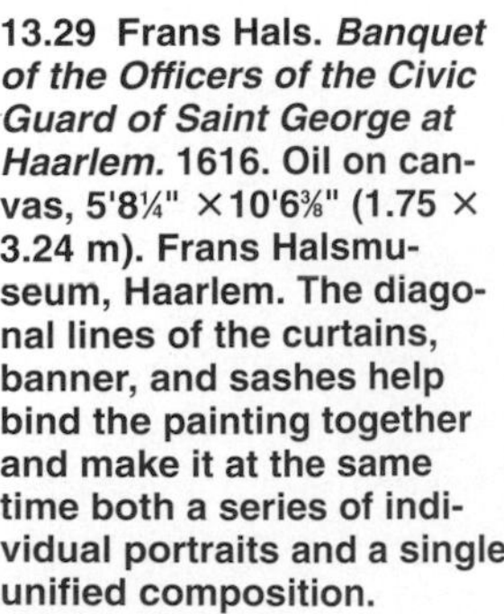

13.29 Frans Hals. *Banquet of the Officers of the Civic Guard of Saint George at Haarlem.* 1616. Oil on canvas, 5'8¼" ×10'6⅜" (1.75 × 3.24 m). Frans Halsmuseum, Haarlem. The diagonal lines of the curtains, banner, and sashes help bind the painting together and make it at the same time both a series of individual portraits and a single unified composition.

13.30 Jan Vermeer. *Woman Reading a Letter.* 1662–1664. Oil on canvas, 18⅛ × 15¼" (46 × 39 cm). Rijksmuseum, Amsterdam. Much of the sense of balance and repose that Vermeer conveys is achieved by his careful color contrasts between blue and yellow and the repetition of rectangular surfaces such as the table, chair backs, and the map of the Netherlands on the wall.

dividuality of each of the participants while conveying the general convivial spirit of the occasion [13.29]. Hals was certainly not the most imaginative or inventive of artists, but his sheer ability to paint, using broad dynamic brush strokes and cleverly organized compositions, makes his works some of the most attractive of that period.

Very different in spirit was Jan Vermeer (1632–1675), who worked almost unknown in the city of Delft and whose art was virtually forgotten after his death. Rediscovered in the 19th century, it is now regarded as second only to Rembrandt's for depth of feeling. At first sight this may seem surprising, since Vermeer's subjects are rather limited in scope. A woman reading a letter [13.30], girls sewing or playing music—through such intimate scenes Vermeer reveals qualities of inner contemplation and repose that are virtually unique in the entire history of art. Unlike Hals, with his loose style, Vermeer built up his forms by applying the paint in the form of tiny dots of color, and then rendering the details with careful precision. Like Velázquez' *Las Meninas* (see Figure 13.24), his paintings are dominated by light so palpable as to seem to surround the figures with its presence. However, where Velázquez' canvas is suffused with a warm, Mediterranean glow, Vermeer's paintings capture the coolness and clarity of northern light. The perfection of his compositions creates a mood of stillness so complete that mundane activities take on a totally unexpected concentration and become endowed with an unexpected sense of importance.

Rembrandt van Rijn (1606–1669) is one of the most deeply loved of all painters. No summary of his achievement can begin to do justice to it. Born in Leiden in the Netherlands, he spent a short time at the university there before beginning his studies as a painter. The early part of his career was spent

13.31 Rembrandt. *The Sortie of Captain Frans Banning Cocq's Company of the Civic Guard (The Night Watch).* 1642. Oil on canvas, 11'9½" × 14'2½" (3.63 × 4.37 m). Rijksmuseum, Amsterdam. Recent cleaning has revealed that the painting's popular name, though conveniently brief, is inaccurate. Far from being submerged in darkness, the principal figures were originally bathed in light and painted in glowing colors.

in Amsterdam, where he moved in 1631 and soon became known as a fashionable portrait painter. His life was that of any successful man of the time, happily married, living in his own fine house.

Rembrandt's interest in spiritual matters and the eternal problems of existence, however, coupled with his researches into new artistic techniques, seem to have prevented his settling down for long to a bourgeois existence of this kind. The artistic turning point of his career came in 1642, the year of the death of his wife, when he finished the painting known as *The Night Watch* [13.31]. Although ostensibly the same kind of group portrait as Hals' *Banquet of the Officers of the Civic Guard* (see Figure 13.29), it is composed with much greater complexity and subtlety. The arrangement of the figures and the sense of depth show how far Rembrandt was outdistancing his contemporaries.

The price Rembrandt paid for his genius was growing neglect, which by 1656 had brought bankruptcy. The less his work appealed to the public of his day, the more Rembrandt retreated into his own spiritual world. About 1645 he set up house with Hendrickje Stoffels, although he never married her, and his unconventional behavior succeeded in alienating him still further from his contemporaries. It was the faithful Hendrickje, however, who together with Titus, Rembrandt's son by his first marriage, helped put his financial affairs in some sort of order. Her death in 1663 left him desolate, and its effect on him is visible in some of the last self-portraits [13.32].

13.32 Rembrandt. *Old Self-Portrait.* 1669. Oil on canvas, 23¼ × 20¾" (59 × 53 cm). Mauritshuis, The Hague. In his last self-portrait, painted a few months before his death, the artist seems drained of all emotion, his expression resigned and gaze fixed.

Throughout his life Rembrandt had sought self-understanding by painting a series of portraits of himself, charting his inner journey through the increasingly tragic events of his life. Without self-pity or pretense he analyzed his own feelings and recorded them with a dispassion that might be called merely clinical if its principal achievement were not the revelation of a human soul. By the time of Hendrickje's death, which was followed in 1668 by that of Titus, Rembrandt was producing self-portraits that evoke not so much sympathy for his sufferings as awe at their truth. The inexorable physical decay, the universal fate, is accompanied by a growth in spiritual awareness that must at least in part have come from Rembrandt's lifelong meditation on the Scriptures.

Throughout his career, Rembrandt used contrast between light and darkness to achieve dramatic and emotional effect. Light also served to build composition and to create depth in his paintings and etchings. In the paintings, he often built up layers of paint to create a richness of color and sense of texture unmatched by any of his contemporaries. In his etchings and engravings he developed ways of varying the lines to produce a similarly elaborate surface. A supremely baroque artist, Rembrandt always used his mastery of composition and texture to deepen and enhance the emotional power of the image.

In the last years of his life Rembrandt turned increasingly to biblical subjects, always using them to explore some aspect of human feelings. In *Jacob Blessing the Sons of Joseph* [13.33] all the tenderness of family affection is expressed in the juxtaposition of the heads of the old man and his son, whose expression of love is surpassed only by that of his wife as she gazes almost unseeingly at her sons.

13.33 Rembrandt. *Jacob Blessing the Sons of Joseph.* 1656. Oil on canvas, 5'8¼" × 6'9" (1.75 × 2.1 m). Staatliche Kunstsammlungen Kassel, Galerie Alte Meister, GK 249. In his very personal version of the biblical story, painted in the year of his financial collapse, Rembrandt includes Asenath, Joseph's wife. Although she is not mentioned in the text, her presence here emphasizes the family nature of the occasion.

The depth of emotion and the dark shadows mark that school of baroque painting initiated by Caravaggio, yet it seems almost an impertinence to categorize so universal a statement. Through this painting Rembrandt seems to offer us a deep spiritual comfort for the tragic nature of human destiny revealed by the self-portraits.

BAROQUE MUSIC

Although the history of music is as long as that of the other arts, the earliest music with which most modern music lovers are on familiar ground is that of the Baroque period. It is a safe bet that many thousands of listeners have tapped their feet to the rhythm of a baroque concerto without knowing or caring anything about its historical context, and with good reason: Baroque music, with its strong emphasis on rhythmic vitality and attractive melody, is easy to respond to with pleasure. Furthermore, in the person of Johann Sebastian Bach, the Baroque period produced one of the greatest geniuses in the history of music, one who shared Rembrandt's ability to communicate profound experience on the broadest level.

The qualities that make baroque music popular today were responsible for its original success: Composers of the Baroque period were the first since classical antiquity to write large quantities of music intended for the pleasure of listeners as well as the glory of God. The polyphonic music of the Middle Ages and the Renaissance, with its interweaving of many musical lines, had enabled composers like Machaut or Palestrina to praise the Lord on the highest level of intellectual achievement, but the result was a musical style far above the heads of most of their contemporary listeners. The Council of Trent, in accordance with Counter-Reformation principles, had even considered prohibiting polyphony in religious works in order to make church music more accessible to the average congregation before finally deciding that this would be too extreme a measure. For once, the objectives of Reformation and Counter-Reformation coincided, for Luther had already simplified the musical elements in Protestant services for the same reason (see page 320).

The time was therefore ripe for a general move toward sacred music with a wider and more universal appeal. Since at the same time the demand for secular music was growing, it is not surprising

13.34 Pieter de Hooch. *The Music Party*. 1663. Oil on canvas, 39 × 47" (99 × 119 cm). Cleveland Museum of Art (Gift of Hanna Fund, 51.355). Some prosperous Dutch citizens are relaxing by both performing and listening to music.

that composers soon developed a style sufficiently attractive and sufficiently flexible not only for the creation of masses and other liturgical works, but also of instrumental and vocal music that could be played and listened to at home [13.34].

The Birth of Opera

Perhaps the major artistic innovation of the 17th century was a new form of musical entertainment that had been formulated at the beginning of the baroque period—*opera,* which consisted of a play in which the text was sung rather than spoken. Throughout the 17th century the taste for opera and operatic music swept Europe, attracting aristocratic and middle-class listeners alike. In the process, the public appetite for music with which it could identify grew even greater. Small wonder that 20th-century listeners have found pleasure and delight in music written to provide our baroque predecessors with precisely those satisfactions.

Like much else of beauty, opera was born in Florence. Ironically enough, an art form that was to become so popular in so short a time was originally conceived of in lofty intellectual terms. Toward the end of the 16th century a number of thinkers, poets, and musicians began to meet regularly at the house of a wealthy Florentine noble, Count Giovanni Bardi. This group, known as the Florentine *Camerata,* objected strongly to the way in which the polyphonic style in vocal music reduced the text to incomprehensible nonsense. They looked back nostalgically to the time of the Greeks, when almost every word of Greek tragedy was both sung and accompanied by instruments, yet remained perfectly understandable to the spectators. Greek music itself was, of course, lost forever; but at least the group could revive what they considered its essence.

The result was the introduction of a musical form known as *monody,* or *recitative,* which consisted of the free declamation of a single vocal line with a simple instrumental accompaniment for support. Thus listeners could follow the text with ease. The addition of music also gave an emotional intensity not present in simple spoken verse, thus satisfying the baroque interest in heightened emotion.

Although in theory monody could be used for either sacred or secular works, its dramatic potential was obvious. In the winter of 1594–1595 the first play set to music, Jacopo Peri's *Dafne,* was performed in Florence. Its subject was drawn from classical mythology and dealt with Apollo's pursuit of the mortal girl Daphne, who turned into a laurel tree to elude him. In the words of a spectator, "The pleasure and amazement of those present were beyond expression." *Dafne* is now lost, but another work of Peri, *Euridice,* has survived to become the earliest extant opera. It too was based on a Greek myth, that of Orpheus and Eurydice. The first performance took place in 1600, again in Florence, at the wedding of Henry IV of France to the same Marie de' Medici whom Rubens was to portray a generation later (see Figure 13.27).

It is, of course, no coincidence that both of Peri's works as well as many that followed were written on classical subjects, since the Camerata had taken its initial inspiration from Greek drama. The story of Orpheus and Eurydice, furthermore, had a special appeal for composers, since it told how the musician Orpheus was able to soften the heart of the King of the Underworld by his music and thereby win back his wife Eurydice from the dead. The theme was treated many times in the music of the next four hundred years, yet no subsequent version is more moving or psychologically convincing than the one by Claudio Monteverdi (1567–1643), the first great genius in the history of opera.

Monteverdi's *L'Orfeo* was first performed in 1607. Its composer brought to the new form not only a complete understanding of the possibilities of monody but in addition an impressive mastery of traditional polyphonic forms such as the madrigal. Equally important for the success of his works was Monteverdi's remarkable dramatic instinct and his ability to transform emotion into musical terms. The contrast between the pastoral gaiety of the first act of *L'Orfeo,* depicting the happy couple's love, and the scene in the second act in which Orpheus is brought the news of his wife's death is achieved with marvellous expressive power.

In *L'Orfeo,* his first opera, Monteverdi was able to breathe real life into the academic principles of the Florentine Camerata, but the work was written for his noble employer, the Duke of Mantua, and intended for a limited aristocratic public. Monteverdi lived long enough to see the new dramatic form achieve widespread popularity at all levels of society throughout Europe. It did not take long for a taste for Italian opera to spread to Germany and Austria and then to England, where by the end of the century Italian singers dominated the London stage. The French showed their usual unwillingness to adopt a foreign invention wholesale; nonetheless, the leading composer at the court of

Louis XIV was a Florentine who tactfully changed his name from Giovanni Batista Lulli to Jean Baptiste Lully (1632–1687). His stately tragedies, which were performed throughout Europe, incorporated long sections of ballet, a custom continued by his most illustrious successor, Jean Philippe Rameau (1683–1764).

It was in Italy itself that opera won its largest public. In Venice alone, where Monteverdi spent the last thirty years of his life, at least sixteen theaters were built between 1637—when the first public opera house was opened—and the end of the century. As in the Elizabethan theater (see Figure 12.29), the design of these opera houses separated the upper ranks of society, who sat in the boxes, from the ordinary citizens, who stood or sat on the ground level.

There is a notable similarity, too, between Elizabethan drama and opera in the way they responded to growing popularity. Just as the groundlings of Shakespeare's day demanded ever more sensational and melodramatic entertainment, so the increasingly demanding and vociferous opera public required new ways of being satisfied. The two chief means by which these desires were met became a feature of most operas written during the following century. The first was the provision of lavish stage spectacles involving mechanical cloud machines that descended from above and disgorged singers and dancers, complex lighting effects that gave the illusion that the stage was being engulfed by fire, apparently magical transformations, and so on—baroque extravagance at its most extreme. The second was a move away from the declamatory recitative of the earliest operas to self-contained musical "numbers" known as *arias.* (In the case of both opera and many other musical forms, we continue to use technical terms like aria in their Italian form—a demonstration of the crucial role played by Italy, and in particular Florence, in the history of music.) The function of music as servant of the drama was beginning to change. Beauty of melody and the technical virtuosity of the singers became the glory of baroque opera, although at the expense of dramatic truth.

Baroque Instrumental and Vocal Music: Johann Sebastian Bach

The development of opera permitted the dramatic retelling of mythological or historical tales. Sacred texts as stories derived from the Bible were set to music in a form known as the *oratorio,* which had begun to appear toward the end of the 16th century. One of the baroque masters of the oratorio was the Italian Giacomo Carissimi (1605–1674), whose works, based on well-known biblical episodes, include *The Judgment of Solomon* and *Job.* By the dramatic use of the chorus, simple textures, and driving rhythms, Carissimi created an effect of strength and power that late-20th-century listeners have begun to rediscover.

The concept of the public performance of religious works, rather than secular operas, made a special appeal to Protestant Germans. Heinrich Schütz (1585–1672) wrote a wide variety of oratorios and other sacred works. In his early *Psalms of David* (1619) he combined the choral technique of Renaissance composers like Gabrieli with the vividness and drama of the madrigal. His setting of *The Seven Last Words of Christ* (1645–1646) uses soloists, chorus, and instruments to create a complex sequence of narrative sections (recitatives), vocal ensembles, and choruses. Among his last works are three settings of the Passion, the events of the last days of the life of Jesus, in the accounts given by Matthew, Luke, and John. Written in 1666, they revert to the style of a century earlier, with none of the instrumental coloring generally typical of Baroque music, both sacred and secular.

Schütz is, in fact, one of the few great Baroque composers who, so far as is known, never wrote any purely instrumental music. The fact is all the more striking because the Baroque period was notable for the emergence of independent instrumental compositions unrelated to texts of any kind. Girolamo Frescobaldi (1583–1643), the greatest organ virtuoso of his day—he was organist at Saint Peter's in Rome—wrote a series of rhapsodic fantasies known as *toccatas* that combined extreme technical complexity with emotional and dramatic expression. His slightly earlier Dutch contemporary Jan Pieterszoon Sweelinck (1562–1621), organist at Amsterdam, built sets of variations out of different settings of a chorale melody, or hymn tune. The writing of *chorale variations,* as this type of piece became known, became popular throughout the Baroque period.

The Danish Dietrich Buxtehude (1637–1707), who spent most of his career in Germany, combined the brilliance of the toccata form with the use of a chorale theme in his *chorale fantasies.* Starting with a simple hymn melody, he composed free-form rhapsodies that are almost improvisational in style. His suites for harpsichord include movements in variation form, various dances, slow lyric pieces, and other forms; like other composers of his day, Buxtehude used the keyboard suite as a kind of compendium of musical forms.

One of the greatest composers of the late Baroque period was Domenico Scarlatti (1685–1757). The greatest virtuoso of his day on the *harpsichord* (the keyboard instrument that was a primary forerunner of the modern piano), he wrote hundreds of *sonatas* (short instrumental pieces) for it and laid down the foundations of modern keyboard technique.

Scarlatti's contemporary Georg Frideric Handel (1685–1759) was born at Halle in Germany, christened with the name he later changed to George Frederick Handel when he settled in England and became a naturalized citizen. London was to prove the scene of his greatest successes, among them *Messiah,* first performed in Dublin in 1742. This oratorio is among the most familiar of all baroque musical masterpieces.

Handel also wrote operas, including a series of masterpieces in Italian that were written for performance in England. Among their greatest glories are the arias, which are permeated by Handel's rich melodic sense; one of the most famous is "Ombra mai fu" from *Xerxes,* often called the "Largo." His best-known orchestral works are probably *The Water Music* and *The Music for the Royal Fireworks,* both originally designed for outdoor performance. Written for a large number of instruments, they were later rearranged for regular concerts.

In the year that saw the births of both Scarlatti and Handel, Johann Sebastian Bach (1685–1750) was born at Eisenach, Germany, into a family that had already been producing musicians for well over a century. With the exception of opera, which as a devout Lutheran did not interest him, Bach mastered every musical form of the time, pouring forth some of the most intellectually rigorous and spiritually profound music ever created.

It is among the more remarkable achievements in the history of the arts that most of Bach's music was produced under conditions of grinding toil as organist and choir director in relatively provincial German towns. Even Leipzig—where he spent twenty-seven years from 1723 to his death, as *kantor* (music director) at the school attached to Saint Thomas' Church—was far removed from the glittering centers of European culture where most artistic developments were taking place. As a result, Bach was little known as a composer during his lifetime and virtually forgotten after his death; only in the 19th century did all his works become known and published. He has since taken his place at the head of the Western musical tradition as the figure who raised the art of polyphony to its highest level.

If the sheer quantity of music Bach wrote is stupefying, so is the complexity of his musical thought. Among the styles he preferred was the *fugue,* a word derived from the Latin word for flight. In the course of a fugue a single theme is passed from voice to voice or instrument to instrument (generally four in number), each imitating the principal theme in turn. The theme thus becomes combined with itself, and in the process the composer creates a seamless web of sound in which each musical part is equally important; this technique is called *counterpoint.* Bach's ability to endow this highly intellectual technique with emotional power is little short of miraculous. The range of emotions Bach's fugues cover can best be appreciated by sampling his two books of twenty-four preludes and fugues each, known collectively as *The Well-Tempered Clavier.* Each of the forty-eight preludes and fugues creates its own mood while remaining logically organized according to contrapuntal technique.

Many of Bach's important works are permeated by a single concern—the expression of his deep religious faith. A significant number were written in his capacity as director of music at Saint Thomas' for performance in the church throughout the year. Organ music, masses, oratorios, motets; in all of these he could use music to glorify God and to explore the deeper mysteries of Christianity. His *chorale preludes* consist of variations on chorales and use familiar and well-loved songs as the basis for a kind of musical improvisation. He wrote some two hundred *cantatas,* short oratorios made up of sections of declamatory recitative and lyrical arias, which contain an almost inexhaustible range of religious emotions, from joyful celebrations of life to profound meditations on death. Most overwhelming of all is his setting of the *Saint Matthew Passion,* the story of the trial and Crucifixion of Jesus as recorded in the Gospel of Matthew. In this immense work Bach asserted his Lutheranism by using the German rather than the Latin translation of the Gospel and by incorporating Lutheran chorales. The use of self-contained arias is Italian, though, and the spirit of deep religious commitment and dramatic fervor can only be described as universal.

It would be a mistake to think of Bach as somehow unworldly and touched only by religious emotions. Certainly his own life had its share of domestic happiness and tragedy. His parents died when he was ten, leaving him to be brought up by an elder brother who treated him with less than complete kindness. At the age of fifteen he jumped at the chance to leave home and become a choirboy in the little town of Luneberg. He spent the next few years moving from place to place, perfecting his skills as organist, violinist, and composer.

In 1707 Bach married his cousin, Maria Barbara Bach, who bore him seven children, of whom four died in infancy. Bach was always devoted to his family, and the loss of these children, followed by the death of his wife in 1720, made a deep impression on him. It may have been to provide a mother for his three surviving sons that he remarried in 1721. At any event his new wife, Anna Magdalena, proved a loving companion, bearing him thirteen more children and helping him with the preparation and copying of his music. One of the shortest but most touching of Bach's works is the little song, *Bist du bei mir,* which has survived copied out in her notebook. The words are: "As long as you are with me I could face my death and eternal rest with joy. How peaceful would my end be if your beautiful hands could close my faithful eyes." (Some scholars now believe that the song may originally have been written by G. H. Stölzel, a contemporary musician whom Bach much admired.)

The move to Leipzig in 1723 was dictated at least in part by the need to provide suitable schooling for his children, although it also offered the stability and security Bach seems to have required. The subsequent years of continual work took their toll, however. Bach's sight had never been good, and the incessant copying of manuscripts produced a continual deterioration. In 1749 he was persuaded to undergo two disastrous operations that left him totally blind. A few months later his sight was suddenly restored, but within ten days he died of apoplexy.

Although the vast majority of Bach's works are on religious themes, the best known of all, the six *Brandenburg Concertos,* were written for the private entertainment of a minor prince, the Margrave of Brandenburg. Their form follows the Italian *concerto grosso,* an orchestral composition in three sections, or *movements,* fast–slow–fast. The form had been pioneered by the Venetian composer Antonio Vivaldi (c. 1676–1741), who delighted in strong contrasts between the orchestra, generally made up of string instruments and a solo instrument, often a violin (as in his well-known set of four concertos *The Four Seasons*) but sometimes a flute, bassoon, or other wind instrument. Four of Bach's six *Brandenburg Concertos* use not one but a group of solo instruments, although the group differs from work to work. The whole set forms a kind of compendium of the possibilities of instrumental color, a true virtuoso achievement requiring equal virtuosity in performance. The musical mood is light, as befits works written primarily for entertainment, but Bach was incapable of writing music without depth, and the slow movements in particular are strikingly beautiful.

The second *Brandenburg Concerto* is written for solo trumpet, recorder, oboe, and violin accompanied by a string orchestra. The first movement combines all of these to produce a brilliant rhythmic effect as the solo instruments now emerge from the orchestra, now rejoin it. The melodic line avoids short themes. Instead, as in much baroque music, the melodies are long, elaborate patterns that seem to spread and evolve, having much of the ornateness of baroque art. It does not require an ability to read music to see as well as hear how the opening theme of the second *Brandenburg Concerto* forms an unbroken line of sound, rising and falling and doubling back as it luxuriantly spreads itself out.

The slow second movement forms a tranquil and meditative interlude. The brilliant tone of the trumpet would be inappropriate here and Bach therefore omits it, leaving the recorder, oboe, and violin quietly to intertwine in a delicate web of sound. After its enforced silence, the trumpet seems to burst out irrepressibly at the beginning of the third movement, claiming the right to set the mood of limitless energy that carries the work to its conclusion.

PHILOSOPHY AND SCIENCE IN THE BAROQUE PERIOD

Throughout the 17th century philosophy, like the visual arts, continued to extend and intensify ideas first developed in the Renaissance by pushing them to new extremes. With the spread of humanism the 16th century had seen a growing spirit of philosophical and scientific inquiry. In the Baroque period that fresh approach to the world and its phenomena was expressed in clear and consistent terms for the first time since the Greeks. It might be said, in fact, that if the Renaissance marked the

TABLE 13.2 Principal Scientific Discoveries of the 17th Century

1609	Kepler announces his first two laws of planetary motion
1614	Napier invents logarithms
1632	Galileo publishes *Dialogue Concerning the Two Chief World Systems*
1643	Torricelli invents the barometer
1660	Boyle formulates his law of gas pressure
1675	Royal Observatory founded at Greenwich, England
1687	Isaac Newton publishes his account of the principle of gravity
1710	Leibnitz invents new notations of calculus
1717	Fahrenheit invents system of measuring temperature

birth of modern philosophy, the 17th century signaled its coming of age.

Briefly put, the chief difference between the intellectual attitudes of the medieval period and those inaugurated by the Renaissance was a turning away from the contemplation of the absolute and eternal to a study of the particular and the perceivable. Philosophy ceased to be the preserve of the theologians and instead became an independent discipline, no longer prepared to accept a supernatural or divine explanation for the world and human existence.

For better or worse, we are still living with the consequences of this momentous change. The importance of objective truth, objectively demonstrated, lies at the heart of all scientific method, and most modern philosophy. Yet great thinkers before the Renaissance, such as Thomas Aquinas (1225–1274), had also asked questions in an attempt to understand the world and its workings. How did 17th-century scientists and philosophers differ from their predecessors in dealing with age-old problems?

The basic difference lay in their approach. When, for example, Aquinas was concerned with the theory of motion, he discussed it in abstract, metaphysical terms. Armed with his copy of Aristotle he claimed that "motion exists because things which are in a state of potentiality seek to actualize themselves." When Galileo wanted to study motion and learn how bodies move in time and space, he climbed to the top of the Leaning Tower of Pisa and dropped weights to watch them fall. It would be difficult to imagine a more dramatic rejection of abstract generalization in favor of objective demonstration [Table 13.2].

Galileo

The life and work of Galileo Galilei (1564–1642) are typical both of the progress made by science in the 17th century and of the problems it encountered. Galileo changed the scientific world in two ways: first, as the stargazer who claimed that his observations through the telescope proved Copernicus right, for which statement he was tried and condemned by the Inquisition; and second as the founder of modern physics. Although he is probably better known for his work in astronomy, from the scientific point of view his contribution to physics is more important.

Born in Pisa, Galileo inherited from his father Vincenzo, who had been one of the original members of the Florentine Camerata, a lively prose style and a fondness for music. As a student at the University of Padua from 1581 to 1592 he began to study medicine but soon changed to mathematics. After a few months back in Pisa, he took a position at the University of Padua as professor of mathematics, remaining there from 1592 to 1600.

In Padua he designed and built his own telescopes [13.35] and saw for the first time the craters of the moon, sunspots, the phases of Venus, and other phenomena which showed that the universe is in a constant state of change, as Copernicus had claimed. From the time of Aristotle, however, it had been a firm belief that the heavens were unalterable, representing perfection of form and movement. Galileo's discoveries thus disproved what had been a basic philosophical principle for 2000 years and so outraged a professor of philosophy at Padua that he refused to shake his own prejudices by having a look through a telescope for himself.

The more triumphantly Galileo proclaimed his findings, the more he found himself involved in something beyond mere scientific controversy. His real opponent was the Church, which had officially adopted the Ptolemaic view of the universe: that the earth formed the center of the universe around which the sun, moon, and planets circled. This theory accorded well with the Bible, which seemed to suggest that the sun moves rather than the earth; for the Church, the Bible naturally took precedence over any reasoning or speculation independent of

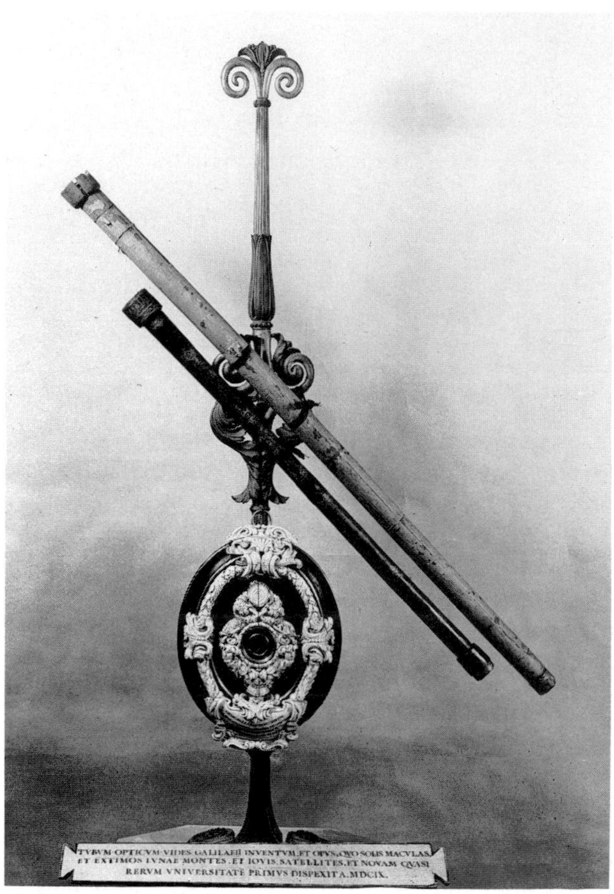

13.35 Galileo Galilei. Telescopes. 1609. Museum of Science, Florence. After his death near Florence in 1642, many of Galileo's instruments, including these telescopes, were collected and preserved. The Museum of Science in Florence, where they can now be seen, was one of the earliest museums to be devoted to scientific rather than artistic works.

theology. Galileo, however, considered ecclesiastical officials incompetent to evaluate scientific matters and refused to give way. When he began to claim publicly that his discoveries had proved what Copernicus had theorized but could not validate, the Church initiated a case against him on the grounds of heresy.

Galileo had meanwhile returned to his beloved Pisa, where he found himself in considerable danger from the Inquisition. In 1615 he left for Rome to defend his position in the presence of Pope Paul V. He failed, and as a result was censured and prohibited from spreading the Copernican theory either by teaching or publication.

In 1632 Galileo returned to the attack when a former friend was elected Pope. He submitted to Pope Urban VIII a *Dialogue Concerning the Two Chief World Systems,* having carefully chosen the dialogue form so that he could put ideas into the mouths of other characters and thereby claim that they were not his own. Once more, under pressure from the Jesuits, he was summoned to Rome. In 1633 he was put on trial after spending several months in prison. His pleas of old age and poor health won no sympathy from the tribunal. He was made to recant and humiliate himself publicly and was sentenced to prison for the rest of his life. (It might well have appealed to Galileo's sense of bitter irony that 347 years later, in 1980, Pope John Paul II, a fellow countryman of the Polish Copernicus, ordered the case to be reopened so that belated justice might be done.)

Influential friends managed to secure Galileo a relatively comfortable house arrest in his villa just outside Florence, and he retired there to work on physics. His last and most important scientific work, *Dialogues Concerning Two New Sciences,* was published in 1638. In it he examined many longstanding problems, including that of motion, always basing his conclusions on practical experiment and observation. In the process he established the outlines of many areas of modern physics.

In all his work Galileo set forth a new way of approaching scientific problems. Instead of trying to understand the final cause or cosmic purpose of natural events and phenomena, he tried to explain their character and the manner in which they came about. He changed the question from *why?* to *what?* and *how?*

Descartes

Scientific investigation could not solve every problem of human existence. While it *could* try to explain and interpret objective phenomena, there remained other more subjective areas of experience involving ethical and spiritual questions. The Counter-Reformation on the one hand and the Protestant churches on the other claimed to have discovered the answers. The debates nevertheless continued, most notably in the writings of the French philosopher René Descartes (1596–1650), often called the "Father of Modern Philosophy" [13.36].

In many ways Descartes' philosophical position was symptomatic of his age. He was educated at a Jesuit school but found traditional theological teaching unsatisfactory. Turning to science and mathematics, he began a lifelong search for reliable evidence in his quest to distinguish truth from falsehood. Attacking philosophical problems, his prime concern was to establish criteria for defining reality. His chief published works, *The Discourse on Method* (1637) and the *Meditations* (1641), contain a

13.36 Frans Hals. *René Descartes.* Oil on panel. Statens Museum for Kunst, Copenhagen. The great French philosopher spent many years in Holland, where his ideas found a receptive audience and where Hals painted this portrait.

step-by-step account of how he arrived at his conclusions.

According to Descartes, the first essential in the search for truth was to make a fresh start by refusing to believe anything that could not be decisively proved to be true. This required that he doubt all his previously held beliefs, including the evidence of his own senses. By stripping away all uncertainties he reached a basis of indubitable certainty on which he could build: that he existed. The very act of doubting proved that he was a thinking being. As he put it in a famous phrase in his second *Meditation*, *Cogito, ergo sum* (I think, therefore I am).

From this foundation Descartes proceeded to reconstruct the world he had taken to pieces by considering the nature of material objects. He was guided by the principle that whatever is clearly and distinctly perceived must exist. He was aware at the same time that our perceptions of the exact nature of these objects are extremely likely to be incorrect and misleading. When, for example, we look at the sun we see it as a very small disk, although the sun is really an immense globe. We must be careful, therefore, not to assume that our perceptions are bound to be accurate. All that they demonstrate is the simple existence of the object in question.

If the idea of the sun comes from the perception, however inaccurate, of something that actually exists, what of God? Is the idea of a divine Being imagined or based on truth? Descartes concluded that the very fact that we who are imperfect and doubting can conceive of a perfect God proves that our conception is based on a reality. In other words, who could ever have imagined God unless God existed? At the center of the Cartesian philosophical system, therefore, lay the belief in a perfect Being, not necessarily to be identified with the God of the Old and New Testaments, who had created a world permeated by perfect (that is, mathematical) principles.

At first sight this may seem inconsistent with Descartes' position as the founder of modern rational thought. It may seem even stranger that, just at the time when scientific investigators like Galileo were explaining natural phenomena without recourse to divine intervention, Descartes succeeded in proving to his own satisfaction the undeniable existence of a divine Being. Yet a more careful look at Descartes' method reveals that both he and Galileo shared the same fundamental confidence in the rational powers of human beings.

Hobbes and Locke

Although Galileo and Descartes represent the major trends in 17th-century thought, other important figures made their own individual contributions. Descartes' fellow countryman Blaise Pascal (1623–1662), for example, launched a strong attack on the Jesuits while providing his own somewhat eccentric defense of Christianity. A more mystical approach to religion was that of the Dutch philosopher Baruch Spinoza (1632–1677), whose concept of the ideal unity of nature later made a strong appeal to 19th-century romantics. The English philosopher Thomas Hobbes (1588–1679), however, had little in common with any of his contemporaries—as he was frequently at pains to make plain. For Hobbes truth lay only in material things: "All that is real is material, and what is not material is not real."

Hobbes is thus one of the first modern proponents of *materialism* and, like many of his materialist successors, was interested in solving political rather than philosophical problems. Born in the year of the Spanish Armada, Hobbes lived through the turbulent English Civil War, a period marked by constant instability and political confusion. Perhaps in consequence, he developed an enthusiasm for the authority of the law, as represented by the king, that verges on totalitarianism.

Hobbes' political philosophy finds its fullest statement in his book *Leviathan,* first published in 1651. The theory of society that he describes there totally denies the existence in the universe of any divinely established morality. (Hobbes never denied the existence of God, not wishing to outrage public and ecclesiastical opinion unnecessarily, although he might as well have.) According to Hobbes, all laws are created by humans to protect themselves from one another—a necessary precaution in view of human greed and violence. Organized society in consequence is arrived at when individuals give up their personal liberty in order to achieve security. As a result, the ideal state is that in which there is the greatest security, specifically one ruled by an absolute ruler.

From its first appearance *Leviathan* created a scandal; it has been subject to continual attack ever since. Hobbes managed to offend both of the chief participants in the intellectual debates of the day: the theologians, by telling them that their doctrines were irrelevant and their terminology "insignificant sound"; and the rationalists, by claiming that human beings, far from being capable of the highest intellectual achievements, are dangerous and aggressive creatures who need to be saved from themselves. Hobbes' pessimism and the extreme nature of his position have won him few wholehearted supporters in the centuries since his death. Yet many modern readers, like others in the time since *Leviathan* first appeared, must reluctantly admit that there is at least a grain of truth in his picture of society, which can be attested to by personal experience and observation. At the very least his political philosophy is valuable as a diagnosis and a warning of some aspects of human potential virtually all of his contemporaries and many of his successors have preferred to ignore.

The leading English thinker of the generation following Hobbes was John Locke (1632–1704), whose work helped to lay the way for the European Enlightenment. The son of a country attorney, his education followed traditional classical lines, but the young Locke was more interested in medicine and the new experimental sciences. In 1666 he became physician and secretary to the future Earl of Shaftesbury, who encouraged Locke's interest in political philosophy.

In his first works, Locke explored the subjects of property and trade, and the role of the monarch in a modern state. He then turned to more general questions: What is the nature of ideas, how do we get them, and what are the limitations of human knowledge? His most influential work, *An Essay Concerning Human Understanding,* appeared in 1690. In it he argued against a theory of innate ideas, proposing instead that our ideas derive from our perceptions. Thus our notions and characters are based on our own individual sense impressions and on our reflections on them, not on inherited values. Rejecting traditional metaphors and metaphysics, Locke advocated an anti-monarchical, property-oriented political philosophy, in which ideas served as a kind of personal property.

For his successors in the 18th century, Locke seemed to have set human nature free from the control of divine authority. Humans were no longer perceived as the victims of innate original sin or the accidents of birth, but derived their ideas and personalities from their experiences. Like many of the spokesmen of the Enlightenment, Voltaire acknowledged the importance of Locke's ideas, while few modern students of education or theory of knowledge have failed to be influenced by him.

LITERATURE IN THE 17TH CENTURY

French Baroque Comedy and Tragedy

It is hardly surprising that the Baroque age, which put so high a premium on the expression of dramatic emotion, should have been an important period in the development of the theater. In France in particular, three of the greatest names in the history of drama were active at the same time, all of them benefiting at one point or another from the patronage of Louis XIV.

Molière was the stage name of Jean-Baptiste Poquelin (1622–1673), who was the creator of a new theatrical form, French Baroque comedy. Having first made his reputation as an actor, he turned to the writing of drama as a means of deflating pretense and pomposity. In his best works, the deceptions or delusions of the principal characters are revealed for what they are with good humor and considerable understanding of human foibles, but dramatic truth is never sacrificed to mere comic effect. Unlike so many comic creations, Molière's characters remain believable. Jourdain, the good-natured social climber of *Le Bourgeois Gentilhomme,* and Harpagon, the absurd miser of *L'Avare,* are by no means mere symbols of their respective vices but victims of those vices, albeit willing ones. Even the unpleasant Tartuffe in the play of that name is a living character with his own brand of hypocrisy.

Classical motifs play a strong part in the works of the two greatest tragic dramatists of the age, Pierre Corneille (1606–1684) and Jean Racine (1639–1699). It was Corneille who created, as counterpart to Molière's comedy, French Baroque tragedy. Most of his plays take as their theme an event in classical history or mythology, which is often used to express eternal truths about human behavior. The themes of patriotism, as in *Horace,* or martyrdom, as in *Polyeucte,* are certainly as relevant today as they were in 17th-century France or in ancient Greece or Rome. However, most people's response to Corneille's treatment of subjects such as these is probably conditioned by the degree to which they enjoy the cut and thrust of rhetorical debate.

Racine may well provide for many modern readers an easier entry into the world of French Baroque tragedy. Although for the most part he followed the dramatic form and framework established by Corneille, he used it to explore different areas of human experience. His recurrent theme is self-destruction: the inability to control one's own jealousy, passion, or ambition and the resulting inability, as tragic as it is inevitable, to survive its effects. Furthermore, in plays like *Phèdre* he explored the psychological state of mind of his principal characters, probing for the same kind of understanding of motivation that Monteverdi tried to achieve in music.

The Novel in Spain: Cervantes

By the middle of the 16th century the writing of fiction in Spain had begun to take a characteristic form that was to influence much later European fiction. The picaresque novel was a Spanish invention; books of this type tell a story that revolves around a rogue or adventurer—in Spanish *pícaro* means a rogue or knave. The earliest example is *Lazarillo de Tormes,* which appeared anonymously in 1554. Its hero, Lazarillo, is brought up among beggars and thieves, and many of the episodes serve as an excuse to satirize priests and church officials—so much so, in fact, that the Inquisition ordered parts omitted in later printings. Unlike prose being written elsewhere at the time, the style is colloquial, even racy, and heavy with irony.

Although *Don Quixote,* by general agreement the greatest novel in the Spanish language, has picaresque elements, its style and subject are both far more subtle and complex. Miguel de Cervantes Saavedra (1547–1616), its author, set out to satirize medieval tales of chivalry and romance by inventing a character—Don Quixote—who is an amiable elderly gentleman looking for the chivalry of storybooks in real life. This apparently simple idea takes on almost infinite levels of meaning, as Don Quixote pursues his ideals, in general without much success, in a world with little time for romance or honor. In his adventures, which bring him into contact with all levels of Spanish society, he is accompanied by his squire Sancho Panza, whose shrewd practicality serves as a foil for his own unworldliness.

The structure of the novel is as leisurely and seemingly as rambling as the Don's wanderings. Yet the various episodes are linked by the constant confrontation between reality and illusion, the real world and that of the imagination. Thus at one level the book becomes a meditation on the relationship between art and life.

By the end of his life Don Quixote has learned painfully that his noble aspirations cannot be reconciled with the realities of the world, and he dies disillusioned. In the last part of the book, where the humor of the hero's mishaps does not conceal their pathos, Cervantes reaches that rare height of artistry where comedy and tragedy are indistinguishable.

The English Metaphysical Poets

In England the pinnacle of dramatic expression had been reached by the turn of the century in the works of Shakespeare, and nothing remotely comparable was to follow. The literary form that proved most productive during the 17th century was that of lyric poetry, probably because of its ability to express personal emotions, although the single greatest English work of the age was John Milton's epic poem *Paradise Lost.*

It might well be argued that the most important of all literary achievements of the 17th century was not an original artistic creation but a translation. It is difficult to know precisely how to categorize the Authorized Version of the Bible, commissioned by King James I and first published in 1611, often called the only great work of literature every produced by a committee. The fifty-four scholars and translators who worked on the task deliberately tried to create a "biblical" style that would transcend the tone of English as it was then generally used. Their success can be measured by the immense influence the King James Bible has had on speakers and writers of English ever since (see page 318). It remained the Authorized Version for English-speaking people until the late 19th century, when it was revised in the light of new developments in biblical studies.

Of all 17th-century literary figures, the group known as the metaphysical poets, with their concern to give intellectual expression to emotional experience, make a particular appeal to modern readers. As is often pointed out, the label *metaphysical* is highly misleading for two reasons. In the first place, it suggests an organized group of poets consciously following a common style. It is true that the earliest poet to write in the metaphysical style, John Donne, exerted a strong influence on a whole generation of younger poets, but there never existed any unified group or school. (Some scholars, in fact, would classify Donne's style as Mannerist.)

Secondly, metaphysical seems to imply that the principal subject of their poetry was philosophical speculation on abstruse questions. It is certainly true that the metaphysical poets were interested in ideas and that they used complex forms of expression and a rich vocabulary to express them. The chief subject of their poems was not philosophy, however, but themselves—particularly their own emotions.

Yet this concern with self-analysis should not suggest a limitation of vision. Indeed, some critics have ranked John Donne (1572–1631) as second only to the Shakespeare of the Sonnets in range and depth of expression. His intellectual brilliance and his love of paradox and ambiguity make his poetry sometimes difficult to follow. Donne always avoided the conventional, either in word or thought, while the swift changes of mood within a single short poem from light banter to the utmost seriousness can confuse the careless reader. Although it sometimes takes patience to unravel his full meaning, the effort is more than amply rewarded by contact with one of the most daring and honest of poets.

Donne's poems took on widely differing areas of human experience, ranging from some of the most passionate and frank discussions of sexual love ever penned to profound meditations on human mortality and the nature of the soul. Born a Catholic, he traveled widely as a young man and seems to have led a hectic and exciting life. He abandoned Catholicism, perhaps in part to improve his chances of success in Protestant England, and in 1601, on the threshold of a successful career in public life, entered Parliament. The same year, however, he secretly married his patron's sixteen-year-old niece, Anne More. Her father had him dismissed and even imprisoned for a few days, and Donne's career never recovered from the disgrace.

Although Donne's marriage proved a happy one, its early years were clouded by debt, ill health, and frustration. In 1615, at the urging of friends, he finally joined the Anglican church and entered the ministry. As a preacher he soon became known as among the greatest of his day. By 1621 he was appointed to one of the most prestigious positions in London, Dean of Saint Paul's. During his last years he became increasingly obsessed with death. After a serious illness in the spring of 1631 he preached his own funeral sermon and died within a few weeks.

Thus the successful worldliness of the early years gave way to the growing somberness of his later career. We might expect a similar progression from light to darkness in his works, yet throughout his life the two forces of physical passion and religious intensity seem to have been equally dominant, with the result that in much of his poetry each is sometimes used to express the other.

The poems of Donne's younger contemporary, Richard Crashaw (1613–1649), blend extreme emotion and religious fervor in a way that is completely typical of much baroque art. Yet Crashaw serves as a reminder of the danger of combining groups of artists under a single label, since although he shares many points in common with the other metaphysical poets, his work as a whole strikes a unique note.

There can be little doubt that Crashaw's obsessive preoccupation with pain and suffering has more than a touch of masochism, and that his religious fervor is extreme even by baroque standards. Some of the intensity is doubtless due to his violent rejection of his father's Puritanism and his own enthusiastic conversion to Catholicism. Stylistically Crashaw owed much to the influence of the flamboyant Italian baroque poet Giambattista Marino (1569–1625), whose virtuoso literary devices he imitated. Yet the eroticism that so often tinges his spiritual fervor gives to his work a highly individual air.

Milton's Heroic Vision

While the past hundred years have seen a growing appreciation for Donne and his followers, the reputation of John Milton has undergone some notable ups and downs. Revered in the centuries following his death, Milton's work came under fire in the early years of the 20th century from major poets like T. S. Eliot and Ezra Pound, who claimed that his influence on his successors had been pernicious and had led much of subsequent English poetry astray. Now that the dust of these attacks has settled, Milton has resumed his place as one of the greatest of English poets. The power of his spiritual vision, coupled with his heroic attempt to wrestle with the great problems of human existence, seem in fact to speak directly to the uncertainties of our own time.

Milton's life was fraught with controversy. An outstanding student with astonishing abilities in languages, he spent his early years traveling widely in Europe and in the composition of relatively lightweight verse—lightweight, that is, in comparison with what was to come. Among his most entertaining early works are the companion poems "L'Allegro" and "Il Penseroso," which compare the cheerful and the contemplative character, with appropriate scenery. They were probably written in 1632, following his graduation from Cambridge.

By 1640, however, he had become involved in the tricky issues raised by the English Civil War and the related problems of church government. He launched into the fray with a series of radical pamphlets that advocated, among other things, divorce on the grounds of incompatibility. (It is presumably no coincidence that his own wife had left him six weeks after their marriage.) His growing support for Oliver Cromwell and the Puritan cause won him an influential position at home but considerable enmity in continental Europe, where he was seen as the defender of those who had ordered the execution of King Charles I in 1649. The strain of his secretarial and diplomatic duties during the following years destroyed his eyesight, but although completely blind he continued to work with the help of assistants.

When Charles II was restored to power in 1660 Milton lost his position and was lucky not to lose his life or liberty. Retired to private life, he spent his remaining years in the composition of three massive works. *Paradise Lost* (1667), *Paradise Regained* (1671), and *Samson Agonistes* (1671).

By almost universal agreement Milton's most important, if not most accessible, work is *Paradise Lost*, composed in the early 1600s and published in 1667. It was intended as an account of the fall of Adam and Eve, and its avowed purpose was to "justify the ways of God to men." The epic is in twelve books (originally ten, but Milton later revised the divisions), written in blank verse.

Milton's language and imagery present an almost inexhaustible combination of biblical and classical reference. From the very first lines of Book I, where the poet calls on a classical Muse to help him tell the tale of The Fall, the two great Western cultural traditions are inextricably linked. Indeed, like Bach, Milton represents the summation of these traditions. In his works, Renaissance and Reformation meet and blend to create the most complete statement in English of Christian humanism, the philosophical reconciliation of humanist principles with Christian doctrine. To the Renaissance Milton owed his grounding in the classics. In composing *Paradise Lost,* an epic poem that touches on the whole range of human experience, he was deliberately inviting comparison with Homer and Vergil. His language is also classical in its inspiration, with its long, grammatically complex sentences and preference for abstract terms. Yet his deeply felt Christianity and his emphasis on human guilt and repentance mark him as a product of the Reformation. Furthermore, although he may have tried to transcend the limitations of his own age, he was as much a child of his time as any of the other artists discussed in this chapter. The dramatic fervor of Bernini, the spiritual certainty of Bach, the psychological insight of Monteverdi, the humanity of Rembrandt—all have their place in Milton's work and mark him, too, as an essentially baroque figure.

SUMMARY

If the history and culture of the 16th century were profoundly affected by the Reformation, the prime element to influence those of the 17th century was the Counter-Reformation, the Catholic Church's campaign to regain its authority and influence. By clarifying and forcefully asserting their teaching, backed up with a vigorous program of missionary work, Church leaders aimed to present a positive and optimistic appearance that would eliminate past discords.

Among the resources used by Counter-Reformation reformers were the arts. Imposing architectural complexes like Saint Peter's Square in Rome, paintings and sculptures, music and verse could all serve to reinforce the glory of the Church. In some cases works were commissioned officially; in others artists responded individually to the spirit of the times. Bernini's *Saint Teresa in Ecstasy,* a statue that reflects the artist's own devout faith, was commissioned for the church in Rome in which it still stands. Richard Crashaw's poetry represents a more personal response to the religious ideas of his day.

For all the importance of religion, the 17th century was also marked by significant developments in philosophy and science. Galileo, the father of modern physics, revolutionized astronomy by proving Copernicus' claims of the previous century correct. Thinkers like Descartes and Hobbes, instead of accepting official Church teachings, tried to examine the problems of human existence by their own intellectual approaches. Descartes was the founder of modern rational thought (although a believer in a supreme Being); Hobbes was the first modern materialist.

The principal artistic style of the 17th century was the baroque, a term originally used for the visual arts but also applied by extension to the other arts of the period. Although the Baroque style was created in Italy, it spread quickly throughout Europe and was even carried to the New World by missionaries.

Baroque art is marked by a wide range of achievements, but there are a number of common features. Artists in the 17th century were concerned to express strong emotions, either religious or personal. This in turn led to an interest in exploring human behavior from a psychological point of view. With the new subjects came new techniques, many of them emphasizing the virtuosity of the artist. These in turn led to the invention of new forms: in music that of opera, in painting that of landscape scenes, to take only two examples.

The chief characteristics of baroque painting were created in Rome around 1600 by two artists. Caravaggio's work is emotional and dominated by strong contrasts of light and darkness. Carracci painted scenes of movement and splendor, many on classical themes. Both strongly influenced their contemporaries and successors. Caravaggio's use of light was the forerunner of the work of artists as diverse as the Spaniard Velázquez and the Dutchman Vermeer, while Carracci's choice of classical subjects was followed by the French Poussin. The two greatest painters of northern Europe, Rembrandt and Rubens, were also influenced by the ideas of their day. Rembrandt used strong contrasts of light and dark to paint deeply felt religious scenes as well as the self-portraits that explore his own inner emotions. Rubens, one of the most versatile of artists, ranged from mythological subjects to historical paintings like the Marie de' Medici cycle to intimate personal portraits.

Although the 17th century saw architects increasingly employed in designing private houses, most of the principal building projects were public. At Rome the leading architect was Bernini, also one of the greatest sculptors of the age, whose churches, fountains, and piazzas changed the face of the city. In his sculpture Bernini drew on virtually all the themes of Counter-Reformation art, including mythological and religious works and vividly characterized portraits. The other great building project of the century was the palace built for Louis XIV at Versailles, where the splendor of the Sun King was reflected in the grandiose decoration scheme.

In music, as in the visual arts, the Baroque period was one of experimentation and high achievement. Counter-Reformation policy required that music for church use should be easily understood and appreciated, as was already the case in the Protestant countries of northern Europe. At the same time there was a growing demand for secular music for performance both in public and at home.

One of the most important innovations of the 17th century was opera. The first opera was performed just before 1600 in Florence, and by the middle of the century opera houses were being built throughout Europe to house the new art form. The first great composer of operas was the Italian Monteverdi, whose *L'Orfeo* is the earliest opera still to hold the stage. Among later musicians of the period to write works for the theater was the German Georg Frideric Handel, many of whose operas were composed to an Italian text for performance in England.

Handel also wrote oratorios, sacred dramas performed without any staging; indeed the most famous of all oratorios is his *Messiah.* The oratorio was a form with a special appeal for Protestant Germans; among its leading exponents was Heinrich Schütz. The greatest of all Lutheran composers, Johann Sebastian Bach, wrote masterpieces in just about every musical form other than opera. Like many of the leading artists of the age, Bach produced works inspired by deep religious faith as well as pieces like the *Brandenburg Concertos* for private entertainment.

The baroque interest in emotion and drama, exemplified by the invention of opera, led to important developments in writing for the theater as well as in the style of poetic composition and the invention of new literary forms. In France the comedies of Molière and the tragedies of Corneille and Racine, written in part under the patronage of Louis XIV, illustrate the dramatic range of the period. The religious fervor of the English metaphysical poets is yet another sign of baroque artists' concern with questions of faith and belief. The more practical problems involved in reconciling ideals with the realities of life are described in *Don Quixote,* one of the first great novels in Western literature. The most monumental of all literary works of the 17th century, Milton's *Paradise Lost,* aimed to combine the principles of Renaissance humanism with Christian teaching. Its drama, spirituality, and psychological insight mark it as a truly baroque masterpiece.

For all the immense range of baroque art and culture, its principal lines were drawn by reactions to the Counter-Reformation. Furthermore, paradoxically enough, by the end of the 17th century a to the Counter-Reformation. Furthermore, paradoxically enough, by the end of the 17th century a movement that had been inspired by opposition to the Reformation had accomplished many of the aims of the earlier reformers: Through art, music, and literature both artists and their audiences were made more familiar with questions of religious faith and more sensitive to aspects of human experience.

Pronunciation Guide

Annibale Carracci: Ann-IB-a-lay Car-AHCH-ee
Baroque: Bar-OAK
Borromini: Bo-roe-MEE-ni
Caravaggio: Ca-ra-VAJ-o
Cervantes: Ser-VAN-teez
Concerto Grosso: Con-CHAIR-owe GRO-sew
Corneille: Cor-NAY
Descartes: Day-CART
Donne: DUN
Don Quixote: Don ki-HOTE-ee
Galileo: Ga-li-LAY-owe
Gentileschi: Gen-ti-LESS-key
Lorrain: Lor-ANN
Molière: Mo-li-AIR
Monteverdi: Mon-te-VAIR-di
Orfeo: Or-FAY-owe
Piazza: pi-AT-sa
Racine: Rah-SEEN
Rameau: Ram-OWE
Rembrandt van Rijn: REM-brant van RHINE
Rubens: RUE-buns
Schütz: SHUETS
Sweelinck: SVAY-link
Theotokopoulos: They-ot-ok-OP-ou-loss
Toccata: To-CA-ta
Velázquez: Ve-LASS-kes
Vermeer: Vur-MERE
Versailles: Ver-SIGH

Exercises

1. What characteristics are common to all the arts in the Baroque period? Give examples.
2. Compare the paintings of Caravaggio and Rembrandt with regard to subject matter and use of contrasts in light.
3. Describe the birth and early development of opera.
4. What were the principal scientific and philosophical movements of the 17th century? To what extent were they the result of external historical factors?
5. Discuss the treatment of religious subjects by Baroque artists, writers, and musicians. How does it contrast with that of the Renaissance?

Further Reading

Boyd, M. *Bach.* London: Dent, 1983. A good recent one-volume study of Bach that interweaves an account of the composer's life with a discussion of his works.

Brown, J. *Images and Ideas in Seventeenth-Century Spanish Painting.* Princeton: Princeton University Press, 1978. Relates the leading Spanish Baroque painters to their cultural world. A chapter is dedicated to an analysis of *Las Meninas.*

Cipolla, C. (ed.). *The Fontana Economic History of Europe,* Vol. II. London: Fontana, 1974. A useful survey of the principal developments in a period marked by widespread economic change and overseas expansion.

Kahr, M. *Dutch Painting in the Seventeenth Century.* New York: Harper & Row, 1978. A concise and readable survey with full discussions of Rembrandt, Vermeer, and Hals.

Knight, R. C. *Racine: Modern Judgments.* New York: Macmillan, 1970. A collection of essays on various aspects of French 17th-century drama, with a good general introductory essay.

Lavin, I. *Bernini and the Unity of the Visual Arts.* New York: Oxford University Press, 1980. A magnificent achievement that analyzes in depth Bernini's process of artistic creation.

McCorquodale, C. *The Baroque Painters of Italy.* New York: Phaidon, 1979. A handy volume especially useful for its excellent color illustrations.

Orrey, L. (rev. R. Milnes). *Opera: A Concise History.* London: Thames and Hudson, 1987. An updated edition of the best brief history of opera, with many interesting photographs.

Palisca, C. V. *Baroque Music.* Englewood Cliffs: Prentice-Hall, 1968. A good survey, not too technical, that places Baroque music in its cultural context.

Sewter, A. C. *Baroque and Rococo.* New York: Harcourt, 1972. A conveniently short and readable introduction to the visual arts of the period, with a good proportion of color plates.

Willey, B. *The Seventeenth-Century Background.* New York: Columbia University Press, 1967. An excellent introduction to 17th-century intellectual developments, including discussions of Galileo, Descartes, Hobbes, and Milton.

	GENERAL EVENTS	LITERATURE & PHILOSOPHY	ART
1700			
DAWN OF THE ENLIGHTENMENT	**1710–c. 1795** Rise of Prussia and Russia **1715** Death of Louis XIV **1715–1774** Reign of Louis XV in France	**1711** Pope, *Essay on Criticism* **1712** Pope, *The Rape of the Lock,* mock-heroic epic **18th cent.** Translations of classical authors; Pope's *Iliad* (1713–1720), *Odyssey* (1725–1726) **1726** Swift, *Gulliver's Travels;* Voltaire exiled from France (returns 1729) **1729** Swift, *A Modest Proposal* **1733–1734** Pope, *Essay on Man* **1734** Voltaire, *Lettres philosophiques* **1739** Hume, *Treatise of Human Nature*	**c. 1715** Rococo style emerges in France **1717** Watteau, *Pilgrimage to Cythera* **c. 1730,** Carriera, *Portrait of a Lady*
1740			
AGE OF ENLIGHTENED DESPOTS	**1740–1786** Reign of Frederick the Great in Prussia **1773–1814** Jesuits disbanded **1774–1792** Reign of Louis XVI and Marie Antoinette in France **1776** American Declaration of Independence **1778–1783** American War of Independence **1788** Collapse of French economy; riots in Paris	**1750–1753** Voltaire at court of Frederick the Great in Potsdam **1751–1772** Diderot's *Encyclopédie* includes writings by Montesquieu and J. J. Rousseau **1758–1778** Voltaire sets up own court in Ferney **1759** Voltaire, *Candide* **1762** J. J. Rousseau, *The Social Contract, Emile* **1772** Political writer Thomas Paine meets Benjamin Franklin in London **1776** In Philadelphia, Paine publishes *Common Sense,* series of pamphlets **1776–1788** Gibbon, *History of the Decline and Fall of the Roman Empire* 	**1743–1745** Hogarth paints satirical series, *Marriage à la Mode* **1748** Excavations begin at Pompeii; interest in ancient classical styles increases Sculpture more virtuosic than profound; Queirolo, *Deception Unmasked* (after 1750) **1754** Boucher, *Cupid Captive* **c. 1765** Gainsborough, *Mary, Countess Howe* **1769** Tiepolo, *The Immaculate Conception,* rococo style applied to religious subject **1771** Houdon, *Diderot* **1773** Fragonard, *Love Letters* **1774** Reynolds, *Three Ladies Adorning a Term of Hymen,* influenced by classical and Renaissance models **c. 1776** Vanvitelli, *The Great Cascade,* fountains at castle of Caserta near Naples **1784–1785** David, *Oath of the Horatii,* establishes official style of revolutionary art **c. 1785** Gainsborough, *Haymaker and Sleeping Girl*
1789			
REVOLUTIONARY AND NAPOLEONIC WARS	**1789** French Revolution begins; new American Constitution **1793** Execution of Louis XVI **1793–1795** Reign of Terror in France **1799–1804** Napoleon rules France as consul **1804–1814** Napoleon rules France as emperor	**1792** Paine, *The Rights of Man*	**c. 1790** Houdon, *George Washington,* statue  **1800** David, *Napoleon Crossing the Alps* **1808** Canova, *Pauline Bonaparte Borghese as Venus*
1815			

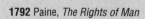

CHAPTER 14

THE 18TH CENTURY: FROM ROCOCO TO REVOLUTION

ARCHITECTURE

1732 Boffrand begins Hôtel de Soubise, Paris; rococo style applied to room decoration

1743 Henry Hoare begins to lay out classical-inspired park at Stourhead

1743–1772 Neumann, Vierzehnheiligen Pilgrim Church near Bamberg

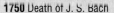

1755–1792 Soufflot converts church of Saint Geneviève into the Panthéon, neoclassical memorial for dead of French Revolution

1785–1796 Jefferson's State Capitol, Richmond, Virginia, modeled on ancient Roman Maison Carée at Nimes

MUSIC

c. 1700–1730 Couperin leading composer of *style galant* music at French court

1750 Death of J. S. Bach

c. 1750 C. P. E. Bach chief representative of emotional *empfindsamer Stil* at court of Frederick the Great

1750–1800 Development of classical style and symphonic form

1752 J. J. Rousseau, *Le Devin du Village,* opera

1759 Death of Handel

1761 Haydn ("Father of the Symphony") begins 30-year service with Esterhazys

1786 First performance of Mozart's *The Marriage of Figaro,* opera based on Beaumarchais play

1788 Mozart, *Symphony No. 40 in G Minor*

1791 Mozart, *Piano Concerto 27 in B flat Major;* opera *The Magic Flute*

1791–1795 Haydn composes 12 symphonies during visits to London, *Symphony No. 104 in D Major* (1795)

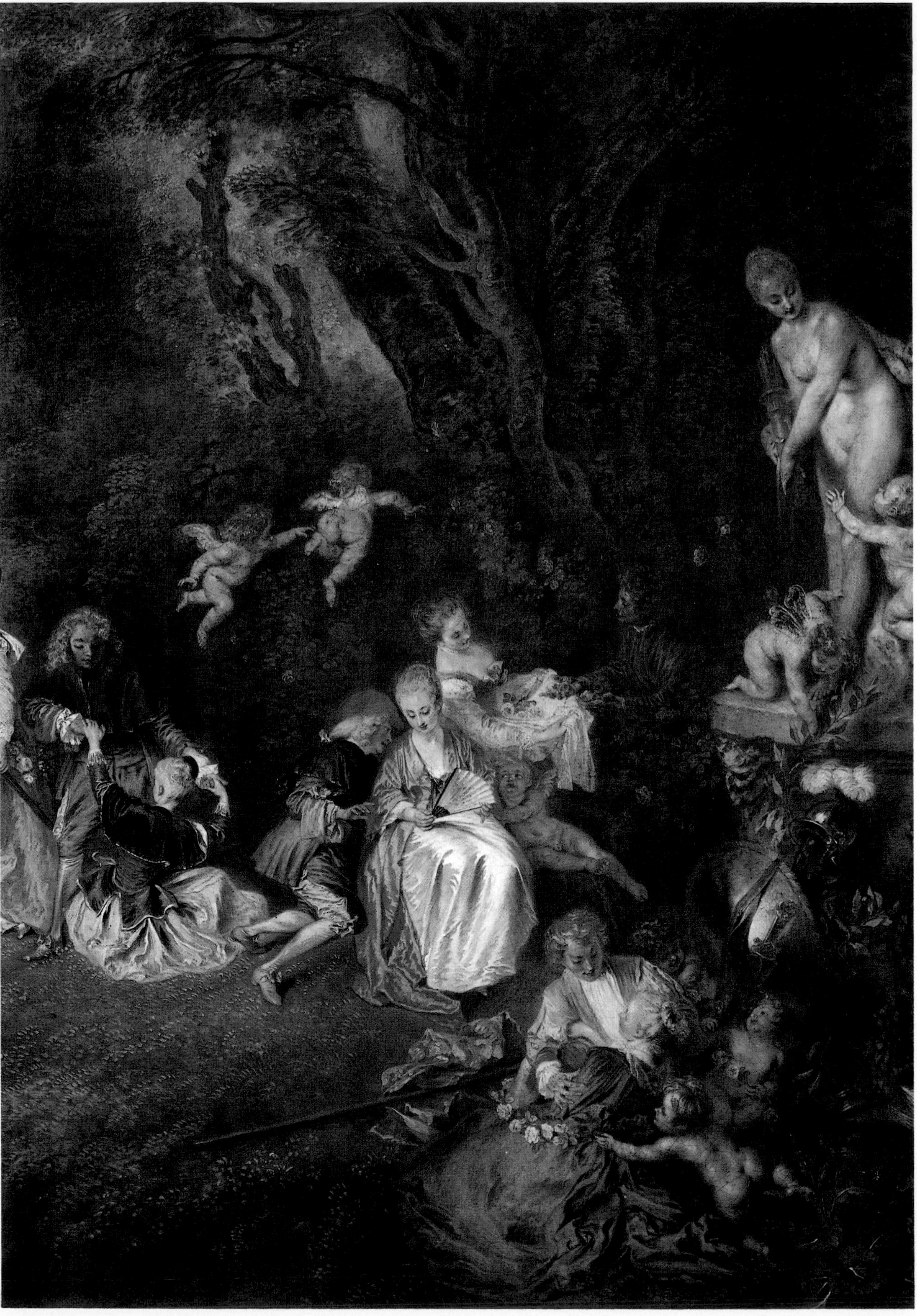

C H A P T E R

14

THE 18TH CENTURY: FROM ROCOCO TO REVOLUTION

AGE OF DIVERSITY

EVEN THE MOST determined cultural historians, fully armed with neat labels for successive stages of Western cultural development, acknowledge serious difficulty in categorizing the 18th century. Although it has often been called the Age of Enlightenment or the Age of Reason, these labels—which do, in fact, describe some of its aspects—fail to encompass the full spirit of the age.

From one perspective, the 18th century was an age of optimism. It had trust in science and in the power of human reason, belief in a natural order, and an overriding faith in the theory of progress—that the world was better than it had ever been and was bound to get better still. Looked at from another perspective, however, the 18th century was marked by pervasive resentment and dissatisfaction with established society. By its end, criticism and the press for reform had actually grown into a desire for violent change, producing the American and then the French revolutions. Furthermore, even these two apparently contradictory views—of unqualified optimism and of extreme discontent—do not cover all aspects of 18th-century culture. For example, one of the most popular artistic styles of the period, the rococo, was characterized by frivolity and lightheartedness. Rococo artists deliberately aimed to create a fantasy world of pleasure into which their patrons could escape from the problems around them.

The 18th century, then, presents an immense variety of artistic and intellectual ideas, seemingly contradictory yet in fact coexistent. Each style or idea seems far easier to grasp and categorize by itself than as part of an overall pattern of cultural development. Nevertheless, it is possible to discern at least one characteristic that links together a number of the diverse artistic achievements of the century: a conscious engagement with social issues. An opera such as Wolfgang Amadeus Mozart's *The Marriage of Figaro*, a series of satiric paintings of daily life such as William Hogarth's *Marriage à la Mode*, a mock epic poem such as Alexander Pope's *The Rape of the Lock*, and revolutionary ideas such as those of Jean-Jacques Rousseau are all examples of ways in which artists and thinkers joined with political leaders to effect social change.

Meanwhile, artists who supported the Establishment and were resistant to change were equally engaged in social issues. They too used their art to express and defend their position. François Boucher's portraits of his wealthy aristocratic patrons, for example, often show them in the guises of Greek gods and goddesses, thus imparting a sense of glamour and importance to an aristocracy that was shortly to be fighting for its survival.

The contrast between revolutionaries and conservatives lasted right to the eve of the French Revolution. Jacques Louis David's famous painting *Oath of the Horatii* of 1784–1785 [14.1], a clarion call to action and resolve, was painted in the same year as Thomas Gainsborough's idealized picture of a *Haymaker and Sleeping Girl* [14.2]. The former, in keeping with the spirit of the times, prefigures the mood of revolution. The latter turns its back on reality, evoking a nostalgic vision of love among the haystacks. In so doing it reinforces the aristocracy's refusal to see the working classes as real people with serious problems of their own. The same contrast occurs in the literature of the age; the conservative stance of Pope or Swift are very different from the views of Enlightenment figures such as Voltaire or Rousseau.

The 18th century opened with Louis XIV still strutting down the Hall of Mirrors at Versailles, but his death in 1715 marked the beginning of the end

14.1 Jacques Louis David, 1748–1785. *Oath of the Horatii.* Oil on canvas, 10'10" × 14' (3.3 × 4.25 m). Louvre, Paris. The story of the Horatii, three brothers who swore an oath to defend Rome even at the cost of their lives, is here used to extol patriotism. Painted only five years before the French Revolution, David's work established the official style of revolutionary art.

14.2 Thomas Gainsborough. Britain, 1727–1788. *Haymaker and Sleeping Girl (Mushroom Girl).* c. 1785. Oil on canvas, 89½ × 59" (227.3 × 149.9 cm). Museum of Fine Arts, Boston (Theresa B. Hopkins and Seth K. Sweetser Fund). These charming and elegant peasants, neither of whom looks exactly ravaged by hard work in the fields, represent the artificial world of rococo art.

TABLE 14.1 European Rulers in the 18th Century

Enlightened Despots	
Frederick II of Prussia	1740–1786*
Catherine the Great of Russia	1762–1796
Gustavus III of Sweden	1771–1792
Charles III of Spain	1759–1788
Joseph II of Austria	1780–1790
Rulers Bound by Parliamentary Government†	
George I of England	1714–1727
George II of England	1727–1760
George III of England	1760–1820
Aristocratic Rulers	
Louis XV of France	1715–1774
Louis XVI of France	1774–1792

* All dates are those of reigns.

† English political life was dominated not by the kings but by two powerful prime ministers: Robert Walpole and William Pitt.

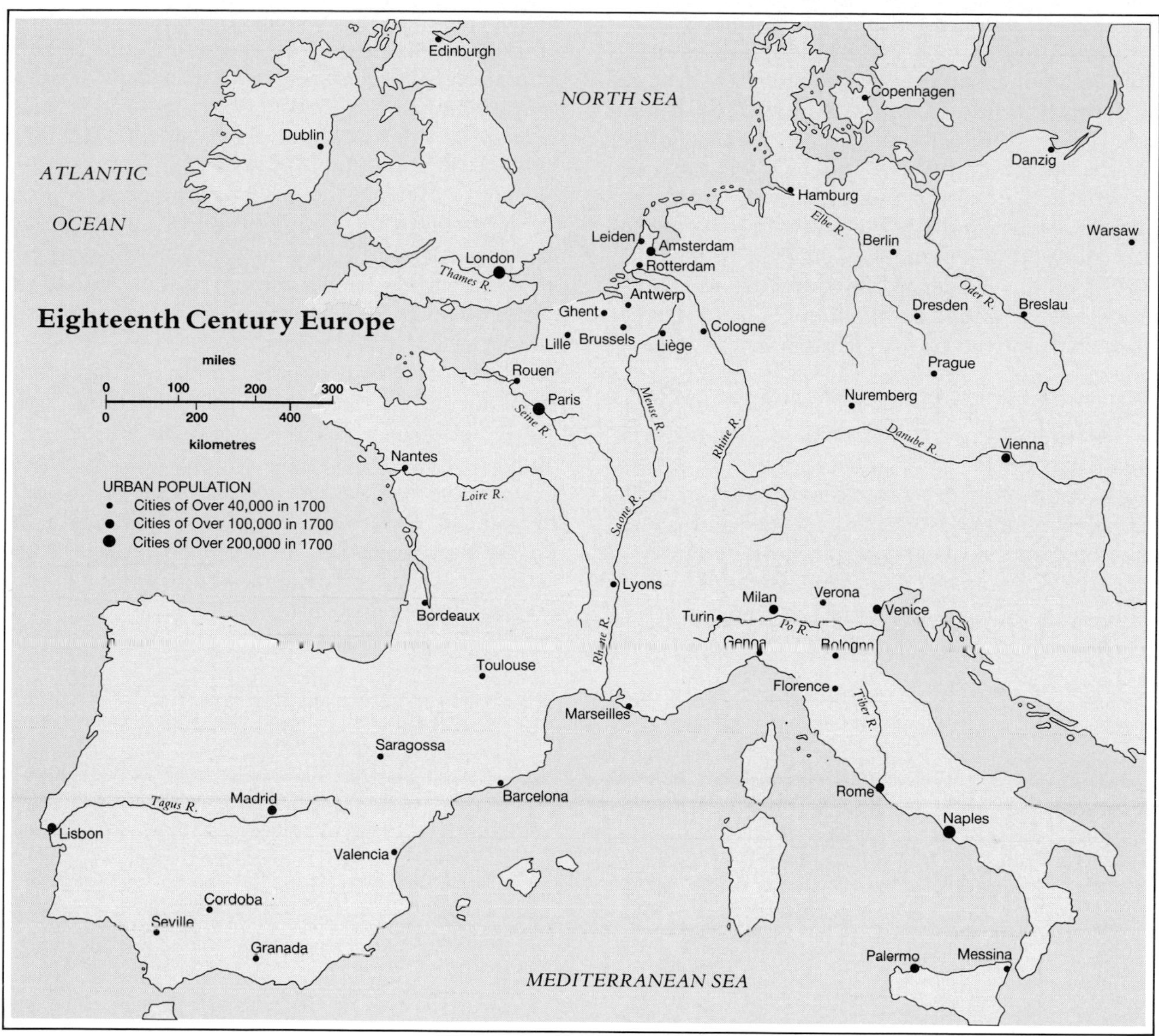

of absolute monarchy. Although most of Europe continued to be ruled by hereditary kings, the former emphasis on splendor and privilege was leavened with a new concern for the welfare of the ordinary citizen. Rulers such as Frederick the Great of Prussia (ruled 1740–1786) were no less determined than their predecessors to retain all power in their own hands, but they no longer thought of their kingdoms as private possessions to be manipulated for personal pleasure. Instead they regarded them as trusts, which required them to show a sense of duty and responsibility. They built new roads, drained marshes, and reorganized legal and bureaucratic systems along rational lines.

Because of their greater concern for the welfare of their people these new more liberal kings, often known as "enlightened despots," undoubtedly postponed for a while the growing demand for change. Inevitably, however, by drawing attention to the injustices of the past they stimulated an appetite for reform that they themselves were in no position to satisfy. Furthermore, for all their claims—Frederick the Great, for example, described himself as "first servant of the state"—their regimes remained essentially autocratic.

THE VISUAL ARTS IN THE 18TH CENTURY

The Rococo Style

In spite of the changing social climate of the time, the vast majority of 18th-century artists still depended on the aristocracy for commissions. The baroque style had been partially evolved to satisfy just these patrons, and throughout the early part of the 18th century many artists continued to produce works following baroque precedents. Yet, despite the continued fondness for the baroque characteristics of richness and elaboration, there was a significant change of emphasis. The new enlightened despots and their courts had less time for pomposity or excessive grandeur. They wanted to be not so much glorified as entertained. In France, too, the death of Louis XIV served as an excuse to escape the oppressive ceremony of life at Versailles; the French court moved back to Paris to live in elegant comfort.

The artistic style that developed to meet these new, less grandiose needs first reached its maturity in France. It is generally called *rococo,* a word derived from the French word *rocaille,* which means a kind of elaborate decoration of rocks and shells that often adorned the grottoes of baroque gardens. Rococo art was conceived of as anti-baroque, a contrast to the weighty grandeur of 17th-century art. It makes plentiful use of shell motifs, along with other decorative elements like scrolls and ribbons, to produce an overall impression of lightness and gaiety. The subject matter is rarely serious, often frivolous, with strong emphasis on romantic dalliance and the pursuit of pleasure.

The style is graceful and harmonious, in contrast to the flamboyant, dramatic effects of much baroque art. It might be said that whereas baroque artists preached or declaimed to their public, rococo art was the equivalent of polite, civilized conversation. Indeed, the 18th century was an age of polite society: a time of letter writing, chamber music, dancing. Clearly such pastimes only represented one aspect of 18th-century life, and the revolutions that shook Europe and the European colonies of North America at the end of the century called on a very different artistic style, the neoclassical, discussed below. Neoclassical artists rejected baroque extravagance and rococo charm in favor of dignity and austerity.

14.3 Jean Antoine Watteau. *Pilgrimage to Cythera.* 1717. Oil on canvas, 4'3" × 6'4½" (1.3 × 1.94 m). Schloss Charlottenburg, Berlin. One ancient Greek tradition claimed the isle of Cythera as the birthplace of Venus, goddess of love; thus the island became symbolic of ideal, tender love. Note that the mood of nostalgia and farewell is conveyed not only by the autumnal colors but also by the late-afternoon light that washes over the scene.

Critics have often said that the only purpose of rococo art was to provide pleasure, but this is a somewhat incomplete view of its social role. The rococo style was aimed for the most part at an aristocratic audience; its grace and charm served the important purpose of shielding this class from the growing problems of the real world. The elegant picnics, the graceful lovers, the Venuses triumphant represent an almost frighteningly unrealistic view of life, and one which met with disapproval from Enlightenment thinkers anxious to promote social change. Yet even the sternest moralist can hardly fail to respond to the enticing fantasy existence that the best of rococo art presents. In a sense the knowledge that the whole rococo world was to be so completely swept away imparts an added (and, it must be admitted, unintentional) poignance to its art. The existence of all those fragile ladies and their refined suitors was to be cut short by the guillotine.

The first and probably the greatest French rococo painter, Jean Antoine Watteau (1684–1721), seems to have felt instinctively the transitoriness and impermanence of the world he depicted. Watteau is best known for his paintings of *fêtes galantes,* elegant outdoor festivals attended by courtly figures dressed in the height of fashion. Yet the charming scenes are always touched with a mood of nostalgia that often verges on melancholy. In *Pilgrimage to Cythera* [14.3], for instance, the handsome young couples are returning home (despite the traditional title of the painting) from a visit to Cythera, the island sacred to Venus and to love. As they leave, a few of them gaze wistfully over their shoulders at the idyllic life, symbolized by the statue of Venus herself, which they must leave behind. Watteau thus emphasizes the moment of renunciation, underscoring the sense of departure and farewell by the autumnal colors of the landscape.

François Boucher (1703–1770), the other leading French rococo painter, was also influenced by Rubens. Lacking the restraint or poetry of Watteau's, Boucher's paintings carry Rubens' theme of voluptuous beauty to an extreme. His canvases often seem to consist of little beyond mounds of pink flesh, as in *Cupid a Captive* [14.4]. It would certainly be difficult to find profundity of intellectual content in most of his work, the purpose of which is to depict only one aspect of human existence. His visions of erotic delights are frankly intended to arouse other than aesthetic feelings.

Among Boucher's pupils was Jean Honoré Fragonard (1732–1806), the last of the great French rococo painters, who lived long enough to see all demand for rococo art disappear with the coming of the French Revolution. Although his figures are generally more clothed than those of Boucher, they are no less erotic. Even more than his master, Fragonard was able to use landscape to accentuate the mood of romance. In *Love Letters* [14.5], for example, the couple flirting in the foreground is

14.4 François Boucher. *Cupid a Captive.* 1754. Oil on canvas, 5'5" × 2'9" (1.64 × .83 m). Wallace Collection, London (reproduced by courtesy of the Trustees). Venus is seen in a relaxed and playful mood as she teases her little son by dangling his quiver of arrows above his head. Nonetheless, the presence of her seductive nymphs reminds us that she is not simply the goddess of motherly love.

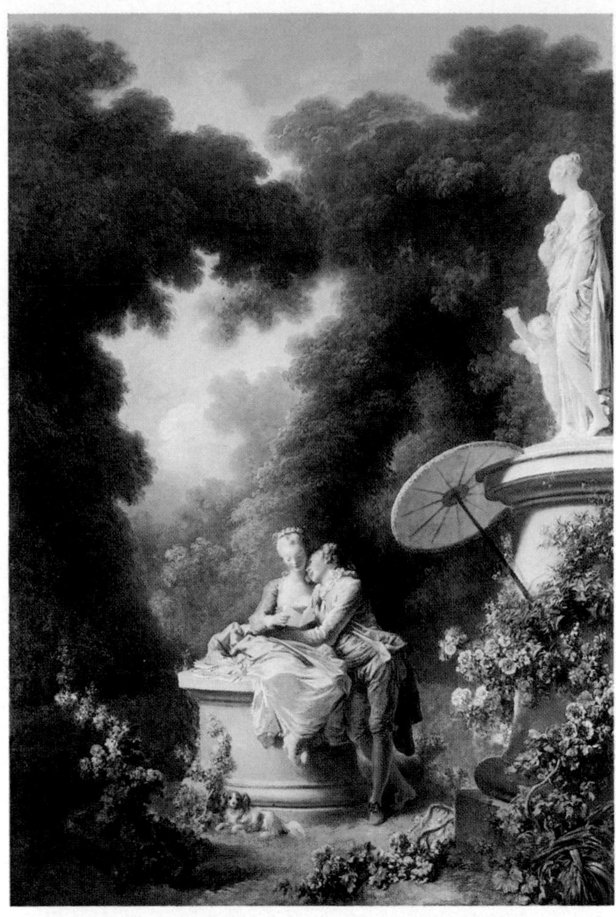

14.5 Jean Honoré Fragonard. *Love Letters*. 1773. Oil on canvas, 10'5" × 7'1" (3.17 × 2.17 m). Copyright Frick Collection, New York. Fragonard's style is much more free and less precise than Boucher's: Compare the hazy, atmospheric landscape of this painting with the background of *Cupid a Captive*.

surrounded by a jungle of trees and bushes that seems to impart a heady, humid air to the apparently innocent confrontation. The end of Fragonard's career is a reminder of how much 18th-century artists were affected by contemporary historical developments. When his aristocratic patrons either died or fled France during the Revolution, he was reduced to complete poverty. It was perhaps because Fragonard supported the ideals of the Revolution, in spite of its disastrous effect on his personal life, that Jacques Louis David, one of the Revolution's chief artistic arbiters, found him a job in the Museums Service. The last representative of the rococo tradition died poor and in obscurity as a minor official in the new French Republic.

Taken together, the three leading representatives of rococo painting provide a picture of the fantasy life of 18th-century aristocratic society. The work of other rococo artists, however, gives us a clearer impression of what life was really like in that aristocratic world. The Venetian artist Rosalba Carriera (1675–1757) traveled widely throughout Europe producing large numbers of portraits in the rather unusual medium of *pastel*, dry sticks of color that disintegrate when rubbed on paper, leaving behind a fine powder. The medium is very delicate, but so, unfortunately, are the works executed in it, since the powder smudges easily and tends to fall off if the paper is shaken. It is unlikely that Carriera was concerned with conveying psychological depths. Her chief aim was to provide her subjects flattering likenesses that reinforced their own favorable visions of themselves. Works like her portrait of the Princess of Modena [14.6] emphasize the delicacy, charm, and sensuality of 18th-century society beauties.

English art in the 18th century was also notable for its artistocratic portraits. The more extreme elements of rococo eroticism had little appeal to the English nobility, but the artists who were commissioned to paint their portraits could hardly help being influenced by the style of their day. Thomas Gainsborough (1727–1788), who together with Sir Joshua Reynolds (1723–1792) dominated the En-

14.6 Rosalba Carriera. *Anna Sofia d'Este, Princess of Modena*. c. 1730. Pastel. Uffizi, Florence. The pale elegance of the subject is typical of most of Carriera's aristocratic sitters, as is the charming untidiness of her dress.

14.7 Thomas Gainsborough. *Mary, Countess Howe*. c. 1765. Oil on canvas, 8 × 5' (2.59 × 1.52 m). London County Councll, Kenwood House (Iveagh Bequest). The wild background and threatening sky set off the subject, but their artificiality is shown by her shoes—hardly appropriate for a walk in the country.

glish art of the time, even studied for a while with a pupil of Boucher. At a time when rococo art had already fallen into disfavor in France, Gainsborough was still producing paintings like *Haymaker and Sleeping Girl* (see Figure 14.2), an idealizing rococo vision that recalls the world of Fragonard. Gainsborough's chief reputation, however, was made by his landscapes and portraits. Most of the portraits are themselves set against a landscape background, as in the case of *Mary, Countess Howe* [14.7]. In this painting, setting and costume are reminiscent of Watteau, but the dignified pose and cool gaze of the subject suggest that she had other than romantic thoughts in mind. There is no lack of poetry in the scene, though, and the resplendent shimmer of the countess' dress is perfectly set off by the more somber tones on the background.

Portraits and landscapes lend themselves naturally to rococo treatment, but what of religious art? One of the very few painters who tried to apply rococo principles to religious subjects was the Venetian painter Giovanni Battista Tiepolo (1696–1770). Many of Tiepolo's most ambitious and best-known works are decorations for the ceilings of churches and palaces, for which projects he was helped by assistants. A more personal work is his painting *The Immaculate Conception* [14.8]. The light colors and chubby cherubs of Boucher and the haughty assurance of Gainsborough's society ladies are here applied to the life of the Virgin Mary.

14.8 Giovanni Battista Tiepolo. *The Immaculate Conception*. 1769. Oil on canvas, 9'2" × 5' (2.79 × 1.52 m). Prado, Madrid. The sense of weightlessness and the wonderful cloud effects are both typical of Tiepolo's style.

14.9 Francesco Queirolo. *Deception Unmasked.* After 1752. Marble, height c. 5'8¼" (1.75 m). Cappella Sansevero, Santa Maria della Pietà di Sangro, Naples. The figure is a Christian sinner freeing himself, with the help of an angel, from the net of deception.

Rococo sculptors were, for the most part, more concerned with displaying their virtuosity in works aimed at a brilliant effect than with exploring finer shades of meaning. For instance, the figure of *Deception Unmasked* [14.9] by the Genoese sculptor Francesco Queirolo (1704–1762) theoretically has serious religious significance; in practice its principal purpose is to dazzle us with the sculptor's skill at rendering such details as the elaborate net in which Deception hides.

Rococo architecture likewise was principally concerned with delighting the eye rather than inspiring noble sentiments. It is most successful in decorative interiors like those of the Hôtel de Soubise in Paris [14.10], where the encrustation of ornament flows from the ceiling down onto the walls, concealing the break between them.

One region of Europe in which the rococo style did exert a powerful influence on religious architecture was southern Germany and Austria. Throughout the 17th century, a series of wars in that area had discouraged the construction of new churches or public buildings; with the return of relatively stable conditions in the German states new building became possible again. By one of those fortunate chances in the history of the arts, the fantasy and complexity of the rococo style provided a perfect complement to the new mood of exuberance. The result is a series of churches that is among the happiest of all rococo achievements.

The leading architect of the day was Balthazar Neumann (1687–1753), who had begun his career as an engineer and artillery officer. Among the many palaces and churches he designed, none is more spectacular than the Vierzehnheiligen (fourteen saints) near Bamberg. The relative simplicity of the exterior deliberately leaves the visitor unprepared for the spaciousness and elaborate decoration of the interior [14.11], with its rows of windows and irregularly placed columns. As in the

14.10 Germain Boffrand. *Salon de la Princesse, Hôtel de Soubise,* Paris. Begun 1732. Oval, 33 × 26' (10.06 × 7.92 m). The decoration is typical of the rococo style. The shape of the room, the paintings that flow from ceiling to walls, and the reflections in the mirrors all create an impression of light and grace.

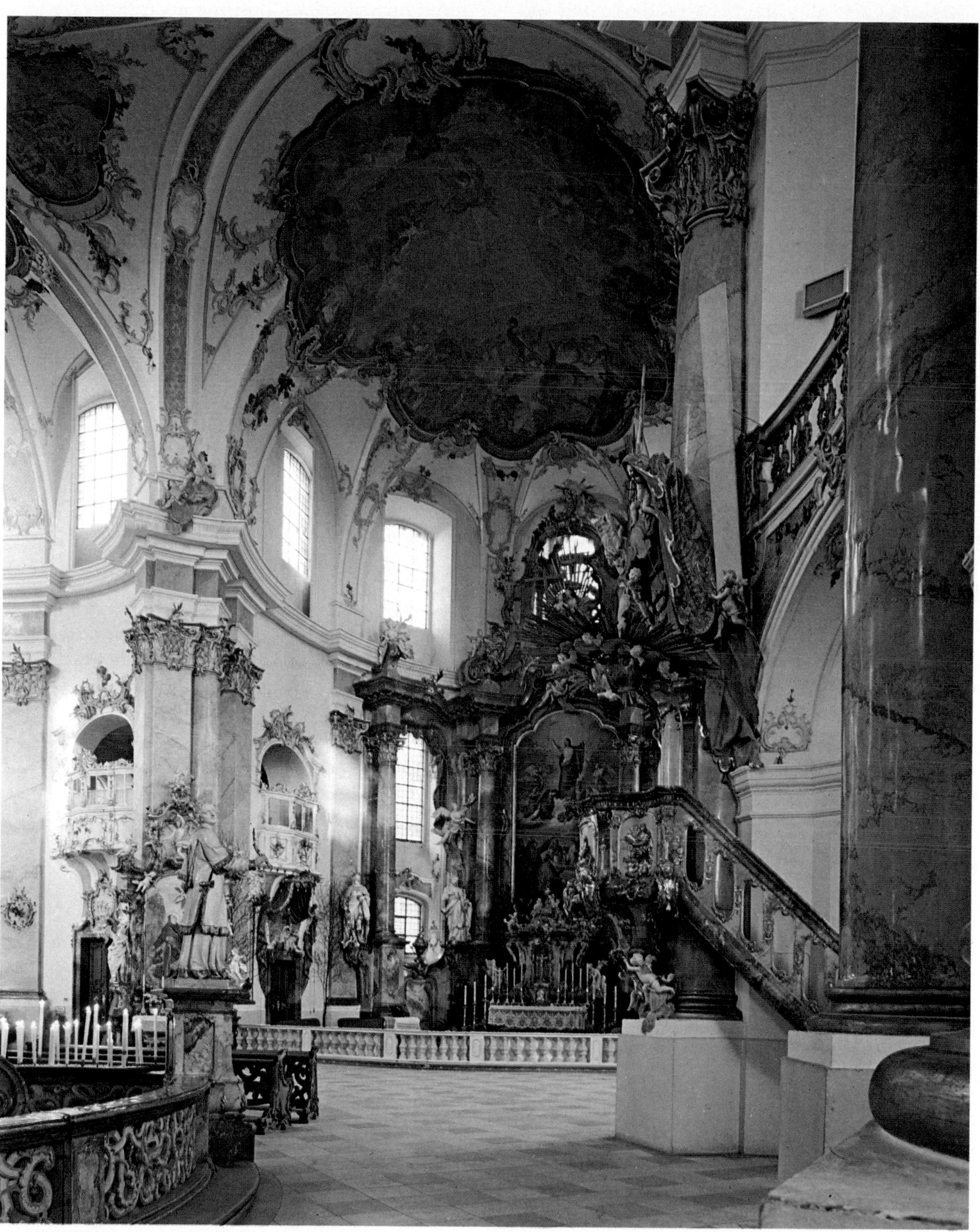

14.11 Balthazar Neumann. The nave of Vierzehnheiligen Pilgrim Church, near Bamberg, Germany. 1743–1772. This view of the interior shows the high altar at the back of the nave (center) and part of the oval altar in the middle of the church (left). The oval altar, the *Gnadenaltar* or "Mercy Altar," is a mark of the pilgrimage churches of southern Germany and Austria. Its shape is echoed in the oval ceiling paintings. The architect deliberately rejected the soaring straight lines of Gothic architecture and the balance and symmetry of the Renaissance style in favor of an intricate interweaving of surfaces, solid volumes, and empty spaces.

Hôtel de Soubise, the joint between the ceiling and walls is hidden by a fresco that, together with its border, spills downward in a series of gracious curves. It is not difficult to imagine what John Calvin would have said of such an interior, but if a church can be allowed to be a place of light and joy, Neumann's design succeeds admirably.

Neoclassical Art

For all its importance, the rococo style was not the only one to influence 18th-century artists. The other principal artistic movement of the age was *neoclassicism,* which increased in popularity as the appeal of the rococo declined.

There were good historical reasons for the rise of neoclassicism. The excavation of the buried cities of Herculaneum and Pompeii, beginning in 1711 and 1748 respectively, evoked immense interest in the art of classical antiquity in general and that of Rome in particular. The wall paintings from Pompeian villas of the 1st century A.D. were copied by countless visitors to the excavations, and reports of the finds were published throughout Europe. The German scholar Johannes Winckelmann (1717–1768), who is sometimes called the Father of Archaeology, played a major part in creating a new awareness of the importance of classical art; in many of his writings he encouraged his contemporaries not only to admire ancient masterpieces but to imitate them.

Furthermore, the aims and ideals of the Roman Republic—freedom, opposition to tyranny, valor—held a special appeal for 18th-century republican politicians, and the evocation of classical models became a characteristic of the art of the French Revolution. The painter who best represents the official revolutionary style is Jacques Louis David (1748–1825). His *Oath of the Horatii* (see Figure 14.1) draws not only upon a story of ancient Roman civic virtue but also upon a knowledge of ancient dress and armor derived from excavations of Pompeii and elsewhere. The simplicity of its message—the importance of united opposition to tyranny—is expressed by the simple austerity of its style and composition, a far cry from the lush, effete world of Fragonard. David used the same lofty grandeur to depict Napoleon soon after his accession to power [14.12], although there is considerable if unintentional irony in the use of the revolutionary style to represent the military dictator.

The austere poses and orderly decorations of ancient art came as a refreshing change for those artists who, regardless of politics, were tired of the excesses of the baroque and rococo styles. One of the most notable painters to introduce a neoclassical sense of statuesque calmness into his works was Sir Joshua Reynolds, Gainsborough's chief rival in England. *Three Ladies Adorning a Term of Hymen* [14.13] shows three fashionable ladies-about-town in the guise of figures from Greek mythology. Their static poses seem derived from actual ancient statues. The classical bust and antique vessel on the right are evidence of a careful attempt to imitate ancient models. Even the stool at center is based on examples found at Pompeii.

Although the rococo and neoclassical styles dominated most of 18th-century painting, a few

TABLE 14.2 The Rediscovery of Classical Antiquity in the 18th Century

1711	First excavations at Herculaneum
1734	Society of Dilettanti formed at London to encourage exploration
1748	First excavations at Pompeii
1753	Robert Wood and James Dawkins publish *The Ruins of Palmyra*
1757	Wood and Dawkins publish *The Ruins of Baalbec*
1762	James Stuart and Nicholas Revett publish the first volume of *The Antiquities of Athens*
1764	Robert Adam publishes *The Ruins of the Palace of Diocletian at Spalato;* Johannes Winckelmann publishes his *History of Ancient Art*
1769	Richard Chandler and William Pars publish the first volume of *The Antiquities of Ionia*
1772	The Hamilton collection of Greek vases bought by the British Museum
1785	Richard Colt Hoare explores Etruscan sites in Tuscany
1801	Lord Elgin receives Turkish permission to work on the Parthenon in Athens

14.12 Jacques Louis David. *Napoleon Crossing the Alps*. 1800. Oil on canvas, 8' × 7'7" (2.44 × 2.31 m). Musée de Versailles. After he took his army across the Alps, Napoleon surprised and defeated an Austrian army. His calm, controlled figure guiding a wildly tearing horse is symbolic of his own vision of himself as bringing order to post-Revolution France.

14.13 Sir Joshua Reynolds. *Three Ladies Adorning a Term of Hymen*. 1773. Oil on canvas, 7'8" × 10'4½" (2.34 × 2.90 m). Tate Gallery, London (reproduced by courtesy of the Trustees). A term is a pillar topped with a bust, in this case of Hymen, god of marriage. Reynolds introduced a marriage theme because the fiancé of one of the ladies, who were the daughters of Sir William Montgomery, commissioned the painting. The neoclassical composition was deliberately chosen by the artist because it gave him "an opportunity of introducing a variety of graceful historical attitudes."

14.14 William Hogarth. *Shortly After the Marriage*, from the *Marriage à la Mode* series. 1743–1745. Oil on canvas, 27 × 35" (69 × 89 cm). National Gallery, London (reproduced by courtesy of the Trustees). Although he achieved his effects through laughter, Hogarth had the serious moral purpose of attacking the corruption and hypocrisy of his day.

important artists avoided both the escapism of the one and the idealism of the other to provide a more truthful picture of the age. The work of William Hogarth, for example, presents its own very individual view of aristocratic society in the 18th century.

As a master of line, color, and composition Hogarth was in no way inferior to such contempo-

SPORTS AND GAMES

Boxing

One of the most popular sports in Hogarth's London was boxing. In 1743, Jack Broughton, the Champion of England, framed the first rules for prize fighting. Four years later he opened a school to train boxers and equipped his pupils with "mufflers"—boxing gloves—"to effectively secure them from the inconveniency of black eyes, broken jaws, and bloody noses." Not all pugilists followed Broughton's rules. Many of the matches fought at fairs and public gatherings were savage occasions for bloodletting, and in 1749 the London borough of Southwark suppressed boxing at the local fair, declaring it barbarous.

Broughton lost his championship in 1750 in a fight that lasted a mere fourteen minutes, blinded by a blow between the eyes. The leading boxer of the latter part of the century was Tom Johnson, a corn porter; he was so strong that he could pick up a sack of corn and swing it around his head. Observers noted that in addition to his physical abilities "he possessed most minute attention to Art." It was in one of Johnson's matches that a raised platform was first introduced. Boxing matches were originally fought on the ground, with the area cordoned off by a rope. Onlookers, particularly those who had wagered on one or the other contestants, tended to force their way into the ring and try to influence the course of the fight. In 1787, at Oakhampton, Berkshire, Johnson and Bill Ware met in a contest staged on a platform six feet high, the first staged in this fashion.

From the beginning, money played an important part in these matches. The most successful boxers were "sponsored" by a wealthy patron—Broughton's backer was none other than the Duke of Cumberland. The patron would put up prize money, and make side bets on his man. Other professional boxers went round to country fairs, offering to "take on" the local talent, and the bystanders wagered on the result. Many of these contests were long drawn out and bloody affairs; in one match, lasting an hour and seventeen minutes, the boxer—who was already blind in one eye from a previous bout—was blinded in the other eye and had to concede. He died a few weeks later.

14.15 Antonio Canova. *Pauline Bonaparte Borghese as Venus Victorious.* 1808. Marble, length 6'6" (1.98 m). Borghese Gallery, Rome. Canova's blend of simplicity and grace was widely imitated by European and American sculptors throughout the 19th century. The apple is the apple of discord, inscribed "to the fairest." According to legend, the goddesses Aphrodite (Venus), Hera, and Athena each offered a tempting bribe to the Trojan Paris, who was to award the apple to one of them. Paris chose Venus, who had promised him the most beautiful of women. The result was the Trojan War, which started when Paris abducted his prize, Helen, wife of a Greek king.

raries as Fragonard or Gainsborough, but he used his skills to paint a series of "moral subjects" that satirized the same patrons his colleagues aimed to entertain and to flatter. In his series of paintings called *Marriage à la Mode* he illustrated the consequences of a loveless marriage between an impoverished earl and the daughter of a wealthy city merchant who wants to improve his social position. By the second scene in the series, *Shortly After the Marriage* [14.14], matters have already started to deteriorate.

The principal neoclassical sculptors, the Italian Antonio Canova (1757–1822) and, the Frenchman Jean Antoine Houdon (1741–1829), succeeded in using classical models with real imagination and creativity (see Figure 14.20, and Figure 14.22). Canova's portrait, *Pauline Bonaparte Borghese as Venus Victorious* [14.15], depicts Napoleon's sister with an idealized classical beauty as she reclines on a couch modeled on one found at Pompeii. The cool worldly elegance of the figure, however, is Canova's own contribution.

For serious projects such as major public buildings, architects tended to follow classical models, as in the portico of the Pantheon in Paris [14.16], the design of which makes use of classical proportions. As might have been expected, the architects of the American Revolution also turned to classical precedents when they constructed their new public buildings. Thomas Jefferson's State Capitol at

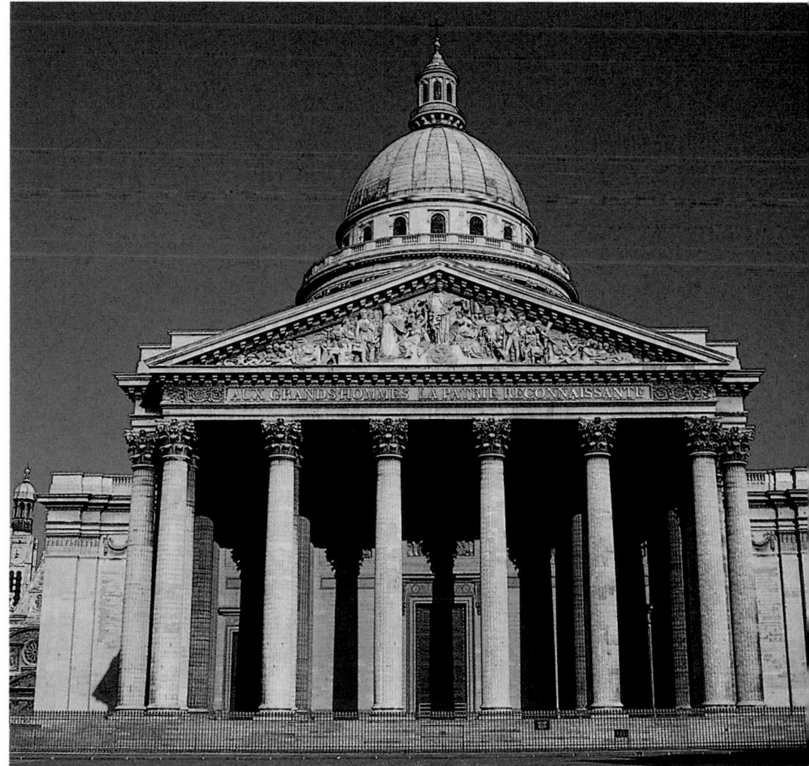

14.16 Germain Soufflot. Pantheon (Sainte Geneviève), Paris. 1755–1792. Originally built as the church of Sainte Geneviève, the building was converted into a memorial to the illustrious dead at the time of the French Revolution. The architect studied in Rome for a time; the columns and pediment were inspired by ancient Roman temples.

14.17 Thomas Jefferson. State Capitol, Richmond, Virginia. 1785–1796. Like the Pantheon, Jefferson's building was modeled on a Roman temple, the Maison Carrée at Nîmes, but the austere spirit of the American Revolution prompted Jefferson to replace the elaborate Corinthian capitals of the original with simpler Ionic ones.

Richmond [14.17], for example, shows a conscious rejection of the rococo and all it stood for in favor of the austere world (as it seemed to him) of ancient Rome.

CLASSICAL MUSIC

For the most part, music in the 18th century followed the example of literature in retaining a serious purpose, and was relatively untouched by the mood of the rococo style. At the French court, it is true, there was a demand for elegant, lighthearted music to serve as entertainment. The leading composer in this *style galant* was François Couperin (1668–1733), whose many compositions for keyboard emphasize grace and delicacy at the expense of the rhythmic drive and intellectual rigor of the best of baroque music. Elsewhere in Europe, however, listeners continued to prefer music that expressed emotion. At the court of Frederick the Great (himself an accomplished performer and composer), for example, a musical style known as *Empfindsamkeit,* or sensitiveness, developed.

The chief exponent of the expressive style was Carl Philipp Emanuel Bach (1714–1788), a son of Johann Sebastian Bach. His works have considerable emotional range and depth; their rich harmonies and contrasting moods opened up new musical possibilities. Like all his contemporaries, C. P. E. Bach was searching for a formal structure with which to organize them. A single piece or movement from a baroque work had first established a single mood and then explored it fully, whether it be joyful, meditative, or tragic. Now composers were developing a musical organization that would allow them to put different emotions side by side, contrast them, and thereby achieve expressive variety.

By the middle of the 18th century a musical style developed that made possible this new range of expression. It is usually called *classical,* although the term is also used in a more general sense, which can be confusing. It would be as well to begin by carefully distinguishing between these two usages.

In its general sense, the term classical is frequently used to distinguish so-called "serious" music from "popular," so that all music likely to be met with in a concert hall or opera house, no matter what its age, is labeled classical. One reason this distinction is confusing is that for many composers before our own time, there was essentially no difference between serious and popular music. They used the same musical style and techniques for a formal composition to be listened to attentively by an audience of music lovers, as for a religious work to be performed in church, or for dance music or background music for a party or festive occasion. Furthermore, used in this sense, classical tells us nothing significant about the music itself or its period or form. It does not even describe its mood, since many pieces of "classical" or "serious" music were in fact deliberately written to provide light entertainment.

The more precise and technical meaning of classical in relation to music denotes a musical style that was in use from the second half of the 18th century and reached its fulfillment in the works of Franz Joseph Haydn (1732–1809) and Wolfgang Amadeus Mozart (1756–1791). It evolved in answer to new musical needs the baroque style could not satisfy and lasted until the early years of the 19th century, when it in turn gave way to the romantic style. The figure chiefly responsible for the change from classical to romantic music was Ludwig van Beethoven (1770–1827). Although his musical roots were firmly in the classical style, he is more appropriately seen as a representative of the new romantic age and will be discussed in Chapter 15.

It is no coincidence that the classical style in music developed at much the same time painters, architects, and poets were turning to Greek and Roman models, for the aims of classical music and neoclassical art and literature were very similar. After the almost obsessive exuberance and display of the Baroque period, the characteristic qualities of ancient art—balance, clarity, intellectual weight—seemed especially appealing. The 18th-century composer, however, faced a different problem than did the artist or writer. Unlike literature or the visual arts, ancient music has disappeared almost without trace. As a result the classical style in music had to be newly invented to express ancient concepts of balance and order. In addition, it had to combine these intellectual principles with the no-less-important ability to express a wide range of emotion. Haydn and Mozart were the two supreme masters of the classical style because of their complete command of the possibilities of the new idiom within which they wrote.

The Classical Symphony

The most popular medium in the classical period was instrumental music. In extended orchestral works, *symphonies,* divided into a number of self-contained sections called *movements,* composers were most completely able to express classical principles.

One reason for this is the new standardization of instrumental combinations. In the Baroque period, composers such as Bach had felt free to combine instruments into unusual groups that varied from composition to composition. Each of Bach's *Brandenburg Concertos* was written for a different set of solo instruments. By about 1750, however, most instrumental music was written for a standard orchestra, the nucleus of which was formed by the string instruments: violins (generally divided into two groups known as first and second), violas, cellos, and double basses. To the strings were added wind instruments, almost always the oboe and bassoon and fairly frequently the flute; the clarinet began to be introduced gradually and by about 1780 had become a regular member of the orchestra. The only brass instrument commonly included was the French horn. Trumpets, along with the *timpani* or kettledrums, were reserved for reinforcing volume or rhythm. Trombones were never used in classical symphonies until Beethoven [14.18].

Orchestras made up of these instruments were capable of rich and varied sound combinations, ideally suited to the new classical form of the symphony. In general, the classical symphony has four movements (as opposed to the baroque concerto's three): a first, relatively fast one, usually the most complex in form; then a slow, lyrical movement, often songlike; a third movement in the form of a *minuet,* a stately dance; and a final one, which brings the entire work to a spirited and usually cheerful conclusion. As time went on, the length and complexity of the movements grew, and many of Haydn's later symphonies last for nearly a half an hour. In most cases, however, the most elaborate musical "argument" was always reserved for the first movement, presumably because during it the listeners were freshest and most able to concentrate.

The structure almost invariably chosen for the first movement of a classical symphony was that called *sonata form.* Since sonata form is not only one of the chief features of classical style but was also a principle of musical organization that remained popular throughout the 19th century, it merits our attention in some detail. The term itself is actually rather confusing, since the word *sonata* is used to describe a work in several movements, like a symphony, but written for one or two instruments rather than an orchestra. Thus a piano sonata is a piece for solo piano, a violin sonata is a piece for violin and an accompanying instrument, almost always a piano, and so on. A symphony is, in fact, a sonata for orchestra.

The term sonata form, however, does not, as might be reasonably expected, describe the form of a sonata but a particular kind of musical organization frequently found in the first movements of both symphonies *and* sonatas as well as other instrumental combinations like string quartets (two violins, viola, and cello). Since these movements are generally played at a fast *tempo* or speed, the term *sonata allegro form* is also sometimes used. (The Italian word *allegro* means "fast"; Italian terms are traditionally used in music, as we have seen.)

Unlike baroque music, with its unity based on the use of a single continually expanding theme (see page 374), sonata form is dominated by the idea of contrasts. The first of the three main sections of a sonata form movement is called the *exposition,* since it sets out, or "exposes," the musical

Percussion
Timpani
Trombones
Trumpets
Harps
Tuba
French Horns
Double Basses
Clarinets
Bassoons
Second Violins
English Horns & Oboes
Flutes
Violas
First Violins
Conductor
Violoncellos

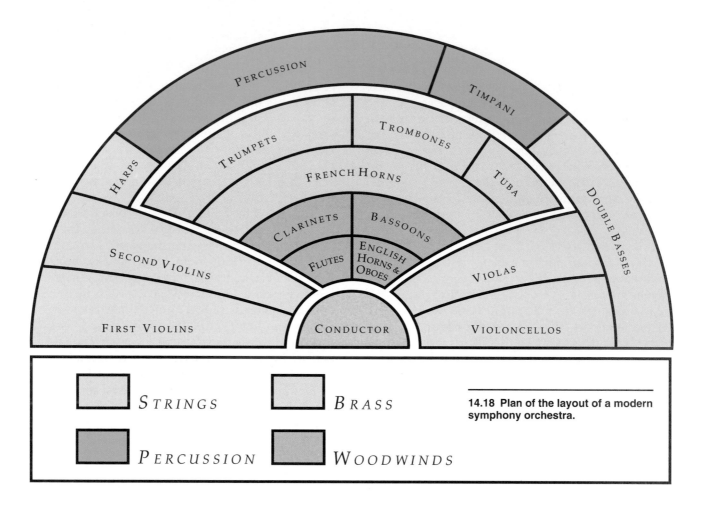

Strings
Brass
Percussion
Woodwinds

14.18 Plan of the layout of a modern symphony orchestra.

material. This consists of at least two themes, or groups of themes, that differ from one another in melody, rhythm, and key. They represent, so to speak, the two principal characters in the drama. If the first theme is lively, the second may be thoughtful or melancholy; or a strong march-like first theme may be followed by a gentle, romantic second one. During the exposition the first of these themes (or *subjects,* as they are often called) is stated, followed by a linking passage leading to the second subject and a conclusion that rounds off the exposition.

During the course of the movement it is of the utmost importance that listeners be able to remember these themes and identify them when they reappear. To help make this easier, classical composers replaced the long, flowing lines of baroque melodies with much shorter tunes, often consisting of only a few notes, comparatively easy to recognize when they recur. The difference between baroque and classical melody is clearly visible even on paper. Compare, for example, the continuous pattern of the melodic line on page 378, from Bach's *Brandenburg Concerto No. 2,* with the following theme from Mozart's *Symphony No. 40 in g minor*. The tune consists basically of a group of three notes *(a)* repeated three times to produce a melodic phrase *(b).* This procedure is then repeated three more times to impress it firmly on our memory.

Just in case their listeners were still not perfectly familiar with the basic material of a movement, composers reinforced it by repeating the entire exposition note for note.

In the second section of a sonata form movement, the *development,* the themes stated in the exposition are changed and varied in whatever way the composer's imagination suggests. One part of the first subject is often detached and treated on its own, passing up and down the orchestra, now loud, now soft, as happens in the first movement of Mozart's *Symphony No. 40* to the notes above *(a).* Sometimes different themes will be combined and played simultaneously. In almost all cases the music passes through a wide variety of keys and moods. In the process the composer sheds new light on what have by now become familiar ideas.

At the end of the development the original themes return to their original form for the third section of the movement, the *recapitulation.* The first section is repeated, or recapitulated, with both first and second subjects now in the same key. In this way the conflict implicit in the development section is resolved. A final "tailpiece" or *coda* (the Italian word for tail) is sometimes added to bring the movement to a suitably firm conclusion.

Sonata form embodies many of the classical principles of balance, order, and control. The recapitulation, which carefully balances the exposition, and the breaking down of the material in the development and its subsequent reassembling both emphasize the sense of structure behind a sonata form movement.

Haydn

The long and immensely productive career of Franz Joseph Haydn (1732–1809) spanned a period of great change in both artistic and social terms. Born in Rohrau on the Austro-Hungarian border, he sang as a child in the choir of Saint Stephen's Cathedral in Vienna. After scraping together a living for a few precarious years, in 1761 he entered the service of a wealthy nobleman, Prince Esterhazy.

Haydn began work for the prince on the same terms as any carpenter, cook, or artisan in his master's employ. That he was a creative artist was irrelevant, since social distinctions were made on grounds of wealth or birth, not talent. By the time he left the Esterhazy family, however, almost thirty years later, the aristocracy was competing for the privilege of entertaining him. The world was indeed changing; in the course of two visits to London he found himself feted and honored, and during his last years in Vienna he was among the most famous figures in Europe. Thus Haydn was one of the very first musicians to attain a high social position solely on the strength of his genius. His success signaled the new relationship between the artist and society that was to characterize the 19th century.

In personal terms Haydn seems to have been little affected by his fame. During the long years of service to Prince Esterhazy and his descendants he used the enforced isolation of the palace where he lived to experiment with all the musical forms available to him. In addition to operas, string quartets, piano sonatas, and hundreds of other pieces, he wrote more than one hundred symphonies that exploit almost every conceivable variation on sonata and other classical forms, winning him the nickname "Father of the Symphony." During his visits to London in 1791–1792 and 1794–1795 he wrote his last twelve symphonies, which are often known as the "London" Symphonies. Although less obviously experimental than his earlier works, they contain perhaps the finest of all his orchestral music; the slow movements in particular manage to express the greatest seriousness and profundity without tragedy or gloom.

14.19 Joseph Lange. *Mozart at the Pianoforte.* 1789. Oil. 13½ × 11½" (35 × 30 cm). Mozart Museum, Salzburg. This unfinished portrait shows the composer for once without the wig customary at the time. Mozart must have liked the painting because he had a copy made and sent to his father.

Mozart

In 1781, in his fiftieth year and at the height of his powers, Haydn met a young man about whom he was to say a little while later to the young man's father: "Before God and as an honest man, I tell you that your son is the greatest composer known to me either in person or by name." Many of us, for whom the music of Wolfgang Amadeus Mozart (1756–1791) represents a continual source of inspiration and joy and a comforting reminder of the heights the human spirit can attain, would see no reason to revise Haydn's judgment [14.19].

Although Mozart's life, in contrast to Haydn's, was to prove one of growing disappointments and setbacks, his early years were comparatively happy. During his childhood he showed extraordinary musical ability. By the age of six he could already play the violin and piano and had begun to compose. His father Leopold, himself a professional musician in the service of the Archbishop of

14.20 ***The Marriage of Figaro*****. Metropolitan Opera, New York, 1975. In this scene from Act II of Mozart's opera, the Count (second from left) is trying to assert his aristocratic authority against the combined arguments of his wife (left), Susanna (second from right), and Figaro (third from right). The singers are Evelyn Lear as the Countess, Wolfgang Brendel as the Count, Judith Blegen as Susanna, and Justino Diaz as Figaro.**

Salzburg, where the family lived, took Wolfgang on a seemingly never-ending series of trips throughout Europe to exhibit his son's musical prowess. The effect of constant travel on the boy's health and temperament can be imagined, but it was during these trips that he became exposed to the most sophisticated and varied musical ideas of the day; the universality of his own musical style must in part be due to the wide range of influences he was able to assimilate, from the *style galant* of the rococo to the Renaissance polyphonies he heard in Rome. From time to time father and son would return to Salzburg, where by this time they both held appointments at the court of the archbishop.

In 1772, however, the old archbishop died. His successor, Hieronymus Colloredo, was far less willing to allow his two leading musicians to come and go as they pleased. Artistic independence of the kind Haydn was to achieve was still in the future, and the next ten years were marked by continued quarreling between Mozart and his aristocratic employer. Finally, in 1781, when Mozart could take no more and asked the archbishop for his freedom, he was literally kicked out of the door of the palace. From 1781 to 1791 Mozart spent the last years of his life in Vienna, trying in vain to find a permanent position while writing some of the most sublime masterpieces in the history of music. When he died at the age of thirty-five, he was buried in a pauper's grave.

The relationship between an artist's life and work is always fascinating. In Mozart's case it raises particular problems. We might expect that continual frustration, poverty, and depression would have left its mark on his music, yet it is a grave mistake to look for autobiographical self-expression in the work of an artist who devoted his life to achieving perfection in his art. In general, Mozart's music reflects only the highest and most noble of human aspirations. Perhaps more than any other artist in any medium Mozart combines ease and grace with profound learning in his art to come as near to ideal beauty as anything can. Nevertheless, his music remains profoundly human. We are reminded many times not of Mozart's own suffering but of the tragic nature of life itself.

A year before his death Mozart wrote the last of his great series of concertos for solo piano and orchestra, the *Piano Concerto No. 27 in B♭*, K. 595 (Mozart's works are generally listed according to the catalogue first made by Köchel; hence the letter K that precedes the catalogue numbers). The wonderful slow movement of this work expresses, with a profundity no less moving for its utter simplicity, the resignation of one for whom the beauty of life is perpetually tinged with sadness. We can only marvel at so direct a statement of so universal a truth.

The need to earn a living, coupled with the inexhaustibility of his inspiration, drew from Mozart works in almost every conceivable category. Symphonies, concertos, masses, sonatas, string quartets are only some of the forms he enriched. It is his operas, however, that many admirers of Mozart would choose if faced with a decision as to what to save if all else were to be lost. Furthermore, his operas provide the clearest picture of his historical position.

Mozart's opera *The Marriage of Figaro* is based on a play of the same name by the French dramatist Pierre-Augustin Beaumarchais (1732–1799). Although a comedy, the play, which was first performed in 1784, contains serious overtones. The plot is too complicated to permit even a brief summary, but among the characters are a lecherous and deceitful, though charming, Count; his deceived wife, the Countess; her maid Susanna, who puts up a determined resistance against the Count's advances; and Susanna's husband-to-be, Figaro, who finally manages to outwit and embarrass the would-be seducer of his future wife, who is also his own employer [14.20]. In other words, the heroes of the play are the servants and the villain their master. Written as it was on the eve of the French Revolution, Beaumarchais' play was interpreted rightly as an attack on the morals of the ruling classes and a warning that the lower classes would fight back. Beaumarchais himself was firmly associated with the moves toward social and political change; he was an early supporter of the American Revolution and helped organize French support for the insurgent colonists.

Mozart's opera was first performed in 1786. It retains the spirit of protest in the original but adds a sense of humanity and subtlety perhaps only music can bring. No one suffered more than Mozart from the high-handedness of the aristocracy, yet when *The Marriage of Figaro* gives voice to the growing mood of revolution, it does so as a protest against the abuse of human rights rather than in a spirit of personal resentment. In the first act, Figaro's aria "Se vuol' ballare" expresses the pent-up frustration of generations of men and women who had endured injustices and who could take no more. The musical form and expression is still restrained, indeed classical, but Mozart pours into it the feelings of the age.

Mozart's ability to create characters who seem real, with whose feelings we can identify, reaches its height in the Countess. Ignored and duped by her husband, the laughingstock of those around her, she expresses the conflicting emotions of a woman torn between resentment and deep attachment. Her aria in the third act, "Dove sono," begins with a recitative in which she gives vent to her bitterness. Gradually it melts into a slow and meditative section where she asks herself what went wrong: "Where are those happy moments of sweetness and pleasure, where did they go, those vows of a deceiving tongue?" The poignant theme to which these words are set returns toward the end of the slow section to provide one of the most affecting moments in all opera. Mozart's gift for expressing human behavior at its most noble is conveyed in the aria's final section, where the Countess decides, in spite of everything, to try to win back her husband's love. Thus, in seven or eight minutes, we have been carried from despair to hope, and Mozart has combined his revelation of a human heart with music that by itself is of extraordinary beauty.

The opera as a whole is far richer than discussion of these two arias can suggest. For instance, among the other characters is one of the composer's most memorable creations, the pageboy Cherubino, whose aria "Non so più" epitomizes the breathless, agonizing joy of adolescent love. An accomplishment of another kind is exemplified by the *ensembles,* scenes in which a large number of characters are involved. Here Mozart combines clarity of musical and dramatic action while advancing the plot at a breakneck pace.

The Marriage of Figaro expresses at the same time the spirit of its age and the universality of human nature, a truly classical achievement. Equally impressively, it illuminates the personal emotions of individual people, and through them teaches us about our own reactions to life and its problems. As one distinguished writer has put it, in this work Mozart has added to the world's understanding of people—of human nature.

LITERATURE IN THE 18TH CENTURY

Intellectual Developments

While painters, poets, and musicians were reflecting the changing moods of the 18th century in their art, social and political philosophers were examining the problems of contemporary society in a more systematic way. Individual thinkers frequently alternated between optimism and despair, since awareness of the greatness of which human beings were capable was always qualified by the perception of the sorry state of the world. The broad range of diagnosis and/or proposed solutions makes it difficult to generalize on the nature of 18th-century intellectual life, but two contrasting trends can be discerned. A few writers, notably Jonathan Swift, reacted to the problems of the age with deep pessimism, bitterly opposing the view that human nature is basically good. Others, convinced that progress was possible, sought to devise new systems of intellectual, social, or political organization. Rational humanists like Diderot and political philosophers like Rousseau based their arguments on an optimistic view of human nature. However, Voltaire, the best-known of all 18th-century thinkers, fitted into neither of these two categories—rather, he moved from one to the other. The answer he finally proposed to the problems of existence is as applicable to the world of today as it was to that of the 18th century, although perhaps no more welcome.

The renewed interest in classical culture, visible in the portraits by Sir Joshua Reynolds and buildings like the Pantheon, also made a strong impression on literature. French writers like Racine (see page 383) had already based works on classical models, and the *Fables* of Jean de La Fontaine. La Fontaine (1621–1695) drew freely on Aesop and other Greek and Roman sources. Elsewhere in Europe, throughout the 18th century poets continued to produce works on classical themes, from the plays of Pietro Metastasio (1698–1782) in Italy to the lyric poetry of Friedrich von Schiller (1759–1805) in Germany.

The appeal of neoclassical literature was particularly strong in England, where major Greek and Roman works like Homer's *Iliad* and *Odyssey* or Vergil's *Aeneid* had long been widely read and admired. In the 17th century, Milton's *Paradise Lost* had represented a deliberate attempt to create an equally monumental epic poem in English. Before the 18th century, however, a number of important works, including the tragedies of Aeschylus, had never been translated into English.

The upsurge of enthusiasm for classical literature that characterized the 18th-century English literary scene had two chief effects: Poets and scholars began to translate or retranslate the most important classical authors, and creative writers began to produce original works on classical forms, deal with classical themes, and include classical references. The general reading public was by now expected to understand and appreciate both the ancient masterpieces themselves and modern works inspired by them.

The principal English writers formed a group calling themselves Augustans. The name reveals the degree to which these writers admired and modeled themselves on the Augustan poets of ancient Rome. In 27 B.C. the victory of the first Roman emperor Augustus ended the chaos of civil war in Rome and brought peace and stability to the Roman world. The principal poets of Rome's Augustan age, writers like Vergil and Horace, had subsequently commemorated Augustus' achievement in works intended for a sophisticated public. In the same way in England the restoration to power of King Charles II in 1660 seemed to some of his contemporaries a return to order and civilization after the tumultuous English Civil War. The founders of the English Augustan movement, writers like John Dryden (1631–1700), explored not only the historical parallel by glorifying English achievement under the monarchy but also the literary one by imitating the highly polished style of the Roman Augustan poets in works intended for an aristocratic audience.

Pope's Rococo Satires

Alexander Pope (1688–1744), the greatest English poet of the 18th century, was one of the Augustans, yet the lightness and elegance of his wit reflect the rococo spirit of his age.

His genius lay precisely in his awareness that the dry bones of classical learning needed to have life breathed into them. The spirit that would awaken art in his own time, as it had done for the ancient writers, was that of Nature—not in the sense of the natural world but in the sense of that which is universal and unchanging in human experience. Pope's conception of the vastness and truth of human experience given form and meaning by rules first devised in the ancient past represents 18th-century thought at its most constructive.

Like Watteau, Pope suffered throughout his life from ill health. At the age of twelve an attack of spinal tuberculosis left him permanently crippled: perhaps in compensation he soon developed the passion for reading and for the beauty of the world around him that shines through his work. A Catholic in a Protestant country, he was unable to make a career for himself in public life or obtain public patronage for his literary work. As a result he was forced to support himself entirely by writing and translating. Pope's literary reputation was first made by the *Essay on Criticism*, but he won economic independence by producing highly successful translations of Homer's *Iliad* (1713–1720) and *Odyssey* (1721–1726) and an edition of the works of Shakespeare (1725). With the money he made from these he abandoned commercial publishing and confined himself, for the most part, to his house on the river Thames at Twickenham, where he spent the rest of his life writing, entertaining friends, and indulging his fondness for gardening.

Pope's range as a poet was considerable, but his greatest achievements were in the characteristically rococo medium of satire. Like his fellow countryman Hogarth, his awareness of the heights to which humans can rise was coupled with an acute sense of the frequency of their failure to do so. In the long poem *Essay on Man* (1733–1734), for example, Pope combines Christian and humanist teaching in a characteristically 18th-century manner to express his philosophical position with regard to the preeminent place occupied by human beings in the divine scheme of life. He is at his best, however, when applying his principles to practical situations and uncovering human folly. His reverence for order and reason made him the implacable foe of those who in his eyes were responsible for the declining political morality and artistic standards of the day. It is sometimes said that Pope's satire is tinged with personal hostility. In fact, a series of literary and social squabbles marked his life, suggesting that he was not always motivated by the highest ideals; nonetheless, in his poetry he nearly always based his moral judgments on what he himself described as "the strong antipathy of good to bad," a standard he applied with courage and wit.

Swift's Savage Indignation

Perhaps the darkest of all visions of human nature in the 18th century was that of Jonathan Swift (1667–1745). In a letter to Alexander Pope he made it clear that, whatever his affection for individuals, he hated the human race as a whole. According to Swift, human beings were not to be defined automatically as rational animals, as so many 18th-century thinkers believed, but as animals *capable* of reason. It was precisely because so many of them failed to live up to their capabilities that Swift turned his "savage indignation" against them into bitter satire, never more so than when the misuse of reason served "to aggravate man's natural corruptions" and provide him with new ones.

Swift was in a position to observe at close quarters the political and social struggles of the times. Born in Dublin, for much of his life he played an active part in supporting Irish resistance to English rule. After studying at Trinity College, Dublin, he went to England and in 1694 was ordained a priest in the Anglican church. For the next few years he moved back and forth between England and Ireland, taking a leading role in the political controversies of the day by publishing articles and pamphlets which, in general, were strongly conservative.

A fervent supporter of the monarchy and of the Anglican church, Swift had good reason to hope that his advocacy of their cause would win him a position of high rank. In 1713 these hopes were partially realized with his appointment as Dean of Saint Patrick's Cathedral in Dublin. Any chances he had of receiving an English bishopric were destroyed in 1714 by the death of Queen Anne and the subsequent dismissal of his political friends from power.

Swift spent the rest of his life in Ireland, cut off from the mainstream of political and cultural life. Here he increasingly emerged as a publicist for the Irish cause. During his last years his mind began to fail, but not before he had composed the epitaph under which he lies buried in Saint Patrick's Cathedral: *Ubi saeva indignatio ulterius cor lacerare nequit* (He has gone where savage indignation can tear his heart no more).

During his years in Ireland Swift wrote his best-known work, *Gulliver's Travels,* first published in 1726. In a sense *Gulliver's Travels* has been a victim of its own popularity, since its surprising success as a work for young readers has distracted attention from the author's real purpose, to satirize human behavior. (It says much for the 18th century's richness that it could produce two writers working in the same genre, the satirists Swift and Pope, with such differing results.) The first two of Gulliver's four voyages, to the miniature land of Lilliput and to Brobdingnag, the land of giants, are the best known. In these sections the harshness of Swift's satire is to some extent masked by the charm and wit of the narrative. In the voyage to the land of the Houyhnhnms, however, Swift draws a bitter contrast between the Houyhnhnms, a race of horses whose behavior is governed by reason, and their slaves the Yahoos, human in form but bestial in behavior. As expressed by the Yahoos, Swift's vision of the depths to which human beings can sink is profoundly pessimistic. His insistence on their deep moral and intellectual flaws is in strong contrast to the rational humanism of many of his contemporaries, who believed in the innate dignity and worth of human beings.

Yet even the Yahoos do not represent Swift's most bitter satire. It took his experience of the direct consequences of "man's inhumanity to man" to draw from his pen a short pamphlet, *A Modest Proposal for Preventing the Children of Poor People in Ireland from Being a Burden to Their Parents or Country, and for Making Them Beneficial to the Public,* the title of which is generally abbreviated to *A Modest Proposal.* First published in 1729, this brilliant and shocking work was inspired by the poverty and suffering of a large section of the population of Ireland. Even today the nature of the supposedly benevolent author's "modest proposal" can take the reader's breath away, both by the calmness with which it is offered and by the devastatingly quiet logic with which its implications are explained. All the irony of which this master satirist was capable is here used to express anger and disgust at injustice and the apparent inevitability of human suffering. Although Swift was writing in response to a particular historical situation, the deep compassion for the poor and oppressed that inspired him transcends its time. Our own world has certainly not lost the need for it.

14.21 Jean Antoine Houdon. *Denis Diderot.* 1771. Terra cotta, height 16" (41 cm). Louvre, Paris. Unlike most official portraiture of the 18th century, Houdon's works aim to reveal the character of his sitters. Here he vividly conveys Diderot's humanity and quizzical humor.

Rational Humanism: The Encyclopedists

Belief in the essential goodness of human nature and the possibility of progress, which had first been expressed by the humanists of the Renaissance, continued to find supporters throughout the 18th century. Indeed, the enormous scientific and technical achievements of the two centuries since the time of Erasmus tended to confirm the opinions of those who took a positive view of human capabilities. It was in order to provide a rational basis for this positive humanism that the French thinker and writer Denis Diderot (1713–1784) [14.21] conceived the project of preparing a vast encyclopedia that would describe the state of contemporary science, technology, and thought and provide a system for the classification of knowledge.

Work on the *Encyclopédie,* as it is generally called, began in 1747; the last of its seventeen volumes appeared in 1765. By its conclusion, what had begun as a compendium of information had become the statement of a philosophical position: that the extent of human powers and achievements conclusively demonstrates that humans are rational beings. The implication of this position is that any political or religious system seeking to control the minds of individuals is to be condemned. It is hardly surprising, therefore, that some years before the conclusion of the project, the *Encyclopédie* had been banned by decree of Louis XV: the last volumes were published clandestinely.

In religious terms the *Encyclopédie* took a position of considerable skepticism, advocating freedom of conscience and belief. Politically, however, its position was less extreme and less consistent. One of the most distinguished philosophers to contribute political articles was Charles Louis Montesquieu (1689–1755), whose own aristocratic origins may have helped mold his relatively conservative views. Both in the *Encyclopédie* and in his own writings Montesquieu advocated the retention of a monarchy, with powers divided between the king and a series of "intermediate bodies" that included parliament, aristocratic organizations, the middle class, and even the church. By distributing power in this way Montesquieu hoped to achieve a workable system of "checks and balances," thereby eliminating the possibility of a central dictatorial government. His ideas proved particularly interesting to the authors of the Constitution of the United States.

A very different point of view was espoused by another contributor to the *Encyclopédie,* Jean Jacques Rousseau (1712–1778), whose own quarrelsome and neurotic character played a considerable part in influencing his political philosophy. Diderot had originally commissioned Rousseau to produce some articles on music, since the latter was an accomplished composer (his opera *Le Devin du Village* is still revived from time to time). After violently quarreling with Diderot and others, however, Rousseau spent much of an unhappy and restless life writing philosophical treatises and novels that expressed his political convictions. Briefly put, Rousseau believed that the natural goodness of the human race had been corrupted by the growth of civilization and that the freedom of the individual had been destroyed by the growth of society. For Rousseau humans were good and society was bad.

Rousseau's praise of the simple virtues like unselfishness and kindness and his high regard for natural human feelings have identified his philosophy with a belief in the "noble savage," but this is misleading. Far from advocating a return to primitive existence in some nonexistent Garden of Eden, Rousseau passionately strove to create a new social order. In *The Social Contract* of 1762 he tried to describe the basis of his ideal state in terms of the General Will of the people, which would delegate authority to individual organs of government, although neither most of his readers nor Rousseau himself seemed very clear on how this General Will should operate.

Although Rousseau's writings express a complex political philosophy, most of his readers were more interested in his emphasis on spontaneous feeling than in his political theories. His contempt for the superficial and the artificial, and his praise for simple and direct relationships between individuals, did a great deal to help demolish the principles of aristocracy and continue to inspire believers in human equality.

Voltaire's Philosophical Cynicism: *Candide*

It may seem extravagant to claim that the life and work of François Marie Arouet (1694–1778), best known to us as Voltaire (one of his pen names), can summarize the events of a period as complex as the 18th century. That the claim can be not only advanced but also supported is some measure of the breadth of his genius. A writer of poems, plays, novels, and history; a student of science, philosophy, and politics; a man who spent time at the courts of Louis XV and Frederick the Great but also served a prison sentence; a defender of religious and political freedom who at the same time supported enlightened despotism, Voltaire was above all a man *engagé*—one committed to the concerns of his age [14.22].

After being educated by the Jesuits, he began to publish writings in the satirical style he was to use throughout his life. His belief that the aristocratic society of the times was unjust must have received strong confirmation when his critical position earned him first a year in jail and then, in 1726, exile from France. He chose to go to England, where he found a system of government that seemed to

14.22 Jean Baptiste Pigalle. *Voltaire.* 1770–1776. Marble, height 4'9⅜" (1.47 m). Louvre, Paris. This most unusual statue of the great philosopher places a powerful head on the torso of an old man. The head was modeled from life when Voltaire was seventy-six; the body is based on that of a Roman statue. The statue seems to represent the triumph of the spirit over the frailty of the body.

him far more liberal and just than the French one. On his return home in 1729 he discussed the advantages of English political life in his *Lettres philosophiques*, published in 1734, and escaped from the scandal and possibility of arrest his work created by spending the next ten years in the country.

In 1744 Voltaire was finally tempted back to the French court but found little in its formal and artificial life to stimulate him. He discovered a more congenial atmosphere at the court of Frederick the Great at Potsdam, where he spent the years from 1750 to 1753. Frederick's warm welcome and considerable intellectual stature must have come as an agreeable change from the sterile ceremony of the French court, and the two men soon established a close friendship. It seems, however, that Potsdam was not big enough to contain two such powerful intellects and temperaments, for after a couple of years Voltaire quarreled with his patron and once again abandoned sophisticated life for that of the country.

In 1758 Voltaire finally settled in the village of Ferney, where he set up his own court. Here the greatest names in Europe—intellectuals, artists, politicians—made the pilgrimage to talk and, above all, listen to the sage of Ferney, while he published work after work, each of which was distributed throughout Europe. Only in 1778, the year of his death, did Voltaire return to Paris, where the excitement brought on by a hero's welcome proved too much for his failing strength.

It is difficult to summarize the philosophy of a man who touched on so many subjects. Nevertheless, one theme recurs continually in Voltaire's writings, the importance of freedom of thought. Voltaire's greatest hatred was reserved for intolerance and bigotry; in letter after letter he ended with the phrase he made famous, *Écrasez l'infâme* (Crush the infamous thing). The "infamous thing" is superstition, which breeds fanaticism and persecution. Those Voltaire judged chiefly responsible for superstition were the Christians, Catholic and Protestant alike.

Voltaire vehemently attacked the traditional view of the Bible as the inspired word of God. He claimed that it contained a mass of anecdotes and contradictions totally irrelevant to the modern world and that the disputes arising from it, which had divided Christians for centuries, were absurd and pointless. Yet Voltaire was far from being an

EAST MEETS WEST

The Slave Trade

At the beginning of the 18th century a new economic system, plantation farming, began to develop rapidly. Plantations were large tracts of land, either in America or on islands such as Jamaica and Haiti, generally belonging to absentee owners in England or France and worked with slave labor imported from Africa. The principal crop was sugar which had been introduced into the New World by Europeans in the form of sugar cane from Asia. The climate was excellent for its growth and the demand for sugar seemed inexhaustible.

Slaves had been imported into Europe from Africa since Roman times. The Muslim world also bought and sold African slaves, although without distinguishing between black and white. The earliest black Africans to be transported to North America were brought to what is now Virginia by Dutch traders in 1619, a year before the arrival in America of the Pilgrim Fathers. With the rise of the plantation economy, slaves became the basis of a substantial and heavily underwritten industry, sugar production, and the numbers of black Africans shipped to America rose sharply. Total figures are impossible to calculate, but some impression can be formed from the numbers imported into the island of Jamaica alone between 1700 and 1786: around 610,000.

The transatlantic slave trade was principally in the hands of English merchants operating either from their home country or from branches in New England; the French provided the fiercest competition. Goods were manufactured in Britain and shipped to Africa, where they were exchanged for slaves. Thus the plantation economy not only produced a valuable commodity but indirectly stimulated production in the home countries. Liverpool, for instance, which at the beginning of the 18th century was a quiet town on the west coast of England, became a transatlantic center of international commerce and would play a major role in the industrial revolution of the 19th century.

By the end of the 18th century the mass exploitation of human labor had begun to concern humane observers. After the American Revolution all states north of Maryland took steps toward the abolition of slavery, and the French revolutionary government abolished it in 1794 throughout French colonies; black Africans in France had already received their civil rights. Not until 1865, however, did the Thirteenth Amendment to the U.S. Constitution prohibit slavery throughout the United States.

CONTEMPORARY VOICES

Horace Walpole

A visit to the court of Louis XV. The English writer and connoisseur Horace Walpole (1717–1797), has been presented to the king and queen and describes the encounter to a friend.

You perceive that I have been presented. The Queen took great notice of me; none of the rest said a syllable. You are let into the King's bedchamber just as he has put on his shirt; he dresses and talks good-humouredly to a few, glares at strangers, goes to mass, to dinner, and a-hunting. The good old Queen, who is like Lady Primrose in the face, and Queen Caroline in the immensity of her cap, is at her dressing-table, attended by two or three old ladies, who are languishing to be in Abraham's bosom, as the only man's bosom to whom they can hope for admittance. Thence you go to the Dauphin, for all is done in an hour. He scarce stays a minute; indeed, poor creature; he is a ghost, and cannot possibly last three months. The Dauphiness is in her bedchamber, but dressed and standing; looks cross, is not civil, and has the true Westphalian grace and accents. The four Mesdames, who are clumsy, plump old wenches, with a bad likeness to their father, stand in a bedchamber in a row, with black cloaks and knitting-bags, looking good-humoured, not knowing what to say, and wriggling as if they wanted to make water. This ceremony too is very short; then you are carried to the Dauphin's three boys, who you may be sure only bow and stare. The Duke of Berry looks weak and weak-eyed: the Count de Provence is a fine boy; the Count d'Artois well enough. The whole concludes with seeing the Dauphin's little girl dine, who is as round and as fat as a pudding.

From *The Letters of Horace Walpole*, ed. P. Cunningham, London, 1892.

atheist. He was a firm believer in a God who had created the world, but whose worship could not be tied down to one religion or another: "The only book that needs to be read is the great book of nature." Only natural religion and morality would end prejudice and ignorance.

Voltaire's negative criticisms of human absurdity are more convincing than his positive views on a universal natural morality. It is difficult not to feel at times that even Voltaire himself had only the vaguest ideas of what natural morality really meant. In fact, in *Candide* (1759), his best-known work, he reaches a much less optimistic conclusion. *Candide* was written with the avowed purpose of ridiculing the optimism of the German philosopher Gottfried von Leibnitz (1646–1716), who believed that "everything is for the best in the best of all possible worlds." Since both intellect and experience teach that this is very far from the case, Voltaire chose to demonstrate the folly of unreasonable optimism, as well as the cruelty and stupidity of the human race, by subjecting his hero Candide to a barrage of disasters and suffering.

Throughout his journeys from Germany to Portugal to the New World and back to Europe, Candide has the opportunity to compare the theory of philosophical optimism with the evil, stupidity, and ignorance that he finds wherever he goes. The conclusion he reaches is expressed in the book's final words, "we must cultivate our gardens." The world is a cruel place where human life is of little account, but to give way to total pessimism is fruitless. Instead, we should try to find some limited activity we can perform well. By succeeding in this small task we can construct a little island of peace and sanity in a hostile world.

This message is, of course, hardly a comforting one. It is a measure of Voltaire's courage that his final advice to "cultivate our gardens" manages to extract something positive from the despair his humor and irony mask.

THE LATE 18TH CENTURY: TIME OF REVOLUTION

Throughout the 18th century Europe continued to prosper economically. The growth of trade and industry, particularly in Britain, France, and Holland, led to a number of significant changes in the life styles of increasing numbers of people. Technological improvements in coal mining and iron casting began to lay the foundations for the Industrial Revolution of the 19th century. The circulation of more books and newspapers increased general awareness of the issues of the day. As states began to accumulate more revenues, they increased both the size of their armies and the number of those in government employment. The Baroque period had seen the exploitation of imported goods and spices from Asia and gold from Latin America; the 18th century was marked by the development of trade with North America and the Caribbean.

Amid such vast changes, it was hardly possible that the very systems of government should remain unaffected. Thinkers like Rousseau and Voltaire began to question the hitherto unquestioned right of the wealthy aristocracy to rule throughout Europe. In Britain, both at home and in the colonies, power was gradually transferred from the king to Parliament. Prussia, Austria, and Russia were ruled by so-called enlightened despots, as we have seen.

In France, however, center of much of the intellectual pressure for change, the despots were not even enlightened. Louis XV, who ruled from 1715 to 1774, showed little interest in the affairs of his subjects or the details of government. The remark often attributed to him, *"Après moi le déluge"* (After me the flood), suggests that he was fully aware of the consequences of his indifference. Subsequent events fully justified his prediction, yet throughout his long reign he remained either unwilling or unable to follow the example of his fellow European sovereigns and impose some order on government. By the time his grandson Louis XVI succeeded him in 1774 the damage was done. Furthermore, the new king's continued reliance on the traditional aristocratic class, into whose hands he put wealth and political power, offended both the rising middle class and the peasants. When in 1788 the collapse of the French economy was accompanied by a disastrous harvest and consequent steep rise in the cost of food in the first phase of the Revolution, riots broke out in Paris and in rural districts. In reaction to the ensuing violence "The Declaration of the Rights of Man and Citizen," which asserted the universal right to "liberty, property, security, and resistance to oppression," was passed on August 26, 1789. Its opening section clearly shows the influence of the American Declaration of Independence (see page 417).

from The Declaration of the Rights of Man

The representatives of the French people, organized in National Assembly, considering that ignorance, forgetfulness, or contempt of the rights of man are the sole causes of public misfortunes and of the corruption of governments, have resolved to set forth in a solemn declaration the natural, inalienable, and sacred rights of man, in order that such declaration, continually before all members of the social body, may be a perpetual reminder of their rights and duties; in order that the acts of the legislative power and those of the executive power may constantly be compared with the aim of every political institution and may accordingly be more respected; in order that the demands of the citizens, founded henceforth upon simple and incontestable principles, may always be directed towards the maintenance of the Constitution and the welfare of all.

Accordingly, the National Assembly recognizes and proclaims, in the presence and under the auspices of the Supreme Being, the following rights of man and citizen.

1. Men are born and remain free and equal in rights; social distinctions may be based only upon general usefulness.

2. The aim of every political association is the preservation of the natural and inalienable rights of man; these rights are liberty, property, security, and resistance to oppression.

3. The source of all sovereignty resides essentially in the nation; no group, no individual may exercise authority not emanating expressly therefrom.

4. Liberty consists of the power to do whatever is not injurious to others; thus the enjoyment of the natural rights of every man has for its limits only those that assure other members of society the enjoyment of those same rights; such limits may be determined only by law.

5. The law has the right to forbid only actions which are injurious to society. Whatever is not forbidden by law may not be prevented, and no one may be constrained to do what it does not prescribe.

6. Law is the expression of the general will; all citizens have the right to concur personally, or through their representatives, in its formation; it must be the same for all, whether it protects or punishes. All citizens, being equal before it, are equally admissible to all public offices, positions, and employments, according to their capacity, and without other distinction than that of virtues and talents.

Declarations alone hardly sufficed, however; after two and a half years of continual political bickering and unrest, the Revolution entered its second phase. On September 20, 1792, a National Convention was assembled. One of its first tasks was to try Louis XVI, by now deposed and imprisoned, for treason. After unanimously finding him guilty, the Convention was divided on whether to execute him or not. He was finally condemned to the guillotine by a vote of 361 to 360 and beheaded forthwith. The resulting Reign of Terror lasted until 1795. During it, utopian theories of a republic based on liberty, equality, and fraternity were ruthlessly put into practice. The revolutionary leaders cold-bloodedly eliminated all opponents, real or potential, and created massive upheaval throughout all levels of French society.

The principal political group in the Convention, the Jacobins, was at first led by Maximilien Robespierre (1758–1794). One of the most controversial figures of the Revolution, Robespierre is viewed by some as a demagogue and bloodthirsty fanatic, by others as a fiery idealist and ardent democrat; his vigorous commitment to revolutionary change is disputed by no one. Following Rousseau's belief in the virtues of natural human feelings, Robespierre aimed to establish a "republic of virtue," democratically made up of honest citizens.

In order to implement these goals, revolutionary courts were set up, which tried and generally sentenced to death those perceived as the enemies of the Revolution. The impression that the Reign of Terror was aimed principally at the old aristocracy is incorrect. Only nobles suspected of political agitation were arrested, and the vast majority of the guillotine's victims—some 70 percent—were rebellious peasants and workers. Nor were revolutionary leaders immune. Georges-Jacques Danton (1759–1794), one of the earliest spokesmen of the Revolution and one of Robespierre's principal political rivals, was executed in March 1794 along with a number of his followers.

Throughout the rest of Europe, events in France were followed with horrified attention. Austria and Prussia were joined by England, Spain, and several smaller states in a war against the revolutionary government. After suffering initial defeat, the French enlarged and reorganized their army and succeeded in driving back the allied troops at the battle of Fleurus in June 1794. Paradoxically, the military victory, far from reinforcing Robespierre's authority, provided his opponents the strength to eliminate him; he was declared an outlaw on July 27, 1794, and guillotined the next day.

By the spring of the following year the country was in economic chaos and Paris was torn by street rioting. Many of those who had originally been in favor of revolutionary change, including businessmen and land-owning peasants, realized that whatever the virtues of democracy, constitutional government was essential. In reply to these pressures the Convention produced a new constitution, known as the Directory. This first formally established French republic lasted only until 1799, when political stability returned to France with the military dictatorship of Napoleon Bonaparte.

Although the French Revolution was an obvious consequence of extreme historical pressures, many of its leaders were additionally inspired by the successful outcome of another revolution, that of the Americans against their British rulers. More specifically, the Americans had rebelled against not the British king but the British parliament. In 18th-century England the king was given little chance to be enlightened or otherwise, since supreme power was concentrated in the legislative assembly, which ruled both England itself and, by its appointees, British territories abroad. A series of economic measures enacted by Parliament succeeded in thoroughly rousing American resentment. The story of what followed the Declaration of Independence of July 4, 1776, is too involved to be summarized here. Its result was the signing of a peace treaty in 1783 and the inauguration of the new American Constitution in 1789.

Although the Declaration of Independence was certainly not intended as a work of literature, its author, generally assumed to be Thomas Jefferson, was as successful as any of the literary figures of the 18th century in expressing the more optimistic views of the age. The principles enshrined in it assume that human beings are capable of achieving political and social freedom. Positive belief in equality and justice is expressed in universal terms like *man* and *nature*—universal for their day, that is—typical of 18th-century enlightened thought [14.23].

from The Declaration of Independence

When in the Course of human events, it becomes necessary for one people to dissolve the political bonds which have connected them with another, and to assume among the Powers of the earth, the separate and equal station to which the Laws of Nature and of Nature's God entitle them, a decent respect to the opinions of mankind requires that they should declare the causes which impel them to the separation.

We hold these truths to be self-evident, that all men are created equal, that they are endowed by their Creator with certain unalienable Rights, that among these are Life, Liberty and the pursuit of

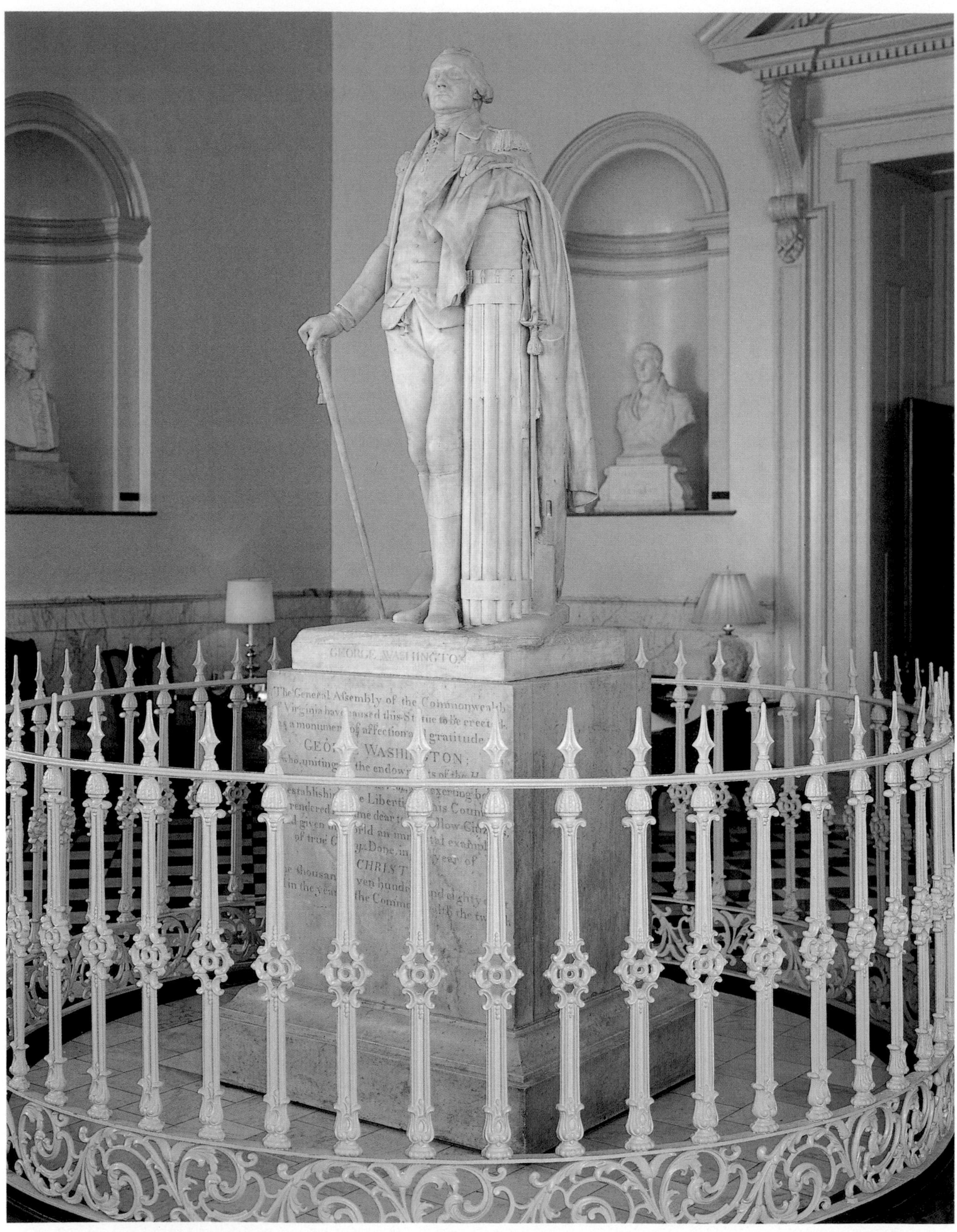

14.23 Jean Antoine Houdon. *George Washington*. 1788. Marble, height 6'8" (2.03 m). Virginia State Capitol, Richmond (courtesy of the Virginia State Library). The sculptor has emphasized the dignity and lofty calm of the first president.

Happiness. That to secure these rights, Governments are instituted among Men, deriving their just powers from the consent of the governed. That whenever any Form of Government becomes destructive of these ends, it is the Right of the People to alter or to abolish it, and to institute new Government, laying its foundation on such principles and organizing its powers in such form, as to them shall seem most likely to effect their Safety and Happiness. Prudence, indeed, will dictate that Governments long established should not be changed for light and transient causes; and accordingly all experience hath shown, that mankind are more disposed to suffer, while evils are sufferable, than to right themselves by abolishing the forms to which they are accustomed. But when a long train of abuses and usurpations, pursuing invariably the same Object, evinces a design to reduce them under absolute Despotism, it is their right, it is their duty, to throw off such Government, and to provide new Guards for their future security. Such has been the patient sufferance of these Colonies; and such is now the necessity which constrains them to alter their former Systems of Government. The history of the present King of Great Britain is a history of repeated injuries and usurpations, all having in direct object the establishment of an absolute Tyranny over these States.

SUMMARY

The 18th century marked the passage in European life from the old aristocratic order to the beginnings of modern society. When the age began Louis XIV was still firmly entrenched; before the century ended Louis XVI and his wife had been executed by the National Convention of the French Revolution—itself inspired, in theory at least, by the American Revolution of a few years earlier.

Elsewhere in Europe enlightened despots like Frederick the Great of Prussia responded to the growing restlessness of their subjects by reorganizing government and improving living conditions. Frederick's court even became one of the leading cultural and intellectual centers of the time; C. P. E. Bach directed the music there and Voltaire spent two years as Frederick's guest.

In the visual arts the principal style to emerge from the baroque splendors of the previous century was the rococo. Lighter and less grandiose, it was wonderfully suited to the civilized amenities of aristocratic life. The chief rococo painters were French and Italian—appropriately enough, since rulers both in France and in the kingdoms of Italy made few concessions to the growing demands for reform. In architecture the builders of Parisian private houses such as the Hôtel de Soubise indulged their taste for fanciful decoration, while the rococo churches of southern Germany and Austria represent some of the happiest of all 18th-century achievements.

The other important artistic style of the period was the neoclassical. Inspired by the increasing quantities of ancient art being excavated at Pompeii and elsewhere, artists began to turn to the style and subjects of classical antiquity, which provided a refreshing contrast to the theatricality of baroque and the artificiality of rococo. Furthermore, in the history of the Roman Republic (at least as they perceived it) revolutionary artists of the later 18th century found a vehicle for expressing their battle for freedom. In many cases painters incorporated into their works discoveries from the various excavations in progress: the French Jacques Louis David in his paintings for the Revolution as well as the English Joshua Reynolds in his portraits of society women.

Ancient sculpture provided a stimulus to some of the leading artists of the day, most notably the Italian Antonio Canova and the French Jean Antoine Houdon. Both of them worked principally during and after the revolutions; Houdon even produced a neoclassical statue of George Washington. Washington and the other leaders of the American Revolution turned naturally to classical architecture for their public buildings. Among the finest examples is Thomas Jefferson's State Capitol at Richmond.

In music the emotional style of baroque composers began to give way to a new way of organizing musical forms. By the middle of the 18th century the classical style was beginning to evolve, and the two greatest composers of the age, Franz Joseph Haydn and Wolfgang Amadeus Mozart (both Austrian), used it to write their symphonies, concertos, and sonatas. Most of these works employed sonata form, a system of musical composition involving contrasts rather than the unity of baroque music. Haydn's hundred or so symphonies show an almost infinitely endless exploration of the possibilities offered by sonata form while also reflecting the evolution of the modern symphony orchestra. His own personal career furthermore illustrates the changing status of the artist: After years of serving in the household of an aristocratic family, he became transformed by his compositions into one of the most famous men in Europe.

Mozart's relations with his noble employers were far less happy. His music, however, transcends the difficulties of his life and achieves the supreme blend of 18th-century art's two chief concerns: beauty and learning. Like Haydn, he explored the possibilities of sonata form and also wrote a number of operas that remain among the best-loved of all musical works for the stage. *The Marriage of Figaro* illustrates Mozart's genius for expressing universal human emotions in music, while in its story it reflects the revolutionary mood of the times.

Like music, the literature of the 18th century was generally serious. Many writers avoided the lightness of the rococo, preferring to produce works based on classical models or themes. They included the Italian dramatist Metastasio and the English historian Edward Gibbon. An exception is provided by the satirical writings of Alexander Pope, which poke fun at the pretensions of 18th-century society, although many of Pope's other works are neoclassical in style. Other writers used satire, in itself a characteristically rococo medium, as a more bitter weapon against human folly. Jonathan Swift's writings present an indictment of his fellow humans that offers little hope for their improvement.

The French Encyclopedists offered a more optimistic point of view. Denis Diderot and most of his colleagues believed in the essential goodness of human nature and the possibility of progress, and their *Encyclopédie* was intended to exalt the power of reason. Not all the contributors agreed, however. Jean Jacques Rousseau claimed that society was an evil that corrupted essential human goodness and called for a new social order. Yet all the leading intellectuals of the day, including the greatest of them all, Voltaire, were united in urging the need for radical social change. In novels, pamphlets, plays, and countless other publications Voltaire attacked traditional religion and urged the importance of freedom of thought.

By the end of the century the battle for freedom had plunged France into chaos and demonstrated to the whole of Europe that the old social order had come to an end. The following century was to see the struggle to forge a new society.

Pronunciation Guide

Beaumarchais: Boe-mar-SHAY
Boucher: Boo-SHAY
Candide: Can-DEED
Cherubino: Ke-ru-BEEN-owe
Cythera: SITH-er-a
David: Da-VEED
Diderot: Di-der-OWE
Fragonard: Fra-gone-ARE
Haydn: HI-dn
Montesquieu: Mont-es-KEW
Mozart: MOTE-sart
Neumann: NOY-man
Robespierre: Robe-spee-AIR
Rococo: Ro-co-COWE
Rousseau: Rue-SEW
Timpani: TIM-pan-ee
Vierzehnheiligen: Fear-tsayn-HI-li-gen
Voltaire: Vol-TARE
Watteau: Wat-OWE
Winckelmann: VIN-kel-man

Exercises

1. Compare and contrast the rococo and neoclassical styles in the visual arts, illustrating your answer with reference to specific works of art.
2. Describe the principles of sonata form and compare it to musical form in the Baroque period.
3. What were the main schools of philosophical thought in 18th-century France? How are they expressed in the writings of Voltaire?
4. Describe the use of satire in the works of Pope and Swift. What are the authors' aims, and how successful are they?
5. How were the social and political developments that led to the French Revolution reflected in the arts?

Further Reading

Brookner, A. *Jacques-Louis David*. New York: Harper & Row, 1980. A short and readable book by a well-known novelist who is also an art historian that interweaves accounts of David's life and works.

Conisbee, P. *Painting in Eighteenth-Century France.* Ithaca: Cornell University Press, 1981. A thoroughly organized survey that sets the great names against the background of their lesser contemporaries.

Kalnein W. and M. Levey. *Art and Architecture of the 18th Century in France.* New York: Penguin, 1972. This well-illustrated book provides an excellent introduction to a rich field. Good bibliographies.

Leppman, W. *Winckelmann.* London: Gollancz, 1971. An absorbing biography of one of the key figures in the rediscovery of classical antiquity and the formation of the neoclassical movement.

Levey, M. *The Life and Death of Mozart.* London: Cardinal, 1973. An original and moving biography that also gives a lively picture of the world in which Mozart moved.

Liebner, J. *Mozart on the Stage.* New York: Praeger, 1972.

A fascinating study that analyzes the revolutionary character of Mozart's operas, in particular the influence on them of the ideas of Rousseau; discusses each of them in detail.

Robbins Landon, H. C. *Essays on the Viennese Classical Style*. New York: Macmillan, 1970. An excellent discussion of the 18th-century classical style; especially good on Haydn.

Rosenblum, R. *Transformations in Late Eighteenth-Century Art*. Princeton: Princeton University Press, 1974. A scholarly survey of a crucial period of transition in Western art.

Rowse, A. L. *Jonathan Swift*. New York: Scribner, 1975. An important biography by a leading historian that describes Swift's life against the background of his times. Interesting illustrations.

Varriano, J. *Italian Baroque and Rococo Architecture*. New York: Oxford, 1986. A good up-to-date survey of 17th- and 18th-century Italian architectural developments.

Waterhouse, E. *Painting in Britain 1530–1790*, 4th ed. New York: Penguin, 1978. The first part of this book covers material outside the strict range of the 18th century, but the accounts of Gainsborough, Reynolds, and Hogarth in the remaining sections should not be missed.

	GENERAL EVENTS	LITERATURE & PHILOSOPHY	ART
1765		**1773** Goethe leads *Sturm und Drang* movement against neoclassicism **1774** Goethe, *The Sufferings of Young Werther*	**c. 1774** Copley leaves Boston to study in England **1784–1785** David, *Oath of the Horatii*
1789 REVOLUTIONARY AND NAPOLEONIC WARS	**1789** French Revolution begins **1793–1795** Reign of Terror in France **1799–1804** Napoleon rules France as consul **1804–1814** Napoleon rules France as emperor **1812** Failure of Napoleon's Russian campaign **1814** Napoleon exiled to Elba. Stephenson's first locomotive. **1814–1815** Congress of Vienna	**1790** Kant, *The Critique of Judgment,* expounding Transcendental Idealism **1794** Blake, "London" **1798** Wordsworth, "Tintern Abbey" **1807–1830** Philosophy of Hegel published in Germany **1808** Goethe's *Faust,* Part I	**1799** David, *The Battle of the Romans and the Sabines*. Goya becomes court painter to Charles IV of Spain; *The Family of Charles IV* (1800) **19th cent.** Romantic emphasis on emotion, nature, exotic images, faraway lands **1814** Goya, *Executions of May 3, 1808,* a retreat from idealism in art
1815 GROWTH OF INDUSTRIALIZATION	**1815** Napoleon escapes Elba; defeated at Battle of Waterloo **1815–1850** Industrialization of England **1816** Wreck of French vessel *Medusa* **1821** Death of Napoleon **1821–1829** Greek War of Independence against Turks **1830–1860** Industrialization of France and Belgium **1837–1901** Reign of Queen Victoria in England **1840–1870** Industrialization of Germany	**1819** Schopenhauer, *The World as Will and Idea;* Keats, *Ode to a Nightingale* **c. 1820** English romantic peak **1820** Shelley, *Prometheus Unbound* **1821** Byron, *Don Juan* **1824** Byron dies in Greece **1829–1847** Balzac, *The Human Comedy,* 90 realistic novels **1832** Goethe, *Faust,* Part II **1836–1860** Transcendentalist movement in New England **1837–1838** Dickens, *Oliver Twist* **1840** Poe, *Tales of the Grotesque* **1846** Sand, *Lucrezia Floriani* **1847** E. Brontë, *Wuthering Heights*	**1818–1819** Géricault, *Raft of the Medusa,* first exhibited 1819 **1820–1822** Goya paints nightmare scenes on walls of his house; *Saturn Devouring One of His Sons* **1824** Delacroix, *Massacre at Chios* **1827** Delacroix, *The Death of Sardanapalus* **c. 1830** Social realism follows romanticism; Daumier, *The Legislative Belly* (1834) **1836** Constable, *Stoke-by-Nayland* **1844** Turner, *Rain, Steam, and Speed* **c. 1847** Development of national styles. American artists influenced by Transcendentalism; Cole, *View of the Falls of Munda* (1847)
1848 AGE OF NATIONALISM	**1848** Revolutionary uprisings throughout Europe **1859** Darwin publishes theory of evolution, *Origin of Species* **1860–1870** Unification of Italy **1861–1865** American Civil War **1866–1871** Unified Germany **1867** Canada granted dominion status; British Factory Act gives workers Saturday afternoons off. **1869** First transcontinental railroad completed in America	**1848** Marx, *Communist Manifesto* **1851** Melville, *Moby-Dick* **1854** Thoreau, *Walden* **1855** First edition of Whitman's *Leaves of Grass* **1856–1857** Flaubert, *Madame Bovary* **1862** Hugo, *Les Misérables* **1869** Tolstoy, *War and Peace*	**1854–1855** Courbet, *The Painter's Studio* **c. 1860** American luminist painting develops; Heade, *Lake George* (1862) **1866** Homer, *Prisoners from the Front,* chronicles Civil War
1870	**1876** Bell patents the telephone **1888** Pasteur Institute founded in Paris	**1873–1877** Tolstoy, *Anna Karenina* **1890** Dickinson's poems first published, four years after her death	**1870** Corot, *Ville d'Avray* **c. 1880** Eakins uses photography and scientific techniques in search for realism; *The Swimming Hole* (1883)
1900			

CHAPTER

15 THE ROMANTIC ERA

	ARCHITECTURE	MUSIC

1808 Girodet, *The Entombment of Atala,* inspired by Chateaubriand's romantic novel *Atala*

1810 Friedrich, *Cloister Graveyard in the Snow*

1811 Ingres, *Jupiter and Thetis*

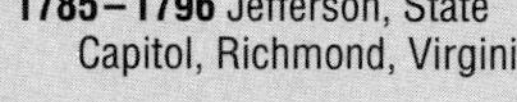

1785–1796 Jefferson, State Capitol, Richmond, Virginia

19th cent. Sequence of revival styles: neoclassical, neo-Gothic, neo-Renaissance; forms affected by growth of industry and technology

1836 Barry and Pugin begin neo-Gothic Houses of Parliament, London

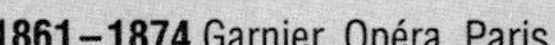

1861–1874 Garnier, Opéra, Paris

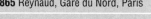

1865 Reynaud, Gare du Nord, Paris

1788 Mozart composes last three symphonies

1795 Debut of Beethoven as pianist

Development from classical to romantic music most evident in work of Beethoven; "Pathetique" *Sonata* (1799)

1804 First performance of Beethoven's "Eroica" *Symphony,* originally meant to honor Napoleon

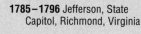

1814 Beethoven's opera *Fidelio* performed

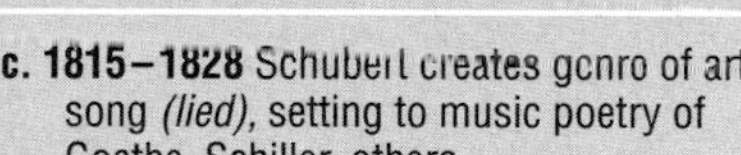

c. 1815–1828 Schubert creates genre of art song *(lied),* setting to music poetry of Goethe, Schiller, others

1822 Schubert, "Unfinished" *Symphony*

1824 First performance of Beethoven's *Symphony No. 9;* finale is choral version of Schiller's "Ode to Joy"

1830 Berlioz, *Fantastic Symphony*

1831 Bellini's *bel canto* opera *Norma* performed

1835 Donizetti, *Lucia di Lammermoor*

c. 1835–c. 1845 Virtuoso performance at peak; brilliant composer-performers create works of immense technical difficulty: Chopin, *Piano Sonata in B♭ Minor,* Op. 35 (1839)

1839 Chopin completes *Twenty-Four Preludes,* Op. 28

1842 Verdi's *Nabucco* performed; symbolic of Italians' suffering under Austrian rule

1846 Berlioz, *The Damnation of Faust*

1853 First performances of Verdi's *Il Trovatore* and *La Traviata,* the latter based on Dumas' novel *The Lady of the Camelias*

1853–1874 Wagner, *The Ring of the Nibelung;* first staged at new Bayreuth opera house 1876

1865 Wagner experiments with harmony in *Tristan and Isolde*

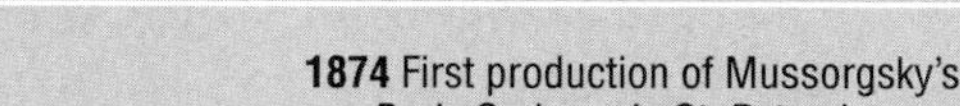

1874 First production of Mussorgsky's opera *Boris Godunov* in St. Petersburg

1876 Brahms, *Symphony No. 1 in C Minor*

1882 Wagner, *Parsifal*

1887 Verdi, *Otello;* Bruckner begins *Symphony No. 8 in C Minor*

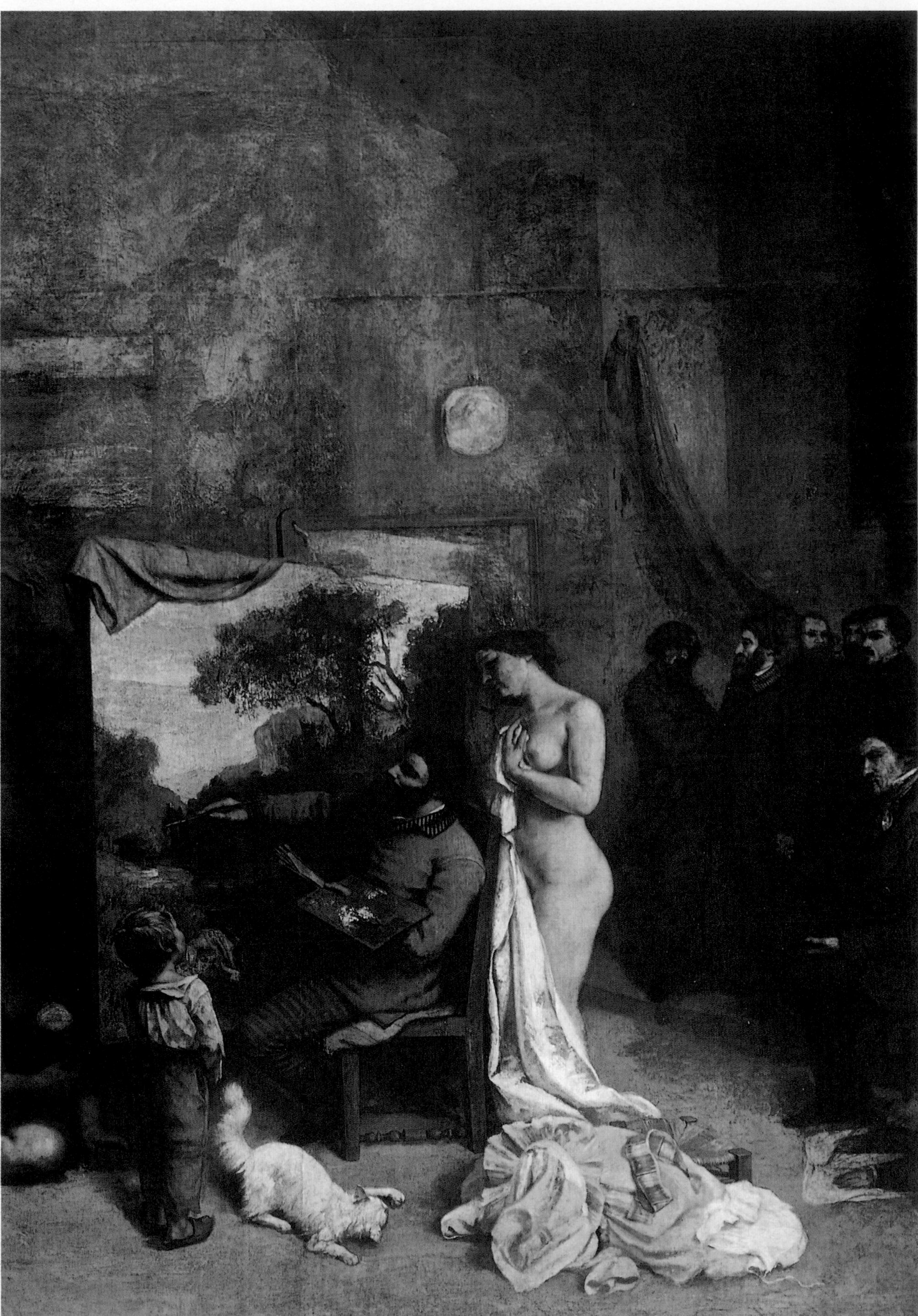

CHAPTER

15 THE ROMANTIC ERA

THE CONCERNS OF ROMANTICISM

THE TIDE of revolution that swept away much of the old political order in Europe and America in the last quarter of the 18th century had momentous consequences for the arts. Both the American and the French revolutions had, in fact, used art as a means of expressing their spiritual rejection of the artistocratic society against which they were physically rebelling, and both had adopted the neoclassical style to do so. Jacques Louis David's images of stern Roman virtue (see Figure 14.1, page 392) and Jefferson's evocation of the simple grandeur of classical architecture (see Figure 14.17, page 404) represented, as it were, the revolutionaries' view of themselves and their accomplishments. Neoclassicism, however, barely survived into the beginning of the 19th century. The movement that replaced it, romanticism, eventually dominated virtually every aspect of 19th-century artistic achievement.

The essence of romanticism is particularly difficult to describe because romanticism is much more concerned with broad general attitudes than with specific stylistic features. Painters, writers, and musicians in the 19th century shared a number of concerns in their approach to their art. First was the important emphasis they placed on personal feelings and their expression. Ironically enough, the very revolutionary movements that had encouraged artists to rebel against the conventional styles of the early 18th century had themselves proved too restricting and conventional.

Second, emphasis on emotion rather than intellect led to the expression of subjective rather than objective visions; after all, the emotions known best are the ones we have experienced. The romantics used art to explore and dissect their own personal hopes and fears (more often the latter) rather than as a means to arrive at some general truth.

This in turn produced a third attitude of romanticism: its love of the fantastic and the exotic, which made it possible to probe more deeply into an individual's creative imagination. Dreams, for example, were a way of releasing the mind from the constraints of everyday experience and bringing to the surface those dark visions reason had submerged, as the Spanish artist Francisco Goya shows us unforgettably in a famous etching [15.1]. Artists felt free to invent their own dream worlds. Some chose to reconstruct such ages long past as the medieval period, which was particularly popular (Britain's Houses of Parliament [15.2] were begun in 1836 in the Gothic style of six centuries earlier). Others preferred to imagine remote and exotic lands and dreamed of life in the mysterious Orient or on a primitive desert island. Still others simply trusted to the powers of their imagination and invented a fantasy world of their own.

A fourth characteristic of much romantic art is a mystical attachment to the world of nature that was also the result of the search for new sensations. Painters turned increasingly to landscape, composers sought to evoke the rustling of leaves in a forest or the noise of a storm, and poets tried to express their sense of union with the natural world. Most 18th-century artists had turned to nature in search of order and reason. In the 19th century the wild unpredictability of nature became emphasized, depicted neither objectively nor realistically but as a mirror of the artist's individual emotions. At the same time, the romantic communion with nature expressed a rejection of the classical notion of a world centered on human activity.

These attitudes, and the new imaginative and creative power they unleashed, had two very different but equally important effects on the relationship between the artist and society. On one hand, many creative artists became increasingly alienated from their public. Whereas they had once filled a

15.1 Francisco Goya. 1797–1798. *Los Caprichos,* plate 43: *El sueño de la razón produce monstruos* (The Sleep of Reason Produces Monsters). Etching and aquatint. 216 × 152 mm. The Metropolitan Museum of Art, Gift of M. Knoedler and Co., 1918 [18.64 (43)]. The precise meaning of the work is not clear, but it evidently represents the inability of Reason to banish monstrous thoughts. Its title is written on the desk below the student, who sleeps with his head on his textbooks.

precise role in providing entertainment or satisfying political and religious demands, now their self-expressive works met no particular needs except their own.

On the other hand, an increasing number of artists sought to express the national characteristics of their people by art. Abandoning the common artistic language of earlier periods and instead developing local styles that made use of traditional folk elements, artists were able to stimulate (and in some cases to initiate) the growth of national consciousness and the demand for national independence (see map, page 428). This was particularly ef-

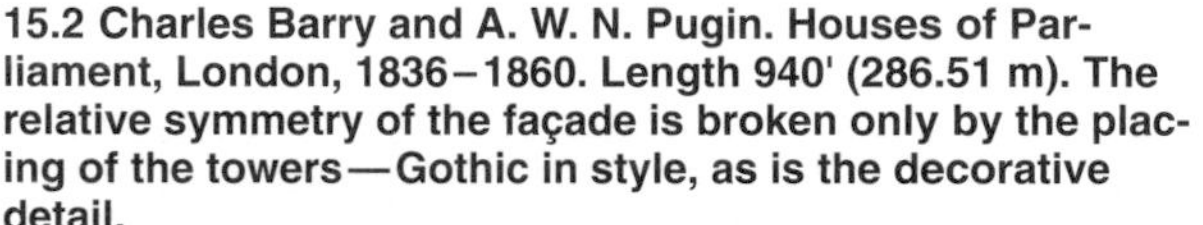

15.2 Charles Barry and A. W. N. Pugin. Houses of Parliament, London, 1836–1860. Length 940' (286.51 m). The relative symmetry of the façade is broken only by the placing of the towers—Gothic in style, as is the decorative detail.

TABLE 15.1 Principal Characteristics of the Romantic Movement

The Expression of Personal Feelings	Interest in Nature
Chopin, *Preludes* (p. 434)	Beethoven, *"Pastoral" Symphony* (p. 433)
Goya, *The Family of Charles IV* [15.11]	Constable, *Hay Wain* [15.23]
Goethe, *The Sufferings of Young Werther* (p. 451)	Poetry of Wordsworth
Self-Analysis	Emerson, *The American Scholar* (p. 456)
Berlioz, *Fantastic Symphony* (p. 433)	Nationalism and Political Commitment
Poetry of Keats	Verdi, *Nabucco* (p. 436)
Whitman, *Leaves of Grass*	Smetana, *My Fatherland* (p. 435)
Love of the Fantastic and Exotic	Goya, *Execution of the Madrileños* [15.10]
Music and performances of Paganini (p. 435)	Byron's support of the Greeks (p. 452)
Girodet, *The Entombment of Atala* [15.13]	Erotic Love and the Eternal Feminine
Delacroix, *Death of Sardanapalus* [15.16]	Goethe, *Faust, Part II* (p. 451)
	Wagner, *Tristan and Isolde* (p. 438)

fective in the Russian and Austrian empires (which incorporated many nationalities) and even in America, which had always been only on the fringe of the European cultural tradition, but it also became an increasingly strong tendency in the art of France and Italy, countries that had hitherto shared the same general culture. Thus at the same time, some artists were retreating into a private world of their own creation, but others were in the forefront of the social and political movements of their own age [Table 15.1].

THE INTELLECTUAL BACKGROUND

It might be expected that a movement like romanticism, which put a high value on the feelings of the moment at the expense of conscious reason, would remain relatively unaffected by intellectual principles. Nonetheless, a number of romantic artists did in fact draw inspiration from contemporary philosophy. A rapid survey of the chief intellectual developments of the 19th century therefore provides a background to the artistic ones.

The ideas that proved most attractive to the romantic imagination had developed in Germany at the end of the 18th century. Their chief spokesman was Immanuel Kant (1724–1804), whose *Critique of Judgment* (1790) defined the pleasure we derive from art as "disinterested satisfaction." Kant conceived of art as uniting opposite principles: It unites the general with the particular, for example, and reason with the imagination. For Kant, the only analogy for the way in which art is at the same time useless and yet useful was to be found in the world of nature.

Even more influential than Kant was Georg Wilhelm Friedrich Hegel (1770–1831), whose ideas continued to affect attitudes toward art and artistic criticism into the 20th century. Like Kant, Hegel stressed art's ability to reconcile and make sense of opposites, and to provide a *synthesis* of the two opposing components of human existence, called *thesis* (pure, infinite being) and *antithesis* (the world of nature). This process, he held, applied to the workings of the mind, and also to the workings of world history, through the development and realization of what he called the "World Spirit." Hegel's influence on his successors lay less in the details of his philosophical system than in his acceptance of divergences and his attempt to reconcile them. The search for a way to combine differences, to permit the widest variety of experience, is still the basis of much contemporary thinking about the arts.

Both Kant and Hegel developed their ideas in the relatively optimistic intellectual climate of the late 18th and early 19th centuries, and their approach both to art and to existence is basically positive. A very different position was that of Arthur Schopenhauer (1788–1860), whose major work, *The World as Will and Idea* (1819), expresses the belief that the dominating will, or power, in the world is evil. At the time of its appearance, Schopenhauer's work made little impression, due in large measure to the popularity of Kant's and Hegel's idealism. Schopenhauer himself did not help matters by launching a bitter personal attack on Hegel. But the failure of the nationalist uprisings of 1848 in many parts of Europe produced a growing mood of pessimism and gloom, against which background Schopenhauer's vision of a world condemned perpetually to be ravaged by strife and misery seemed more convincing. Thus his philosophy, if it did not mold the romantic movement, came to reflect its growing despondency.

It must be admitted, of course, that many of the major developments in 19th-century thought had little direct impact on the contemporary arts. The

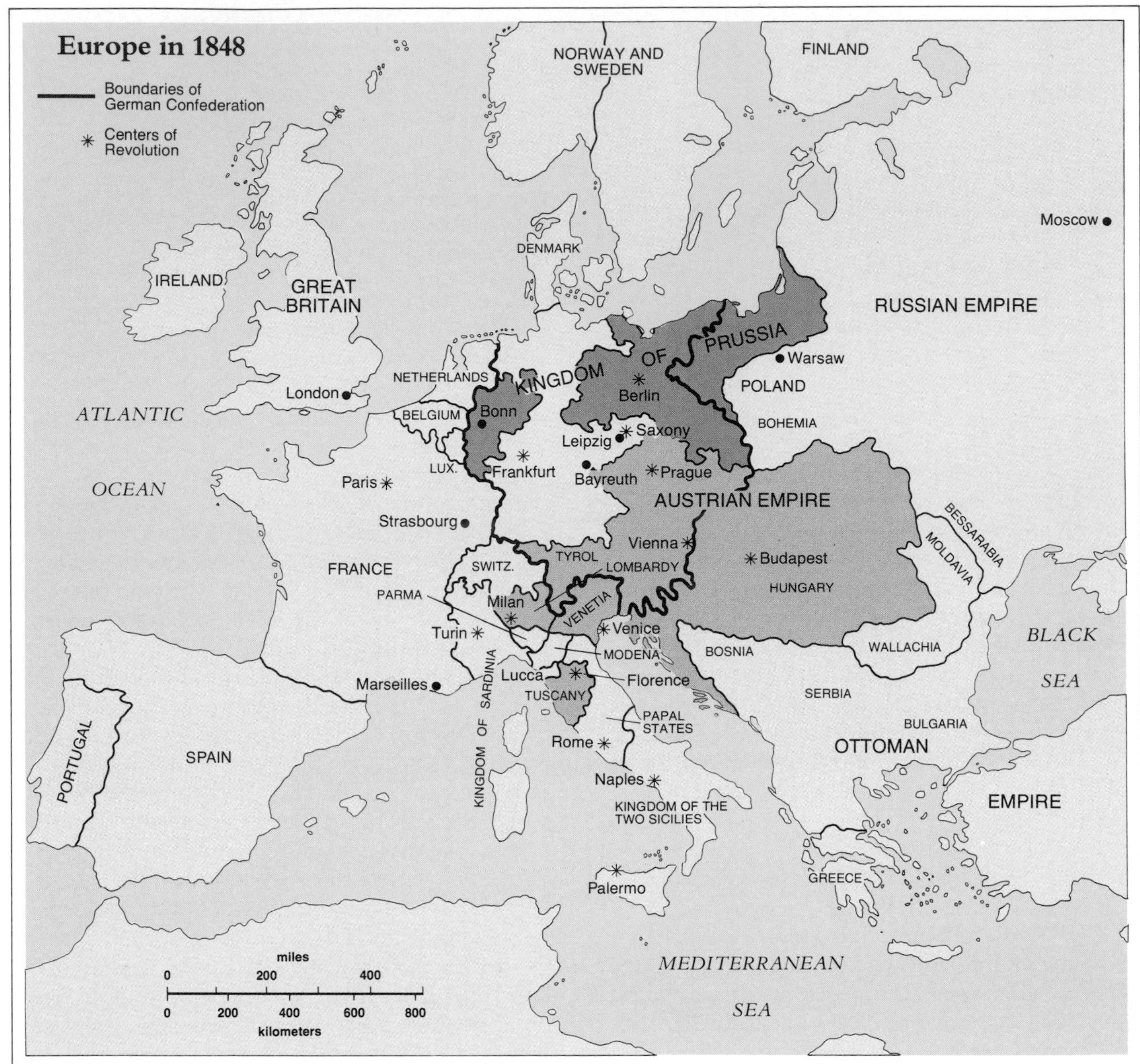

most influential of all 19th-century philosophers was probably Karl Marx (1818–1883), whose belief in the inherent evil of capitalism and in the historical inevitability of the proletarian revolution was powerfully expressed in the *Communist Manifesto* of 1848.

Marx's belief that revolution was both unavoidable and necessary was based at least in part on his own observation of working conditions in industrial England, where his friend and fellow Communist Friedrich Engels (1820–1895) had inherited a textile factory. Marx and Engels both believed that the factory workers, although creating wealth for the middle classes, received no benefit from it for themselves. Living in overcrowded, unsanitary conditions, the workers were deprived of any effective political power, and only kept quiet by the drug of religion, which offered them the false hope of rewards in a future life. The plight of the working classes seemed to Marx to transcend all national boundaries and create a universal proletariat that could only achieve freedom through revolution: "Workers of the world, unite! You have nothing to lose but your chains!"

The drive to political action was underpinned by Marx's economic philosophy, with its emphasis on the value of labor and, more generally, on the supreme importance of economic and social conditions as the true moving forces behind historical events. This so-called materialist concept of history was to have worldwide repercussions in the century that followed Marx's death. In our own time, writers such as Bertolt Brecht (1898–1956) have embraced Marxist principles, and Marxist critics have developed a school of aesthetic criticism that applies standards based on Marxist doctrines. For the 19th and early 20th centuries, however, Marx's influence was exclusively social and political.

Marx clearly laid out his views on the arts. Art has the ability to contribute to important social and political changes, and is thus a determining factor in history. Nor is artistic output limited to the upper or more prosperous social classes; according to the "principle of uneven development" a higher social order does not necessarily produce a correspondingly high artistic achievement. Capitalism, in fact, is hostile to artistic development because of its obsession with money and profit. As for styles, the only one appropriate for the class struggle and the new state is realism, which would be understood by the widest audience. Lenin inherited and developed this doctrine further, when he ordered that art should be a specific "reflection" of reality, and used the Party to enforce the official cultural policy.

The 19th century saw vast changes in the lives of millions of people, as industrial development and scientific progress overthrew centuries-old ways. The railroad, using engines powered by steam, first appeared in 1825 between Stockton and Darlington in England. By 1850, there were 6,000 miles of track in Britain, 3,000 in Germany, 2,000 in France, and the beginnings of a rail system in Austria, Italy, and Russia. The economic impact was overwhelming. The railroad represented a new industry which fulfilled a universal need; it provided jobs and offered opportunities for capital investment. At the same time, it increased the demand for coal and iron.

Industry soon overtook agriculture as the source of national wealth. With the growth of mass production in factories, the cities which the railroad connected became vast urban centers, attracting wholesale migration from the countryside. The numbers of people living in them rose dramatically. The population of Turin, in northern Italy, was 86,000 in 1800, 137,000 by 1850, and over 200,000 by 1860. By 1850, half of Britain's inhabitants lived in cities, the first time in history that this was true for any large society. The results were by no means always happy; one Londoner described his city in the 1820s as "a wilderness of human beings."

In science, constant research brought a host of new discoveries. Experiments in magnetism and electricity advanced physics. Using new chemical elements, the French chemist Louis Pasteur (1822–1895) explored the process of fermentation and invented "pasteurization"—a discovery that helped to improve diet. Equally beneficial was Pasteur's demonstration that disease is spread by living but invisible (to the naked eye, at least) germs, that can be combatted by vaccination and the sterilization of medical equipment.

No single book affected 19th-century readers more powerfully than *The Origin of Species* by Charles Darwin, which appeared in 1859. As a student at Cambridge, in 1831 Darwin was offered the post of naturalist aboard H.M.S. *Beagle,* a ship about to leave on a surveying expedition around the world. In the course of the voyage, he studied geological formations, fossils, and the distribution of plant and animal types. On examining his material, he became convinced that species were not fixed categories, as had always been held, but were capable of variation. Drawing on the population theories of Malthus, and the geological studies of Sir Charles Lyell, Darwin developed his theory of evolution, as an attempt to explain the changes, disappearances, and new appearances in various species.

According to Darwin, animals and plants evolve by a process of natural selection (he chose the term to contrast it with the "artificial selection" used by animal breeders). Over time, some variations of each species survive while others die out. Those likely to survive are those best suited to prevailing environmental conditions—a process called by one of Darwin's followers "the survival of the fittest." Changes in the environment would lead to adjustments within the species. The first publication of this theory appeared in 1858, in the form of a short scientific paper; *The Origin of Species* appeared a year later. In 1871, Darwin published *The Descent of Man,* in which he claimed that the human race is descended from an animal of the anthropoid group.

The impact of both books was spectacular. Their author quietly continued his research and tried to avoid the popular controversy surrounding his work. Church leaders thundered their denunciations of a theory that utterly contradicted the notion that humans, along with everything else, had been created by God in accordance with a divine plan. Scientists and freethinkers stoutly defended Darwin, often enlarging his claims. Others held that the development of modern capitalism and industrial society represented a clear demonstration of the "survival of the fittest," although Darwin himself never endorsed this "social Darwinism" [Table 15.2].

Achievements in science and technology are reflected to a certain extent in romantic art, although

TABLE 15.2 19th-Century Scientific and Technological Developments

1814	Stephenson builds first locomotive
1821	Faraday discovers principle of electric dynamo
1825	Erie Canal opened in the United States
	First railway completed (England)
1839	Daguerre introduces his process of photography
1844	Morse perfects the telegraph
1853	First International Exhibition of Industry (New York)
1858	Transatlantic cable begun (completed 1866)
1859	Darwin publishes *The Origin of Species*
	First oil well drilled (in Pennsylvania)
1867	Nobel invents dynamite
1869	Transcontinental Railway completed in the United States
	Suez Canal opened
1876	Bell patents the telephone
1877	Edison invents the phonograph
1885	First internal combustion engines using gasoline

chiefly from a negative point of view. The growing industrialization of life in the great cities, and the effect of inventions like the railway train on urban architecture served to stimulate a "back-to-nature" movement, as romanticism provided an escape from the grim realities of urbanization and industrialization. Furthermore, at a time when many people felt themselves submerged and depersonalized in overcrowded cities, the romantic emphasis on the individual and on self-analysis found an ap-

SPORTS AND GAMES

Football

Modern sport, organized on a nationwide basis, began in Britain around 1850. Until then it had been an upper-class activity, limited to those sports which appealed to aristocratic tastes and pockets: hunting, horse racing, cricket. With the rise of the middle classes and the spread of popular education, other kinds of games began to attract both players and spectators; often based on traditional pastimes, they did not require expensive equipment.

By far the most popular of these was football, the European version of which—soccer—has now become the most widely played game in the world. The stimulus to the formation of local teams which could compete with one another was the passing of the British Factory Act in 1867, which gave factory employees Saturday afternoon off work; this created what was called "the English weekend." Few workers had had the energy after an exhausting day in the factory to play sports. By institutionalizing the concept that everyone was entitled to some leisure time, the Act promoted the formation of a series of sporting organizations, including the Football Association and the Rugby Union. By 1890, the Football League had organized English football teams into a series of matches, played for a national championship. With the growth of the popular press, the annual Football League contest was followed by hundreds of thousands of football fans. Many of those who cheered on their team on a Saturday afternoon also played themselves: All the game required was a bit of empty land, or the square in front of a church, and a ball.

Soccer has remained a game with strong working-class associations. Rugby, in which the ball is picked up and carried, was invented at one of England's aristocratic public schools, and, like cricket, never achieved the universal popularity of soccer. In the United States, however, the inventors of American football used rugby as their model. The main rules and tactics were devised by Walter Camp in the 1880s at Yale. The new game became popular, but drew public criticism for its physical violence. In 1906, President Theodore Roosevelt met with team representatives, and agreed on a ban of dangerous practices. Modern professional soccer was introduced for the first time in the United States in 1967. The game's increasing attraction can be judged by the staging of the World Cup—the highest international competition—in the United States in 1994.

preciative audience. Many artists contrasted the growing problems of urban life with an idyllic (and highly imaginative) picture of rustic bliss.

Scientific ideas had something of the same negative effect on 19th-century artists. The English Victorian writers (so called after Queen Victoria, who reigned from 1837 to 1901) responded to the growing scientific materialism of the age. Although few were, strictly speaking, romantics, much of their resistance to progress in science and industry and their portrayal of its evil effects has its roots in the romantic tradition.

MUSIC IN THE ROMANTIC ERA

Beethoven

For many of the romantics, music was the supreme art. Free from the intellectual concepts involved in language and the physical limits inherent in the visual arts, it was capable of the most wholehearted and intuitive expression of emotion. Since Ludwig van Beethoven (1770–1827), widely regarded as the pioneer of musical romanticism, also manifested many characteristically romantic attitudes—such as love of nature, passionate belief in the freedom of the individual, and fiery temperament—it is not surprising that he has come to be regarded as the prototype of the romantic artist [15.3]. When he wrote proudly to one of his most loyal aristocratic supporters "There will always be thousands of princes, but there is only one Beethoven," he spoke for a new generation of creators. When he used the last movement of his *Symphony No. 9* to preach the doctrine of universal brotherhood he inspired countless ordinary listeners by his fervor. Even today familiarity with Beethoven's music has not dulled its ability to give dramatic expression to the noblest of human sentiments.

15.3 Ferdinand Georg Waldmüller. *Ludwig van Beethoven.* 1823. 28 × 22¾" (72 × 58 cm). Painting now lost. Painted a year before the first performance of Beethoven's *Symphony No. 9 in d minor,* the portrait emphasizes the composer's stubborn independence by both the set of the mouth and the casual, even untidy, dress and hair. Beethoven, who had become irascible in his later years, allowed the artist only one sitting for this portrait commissioned by one of his music publishers.

Although Beethoven's music served as the springboard for the Romantic movement in music, his own roots were deep in the classical tradition. He pushed to the limits classicism through use of the sonata allegro form. In spirit, furthermore, his work is representative of the Age of Enlightenment and the revolutionary mood of the turn of the century, as is proved by both the words and music of his opera *Fidelio.* A complex and many-sided genius, Beethoven transcended the achievements of the age in which he was born and set the musical tone for the 19th century.

Beethoven was born in Bonn, Germany, where he received his musical training from his father. An alcoholic, Beethoven's father saw the possibility of producing a musical prodigy in his son. He forced him to practice hours at the keyboard, often locking him in his room and beating him on his return from drinking bouts. All possibilities of a happy family life were brought to an end in 1787 by the death of Beethoven's mother and his father's subsequent decline into advanced alcoholism. Beethoven sought compensation in the home of the von Breuning family, where he acted as private tutor. It was there that he met other musicians and artists and developed a love of literature that he kept throughout his life. He also struck up a friendship with a local minor aristocrat, Count Waldstein, who remained his devoted admirer until the composer's death.

In 1792 Waldstein was one of the aristocrats who helped Beethoven go to Vienna to study with Haydn, then regarded as the greatest composer of his day; but although Haydn agreed to give him lessons, the young Beethoven's impatience and suspicion, and Haydn's deficiencies as a teacher, did not make for a happy relationship. Nevertheless, many of the works Beethoven wrote during his first years in Vienna are essentially classical in both form and spirit; only by the end of the century had he begun to extend the emotional range of his music.

One of the first pieces to express the characteristically Beethovenian spirit of rebellion against Fate and the determination to struggle on is his *Piano Sonata No. 8 in c minor,* Op. 13, generally known as the "Pathétique." The first movement begins with a slow introduction, but unlike similar introductions in the classical music of Haydn, it sets the emotional tone of the entire piece rather than merely capturing the listener's attention. As is so often the case, the significance of Beethoven's music is as easy to grasp on hearing as it is difficult to express in words. The heavy, foreboding chords seem to try to pull themselves up, only to fall back again and again in defeat, until finally they culminate in a burst of defiant energy that sets the main *allegro* (fast) portion of this movement on its stormy way. Just before the very end of the movement the ghost of the slow introduction returns briefly, as if to emphasize the odds against which the struggle has been—and will be—waged.

It is important to understand precisely how Beethoven used music in a new and revolutionary way. Other composers had written music to express emotion long before Beethoven's time, from Bach's outpouring of religious fervor to Mozart's evocation of human joy and sorrow. What is different about Beethoven is that his emotion is autobiographical. His music tells us how he feels, what his succession of moods is, and what conclusion he reaches. It does other things at the same time, and at this early stage in his career for the most part it self-consciously follows classical principles of construction, but the vivid communication of personal emotions is its prime concern. That Beethoven's range was not limited to anger and frustration is immediately demonstrated by the beautiful and consoling middle slow movement of the "Pathétique," with its lyrical main theme, but the final movement returns to turbulent passion.

Parallels for the turbulent style of the "Pathétique" can be found in other contemporary arts, especially literature, but although to some extent Beethoven was responding to the climate of the times, there can be no doubt that he was also expressing a personal reaction to the terrible tragedy that had begun to afflict him as early as 1796. In that year the first symptoms of his deafness began to appear; by 1798 his hearing had grown very weak, and by 1802 he was virtually totally deaf.

Nonetheless, although obviously affected by his condition, Beethoven's music was not exclusively concerned with his own fate. The same heroic attitude with which he faced his personal problems was also given universal expression, never more stupendously than in the *Symphony No. 3 in E♭,* Op. 55, subtitled the "Eroica," the Heroic Symphony. As early as 1799 the French ambassador to Vienna had suggested that Beethoven write a symphony in honor of Napoleon Bonaparte. At the time Napoleon was widely regarded as a popular hero who had triumphed over his humble origins to rise to power as a champion of liberty and democracy. Beethoven's own democratic temperament made him one of Napoleon's many admirers. The symphony was duly begun, but in 1804, the year of its completion, Napoleon had himself crowned emperor. When Beethoven heard the news, he angrily crossed out Napoleon's name on the title page. The first printed edition, which appeared in 1806, bore only the dedication "to celebrate the memory of a great man."

It would be a mistake to see the "Eroica" merely as a portrait of Napoleon. Rather, inspired by what he saw as the heroic stature of the Frenchman, Beethoven created his own heroic world in sound, in a work of vast dimensions. The first movement alone lasts for almost as long as many a classical symphony. Its complicated structure requires considerable concentration on the part of the listener. The form is basically the old classical sonata allegro form (see page 406), but on a much grander scale and with a wealth of musical ideas. Yet the principal theme of the movement, which the cellos announce at the very beginning, after two hammering, impatient chords demand our attention, is of a rocklike sturdiness and simplicity:

Beethoven's genius emerges as he uses this and other similarly straightforward ideas to build his mighty structure. Throughout the first movement his use of harmony and, in particular, discord, adds to the emotional impact, especially in the middle of the development section, where slashing dissonances seem to tear the orchestra apart. His classical grounding emerges in the recapitulation, where the infinite variety of the development section gives way to a restored sense of unity; the movement ends triumphantly with a long and thrilling coda. The formal structure is recognizably classical, but the intensity of expression, depth of personal commitment, and heroic defiance are all totally romantic.

The second movement of the "Eroica" is a worthy successor to the first. A funeral march on the same massive scale, it alternates a mood of epic tragedy, which has been compared, in terms of impact with the works of the Greek playwright Aeschylus, with rays of consolation that at times achieve a transcendental exaltation. Although the many subtleties of construction deserve the closest attention, even a first hearing will reveal the grandeur of Beethoven's conception.

The third and fourth movements relax the tension. For the third, Beethoven replaces the stately minuet of the classical symphony with a scherzo—the word literally means joke and is used to describe a fast-moving, generally lighthearted piece of music. Beethoven's introduction of this kind of music, which in his hands often has something of the crude flavor of a peasant dance, is another illustration of his "democratization" of the symphony. The last movement is a brilliant and energetic series of variations on a theme Beethoven had composed a few years earlier for a ballet he had written on the subject (from classic mythology) of Prometheus, who defied the ancient gods by giving mortals the gift of fire, for which he was punished by Zeus—a final reference to the heroic mood of the entire work.

Many of the ideas and ideals that permeate the "Eroica" reappear throughout Beethoven's work. His love of liberty and hatred of oppression are expressed in his only opera, *Fidelio,* which describes how a faithful wife rescues her husband who has been unjustly imprisoned for his political views. A good performance of *Fidelio* is still one of the most uplifting and exalting experiences music has to offer. The concept of triumph over Fate recurs in his best-known symphony, *No. 5,* Op. 67, while *Symphony No. 6,* Op. 68, the "Pastoral," consists of a romantic evocation of nature and the emotions it arouses. *Symphony No. 9,* Op. 125, is perhaps the most complete statement of the human striving to conquer all obstacles and win through to universal peace and joy. In it Beethoven introduced a chorus and soloists to give voice to the "Ode to Joy" by his compatriot Friedrich Schiller (1759–1805). The symphony represents the most complete artistic vindication of Kant's Transcendental Idealism. It is also one of the most influential works of the entire romantic movement.

Instrumental Music after Beethoven

After Beethoven, music could never again return to its former mood of classical objectivity. Although Beethoven's music may remain unsurpassed for its universalization of individual emotion, his successors tried—and in large measure succeeded—to find new ways to express their own feelings. Among the first to follow Beethoven was Hector Berlioz (1803–1869), the most distinguished French romantic composer who produced, among other typically romantic works, the *Fantastic Symphony,* which describes the hallucinations of an opium-induced dream, and *The Damnation of Faust,* a setting of Part One of Goethe's work. In both of these he used the full romantic apparatus of dreams, witches, demons, and the grotesque to lay bare the artist's innermost feelings—although, like Goethe, he never lost an innately classical streak.

A much more intimate and poetic form of romantic self-revelation is the music of Franz Schubert (1797–1828), who explored in the few years before his premature death the new possibilities opened up by Beethoven in a wide range of musical forms. In general he was happiest when working on a small scale, as evidenced by his more than six hundred *Lieder* (songs), which are an inexhaustible store of musical and emotional expression.

On the whole, the more rhetorical nature of the symphonic form appealed to Schubert less, although the wonderful *Symphony No. 8 in b minor,* called the "Unfinished" because he only completed two movements, combines great poetic feeling with a genuine sense of drama. His finest instrumental music was written for small groups of instruments. The two *Trios for Piano, Violin, and Cello,* Op. 99 and 100, are rich in the heavenly melodies that seemed to come to him so easily; the second, slow movement of the *Trio in E♭,* Op. 100, touches profound depths of romantic expression. Like the slow movement of Mozart's *Piano Concerto No. 27 in B♭* (see page 408), its extreme beauty is tinged with an unutterable sorrow. But whereas Mozart seems to speak for humanity at large, Schubert moves us most deeply by communicating his own personal feelings.

Most 19th-century composers followed Beethoven in using the symphony as the vehicle for their most serious musical ideas. Robert Schumann (1810–1856) and Johannes Brahms (1833–1897) regarded the symphonic form as the most lofty means of musical expression, and each as a result wrote only four symphonies. Brahms did not even dare to write a symphony until he was forty-four, and is said to have felt the presence of Beethoven's works "like the tramp of a giant" behind him. When it finally appeared, Brahms' *Symphony No. 1 in c minor,* Op. 68, was inevitably compared with Beethoven's symphonies. Although Brahms' strong sense of form and conservative style won him the hostility of the arch-romantics of the day, other critics hailed him as the true successor to Beethoven.

Both responses were, of course, extreme. Brahms' music certainly is romantic—with its emphasis on warm melody and a passion no less present for being held tightly in rein—but far from echoing the heaven-storming mood of many of the symphonies of his great predecessor, Brahms was really more at home in a relaxed vein. Although the *Symphony No. 1* begins with a gesture of defiant grandeur akin to Beethoven's, the first movement ends by fading dreamily into a glowing tranquility. The lovely slow movement is followed not by a scherzo but by a quiet and graceful intermezzo or interlude, and only in the last movement do we return to the mood of the opening.

Closer to the more cosmic mood of the Beethoven symphonies are the nine symphonies of Anton Bruckner (1824–1896). A deeply religious man imbued with a romantic attachment to the beauties of nature, Bruckner combined his devout Catholicism and mystical vision in music of epic grandeur. It has often been remarked that Bruckner's music requires time and patience on the listener's part. His pace is leisurely and he creates huge structures in sound that demand our full concentration if we are to appreciate their "architecture." There is no lack of incidental beauty, however, and the rewards are immense. No other composer has been able to convey quite the tone of mystical exaltation that Bruckner achieves, above all in the slow movements of his last three symphonies. The *adagio* movement from the *Symphony No. 8 in c minor,* for instance, moves from the desolate romanticism of its opening theme to a mighty, blazing climax as thrilling and stirring as anything in 19th-century music.

The Age of the Virtuosos

Beethoven's emphasis on the primacy of the artist inspired another series of romantic composers to move in a very different direction from that of the symphony. Beethoven himself had first made his reputation as a brilliant pianist, and much of his music, both for piano and for other instruments, was of considerable technical difficulty. As composers began to demand greater and greater feats of virtuosity from their performers, performing artists themselves came to attract more attention. Singers had already, in the 18th century, commanded high fees and attracted crowds of fanatical admirers, and continued to do so. Now, however, they were joined by instrumental virtuosos, some of whom were also highly successful composers.

The life of Frédéric Chopin (1810–1849) seems almost too romantic to be true [15.4]. Both in his piano performances and in the music he composed he united the aristocratic fire of his native Poland with the elegance and sophistication of Paris, where he spent much of his life. His concerts created a sensation throughout Europe, while his piano works exploited (if they did not always create) new musical forms like the *nocturne,* a short piano piece in which an expressive, if melancholy, melody floats over a murmuring accompaniment. Chopin is characteristically romantic in his use of music to express his own personal emotions. The structure of works like the twenty-four *Preludes,* Op. 28, is dictated not by formal considerations but by the feeling of the moment. Thus the first three take us from excited agitation to brooding melancholy to bubbling high spirits in just over three minutes.

In private, Chopin's life was dominated by a much-talked-about liaison with the leading French woman author of the day, George Sand (1804–1876). His early death from tuberculosis put the final romantic touch to the life of a composer who has been described as the soul of the piano.

15.4 Eugène Delacroix. 1789–1863. *Frédéric Chopin.* 1838. Oil on canvas, 18 × 15" (45 × 38 cm). Louvre, Paris. Delacroix's portrait of his friend captures Chopin's romantic introspection. Delacroix himself was a great lover of music, though perhaps surprisingly the great romantic painter preferred Mozart to Beethoven.

Franz Liszt (1811–1886) shared Chopin's brilliant skill at the keyboard and joined to it his own more robust temperament. A natural romantic, he ran the gamut of romantic themes and experiences. After beginning his career as a handsome, impetuous young rebel, the idol of the salons of Paris, he conducted a number of well-publicized affairs and ended up by turning to the consolations of religion. His vast musical output includes some of the most difficult of all piano works (many of them inspired by the beauties of nature), two symphonies on the characteristically romantic subjects of Faust and Dante (with special emphasis, in the latter case, on the *Inferno*), and a host of pieces that made use of the folk tunes of his native Hungary.

Assessment of Liszt's true musical stature is difficult. He was probably a better composer than his present reputation suggests, although not so great a one as his contemporaries (and he) thought. As a virtuoso performer even *he* takes second place to Nicolò Paganini (1782–1840), the greatest violinist of the age, if not of all time.

Like Chopin and Liszt, Paganini also composed, but it was his public performances that won him his amazing reputation. So apparently impossible were the technical feats he so casually executed that rumor spread that, like Faust, he had sold his soul to the devil. This typically romantic exaggeration was, of course, assiduously encouraged by Paganini himself, who cultivated a suitably ghoulish appearance to enhance his public image. Nothing more clearly illustrates the 19th century's obsession with music as emotional expression (in this case diabolical) than the fact that Paganini's concerts earned him both honors throughout Europe and a considerable fortune.

Musical Nationalism

Both Chopin and Liszt introduced the music of their native lands into their works, Chopin in his *mazurkas* and *polonaises* (traditional Polish dances) and Liszt in his *Hungarian Rhapsodies*. For the most part, however, they adapted their musical styles to the prevailing international fashions of the day.

Other composers placed greater emphasis on their native musical traditions. In Russia a group of five composers (Moussorgsky, Balakirev, Borodin, Cui, and Rimsky-Korsakov) consciously set out to exploit their rich musical heritage. The greatest of the five was Modest Moussorgsky (1839–1881), whose opera *Boris Godunov* (1874) is based on an episode in Russian history. It makes full use of Russian folk songs and religious music in telling the story of Tsar Boris Godunov, who rises to power by killing the true heir to the throne. Although Boris is the opera's single most important character, the work is really dominated by the chorus, which represents the Russian people. Moussorgsky powerfully depicts their changing emotions, from bewilderment to awe, to fear, to rage, and in doing so gives voice to the feelings of his nation.

Elsewhere in Eastern Europe composers were finding similar inspiration in national themes and folk music. The Czech composer Bedřich Smetana (1824–1884), who aligned himself with his native Bohemia in the uprising against Austrian rule in 1848, composed a set of seven pieces for orchestra that bear the collective title of *Má Vlast (My Fatherland)*. The best known, *Vltava (The Moldau)*, depicts the course of the river Vltava as it flows from its source through the countryside to the capital city of Prague. His fellow countryman Antonin Dvořák (1841–1904) also drew on the rich tradition of folk music in works like his *Slavonic Dances*, colorful settings of Czech folk tunes.

Opera in Italy: Verdi

Throughout the 19th century opera achieved new heights of popularity in Europe and "operamania" began to spread to America, where opera houses opened in New York in 1854 and Chicago in 1865. On both sides of the Atlantic opera houses are still dominated by the works of the two 19th-century giants in the history of opera—the Italian Giuseppe Verdi and the German Richard Wagner.

When Giuseppe Verdi (1813–1901) began his career, the Italian operagoing public was interested in beautiful and brilliant singing rather than realism of plot or action. This love of what is often called *bel canto* (beautiful singing) should not be misunderstood. Composers like Gaetano Donizetti (1797–1848) and Vincenzo Bellini (1801–1835) used their music to express sincere and deep emotions and even drama, but the emotional expression was achieved primarily by means of song and not by a convincing dramatic situation. The plots of their operas serve only as an excuse for music; thus characters in *bel canto* operas are frequently given to fits of madness in order to give musical expression to deep emotion. Within the necessary framework provided by the plot a great singer, inspired by great music, could use the magic of the human voice to communicate a dramatic emotion that transcended the time and place of the action. Under the inspiration of Verdi and Wagner, however, opera began to move in a different direction. The subjects composers chose remained larger than

15.5 Maria Callas as Norma in Bellini's opera of the same title. Covent Garden, London, 1957. The Greek-American Maria Callas (1923–1977), one of the great sopranos of this century, made her professional debut in Verona in 1947. Her first appearances at La Scala, Milan, Covent Garden, London, and the Metropolitan Opera, New York, followed in 1950, 1952, and 1956.

life, but dramatic credibility became increasingly important.

Beginning in the 1950s, however, many music lovers began to discover a rich source of musical beauty and even drama in a work like Bellini's *Norma,* first performed in 1831. The revival and subsequent popularity of much early 19th-century opera are due in large measure to the performances and recordings of Maria Callas [15.5], whose enormous talent showed how a superb interpreter could bring such works to life. Following her example, other singers turned to *bel canto* opera, with the result that performances of *Norma* and of Donizetti's best-known opera, *Lucia di Lammermoor* (1835), have become a regular feature of modern operatic life, while lesser-known works are revived in increasing numbers.

The revival of *bel canto* works has certainly not been at the expense of Verdi, perhaps the best-loved of all opera composers. His works showed a new concern for dramatic and psychological truth. Even in his early operas like *Nabucco* (1842) or *Luisa Miller* (1849) Verdi was able to give convincing expression to human relationships. At the same time his music became associated with the growing nationalist movement in Italy. *Nabucco,* for example, deals ostensibly with the captivity of the Jews in Babylon and their oppression by Nebuchadnezzar, but the plight of the Jews became symbolic of the Italians' suffering under Austrian rule. The chorus the captives sing as they think of happier days, "*Va, pensiero . . .*" ("Fly, thought, on golden wings, go settle on the slopes and hills where the soft breezes of our native land smell gentle and mild"), became a kind of theme song for the Italian nationalist movement, the Risorgimento, in large measure because of the inspiring yet nostalgic quality of Verdi's tune.

Verdi's musical and dramatic powers reached their first great climax in three major masterpieces, *Rigoletto* (1851), *Il Trovatore* (1853), and *La Traviata* (1853), which remain among the most popular of all operas. They are very different in subject and atmosphere. *Il Trovatore* is perhaps the most traditional in approach, with its gory and involved plot centering around the troubadour Manrico and its abundance of superb melodies. In *Rigoletto* Verdi achieved one of his most convincing character portrayals in the hunchback court jester Rigoletto, who is forced to suppress his human feelings and play the fool to his vicious and lecherous master, the Duke of Mantua. With *La Traviata* Verdi broke new ground in the history of opera by dealing with contemporary life rather than a historical or mythological subject.

The principal character of *La Traviata* is Violetta, a popular courtesan in Paris, who falls in love with Alfredo Germont, a young man from the provinces, and decides to give up her sophisticated life in the capital for country bliss. Her reputation follows her there, however, in the form of Alfredo's father. In a long and emotional encounter he persuades her to abandon his son and put an end to the disgrace she is bringing on his family [15.6]. Violetta, who is aware that she is suffering from a fatal illness, returns alone to the cruel glitter of her life in Paris. By the end of the opera, her money gone, she lies dying in poverty and solitude. At this tragic moment Verdi gives her one of his most moving arias, "Addio del passato" ("Goodbye bright dreams of the past"), as she thinks back over her earlier life. Alfredo, who has finally learned of the sacrifice she has made for his sake, rushes to find her, only to arrive for a final farewell—Violetta dies in his arms.

Throughout the later part of his career Verdi's powers continued to develop and enrich, until in 1887 he produced in *Otello,* a version of Shake-

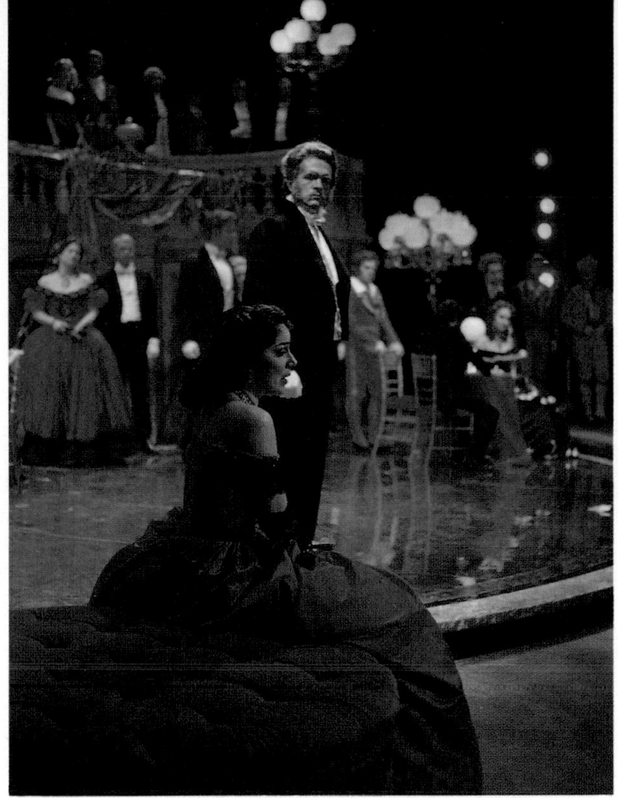

15.6 *La Traviata.* Metropolitan Opera, New York, 1981. Alfredo's father begs Violetta to leave his son. This is the scene in Act II of Verdi's opera, set in the salon of Violetta's and Alfredo's country house. The singers are Cornell MacNeil as Giorgio Germont and Catherine Malfitano as Violetta. *La Traviata* was first performed in Venice in 1853 and in New York in 1856. Many noted sopranos have taken the role of Violetta, including Maria Callas (Figure 15.5).

speare's tragedy *Othello,* perhaps the supreme work in the entire Italian operatic tradition. From the first shattering chord that opens the first act to Otello's heartbreaking death at the end of the last, Verdi rose to the Shakespearean challenge with music of unsurpassed eloquence. In a work that is so consistently inspired it seems invidious to pick out highlights, but the ecstatic love duet of Act I between Otello and Desdemona deserves mention as one of the noblest and most moving of all depictions of romantic passion.

Opera in Germany: Wagner

The impact of Richard Wagner (1813–1883) on his times went far beyond the opera house. Not only did his works change the course of the history of music, but many of his ideas had a profound effect on writers and painters [15.7]. This truly revolutionary figure even became actively involved with the revolutionary uprisings of 1848 and spent a number of years in exile in Switzerland.

It is difficult to summarize the variety of Wagner's ideas, which ranged from art to politics to vegetarianism and in general are not noted for their tolerance. Behind many of his writings on

15.7 Wilhelm Beckmann. *Richard Wagner at His Home in Bayreuth.* 1880. Oil on canvas, 4'¾" × 5'1⅝" (1.25 × 1.58 m). Richard Wagner Museum, Triebschen-Luzern, Switzerland. Characteristically, Wagner is holding forth to his wife and friends, in this case Liszt in his abbé garb and the author Hans von Wolzogen. At lower left are some stage designs for Wagner's last work, *Parsifal.*

opera and drama lay the concept that the most powerful form of artistic expression was one that united all the arts, music, painting, poetry, movement, in a single work of art, the *Gesamtkunstwerk* (complete-art work). To illustrate this theory Wagner wrote both the words and music of what he called "music dramas" and even designed and built a special theater for their performance at Bayreuth, where they are still performed every year at the Bayreuth Festival.

A number of characteristics link all Wagner's mature works. First, he abolished the old separation between recitatives (in which the action was advanced) and arias, duets, or other individual musical numbers (which held up the action). Wagner's music flowed continuously from the beginning to the end of each act with no pauses. Second, he eliminated the vocal display and virtuosity that had been traditional in opera. Wagner roles are certainly not easy to sing, but their difficulties are always for dramatic reasons and not to show off a singer's skill. Third, he put a new emphasis on the orchestra, which not only accompanied the singers but also provided a rich musical argument of its own. This was enhanced by his fourth contribution, the famous device of the *leitmotiv* (leading motif), which consisted of giving each of the principal characters, ideas, and even objects an individual theme of his, her, or its own. By recalling these themes and by combining them or changing them Wagner achieved highly complex dramatic and psychological effects.

Wagner generally drew his subjects from German mythology. By peopling his stage with heroes, gods, giants, magic swans, and the like, he aimed to create universal dramas that would express universal emotions. In his most monumental achievement, *The Ring of the Nibelung,* written between 1851 and 1874, he even represented the end of the world. *The Ring* consists of four separate music dramas, *The Rhinegold, The Valkyrie, Siegfried,* and *The Twilight of the Gods,* the plot of which defies summary. In music of incredible richness Wagner depicted not only the actions and reactions of his characters but also the wonders of nature. In *Siegfried,* for example, we hear the rustling of the forest and the songs of woodbirds, while throughout *The Ring* and especially in the well-known "Rhine Journey" from *The Twilight of the Gods* the mighty river Rhine sounds through the music. At the same time *The Ring* has a number of philosophical and political messages, many of them derived from Schopenhauer (see page 427). One of its main themes is that power corrupts, while Wagner also adopted Goethe's idea of redemption by a woman in the final resolution of the drama.

No brief discussion can begin to do justice to so stupendous a work. It is probably easier to see Wagner's genius in operation by looking at a work on small scale, a single self-contained music drama—albeit one of some four hours' duration. *Tristan and Isolde* was first performed in 1865, and its very first notes opened a new musical era. Its subject is the overwhelming love of the English knight Tristan and the Irish princess Isolde, so great that the pair betray his dearest friend and lord and her husband, King Mark of Cornwall, and so overpowering that it can achieve its complete fulfillment only in death.

Wagner's typically romantic preoccupation with love and death may seem morbid and farfetched, but under the sway of his intoxicating music it is difficult to resist. The sense of passion awakened but unfulfilled is expressed in the famous opening bars of the Prelude, with their theme that yearns upward and the discords that dissolve into one another only to hang unresolved in the air:

The music gives the sense of having no settled harmony or clear direction. This lack of *tonality,* used here for dramatic purpose, was to have a considerable influence on modern music.

The core of *Tristan and Isolde* is the long love scene at the heart of the second act, where the music reaches heights of erotic ecstasy too potent for some listeners. Whereas Verdi's love duet in *Otello* presents two noble spirits responding to one another with deep feeling but with dignity, Wagner's characters are racked by passions they cannot begin to control. If ever music expressed what neither words nor images could depict it is in the overwhelming physical emotion of this scene [15.8]. The pulsating orchestra and the surging voices of the lovers build up an almost unbearable tension that Wagner suddenly breaks with the arrival of King Mark. Once again, as in the Prelude, fulfillment is denied both to the lovers and to us.

That fulfillment is reached only at the very end of the work in Isolde's *"Liebestod"* ("Love Death"). Tristan has died, and over his body Isolde begins to sing a kind of incantation. She imagines she sees the spirit of her beloved, and in obscure, broken words describes the bliss of union in death before sinking lifeless upon him. Although the *"Liebestod"* makes its full effect only when heard at the end of the entire work, even out of context the emotional power of the music as it rises to its climax can hardly fail to affect the sensitive listener.

15.8 Scene from *Tristan and Isolde,* Act II. This is the Bayreuth staging designed and produced by Wagner's grandson, Wieland Wagner. First mounted in 1962, the production starred Wolfgang Windgassen and Birgit Nilsson as the lovers. The abstract sets and complex lighting have influenced much stage design since then.

ROMANTIC ART

Painting at the Turn of the Century: Goya

Just as Beethoven and his Romantic successors rejected the idealizing and universal qualities of classical music to achieve a more intense and personal communication, so painters began to abandon the lofty, remote world of neoclassical art for more vivid images. In the case of painting, however, the question of style was far more related to political developments. We have already seen in Chapter 14 that neoclassicism had become, as it were, the official artistic dress of the Revolution, so it was not easy for a painter working in France, still the center of artistic life, suddenly to abandon the revolutionary style. The problem is particularly visible in the works of Jacques Louis David (1748–1825), whose *Oath of the Horatii* (see Figure 14.1, page 392) had been inspired by the prerevolutionary longing for austere Republican virtue. By the end of the Revolution, David had come to appreciate the advantages of peace; his painting *The Battle of the Romans and the Sabines* of 1799 [15.9] expresses his desire for an end to violence and bloodshed. The subject is drawn from Roman mythology and focuses on that moment when Hersilia, wife of the Roman leader Romulus, interrupts the battle between Romans and Sabines and begs for an end to war. Its significance is precisely the reverse of the *Oath of the Horatii.* In place of a masculine call to arms and sacrifice, David shows his heroine making an impassioned plea for peace. The style, however, remains firmly neoclassical, not only in the choice of subject but also in its execution. For all the weapons and armor, there is no sign of actual physical violence. The two opponents, with their heroic figures and noble brows, are idealized along typical neoclassical lines. The emotional gestures of Hersilia and others are also stylized and frozen. The painting is powerful, but it depicts a concept rather than individual human feelings.

The contrast between the neoclassical representation of the horrors of war and a romantic treatment of the same theme can be seen by comparing David's painting with *Execution of the Madrileños on*

15.9 Jacques Louis David. *The Battle of the Romans and the Sabines.* 1799. Oil on canvas, 12'8" × 17'¾" (3.86 × 5.2 m). Louvre, Paris. David may have intended his depiction of feminine virtue as a tribute to his wife, who had left him when he voted for the execution of Louis XVI but returned to him when he was imprisoned for a time.

15.10 Francisco Goya. *Execution of the Madrileños on May 3, 1808.* 1814. Oil on canvas, 8'8¾" × 11'3¾" (2.66 × 3.45 m). Prado, Madrid. The painting shows the execution of a group of citizens of Madrid who had demonstrated against the French occupation by Napoleon's troops. The Spanish government commissioned the painting after the expulsion of the French army.

May 3, 1808 [15.10] by Francisco Goya (1746–1828). In Goya's painting, nothing is idealized. The horror and the terror of the victims, their faceless executioners, the blood streaming in the dust all combine to create an almost unbearable image of protest against human cruelty. Goya's painting is romantic because it conveys to us his own personal emotions at the thought of the executions and because, great artist that he was, his emotions become our own.

As Beethoven convinces us of the necessity to struggle against the injustices of human beings and of Fate by his own passionate commitment, so Goya by his intensity urges us to condemn the atrocities of war. Furthermore, both Beethoven and Goya shared a common sympathy with the oppressed and a hatred of tyranny. The soldiers firing their bayoneted guns in Goya's painting were serving in the army of Napoleon; the event shown took place some four years after Beethoven had seen the danger Napoleon presented to the cause of liberty and had erased his name from the "Eroica."

It was, of course, easier for an artist outside France to abandon the artistic language of neoclassicism for more direct ways of communication. Although from 1824 to his death Goya lived in France, he was born in Spain and spent most of his working life there. Removed from the mainstream of artistic life, he seems never to have been attracted by the neoclassical style. Some of his first paintings were influenced by the rococo style of Tiepolo (see Figure 14.8, page 397), who was in Spain from 1762 until 1770, but his own introspective nature and the strength of his feelings seem to have driven him to find more direct means of expression. Personal suffering may have played a part also, since Goya, like Beethoven, became totally deaf.

In 1799 Goya became official painter to Charles IV, the king of Spain, and was commissioned to produce a series of formal court portraits. The most famous of these, *The Family of Charles IV* [15.11], was deliberately modeled on Velásquez' *Las Meninas* (see Figure 13.24, page 367). Goya shows us the royal family—king, queen, children, and grandchildren—in the artist's studio, where they have come to visit. The comparison he intends us to make between his own painting and that of his distinguished predecessor is devastating. At first glance Goya's painting may seem just another official portrait, but it does not take a viewer very long to realize that something is very wrong at the court of Spain. Instead of grace and elegance,

15.11 Francisco Goya. *The Family of Charles IV.* 1800. Oil on canvas, 9'2" × 11' (2.79 × 3.35 m). Prado, Madrid. In this scathing portrayal of the Spanish royal family the artist himself is working away quietly at the far left. The French writer Alphonse Daudet said the painting showed "the grocer and his family who have just won top prize in the lottery."

15.12 Francisco Goya. *Saturn Devouring One of His Sons*. c. 1821. Fresco detached on canvas, 4'9½" × 2'8⅛" (1.46 × .83 m). Prado, Madrid. The painting originally decorated a wall in Goya's country house, La Quinta del Sordo (Deaf Man's Villa).

Goya's patrons radiate arrogance, vanity, and stupidity. The king and queen, in particular, are especially unappealing.

The effect of Goya's painting is not so much one of realism as of personal comment, although there is every reason to believe that the queen was in fact quite as ugly as she appears here. The artist is communicating his own feelings of disgust at the emptiness, indeed the evil, of court life. That he does so through the medium of an official court portrait that is itself a parody of one of the most famous of all court portraits is of course an intentional irony.

Even at the time of his official court paintings Goya was obsessed by the darker side of life. His engraving *The Sleep of Reason Produces Monsters* (see Figure 15.1) foreshadowed the work of his last years. Between 1820 and 1822 he covered the walls of his own house with paintings that depict a nightmare world of horror and despair. *Saturn Devouring One of His Sons* [15.12] makes use of a classical myth to portray the god of Time in the act of destroying humanity, but the treatment owes nothing to neoclassicism. Indeed, no simple stylistic label seems adequate to describe so personal a vision. The intensity of expression, the fantastic nature of the subject, and the mood of introspection are all typically romantic, yet the totality transcends its components. No one but Goya has ever expressed a vision of human existence in quite these terms.

Painting and Architecture in France: Romantics and Realists

Although the events of the French Revolution and Napoleon's subsequent dictatorship had an immediate impact on artists, writers, and musicians outside France, their effect on French artists was more complex. As we have seen earlier in this chapter, David was never able to throw off the influence of neoclassicism, and his immediate successors had a hard time finding a style that could do justice to romantic themes while remaining within neoclassical limits. One solution was offered by Anne-Louis Girodet-Trioson (1767–1824), whose painting *The Entombment of Atala* [15.13] depicts a highly romantic subject acted out, as it were, by classical figures.

The subject is from a popular novel by the French romantic novelist René de Chateaubriand (1768–1848) and depicts the burial of its heroine, Atala, in the American wilderness where the book is set. The other figures are her Indian lover, Choctas, and a priest from a nearby mission in the Florida swamps. The story of the painting therefore contains just about every conceivable element of romanticism: an exotic location, emphasis on personal emotion, the theme of unfulfilled love. Girodet provides for his characters a romantic setting, with its dramatic light and mysterious jungle background, but the figures themselves are idealized in a thoroughly classical way. Atala's wan beauty and elegant drapery and the muscular nudity of her lover are obviously reminiscent of clas-

15.13 Anne-Louis Girodet-Trioson. ***The Entombment of Atala.*** **1808. Oil on canvas, 6'11¾" × 8'9" (2.13 × 2.67 m). Louvre, Paris. The anticlassical nature of the subject is emphasized by the Christian symbolism of the two crosses, one on Atala's breast and the other rather improbably placed high up in the jungle outside the cave.**

sical models. Only the mysterious figure of the old priest provides a hint of romantic gloom.

It took a real-life disaster and a major national scandal to inspire the first genuinely romantic French painting. In 1816 a French government vessel, the *Medusa,* bound for Africa with an incompetent political appointee as captain, was wrecked in a storm. The 149 passengers and crew members were crowded onto a hastily improvised raft that drifted for days under the equatorial sun. Hunger, thirst, madness, and even, it was rumored, cannibalism had reduced the survivors to fifteen by the time the raft was finally sighted.

The young French painter Théodore Géricault (1791–1824), whose original enthusiasm for Napoleon had been replaced by adherence to the liberal cause, depicted the moment of the sighting of the raft in his painting *Raft of the Medusa* [15.14].

15.14 Théodore Géricault. 1791–1824. *Raft of the Medusa.* 1818. Oil on canvas, 16'1¼" × 23'6" (4.91 × 7.16 m). Louvre, Paris. Note the careful composition of this huge work, built around a line that leads from the bottom left corner to the top right, where a survivor desperately waves his shirt.

EAST MEETS WEST

European Perceptions of the American Indian

Chateaubriand and Girodet were by no means the first Europeans to be impressed by the nobility and simple grandeur of North America's native Indian population. In 1687 the governor of French Canada captured a group of Iroquois chieftains and shipped them to Louis XIV. The king, scandalized by so shocking a breach of protocol against fellow rulers, ordered them to be immediately released, entertained them as distinguished visitors, and had them sent home in style. In general the Indians fared better at the hands of the French colonists in North America than at those of the British; the French did not expropriate Indian territory, and their missionaries encouraged peaceful settlement.

By the beginning of the 19th century European travelers were beginning to see for themselves the superb natural setting of Indian culture, untouched by industrialization or the plagues of civilized life; their general reaction can be summed up in the words of one visitor to the Mohawk, near modern Utica, N.Y.: "No more roads, no more towns, no monarchy, no republic, no presidents, no kings. . . !"

In the course of traveling round America to provide himself with background material for *Atala,* Chateaubriand sailed down the Ohio River into Tennessee, where he met some Seminole Indians from Florida (he calls them Siminoles). They were horsetraders by profession, but, according to the great romantic novelist they were driven by passions, "not of rank, education, or prejudice, but of nature, untrammelled and unimpaired, proceeding only to their goal, a valley that could never be discovered, a river without name." The Seminoles told him of Indian girls abandoned by white lovers in Pensacola and of others who had managed to exploit their European exploiters.

The early-19th-century American writers like James Fenimore Cooper (1789–1851) convey an equal respect for the Indians' life at one with nature; and in his poem *Hiawatha* Henry Wadsworth Longfellow (1807–1882) used Indian myths to try to provide America a legendary past. By the end of the century, however, the "noble savage" had become the "ruthless savage," as American and European pioneers in the Far West struggled to conquer and hold on to Indian territory. In the process the Indians became perceived as the enemies of progress, and their remoteness from "civilization" as a weakness. The white settlers, in order to justify the wholesale slaughter of the native population or depopulation of vast tracts of the country, portrayed their Indian enemies as cruel and cunning. The consequence was the stereotyped image of popular fiction and movies.

Horror at the suffering of the victims and anger at the corruption and incompetence of the ship's officers (and their political supporters) inspired a work that, from its first exhibition in 1819, created a sensation in artistic circles. Even the general public flocked to see a painting that so dramatically illustrated contemporary events. In the process they became exposed to the principles of romantic painting. Géricault's work deliberately rejects the ideal beauty of classical models. The agonizing torment of the survivors is powerfully rendered, and the dramatic use of lighting underlines the intense emotions of the scene.

When Géricault died following a fall from a horse, the cause of romanticism was taken up by his young friend and admirer, Eugène Delacroix (1798–1863), whose name has become synonymous with romantic painting. Although the subjects of many of his paintings involve violent emotions, Delacroix himself seems to have been aloof and reserved. He never married, or for that matter formed any lasting relationship. His *Journal* reveals him as a man constantly stimulated by ideas and experience but he preferred to live his life through his art, a true romantic. Among his few close friends was Chopin; his portrait of the composer (see Figure 15.4) seems to symbolize the introspective creative vision of the romantic artist.

Like his mentor Géricault, Delacroix supported the liberal movements of the day. His painting *Massacre at Chios* [15.15] depicted a particularly brutal event in the Greek War of Independence. In 1824, the year in which Lord Byron died while supporting the Greek cause, the Turks massacred some 90 percent of the population of the Greek island of Chios, and Delacroix' painting on the subject was intended to rouse popular indignation. It certainly roused the indignation of the traditional artists of the day, one of whom dubbed it "the massacre of painting," principally because of its revolutionary use of color. Whereas David and other neoclassical painters had drawn their forms and then filled

15.15 Eugène Delacroix. *Massacre at Chios.* 1824. Oil on canvas, 13'7" × 11'10" (4.19 × 3.64 m). Louvre, Paris. Rather than depict a single scene, the painter chose to combine several episodes, contrasting the static misery of the figures on the left with a swirl of activity on the right.

them in with color, Delacroix used color itself to create form. The result is a much more fluid use of paint.

Lord Byron figures again in another of Delacroix' best-known paintings, since it was on one of the poet's works that the artist based *The Death of Sardanapalus* [15.16]. The Assyrian king, faced with the destruction of his palace by the Medes, decided to prevent his enemies from enjoying his possessions after his death by ordering that his wives, horses, and dogs be killed and their bodies piled

15.16 Eugène Delacroix. *The Death of Sardanapalus.* 1826. Oil on canvas, c. 12'1" × 16'3" (3.68 × 4.95 m). Louvre, Paris. The painting makes no attempt to achieve archaeological accuracy but concentrates on exploiting the violence and cruelty of the story. Delacroix himself called this work "Massacre No. 2," a reference to his earlier painting, the *Massacre at Chios* (Figure 15.15). Although this suggests a certain detachment on the artist's part, there is no lack of energy or commitment in the free, almost violent, brush strokes.

15.17 Jean-Auguste-Dominique Ingres. *Jupiter and Thetis.* 1811. Oil on canvas, 10'10" × 8'5" (3.3 × 2.57 m). Musée Granet, Aix-en-Provençe. The figure of Jupiter, with his youthful face surrounded by a vast wreath of beard and hair, is highly unconventional. Thetis' arms and throat are purposely distorted to emphasize her supplication.

up, together with his treasures, at the foot of the funeral pyre he intended for himself. The opulent, violent theme is treated with appropriate drama; the savage brutality of the foreground contrasts with the lonely, brooding figure of the king reclining on his couch above. Over the whole scene, however, hovers an air of unreality, even of fantasy, as if Delacroix is trying to convey not so much the sufferings of the victims as the intensity of his own imagination.

Although with Delacroix' advocacy romanticism acquired a vast popular following, not all French artists joined the romantic cause. A fierce and bitter rear-guard action was fought by the leading neoclassical proponents, headed by Jean-Auguste-Dominique Ingres (1780–1867), who was, in his own very different way, as great a painter as Delacroix. The self-appointed defender of classicism, Ingres once said of Delacroix that "his art is the complete expression of an incomplete intelligence." Characteristically, his war against romantic painting was waged vindictively and on the most personal terms. Now that the dust has settled, however, it becomes clear that Ingres himself, far from religiously adhering to classical doctrines, was unable to suppress a romantic streak of his own. His extraordinary painting *Jupiter and Thetis* [15.17] deals with an event from Homer's *Iliad* and shows Thetis, the mother of Achilles, begging the father of gods and mortals to avenge an insult by the Greek commander Agamemnon to her son by allowing the Trojans to be victorious. The subject may be classical, but Ingres' treatment of it is strikingly personal, even bizarre. Sensuality blends with an almost hallucinatory sharpness of detail to create a memorable if curiously disturbing image. Even in his more conventional portraits [15.18] Ingres' stupendous technique endows subject and setting with an effect that is the very reverse of academic.

The style that in the end succeeded in replacing the full-blown romanticism of Delacroix and his followers was not that of the neoclassical school,

15.18 Jean-Auguste-Dominique Ingres. *La Comtesse d'Haussonville.* 1845. Oil on canvas, 4'5½" × 3'¼" (1.36 × .92 m). Frick Collection, New York. The artist seems to have been more interested in his subject's dress, which is marvelously painted, than in her personality. The reflection in the mirror reinforces the highly polished air of the painting.

15.19 Honoré Daumier. ***Le Ventre législatif (The Legislative Belly).*** **1834. Lithograph, $11\frac{1}{16} \times 17\frac{1}{16}$" (28.1 × 43.3 cm). Philadelphia Museum of Art (gift of Carl Zigrosser). Although obviously caricatures, the politicians ranged in tiers are recognizable as individual members of the legislative assembly of the time.**

with its emphasis on idealism, but a style that stressed precisely the reverse qualities. The greatest French painters of the second half of the 19th century were realists, who used the everyday events of the world around them to express their views of life. One of the first realist artists was Honoré Daumier (1808–1879), who followed the example of Goya in using his work to criticize the evils of society in general and government in particular. In *The Legislative Body*—or, more accurately, *Belly* [15.19]—he produced a powerful image of the greed and corruption of political opportunists that has lost neither its bitterness nor, unfortunately, its relevance.

Equally political was the realism of Gustave Courbet (1819–1877), a fervent champion of the working class, whose ability to identify with ordinary people won him the label of Socialist. Courbet tried to correct this political impression of his artistic and philosophical position in a vast and not entirely successful allegorical work, *The Studio* [15.20]. Like Goya's royal portrait (see Figure 15.11), the painting deliberately evokes memories of Velásquez' *Las Meninas* (see Figure 13.24, page

15.20 Gustave Courbet. ***The Studio: A Real Allegory of the Last Seven Years of My Life.*** **1855. Oil on canvas, $11'9\frac{3}{4}" \times 19'6\frac{5}{8}"$ (3.6 × 5.96 m). Louvre, Paris. Although most of the figures can be convincingly identified as symbols or real people, no one has ever satisfactorily explained the small boy admiring Courbet's work or the cat at his feet.**

15.21 Charles Garnier. Opéra, Paris. 1861–1875. The incredibly rich and complex ornamentation has earned this style of architecture the label neo-baroque.

367), although the artist is now placed firmly in the center of the picture, hard at work on a landscape, inspired by a nude model who may represent Realism or Truth. The various other figures symbolize the forces that made up Courbet's world. There is some doubt as to the precise identification of many of them, and it is not even clear that Courbet himself had any single allegory in mind. The total effect of the confusion, unintentional though it may be, is to underline the essentially romantic origins of Courbet's egocentric vision.

Neither romanticism nor its realistic vision made much impression on architectural styles in 19th-century France. French architects retained a fondness for classical forms and abandoned them only to revive the styles of the Renaissance. In some of the public buildings designed to meet the needs of the age, however, the elaborate decoration makes use of classical elements to achieve an ornateness

15.22 Caspar David Friedrich. *Cloister Graveyard in the Snow.* 1810. Oil on panel, 3'11⅝" × 5'10" (1.21 × 1.78 m). Formerly Nationalgalerie, Berlin (now lost). The vast bare trees in the foreground and the ruined Gothic abbey behind emphasize the insignificance of the human figures.

of effect that is not very far from the opulent splendor of Delacroix' *Death of Sardanapalus.*

The most ornate of all 19th-century French buildings was the Paris Opera [15.21] of Charles Garnier (1824–1898). The new opera house had to be sufficiently large to accommodate the growing public for opera and sufficiently ostentatious to satisfy its taste. Garnier's building, designed in 1861 and finally opened in 1875, makes use of classical ornamentation like Corinthian columns and huge winged Victories, but the total effect is highly unclassical, a riot of confusion that would surely have appalled classical and Renaissance architects alike.

Painting in Germany and England

Unlike their French counterparts, romantic artists in both England and Germany were particularly attracted by the possibilities offered by landscape painting. The emotional range of their work illustrates once again the versatility of the romantic style. The German painter Caspar David Friedrich (1774–1840) seems to have drawn some of his Gothic gloom from a tradition that had been strong in Germany since the Middle Ages, although he uses it to romantic effect. His *Cloister Graveyard in the Snow* [15.22], in fact, illustrates a number of romantic preoccupations, with its ruined medieval architecture and melancholy dreamlike atmosphere.

The English painter John Constable (1776–1837), on the other hand, shared the deep and warm love of nature expressed by Wordsworth. His paintings convey not only the physical beauties of the landscape but also a sense of the less tangible aspects of the natural world. In *Hay Wain* [15.23], for example, we not only see the peaceful rustic scene, with its squat, comforting house on the left, but we can even sense that light and quality of atmosphere, prompted by the billowing clouds that, responsible for the fertility of the countryside, seem about to release their moisture.

Constable's use of color pales besides that of his contemporary, Joseph Mallord William Turner (1775–1851). In a sense, the precise subjects of

15.23 John Constable. *Hay Wain.* 1821. Oil on canvas, 4'2½" × 6'1" (1.28 × 1.85 m). National Gallery, London (reproduced by courtesy of the Trustees). Note Constable's bold use of color, which impressed Delacroix.

15.24 Joseph Mallord William Turner. British, 1775–1851. *The Slave Ship.* 1840. Oil on canvas, 35¾ × 48¼" (90.8 × 122.6 cm). Museum of Fine Arts, Boston (Henry Lillie Pierce Fund). The title of this painting is an abbreviation of a longer one: *Slavers Throwing Overboard the Dead and Dying; Typhoon Coming On.* Turner includes a horrifying detail at lower center: the chains still binding the slaves whose desperate hands show above the water. Note the extreme contrast between Turner's interpretation of color and light and that of the American luminists as shown in Heade's painting (Figure 15.31).

Turner's paintings are irrelevant. All his mature works use light, color, and movement to represent a cosmic union of the elements in which earth, sky, fire, and water dissolve into one another and every trace of the material world disappears. His technique is seen at its most characteristic in *The Slave Ship* [15.24].

Like Géricault's *Raft of the Medusa* (see Figure 15.14), Turner's *Slave Ship* deals with a social disgrace of the time; in this case the horrifyingly common habit of the captains of ships loaded with slaves to jettison their entire cargo if an epidemic broke out. Turner only incidentally illustrates his specific subject—the detail of drowning figures in the lower right corner seems to have been added as an afterthought—and concentrates instead on conveying his vision of the grandeur and mystery of the universe.

LITERATURE IN THE 19TH CENTURY

Goethe

The towering figure of Johann Wolfgang von Goethe (1749–1832) spans the transition from neoclassicism to romanticism in literature like a colossus. So great was the range of his genius that in the course of a long and immensely productive life he wrote works in a bewildering variety of disciplines. One of the first writers to rebel against the principles of neoclassicism, he used both poetry and prose to express the most turbulent emotions; yet he continued to produce works written according to neoclassical principles of clarity and balance until his last years, when he expressed in his writing a profound if abstruse symbolism.

Although the vein of romanticism is only one of many that runs through Goethe's work, it is an important one. As a young man Goethe studied law, first at Leipzig and then at Strasburg, where by 1770 he was already writing lyric poetry of astonishing directness and spontaneity. By 1773 he was acknowledged as the leader of the literary movement known as *Sturm und Drang* (Storm and Stress). This German manifestation of romanticism rebelled against the formal structure and order of neoclassism, replacing it with an emphasis on originality, imagination, and feelings. Its chief subjects were nature, primitive emotions, and protest against established authority. Although the Storm and Stress movement was originally confined to literature, its precepts were felt elsewhere. For instance, it was partly under the inspiration of this movement that Beethoven developed his fiery style.

The climax of this period in Goethe's life is represented by his novel *The Sufferings of Young Werther* (1774), which describes how an idealistic young man comes to feel increasingly disillusioned and frustrated by life, develops a hopeless passion for a happily married woman, and ends his agony by putting a bullet through his head. All of these events but the last were autobiographical. Instead of committing suicide, Goethe left town and turned his life experiences into the novel that won him international fame. Not surprisingly it became a key work of the romantic movement. Young men began to dress in the blue jacket and yellow trousers Werther is described as wearing, and some, disappointed in love, even committed suicide with copies of the book in their pockets—a dramatic if regrettable illustration of Goethe's ability to communicate his own emotions to others [15.25].

15.25 Tony Johannot. Illustration for a later edition of *The Sufferings of Young Werther.* 1852. By permission of Houghton Library, Harvard University. The hero has just declared his hopeless passion for Charlotte.

The years around the turn of the century found Goethe extending the range of his output. Along with such plays as the classical drama *Iphigeneia in Tauris,* which expressed his belief in purity and sincere humanity, were stormy works like *Egmont,* inspired by the idea that human life is controlled by demonic forces. The work for which Goethe is probably best known, *Faust,* was begun at about the turn of the century, although its composition took many years. Part One was published in 1808 and Part Two was only finished in 1832, shortly before his death.

The subject of Dr. Faustus and his pact with the devil had been treated before in literature, notably in the play by Christopher Marlowe (see page 339). The theme was guaranteed to appeal to the romantic sensibility with its elements of the mysterious and fantastic, and in Part One Goethe put additional stress on the human emotions involved. The chief victim of Faust's lust for experience and power is the pure and innocent Gretchen, whom he callously seduces and then abandons. She becomes deranged as a result. At the end of Part One of *Faust,* Gretchen is accused of the murder of her illegitimate child, condemned to death, and executed. Moving from irony to wit to profound compassion, the rich tapestry of Part One shows Goethe, like Beethoven and Goya, on the side of suffering humanity.

Part Two of *Faust* is very different. Its theme, expressed symbolically through Faust's pact with the devil, is nothing less than the destiny of Western culture. Our civilization's unceasing activity and thirst for new experience inevitably produces error and suffering; at the same time, it is the result of the divine spark within us and will, in the end, guarantee our salvation. In his choice of the agent of this salvation Goethe established one of the other great themes of romanticism, the Eternal Feminine. Faust is finally redeemed by the divine love of Gretchen, who leads him upward to salvation.

Romantic Poetry

English romantic poetry of the first half of the 19th century represents a peak in the history of English literature. Its chief writers, generally known as the romantic poets, touched on a number of themes characteristic of the age. William Wordsworth's deep love of the country led him to explore the relationship between human beings and the world of nature; Percy Bysshe Shelley and George Gordon, Lord Byron, probed the more passionate, even demonic aspects of existence; and John Keats expressed his own sensitive responses to the eternal problems of art, life, and death.

William Wordsworth (1770–1850), often called the founder of the romantic movement in English poetry, clearly described his aims and ideals in his critical writings. For Wordsworth, the poet was a person with special gifts, "endowed with more lively sensibility, more enthusiasm and tenderness, who has a greater knowledge of human nature, and a more comprehensive soul" than ordinary people. Rejecting artificiality and stylization, Wordsworth aimed to make his poetry communicate directly in easily comprehensible terms. His principal theme was the relation between human beings and nature, which he explored by thinking back calmly on experiences that had earlier produced a violent emotional reaction: his famous "emotion recollected in tranquility."

Wordsworth's emotion recollected in tranquility is in strong contrast to the poetry of George Gordon, Lord Byron (1788–1824), who filled both his life and work with the same moody, passionate frenzy of activity [15.26]. Much of his time was spent wandering throughout Europe, where he became a living symbol of the unconventional, homeless, tormented romantic hero who has come to be called Byronic after him. Much of his flamboyant behavior was no doubt calculated to produce the effect it did, but his personality must indeed have been striking for no less a figure than Goethe to describe him as "a personality of such eminence as has never been before and is not likely to come again." Byron's sincere commitment to struggles for liberty like the Greek war of independence against the Turks can be judged by the fact that he died while actually on military duty in Greece.

Percy Bysshe Shelley (1792–1822), who like Byron spent many of his most creative years in Italy, lived a life of continual turmoil. After being expelled from Oxford for publishing his atheist views, he espoused the cause of anarchy and eloped with the daughter of one of its chief philosophical advocates. The consequent public scandal, coupled with ill health and critical hostility to his works, gave him a sense of bitterness and pessimism that lasted until his death by drowning.

15.26 Thomas Phillips. *Lord Byron in Albanian Costume.* 1814. Oil on canvas, 29½ × 24½" (75 × 62 cm). National Portrait Gallery, London. Byron is shown during his first visit to Greece, approximately dressed for the role of romantic sympathizer with exotic lands and peoples.

Shelley's brilliant mind and restless temperament produced poetry that united extremes of feeling, veering from the highest pitch of exultant joy to the most extreme despondency. His belief in the possibility of human perfection is expressed in his greatest work, *Prometheus Unbound* (1820), where the means of salvation is love, the love of human beings for one another expressed in the last movement of Beethoven's *Ninth Symphony,* rather than the redeeming female love of Goethe and Wagner. His most accessible works, however, are probably the short lyrics in which he seized a fleeting moment of human emotion and captured it by his poetic imagination.

Even Shelley's sensitivity to the poetic beauty of language was surpassed by that of John Keats (1795–1821), whose life, clouded by unhappy love and by the tuberculosis that killed him so tragically young, inspired poetry of rare poignance and sensitivity. In his *Odes* (lyric poems of strong feeling), in particular, he conveys both the glory and the tragedy of human existence and dwells almost longingly on the peace of death. In the wonderful "Ode to a Nightingale" the song of a bird comes to represent a permanent beauty beyond human grasp. The sensuous images, the intensity of emotion, and the flowing rhythm join to produce a magical effect.

The Novel

Although great novels have been written in our own time, the 19th century probably marked the high point in the creation of fiction. Increase in literacy and a rise in the general level of education resulted in a public eager for entertainment and instruction, and the success of such writers as Charles Dickens and Leo Tolstoy was due in large measure to their ability to combine the two. The best of 19th-century novels were those rare phenomena, great works of art that achieved popularity in their own day. Many of them are still able to enthrall the modern reader by their humanity and insight.

Most of the leading novelists of the mid-19th century wrote within a tradition of realism that came gradually to replace the more self-centered vision of romanticism. Instead of describing an imaginary world of their own creation, they looked outward to find inspiration in the day-to-day events of real life. The increasing social problems produced by industrial and urban development produced not merely a lament for the spirit of the times but a passionate desire for the power to change them as well. In some cases writers were able to combine a romantic style with a social conscience, as in the case of the French novelist Victor Hugo (1802–1885), whose *Les Misérables* (1862) describes the plight of the miserable victims of society's injustices. The hero of the novel, Jean Valjean, is an ex-convict who is rehabilitated through the agency of human sympathy and pity. Hugo provides graphic descriptions of the squalor and suffering of the poor, but his high-flown rhetorical style is essentially romantic.

Increasingly, however, writers found that they could best do justice to the problems of existence by adopting a more naturalistic style and describing their characters' lives in realistic terms. One of the most subtle attacks on contemporary values is *Madame Bovary* (1856–1857) by Gustave Flaubert (1821–1880). Flaubert's contempt for bourgeois society finds expression in his portrait of Emma Bovary, who tries to discover in her own provincial life the romantic love she reads about in novels. Her shoddy affairs and increasing debts lead to an inevitably dramatic conclusion. Flaubert is at his best in portraying the banality of her everyday existence.

Honoré de Balzac (1779–1850) was the most versatile of all French novelists. He created a series of some ninety novels and stories, under the general title of *The Human Comedy,* in which many of the same characters appear more than once. Above all a realist, Balzac depicted the social and political currents of his time while imposing on them a sense of artistic unity. His novels are immensely addictive. The reader who finds in one of them a reference to characters or events described in another novel hastens there to be led on to a third, and so on. Balzac thus succeeds in creating a fictional world that seems, by a characteristically romantic paradox, more real than historical reality.

Among the leading literary figures of Balzac's Paris, and a personal friend of Balzac himself, was the remarkable Aurore Dupin (1804–1876), better known by her pseudonym George Sand. This redoubtable defender of women's rights and attacker of male privilege used her novels to wage war on many of the accepted conventions of society. In her first novel, *Lélia* (1833) she attacked, among other institutions, the church, marriage, the laws of property, and the double standard of morality whereby women were condemned for doing what was condoned for men.

Unconventional in her own life, Sand became the lover of Chopin, with whom she lived from 1838 to 1847. Her autobiographical novel *Lucrezia Floriani* (1846) chronicles as thinly disguised fiction the remarkable course of this relationship, albeit very much from its author's point of view.

If France was one of the great centers of 19th-century fiction, another was Russia, where Leo Tolstoy (1828–1910) produced, among other works, two huge novels of international stature, *War and Peace* (1863–1869) and *Anna Karenina* (1873–1877). The first is mainly set against the background of Napoleon's invasion of Russia in 1812. Among the vast array of characters is the Rostov family, aristocratic but far from wealthy, who, together with their acquaintances, have their lives permanently altered by the great historical events through which they live. Tolstoy even emphasizes the way in which the course of the war affects his characters by combining figures he created for the novel with real historical personages, including Napoleon himself, and allowing them to meet.

At the heart of the novel is the young and impressionable Natasha Rostov, whose own confused love life seems to reflect the confusion of the times. Yet its philosophy is profoundly optimistic, in spite of the tragedies of Natasha's own life and the horrors of war that surround her. Her final survival and triumph represent the glorification of the irrational forces of life, which she symbolizes as the "natural person," over sophisticated and rational civilization. Tolstoy's high regard for irrationality and contempt for reason link him with other 19th-century romantics, and his ability to analyze character through the presentation of emotionally significant detail and to sweep the reader up in the panorama of historical events make *War and Peace* the most important work of Russian realistic fiction.

Toward the end of his life Tolstoy gave up his successful career and happy family life to undertake a mystical search for the secret of universal love. Renouncing his property, he began to wear peasant dress and went to work in the fields, although at the time of his death he was still searching in vain for peace. Russia's other great novelist, Feodor Dostoyevsky (1821–1881), although he died before Tolstoy, had far more in common with the late 19th century than with the romantic movement, and he is accordingly discussed in Chapter 16.

The riches of the English 19th-century novel are almost unlimited. They range from the profoundly intellectual and absorbing works of George Eliot, the pen name of Mary Ann Evans (1819–1880), to *Wuthering Heights* (1847), the only novel by Emily Brontë (1818–1848) and one of the most dramatic and passionate pieces of fiction ever written. The book's brilliant evocation of atmosphere and violent emotion produces a shattering effect. Like the two already mentioned, many of the leading novelists of the time were women, and the variety of their works soon puts to flight any facile notions about the feminine approach to literature. Elizabeth Gaskell (1810–1865), for example, was one of the leading social critics of the day; her novels study the effects of industrialization on the poor.

If one figure stands out in the field of the English novel, it is Charles Dickens (1812–1870), immensely popular in his own lifetime and widely read ever since. It is regrettable that Dickens' best-known novel, *A Tale of Two Cities* (1859), is one of his least characteristic, since its melodramatic and not totally successful historical reconstruction of the French Revolution may have deterred potential readers from exploring the wealth of humor, emotion, and imagination in his more successful books. Each of Dickens' novels and short stories creates its own world, peopled by an incredible array of characters individualized by their tics and quirks of personality. His ability to move us from laughter to tears and back again gives his work a continual human appeal, although it has won him the censure of some of the severer critics.

15.27 George Cruikshank. *"Please sir, I want some more."* 1838. From *Oliver Twist, or The Parish Boy's Progress* by "Boz," published by Richard Bentley, London. New York Public Library. In the workhouse, young Oliver Twist dares to ask for a second bowl of gruel. George Cruikshank (1792–1878), a famed illustrator and caricaturist of the 19th century, illustrated more than 850 books; probably his best-known work is that for *Oliver Twist.*

Throughout his life Dickens was an active campaigner against social injustices and used his books to focus on individual institutions and their evil effects. *Oliver Twist* (1837–1838) attacked the treatment of the poor in workhouses and revealed Dickens' view of crime as the manifestation of a general failing in society [15.27]. In *Hard Times* (1854) he turned, like Mrs. Gaskell, to the evils of industrialization and pointed out some of the harm that misguided attempts at education can do.

THE ROMANTIC ERA IN AMERICA

The early history of the arts in America was intimately linked to developments in Europe. England, in particular, by virtue of its common tongue and political connections, exerted an influence on literature and painting that even the War of Independence did not end. American writers

15.28 John Singleton Copley. *Portrait of Nathaniel Hurd.* c. 1765. Oil on canvas, 30 × 25½" (76 × 65 cm). Cleveland Museum of Art (gift of the John Huntington Art and Polytechnic Trust). In this portrait of a friend Copley avoids technical tricks. The result is an attractive simplicity of style that still lets him reveal something of the subject's personality.

sought publishers and readers there, and modeled their style on that of English writers. American painters went to London to study, sometimes with less than happy results. John Singleton Copley (1738–1815), for example, produced a series of portraits in a simple, direct style of his own [15.28] before leaving Boston for England, where he fell victim to Sir Joshua Reynolds' Grand Manner (see Figure 14.13, page 401). Of American music we cannot say much, since the earliest American composers confined their attention to settings of hymns and patriotic songs. A recognizably American musical tradition of composition did not develop before the very end of the 19th century, although much earlier European performers found a vast and enthusiastic musical public in the course of their American tours [15.29].

In the case of literature and the visual arts, the French Revolution provided a change of direction, for revolutionary ties inevitably resulted in the importation of neoclassicism into America. With the dawning of the Romantic Era, however, American artists began to develop for the first time an authentic voice of their own. In many cases they still owed much to European examples. Indeed, the tradition of the expatriate American artist who left home to study in Europe and remained there had been firmly established by the 18th century. Throughout the 19th century writers like Washington Irving (1783–1859) and painters like

15.29 Nathaniel Currier. First Appearance of *Jenny Lind in America: At Castle Garden, September 11, 1850,* detail. 1850. Lithograph. J. Clarence Davies Collection, Museum of the City of New York. The great soprano, inevitably known as the Swedish Nightingale, made a very successful tour of America under the management of P. T. Barnum in 1850–1851, during which she earned the staggering sum of $120,000 (multiply by ten for present value). At this first appearance in New York, the total receipts were $26,238. Nathaniel Currier (1813–1888) and James Merritt Ives (1824–1895), who became his partner in 1857, were lithographers who sold thousands of hand-colored prints that show many aspects of 19th-century American life.

CONTEMPORARY VOICES

Isabella Bird Meets a Mountain Man

Isabella Bird (1831–1904), the English travel writer, meets Rocky Mountain Jim in Colorado in 1873—"a man who any woman might love, but who no sane woman would marry." A tireless traveler throughout America, Asia, and Australia, Isabella finally did settle down for a while and get married; her husband observed that he "had only one formidable rival in Isabella's heart, and that is the high Table Land of Central Asia."

Roused by the growling of the dog, his owner came out, a broad, thickset man, about the middle height, with an old cap on his head, and wearing a grey hunting-suit much the worse for wear (almost falling to pieces, in fact), a digger's scarf knotted round his waist, a knife in his belt, and a bosom friend, a revolver, sticking out of the breast-pocket of his coat; his feet, which were very small, were bare, except for some dilapidated moccasins made of horse hide. The marvel was how his clothes hung together, and on him. The scarf round his waist must have had something to do with it. His face was remarkable. He is a man about 45, and must have been strikingly handsome. He has large grey-blue eyes, deeply set, with well-marked eyebrows, a handsome aquiline nose, and a very handsome mouth. His face was smooth shaven except for a dense moustache and imperial. Tawny hair, in thin uncared-for curls, fell from under his hunter's cap and over his collar. One eye was entirely gone, and the loss made one side of the face repulsive, while the other might have been modelled in marble. "Desperado" was written in large letters all over him. I almost repented of having sought his acquaintance.

His first impulse was to swear at the dog, but on seeing a lady he contented himself with kicking him, and coming up to me he raised his cap, showing as he did so a magnificently formed brow and head, and in a cultured tone of voice asked if there were anything he could do for me? I asked for some water, and he brought some in a battered tin, gracefully apologizing for not having anything more presentable. We entered into conversation, and as he spoke I forgot both his reputation and appearance, for his manner was that of a chivalrous gentleman, his accent refined, and his language easy and elegant. I inquired about some beavers' paws which were drying, and in a moment they hung on the horn of my saddle. Apropos of the wild animals of the region, he told me that the loss of his eye was owing to a recent encounter with a grizzly bear, which after giving him a death hug, tearing him all over, breaking his arm and scratching out his eye, had left him for dead.

From *A Lady's Life in the Rocky Mountains*, London, 1879; reprinted by Virago Press, London, 1982.

Thomas Eakins (1844–1916) continued to bring back to America themes and styles they had acquired during their European travels. Something about the very nature of romanticism, however, with its emphasis on the individual, seemed to fire the American imagination. The romantic love of the remote and mysterious reached a peak in the macabre stories of Edgar Allan Poe (1809–1849). For the first time, in the Romantic Era American artists began to produce work that was both a genuine product of their native land and at the same time of international stature.

American Literature

In a land where daily existence was lived so close to the wildness and beauty of nature, the romantic attachment to the natural world was bound to make a special appeal. The romantic concept of the transcendental unity of humans and nature was quickly taken up in the early 19th century by a whole group of American writers who even called themselves the Transcendentalists. Borrowing ideas from Kant and from his English followers such as Coleridge and Wordsworth, they developed notions of an order of truth that transcends what we can perceive by our physical senses and which unites the entire world. One of their leading representatives, Ralph Waldo Emerson (1803–1882), underlined the particular importance of the natural world for American writers in his essay *The American Scholar,* first published in 1837. In calling for the development of a national literature, Emerson laid down as a necessary condition for its success that his compatriots should draw their inspiration from the wonders of their own country. A few years later he was to write: "America is a poem in our eyes; its ample geography dazzles the imagination, and it will not wait long for metres."

Emerson always tried to make his own work "smell of pines and resound with the hum of insects," but although his ideas have exerted a profound effect on the development of American culture, Emerson himself was a better thinker than creative artist. Far more successful as a literary practitioner of Transcendentalist principles was Henry David Thoreau (1817–1862), whose masterpiece *Walden* (1854) uses his day-to-day experiences as he lived in solitude on the shore of Walden Pond to draw general conclusions about the nature of existence. Thoreau's passionate support of the freedom of the individual led him to be active in the antislavery movement, and by the end of his life he had moved from belief in passive resistance to open advocacy of violence against slavery.

Ideas of freedom, tolerance, and spiritual unity reached their most complete poetic expression in the works of America's first great poet, Walt Whitman (1819–1892). His first important collection of poems was published in 1855 under the title *Leaves of Grass*. From then until his death he produced edition after edition, retaining the same title but gradually adding many new poems and revising the old ones.

Whitman was defiantly, even aggressively, an American poet, yet the central theme of most of his work was the importance of the individual. The contradiction this involves serves as a reminder of the essentially romantic character of Whitman's mission, since by describing the details of his own feelings and reactions he hoped to communicate a sense of the essential oneness of the human condition. Much of the time the sheer vitality and flow of his language helps to make his experiences our own, although many of his earlier readers were horrified at the explicit sexual descriptions in some of his poems. Above all, Whitman was a fiery defender of freedom and democracy. His vision of the human race united with itself and with the universe has a special significance for the late 20th century.

Emily Dickinson (1830–1881) was as private in her life and work as Whitman was public in his. Only seven of her poems appeared in print during her lifetime, and the first complete edition was published as late as 1958. Yet by the end of the 20th century, few American poets are better known or better loved. Her work tries to create a balance between passion and the promptings of reason, while her interest in psychological experience appeals to modern readers. Many, too, are attracted by her desire for a secure religious faith, equalled only by her stubborn skepticism.

The essential optimism of the Transcendentalists, especially as interpreted by Whitman, is absent from the work of the two great American novelists of the 19th century, Nathaniel Hawthorne (1804–1864) and Herman Melville (1819–1891). Hawthorne in particular was deeply concerned with the apparently ineradicable evil in a society dedicated to progress. In *The Scarlet Letter* (1850), his first major success, and in many of his short stories he explored the conflicts between traditional values and the drive for change.

Melville imitated Hawthorne's example in combining realism with allegory and in dealing with profound moral issues. His subjects and style are both very different, however. *Moby-Dick* (1851), his masterpiece, is often hailed as the greatest of all American works of fiction. It shares with Goethe's *Faust* the theme of the search for truth and self-discovery, which Melville works out by using the metaphor of the New England whaling industry. Both Melville and Hawthorne were at their greatest when using uniquely American settings and characters to shed light on universal human experience.

American Painting

Under the influence of the Transcendentalists, landscape painting in America took on a new significance. Emerson reminded the artist who set out to paint a natural scene that "landscape has a beauty for his eye because it expresses a thought which to him is good, and this because the same power which sees through his eyes is seen in that spectacle." Natural beauty, in other words, is moral beauty, and both of them demonstrate the transcendental unity of the universe.

The earliest painters of landscapes intended to glorify the wonders of nature are known collectively as the Hudson River School. The foundations of their style were laid by Thomas Cole (1801–1848), himself born in England, whose later paintings combine grandeur of effect with accurate observation of details. His *Genesee Scenery* [15.30] is particularly successful in capturing a sense of atmosphere and presence.

By midcentury a new approach to landscape painting had developed. Generally called luminism, it aimed to provide the sense of artistic anonymity Emerson and other Transcendentalists demanded. In a way this is the exact antithesis of romanticism. Instead of sharing with the viewer their own reactions, the luminists tried by realism to eliminate their own presence and let nothing stand between the viewer and the scenes. Yet the results, far from achieving only a photographic realism, have an utterly characteristic and haunting beauty that has no real parallel in European art of the time. The painting *Lake George* [15.31] by Martin J. Heade (1819–1904), one of the leading luminists,

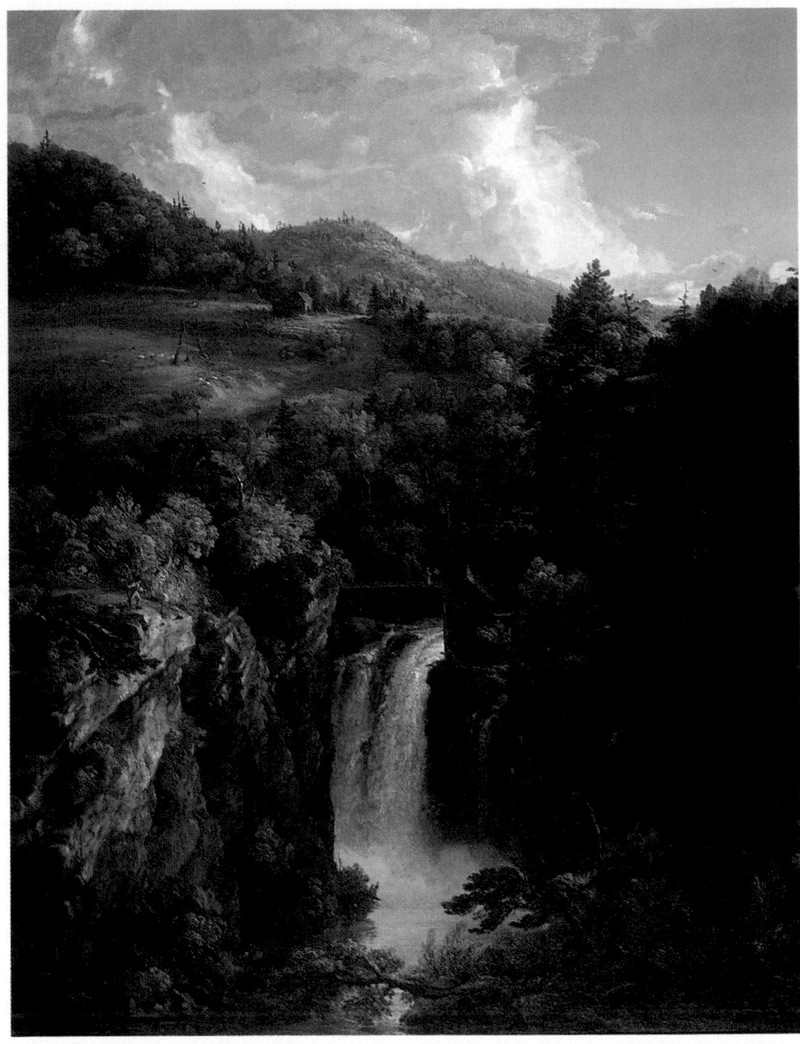

15.30 Thomas Cole. American, 1801–1848. *Genesee Scenery (Landscape with Waterfall).* 1847. Oil on canvas, 51" × 39½" (1.3 × 1 m). Museum of Art, Rhode Island School of Design, Providence (Jesse Metcalf Fund). One of Cole's last works, this shows a meticulous care for detail that is never allowed to detract from the broad sweep of the view.

15.31 Martin Johnson Heade. American, 1819–1904. *Lake George.* 1862. Oil on canvas, 26 × 49¾" (66 × 126.3 cm). Museum of Fine Arts, Boston (bequest of Maxim Karolik). Note the smooth surface of the painting, which reveals no trace of the artist's brush strokes, and the extreme precision of the rendering of the rocks at right.

15.32 Winslow Homer. *Eagle Head, Manchester, Massachusetts.* 1870. Oil on canvas, 26 × 38" (66 × 97 cm). Metropolitan Museum of Art, New York (gift of Mrs. William F. Milton, 1923). This painting, produced after Homer's visit to France, shows a new, more impressionistic approach to light and to the sea.

seems almost to foreshadow the surrealist art of the 20th century.

The two great American painters of the later 19th century, Winslow Homer (1836–1910) and Thomas Eakins (1844–1916), both used the luminist approach to realism as a basis for their own very individual styles. In the case of Homer, the realism of his early paintings was in large measure the result of his work as a documentary artist, recording the events of the Civil War. His style underwent a notable change as he became exposed to contemporary French impressionist painting (discussed in Chapter 16). His mysterious *Eagle Head* [15.32] is certainly far more than a naturalistic depiction of three women and a dog on a beach. By the way in which he has positioned the figures, Homer suggests rather than spells out greater emotional depths than initially meet the eye. The sense of restrained drama occurs elsewhere in his work, while the sea became a growing obsession with him and provided virtually the only subject of his last works.

Thomas Eakins used realism as a means of achieving objective truth. His pursuit of scientific accuracy led him to make a particular study of the possibilities of photography. Animals and, more particularly, humans in motion continually fascinated him. This trait can be observed in *The Swimming Hole* [15.33], where the variety of poses and actions produces a series of individual anatomical studies rather than a unified picture.

In his own day Eakins' blunt insistence on accuracy of perception did not endear him to a public that demanded more glamorous art. Yet if many of his works seem essentially antiromantic in spirit, foreshadowing as they do the age of mechanical precision, in his portraits he returns to the romantic tradition of expressing emotions by depicting them. The sitter in *Miss Van Buren* [15.34], as in most of his portraits, turns her eyes away from us, rapt in profound inner contemplation. The artist's own emotional response to the mood of his subject is made visible in his painting.

15.33 Thomas Eakins. *The Swimming Hole.* 1883. Oil on canvas, 27⅜ × 36⅜" (69.5 × 92.4 cm). Fort Worth Art Museum, Texas. Purchased by the Friends of Art, Fort Worth Art Association, 1925. Presented to the Amon Carter Museum, 1990, by the Modern Art Museum of Fort Worth through pledges from The Amon G. Carter Foundation, The Sid W. Richardson Foundation, The Anne Burnett and Charles Tandy Foundation, Capital Cities/ABC Foundation, Fort Worth Star-Telegram, The R. D. and Joan Dale Hubbard Foundation and the people of Fort Worth. Eakins painted figures directly from models placed in poses from Greek sculpture in order to try to see nature as the Greeks saw it, but without the Greeks' idealization. The figure swimming in the bottom right-hand corner is Eakins himself.

Painters such as Homer and Eakins, like Whitman and other writers discussed here, are important in the history of American culture not only for the value of their individual works. Their achievements demonstrated that American society could at last produce creative figures capable of absorbing the European cultural experience without losing their individuality.

15.34 Thomas Eakins. *Miss Van Buren.* c. 1889–1891. Oil on canvas, 45 × 32" (114 × 81 cm). Phillips Collection, Washington. Note how, in contrast to the portraits by Ingres (Figure 15.18), and Copley (Figure 15.28), Eakins achieves deep feeling and sensitivity by the angle of his subject's head and her position in the chair.

SUMMARY

The revolutionary changes that ushered in the 19th century, and that were to continue throughout it, profoundly affected society and culture. The industrialization of Europe produced vast changes in the life styles of millions of people. The Greek struggle for independence, the unification of Italy and of Germany, and the nationalist revolutionary uprisings of 1848 in many parts of Europe all radically changed the balance of power and the nature of society. The same period, furthermore, saw the gradual assertion of the United States, tested and tried by its own Civil War, as one of the leading Western nations. By the end of the 19th century America had not only established itself as a world power; it had produced artists, writers, and musicians who created works with an authentically American spirit.

A period of such widespread change was naturally also one of major intellectual ferment. The political philosophy of Karl Marx and the scientific speculations of Charles Darwin, influential in their day, remain powerful and controversial in the late 20th century. The optimism of Immanuel Kant and Friedrich Hegel and the pessimism of Arthur Schopenhauer were reflected in numerous works of art.

The artistic movement that developed alongside these ideas was romanticism. The romantics, for all their divergences, shared a number of common concerns. They sought to express their personal feelings in their works rather than search for some kind of abstract philosophical or religious "truth." They were attracted by the fantastic and the exotic, and by worlds remote in time—the Middle Ages—or in place—the mysterious Orient. Many of them felt a special regard for nature, in the context of which human achievement seemed so reduced. For some, on the other hand, the new age of industry and technology was itself exotic and exciting. Many romantic artists identified with the nationalist movements of the times and either supported their own country's fight for freedom (as in the case of Verdi) or championed the cause of others (as did Byron).

In music the transition from the classical to the romantic style can be heard in the works of Ludwig van Beethoven. With roots deep in the classical tradition, Beethoven used music to express emotion in a revolutionary way, pushing traditional forms like the sonata to their limits. Typical of the age is his concern with freedom, which appears in *Fidelio* (his only opera), and human unity, as expressed in the last movement of the *Ninth Symphony*.

Many of Beethoven's successors in the field of instrumental music continued to use symphonic forms for their major works. Among the leading symphonists of the century were Hector Berlioz, Johannes Brahms, and Anton Bruckner. Other composers, although they wrote symphonies, were more at home in the intimate world of songs and chamber music; they included Franz Schubert and Robert Schumann. The romantic emphasis on personal feelings and the display of emotion encouraged the development of another characteristic of 19th-century music: the virtuoso composer-performer. Frédéric Chopin, Franz Liszt, and Niccolò Paganini all won international fame performing their own works. The nationalist spirit of the times was especially appealing to musicians who could draw on a rich tradition of folk music. The Russian Modest Moussorgsky and the Czech Bedřich Smetana both wrote works using national themes and folk tunes.

The world of opera was dominated by two giants, Giuseppi Verdi and Richard Wagner. The former took the forms of early-19th-century opera and used them to create powerful and dramatic masterpieces. An enthusiastic supporter of Italy's nationalist movement, Verdi never abandoned the basic elements of the Italian operatic tradition—expressive melody and vital rhythm—but he infused them with new dramatic truth. Wagner's quest for "music drama" led him in a very different direction. His works break with the operatic tradition of individual musical numbers; the music, in which the orchestra plays an important part, runs continuously from the beginning to the end of each act. In addition, the use of leading motifs to represent characters or ideas makes possible complex dramatic effects. Wagner's works revolutionized the development of both operatic and nonoperatic music, and his theoretical writings on music and much else made him one of the 19th century's leading cultural figures.

Just as Beethoven spanned the transition from classical to romantic in music, so Francesco Goya, some of whose early works were painted in the rococo style, produced some of the most powerful of romantic paintings. His concern with justice and liberty, as illustrated in *Execution of the Madrileños on May 3, 1808* and with the world of dreams, as in *The Sleep of Reason Produces Monsters*, was prototypical of much romantic art.

In France, painters were divided into two camps. The fully committed romantics included Théodore Géricault, also concerned to point out injustice, and Eugène Delacroix, whose work touched on virtually every aspect of romanticism:

nationalism, exoticism, eroticism. The other school was that of the realists. Honoré Daumier's way of combating the corruption of his day was to portray it as graphically as possible. In the meantime Ingres waged *his* campaign against both progressive movements by continuing to paint in the academic neoclassical style of the preceding century—or at least his version of it.

Painters in England and Germany were particularly attracted by the romantic love of nature. Caspar David Friedrich used the grandeur of the natural world to underline the transitoriness of human achievement, while in John Constable's landscapes there is greater harmony between people and their surroundings. Joseph M. W. Turner, Constable's contemporary, falls into a category by himself. Although many of his subjects were romantic, his use of form and color make light and movement the real themes of his paintings.

In literature no figure dominated his time more than Johann Wolfgang von Goethe, the German poet, dramatist, and novelist. One of the first writers to break the fetters of neoclassicism, he nonetheless continued to produce neoclassical works as well as more romantic ones. The scale of his writings runs from the most intimate love lyrics to the monumental two parts of his *Faust* drama.

The work of the English romantic poets William Wordsworth, Percy Bysshe Shelley, John Keats, and George Gordon, Lord Byron touched on all the principal romantic themes. Other English writers used the novel as a means of expressing their concern with social issues, as in the case of Charles Dickens, or their absorption with strong emotion, as did Emily Brontë. Indeed, the 19th century was the great age of the novel, with Honoré de Balzac and Gustave Flaubert writing in France and—above all—Leo Tolstoy in Russia.

The Romantic Era was the first period in which American artists created their own original styles rather than borrow them from Europe. Love of nature inspired writers like Henry David Thoreau and painters like Thomas Cole. The description of strong emotions, often personal ones, characterizes the poetry of Walt Whitman and many of the paintings of Winslow Homer. Thomas Eakins, with his interest in realism, made use of a 19th-century invention that had an enormous impact on the visual arts: photography.

By the end of the century the audience for art of all kinds had expanded immeasurably. No longer commissioned by the church or the aristocracy, artworks expressed the hopes and fears of individual artists and of humanity at large. Furthermore, as the revolutionaries of the 18th century had dreamed, they had helped bring about social change.

Pronunciation Guide

Balzac: Bal-ZAK
Berlioz: BARE-li-owes
Bruckner: BROOK-ner
Chios: KEY-os
Chopin: Show-PAN
Courbet: Coor-BAY
Daumier: Doe-MYAY
Delacroix: De-la-KRWA
Eakins: ACHE-ins
Fidelio: Fi-DAY-li-owe
Géricault: Jay-rick-OWE
Goethe: GUR-te
Ingres: ANG
Kant: CANT
Leitmotiv: LITE-mow-teef
Liebestod: LEE-bis-tote
Liszt: LIST
Moussorgsky: Mus-ORG-ski
Nabucco: Na-BOO-ko
Sardanapalus: Sar-dan-AP-al-us
Scherzo: SCARE-tsow
Schopenhauer: SHOWP-en-how-er
Thoreau: Thoh-ROW
Traviata: Tra-vi-AH-ta
Wagner: VAHG-ner
Waldstein: VALD-stine

Exercises

1. Analyze the elements of the romantic style and compare its effect on the various arts.
2. Discuss the career of Beethoven and assess his influence on the development of music in the 19th century.
3. What were the principal schools of French romantic painting, and who were their leaders? What kinds of subject did they choose and why?
4. What factors—historical, cultural, social—favored the popularity of the novel in the 19th century? How do they compare to present conditions, and what is the status of the novel today?
5. Discuss the American contribution to the romantic movement.

Further Reading

Canaday, J. *Mainstreams of Modern Art,* 2nd ed. New York: Holt, 1981. A survey that combines scholarship, deep feeling, and unusually enjoyable prose. Many excellent illustrations.

Chissell, J. *Clara Schumann: A Dedicated Spirit.* London: Hamish Hamilton, 1983. An absorbing biography of a woman whose life was divided between her composer-husband and her own career as pianist and composer.

Clark, K. *The Romantic Rebellion.* New York: Harper & Row, 1986. The latest edition of a magisterial survey of the Romantic movement, plentifully illustrated.

Cooper, M. *Beethoven: The Last Decade.* New York: Oxford University Press, 1985. An unusually detailed study of the events and compositions of Beethoven's last years, with an interesting appendix on his medical history.

Fischer-Dieskau, D. *Schubert: A Biographical Study of His Songs.* London: Cassell, 1976. In this fascinating book one of the greatest singers (and Schubert interpreters) of this century traces the composer's life through his songs.

Gage, J. (ed. and trans.). *Goethe on Art.* Berkeley: University of California Press, 1980. This book contains many of Goethe's observations on art and throws considerable light on the poet's own work.

Johnson, E. *Charles Dickens. His Tragedy and Triumph.* New York: Viking, 1977. An updated and abridged edition of an earlier work, this fine biography is particularly good on Dickens' visits to America.

Kerman, J. and A. Tyson. *Beethoven.* London: Macmillan, 1983. Based on the entry in the *New Grove Dictionary of Music,* this provides a great deal of information, including a complete catalogue of Beethoven's works.

Osborne, C. *The Complete Operas of Verdi.* New York: Knopf, 1970. An engrossing book that combines synopses and analyses of all Verdi's operas with an account of his life and excerpts from his letters.

Paulson, R. *Literary Landscape: Turner and Constable.* New Haven: Yale University Press, 1982. A cross-discipline study, this difficult but rewarding work attempts to "read" the landscape paintings of Turner and Constable by finding literary meanings for them.

Wolf, B. *Romantic Re-Vision: Culture and Consciousness in Nineteenth Century Painting and Literature.* Chicago: University of Chicago Press, 1982. A sophisticated discussion of 19th-century American art, using the critical tools of the late 20th century—structuralism, semiotics, and psychoanalysis.

	GENERAL EVENTS	LITERATURE & PHILOSOPHY	ART
1860			
GROWTH OF BIG BUSINESS	**1876** Speech first transmitted through telephone by Alexander Graham Bell **1880–1914** Height of European colonialism **1886** Dedication of Statue of Liberty, presented by France to America **1889** International League of Socialist Parties founded	**1866** Dostoyevsky, *Crime and Punishment* **1870–1914** New areas explored in writing: impact of subconscious on human behavior, the role of women **1879** First performance of Ibsen's realistic drama *A Doll's House* **1881** Death of Dostoyevsky **1883–1892** Nietzsche, *Thus Spoke Zarathustra*	**1863** Manet exhibits *Déjeuner sur l'Herbe* to public outrage **1869–1872** Degas, *Degas' Father Listening to Lorenzo Pagans Singing* **1874** Impressionism emerges when Monet and others exhibit at Café Guerbois, Paris; *Impression: Sunrise* (1872) **1875** Monet, *Red Boats at Argenteuil* **1876** Renoir, *Le Moulin de la Galette* **c. 1880** Postimpressionists reject impressionism **1881–1882** Manet, *Bar at the Folies-Bergère* **1884–1886** Seurat, *A Sunday Afternoon on the Island of La Grande Jatte* **c. 1885** Protocubist experiments of Cézanne; *Still Life with Commode* **1886** Rodin, *The Kiss;* Degas, *The Tub* **1888** van Gogh, *The Night Café* **1889** van Gogh, *The Starry Night;* Cassatt, *Mother and Child*
1890			
HEIGHT OF EUROPEAN COLONIALISM	**1890–1914** Industrialization of Russia **1899–1902** Boer War	**1891** Shaw, drama critic for *Saturday Review,* champions Ibsen **1893** Wilde, *Salome* **1894** Kate Chopin, *The Story of an Hour* **1899** Kate Chopin, *The Awakening*	**1891** Gauguin, *Ia Orana Maria;* Mary Cassatt's first solo exhibition in Paris **1893** Munch, *The Scream;* Rodin begins *Balzac* **1894–1898** Kollwitz, *The Weavers,* etching based on Hauptmann play
1900			
RISE OF GERMAN MILITARY POWER	**1901** Death of Queen Victoria of England; reign of Edward VII begins. First message sent over Marconi's transatlantic wireless telegraph **1903** Wright brothers make first airplane flight **1904** Russo-Japanese War **1905** First Revolution breaks out in Russia; Einstein formulates theory of relativity; first motion-picture theater opens in Pittsburgh **1908** Model T touring car introduced by Ford **1911** Revolution in China establishes republic **1914** World War I begins	**1900** Freud, *Interpretation of Dreams* **1904** Death of Chekov **1913** Publication of *Swann's Way,* first volume of Proust's *Remembrance of Things Past;* final volume published posthumously (1927)	**c. 1902–1906** Cézanne paints last series of landscapes depicting *Mont Sainte-Victoire* **1903–1913** German expressionist movement *Die Brücke* **1905** First Fauve exhibition in Paris; Matisse, *The Joy of Living* (1905–1906) **1907–1914** Picasso and Braque develop cubism in Paris **1911** Matisse, *The Red Studio.* German expressionist group *Der Blaue Reiter* formed
1914			

CHAPTER 16 TOWARD THE MODERN ERA: 1870–1914

	ARCHITECTURE	MUSIC
		**mid-19th cent.** Liszt's symphonic poems precursors of *program music*
	1883 Birth of Gropius	
		1886 R. Strauss begins tone poem *Don Juan*
	**1890–1891** Sullivan, Wainwright Building, St. Louis, first skyscraper	
		**1893** Tchaikovsky, "Pathetique" *Symphony*, precedes composer's suicide. Mahler's *Symphony No. 1 in D* marks transition from romantic to modern music. **1894** Debussy, musical impressionist, composes *Prélude à l'après-midi d'un faune* **1895** R. Strauss, *Till Eulenspiegel* **1896** Puccini champions *verismo* in Italian opera; *La Bohème* **1899** R. Strauss, *A Hero's Life*
	1905–1907 Gaudí, Casa Milá, Barcelona	**1900–1904** Puccini, *Tosca; Madama Butterfly* **1905** First performance of R. Strauss' opera *Salome*, based on Wilde's play; Debussy, *La Mer*
		1908 Schoenberg, *Three Piano Pieces*, Op. 11, first major atonal work
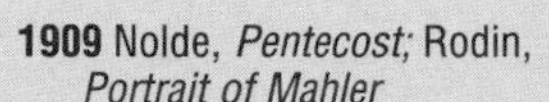 **1909** Nolde, *Pentecost;* Rodin, *Portrait of Mahler*	**1909** Robie House, Chicago, Frank Lloyd Wright's first big success	**1909–1910** Mahler, *Symphony No. 9* **1910–1913** Stravinsky composes *Firebird, Petrouchka, Rite of Spring* for Diaghilev's Ballet Russe in Paris
1912 Heckel, *Two Men at a Table (To Dostoyevsky)*		**1911–1915** R. Strauss, *Alpine Symphony* **1912** Schoenberg, *Pierrot Lunaire* **1913** Ravel composes *Daphnis and Chloe* for Diaghilev

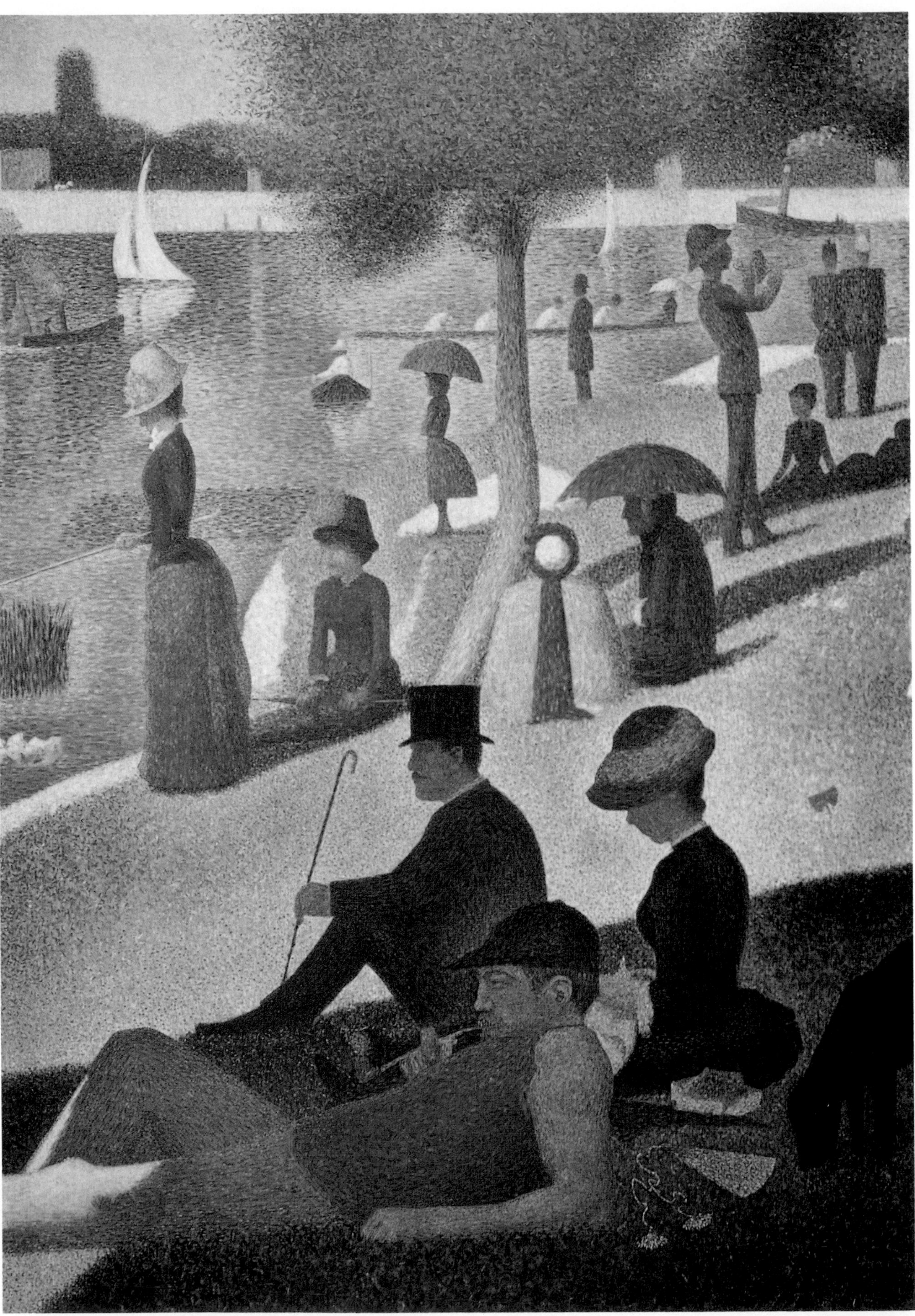

C H A P T E R

16
TOWARD THE MODERN ERA: 1870–1914

DISTANCE LENDS perspective in human experience. The more intimately we are affected by events, the more difficult it is to evaluate them objectively. Looking back, we can see that the world in which we live, with its great hopes and even greater fears, began to take its present shape in the early years of the 20th century. The First World War of 1914 to 1918 marked an end to almost three thousand years of European political and cultural supremacy as well as the beginning of a world in which events in any corner of the globe could—and still do—have immense consequences for good or ill for the entire human race. The effects on the humanities of so vast a change in direction are the subject of chapters 17 and 18. Here we will consider some of the causes and early symptoms of the change.

Although the period in which the modern world was formed is the historical era that directly affects our daily lives, our cultural traditions go back to ancient Greece and Rome. Yet even if the cataclysmic events of the 20th century have not destroyed the value of centuries of accumulated experience, we naturally feel more intimately linked to the generation of our parents and grandparents than to more distant generations of ancestors of which we are also the product. Nevertheless, our parents and grandparents are the very people whose nearness to us in time and emotional impact makes them and their world more difficult to understand objectively.

Our own responses to the increasing complexity of historical forces during the formative stages of modern culture are still so confused that it is helpful to turn to the reactions of individual artists and thinkers who themselves lived through the times and can to some extent interpret them to us. Further, within the relatively limited sphere of artistic creativity we can observe at work forces that also operated on a much larger scale. As so often in the history of Western civilization, the arts provide a direct and powerful, if incomplete, expression of the spirit of an age—in this case an age that happens to be our own. It may even be that the enduring importance of the humanities as a reflection of human condition is one of the few aspects of Western civilization to survive a century of global turmoil, and help us on our way into the 21st century.

THE GROWING UNREST

By the last quarter of the 19th century there was a widespread if unfocused feeling in Europe that life could not continue as before. Social and political revolutions had replaced the old monarchies with more nearly equitable forms of government. Scientific and technological developments had affected millions of ordinary people, bringing them improved standards of living and a more congenial existence. As a result, a new mood of cheerfulness began to make itself felt in the great cities of Europe; in Paris, for example, the period became known as the *belle époque* (beautiful age).

But the apparent gaiety was only superficial. The price of the immense changes that made it possible had been unrest and violence, and the forces that had been built up to achieve them remained in existence. Thus, in a period of nominal peace, most of the leading countries in Europe were maintaining huge armies and introducing compulsory military service. Long before 1914 a growing mood of frustration led many people to assume that sooner or later war would break out—a belief that certainly did not help to avert it [16.1].

The many historical causes of this mood are beyond the scope of this book but some of the more

16.1 Ludwig Meidner. *The Eve of the War*. 1914. Stadtische Kunsthalle, Recklinghausen. The distorted faces and violent, heaving composition reflect the spirit of a world on the point of collapse.

important underlying factors are easy enough to perceive. In the first place, the growth of democratic systems of government had taught increasing numbers of people that they had a right to share in the material benefits made possible by the Industrial Revolution. Discontent grew on all sides. In the richest countries in Europe—France, England, and Germany—the poor compared their lot with that of the more affluent. At the same time, in the poorer European countries, including Ireland, Spain, Portugal, and all of Eastern Europe, everyone looked with envy at their wealthier neighbors. Even more significantly, those vast continents that the empire-building European powers were introducing to European civilization for the first time, including parts of Africa, Asia, and South America, began increasingly to resent European domination.

In the second place, the scientific progress that made possible improvements in people's lives created problems of its own. New medical advances reduced the rate of infant mortality, cured hitherto fatal diseases, and prolonged life expectancy. As a result the population of most of Europe soared to a record level, creating food and housing shortages. New forms of transport and new industrial processes brought vast numbers of workers to the cities. In consequence the lives of many people were uprooted and their daily existence became anonymous and impersonal.

Third, the growth of a world financial market, dependent primarily on the value of gold, gave new power to the forces of big business. In turn, the rise of capitalism, fiercely opposed by the growing forces of socialism [16.2], provoked the development of trade unions to protect the interests of the workers.

Finally, at a time when so many political and social forces were pitted against one another there seemed to be no certainty on which to fall back. Religion had lost its hold over intellectual circles by

16.2 Käthe Kollwitz. *March of the Weavers*, from *The Weavers Cycle*. 1897. Etching, 8⅜ × 11⅝" (21 × 29 cm). University of Michigan Museum of Art, Ann Arbor, 1956/1.21. This print is based on a play, *The Weavers*, by the German playwright Gerhart Hauptmann (1862–1946) dealing with the misery and helplessness of both workers and owners in the industrial age. The axes and mattocks in the workers' hands point to the coming violence.

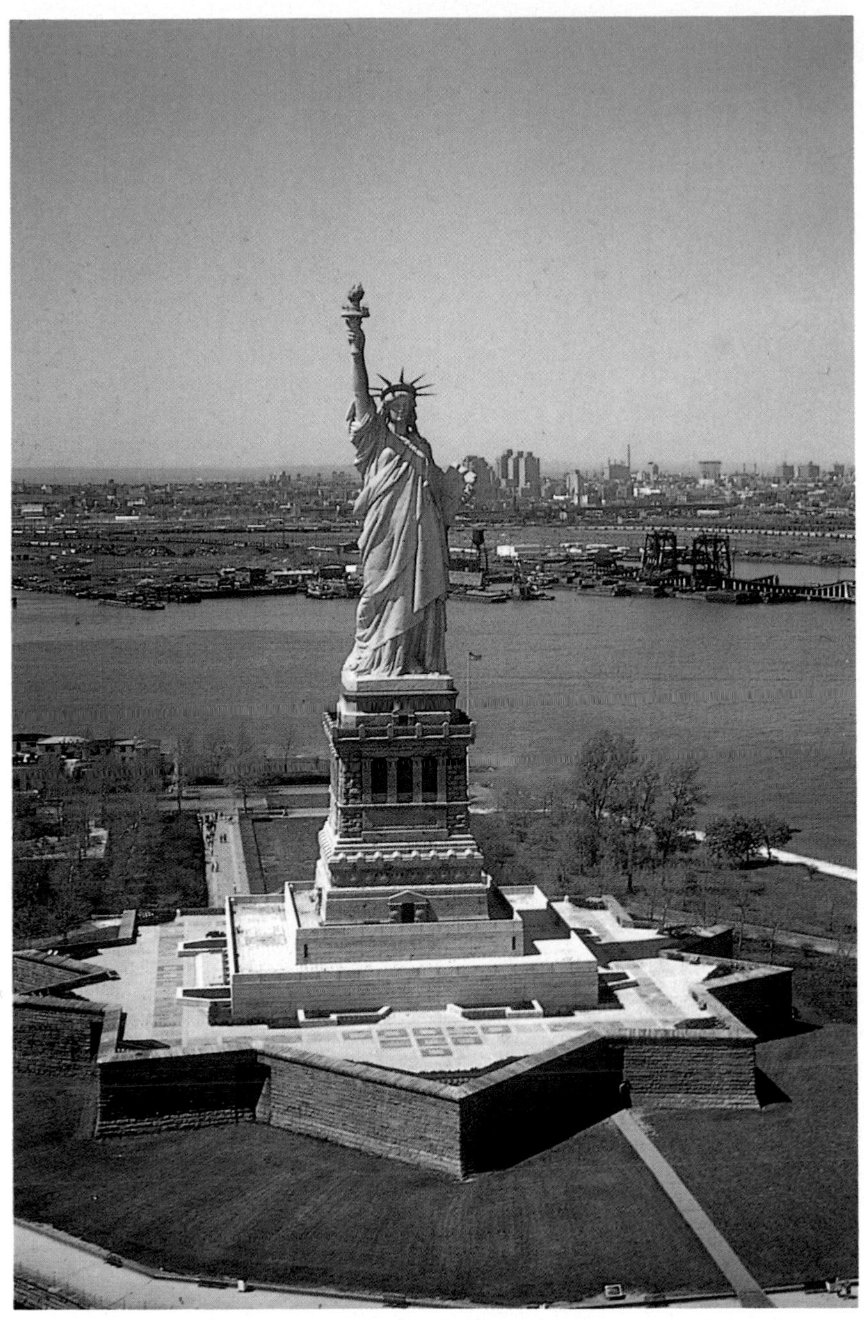

16.3 Frédéric-Auguste Bartholdi. Statue of Liberty *(Liberty Enlightening the World)*. Constructed and erected in Paris, 1876–1884; disassembled, shipped to New York, re-erected, dedicated 1886. Hammered copper sheets over iron trusswork and armature; height of figure 151' (46 m), total height, including pedestal, above sea level 306' (93 m). This famous monument, which still dominates New York's harbor, became the symbol to European immigrants in the late 19th century of the welcome they would find in the New World. The colossal statue (the head alone is 13'6", or 4.4 m, high) was a gift from France to the United States. It was designed by the French sculptor Frédéric-Auguste Bartholdi (1834–1904); its supporting framework was designed by the French engineer Gustave Eiffel (1832–1923), known mainly for his Eiffel Tower in Paris, France's national monument, completed in 1889.

the 18th century, and by the end of the 19th century strong religious faith and its manifestation in churchgoing had begun to fall off drastically at all levels of society. The newly developing fields of anthropology and psychology, far from replacing religion, provided fresh controversy with their radically different explanations of human life and behavior.

In a state of such potential explosiveness it is hardly surprising that a major collapse of the fabric of European civilization seemed inevitable. Only in America, where hundreds of thousands of Europeans emigrated in the hope of making a new start, did optimism seem possible [16.3]. Events were moving at so fast a pace that few thinkers were able to detach themselves from their times and develop a philosophical basis for dealing with them. One of the few who did was Friedrich Nietzsche (1844–1900), whose ominous diagnosis of the state of Western civilization in *Thus Spake Zarathustra* (1883–1892) and other works led him to propose drastic remedies.

For Nietzsche Christianity was a slave religion, extolling feeble virtues such as compassion and

EAST MEETS WEST

The Emergence of Japan

From the 16th century, traders and missionaries maintained links between Europe and China that were to have profound effects on later Chinese economic and political developments. Their Japanese neighbors, by contrast, maintained a careful policy of self-imposed isolation. The few Jesuits who had arrived there were driven out in the early 17th century, and in 1640 all Europeans were expelled, apart from a small group of Dutch merchants confined to Nagasaki under strict supervision. Japan was ruled by the emperor's commander-in-chief, a *shogun*, in a system of government that was principally feudal. The great lords, or *daimyo*, used their private armies of *samurai* warriors to impose order and advance their own interests.

In 1853 the American commodore Matthew Perry led a mission to Japan to establish commercial relations between the Japanese and the United States; the imposing fleet of steam warships he took with him no doubt played its part in persuading Japan to open its ports to foreign trade. Other nations hastened to take advantage of the new market, and Japan's seclusion was over.

The period of Japan's westernization is known as the Meiji era, the name given to the reign of the emperor Mutsuhito (1858–1912). Feudalism was abolished, and the country became a modern nation-state. Universal education and national service played their part in transforming illiterate peasants into trained and efficient workers. The result was the development of an economy that has become among the world's most powerful market forces.

The Japanese had been able to satisfy their limited curiosity about events elsewhere in the world, but the internal affairs of the island nation remained shrouded in mystery for Westerners. Not surprisingly, therefore Japan's emergence into the modern world caused a considerable stir. In artistic circles Japanese woodcuts, with their elegant simplicity, became prized collector's pieces; Degas was an enthusiastic connoisseur, and works like *The Tub* [16.12] show their influence. On a less sophisticated level, Western delight at the "quaintness" of Japanese life, dress, and customs was expressed in William Gilbert and Arthur Sullivan's operetta *The Mikado* (1885), while Japanese vulnerability to insensitive Western ways was the subject of Giacomo Puccini's popular opera *Madama Butterfly* (1904).

self-sacrifice, the greatest curse of Western civilization. He viewed democracy as little better, calling it the rule of the mediocre masses. The only valid life force, according to Nietzsche, is the "will to power," the energy that casts off all moral restraints in its pursuit of independence. Anything that contributes to power is good. Society can only improve if strong and bold individuals who can survive the loss of illusions, by the free assertion of the will, establish new values of nobility and goodness. Nietzsche called this superior individual an *Übermensch* (literally "overperson"). Like Schopenhauer in the early 19th century (see page 427), Nietzsche is valuable principally for the way in which he anticipated future ideas rather than because he was the leader of a movement. Unfortunately, his concepts were later taken up in a distorted form by many of the would-be world rulers of the 20th century, most notoriously the leaders of Nazi Germany.

Cut adrift from the security of religion or philosophy, the arts responded to the restless mood of the times by searching for new subjects and styles. Often these subjects and styles challenged principles that had been accepted for centuries. In music traditional concepts of harmony and rhythm were first radically extended and then, by some composers at least, completely discarded. In literature new areas of experience were explored, including the impact of the subconscious on human behavior, and traditional attitudes like the role of women were examined afresh. In the visual arts, the impressionists found a totally new way of looking at the world, which in turn opened up other exciting new fields of artistic expression. Whatever their defects, the formative years of the modern world were certainly not dull with respect to the arts.

NEW MOVEMENTS IN THE VISUAL ARTS

Something of the feverish activity in the visual arts during this period can be gauged by the sheer number of movements and styles that followed one another in rapid succession: impressionism, post-impressionism, fauvism, expressionism, culminating in the birth of cubism around the time of World War I. Cubism is discussed in Chapter 17 because of its effects on the whole of 20th-century art, but all the other movements form important stages in the transition from traditional artistic styles to the art of our own time, much of which rejects any attempt at realism in favor of abstract values of line, shape, and color. An understanding of their significance is thus a necessary prerequisite for a full appreciation of modern abstract art. Quite apart from their historical interest, however, the artistic movements of the late 19th and 20th centuries have much visual pleasure to offer.

As so often in the past, the center of artistic activity was Paris, where Édouard Manet (1832–1883) had created a sensation in 1863 with his painting *Le Déjeuner sur l'Herbe (Luncheon on the Grass)* [16.4]. Public outcry had been directed against the subject of the painting, which shows a female nude among two fully clothed young men and another clothed female figure. Other artists had combined nude females and clothed males before in a single picture, but Manet's scene has a particular air of reality; the way the unclad young woman stares out from the canvas and the two smartly dressed young men appear nonchalantly indifferent to her condition can still take the spectator by surprise. The true break with tradition, however, lay not in the picture's subject but its style. The artist is much less interested in telling us what his characters are doing than in showing us how he sees them and their surroundings. Instead of representing them as rounded, three-dimensional forms, he has painted them as a series of broad, flat areas in which the brilliance of color is unmuted. In creating this style, Manet laid the philosophical foundations that made impressionism possible.

The massive, almost monumental human form reappears in one of Manet's last paintings, *A Bar at the Folies-Bergère* of 1881 [16.5], where the barmaid amid her bottles and dishes presents the same solid appearance as the nude in *Déjeuner*. If we glance over her shoulder, however, and look into the mirror as it reflects her back and the crowded scene of which we have temporarily become a part, the style changes. The sharp outlines and fully defined forms of the foreground are replaced by a blur of shapes and colors that conveys the general impression of a crowded theater without reproducing specific details. A comparison between the background of the two pictures makes it clear that between 1863 and 1881 something drastic had occurred in the way painters looked at scenes and then reproduced them.

SPORTS AND GAMES

Baseball

When the European immigrants of the late 19th century arrived in America and settled down there, they found that the American national sport, baseball, was unfamiliar to them. Popular tradition ascribes the invention of baseball to Abner Doubleday (1819–1893), a Union general who, it is said, organized the first baseball game in 1839 at Cooperstown, N.Y. A hybrid, the game is loosely based on two English games, cricket and rounders. Most of its rules were first set down by the New York Knickerbocker Club, founded in 1845.

Even the Civil War did not prevent the new sport from rapidly spreading throughout the country. Cities generally acquired a team at about the same time that they obtained a rail link; Chicago's first team was formed in 1856, two years after the city was connected to Baltimore by rail. In 1869, the Cincinnati Red Stockings, the first fully professional team, were the first players to make a transcontinental tour from Maine to California. One of those accompanying them reported back: "The boys have received every attention from the officers of the different railroads. . . . At all the stations groups stare us almost out of countenance." A year later, it was Harvard's turn; their tour included Syracuse, Cleveland, Chicago, Milwaukee, Indianapolis, Washington, and New York. The English-born U.S. sports journalist Henry Chadwick wrote of the Harvard tour, almost twenty years later, that it was "the most brilliant in the history of college baseball." Chadwick himself played an important part in popularizing the game, writing on it in the New York *Times,* and compiling an annual handbook; Albert Spalding (1850–1915), who played for Boston and Chicago, eventually took over the production of the handbook.

The National League of Baseball Clubs was founded in 1876, the year of the first performance of Wagner's *Ring*. Attempts to form a rival league were unsuccessful until the turn of the century, when the American League was set up. The first World Series between the leading teams in each league was played in 1903. By the 1980s, the National League had twelve teams and the American League fourteen.

After World War II, with American forces still in Europe, some European sports fans began to develop an interest in the game, and some schools introduced baseball as an alternative to soccer. On the whole, however, it has proved resistant to transplantation. Italian and French teenagers collect baseball caps, and some even play the game, but as a mass spectator sport baseball remains quintessentially American.

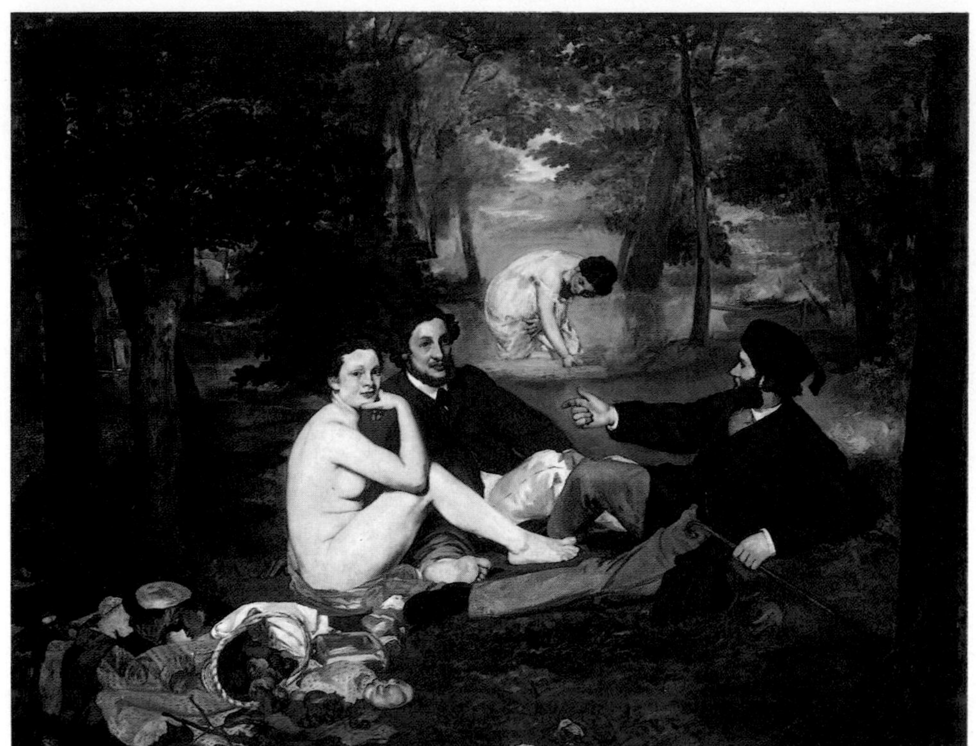

16.4 Édouard Manet. *Le Déjeuner sur l'Herbe*. 1863. Oil on canvas, 7'¾" × 8'10⅞" (2.15 × 2.7 m). Musée d'Orsay, Paris. Manet probably based the landscape on sketches made out-of-doors but painted the figures from models in his studio, something a careful look at the painting seems to confirm.

16.5 Édouard Manet. *A Bar at the Folies-Bergère.* 1881–1882. Oil on canvas, 3'1½" × 4'3" (.95 × 1.3 m). Courtauld Institute Galleries, London (Courtauld Collection). Note the very impressionistic way in which Manet painted the girl's top-hatted customer, reflected in the mirror at right.

Impressionism

In 1874 a group of young artists organized an exhibition of their work during conversations at the Café Guerbois in Paris. Their unconventional approach to art and their contempt for traditional methods meant that normal avenues of publicity were closed to them; they hoped that the exhibition would succeed in bringing their work to public attention. It certainly did. One of the paintings, *Impression: Sunrise* [16.6] by Claude Monet (1840–1926), particularly scandalized the more conventional critics, some of whom derisively borrowed its title and nicknamed the whole group impressionists. Within a few years the impressionists had revolutionized European painting.

Although impressionism seemed at the time to represent a radical break with the past, it first de-

16.6 **Claude Monet. *Impression: Sunrise.* 1872. Oil on canvas, 19½ × 24½" (50 × 62 cm). Musée Marmottan, Paris. Although this was the painting after which the impressionist movement was named, its use of impressionist techniques is relatively undeveloped compared with Figures 16.7 and 16.8.**

16.7 **Claude Monet. French, 1840–1926. *Red Boats at Argenteuil.* 1875. Oil on canvas (61.9 × 82.4 cm). Courtesy of the Harvard University Art Museum. Fogg Art Museum (bequest—Collection of Maurice Wertheim, Class of 1906). Painted the year after the first impressionist exhibition in Paris, this shows Monet's characteristic way of combining separate colors to reproduce the effect of light.**

veloped out of yet another attempt to achieve greater realism, a tradition that had begun at the dawn of the Renaissance with Giotto. The impressionists concentrated, however, on realism of light and color rather than realism of form and sought to reproduce with the utmost fidelity the literal impression an object made on their eyes. If, for example, we look at a house or a human face from a distance, we automatically interpret it on the basis of our mental knowledge, and "see" details that are not really visible. Impressionist painters tried to banish all such interpretations from their art and to paint with an "innocent eye." In *Red Boats at Argenteuil* [16.7] Monet has recorded all the colors he saw in the water and the reflections of the boats without trying to blend them together conventionally (or intellectually). The result is not a painting of boats at anchor but a representation of

16.8 Claude Monet. *Nymphéas (Water Lilies).* 1920–1921. Oil on canvas, 6'6" × 19'7" (1.98 × 5.97 m). The Carnegie Museum of Art, Pittsburgh (acquired through the generosity of Mrs. Alan M. Scaife, 1962). This is one of a number of huge paintings (in this case almost 20' long) that Monet produced in the garden of his house in Giverny. Note the contrast with his *Red Boats at Argenteuil* of forty-five years earlier (Figure 16.7); in *Water Lilies* there is a very different attitude to realism of form. The greatly enlarged detail at right gives an idea of Monet's technique—one that looks simple at first glance but actually results from many separate, complex decisions. In every case the artist was guided by purely visual factors rather than formal or intellectual ones.

the instantaneous impact on the eye of the lights and colors of those boats—that is, what the artist saw rather than what he knew.

Throughout his long career Monet retained a total fidelity to visual perception. His fellow painter Paul Cézanne is said to have called him "only an eye, but my God what an eye!" His preoccupation with the effects of light and color reached its most complete expression in his numerous paintings of water lilies in his garden. In version after version he tried to capture in paint the effect of the shimmering, ever-changing appearance of water, leaves, and blossoms. The result, as in the *Water Lilies* of 1920 [16.8], reproduces not so much the actual appearance of Monet's lily pond as an abstract symphony of glowing colors and reflecting lights. Paradoxically, the most complete devotion to naturalism was to pave the way for abstraction and for what we know as modern art.

Monet's art represents impressionism in its purest form. Other painters, while preserving its general principles, devised variants on it. Pierre-Auguste Renoir (1841–1919) shared Monet's interest in reproducing the effects of light in patches of color, but he brought to his subjects a human interest that derived from his own joy in life. It is a refreshing change, in fact, to find an artist whose work consistently explored the beauty of the world around him rather than the great problems of human existence. Nor was Renoir's interest limited, as was Monet's, to the wonders of nature. His most enduring love was for women as symbols of life itself; in his paintings they radiate an immense warmth and charm. His painting of *Le Moulin de la Galette* [16.9], a popular Parisian restaurant and dance hall, captures the spirit of the crowd by means of the same fragmentary patches of color Manet had used in the background of *A Bar at the Folies-Bergère* (see Figure 16.5), but Renoir adds his own sense of happy activity. The group in the foreground is particularly touching, with its sympathetic depiction of adolescent love. The boy leans impetuously forward, nervously fingering his chair, while the girl who has attracted his attention leans back and looks gravely yet seductively into his face, restrained by the protective arm of an older companion. Although the encounter may be commonplace, Renoir endows it with a significance and a humanity far different from Monet's more austere, if more literal, vision of the world by setting it against the warmth and movement of the background.

Unlike many other impressionists, Renoir traveled widely throughout Europe in order to see the paintings of the great Renaissance and baroque masters. The influence of artists like Raphael,

16.9 Auguste Renoir. *Le Moulin de la Galette*. 1876. Oil on canvas, 4'3½" × 5'9" (1.31 × 1.75 m). Musée d'Orsay, Paris. By using small patches of color, Renoir achieves the impression of dappled sunlight filtering through the trees.

Velázquez, and Rubens is visible in his work. This combination of an impressionist approach to color with a more traditional attitude to form and composition emerges in *Two Girls at the Piano* [16.10], where the girls' arms have a genuine sense of roundness and weight. This painting is not a mere visual exercise, for Renoir endows his figures with a sense of self-assurance that only emphasizes their vulnerability.

The artist Edgar Degas (1834–1917) shared Renoir's interest in people, but unlike Renoir (who emphasized the positive side of life) he simply

16.10 Auguste Renoir. 1841–1919. *Two Girls at the Piano*. 1892. Oil on canvas, 45½ × 34½" (116 × 90 cm). Musée d'Orsay, Paris. The position of the two girls, one leaning forward and resting her arm on the shoulder of the other, is almost exactly the same as that of the woman and the girl in the center of Figure 16.9; this position seems to have appealed to Renoir as a gesture of affection.

16.11 Edgar Degas. *The Rehearsal.* 1874. Oil on canvas, 26 × 32¼" (66 × 82 cm). Musée d'Orsay, Paris. Degas' careful observation extends even to the director of the ballet troupe at the right-hand edge of the stage, hat almost over his eyes, holding the back of his chair.

reported what he saw, stressing neither the good nor the bad. By showing us intimate moments in other people's lives, revealed by a momentary gesture or expression, his frankness, far from being heartless, as some of his critics have claimed, conveys the universality of human experience. Although Degas exhibited with the impressionists and, like them, chose to paint scenes from the everyday events of life, his psychological penetration distinguishes his art from their more literal approach to painting. Even the impressionist principle of capturing a scene spontaneously, in action, becomes in Degas' hands a powerful means of expression. One of the themes he turned to again and again was ballet, perhaps because of the range of movement it involved, although he also often underlined the gulf between the romantic façade of ballet and its down-to-earth reality. In *The Rehearsal* [16.11] we are left in no doubt that neither ballet nor ballet dancers are entirely glamorous. Degas' point of view is emphasized by the unusual vantage point from which the stage is shown: close to and from a position high up on the side. Far from coldly observing and reproducing the scene, Degas creates an instant bond between us and the hard-worked dancers, based on our perception of them as human beings.

Degas' honesty won him the reputation of being a woman hater, since many of his representations of female nudes lack the idealizing qualities of Renoir's and other painters' work. In a series of pastels he shows women caught unawares in simple natural poses. *The Tub* [16.12], with its unusual angle of vision, shows why these were sometimes called "key-hole visions." Far from posing, his subjects seem to be spied on while they are engrossed in the most intimate and natural activities.

16.12 Edgar Degas. *The Tub.* c. 1886. Pastel, 27⅝" (70 cm) square. Hill-Stead Museum, Farmington, Connecticut. The beautiful simplicity of Degas' drawing gives an impression of action glimpsed momentarily, as if by one passing by.

16.13 Mary Cassatt. *Mother and Child.* c. 1889. Oil on canvas, 29 × 23½" (74 × 60 cm). Cincinnati Art Museum (John J. Emery Endowment, 1928). By turning the mother's face away the artist concentrates attention on the child, an effect enhanced by the vague background.

One of Degas' closest friends was the American artist Mary Cassatt (1844–1926), who, after overcoming strong opposition from her father, settled in Europe to pursue an artistic career. Like Degas she painted spontaneous scenes from daily life, particularly situations involving mothers and children. *Mother and Child* [16.13] shows the mother turned away from us and a child who is saved from sentimentality by his complete unawareness of our presence. Cassatt herself never married, but there is no reason to think that her paintings of children were created out of frustration. She seems to have had a rich and happy life, and her championship of the impressionist cause among her American friends led to many of them buying impressionist works and taking them home with them. Cassatt's artist friends had much to thank her for, and so do the curators of many American museums and galleries, which have inherited collections of impressionist paintings.

Another member of the same circle was Berthe Morisot (1841–1895) whose early painting career was encouraged by Corot. In 1868 she met Manet and they became warm friends; a few years later she married his younger brother. An active member of the impressionist group, she exhibited works in almost all their shows.

Morisot's work has often been labeled "feminine," both by her contemporaries and by more recent critics. Like Cassatt, a close friend, she often painted women and children. Yet she also produced works of considerable breadth. *Paris Seen from the Trocadero* [16.14] presents a panoramic view of the city. The sense of light and atmosphere is conveyed by loose, fluid brushstrokes, while the figures in the foreground do not seem part of any story or incident: they help focus the scale of the view, which is seen as if from a height.

16.14 Berthe Morisot. *View of Paris from the Trocadero.* 1872. Oil on canvas, 18⅛ × 32$\frac{1}{16}$" (46.3 × 81.3 cm). Santa Barbara Museum of Art (gift of Mrs. Hugh N. Kirkland). The separation between the various planes of the view produces an effect of breadth and tranquility.

16.15 Auguste Rodin. *Monument to Balzac.* 1897–1898. Bronze (cast 1954), 9'3" × 48¼" × 41" (2.7 m). Collection, The Museum of Modern Art, New York. Presented in memory of Curt Valentin by his friends. Unlike most sculptors who worked in bronze, Rodin avoided a smooth surface by roughening and gouging the metal.

The impact of impressionism on sculptors was inevitably limited, since many of its principles were dependent on color and light and could only be applied in paint. Nevertheless, the greatest sculptor of the age (according to many, the greatest since Bernini), Auguste Rodin (1840–1918), reproduced in bronze something of the impressionist love of shifting forms and light and shadow. His remarkable figure of Balzac [16.15] demonstrates the irregularity of surface by which Rodin converted two-dimensional impressionist effects to a three-dimensional format. It also reveals one of the ways in which he differed from his impressionist contemporaries, since his themes are generally massive and dramatic rather than drawn from everyday life. The portrait of Balzac shows the great novelist possessed by creative inspiration, rather than his actual physical appearance. The subject of this sculpture is really the violent force of genius (a concept also illustrated in his portrait of the composer Gustav Mahler (see Figure 16.31) and Rodin conveys it with almost elemental power.

It should perhaps not be surprising that critics of the day were unprepared for such burning intensity. One of them dubbed the statue a "toad in a sack." But in retrospect Rodin breathed new life into sculpture. The "primitive" grandeur of his images formed a powerful attraction for 20th-century sculptors.

In general Rodin's works in marble are less impressionistic than those in bronze, but his famous *The Kiss* [16.16] achieves something of Renoir's blurred sensuality by the soft texture of the stone and the smooth transitions between the forms of the figures. Yet even though Rodin at times seems to strive for an impressionistic surface effect, the drama and full-blooded commitment of many of his works show the inadequacy of stylistic labels. We can only describe Rodin as a sculptor who used the impressionist style in works that foreshadow modern developments—that is, as a great original.

Post-Impressionism

As a stylistic category *post-impressionism* is one of the least helpful or descriptive terms in art history. The artists who are generally grouped together un-

16.16 Auguste Rodin. *The Kiss.* 1886. Marble, height 6'2" (1.9 m). Musée Rodin, Paris. As in his Balzac, the artist used the texture of his material to enhance the appearance of his work. But the smooth, slightly blurred surface of the marble here, in contrast to the rough surface of the portrait, produces a glowing effect.

16.17 Georges Seurat. French, 1859–1891. *A Sunday on La Grande Jatte.* 1884–1886. Oil on canvas, 6'9" × 10'⅜" (207.6 × 308 cm). The Art Institute of Chicago (Helen Birch Bartlett Memorial Collection), 1926.224. For all the casual activity in this scene of strollers in a park on an island in the river Seine, Seurat's remarkable sense of form endows it with an air of formality. Both shape and color (applied in minute dots) are rigorously ordered.

der it have as their only real common characteristic a rejection of impressionism for new approaches to painting. All of them arrived at their own individual styles. Their grouping together is therefore more a matter of historical convenience than critical judgment. The scientific precision of Georges Seurat (1859–1891), for example—whose paintings, based on the geometric relationship of forms in space, are made up of thousands of tiny dots of paint applied according to strict theories of color [16.17]—has little in common with the flamboyant and exotic art of Paul Gauguin (1848–1903). Particularly in his last paintings, based on his experiences in Tahiti, Gauguin attacked primitive subjects in a highly sophisticated manner, producing results like *Ia Orana Maria* [16.18], which may attract or repel viewers but rarely leave them indifferent.

The greatest post-impressionist painter was Paul Cézanne (1839–1906). It would be difficult to overestimate the revolutionary quality of Cézanne's art, which has been compared to that of the proto-Renaissance Florentine painter Giotto as an influence on Western art. Cézanne's innovations brought to an end the six-hundred-year attempt since Giotto's time to reproduce nature in painting. In place of nature Cézanne looked for order; or rather he tried to impose order on nature, without worrying if the results were realistic. It is not easy to comprehend or express in intellectual terms the character of Cézanne's vision, although, as so often

16.18 Paul Gauguin. *Ia Orana Maria.* 1891. Oil on canvas, 44¾ × 34½" (114 × 88 cm). Metropolitan Museum of Art, New York (bequest of Samuel A. Lewisohn, 1951). The title means "We hail thee, Mary"; the painting shows a Tahitian Madonna and Child being worshiped by two women with an angel standing behind them. The whole scene presents a fusion of Western spiritual values and the simple beauty of primitive Polynesian life.

16.19 Paul Cézanne. French, 1839–1906. *Still Life with Commode.* c. 1887–1888. Oil on canvas (65.1 × 80.8 cm). Courtesy of the Harvard University Art Museums. Fogg Art Museum (bequest—Collection of Maurice Wertheim, Class of 1906). So painstakingly did the artist work on the precise arrangement of the objects in his still lifes and on their depiction that the fruit usually rotted long before a painting was complete.

in the arts, the works speak for themselves. He claimed that he wanted to "make of Impressionism something solid and durable," and many of his paintings have a monumental air; they convey the mass and weight, in terms of both shape and color, of his subject matter rather than its literal physical appearance. His *Still Life with Commode* [16.19] does not try to show how the fruit, vase, and cloth really look or reproduce their actual relationship to one another. On the contrary, the painter has deliberately distorted the surface of the table and oversimplified the shape of the objects to achieve a totally satisfying design. Abstract considerations, in other words, take precedence over fidelity to nature. Cézanne believed that all forms in nature are based on the cone, the sphere and the cylinder, and he shapes and balances the forms to make them conform to this, using vigorous, rhythmical brush strokes. In the process a simple plate of fruit takes on a quality that can only be called massive.

The miracle of Cézanne's paintings is that for all their concern with ideal order they are still vibrantly alive. *Mont Sainte-Victoire* [16.20] is one of a number of versions Cézanne painted of the same scene, visible from his studio window. Perhaps the contrast between the peaceful countryside and the grandeur of the mountain beyond partially explains the scene's appeal to him. He produced the transition from foreground to background and up to the sky by the wonderful manipulation of planes of pure color. It illustrates his claim that he tried to give the style of impressionism a more solid appearance by giving his shapes a more continuous surface, an effect produced by broad brushstrokes. Yet equally the painting conveys the vivid colors of

16.20 Paul Cézanne. *Mont Sainte-Victoire.* 1904–1906. Oil on canvas, 28⅞ × 36¼" (73 × 92 cm). Philadelphia Museum of Art (George W. Elkins Collection). The reduction of the elements in the landscape to flat planes and the avoidance of the effect of perspective give the painting a sense of concentrated intensity.

16.21 Vincent van Gogh. *The Starry Night*. 1889. Oil on canvas, 29 × 36¼" (74 × 92 cm). Collection, The Museum of Modern Art, New York (acquired through the Lillie P. Bliss bequest). The impression of irresistible movement is the result of the artist's careful use of line and shape. The scene is dominated by spirals, vertical ones formed by the cypress trees and horizontal ones in the sky, which create a sense of rushing speed.

a Mediterranean landscape, with particular details refined away so as to leave behind the pure essence in all its beauty.

Nothing could be in greater contrast to Cézanne's ordered world than the tormented vision of Vincent van Gogh (1853–1890), the tragedy of whose life found its expression in his work. The autobiographical nature of van Gogh's painting, together with its passionate feelings, has a special appeal to modern sensibilities. In fairness to van Gogh, however, we should remember that by giving expression to his desperate emotions the artist was, however briefly, triumphing over them. Further, in a way that only the arts make possible, the suffering of a grim, even bizarre life became transformed into a profound if admittedly partial statement on the human condition. Desperate ecstasy and passionate frenzy are not emotions common to most people, yet *The Starry Night* [16.21] communicates them immediately and unforgettably.

The momentum of swirling, flickering forms in *The Starry Night* is intoxicating, but for the most part van Gogh's vision of the world was profoundly pessimistic. *The Night Café* [16.22] was described by the artist himself as "one of the ugliest I have done," but the ugliness is deliberate. Van Gogh's subject was "the terrible passions of humanity," expressed by the harsh contrasts between red, green, and yellow, which were intended to convey the idea that "the café is a place where one can ruin oneself, go mad, or commit a crime."

Much of van Gogh's pessimism was undoubtedly the result of the unhappy circumstances of his

16.22 Vincent van Gogh. *The Night Café.* 1888. Oil on canvas, 28½ × 36¼" (72 × 92 cm). Yale University Art Gallery, New Haven (bequest of Stephen C. Clark). Compare the lack of perspective in Cézanne's *Mont Sainte-Victoire* (Figure 16.20) with the highly exaggerated perspective used by van Gogh here to achieve a sense of violent intensity.

16.23 Vincent van Gogh. *Portrait of Dr. Gachet.* 1890. Oil on canvas, 26¼ × 22½" (67 × 57 cm). Private collection, U.S.A. Gachet was an amateur artist and friend of van Gogh who often provided medical treatment for his painter acquaintances without taking any fee. Mentally ill and in despair, van Gogh committed suicide while staying with Gachet.

own life, but it is tempting to place it in the wider context of his times and see it also as a terrifying manifestation of the growing social and spiritual alienation of society in the late 19th century. That van Gogh was actually aware of this is shown by a remark he made about his Portrait of Dr. Gachet [16.23], the physician who treated him in his last illness. He had painted the doctor, he said, with the "heartbroken expression of our times."

Fauvism and Expressionism

By the early years of the 20th century the violent mood of the times had intensified still further, and artists continued to express this in their art. The impact of post-impressionists like van Gogh inspired several new movements of which the most important was *fauvism,* which developed in France, and *expressionism,* which reached its high point in Germany.

The origin of the term fauvism reveals much of its character. In 1905 a group of artists exhibited paintings that broke with tradition so violently in their use of color and form that a critic described the painters as *les fauves* (the wild beasts). These painters had little in common apart from their desire to discard all traditional values; not surprisingly, the group broke up after a short while. But

TABLE 16.1 Principal Characteristics of Fauvism and Expressionism

Fauvism:	Violent, startling color contrasts Paintings reflect the effect of visual contact on the psyche Nature interpreted and subjected to the spirit of the artists Composition a decorative arrangement of elements to express the artist's feelings Technique deliberately crude to disturb the form of objects No effect of light or depth Art for art's sake
Expressionism:	Brilliant, clashing colors Paintings reflect mysticism, self-examination, speculation on the infinite Nature used to interpret the universe Composition: distorted forms in a controlled space, derived from late Gothic woodcut tradition Technique influenced by medieval art and the primitivistic art of Africa and Oceania No use of traditional perspective Art to convey emotional or psychological truth

one of their number, Henri Matisse (1869–1954), became a major force in 20th-century art.

Henri Matisse was the leading spirit of the fauves. His works are filled with the bold accents and brilliant color typical of fauvist art. Yet the flowing images of Matisse's paintings strike an individual note, expressing a mood of optimism and festivity curiously at odds with the times. One of his first important paintings, *The Joy of Life* [16.24], shows fields and trees in bright sunlight, where men and women are sleeping, dancing, and making music and love. It is difficult to think of any work of art further removed from the anguish of the years immediately preceding World War I than this image of innocent joy painted in 1905 and 1906.

16.24 Henri Matisse. *The Joy of Life*. 1905–1906. Oil on canvas, 5'8" × 7'9¾" (1.74 × 2.38 m). Barnes Foundation, Merion Station, Pennsylvania. By varying the sizes of the figures without regard to the relationship of one group to another the artist accentuates the sense of dreamlike unreality. Note Matisse's characteristically simple, flowing lines.

16.25 Henri Matisse. *The Red Studio*. Issy-les-Molineaux. 1911. Oil on canvas, 71¼" × 7'2¼" (1.81 × 2.19 m). Collection, The Museum of Modern Art, New York (Mrs. Simon Guggenheim Fund). The paintings and small sculptures in the studio are actual works by Matisse himself; they show the brilliant colors typical of fauve art.

16.26 Edvard Munch. *The Scream*. 1893. Oil on cardboard, 35½ × 28¾" (91 × 74 cm). Nasjonalgalleriet, Oslo. Munch himself once said, "I hear the scream in nature," and in this painting the anguish of the human figure seems to be echoed by the entire world around.

Matisse was saved from the gloom of his contemporaries by his sheer pleasure in seeing and painting; his work eloquently communicates the delight of visual sensation. His still-life paintings, like those of Cézanne, sacrifice realism in effective and satisfying design, but his use of color and the distortion of the natural relationships of the objects he paints are even greater than Cézanne's. In *The Red Studio* [16.25] every form is clearly recognizable but touched by the painter's unique vision. It is as if Matisse compels us to look through his eyes and see familiar objects suddenly take on new, vibrant life.

Matisse's sunny view of the world was very unusual, however. In northern Europe, particularly, increasing social and political tensions inspired a group of artists who are generally known as the expressionists to produce works that are at best gloomy and foreboding, sometimes chilling.

The forerunner of expressionist art was the Norwegian painter Edvard Munch (1863–1944), whose influence on German painting was comparable to that of Cézanne on French. The morbid insecurity that characterized Munch's own temperament emerges with horrifying force in his best-known work, *The Scream* [16.26], from which the lonely figure's cry seems to reverberate visibly through space. This painting is more than autobio-

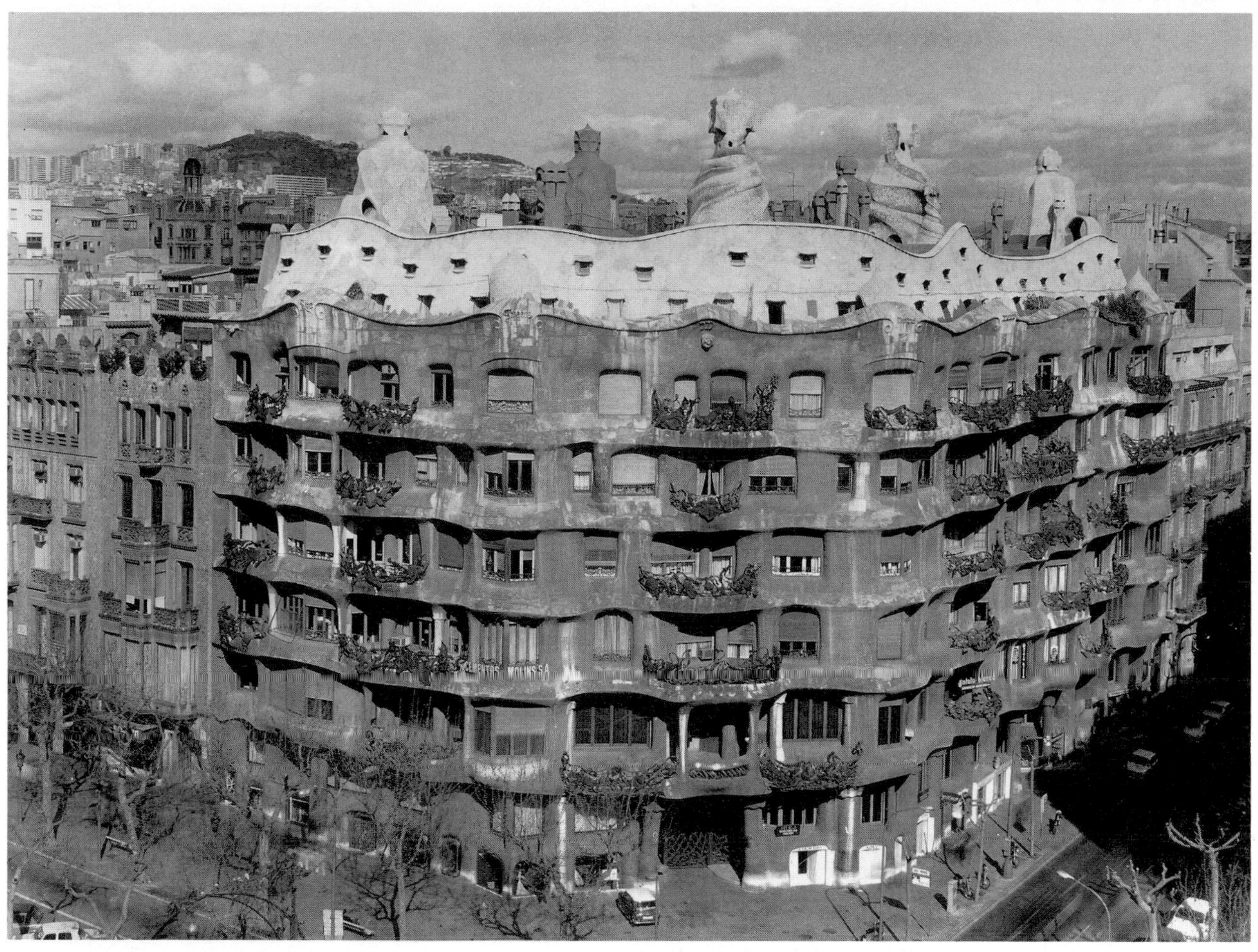

16.27 Antonio Gaudí. Casa Milá, Barcelona. 1907. Note the rough surface of the stone and the absence of any straight lines.

graphical, however, since it reflects a tendency on the part of Norwegian and other Scandinavian artists and writers to explore social and psychological problems. Elsewhere in Europe the Spanish architect Antonio Gaudí (1852–1926) applied the same artistic principles to his buildings, with often startling results. His Casa Milá [16.27], an apartment house in Barcelona, like *The Scream,* makes use of restless, waving lines that seem to undulate as we look. The sense of disturbance is continued by the spiraling chimneys—although Gaudí's intention was neither to upset nor necessarily to protest.

By 1905 expressionist artists in Germany were using the bold, undisguised brushstrokes and vivid colors of fauvism to paint subjects with more than a touch of Munch's torment. The German expressionists, many of them grouped in "schools" with such names as *Die Brücke* (The Bridge) and *Der blaue Reiter* (The Blue Rider), were relatively untouched by the intellectual and technical explorations of their contemporaries elsewhere. Instead, they were concerned with the emotional impact that a work could produce on the viewer. They were fascinated by the power of color to express mood, ideas, and emotion. They wanted their art to affect not only the eye but the viewer's inner sense. When they succeeded, as they often did, their works arouse strong emotions.

One of their principal themes was alienation and loneliness, so it is not surprising that they often turned to the writings of Dostoyevsky (see page 493) for inspiration. *Two Men at a Table* [16.28], by Erich Heckel (1883–1970), is in fact subtitled *To Dostoyevsky*.

Emil Nolde (1867–1956), who identified himself with Die Brücke after 1906, was one of the few expressionists to paint biblical scenes. To these he brought his own ecstatic, barbaric intensity. *Pentecost* [16.29] shows the apostles seated around the table literally burning with inspiration; the tongues of flame of the biblical account are visible above

16.28 Erich Heckel. *Two Men at a Table (To Dostoyevsky).* 1912. Kunsthalle, Hamburg. The two figures seem separated from one another by doubt and distrust, each wrapped up in his own isolation. Behind them is a distorted image of the crucified Christ.

16.29 Emil Nolde. *Pentecost.* 1909. Oil on canvas, 2'8" × 3'6" (87 × 107 cm). Staatliche Musseen Preussischer Kulturbesitz, National-galerie, Berlin. The broad, simplified faces and the powerful gestures of Christ in the center and of the two apostles clasping hands impart to the scene a concentration of emotional intensity.

their heads. Their faces have a masklike simplicity, but the huge eyes and heavy eyebrows convey frighteningly intense emotion. The image is far more disturbing than inspiring. Even in a religious context, expressionist art touches chords of alarm, even hysteria, unhappily appropriate to the times.

NEW STYLES IN MUSIC

The impressionists had forced both artists and public to think afresh about painting and about seeing; by the early years of the 20th century musicians and music lovers, too, were to have many of their preconceptions challenged. Not only were traditional forms like the symphony either discarded or handled in a radically new way, but even the basic ingredients of musical expression, *melody, harmony,* and *rhythm,* were subject to startling new developments. Few periods in the history of music are more packed with change, in fact, than those between 1870 and 1914, which saw a fresh approach to symphonic form, the rise of a musical version of impressionism, and the revolutionary innovations of the two giants of modern music, Schoenberg and Stravinsky.

Orchestral Music at the Turn of the Century

Although many extended orchestral works written in the last years of the 19th and the early 20th centuries were called symphonies by their composers, they would hardly have been recognizable as such to Haydn or Beethoven. The custom of varying the traditional number and content of symphonic movements had already begun during the romantic period; Berlioz had written his *Fantastic Symphony* as early as 1829 (see page 433). Nonetheless, by the turn of the century, so-called symphonies were being written that had little in common with one another, much less the classical symphonic tradition.

The driving force behind many of these works was the urge to communicate something beyond purely musical values. From the time of the ancient Greeks, many composers have tried to write instrumental music that tells a story or describes some event, including Vivaldi and his *Four Seasons* and Beethoven in his curious work known as the *Battle Symphony*. By the mid-19th century, however, composers had begun to devise elaborate *programs,* or plots, which their music would then describe. Music of this kind is generally known as *program music,* the first great exponent of which was Liszt (see page 435), who wrote works with titles like *Hamlet, Orpheus,* and *The Battle of the Huns,* for which he invented the generic description "symphonic poem."

The principle behind program music is no better or worse than many another. The success of any individual piece naturally depends on the degree to which narrative and musical interest can be combined. There are, to be sure, some cases where a composer has been carried away by eagerness for realism. Ottorino Respighi (1879–1936), for example, incorporated the sound of a nightingale by including a record player and a recording of live birdsong in a score.

No one was more successful at writing convincing program symphonies and symphonic poems (*tone poems,* as he called them) than the German composer Richard Strauss (1864–1949). One of his first successful tone poems, *Don Juan,* begun in 1886, deals with the familiar story of the compulsive Spanish lover from a characteristically late-19th-century point of view. Instead of the unrepentant Don Giovanni of Mozart or Byron's amused (and amusing) Don Juan, Strauss presents a man striving to overcome the bonds of human nature, only to be driven by failure and despair to suicide. The music, gorgeously orchestrated for a vast array of instruments, moves in bursts of passion, from the surging splendor of its opening to a bleak and shuddering conclusion.

Strauss was not limited to grand and tragic subjects. *Till Eulenspiegel* is one of the most successful examples of humor in music. It tells the story of a notorious practical joker and swindler. Even when Till goes too far in his pranks and ends up on the gallows (vividly depicted by Strauss' orchestration), the music returns to a cheerful conclusion.

One of Strauss' most remarkable works, and one that clearly demonstrates the new attitude toward symphonic form, is his *Alpine Symphony,* written between 1911 and 1915. In one huge movement lasting some fifty minutes it describes a mountain-climbing expedition, detailing the adventures on the way (with waterfalls, cowbells, glaciers all in the music) and, at its climax, the arrival on the summit. The final section depicts the descent, during which a violent storm breaks out, and the music finally sinks to rest in the peace with which it opened. All this may sound more like the sound track to a movie than a serious piece of music, but skeptical listeners should try the *Alpine Symphony* for themselves. It is as far from conventional notions of a symphony as Cézanne's painting of *Mont*

Sainte-Victoire (see Figure 16.20) is from a conventional landscape, but genius makes its own rules. Strauss' work should be taken on its own terms.

Not surprisingly, a composer capable of such exuberant imagination was also fully at home in the opera house. Several of Strauss' operas are among the greatest of all 20th-century contributions to the repertoire. In some of them he was clearly influenced by the prevailingly gloomy and morbid mood of German expressionist art. His first big success, for example, was a setting of the English writer Oscar Wilde's play *Salome,* based on the biblical story, first performed to a horrified audience in 1905. After one performance in 1907 at the Metropolitan Opera House in New York, it was banned in the United States for almost thirty years. The final scene provides a frightening yet curiously moving depiction of erotic depravity, as Salome kisses the lips of the severed head of John the Baptist. This subject had been gruesomely represented by the German expressionist painter Lovis Corinth (1858–1925) in 1899 [16.30].

Works like *Don Juan* and the *Alpine Symphony* deal with stories we know or describe events with which we are familiar. In other cases, however, Strauss took as his subject his own life, and a number of his pieces, including the *Domestic Symphony* and the somewhat immodestly entitled *Hero's Life,* are frankly autobiographical. In this he was following a custom that had become increasingly popular in the late 19th century—the composition of music concerned with the detailed revelation of its composer's inner emotional life.

16.30 Lovis Corinth. *Salome.* 1899. Oil on canvas (76.2 × 83.3 cm). Courtesy of Busch-Reisinger Museum, Harvard University (gift of Hans H. A. Meyn). Note the strikingly modern look of Salome, here representing the degeneracy of the artist's own times.

One of the first musicians to make his personal emotions the basis for a symphony was the late-romantic composer Peter Ilych Tchaikovsky (1840–1893), whose *Symphony No. 6 in b minor,* known as the "Pathétique," was written in the year of his death. An early draft outline of its "story" was found among his papers, describing its "impulsive passion, confidence, eagerness for activity," followed by love and disappointments, and finally collapse and death. It is now believed that the Russian composer's death from cholera was not, as used to be thought, accidental, but deliberate suicide. The reasons are still not clear, but they perhaps related to a potentially scandalous love affair in high places with which Tchaikovsky had become involved. In the light of this information the *"Pathétique" Symphony* takes on new poignance. Its last movement sinks mournfully into silence after a series of climaxes that seem to protest bitterly if vainly against the injustices of life.

The revelation of a composer's life and emotions through his music reached its most complete expression in the works of Gustav Mahler (1860–1911). Until around 1960, the centenary of his birth in Bohemia, Mahler's music was almost unknown and he was generally derided as unoriginal and overambitious. Now that he has become one of the most frequently performed and recorded of composers, we can begin to appreciate his true worth and learn the danger of hasty judgments.

The world of Mahler's symphonies is filled with his own anxieties, triumphs, hopes, and fears, but it also illuminates our own problem-ridden age. It may well be that Mahler speaks so convincingly and so movingly to a growing number of ordinary music lovers because his music touches on areas of human experience unexplored before his time and increasingly significant to ours. In purely musical terms, however, Mahler can now be seen as a profoundly original genius. Like Rodin, who produced a marvelous portrait of him [16.31], he stands as both the last major figure of the 19th century in his field and a pioneer in the modern world. Indeed, it was precisely his innovations that won him the scorn of earlier listeners: his deliberate use of popular, banal tunes, for example, and the abrupt changes of mood in his music. A symphony, he once said, should be like the world; it should contain everything. His own nine completed sym-

CONTEMPORARY VOICES

Gustav Mahler

A letter from Mahler to his wife Alma reporting on a meeting with Richard Strauss. Mahler had heard *Salome,* and was impressed. The *she* in the second line is Pauline, Strauss' wife.

Berlin, January 1907

My dear, good Almschili:

Yesterday afternoon I went to see Strauss. She met me at the door with pst! pst! Richard is sleeping, pulled me into her (very slovenly) boudoir, where her old mama was sitting over some mess (not coffee) and filled me full of nonsensical chatter about various financial and sexual occurrences of the last two years, in the meantime asking hastily about a thousand and one things without waiting for a reply, would not let me go under any circumstances, told me that yesterday morning Richard had had a very exhausting rehearsal in Leipzig, then returned to Berlin and conducted *Götterdämmerung* in the evening, and this afternoon, worn to a frazzle, he had gone to sleep, and she was carefully guarding his sleep. I was dumbfounded.

Suddenly she burst out: "Now we have to wake up the rascal!" Without my being able to prevent it, she pulled me with both her fists into his room and yelled at him in a very loud voice: "Get up, Gustav is here!" (For an hour I was Gustav—then suddenly Herr Direktor again.) Strauss got up, smiled patiently, and then we went back to a very animated discussion of all that sheer bilge. Later we had tea and they brought me back to my hotel in their automobile, after arranging for me to take lunch with them at noon Saturday.

There I found two tickets for parquet seats in the first row for *Salome* and I took Berliner along. The performance was excellent in every respect—orchestrally, vocally, and scenically it was pure Kitsch and Stoll, and again it made an extraordinary impression on me. It is an extremely clever, very powerful piece, which certainly belongs among the most significant of our time! Beneath a heap of rubbish an infernal fire lives and burns in it—not just fireworks.

That's the way it is with Strauss's whole personality and it's difficult to separate the wheat from the chaff. But I had felt tremendous respect for the whole manifestation and his was confirmed again. I was tremendously pleased. I go the whole hog on that. Yesterday Blech conducted—excellently. Saturday Strauss is conducting and I am going again. Destinn was magnificent; the Jochanaan (Berger) very fine. The others, so-so. The orchestra really superb.

From G. Norman and M. L. Shrifte: *Letters of Composers* (New York: Grosset & Dunlap, 1946), p. 301.

16.31 Auguste Rodin. *Gustav Mahler.* 1909. Bronze, height 13" (34 cm). Musée Rodin, Paris. As in his *Monument to Balzac* (Figure 16.15), Rodin deliberately roughened the surface of the bronze for dramatic effect. In this case Mahler's hollow cheeks and intense gaze are powerfully suggested.

phonies (he left a tenth unfinished), and *The Song of the Earth,* a symphony for two singers and orchestra, certainly contain just about every human emotion.

As early as the *Symphony No. 1 in D,* we can hear the highly individual characteristics of Mahler's music. The third movement of the symphony is a funeral march, but its wry, ironic tone is totally unlike any other in the history of music. The movement opens with the mournful sound of a solo double bass playing the old round "Frère Jacques," which is then taken up by the rest of the orchestra. There are sudden bursts of trite nostalgia and violent aggression until the mood gradually changes to one of genuine tenderness. After a gentle middle section the movement returns to the bizarre and unsettling spirit of the opening.

By the end of his life Mahler was writing much less optimistic music than *Symphony No. 1,* which—despite its third-movement funeral march—concludes with a long finale ending in a blaze of triumphant glory. Mahler's last completed works, *The Song of the Earth* and the *Symphony No. 9,* composed under the shadow of fatal heart disease and impending death, express all the beauty of the world together with the sorrow and ultimate resignation of one who has to leave it. The final movement of the *Symphony No. 9,* in particular, is a uniquely eloquent statement of courage in the face of human dissolution. Opening with a long, slow theme of great passion and nobility, the movement gradually fades away as the music dissolves into fragments and finally sinks into silence. Like all Mahler's music, and like the paintings of van Gogh or Munch, the *Symphony No. 9* does not turn its back on the ugliness and tragedy of life; but Mahler, unlike many of his contemporaries, was able to see beyond them and express something of the painful joy of human existence. Perhaps that is why his music has become so revered in our own times.

Impressionism in Music

At about the same time painters in France were developing the style we call impressionist, Claude Debussy (1862–1918), a young French composer, began to break new musical ground. Abandoning the concept of the development of themes in a systematic musical argument, which lies behind classical sonata form and romantic symphonic structure, he aimed for a constantly changing flow of sound. Instead of dealing with human emotions, his music evoked the atmosphere of nature, the wind and rain and the sea. The emphasis on shifting tone colors led inevitably to comparisons with impressionist painting. Like Monet or Renoir, he avoided grand, dramatic subjects in favor of ephemeral, intangible sensations and replaced romantic opulence with refinement.

These comparisons should nevertheless not be exaggerated. Debussy and the impressionists shared a strong reaction against tradition in general and the romantic tradition in particular, in response to which they created a radically new approach to their respective arts, but impressionism permanently changed the history of painting, while the only really successful impressionist composer was Debussy himself. Later musicians have borrowed some of Debussy's musical devices, including his very fluid harmony and frequent dissonances, but Debussy never really founded a school. The chief developments in 20th-century music after Debussy took a very different direction, summed up rather unsympathetically by the French writer Jean Cocteau (1891–1963): "After music with the silk brush, music with the axe." These developments represent a more determined break with tradition than the refined style of Debussy. Indeed, with the passing of time Debussy's musical style appears increasingly to represent the last gasp of romanticism rather than the dawn of a new era.

Whatever his historical position, Debussy was without doubt one of the great creative musical figures in the last hundred years. He is at his best and most impressionist in orchestral works like *La Mer (The Sea),* which Debussy himself called symphonic sketches—a rather curious term that shows the composer for once willing to accept a traditional label. This marine counterpart of Strauss' *Alpine Symphony* is in three movements, the titles of which ("From Dawn to Noon on the Sea," "Play of the Waves," and "Dialogue of the Wind and the Sea") describe the general atmosphere that concerned Debussy rather than literal sounds. There are no birdcalls or thunderclaps in the music; instead the continual ebb and flow of the music suggest the mood of a seascape. The second movement, for example, depicts the sparkling sunlight on the waves by means of delicate, flashing violin scales punctuated by bright flecks of sound color from the wind instruments. It is scarcely possible to resist a comparison with the shimmering colors of Monet's *Water Lilies* (see Figure 16.8).

Elsewhere Debussy's music is less explicitly descriptive. His piano music, among his finest, shows an incredible sensitivity to the range of sound effects that instrument can achieve. Many of his pieces have descriptive titles—"Footsteps in the Snow," "The Girl with the Flaxen Hair," and so on—but often these were added after their composition as the obligatory touch of musical impressionism. Sometimes they were even suggested by Debussy's friends as their own personal reactions to his music.

The only composer to make wholehearted use of Debussy's impressionistic style was his fellow countryman Maurice Ravel (1875–1937), who, however, added a highly individual quality of his own. Ravel was far more concerned with classical form and balance than Debussy. His musical god was Mozart, and something of the limpid clarity of Mozart's music can be heard in many of his pieces—although certainly not in the all-too-familiar *Bolero*. His lovely *Piano Concerto in G* alternates a Mozartian delicacy and grace with an exuberance born of Ravel's encounters with jazz. Even in his most overtly impressionistic moments, like the scene in his ballet *Daphnis and Chloe* that describes dawn rising, he retains an elegance and verve distinctly different from the veiled and muted tones of Debussy.

The Search for a New Musical Language

In 1908 the Austrian composer Arnold Schoenberg (1874–1951) wrote his *Three Piano Pieces,* Op. 11, in which he was "conscious of having broken all restrictions" of past musical traditions. After their first performance one critic described them as "pointless ugliness" and "perversion." In 1913 the first performance of *The Rite of Spring,* a ballet by the Russian-born composer Igor Stravinsky (1882–1971), was given in Paris, where he was then living. It was greeted with hissing, stamping, and yelling, and Stravinsky was accused of the "destruction of music as an art." Stravinsky and Schoenberg are now justly hailed as the founders of modern music, but we can agree with their opponents in at least one respect: Their revolutionary innovations permanently changed the course of musical development.

It is a measure of their achievement that today listeners find *The Rite of Spring* exciting, even explosive, but perfectly approachable. If Stravinsky's ballet score has lost its power to shock and horrify, it is principally because we have become accustomed to music written in its shadow. *The Rite of Spring* has created its own musical tradition, one without which the music of the 20th century at all levels of popularity would be unthinkable. Schoenberg's effect has been less widespread and more subtle; nonetheless, no serious composer writing since his time has been able to ignore his music. It is significant that Stravinsky himself, who originally seemed to be taking music down a radically different "path to destruction," eventually adopted principles of composition based on Schoenberg's methods.

As is true of all apparently revolutionary breaks with the past, Stravinsky and Schoenberg were really only pushing to extreme conclusions developments that had been under way for some time. Traditional harmony had been collapsing since the time of Wagner, and Schoenberg only dealt it a death blow by his innovations. Wagner's *Tristan and Isolde* had opened with a series of chords that were not firmly rooted in any key and had no particular sense of direction (see page 438), a device Wagner used to express the poetic concept of restless yearning. Other composers followed him in rejecting the concept of a fixed harmonic center from which the music might stray as long as it returned there, replacing it with a much more fluid use of harmony. (Debussy, in his attempts to go beyond the bounds of conventional harmony, often combined chords and constructed themes in such a way as to avoid the sense of a tonal center; the result can be heard in the wandering, unsettled quality of much of his music.)

Schoenberg believed that the time had come to abandon a harmonic (or tonal) system that had served music well for over three hundred years but had simply become worn out. He therefore began to write *atonal* music—music that deliberately avoided traditional chords and harmonies. Thus Schoenberg's atonality was a natural consequence of earlier musical developments. At the same time, it was fully in accordance with the spirit of the times. The sense of a growing rejection of traditional values, culminating in a decisive and violent break with the past, can be felt not only in the arts but also in the political and social life of Europe; Schoenberg's drastic abandonment of centuries of musical tradition prefigured by only a few years the far more drastic abandonment of centuries of tradition brought by World War I.

There is another sense in which Schoenberg's innovations correspond to contemporary developments. One of the principal effects of atonality is a mood of instability, even disturbance, which lends itself to the same kind of morbid themes that attracted expressionist painters—in fact, many of Schoenberg's early atonal works deal with such themes. Schoenberg himself was a painter of some ability and generally worked in an expressionist style.

One of Schoenberg's most extraordinary pieces is *Pierrot Lunaire,* finished in 1912, a setting of twenty-one poems for women's voice and small instrumental group. The poems describe the bizarre experiences of their hero, Pierrot, who is an expressionist version of the eternal clown, and their mood is grotesque and at times demonic. The eighth poem, for example, describes a crowd of gigantic black moths flying down to block out the sunlight, while in the eleventh, entitled "Red Mass," Pierrot holds his own heart in his blood-stained fingers to use as a "horrible red sacrificial wafer." Schoenberg's music clothes these verses in appropriately fantastic and macabre music. The effect is enhanced by the fact that the singer is instructed to *speak* the words at specific pitches. This device of

Sprechstimme (voiced speech), invented by Schoenberg for *Pierrot Lunaire,* is difficult to execute, but when it is done properly by a skilled performer, it imparts a wistfully dreamlike quality to the music.

The freedom atonality permitted the composer became something of a liability, and by the 1920s Schoenberg replaced it with a system of composition as rigid as any earlier method in the history of music. His famous *twelve-tone technique* makes use of the twelve notes of the chromatic scale (on the piano, all the black and white notes in an octave), which are carefully arranged in a *row* or *series,* the latter term having given rise to the name *serialism* to describe the technique. The basic row, together with variant forms, then serves as the basis for a movement or even an entire work, with the order of the notes remaining always the same. The following example presents the row used in the first movement of Schoenberg's *Piano Suite,* Op. 25, together with three of its variant forms. No. 1 is the row itself, No. 2 its inversion (that is, the notes are separated by the same distance but in the opposite direction, down instead of up, and up instead of down); No. 3 is the row retrograde or backward, and No. 4 the inversion of this backward form, known as retrograde inversion.

Just as with program music, the only fair way to judge the twelve-tone technique is by its results. Not all works written in it are masterpieces, but we can hardly expect them to be. It is not a system that appeals to all composers or brings out the best in them, but few systems ever have universal application. A number of Schoenberg's own twelve-tone works, including his unfinished opera *Moses and Aaron* and the *Violin Concerto* of 1934, demonstrate that serial music can be both beautiful and moving. The 21st century will decide whether the system has permanent and enduring value.

Like *Pierrot Lunaire,* Stravinsky's *The Rite of Spring* deals with a violent theme. It is subtitled "Pictures from Pagan Russia" and describes a springtime ritual culminating in the sacrifice of a chosen human victim. Whereas Schoenberg had jettisoned traditional harmony, Stravinsky used a new approach to rhythm as the basis of his piece. Constantly changing, immensely complex, and frequently violent, his rhythmic patterns convey a sense of barbaric frenzy that is enhanced by the weight of sound obtained from the use of a vast orchestra. There are some more peaceful moments, notably the nostalgic opening section, but in general the impression is of intense exhilaration. Something of the rhythmic vitality of *The Rite of Spring* can be seen in this brief extract from the final orgiastic dance. The same melodic fragment is repeated over and over again, but in a constantly fluctuating rhythm that changes almost from bar to bar.

The *Rite of Spring* was the last of three ballets (the others were *The Firebird* and *Petrouchka*) that Stravinsky based on Russian folk subjects [16.32].

16.32 Vaslav Nijinsky as the puppet Petrouchka in Igor Stravinsky's ballet of that name, as choreographed by Michel Fokine and performed by the Ballet Russe. Paris, 1911. New York Public Library at Lincoln Center (Roger Pryor Dodge Collection). Nijinsky (1890–1950), a Russian, was one of the greatest dancers of all time. Fokine (1880–1942), also a Russian, was a choreographer who broke new ground in the ballet just as the impressionists did in art and music.

In the years following World War I he wrote music in a wide variety of styles, absorbing influences as varied as Bach, Tchaikovsky, and jazz. Yet a characteristically Stravinskian flavor pervades all his best works, with the result that his music is almost always instantly recognizable. Short, expressive melodies and unceasing rhythmic vitality, both evident in *The Rite of Spring,* recur in works like the *Symphony in Three Movements* in 1945. Even when, in the 1950s, he finally adopted the technique of serialism he retained his own unique musical personality. Indeed, Stravinsky is a peculiarly 20th-century cultural phenomenon, an artist uprooted from his homeland, cut off (by choice) from his cultural heritage, and exposed to a barrage of influences and counterinfluences. That he never lost his sense of personal identity or his belief in the enduring value of art makes him a 20th-century hero.

NEW SUBJECTS FOR LITERATURE

Psychological Insights in the Novel

At the end of the 19th century many writers were still as concerned with exploring the nature of their own individual existences as they had been when the century began. In fact, the first years of the 20th century saw an increasing interest in the effect of the subconscious on human behavior, a result in large measure of the work of the Austrian psychoanalyst Sigmund Freud (1856–1939); the general conclusions Freud reached are discussed in Chapter 17. In many ways his interest in the part played by individual frustrations, repressions, and neuroses (particularly sexual) in creating personality was prefigured in the writing of two of the greatest novelists of the late 19th century. Fyodor Dostoyevsky (1821–1881) and Marcel Proust (1871–1922).

Self-knowledge played a major part in Dostoyevsky's work, and his concern for psychological truth led him into a profound study of his characters' subconscious motives. His empathy for human suffering derived in part from his identification with Russian Orthodox Christianity, with its emphasis on suffering as a means to salvation. Although well aware of social injustices, he was more concerned with their effect on the individual soul than on society as a whole. His books present, to be sure, a vivid picture of the Russia of his day, with characters at all levels of society brought brilliantly to life. Nevertheless, he was able to combine realism of perception with a deep psychological understanding of the workings of the human heart. Few artists have presented so convincing a picture of individuals struggling between good and evil.

The temptation to evil forms a principal theme of one of his most powerful works, *Crime and Punishment*. In it he tells the story of a poor student, Raskolnikov, whose growing feeling of alienation from his fellow human beings leads to a belief that he is superior to society and above conventional morality. To prove this to himself Raskolnikov decides to commit an act of defiance: the murder of a defenseless old woman, not for gain but as a demonstration of his own power.

He murders the old woman and also her younger sister, who catches him in the act. Crime is followed immediately, however, not by the punishment of the law but by the punishment of his own conscience. Guilt and remorse cut him off even further from human contact until finally, in utter despair and on the verge of madness, he goes to the police and confesses to the murder. Here and in his other works Dostoyevsky underlines the terrible dangers of intellectual arrogance. The world he portrays is essentially cruel, one in which simplicity and self-awareness are the only weapons against human evil, and suffering is a necessary price for victory.

If Dostoyevsky used violence to depict his view of the world, his contemporary and fellow Russian Anton Chekhov (1860–1904) used irony and satire to show the passivity and emptiness of his characters. In plays and short stories, Chekhov paints a provincial world whose residents dream of escape, filled with a frustrated longing for action. The three sisters who are the chief characters in the play of that name never manage to achieve their ambition to go "To Moscow, to Moscow!" In stories such as "The Lady with the Dog," Chekhov uses apparent triviality to express profound understanding, while in "The Bet" he ironically challenges most of our basic values.

One of the most influential of all modern writers was the French novelist Marcel Proust. Proust's youth was spent in the fashionable world of Parisian high society, where he entertained lavishly and mixed with the leading figures of the day while writing elegant if superficial poems and stories. The death of his father in 1903 and of his mother in 1905 brought a complete change. He retired to his house in Paris and rarely left his soundproofed bedroom, where he wrote the vast work for which he is famous, *Remembrance of Things Past.* The first volume appeared in 1913; the eighth and last volume was not published until 1927, five years after his death.

It is difficult to do justice to this amazing work. The lengthy story is told in the first person by a narrator who, though never named, obviously has much in common with Proust himself. Its entire concern is to recall the narrator's past life, from earliest childhood to middle age, by bringing to mind the people, places, things, and events that have affected him. In the course of the narrator's journey back into his past he realizes that all of it lies hidden inside him and that the tiniest circumstance—a scent, a taste, the appearance of someone's hair—can trigger a whole chain of memory associations. By the end of the final volume the narrator has decided to preserve the recollection of his past life by making it permanent in the form of a book—the book the reader has just finished.

Proust's awareness of the importance of the subconscious and his illustration of the way in which it can be unlocked have had a great appeal to modern writers, as has his *stream of consciousness* style, which appears to reproduce his thought processes as they actually occur rather than as edited by a writer for logical connections and development. Further, as we follow Proust's (or the narrator's) careful and painstaking resurrection of his past, it is important to remember that his purpose is far more than a mere intellectual exercise. By recalling the past we bring it back to life in a literal sense. Memory is our most powerful weapon against death.

TABLE 16.2 Social and Intellectual Developments 1870–1914

1875	German Social Democratic party founded
1879	Edison invents electric lightbulb
1881	Pasteur and Koch prove German theory of disease
1883	Social insurance initiated by Bismarck in Germany
1888	Brazil abolishes slavery, the last nation to do so
1889	International league of Socialist parties founded, the so-called Second International
1894–1906	Dreyfus affair in France reveals widespread anti-Semitism and leads to separation of church and state
1895	Roentgen discovers x-rays Marconi invents wireless telegraphy
1900	Freud publishes *The Interpretation of Dreams*
1903	Wright brothers make first flight with power-driven plane
1905	Einstein formulates theory of relativity Revolution in Russia fails to produce significant social change
1906–1911	Social insurance and parliamentary reform enacted in Britain
1909	Ford produces assembly line–made automobiles
1911	Revolution in China establishes republic Rutherford formulates theory of positively charged atomic nucleus

Responses to a Changing Society: The Role of Women

Not all writers in the late 19th and early 20th centuries devoted themselves to the kind of psychological investigation found in the works of Dostoyevsky and Proust. The larger question of the nature of society continued to attract the attention of more socially conscious writers who explored the widening range of problems created by industrial life as well as a whole new series of social issues [Table 16.2].

One of the most significant aspects of the development of the modern world has been the changing role of women in family life and in society at large. The issue of women's right to vote was bitterly fought out in the early years of the 20th century, and not until 1918 in Great Britain and 1920 in the United States were women permitted to participate in the electoral process. On a more personal basis, the growing availability and frequency of divorce began to cause many women (and men) to rethink the nature of the marriage tie. The pace of women's emancipation from the stock role assigned to them over centuries was, of course, extremely slow, and the process is far from complete. A beginning had to be made somewhere, however, and it is only fitting that a period characterized by cultural and political change should also be marked by social change in this most fundamental of areas.

In the same way Dickens had led the drive against industrial oppression and exploitation in the mid-19th century, writers of the late 19th and early 20th centuries not only reflected feminist concerns but actively promoted them as well. They tackled a range of problems so vast that we can do no more than look at just one area, marriage, through the eyes of two writers of the late 19th century. One of them, Henrik Ibsen (1828–1906), was the most famous playwright of his day and a figure of international renown. The other, Kate Chopin (1851–1904), was ignored in her own lifetime even in her native America.

Ibsen was born in Norway, although he spent much of his time in Italy. Most of his mature plays deal with the conventions of society and their consequences, generally tragic. Although many of them are technically set in Norway their significance was intended to be universal. The problems Ibsen explored were frequently ones regarded as taboo, including venereal disease, incest, and insanity. The realistic format of the plays brought issues like these home to his audience with shocking force. At first derided, Ibsen eventually became a key figure in the development of drama, particularly in the English-speaking world, where his work was championed by George Bernard Shaw (1856–1950), himself later to inherit Ibsen's mantle as a progressive social critic.

In one of his first important plays, *A Doll's House* (1879), Ibsen dealt with the issue of women's rights. The principal characters, Torvald Helmer and his wife Nora, have been married for eight years, apparently happily enough. Early in their marriage, however, before Helmer had become a prosperous lawyer, Nora had secretly borrowed some money from Krogstad, a friend, to pay for her husband's medical treatment; she had told Torvald that the money came from her father, for Helmer himself was too proud to borrow. As the play opens, Krogstad, to whom Nora is still in debt, threatens to blackmail her if she does not persuade Helmer to find him a job. When she refuses to do so Krogstad duly writes a letter to Helmer revealing the truth. Helmer recoils in horror at his wife's deception. The matter of the money is eventually settled by other means and Helmer eventually forgives Nora, but not before the experience has given her a new and unforgettable insight into her relationship with her husband. In the final scene, she walks out the door, slams it, and leaves him forever.

Nora decides to abandon her husband on two grounds. In the first place she realizes how small a part she plays in her husband's real life. As she says, "Ever since the first day we met, we have never exchanged so much as one serious word about serious things." The superficiality of their relationship horrifies her. In the second place, Helmer's inability to rise to the challenge presented by the discovery of his wife's deception and prove his love for her by claiming that it was he who had borrowed and failed to repay the debt diminishes him in Nora's eyes. Ibsen tries to express what he sees as an essential difference between men and women when, in reply to Helmer's statement "One doesn't sacrifice one's honor for love's sake," Nora replies, "Millions of women have done so." Nora's decision not to be her husband's childish plaything—to leave the doll's house in which she was the doll—was so contrary to accepted social behavior that one noted critic remarked: "That slammed door reverberated across the roof of the world."

In comparison with the towering figure of Ibsen, the American writer Kate Chopin found few readers in her own lifetime; even today she is not widely known. Only recently have critics begun to do justice to the fine construction and rich psychological insight of her novel *The Awakening*, denounced as immoral and banned when first published in 1899. Its principal theme is the oppressive role women are forced to play in family life. Edna, its heroine, like Nora in *A Doll's House*, resents the meaninglessness of her relationship with her husband and the tedium of her daily existence. Her only escape is to yield to her sexual drives and find freedom not in slamming the door behind her but by throwing herself into a passionate if unloving affair.

In her short stories Kate Chopin dealt with the same kind of problem, but with greater delicacy and often with a wry humor. Frequently on the smallest of scales, these stories examine the prison that marriage seems so often to represent. In the course of a couple of pages Chopin exposes an all-too-common area of human experience and, like Ibsen, touches a chord that rings as true now as it did at the turn of the century.

SUMMARY

The last years of the 19th century saw the threat of war gathering with increasing speed over Europe. The gap between the prosperous and the poor, the growth of the forces of big business, overcrowding and food shortages in the cities all tended to create a climate of unease that the rivalries of the major European powers exacerbated. Many emigrated to America in search of a new start. For the philosopher Friedrich Nietzsche only drastic remedies could prevent the collapse of Western civilization.

In each of the arts the years leading up to World War I were marked by far-reaching changes. In the case of painting, the impressionist school developed in Paris. Foreshadowed in the work of Édouard Manet, impressionist art represented a new way of looking at the world. Painters like Claude Monet, Auguste Renoir, and Berthe Morisot reproduced what they saw rather than visually interpret their subjects. The depiction of light and atmosphere became increasingly important. The figure studies of Edgar Degas and Mary Cassatt avoided the careful poses of earlier times in favor of natural, intimate scenes.

The various schools that developed out of impressionism are collectively known as post-impressionist although they have little in common with one another. Among the leading artists were Paul Gauguin, with his love of exotic subjects, and Vincent van Gogh, whose deeply moving images have made him perhaps the best-known of all

19th-century painters. In historical terms, the most important figure was probably Paul Cézanne: His works are the first since the dawn of the Renaissance to eliminate perspective and impose order on nature rather than try to reproduce it.

In the early years of the 20th century two movements began to emerge: fauvism and expressionism, the former in France and the latter in Germany and Scandinavia. Both emphasized bright colors and violent emotions, and the works of Edvard Munch and other expressionists are generally tormented in spirit. Henri Matisse, the leading fauve artist, however, produced works that are joyous and optimistic; he was to become a major force in 20th-century painting.

Composers of orchestral music in the late 19th and early 20th centuries turned increasingly to the rich language of post-Wagnerian harmony and instrumentation to express either extra-musical "programs" or to compose "autobiographical" works. The leading figures of the period included Richard Strauss and Gustav Mahler. Many of Strauss' operas have held the stage since their first performances, while his tone poems use a vast orchestra either to tell a story (as in *Don Juan*) or to describe his own life *(Domestic Symphony)*. Mahler's symphonies, neglected in the composer's lifetime, have come to represent some of the highest achievements of the symphonic tradition. Openly autobiographical, they reflect at the same time the universal human problems of loss and anxiety.

In France the music of Claude Debussy, and to a lesser extent Maurice Ravel, set out to achieve the musical equivalent of impressionism. In works like *La Mer* Debussy used new harmonic combinations to render the atmosphere of a seascape.

The experiments of composers like Mahler and Debussy at least retained many of the traditional musical forms and modes of expression, although they vastly extended them. In the early years of the 20th century Arnold Schoenberg and Igor Stravinsky wrote works that represented a significant break with the past. Schoenberg's atonal and, later, serial music sought to replace the traditional harmonic structure of Western musical style with a new freedom, albeit one limited by the serial system. In *The Rite of Spring* and other works Stravinsky revealed a new approach to rhythm. Both composers profoundly influenced the development of 20th-century music.

Like the other arts, literature also underwent revolutionary change in the last decades of the 19th century. In the hands of Fyodor Dostoyevsky and Marcel Proust the novel became a vehicle to reveal the effects of the subconscious on human behavior. In Dostoyevsky's books self-knowledge and psychological truth are combined to explore the nature of human suffering. Proust's massive exploration of the past not only seeks to uncover his own memories; it deals with the very nature of time itself. Both writers, along with many of their contemporaries, joined painters and musicians in pushing their art to its limits in order to extend its range of expression.

A more traditional aim of literature was to effect social change. At a time when society was becoming aware of the changing role of women in the modern world, writers aimed to explore the implications for marriage and the family of the gradual emancipation of women and the increasing availability of divorce. The plays of Henrik Ibsen not only described the issues of his day, including feminist ones; they were also intended to open up discussion of topics—venereal disease, incest—that his middle-class audience would have preferred to ignore.

With the outbreak of war in 1914, the arts were wrenched from their traditional lines of development to express the anxieties of the age. Nothing—in art, culture, politics, or society—was ever to return to its former state.

Pronunciation Guide

Belle Epoque: Bell Ep-OCK
Cézanne: Say-ZAN
Degas: Deh-GA
Dostoyevsky: Doh-stoy-EV-ski
Gauguin: Go-GAN
Ibsen: IB-sun
Manet: Ma-NAY
Monet: Mo-NAY
Morisot: Mo-ri-SEW
Munch: MOONK
Nietzsche: NEE-che
Proust: PROOST
Renoir: Ren-WAAR
Rodin: Roe-DAN
Schoenberg: SHURN-burg
Till Eulenspiegel: til OY-lin-shpee-gull
van Gogh: van GO

Exercises

1. Assess the impact of political and philosophical developments on the arts in the late 19th century.
2. Describe the goals and achievements of the impressionist movement in painting. How do you account for the enormous popularity of impressionist art ever since?
3. How did Arnold Schoenberg's music break with the

past? How does his serial system function, and what is its purpose?

4. In what ways is the changing role of women reflected in art and literature at the turn of the century?
5. Compare the fiction of Dostoyevsky and Proust. How does it differ from earlier 19th-century novels discussed in Chapter 15?

Further Reading

Clark, T. J. *The Painting of Modern Life: Paris in the Art of Manet and His Followers.* New York: Knopf, 1984. A Marxist analysis of impressionist art and the society in which it was created, with much valuable information about the development of urban life. Controversial but stimulating.

Goldwater, R. *Symbolism.* New York: Harper & Row, 1979. A thoughtful and absorbing account of the ideas and principles behind much of early-20th-century art. Among the artists discussed are van Gogh, Gauguin, and Rodin.

Grossman, L. *Dostoyevsky: His Life and Work.* Indianapolis: Bobbs-Merrill, 1975. As the title suggests, this book combines biography with a critical discussion of Dostoyevsky's works. Authoritative and perceptive, it incorporates important information its author gained from conversations with Dostoyevsky's widow.

Hamilton, G. H. *Manet and His Critics.* New Haven: Yale University Press, 1986. The latest edition of an important study of the origins of impressionism.

Holloway, R. *Debussy and Wagner.* London: Eulenburg, 1979. A groundbreaking analysis of connections between two of the most influential figures in the development of modern music.

Kroegger, M. E. *Literary Impressionism.* New Haven: Yale College and University Press, 1973. A useful guide to the main literary movements of the impressionist period.

Lipton, E. *Looking into Degas: Uneasy Images of Women and Modern Life.* Berkeley: University of California Press, 1986. A feminist analysis of Degas' art, cogently argued and profusely illustrated.

Meyer, M. *Ibsen.* Garden City: Doubleday, 1971. This massive book provides a highly readable account of the great dramatist's life and work and at the same time conveys much of the intellectual atmosphere of the age.

Mitchell, D. *Gustav Mahler: The Wunderhorn Years.* Berkeley: University of California Press, 1975. A rich and detailed study of Mahler's crucial middle years, which reveals much about his techniques of composition.

Newlin, D. *Bruckner, Mahler, Schoenberg.* New York: Norton, 1978. An updated edition of a classic account of the formation of Schoenberg's musical style, with valuable insights into the music of the other composers discussed.

Rewald, J. *Cézanne: A Biography.* New York: Abrams, 1986. A lavish new biography of one of the founding fathers of modern art. Excellent illustrations, a high proportion of them in color.

	GENERAL EVENTS	LITERATURE & PHILOSOPHY	ART
1901 EDWARDIAN AGE IN ENGLAND 1910	**1900–1905** Einstein researches the theory of relativity	**1900–1905** Freud formulates basic ideas of psychoanalysis; *The Interpretation of Dreams* (1900) **1908–1915** Marinetti publishes futurist manifestos	**1907** African sculpture fascinates artists in Paris: Picasso, *Les Demoiselles d'Avignon.* Retrospective of Cézanne's work in Paris. Picasso and Braque begin cubist experiments: Braque, *Violin and Palette* (1909–1910); Picasso, *Daniel-Henry Kahnweiler* (1910) **1909–1915** Italian futurists glorify technological progress
THE CALM AND THE "GREAT WAR" 1918	**1910** Death of Edward VII of England **1914** World War I begins; European colonialism wanes **1917** Bolshevik Revolution ends tsarist rule in Russia	**1910** Death of Tolstoy **1910–1941** British Bloomsbury Group around Virginia and Leonard Woolf rejects Edwardian mentality **1913** Carl Jung breaks with Freud **1915–1916** Dada movement founded Café Voltaire in Zurich; Dada manifesto by Tristan Tzara (1918) **1917** Cocteau, scenario for ballet *Parade;* Wilfred Owen, "Dulce et Decorum Est." Leonard Woolf begins Hogarth Press	**1910** Roger Fry's First Post-Impressionist Exhibition scandalizes London **c. 1911** German expressionism flourishes **1912** Kandinsky, *Concerning the Spiritual in Art* **1912–1914** Mondrian in Paris influenced by cubists; *Color Squares in Oval* (1914–1915) **1913** New York Armory Show brings avant-garde art to attention of American public **1915** End of futurist movement; Severini, *Armoured Train in Action* **1915–1916** Dada artists begin assault on traditional concepts of art; Duchamp *L.H.O.O.Q.* (1919) **1916** Arp, *Fleur Marteau* **1917** Picasso designs *Parade* set
BETWEEN THE WORLD WARS 1939	**1918** World War I ends; women granted right to vote in Great Britain **1920** Women granted right to vote in United States **1922** Fascists come to power in Italy after Mussolini's march on Rome **1927** Lindbergh's solo flight across Atlantic **1928** First sound movie produced **1929** Great Depression begins in Europe and America **1933** Nazis come to power in Germany under Hitler; first refugees leave country **1936–1939** Spanish Civil War; Guernica bombed 1937	**1919** Yeats, "The Second Coming" **1922** Alienation and cultural despair themes in postwar literature: T. S. Eliot, *The Waste Land;* Joyce, *Ulysses.* Sinclair Lewis satirizes American middle class in *Babbitt* **1924** Freudian theory and dadaism foster surrealism; Breton, *First Surrealist Manifesto.* Freudian themes appear in American drama; O'Neill, *Desire Under the Elms* (1924) **c. 1925** Black cultural regeneration, "Harlem Renaissance," in Northern U.S. cities **1925** Eliot, *The Hollow Men;* Kafka, *The Trial* **1926** Kafka, *The Castle* **1929** V. Woolf, *A Room of One's Own* **1930** Freud, *Civilization and Its Discontents* **1932** Huxley warns against unrestrained growth of technology in *Brave New World*	**1921** Picasso, *Three Musicians* **1921–1931** Klee teaches at Bauhaus; Kandinsky appointed professor in 1922 **1924** Surrealism begins; Buñuel and Dali collaborate on films *Un Chien Andalou* (1929), *L'Age d'Or* (1930) **1925** Eisenstein completes influential film *Potemkin* **1926** Gris, *Guitar and Music Paper;* Kandinsky, *Several Circles, No. 323;* Klee, *Around the Fish* **1927** Rouault, *This will be the last time, little Father!* (*Miserere* series) **1928** Magritte, *Man with a Newspaper* **1930** Cocteau film *Blood of a Poet* **1931** Dali, *The Persistence of Memory*
WORLD WAR II 1945	**1939** Germany invades Poland; World War II begins **1939** First commercial TV **1941** United States enters war	**1939** Death of Freud; Auden, *In Memory of Sigmund Freud*	**1942–1943** Mondrian, *Broadway Boogie-Woogie* **1944–1946** Eisenstein, *Ivan the Terrible,* parts I and II
	1945 World War II ends	**1945** Orwell, *Animal Farm* **1949** Orwell, *1984*	

CHAPTER 17 BETWEEN THE WORLD WARS

CHAPTER 17 BETWEEN THE WORLD WARS

ARCHITECTURE | **MUSIC**

c. 1900 Jazz originates among black musicians of New Orleans

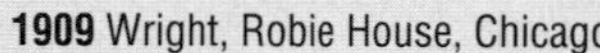

1909 Wright, Robie House, Chicago

c. 1910 Peak and decline of ragtime music; jazz becomes fully developed

1911 Piano rag composer Scott Joplin completes opera *Treemonisha*

1913 Stravinsky's *Rite of Spring* first performed in Paris

1916 Death of futurist architect Antonio Sant' Elia in World War I

1917 Satie composes score for ballet *Parade*

1918 Chagall, *The Green Violinist*

1919 Bauhaus design school founded at Weimar; Bauhaus ideas find wide acclaim in architecture and many industrial fields

1919–1920 Russian constructivist sculptor and visionary architect Tatlin builds model for *Monument to the Third International*

Avant-garde composers come under influence of jazz and ragtime: Stravinsky, *L'Histoire du Soldat* (1918), Hindemith, *Klaviersuite* (1922)

c. 1920 Chicago becomes jazz center; in New York's Harlem, Cotton Club provides showcase for jazz performers

1920s Josephine Baker and other American performers bring jazz and blues to Paris

1923 Schoenberg perfects twelve-tone technique (serialism)

1924 Gershwin, *Rhapsody in Blue*

1926 Gershwin, *Concerto in F Major* for piano

late 1930s Bauhaus architects Gropius and van der Rohe flee Nazi Germany for U.S.

1930 Weill, *The Threepenny Opera,* text by Bertolt Brecht

1935–1940 WPA photographers active

1936 Riefenstahl, *Triumph of the Will,* film glorifying Nazis

1937 Picasso paints *Guernica* in protest against war; Dali uses Freudian symbolism in *Inventions of the Monsters*

1938 Eisenstein film *Alexander Nevský,* score by Prokofiev; Riefenstahl, *Olympia*

1935 Gershwin's *Porgy and Bess,* first widely successful American opera

1943 Duke Ellington's symphonic suite *Black, Brown, and Beige* premieres at Carnegie Hall

1945 Stravinsky, *Symphony in Three Movements*

C H A P T E R

17 BETWEEN THE WORLD WARS

THE "GREAT WAR" AND ITS SIGNIFICANCE

THE ARMED CONFLICT that raged in Europe from 1914 to 1918 put to rest forever the notion that war was a heroic rite of passage conferring nobility and glory. The use of technology—especially poison gas, tanks, and planes—made possible slaughter on a scale hitherto only imagined by storytellers. The sheer numbers of soldiers killed in the major battles of World War I continue to stagger the imagination. By the end of the war the Germans had lost three and a half million men and the Allies five million.

The sociopolitical consequences of the "Great War" were monumental. The geopolitical face of Europe was considerably altered. The October Revolution of 1917 led by V. I. Lenin toppled the tzarist regime and produced a Communist government in Russia; it was a direct result of Russia's humiliation in the war. The punitive attitude of the Allies and the stricken state of Germany's economy after the war provided the seedbed from which Hitler's National Socialist movement (Nazism) sprang. Postwar turmoil led to Mussolini's ascendancy in Italy. England had lost many of its best young men in the war. Those who survived leaned toward either frivolity or pacifism.

Culturally, World War I sounded the death knell for the world of settled values. The battle carnage and the senseless destruction, in no small part the result of callous and incompetent military leadership, made a mockery of patriotic slogans, appeals to class, and the metaphysical unity of nations. One result of this disillusionment was a spirit of frivolity but another was bitterness and cynicism about anything connected with military glory. A whole school of poets, many of whom did not survive the war, gave vent to their hatred and disgust with this first modern war. English poets like Rupert Brooke (1887–1915) and Wilfred Owen (1893–1918) both died in the war but not before penning powerful poems about the stupidity, the carnage, and the waste of the battles.

The political upheavals and cultural tremors of the immediate postwar period coincided with a technological revolution in transportation and communications. After World War I radio came into its own. It is hard for us to comprehend what this information linkup meant for people previously isolated by lack of access to the larger world of information and culture. Similarly, the mass production of the automobile, made possible by the assembly-line techniques of Henry Ford in the United States, provided mobility to many who a generation before were confined to an urban neighborhood or a rural village. The widespread popularity of the cinema gave new forms of entertainment and instruction to those who already were accustomed to the voices of the radio coming into their homes each evening.

LITERARY MODERNISM

At the end of World War I the Irish poet William Butler Yeats (1865–1939), profoundly moved by unrest in his own country (particularly the Easter Rebellion of 1916) and the rising militarism on the Continent, wrote one of the most extraordinarily beautiful and prophetic poems of modern times, "The Second Coming." The title of the poem is deeply ironic because the title refers not to the glorious promised return of the Savior but an event the poet only hints at in an ominous manner. A line from that poem with its prescient look into the future is as strikingly relevant for our times as it was for Yeats:

Things fall apart; the centre cannot hold;
Mere anarchy is loosed upon the world,
The blood-dimmed tide is loosed, and everywhere
The ceremony of innocence is drowned;
The best lack all conviction, while the worst
Are full of passionate intensity.

T. S. Eliot and James Joyce

The year 1922 was a turning point for literary modernism. In that year T. S. Eliot (1888–1965), an expatriate American living in England, published his poem *The Waste Land* and James Joyce (1882–1941), an expatriate Irish writer living on the Continent, published his novel *Ulysses.* In their respective works Eliot and Joyce reflect some of the primary characteristics of what is called the modernist temper in literature. There is fragmentation of line and image, the abandonment of traditional forms, and overwhelming sense of alienation and human homelessness (both authors were self-imposed exiles), an ambivalence about the traditional culture, an intense desire to find some anchor in a past that seems to be escaping, a blurring of the distinction between reality "out there" and the world of subjective experience, and, finally, a straining and pushing of language to provide new meanings for a world they see as exhausted.

Both Eliot and Joyce reflect the conviction that, in Yeats' phrase, "the centre cannot hold." For Joyce, only art would give people a new worldview that would provide meaning. Eliot felt that, if culture was to survive, one had to recover a sense of cultural continuity through a linkage of the artistic and religious tradition of the past. That perceived need for past cultural links helps explain why Eliot's poems are filled with allusions to works of art and literature as well as fragments from Christian rituals.

The gradual shift from cultural despair in *The Waste Land* can be traced in Eliot's later poems beginning with *The Hollow Men* (1925) and *Ash Wednesday* (1930) and culminating in *Four Quartets,* which were finished in the early forties. The *Quartets,* were Eliot's mature affirmation of his Christian faith as a bulwark against the ravages of modernist culture. To read *The Waste Land* and the *Four Quartets* in tandem is to see one way in which a sensitive mind moved from chaos to stability in the period between the wars.

Before the First World War Joyce had already published his collection of short stories under the title *Dubliners* (1912) and his *Portrait of the Artist as a Young Man* (1916). The former was a series of linked short stories in which persons come to some spiritual insight (which Joyce called an "epiphany"), while the latter was a thinly disguised autobiographical memoir of his own youth before he left for the Continent in self-imposed exile after his graduation from college. With the 1922 publication of *Ulysses,* Joyce was recognized as a powerful innovator in literature. In 1939, two years before his death, Joyce published the dauntingly difficult *Finnegans Wake.* Joyce once said that *Ulysses* was a book of the day (it takes place in one day) while *Finnegans Wake* was a haunting dream book of the night.

Joyce's blend of myth and personal story, his many-layered puns and linguistic allusions, his fascination with stream of consciousness, his sense of the artist alienated from his roots, and his credo of the artist as maker of the world have all made him one of the watershed influences on literature in the 20th century.

TABLE 17.1 Some American Poets Active Between the Wars

Edgar Lee Masters (1868–1950)
Robert Frost (1874–1963)
Carl Sandburg (1878–1967)
Wallace Stevens (1879–1955)
William Carlos Williams (1883–1963)
Ezra Pound (1885–1972)
Robinson Jeffers (1887–1962)
Marianne Moore (1887–1972)
Claude McKay (1890–1948)
e. e. cummings (1894–1962)
Edna St. Vincent Millay (1892–1950)
Hart Crane (1899–1932)
Langston Hughes (1902–1967)
Countee Cullen (1903–1946)
Richard Wright (1908–1960)
Elizabeth Bishop (1911–1979)

Franz Kafka

Perhaps the quintessential modernist in literature is the Czech writer Franz Kafka (1883–1924). A German-speaking Jew born and raised in Prague, Kafka was by heritage alienated both from the majority language of his city and its predominant religion. An obscure clerk for a major insurance company in Prague, he published virtually nothing during his lifetime. He ordered that his works be destroyed after his death, but a friend did not accede to his wish. What we have from Kafka's pen is so unique that it has contributed the adjective

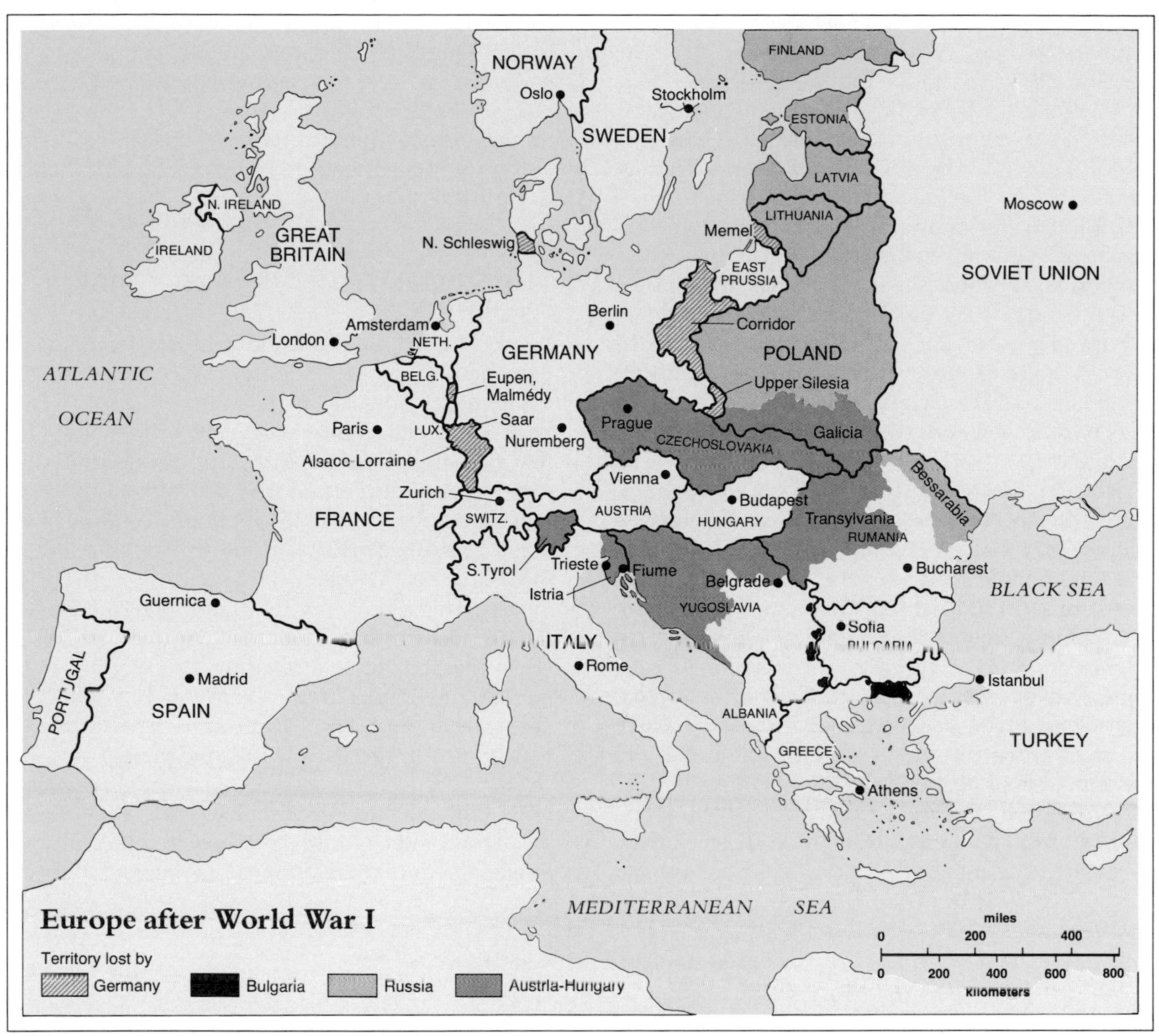

Europe after World War I

Kafkaesque to our language. A Kafkaesque experience is one in which a person feels trapped by forces that seem simultaneously ridiculous, threatening, incomprehensible, and dangerous.

This is precisely the tone of Kafka's fiction. In Kafka's *The Trial* (1925) Joseph K. (note the near-anonymity of the name) is arrested for a crime that is never named by a court authority that is not part of the usual system of justice. At the end of the novel the hero (if he can be called that) is executed in a vacant lot by two seedy functionaries of the court. In *The Castle* (1926) a land surveyor known merely as K., hired by the lord of a castle overlooking a remote village, attempts in vain to approach the castle, to communicate with its lord, to learn of his duties. In time, he would be satisfied just to know if there actually is a lord who has hired him.

No critic has successfully uncovered the meaning of these novels—if in fact they should be called novels. Kafka's works might better be called extended parables that suggest, but do not explicate, a terrible sense of human guilt, a feeling of loss, and an air of oppression and muted violence.

Virginia Woolf

Virginia Woolf (1882–1941) is one of the most important writers in the period of literary modernism. Novels like *Mrs. Dalloway* (1925), *To the Lighthouse* (1927), and *The Waves* (1931) have been justly praised for their keen sense of narrative, sophisticated awareness of time shifts, and profound feeling for the textures of modern life.

Woolf's reputation would be secure if she had only been known for her novels but she was also an accomplished critic, a founder (with her husband Leonard Woolf) of the esteemed Hogarth Press, and a member of an intellectual circle in London known as the Bloomsbury Group. That informal circle of friends was at the cutting edge of some of the most important cultural activities of the period. Lytton Strachey, the biographer, was a member, as was John Maynard Keynes, the influential economist. The group also included the art critics Roger Fry and Clive Bell, who championed the new art coming from France. The Bloomsbury Group also had close contacts with the mathematician-philosopher Bertrand Russell and the poet T. S. Eliot.

Two small books, written by Woolf as polemical pieces, are of special contemporary interest. *A Room of One's Own* (1929) and *Three Guineas* (1938) were passionate but keenly argued polemics against the discrimination of women in public intellectual life. Woolf argued that English letters had failed to provide the world with a tradition of great women writers not because women lacked talent but because social structures never provided them with a room of their own, that is, the social and economic aid to be free to write and think or the encouragement to find outlets for their work. Woolf, a brilliant and intellectually restless woman, passionately resented the kind of society that had barred her from full access to English university life and entry to the professions. Her books were early salvos in the coming battle for women's rights. Woolf is rightly seen as one of the keenest thinkers of the modern feminist movement whose authority was enhanced by the position she held as a world-class writer and critic.

THE REVOLUTION IN ART: CUBISM

Between 1908 and 1914 two young artists, the Frenchman Georges Braque (1882–1963) and the expatriate Spaniard, Pablo Ruiz Picasso (1881–1973), began a series of artistic experiments in Paris that revolutionized the direction of Western painting. For nearly five hundred years painting in the West had attempted a reconstruction on canvas of a real or ideal world "out there" by the use of three-dimensional perspective and the rules of geometry. This artistic tradition, rooted in the ideas of the Italian Renaissance, created the expectation that when one looked at a painting one would see the immediate figures more clearly and proportionately larger while the background figures and the background in general would be smaller and less clearly defined. After all, it was reasoned, that is how the eye sees the real world. Braque and Picasso challenged that view as radically as Einstein, a decade before, had challenged all of the

EAST MEETS WEST

"Primitive" Arts

A great deal of art from the world of the native peoples of Africa, Oceania, and North and South America came into Europe in the 19th and 20th centuries as a result of the colonial presence of Europe in those regions. At first, this material was of interest only to ethnographers and anthropologists. Before too long, however, artists began to take a keen interest in and become influenced by this art. Pablo Picasso's homage to African sculptured masks must be noted. Picasso and other cubists were struck by the formal power of this art to distort and saw it as a new alternative to the Western tradition of seeing the human figure.

The fascination with these cultures triggered a mania for collecting such art and, in turn, this interest touched a wide range of artists. The English sculptor Henry Moore was deeply moved by the simplicity and suggestiveness of prehistoric art. In the 1920s, when he was beginning his career as a sculptor, he haunted the museums of England studying the pre-Columbian art of Mexico and the sculpture of Africa. The monumental works found in many major cities today reflect his deep debt to those great works of the Aztecs, Incas, and Africans.

The enormous popularity of jazz in the 1920s both in the United States and abroad led to a fresh appreciation of African motifs in everything from painting to the graphic arts. Painting and sculpture of the Harlem Renaissance looked to Africa in the 1920s and 1930s to recover the roots of their own tradition as they carved out an identity as Afro-Americans. That interest in things African, begun between the wars, continues to influence Afro-American artists.

The roots of the Western interest in the arts of other cultures began, largely, as a by-product of Western colonialism but, in time, came to be appreciated as a rich source of artistic inspiration so that, like many things in the 20th century, the visual arts began to move away from narrow cultural interests into a more global consciousness.

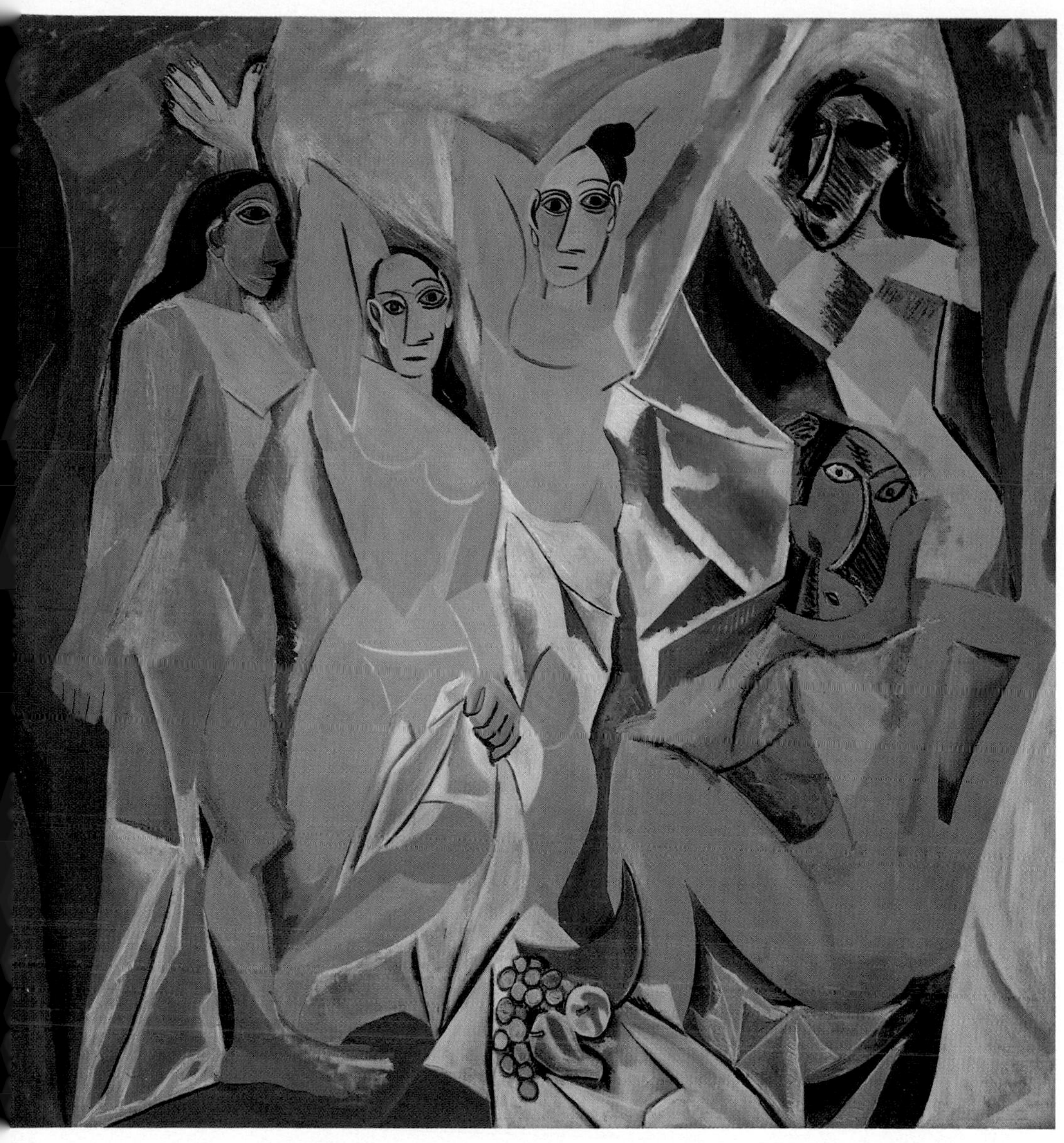

17.1 Pablo Picasso. *Les Demoiselles d'Avignon*, Paris (June–July 1907). Oil on canvas, 8' × 7'8" (2.43 × 2.33 m). Collection, The Museum of Modern Art, New York (acquired through the Lillie P. Bliss bequest). Note the increasing distortion of the faces as one's eyes move from left to the right.

classical assumptions we had made about the physical world around us.

To Braque and Picasso, paint on an essentially two-dimensional and flat canvas represented a challenge: how could one be faithful to a medium that by its very nature was not three-dimensional while still portraying objects which by their very nature *are* three-dimensional? Part of their answer came from a study of Paul Cézanne's many paintings of Mont Sainte-Victoire executed the century before. Cézanne saw and emphasized the geometric characteristics of nature; his representations of the mountain broke it down as a series of geometrical planes. With the example of Cézanne and their own native genius, Braque and Picasso began a series of paintings to put this new way of "seeing" into practice. These experiments in painting began an era called "analytical cubism" since the artists were most concerned with exploring the geometric qualities of objects seen without reference to linear perspective.

Picasso's *Les Demoiselles d'Avignon* [17.1], painted in 1907, is regarded as a landmark of 20th-century painting. Using the traditional motif of a group of bathers (the title of the painting is a sly joke; it alludes to a brothel on Avignon Street in Barcelona), Picasso moves from poses that echo classical sculpture on the left to increasingly fragmented and distorted figures on the right. His acquaintance with African art prompted him to repaint the faces the same year to reflect his delight with the highly angular and "primitive" African masks he had seen in a Paris exhibition. The importance of this work rests in its violently defiant move away from both the classical perspective of Renaissance art and the experiments of Cézanne in the preceding century. It heralds the cubism with which both Picasso and Braque became identified the following year.

A look at representative paintings by Braque and Picasso will help to clarify the aim of the cubists. In *Violin and Palette* [17.2] Braque depicts a violin so that the viewer sees, simultaneously, the front, the sides, and the back of the instrument while at the same time they appear on a single flat plane. The ordinary depth of the violin has disappeared. The violin is recognizable but the older notion of the violin as appearing "real" has been replaced by the artist's vision of the violin as a problem to be solved according to his vision and through his analysis.

In Picasso's portrait of *Daniel-Henry Kahnweiler* [17.3] the entire picture plane has become a geometric grid in which the traditional portrait form has been broken into separate cubelike shapes and scattered without reference to traditional propor-

17.2 Georges Braque. *Violin and Palette.* 1909–1910. Oil on canvas, 36⅛ × 16⅛" (92 × 43 cm). Solomon R. Guggenheim Museum, New York. The cubist strategy of breaking up planes can be seen clearly by attempting to reconstruct the normal shape of the violin with the eye.

17.3 Pablo Picasso. Spanish, 1881–1973. *Daniel-Henry Kahnweiler.* 1910. Oil on canvas, 39⅝ × 28⅝" (100.6 × 72.8 cm). The Art Institute of Chicago (gift of Mrs. Gilbert W. Chapman, 1948.561). Note the intensely two-dimensional plane of the painting.

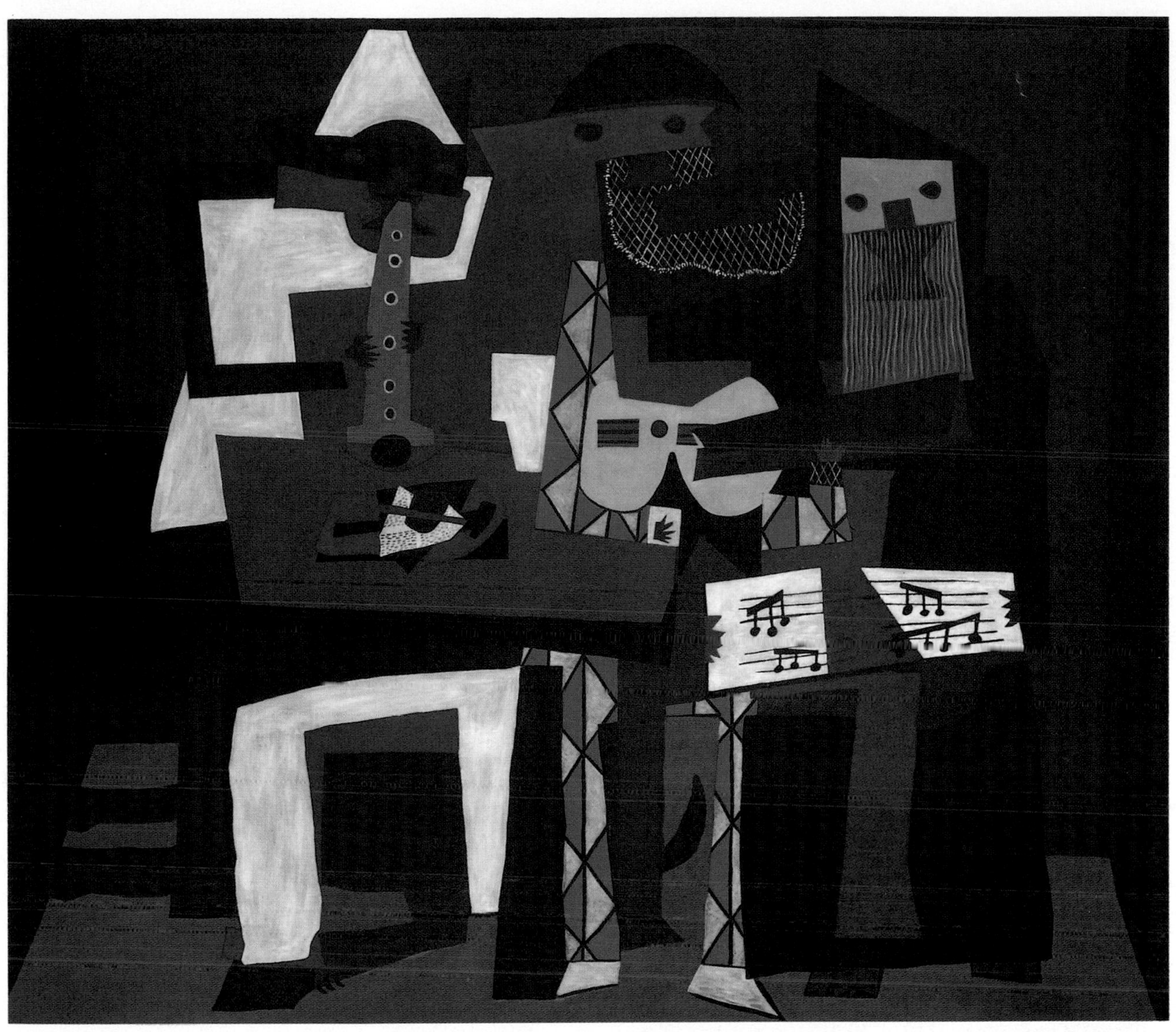

17.4 Pablo Picasso. *Three Musicians.* Fontainebleau, summer 1921. Oil on canvas, 6'7" × 7'3¾" (2.7 × 2.23 m). Collection, The Museum of Modern Art, New York (Mrs. Simon Guggenheim Fund). Another, more severe, version of this painting done in the same year now hangs in New York's Museum of Modern Art.

tion. The viewer must reconstruct the portrait from the various positions on the cubist grid. Within the picture one detects here a face, there a clasped hand, and a table with a bottle on it. The intense preoccupation in this work with line and form can be noted by a close examination of the tiled surface facets that provide the painting with its artistic unity.

In the postwar period the impact of cubism on the artistic imagination was profound and widespread. Picasso himself moved away from the technically refined yet somewhat abstractly intellectual style of analytic cubism to what has been called synthetic cubism. In *Three Musicians* [17.4] he still employs the flat planes and two-dimensional linearity of cubism, as the geometric masks of the three figures and the way they are lined up clearly show, but their color, vivacity, playfulness, and expressiveness somehow make us forget that they are worked out in terms of geometry. These postwar paintings seem more humane, alive, and less intellectually abstract.

The visual revolution of cubism stimulated other artists to use the cubist insight in a variety of ways. Only a close historical analysis could chart the many ways in which cubism made its mark on

17.5 Juan Gris. *Guitar and Music Paper.* 1926. Oil on canvas, 25⅝ × 31⅞" (65 × 81 cm). Private collection. It is instructive to compare this work with Braque's painting of a similar subject (Figure 17.2) to see how a similar theme was handled differently by another cubist painter.

17.6 Piet Mondrian. *Color Planes in Oval.* 1913–1914. Oil on canvas, 42⅜ × 31" (108 × 79 cm). Collection, The Museum of Modern Art, New York (purchase). Color experiments of this kind would exert an enormous influence on clothing design and the graphic arts in subsequent decades.

subsequent art, but a sampling shows both the richness and the diversity of art in the West after the Great War.

Some painters, like Juan Gris (1887–1927), continued to experiment rather faithfully with the problems Picasso and Braque explored before the war. His *Guitar and Music Paper* [17.5] demonstrates that such experimentation was not merely an exercise in copying. Other artists followed along the lines of Gris. The Dutch painter Piet Mondrian (1872–1944), after visits to Paris, where he saw cubist work, abandoned his earlier naturalistic works for paintings like *Color Planes in Oval* [17.6], a work whose main focus is on line and square highlighted by color.

The influence of cubism was not confined to a desire for simplified line and color even though such a trend has continued to our day in minimalist and hard edge art. The *Green Violinist* [17.7] by Marc Chagall (1889–1985) combines cubist touches (in the figure of the violinist) with the artist's penchant for dreamy scenes evoking memories of Jewish village life in Eastern Europe.

Although cubism was the most radical departure in modern art, it was not the only major art trend that overarched the period of the Great War. German painters continued to paint works in the expressionist style of the early years of the century. Perhaps the most accomplished exponent of expressionism was Wassily Kandinsky (1866–1944),

17.7 Marc Chagall. *Green Violinist.* 1923–1924. Oil on canvas, 6'8" × 3'6¼" (1.98 × 1.09 m). Solomon R. Guggenheim Museum, New York. This highly complex work blends cubist, primitivist, and dreamlike characteristics. Chagall's work blends memories of his Russian past and Jewish mysticism in a highly formal manner.

who was also one of the few painters of his time who attempted to state his theories of art in writing. Kandinsky's *Concerning the Spiritual in Art* (1910) argued his conviction that the inner, mystical core of a human being is the truest source of great art. That attitude, together with Kandinsky's conviction that the physical sciences were undermining confidence in the solidity of the world as we see it, led him closer to color abstraction and further away from any form of representation. By 1926 he was attempting to express the infinity and formlessness of the world (indeed, the cosmos) in paintings like *Several Circles* [17.8] without appeal to any representative figures or sense of narration.

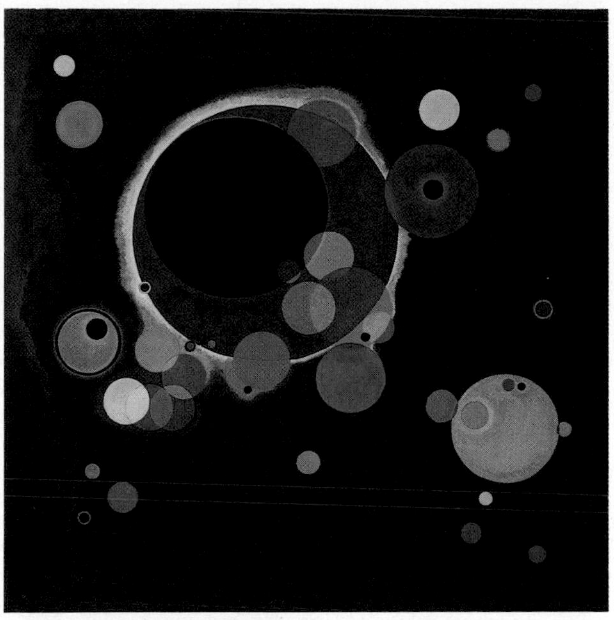

17.8 Wassily Kandinsky. *Several Circles.* 1926. Oil on canvas, 4'7¼" (1.4 m) square. Solomon R. Guggenheim Museum, New York.

FREUD, THE UNCONSCIOUS, AND SURREALISM

In 1900, on the very threshold of the century, a Viennese physician, Sigmund Freud (1856–1939), published *The Interpretation of Dreams*—one of the most influential works of modern times, Freud argued that deep in the unconscious, which Freud called the *Id,* were chaotic emotional forces of life and love (called *Libido* or *Eros*) and death and violence (called *Thanatos*). These unconscious forces, often at war with each other, are kept in check by the *Ego,* which is the more conscious self, and the *Super Ego,* which is the formally received training of parental control and social reinforcements. Human life is shaped largely by the struggle of the Ego and Super Ego to prevent the deeply submerged drives of the *Unconscious* from emerging. One way to penetrate the murky realm of the human unconscious, according to Freud, was through the dream. In the life of sleep and dreams the Ego and Super Ego are more vulnerable in their repressive activities. "The dream," Freud wrote, "is the royal road to the Unconscious." To put it simply, Freud turned the modern mind inward to explore those hidden depths of the human personality where the most primitive and dynamic forces of

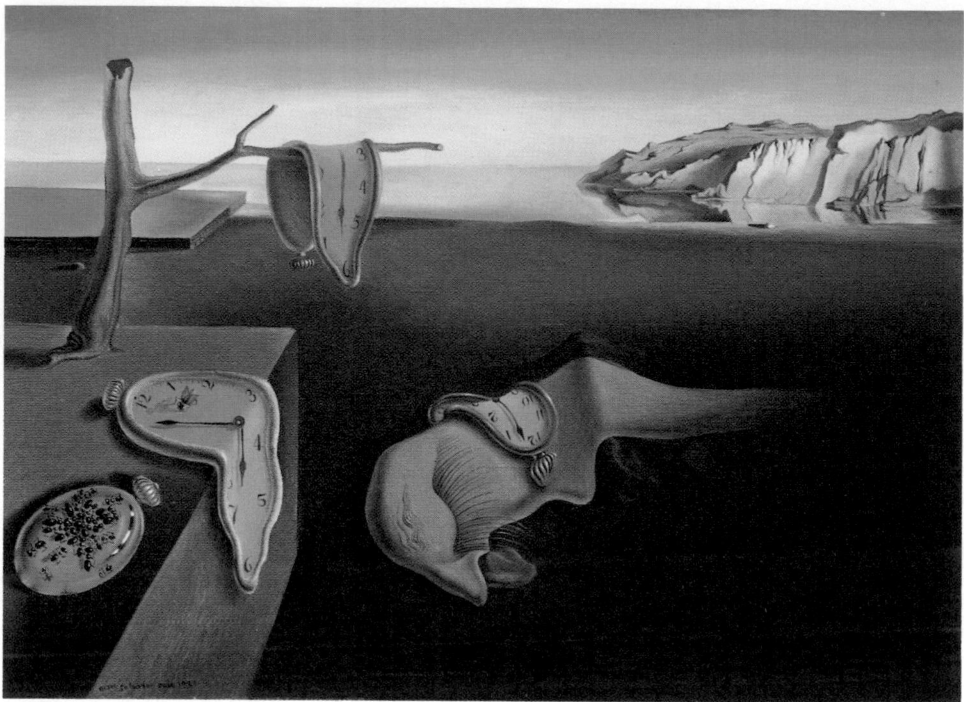

17.9 Salvador Dali. *The Persistence of Memory.* 1931. Oil on canvas, 9½ × 13" (24 × 33 cm). Collection, The Museum of Modern Art, New York (given anonymously).

life dwell. Freudian psychoanalysis was not only a therapeutic technique to help anxious patients but also a descriptive philosophy that proposes to account both for human behavior and for culture in general.

After the Great War, Freud's ideas were readily accessible to large numbers of European intellectuals. His emphasis on nonrational elements in human behavior exercised a wide influence on those who had been horrified by the carnage of the war. One group in particular was anxious to use Freud's theories about the dream world of the Unconscious as a basis for a new aesthetics. The result was the movement known as *surrealism.*

Surrealism was both a literary and artistic movement, gathered around the journal *Littérature,* edited in Paris by the French critic André Breton. In 1924 Breton published his first *Manifesto of*

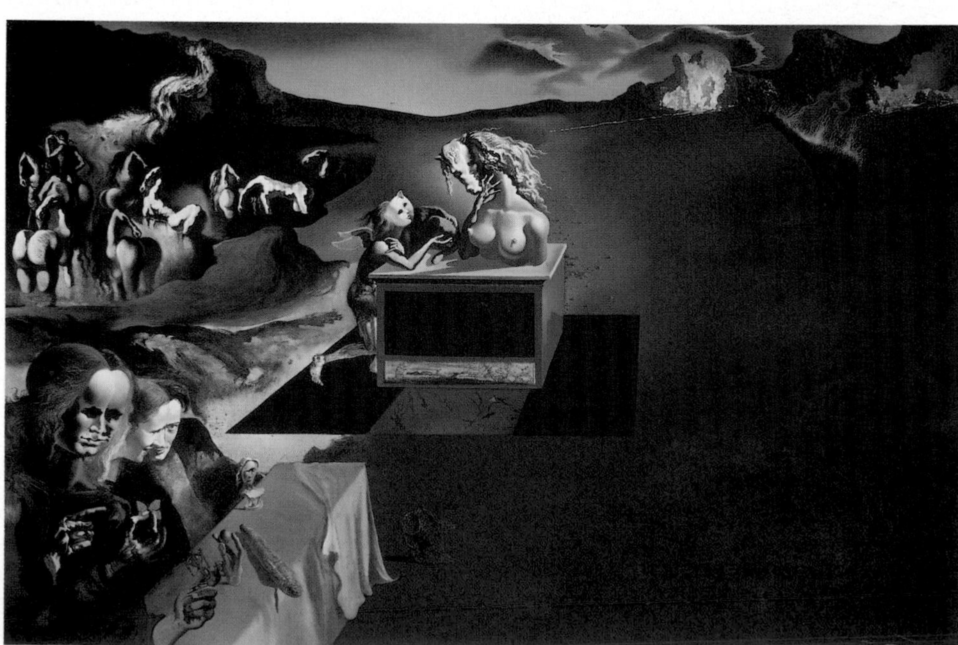

17.10 Salvador Dali. Spanish, 1904–1989. *Inventions of the Monsters.* 1937. Oil on canvas, 20⅛ × 30⅞" (51.2 × 78.4 cm). The Art Institute of Chicago (Joseph Winterbotham Collection, 1943.798). Note the highly charged erotic character of the painting.

SPORTS AND GAMES

Swimming

Although swimming is a skill as old as humanity itself it is only in the modern period that it has become a competitive sport open to both men and women. Swimming became an Olympic sport in 1896 but it was only in 1912 that it became an event for women; in the same year women's diving was added to the Olympic program whereas men's diving had been a competitive sport since 1904.

In the period between the world wars, swimming, while always a minor sport, nonetheless took on a certain aura of glamour. Olympic swimmers like the Americans Johnnie Weissmuller, Buster Crabbe, and Esther Williams later turned their skills into lucrative and successful Hollywood film careers. The American long-distance swimmer Gertrude Ederle was the first woman (in 1926) to swim the English Channel, a feat which had been accomplished by a man in 1875. Ederle's feat made her an international celebrity.

The most important developments in competitive swimming and diving were the improvement of new techniques (such as the perfection of the "crawl" stroke first used in Australia and later perfected in the United States) and more scientifically styled training techniques. In the period between the wars Americans and Australians dominated swimming to be challenged, after World War II, by the countries of the Eastern bloc, most notably what was then East Germany.

On the contemporary scene, the recognition of how beneficial swimming is for cardiovascular health has led to a widspread interest in swimming as a noncompetitive form of recreation. At the same time swimming has been combined with running and cycling (the *triathlon*) as a new form of competitive sport. The accessibility of more pools has led to a greater number of swiming opportunities for clubs, schools, colleges and universities. Older Americans are also now swimming competitively through the "Master's" program, which has gained great popularity.

Competitive diving is now seen as a different sport with its own particular training and ethos. A part of Olympic competition since 1904 (for men; 1912 for women), it is an exacting discipline requiring great conditioning and thorough training in gymnastics.

Surrealism, which paid explicit homage to Freud's ideas on the subjective world of the dream and the unconscious. "Surrealism," Breton declared, "is based on the belief in the superior reality of certain forms of association hitherto neglected, in the omnipotence of the dream, and in the disinterested play of thought."

The painters first associated with surrealism are familiar to every museumgoer: Jean Arp, Giorgio de Chirico, Max Ernst, Paul Klee, Joan Miró, Pablo Picasso. The Spanish artist Salvador Dali (1904–1989), who joined the movement in its later period, however, was to become almost synonymous with surrealism. His *The Persistence of Memory* [17.9] is perhaps the most famous surrealist painting. Its dreamlike quality comes from the juxtaposition of almost photographic realism with a sense of infinite quiet space and objects that seem unwilling to obey the laws of physics. The soft watches seem to melt in their plasticity. It is the very juxtaposition of solidity and lack of solidity that contributes to the "surreal" tone of the painting, In other paintings, like *Inventions of the Monsters* [17.10], Dali's surreal world has more conscious allusions to the Freudian unconscious. There are open references to terror, violence, and sexuality. The double portrait is an allusion to the male/female principles that constitute each person, and Dali frequently alludes to this bisexual dynamic in his work.

Dali utilized strong realist draftmanship to set out his dream world. The iconography of his work, at least in the 1930s, was orthodox in its Freudianism. Another surrealist, René Magritte (1898–1967), was no less a draftsman but was less concerned with the dark side of the unconscious. His work, done with scrupulous attention to realistic detail, calls into question our assumptions about the reality of our world. In his *Man with a Newspaper* [17.11] even the title of the painting misleads us since the man, like a figure in the frame of a moving-picture film, has disappeared after the first frame.

Film was a major influence on Magritte's development—as it was on other surrealists. The motion picture camera could be used to make images that corresponded closely with surreal intentions. Figures could dissolve, blend into other figures, be elongated, or slowly disappear. Some of the first artists associated with surrealism like the American Man Ray experimented with both still photography and moving pictures. Dali collaborated with his compatriot film director Luis Buñuel to produce two famous surrealistic films: *Un Chien Andalou*

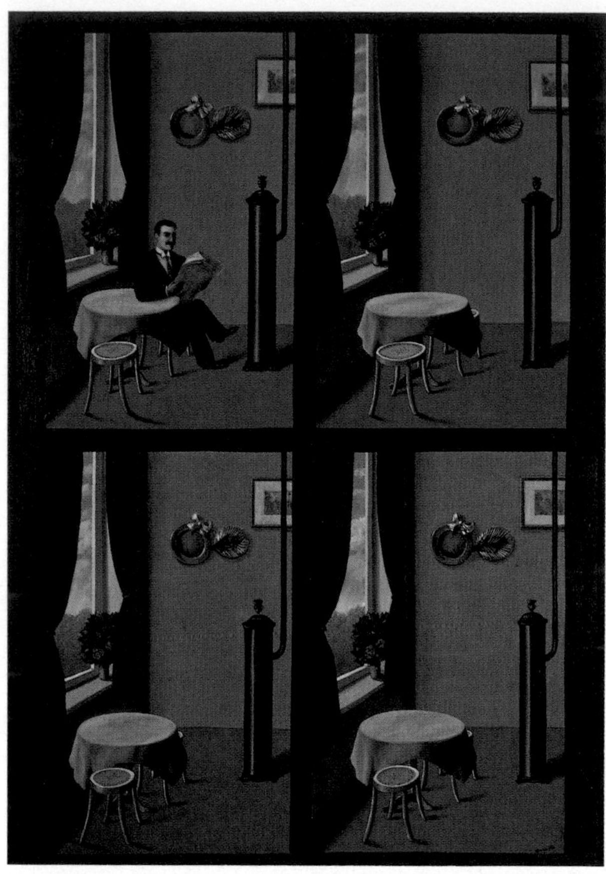

17.11 René Magritte. *Man with a Newspaper.* 1928. Oil on canvas, 45½ × 32" (116 × 81 cm). Tate Gallery, London (reproduced by courtesy of the Trustees). Magritte's power to invoke solitude is evident in this picture.

(1929) and *L'Âge d'Or* (1930). The French poet Jean Cocteau also produced a famous surrealistic film in 1931, *Blood of a Poet.*

One artist deserves a separate mention; although his association with the surrealist movement was important, it does not adequately define his originality. The Swiss painter Paul Klee (1879–1940) had touched most of the major art movements of his day. He knew the work of Picasso in Paris; he exhibited for a time with the Blaue Reiter in Germany; after the war he taught at the famous design school in Germany called the Bauhaus. Finally, he showed his work at the first surrealist exhibition of art in Paris. It was characteristic of Klee's talent that he could absorb elements of cubist formalism, expressionist colorism, and the fantasy of the surrealists without being merely a derivative painter. He was, in fact, one of the most original and imaginative artists of the first half of the century. A painting like his 1926 *Around the Fish* [17.12] is typical. The cylindrical forms hint at cubism but the floating shapes, some enigmatic, and the brilliant coloring evoke the dreamlike world of the surreal.

We have already noted that Freud's pioneering researches into the nature of the unconscious profoundly impressed those writers associated with André Breton. Other writers more fully explored the implication of Freud and his followers throughout this century in fiction, poetry, drama, and criticism. The great American dramatist Eugene O'Neill (1888–1953) restated basic Freud-

17.12 Paul Klee. *Around the Fish.* 1926. Oil on canvas, 18⅜" × 25⅛" (47 × 64 cm). Collection, The Museum of Modern Art, New York (Abby Aldrich Rockefeller Fund). The figures in the painting seem to float freely in an indeterminate space.

ian themes of love and hate between children and parents (the so-called Oedipus and Electra complexes) in plays like *Desire under the Elms* and *Mourning Becomes Electra.* Other writers of world repute like Franz Kafka and the American novelist William Faulkner (1897–1962) may not have been directly dependent on Freud's writings but their works are more accessible when we understand that they are dealing with similar issues and problems.

THE AGE OF JAZZ

Jazz is a peculiarly American contribution to Western culture, born out of the unique experience of American blacks. The matrix out of which jazz was born is an imperfectly documented history of a process that includes, among other elements: (1) certain intonations, rhythmic patterns (such as love of repetition), and melodic lines that come ultimately from the African ancestors of American blacks; (2) the tradition of the spirituals, Christian hymns sung both in the slave culture of the South and in the free churches of blacks after the Civil War; (3) the ineffable music of the blues, developed in the Deep South with its characteristic *blue note,* the lowering by a half step of a note in the melodic line, which produces a sound hard to describe but instantly recognized; and (4) adaptations of certain European songs, especially French quadrilles and polkas, into a slightly different style of music that became known as ragtime.

Jazz made its first organized appearance in New Orleans around the turn of the century. The musicians, who were all black, performed without written music and were self-taught. They formed bands and played in the streets and in the cabarets of the city. By the end of World War I many of these musicians had migrated north to Chicago—which, in the early 1920s, was the center of jazz music. From there jazz spread to Harlem in New York City and to other urban centers of both coasts.

The influence of black jazz (and its white counterpart) on American culture is hard to overestimate. In fact, that period directly after World War I has been called "The Jazz Age," borrowing from an F. Scott Fitzgerald title. Some of the musicians of that era have permanent niches in American culture: the great blues singer Bessie Smith (1895–1937) and the trumpeter Louis Armstrong (1900–1975), along with such rediscovered masters as Eubie Blake (1883–1983) and Alberta Hunter. Jazz figures who reach down into contemporary culture would include such classic masters as Duke Ellington (1899–1974), Count Basie (1906–1984), and Lionel Hampton (1913–).

The popularity of jazz, a peculiarly black musical idiom, was soon appropriated by the predominant white culture in America so that often white jazz bands and the mass media (the first talking motion picture in this country starred a white actor, Al Jolson, portraying a black man in *The Jazz Singer*) overshadowed the unheralded black musicians of the time. Only more recently have serious and systematic attempts been made to recover early jazz recordings (since written music is, by and large, nonexistent) and to bring out of retirement or obscurity the now-old blues singers who are the most authentic exponents of this art form.

Jazz as a musical and cultural phenomenon was not limited to the United States in the period after World War I. Jazz had a tremendous following in Paris in the 1920s, where one of the genuine celebrities was the black American singer Josephine Baker [17.13].

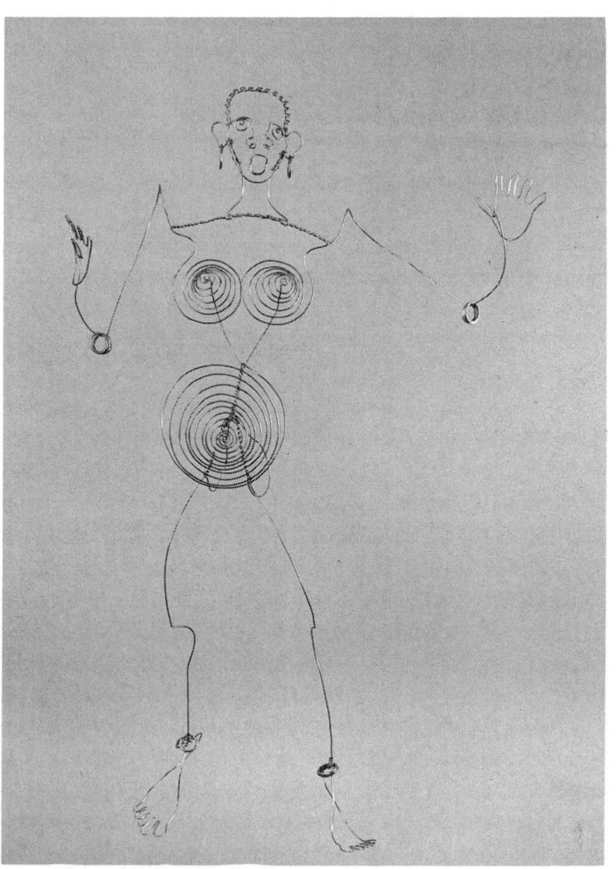

17.13 Alexander Calder. *Josephine Baker.* 1927–1929. Iron-wire construction, 39 × 22⅜ × 9¾" (99 × 57 × 25 cm). Collection, The Museum of Modern Art, New York (gift of the artist). This is one of many such works Calder made during his stay in Europe in the late 1920s.

Just as Pablo Picasso had assimilated African sculptural styles in his painting, so serious musicians on the Continent began to understand the possibilities of this American black music for their own explorations in modern music. As early as 1913, Igor Stravinsky (1882–1971) utilized the syncopated rhythms of jazz in his pathbreaking ballet *The Rite of Spring.* His *L'Histoire du soldat* (1918) incorporates a "ragtime" piece Stravinsky composed based only on sheet-music copies he had seen of such music. Other avant-garde composers in Europe also came under the influence of jazz. Paul Hindemith's 1922 *Klaviersuite* shows the clear influence of jazz. Kurt Weill's 1928 *Dreigroschenoper (Threepenny Opera),* with a libretto by Bertolt Brecht, shows a deep acquaintance with jazz—demonstrated notably in the song "Mack the Knife."

By the 1930s in the United States the influence of jazz had moved into the cultural consciousness of the country at large. Jazz was now commonly referred to as *swing,* and swing bands toured the country and were featured in films. The bands of Duke Ellington (see below) and Count Basie were well known even though their members, on tour, had to put up with the indignities of racial segregation: They often played in hotels and clubs which they themselves would have been unable to patronize. By the late 1930s there was even a renewed interest in the older roots of jazz. In 1938, for example, Carnegie Hall in New York City was the site of the "Spirituals to Swing" concert, which presented a range of musicians from old-time New Orleans–style jazz performers to such avant-garde performers as Lester Young.

Many of the musicians of the swing era were extremely talented musicians who were quite able to cross musical boundaries. The great clarinetist Benny Goodman recorded the Mozart *Clarinet Quintet* with the Budapest String Quartet in 1939, the year he commissioned a composition from classical composer Béla Bartók (1881–1945). The black jazz musician Fats Waller, in the same year, wrote his *London Suite,* his impressionistic tribute to that city.

Such crossovers were the exception rather than the rule, but they do underscore the rich musical tradition of the jazz movement. In the period after the Second World War there would be a new wave of experiments in avant-garde, new wave, and cool jazz that would give performers the opportunity to extend the definition and range of jazz to where it would intersect with other forms of avant-garde music, as is evident in the musical career of the late Charlie ("Bird") Parker and the late Miles Davis.

George Gershwin

The most persistent effort to transpose jazz into the idiom of symphonic and operatic music was that made by the American composer George Gershwin (1898–1937). In large symphonic works like *Rhapsody in Blue* (1924) and *Concerto in F Major* (1926), for piano and orchestra Gershwin utilized such jazz characteristics as blue notes, syncopation, and seemingly improvised variations (riffs) on a basic theme along with the more classically disciplined form for large orchestral music.

It is certainly appropriate, perhaps inevitable, that the first widely successful American opera should have a jazz background. George Gershwin's *Porgy and Bess* (1935) incorporated jazz and other black musical material such as the "shouting" spirituals of the Carolina coastal black churches to a libretto written by the Southern novelist DuBose Heyward and Gershwin's brother, Ira. *Porgy and Bess* was not an immediate success in New York, but later revivals in the 1940s and after World War II established its reputation. In 1952 it had a full week's run at the La Scala opera house in Milan; in 1976 the Houston Opera mounted a full production, with earlier cuts reintroduced into the text, that subsequently was seen at the Metropolitan Opera in New York. It now ranks as a classic. Some of its most famous songs (such as "Summertime" and "It Ain't Necessarily So") have also become popular favorites.

Gershwin was white and thus had easier access to the world stage than did many of the black musicians in the first half of this century. It has only been in the last two decades or so that a fine composer like Scott Joplin (1868–1917), for example, has achieved any wide recognition in this country. The great blues singer Bessie Smith died after an automobile accident in the South because of delays in finding a hospital that would treat blacks. Many other singers and instrumentalists have remained in obscurity all their lives, although some—artists like the late Louis Armstrong—were so extraordinarily gifted that not even the hostile and segregated culture of the times could repress their talent.

Duke Ellington

One black American who managed to emerge decisively from the confines of black nightclubs into international fame was Edward Kennedy ("Duke") Ellington (1899–1974). Ellington gained fame at the Cotton Club in Harlem in the 1920s both for his virtuoso orchestral skills and for his prolific output as a composer. He was not only a successful writer of such popular musical pieces as "Take the A Train" and "Mood Indigo" but also a true original in his attempt to extend the musical idiom of jazz into a larger arena. Beginning after World War II, he produced any number of works for symphonic settings. His symphonic suite *Black, Brown, and Beige* had its first hearing at Carnegie Hall in 1943. This work was to be followed by others whose titles alone indicate the ambition of his musical interests: *Shakespearean Suite* (1957), *Nutcracker Suite* (1960), *Peer Gynt Suite* (1962), and his ballet *The River* (1970), which he wrote for the dance company of Alvin Ailey, a notable black choreographer.

The Harlem Renaissance

Jazz is an American or, more specifically, a distinctively African-American contribution to world culture. It was not the only cultural movement among African-Americans in the period between the wars. In the section of New York City known as Harlem there was a concentration of African-American writers, artists, intellectuals, and musicians who produced such a conspicuous body of specifically African-American work that they are known collectively as the Harlem Renaissance. There were explorers of African-American culture like Zora Neale Huston, James Weldon Johnson, and Alain Locke; poets like Countee Cullen, Helene Johnson, Langston Hughes, and Claude McKay; artists like Hale Woodruff and Sargent Johnson. When one reads the poetry and fiction produced during the 1920s and 1930s by the Harlem Renaissance writers it is easy to to detect abiding themes of the African-American experience: the ancestral roots of Africa; the quest for dignity in a culture of racism; a debate over the degree to which African-American values should be part of—as opposed to distinct from—the majority culture; and the role of the church in life.

Behind most of these questions was the one posed at the very beginning of the century by the African-American intellectual W. E. B. DuBois: What self-identity does an African-American affirm who must hold in balance his identity as being African, his place in American life, and the racism he endures? Those issues burn at the heart of what the Harlem Renaissance debated.

BALLET: COLLABORATION IN ART

In the period between the world wars one form of culture where the genius of the various arts most easily fused was the ballet. The most creative experiments took place in Paris through the collaboration of a cosmopolitan and talented group of artists.

The driving force behind ballet in this period in Paris was Serge Diaghilev (1872–1929), a Russian-born impresario who founded a dance company called the Ballet Russe, which opened its first artistic season in 1909. Diaghilev brought from Russia two of the most famous dancers of the first half of the century: Vaslav Nijinsky (1890–1950) and Anna Pavlova (1881–1931).

Diaghilev had a particular genius for recruiting artists to produce works for his ballet. Over the years the Ballet Russe danced to the commissioned music of Igor Stravinsky, Maurice Ravel, Serge Prokofiev, Claude Debussy, Erik Satie, and Darius Milhaud. In that same period sets, costumes, and stage curtains were commissioned from such artists as Pablo Picasso, Georges Rouault, Naum Gabo, Giorgio de Chirico, and Jean Cocteau.

In 1917 Diaghilev produced a one-act dance called *Parade* in Paris. This short piece (revived in 1981 at the Metropolitan Opera with sets by the young English painter David Hockney) is an excellent example of the level of artistic collaboration Diaghilev could obtain. The story of the interaction of street performers and men going off to war was by the poet Jean Cocteau (1891–1963); the avant-garde composer Erik Satie (1866–1925) contributed a score replete with street sounds, whistles, horns, and other accouterments of urban life. Pablo Picasso designed the curtain drop, the sets, and the costumes [17.14]. *Parade* had much to say about musicians, players, and street performers, so the production was readymade for Picasso's well-known interest in these kinds of people.

The collaborative effort of these important figures was a fertile source of artistic inspiration. Picasso had a great love for such work and returned to it on a number of other occasions. He designed the sets for *Pulcinella* (1920), which had music by Igor Stravinsky. He designed sets for a balletic interpretation of Euripides' tragedy *Antigone* done from a translation of the play from the Greek into French by Jean Cocteau. In 1924 he also did designs for a ballet, which had original music written by Erik Satie, called *Mercury*.

Ballet, like opera, is an art form that lends itself to artistic integration. To enjoy ballet one must see the disciplined dancers in an appropriate setting, hear the musical score that at once interprets and guides the movements of the dancers, and follow the narrative or "book" of the action. It is no wonder that an organizational genius like Diaghilev would seek out and nurture the efforts of the most creative artists of his era.

17.14 Pablo Picasso. Curtain for the ballet *Parade.* Paris, 1917. Tempera on cloth, 34'9" × 56'¾" (10.6 × 17.3 m). Musée National d'Art Moderne, Centre Georges Pompidou, Paris. Many critics agree that both the music and the choreography of the ballet were overwhelmed by Picasso's brilliant sets, which dominated the production.

Art as Escape: Dada

A group of artists, writers, and musicians who gathered around the tables of the Café Voltaire in Zurich in 1915 founded a movement to protest what they considered the madness of the war and its senseless slaughter. They decided to fight the "scientific" and "rational" warmakers and politicians with nonsense language, ugly dissonant music, and a totally irreverent and iconoclastic attitude toward the great masterpieces of past culture. It was called *dada,* a nonsense word of disputed origin that could be a diminutive of "father" or the word for "yes" or a child's word for a hobbyhorse. One of its poets, Tristan Tzara, wrote a dada manifesto in 1918 that called for, among other things, a destruction of good manners, the abolition of logic, the destruction of memory, forgetfulness with respect to the future, and the elevation of the spontaneous to the highest good.

One of the most representative and creative of the dada artists was Marcel Duchamp (1887–1968), who after 1915 was associated with an avant-garde art gallery in New York founded by the American photographers Alfred Stieglitz (1864–1946) and Edward Steichen (1879–1973). Duchamp was a restless innovator who originated two ideas in sculpture that became part of the common vocabulary of modern art: sculptures with moving parts (*mobiles*) and sculptures constructed from preexisting fabricated material originally intended for other purposes (*readymades*). Besides these important innovations Duchamp also has gained notoriety for his whimsically irreverent attitude toward art, illustrated by his gesture of exhibiting a urinal at an art show as well as his humorous but lacerating spoofs of high culture, the most "dada" of which is his famous defacement of the *Mona Lisa* [17.15].

The dadaists could not maintain the constant energy of their anarchy, so it was inevitable that they would move individually into other directions. Dada was a movement symptomatic of the crisis of the times, a reaction to chaos but no adequate answer to it. It is no small irony that while the dada theater group performed in Zurich's Voltaire cab-

17.15 Marcel Duchamp. L.H.O.O.Q. 1919. Rectified ready-made, pencil on colored reproduction of Leonardo da Vinci's *Mona Lisa;* 7¾ × 4⅞" (20 × 12 cm). Private collection. The French pronunciation of the letters under the picture sound like an off-color expression.

aret in 1916, there lived across the street an obscure Russian political activist in exile from his native land. He also would respond to the chaos of the time but in a far different way. His name was V. I. Lenin.

Art as Protest: *Guernica*

The late Protestant theologian Paul Tillich once called Picasso's *Guernica* [17.16] *the* great Protestant painting. He said this not because Picasso was religious (which he was not) but because of the quality and depth of Picasso's protest against inhumanity. The title of the painting comes from the name of a small Basque town that was saturation-bombed by Germany's Condor Legion in the service of Franco's Fascist rebel forces during the Spanish Civil War. Picasso completed the huge canvas in two months—May and June 1937—so that he could exhibit it at the Paris World's Fair for that year.

There have been intense studies of the genesis and development of *Guernica* in order to "unlock" its symbolism, but it would be safe to begin with Picasso's particular images. Many of these images recur over and over again in his work to convey

17.16 Pablo Picasso. *Guernica.* 1937. Oil on canvas, 11'5½" × 25'5¼" (3.49 × 7.77 m). Prado Museum, Madrid. This monumental painting was on extended loan in New York until after the death of General Francisco Franco, when Picasso agreed to its return to his native Spain.

Picasso's sense of horror at the destruction of war together with his muted affirmation of hope in the face of the horror. His iconography is reinforced by its somber palette—gradations of black, brown, and white.

The very complexity of images in *Guernica* at first glance seems chaotic, but prolonged looking reveals a dense and ordered rhythm. Starting at the left with the bull—Picasso's symbol of brute force, of Spain, and at times of the artist himself—we see beneath the animal a woman with the broken body of a child. The echo of the *Pietà* theme is obvious. In the lower center and to the right is a dismembered figure, in the cubist style, over whom rears up a "screaming" horse. At the top right of the work are Picasso's only hints of hope in the face of such evil: a small open window above a supplicant figure and an emerging figure holding a lamp. Over the center is an *oculus* (eye) in which a lamp burns and casts off light.

As a social document the importance of *Guernica* cannot be overestimated. The German bombing of the little town was an experiment in a new style of warfare, a style that would be refined into a deadly technique in World War II. In *Guernica* Picasso innovatively combines various stylistic techniques that were employed on the eve of World War I—expressionistic distortion and cubist abstraction—to protest a technological development that became a commonplace in the next war. In this sense, *Guernica* is a pivotal document—it straddles two cataclysmic struggles in the century. *Guernica's* cry of outrage provides an important observation about human culture. The painting reminds us that at its best the human imagination calls up the most primordial symbols of our collective experience (the woman and child, the horse and bull, the symbol of light) and invests them with new power and expressiveness fit for the demands of the age.

Art as Propaganda: Film

Propaganda is the diffusion of a point of view with the intention to persuade and convince. We usually think of it in political terms. Throughout history propagandists have used books, art, and music to spread their ideas. Inventions in the early part of the 20th century, however, added immeasurably to the propagandist's weapons.

Besides the radio, the other medium that most successfully blended propaganda with attempts at some artistic vision in the first half of this century was film. Two acknowledged masters of the use of film for propaganda need to be singled out since they set such a standard of excellence that, at least through their finest work, propaganda became high art.

Sergei Eisenstein (1898–1948) remains not only the greatest filmmaker the Soviet Union has produced but one of the most influential artists in the history of the cinema as well.

A dedicated supporter of the Russian Revolution, Eisenstein fully appreciated Lenin's observation that the cinema would become the foremost cultural weapon in winning the proletariat to the Revolution. From his early film *Strike!* (1925) to his last works, *Ivan the Terrible, Parts I and II* (1944/1946), Eisenstein was conscious of the class struggle, the needs of the working class, and the inevitable advance of socialism in history—themes dear to the official line of Stalin's U.S.S.R. Despite this orthodox line, Eisenstein was never an ideological hack. His films were meticulously thought out and he brought to bear his own considerable culture and learning to make films of high art. His *Alexander Nevskÿ* (1938) had an impressive musical score by Serge Prokofiev, and the two men worked closely to integrate musical and visual concepts. His vast *Ivan the Terrible* was deeply indebted to a study of El Greco's paintings; Eisenstein was struck by the cinematic possibilities in that artist's striking canvases.

Eisenstein's most influential film was *Potemkin* (finished at the end of 1925), the story of the 1905 naval mutiny on the battleship *Potemkin* and the subsequent riot in Odessa that was put down by the tsarist police. The Communists saw in that historical incident a major foreshadowing of the October Revolution of 1917, which brought the Bolsheviks to power.

The scene in *Potemkin* of the crowd cheering the mutineers on a broad flight of stairs in Odessa and the subsequent charge of the police is a classic sequence in film history. In that sequence Eisenstein used the device of *montage,* the sharp juxtaposition of shots by film cutting and editing, with such power that the scene would become a benchmark for subsequent filmmakers. His close-ups were meant to convey a whole scene quickly: A shot of a wounded woman cuts to a close-up of a clenched hand that slowly opens, telling the story of death in a moment. A crazily moving baby carriage is a macabre metaphor for the entire crowd in panic and flight. Shattered eyeglasses and blood pouring from an eye [17.17] become a terrible shorthand statement of police violence.

For sheer explicit propaganda one must turn to two documentary films made in Nazi Germany in the 1930s by the popular film actress and director

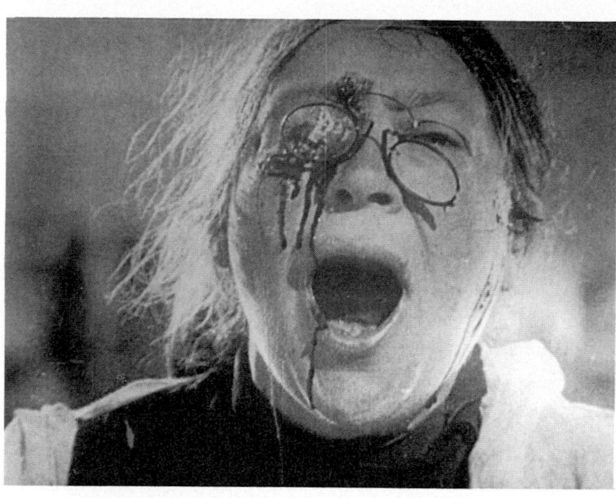

17.17 Sergei Eisenstein. Still from the Odessa Steps sequence of the film *Potemkin.* 1925. Museum of Modern Art, Film Stills Archive, New York. This close-up is a classic shot in the history of film. The single image stands for the horror of the entire scene.

Leni Riefenstahl (1902–1987). Her first great film was a documentary of the 1934 Nazi Congress in Nuremburg called *Triumph of the Will* (1936). Designed to glorify the Nazi party and to impress the rest of the world, the film made ample use of the great masses of party stalwarts who gathered for their rally. That documentary allowed the young filmmaker to show the party congress as a highly stylized and ritualistic celebration of the Nazi virtues of discipline, order, congregated might, and the racial superiority of the Teutonic elite of the party members.

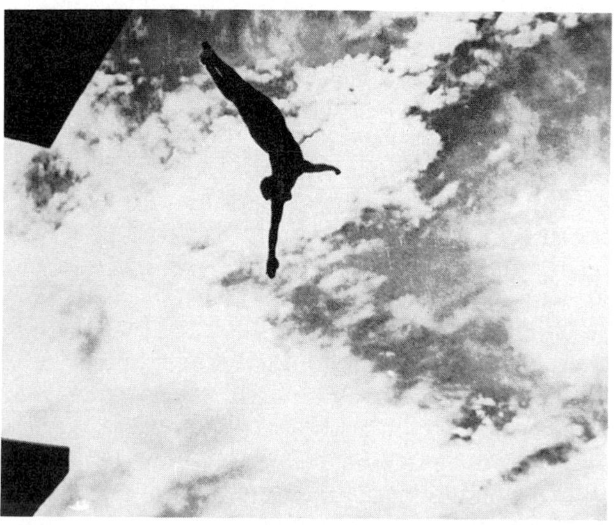

17.18 Leni Riefenstahl. Still shot from the diving sequence of *Olympia.* 1938. This still shows the uniquely original camera angles Riefenstahl used. Such angles became a model for documentary filmmakers.

Riefenstahl's other great film, and arguably her masterwork, was a long documentary made at the Berlin Olympics of 1936 and issued in 1938 under the title *Olympia.* Riefenstahl used five camera technicians and thirty-eight assistants as well as footage shot by news agency photographers to make her film. The completed documentary, divided in two parts, pays tribute to the Olympic spirit of ancient Greece, develops a long section on the carrying of the Olympic torch to Berlin, records the homage to Hitler and the Nazi party, and shows most of the major athletic competitions.

As a film *Olympia* is matchless in its imaginative use of the camera to catch the beauty of sport [17.18]. The vexing question is to what degree the film is political beyond the obvious homage paid to the German Reich, which sponsored the Olympics in 1936. Many critics note its elitist attitude to justify their contention that it is propaganda, albeit of a very high and subtle quality. Athletes are depicted as superior beings who act beyond the range of the ordinary mortal. They give all and seem almost demigods. The film praises the heroic, the conquest, the struggle. It praises the ritualized discipline of the crowds and lovingly seeks out examples of the adoring Berlin masses surrounding the party leaders.

Photography

Photography is a 19th-century invention, as we have seen. During the 19th century photography had a complex technological evolution as photographers sought ways to make cameras and photographic equipment more mobile. As this mobility increased, photography developed a number of specialties: portraiture, landscapes, documentation, and reportage. More important and more basic, photography gave to the world what no other visual medium could: immediacy. Before the advent of photography it was the job of the field artist to transcribe an event in sketches and then transfer those drawings onto etching plates for reproduction in newspapers and magazines. With the photograph people could "see" events as they were actually happening. The idea that "a picture is worth a thousand words" has become a tired cliché, but it is difficult for us today to comprehend the impact the first photographs of war must have made when traveling photographers sent back to England pictures of dying soldiers in the Crimean War of the 1850s or when the American public first saw the pictures of death and devastation made by Mathew Brady (1823–1896) and his assistants during the Civil War in the 1860s.

17.19 Walker Evans. *The Bud Fields Family at Home, Alabama.* 1935. Evans and James Agee often visited this family. Agee wrote about the family in *Let Us Now Praise Famous Men.* With Bud Fields, a one-mule tenant farmer, aged fifty-nine, are his second wife, Ivy (mid-twenties), their daughter (twenty months), Ivy's daughter by an earlier common-law marriage (eight), Bud's and Ivy's son (three), and Ivy's mother (early fifties).

Further technical advances, like the small portable Kodak camera invented by the American George Eastman in the late 19th century and 35mm cameras (including the famous Leica) invented in the early 20th century in Germany, contributed to the advance of photography in our century. In the period after World War I there was an intense interest in photography as a new instrument for art. Man Ray (1890–1976), an American artist living in Paris, experimented with darkroom manipulations to produce what he called *rayograms.* László Moholy-Nagy (1895–1946) taught a wide range of techniques in photography while he was an instructor at the influential Bauhaus school of design in Germany. When the school was closed by the Nazis, Moholy-Nagy came to the United States in 1933, where he continued to be a great influence on the development of American photography. A group of American photographers loosely connected with what was called the "f/64 Group" included pioneer photographers who are now recognized as authentic geniuses of the medium: Edward Weston (1886–1958), Ansel Adams (1902–1984), and Imogen Cunningham (1883–1975). We have already noted the influence of Alfred Stieglitz on the avant-garde art of New York. These photographers, and others like them, emphasized direct, crisp, and nonmanipulative pictures that set the standard for much of modern photography.

In the United States the most powerful pictures between the world wars that were produced for social purposes were those photographs made to show the terrible economic deprivations of the

Great Depression of the 1930s. In the mid-1930s the Farm Security Administration of the United States Department of Agriculture commissioned a number of photographers to record the life of America's rural poor. The resulting portfolios of these pictures taken by such photographers as Dorothea Lange, Arthur Rothstein, and Walker Evans have become classics of their kind. In 1941 the Pulitzer Prize-winning writer James Agee wrote a prose commentary on some of the photographs of Walker Evans. The photos of Evans and the text of James Agee were published together under the title *Let Us Now Praise Famous Men* [17.19]. Along with John Steinbeck's novel *The Grapes of Wrath* (itself turned into an Academy Award–winning film), Agee's book is one of the most moving documents of the Great Depression, as well as a model of how word and picture can be brought together into an artistic whole for both social and aesthetic purposes.

Art as Prophecy: From Futurism to *Brave New World*

Great art always has a thrust to the future. This chapter began with the observation of William Butler Yeats that "the centre cannot hold"—a prescient observation, as the aftermath of World War I was to show.

Not all artists were either so pessimistic or so prophetic as Yeats. A small group of painters, sculptors, architects, and intellectuals in Italy looked to the future with hope and to the past with contempt. Known as the *futurists,* they exalted the values of industrial civilization, the power of urban accomplishment, and (with equal intensity) despised the artistic culture of the past. The theorist of the movement was a Milanese poet and writer, Filippo Tommaso Marinetti (1876–1944), who issued a long series of futurist manifestos between 1908 and 1915.

In the few years during which futurism flourished its followers produced some significant painting, sculpture, and ideas about city planning and urban architecture. World War I was to end their posturings; the sculptor Umberto Boccioni and the futurist architect Antonio Sant'Elia were both to die in 1916, victims of the war. Some of the futurists, including Marinetti, true to their fascination with power, war, destruction, and the exaltation of might, would be increasingly used as apologists for the emerging Fascist movement in Italy. Thus a painting like Gino Severini's *Armored Train in Action* [17.20] proved prophetic in ways not quite appreciated in 1915.

The futurist romance with industrial culture and the idea of technological "progress" was not shared by all artists of the 20th century. We have already noted that T. S. Eliot pronounced his world a waste land. The American novelist Sinclair Lewis (1885–1951) viciously satirized American complacency in the postwar period. His novel *Babbitt* (1922) was a scathing indictment of the middle-class love for the concept of "a chicken in every pot and two cars in every garage." His philistine hero, George Babbitt, became synonymous with a mindless materialism in love with gadgets, comfort, and simplistic Midwestern values.

By contrast, the English novelist Aldous Huxley (1894–1963) saw the unrestrained growth of technology as an inevitable tool of totalitarian control over individuals and society. His 1932 novel *Brave New World* was a harbinger of a whole literature of prophetic warning about the dangers in our future. The two most famous prophetic works of the post–World War II era are *Animal Farm* (1945) and *1984* (1949), both by the English writer George

17.20 Gino Severini. *Armored Train in Action.* 1915. Oil on canvas, 45⅝" × 34⅞" (177 × 88 cm). Collection, The Museum of Modern Art, New York (gift of Richard S. Zeisler). The influence of cubism in the composition is obvious.

CONTEMPORARY VOICES

Virginia Woolf

Then Joyce is dead: Joyce about a fortnight younger than I am. I remember Miss Weaver, in wool gloves, bringing *Ulysses* in typescript to our teatable at Hogarth House . . . One day Catherine [sic] Mansfield came, and I had it out. She began to read, ridiculing: then suddenly said: But there's something in this: a scene that should figure I suppose in the history of literature . . . Then I remember Tom [T. S. Eliot] saying: how could anyone write again after the immense prodigy of that last chapter?

We were in London on Monday. I went to London Bridge. I looked at the river; very misty; some tufts of smoke, perhaps from burning houses. There was another fire on Saturday. Then I saw a cliff of wall, eaten out, at one corner; a great corner all smashed: a bank; the monument erect: tried to get a bus; but such a block I dismounted; and the second bus advised me to walk. A complete jam of traffic; for streets were being blown up. So by Tube to the Temple; and there wandered in the desolate ruins of my old squares: gashed, dismantled; the old red bricks all white powder, something like a builder's yard. Grey dirt and broken windows. Sightseers; all that completeness ravished and demolished.

An abridged entry in Virginia Woolf's diary for January 15, 1941, describing the results of the German bombing of London. Shortly after this entry Virginia Woolf committed suicide.

Orwell, the pen name used by Eric Arthur Blair (1903–1950).

Huxley's *Brave New World* is set in the far distant future—600 A.F. (After [Henry] Ford, who had been deified as the founder of industrial society because he developed the assembly line.) In this society babies are raised in state hatcheries according to the needs of the state. They are produced in five classes (from Alpha to Epsilon) so that the exact numbers of needed intellectuals (Alphas) and menials (Epsilons) are produced. The goal of society is expressed in three words: Community/Identity/Stability. All sensory experience is supplied either by machines or a pleasure-drug called *soma*. Individuality, family relationships, creativity, and a host of other "unmanageable" human qualities have been eradicated from society either by coercion or programming.

Toward the end of the novel there is a climactic conversation between John Savage, a boy from the wilds of New Mexico raised outside the control of society, and Mustapha Mond, one of the controllers of the "brave new world" of the future. Patiently, Mustapha Mond explains to the uncivilized young man the reasons why certain repressions are inevitable and necessary in the society of the future. The reader sees rather clearly how aware Huxley is that the great humanistic achievements of the past—literature, art, religion—are threatening forces to any totalitarian society and as such are logical targets for a "scientifically" constructed society. His explanations now have a prescient and somber reality to us in the light of what we know about the real totalitarian societies of our own time.

SUMMARY

What made World War I so terrible was the advanced technologies used in the service of death. The old military charge against an enemy was obsolete with the invention of the machine gun just as the use of poison gas (not outlawed until after the war) made a mockery of military exercises of strategy. The result was an appalling slaughter of youth on a scale unparalleled in human history.

In the period between the wars the memory of that slaughter shook intellectuals to the core. Their response to it was predictable enough: protest or pacifism or a total distrust of the powers of rationality to cope with human evil. The reaction to the Great War ranged, in short, from T. S. Eliot's combination of pessimism and faith to the playful nonsense of the dada artists and the inner retreat of the surrealists.

The technological advances that had made the war so terrible also gave promise of new forms of communication that would radically advance the arts into new and different fields. The widespread development of radio networks, the transition of the movies from the silent screen to the "talkies," the increased mobility brought about by the automobile, and the advances in photography would not only produce new art forms but provide their availability to larger audiences.

Coupled with these advances were some profound shifts in social status. People were leaving rural areas in great numbers for the factories of the cities of America and Europe. The old social stratification of the classes was beginning to break down in Europe. The economic dislocations brought on by the war caused urban poverty in Europe and, after a giddy decade of prosperity in the 1920s, the depression years in the United States. In response to these social and economic dislocations new political movements seemed attractive and compelling. Hitler's National Socialist party rose against the background of Germany's defeat, as did Mussolini's Fascists. The period between the wars also saw the consolidation of Communist power in Russia and the rise of the totalitarian state under Stalin.

Finally, we should note some other fundamental (and radical) ideas that were beginning to gain currency. Einsteinian physics were changing the picture of the world in which we lived while containing the seeds of the atomic era. Sigmund Freud's ideas were also radically reshaping our notions of the interior landscape of the human soul.

All of these forces—political, technological, scientific, social, and artistic—gave a shape to a culture that in its richness (and sadness) we call the Western world between the two great wars.

Pronunciation Guide

Braque: BRAK
Breton: Bre-TAN
Buñuel: BON-well
Chagall: Sha-GAL
Diaghilev: DIAG-i-leff
Duchamp: Dew-SHAWM
Guernica: GHER-knee-ka
Kafka: KAF-ka
Mustapha Mond: MUS-taw-fa MOND
Nijinsky: Nidge-IN-ski
Riefenstahl: REEF-in-stall
Stravinsky: Stra-VIN-ski

Exercises

1. Look carefully at a cubist painting. Can you analyze the precise manner in which a Picasso or a Braque tries to get us to see in a new and unaccustomed way?
2. Some people have called Kafka a surrealist writer. Is that an apt description of his writing? Is "dreamlike" ("nightmarish"?) an apt way to think of his writing?
3. Jazz is still a much-respected art form today. Give a description of what you understand by jazz and distinguish it from rock music.
4. Discuss ways in which photography and film are used for propaganda purposes and/or political ends. You could begin by exploring how election films are used in our culture or television commercials made for public persuasion either as advertisements or for public-service spots.
5. Discuss *Brave New World* as an antitotalitarian novel. Tell about other books you have read or films you have seen that attempt to convey the same message.
6. Identify the religious message of Eliot's poems. How do they relate to the protest that is so much a part of the culture of the time?
7. Make (or describe) a dada art work that would outrage a contemporary viewer.

Further Reading

Arnason, H. H. *History of Modern Art.* Englewood Cliffs: Prentice-Hall, 1977. The standard basic survey of modern art in English.

Berman, Marshall. *All That Is Solid Melts into Air: The Experience of Modernity.* New York: Simon & Schuster, 1981. An ambitious account of modernity in the 20th century.

Ellmann, Richard, and Feidelson R., eds. *The Modern Tradition: Backgrounds of Modern Literature.* New York: Oxford University Press, 1965. A somewhat dated but still useful and wide-ranging collection of texts.

Fussell, Paul. *The Great War and Modern Memory.* New York: Oxford University Press, 1976. A brilliant study of how World War I changed the artistic life of Europe and America.

Harrison, Max. "Jazz" in *The New Grove Dictionary of Music and Musicians,* edited by S. Sadie (New York: Macmillan, 1980). A panoramic treatment with full bibliographies of books and journals as well as discographies. Grove is the standard reference in English for music.

Hayman, Ronald. *Kafka: A Biography.* New York: Oxford, 1981. A readable biography. Good for the intellectual background of German culture between the wars.

Huggins, Nathan. *Voices from the Harlem Renaissance.* New York: Oxford University Press, 1976. Comprehensive anthology of texts. Useful.

Hughes, Robert. *The Shock of the New.* New York: Knopf, 1981. A provocative study of modern art developed from the television series of the same name.

Newhall, Beaumont. *The History of Photography from 1839 to the Present Day,* rev. ed. New York: New York Graphic Society, 1978. An excellent survey.

Richardson, John. *Pablo Picasso* vol. 1. New York: Knopf, 1991. A fundamental study which takes up the life of Picasso to the painting of *Demoiselles.*

Wilson, Edmund. *Axel's Castle.* New York: Scribner, 1936. The classic critical work on literary modernism; still useful.

THE ATOMIC ERA

Period	GENERAL EVENTS	LITERATURE & PHILOSOPHY	ART
1939–1950 World War II and Aftermath	**1939** World War II begins; start of commercial television **1941** Japanese attack Pearl Harbor **1945** First atomic bombs used in warfare against Japan; World War II ends; Nazi extermination of Jews becomes widely known **1946** First meeting of UN General Assembly in London **1948** Israel becomes independent state; Berlin airlift marks beginning of "cold war" **1949** China becomes communist under leadership of Mao Zedong	**1945** Salinger, *The Catcher in the Rye* **1946** Orwell, *1984;* Sartre, *Existentialism as a Humanism* Existentialist philosophy influences writers and dramatists: Camus, *The Stranger* (1946); Beckett, *Waiting for Godot* (1953) **1949** Miller's *Death of a Salesman* given Pulitzer Prize for Drama; Faulkner awarded Nobel Prize for Literature	**late 1930s** Refugee artists Hoffman, Albers, Grosz bring ideas to America **1942** Cornell, *Medici Slot Machine.* Peggy Guggenheim exhibits European art at New York Gallery **1943** Pollock's first exhibition **c. 1945** New York becomes international art center; New York School includes abstract expressionism, color-field painting **1948** Pollock, *Number 1* **1949** Shahn, *Death of a Miner*
1950–1960 The Beat Generation	**1950** Korean War begins; FCC approves first commercial transmission of color TV **1952** U.S. explodes first hydrogen bomb **1954** School segregation outlawed by Supreme Court **1955** Civil Rights Movement starts in South **1957** First earth satellite launched by USSR	**1950** Sociologist David Riesman writes *The Lonely Crowd* **1951** Langston Hughes, "Harlem," "Theme for English B" **1950s** Alienation and anxiety become major themes of "Beat" writers Kerouac and Ginsberg 	**1951** Frankenthaler begins stained canvases: *The Bay* (1963); Moore, *Reclining Figure* **1950s** Rauschenberg experiments with "combine" paintings and, with Cage, "happenings" **1953–1954** Motherwell, *Elegy to the Spanish Republic XXXIV* **c. 1955** Reaction to abstract expressionism results in "Pop" art; Johns, *Flag* (1954–1955); Warhol *Soupcans* **1956** Hopper, *Office in a Small City;* Bergman film *Wild Strawberries* **1957–1960** Nevelson, *Sky Cathedral – Moon Garden + One* **1959** Rauschenberg, *Monogram;* Gottlieb, *Thrust;* Calder, *Big Red*
1960–1975 The Youth Movement	**1961** East Germans erect Berlin Wall; Soviets put first person in space **1962** First American orbits earth in space; transatlantic transmission of television signal via earth satellite **1963** President John F. Kennedy assassinated **1964** Massive buildup of American troops in Vietnam; Cultural Revolution in Communist China **1966** Founding of National Organization for Women in U.S. **1968** Assassination of Martin Luther King, Jr., and Robert F. Kennedy; youth movement at apex **1969** First walk on moon	**1960** Wiesel, *Night,* memoir of Nazi concentration camps **1961** Heller, *Catch-22,* satire on absurdity of war **1963** Flannery O'Connor, "Revelation" **1964** Stoppard, *Rosenkrantz and Guildenstern Are Dead* **1970** Solzhenitsyn awarded Nobel Prize for Literature; Toffler, *Future Shock;* Nikki Giovanni, "Ego Tripping" **1971** Plath, *The Bell Jar,* published posthumously **1973** Pynchon, *Gravity's Rainbow*	**1960** Johns, beer cans *Painted Bronze* **1960s** Rothko panels for Houston Chapel, opened 1971 **1962** Chamberlain, *Velvet White,* sculpture of crushed auto parts **1963** Smith, *Cubi I:* Manzù, Doors of Saint Peter's **1964** Kubrick, film *Dr. Strangelove* **1964–1966** Segal, *The Diner;* Kienholz, *The State Hospital* **1964** Romane Bearden, *The Prevalence of Ritual* **1966** Oldenburg, *Soft Toilet* **1970s** Resurgence of realism; incorporation of technology in art: videotapes, computers, lasers **1974** Kelly, *Grey Panels 2;* Pearlstein. *Two Female Models on Regency Sofa*
1975–1993	**1975** American withdrawal from Vietnam **1977** New Chinese government allows art previously banned **1981** First space shuttle flight **1989** Berlin Wall breached **1991** Soviet Union dissolved at the end of 1991		**1976** Leslie, *The 7 A.M. News* **1976–1982** *Backs* by Magdalena Abramowicz **1976** *Cabin Fever* by Susan Rothenberg **1981** Picasso's *Guernica* "returned" to Spain **1981** Anselm Kiefer's *Innerraum* **1987** Jean Lacy's *Little Egypt Condo*

CHAPTER **18** THE CONTEMPORARY CONTOUR

CHAPTER 18 THE CONTEMPORARY CONTOUR

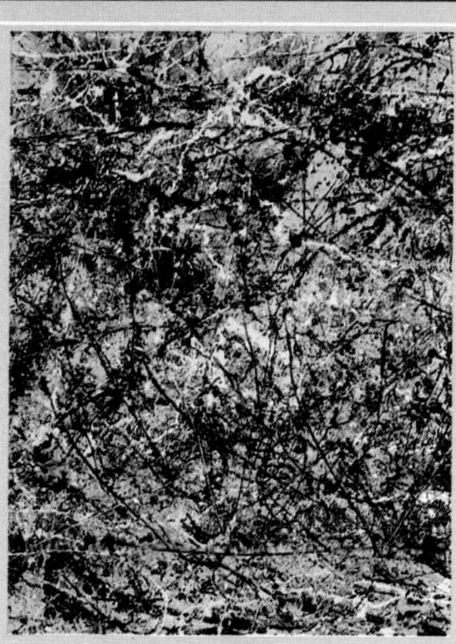

ARCHITECTURE

late 1930s Bauhaus architects Gropius and van der Rohe flee Nazi Germany for U.S.

1943 Wright designs Guggenheim Museum, New York

c. 1947 Buckminster Fuller develops geodesic dome

1952 Le Corbusier, *L'Unité d'Habitation,* Marseilles

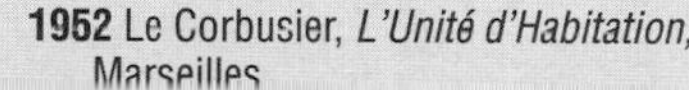

Reinforced concrete technology results in building as sculpture: Nervi and Vitellozzi, *Palazzo dello Sport,* Rome (1956–1957)

1958 van der Rohe and Johnson, Seagram Building, New York

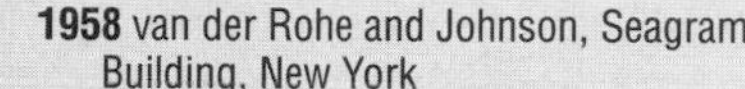

1959 Guggenheim Museum completed

1959–1972 Utzon, Opera House, Sydney

1960 Niemeyer completes government buildings at Brasilia

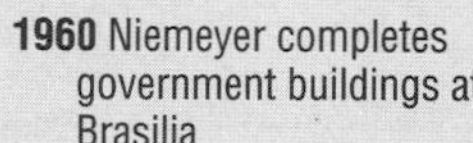

1962 Saarinen, TWA Flight Center, New York

1970 Soleri begins utopian city Arconsanti in Arizona

1977 Piano and Rogers, Pompidou Center, Paris

1978 Pei, East Wing of National Gallery of Art, Washington, D.C.

1991 Seattle Art Museum by Brown/Venturi

MUSIC

1945 Britten composes opera *Peter Grimes*

1948 Structuralist Boulez composes *Second Piano Sonata;* LP recordings become commercially available

1950s Beginnings of electronic music; first use of synthesizer

1952 Boulez, *Structures;* Cage experiments with aleatoric music: *4′3″*

1955–1956 Stockhausen, *Song of the Boys*

1958 Cage, *Concert for Piano and Orchestra*

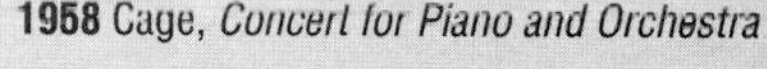

1960 Penderecki, *Threnody for the Victims of Hiroshima*

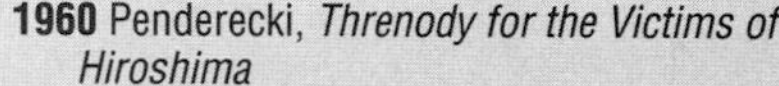

1962 Britten, *War Requiem;* Shostakovich, *Symphony No. 13,* text from poems by Yevtushenko

1965 Stockhausen, *Mixtur*

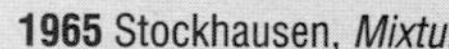

c. 1965 Baez, Seeger, Dylan entertain with protest songs; height of rock music and Beatles; Lennon, *Yesterday;* eclectic music of Zappa and Mothers of Invention

1971 Shostakovich, *Symphony No. 15*

1973 Stockhausen, *Stop;* Britten, opera *Death in Venice*

1978 Penderecki, opera *Paradise Lost*

1983 Steve Reich's "Desert Music"

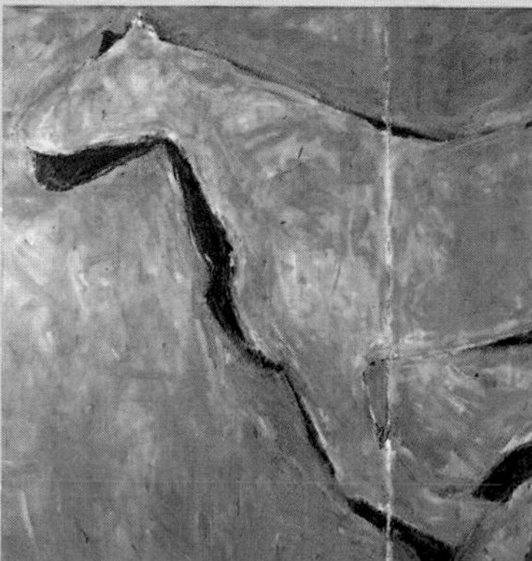

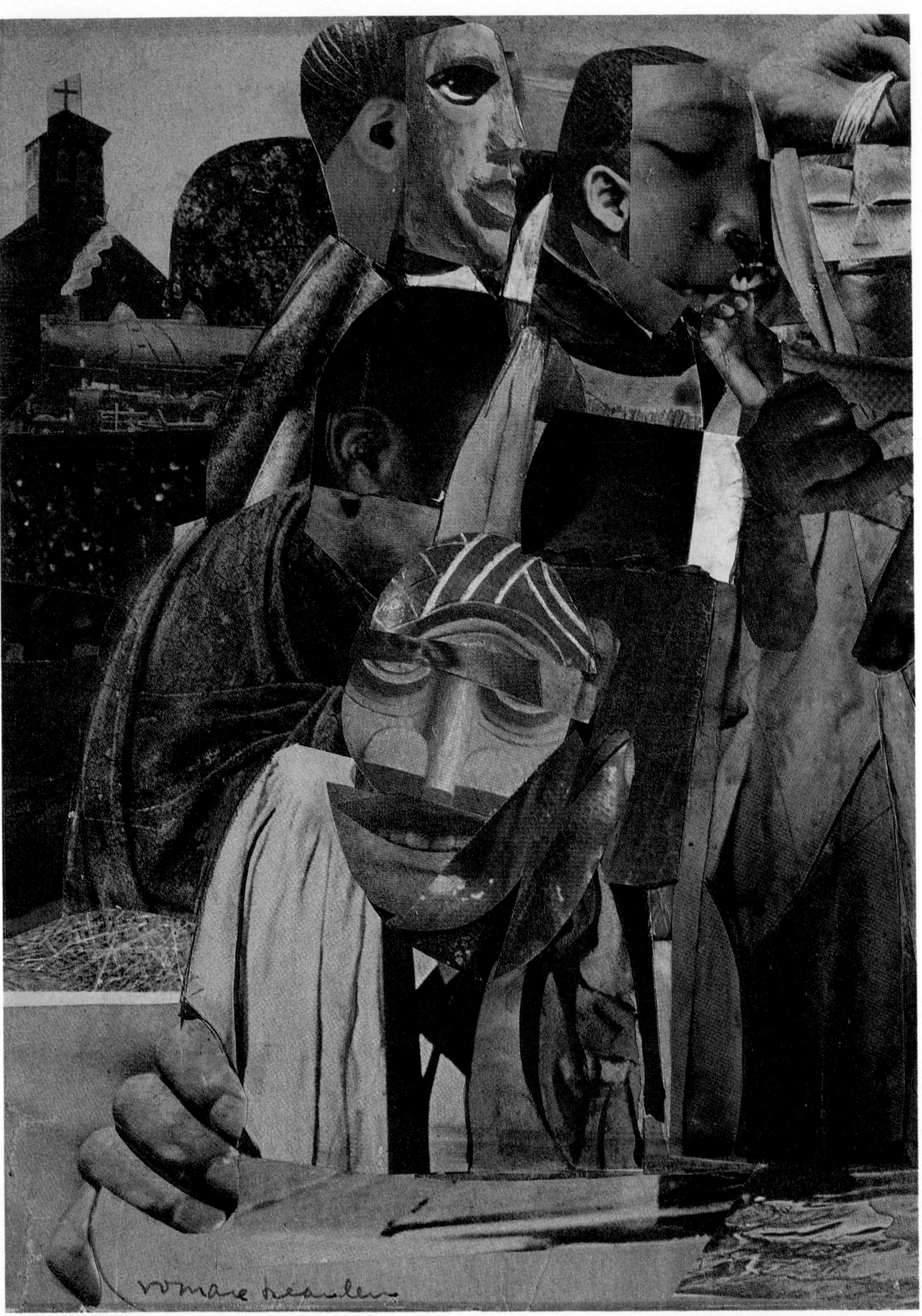
romare bearden

CHAPTER

18 THE CONTEMPORARY CONTOUR

TOWARD A GLOBAL CULTURE

As we approach the end of the 20th century the period after 1945 seems to recede into history. It is difficult to remember what has happened to us as a culture in the two generations since the end of World War II. Events that have happened in the past decade or two are perhaps too close for us to know whether or not they have permanently changed us as a people. Was the moon landing of 1969 really a watershed in our consciousness as humans? Is the "American Century" so proudly forecast by commentators at the end of World War II slowly coming to an end? Has the revolution in communications already radically changed the way we learn things? Is the age of microtechnology and computers going to bring in a new, wonderful era or an antiutopia?

The postwar period is rightly called *The Atomic Era*. Developed largely by refugee scientists during World War II, atomic weaponry looms like an ominous shadow over all international tensions and all potentially belligerent situations. It is not simply a question of atomic bombs being bigger or more deadly weapons, although they are surely that. Atomic weapons can have long-term and little-understood consequences both for nature and for individuals who happen to survive their first devastation.

Because modern war is so far beyond the power of the human imagination to depict, contemporary artists have turned to satire as a way of expressing their fear and hatred of it. Novels like Joseph Heller's *Catch-22* and Thomas Pynchon's *Gravity's Rainbow* sketched out war in terms of insanity, irrationality, and the blackest of humor while Stanley Kubrick's brilliant movie *Doctor Strangelove* mounts a scathing attack on those who speak coolly about "megadeaths" and "mutual assured destruction" (MAD in military lingo). Any attempt at mere realism, these artists seem to say, pales into triviality.

Second, at the end of World War II the United States emerged both as a leading economic power in the world and as the leader of the "Free World" in its struggle against communism. This preeminence explains both the high standard of living in the West and the resentment of those who do not share it. Only lately have we understood that economic supremacy does not permit a nation to live free from outside forces. The energy crisis, the need for raw materials, the quest for labor, and the search for new markets bind many nations together in a delicate economic and social network of political relationships. The United States depends on other countries; the shifting patterns of economic relationships between North America, Europe, the Third World, Japan, and the oil producers are all reminders of how fragile that network really is. With the collapse of communism in Eastern Europe new patterns of culture slowly emerge. We do not know what the "New World Order" will look like.

The material satisfactions of Western life have spawned other kinds of dissatisfaction. While we may be the best-fed, best-housed, and best-clothed people in history, the hunger for individual and social meaning remains a constant in our lives. For instance, the many movements in this country—for civil rights, the rights of women, for minority recognition—are signs of that human restlessness that will not be satisfied by bread alone. Those movements are not peculiar to North America as democratic movements in other parts of the world so readily attest.

The incredible achievements of modern society have exacted their price. Sigmund Freud shrewdly pointed out in *Civilization and Its Discontents* (1929) that the price of advanced culture is a certain repression of the individual together with the need of that individual to conform to the larger will of the community. North Americans have always been sensitive to the constraints of the state, since their history began as a revolt against statist domination.

The Western world tends to see repression in terms that are more social than political. The very complexity of the technological management of modern life has led many to complain that we are becoming mere numbers or ciphers under the indifferent control of data banks and computers. Such warnings began as early as George Orwell's political novel *1984* (1946), written right after the war, and progress through David Riesman's sociological tract of the 1950s, *The Lonely Crowd,* to the futurist predictions of Alvin Toffler's *Future Shock* in the 1970s. As we inch towards a new millenium, many such analyses are sure to appear.

Art, of course, reflects not only the materials of its age but also its hopes and anxieties. The art, literature, and music of our times attempt to diagnose our ills, protest our injustices, and offer alternative visions of what life might be. On very exceptional occasions the voice of the artist can sum up a cultural condition in such a way that change can come. Who would have thought that an obscure convict, buried in the vast prison complex of the Siberian wasteland, would raise his voice against injustice and repression in such a way as radically to change the way a whole society is understood? That is surely what Alexsandr Solzhenitsyn has done in our own time with respect to the ominous character of a now collapsed Soviet communism.

Finally, the true artist can articulate a vision of what humanity can trust. In the midst of alienation, the artist can bring community and in the midst of ugliness, beauty. The artist, in short, acts not only as a voice of protest but as a voice of hope. The American novelist William Faulkner (1897–1962) spent a lifetime chronicling the violence, decay, injustice, poverty, and lost dreams of the American South. His novels are difficult to read, for they reflect the modernist sense of dislocated place and fragmented time. His most famous novel, *The Sound and the Fury* (1929), was notorious for its depiction of defective children, incestuous relationships, loutish drunkenness, and violence. In that sense it reflects the bleak landscape of the modern literary imagination. Yet Faulkner insisted that beneath the horror of modern life was a strong residue of human hope and goodness. Faulkner

EAST MEETS WEST

A Global Culture

While nationalism is still a fact of life, it is clear that we are rapidly becoming a global culture. New forms of information technology, intercontinental travel, and the complex nature of economics are all elements in such a change. Japan, an ancient Eastern culture, now dominates the West economically while its own traditional culture is rapidly becoming westernized in the process.

It does not take a great deal of analysis to see the vast interchanges of cultural influences in the world today. The thirst for Western fashions, popular music, and the other elements of consumer culture make great inroads in non-Western lands while the West seeks out everything from the religious traditions of the East to the art and music these countries produce. In the field of literature, to cite one conspicuous example, contemporary readers seek books beyond those of the West. Latin American authors, as well as those from Africa, Asia, and India, now find appreciative audiences.

A global culture does not mean a unitary or "one world" culture. It does mean that people are increasingly aware of the diversity of culture. World events enter our living rooms so that things that may once have been thought of as distant events now greet us immediately and in color. We may watch those events on a television made in Japan while wearing clothes sewn in Thailand and shoes made in Hungary while snacking on food grown in Mexico. Such an economic interdependence reflects the reality of a global banking system, the globalization of the economy, and the increasing globalization of information and information technologies.

Nowhere has this shrinking of distances (and attitudes) become more clear than in the academic debates over what constitutes a liberal arts education today. Is it possible (or desirable) to have the Western core of humanities as the centerpiece of a curriculum? The place of non-Western and nontraditional cultures as part of the general education of a student is hotly argued in educational circles. The very fact of that discussion points to the emergence of a global consciousness with a continued shrinking of parochial attitudes. The fact that such globalization is hotly debated only emphasizes the profound nature of the changes taking place in our culture.

reaffirmed it ringingly in his acceptance speech when awarded the Nobel Prize for Literature in 1949: "I believe that man will not merely endure; he will prevail."

In the rapidly shifting contours of our contemporary world we might reflect upon the ways in which artists have participated in the restructuring of societies. Many of those who strggled for human rights in what was the Soviet Union and the Eastern bloc were poets, novelists, filmmakers, musicians, and playwrights. The redefinition of the status of women or others who suffer minority status in our own country expresses their plight in everything from films to poetry. The "subversive" quality of popular music is not only a part of our culture but has become a worldwide phenomenon. The role of artists in the changing of society is very much a part of the fabric of this chapter; history teaches that it will also be true in the next millenium.

Existentialism

The philosophy that most persistently gripped the intellectual imagination of the Western world in the postwar period was *existentialism.* Existentialism is more an attitude than a single philosophical system. Its direct ancestry can be traced to the 19th-century Danish theologian and religious thinker Sören Kierkegaard (1813–1855), who set out its main emphases. Kierkegaard strongly reacted against the great abstract philosophical systems developed by such philosophers as Georg Hegel (1770–1831) in favor of an intense study of the individual person in his or her actual existing situation in the world. Kierkegaard emphasized the single individual ("the crowd is untruth") who exists in a specific set of circumstances at a particular time in history with a specific consciousness. Philosophers like Hegel, Kierkegaard once noted ironically, answer every question about the universe except "Who am I?," "What am I doing here?," and "Where am I going?"

This radically subjective self-examination was carried on all through the last century by philosophers like Friedrich Nietzsche and novelists like Fyodor Dostoyevsky, who are regarded as forerunners of modern existentialist philosophy. In our own century writers like Franz Kafka, the German poet Rainer Maria Rilke, the Spanish critic Miguel de Unamuno, and, above all, the German philosopher Martin Heidegger gave sharper focus to the existentialist creed. The writer who best articulated existentialism both as a philosophy and a style of life, however, was the French writer and philosopher Jean-Paul Sartre (1905–1980).

Sartre believed it the task of the modern thinker to take seriously the implications of atheism. If there is no God, Sartre insisted, then there is no blueprint of what a person should be and there is no ultimate significance to the universe. People are thrown into life and their very aloneness forces them to make decisions about who they are and what they shall be. "People are condemned to be free," Sartre wrote. Existentialism was an attempt to help people understand their place in an absurd world, their obligation to face up to their freedom, and the kinds of ethics available to people in a world bereft of any absolutes.

Sartre began his mature career just as Germany was beginning its hostilities in the late 1930s. After being a prisoner of war in Germany Sartre lived in occupied France, where he was active in the French Resistance, especially as a writer for the newspaper *Combat.* With the novelist Albert Camus (1913–1960) and the writer Simone de Beauvoir (1908–1986) his was the major voice demanding integrity in the face of the absurdities and horrors of war-torn Europe. Such an attitude might be considered a posture if it were not for the circumstances in which these existentialist writers worked.

The appeal of existentialism was its marriage of thought and action, its analysis of modern anxiety, and its willingness to express its ideas through the media of plays, novels, films, and newspaper polemics. After the close of the war in 1945 there was a veritable explosion of existentialist theater (Samuel Beckett, Harold Pinter, Jean Gênet, Eugène Ionesco) and existentialist fiction (Camus, Sartre, Beauvoir) in Europe. In the United States

TABLE 18.1 Some Writers in the Existentialist Tradition

Fyodor Dostoyevsky (1821–1881)—Russian
Sören Kierkegaard (1813–1855)—Danish
Friedrich Nietzsche (1844–1900)—German
Miguel de Unamuno (1864–1936)—Spanish
Rainer Maria Rilke (1875–1926)—Czech/German
Franz Kafka (1883–1924)—Czech/German
Martin Heidegger (1889–1976)—German
Jean-Paul Sartre (1905–1980)—French
José Ortega y Gasset (1883–1955)—Spanish
Albert Camus (1913–1960)—French
Nicholas Berdyaev (1874–1948)—Russian
Martin Buber (1878–1965)—Austrian/Israeli
Karl Jaspers (1883–1969)—German
Jacques Maritain (1882–1973)—French

existentialist themes were eagerly taken up by intellectuals and writers who were attracted to its emphasis on anxiety and alienation.

The so-called "beat writers" of the 1950s embraced a rather vulgarized style of existentialism filtered through the mesh of jazz and the black experience. Such beat writers as the late Jack Kerouac, Gregory Corso, and Allan Ginsberg embraced the existentialist idea of alienation even though they rejected the austere tone of their European counterparts. Their sense of alienation was united with the idea of experience heightened by ecstasy either of a musical, sexual, or chemical origin. The beats, at least in that sense, were the progenitors of the hippies of the 1960s.

The existentialist ethic has remained alive mainly through the novels of Albert Camus. In works like *The Stranger* (1942), *The Plague* (1947), and *The Fall* (1956), Camus, who disliked being called an existentialist, continues to impress his readers with heroes who fight the ultimate absurdity of the world with lucidity and dedication and without illusion.

Today, existentialism is mainly an historical moment in the postwar culture of Europe and America. Its importance, however, rests in its capacity for formulating some of the most important ideas of modernity: the absence of religious faith; the search for meaning; the dignity of the individual; the concern with human subjectivity.

PAINTING SINCE 1945

Art critic Barbara Rose has written that the history of world art in the second half of the 20th century bears an unmistakable American stamp. It is hard to quarrel with that historical judgment since in the 1940s the United States, and more specifically New York, became the center of new impulses in art, much the way Paris had been in the first half of the century. As we come to the end of the century, however, it is also clear that American supremacy may well be diluted as art takes on an international and transnational character.

Part of this geographic shift from Paris to New York can be explained by the pressures of World War II. Numerous artists and intellectuals fled the totalitarian regimes of Europe to settle in America. Refugee artist/teachers like Hans Hofmann (1880–1966), Josef Albers (1888–1976), and George Grosz (1893–1959) brought European ideas to a new generation of American painters. The American patron and art collector Peggy Guggenheim, then married to the surrealist painter Max Ernst, fled her European home when war broke out to return to New York City, where at her Art of This Century gallery she exhibited such European painters as Braque, Léger, Arp, Brancusi, Picasso, Severini, and Miró. She quickly became patron to American painters who eventually led the American avant-garde. Peggy Guggenheim's support of this group in New York was crucial to the "Americanization" of modern art.

History nevertheless rarely records total and immediate shifts in artistic style. Thus, while a revolution was taking place in American art and, for that matter, in world art, some excellent artists continued to work in an older tradition relatively untouched by this revolution. Edward Hopper (1882–1967), for instance, continued to produce paintings that explored his interest in light and his sensitivity to the problems of human isolation and loneliness. His *Office in a Small City* [18.1] is a late example of Hopper's twin concerns. Ben Shahn (1898–1969) never lost the social passion that had motivated his work all through the 1930s. His *Death of a Miner* [18.2] is both a tribute to and an outcry against the death of a workingman in a senseless accident.

Another painter who remained untouched by the American revolution in painting is Georgia O'Keeffe (1887–1987), who had her first show in New York in 1916 at the galleries of Alfred Stieglitz, the photographer she married in 1924. Her early paintings, like *Calla Lily with Red Roses* [18.3], show both a masterful sense of color and a precise sense of line. She belonged to the early strain of American modernism but continued in her own style. O'Keeffe has not only been recognized as a major artist in her own right but as the focus for serious discussion about a feminist aesthetic in art for our time.

Abstract Expressionism

The artists mentioned above have a secure reputation in the history of art, but it was the abstract expressionists who gave art in the period after 1945 its "unmistakable American stamp." The term *abstract expressionism* is useful because it alludes to two characteristics fundamental to the work of these artists: It was devoid of recognizable content (and thus abstract) and it used color, line, and shape to express interior states of subjective aesthetic experience. *Action painting* and *New York School* are two other terms used to classify these painters.

The acknowledged leader of the abstract expressionists was the Wyoming-born painter Jackson

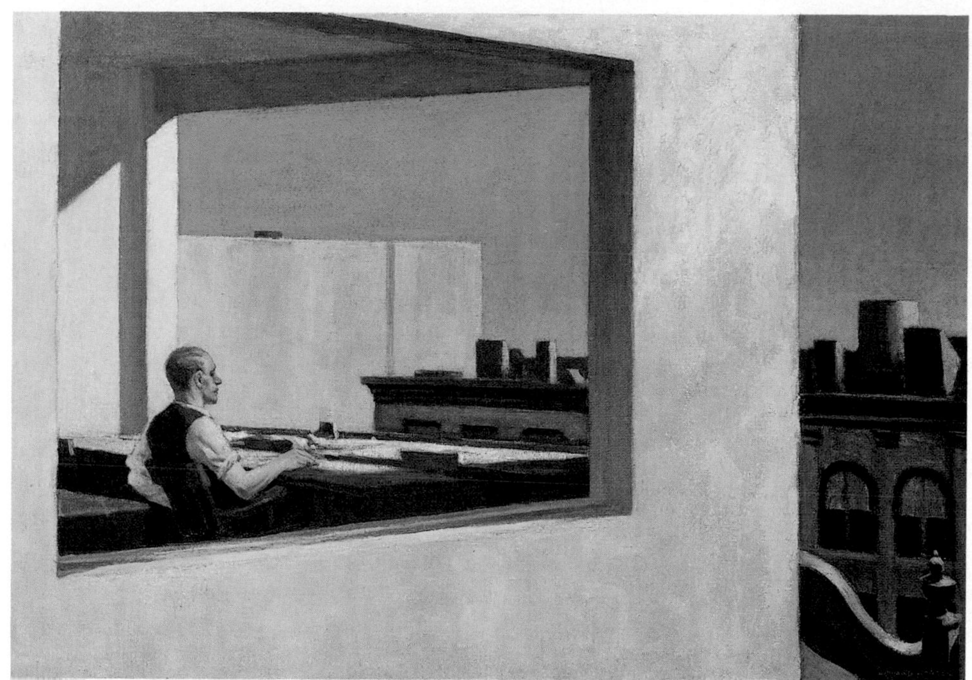

18.1 Edward Hopper. *Office in a Small City.* 1953. Oil on canvas, 28 × 40" (71 × 102 cm). Metropolitan Museum of Art, New York (George A. Hearn Fund). Hopper's style, set by the 1920s, used light to set the tone of emotional isolation.

18.2 Ben Shahn. *Death of a Miner.* 1949. Tempera on muslin treated with gesso, on panel; 2'3" × 4' (.69 × 1.22 m). Metropolitan Museum of Art, New York (Arthur H. Hearn Fund, 1950).

18.3 Georgia O'Keeffe. *Calla Lily with Red Roses.* 1927. Oil on canvas, 30 × 48" (76 × 122 cm). Private collection. The artist took the common subject of flowers and, through her profound line and strong sense of color, turned them into mysterious, nearly abstract, shapes of feminine power.

CONTEMPORARY VOICES

Georgia O'Keeffe

I have picked voices where I have found them—Have picked up sea shells and rocks and pieces of wood where there were sea shells and rocks and pieces of wood that I liked.

When I found beautiful white bones in the desert I picked them up and took them home too.

I have used these things to say what it is to me the wideness and the wonder of the world as I live in it.

A pelvis bone has always been useful in any animal that has it—quite as useful as a head I suppose. For years in the country the pelvis bones lay about the house indoors and out—always underfoot—seen and not seen as such things can be—seen in many different ways. . . .

I was the sort of child that ate around the raisin on the cookie and ate around the hole in the doughnut saving either the raisin or the hole for the last and best.

So probably—not having changed much—when I started painting the pelvis bones I was most interested in the holes in the bones—what I saw through them—particularly the blue from holding them up to the sun against the sky as one is apt to do when one seems to have more sky than earth in one's world—

They were most wonderful against the Blue—the Blue that will be there as it is now after all men's destruction is finished.

I have tried to paint the Bones and the Blue.

A catalogue statement of Georgia O'Keeffe about her desert paintings, 1944.

18.4 Jackson Pollock. *Number 1, 1948.* 1948. Oil and enamel on unprimed canvas, 5'8" × 8'8" (76 × 122 cm). Collection, The Museum of Modern Art, New York (purchase). The theoretical basis for such random painting can be traced to the Freudian idea of free association and the surrealist adaptation of that technique for art called *psychic automatism.*

18.5 Adolph Gottlieb. *Thrust.* 1959. Oil on canvas, 9' × 7'6" (2.74 × 2.29 m). Metropolitan Museum of Art, New York (George A. Hearn Fund). Gottlieb's art is partly inspired by a year he spent in Arizona studying the Native American tradition of pictographs. The paintings also have a strong sexual undercurrent.

Pollock (1912–1956), who had his first one-man show at Peggy Guggenheim's Art of This Century gallery in 1943. Pollock's early work was characterized by an interest in primitive symbolism, deriving from the artist's long encounter with the psychology of Carl Jung. By the early 1940s, under the influence of the surrealists and their technique of automatic creation—in which the artist allows the unconscious rather than the conscious will to stimulate the act of creation—he had begun to depart radically from traditional ways of painting.

At first Pollock discarded brush and palette for sticks, small mops, and sponges to apply paint in coarse, heavy gestures. Then he set aside instruments altogether and poured, dripped, and spattered paint directly on the canvas in nervous gestural lines rather than enclosed shapes. For his colors he mixed the expensive oils of the artists with the utilitarian enamels used by house painters. Perhaps most radically, instead of using an easel he rolled out large expanses of canvas on the floor of his studio and applied paint in his unusual manner as he walked around and on them. The dimensions of the finished painting were fixed when Pollock decided to cut out from this canvas a particular area and then attach it to the traditional wooden support or stretcher.

The result of these unorthodox procedures was huge paintings composed of intricate patterns of dribbles, drops, and lines—webs of color vibrant in their complexity [18.4]. The energy-filled nets of paint extended to the limits of the stretched canvas and by implication beyond, seeming to have no beginning or end and hence attracting the stylistic label *over-all painting*. Neither did these colors and lines suggest the illusion of space receding in planes behind the surface of the picture, although they did create a sense of continuous rhythmic movement.

Other painters of the New York School in the 1940s and 1950s were more interested in the potentialities of large fields of color and abstract symbol systems, often with obvious psychological meanings. Adolph Gottlieb (1903–1974) painted a series of "bursts" in the 1950s in which a luminous sunlike color field hung over a primordial exploding mass [18.5]. Robert Motherwell (1915–1991) did hundreds of paintings in which huge primitive black shapes are in the foreground of subtle, broken color fields [18.6]. Mark Rothko (1903–1970)

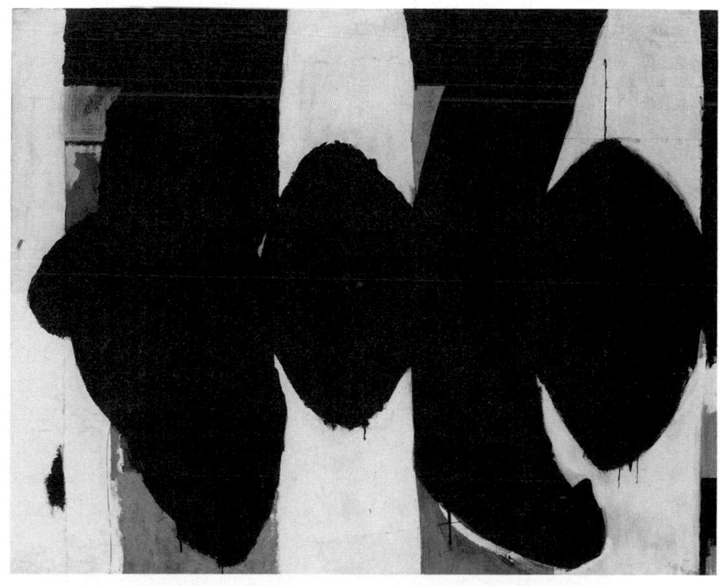

18.6 Robert Motherwell. *Elegy to the Spanish Republic #34.* 1953–1954. Oil on canvas, 80 × 100", Albright-Knox Art Gallery, Buffalo, New York (gift of Seymour H. Knox, 1957). The title of the painting was inspired by the poetry of Federico García Lorca, but no direct literary reference should be seen in the painting. Motherwell insists that the "painter communes with himself."

18.7 The Rothko Chapel, Rice University, Houston. Consecrated 1971. Chapel design by Philip Johnson. Murals by Mark Rothko. This ecumenical chapel contains fourteen panels finished several years before the artist's death. The fourteen panels may make an oblique reference to the traditional fourteen stations of the cross, but the artist desired their brooding simplicity to be a focus for the personal meditation of each viewer.

experimented restlessly with floating color forms of the most subtle variation and hue. In the 1960s Rothko painted a series of panels for a chapel in Houston [18.7] in which he attempted with some success to use color variations alone to evoke a sensibility of mystical awareness of transcendence.

What did these artists have in common? Their energy and originality make it difficult to be categorical although some generalizations are possible. They all continued the modernist tendency to break with the older conventions of art. As the cubists turned away from traditional perspective so the abstract expressionists turned away from recognizable content to focus on the implications of color and line. Second, they were *expressionists,* which is to say that they were concerned with the ability of their paintings to express not what they saw but what they felt and what they hoped to communicate to others. As one critic has put it, in an age when organized religion could no longer compel people with the notion of revelation, these artists wished to express their sense of ultimate meaning and their thirst for the infinite. "Instead of making cathedrals out of Christ, Man, or 'Life,'" painter Barnett Newman wrote, "we are making them out of ourselves, out of our own feeling."

The desire to expand the possibilities of pure color detached from any recognizable imagery has been carried on and extended by a second generation of color-field painters, the most notable of whom is Helen Frankenthaler (1928–). Around 1951 Frankenthaler began to saturate unprimed canvases with poured paint so that the figure (the paint) merged into the ground (the canvas) of the work. By staining the canvas she carried Pollock's action painting one step further, emphasizing the pure liquidity of paint and the color that derives from it. Frankenthaler uses the thinnest of paints to take advantage of the light contrast between the

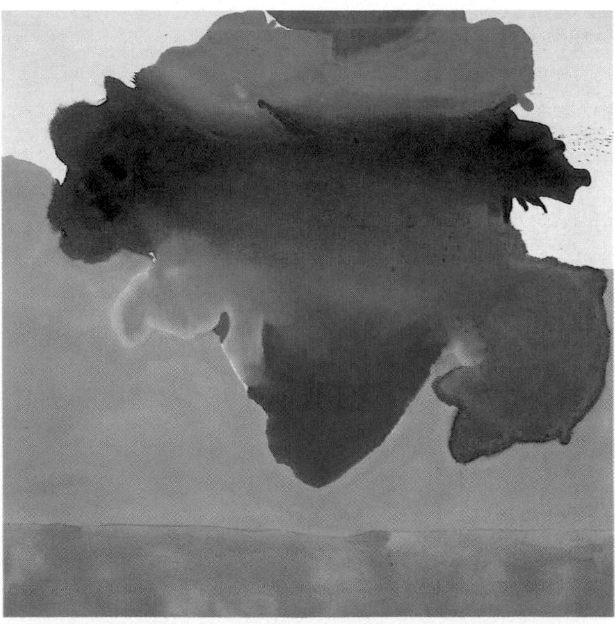

18.8 Helen Frankenthaler. *The Bay.* 1963. Acrylic resin on canvas, 6'8¼" × 6'9¼" (2.02 × 2.08 m). Detroit Institute of Arts (gift of Dr. Hilbert D. Delawter). Frankenthaler's work gains its almost watercolor luminosity by her practice of thinning her paints to the consistency of washes.

paint and the unstained canvas (unlike Pollock she does not paint "all over" her ground). The result has been paintings with the subtlety of watercolors but distinctively and inescapably different [18.8].

The Return to Representation

It was inevitable that some artists would break with abstract expressionism and return to a consideration of the object. This reaction began in the middle 1950s with painters like Jasper Johns (1930–), whose *Flag* series [18.9] heralded a new appreciation of objects. Further, Johns' art focused on objects taken from the mundane world. Johns went on to paint and sculpt targets, toothbrushes, beer cans, and even his own artist's brushes. This shift signaled a whimsical and ironic rejection of highly emotive, content-free, and intellectualized abstract art.

18.9 Jasper Johns. *Flag.* 1954. Encaustic, oil, and collage on fabric mounted on plywood; 3'6¼" × 5'⅝" (1.07 × 1.54 m). Museum of Modern Art, New York (gift of Phillip Johnson in honor of Alfred Barr, Jr.). The rather banal subject should not detract from Johns' phenomenal technique. Encaustic is painting done with molten colored wax.

Robert Rauschenberg (1925–) was another artist who helped define the sensibility emerging as a counterforce to abstract expressionism in the 1950s. Rauschenberg had studied at Black Mountain College, an experimental school in North Carolina, under the tutelage of the refugee Bauhaus painter Josef Albers. A more important influence from his Black Mountain days was the avant-garde musician and composer John Cage (1912–1992), who encouraged experiments combining music, drama, dance, art, and other media into coherent artistic wholes which were called *happenings.* Rauschenberg began to experiment with what he called "combine" paintings that utilized painting combined with any number of assembled objects in a manner that had deep roots in the avant-garde. By 1959 he was doing large-scale works like his *Monogram* [18.10], which combined an assortment of elements (including a stuffed goat!) in an outrageous yet delightful collage.

18.10 Robert Rauschenberg. *Monogram.* 1955–1959. Freestanding combine, 5'4½" × 3'6" × 5'3¼" (1.64 × 1.07 × 1.61 m). Moderna Museet, Stockholm. Although Rauschenberg's work was once considered a spoof of abstract art—a sort of contemporary dada—he is now regarded as one of the most inventive of American artists.

The third artist who emerged in the late 1950s is Andy Warhol (1930–1987). Warhol became notorious for his paintings of soup cans, soap boxes, cola bottles, and the other throwaway detritus of our society, which made his name synonymous with *pop art,* a term first used in England to describe the art of popular culture. The long-range judgment on Warhol as a serious artist may be harsh, but he understood one thing very well: taste today is largely shaped by the incessant pressure of advertising, the mass media, pulp writing, and the transient culture of fads. Warhol, who started his career as a commercial illustrator, exploited that fact relentlessly.

Over the years Warhol increasingly turned his attention away from painting and toward printmaking, videotapes, movies, and Polaroid photography. His subjects tended to be the celebrities of the film and social world. Whether his art is a prophetic judgment on our culture or a subtle manipulation of it is difficult to answer since Warhol could be bafflingly indirect. His lightly retouched silkscreen prints of entertainment celebrities [18.11] seem banal and of little permanent value, but that may be exactly what he wished to express.

Painting from the 1970s is difficult to categorize. Some artists continue to explore color-field painting with great verve. Others, such as Ellsworth Kelly, Kenneth Noland, and Frank Stella, explore more formal elements with carefully drawn "hard edges," primary colors, and geometrically precise compositions. They are almost ascetic in their use of line and color, as recent "minimalist" works of an artist like Ellsworth Kelly show [18.12].

18.11 Andy Warhol. *Mick Jagger.* 1975. Acrylic paint and silkscreen enamel on canvas, 40" (102 cm) square. Private collection. Warhol incorporated into high art the world of the media, money, and fashion. Until his death in 1987 he incarnated the notion of the artist as celebrity figure with his explorations in video, film, photography, magazine publishing, graphics, and painting.

18.12 Ellsworth Kelly. *Grey Panels 2.* 1974. Oil on canvas, 7'8" × 8'6" (2.34 × 2.59 m). Leo Castelli Gallery, New York. By comparing this work with Frankenthaler's (Figure18.8) one can see the different approaches to color in the post–abstract expressionist period.

Another group of painters has gone back totally to the recognizable object painted in a manner so realistic that critics have called them "photorealists." Less glossy than the photorealists but almost classical in their fine draftsmanship are the erotically charged nudes of Philip Pearlstein, who takes a position somewhere between the fragmented world of cubism and the slick glossiness of popular magazines. His *Two Female Models on Regency Sofa* [18.13] is a serious and unsentimental study of the female figure.

For Alfred Leslie (1927–) the past can still be a teacher for the modern painter. In a work like *7 A.M. News* [18.14] Leslie combines an eye for contemporary reality and the use of *chiaroscuro,* a technique he consciously borrows directly from the 17th-century painter Caravaggio. With Alfred Leslie we have come, as it were, full circle from the abstract expressionist break with tradition to a contemporary painter who consciously looks back to the 17th-century masters for formal inspiration.

One can say that two intellectual trends seem to have emerged in American painting in this period. One strain, abstract expressionism and its various offspring, is heavily indebted to the modernist in-

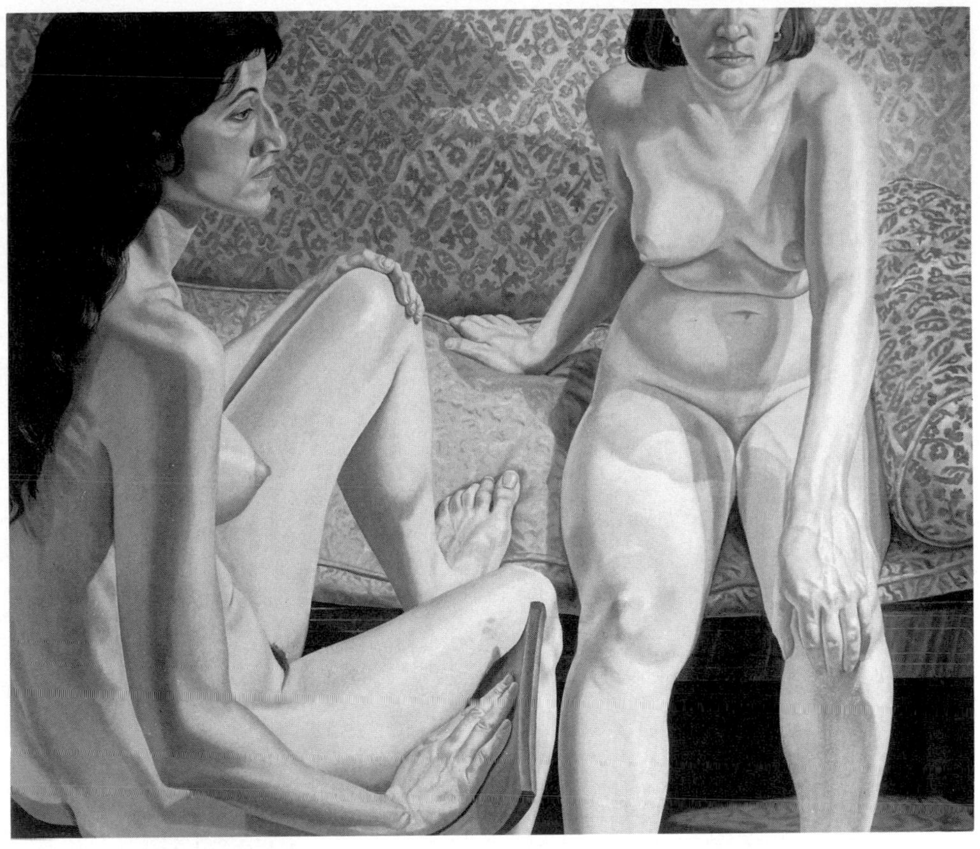

18.13 Philip Pearlstein. *Two Female Models on Regency Sofa.* 1974. Oil on canvas, 5' × 5'10" (1.52 × 1.78 m). Private collection, New York. Compare Pearlstein's nudes with those of the Renaissance tradition represented by an artist like Titian to get a feeling for the modern temper.

18.14 Alfred Leslie. *7 a.m. News.* 1976–1978. Oil on canvas, 7 × 5' (2.13 × 1.52 m). Allan Frumkin Gallery, New York. Leslie uses the technique of *chiaroscuro* in conscious homage to the baroque masters like Caravaggio and Rembrandt.

tellectual tradition, with its many roots in psychological theories of Jung and Freud and the existentialist vocabulary of anxiety and alienation. By contrast, the work of painters like Johns, Warhol, Rauschenberg, and others is far more closely linked to the vast world of popular culture in post-industrial America. Its material, its symbols, and its intentions reflect the values of consumer culture more than the work of the New York School of the 1940s. Pop art, largely free from the brooding metaphysics of the abstract expressionists, can be seen—perhaps simultaneously—as a celebration and a challenge to middle-class values.

One sees that same blend of "isms" and references to popular culture in the work of African-American artists. A painter like Romare Bearden (1914–1988) produced a body of work which absorbed collage, cubism, and tendencies to abstraction in order to make a body of art that was distinctively his own. A painting like *The Prevalence of*

18.15 Romare Bearden. *The Prevalence of Ritual: Baptism.* 1964. Collage on board. 9 × 12" (23 × 30 cm). The Hirshhorn Museum and Sculpture Garden, Smithsonian Institution. Washington, D. C.

Ritual: Baptism [18.15] celebrates a traditional religious ritual with references to Africa done in a cubist style. By contrast, the painter Jean Lacy (1932–) utilizes mixed media in a work like *Little Egypt Condo/New York City* to celebrate her racial heritage and, at the same time, celebrate the energy of city life [18.16].

Painting in the late 1970s and 1980s has gone in many directions. Critics are agreed on one point: There is no predominant "ism" that defines con-

18.16. Jean Lacy. *Little Egypt Condo/New York City.* 1987. Mixed media on museum board. 10½" × 13½" (26.6 × 33.5 cm). Collection of the artist.

18.17 Frank Stella. *Shoubeegi (Firebirds).* 1978. Mixed media on metal relief, 94 × 120 × 32½" (2.39 × 3.5 × .82 m). Private collection (courtesy of Leo Castelli Gallery, New York). Stella has been the foremost and most persistent defender of abstract art on the American scene today.

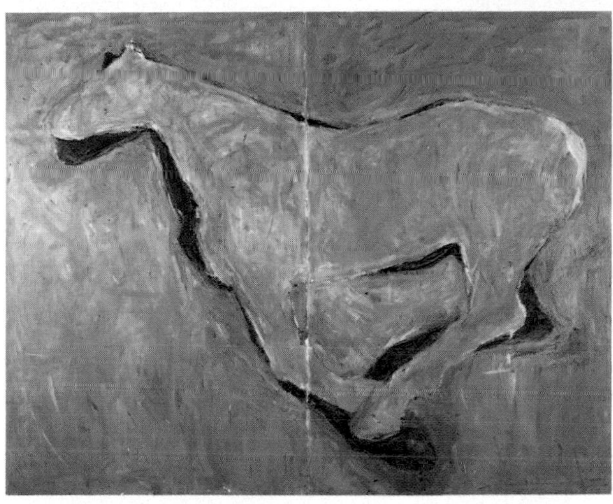

18.18 Susan Rothenberg. *Cabin Fever.* 1976. Acrylic and tempera on canvas, 67 × 84". Collection of the Modern Art Museum of Fort Worth, Museum Purchase, Sid W. Richardson Foundation Endowment Fund and an Anonymous Donor.

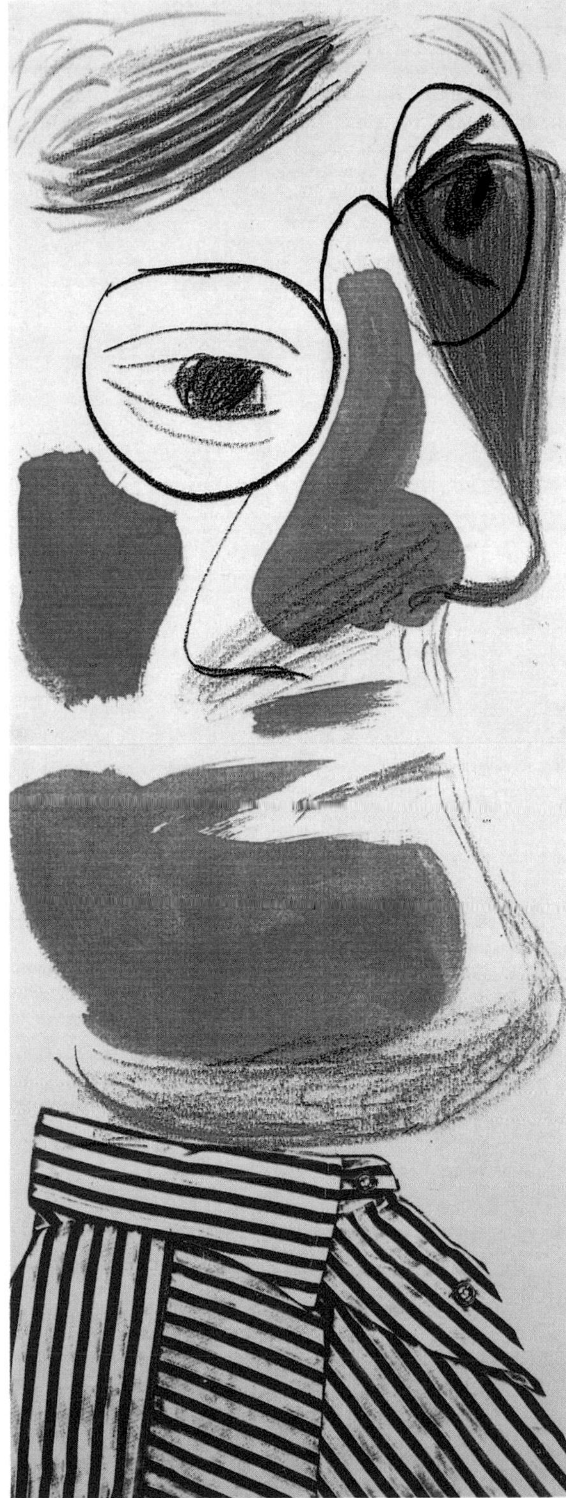

18.19 David Hockney. *Self Portrait.* 1986. Collection of the artist. This work was done by running the page through commercial copying machines to get the various colors of the finished portrait.

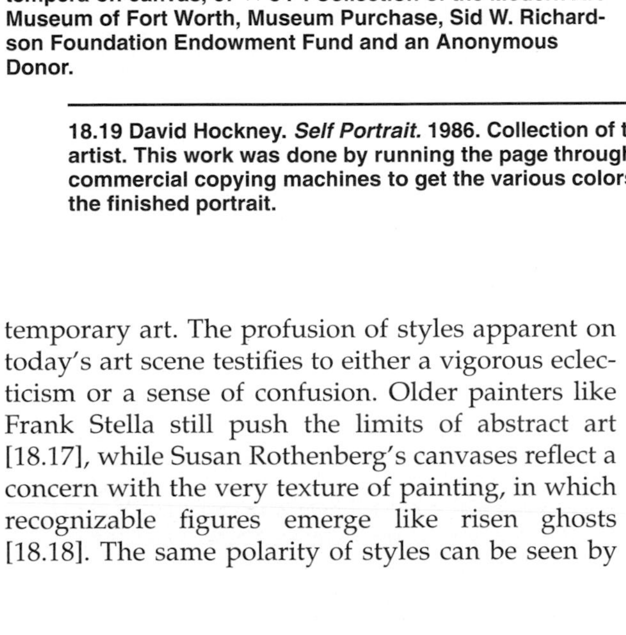

temporary art. The profusion of styles apparent on today's art scene testifies to either a vigorous eclecticism or a sense of confusion. Older painters like Frank Stella still push the limits of abstract art [18.17], while Susan Rothenberg's canvases reflect a concern with the very texture of painting, in which recognizable figures emerge like risen ghosts [18.18]. The same polarity of styles can be seen by contrasting the sunny optimism of the English-born David Hockney (now living in California) [18.19] with the brooding work of the German expressionist painter, Anselm Kiefer [18.20]. These artists work in a time when the older "masters" like Johns, Rauschenberg, and others still push the limits of their original insights and flights of imagination.

18.20 Anselm Kiefer. *Inneraum.* 1981. Oil, paper, and canvas; 113' × 122' (34.45 × 37.2 m). Stedelijk Museum, Amsterdam. Kiefer's monumental paintings have echoes of past masters combined with a brooding sense of Germany's own past, mythic and historical.

18.21 Giacomo Manzù. Doors of Saint Peter's. 1963. Cast bronze, 24'3" × 11'9" (7.4 × 3.6 m). Vatican City, Rome. These doors are on the extreme left of the portico of the basilica. (Opposite is the entrance opened only for Holy Year celebrations, every quarter-century.)

CONTEMPORARY SCULPTURE

Sculpture since 1945 shows both continuities and radical experimentation. The Italian sculptor Giacomo Manzù (1908–1990) still worked with traditional forms of bronze-casting to produce works like the doors of Saint Peter's [18.21] commissioned by the Vatican in the 1950s and cast in the 1960s. While his style is modern, the overall concept and the nature of the commission hark back to the Italian Renaissance and earlier.

Much of contemporary sculpture has utilized newer metals (stainless steel or rolled steel, for instance) and welding techniques to allow some freedom from the inherent density of cast bronze, the traditional metal of the sculptor. David Smith (1906–1965) used his skills as a onetime autobody assembler to produce simple and elegant metal sculptures that reflected his not inconsiderable technical skills with metal as well as his refined

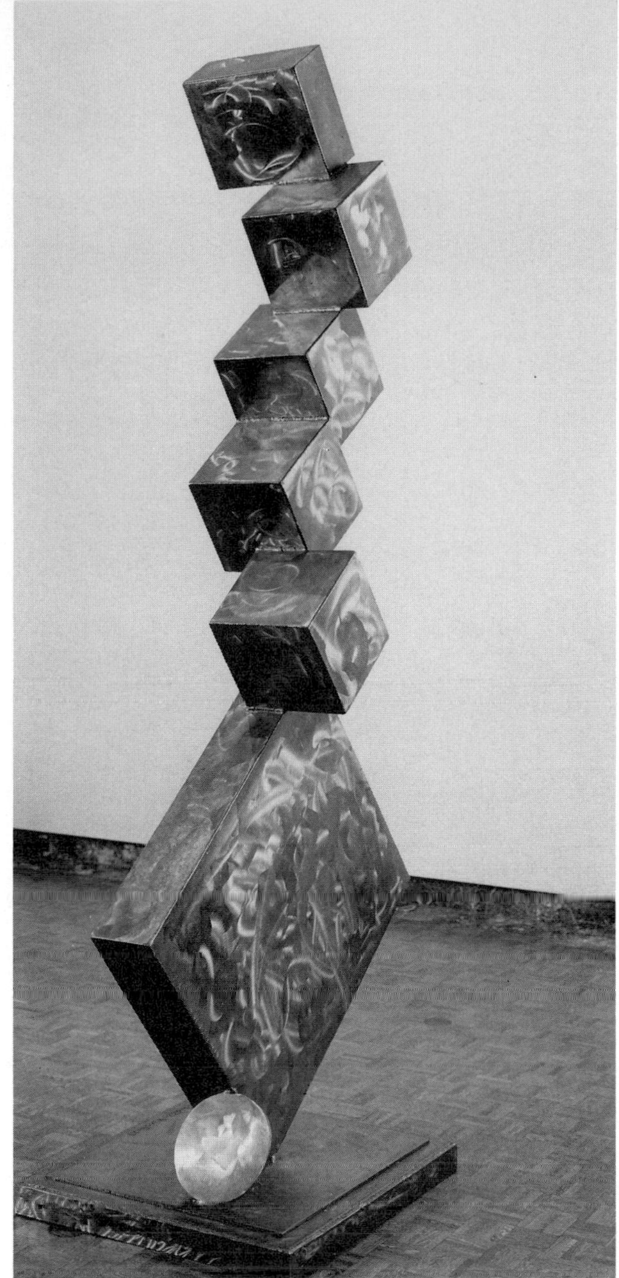

18.22 David Smith. *Cubi I.* 1963. Stainless steel, height 10'4" (3.15 m). Detroit Institute of Arts (Founders Society Purchase Fund). Critics recognize Smith as one of the most important sculptors of the century. Smith took this photograph at his studio in Bolton Landing, New York.

sense of aesthetic balance. In works like *Cubi I* [18.22] he utilized stainless steel to produce a geometrically balanced work of solidity that conveys a sense of airy lightness.

Alexander Calder (1898–1976) used his early training as a mechanical engineer to combine the weightiness of metal with the grace of movement. Mobiles like *Big Red* [18.23] are made of painted sheet metal and wire; these constructions move because they are so delicately balanced that they respond to even the slightest currents of air. Calder once said that people think monuments "come out of the ground, never out of the ceiling", his mobiles were meant to demonstrate just the opposite.

Other contemporary sculptors have expanded the notion of assembling disparate materials into a coherent artistic whole. Employing far from traditional materials, these artists utilize a variety of found and manufactured articles of the most amazing variety to create organic artistic wholes. Louise Nevelson (1900–1988), for example, used pieces of wood, many of which had been lathed or turned for commercial uses, to assemble large-scale

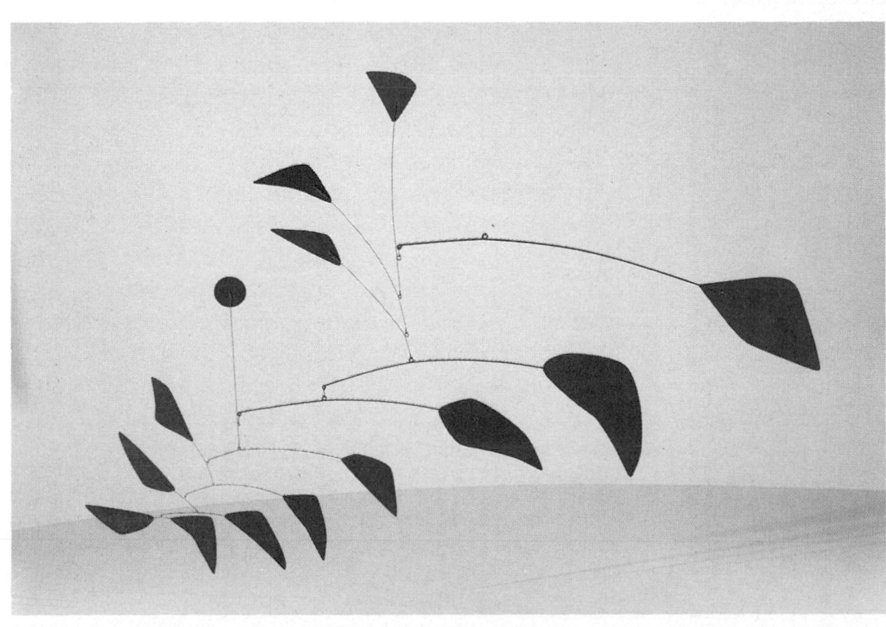

18.23 Alexander Calder. *Big Red.* 1959. Painted sheet metal and steel wire, 6'2" × 9'6" (1.9 × 2.9 m). Whitney Museum of American Art, New York (purchased with funds from the Friends of the Whitney Museum of American Art).

18.24 Louise Nevelson. *Sky Cathedral—Moon Garden + One.* 1957–1960. Painted wood, 9'1" × 10'10" × 19" (2.77 × 3.3 × 48 m). Milly and Arnold Glimcher Collection. This detail shows the intricate and complex nature of Nevelson's work. At her death in 1988, she was considered one of the most accomplished sculptors in the world.

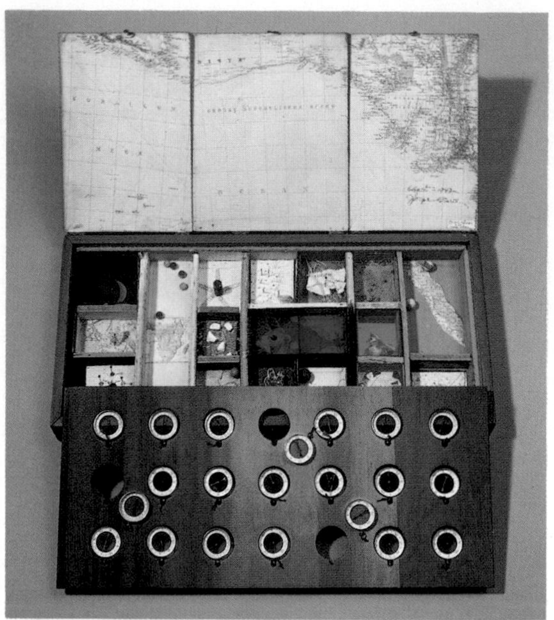

18.25 Joseph Cornell. *Object Roses des Vents.* 1942–1953. Wooden box with 21 compasses set into a wooden tray, resting on Plexiglas-topped-and-partitioned section, divided into 17 compartments containing small miscellaneous objects and three-part hinged lid covered inside with parts of maps of New Guinea and Australia, 2⅝ × 21¼ × 10⅜". The Museum of Modern Art, New York (Mr. and Mrs. Gerald Murphy Fund).

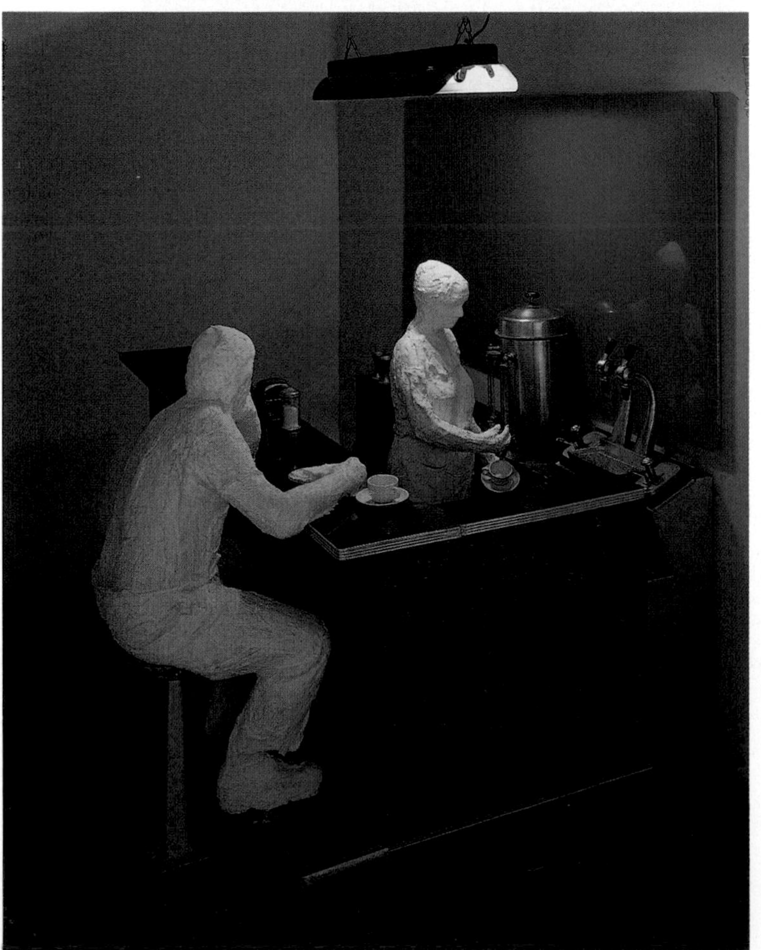

18.26 George Segal. *The Diner.* 1964–1966. Plaster, wood, chrome, Formica, masonite, fluorescent lights; 8'6" × 9' × 7'3" (2.59 × 2.75 × 2.14 m). Walker Art Center, Minneapolis (gift of the T. B. Walker Foundation). More recently, Segal has been experimenting with colored plasters and large bronze cast outdoor pieces.

structures that seem at the same time to function as walls closing off space and as containers to hold the items that make up her compositions [18.24]. Joseph Cornell (1903–1972), early influenced by both surrealism and dada, constructed small boxes that he filled with inexpensive trinkets, maps, bottles, tops, stones, and other trivia. In contrast to the larger brooding, almost totemic spirit of Nevelson, Cornell's painstakingly organized boxes [18.25] allude to a private world of fantasy.

The sculptural interest in *assemblage* has been carried a step further by such artists as George Segal (1924–) and Edward Kienholz (1927–). Their works recreate entire tableaux into which realistically sculptured figures are placed. Segal, once a painting student of Hans Hofmann in New York, likes to cast human figures in plaster of Paris and then set them in particular but familiar settings [18.26]. The starkness of the lone white figures evokes a mood of isolation and loneliness not unlike that of the paintings of Edward Hopper. Kienholz, a California-based artist, is far better prepared to invest his works with strong social comment. His *State Hospital* [18.27] is a strong, critical indictment of the institutional neglect of the mentally ill. The chained figure at the bottom of the tableau "dreams" of his own self-image (note the cartoon-like bubble) on the top bunk. In the original version of this powerful piece goldfish were swimming in the plastic-enclosed faces of the two figures.

Both Segal and Kienholz have certain ties to pop art but neither works within its whimsical or humorous vein. Claes Oldenburg (1929–), however, is one of the more humorously outrageous and inventively intelligent artists working today. He has proposed (and, in some cases, executed) monumental outdoor sculptures depicting teddy bears, ice-cream bars, lipsticks, and baseball bats. From the 1960s on he has experimented with sculptures that turn normally rigid objects into "soft" or "collapsing" versions made from vinyl or canvas and stuffed with kapok. A piece like his *Soft Toilet* [18.28] is at the same time humorous and mocking. It echoes pop art and recalls the oozing edges so characteristic of surrealism.

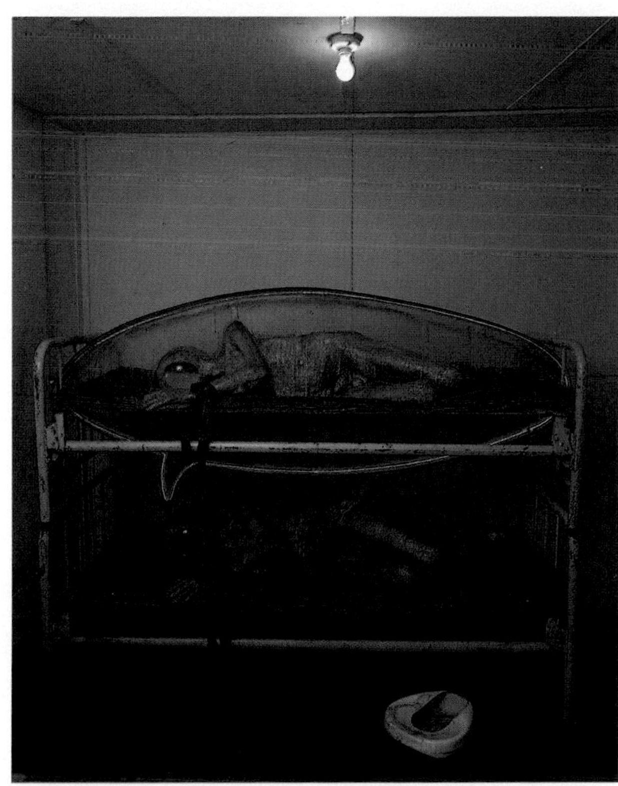

18.27 Edward Kienholz. *The State Hospital,* detail. 1966. Mixed media, 8 × 12 × 10" (2.44 × 3.66 × 3.05 m). Moderna Museet, Stockholm. Kienholz's work provokes such violent reactions that in 1966 some works were threatened with removal from a one-person show he had in Los Angeles.

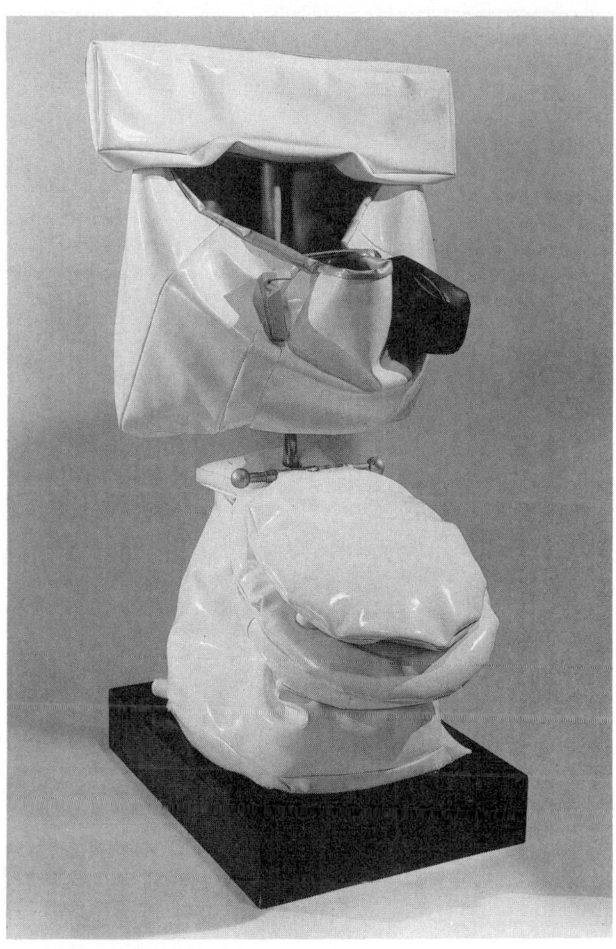

18.28 Claes Oldenburg. *Soft Toilet.* 1966. Vinyl filled with kapok painted with liquitex, and wood; height 4'4" (1.27 m). Whitney Museum of Modern Art, New York (50th anniversary gift of Mr. and Mrs. Victor W. Ganz). Oldenburg's humor derives from the well-known device of taking the expected and rendering it in an unexpected self-parodying form.

Overarching these decades of sculptural development is the work of the British sculptor Henry Moore (1898–1986). Moore's work, which extends back into the 1920s, is a powerful amalgam of the monumental tradition of Western sculpture deriving from Renaissance masters like Michelangelo and his love for the forms coming from the early cultures of Africa, Mexico, and pre-Columbian Latin America. From these two sources Moore worked out hauntingly beautiful works—some on a massive scale—that speak of the most primordial realities of art.

Moore's *Reclining Figure* [18.29] is a complex work that illustrates many of the sculptor's mature interests. The outline is obviously that of a woman in a rather abstract form. There is also the hint of bone-like structures, a favorite motif in Moore's abstract sculpture, and holes pierce the figure. The

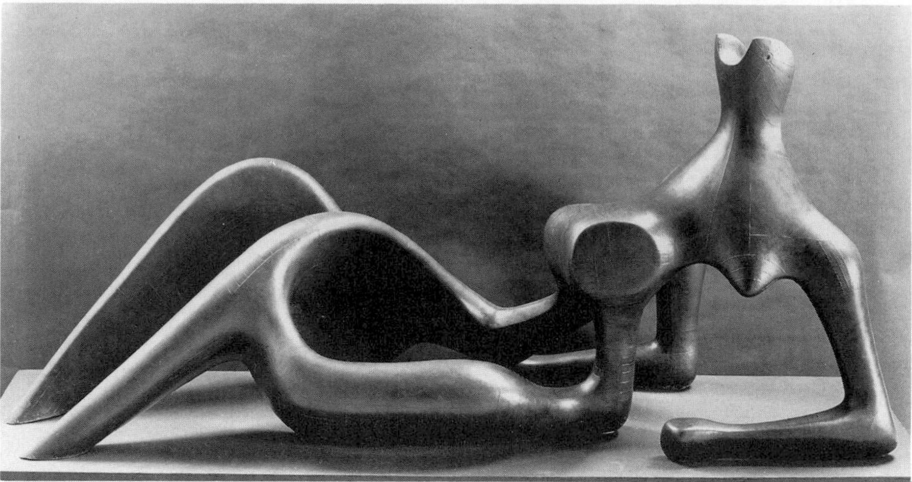

18.29 Henry Moore. *Reclining Figure.* 1951. Bronze, length 7'5" (2.25 m). Musée National d'Art Moderne, Centre Georges Pompidou, Paris. Note the allusions to bones in the figure, allusions that serve as a counterpoint to the curved character of the figure.

holes, Moore once said, reminded him of caves and openings in hillsides with their hint of mystery, and critics have also noted their obvious sexual connotations. The figure reclines after the fashion of Etruscan and Mexican burial figures. In a single work Moore hints at three primordial forces in the universal human experience: life (the female figure), death (the bone-like configurations), and sexuality (the holes). It is a sculpture contemporary in style but timeless in its message.

Most of the sculpture just discussed was made for a gallery or a collector. Thanks to increased government and corporate patronage in recent decades it is possible for the average citizen to see outdoor

18.30 Christo. *Valley Curtain.* Rifle, Colorado. 1970–1972. Span 1250' (381 m). Height 365' to 182' (111 m to 56 m). 142,000 square feet (12,780 m) of woven nylon fabric; 110,000 pounds of steel cables. Project direction: Jan van der Marck. Since that project, Christo's realized projects include a 24½-mile *Running Fence* in California, 11 *Surrounded Islands* in Florida, *The Pont Neuf Wrapped* in Paris and *The Umbrellas, Japan–USA, 1984–92.*

18.31 Magdalena Abakanowicz. *Backs.* 1976–1982. Burlap and plaster. These figures speak of human degradation, the horrors of war and servitude, and inhumanity. Abakanowicz has pushed fiber arts to new and profound directions beyond the mere designation of "craft art."

sculpture as part of the urban environment. A walk in the downtown area of Chicago, for example, provides a chance to see monumental works of Picasso, Chagall, Bertoia, Calder, and Oldenburg. The fact that the federal government had set aside a certain percentage of its building budget for works of art to enhance public buildings has been an impetus for wider diffusion of modern art and sculpture. In one sense, the government, the large foundations, and the corporation have supplanted the church and the aristocracy as patrons for monumental art in our time.

As we move into the 1980s sculpture demonstrates a variety not unlike that of contemporary painting. The Bulgarian-born Christo still seeks out large natural sites to drape with various fabrics for temporary alteration of our perception of familiar places [18.30]. By contrast, the haunting work of Magdalena Abakanowicz uses basic fibers to make pieces that have fearful references to the human disasters of 20th-century history [18.31]. The American sculptor Duane Hanson takes advantage of new materials like polyvinyl to create hyperrealistic visions of ordinary people in ordinary experiences [18.32]. All these sculptors draw on the most

18.32 Duane Hanson. *The Dockman.* 1979. Polyvinyl, polychromed in oil. Life-size. Collection Yellow Freight System, Inc. Compare this work with George Segal's casts in Figure 18.26.

18.33a Jennifer Bartlett. *House.* 1984. White painted wood with copper roof.

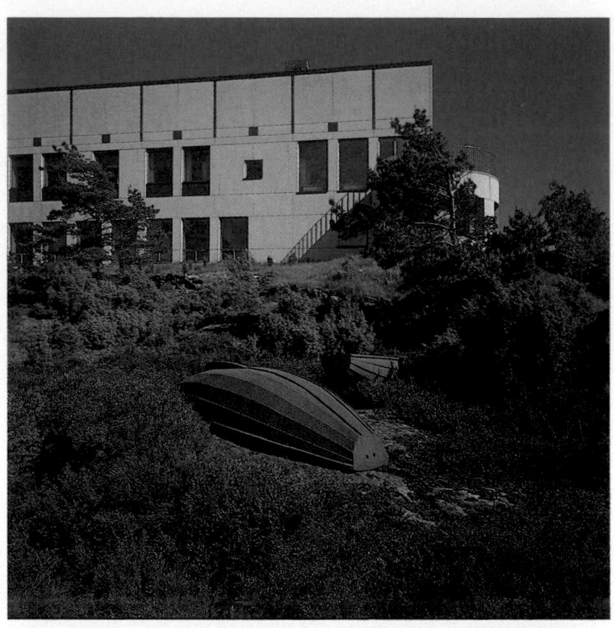

18.33b Jennifer Bartlett. *Two Boats.* 1984. Cor-ten steel. Volvo Corporate Headquarters. Göteborg, Sweden.

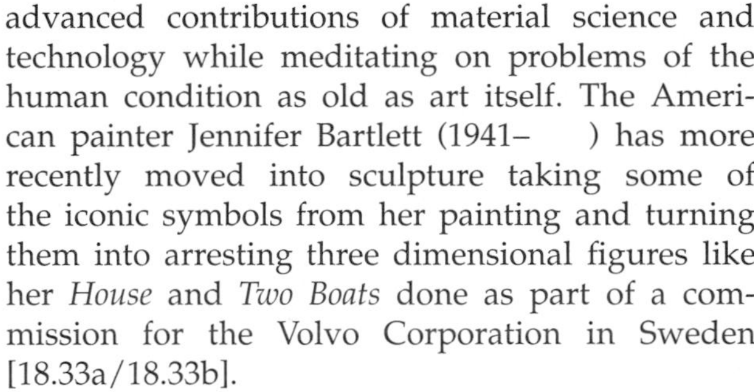

advanced contributions of material science and technology while meditating on problems of the human condition as old as art itself. The American painter Jennifer Bartlett (1941–   ) has more recently moved into sculpture taking some of the iconic symbols from her painting and turning them into arresting three dimensional figures like her *House* and *Two Boats* done as part of a commission for the Volvo Corporation in Sweden [18.33a/18.33b].

By contrast Mary Frank (1932–   ) has stepped into the world of ceramics to use terra cotta to create large-scale sculptures of women that reflect a haunting beauty and an almost primitive power [18.34].

ARCHITECTURE

The most influential American architect of this century was Frank Lloyd Wright (1869–1959). Wright was a disciple of Louis Sullivan (1856–1924), who had built the first skyscrapers in the United States in the last decade of the 19th century. Like Sullivan,

18.34 Mary Frank. *Chant.* 1984. Ceramic. 40 × 60 × 38". Collection of Virginia Museum of Fine Arts. Richmond, Va.

18.35 Frank Lloyd Wright. Solomon R. Guggenheim Museum, New York. 1957–1959. Reinforced concrete; diameter at ground level c. 100' (30.48 m), at roof level 128' (39 m), height of dome 92' (28 m). One of the most discussed American buildings of the century, it is hard to realize that it sits in the midst of New York's Fifth Avenue buildings. A rectangular addition behind the museum is now under construction.

Wright championed an architecture that produced buildings designed for their specific function with an eye to the natural environment in which the building was to be placed and with a sensitivity to what the building should "say." "Form follows function" was Sullivan's famous aphorism for this belief. For Wright and his disciples there was something ludicrous about making a post office look like a Greek temple and then building it in the center of a Midwestern American city. Wright wanted an *organic* architecture—an architecture that grows out of its location rather than being superimposed on it.

For decades Wright designed private homes, college campuses, industrial buildings, and churches that reflected this basic philosophy. In the postwar period Wright finished his celebrated Solomon R. Guggenheim Museum [18.35] in New York City from plans he had made in 1943. This building, one of Wright's true masterpieces, is a capsule summary of his architectural ideals. Wright was interested in the flow of space rather than its obstruction ("Democracy needs something basically better than a box"), so the Guggenheim Museum interior tries hard to eliminate corners and angles. The interior is essentially one very large room with an immensely airy central space. Rising from the floor in a continuous flow for six stories is a long simple spiraling ramp cantilevered off the supporting walls. A museumgoer can start walking down the ramp to view an exhibition without ever encountering a wall or partition. The viewing of the art is a continuous unwinding experience. Thus the *function* of the museum (to show art) is accomplished by the *form* of the building.

The exterior of the Guggenheim Museum vividly demonstrates the possibilities inherent in the new building materials becoming available in this century. By the use of reinforced or ferroconcrete one can model or sculpt a building easily. The Guggenheim Museum, with its soft curves and cylindrical forms, seems to rise up from its base. The

18.36 Pier Luigi Nervi and Annibale Vitellozi. Palazzetto dello Sport, Rome. 1956–1957. The walls beneath the dome are of glass. The Y-shaped ferroconcrete columns are reminiscent of caryatids; their outstretched "arms" support the dome.

undulating lines stand in sharp contrast to the boxy angles and corners of most of the buildings found in New York City. By using such a design, made to fit a rather restricted urban space, the Guggenheim almost takes on the quality of sculpture.

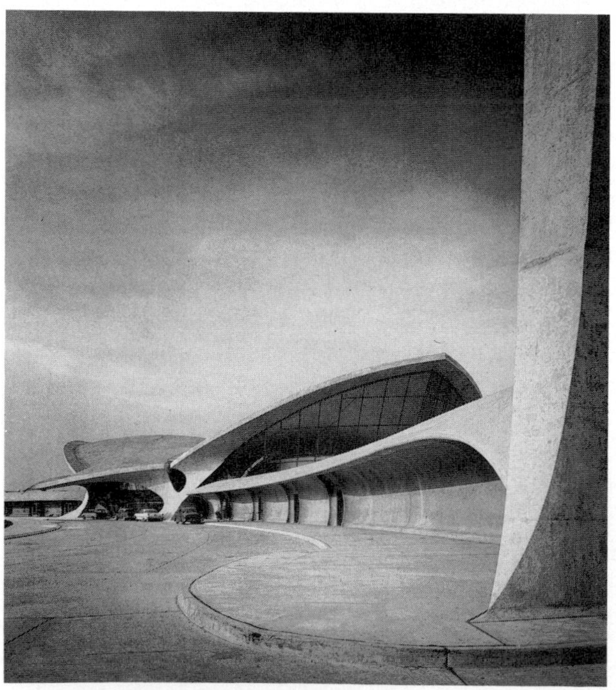

18.37 Eero Saarinen. Trans World Flight Center, Kennedy International Airport, New York. 1962. The building brilliantly shows the sculptural possibilities of concrete. There is a hint of a bird in flight in the general configuration of the roof as it flares out on both sides.

The sculptural possibilities of reinforced and prestressed concrete have given other architects the means to "model" buildings in dramatically attractive ways. The Italian engineer and architect Pier Luigi Nervi (1891–1979) demonstrated the creative use of concrete in a series of buildings he designed for the 1960 Olympic Games in Rome [18.36]. Eero Saarinen (1910–1961) showed in the TWA Flight Center at John F. Kennedy Airport in New York City [18.37] that a building can become almost pure sculpture; Saarinen's wing motif is peculiarly appropriate for an airport terminal. That architects have not exhausted the potentialities of this modeled architecture seems clear from the recently opened Opera House complex in Sydney, Australia [18.38]. Here the Danish architect Jörn Utzon utilized Saarinen's wing motif, but it is not a slavish copy since Utzon gives it a new and dramatic emphasis.

The influential French architect Le Corbusier (1887–1965; born Charles Édouard Jeanneret-Gris) did not share Wright's enthusiasm for "organic" architecture. Le Corbusier saw architecture as a human achievement that should stand in counterpoint to the world of nature. During his long career Le Corbusier designed and oversaw the construction of both individual buildings and more ambitious habitations ranging from apartment complexes to an entire city. One of his most important contributions to architecture is his series of Unités d'Habitation in Marseille (1952) and Nantes [18.39]. These complexes were attempts to make large housing units into livable modules that would not

18.38 Jörn Utzon. Opera House, Sydney, Australia. 1959–1972. Reinforced concrete, height of highest shell 200' (60.96 m). The building juts dramatically into Sydney's harbor. Structural technology was pushed to the limit by the construction of the shells, which are both roof and walls. The openings between the shells are closed with two layers of amber-tinted glass to reduce outside noise and to give views to people in the lobbies of the buildings.

only provide a living space but would also be sufficiently self-contained to incorporate shopping, recreation, and walking areas. Le Corbusier used basic forms (simple squares, rectangles) for the complexes and set them on pylons both to give more space beneath the buildings and to break up their rather blocky look. Many of these buildings would be set in green park areas situated to capture something of the natural world and the sun. The basic building material was concrete and steel (often the concrete was not finished or polished since Le Corbusier liked the texture of the material). Less inspired architects have utilized these same concepts for public housing with indifferent success—as visits to the peripheries of most urban centers will attest. Indeed, time has been a harsh judge of Le Corbusier's vision of human living space.

18.39 Le Corbusier. L'Unité d'Habitation. Marseille, France. 1947–1952. Length 550' (167.64 m), height 184' (56.08 m), width 79' (24.08 m). The individual balconies have colored panels to break up the stark rough concrete exterior. Imitation of this style has resulted in much soulless public housing in the large cities of the world.

Le Corbusier's influence in North America has mainly been derivative. Two other European architects, however, have had an immense impact on American architecture. Walter Gropius (1883–1969) and Ludwig Miës van der Rohe (1896–1969) came to this country in the late 1930s, refugees from Nazi Germany. Both men had long been associated with the German school of design, the Bauhaus.

Miës van der Rohe's Seagram Building [18.40] in New York City, designed with Philip Johnson (1906–1991), beautifully illustrates the intent of Bauhaus design. It is a severely chaste building of glass and anodized bronze set on stainless steel pylons placed on a wide granite platform. The uncluttered plaza (broken only by pools) contrasts nicely with the essentially monolithic glass building that rises up from it. The lines of the building are austere in their simplicity while the materials are few and well chosen, with a resultant integration of the whole. It illustrates the "modern" principle of the Bauhaus that simplicity of design results in an aesthetically harmonic whole—"less is more" according to the slogan of this art.

The Seagram Building now seems rather ordinary to us, given the unending procession of glass-and-steel buildings found in most of our large city centers. That many of these buildings are derivative cannot be denied; that they may result in sterile jungles of glass and metal is likewise a fact. Imitation does not always flatter the vision of the artist but excesses do not invalidate the original goal of the Bauhaus designers. They were committed to crispness of design and the imaginative use of material. In the hands of a master architect that idea is still valid, as the stunning new East Wing of

18.40 Ludwig Miës van der Rohe and Philip Johnson. Seagram Building. New York. Height 512' (156.2 m). Compare the cleanly severe lines of this building with those of the more ornate buildings in the background.

18.41 I. M. Pei. East Building of the National Gallery of Art, Washington, (c) 1992. National Gallery of Art, Washington, opened 1978. Pei combined a "modernist" look with a "classical" one that prevents the edifice from clashing with the older buildings on the mall leading to the Capitol.

18.42 Renzo Piano and Richard Rogers. Georges Pompidou National Center for Arts and Culture, Paris. 1977. In the last few years this center has taken on a lively bohemian air; nearby streets are lined with galleries and adjoining squares are dotted with street performers and musicians.

SPORTS AND GAMES

Ice Hockey

Ice hockey, the modern version of field hockey, has acquired a new popularity in the age of television. A fast and sometimes violent game, it places a premium on speed, stamina, strength and mobility. Players, divided into two teams of six skaters, use wooden sticks in order to score goals by hitting the puck (a hard rubber disc) into the opponents' goal. The game originated in Canada, where it has become a national sport, and Canadian and United States teams compete in the National Hockey League (NHL); international events are organized by the International Ice Hockey Federation.

Most of the games and sports described in the earlier chapters of this book developed in Europe and spread to the New World. Ice hockey, by contrast, is a North American invention which has taken Europe by storm. Because of climate it is especially popular in northern Europe. Among the leading European teams are the Swedes, the Finns and, in particular, the Russians. Clashes between the Russian and American teams dominated the Olympic ice hockey competitions of the 1970s and 1980s. In the early 1990s, with the fall of the Berlin Wall and the collapse of East European regimes, many of the best East European players moved to the US and Canada. In the 1993 season, Europeans made up 17 percent of the members of North American teams, and scouts predicted that by the end of the century as many as 40 percent of NHL players could be European; the New Jersey Devils has become known as the United Nations Team—Team UN—because its 20-man roster includes as many as nine Europeans.

The combination of North American and European sporting cultures has had its problems. On the whole, Czech and Russian players, for example, are more noted for their finesse than for their combativeness or their willingness to "get physical" in the battle for the puck. Nor do North American players always welcome foreign competition: in September 1992, at the Detroit Red Wings training camp, Russian and Canadian players battled with fists and sticks. The NHL has done its best to ease the adjustment, by introducing strict rules against violence.

By the end of the century, teams have learned to combine the offensive creativity and finesse of European players with North American toughness and speed. As a result, the NHL game series, followed by a growing number of television fans, provides an exciting blend of sporting culture and values from both sides of the Atlantic.

the National Gallery of Art in Washington, D.C., clearly demonstrates [18.41]. This building, designed by I. M. Pei (1917–), utilizes pink granite and glass within the limits of a rather rigid geometric design to create a building monumental in scale without loss of lightness or crispness of design.

One can profitably contrast the chaste exterior East Wing of Washington's National Gallery with the Georges Pompidou National Center for Arts and Culture in Paris [18.42], designed by Renzo Piano and Richard Rogers. The Pompidou Center was opened in 1977 as a complex of art, musical research, industrial design, and public archives. The architects eschewed the clean lines of classical sculpture, covering the exterior with brightly colored heating ducts, elevators, escalators, and building supports. It has been an extremely controversial building since its inception but Parisians (and visitors) have found it a beautiful and intriguing place. Whether its industrial style will endure is, of course, open to question, but for now its garishness and nervous energy have made it a cultural mecca for visitors to Paris. It may even in time rival that other monument once despised by Parisians and now practically a symbol for the city, the Eiffel Tower.

Since the 1970s a number of architects, including Philip Johnson and Robert Venturi, have moved beyond the classic modern design of large buildings to reshape them with decorative elements and more broken lines; this break with the severe lines of modernist taste has come to be called postmodernism in architecture. The country now has many such buildings but one, a skyscraper in Seattle, Washington, well illustrates the postmodern sensibility [18.43]. The designer, William Pederson, retains the severe lines and the ample use of glass characteristic of most modern business buildings, but he breaks those lines up with a bowed center of the building that stands in contrast to the classical sides. The last floors break up the design of the lower floors, and in an almost postmodern signature, he caps the building with a half-arch students will remember seeing on the façades of Renaissance and baroque buildings but whose ultimate inspiration is the Roman half-arch. One architectural critic has said that this building sums up what is best in innovative skyscraper design today.

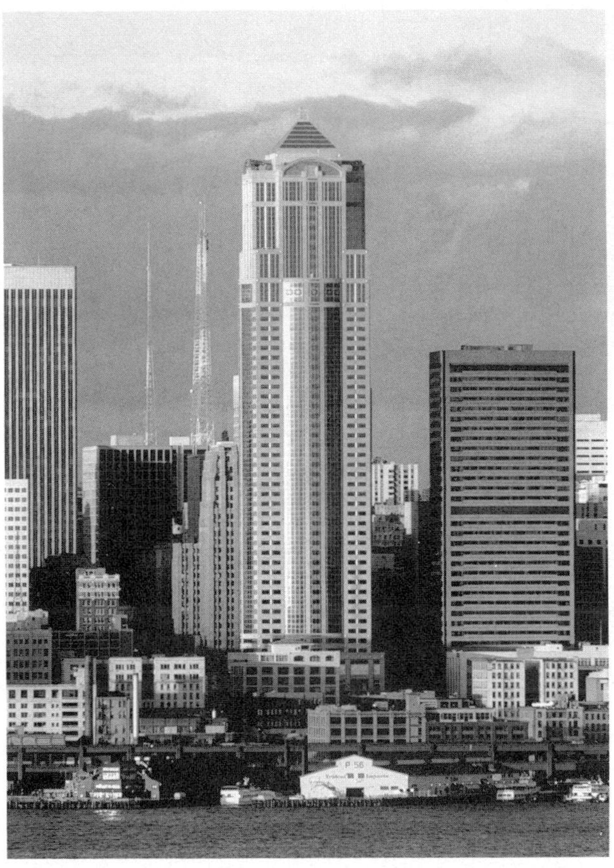

18.43 Kohn Pederson Fox. 1201 Third Avenue in Seattle. Seattle, Washington, 1988. The postmodern character of the building may be seen clearly by contrasting this building with the two office towers to the right and left in the photograph.

18.44 Robert Venturi and Scott Brown. Seattle Art Museum (interior corridor). 1991. Notice the almost oriental-looking arches and the perspectival view enhanced by the hidden lighting.

Its sense of color (the stone is a pinkish granite); its homage to classical decorative motifs; its advance upon Bauhaus severity (without a firm rejection of it)—all summarize what is known as the postmodern in architecture.

The Seattle Art Museum (1991), designed by the husband and wife team of Robert Venturi and Scott Brown, has many of the same postmodern characteristics with its bold use of color and modification of traditional architectural motifs to provide a startling new vision which is an advance beyond the modernist ideal [18.44].

SOME TRENDS IN CONTEMPORARY LITERATURE

By the end of World War II, literary figures who had defined the modernist temper—writers like T. S. Eliot, James Joyce, Thomas Mann, Ezra Pound—were either dead or had already done their best work. Their passionate search for meaning in an alienated world, however, still inspired the work of others. The great modernist themes received attention by other voices in other media. The Swedish filmmaker Ingmar Bergman (1918–) began a series of classic films starting with *Wild Strawberries* in 1956, done in black and white, which explored the loss of religious faith and the demands of modern despair. The enigmatic Irish playwright (who lives in France and writes in French and English) Samuel Beckett (1906–1989) has produced plays like *Waiting for Godot* (1952) that explore an absurdist world beyond logic, decency, and the certainty of language itself.

Waiting for Godot, for all its apparent simplicity, is maddeningly difficult to interpret. Two characters, Vladimir and Estragon, wait at an unnamed and barren crossroads for Godot. Their patient wait is interrupted by antic encounters with two other characters. In the two acts, each representing one day, a young boy announces that Godot will arrive the next day. At the end of the play Vladimir and Estragon decide to wait for Godot although they toy momentarily with the idea of splitting up or committing suicide if Godot does not come to save them.

The language of *Godot* is laced with biblical allusions and religious puns. Is Godot God and does the play illuminate the nature of an absurd world without final significance? Beckett does not say and critics do not agree, although they are in accord with the judgment that *Waiting for Godot* is a classic—if cryptic—statement about language, human relations, and the ultimate significance of the world.

Gradually, as the war receded in time, other voices that told us of the horrors of the war experience began to be heard. The most compelling atrocity of the war period, the extermination of six million Jews and countless other dissidents or enemies in the Nazi concentration camps, has resulted in many attempts to tell the world that story. The most significant voice of the survivors of the event is the European-born Elie Wiesel (1928–), himself a survivor of the camps. Wiesel describes himself as a "teller of tales." He feels a duty, beyond the normal duty of art, to keep alive the memory of the near-extermination of his people. Wiesel's autobiographical memoir *Night* (1960) recounts his own years in the camps. It is a terribly moving book with its juxtaposition of a young boy's fervent faith with the demonic powers of the camp.

In the United States an entirely new generation of writers has defined the nature of the American experience. Arthur Miller's play *Death of a Salesman* (1949) explores the failure of the American dream in the person of its tragic hero, Willie Loman, an ordinary man defeated by life. J. D. Salinger's *Catcher in the Rye* (1951) documented the bewildering coming of age of an American adolescent in so compelling a manner that it was, for a time, a cult book for the young. Southern writers like Eudora Welty, William Styron, Walker Percy, and Flannery O'Connor have continued the meditations of William Faulkner about an area of the United States that has tasted defeat in a way no other region has. Poets like Wallace Stevens, Theodore Roethke, William Carlos Williams, and Marianne Moore continued to celebrate the beauties and terrors of both nature and people.

We have already noted that existentialism was well suited to the postwar mood. One aspect of existentialism's ethos was its insistence on protest and human dissatisfaction. That element of existential protest has been very much a part of the postwar scene. The civil rights movement of the late 1950s and early 1960s became a paradigm for other more recent protests such as those against the Vietnam War; in favor of the rights of women; for the rights of the dispossessed, underprivileged, or the victims of discrimination. The literature of protest has been very much a part of this cry for human rights.

First and foremost, one can trace the African-Americans' struggle for dignity and full equality through the literature they produced, especially in the period after the First World War. The great pioneers were those writers who are grouped loosely under the name "Harlem Renaissance," whom we discussed in the last chapter. They refused the stereotype of the Negro but crafted an eloquent literature demanding humanity and unqualified justice. The work of these writers presaged the powerful torrent of black fiction chronicling racial injustice in America. Two novels in particular, Richard Wright's *Native Son* (1940) and Ralph Ellison's *Invisible Man* (1952), have taken on the character of American classics. Younger writers followed, most notably James Baldwin, whose *Go Tell It On the Mountain* (1953) fused vivid memories of black Harlem, jazz, and the intense religion of the black church into a searing portrait of growing up black in America. Alice Walker has explored her Southern roots in the explosively powerful *The Color Purple* (1982).

For many of the younger black writers in America the theme of black pride has been linked with the consciousness of being a woman. Nikki Giovanni (1936–) has produced a whole body of poetry celebrating both her sense of "blackness" and her pride in her femininity. Her poetry has been a poetic blend of black history and female consciousness done in an American mode. Similarly, Maya Angelou has become an enormously important voice for the African-American community as has Gwendolyn Brooks, who has ties that go back to the writers of the Harlem Renaissance.

The rightful claims of women have been advanced in our day by an activist spirit that seeks equality of women and men, free from any sexual discrimination. The battle for women's rights began in the last century. It was fought again in the drive for women's suffrage in the first part of this century and continues today in the feminist movement. The cultural oppression of women has been a major concern of the great women writers of our time. Writers like Doris Lessing, Margaret Atwood, Adrienne Rich, Maxine Kumin, and others continue to explore feminine consciousness in great depth and from different angles of vision.

Two contemporary poets deserve particular mention, since both of them dealt so clearly with the dissatisfaction of women. Sylvia Plath (1932–1963) and Anne Sexton (1928–1974) used the imagery of traditional sexual roles to complain about the restraints of their position. Ironically enough, the precociously talented Sylvia Plath and Anne Sexton briefly knew each other when they studied poetry together. Sylvia Plath not only produced an important body of poetry but a largely autobiographical novel *The Bell Jar* (1962), describing most of her short and unhappy life. Anne Sexton, by contrast, wrote only poetry. Both, alas, died by their own hand after tortured lives of emotional upheavals.

A Note on the Postmodern

For the past decade or so some literary critics have been insisting, with varying degrees of acceptance, that much of contemporary literature has moved beyond the modernist preoccupation with alienation, myth, fragmentation of time, and the interior states of the self. The most debated question now is: What exactly has followed modernism (by definition it is postmodern) and does it have a shaping spirit? Further, who are its most significant practitioners? The latter question seems to be the easier of the two. Many critics would mention the following among those who are setting and defining the postmodernist literary agenda: Italo Calvino in Italy; Jorge Luis Borges in Argentina; Gabriel García Márquez in Colombia; and a strong group of American writers that includes Donald Barthelme, Robert Coover, John Barth, Stanley Elkin, Thomas Pynchon, Renata Adler, Susan Sontag, and Kurt Vonnegut, Jr. Borges is perhaps the writer most influential in shaping the postmodern sensibility.

That list of writers represents far-ranging and diverse sensibilities. What do they hold in common that permits them to be considered representative postmodernists? Some critics see the postmodernists as those who push the modernist world view to its extreme limit. Postmodernist writing, these critics would say, is less concerned with traditional plot lines, more antirational, more private in its vision, more concerned to make the work a private world of meanings and significations. This is hardly a satisfactory definition since it merely defines the postmodern as more of the same. It does not define, it merely extends the definition. Postmodernism is a form of literary art in the process of birth. It must build on what modernism has accomplished but it must find its own voice.

It is impossible to make art today as if cubism or abstract expressionism had never existed, just as it is impossible to compose music as if Stravinsky had never lived. Further, we cannot live life (or even look at it) as if relativity, atomic weapons, and Freudian explorations of the unconscious were not part of our intellectual and social climate. If art is to be part of the human enterprise it must surely reflect its past without being a prisoner of it. In fact, most of the great achievements in the arts have done precisely that; they have mastered the tradition and then extended it. The terrain of modernism has been fairly well mapped; it is time to move on. But in what direction?

MUSIC SINCE 1945

Avant-Garde Developments

Since World War II many avant-garde composers have been moving toward greater and greater complexity of musical organization, coupled with an increasing use of new kinds of sound. At the same time other musicians, disturbed by their colleagues' obsessive concern for order, have tried to introduce an element of chance, even chaos, into the creation of a work of music. Both the "structuralists" and the advocates of random music have attracted followers, and only time will tell which approach will prove more fruitful.

Before considering the nature of these two schools in detail, some general observations are in order. It must be admitted that advanced contemporary music presents a tough challenge to the patience and sympathy of many sincere music lovers. Unlike the visual arts and literature, modern music seems, superficially at least, to have made a virtually complete break with past traditions. Furthermore, much of it seems remote from our actual experience. Developments in painting or architecture are visible around us in one form or another on a daily basis, and modern writers deal with problems that affect us in our own lives. Many creative musicians, however, have withdrawn to the scientific laboratory, where they construct their pieces with the aid of machines and in accordance with mathematical principles. It is hardly surprising that the results may seem sterile at first.

Yet it is well worth making an effort to understand and enjoy the latest developments in music. Concentration and open-mindedness will remove many of the barriers. So will persistence. Music lovers who listen twenty times to a recording of a Chopin waltz or a Mahler symphony for every one time they listen to a work by Boulez or Stockhausen can hardly expect to make much progress in understanding a new and admittedly difficult idiom. Much of today's music may well not survive the test of time, but it is equally probable that some pieces will become the classics of the 21st century. By discriminating listening we can play our own part in judging which music is worthless and which will be of permanent value.

The principle of precise musical organization had already become important in 20th-century music with the serialism of Arnold Schoenberg. Schoenberg's ordering of pitch (the melodic and harmonic element of music) in rigidly maintained twelve-tone rows has been extended by recent composers to other elements. Pierre Boulez (1925–), for example, constructed rows of twelve note-durations (the length of time each note sounds), twelve levels of volume, and twelve ways of striking the keys for works like his *Second Piano Sonata* (1948) and *Structures* for two pianos (1952). In this music every element (pitch, length of notes, volume, and attack) is totally ordered and controlled by the composer in accordance with his predetermined rows, since none of the twelve components of each row can be repeated until after the other eleven.

The effect of this "total control" is to eliminate any sense of traditional melody, harmony, or counterpoint along with the emotions they evoke. Instead the composer aims to create a pure and abstract "structure" that deliberately avoids any kind of subjective emotional expression.

There remains, however, one element in these piano works that even Boulez cannot totally control—the human one. All the composer's instructions, however precise, have to be interpreted and executed by a performer, and as long as composers are dependent on performers to interpret their works they cannot avoid a measure of subjectivity. Different pianists will inevitably produce different results, and even the same pianist will not produce an identical performance on every occasion.

It was to solve this problem that in the 1950s some composers began to turn to *electronic music*, the sounds of which are produced not by conventional musical instruments but by an electronic oscillator, a machine that produces pure sound waves. A composer can order the sounds by means of a computer and then transfer them to recording tape for playback. In the last few years the process of manipulating electronic sound has been much simplified by the invention of the *synthesizer*, a piece of equipment that can produce just about any kind of sound effect. In combination with a computer, machines like the Moog synthesizer can be used either for original electronic works or for creating electronic versions of traditional music, as in the popular "Switched-on Bach" recordings.

From its earliest days, electronic music has alarmed many listeners by its apparent lack of humanity. The whistles, clicks, and hisses that characterize it may be eerily appropriate to the mysteries of the space age, but they have little to do with traditional musical expression. Indeed, composers of electronic music have had considerable difficulty in inventing formal structures for organizing the vast range of sounds available to them. In addition, there still exists no universally agreed-on system of writing down electronic compositions; most of them exist only on tape. It is probably significant that even Karlheinz Stockhausen (1928–), one of the leading figures in electronic music, has tended to combine electronic sounds with conventional musical instruments [18.45]. His *Mixtur* (1965), for example, is written for five orchestras, electronic equipment, and loudspeakers. During performance the sounds produced by the orchestral instruments

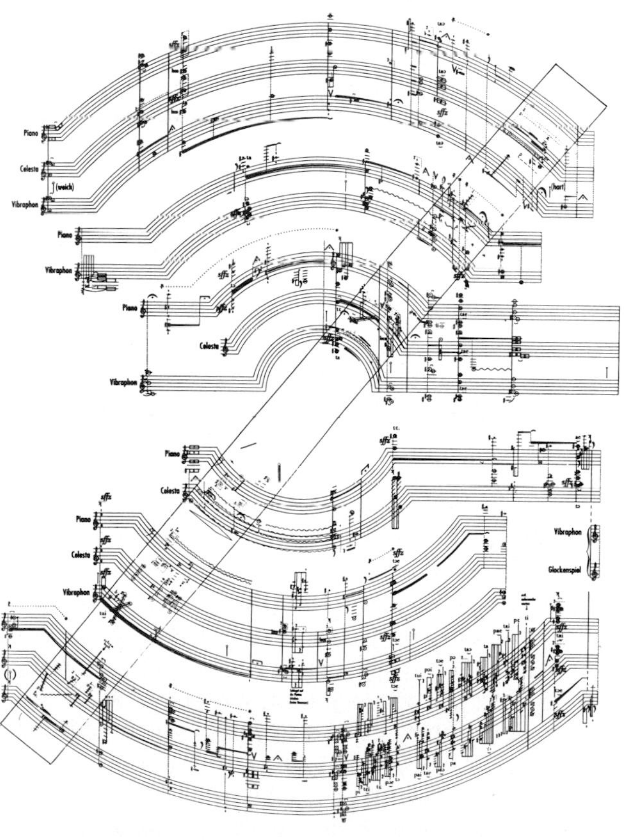

18.45 From Karlheinz Stockhausen. *Nr. 11 Refrain.* © 1961 by Universal Editions (London), Ltd. London. Used by permission. This portion of the score was reproduced in the composer's own work, *Test on Electronic and Instrumental Music.* The system of musical notation that Stockhausen devised for this piece is as revolutionary as the music itself; it is explained in a preface to the score.

are electronically altered and simultaneously mixed with the instrumental sound and with a prerecorded tape. In this way an element of live participation has been reintroduced.

For all its radical innovations, however, *Mixtur* at least maintains the basic premise of music in the Western tradition: that composers can communicate with their listeners by predetermining ("composing") their works according to an intellectual series of rules. The laws of baroque counterpoint, classical sonata form, or Stockhausen's ordering and altering of sound patterns all represent systems that have enabled composers to plan and create musical works. One of the most revolutionary of all recent developments, however, has been the invention of *aleatoric* music. The name is derived from the Latin word *alea* (a dice game) and is applied to music in which an important role is played by the element of chance.

One of the leading exponents of this kind of music is the American composer John Cage (1912–1992), who has been much influenced by Zen philosophy. Adopting the Zen attitude that one must go beyond logic in life, Cage has argued that music should reflect the random chaos of the world around us and so does not seek to impose order on it. His *Concert for Piano and Orchestra* of 1958 has a piano part consisting of eighty-four different "sound events," some, all, or none of which are to be played in any random order. The orchestral accompaniment consists of separate pages of music, some, all, or none of which can be played by any (or no) instrument, in any order and combination. Clearly every performance of the *Concert* is going to be a unique event, largely dependent on pure chance for its actual sound. In other pieces Cage has instructed the performers to determine the sequence of events by even more random methods, including the tossing of coins.

Works like these are, of course, more interesting for the questions they ask about the nature of music than for any intrinsic value of their own. Cage has partly reacted against what he regards as the excessive organization and rigidity of composers like Boulez and Stockhausen, but at the same time he has also raised some important considerations. What is the function of the artist in the modern world? What is the relationship between creator and performer? And what part, if any, should the listeners themselves play in the creation of a piece of music? Need it always be a passive one? If Cage's own answers to questions like these may not satisfy everyone, he has at least posed the problems in an intriguing form.

The New Minimalists

A very different solution to the search for a musical style has been proposed by a younger generation of American composers. Steve Reich (1936–) was one of the first musicians to build lengthy pieces out of the multiple repetition of simple chords and rhythms. Critics have sometimes assumed that the purpose of these repetitions is to achieve a hypnotic effect by inducing a kind of state of trance. Reich himself has stated that his aim is, in fact, the reverse: a state of heightened concentration.

In *The Desert Music,* a composition for chorus and instruments completed in 1983, Reich's choice of texts is helpful to an understanding of his music. The work's central section consists of a setting of words by the American poet William Carlos Williams (1883–1963):

> It is a principle of music
> to repeat the theme. Repeat
> and repeat again,
> as the pace mounts. The
> theme is difficult
> but no more difficult
> than the facts to be
> resolved.

The piece begins with the pulsing of a series of broken chords, which is sustained in a variety of ways, chiefly by tuned mallets. This pulsation, together with a wordless choral vocalise, gives the work a rhythmical complexity and richness of sound which at times are reminiscent of some African or Balinese music.

The works of Philip Glass (1937–) are even more openly influenced by non-Western music. Glass himself studied the Indian tabla drums for a time; he is also interested in West African music, and he has worked with Ravi Shankar, the great Indian sitar virtuoso. Many of Glass' compositions are based on combinations of rhythmical structures derived from classical Indian music. They are built up into repeating modules, the effect of which has been likened by unsympathetic listeners to a needle stuck in a record groove.

Length plays an important part in Glass' operas, for which he has collaborated with the American dramatist Robert Wilson. Wilson, like Glass, is interested in "apparent motionlessness and endless durations during which dreams are dreamed and significant matters are understood." They have produced together three massive stage works in the years between 1975 and 1985: *Einstein on the Beach, Satyagraha,* and *Akhnaten.* The performances involve a team of collaborators that includes directors, designers, and choreographers; the results have the quality of a theatrical "happening." Although a description of the works makes them sound remote and difficult, performances of them have been extremely successful. Even New York's Metropolitan Opera House, not famous for its adventurousness in repertory, was sold out for two performances of *Einstein on the Beach.* Clearly, whatever its theoretical origins, the music of Glass touches a wide public.

Traditional Approaches to Modern Music

Not all composers have abandoned the traditional means of musical expression. Musicians like Benjamin Britten (1913–1976) and Dmitri Shostakovich (1906–1975) demonstrated that an innovative approach to the traditional elements of melody, harmony, and rhythm can still produce exciting and moving results. Nor can either of them be accused of losing touch with the modern world. Britten's *War Requiem* (1962) is an eloquent plea for an end to the violence of contemporary life, while Shostakovich's entire musical output reflects his uneasy relationship with Soviet authority. His *Symphony No. 13* (1962) includes settings of poems by the Russian poet Yevtushenko on anti-Semitism in Russia and earned him unpopularity in Soviet artistic and political circles.

Both Britten and Shostakovich did not hesitate to write recognizable "tunes" in their music. In his last symphony, *No. 15* (1971), Shostakovich even quoted themes from Rossini's *William Tell Overture* (the familiar "Lone Ranger" theme) and from Wagner. The work is at the same time easy to listen to and deeply serious. Like much of Shostakovich's music, it is concerned with the nature of death (a subject also explored in his *Symphony No. 14*). Throughout its four movements, Shostakovich's sense of rhythm is much in evidence, as is his feeling for orchestral color, in which he demonstrates that the resources of a traditional symphony orchestra are far from exhausted. The final mysterious dying close of *Symphony No. 15* is especially striking in its use of familiar ingredients—repeating rhythmic patterns, simple melodic phrases—to achieve an unusual effect.

If Shostakovich demonstrated that a musical form as old-fashioned as the symphony can still be used to create masterpieces, Britten did the same for opera. His first great success, *Peter Grimes* (1945), employed traditional operatic devices like arias, trios, and choruses to depict the tragic fate of its hero, a man whose alienation from society leads to his persecution at the hands of his fellow citizens. In other works Britten followed the example of many of his illustrious predecessors in turning to earlier literary masterpieces for inspiration. *A Midsummer Night's Dream* (1960) is a setting of Shakespeare's play, while *Death in Venice* (1973) is based on the story by Thomas Mann. In all of his operas Britten writes music that is easy to listen to (and, equally important, not impossible to sing), but he never condescends to his audience. Each work deals with a recognizable area of human experience and presents it in a valid musical and dramatic form. It is always dangerous to make predictions about the verdict of posterity, but from today's vantage point the music of Britten seems to have as good a chance as any of surviving into the next century.

Popular Music

No discussion of music since 1945 would be complete without mention of pop music, the worldwide appeal of which is a social fact of our times. Much of pop music is American in origin, although its ancestry is deeply rooted in the larger Western musical tradition. Its development both in this country and abroad is so complex as to be outside the scope of this book. One cannot adequately describe in a few pages the character of folk music, rhythm and blues, country and western, and the various shades of rock, much less sketch out their tangled interrelationships.

A single example demonstrates this complexity. During the 1960s, protest singers like Joan Baez, Pete Seeger, and Bob Dylan had in their standard repertoire a song called "This Land Is Your Land." The song had been written by Woody Guthrie as an American leftist reaction to the sentiments expressed in Irving Berlin's "God Bless America." Guthrie had adapted an old mountain ballad sung by the Carter Family, who had been a formative part of country and western music at the Grand Ol' Opry since the late 1920s. The Carters played and sang mountain music that was a complex blending of Old English balladry, Scottish drills, some black music, and the hymn tradition of the mountain churches.

The worldwide appeal of pop music must be recognized. The numbers in themselves are staggering. Between 1965 and 1973 nearly twelve hundred different recorded versions of the Beatles' song "Yesterday" (written by Paul McCartney and John Lennon) were available. By 1977 the Beatles had sold over one hundred million record albums and the same number of singles. Elvis Presley had sold more than eighty million singles at the time of his death in 1977; today, some years after his death, all his major albums remain in stock in record stores. Bootleg tapes and cassettes are prized in those places of the world where political and social oppression are facts of life.

The very best of popular music, both folk and rock, is sophisticated and elegant. Classic rock albums of the Beatles like *Revolver* reflect influences from the blues, ballads, the music of India, jazz harmonies, and some baroque orchestrations. The talented (and outrageous) Frank Zappa and the Mothers of Invention dedicated their 1960s album *Freak Out* to "Charles Mingus, Pierre Boulez, Anton Webern, Igor Stravinsky, Willie Dixon, Guitar Slim, Edgar Varèse, and Muddy Waters." Zappa's experiments with mixing rock and classical music were deemed serious enough for Zubin Mehta and the Los Angeles Philharmonic to have attempted some joint concerts. The popular folk singer Judy Collins' most successful album of the 1960s—*Wildflowers*—was orchestrated and arranged by Joshua Rifkin, a classical composer once on the music faculty of Princeton University. The crossbreeding of folk, rock, and classical modes of music continues with increasing interest in the use of electronic music and advanced amplification systems.

The folk and rock music of the 1960s saw itself in the vanguard of social change and turmoil. Rock music was inextricably entwined with the youth culture. In fact, popular music provided one of the most patent examples of the so-called generation gap. If the Beatles upset the older generation with their sunny irreverence, their coded language about drugs, and their open sexuality, groups like the Rolling Stones were regarded by many as a clear menace to society. With their hard-driving music, their aggressive style of life, their sensuality, and their barely concealed flirtation with violence and nihilism, the Stones were seen by many as a living metaphor for the anarchy of the turbulent 1960s. It was hardly reassuring for parents to see their young bring home a Stones album entitled *Their Satanic Majesties Request* inside the cover of which is an apocalyptic collage of Hieronymus Bosch, Ingres, Mughal Indian miniatures, and pop photography. Nor were many consoled when the violence of the music was translated into actual violence as rock stars like Jimi Hendrix, Janis Joplin, Phil Ochs, and Jim Morrison destroyed themselves with alcohol or drugs. Contemporary concerns with the social consequences of everything from Heavy Metal to Rap music must be seen against the background of criticism of popular music that goes back far into our past.

Whatever the long-range judgment of history may be, pop music in its variegated forms is as much an indicator of our present culture as the novels of Dickens were of the 19th century. It partakes of both brash commercial hype and genuine social statement. The record album of a major rock group today represents the complex interaction of advanced technology, big business, and high-powered marketing techniques as well as the music itself. Likewise, a rock concert is not merely the live presentation of music to an audience but a multimedia "happening" in which the plastic arts, dramatic staging, sophisticated lighting and amplification, and a medley of other visual and aural aids are blended to create an artistic whole with the music. Beyond (or under) this glitter, notoriety, and hype, however, is a music arising from real issues and expressing real feelings. New wave and punk rock, for instance, reflected the alienation of the working-class youth of Great Britain in the 1970s and 1980s.

Finally, pop music is not a phenomenon of the moment alone. Its roots are in the tribulations of urban blacks, the traditionalism of rural whites, the protest of activists, and the hopes and aspirations of the common people, causes with a lengthy history in the United States yet still alive today. Pop music, then, is both a social document of our era and a record of our past.

The very best pop music hymns the joy of love, the anxiety of modern life, the yearning for ecstasy, and the damnation of institutionalized corruption. Rock music in particular creates and offers the possibility of ecstasy. For those who dwell in the urban wastelands of post-technological America or the stultifying structures of post-Stalinist Eastern Europe the vibrant beat and incessant sound of rock music must be a welcome, if temporary, refuge from the bleakness of life.

As we move to the end of the 20th century the popular music scene has shown two new trends that coincide with some of the themes we have noted in this chapter.

In the first place, advances in communication technology have not only spawned the music video (in which the visual arts, drama, and music can be joined in a single art experience) but—with the easy access of television linkups—it is now possible to put on transcontinental shows (like the famous Live Aid show of 1985) in which rock concerts take on a simultaneous character and showcase the international idiom of rock music.

Secondly, and closely allied to the first trend, there has been a powerful crossfertilization of music brought about through easy communication. Rock music, with its old roots in American forms of music, has now expanded to absorb everything from Caribbean and Latin American music to the music of West Africa and Eastern Europe. If there is any truth in the thesis of the global culture it is most easily seen, in its infant stages, in the world of popular music.

SUMMARY

This chapter deals with Western culture after the time of the Second World War. In the postwar period, with Europe in shambles and the Far East still asleep, we confidently felt that the 20th was the American century; many people, not always admiringly, spoke of the "Coca-Colazation" of the world. From the vantage point of the near-end of the century we now see that, however powerful the United States may be, there now exist other countervailing powers, as the economic power of Japan readily demonstrates.

This period has also seen some dramatic shifts in the arts. The modernist temper that prevailed both in literature and in the arts has had its inevitable reaction. The power of the New York School of painting (abstract expressionism/color field painting/minimalism) has been challenged by new art forces, mainly from Europe, that emphasize once again the picture plane and the expressive power of emotion. In literature, the modernist temper exemplified in writers like Eliot, Woolf, and others has now given way to a postmodern sensibility represented in writers who are from Latin America, Japan, and Europe. Increasing attention is being paid to the writers both from Eastern Europe and from Africa.

Out of the human rights movement of the past decades has arisen a determined effort to affirm the place of women in the world of the arts both by retrieving their overlooked work from the past and by careful attention to those who work today. Similarly, peoples of color, both male and female, have come to the attention of large audiences as the arts democratize. Contemporary debates over the core humanities requirements in universities (Should they restrict themselves to the old "classics" or should they represent many voices and many cultures?) simply reflect the pressures of the culture, which is no longer sure of its older assumptions.

No consensus exists on a humanistic worldview. The power of existentialism after the war sprang both from its philosophical ideas and from its adaptability to the arts, especially the literary arts. While the writings of Albert Camus are still read and the plays of Beckett and Ionesco are still performed, they now reflect a settled place in the literary canon with no new single idea providing the power to energize the arts as a whole.

It may well be that the key word to describe the contemporary situation is *pluralism:* a diversity of influences, ideas, and movements spawned by an age of instant communication and ever-growing technology. The notion of a global culture argues for a common culture growing out of mutual links. There is some evidence of commonality, but it must be said that in other areas there are regional differences and even antagonisms. What we seem to be seeing in an age when more people buy books, see films, watch television, listen to tapes and records, go to plays and concerts than ever before is a situation the Greek philosophers wrote about millennia ago: the curious puzzle about the relationship of unity and diversity in the observable world: We are one, but we are also many.

Pronunciation Guide

Borges: BOR-hays
Boulez: Boo-LEZ
Camus: Cam-OO
existentialism: eggs-es-TEN-shall-ism
Godot: go-DOUGH
Sören Kierkegaard: SORE-en KEER-ke-jar
Le Corbusier: luh cor-BOO-see-ay
Miës van der Rohe: MEESE van-der-ROW-eh
Rauschenberg: RAU-shen-berg
Shostakovich: Shah-stah-KO-vich
Wiesel: Vee-ZELL

Exercises

1. When we look at abstract expressionist art it is tempting to think that "anyone could do that." But *can* "anyone" do it? How does one go about describing in writing the character of abstract art?
2. Look closely at a work by Alexander Calder. Would a classical sculptor (Rodin, Michelangelo) have recognized his work as "sculpture"? What makes it different and why is it sculpture?
3. After reading Sartre's essay on existentialism, ask yourself: Is this a philosophy that could serve as a guide to my life? Give the reasons for your answer.
4. Look carefully at your campus buildings. Does "form follow function"? Is "less more"? Can you detect the styles that have influenced the campus architect?
5. A classic is said to have a "surplus of meaning"—it is so good that one can always go back and learn more from it. Are there compositions in popular music which are now "classics" in that sense? List five records or songs that still inspire musicians today.
6. Have the new forms of communication (especially

television) made you less of a reader? How does reading differ from watching television? How does looking at art differ from looking at television? Listening to music?

Further Reading

Armstrong, Tom, et al. *200 Years of American Sculpture.* New York: Whitney Museum, 1976. This well-illustrated catalogue has abundant bibliographies. A good first look at sculpture in this country from a historical perspective.

Cage, John. *Silence.* Cambridge: MIT Press, 1969. A manifesto from one of the leaders of the artistic avant-garde.

Cantor, Norman F. *Twentieth Century Culture: Modernism to Deconstruction.* New York: Peter Lang, 1988. A survey of critical theory in this century that includes developments after structuralism.

Glass, Philip, and R. T. Jones. *Music by Philip Glass.* New York: Harper & Row, 1987. A good introduction to the minimalist spirit in music, with a discography.

Hilberg, Raoul. *The Destruction of the European Jews.* Chicago: Quadrangle, 1967. The standard history of the subject; essential background for reading Wiesel and other Holocaust authors.

Kaufmann, Walter (ed.). *Existentialism from Dostoevsky to Sartre.* New York: New American Library, 1975. A standard anthology, although not everyone agrees that "revolt" is the prime category for understanding the movement.

Rubin, William. *Pablo Picasso: A Retrospective.* New York: Museum of Modern Art, 1980. This profusely illustrated catalogue sums up a good deal of the 20th century with its scholarly concentration on the century's major figure in art.

Sandler, Irving. *The Triumph of American Painting.* New York: Praeger, 1970. Sandler is the best chronicler of the New York school of painting.

Yates, Gayle Graham. *What Women Want: The Idea of the Movement.* Cambridge: Harvard University Press, 1975. A good introduction to the feminist movement considered historically.

GLOSSARY

Terms *italicized* within the definitions are themselves defined within the Glossary.

a capella Music sung without instrumental accompaniment.

abacus (1) The slab that forms the upper part of a *capital*. (2) A computing device using movable counters.

Academy Derived from Akademeia, the name of the garden where Plato taught his students; the term came to be applied to official (generally conservative) teaching establishments.

accompaniment The musical background to a melody.

acoustics The science of the nature and character of sound.

acropolis Literally, the high point of a Greek city, frequently serving as refuge in time of war. The best known is the Acropolis of Athens.

acrylic A clear plastic used to make paints and as a casting material in sculpture.

adagio Italian for "slow"; used as an instruction to musical performers.

aesthetic Describes the pleasure derived from a work of art, as opposed to any practical or informative value it might have. In philosophy, aesthetics is the study of the nature of art and its relation to human experience.

agora In ancient Greek cities, the open marketplace, often used for public meetings.

aisle In church *architecture,* the long open spaces parallel to the *nave.*

aleatory music Music made in a random way after the composer sets out the elements of the musical piece.

allegory A dramatic or artistic device in which the superficial sense is accompanied by a deeper or more profound meaning.

allegro Italian for "merry" or "lively"; a musical direction.

altar In ancient religion, a table at which offerings were made or victims sacrificed. In Christian churches, a raised structure at which the sacrament of the Eucharist is consecrated, forming the center of the ritual.

altarpiece A painted or sculptured *panel* placed above and behind an altar to inspire religious devotion.

alto The lowest range of the female voice, also called contralto.

ambulatory Covered walkway around the *apse* of a church.

amphora Greek wine jar.

anthropomorphism The endowing of nonhuman objects or forces with human characteristics.

antiphony Music in which two or more *voices* alternate with one another.

apse Eastern end of a church, generally semicircular, in which the *altar* is housed.

architecture The art and science of designing and constructing buildings for human use.

architrave The lowest division of an *entablature.*

archivault The molding that frames an arch.

aria Song for a solo voice in an *opera,* an *oratorio,* or a *cantata.*

Ars Nova Latin for "the New Art." Describes the more complex new music of the 14th century, marked by richer harmonies and elaborate rhythmic devices.

assemblage The making of a sculpture or other three-dimensional art piece from a variety of materials. Compare *collage, montage.*

atelier A workshop.

atonality The absence of a *key* or tonal center in a musical composition.

atrium An open court in a Roman house or in front of a church.

augmentation In music, the process of slowing down a melody or musical phrase by increasing (generally doubling) the length of its notes.

aulos Greek wind instrument, similar to an oboe but consisting of two pipes.

avant-garde French for advance-guard. Term used to describe artists using innovative or experimental techniques.

axis An imaginary line around which the elements of a painting, sculpture or building are organized; the direction and focus of these elements establishes the axis.

ballad A narrative poem or song with simple stanzas and a refrain which is usually repeated at the end of each stanza.

ballet A dance performance, often involving a narrative or plot sequence, usually accompanied by music.

band A musical performance group made up of *woodwind, brass,* and *percussion,* but no *strings.*

baritone The male singing voice of medium register, between *bass* and *tenor.*

barrel vault A semicircular *vault* unbroken by ribs or groins.

basilica Originally a large hall used in Roman times for public meetings, law courts, etc.; later applied to a specific type of early Christian church.

bas-relief Low relief; see *relief.*

bass The lowest range of the male voice.

beat The unit for measuring time and *meter* in music.

binary form A two-part musical form in which the second part is different from the first, and both parts are usually repeated.

bitonality A musical technique involving the simultaneous performance of two melodies in different *tonalities.*

black figure A technique used in Greek vase painting which involved painting figures in black paint in silhouette and incising details with a sharp point. It was used throughout the Archaic period. Compare *red figure.*

blank verse Unrhymed verse often used in English *epic* and dramatic poetry. Its meter is *iambic pentameter.* Compare *heroic couplet.*

blue note A flattened third or seventh note in a *chord,* characteristic of jazz and blues.

brass instruments The French horn, trumpet, trombone, and tuba, all of which have metal mouthpieces and bodies.

Bronze Age The period during which bronze (an alloy of copper and tin) was the chief material for tools and weapons. It began in Europe around 3000 B.C. and ended around 1000 B.C. with the introduction of iron.

burin Steel tool used to make copper *engravings.*

buttress An exterior architectural support.

cadenza In music, a free or improvised passage, usually inserted toward the end of a *movement* or *aria,* intended to display the performer's technical skill.

caliph An Arabic term for leader or ruler.

calligraphy The art of penmanship and lettering.

campanile In Italy the bell tower of a church, often standing next to but separate from the church building.

canon From the Greek meaning a "rule" or "standard." In *architecture* it is a standard of proportion. In literature it is the authentic list of an author's works. In music it is the melodic line sung by overlapping voices in strict *imitation.* In religious terms it represents the authentic books in the Bible or the authoritative prayer of the Eucharist in the Mass or the authoritative law of the church promulgated by ecclesiastical authority.

cantata Italian for a piece of music that is sung rather than played; an instrumental piece is known as a *sonata.*

cantus firmus Latin for "fixed song," a system of structuring a *polyphonic* composition around a preselected melody by adding new melodies above and/or below. The technique was used by medieval and Renaissance composers.

canzoniere The Italian word for a songbook.

capital The head, or crowning part, of a column, taking the weight of the *entablature.*

capitulary A collection of rules or regulations sent out by a legislative body.

cartoon (1) A full-scale preparatory drawing for a picture, generally a large one such as a wall painting. (2) A humorous drawing.

caryatid A sculptured female figure taking the place of a column.

cast A moulded replica made by a process whereby plaster, wax, clay, or metal is poured in liquid form into a mold. When the material has hardened the mold is removed, leaving a replica of the original from which the mold was taken.

catharsis Literally, "purgation." Technical term used by Aristotle to describe the emotional effect of a tragic drama upon the spectator.

cathedra The bishop's throne. From that word comes the word cathedral, i.e., a church where a bishop officiates.

cella Inner shrine of a Greek or Roman temple.

ceramics Objects made of baked clay, such as vases and other forms of pottery, tiles, and small sculptures.

chamber music Music written for small groups.

chancel The part of a church that is east of the *nave* and includes *choir* and *sanctuary.*

chant A single line of melody in free rhythm and unaccompanied. The term is most frequently used for liturgical music such as Gregorian or Ambrosian chant.

chapel A small space within a church or a secular building such as a palace or castle, containing an *altar* consecrated for ritual use.

chevet The eastern *(altar)* end of a church.

chiaroscuro In painting, the use of strong contrasts between light and dark.

choir The part of a church *chancel* between *nave* and *sanctuary* where the monks sing the Office; a group of singers.

chorale A simple hymn tune sung either in unison or harmonized.

chord Any combination of three or more notes sounded together.

chorus In ancient Greek drama, a group of performers who comment collectively on the main action. The term came to be used, like *choir,* for a group of singers.

cithara An elaborate seven-string *lyre* used in Greek and Roman music.

classical Generally applied to the civilizations of Greece and Rome; more specifically to Greek art and culture in the 5th and 4th centuries B.C. Later imitations of classical styles are called neoclassical. Classical is also often used as a broad definition of excellence: a "classic" can date to any period.

clavecin French for "harpsichord."

clef French for "key." In written music the term denotes the sign placed at the beginning of the *staff* to indicate the range of notes it contains.

clerestory A row of windows in a wall above an adjoining roof.

cloister The enclosed garden of a monastery, surrounded by a covered walkway; by extension the monastery itself. Also, a covered walkway alone.

coda Italian for "tail." Final section of a musical *movement* in sonata form, summing up the previous material.

codex A manuscript volume.

coffer In *architecture,* a recessed panel in a ceiling.

collage A composition produced by pasting together disparate objects such as train tickets, newspaper clippings, or textiles. Compare *assemblage, montage.*

colonnade A row of columns.

comedy An amusing and lighthearted play or narrative intended to provoke laughter on the part of the spectator; or a work with a happy ending.

composer The writer of a piece of music.

composition Generally, the arrangement or organization of the elements that make up a work of art. More specifically, a piece of music.

concerto A piece of music for one or more solo instruments and *orchestra,* usually with three contrasting *movements.*

concerto grosso A piece of music similar to a *concerto* but designed to display the *orchestra* as a whole.

concetto Italian for "concept." In Renaissance and Baroque art, the idea that undergirds an artistic ensemble.

consul One of two Roman officials elected annually to serve as the highest state magistrates in the Republic.

contralto See *alto.*

contrapposto In sculpture, placing a human figure so that one part (e.g., the shoulder) is turned in a direction opposite to another part (e.g., the hip and leg).

cori spezzati Italian for "split choirs." The use of two or more choirs for a musical performance.

Corinthian An order of *architecture* that was popular in Rome, marked by elaborately decorated *capitals* bearing acanthus leaves. Compare *Doric, Ionic.*

cornice The upper part of an *entablature.*

counterpoint Two or more distinct melodic lines sung or played simultaneously in a single unified composition.

crescendo In music, a gradual increase in volume.

cruciform Arranged or shaped like a cross.

crypt A *vaulted* chamber, completely or partially underground, which usually contains a *chapel.* It is found in a church under the *choir*.

cult A system of religious belief and its followers.

cuneiform A system of writing, common in the ancient Near East, using characters made up of wedge shapes. Compare *hieroglyphics*.

da capo Italian for "from the beginning." In a musical performance, return to and repetition of the beginning section.

daguerreotype Early system of photography in which the image is produced on a silver-coated plate.

decrescendo In music, a gradual decrease in volume.

design The overall conception or scheme of a work of art. In the visual arts, the organization of a work's *composition* based on the arrangement of lines or contrast between light and dark.

development Central section of a *sonata-form* movement, in which the themes of the exposition are developed.

dialectics A logical process of arriving at the truth by putting in juxtaposition contrary propositions; a term often used in medieval philosophy and theology, and also in the writings of Hegel and Marx.

diatonic The seven notes of a major or minor *scale*, corresponding to the piano's white *keys* in an *octave*.

diminuendo In music, a gradual decrease in volume.

diminution The speeding up of a musical phrase by decreasing (usually halving) the length of the notes.

dithyramb Choral hymn to the Greek god Dionysus, often wild and violent in character. Later, any violent song, speech, or writing. Compare *paean*.

dome A hemispherical *vault*.

dominant The fifth note of a *diatonic scale*.

Doric One of the Greek orders of *architecture*, simple and austere in style. Compare *Corinthian, Ionic*.

dramatis personae Latin for characters in a play.

dynamics In music, the various levels of loudness and softness of sound, together with their increase and decrease.

echinus The lower part of the *capital*.

elevation In *architecture*, a drawing of the side of a building which does not show perspective.

encaustic A painting technique using molten wax colored by pigments.

engraving (1) The art of producing a depressed design on a wood or metal block by cutting it in with a tool. (2) The impression or image made from such a wood or metal block by ink that fills the design. Compare *burin, etching, woodcut*.

entablature The part of a Greek or Roman temple above the columns, normally consisting of *architrave, frieze*, and *cornice*.

entasis The characteristic swelling of a Greek column at a point about a third above its base.

epic A long narrative poem celebrating the exploits of a heroic character.

Epicurean A follower of the Greek philosopher Epicurus, who held that pleasure was the chief aim in life.

epithet Adjective used to describe the special characteristics of a person or object.

essay A short literary composition, usually in prose, dealing with a specific topic.

etching (1) The art of producing a depressed design on a metal plate by cutting lines through a wax coating and then applying corrosive acid that removes the metal under the lines. (2) The impression or image made from such a plate by ink that fills the design. Compare *engraving, woodcut*.

ethos Greek word meaning "character." In general, that which distinguishes a particular work of art and gives it character. More specifically, a term used by the Greeks to describe the moral and ethical character that they ascribed to music.

evangelist One of the authors of the four *Gospels* in the Bible: Matthew, Mark, Luke, and John.

exposition In music, the statement of the themes or musical ideas in the first section of a *sonata-form movement*.

façade The front of a building.

ferroconcrete A modern building material consisting of concrete and steel reinforcing rods or mesh.

finale In music, the final section of a large instrumental composition or of the act of an *opera*.

flat A symbol (♭) used in music to signify that the note it precedes should be lowered by one half-step.

flute Architectural term for the vertical grooves on Greek (and later) columns generally.

foot In poetry, the unit for measuring *meter*.

foreshortening The artistic technique whereby a sense of depth and three-dimensionality is obtained by the use of receding lines.

form The arrangement of the general structure of a work of art.

forte Italian for "loud."

fresco A painting technique that employs the use of pigments on wet plaster.

friar A member of one of the religious orders of begging brothers founded in the Middle Ages.

frieze The middle section of an *entablature*. A band of painted or carved decoration, often found running around the outside of a Greek or Roman temple.

fugue A *polyphonic* composition, generally for two to four voices (vocal or instrumental), in which the same themes are passed from voice to voice and combined in *counterpoint*.

gallery A long, narrow room or corridor, such as the spaces above the *aisles* of a church.

genre A type or category of art. In the visual arts, the depiction of scenes from everyday life.

Gesamtkunstwerk German for "complete work of art." The term, coined by Wagner, refers to an artistic ensemble in which elements from literature, music, art, and the dance are combined into a single artistic totality.

glaze In oil painting a transparent layer of paint laid over a dried painted canvas. In ***ceramics*** a thin coating of clay fused to the piece by firing in a kiln.

gospels The four biblical accounts of the life of Jesus, ascribed to Matthew, Mark, Luke, and John. Compare *evangelist*.

gouache An opaque watercolor medium.

graphic Description and demonstration by visual means.

Greek cross A cross with arms of equal length.

Gregorian chant *Monophonic* religious music usually sung without accompaniment. Called *plainsong*. Compare *melisma, neum, trope*.

ground A coating applied to a surface to prepare it for painting.

guilloche A decorative band made up of interlocking lines of design.

hadith Islamic law/traditions outside of the Qu'ran.
haj The Islamic pilgrimage to Mecca.
hamartia Literally Greek for "missing the mark," "failure," or "error." Term used by Aristotle to describe the character flaw that would cause the tragic end of an otherwise noble hero.
happening In art, a multimedia event performed with audience participation so as to create a single artistic expression.
harmony The *chords* or vertical structure of a piece of music; the relationships existing between simultaneously sounding notes and chord progressions.
hedonism The philosophical theory that material pleasure is the principal good in life.
hegira Muhammad's flight from Mecca to Medina; marks the beginning of the Islamic religion.
heroic couplet The *meter* generally employed in *epic* poetry, consisting of pairs of rhyming *iambic pentameter* lines. Compare *blank verse*.
hierarchy A system of ordering people or things which places them in higher and lower ranks.
hieroglyphics A system of writing in which the characters consist of realistic or stylized pictures of actual objects, animals, or human beings (whole or part). The Egyptian hieroglyphic script is the best known, but by no means the only one. Compare *cuneiform*.
high relief See *relief*.
hippodrome A race course for horses and chariots. Compare *spina*.
homophony Music in which a single melody is supported by a harmonious accompaniment. Compare *monophonic*.
hubris The Greek word for "insolence" or "excessive pride."
humanist In the Renaissance, someone trained in the humane letters of the ancient classics and employed to use those skills. More generally, one who studies the humanities as opposed to the sciences.
hymn A religious song intended to give praise and adoration.

iambic pentameter Describes the *meter* of poetry written in lines consisting of five groups (pentameter) of two syllables each, the second syllable stressed more than the first (iambic *foot*).
icon Greek word for "image." Panel paintings used in the Orthodox church as representations of divine realities.
iconography The set of symbols and allusions that gives meaning to a complex work of art.
ideal The depiction of people, objects, and scenes according to an idealized, preconceived model.
idol An image of a deity that serves as the object of worship.
image The representation of a human or nonhuman subject, or of an event.
imitation In music, the restatement of a melodic idea in different voice parts of a *contrapuntal* composition.
impasto Paint laid on in thick textures.
improvisation In musical performance, the spontaneous invention of music for voice or instrument.
incising Cutting into a surface with a sharp instrument.
intercolumniation The horizontal distance between the central points of adjacent columns in a Greek or Roman temple.
interval Musical term for the difference in pitch between two musical notes.
Ionic One of the Greek orders of *architecture*, elaborate and graceful in style. Compare *Doric*, *Corinthian*.
Iron Age The period beginning in Europe around 1000 B.C. during which iron was the chief material used for tools and weapons.
isorhythmic *Polyphonic* music in which the various sections are unified by repeated rhythmic patterns, but the melodies are varied.
italic The type face *like this* designed during the Renaissance that was based on a form of handwriting often used in manuscript copying.

jamb Upright piece of a window or a door frame, often decorated in medieval churches.
jazz Form of American music first developed in the Black community in the early 20th century, consisting of improvisation on a melodic theme.
jongleur In French, a wandering minstrel. A professional musician, actor, or mime who went from place to place, offering entertainment.

key (1) The tonal center around which a composer bases a musical work. (2) The mechanism by which a keyboard instrument (piano, organ, etc.) or wind instrument (clarinet, bassoon, etc.) is made to sound.
keystone Central stone of an arch.
kore Type of standing female statue produced in Greece in the Archaic period.
kouros Type of standing male statue, generally nude, produced in Greece in the Archaic period.

lancet A pointed window frame of a medieval Gothic cathedral.
landscape In the visual arts, the depiction of scenery in nature.
Latin cross A cross with the vertical arm longer than the horizontal arm.
legato Italian for "tied." In music, the performance of notes in a smooth line. The opposite, with notes detached, is called *staccato*.
Leitmotif German for "leading motif." A system devised by Wagner whereby a melodic idea represents a character, an object, or an idea.
lekythos Small Greek vase for oil or perfume, often used during funeral ceremonies.
libretto Italian for "little book." In music, the text or words of an *opera*, *oratorio*, or other musical work involving text.
lied German for "song."
line engraving A type of *engraving* in which the image is made by scored lines of varying width.
lintel The piece that spans two upright posts.
lithography A method of producing a print from a slab of stone on which an image has been drawn with a grease crayon or waxy liquid.
liturgy The rites used in public and official religious worship.
loggia A gallery open on one or more sides, often with arches.
low relief See *relief*.
lunette Semicircular space in wall for window or decoration.
lyre Small stringed instrument used in Greek and Roman music. Compare *cithara*.
lyric (1) Words or verses written to be set to music. (2) Description of a work of art that is poetic, personal, even ecstatic in spirit.

Madonna Italian for "My Lady." Used for the Virgin Mary.

madrigal *Polyphonic* song for three or more voices, with verses set to the same music and a refrain set to different music.

mandorla Almond-shaped light area surrounding a sacred personage in a work of art.

Mass The most sacred rite of the Catholic *liturgy.*

matroneum Gallery for women in churches, especially churches in the Byzantine tradition.

mausoleum Burial chapel or shrine.

meander Decorative pattern in the form of a maze, commonly found in Greek Geometric art.

melisma In *Gregorian chant,* an intricate chain of notes sung on one syllable. Compare *trope.*

meter A systematically arranged and measured rhythm in poetry or music.

metopes Square slabs often decorated with sculpture which alternated with *triglyphs* to form the *frieze* of a *Doric* temple.

michrab A recessed space or wall design in a mosque to indicate direction of Mecca for Islamic worshippers.

minnesingers German medieval musicians of the aristocratic class who composed songs of love and chivalry. Compare *troubadors.*

minuet A French 17th-century dance, the form of which was eventually incorporated into the *sonata* and *symphony* as the third *movement.*

mobile A sculpture so constructed that its parts move either by mechanical or natural means.

mode (1) In ancient and medieval music an arrangement of notes forming a scale which, by the character of intervals, determines the nature of the composition. Compare *tetrachord.* (2) In modern music one of the two classes, major or minor, into which musical scales are divided.

modulation In music, movement from one *key* to another.

monastery A place where monks live in communal style for spiritual purposes.

monochrome A single color, or variations on a single color.

monody A *monophonic* vocal piece of music.

monophonic From the Greek meaning "one voice." Describes music consisting of a single melodic line. Compare *polyphonic.*

montage (1) In the cinema, the art of conveying an idea and/or mood by the rapid juxtaposition of different images and camera angles. (2) In art, the kind of work made from pictures or parts of pictures already produced and now forming a new composition. Compare *assemblage, collage.*

mosaic Floor or wall decoration consisting of small pieces of stone, ceramic, shell, or glass set into plaster or cement.

mosque Islamic house of worship.

motet (1) Musical composition, developed in the 13th century, in which words (French "mots") were added to fragments of *Gregorian chant.* (2) 16th-century composition: four- or five-voiced sacred work, generally based on a Latin text.

movement In music, an individual section of a *symphony, concerto,* or other extended composition.

mullions The lines dividing windows into separate units.

mural Wall painting or mosaics attached to a wall.

myth Story or legend whose origin is unknown; myths often help to explain a cultural tradition or cast light on a historical event.

narthex The porch or vestibule of a church.

natural In music, the sign (♮) which cancels any previously indicated *sharp* (♯) or *flat* (♭).

nave From the Latin meaning "ship." The central space of a church.

Neanderthal Early stage in the development of the human species, lasting from before 100,000 B.C. to around 35,000 B.C.

Neolithic Last part of the Stone Age, when agricultural skills had been developed but stone was still the principal material for tools and weapons. It began in the Near East around 8000 B.C. and in Europe around 6000 B.C.

neum The basic symbol used in the notation of *Gregorian chant.*

niche A hollow recess or indentation in a wall to hold a statue or other object.

notation The system of writing out music in symbols that can be reproduced in performance.

obelisk A rectangular shaft of stone that tapers to a pyramidal point.

octave The *interval* from one note to the next with the same pitch; e.g., from C to the C above or below.

oculus A circular eye-like window or opening.

ode A lyric poem, usually exalted and emotional in character.

oil painting Painting in a medium made up of powdered colors bound together with oil, generally linseed.

opera Theatrical performance involving a drama, the text of which is sung to the accompaniment of an orchestra.

opus Latin for "work." Used for chronological lists of composers' works.

Opus Dei Latin for "work of God." Used to describe the choral offices of monks, which are sung during the hours of the day.

oral composition The composition and transmission of works of literature by word of mouth, as in the case of the Homeric epics.

oratorio An extended musical *composition* for solo singers, *chorus,* and *orchestra* on a religious subject. Unlike *opera,* the oratorio is not staged.

orchestra (1) In Greek theaters, the circular space in front of the stage in which the *chorus* moves. (2) A group of instrumentalists who come together to perform musical *compositions.*

order (1) In *classical architecture* a specific form of column and *entablature;* see *Doric, Ionic,* and *Corinthian.* (2) More generally, the arrangement imposed on the various elements in a work of art.

organum An early form of *polyphonic* music in which one or more melody lines were sung along with the song line of plainsong. Compare *Gregorian chant.*

Orientalizing Term used to describe Greek art of the 7th century B.C. that was influenced by Eastern artistic styles.

overture An instrumental *composition* played as an introduction to a *ballet, opera,* or *oratorio.*

paean A Greek hymn to Apollo and other gods, either praying for help or giving thanks for help already received. Later generally applied to any song of praise or triumph. Compare *dithyramb.*

Paleolithic The Old Stone Age, during which human beings appeared and manufactured tools for the first time. It began around two and a half million years ago.

palette (1) The tray on which a painter mixes colors. (2) The range and combination of colors typical of a particular painter.

panel A rigid, flat support, generally square or rectangular, for a painting; the most common material is wood.

pantheon The collected gods. By extension, a temple to them. In modern usage a public building containing the tombs or memorials of famous people.

pantocrator From the Greek meaning "one who rules or dominates all." Used for those figures of God and/or Christ found in the *apses* of Byzantine churches.

parable A story told to point up a philosophical or religious truth.

parallelism A literary device, common in the psalms, of either repeating or imaging one line of poetry with another that uses different words but expresses the same thought.

pastel A drawing made by rubbing colored chalks on paper.

pathos That aspect of a work of art that evokes sympathy or pity.

pediment The triangular space formed by the roof *cornices* on a Greek or Roman temple.

pendentives Triangular architectural devices used to support a dome of a structure; the dome may rest directly on the pendentives. Compare *squinches*.

percussion instruments Musical instruments that are struck or shaken to produce a sound, e.g., drums, tambourine, cymbals.

peripatetic Greek for "walking around." Specifically applied to followers of the philosopher Aristotle.

peristyle An arcade (usually of columns) around the outside of a building. The term is often used of temple *architecture*.

perspective A technique in the visual arts for producing on a flat or shallow surface the effect of three dimensions and deep space.

piano Italian for "soft."

piazza Italian term for a large, open public square.

pietà An image of the Virgin with the dead Christ.

pietra serena Italian for "serene stone." A characteristic building stone often used in Italy.

pilaster In *architecture* a pillar in *relief*.

pitch In music the relative highness or lowness of a note as established by the frequency of vibrations occurring per second within it.

pizzicato Italian for "plucked." An instruction to performers on *string* instruments to pluck instead of bow their strings.

plainsong See *Gregorian chant*.

plan An architectural drawing showing in two dimensions the arrangement of space in a building.

podium A base, platform, or pedestal for a building, statue, or monument.

polis The Greek word for "city," used to designate the independent city-states of ancient Greece.

polychrome Several colors. Compare *monochrome*.

polyphonic From the Greek meaning "many voices." Describes a musical composition built from the simultaneous interweaving of different melodic lines into a single whole. Compare *monophonic*.

portal A door, usually of a church or cathedral.

portico A porch with a roof supported by columns.

prelude In music, a short piece that precedes a large-scale *composition*.

pre-Socratic Collective term for all Greek philosophers before the time of Socrates.

presto Italian for "fast."

program music Instrumental compositions that imitate sound effects, describe events, or narrate a dramatic sequence of events.

prophet From the Greek meaning "one who speaks for another." In the Hebrew and Christian tradition it is one who speaks with the authority of God. In a secondary meaning, it is one who speaks about the future with authority.

proportion The relation of one part to another, and each part to the whole, in respect of size, whether of height, width, length, or depth.

prosody The art of setting words to music.

prototype An original model or form on which later works are based.

psalter Another name for the Book of Psalms from the Bible.

Qur-an The sacred scriptures of Islam.

realism A 19th-century style in the visual arts in which people, objects, and events were depicted in a manner that aimed to be true to life. In film, the style of Neorealism developed in the post–World War II period according to similar principles.

recapitulation The third section of a *sonata-form* movement in which the ideas set out in the *exposition* are repeated.

recitative A style of musical declamation that is halfway between singing and ordinary speech.

red figure A technique used in Greek vase painting which involved painting red figures on a black background and adding details with a brush. Compare *black figure*.

register In music, the range of notes within the capacity of a human voice or an instrument.

relief Sculptural technique whereby figures are carved out of a block of stone, part of which is left to form a background. Depending on the degree to which the figures project, the relief is described as either high or low.

reliquary A small casket or shrine in which sacred relics are kept.

requiem A *mass* for the dead.

rondo A musical form in which one main theme recurs in alternation with various other themes. The form was often used in the last *movement* of a *sonata* or *symphony*.

sanctuary In religion, a sacred place. The part of a church where the altar is placed.

sarcophagus From the Greek meaning "flesh eater." A stone (usually limestone) coffin.

satire An amusing exposure of folly and vice, which aims to produce moral reform.

satyr Greek mythological figure usually shown with an animal's ears and tail.

scale (1) In music, a succession of notes arranged in ascending or descending order. (2) More generally, the relative or proportional size of an object or image.

scherzo Italian for "joke." A lighthearted and fast-moving piece of music.

score The written form of a piece of music in which all the parts are shown.

scriptorium That room in a medieval *monastery* in which manuscripts were copied and illuminated.

section An architectural drawing showing the side of a building.

secular Not sacred; relating to the worldly.
sequence In music, the repetition of a melodic phrase at different *pitches*.
serenade A type of instrumental *composition* originally performed in the 18th century as background music for public occasions.
serial music A type of 20th-century musical *composition* in which various components (notes, rhythms, dynamics, etc.) are organized into a fixed series.
sharp In music, a sign (♯) which raises the note it precedes by one half-step.
silhouette The definition of a form by its outline.
skolion Greek drinking song, generally sung at banquets.
soliloquy A speech delivered by an actor either while alone on stage or unheard by the other characters, generally so constructed as to indicate the inner feelings of a character.
sonata An extended instrumental *composition,* generally in three or four *movements*.
sonata form A structural form for instrumental music that employs *exposition, development,* and *recapitulation* as its major divisions.
sonnet A fourteen-line poem, either eight lines (octave) and six lines (sextet) or three quatrains of four lines and an ending couplet. Often attributed to Petrarch, the form—keeping the basic fourteen lines—was modified by such poets as Spenser, Shakespeare, and Milton.
soprano The highest *register* of the female voice.
spandrel A triangular space above a window in a *barrel vault* ceiling, or the space between two arches in an arcade.
spina A monument at the center of a stadium or *hippodrome,* usually in the form of a triangular *obelisk*.
squinches Either columns or *lintels* used in corners of a room to carry the weight of a superimposed mass. Their use resembles that of *pendentives*.
staccato See *legato*.
staff The five horizontal lines, with four spaces between, on which musical notation is written.
stele Upright stone slab decorated with relief carvings, frequently used as a grave marker.
still life A painting of objects such as fruit, flowers, dishes, etc., arranged to form a pleasing composition.
stoa A roofed *colonnade,* generally found in ancient Greek open markets, to provide space for shops and shelter.
stoic School of Greek philosophy, later popular at Rome, which taught that the universe is governed by Reason and that Virtue is the only good in life.
stretcher A wooden or metal frame on which a painter's canvas is stretched.
string quartet A performing group consisting of two violins, viola, and cello; a *composition* in *sonata form* written for such a group.
string instruments The violin, viola, violoncello (or cello), and double bass. All of these have strings that produce sound when stroked with a bow or plucked.
stylobate The upper step on which the columns of a Greek temple stand.
suite In music, a collection of various *movements* performed as a whole, sometimes with a linkage in *key* or theme between the movements.
summa The summation of a body of learning, particularly in the fields of philosophy and theology.
sura A chapter division in the Qur-an, the scripture of Islam.
symmetry An arrangement in which various elements are so arranged as to parallel one another on either side of an *axis*.
symphonic poem A one-movement orchestral work meant to illustrate a non-musical object like a poem, painting, or view of nature. Also called a tone poem.
symphony An extended orchestral *composition,* generally in three or four movements, in *sonata form*.
syncopation In music, the accentuation of a beat that is normally weak or unaccented.
synthesizer An electronic instrument for the production and control of sound that can be used for the making of music.

tabernacle A container for a sacred object; a receptacle on the altar of a Catholic church to contain the Eucharist.
tambour The drum that supports the cupola of a church.
tempera A painting technique using coloring mixed with egg yolk, glue, or casein.
tempo In music, the speed at which the notes are performed.
tenor The highest range of the male voice. In medieval *organum,* it is the voice that holds the melody of the plainsong.
ternary form A musical form composed of three separate sections, with the second in contrast to the first and third, and the third a modified repeat of the first.
terra cotta Italian meaning "baked earth." Baked clay used for *ceramics*. Also sometimes refers to the reddish-brown color of baked clay.
tesserae The small pieces of colored stone used for the creation of a *mosaic*.
tetrachord Musical term for a series of four notes. Two tetrachords formed a *mode*.
theme In music, a short melody or a self-contained musical phrase.
tholos Term in Greek *architecture* for a round building.
timbre The particular quality of sound produced by a voice or instrument.
toccata In music, a *virtuoso composition* for a keyboard instrument characterized by a free style with long, technically difficult passages.
toga Flowing woolen garment worn by Roman citizens.
tonality In music, the organization of all tones and chords of a piece in relation to the first tone of a *key*.
tonic The first and principal note of a *key,* serving as a point of departure and return.
tragedy A serious drama in which the principal character is often brought to disaster by his/her *hamartia,* or tragic flaw.
transept In a cruciform church, the entire part set at right angles to the *nave*.
treble In music, the higher voices, whose music is written on a *staff* marked by a treble *clef*.
triglyphs Rectangular slabs divided by two vertical grooves into three vertical bands; these alternated with *metopes* to form the *frieze* of a *Doric* temple.
triptych A painting consisting of three panels. A painting with two panels is called a diptych; one with several panels is a polyptych.
trompe l'oeil From the French meaning "to fool the eye." A painting technique by which the viewer seems to see real subjects or objects instead of their artistic representation.

trope In *Gregorian chant,* words added to a long *melisma.*

troubadors Aristocratic southern French musicians of the Middle Ages who composed *secular* songs with themes of love and chivalry; called trouvères in northern France. Compare *minnesingers.*

trumeau A supporting pillar for a church *portal,* common in medieval churches.

twelve-tone technique A *serial* method of *composition* devised by Schönberg in the early 20th century. Works in this style are based on a tone row consisting of an arbitrary arrangement of the twelve notes of the *octave.*

tympanum The space, usually decorated, above a *portal,* between a *lintel* and an *arch.*

unison The sound that occurs when two or more voices or instruments simultaneously produce the same note or melody at the same *pitch.*

value (1) In music, the length of a note. (2) In painting, the property of a color that makes it seem light or dark.

vanishing point In perspective, the point at which receding lines seem to converge and vanish.

vault A roof composed of arches of masonry or cement construction.

virginal A stringed keyboard instrument, sometimes called a spinet, which was a predecessor of the harpsichord.

virtuoso A person who exhibits great technical ability, especially in music. As an adjective, it describes a musical performance that exhibits, or a music composition that demands, great technical ability.

vivace Italian for "lively" or "vivacious."

volutes Spirals that form an *Ionic capital.*

votive An offering made to a deity either in support of a request or in gratitude for the fulfillment of an earlier prayer.

voussoirs Wedge-shaped blocks in an arch.

waltz A dance in triple rhythm.

woodcut (1) A wood block with a raised design produced by gouging out unwanted areas. (2) The impression or image made from such a block by inking the raised surfaces. Compare *engraving, etching, lithograph.*

woodwind instruments The flute, oboe, English horn, clarinet, bass clarinet, bassoon, contrabassoon, and saxophone. All of these are pipes perforated by holes in their sides which produce musical sound when the columns of air within them are vibrated by blowing on a mouthpiece.

ziggurat An Assyrian or Babylonian stepped pyramid.

INDEX

Page numbers in italics refer to illustrations.

COPYRIGHTS AND ACKNOWLEDGMENTS

PHOTOGRAPHIC CREDITS

Copyright in the photograph is property of the photographer unless otherwise noted.

AA&A: Ancient Art and Architecture Collection, Harrow-on-the-Hill, England
A/AR: Alinari/Art Resource, New York
BPK: Bildarchiv Preussischer Kulturbesitz, Berlin
G/AR: Giraudon/Art Resource, New York
H: Hirmer Fotoarchiv, Munich
NYPL: New York Public Library; Astor, Lenox & Tilden Foundations
PR: Photo Researchers, New York
RMN: © Photo by Service de Documentation Photographique de la Reunion des Musées Nationaux, Paris
S/AR: Scala/Art Resource, New York

1.1: Colorphoto Hans Hinz, Allschwil/Basel. **1.2 & TL:** H. **1.4:** Frank Schneider/PR. **1.5 & 1.6:** H. **1.7, 1.8 & TL:** BPK. **1.9:** S/AR. **1.10:** Boltin Picture Library, Croton-on-Hudson, New York. **1.11 & TL:** George Holton/PR. **1.12** (center and bottom), **1.13 & TL, 1.14, & 1.15:** H. **1.16:** Superstock. **1.17:** H. **1.18 & TL:** G/AR. **1.20:** Erich Lessing/AR. **1.22:** Borromeo/AR. **1.23:** H. **1.24:** Robert Harding Picture Library, London. **1.25 & 1.26:** AA&A. **1.27:** AR. **1.28 & TL:** H. **1.29:** Alton S. Tobey, Larchmont, NY.

2.1 & TL: Erich Lessing/AR. **2.2 & TL:** Deutsches Archaeologisches Institut, Athens. **2.3:** Colorphoto Hans Hins, Allschwil/Basel. **2.4:** Ingrid Geske-Heiden/Antikenmuseum/BPK. **2.5:** H. **2.6:** Deutsches Archaeologisches Institut, Athens. **2.8 & TL, 2.9, & 2.10:** H. **2.11:** A/AR. **2.12:** AA&A. **2.13:** S/AR. **2.14:** H. **2.16:** John Lewis Stage/The Image Bank. **2.19 & TL:** H. **2.20:** Deutsches Archaeologisches Institut, Athens.

3.1: Paul Warchol/AR. **3.2:** A/AR. **3.3 & TL:** PhotoEdit, Tarzana, CA. **3.4:** William Francis Warden Fund. Courtesy, Museum of Fine Arts, Boston. **3.5:** PhotoEdit, Tarzana, CA. **3.6:** A/AR. **3.7:** S/AR. **3.9 & TL, 3.10, & 3.11:** H. **3.12:** AR. **3.14:** PhotoEdit, Tarzana, CA. **3.15:** H. **3.16:** Bridgeman Art Library, London/Superstock. **3.17:** H. **3.18:** AR. **3.19 & TL, & 3.21:** S/AR. **3.22:** A/AR. **3.23:** Barbara Malter, Capitoline Museums, Rome. **3.25:** SEF/AR. **3.26:** H. **3.27:** From Hermann Thiersch, *Pharos Antike, Islam und Occident* (Leipzig: B. G. Teubner, 1909), opp. title page/NYPL. **3.29:** Jurgen Liepe/BPK. **3.30 & TL:** S/AR.

4.2 & TL: Mauro E. Mujica/AR. **4.3 & TL:** S/AR. **4.5:** A/AR. **4.6:** Graziano Paiella, Milan. **4.7 & TL:** A/AR. **4.10:** S/AR. **4.11:** A/AR. **4.12 & TL:** AR. **4.13:** Erich Lessing/AR. **4.14:** Fototeca Unione, American Academy in Rome. **4.15:** A/AR. **4.16:** AR. **4.17 & 4.18:** S/AR. **4.19:** Fototeca Unione, American Academy in Rome. **4.20:** A/AR. **4.22:** PR/Jan Halaska. **4.24 & TL:** Fototeca Unione, American Academy in Rome. **4.25:** AR. **4.26:** Fototeca Unione, American Academy in Rome. **4.27 & TL:** S/AR. **4.28, 4.29, & 4.30:** A/AR. **Interlude: 1a:** Culver Pictures. **1b:** Angus McBean Photo/Harvard Theatre Collection. **2a:** Bibliotheque Nationale, Paris.

5.1 & TL: Lee C. Ellenberger for The American Schools of Oriental Research, Philadelphia. **5.2 & TL:** A/AR. **5.3 & TL:** Andre Held, Ecublens, Switzerland. **5.4:** S/AR. **5.6:** A/AR, 1875—Roma, Sarcofago Cristiano—Museo Laterano. **5.8 & TL:** Robert Harding Picture Library, London. **5.9:** Zev Radovan, Jerusalem.

6.2 & TL: Ara Guler, Istanbul. **6.3:** Wim Swaan, New York. **6.4:** H. **6.5 & TL, 6.6, & 6.7:** S/AR. **6.8:** A/AR. **6.9 & 6.10:** Estate of Leonard von Matt, Stansstad, Switzerland. **6.11:** AA&A. **6.12:** AR. **6.13:** S/AR. **6.14:** Fotocielo, Rome. **6.15:** S/AR. **6.16, 6.17, & 6.18:** S/AR. **6.19 & TL:** Estate of Leonard von Matt, Stansstad, Switzerland. **6.20:** H. **6.21 & TL:** Reproduced through the courtesy of the Michigan-Princeton-Alexandria Expedition to Mount Sinai. **6.22:** AA&A. **6.23:** Mehmet Biber/Photopress © 1992 Biber. **6.24:** BPK. **6.25:** Israel Ministry of Tourism.

7.1: Archives Nationales de France. **7.3 & TL, 7.4 & TL:** Domkapitel Aachen (photo Ann Munchow). **7.7 & TL:** Austrian National Library. **7.8:** G/AR. **7.10 & TL:** Domkapitel Aachen (photo Ann Munchow). **7.11:** Walter Horn and Ernest Born. *Plan of St. Gall,* vol. II, p. XII. Copyright © 1979 Walter Horn and Ernest Born. **7.13 & TL:** G/AR. **7.14:** Marburg/AR. **7.15 & 7.16:** Archives Photographiques, Paris/SPADEM. **7.17 & TL:** J. E. Bulloz Editions, Paris.

8.1: After Professor Sumner McK. Crosby, Yale University. **(8.1):** Marburg/AR. **8.2:** Mikael Audrain/Editions Arthaud, Paris. **8.3:** RIBA, London. **8.4:** Sonia Halliday and Laura Lushington, Weston Turville, England. **8.5 & TL:** Wim Swaan, New York. **8.6:** Archives Photographiques, Paris/SPADEM. **8.7:** A/AR. **8.8 & TL:** The Image Bank. **8.9:** Fischer/AR. **8.10:** Bibliotheque Nationale, Paris. **8.12:** BPK. **8.13, 8.14, & 8.15:** S/AR. **8.16:** Colorphoto Hans Hinz, Allschwil/Basel. **8.17 & TL, 8.18:** S/AR. **Interlude: 1a & 1b:** Bibliotheque Nationale, Paris. **2a:** Theatre World Collection, New York.

9.1: Archives Photographiques, Paris/SPADEM. **9.2 & 9.3:** AR. **9.4 & TL:** A/AR. **9.5, 9.6, & 9.7:** S/AR. **9.8:** A/AR. **9.9, 9.10, 9.11, 9.12, 9.13, 9.14:** S/AR. **9.16:** AR. **9.17 & TL:** Elsa Peterson, New York. **9.18 & 9.19 & TL:** G/AR. **9.20, 9.21 & TL, & 9.22 & TL:** S/AR. **9.23:** G. Barone/Superstock, Inc. **9.24 & TL:** Woodmansterne, London. **9.26 & TL:** S/AR.

10.1 & TL: S/AR. **10.2:** Marburg/AR. **10.3:** S/AR. **10.4:** Erich Lessing/S/AR. **10.5, 10.6 & TL:** A/AR. **10.7:** S/AR. **10.8 & 10.9:**

MIT Press. **10.10:** A/AR. **10.11 & TL:** Nicholas Sapieha/AR. **10.13:** S/AR. **10.15:** A/AR. **10.16 & TL, 10.17, 10.18, 10.19, 10.20, 10.21 & TL, 10.23, & 10.24:** S/AR. **10.25 & 10.26:** A/AR. **10.27 & TL:** S/AR.

11.1: Kunsthistorisches Museum, Vienna. **11.2 & TL, 11.3, 11.4 & TL:** S/AR. **11.7, 11.9 & TL, 11.10:** Photo Vatican Museums. **11.11, 11.12, & 11.14:** A/AR. **11.15:** S/AR. **11.16:** RMN. **11.17:** Erich Lessing/AR. **11.18 & TL:** S/AR. **11.19 & 11.20:** A/AR. **11.21:** S/AR. **11.22:** A/AR. **11.23:** RMN. **11/24 & TL:** A/AR.

12.3 & TL: A/AR. **12.4 & TL:** S/AR. **12.5:** NYPL. **12.8:** RMN. **12.10 & TL:** Artothek. **12.14 & 12.15:** G/AR. **12.16:** J. Blauel/Artothek. **12.21:** RMN. **12.22 & TL:** Caisse Nationale des Monuments et des Sites, France. **12.23 & 12.25:** RMN. **12.28:** © 1948 NYPL. **12.29:** NYPL.

13.1 & 13.2: The Image Bank. **13.3, 13.4 & TL:** S/AR. **13.5:** AR. **13.6 & TL:** A/AR. **13.7:** S/AR. **13.8:** AR. **13.9 & 13.10:** A/AR. **13.11:** Barbara Malter, Rome. **13.12 & TL:** A/AR. **13.13:** Jorg P. Anders. **13.14:** Reproduced by permission of the Chatsworth Settlement Trustees. **13.16, 13.18 & TL:** RMN. **13.19:** French Government Tourist Office. **13.20:** Archives Photographiques, Paris/SPADEM. **13.21:** © Museo del Prado. **13.22:** Ampliaciones y Reproducciones MAS, Barcelona. **13.23:** A/AR. **13.25:** RMN. **13.26:** J. Blauel/Artothek. **13.27:** RMN. **13.29:** Tom Haartsen. **13.35:** S/AR. **13.36:** Hans Petersen, Copenhagen.

14.1 & TL: RMN. **14.9:** A/AR. **14.10:** H. **14.11 & TL:** A. F. Kersting, London. **14.12 & TL, 14.13:** AR. **14.15 & TL:** S/AR. **14.16 & TL:** Sylvain Grandadam/Pantheon Paris/PR. **14.17 & TL:** Virginia Tourism Group. **14.20:** © 1993 Beth Bergman. **14.21:** RMN. **14.22:** G/AR **14.23:** Virginia State Library and Archives.

15.2: Robert Harding Picture Library. **15.3 & TL:** Archiv fur Kunst und Geschichte, Berlin. **15.4:** RMN. **15.5:** Marc Wisneski, Bricktown, NJ. **15.6:** © 1993 Beth Bergman, New York. **15.8:** Jack Vartoogian, New York. **15.9:** G/AR. **15.11:** S/AR. **15.12:** A/AR. **15.13, 15.14, & 15.15:** RMN. **15.16:** S/AR. **15.17:** Erich Lessing/AR. **15.20:** S/AR. **15.21 & TL:** The Image Bank. **15.22:** BPK. **15.27:** NYPL. **Interlude: 1a:** H. Roger-Viollet, Paris. **1b:** Françoise Foliot, Paris. **2a:** H. Roger-Viollet, Paris. **2b:** Archives Photographiques, Paris/SPADEM.

16.3: United States National Park Service. **16.4 & TL:** G/AR. **16.6:** RMN. **16.9, 16.10, & 16.11:** RMN. **16.16:** Bruno Jarret/ © ARS, New York/ADAGP, Paris. **16.17:** © 1992, The Art Institute of Chicago. All Rights Reserved. **16.23:** Hideto Ko bayashi, Tokyo. **16.24:** © Copyright 1993 by The Barnes Foundation. BF No. 719. **16.26 & TL:** © Copyright Munch Museum, Oslo 1992. **16.27 & TL:** MAS, Barcelona. **16.28:** © Elke Walford. **16.31 & TL:** Bruno Jarret. © ARS, New York/ADAGP, Paris. **16.32 & TL:** Billy Rose Theatre Collection, The New York Public Library for the Performing Arts. Astor, Lenox and Tilden Foundations.

17.2: David Heald/© The Solomon R. Guggenheim Foundation, New York (FN 54.1412). **17.3:** © 1992, The Art Institute of Chicago. All Rights Reserved. **17.5:** Saidenberg Gallery. **17.7 & 17.8 & TL:** David Heald/ © The Solomon R. Guggenheim Foundation, New York. **17.10:** © 1992, The Art Institute of Chicago. All Rights Reserved. **17.11:** Tate Gallery, London/AR. **17.15:** Alain Tarica. **17.18:** Phoenix Films. **17.19:** The Library of Congress, Washington, D.C.

18.3: Hirschl and Adler Galleries, Inc., New York. **18.5:** George A. Hearn Fund, 1959. Photo by Malcom Varon. **18.7:** The Rothko Chapel. **18.8:** Gift of Dr. Hilbert and Mrs. H. Delawter. **18.10:** Statens Konstmuseen, Stockholm. **18.11:** © 1985 Harry Shunk, New York. **18.12:** Leo Castelli Gallery, New York. **18.13:** Frumkin/Adams Gallery. **18.14:** eeva-inkeri, New York, Frumkin/Adams Gallery. **18.15:** Photo Lee Stalsworth / Gift of Joseph H. Hirshorn, 1966. **18.16:** Dallas Museum of Arts, gift of the Dallas Chapter of the LINKS, Inc. **18.17:** Bevan Davies. **18.18 & TL:** © David Hockney, 1986. **18.21:** Fabbrica di San Pietro. **18.24:** Pace Gallery. **18.30:** Harry Shunk / © Christo 1972. **18.31 & TL:** VAGA. **18.32:** Courtesy of O.K. Harris Works of Art, New York, NY. © Copyright 1990 Duane Hanson. **18.35 & TL:** Mid-Town Payson Gallery. **18.36:** David Heald/ © The Solomon R. Guggenheim Foundation, New York. **18.37:** A/AR. **18.38:** Ezra Stoller/© Esto. All Rights Reserved. **18.39:** Guido Rossi/The Image Bank. **18.40 & TL, 18.41:** Ezra Stoller/© Esto. All Rights Reserved. **18.43:** Dimitri Kessel, Paris. **18.44:** James E. House/ Kohn Pederson Fox Associates. **18.45:** Susan Dirk. **18.46:** Stockhausen NR.11 REFRAIN. © Universal Edition (London) Ltd., London, 1961 © Renewed. All Rights Reserved. Used by permission of European American Music Distributors Corporation, Sole U.S. and Canadian agent for Universal Edition London.

LITERARY ACKNOWLEDGMENTS

Harcourt Brace wishes to thank the copyright owners for permission to reproduce the following copyrighted literature.

1.16: From *Life under the Pharaohs* by Leonard Cottrell, 1960. Reprinted by permission of Henry Holt & Company, Inc. **1.16:** "A Father's Advice to His Son" from *Temples, Tombs and Heiroglyphics* by Barbara Mertz, 1964. Copyright © 1964, 1978 by Barbara Mertz. All rights reserved. Reproduced by permission of Peter Bedrich Books, 2112 Broadway, New York, NY 10023. **1.23:** From *The Law Code of Hammurabi.* Reprinted by permission of University of Chicago Press.

2.65: From Book XVIII of *The Iliad* by Homer, trans. Richmond Lattimore. Copyright by the University of Chicago Press, 1951. Reprinted by permission of University of Chicago Press. All rights reserved.

3.187: Herondas excerpt from *Greek Literature in Translation,* trans. George Howe & Gustave Adolphus Harrer, 1924. Reprinted by permission of the Estate of George Howe.

4.324: Letter by Cicero, trans. John Reich. **4.354:** From *The Satyricon* by Petronius, translation formerly attributed to Oscar Wilde. Privately printed, 1928.

5.448: From I Corinthians and II Timothy of *Revised Standard Version Bible.* Copyright © 1946, 1952, 1971 by the Division of Christian Education of the National Council, Churches of Christ in the USA.

6.521: From *Procopius of Caesarea, Buildings* by Procopius, trans. H. B. Dewing with the collaboration of Glanville Downey. Reprinted by permission of Harvard University Press. **6.527–528:** From Book I of *History of the Wars* by Procopius, trans. H. B. Dewing with the collaboration of Glanville Downey. Reprinted by permission of Harvard University Press.

7.603: "Quem Qu(ae)ritis" trope from *Saint Gall Manuscript* in *Chief Pre-Shakespearean Dramas* by John Quincy Adams (ed.). Copyright © 1924 by Houghton Mifflin Company. Reprinted by permission of the publisher.

8.696–697: From "General Prologue" of *The Canterbury Tales* by Geoffrey Chaucer, trans. David Wright. Translation © David Wright 1985. Reprinted by permission of the Peters Fraser & Dunlop Group Ltd.

12.126: Letter by Katherine Zell (1508) from *Women of the Reformation in Germany and Italy* by Roland H. Bainton. Copyright © 1971 Augsburg Publishing House. Reprinted by permission of Augsburg Press.

13.318: From *Born Under Saturn* by Giambattista Passeri, trans. Rudolf and Margot Wittkower. Copyright © 1963 by Rudolf and Margot Wittkower and renewed 1991 by Margot Wittkower. Reprinted by permission of Random House, Inc.

16.658: Letter of Gustav Mahler to his wife from *Letters of Composers* by G. Norman and M. L. Shrifte.

17.705: "The Second Coming" by W. B. Yeats from *The Poems of W. B. Yeats: A New Edition* by Richard J. Finneran. Copyright 1924 by Macmillan Publishing Company, renewed 1952 by Bertha Georgie Yeats. Reprinted by permission of Macmillan Publishing Company. **17.752:** From "The Hollow Men" in *Collected Poems 1909–1962* by T. S. Eliot. Copyright 1963 by Harcourt Brace Jovanovich, Inc., copyright © 1963 by T. S. Eliot. Reprinted by permission of Harcourt Brace Jovanovich, Inc. and Faber & Faber, London.

18.807: Statement by Georgia O'Keeffe, 1944. Reprinted by permission of the Georgia O'Keeffe Foundation. **18.836:** From *The Collected Poems of William Carlos Williams, 1909–1939,* Vol. I by William Carlos Williams. Copyright 1938 by New Directions Publishing Corporation. Reprinted by permission of the publisher.